Oxford Handbook of Political Psychology

EDITED BY

David O. Sears

Leonie Huddy

Robert Jervis

OXFORD
UNIVERSITY PRESS

2003

OXFORD

UNIVERSITY PRESS

Oxford   New York
Auckland   Bangkok   Buenos Aires   Cape Town   Chennai
Dar es Salaam   Delhi   Hong Kong   Istanbul   Karachi   Kolkata
Kuala Lumpur   Madrid   Melbourne   Mexico City   Mumbai   Nairobi
São Paulo   Shanghai   Taipei   Tokyo   Toronto

Copyright © 2003 by Oxford University Press, Inc.

Published by Oxford University Press, Inc.
198 Madison Avenue, New York, New York 10016

www.oup.com

Oxford is a registered trademark of Oxford University Press

Library of Congress Cataloging-in-Publication Data
Oxford Handbook of political psychology / edited by David O. Sears,
Leonie Huddy, and Robert Jervis.
    p. cm.
Includes bibliographical references and index.
    ISBN-13 978 0-19-515220–3; 978-0-19-516220-2 (pbk.)

    1. Political psychology. I. Sears, David O. II. Huddy, Leonie. III.
Jervis, Robert, 1940–
    JA74.5 .H355 2003
    320'.01'9—dc21   2002012893

9 8

Printed in the United States of America
on acid-free paper

Acknowledgments

This *Oxford Handbook of Political Psychology* is officially sponsored by the International Society of Political Psychology (ISPP). At the 1999 annual meeting in Amsterdam, the president of ISPP, Daniel Bar-Tal, approached us, suggesting that the rapid evolution of the field of political psychology required fresh reexamination. He proposed that we edit a successor volume to two earlier comprehensive treatments of the field, the *Handbook of Political Psychology*, edited by Jeanne Knutson (1973) and *Political Psychology*, edited by Margaret Hermann (1986). We then developed a proposal and solicited authors. We were fortunate in being able to enlist a roster of the very best of contemporary political psychologists. The new president of ISPP and its governing council endorsed our plan a year later at the 2000 annual meeting in Seattle. It has been an exciting challenge for us to bring the richness and diversity of the multidisciplinary and far-ranging field of political psychology into a single volume. There are some important areas that we did not have space to include, whose omission we regret. But the ultimate success of our venture will be judged by our readers. We want to express particular thanks to the officers and members of ISPP who provided particular support, especially Daniel Bar-Tal and Ervin Staub, and Robert E. Lane, George Marcus, Stanley Renshon, Charles Taber, and David Winter. We owe much gratitude to our editor at Oxford University Press, Dedi Felman, and to her colleagues who helped with the production, especially Jennifer Rappaport and Jessica Ryan. Our most special appreciation is reserved for the tireless efforts of Marilyn Hart of the Institute for Social Science Research at UCLA, who remarkably managed to keep a lengthy and complex project organized and on track throughout its course, while always maintaining her own usual fine humor and the good cheer of everyone else.

Contents

Daniel Bar-Tal is Professor of Education at Tel Aviv University.

Michael Billig is Professor of Social Sciences at Loughborough University.

John Duckitt is Senior Lecturer in the Department of Psychology at the University of Auckland.

Stanley Feldman is Professor of Political Science at Stony Brook University.

Ronald J. Fisher is Professor of International Relations in the School of International Service at American University.

Richard K. Herrmann is Professor of Political Science at Ohio State University.

Leonie Huddy is Associate Professor of Political Science at Stony Brook University.

Orit Ichilov is Professor of Education at Tel Aviv University.

Robert Jervis is Professor of Political Science at Columbia University.

Herbert C. Kelman is Research Professor of Psychology at Harvard University.

Donald R. Kinder is Professor of Political Science and Psychology at the University of Michigan.

Bert Klandermans is Professor of Applied Social Psychology at Free University, Amsterdam.

Robert Kurzban is Assistant Professor of Psychology at the University of Pennsylvania.

Robert E. Lane is Professor Emeritus of Political Science at Yale University.

Richard R. Lau is Professor of Political Science at Rutgers University.

Jack S. Levy is Professor of Political Science at Rutgers University.

Sheri Levy is Assistant Professor of Psychology at Stony Brook University.

George E. Marcus is Professor of Political Science at Williams College.

Kathleen M. McGraw is Professor of Political Science and Psychology at Ohio State University.

Virginia Sapiro is Professor of Political Science at the University of Wisconsin, Madison.

David O. Sears is Professor of Psychology and Political Science at the University of California, Los Angeles.

Jim Sidanius is Professor of Psychology at the University of California, Los Angeles.

Ervin Staub is Professor of Psychology at the University of Massachusetts, Amherst.

Charles S. Taber is Professor of Political Science at Stony Brook University.

David G. Winter is Professor of Psychology at the University of Michigan.

1 David O. Sears, Leonie Huddy, and Robert Jervis

The Psychologies Underlying Political Psychology

Political psychology is, at the most general level, an application of what is known about human psychology to the study of politics. From psychology it draws on theory and research on personality, psychopathology, social psychology, developmental psychology, cognitive psychology, and intergroup relations. It addresses political phenomena such as individual biography and leadership, mass political behavior, mass communication effects, political socialization and civic education, international conflict, foreign policy decision-making, conflict resolution, intergroup conflicts involving race, gender, nationality, and other groupings, political movements, and political mobilization. Although many of its practitioners are drawn from the disciplines of psychology and political science, they also include historians, sociologists, anthropologists, psychiatrists, communications researchers, educators, and lawyers.

The field of political psychology as a self-conscious specialty dates from the late 1960s. As far as we know, the first undergraduate and graduate courses taught under that title began in 1970 (Funk & Sears, 1991; Sears & Funk, 1991). Political psychology is now taught at both the graduate and undergraduate levels at most major universities in the United States, although not in every case under that exact title, and increasingly at smaller liberal arts colleges and in universities around the globe. The International Society of Political Psychology (ISPP), the core professional society for political psychology, was founded in 1978 under the strong leadership of Jeanne Knutson. It developed a journal, *Political Psychology*, published since 1980; research in the field is of course published in a wide variety of other outlets, as the bibliographies for the individual chapters here demonstrate.

As with any other academic specialty, the field of political psychology should be drawn together periodically to assess its standing, progress, and direction. Within the disciplines of psychology particularly, and political science as well, there is a tradition of periodic handbooks (see Greenstein & Polsby, 1975; Gilbert, Fiske, & Lindzey, 1998). There are two such previous books on political psychology: the *Handbook of Political Psychology* (Knutson, 1973) and *Political Psychology* (Hermann, 1986). The field has grown considerably since then. As a result, Daniel Bar-Tal and Ervin Staub, as president and president-elect of ISPP, suggested in 1999 that we prepare a new edition.

In this handbook a group of widely respected political scientists and psychologists summarize what psychology has contributed to our understanding of the political behavior of both political elites and ordinary citizens. Drawing on a diverse set of psychological theories, the contributors to this handbook shed light on central issues such as the effects of personality on leadership style, the development of biases that distort political decision-making, the origins of racial prejudice, and the etiology of violent communal conflicts. Our goal is to present the main contemporary content of political psychology. We strove to make the presentation comprehensive, cumulative, and international. First of all, it is intended to systematically review current knowledge; it is comprehensive, embracing all the fields of political psychology; and it is contemporary, emphasizing the latest and most current knowledge. Second, in soliciting authors we sought first and foremost prominent scholars in each area of political psychology. Third, we sought to make the book fully interdisciplinary, and indeed the authors come approximately equally from psychology and political science backgrounds. Fourth, we sought to make the book international, not merely a product of the United States, and we have included a significant number of authors from other nations. The chapters in each provide an up-to-date account of cutting-edge research within both psychology and political science and will be an essential reference for scholars and students interested in the intersection of these two fields. This handbook should allow one-stop shopping for what is currently known about political psychology in all its many forms.

◤ Psychological Approaches to Politics

The chapters that follow will make it clear that there is no one "political psychology." Rather, there are a number of political phenomena that have been investigated from a psychological approach, and using a number of different psychological theories. In that sense there are a number of "political psychologies," though of course every theory is more appropriate for some phenomena than for others. It may be helpful if we here lay out the major psychological theoretical approaches that have been applied to the study of politics (see also Sullivan, Rahn, & Rudolph, 2002).

Personality

One approach that is sometimes mistakenly identified as *the* psychological approach uses individual personality or characterological predispositions as the primary explanatory variable. Personality is usually defined as a stable individual difference variable that transcends specific situations. For example, we might describe a national leader as "highly aggressive," by which we mean that she has a tendency, in most situations and more than most people, to initiate action rather than passively respond and to be angry and hostile rather than gentle and sweet.

Sigmund Freud had a great deal of influence on early political psychologists because his psychoanalysis of specific individuals lent itself well to the analysis of the personalities of specific political leaders. Harold Lasswell, in his *Psychopathology and Politics* (1930), was a pioneer in analyzing the personalities of political activists in terms of the unconscious conflicts that motivated their political activities. This approach led to numerous psychobiographies of famous leaders, such as the analysis of Woodrow Wilson by George and George (1956) and of Martin Luther by Erik Erikson (1958). A natural extension of this examination of individuals has been to classify individuals into personality or character categories, such as Barber's (1972) fourfold classification of presidents as active or passive and positive or negative. This intensive analysis of specific individuals also was extended to the analysis of ordinary people. Smith, Bruner, and White (1956) examined the psychological functions that political attitudes serve for ordinary citizens, and Lane (1962) the values and ideologies ordinary citizens use in thinking about politics.

This "idiographic" approach to personality and politics, examining the idiosyncracies of specific individuals, contrasts with the "nomothetic" approach, which statistically places larger numbers of people at various positions on a specific dimension of personality. The most famous is perhaps the book *The Authoritarian Personality* (Adorno, Frenkel-Brunswick, Levinson, & Sanford, 1950), an ambitious and influential effort to distinguish authoritarian, antidemocratic people from more egalitarian, democratic personalities, with a single questionnaire. For example, high authoritarians are more likely than low authoritarians to agree that "any good leader should be strict with people under him in order to gain their respect."

The personality approach dominated political psychology in the 1940s and 1950s (Sullivan et al., 2002). Greenstein (1987) offers a most perceptive analysis of how and when personality analyses are most telling in political psychology (also see Runyan, 1984). Though somewhat less prominent today, the personality approach continues to influence research on mass and elite political behavior, as seen in John Duckitt's review of explanations for prejudice and David Winter's analysis of individual differences in elite behavior and decision-making.

Behaviorist Learning Theories

Another general approach has evolved from the behaviorist theories that were much in vogue in the middle half of the twentieth century. One version of behaviorist theories emphasizes the learning of longlasting habits, which in turn guide later behavior. They were inspired by the classical conditioning studies of Pavlov, who showed that dogs could be conditioned to salivate at the sound of a bell if it were always followed by food, by the instrumental conditioning studies of Watson and Skinner, who showed that animals could develop complex habits if their behavior proved instrumental to the satisfaction of their basic needs such as hunger or thirst, and the imitative learning examined by Bandura, who showed that children would engage in imitative behavior without any involvement of need satisfaction. Such theories long dominated the analysis of mass political attitudes. The field of political socialization, as described by Sears and Levy, developed from the assumption that children learned basic political attitudes (such as party identification or racial prejudice) from their families and friends, and that the residues of these early attitudes dominated their later political attitudes in adulthood, such as their presidential vote preferences. Mass communication effects were analyzed in terms of the "reinforcement" of a prior position by exposure to congruent communications (Klapper, 1960; Zaller, 1992; see Kinder, chapter 11).

Developmental Theory

An important counterweight to the behaviorist emphasis on social learning was the theory of childhood cognitive development originally proposed by Piaget and later elaborated by Kohlberg and others. As children get older, they pass through various cognitive stages in their understanding of the social world, initially understanding only the positive or negative effects of an action, then focusing more on the views of authority, and finally being able to reason in terms of either relativistic or absolute moral values (Tapp & Kohlberg, 1971). Some have suggested that progress through these stages is usually incomplete by the time people reach adulthood, giving rise to the possibility of individual differences among adults in level of cognitive or moral development (Rosenberg, 1988). This developmental approach has had its primary application to preadult political socialization, defined broadly. Sears and Levy discuss different theoretical approaches to attitude acquisition among children.

Incentive Theories

A second general behaviorist idea is that behavior is governed by the structure of incentives in the individual's current situation. For example, a rat in a t-maze would turn to the alternative that provided the most reward and the least punishment and avoid the less favorable alternative. Later variants of these theories emphasized the positive and negative incentives that induced people toward specific behaviors or repelled them. Kurt Lewin developed a variant on these that he described as "field theory," which placed individuals in a field in which internal and external forces pushed and pulled them into specific behaviors.

These too have long influenced the study of mass political behavior. Mass electoral behavior was analyzed in terms of "pressures" on a voter to vote in a particular direction, such as those associated with the dominant political preferences of their demographic groups (Lazarsfeld, Berelson, & Gaudet, 1948) or "short-term forces" such as candidate appeal or foreign policy issue preferences (Campbell, Converse, Miller, & Stokes, 1960; also see chapter 12). Basic values can also provide incentives for or against specific political actions (see chapter 14). Collective action and violence is often analyzed in terms of incentives for and against it (see chapter 20).

A variant on the incentive approach adds subjective appraisals of the most important incentives. For example, "expectancy-value" theory predicts that choices will favor alternatives that hold the highest potential hedonic value to the individual, multiplied by the individual's subjective expectation of the probability of that value being produced by that choice alternative (Edwards, 1954; see chapter 2). The similarity between such theories and the rational choice theory that is central to neoclassic economics, and now very popular in political science, is evident; that link is discussed further hereafter.

Social Cognition

The Gestalt movement that migrated from Germany to the United States before World War II began with the assumption that people had needs for understanding and perceptual order and so would spontaneously develop perceptions and cognitions that simplified a disorderly perceptual world (Asch, 1952; Krech & Crutchfield, 1948). In the hands of Heider (1958) and Festinger (1957) and others this was applied to the study of attitudes, with the presumption that people were motivated to seek cognitive consistency (Abelson, Aronson, McGuire, Newcomb, Rosenberg, & Tannenbaum, 1968). Many of the phenomena of electoral behavior and mass communications were subsequently analyzed in terms of individuals' tendencies to develop electoral and other political preferences that were consistent with their other strong attitudes (e.g., Sears, 1969; Sears & Whitney, 1973).

Later this cognitive consistency approach was subsumed under the field of "social cognition," which analyzes individuals as seeking to develop simplifying views of the external world, easily capable of learning new information but also needing to economize on cognitive processing because of limited processing capacities (Fiske & Taylor, 1991). The field of social cognition was also influenced by the more general cognitive revolution in psychology that emerged in the 1980s, based on the application of computer analogies to the structure and processes of the cognitive system. It led to a series of key insights into the strengths and limitations of human information processing that were readily applicable to political reasoning.

The need for cognitive economy helped to explain the tendency toward cognitive consistency. It also pointed to the use of cognitive heuristics or shortcuts, which could potentially distort both elites' decision-making (Jervis, 1976; Larson, 1985) and the mass public's preferences. Levy (chapter

8) reviews the impact of a psychological approach on foreign policy decision-making and explores these biases in greater detail, drawing a distinction between "cold" biases based on the application of cognitive heuristics and "hot" motivated biases, such as wishful thinking and cognitive consistency. Lau (chapter 2) reviews work on behavioral decision theory, contrasting normative models with behavioral descriptions of how ordinary people actually do make political decisions, with a particular focus on voting decisions. Here too the cognitive limits on rationality lead to a variety of problem-solving stratgeies involving cognitive shortcuts. Taber (chapter 13) similarly develops an information-processing model of voter decision-making.

An emphasis on cognitive shortcuts also allows for elite manipulation of mass publics, as elites determine how an issue is to be framed or what predispositions are to be primed, through their agenda-setting powers (Iyengar & Kinder, 1987; see chapter 17). But as McGraw (chapter 12) notes in her discussion of the dynamic process of impression formation, when voters assess political candidates via on-line processes they often forget the details but arrive at the "right" decision about the candidate consistent with their preferences. In this instance, the need for cognitive economy does not bias political decision-making. Taber (chapter 13) and Lau (chapter 2) too conclude that the use of cognitive shortcuts may often not bias the ordinary voter's decision making as much as was once feared (also see Lau & Redlawsk, 1997).

In recent years, the centrally cognitive emphasis of social cognition has been questioned to some extent and so the role of emotions and affect has begun to play a larger role, as described by George Marcus (chapter 6).

Intergroup Relations

Intergroup relations is a particularly active area within political psychology at present and this emphasis is reflected across the chapters of this handbook. In addition to the discussions by Huddy (chapter 15) and Duckitt (chapter 16) that deal directly with group-linked research, Sears and Levy (chapter 3) include a section on the childhood development of racial identity, Billig (chapter 7) discusses the use of group-linked pronouns in his contribution of political rhetoric, McGraw explores the impact of race on candidate evaluations in her discussion of political impressions, and Klandermans (chapter 19) discusses the role of group identification in intensifying commitment to social movements.

The field of intergroup relations does not embody a single theoretical approach; rather it draws on diverse psychological theories. Early research on intergroup relations conducted in the 1950s and 1960s focused primarily on outgroup animosity, especially toward Jews and Negroes (Allport, 1954). Research on the authoritarian personality emphasized the importance of personality factors on the development of racial prejudice and anti-Semitism

(Adorno et al., 1950). More recently, research on racial prejudice has been dominated by theories that stress the role of social learning in the acquisition of negative racial attitudes, stereotypes, and authoritarian beliefs (Altemeyer, 1988; Ashmore & Del Boca, 1981; Sears, 1988).

Yet theories in the area of intergroup relations have increasingly emphasized the distinctive psychological power of group boundaries and group attachments. For example, contemporary research has devoted increasing research to ingroup loyalties. This work has focused less on individual differences and more on group-related factors to account for the development of both ingroup attachments and outgroup antipathies. Huddy (chapter 15) highlights the important distinction between two key group-related approaches: social identity theory, which stresses social prestige and intergroup respect as motives for the development of identity and ingroup favoritism (Tajfel, 1981; Tajfel & Turner, 1986), and realistic interest theories, which place emphasis on shared material interests and conflict over tangible resources as the origins of ingroup attachments and outgroup antipathy (Blumer, 1958; Bobo, 1983; LeVine & Campbell, 1972; Sidanius & Pratto, 1999). She concludes that the political impact of strong group identities is usually more closely tied to symbolic than to realistic interests. Duckitt attempts to reconcile the group and individual levels of theories about the development of prejudice. He develops a combined model in which group inequality leads to a desire to dominate other groups (consistent with social dominance theory) whereas intergroup threat leads individuals to an overt dislike of threatening group members (akin to findings on authoritarianism).

◤ New Developments

Both evolutionary psychology and neuroscience are beginning to influence research on an array of questions linked to political psychology. Sidanius and Kurzban explore evolutionary psychology in some detail as they discuss the origins of ethnocentrism, gender differences in political behavior, and the development of group-based hierarchies. Developments in evolutionary psychology are closely tied to recent developments in neuropsychology. Sidanius and Kurzban (chapter 5), for example, describe the brain as a system of "functionally specialized circuits" designed through the process of evolution to handle distinct tasks. This insight from neuropsychology forms the basis for George Marcus's approach to emotions. He emphasizes different types of emotional responses, such as enthusiasm, anxiety, and aversion, that may be under the control of different neutral processes. This, too, holds important insight for political psychology. Anxiety, for example, motivates a search for new information, shattering the traditional view of emotion as something that interferes with rational decision-making. In contrast, enthusiasm or aversion results in a tendency to rest on one's existing tendencies without initiating a search for new information.

Billig draws from an approach more commonly used in qualitative social sciences—discourse analysis—to reconceptualize central psychological variables, such as identity, as a product of conversation that is nested within a specific context. This leads to the view that political attitudes need to be studied within a controversial or argumentative setting.

Political psychologists have also paid growing attention to the complex theoretical and empirical role of gender. Sapiro (chapter 17) provides an overview of this research, drawing from a wide array of sources in political science and psychology. She challenges the notion that gender has obvious and consistent effects and argues instead that its political effects are variable and contingent. Under some circumstances, women and men react differently to political events, and gendered political objects (such as politicians or policies) can elicit clear reactions based on gender stereotypes.

Another important trend concerns an examination of the interplay between political elites and publics. Frames have become an increasingly important concept within the study of mass politics. Both Kinder (chapter 11) and Klandermans (chapter 19) discuss the uses of frames by political elites and social movement leaders to shape public opinion on an issue or key problem. And McGraw reviews politicians' attempts and success at manipulating their public image. But this is a relatively new approach to political behavior that is ripe for further development.

One tension within political psychology concerns the relative emphasis on the stability, as opposed to the changeability, of attitudes and behavior. Research in a number of areas has begun to address this divide. For example, research on threat highlights the way in which an external stimulus can provoke the application of a preexisting belief such as authoritarianism (Duckitt) or strengthen a preexisting group attachment (Huddy). This interaction between people and situations provides a more compelling psychological view of the political process that accounts for variations in political attitudes and behavior across situations, and provides a potentially useful framework for future research.

▶ Alternative Theories

One particularly vexing question is whether there is an alternative to psychological theories of politics. It is obvious that there is no single accepted theory of human psychology. Whether we could ever develop such a theory, whether the barriers to it are potentially surmountable with greater research or are inherent in the complex and changing nature of human behavior, is as yet unanswerable. But at least as basic is the question of whether we can ever have a sensible theory that is completely nonpsychological.

At first glance, it would seem that important and indeed dominant theories in political science have no place for psychology of any kind. This would seem to be true for theories that can be labeled materialist in that they argue that people pursue material self-interest (most obviously in the form of wealth) by the means that are best designed to reach those objectives at lowest cost. The obvious categories of theories here are rational choice and game theory.

The question is not whether theories like this are correct or not but a more conceptual one of whether they can be considered nonpsychological. We do not think that they can be. While they embody a psychology that is different from and perhaps simpler than that portrayed in the literatures reviewed in this book, they still rest on assumptions, usually implicit, about how people think and feel. Interests stem from what people value, and while these may be material, few can be understood without some sort of psychology. While human survival requires a minimal level of food and protection, most human behavior cannot be encompassed in these terms, and people seek much more than this. Most materialist theories take people's values, goals, and preferences as a given. This is not foolish, since no theory can explore everything. But it should not lead us to forget that explaining these things is a central part of social science and it is hard to see how this could be done without some form of psychology. Furthermore, the psychology almost certainly would have a large social component to it, because values and preferences stem in part from how people are socialized and take form in imitation, response to, and reaction against what others value and seek.

Preferences do not automatically lead to behavior, of course. To know how people will act in order to reach their goals, we have to know what their means-ends beliefs are. For example, knowing that a national leader desires peace cannot explain her behavior without also explaining how she thought it could be obtained. To say that politicians are primarily motivated to remain in power, as is assumed in rational choice theories, does not tell us what they think they need to do to reach this objective. Strategies and lines of policy are rarely obvious, which is shown by the twin facts that they are often hotly disputed and the ones pursued frequently turn out to be in error. Voters and elite decision-makers who want certain outcomes have to decide what policies are most likely to reach them. Debates about whether they are rational or not at best scratch the surface and at worst are misleading because there is no single rational way to go about their tasks.

The role of psychology is even clearer—although often overlooked—in contexts such as international politics, where we are dealing with small numbers of actors that are engaged in strategic interaction. That is, the outcome depends not on what each actor does separately but on the interaction of actors' behaviors, and each sets her behavior anticipating what the other will do, knowing that the other is engaged in a similar exercise. This is the essence of game theory. But far from being antithetical to psychology, game theory is highly psychological, as its best practitioners fully understand

(Kreps, 1990; O'Neill, 1999; Schelling, 1960). Each side has to develop expectations about what the other will do. There is no way to separate these processes into strategic and psychological parts, let alone to oppose a strategic theory to a psychological one. Rather, psychology and strategy are conjoined.

In general, rational choice or "positive theory" or "formal theory" approaches seek to model human behavior in mathematical terms, presupposing "rational" behavior based on maximizing material self-interest. This has in turn inspired efforts to identify psychological factors that cause people to behave inconsistently from rational choice, whether in individual decision-making (see especially Lau and Levy) or in interaction (see Kelman & Fisher, chapter 10).

◣ Other Disciplines

We do not mean to imply that the field of political psychology simply borrows its ideas from psychology. Krosnick and McGraw (2002; Krosnick, 2002) argue that political psychologists have much to contribute to the development of psychological theory by refining theories so that their predictions generalize beyond a laboratory setting. This potential is evident throughout the chapters of this handbook.

Moreover, other disciplines have made important contributions to political psychology. As the preceding section implies, economics has made the important contribution of providing a major alternative to psychological approaches. Sociology has especially provided models for collective behavior (see, Klandermans chapter 19, and Staub & Bar-Tal, chapter 20), and social structural analyses both of institutional behavior (see Ichilov, chapter 18) and of individual behavior, especially in the area of intergroup relations (see Huddy, chapter 15, Sidanius & Kurzban, chapter 5, and Duckitt, chapter 16). The field of communications has provided analyses of rhetoric and discourse that can help to explain elite rhetoric (see Billig, chapter 7). And the field of history has provided a great deal of grist for the political psychologist's mill, whether in the form of psychodynamic (George & George, 1956) or cognitive (Jervis, 1976; Larson, 1985) studies of individuals or studies of the behavior of small (Janis, 1982) and large (Volkan, 1988) groups.

One particularly noteworthy feature of political psychology is how much of its theoretical and empirical content has been stimulated by the search for explanations of events that occur in the real political world, not just the posing and testing of abstract academic theories. The regularly scheduled American national elections have stimulated much of the work on voting behavior, just as the Cold War stimulated much of the work on foreign policy decision-making and international relations.

◣ *Organization of This Book*

Part I of this book focuses on psychological theories themselves. This part includes basic psychological theories and their application to decision-making, childhood and adult development, personality, evolutionary psychology, the study of emotion, and a discourse analysis approach to rhetoric. Then we move to the substantive focus of different areas of political psychological research that tend to cut across theoretical approaches. In Part II we start with elite behavior in the area of international relations focusing on models of foreign policy decision-making, strategic interaction, and conflict resolution. Part III focuses on the interplay of elites and masses, through the media and voters' responses to political candidates. Part IV focuses on mass political behavior, including an analysis of political reasoning, the role of values, intergroup relations, and the political role of gender. Part V considers collective behavior: the effects of civic education, collective political action, and the effects of politics on the larger society. And the epilogue offers with some observations by one of the pioneers of political psychology, Robert E. Lane, who ponders the differences just alluded to between psychological and economic approaches to the analysis of political behavior.

Before closing, we also want to refer the reader with a further interest in political psychology to several other more specialized books with different goals from our own but somewhat similar titles. This handbook is intended as a comprehensive statement of the current state of knowledge in political psychology. Three other books (Kuklinski [2002b]; Monroe [2000], and Renshon and Duckitt [2000]) do not attempt such comprehensive overviews of research in specific subfields of political psychology. Rather, each has two more specific goals. Each includes essays reviewing the research programs of a few selected authors. Each also includes essays expressing opinions about how political psychological research ought to be done. The latter also presents examples of research at the intersection of political psychology and culture; for example, from Japan, Latin America, the Middle East, eastern Europe, and so on. Each would be of more value to political psychologists who want thoughtful perspectives on the field as a whole than to scholars seeking a current assessment of knowledge of the field, or to beginning researchers. Finally, Kuklinski (2002a) contains chapters from researchers describing their own research. This book too does not aspire to be comprehensive about the field of political psychology; each essay describes a specific research program rather than canvassing an entire topical area.

In other words, despite the similarities in titles, this handbook has a quite different purpose, and value, from these other recent books. This handbook is intended as the primary reference source to the many different fields under the umbrella topic of "political psychology."

▶ References

Abelson, R. P., Aronson, E., McGuire, W. J., Newcomb, T. M., Rosenberg, M. J., & Tannenbaum, P. H. (Eds.). (1968). *Theories of cognitive consistency: A sourcebook.* Chicago: Rand McNally.

Adorno, T. W., Frenkel-Brunswik, E., Levinson, D. J., & Sanford, R. N. (1950). *The authoritarian personality.* New York: Harper & Row.

Allport, G. W. (1954). *The nature of prejudice.* Garden City, NY: Doubleday Anchor.

Altemeyer, B. (1988). *Enemies of freedom: Understanding right-wing authoritarianism.* San Francisco: Jossey-Bass.

Asch, S. E. (1952). *Social psychology.* Englewood Cliffs, NJ: Prentice-Hall.

Ashmore, R. D., & Del Boca, F. K. (1981). Conceptual approaches to stereotypes and stereotyping. In D. L. Hamilton (Ed.), *Cognitive processes in stereotyping and intergroup behavior* (pp. 1–35). Hillsdale, NJ: Erlbaum.

Barber, J. D. (1972). *Presidential character: Predicting performance in the White House.* Englewood Cliffs, NJ: Prentice-Hall.

Blumer, H. (1958). Race prejudice as a sense of group position. *Pacific Sociological Review, 1,* 3–7.

Bobo, L. (1983). Whites' opposition to busing: Symbolic racism or realistic group conflict? *Journal of Personality and Social Psychology, 45,* 1196–1210.

Campbell, A., Converse, P. E., Miller, W. E., & Stokes, D. E. (1960). *The American voter.* New York: Wiley.

Edwards, W. (1954). The theory of decision-making. *Psychological Bulletin, 51,* 380–417.

Erikson, E. H. (1958). *Young man Luther: A study in psychoanalysis and history.* New York: Norton.

Festinger, L. (1957). *A theory of cognitive dissonance.* Evanston, IL: Row, Peterson.

Fiske, S. T., & Taylor, S. E. (1991). *Social cognition* (2nd ed.). New York: McGraw-Hill.

Funk, C. L., & Sears, D. O. (1991). Are we reaching undergraduates? A survey of course offerings in political psychology. *Political Psychology, 12,* 559–572.

George, A. L., & George, J. L. (1956). *Woodrow Wilson and Colonel House: A personality study.* New York: Dover.

Gilbert, D. T., Fiske, S. T., & Lindzey, G. (Eds.). (1998). *The handbook of social psychology.* Boston: McGraw-Hill.

Greenstein, F. I. (1987). *Personality and politics: Problems of evidence, inference, and conceptualization.* Princeton: Princeton University Press.

Greenstein, F. I., & Polsby, N. W. (Eds.). (1975). *Handbook of political science.* Reading, MA: Addison-Wesley.

Heider, F. (1958). *The psychology of interpersonal relationships.* New York: Wiley.

Hermann, M. G. (1986). *Political psychology.* San Francisco: Jossey-Bass.

Iyengar, S., & Kinder, D. R. (1987). *News that matters: Television and American opinion.* Chicago: University of Chicago Press.

Janis, I. L. (1982). *Groupthink.* New York: Free Press.

Jervis, R. (1976). *Perception and misperception in international politics.* Princeton: Princeton University Press.

Klapper, J. T. (1960). *The effects of mass communications.* Glencoe, IL: Free Press.

Knutson, J. N. (Ed.) (1973). *Handbook of political psychology.* San Francisco: Jossey-Bass.

Krech, D., & Crutchfield, R. A. (1948). *Theory and problems of social psychology*. New York: McGraw-Hill.

Kreps, D. M. (1990). *Game theory and economic modelling*. New York: Oxford University Press.

Krosnick, J. A. (2002). The challenges of political psychology: Lessons to be learned from research on attitude perception. In J. H. Kuklinski (Ed.), *Thinking about political psychology* (pp. 115–152). Cambridge: Cambridge University Press.

Krosnick, J. A., & McGraw, K. M. (2002). Psychological political science versus political psychology true to its name: A plea for balance. In K. R. Monroe (Ed.), *Political psychology* (pp. 79–94). Mahwah, NJ: Erlbaum.

Kuklinski, J. H. (2002a). *Citizens and politics: Perspectives from political psychology*. Cambridge: Cambridge University Press.

Kuklinski, J. H. (Ed.).(2002b). *Thinking about political psychology*. Cambridge: Cambridge University Press.

Lane, R. E. (1962). *Political ideology: Why the American common man believes what he does*. Glencoe, IL: Free Press.

Larson, D. (1985). *Origins of containment*. Princeton: Princeton University Press.

Lasswell, Harold D. (1930). *Psychopathology and politics*. New York: Viking.

Lau, R. R., & Redlawsk, D. P. (1997). Voting correctly. *American Political Science Review, 91*, 585–598.

Lazarsfeld, P. F., Berelson, B., & Gaudet, H. (1948). *The people's choice* (2nd ed). New York: Columbia University Press.

LeVine, R. A., & Campbell, D. T. (1972) *Ethnocentrism: Theories of conflict, ethnic attitudes, and group behavior*. New York: Wiley.

Monroe, K. R. (Ed.). (2002). *Political psychology*. Mahwah, NJ: Erlbaum.

O'Neill, B. (1999). *Honors, symbols, and war*. Ann Arbor: University of Michigan Press.

Renshon, S. A., & Duckitt, J. (Eds.). (2000). *Political psychology: Cultural and crosscultural foundations*. New York: New York University Press.

Rosenberg, S. (1988). *Reason, ideology, and politics*. Princeton: Princeton University Press.

Runyan, W. M. (1984). *Life histories and psychobiography: Explorations in theory and method*. New York: Oxford University Press.

Schelling, T. C. (1960). *The strategy of conflict*. Cambridge, MA: Harvard University Press.

Sears, D. O. (1969). Political behavior. In G. Lindzey & E. Aronson (Eds.), *Handbook of social psychology* (Vol. 5, rev. ed., pp. 315–458). Reading, MA: Addison-Wesley.

Sears, D. O. (1988). Symbolic racism. In P. A. Katz & D. A. Taylor (Eds.), *Eliminating racism: Profiles in controversy* (pp. 53–84). New York: Plenum Press.

Sears, D. O., & Funk, C. L. (1991). Graduate education in political psychology in the United States. *Political Psychology, 12*, 345–362.

Sears, D. O., & Whitney, R. E. (1973). Political persuasion. In I. de S. Pool, W. Schramm, F. W. Frey, N. Maccoby, & E. B. Parker (Eds.), *Handbook of communication* (pp. 153–289). Chicago: Rand-McNally.

Sidanius, J. & Pratto, F. (1999). *Social dominance: An intergroup theory of social hierarchy and oppression*. New York: Cambridge University Press.

Smith, M. B., Bruner, J. S., & White, R. W. (1956). *Opinions and personality*. New York: Wiley.

Sullivan, J. L., Rahn, W. M., & Rudolph, T. J. (2002). The contours of political psychology: Situating research on political information processing. In J. H. Kuklinski (Ed.), *Thinking about political psychology* (pp. 23–47). Cambridge: Cambridge University Press.

Tajfel, H. (1981). *Human groups and social categories: Studies in social psychology.* Cambridge: Cambridge University Press.

Tajfel, H., & Turner, J. C. (1986). The social identity theory of intergroup behavior. In S. Worchel & W. G. Austin (Eds.), *Psychology of intergroup relations* (2nd ed., pp. 7–24). Chicago: Nelson-Hall.

Tapp, J. L., & Kohlberg, L. (1971). Developing senses of law and legal justice. *Journal of Social Issues, 27,* 65–92.

Volkan, V. D. (1988). *The need to have enemies and allies: From clinical practice to international relationships.* Northvale, NJ: Aronson.

Zaller, J. (1992). *The nature and origins of mass opinion.* New York: Cambridge University Press.

Theoretical Approaches

2   Richard R. Lau

Models of Decision-Making

If politics involves the "authoritative allocation of values" (Easton, 1953), as one classic definition holds, then the *study* of politics must certainly involve, as a central organizing theme, how those authoritative allocation decisions are made. This question can be addressed from a number of different perspectives. One concerns how *individual* political actors, be they kings or dictators, politicians or ordinary citizens, make political decisions. Few decisions are made in total isolation from others, but for the most part this first perspective views decision-making as a question of individual psychology: individual preferences, information search, memory, and choice. A second perspective considers how the *institutions* of government—the legislative, executive, and judicial branches, and the various organizations in the larger governmental bureaucracy—make decisions. All institutions are made up of individuals, of course, but all institutions also have their own particular ways—laws, traditions, "standard operating procedures"—for gathering information, aggregating preferences, and taking actions. In many instances, institutional norms and procedures can overwhelm individual decision-making processes. March (1994) tries to capture this difference in perspectives by asking whether decision-makers are generally seen as autonomous actors or as being primarily guided by the "systematic properties of an interacting ecology" (p. ix).

Without meaning to minimize the importance of institutional factors in understanding political decisions, this chapter will focus on how individual political actors make decisions. Individual decision-making has been the primary concern of psychologists, while economists, sociologists, and organizational theorists have more frequently studied larger aggregates like institutions and firms. The literatures are largely distinct; both are voluminous. I will narrow my focus and concentrate on the individual perspective. For good overviews of research aimed more at the institutional level, the reader is referred to the many works of March (e.g., 1988, 1994; March & Olsen, 1989; March & Simon, 1958) and the earliest research of Simon (1947). Allison (1971; Allison & Zelikow, 1999) does an excellent job of contrasting the two perspectives in the context of the Cuban missile crisis.

Even limiting our attention to individual political decision-makers, democratic systems provide two important categories of decision-makers: politicians and other government elites, and ordinary citizens. If democracy is to work the way it is supposed to work, both types of individuals must be making reasonably frequent political decisions. One obvious dimension along which these two categories of decision-makers differ is their level of expertise or knowledge about politics. Almost by definition, political elites are political experts: they generally have far more relevant knowledge and experience than ordinary people. Everyday citizens, on the other hand, vary greatly in how much they know and care about the topics that they are regularly asked to make decisions about as part of their role as citizens.

In this chapter I will try to provide a general framework for studying decision-making that applies to both everyday citizens (i.e., the "mass") and to political elites. Political elites and common citizens differ not only in the amount of expertise they typically bring to the decision-making task, however, but also in the type of decisions they are generally asked to make. I will try to point out some of the more obvious differences. In my examples and extensions of the basic decision-making framework, I will concentrate on the decision-making of everyday citizens. (One very important topic of elite decision-making, foreign policy, is the specific focus of chapter 8.)

It is useful at the outset to distinguish between "judgment" and "decision-making." The two have often been linked (e.g., Slovic & Lichtenstein, 1971), and normatively they are equivalent in the sense that a decision-maker should choose an alternative if and only if it is liked more than any other. Still, judgment and decision-making are not the same thing. A judgment involves an evaluation of a single entity along some dimension: how heavy or light, or bright or dark, an object is (psychophysical judgment); how attractive/funny/likable/smart a person is (person judgment); how likely some event is to occur (probabilistic judgment). Judgment involves the mapping of some ambiguous stimuli onto a perceptual system. The tendency to make judgments is particularly true of entities—that is, people—in the social world. Kathleen McGraw reviews this literature as it applies to political actors in chapter 12. (See also Druckman & Lupia, 2000.) A decision, in contrast, involves a *choice* between two or more alternatives: *whether* to take drugs, *who* to marry, *when* to retire, *which* candidate to support in the election. Making a choice implies more *commitment* to the chosen alternative than making a judgment suggests about the judged entity, and may well also involve searching for reasons to *justify* the choice (Slovic, Fischhoff, & Lichtenstein, 1982). People make judgments all the time without necessarily "putting those judgments into action."

Decisions are often treated as if they are nothing more than choosing the most highly evaluated alternative. This is a mistake, for at least two reasons. First, people (and institutions) make all sorts of decisions without first evaluating the alternatives on some global dimension. "Spur of the moment" decisions are certainly of this type, as are habitual or "standing" decisions (Quadrel, Fischhoff, & Davis, 1993), but the problem is much broader than this. If I knew I was going to die tomorrow I might very well think about what is my favorite restaurant and decide to eat my last meal there; but most of the time I decide whether I want to eat Chinese or Italian or Mexican food not because of any judgment about the quality or tastiness or healthiness of these different cuisines and not because of any judgment about the quality of the service or the skill of the chef in any of the nearby restaurants that serve these different types of food, but rather because I "feel" like having Chinese tonight.

I suspect, however, that the vote decision in particular—or any choice between different *people*—is rarely made without first forming some global evaluation of the different candidates for the position. Hence candidate evaluation is intimately involved in the vote choice. But a second reason that it is wrong to equate judgment and decision-making is that global evaluations, even when they are made, do not necessarily dictate choice. People may vote "strategically"—that is, choose a less preferred alternative because their most preferred candidate has no chance of winning (Abramson, Aldrich, Paolino, & Rohde, 1992). People may vote for a candidate they do not particularly like for some reason largely external to the decision itself (acting "against my better judgment"), for example to please a parent or girlfriend. In any case, I will leave the literature on person (candidate) impression to chapter 12, and focus almost exclusively here on clear choices or decisions.

This chapter begins by laying out more fully a general framework for what constitutes a "decision," a discussion that segues nicely into the classic economic rational choice approach to decision-making associated with von Neuman and Morgenstern (1947). This approach provides a standard against which particular decisions can be judged. No one who has actually observed decision-making believes that the classic approach provides an accurate description of how decision-makers actually behave, however, and this chapter will spend more time discussing an approach that takes accurate description as its primary goal: behavioral decision theory. As I will show, behavioral decision theory takes as its starting point a very different (and more limited) view of human cognitive abilities than the classic approach. Ironically, this more limited starting point provides many more dimensions along which to study decision-making. Consequently I will spend some time discussing the methods for studying decision-making that have been developed with this approach, particularly process tracing methods. Finally I will consider briefly one very common political decision made by everyday citizens many times during their adult lives: whether, and how, to vote in an election.

▶ *A General Framework for Studying Decision-Making*

As already noted, any decision involves a *choice*, and a choice requires at least two *alternatives* that could be chosen. Each alternative is associated with a set of beliefs about the *outcomes* that are potentially associated with each alternative—beliefs that can be idiosyncratic to every decision-maker. Every outcome must be associated with a *value* or preference, which again can be unique to every decision-maker. But these three characteristics—alternatives (plural), beliefs about outcomes, and values associated with those outcomes—provide the general framework of any decision (Hastie, 2001).

Within this general framework, decisions can be categorized along a whole slew of dimensions. Two of the most important involve

- Whether the alternatives are fixed and presented as such to the decision-maker, in which case the decision is "well defined" or "well structured" (Langley, Simon, Bradshaw, & Zytkow, 1987) or whether the alternative courses of action must be *sought out* or *constructed* by the decision-maker (which is more often the case in organizational contexts and with fairly complicated policy problems), in which case the decision is "ill defined" or "ill structured."
- Whether the outcomes associated with each alternative will occur with certainty (if I pay $50 for a U.S. savings bond today, I will be able to cash it in for $100 in 15 years), in which case the decision is *riskless*, or will occur only with some probability (if George W. Bush is elected president, he will cut taxes, increase defense spending, and be compassionate toward people outside of the Republican coalition), in which case the decision is *risky*.

The theories and techniques for studying decision-making that have been developed in psychology have typically focused on well-defined decisions, and I will limit my discussion to those types of decisions. A largely independent set of theories and methods must be invoked to study the generation or discovery of alternatives, and they are beyond the scope of this chapter (but see Gettys, Pliske, Manning, & Casey, 1987; Keller & Ho, 1988). Even ill-defined decisions can usually be studied as if they occur in stages, however, with the data gathering and alternative generation stage logically occurring first. The theories and methods discussed here could then be applied to the alternatives "on the table" at the time the choice must be made.

Psychologists have studied both risky and riskless decisions, and uncertainty can easily be incorporated into most common models of decision-making. For example, beliefs about the outcomes or consequences associated with some alternative involve not only what those consequences are but how likely they are to occur. Thus the uncertainty dimension falls easily within the purview of this chapter. At some level all decisions involve risk (the U.S. government could go belly-up before it is time to cash in my savings bond), but the probabilities of such outcomes are usually so minuscule that it is reasonable to consider them riskless. Many decisions involve alternatives that truly do involve a great deal of uncertainty, however, and that uncertainty must be taken into consideration when considering those decisions.

Table 2.1
A General Structural Framework for Analyzing Decision-Making

Multiple alternatives	Each associated with one or more outcomes	That have fixed values to the decision-maker	Which may have differential importance	And/or occur probabilistically
A_1	O_1	$+$	W_1	P_{11}
	O_2	$-$	W_2	P_{12}
	O_3	$+$	W_3	P_{13}
A_2	O_1	$+$	W_1	P_{21}
	O_2	$-$	W_2	P_{22}
	O_3	$+$	W_3	P_{23}
A_3	O_1	$+$	W_1	P_{31}
	O_2	$-$	W_2	P_{32}
	O_3	$+$	W_3	P_{33}
A_4	O_1	$+$	W_1	P_{41}
	O_2	$-$	W_2	P_{42}
	O_3	$+$	W_3	P_{43}

Table 2.1 provides a general framework for analyzing decisions that contains the major structural features of decisions just laid out: multiple alternatives, outcomes, and values. The table also incorporates the possibility of risky decisions and, as one further complication, the possibility that different outcomes may be of varying importance to the decision-maker. If all outcomes are equally important, the weights in this column would all be set to 1.0 (or just ignored). Likewise, with riskless decisions the probabilities would all be set to 1.0. For simplicity, the table assumes that every outcome associated with any alternative is associated with every alternative. In practice this very well might not be the case, but then the probability could be set to zero for any such outcome. For the well-defined decision problems I am focusing on here, alternatives and outcomes are "provided to" the decision-maker by the problem itself. The values, importance weights, and probabilities associated with each outcome are subjective in nature and must be determined by the decision-maker herself.

▲ Rational Choice/Economic Theories of Decision-Making

The first major social science theories of decision-making, developed within the field of economics, were explicitly normative in orientation, describing how decision-makers *should* behave. If the theory considers uncertainty, it has an "expected value" framework. This general approach holds that decision-makers should gather sufficient information about every plausible course of action to evaluate it. Every consequence or outcome associated with each alternative is assumed to have a certain fixed value for the decision-maker. The value of the outcomes associated with each alternative, weighted by their expected probability of occurring, are combined in a simple additive fashion to determine the overall value associated with each alternative. After going through this process of information gathering and alternative evaluating, decision-makers are assumed to choose among alternatives by some value-maximizing process (e.g., choose the alternative with the greatest expected value; choose the alternative that minimizes the worst thing that would be associated with every alternative—that is, minimizes maximum regret).[1] This standard economic perspective on rationality views humans (*homo economicus*) as "omniscient calculators" (Lupia, McCubbins, & Popkin, 2000) or demons (Gigerenzer & Todd, 1999) who can easily perform all of the cognitive manipulations required to reach a decision.

The term "rational" has become fairly loaded and has many different meanings (see Converse, 1975; March, 1978; Rubenstein, 1998). In this chapter I will restrict my meaning to *procedural rationality*, that is, to the process by which the choice is made. A "rational choice" is one that is based on relatively fixed preferences and follows a *logic of consequence*, by which current actions are dictated by anticipation of the value associated with future outcomes (March, 1994). Rational decision-makers are motivated to maximize their "interests," although the theory is silent about what those interests ought to be. This restriction on the meaning of rationality also draws attention to the fact that rational choice does not guarantee that the value-maximizing outcome *will* be obtained, only that it is the most likely to be obtained.

Consider as an example the decision of whether I should play the Pick-3 game in my state's lottery. It costs $1 to play, where playing, in essence, means picking a three-digit number between 0 and 999. If I pick the right number, I win $499 ($500 minus the $1 it cost to play); if I pick any other number, I win nothing but am still out the $1 price of a ticket. Let's assume lottery tickets are sold in the convenience store where I buy my coffee on the way to work every morning, and I have the computer automatically select a random number for me, so I accrue no tangible costs in either time (agonizing over which numbers to choose) or effort (getting to a place lottery tickets are sold) to buy a ticket in the first place, nor do I receive any noticeable psychic benefits from fantasizing about what I would do with the money if I won. If I choose to play, I either win $499 with some small probability p, or lose $1 with probability $1-p$. If I choose not to play, on the other hand, I have the status quo in my wallet with 100 percent certainty. There is little room for idiosyncratic beliefs in this choice, as the outcomes associated with each alternative are few and easy to determine, and the probabilities associated with each outcome are also simple to compute. My decision algorithm—and that of anyone else making the same decision—can be faithfully represented by table 2.2.

Table 2.2
Expected Value Analysis of Whether it is "Rational" to Play the Pick-3 Lottery

Multiple alternatives	Each associated with one or more outcomes	That have fixed Values to the decision-maker	Which may occur probabilistically	Expected value
A_1: Play	O_1: Win	$499	$P_{11} = .001$	$EV_1 = .001^*(\$499)$
	O_2: Lose	−$1	$P_{12} = .999$	$+ .999^*(-\$1) =$
	O_3: Status Quo	$0	$P_{13} = 0$	−50¢
A_2: Don't Play	O_1: Win	$499	$P_{21} = 0$	$EV_2 = \$0$
	O_2: Lose	−$1	$P_{22} = 0$	
	O_3: Status Quo	$0	$P_{23} = 1.0$	

Note. This example assumes that any nonmonetary values associated with the decision are so small they can be ignored.

This decision perfectly fits the general framework just laid out. For simplicity, table 2.2 ignores the differential importance column. There are multiple alternatives to choose from (Play, Don't Play), outcomes associated with each alternative (only one outcome, with certainty, for the second alternative; and two possible outcomes for the first, each associated with some uncertainty), and a value associated with each outcome (the amount of money I will win or lose). The expected value associated with 100 percent certainty with the second outcome is the status quo, or $0. There is uncertainty associated with the first alternative of playing the lottery, and the expected value of that alternative is the sum of the value of the first outcome (win $499), multiplied by its probability (.001), plus the expected value of the second outcome (lose $1) multiplied by *its* probability (.999). When you do the simple math, the expected value associated with playing this game is minus 50¢.[2] Rationally, then, no one should ever play the Pick-3 lottery, because it is a losing bet. If my choice about playing the lottery were to be described as (procedurally) "rational," I must follow the steps outlined here to reach my decision.

The most general expectancy-value theory is *subjective expected utility* (SEU) theory (von Neuman and Morgenstern, 1947; see also Luce & Raiffa, 1957; Raiffa, 1968; Savage, 1954). The concept of "utility" is a clever solution to a very tricky analytic problem, and it deserves some discussion.[3] The preceding decision of whether one should play the Pick-3 lottery was fairly simple because it was assumed the only values associated with any outcome were monetary. But consider just about any proposal a candidate might make during political campaign. Say Roger Republican is running against Debra Democrat for governor of my state, and he proposes a one-time, across-the-board $100 cut in state income taxes for all taxpayers in the state as a spur to the sluggish economy. If Roger's proposal becomes law, what would be its consequences for me?

- First, I would receive a reduction in taxes of $100. That is nice, that is a plus, I like it; all else equal, I would rather have $100 than not. Money is very tangible and easy to comprehend.
- At the same time, the state's revenue will be significantly less, at least in the short run, even if this proposal did stimulate the state's economy and thus generate additional revenue in the long term. This reduction probably would have some negative impact on my life, in terms of reduced state services from which I benefit. For example, the potholes in my streets may take longer to repair, there may be fewer police on the streets, and the science labs in my state's older schools might have to make due with outdated equipment for a little longer. This could then result in my having to have my car realigned more frequently, or a burglar alarm installed in my home, or even put my children in private schools. Although more long-term and harder to "see" precisely, I can still understand these costs in dollar terms, and they can figure into my decision.
- But what else will result from this tax cut? There certainly will be less money in the public till to help preserve open space in my state, a local issue that is very important to me. More development means more jobs but also more traffic, more pollution, and less "wilderness" around me. I could translate some of these results into consequences for my economic well-being, but that activity simply misses the point. My opposition is largely *symbolic* in nature and not translatable to some consequence for my pocketbook.
- And how about the poor in my state, who do not pay taxes and thus receive no immediate benefit, but who are undoubtedly much more dependent on state services than I am? I am not among them, but the problem has nothing to do with my material self-interest. I simply do not like the fact that I live in a state which tries to solve its economic hard times on the backs of the poor. Similarly, while the schools in my neighborhood have nice new science labs, those in the poorer areas of the state do not, and this bothers me because I think it is not fair, and wrong. Again, my opposition is largely symbolic in nature.

I could go on, but the point is, how can these various costs and benefits that I believe will occur if this proposed tax cut becomes law be combined in any rational manner into a decision? That is, dollars are easy to compare, but how can I weigh a $100 gain to my pocketbook against the various symbolic costs I will accrue if this tax cut becomes law? The problem is one of *incommensurability*—the inability to compare the various outcomes associated with this program. And the clever solution of subjective expected utility theory is to invent the hypothetical concept of subjective "utility" into which all costs and benefits can be translated. With this assumption, all values (i.e., utilities) become commensurable, and an expected value analysis can proceed. I can associate some positive utility with the $100, some negative utility with living in a state with deteriorating schools, real suffering by its poor, and less open space, and perform my calculations.

But would anyone actually do this? I know a lot about politics, and it was easy for me to generate the preceding list of potential costs and benefits of the Roger Republican's proposed tax cut. I could have easily come up with several more. But how much information about this policy should I try to learn? Rationally, I must seek out all relevant information.[4] Even assuming I have a "utility register" in my brain that can easily assign utilities to different outcomes, once there are more than a few outcomes or considerations to keep in mind, each weighed by some subjective probability of occurring, keeping track of the different calculations becomes quite challenging. And so far we are talking about only one alternative. If I were making a decision between Roger's proposal and some alternative plan(s), I would rationally have to seek out exactly the same relevant information about every other proposal under consideration. The calculation difficulties multiply rapidly. Worse yet, suppose I were deciding whether to vote for Roger or Debra in an upcoming election, and this tax cut proposal was one of a dozen different policies the candidates were debating during the campaign. Now the level of calculations required to make a "rational" decision becomes exponentially more difficult, particularly when we acknowledge that policy differences are only one dimension across which candidates can be compared. If people actually made decisions in this manner, they could be truly characterized as demonic in their cognitive abilities.

There are two issues here, one concerning ability, the second concerning motivation. Is it *possible* for the unaided decision-maker (i.e., one without a computer, or even a pencil and paper and a calculator) to make anything but the simplest decisions in the manner directed by the rational choice approach? Given the number of computations involved, and the limitations of working memory (see hereafter), the answer must be No. Okay, fine, but how about the "aided" decision-maker? The human race has, after all, had paper and writing implements (if not computers) available to it for several thousands of years. The answer now is probably yes—for the most part the computational demands are within reason, and the memory problem can be overcome by simply making lists of pluses and minuses associated with any alternative (e.g., Kelley & Mirer, 1974).[5]

But *would I* go to all this effort to make a decision? Here the issue of motivation arises, and it is a serious challenge to the rational choice approach. I *could*, probably, follow most of the dictates of subjective expected utility theory for arriving at a good decision about which candidate to support in an election, say—but why would I bother? It is a lot of work to learn everything I want to know about the competing candidates. And according to the theory, it is only rational for me to expend all of this effort if the expected value of making the correct vote choice is greater than the costs of all of this information gathering and computation. It is important to realize that we are not just trading off the greater expected utility to me of, say, Roger Republican winning rather than Debra Democrat against the information gathering and computation costs it takes for me to figure out which candidate to support. That utility could be substantial. But it must be weighed against the probability that my vote would determine the outcome of the election—and that probability is, for all practical purposes, nil. In other words, even if the difference in utilities associated with a Roger victory or a Debra victory is quite large, I am still going to receive one or the other of those utilities irrespective of what I do. Just as playing the Pick-3 lottery is always a losing bet, figuring out which candidate to vote for—indeed, going to the polls at all—is, according to the rational choice approach, an irrational activity. This argument can be pushed further (see for example Meehl, 1977), but the only way "rationality" can be saved is by adopting the economist's notion of "revealed preferences": because people *do* vote, we know the utility of voting must be greater than the costs. Thus notions like fulfilling one's "civic duty" are given great utility (Riker & Ordeshook, 1968). Unfortunately, this "solution" quickly makes the entire approach tautological.[6]

That so many people nonetheless do play the lottery every week, and do bother to vote, suggests either that many people are irrational or that the rational choice perspective is somehow flawed.[7] The flaw, I think, is not in assuming that people want to be rational, but in pretending that people actually make decisions in the way that they must if they are to ensure that they will make a value-maximizing decision. March (1994) captures this issue perfectly when he asks whether "decision makers pursue a logic of consequence, making choices among alternatives by evaluating their consequences in terms of prior preferences" (p. viii). A "logic of consequence" simply does not describe how people make the vast majority of the decisions they make in all aspects of their lives, including (but certainly not restricted to) the political realm.

The rational choice subjective expected utility approach need not—and should not—be applied as a behavioral description of how people (or organizations) actually make decisions. Nor should this limitation eliminate the most attractive aspects of the perspective, its strong normative component. If a decision-maker were to follow the dictates of the rational choice approach, he can rest assured that he will make what is, for him, the "best" decision. Given certain reasonable (but not indisputable) assumptions, such as maximizing the interests of the most people, the rationality of individual decision-making can also be "aggregated up" to make normative judgments about institutional arrangements for decision-making (see Jones, 1994).

▲ Behavioral Decision Theory

In contrast to the normative focus of classical decision theory, behavioral decision theory has always taken as its primary goal a description and understanding of how people actually make decisions. And every study of decision-making in the real world has shown that rarely are all alternatives known, all outcomes considered, or all values evoked at the same time. People generally settle for alternatives that are "good enough" rather than seeking out the value-maximizing alternative.

The behavioral decision theory approach begins with the view of humans as *limited information processors*, with neither the inclination nor the ability to make the sort of "consequential" calculations described by a rational choice perspective (Anderson, 1983; Hastie, 1986; Simon, 1979). The term "cognitive miser" was once popular to represent this view (Taylor, 1981), but that term is somewhat misleading in that it suggests a conscious hoarding of cognitive resources, which is simply inaccurate. "Bounded rationality," first coined by Simon (1947, 1957) is probably a better term to characterize human cognition.

Cognitive Limits on Rationality

But what, exactly, are the bounds or limits on information processing? Lupia, McCubbins, and Popkin (2000) complain that "Simon's bounded rationality offers little systematic guidance as to where the bounds of rationality are" (p. 10). I cannot imagine what Lupia and colleagues were thinking of when they wrote this, but the statement could not be more wrong. Charles Taber more thoroughly discusses bounded rationality in chapter 13, but let me highlight where some of the bounds on omniscient rationality occur. They can be categorized as limitations on processing and limitations on retrieval. Processing limitations begin with the physical orientations of our sense organs. Unlike Madeye-Moody, one of the succession of dark arts teachers at Harry Potter's wizarding school Hogwarts, human beings (a.k.a. muggles) do not have eyes that can see in all directions or ears that can distinguish more than one or two simultaneous sounds. Even limiting consideration to sights that are somehow before our eyes and sounds that are nearby, there is almost always more in our visual and auditory fields than can be processed because all incoming stimuli must pass through "short-term" or "working" memory, and short-term memory has a very limited capacity (of approximately 7, $\pm$ 2, bits of information; Miller, 1956). This bottleneck of short-term memory is in practice the most important "bound" on classic rationality. Its consequence is that *attention*, and factors that influence it, become crucially important to information processing. The limited nature of working memory also dictates that most information processing will occur serially, that is, one goal at a time.

Now, if incoming stimuli is processed by working memory—and again, that is a big *if*—it can be stored more or less permanently in long-term memory. Long-term memory is usually envisioned as an associative network of nodes and the connections between them that for all practical purposes has an unlimited capacity. Retrieval from long-term memory, on the other hand, is far from perfect and is a function of how the initial stimulus was processed (that is, what else it was associated with), preexisting memory structures (schemas) with which it could be associated, how often and how recently one has been exposed to the same stimuli (which influences the strength of the connections between nodes), and so on (see Anderson, 1983; Hastie, 1986; Simon, 1957, 1979; Smith, 1998). Limited retrieval from memory means that one of the fundamental assumptions of rational decision-making, that people have preexisting preferences for outcomes and that they are relatively *fixed* and immediately available, is frequently not going to be the case. Together, these cognitive limitations make the omniscient calculator of *homo economicus* an unapproachable ideal.

So How Do People Cope?

If humans have so many limitations on their information processing, how can they possibly cope with a world that can overwhelm the senses with incoming stimulation? People still want to make good decisions—they just cannot do so in the ideal manner described by rational choice. The answer is that human beings have developed a number of cognitive mechanisms or rules for dealing with information overload. These mechanisms are typically employed automatically without any conscious forethought. Most of these mechanisms are quite general and have ramifications for many aspects of human life. For example, *categorization* or grouping seems to be a basic property of human perception, such that when new stimuli are perceived, the first thing people try to do is categorize the stimuli as another instance of some familiar group (Cantor & Mischel, 1979; Rosch, 1978). A "schema" is a memory structure, a hierarchical organization of knowledge in a particular domain, which usually includes a category label, specific attributes of the stimulus domain, particular instances of the category, and links between all of these (Fiske & Taylor, 1991; Lau & Sears, 1986). Category- and schema-based processing are cognitively efficient because once a stimulus is perceived as another instance of some preexisting schema, the details of the new stimulus can be largely ignored and "default values" associated with the schema assumed to hold.[8] Conover and Feldman (1984, 1986, 1989) and Lodge (Hamill, Lodge, & Blake, 1985; Lodge & Hamill, 1986) provide many political examples of schema-based processing.

Turning to the topic of specific interest in this chapter, decision-makers seem to simplify their task in at least three fundamental ways: decomposition, editing, and heuristic use.

- *Decomposition* refers to breaking a decision down into its component parts, each of which are presumably easier to evaluate than the entire decision. A candidate running for some political office might try to devise a campaign strategy by making separate decisions about television advertising, personal appearances, and policy positions. Problem decomposition is closely related to the specialization and division of labor that is essential in any successful organization.
- *Editing* refers to simplifying a decision by eliminating (i.e., ignoring) relevant aspects of the decision. Voters might simplify their decision task by restricting attention to familiar candidates, thus effectively removing one or more alternatives from the choice set. "Single issue voters" limit the number of "outcomes" associated with each candidate that must be considered to a manageable number, thus also largely avoiding the need to resolve goal conflicts. A decision-maker could simply count the number of pluses and minuses associated with each alternative rather than trying to weight them by importance or devise an evaluative scale with more than two levels. All of these procedures would greatly simplify any decision.
- *Heuristics* are problem solving strategies (often employed automatically or unconsciously) that serve to "keep the information processing demands of the task within bounds" (Abelson & Levi, 1985, p. 255). They are cognitive shortcuts, rules of thumb for making certain judgments or inferences that are useful in decision-making with considerably less than the complete search for alternatives and the consequences associated with alternatives dictated by rational choice. Kahneman and Tversky (1972, 1973, 1984; Tversky & Kahneman, 1973, 1974) have identified three common cognitive heuristics that decision-makers employ in lieu of detailed information gathering and analysis, heuristics that allow decision-makers to simplify complex judgments by focusing attention on a small subset of all possible information. These heuristics include *availability*—judging frequency, probability, and causality by how accessible or available concrete examples are in memory, or how easy it is to generate a plausible scenario;[9] *representativeness*—assigning specific instances to specific categories (stereotypes, schemata) according to how well the particular instance fits or matches the essential properties of one category rather than another; and *anchoring and adjustment*—forming a tentative response and then adjusting by reviewing relevant data.

These three simplification mechanisms all help solve the problems of bounded rationality. These are very general mechanisms that are applied to many different types of decisions by all different types of people. We can adopt a Darwinian perspective and conclude that these simplifications must, in general, "work," in the sense of producing choices that are, if not optimal, at least "good enough" most of the time to encourage their reproduction—and rarely bad enough to lead to extinction. Nonetheless, it is important to recognize that all three of these simplification mechanisms can at times lead to poor decisions. Decomposition, for example, can lead to very embarrassing decisions when the components of a decision are treated as independent when in fact they are not. A candidate who stresses one set of policies in her personal appearances and another set of policies in her political advertisements at best puts forth a very diffuse and unfocused message and at worst can be caught espousing contradictory policies. Editing can lead to poor decisions when the ignored aspects of the decision would result, cumulatively, in a new preference order across alternatives if those ignored aspects had been considered. And heuristics can lead to systematic biases when the reason the heuristic is generally effective (e.g., more frequent occurrences really are easier to recall; numerical anchors provided by the decision context usually are reasonable) is not true in some particular instance.

Thus decision-makers face a real dilemma in coping with cognitive limitations. On the one hand, because we are not demonic omniscient calculators we simply *need* to develop some cognitive shortcuts, some means of simplifying decisions so that a choice can be made. Both information acquisition and information processing can be very costly in terms of time and cognitive effort. On the other hand, whatever shortcuts and simplifications we adopt also come with a potential cost: inaccurate judgments and something short of value-maximizing decisions. Thus I can make sense of many of the diverse findings in behavioral decision theory by suggesting that decision-makers are generally guided by two competing goals: (1) the desire to make a good decision; and (2) the desire to reach a decision with the minimal cognitive effort (see for example Hogarth, 1975; Payne, Bettman, & Johnson, 1993; Shugan, 1980; Wright, 1975).

This view leads to another important distinction between the rational choice and behavioral decision theory approaches. Rational choice focuses attention on the *structure* or *elements* of a decision—the multiple alternatives, and the value of the different outcomes that are associated, with some probability, with each alternative. Behavioral decision theories, in contrast, are much more likely to be concerned with the dynamic processes of *how decisions are made*, with information search and with strategies for making choices. Not surprisingly, behavioral decision theory researchers have developed methodologies that are particularly suited to observing decision-making, with the underlying assumption that the best way to study decision-making is to observe it while the decision is being made (Svenson, 1979). These *process tracing* methodologies keep track of what information was obtained and the order in which it was obtained to make inferences about the strategies employed in making the choice.

▶ Process Tracing Methodologies for Studying Decision-Making

Behavioral decision theorists have utilized two primary strategies for studying decisions "while they happen," verbal protocols and information boards. With verbal protocols, the decision-maker is asked to "think aloud" while she is making some decision, to vocalize "every passing thought" (Ericsson & Simon, 1984). The decision-maker is thus assumed to be able to report on the contents of working memory as a decision is being made.[10] Verbal protocols are an excellent technique for exploratory research, for developing models of how people go about making a particular type of decision. Because verbal reports are less easily quantifiable, however, verbal protocols are generally a less powerful technique for testing hypotheses.

The second major process tracing technique for studying decision-making is the information board (Carroll & Johnson, 1990). If studying verbal protocols resembles eavesdropping on a decision as it is being made, information boards are more like voyeurism. Information boards present subjects with some sort of matrix on a computer screen, where the alternatives under consideration are typically the columns of the matrix, and the different attributes of choice (i.e., the outcomes associated with every alternative) are the rows. The actual information is hidden from view (i.e., the cells of the matrix are blank), and decision-makers must *actively* decide to learn any specific bit of information by clicking on a particular cell of the matrix with a mouse. Every action the decision-maker takes is recorded by the computer, so that at the end there is a complete record of what the decision-maker accessed, how long every bit of information was considered, and the order in which every bit of information was examined.

Decision Strategies

A decision strategy is a set of mental and physical operations that an individual uses to reach a decision. In the most general sense, it includes identifying alternatives, searching for information about the possible outcomes associated with the different alternatives, making probabilistic judgments about the likelihood of those different outcomes, searching through memory to determine how much each of those outcomes is valued, and how important it is in this particular context, and so on. A decision strategy also includes a method for choosing among the alternatives. With process tracing methodologies it is possible to observe decision strategies in action.

Behavioral decision theory researchers have identified a number of different decision strategies or "rules" that can be used by decision-makers to reach a decision. These strategies differ in terms of how cognitively difficult they are to use, how much of the available information they consider, and their likelihood of reaching a "best" decision. I will refer to strategies that employ all available information as decision *rules* and those that ignore some information as decision *heuristics*.

The major way decision strategies are categorized in the behavioral decision theory literature is by the extent to which they confront or avoid conflict (Billings & Marcus, 1983; Ford, Schmitt, Schechtman, Hults, & Doherty, 1989). When one alternative is preferred on one dimension of judgment but a different alternative is preferred on another dimension of judgment, the potential for value conflict or tradeoffs exists.[11]

- *Compensatory* strategies are cognitively complex information integration rules where decision-makers are assumed to assign a value to every-attribute associated with each alternative. Some of those values can be positive and others negative, but when they are combined into an overall evaluation or decision, a positive value on one dimension can *compensate for* or trade off against a negative value on another dimension. Conflict is confronted and resolved in the process of integrating the positive and negative information or values associated with a choice. Compensatory strategies require commensurable outcomes or values. To avoid confusion, we should employ the term "utility."
- *Noncompensatory* strategies, on the other hand, rely on incomplete information search to avoid conflicts. Negative values on one attribute or possible outcome cannot trade off against positive values on another attribute or outcome; instead, alternatives are usually eliminated once negative information about them is obtained. Incommensurability typically is not a problem.

A great deal of research has shown that most decision-makers, most of the time, try to avoid value tradeoffs (Hogarth, 1987; Jervis, 1976). But again this avoidance has a cost: potentially less accurate decisions. I review some of the major decision strategies here.

Compensatory Decision Strategies

The *weighted additive rule* (WAdd) and the *expected utility rule* (EU) are both formal variants of rational choice and are thus often considered normative standards. They both suggest that decision-makers evaluate each alternative according to the utilities of all relevant attributes or outcomes associated with it, form an overall evaluation of each alternative, and then choose the most highly evaluated one. A linear regression model would be a perfect example of such a strategy. The WAdd rule assumes that decision-makers further consider the relative importance of each attribute, whereas EU assumes that decision-makers consider the probability that each outcome will occur. Hence they both involve great cognitive complexity. Both of these rules assume that conflicts are explicitly confronted and resolved via the different weights or probabilities.

The *equal weights heuristic* (EqW) is a simplified version of WAdd and

EU where all the weights and/or probabilities are assumed to equal 1.0. It is considerably less complex than either WAdd or EU, although the rule still assumes that all relevant attributes are considered about every alternative and that conflicts are confronted and reconciled. Because of the information that is ignored (i.e., importance weights and probabilities), the EqW rule should not be quite as likely as either WAdd or EU to reach the value-maximizing decision, although several researchers have argued that in practice, EqW is nearly as accurate as WAdd and EU (Dawes, 1979; Einhorn & Hogarth, 1975).

The *frequency of good and bad features heuristic* (FreqGB) is an even simpler strategy that ignores not only importance weights and probabilities but also fine discriminations of utility (Alba & Marmorstein, 1987). Every attribute of judgment is assumed to have only two levels, good and bad, and decision-makers are assumed to simply count up the number of good and bad features associated with each alternative. Any problems with incommensurability disappear.

The *additive difference rule* (AddDif) is logically equivalent to the Add model. Here decision-makers are assumed to compare alternatives one attribute at a time and to calculate and retain the differences between alternatives. As with WAdd, all information is assumed to be considered, and the differences are weighed in terms of their relative importance to the decision-maker. If more than two alternatives are available this decision rule is exceedingly complex, but Aschenbrenner, Bockenholt, Albert, and Schmalhofer (1986) have suggested a more plausible variant of this rule where alternatives are considered two at a time, with the losing alternative eliminated and the winning alternative compared in a pairwise manner to a third alternative, and so one, until the best alternative is determined.

The *majority of confirming dimensions heuristic* (MCD) is a simplified version of the AddDif procedure, where alternatives are compared in a pairwise fashion on every dimension of judgment, but those comparisons only result in a judgment of which alternative is preferred. The alternative with a majority of winning or "confirming" judgments is retained and compared to another alternative. This procedure continues until all alternatives have been considered.

Noncompensatory Decision Strategies

The *satisficing heuristic* (SAT) is one of the first and most famous decision heuristics identified in the behavioral decision theory literature (Simon, 1957). It assumes that decision-makers set aspiration levels for every attribute of judgment they care about, and considering alternatives one at a time in random order, keep searching until an alternative is discovered that meets or exceeds the aspiration level for every criteria. Search then stops and this alternative is chosen. If no such alternative is found, aspiration levels must be lowered and the process repeated until an alternative that "satisfies" all criteria is found. Because a chosen alternative must satisfy the criterion on the first attribute *and* the second attribute *and* the third attribute, and so on, strategies such as SAT are sometimes called conjunctive strategies. Satisficing involves relatively simple cognitive processes. Conflict and incommensurability are avoided by seeking an alternative that is satisfactory on every criterion of judgment, and by *not* comparing the alternatives to each other. Indeed, some alternatives may be totally ignored, and there is no guarantee that anything approaching the "best" alternative will be selected. Obviously the order in which alternatives are considered can completely determine which alternative is selected.

The *lexicographic heuristic* (LEX) considers the value of every alternative on the most important attribute of judgment, and selects the alternative with the highest value (Tversky, 1969). If two or more alternatives are tied for the highest value, the remaining alternatives are compared on the second most important attribute, and so on until only one remains.[12] The LEX rule can involve fairly complex cognitive processes if there are many alternatives in the choice set, but it produces cognitive savings by restricting the number of attributes under consideration to a relative few. Conflict is avoided by considering attributes one at a time and eliminating alternatives that are not the best on the attribute under consideration. Any incommensurability across attributes is not a problem. Again there is no guarantee that the "best" decision will be reached, as an alternative that is not quite as good as another alternative on the most important criterion might be far superior to it on every other criterion. In practice, however, if a decision-maker's preferences are structured in a conventional manner (a voter has consistently liberal or conservative positions on a set of policy issues, say) and the alternatives are similarly structured in a stereotypic manner (the Democratic candidates takes mostly liberal positions, the Republican mostly conservative ones), the LEX rule will usually select the "correct" alternative. (See Lau & Redlawsk, 2001a, for an instance where this is not the case.)

The *elimination-by-aspects heuristic* (EBA) is a combination of satisficing and the lexicographic strategies and generally simpler than both of them (Tversky, 1972). As with LEX, decision-makers are assumed to rank the attributes of judgment in terms of importance, and consider the most important attribute first. As with SAT, decision-makers are assumed to have something like an aspiration level of every attribute, and alternatives are eliminated if they do not meet or exceed the aspiration level. The procedure continues with additional attributes of judgment in decreasing order of importance until only one alternative remains. Like SAT and LEX, EBA avoids conflicts by eliminating alternatives before conflicts occur.

The preceding descriptions of different decision strategies are idealized accounts, of course, and would rarely be observed in such pure states.[13] One may well ask, then, How can you tell which strategy a decision-maker is using? A very important finding of much behavioral decision theory research is that different patterns of information acquisition clearly reflect distinguishable choice strategies. Thus a key to understanding any decision is observing how people acquire information, because this in turn sheds light on the decision rules or heuristics that people follow in making their choices.

Measures of Information Search

Information boards provide a large amount of detailed information about the process of decision-making, particularly information search. If decision-makers are omniscient calculators who seek out and process all relevant information, the order in which information is acquired is irrelevant. But if decision makers are limited information processors who almost certainly will make a decision before all possible information has been obtained, then the order of information acquisition can be crucially important. It should be obvious that how much information is obtained can influence choice. Somewhat less obviously, even controlling on amount of information, *how* information comes to a decision-maker can also influence choice. As summarized in table 2.3, each of the decision strategies just discussed specifies a particular depth and order of information search. Thus if we can develop standard measures of information search, they can be used to infer which decision strategy is being employed.

Consider first the depth of information search. Rationally, all relevant information about every alternative should be obtained. In practice it rarely is, but with information boards it is easy to calculate the proportion of all alternatives that are considered, the proportion of all attributes that are considered, the proportion of all possible information about every alternative that is considered, and so on—all reasonable measures of the depth of information search. All of the compensatory decision strategies just considered assume that all relevant information about every alternative will be considered, and thus that search will be relatively deep. Each of the non-compensatory strategies allow for much shallower search, although the choice set and aspiration levels could be such that all information must be considered before a satisfactory alternative is found, or all but one alternative eliminated.

We can also consider the sequence of information acquisition. Irrespective of how much information is gathered, the search sequence can be relatively ordered, or largely haphazard. With information boards it can be studied formally with a "transition analysis" (Jacoby, Chestnut, Weigl, & Fischer, 1976). *Ordered search* is of two types, as follows.

- With *alternative-based* search (more formally, intraalternative, interattribute), sometimes also called holistic search, decision-makers consider the different alternatives sequentially. A voter following this search strategy would learn about the issue stands, political experience, personal values, and whatever else he considered important

Table 2.3
Characteristics of Different Decision Strategies

Decision rule	Type	Depth of search	Variance of search	Sequence of search	Cognitive effort
Weighted additive rule (WAdd) or expected utility rule (EU)	Compensatory	Very deep	Equal	Alternative-based	Very high
Equal weights heuristic (EqW)	Compensatory	Deep	Equal	Alternative-based	Moderately high
Frequency of good and bad features heuristic (FreqGB)	Compensatory	Deep	Equal	Alternative-based	Moderate
Additive difference rule (AddDif)	Compensatory	Very deep	Equal	Attribute-based	Very high
Majority confirming dimensions heuristic (MCD)	Compensatory	Deep	Equal	Attribute-based	Moderately high
Satisficing heuristic (SAT)	Noncompensatory	Depends: shallow to deep	Generally unequal	Alternative-based	Moderately low
Lexicographic heuristic (LEX)	Noncompensatory	Generally shallow	Generally unequal	Attribute-based	Moderately low
Elimination-by-aspects heuristic (EBA)	Noncompensatory	Generally shallow	Generally unequal	Attribute-based	Low

about one candidate in an election, before trying to learn the same information about a second candidate, and so on, until all of the competing candidates were explored. WAdd, EU, EqW, FreqGB, and SAT all assume alternative-based searching.

- With *attribute-based* search (intraattribute, interalternative), sometimes also called dimensional search, a decision-maker chooses one attribute for consideration and compares the values of all competing candidates on that issue, before turning to another attribute and comparing all of the competing alternatives on it. AddDif, MCA, LEX, and EBA all assume attribute-based searching.

Haphazard search then is everything else—interattribute, interalternative transitions.[14]

Most research with decision boards considers the relative proportion of alternative-based to attribute-based search, with the latter usually being considered cognitively easier (Russo & Dosher, 1983; Rahn, 1993). This focus obscures the larger point that either type of ordered search must be much simpler, cognitively, than haphazard search. When information acquisition is completely under the decision-maker's control, as it is with decision boards, the great majority of all transitions are ordered, as I have defined them (Jacoby, Jaccard, Kuss, Troutman, & Mazursky, 1987; Payne & Braunstein, 1978), reflecting the decision-maker's overriding goal of minimizing cognitive effort. Ordered information can be processed and stored more efficiently, and it should be a big aid to decision-making. When information acquisition is not entirely controllable, however, the sequence in which information becomes available, the structure of that information in the environment, and the decision-maker's ability to at least partially restructure that sequence in some coherent manner can have important effects on decision-making, even changing preferences among alternatives (Tversky & Sattath, 1979).

The various decision strategies make specific statements not only about the depth and order of information search but also about the variance of information search across alternatives. The various compensatory strategies all assume that the same information should be considered about every alternative, whereas the three noncompensatory strategies all allow for unequal search across alternatives. Thus the within-subject *variance* in the amount of information considered about each alternative is another way to distinguish between choice strategies. Compensatory strategies dictate equal variance, while noncompensatory strategies allow for unequal search. Variance measures are particularly useful in distinguishing between decision strategies when task constraints (e.g., time) make it impossible for all information to be considered.

Comparable alternatives are those about which the same attribute information is known, as is always possible with a standard information board. *Noncomparable alternatives,* on the other hand, are those with at least some attributes that are unique to each alternative (Johnson, 1984, 1986). Alternatives can be *inherently* noncomparable—guns versus butter, say—or de facto noncomparable because of information about some alternatives that exists but is unknown to the decision-maker. Rationally, information that is available about some but not all alternatives should be ignored in making a choice—but I suspect it rarely is. Instead, people use what information they have and whenever possible make category-based inferences about the missing information. More generally, however, the possibility (probability, in most instances) of incomplete search of available information means that virtually any decision could involve noncomparable alternatives.

▶ Determinants of Choice Strategies— Deciding How to Decide

Having described a number of different decision strategies, and various means of determining when a particular strategy is being employed, it is worth asking whether these strategies are available to and used by almost everyone, or if instead different people tend to specialize in the use of one or another strategy, employing it for many different types of decisions. Asked differently, are there some people who tend to be very rational and methodical in their decision-making, while others typically employ more intuitive and heuristic-based decision strategies? The broad answer to this question is that there is little evidence for systematic individual differences in use of these different strategies. Instead, almost all people seem to have available a wide variety of different decision strategies that they can and do employ in making decisions. Choice of decision strategy seems to be highly contingent on the nature of the decision task (Payne, Bettman, & Johnson, 1993). Hence research in behavioral decision theory, rather than searching for individual differences in decision-making, has instead focused on situational or contextual factors that make it more likely that one or another strategy will be employed.[15] I will highlight several of these factors here.

One very important set of factors involve the complexity or size of the decision task. Task complexity is usually defined in terms of the number of alternatives under consideration and the number of different attributes across which they vary, with the general finding being that people rely more heavily on simplifying decision heuristics the more complex the task. This is true for both variation in the number of alternatives (Biggs, Bedard, Gaber, & Linsmeier, 1985; Billings & Marcus, 1983; Klayman, 1985; Lau & Redlawsk, 2001b; Olshavsky, 1979; Payne, 1976) and the number of attributes under consideration (Jacoby, Speller, & Kohn, 1974; Keller & Staelin, 1987; Malhotra, 1982), although the former seems to have much more consistent effects than the latter. Generally speaking, decision-makers rely on noncompensatory decision strategies when there are more than two alternatives, but they may use more compensatory strategies if there are only two alternatives (Einhorn, 1970; Tversky, 1972).

There are additional factors that can affect the difficulty of the choice facing decision-makers, holding task size constant. One such factor that can characterize many political decisions is time pressure, which could shift a decision-maker's goals from accuracy to efficiency. Thus decision-makers faced with time pressure may accelerate processing (that is, work faster); reduce the total amount of information considered, focusing on the most important factors; or change decision strategies, shifting from a compensatory to a noncompensatory strategy (Ben Zur & Breznitz, 1981; Holsti, 1989; Holsti & George, 1975; Payne, Bettman, & Johnson, 1988). Another factor that affects task complexity is the similarity of the alternatives to each other. When alternatives are very dissimilar, it is relatively easy to distinguish between them and choose the best one. A noncompensatory choice strategy might very well lead to a different choice than a compensatory strategy, however. When alternatives are relatively similar to each other, it is much more difficult to find the best alternative (Lau & Redlawsk, 2001). Depth of search should increase (Bockenholt, Albert, Aschenbrenner, & Schmalhofer, 1991), and decision-makers may be more likely to employ a compensatory decision strategy (Biggs et al., 1985). On the other hand, it usually doesn't matter very much if one picks the second- or third-best alternative if they are all very similar to each other.

It is reasonable to hypothesize that the more important the decision is to the decision-maker, the more she will be motivated by decision accuracy rather than decision ease, and the greater will be the effort expended in making the decision (Payne et al., 1993). Thus information search should be deeper, and compensatory decision strategies are more likely to be employed (Lindberg, Garling, & Montgomery, 1989). This reasoning assumes that deeper information search leads to better decisions, a conclusion that is easy to reach granted omniscient rationality and demonic abilities but may not actually hold for limited information processors. Indeed, Gigerenzer & Goldstein (1999; Czerlinski, Gigerenzer, and Goldstein, 1999) have demonstrated at least some instances when additional information actually results in lower-quality judgments.

Variations in how information is displayed or becomes available have also been shown to affect decision-making. The alternatives-by-attributes matrix of a standard information board provides an ideal world where all information is organized and easily available to decision-makers. But information about real decisions rarely becomes available in such an orderly, controllable manner. Obviously, if information is displayed about alternatives sequentially, the decision-maker has little choice but to engage in alternative-based decision strategies, while simultaneous presentation of information about several alternatives makes attribute-based search possible (Tversky, 1969). More subtle variations of information display can also make alternative-based or attribute-based processing more likely (e.g., Herstein, 1981) and even determine whether particular information is utilized at all (Russo, 1977). During an election campaign, watching a rally or speech or party convention for a single candidate provides primarily alternative-based information; a political debate, on the other hand, provides largely attribute-based information (Rahn, Aldrich, & Borgida, 1994). The *completeness* of the information display—that is, whether the same information is available about every alternative—determines whether inferences about the missing data are necessary (Ford & Smith, 1987) but can also influence whether information "outside of the box" is even considered in making the decision (Fischhoff, Slovic, & Lichtenstein, 1978).

Finally, there is a great deal of research in behavioral decision theory on *response mode* effects, that is, whether a choice among, a ranking of, or an evaluation of different alternatives is required. This topic has received so much research because different response modes can lead to preference reversals, which violates one of the fundamental propositions of rational choice, that of *procedure invariance*—that strategically equivalent ways of eliciting a preference should reveal the same preference (Tversky, Sattath, & Slovic, 1988). The leading explanations for the observed preference reversals have to do with processing differences associated with the different response modes. The need to evaluate alternatives leads to alternative-based searching and more quantitative thinking, while choosing among alternatives leads to more attribute-based searching and more qualitative thinking (Fischer & Hawkins, 1993; Lichtenstein & Slovic, 1971; Tversky, 1969; Tversky et al., 1988).

This research is yet another reason to distinguish between decision-making and judgment, but it is one that has largely been ignored in political science. Could the processes by which citizens form evaluations of their leaders—for example, judging how good a job the president has been doing—be fundamentally different from how they choose among candidates in an election? Virtually all political science models of the vote decision involve overall liking of the candidates and/or performance evaluations as crucial components, yet such judgments might have little to do with how most people decide how to vote.[16] I will conclude this chapter by turning attention explicitly to the most fundamental decision that citizens in a democracy make on a regular basis—the vote choice.

Studying the Vote Decision

When political scientists have attempted to understand individual vote decisions, they have almost universally turned to the sample survey as their methodology of choice (e.g., Campbell, Converse, Miller, & Stokes, 1960; Fiorina, 1981; Kelley & Mirer, 1974; Lazarsfeld, Berelson, & Gaudet, 1948; Markus & Converse, 1979; Miller & Shanks, 1998; Nie, Verba, & Petrocik, 1976). Surveys do an excellent job of recording what decision was made (e.g., Are you going to vote in the upcoming election? Which candidate do you support?), but they are a poor vehicle for studying *how* that decision was reached. For most respondents, surveys ask about opinions or decisions that were reached some time in the past, and thus the information provided is based on respondents' memories. Moreover, the reasons people provide on surveys for why they might vote for or against one or another candidate have been shown to be justifications of a decision already reached rather than a veridical representation of the information that went into that decision (Lau, 1982; Rahn, Krosnick, & Breuning, 1994). A very popular model of candidate impression suggests that people keep an "on-line running tally" or summary evaluation of familiar candidates in their heads, which they update whenever new information is encountered, but forgetting the details of that new information (Lodge, McGraw, & Stroh, 1989;

Lodge, Steenbergen, & Broh, 1995). Indeed, people are notoriously poor at providing the reasons for their own actions, even those in the recent past (Nisbett & Wilson, 1977). Memory, then, usually provides a poor trace of how a decision was reached.

The shortcomings of the sample survey for studying how decisions are made suggests that researchers must look elsewhere, and the process tracing methodologies described earlier seem an obvious starting point. A few researchers have already provide some evidence on the vote decision from experiments based on information boards (Herstein, 1981; Huang, 2000; Riggle & Johnson, 1996). Yet in many ways, a standard information board provides a poor analog to a political campaign. With a decision board the decision-maker can access any information any time he wants, while campaigns have a dynamic quality about them such that information easily available today might be harder to find tomorrow and almost completely gone by the following day. All information on a standard information board is equally easy to access, while in a political campaign certain types of information (e.g., hoopla and horse race) are much easier to find than others (e.g., detailed issue stands). Decision-makers must actively choose to learn everything they find out about the alternatives with a standard information board, but much information during political campaigns (e.g., political commercials) comes to us without any active effort by the decision-maker to learn that information. And, most important, decision-making with an information board is far too "manageable," too controllable, too easy; while during a typical high-level political campaign (e.g., presidential elections and many statewide races), voters are overwhelmed by far more information than they can possibly process. In many ways the static information board represents an "ideal world" for decision-making that can be contrasted to voting in an actual political campaign.

There is an epistemological argument for studying any phenomenon in a simplified, ideal state (Henshel, 1980), and the tradeoffs between internal and external validity with any methodology are well known (Campbell & Stanley, 1963). David Redlawsk and I have sought a middle ground for studying the vote decision, trying to devise a more ecologically valid research technique that would better approximate the realities of modern political campaigns while still providing the experimental control and detailed evidence on information search that is available from a traditional information board (Lau, 1995; Lau & Redlawsk, 1992, 1997, 2001a, 2001b; Redlawsk, 2001). To accomplish these goals we have designed a dynamic process tracing methodology, which retains the most essential features of the standard information board while making it a better analog of an actual political campaign. This new methodology has the information boxes scroll down a computer screen rather than sitting in a fixed location. If a standard information board is artificial because it is static and therefore too "manageable," our procedure overwhelms subjects (voters) with information. If the standard information board is unrealistic by making all information available whenever a subject wants it, we mimic the ongoing flow of information during a campaign with the scrolling, where information available today might be much harder to find tomorrow. If the standard information board is artificial because all different types of information are equally available, our procedure models in a realistic way the relative ease or difficulty of finding different types of information during a campaign. And if a standard information board only allows for information that is actively accessed by the decision-makers, we provide voters with a good deal of relevant information "free of charge" in the form of campaign advertisements that occasionally take over the computer screen without any active decision on the voter's part to learn that information. Our research program aims to discover which of the various findings of the behavioral decision theory literature apply to voting during political campaigns. A forthcoming book provides an overview of this research (Lau & Redlawsk, in preparation).

Methodology aside, elections have typically been studied by historians, journalists, and political scientists, all of whom are chiefly concerned with which candidate or which party won the most votes. Such a focus is understandable, and quite appropriate. Yet there is another way to look at the vote decision that is more compatible with a behavioral decision theory perspective: Did the voter choose *correctly*—that is, did the voter select the candidate who, in some normative sense, and from the voter's own perspective, was the best one? This is the primary focus of my and Redlawsk's (1997, 2001a) research, and I would hope this question could become the concern of many political psychologists.

I do not have the space to go into much detail in discussing how voters decide how to vote, and I will only try to sketch out the most important features. I want to briefly describe seven heuristics or cognitive shortcuts that I believe people utilize in making vote decisions. These heuristics provide great cognitive efficiency while probably still yielding reasonably accurate decisions most of the time. I say "probably" because there is in fact little empirical research addressing how people go about making a vote decision and how likely they are to choose the candidate who, for them, is best. Thus the use of these seven cognitive shortcuts should better be considered testable hypotheses rather than statements of fact.

> *Affect referral* (Wright, 1975): If an election involves several candidates with whom you are already quite familiar, vote for the most highly evaluated candidate. This heuristic can only be used for candidates who have been around for multiple elections, but it could be used in a general election campaign if voters have already formed impressions of the candidates from primary elections.
>
> *Endorsements*: Follow the recommendations of close acquaintances, trusted political elites (Carmines & Kuklinski, 1990; Mondak, 1993; Sniderman, Brody, & Tetlock, 1991), or social groups (Brady & Sni-

derman, 1985; Lau & Redlawsk, 2001a; Sniderman et al., 1991) with whom one identifies. In other words, let someone else do the hard work of figuring out how to vote.

Familiarity (Gigerenzer & Goldstein 1999): If you have heard of one candidate but not any of the others, and your evaluation of that one candidate is neutral or better, vote for the candidate with whom you are already familiar. This heuristic is a variant of Tversky and Kahneman's (1973) availability heuristic. It is probably the most important explanation of the powerful incumbency effects that characterize most legislative elections.

Habit: Vote how you voted the last time. Make a "standing decision" (e.g., always vote Republican) and stick to it (Quadrel, 1990).

Apply *partisan and ideological schemata* (Conover & Feldman, 1986, 1989; Hamill, Lodge, & Blake, 1985; Lau & Redlawsk, 2001a; Lodge & Hamill, 1986; Rahn, 1993; Sniderman, Hagen, Tetlock, & Brady, 1986): When you are relatively unfamiliar with the candidates in an election, categorize them according to widely available political schemata, assume schema-consistent detailed (default) information, and apply category-based affect (Fiske & Pavelchak, 1986). Voting one's party identification is probably the most important reason for a vote choice (in partisan elections, for the large majority of people with some partisan leanings), particularly if you include the indirect effect of partisanship on selective exposure and selective evaluation.

Likewise, apply *person stereotypes* concerning gender, race, age, appearance, and so on to "flesh out" your impression of the candidates (Fiske & Taylor, 1991; Miller, Wattenberg, & Malanchuk, 1986; Riggle, Ottati, Wyer, Kuklinski, & Schwartz, 1992; Rosenberg, Kahn, & Tran, 1991). Stereotype- and/or schema-based inferences are applications of Kahneman and Tversky's (1972) representativeness heuristic.

Viability (Aldrich, 1980; Bartels, 1988; Lau & Redlawsk, 2001a): Only consider candidates who have a good chance of winning.

Although most citizens in almost all democracies feel it is sufficiently important to participate in politics that they get to the polls at least some of the time, still it should be obvious that the vote decision is not nearly as momentous to most people as buying a house or a car, deciding what college to attend, who to marry, where to work, and so on. Thus we must assume that the goal of efficiency rather than accuracy will dominate the decision strategies of most voters. Hence some noncompensatory decision strategy will almost certainly be applied. This tendency should be particularly strong in multiple (i.e., more than two) candidate elections. A simplified compensatory strategy is more feasible in a two-candidate election. And of course combined strategies are very possible—for example, beginning with a noncompensatory heuristic like viability, and then switching to some simplified compensatory strategy such as the EqW heuristic or the FreqGB heuristic. Table 2.4 summarizes this reasoning.

We also should consider how the political information environment typically structures information. I know of no hard data on this point, but I will tentatively assert that the great bulk of all political information concerning elections becomes available in a candidate-centered format, thus almost requiring alternative-based searching. Citizens can actively choose to process more or less of that candidate-centered information, but attribute-based information—for example, charts in newspapers comparing the candidates' stands on selected issues—is much harder to come by (Lodge, Steenbergen, & Brau, 1995; Rahn, Aldrich, & Borgida, 1994). This is an important area for future research.

◣ Conclusion

This chapter began by considering the classic, rational choice perspective on decision-making and suggested that a more behaviorally oriented approach based on a view of humans as limited information processors was a more useful and accurate perspective. I have tried to shape my review of

Table 2.4
A General Procedural Framework for Analyzing Political Decision-Making

Problem determination and preliminary information search	Do I have a standard or simple way to decide?	If not, how can I simplify this decision?	Is accuracy sufficiently important that I must employ a more complicated strategy?
Is this problem familiar or new?	Affect referral	Endorsements	Compensatory strategy (EqW, FreqGB, MCD)
	Familiarity heuristic	Person stereotypes	to reach final decision
Is it relatively simple or complex?	Habit	Political schemata	
How important is it to make an accurate decision?		Viability	
		Use noncompensatory decision strategy (SAT, LEX, EBA) to eliminate alternatives and/or attributes	

the behavioral decision theory literature in a manner that highlights issues that should be of use to political psychologists. The focus on description in the behavioral decision theory literature can leave the casual reader of summaries of that literature (e.g., Abelson & Levi, 1985; Dawes, 1998; Einhorn & Hogarth, 1981; Hastie, 2001; Mellers, Schwartz, & Cooke, 1998; Payne, Bettman, & Johnson, 1992; Pitz & Sachs, 1984; Slovic, Fischoff, & Lichtenstein, 1977) with a view more of the trees than the forest. I have tried to provide a map of the forest rather than describe all the trees, because the latter obscure the fact that while the process of making a decision is much more varied than the single ideal procedure suggested by the rational choice approach, it is still far from random (Jacoby et al., 1987). The regularities in human behavior are what social scientists must study, and there are more than enough in the decision-making field to go around.

One topic that is largely absent from this chapter is any discussion of the role of emotions or motivation on decision-making. My focus in this chapter has been on the rational choice and behavioral decision theory literatures, and there is very little research in either of those fields on emotions or motivations—except for the overarching motivation of self-interest that the rational choice perspective presumes universally guides behavior. I suspect this will change, and one can point to at least two areas in political science where it already has: the study of "motivational biases" in foreign policy decision-making (Janis & Mann, 1977; Jervis, 1976, 1985; again, see chapter 8); and the work of Marcus, MacKuen, & Neuman on the role of emotions on political behavior (Marcus, 1988; Marcus & MacKuen, 1993; Marcus, Neuman, & MacKuen, 2000). I do not have the space here to adequately address this topic, and motivational biases are discussed in chapter 8. The gist of Markus's argument is that the emotional system, particularly anxiety, can provide the increased motivation for more thorough (procedurally rational) information processing and decision-making. As such, it influences answers to questions in the first stage of the general model presented in table 2.4.

I will conclude this chapter by addressing whether rational choice and behavioral decision theory approaches could ever be reconciled. At some level, it is fairly easy to integrate the notion of bounded rationality into a rational choice perspective. Information costs have been recognized as an integral part of the approach (e.g., Downs, 1957; Fiorina, 1981). Bounded rationality provides a more complete understanding, not only in terms of the costs of gathering the information but also in terms of the costs of utilizing it once it has been gathered. More recent versions of rational choice view decision-makers as "intendedly rational," as doing the best they can under the circumstances and with acknowledged cognitive limitations. Jones (1994) and Lupia et al. (2000) seem to adopt this position. I think this reconciliation misses the boat (see also Simon, 1985). Sometimes people *are* intendedly rational; but much more often they make decisions automatically or semiautomatically with no conscious consideration or how or why they are choosing as they are. The view of decision-makers as "omniscient calculators," even as an ideal, should probably be dropped: it can be misleading, when people confuse "ought" with "is," and a consequence set unrealistically high standards (Lau & Redlawsk, 1997). But the normative concerns of a rational choice approach are important, and the guidelines of procedural rationality are worthwhile standards for making good decisions. Rather than intendedly rational behavior, however, I would characterize most decision-making—and certainly most political decision-making—as *semiautomatic rule following*, with any conscious deliberation focused on determining which heuristic it is appropriate to apply rather than value-maximization.

I would echo Kahneman (1994) in arguing that rather than asking *whether* decisions are rational or not, or revising our definition of "rationality" so that it can include more actual choice behavior, a better question for future decision research to address is *under what conditions* decision-makers are at least "reasonably" rational in their decision processes;[17] and when they are not, what cognitive shortcuts or heuristics do they employ in lieu of thorough information search and value-maximizing choice strategies, and what consequences do those strategies hold for the quality of the decisions that are made? People can, and often do, follow a logic of consequence, if not omnisciently, at least reasonably, given their cognitive limitations. And people can, and often do, make many decisions automatically, by unconsciously following well-learned rules for making decisions. The question that political psychologists should consider is not whether people are always or ever procedurally rational in their decision processes but what they do when they are not, and what effect it has on the quality of the decision that is reached.

▲ Notes

I would like to thank Jamie Druckman, Jack Levy, Kathleen McGraw, David Redlawsk, and the editors for comments on an earlier draft of this manuscript, which was written while I was a fellow at the Center for the Study of Democratic Politics at Princeton University. I am indebted to the Center's director, Larry Bartels, and Princeton University and Rutgers University, for providing support for this research.

1. When people refer to a "best" or "ideal" solution, they usually mean the value-maximizing alternative. The rational choice approach also assumes that decision-makers follow a number of formal mathematical principles in making their probability judgments and value assessments, including regularity, independence from irrelevant alternatives, transitivity, procedure invariance, dominance, and all the dictates of Bayes's theorem. Although these principals can sound intimidating, for the most part they are quite logical and intuitive, and are widely accepted by decision-makers when they are explained. Dawes (1988) summarizes these principals more simply by saying that a decision can be considered "rational" if it is (1) based on the status quo of current assets such that losses or foregone gains are equivalent; (2) based on all possible/ plausible

outcomes associated with the choice; and (3) where uncertainty is involved, does not violate any of the basic rules of probability.

2. Notice that −50¢ is never a value associated with any outcome that ever occurs when choosing to play the lottery. When outcomes are uncertain, expected value takes on an "in the long run" meaning: if one plays the Pick-3 lottery over and over again, on average you will lose 50¢ for every time you play.

3. Economists contrast "utility" to straightforward numeric value, because most people view the difference between $0 and $100 to be much greater than the difference between $10,000 and $10,100. Thus the "subjective utility" curve for increased wealth is concave (i.e., sloping downward). This is an important empirical refinement, but its implications are much narrower in scope than the incommensurability problem I discuss hereafter. The real advantage of von Neuman and Morgenstern's subjective expected utility theorem to economists, however, is its method for turning ordinal preferences into cardinal utility functions, which then allows much more powerful mathematics to come into play.

The implications of *this* change are huge, for it is the basis of most of modern microeconomics, and it has allowed the development of game theory. The SEU theorem begins by assuming away incommensurability.

4. "Relevance" is again typically defined subjectively, as including everything I "care" about that is affected by this policy. Many rational choice models, most notably Downs (1957), consider the cost of gathering information as a means of limiting the burdens on the decision-maker. Such models can be viewed as "optimization under constraints." New information should be gathered until the marginal costs of additional information exceed the marginal returns from that information. Although considering information costs seems at first glance a plausible way of limiting cognitive effort, in fact any stopping rule actually takes more cognitive effort to employ (Gigerenzer & Todd, 1999; Vriend, 1996). In practical terms, information search—data gathering—is probably the most effortful and influential aspect of decision-making, yet it is outside the realm of many rational choice models.

5. From an evolutionary perspective, the availability of ink and paper for several thousand years would not be anywhere near long enough for the human brain to have adapted accordingly. Thus, functionally speaking, the brains we are all using today to make decisions were developed at a time when the best our ancestors could do vis-à-vis any calculating was make a few marks in the dirt with a stick—if that activity would have occurred to anyone.

6. See Green and Shapiro (1994) for an elaborate presentation of this argument, Simon (1985, 1995) for its essence, and Aldrich (1993) or Friedman (1995) for various responses from the rational choice perspective.

7. Kahneman and Tversky's (1979; Tversky & Kahneman, 1992) prospect theory provides an alternative framework that is better suited to explain why some seemingly "irrational" behavior like playing the Pick-3 lottery occurs (see Levy, 1997, and chapter 8).

8. Cognitive efficiency results from being able to ignore the details of some particular stimulus that are present in the information environment if the stimulus has been categorized as another instance of some familiar group. Efficiency also results from being able to make category-based inferences about the particular stimulus even when the detailed information is *not* actually present in the information environment—thus avoiding additional information search.

9. The generation of possible causal scenarios is sometimes distinguished from availability as the "simulation" heuristic (Kahneman and Tversky, 1982).

10. It takes some practice to be able to do this without noticeably interfering with the decision-making itself. Ericsson and Simon distinguish between concurrent verbalizations, where decision-makers try to report on their thoughts as they are making a decision, and retrospective verbal protocols, where decision-makers try to describe cognitive processes that occurred earlier in time. The latter procedure should not be considered a process tracing methodology at all, for it must rely on long-term rather than short-term memory, and people are notoriously poor after-the-fact reporters on what has influenced their own behavior (Nisbett & Wilson, 1977). People can give plausible rationalizations for their behavior, but those explanations may have little association with why people actually did what they did.

11. If one alternative is preferred to all other alternatives on every dimension of judgment, it is said to "dominate" the other alternatives (Dawes, 1998), and there should be no conflict in making a decision.

12. The LEX heuristic is sometimes combined with the psychological notion of "just noticeable differences" (JNDs), which recognizes that human perceptual abilities cannot discriminate among very many distinct levels on most dimensions of judgment. Alternatives are then selected only if they are "greater than one JND" better than the other alternatives. This results in many more "ties" when applying the LEX heuristic, which can lead to intransitivities in preferences such that option A is preferred to option B, B is preferred to C, but C is preferred to A (see Payne et al., 1993). FreqGB, SAT, and LEX all assumed that decision-makers consider only a single JND for all attributes of judgment, and thus only two values—good or bad, satisfactory or unsatisfactory—are possible.

13. Taber and Steenbergen (1995) attempted to model several pure decision strategies with a procedure they called computational process tracing in order to predict the choices subjects made in a mock election study. No process tracing data were gathered, but Taber and Steenbergen did know the political beliefs of their subjects and which of two hypothetical congressional candidates they preferred. Thus the authors asked the question "Had subjects used this strategy, what choice should they have made?" Unfortunately all of the rules Taber and Steenbergen considered did a good job of predicting subjects' actual vote choices, which make it difficult to use this procedure to determine which strategies were most likely to have been employed.

14. One other type of transition is possible: intraattribute, intraalternative, that is, reaccessing the same item of information. Whenever this type of transition occurs it can usually be considered a random error.

15. The one exception to this statement is expertise, which has been a major focus of attention in the field; see for example Chase & Simon, 1973; Fiske, Kinder, & Larter, 1983; Fiske, Lau, & Smith, 1990; Lau & Erber, 1985; Reder & Anderson, 1980.

16. Most of the political science models that attempt to predict the outcome of presidential elections had Al Gore winning about 55 percent of the popular vote in 2000—about 5 percent more than he actually received (e.g., Holbrook, 1996; Lewis-Beck & Rice, 1992; Rosenstone, 1983). All of these models include evaluations of the incumbent administration's job performance as a crucial predictor. Evidently enough voters were *deciding* between Bush and Gore on some other basis to throw these models off.

17. Marcus et al. (2000) have supplied one answer to this question: people are more "rational" when they are more anxious.

◣ References

Abelson, R. P., & Levi, A. (1985). Decision making and decision theory. In G. Lindzey & E. Aronson (Eds.), *Handbook of social psychology* (3rd ed., vol.1, pp. 231–309). New York: Random House.

Abramson, P. R., Aldrich, J. H., Paolino, P., & Rohde, D. W. (1992). "Sophisticated" voting in the 1988 presidential primaries. *American Political Science Review, 86,* 55–69.

Alba, J. W., & Marmorstein, H. (1987). The effects of frequency knowledge on consumer decision making. *Journal of Consumer Research, 14,* 14–26.

Aldrich, J. H. (1980). *Before the convention: Strategies and choices in presidential nomination campaigns.* Chicago: University of Chicago Press.

Aldrich, J. H. (1993). Rational choice and turnout. *American Journal of Political Science, 37,* 246–276.

Allison, G. T. (1971). *Essence of decision: Explaining the Cuban missile crisis.* Boston: Little, Brown.

Allison, G. T., & Zelikow, P. D. (1999). *Essence of decision: Explaining the Cuban missile crisis* (2nd ed.). New York: Longman.

Anderson, J. R. (1983). *The architecture of cognition.* Cambridge, MA: Harvard University Press.

Aschenbrenner, K. M., Bockenholt, U., Albert, D., & Schmalhofer, F. (1986). The selection of dimensions when choosing between multiattribute alternatives. In R. W. Scholz (Ed.), *Current issues in West German decision research* (pp. 63–78). Frankfurt: Lang.

Bartels, L. M. (1988). *Presidential primaries and the dynamics of public choice.* Princeton: Princeton University Press.

Ben Zur, H., & Breznitz, S. J. (1981). The effects of time pressure on risky choice behavior. *Acta Psycologica, 47,* 89–104.

Biggs, S. F., Bedard, J. C., Gaber, B. G., & Linsmeier, T. J. (1985). The effects of task size and similarity on the decision behavior of bank loan officers. *Management Science, 31,* 970–987.

Billings, R. S., & Marcus, S. A. (1983). Measures of compensatory and noncompensatory models of decision behavior: Process tracing versus policy capturing. *Organizational Behavior and Human Performance, 31,* 331–352.

Bockenholt, U., Albert, D., Aschenbrenner, M., & Schmalhofer, F. (1991). The effects of attractiveness, dominance and attribute differences on information acquisition in multiattribute binary choice. *Organizational Behavior and Human Decision Processes, 49,* 258–281.

Brady, H. E., & Sniderman, P. M. (1985). Attitude attribution: A group basis for political reasoning. *American Political Science Review, 79,* 1061–1078.

Campbell, A., Converse, P. E., Miller, W. E., & Stokes, D. E. (1960). *The American voter.* Chicago: University of Chicago Press.

Campbell, D. T., & Stanley, J. C. (1963). *Experimental and quasi-experimental designs for research.* Chicago: Rand McNally.

Cantor, N., & Mischel, W. (1979). Prototypes in person perception. In L. Berkowitz (Ed.), *Advances in experimental social psychology* (vol. 12, pp. 3–25). New York: Academic Press.

Carmines, E. G., & Kuklinski, J. H. (1990). Incentives, opportunities, and the logic of public opinion in American political representation. In J. A. Ferejohn &

J. H. Kuklinski (Eds.), *Information and democratic processes* (pp. 240–268). Urbana: University of Illinois Press.

Carroll, J. S., & Johnson, E. J. (1990). *Decision research: A field guide.* Beverly Hills, CA: Sage.

Chase, W. G., & Simon, H. A. (1973). Perception in chess. *Cognitive Psychology, 4,* 55–81.

Conover, P. J., & Feldman, S. (1984). How people organize their political world: A schematic model. *American Journal of Political Science, 28,* 95–126.

Conover, P. J., & Feldman, S. (1986). The role of inference in the perception of political candidates. In R. R. Lau & D. O. Sears (Eds.), *Political cognition: The nineteenth annual Carnegie symposium on cognition* (pp. 127–158). Hillsdale, NJ: Erlbaum.

Conover, P. J., & Feldman, S. (1989). Candidate perception in an ambiguous world: Campaigns, cues, and inference processes. *American Journal of Political Science, 33,* 912–940.

Converse, P. E. (1975). Public opinion and voting behavior. In F. Greenstein & N. Polsby (Eds.), *Handbook of political science* (vol. 4, pp. 75–170). Reading, MA: Addison-Wesley.

Czerlinski, J., Gigerenzer, G., & Goldstein, D. G. (1999). How good are simple heuristics? In G. Gigerenzer, P. M. Todd, & the ABS Research (Eds.), *Simple heuristics that make us smart* (pp. 97–118). New York: Oxford University Press.

Dawes, R. M. (1979). The robust beauty of improper linear models in decision making. *American Psychologist, 34,* 571–582.

Dawes, R. M. (1988). *Rational choice in an uncertain world.* New York: Harcourt Brace Jovanovich.

Dawes, R. M. (1998). Behavioral decision making and judgment. In D. T. Gilbert, S. T. Fiske, & G. Lindzey (Eds.), *The handbook of social psychology* (4th ed., vol. 1, vol. pp. 497–548). Boston: McGraw-Hill.

Downs, A. (1957). *An economic theory of democracy.* New York: Harper and Row.

Druckman, J. N., & Lupia, A. (2000). Preference formation. *Annual Review of Political Science, 3,* 1–24.

Easton, D. (1953). *The political system: An inquiry into the state of political science.* New York: Knopf.

Einhorn, H. J. (1970). The use of nonlinear, noncompensatory models in decision making. *Psychological Bulletin, 73,* 211–230.

Einhorn, H. J., & Hogarth, R. M. (1975). Unit weighting schemes for decision making. *Organizational Behavior and Human Performance, 13,* 171–192.

Einhorn, H J., &. Hogarth, R. M. (1981). Behavioral decision theory: Processes of judgment and choice. *Annual Review of Psychology, 32,* 53–88.

Ericsson, K. A., & Simon, H. A. (1984). *Protocol analysis: Verbal reports as data.* Cambridge, MA: MIT Press.

Fiorina, M. P. (1981). *Retrospective voting in American national elections.* New Haven: Yale University Press.

Fischer, G. W., & Hawkins, S. A. (1993). Strategy compatibility, scale compatibility, and the prominence effect. *Journal of Experimental Psychology: Human Perception and Performance, 19,* 580–597.

Fischoff, B., Slovic, P., & Lichtenstein, S. (1978). Fault trees: Sensitivity of estimated failure probabilities to problem representation. *Journal of Experimental Psychology: Human Perception and Performance, 4,* 330–344.

Fiske, S. T., Kinder, D. R., & Larter, W. M. (1983). The novice and the expert: Knowledge-based strategies in political cognition. *Journal of Experimental Social Psychology, 19,* 381–400.

Fiske, S. T., Lau, R. R., & Smith, R. A. (1990). On the variety and utility of political knowledge structures. *Social Cognition, 8,* 31–48.

Fiske, S. T., & Pavelchak, M. A. (1986). Category-based versus piecemeal-based affective responses: Developments in schema-triggered affect. In R. M. Sorrentino & E. T. Higgins (Eds.), *The handbook of motivation and cognition: Foundations of social behavior* (pp. 167–203). New York: Guilford.

Fiske, S. T., & Taylor, S. E. (1991). *Social cognition* (2nd ed.). New York: McGraw-Hill.

Ford, J. K., Schmitt, N., Schechtman, S. L., Hults, B. M., & Doherty, M. L. (1989). Process tracing methods: Contributions, problems, and neglected research questions. *Organizational Behavior and Human Decision Processes, 43,* 75–117.

Ford, J. K., & Smith, R. A. (1987). Inferential beliefs in consumer evaluations: An assessment of alternative processing strategies. *Journal of Consumer Research, 14,* 363–371.

Friedman, J. (Ed.). (1995). *The rational choice controversy.* New Haven: Yale University Press.

Gettys, C. F., Pliske, R. M., Manning, C., & Casey, J. T. (1987). An evaluation of human act generation performance. *Organizational Behavior and Human Decision Processes, 39,* 23–51.

Gigerenzer, G., & Goldstein, D. G. (1999). Betting on one good reason: The take the best heuristic. In G. Gigerenzer, P. M. Todd, & the ABS Research (Eds.), *Simple heuristics that make us smart* (pp. 75–95). New York: Oxford University Press.

Gigerenzer, G., & Todd, P. M. (1999). Fast and frugal heuristics: The adaptive toolbox. In G. Gigerenzer, P. M. Todd, & the ABS Research (Eds.), *Simple heuristics that make us smart* (pp. 3–34). New York: Oxford University Press.

Green, D. P., & Shapiro, I. (1994). *Pathologies of rational choice theory: A critique of applications in political science.* New Haven: Yale University Press.

Hamill, R., Lodge, M., & Blake, F. (1985). The breadth, depth, and utility of class, partisan, and ideological schemata. *American Journal of Political Science, 29,* 850–870.

Hastie, R. (1986). A primer of information-processing theory for the political scientist. In R. R. Lau & D. O. Sears (Eds.), *Political cognition: The nineteenth annual Carnegie Symposium on Cognition* (pp. 11–39). Hillsdale, NJ: Erlbaum.

Hastie, R. (2001). Problems for judgment and decision making. *Annual Review of Psychology, 52,* 653–683.

Henshel, R. L. (1980). The purposes of laboratory experimentation and the virtues of deliberate artificiality. *Journal of Experimental Social Psychology, 16,* 466–478.

Herstein, J. A. (1981). Keeping the voter's limits in mind: A cognitive process analysis of decision making in voting. *Journal of Personality and Social Psychology, 40,* 843–861.

Hogarth, R. M. (1975). Cognitive processes and the assessment of subjective probability distributions. *Journal of the American Statistical Association, 70,* 271–289.

Hogarth, R. M. (1987). *Judgment and choice* (2nd ed.). New York, NY: Wiley.

Holbrook, T. M. (1996). Reading the political tea leaves: A forecasting model of contemporary presidential elections. *American Politics Quarterly, 24,* 506–519.

Holsti, O. R. (1989). Crisis decision making. In P. E. Tetlock, National Research Council Committee on Contributions of Behavioral and Social Science to the Prevention of Nuclear War, and the Committee on International Conflict and Cooperation (Eds.), *Behavior, society, and nuclear war* (vol. 1, pp. 8–84). New York: Oxford University Press.

Holsti, O. R., & George, A. L. (1975). The effects of stress on the performance of foreign policy–makers. In C. P. Cotter (Ed.), *Political science annual* (pp. 255–319). Indianapolis: Bobbs-Merrill.

Huang, L-N. (2000). Examining candidate information search processes: The impact of processing goals and sophistication. *Journal of Communication, 50,* 93–114.

Jacoby, J., Chestnut, R. W., Weigl, K. C., & Fischer, W. (1976). Pre-purchasing information acquisition: Description of a process methodology, research paradigm, and pilot investigation. *Advances in Consumer Research, 5,* 546–554.

Jacoby, J., Jaccard, J., Kuss, A., Troutman, T., & Mazursky, D. (1987). New directions in behavioral process research: Implications for social psychology. *Journal of Experimental Social Psychology, 23,* 146–175.

Jacoby, J., Speller, D. E., & Kohn, C. A. (1974). Brand choice behavior as a function of information load. *Journal of Marketing Research, 11,* 63–69.

Janis, I. L., & Mann, L. (1977). *Decision making: A psychological analysis of conflict, choice, and commitment.* New York: Free Press.

Jervis, R. (1976). *Perception and misperception in international politics.* Princeton: Princeton University Press.

Jervis, R. (1985). Perceiving and coping with threat. In R. Jervis, R. N. Lebow, & J. G. Stein (Eds.), *Psychology and deterrence* (pp. 13–33). Baltimore: Johns Hopkins University Press.

Johnson, M D. (1984). Consumer choice strategies for comparing noncomparable alternatives. *Journal of Consumer Research, 11,* 741–753.

Johnson, M D. (1986). Modeling choice strategies for noncomparable alternatives. *Marketing Sciences, 5,* 37–54.

Jones, B. D. (1994). *Reconceiving decision-making in democratic politics: Attention, choice, and public policy.* Chicago: University of Chicago Press.

Jones, B. D. (1999). Bounded rationality. *Annual Review of Political Science, 2,* 297–321.

Kahneman, D. (1994). New challenges to the rationality assumption. *Journal of Institutional and Theoretical Economics, 150,* 18–36.

Kahneman, D., & Tversky, A. (1972). Subjective probability: A judgment of representativeness. *Cognitive Psychology, 3,* 430–454.

Kahneman, D., & Tversky, A. (1973). On the psychology of prediction. *Psychological Review, 80,* 237–251.

Kahneman, D., & Tversky, A. (1979). Prospect theory: An analysis of decision under risk. *Econometrica, 47,* 263–291.

Kahneman, D., & Tversky, A. (1982). The psychology of preferences. *Scientific American, 246,* 160–173.

Kahneman, D., & Tversky, A. (1984). Choices, values, and frames. *American Psychologist, 39,* 341–350.

Keller, K. L., & Staelin, R. (1987). Effects of quality and quantity of information on decision effectiveness. *Journal of Consumer Research, 14,* 200–213.

Keller, L. R., & Ho, J. L. (1988). Decision problem structuring: Generating options. *IEEE Transactions on System, Man, and Cybernetics, 18,* 715–728.

Kelley, S., Jr., & Mirer, T. W. (1974). The simple act of voting. *American Political Science Review, 68,* 572–591.

Klayman, J. (1985). Children's decision strategies and their adaptation to task characteristics. *Organizational Behavior and Human Decision Processes, 35,* 179–201.

Langley, P., Simon, H. A., Bradshaw, G. L., & Zytkow, J. M. (1987). *Scientific Discovery.* Cambridge, MA: MIT Press.

Lau, R. R. (1982). Negativity in political perception. *Political Behavior, 4,* 353–378.

Lau, R. R. (1995). Information search during an election campaign: Introducing a process tracing methodology to political science. In M. Lodge & K. McGraw (Eds.), *Political judgment: Structure and process* (pp. 179–205). Ann Arbor: University of Michigan Press.

Lau, R. R., & Erber, R. (1985). An information processing perspective on political sophistication. In S. Kraus & R. Perloff (Eds.), *Mass media and political thought* (pp. 17–39). Beverly Hills, CA: Sage.

Lau, R. R., & Redlawsk, D. P. (1992 August). How voters decide: A process tracing study of decision making during political campaigns. Paper presented at the eighty-eighth annual meeting of the American Political Science Association, Chicago.

Lau, R. R., & Redlawsk, D. P. (1997). Voting correctly. *American Political Science Review, 91,* 585–599.

Lau, R. R., & Redlawsk, D. P. (2001a). Advantages and disadvantages of cognitive heuristics in political decision making. *American Journal of Political Science, 45,* 951–971.

Lau, R. R., & Redlawsk, D. P. (2001b). An experimental study of information search, memory, and decision making during a political campaign. In J. H. Kuklinski (Ed.), *Citizens and politics: Perspectives from political psychology* (pp. 136–159). Cambridge: Cambridge University Press.

Lau, R. R., & Redlawsk, D. P. (in preparation). *How voters decide: Information processing during an election campaign.*

Lau, R. R., & Sears, D. O. (1986). Social cognition and political cognition. In R. R. Lau & D. O. Sears (Eds.), *Political cognition: The nineteenth annual Carnegie symposium on cognition* (pp. 347–366). Hillsdale, NJ: Erlbaum.

Lazarsfeld, P. F., Berelson, B. R., & Gaudet, H. (1944). *The people's choice.* New York: Columbia University Press.

Levy, J. (1997). Prospect theory, rational choice, and international relations. *International Studies Quarterly, 41,* 87–112.

Lewis-Beck, M. S., & Rice, T. W. (1992). *Forecasting elections.* Washington, DC: CQ Press.

Lichtenstein, S., & Slovic, P. (1971). Reversals of preference between bids and choices in gambling decisions. *Journal of Experimental Psychology, 89,* 46–55.

Lindberg, E., Garling, T., & Montgomery, H. (1989). Differential predictability of preferences and choices. *Journal of Behavioral Decision Making, 2,* 205–219.

Lodge, M., & Hamill, R. (1986). A partisan schema for political information processing. *American Political Science Review, 80,* 505–519.

Lodge, M., McGraw, K. M., & Stroh, P. (1989). An impression-driven model of candidate evaluation. *American Political Science Review, 83,* 399–420.

Lodge, M., Steenbergen, M. R., & Brau, S. (1995). The responsive voter: Campaign information and the dynamics of candidate evaluation. *American Political Science Review, 89*, 309–326.

Luce, R. D., & Raiffa, H. (1957). *Games and decisions: Introduction and critical survey.* New York: Wiley.

Lupia, A., McCubbins, M. D., & Popkin, S. L. (2000). Beyond rationality: Reason and the study of politics. In A. Lupia, M. D. McCubbins, & S. L. Popkin (Eds.), *Elements of reason: Cognition, choice, and the bounds of rationality* (pp. 1–20). New York: Cambridge University Press.

Malhotra, N. K. (1982). Information load and consumer decision making. *Journal of Consumer Research, 8*, 419–430.

March, J. G. (1978). Bounded rationality, ambiguity, and the engineering of choice. *Bell Journal of Economics, 9*, 578–608.

March, J. G. (1988). *Decisions and organizations.* Oxford: Blackwell.

March, J. G. (1994). *A primer on decision making.* New York: Free Press.

March, J. G., & Olson, J. P. (1989). *Rediscovering institutions: The organizational basis of politics.* New York: Free Press.

March, J. G., & Simon, H. A. (1958). *Organizations.* New York: Wiley.

Marcus, G. E. (1988). The structure of emotional response: 1984 presidential candidates. *American Political Science Review, 82*, 737–761.

Marcus, G. E., & MacKuen, M. B. (1993). Anxiety, enthusiasm, and the vote: The emotional underpinnings of learning and involvement during presidential campaigns. *American Political Science Review, 87*, 672–685.

Marcus, G. E., Neuman, W. R., & MacKuen, M. (2000). *Affective intelligence and political judgment.* Chicago: University of Chicago Press.

Markus, G. B., & Converse, P. E. (1979). A dynamic simultaneous equation model of electoral choice. *American Political Science Review, 73*, 1055–1070.

Meehl, P. E. (1977). The selfish voter and the thrown-away vote argument. *American Political Science Review, 71*, 11–30.

Mellers, B. A., Schwartz, A., & Cooke, A. D. J. (1998). Judgment and decision making. *Annual Review of Psychology, 49*, 447–477.

Miller, A. H., Wattenberg, M. P., & Malanchuk, O. (1986). Schematic assessments of presidential candidates. *American Political Science Review, 80*, 521–540.

Miller, G. A. (1956). The magical number seven, plus or minus two: Some limits on our capacity for processing information. *Psychological Review, 63*, 81–97.

Miller, W. E., & Shanks, J. M. (1996). *The new American voter.* Cambridge, MA: Harvard University Press.

Mondak, J. J. (1993). Public opinion and heuristic processing of source cues. *Political Behavior, 15*, 167–192.

Nie, N. H., Verba, S., & Petrocik, J. R. (1976). *The changing American voter.* Cambridge, MA: Harvard University Press.

Nisbett, R. E., & Wilson, T. D. (1977). Telling more than we can know: Verbal reports on mental processes. *Psychological Review, 84*, 231–259.

Olshavsky, R. W. (1979). Task complexity and contingent processing in decision making: A replication and extension. *Organization Behavior and Human Performance, 249*, 300–316.

Payne, J. W. (1976). Task complexity and contingent processing in decision making: An information search and protocol analysis. *Organizational Behavior and Human Performance, 16*, 366–387.

Payne, J. W., Bettman, J. R., & Johnson, E. J. (1988). Adaptive strategy selection in decision making. *Journal of Experimental Psychology: Learning, Memory, and Cognition, 14,* 534–552.

Payne, J. W., Bettman, J. R., & Johnson, E. J. (1992). Behavioral decision research: A constructive processing perspective. *Annual Review of Psychology, 43,* 87–131.

Payne, J. W., Bettman, J. R., & Johnson, E. J. (1993). *The adaptive decision maker.* New York: Cambridge University Press.

Payne, J. W., & Braunstein, M. L. (1978). Risky choice: An examination of information acquisition behavior. *Memory and Cognition, 6,* 554–561.

Pitz, G., & Sachs, N. (1984). Judgment and decision: Theory and application. *Annual Review of Psychology, 35,* 139–163.

Quadrel, M. J. (1990). *Elicitation and Evaluation of Adolescents' Risk Perceptions: Quantitative and Qualitative Dimensions.* Ph.D. Dissertation, Carnegie Mellon University.

Quadrel, M. J., Fishhoff, B., & Davis, W. (1993). Adolescent (in)vulnerability. *American Psychologist, 48,* 102–116.

Rahn, W. M. (1993). The role of partisan stereotypes in information processing about political candidates. *American Journal of Political Science, 37,* 472–496.

Rahn, W. M., Aldrich, J. H., & Borgida, E. (1994). Individual and contextual variations in political candidate appraisal. *American Political Science Review, 88,* 193–199.

Rahn, W. M., Krosnick, J. A., & Breuning, M. (1994). Rationalization and derivation processes in survey studies of political candidate evaluation. *American Journal of Political Science, 38,* 582–600.

Reder, L. M., & Anderson, J. R. (1980). A partial resolution of the paradox of interference: The role of integrating knowledge. *Cognitive Psychology, 12,* 447–472.

Redlawsk, D. P. (2001). You must remember this: A test of the on-line model of voting. *Journal of Politics, 63,* 29–58.

Raiffa, H. (1968). *Decision analysis: Introductory lectures on choices under uncertainty.* Reading, MA: Addison-Wesley.

Riggle, E. D., & Johnson, M. M. S. (1996). Age differences in political decision making: Strategies for evaluating political candidates. *Political Behavior, 18,* 99–118.

Riggle, E. D., Ottati, V., Wyer, R. S., Kuklinski, J., & Schwartz, N. (1992). Bases of political judgments: The role of stereotypic and nonstereotypic information. *Political Behavior, 14,* 67–87.

Riker, W. H., & Ordeshook, P. C. (1968). A theory of the calculus of voting. *American Political Science Review, 62,* 25–42.

Rosch, E. (1978). Principles of categorization. In E. Rosch & B. B. Lloyd (Eds.), *Cognition and categorization* (pp. 28–50). Hillsdale, NJ: Erlbaum.

Rosenberg, S. W., Kahn, S., & Tran, T. (1991). Creating a political image: Shaping appearance and manipulating the vote. *Political Behavior, 13,* 345–367.

Rosenstone, S. J. (1983). *Forecasting presidential elections.* New Haven: Yale University Press.

Rubenstein, A. H. (1998). *Modeling bounded rationality.* Cambridge, MA: MIT Press.

Russo, J. E. (1977). The value of unit price information. *Journal of Marketing Research, 14,* 193–201.

Russo, J. E., & Dosher, B. A. (1983). Strategies for multiattribute binary choice. *Journal of Experimental Psychology: Learning, Memory and Cognition, 17,* 676–696.

Savage, L. J. (1954). *The foundations of statistics.* New York: Wiley.

Shugan, S. M. (1980). The cost of thinking. *Journal of Consumer Research, 7,* 99–111.

Simon, H. A. (1947). *Administrative behavior.* New York: Macmillan.

Simon, H. A. (1957). *Models of man: Social and rational.* New York: Wiley.

Simon, H. A. (1979). Information processing models of cognition. *Annual Review of Psychology, 30,* 363–396.

Simon, H. A. (1985). Human nature in politics: The dialogue of psychology with political science. *American Political Science Review, 79,* 293–304.

Simon, H. A. (1995). Rationality in political behavior. *Political Psychology, 16,* 45–61.

Slovic, P., Fischoff, B., & Lichtenstein, S. (1977). Behavioral decision theory. *Annual Review of Psychology, 28,* 1–39.

Slovic, P., Fischhoff, B., & Lichtenstein, S. (1982). Response mode, framing, and information processing effects in risk assessment. In R. Hogarth (Ed.), *New directions for methodology of social and behavioral science: The framing of questions and the consistency of response* (pp. 21–36). San Francisco: Jossey-Bass.

Slovic, P., & Lichtenstein, S. (1971). Comparison of Bayesian and regression approaches to the study of information processing in judgment. *Organizational Behavior and Human Performance, 6,* 649–744.

Smith, E. R. (1998). Mental representation and memory. In D. T. Gilbert, S. T. Fiske, & G. Lindzey, (Eds.), *The handbook of social psychology* (4th ed., vol. 1, pp. 391–445). Boston: McGraw-Hill.

Sniderman, P. M., Brody, R. A., & Tetlock, P. E. (1991). *Reasoning and choice: Explorations in political psychology.* New York: Cambridge University Press.

Sniderman, P. M., Hagen, M. G., Tetlock, P. E., & Brady, H. E. (1986). Reasoning chains: Causal models of policy reasoning in mass publics. *British Journal of Political Science, 16,* 405–430.

Svenson, O. (1979). Process descriptions of decision making. *Organizational Behavior and Human Performance, 23,* 86–112.

Taber, C. S., & Steenbergen, M. R. (1995). Computational experiments in electoral behavior. In M. Lodge & K. M. McGraw (Eds.), *Political judgment: Structure and process* (pp. 141–178). Ann Arbor: University of Michigan Press.

Taylor, S. E. (1981). The interface of cognitive and social psychology. In J. Harvey (Ed.), *Cognition, social behavior, and the environment* (pp. 189–211). Hillsdale, NJ: Erlbaum.

Tversky, A. (1969). Intransitivity of preferences. *Psychological Review, 76,* 31–48.

Tversky, A. (1972). Elimination by aspects: A theory of choice. *Psychological Review, 79,* 281–299.

Tversky, A., & Kahneman, D. (1973). Availability: A heuristic for judging frequency and probability. *Cognitive Psychology, 5,* 207–232.

Tversky, A., & Kahneman, D. (1974). Judgment under uncertainty: Heuristics and biases. *Science, 185,* 1124–1131.

Tversky, A., & Kahneman, D. (1981). The framing of decisions and the psychology of choice. *Science, 211,* 453–463.

Tversky, A., & Kahneman, D. (1986). Rational choice and the framing of decisions. *Journal of Business, 59,* S251–S278.

Tversky, A., & Kahneman, D. (1992). Advances in prospect theory: Cumulative representation of uncertainty. *Journal of Risk and Uncertainty, 5,* 297–323.

Tversky, A., & Sattath, S. (1979). Preference trees. *Psychological Review, 86,* 542–573.

Tversky, A., Sattath, S., & Slovic, P. (1988). Contingent weighting in judgment and choice. *Psychological Review, 95,* 371–384.

Wright, P. (1975). Consumer choice strategies: Simplifying vs. optimizing. *Journal of Marketing Research, 12,* 60–67.

von Neuman, J., & Morgenstern, O. (1947). *Theory of games and economic behavior.* Princeton: Princeton University Press.

Vriend, N. J. (1996). Rational behavior and economic theory. *Journal of Economic Behavior & Organization, 29,* 263–285.

3 David O. Sears and Sheri Levy

Childhood and Adult Political Development

If the study of history revolves centrally around time as an independent variable, the study of childhood and adult development revolves most centrally around life history, the study of time within the human life span. "Taking time seriously," as Alwin (1995) puts it. This chapter examines political orientations as they evolve through the life history from early childhood through old age.

Why should we care about the life histories of social and political orientations? At the most basic level, it is because the constant tension between continuity and change is played out throughout an individual's life span. This is a piece of the broader question for psychological theory about the lasting effects of formative early experiences on adult behavior. This historical emphasis contrasts markedly with that of the more ahistorical rational choice theories drawn from the field of economics, or even the more psychological behavioral decision theories. Both emphasize the appraisal of available information at decision points in adulthood, even if they less obtrusively also incorporate provisions for "preferences" with unexamined origins and inertial power in adult decision-making. A second motive is also theoretical but more political, to understand the origins of orientations that are politically consequential among adults, whether concerning politics specifically (see chapters 13 and 14) or intergroup relations (see chapters 15 and 16). Perhaps understanding the trajectory of party identification or prejudice or basic values through the life course will give us leverage on understanding their antecedents and consequences. A third motive has been more purely political, often stemming from liberal social scientists' idealistic hopes that social and political evils might be prevented by better early socialization experiences. They have thought that tolerance and good citizenship, if taught early, might dampen ethnocentrism (see chapter 15) and prejudice (see chapter 16), so mass oppression and even genocide (see chapter 20) might thereby be reduced or even avoided.

� Thinking about Time and the Political Life History

From a psychological point of view, there are three general ways of thinking about time and the political life history. The first concerns the persisting effects of early experiences. Early theories about political socialization saw those effects as lasting indeed, with research on the origins of racial prejudice, national identity, and hostility toward other countries in children (Harding, Proshansky, Kutner, & Chein, 1969; Lambert & Klineberg, 1967), on the lasting stigma associated with minority identity among black children (Clark & Clark, 1939), and on the youthful origins of party identification and ideology (Hyman, 1959) or diffuse support for a democratic political system (Easton & Dennis, 1969; Greenstein, 1965). The lasting influence of such early attitudes was largely assumed rather than tested directly, perhaps sustained by the then-widespread conviction, derived from psychoanalytic and learning theories, that "great oaks from little acorns grow." This assumption soon encountered robust criticism, however (e.g., Marsh, 1971; Searing, Schwartz, & Lind, 1973; Searing, Wright, & Rabinowitz, 1976; Vaillancourt, 1973), along with considerable research (e.g., Jennings & Markus, 1984; for reviews see D. Sears, 1975, 1990).

A contrasting focus is on "the times." They may change or stay the same, and with them, individuals' orientations. What happens within individuals' life histories is inextricably connected to what happens in the broader environment, which is a product of "the times." American children reported considerable increases in anxiety during the last half of the twentieth century (Twenge, 2000). Support for Jim Crow racism dropped precipitously during the same period (Schuman, Steeh, Bobo, & Krysan, 1997). Political systems change with time, and within them party systems change as well (Converse, 1969), as has been shown most dramatically by the abrupt collapse of the Soviet Union and more subtly by the partisan realignment of the white South and the Mountain states in the United States since the 1960s (Carmines & Stimson, 1989; Marchant-Shapiro & Patterson, 1995).

A third general approach looks for politically distinctive features of different life stages. Young children may have difficulty interlinking various aspects of events (Newcombe, Drummey, Fox, Lie, & Ottinger-Alberts, 2000); the concreteness of their thinking may delay their appreciation of abstract concepts such as Congress or the Supreme Court (Hess & Torney, 1967); and their thinking about moral choices may progress in turn through hedonic, authoritarian, and more principled stages (Adelson, 1972; Tapp & Kohlberg, 1971). Adolescents may be especially vulnerable to "storm and stress" (Arnett, 1999), and drawn to unconventional behavior (Watts, 1999) and political rebellion (Feuer, 1969). Young adults may be especially concerned about their own independent identity (Erikson, 1968) and somewhat unmoored in society (Arnett, 2000; Carlsson & Karlsson, 1970) and so more open to influence. The elderly may flag in mental and physical energy, with consequences for the consistency and stability of their attitudes (Sears, 1981).

Early research on the political life history also grew out of all the major theories of political behavior, though sometimes only implicitly (Merelman, 1986). Systems theory gave rise to a concern with how people become attached to their political system and developed trust in political authority, especially in mature democracies (Easton & Dennis, 1969; Greenstein, 1965). Hegemonic or Marxist theories gave rise to an interest in how schools and the media produce a compliant citizenry, especially in the lower and working classes (Hochschild, 1981). Theories of democratic pluralism assumed that stable democracies are built on a foundation of public attachments to political parties, a sense of citizen duty, support for "the rules of the game," and political tolerance (Campbell, Converse, Miller, & Stokes, 1960; Sullivan, Piereson, & Marcus, 1982). Sociological conflict theories focus on class and other versions of group consciousness (Miller, Gurin, Gurin, & Malanchuk, 1981).

Review essays in the previous handbooks of political psychology have been titled "political socialization" and have focused largely on the childhood acquisition of specifically political orientations (Merelman, 1986; Niemi, 1973). We broaden our scope to the full life span and to a broader array of political and social orientations. We begin with a discussion of the acquisition of basic dispositions in preadult life, with particular focus on moral and cognitive development, ethnic and racial identity, ethnic and racial prejudices, and basic partisanship. We then consider the later life history of such dispositions, with particular attention to their persistence, as well as susceptibility to change in an "impressionable" period lasting up through early adulthood. Finally we take up applications of these ideas to the question of political generations and to the case of immigrants to another country.

▶ Preadult Acquisition

Moral and Cognitive Development

Children construct principles of morality through interactions with parents, teachers, siblings, and peers. Researchers have conceptualized morality in terms of justice ("Do unto others as you would have them do unto you"), fairness, rights, and interpersonal reciprocity ("Love thy neighbor as thyself"; see Gilligan, 1982; Kohlberg & Candee, 1984). Two predominant orientations to the study of moral judgment and moral decision-making by developmental psychologists have generated most of the empirical research over the past four decades. The first model was reflected by the pioneering stage models of moral development, first formulated by Piaget (1932/1965) and then elaborated by American psychologists, most notably by Kohlberg (1969, 1984; see also Damon, 1977; Selman, 1980). The stage approach characterized children's moral understanding as a series of progressively more advanced stages of moral thinking and behavior. The second model, referred to as a social-cognitive domain model, was first formulated by Turiel (1983, 1998) and expanded on by his colleagues (for reviews, see Smetana, 1995; Tisak, 1995; Turiel, Killen, & Helwig, 1987). The domain model characterized moral reasoning as one of several domains of knowledge that emerge in early social development. We will first discuss the stage model, which set the foundation for a structural-developmental approach to moral thinking, and then describe more current work, which has made use of the domain-specific model of social knowledge.

Stage Theories

Piaget (1932/1965) proposed a two-stage model of moral development in which children move from heteronomy, or relying entirely on externally imposed rules, in early childhood to a more autonomous and flexible moral orientation in middle childhood. Elaborating on Piaget's model, Kohlberg (1969, 1976) offered a three-stage model of development from early to middle childhood, extending the model with three additional stages to account for moral reasoning into adolescence and adulthood (also see Kohlberg, 1984, and Tapp & Kohlberg's 1971 model of legal reasoning). Like Piaget, Kohlberg suggested that children in early and middle childhood moved from a heteronomous orientation to one more flexible, although Kohlberg outlined rules or goals governing the "flexibility" of the moral principles (e.g., avoid punishment, gain approval). The later stages proposed by Kohlberg stressed moving from a focus on the utility of laws for societal functioning to a recognition that universal ethical principles transcend and may contradict laws. Kohlberg's methodology for studying moral reasoning was novel, as he asked children about moral dilemmas that were concrete, dramatic, and engaging, which addressed abstract moral issues (e.g., whether a husband should steal the medication he cannot afford to save his dying wife). Studies show that some children regress in their development or skip a stage (e.g., Kuhn, 1976; Kurtines & Grief, 1974) and few adolescents achieve the final stages (Colby & Kohlberg, 1984; Colby, Kohlberg, Gibbs, & Lieberman, 1983). Kohlberg's theory has been criticized for its inability to demonstrate relations between hypothetical reasoning about moral dilemmas and actual moral behavior (Rest, 1983), for being male-centered (Gilligan 1977, 1982), and for being culture-specific (e.g., Schweder, 1982).

In contrast to Kohlberg's approach, which characterized all forms of moral reasoning as decisions about the value of human life, Damon (1975, 1977, 1980) proposed a stage theory of positive justice, which delineates children's decisions to divide resources or distribute rewards fairly. In studies in the United States, Israel, Puerto Rico, and Europe, Damon (1983) found that children's positive justice reasoning, demonstrated through their choices of allocations, progressed through six stages in which choices were first based on wishes and desires (age 4–5), then on equality and reciprocity of actions (age 5–9), and finally on demands of persons and situations (age 8 and older). Subsequent research showed that even children as young as 6 years old can weigh relevant person and situation factors when the judgment context is familiar to them (Thorkildsen, 1989). Addressing a criticism of

Kohlberg's theory, Damon (1977) showed that children's hypothetical reasoning related to their behavior in a real situation (e.g., dividing rewards on the basis of their performance in an activity).

Also departing from Kohlberg's focus on reasoning about law violations, Adelson and colleagues (Adelson, Green, & O'Neil, 1969; Adelson & O'Neil, 1966) studied children's thoughts about rule development. Consistent with cognitive-developmental stage theories, Adelson and colleagues showed that children and adolescents progress from understanding society in terms of concrete people and events to an understanding based on abstract principles (also see Tapp & Levine, 1972). They examined reasoning about laws in situations that involved conflicts between individual autonomy and community benefits. This work showed that, with age, children move from thinking about laws as social control (deciding to increase punishment for laws that are not working) to an increased awareness of the social benefits of law (suggesting that if a law is not working, the law itself should be altered).

Contemporary Models of Morality

Contemporary work has departed from the aforementioned work in two ways. First, contemporary researchers have shown that even very young children are capable of making moral judgments about fairness (unlike Piaget's and Kohlberg's theories, which found that young children reasoned in terms of authority or avoiding punishment) and, second, that children's reasoning varies with the context, referred to as a domain-specificity approach. In the domain model, moral reasoning is distinct from, but coordinated with, social-conventional reasoning and personal reasoning (Nucci, 1981; Turiel, 1983, 1998; Turiel, Killen, & Helwig, 1987).

Contrary to Piaget's theorizing, researchers found that young children do not merely show a heteronomous orientation toward authority; rather, their reasoning is complex and context-specific; children consider variables such as status, experience, and knowledge as important for determining when to obey someone (Laupa, 1991, Laupa, Turiel, & Cowan, 1995). In addition, contrary to Kohlberg's theorizing (Tapp & Kohlberg, 1971), researchers found that young children believe law violation is acceptable under certain circumstances. For example, Helwig and Jasiobedzka (2001) presented Canadian children (age 6–11) with real and fictitious laws that either had social benefits (mandatory vaccinations), but could infringe on personal rights, or were unjust (discriminatory) and clearly infringed on personal rights. Children were provided with examples of law violations and their reasons (e.g., religion dictates familial control over education). Rather than mandating a strict adherence to laws, or even only allowing exceptions in extreme (e.g., life threatening) circumstances, even young children recognized that minor infringements on people's rights (e.g., being forced to stand on a bus because of age) sometimes justified breaking the law. In another study, Helwig and Prencipe (1999) asked Canadian children 6 to 11 years old to evaluate several vignettes concerning flag burning. Younger children were more likely to focus on the functional, as opposed to symbolic, importance of the flag (e.g., marking the location of the country as opposed to representing shared values) and also to be less responsive to social context changes that might alter the meaning of the burning (e.g., the country has unfair practices). However, young children were sensitive to the intentions of the burner and to the potential consequences of the acts, as they disapproved of accidental and private transgressions than symbolic and public burning.

Turiel and colleagues' social-cognitive domain model has been a highly influential developmental model of reasoning (e.g., Nucci & Lee, 1993; Smetana, 1995; Turiel, 1983, 1998; Turiel & Davidson, 1986; Turiel, Killen, & Helwig, 1987). By age 3–4, children can differentiate moral rules and social conventions (Turiel, 1983). By middle childhood, children can make explicit judgments about the importance of different kinds of rules (Nucci & Killen, 1991). Turiel and colleagues' model specifies that children conceptualize their world in three structured domains or subsystems: (1) social conventions (e.g., traditions, customs, and rituals; alterable and non-generalizable acts); (2) morality (e.g., fairness, rights, and equal treatment; unalterable and generalizable acts); and (3) psychological factors (e.g., autonomy, personal goals, and personal prerogatives; acts of personal choice). Evidence for reasoning in these three domains comes from studies in different cultures (e.g., Brazil, Canada, Germany, India, Israel, Japan, Nigeria, Turkey), different settings (urban, rural), and different socioeconomic status levels (high, low; see Killen, McGlothlin, & Lee-Kim, 2002, for a recent review).

To investigate children's underlying reasoning and judgment, these researchers have used individually administered interviews, similar to Piaget's and Kohlberg's, but have improved them by adding closed-ended formats and more straightforward vignettes (e.g., Helwig, 1998). They have examined numerous multifaceted and controversial issues (e.g., abortion, incest, pornography, drug use; see Killen, Leviton, & Cahill, 1991; Turiel, Hildebrandt, & Wainryb, 1985). Recently, Killen and her colleagues (Killen et al., 2002) have used the social-cognitive domain model to examine children's evaluations of intergroup inclusion and exclusion in the context of situations that involve stereotypes and fairness considerations. In one study, Killen and Stangor (2001) evaluated children' and adolescents' (age 7–13) decisions whether to exclude an individual from a race-typed after-school peer club (e.g., "white" math club, "black" basketball team) on the basis of the individual's race, as well as on exclusion from a gender-typed after-school peer club (e.g., ballet for girls, baseball for boys) on the basis of gender. When the scenario was a straightforward exclusion scenario (e.g., decide whether to include child), the vast majority of participants (all grade levels) felt that it was morally wrong to exclude the basis of race. Children also were presented with more complex scenarios in which two children wanted to join a group with one opening. When presented with equally qualified children, fourth- and seventh-graders picked the child who did not fit the stereotype, providing equal treatment reasons. When qualifications differed (e.g., the black child had more experience in playing basketball than the white child), seventh-graders tended to pick the better-qualified (stereotypic) child, giving group functioning reasons, whereas fourth-graders continued to choose the nonstereotypical child. More research is needed to understand the prodiversity selections of the children, how group functioning, opposed to individual merit, justifications are weighed, and how members of traditionally excluded groups respond to such dilemmas (see Killen et al., 2002).

Future Directions

Future work is needed to investigate how children's reasoning relates to their actual behavior. For example, contemporary theorizing could be enriched by a greater focus on on-line behavior (e.g., unobtrusive observations of children's moral-relevant behavior on the playground) in addition to the current focus on reports of retrospective and intended behavior. In addition, we anticipate that social-cognitive domain researchers will increasingly put their growing body of findings into action by developing reasoning-based interventions that improve social relations and tolerance (Aboud & Levy, 2000; Helwig & Jasiobedzka, 2001).

Development of Ethnic and Racial Identity

In a diverse society, ethnicity and race are important components of people's identities and greatly influence social and academic opportunities. In this section, we consider the development of racial and ethnic identification among different groups and how this identification relates to the attitudes children and adolescents develop toward themselves, their group, and other groups. Although there are distinctions between race and ethnicity (e.g., see Ocampo, Bernal, & Knight, 1993; Quintana, 1998), racial and ethnic identities appear to have similar implications; thus we will discuss the findings of research on racial and ethnic identities together.

Racial/ethnic identity and its consequences were brought to public attention by the work of Clark and Clark (1939, 1940), who found that young U.S. black children preferred white dolls to black dolls (e.g., wanting to play with them and liking them), suggesting that identification with a low-status ethnic group could reduce one's self-esteem. Preference for the race-majority group was replicated in studies with Native Americans (Annis & Corenblum, 1987) and Bantu in South Africa (Gregor & McPherson, 1966). Subsequent research showed that preference for the majority group does not necessarily translate into low self-esteem (Cross, 1991; Spencer,

1984). Work by Beuf (1977) with Native American children, for example, suggests that minority children's preferences for the majority group may have more to do with desiring the majority group's wealth and power and less to do with having a negative self-concept.

Contemporary Research

Children's ethnic cognitions seem to begin with an understanding of race, or the physical features that differentiate groups (Aboud, 1987). Racial awareness then leads to ethnic identity (Rotheram & Phinney, 1987). Children's understanding of ethnicity and race also is thought to derive from their families (Knight, Bernal, Garza, Cota, & Ocampo, 1993), naïve theories of biology (e.g., Hirschfeld, 1995), and the linguistic negative connotation of "black" and positive connotation of "white" (e.g., Williams & Morland, 1976). Recently, Quintana (1994, 1998) proposed a five-stage model of ethnic development and found support for it by studying Mexican-American, African-American, white, Latino, and Quiche and Ladion Guatemalan children. Quintana's early childhood stages (stages 0 and 1) integrate findings from other researchers and thus serve as an excellent organizational framework in which to broadly summarize findings in the field. In level 0, "integration of affective and perceptual understandings of ethnicity" (age 3–6), children's awareness of race is based on observable, biological features; thus children learn and use terms that are both descriptive and racial (e.g., white, black) before terms that only have racial or ethnic meaning (e.g., African-American, Hispanic; see Alejandro-Wright, 1985; Quintana, 1994). Also during this stage, children's affective differentiation of races tends to be promainstream culture (e.g., prowhite), probably because early understanding of race derives from mainstream culture, where the majority is represented more often and more positively (e.g., Aboud, 1988). In level 1, "literal understanding of ethnicity" (age 6–10), children understand more subtle aspects of ethnicity (language, customs, food preferences; Alejandro-Wright, 1985; Bernal et al., 1990).

To understand children's identity development from middle childhood to adolescence, we turn to Phinney's (1989) and Cross's (1978) classic three-stage models of ethnic identity, which are similar to each other and to Quintana's later stages and derive from work on ego-identity theory (Erikson, 1968; Marcia, 1980). In the first stage, "unexamined ethnic identity" (Phinney) or "preencounter" (Cross), children have not explored their ethnic identity. Phinney (1989) found that about one half of Asian-American, black, and Hispanic tenth-graders were in stage 1. Children who have not examined their ethnic identity might have negative feelings toward their own group (Cross, 1978; see Phinney, 1989). In the second stage, "ethnic identity search" (Phinney) or "encounter and immersion," young persons seek out information about their group (e.g., reading books on ethnicity, visiting ethnic museums). This stage is considered a turning point akin to an "identity crisis" (Erikson, 1968). Active identity exploration often begins in high school or college but may begin in middle school or even younger as children express identity through joining ethnicity-based peer groups (Rotheram-Borus, 1993). Phinney (1989) found that over one fifth of Asian-American, black, and Hispanic tenth-graders were in stage 2. During this stage, minority-ethnic and immigrant youth often grapple with contradictory norms of mainstream and nonmainstream cultures as well as with the mainstream's ethnic group stereotypes (Berry, 1980; Phinney, 1990). In fieldwork in central California, Matute-Bianchi (1986) found that Mexican-descent students seemed to identify more with their ethnic heritage than Japanese-descent students, presumably because collective group identity helped combat the relatively negative stereotypes about their group in that environment. However, even though in the United States there is seemingly a positive stereotype of Asian Americans as the "model minority," Asian Americans also strongly identify with their ethnic group for protection from mainstream racism (Chan & Hune, 1995). Clashes between one's native ethnicity and mainstream culture can, alternatively, instigate immersion in the mainstream culture. For example, in research with Cambodian adolescent girls in the United States, Lee (1999) found that some embraced the mainstream culture to avoid their native group's limiting gender roles.

In stage 3, "achieved ethnic identity (Phinney) or "internalization" (Cross), adolescents have developed positive self-concepts as members of their group. Phinney (1989) found that about one-fourth of the Asian-American, black, and Hispanic tenth-graders were in stage 3. With acceptance of one's own ethnicity, adolescents may develop a greater acceptance of and respect for other groups. That is, contrary to traditional views, contemporary researchers suggest that having a secure ethnic identity can undermine prejudice (Aboud & Doyle, 1993; Gonzales & Cauce, 1995).

Social context is an important variable in children's acquisition of racial and ethnic identities. "Enculturation refers to the cultural teaching that parents, families, peers, and the rest of the ethnic community provide to children during the childhood years" (Bernal & Knight, 1993, p. 3). Parents were identified as an important variable, beginning with the followup studies of Clark and Clark's classic doll study (Beuf, 1977; Spencer & Horowitz, 1973). Beuf (1977) found, for example, that Native American children whose parents were more active in cultural and civil rights were more likely to prefer a Native American doll to a white doll. Large-scale sociocultural changes across ethnic communities also can change the very identities that adolescents are forming. For example, structurally, linguistically, and culturally different Asian groups (Japanese, Chinese, Filipinos, Korean, Asian Indian) living in the United States came together in the 1960s to forge an Asian-American identity and to collectively combat discrimination (Chan & Hune, 1995; Espiritu, 1992). Context may be particularly relevant for multiracial or biracial youth as their ethnic/racial identity may vary with environments.

Acculturation is defined as "the adaptation of ethnic minority people to the dominant culture and its members" (Bernal & Knight, 1993, p. 3), or, more broadly, as "encompassing a wide range of behaviors, attitudes and values that change with contact between cultures" (Phinney, Romero, Nava, & Huang, 2001, p. 495). The definitions lead to two acculturation models—a linear model, assuming that individuals must either identify with their native culture or the mainstream culture (e.g., Rogler, Cortes, & Malgady, 1991), or the bidirectional model, which assumes that individuals can have distinct relations with their native and the mainstream cultures, thereby allowing for multiculturalism (Berry, Trimble, & Olmedo, 1986; Berry, 1999; Phinney et al., 2001). A key remaining question is: How do children negotiate all the contexts that might be giving them mixed messages? (For a discussion see Phelan, Davidson, & Yu, 1998.)

Consequences of Group Identification

Contemporary research has shown that greater identification with one's ethnicity is related to a host of positive outcomes, including greater self-esteem (Phinney & Chavira, 1992), ego-identity (Markstrom & Hunter, 1999), and school involvement (Taylor, Casten, Flickinger, Roberts, & Fulmore, 1994). For example, in a study of African-American eighth- and ninth-graders, Gonzales and Cauce (1995) found that ethnic pride was positively related to boys' and girls' confidence as potential dating partners and boys' grade point averages. Cross (1995), discussing blacks in the United States, views a strong ethnic identity as serving the protective function of filtering one's social worldview so as to be make it less dehumanizing. The protection comes from accepting that racism exists and affects all blacks, that negative outcomes are because of a racist system and not the self, and that one can use various strategies to deal with racism (withdrawal, assertion, avoidance, passivity). Other functions that a strong identity may serve include providing purpose, meaning, and affiliation, often expressed in celebration of accomplishments of the black community (Cross, 1995).

Greater ethnic identification can also have potentially negative consequences such as leading to greater separation from the majority group (e.g., less intergroup contact and greater conflict when contact does occur), which tends to occur in the immersion stage when adolescents seek out information about their own group (e.g., Phinney, 1990). Although self-protective, such behavior can limit children's social and academic opportunities and experiences. For this reason, researchers have explored whether school performance differences between race-majority and minority groups are in part explained by student ethnic identification. For example, in the United States, Fordham and Ogbu (1986, see Cross, 1995) considered whether school failure of race-minority adolescents is due to the development of an "oppositional identity" (rejecting dominant groups' dress, speech, attitudes). In a study of black students from low-income families, they found that in middle and high school, the students increasingly sought to disidentify with "acting white," which included doing well in school. Alternatively, Spencer (2001) has shown that African-American youth do not necessarily associate high achievement with "acting white." Drawing on data from sixth-, seventh-, and eighth-grade African-American youth, Spencer (2001) noted that "high-achieving African American adolescents are not only failing to identify with acting white values, but more than likely have a better understanding of the irrelevance of the comparison for blacks and in what seems to be the term's lack of meaning, even for whites" (p. 29).

Why might some minority youth shy away from academics, whereas other minority groups might actively pursue it? Chan and Hune (1995) suggest that "among Asian American children and their families, the reaction to racialized behavior may be intense concentration on school achievement at the risk of their mental health and personality—a reaction that can been as adaptive from one perspective and limiting from another" (p. 226). In addition, work on interpersonal expectancies (e.g., McKown & Weinstein, 2002) and on "stereotype threat" (e.g., Steele & Aronson, 1995) provides a better understanding of why high-performing minority youth may experience school failure. For example, stereotype threat is a social-psychological threat in situations in which a stereotype of one's group applies (e.g., the threat of being judged as poor in math for girls). Ambady, Shih, Kim, and Pittinsky (2001) activated children's Asian or gender identity and then had them complete part of a standardized math test. Relative to a control condition, girls in kindergarten and middle school who were in the Asian identity activation condition showed facilitated performance, while the gender identity condition inhibited girls' performance. Thus, Asian-American girls who are disadvantaged in the math arena because of the female stereotype can draw on the Asian identity as a self-protective factor in those situations. These findings suggest that salient negative academic stereotypes about one's ethnic or racial group would diminish one's academic performance.

Future directions. Stage models have dominated work on ethnic and racial identity development. Research using these models has illustrated how most children initially show a preference for the mainstream racial group but eventually work toward a positive self-concept as members of their own groups. Although this line of research has tended to focus on nonwhite ethnic groups, as victims of the racism perpetuated by whites, some aspects of the models (e.g., immersing oneself in one's ethnicity, developing a respect for other groups) apply to whites and other mainstream groups. For instance, Helms (1993) proposed a stage model of white identity development, which included stages of discarding racism and learning to be white without racism (see also Rowe, Bennett, & Atkinson, 1994).

The stage model approach has shed light on some seemingly contradictory findings. For example, research shows that a strong ethnic identity can lead to both outgroup prejudice and outgroup tolerance. This seeming contradiction can be explained by the identity stage children are in (e.g., immersion vs. internalization). Despite this, a current shortcoming of stage models is their inability to clearly specify the ages at which children and adolescents will be at different stages of the identity process. This will probably be addressed in future work as researchers expand their study of different racial and ethnic groups and their focus on these groups in different contexts (Gonzales & Cauce, 1995).

Another pressing issue for identity researchers is helping educators address the ethnic and racial diversity of their students. The "colorblind" practice of ignoring racial and ethnic differences seeks a laudable social outcome—fair and equal treatment (see Neville, Lilly, Duran, Lee, & Browne, 2000; Schofield, 1986). Yet a colorblind approach to education is controversial because race and other characteristics do affect children's lives (e.g., Jones, 1997; West, 1992), and some efforts to assimilate immigrants and ethnic groups into the dominant culture have failed in the short term, leading to high dropout rates (e.g., Garcia & Hurtado, 1995). Multicultural education, an alternative approach, suggests "a restructuring and transformation of the total school environment so that it reflects the racial and cultural diversity that exists within U.S. society and helps children from diverse groups to experience educational equality" (Banks, 1995, p. 329, also see Hollins, 1999). Multicultural programs also are controversial because they often do not teach the rich nuances of culture, ethnicity, nationality, and race (Lee, 1999) or may exaggerate differences across groups, both of which may produce and perpetuate stereotyping among children (Bigler, 1999). Schools and communities that work collaboratively will probably be able to develop the most effective education programs (Banks, 1995; Phelan, Davidson, & Yu, 1998), for example, drawing on the different strengths of colorblind and multicultural programs.

Development of Ethnic and Racial Prejudice

In a racially and ethnically diverse world with limited social and economic resources, intergroup conflict seems inevitable. Despite a decline in the reporting of racial and ethnic prejudice over the past few decades (e.g., in the U.S., see Dovidio & Gaertner, 2000), group disparities and intergroup conflict continue to make headlines across the globe. In this section, we review traditional theories of racial and ethnic prejudice among children and then highlight contemporary theories such as the cognitive-developmental approach and the evolutionary approach (also see Aboud, 1988; Brown, 1995). Although prejudice is to some degree inevitable because of limited resources in the environment and within the person, researchers have made tremendous strides in understanding how to reduce prejudice, which we mention at the end of this section.

Traditional Theories of Prejudice among Children

An early theory of explaining prejudice among children evolved from a psychodynamic framework (e.g., Adorno, Frenkel-Brunswick, Levinson, & Sanford, 1950; Bettleheim & Janowitz, 1950). For example, Adorno and colleagues (1950) suggested that parents' threatening and punishing responses to their children's "unconventional" behavior produced an inadequate ego, which relied on the use of defense mechanisms (such as projection of anger toward outgroups rather than toward parents) to release the aggressive and sexual impulses of children's poorly controlled "ids," resulting in the "authoritarian personality." This work was criticized on theoretical, conceptual, and methodological grounds. In the 1980s a newer version of this research showed that authoritarianism is related to prejudice toward a wide variety of groups, at least in college-age samples (see Altemeyer, 1998).

The traditional social-learning approach to prejudice (also referred to as social reflection theory, Allport, 1954) suggested that children become gradually more prejudiced with age as they try to imitate and to please their parents. Research on the link between children's attitudes and those of others in their environment, however, has not revealed consistent results. For example, Carlson and Iovini (1985) found a significant relation between the racial attitudes of white fathers and their adolescent sons but not between the racial attitudes of black fathers and sons. Branch and Newcombe (1986) found that as black children get older, their attitudes toward whites and blacks become more similar to their parents' attitudes. Aboud and Doyle (1996b) found that third-grade children's racial attitudes were not strongly related to their mothers' attitudes. Studies also have examined whether children's racial attitudes are related to their peers' attitudes. Patchen (1983) found that both black and white ninth-graders' attitudes and behaviors were not significantly related to their peers' racial attitudes. Similarly, Aboud and Doyle (1996b) found that a multiracial group of third- and fourth-graders perceived their peers to hold attitudes similar to their own; however, in actuality their peers generally did not report similar racial attitudes to their own (see also Aboud & Doyle, 1996a). These results may suggest that children often do not discuss their racial attitudes very much with their parents and peers. Parents (particularly members of race-majority groups) also may not discuss prejudice much with their children (Knight et al., 1993; Kofkin, Katz, & Downey, 1995). However, when adults and peers discuss prejudice in ways that address its cognitive underpinnings, prejudice is decreased (Aboud & Doyle, 1996a). For example, Aboud and Doyle (1996a) found that low-prejudice white third- and fourth-graders who discussed their racial attitudes with a high-prejudice peer were able to lower their peer's prejudice by pointing out instances of cross-race similarity (how members of all groups can be mean sometimes) and within-race trait variability (how whites exhibit negative and positive traits).

Contemporary Theories

Children's attitudes toward racial and ethnic groups are influenced not only by their social environment but also by their social cognitive skills. According to the cognitive-developmental approach as articulated by Aboud (1988) and Katz (1976; also see Piaget & Weil, 1951), children's racial/ethnic prejudice decreases from early to middle childhood in part because of their acquisition of particular cognitive skills (e.g., Bigler & Liben, 1993; Doyle, Beaudet, & Aboud, 1988; Katz & Zalk, 1978). As early as preschool and kindergarten, majority group children exhibit prejudice; examples include English Canadians judging French Canadians (Doyle et al., 1988), Euro-Australians judging Aboriginal Australians (Black-Gutman & Hickson, 1996), and Jewish Israelis judging Arabs (for a review, see Bar-Tal, 1996). Young majority children typically assign more positive and less negative attributes to their own group than to other groups (outgroups) but show a decline in prejudice at around age 7 (Doyle & Aboud, 1995; Doyle et al., 1988; Powlishta, Serbin, Doyle, & White, 1994). Race-minority children (e.g., Native American, Beuf, 1977; African-American, Spencer, 1982) have shown a bias against their racial group in preschool, but after age 7, they tend to have more positive attitudes toward their own group (Aboud, 1988).

These age-related declines in prejudice have been shown to reflect the influence of specific cognitive skills such as classifying others on multiple dimensions (e.g., Bigler & Liben, 1992, 1993; Katz, Sohn, & Zalk, 1975), taking on differing perspectives (e.g., Black-Gutman & Hickson, 1996; Doyle & Aboud, 1995), perceiving similarities between different groups (e.g., Black-Gutman & Hickson, 1996; Doyle & Aboud, 1995; Doyle et al., 1988; Powlishta et al., 1994), and perceiving differences within the same group (e.g., Black-Gutman & Hickson, 1996; Doyle & Aboud, 1995; Katz et al., 1975). For example, Doyle and Aboud (1995) found that between ages 6 and 9, white Canadian children developed more positive attitudes of blacks and more negative attributes of whites, although the number of negative attributions toward blacks and positive attributions toward whites did not change. Thus children could conceive of both groups on multiple overlapping dimensions. Another cognitive limitation of children worth noting is their limited attention to stereotype-inconsistent information (e.g., Bigler, 1999). Bigler and Liben (1993) showed that when white children were read stories, they remembered stereotype-consistent more than stereotype-inconsistent information about blacks (see also Martin & Halverson, 1981). Children who are skillful in classifying people on multiple dimensions, however, have a better memory for counterstereotypic stories.

These cognitive skills that are acquired with age yield individual differences among late adolescents, and influence prejudice levels (for a review, see Levy, 1999). For example, several individual difference constructs (e.g., need for cognition, attributional complexity) are conceptually similar to the abilities to classify others on multiple dimensions and to reconcile differing perspectives, which most children acquire by age 9 or 10 (e.g., Bigler & Liben, 1993; Doyle & Aboud, 1995). Thus, with age, people probably draw differentially on cognitive skills relevant to prejudice.

Although given minimal attention thus far, evolutionary perspectives will probably be given increasing treatment in developmental theorizing on prejudice (e.g., Fishbein, 1996; Hirschfeld, 2001; also see chapter 5). Fishbein (1996) argues that evolutionary processes that produce prejudice began in hunter-gatherer tribes and were incorporated in human's epigenetic systems. Hypothesized evolutionary processes include: inclusive fitness, which leads children to give preferential treatment toward relatives, authority-bearing systems, which encourage children to almost blindly accept whatever they hear about outgroup members from ingroup authority figures, and intertribal hostility, which encourages protection of limited resources. Consistent with cognitive-developmental theories, Fishbein argues that identification with a group is often a precursor to prejudice.

Another evolutionary perspective draws on cognitive developmental work on children's competencies in physics, mathematics, and folk biology (e.g., Hauser & Carey, 1998). Hirschfeld (1995, 2001) argues that children's thinking about human social aggregates derives from a theorylike knowledge structure, which is governed by an endogenous preorganized acquisition device. Children's theorylike competence, or *naive sociology*, helps them decide which group affiliations to weigh more heavily than others and thus helps children reduce the cognitive demands of equally weighing all social information in their environment.

Evolutionary approaches have generally been criticized for suggesting that prejudice is natural and thus should be condoned. Yet aspects of evolutionary explanations overlap considerably with cognitive approaches that suggest that categorizing is inevitable, at least at some ages, and with sociocultural interpretations that suggest that prejudice grows out of social forces and limited resources. Evolutionary perspectives cannot be disentangled from these other approaches. For example, the finding that children and adults see race as a relevant social category for hierarchically organizing their world could be evidence for the endogenous module or evidence that children learned the relevant category from their environment. Evolutionary approaches are probably best thought of as illuminating potential distal causes of prejudice, whereas these other approaches (cognitive, social learning) focus on and test more proximal causes of prejudice.

Prejudice-Reduction Interventions

With a greater understanding of prejudice among children, there is increasing dialogue between basic and applied researchers of prejudice (see Aboud & Levy, 1999). Cooperative learning programs have become a popular, successful intervention strategy in schools (Johnson & Johnson, 2000;

Slavin & Cooper, 1999). Multicultural programs also have become extremely popular in schools, but their effectiveness has been questioned, as discussed in the previous section on racial and ethnic identity (also see Bigler, 1999). Researchers also have developed successful mediation programs to resolve interethnic conflicts in schools (Johnson & Johnson, 2000; also see Coleman & Deutsch, 1995; Deutsch, 1993). Relatively new intervention strategies in schools, such as social-cognitive retraining (e.g., Aboud & Fenwick, 1999; for a review see Aboud & Levy, 2000) and bilingual education programs (e.g., Genesee & Gandura, 1999) show promise. Media interventions such as television programs (e.g., *Sesame Street*) have been revised to more effectively reduce prejudice among viewers (Graves, 1999). Because prejudice is multifaceted, different intervention strategies are probably needed to tackle each component of prejudice.

Future directions. Over the past few decades, cognitive-developmentalists have shown that age-related cognitive abilities make young children more receptive to categorical (prejudice-increasing) information and less receptive to individuating (prejudice-reducing) information. However, researchers from other theoretical traditions have continued to show that children's levels of prejudice also reflect social and emotional factors. Because of this, contemporary research is moving toward an integrative approach, combining elements of cognitive development and social learning theories (e.g., Aboud & Amato, 2001). These new avenues can be seen in research on dyadic discussion (Aboud & Doyle, 1996a), assertive bystander training in the face of racial bullying (Aboud & Fenwick, 1999), and exclusion from social clubs on the basis of racial group membership (Killen et al., 2002). In doing so, researchers are incorporating theorizing and methodology from experimental social psychology (e.g., Levy, 1999), such as the identification of individual differences in children's lay theories relevant to prejudice (Cameron, Alvarez, Ruble, & Fuligni, 2001; Levy & Dweck, 1999) and the variables that contribute to stereotyping in adulthood (see Oskamp, 2000). In future work, developmentalists will probably draw on social psychology research on implicit and subtle forms of prejudice in college students (see Dovidio & Gaertner, 1986). There is already some evidence of implicit prejudice among children (Verna, 1982) and of children expressing weaker prejudice in nonambiguous situations, compared to ambiguous situations where their responses cannot easily be attributed to prejudice (Lawrence, 1991; Sagar & Schofield, 1980). Since implicit prejudice assesses the strength of the internal associations between attributes and a target group, children will probably develop higher levels of implicit prejudice with age because of the corresponding increase in their experiences with groups.

Party Identification

The aforementioned developmental work focuses on children's and young adolescents' attitudes about social groups, which can lay the foundation for political awareness and action in adulthood. Now we turn to explicitly political attitudes, first to their acquisition by preadults and then to their later life histories. The paradigmatic case of the development of political attitudes among preadults has from the beginning been Americans' party identification. In large part that is because party identification turns out to be by far the strongest and most consistent prediction of Americans' voting preferences, and seems to have been so for over a century (e.g., Campbell et al., 1960; Miller & Shanks, 1996).

The early conventional wisdom was that "a man is born into his political party just as he is born into probable future membership in the church of his parents" (Hyman, 1959, p. 74). The more complex theory developed in *The American Voter* (Campbell et al., 1960) is perhaps the most influential in the study of political behavior. It is based on a simple two-question series asked of each survey respondent: "Generally speaking, do you usually think of yourself as a Republican, a Democrat, an Independent, or what?" Those giving either of the first two responses were then asked: "Would you call yourself a strong (X) or a not very strong (X)?" Those giving the third response were asked, "Do you think of yourself as closer to the Republican party or to the Democratic party?" Those saying "closer to the Republican party" were classified as "Independent leaning to the Republicans," a parallel classification generated "Independent leaning to the Democrats," and those selecting neither were regarded as "pure Independents." This generated a simple seven-point scale running from strong Republican through Pure Independent to strong Democrat.

The theory described the *direction* of party identification as an attitudinal predisposition typically acquired in preadult life, often from the parental family; as usually acquired without an elaborate accompanying ideology about the relative merits of the two parties; as highly stable over the life span; and as the most powerful single factor in determining candidate evaluations and voting choices in partisan elections, and often issue preferences as well. The *strength* of party identification was thought to increase through the life cycle as the individual accumulated experience with the partisan electoral system (Converse, 1969, 1976). Party identification was originally conceptualized in terms that grew out of reference group theory, though more recently there have been efforts to conceptualize it in terms of social identity theory (Greene, 1999; Miller & Shanks, 1996, p. 127; see chapter 15). It is not clear that such a reformulation has so far led to any very different predictions or empirical findings.

The observation that *family transmission* was crucial to the development of party identification was most thoroughly tested by Jennings and Niemi (1974, 1981) in their classic "Michigan socialization study." They conducted interviews with a national sample of high school seniors and their parents in 1965, with both samples again in 1973 and 1982, and with the student cohort along with children of the former students in 1997 (Jennings, Stoker, & Bowers, 1999). They found substantial, though not perfect, parental transmission of party identification to their adolescent children, and lesser transmission of other political attitudes. Parent-child similarity of partisanship declined through the offsprings' early adulthood (though not thereafter), as the offsprings' own issue preferences played an increasing role in their party identifications (Beck & Jennings, 1991; Niemi & Jennings, 1991).

Plainly families vary considerably in their ability to pass their partisanship on to their offspring. Variations in parent-child relationships seem not to be central in success of transmission; e.g., politics has not been found to be a central vehicle for rebellion against parents (Jennings & Niemi, 1974; Niemi, 1974), even among student protestors (D. Sears, 1975, pp. 126–127). However, the most politicized parents and those with the most stable attitudes were consistently the most successful at socializing their offspring even through the latter's middle age (Beck & Jennings, 1991; Jennings, et al., 1999). The main reason seems to be that such parents are most successful in accurately communicating their political positions to their children (Tedin, 1974, 1980). In fact offspring usually exaggerate the true level of parent-child political similarity (Westholm, 1999). Accuracy of perception of parental positions also helps to explain differences in transmission across attitude domains: parental attitudes are communicated more clearly in some domains (e.g., hotly contested elections) than others (e.g., political efficacy). As indicated earlier, young children's racial/ethnic attitudes are not as similar to their parents' attitudes, apparently because parents (at least those in the racial majority) often do not discuss them with their children. There is also evidence that offspring sometimes influence parental attitudes, especially in domains in which offspring introduce more "modern" attitudes to families (e.g., Glass, Bengtson, & Dunham, 1986). And, more generally, parental political information has a major effect on the flow of political information to offspring (Jennings, 1996).

The centrality of family transmission was originally proposed in an era of more common intact two-parent families than is the case now, with higher rates of divorce, never-married mothers, and so on. Even so, the extension of the Michigan socialization study to the children of the original students shows quite convincingly that parent-child transmission in those families shows very much the same pattern as it did in the original families (Jennings et al., 1999). Indeed in some domains it is even higher, such as in political ideology and racial attitudes. Unstable families do take their toll, however. College students report both less political agreement between divorced parents and weaker family transmission (Hardy, Carrier, & Endersby, 2000).

The original theory implied that party identification was transmitted in piecemeal fashion as part of daily life. But if the key to successful political socialization is clear communication of stable parental attitudes, vivid *political events* should be important catalysts because they stimulate heavy information flow, and so provide occasions for such communication. Presidential elections should be one such regular occasion. Consistent with the catalyst hypothesis, Sears and Valentino (1997) found that the strength of adolescents' partisan attitudes increased dramatically from before the beginning to the end of such a campaign, almost to their parents' levels. No such increase occurred in adults' partisanship, which was already at high levels; or in attitudes about objects more peripheral to the campaign; or during the less information-intense year following the campaign. Also consistent with the catalyst idea, the surge in partisanship was greatest among adolescents most involved in interpersonal political communication (Valentino & Sears, 1998).

Another example of a vivid and socializing political event was the year-long controversy over President Bill Clinton's relationship to the intern Monica Lewinsky. Parents reported that their adolescent children found the scandal quite interesting, that it catalyzed increased conversation about politics in their families, and gave parents an opportunity to express their own views to their children about Clinton and about sex, morals, and values in general (Pew Research Center, 1998). Republicans felt especially successful in passing on their own views to their children. Although about half the parents reported being "very upset" by the allegations, the children's predominant response was described as being "interested" in what would happen to the president, and they did not seem to be too disturbed by the whole affair. Overall parents felt it more likely to help than to "harm" their children's interest in politics.

The mass media are, of course, important for providing contact between children and the world of politics. Indeed, longer term interest in politics may be sparked if preadults enter the age of political awareness at times of heightened activity in the political arena (Danowski & Ruchinskas, 1983). Children's first contact with politics is usually via television, although their degree of political knowledge seems to be suppressed somewhat by heavy viewing of entertainment television. It seems better explained by their level of exposure to the print media (see the review by Chaffee and Yang, 1990).

◣ Adult Life History

The original theory of party identification, with its focus on early learning and later persistence, provided a clear and quite influential paradigm. Is it a useful model for thinking about political life histories more generally? To address this question, we return to the three ways of thinking about time noted at the outset. Four distinctive models of the political life cycle have been most common and will be discussed in turn. Two reflect the persisting effects of early experience: (1) a *persistence* model, in which the residues of preadult learning persist through life, perhaps even hardening with time; and (2) a variant on it, an *impressionable years* model, in which attitudes are particularly susceptible to influence in late adolescence and early adulthood but tend to persist thereafter. These models are normally contrasted with one that, loosely speaking, views adults as more responsive to the events of their "times," (3) a *lifelong openness* model, in which individuals remain open to influence throughout later life. A fourth model, somewhat orthogonal to the others, picks up on the idea of distinctive political life stages: (4) a *life cycle* model, in which people are attracted to certain attitudes at specific life stages, such as radical ideas in their youth and conservatism in old age (Alwin, 1994; Jennings & Niemi, 1981; D. Sears, 1975).

Persistence over the Life Span

The persistence hypothesis is important from both the psychological and political points of view. There is the psychological question of the trajectory of important political and social attitudes through the life cycle. Is there generally a "critical period" in an individual's life for acquisition of political attitudes? What is the plasticity of those attitudes as the individual ages (see Alwin, 1993; Alwin, Cohen, & Newcomb, 1991; D. Sears, 1975, 1983, 1990)? From a political perspective, if the most important attitudes are essentially static after early life, change would occur primarily by replacing older cohorts with younger ones holding fresher attitudes rather than by conversion of mature adults to new points of view (see Alwin, 1993). So widespread persistence would mean that political change depends to a considerable degree on cohort replacement. A system in which political loyalties are essentially static through adulthood would yield a very different politics from one in which they are regularly formed anew on the merits of each circumstance.

Longitudinal Studies

The most straightforward way of assessing persistence, though the most expensive and difficult to execute well, is to measure a given attitude from a given set of respondents at multiple points in time. Psychologists tend to call such studies "longitudinal studies" (e.g., R. Sears, 1975; 1984) while political scientists and sociologists call them "panel studies" (e.g., Converse & Markus, 1979). The most extensive work has been done using two 4-year National Election Studies (NES) panel studies done in the 1950s and 1970s. Party identification was the most stable attitude measured in those studies, indeed almost perfectly stable, with some correction for measurement unreliability (Converse & Markus, 1979). Similar conclusions have emerged from other studies in the United States (Green & Palmquist, 1994; Green & Schickler, 1993; Jennings & Stoker, 1999) and in Canada, Britain, and Germany (Schickler & Green, 1997).

Two studies of more specialized populations yield evidence of stability across much longer periods of adulthood. Newcomb (1943) studied a cohort of women attending Bennington College during the 1930s. They generally came from affluent, politically conservative families, but many changed in a liberal direction while attending that politically progressive college. Followup studies showed extremely high long-term stability of partisanship from college graduation through adulthood: "attitudes, once formed, can be incredibly stable. . . . The stability coefficient linking a latent attitude variable over roughly 50 years of the life-span is in the .70 to .80 range" (Alwin, 1993, p. 68; also see Alwin et al., 1991). The long-term Terman gifted children study tested a considerably larger and more heterogeneous sample, selected from high-IQ children in California public elementary schools after World War I. Their party identifications were quite stable from approximately age 30 to 67, with a coefficient of .65 corrected for measurement error (Sears & Funk, 1999).

Variations across Attitude Objects

In longitudinal studies, then, party identification became the paradigmatic case for attitudinal persistence. What about other attitudes? The conventional wisdom is that racial policy attitudes are among the most stable of whites' policy attitudes, though less stable than party identification (Converse, 1964; Converse & Markus, 1979; Jennings & Stoker, 1999; Kinder & Sanders, 1996; Sears, 1983). Basic political ideology has also been found to be quite stable (Alwin et al., 1991; Jennings & Stoker, 1999; Sears, 1983; Sears & Funk, 1999). For example, only 13 percent changed from "liberal" to "conservative," or vice versa, over the 37-year span of the Terman gifted children study (Sears & Funk, 1999). Moral attitudes, such as those toward abortion and marijuana, have also been found to be highly stable in some of these studies. On the other hand, attitudes in many domains intensely debated by political elites seem to show much less stability over time in the mass public (Converse, 1964; Converse & Markus, 1979; Jennings et al., 1999; Sears, 1983).

Why do some attitudes persist for so long whereas others seem to be much more unstable? To start with, their observed stability only reflects the external outcome of a series of internal collisions between the individual's predispositions and external pressures to change. Both can vary a good bit. In addition, the normal criterion for stability, a high test-retest correlation, can be somewhat misleading if the marginal frequencies have changed. The conclusion that party identification is highly stable was based on high stability coefficients during a period in which party divisions remained more or less constant (Converse, 1976). However, some older racial attitudes would look misleadingly stable by the same criterion. In that period of great social change the public as a whole became markedly more liberal; presumably, many people shifted to the left but maintained their approximate rank order (Firebaugh & Davis, 1988; Schuman et al., 1997). Rather than one model of the political life cycle fitting all, then, the trajectories of both any given individual's attitudes and the attitudes of people in the aggregate are likely to vary across attitude objects.

How can one explain such variations? One theory looks both to learning factors, such as the volume and one-sidedness of communication in the individual's microenvironment, or the opportunity to practice the attitude in conversation and behavior, and to cognitive factors, such as the constancy of meaning of the attitude object and connectedness of attitudes to other attitudes and values, as general factors that enhance attitude stability (Sears, 1983). Americans' party identifications and racial attitudes are cases of relatively high levels of information flow and thus are presumably sources of conversation and opportunities for behavioral practice. But many policy issues scarcely come to public attention at all and thus involve considerably lower levels of all these contributors to persistence.

Persistence also should be greater for attitudes toward objects that are salient in early life than toward those that only become salient later in life, even if in the same general domain. Adulthood migration between the relatively racially tolerant North and the more racially conservative South affected whites' racial attitudes selectively (Glaser & Gilens, 1997). Region of origin dominated whites' adult attitudes about the issues, such as racial intermarriage, that were most salient in the civil rights era of the 1950s and 1960s, when they were relatively young. Region of adult residence had a stronger effect on the issues more salient in their adulthood, such as busing for school integration or special aid to minorities.

Another possibility raised by Achen (1975) is that some observed attitude instability may simply be due to measurement error. Though he did not precisely specify the source of the error, he implied that it resulted especially from ambiguous survey items. As noted by Converse and Markus (1979), it is not obvious why the same question-writers systematically did so well in some domains and so badly in others, or why political elites and more educated citizens show much higher stability on the same presumably flawed items than does the full mass public. Following Achen's logic, Alwin and Krosnick (1991), using structural equation models to correct for measurement error, estimated that almost all attitudes measured in the 4-year NES panel studies were nearly perfectly stable, which seems unlikely. They concede that their models make assumptions that may be untenable.

Zaller and Feldman (1992) offer another interpretation of "measurement error": that a person might give contradictory answers to the same question in two interviews because of "ambivalence." Different "considerations" might come to mind each time, leading to unstable overall responses because they are based on different subsets of "considerations" at different times. This may not help explain differences in stability across attitude objects very much, however. For example, abortion is an issue that creates a great deal of ambivalence (Alvarez & Brehm, 1995). Attitudes about it nevertheless have among the greatest over-time attitude stability of all contemporary political issues (Converse & Markus, 1979).

Other Assessments of Persistence

One problem with longitudinal studies is they tend to be limited to one historical era, and often to one cohort, which limits their ability to distinguish levels of stability across the life course from particular historical circumstances. Another tool for assessing persistence that is not so limited to historical period and cohort is cohort analysis. This requires a series of cross-sectional surveys conducted at different times with different samples but including the same measures. If each birth cohort, as a whole, does not maintain the same distribution of opinion as it ages, high levels of attitudinal persistence at the individual level are unlikely. On the other hand, cohort analysis yields less direct evidence about individual-level stability than do longitudinal studies.

Moreover, this generality across cohorts and periods creates its own problems. Any correlations of age with political attitudes potentially reflect three different confounded effects: cohort (birth cohort), life cycle (age at measurement), and period (year of measurement). To assess these three effects, researchers can extract only two pieces of information from any given survey—respondent age and year of survey. Age and birth cohort are perfectly correlated in any given survey, and age and chronological time are perfectly correlated across a series of surveys. Therefore, assigning variance to any one of these three effects is indeterminate, in a strict sense, unless "side information" is available from other sources to rule out one of these potential sources of variance (Mason, Mason, Winsborough, & Poole, 1973). For example, in the "steady state" period of the American party system from 1952 to 1964, the aggregate distribution of party identification among whites did not change, allowing period effects to be set at zero (Cassel, 1999; Converse, 1976).

A useful application of cohort analysis has been to explain the reasons for the greatly increased support for general principles of racial equality among white Americans since World War II (see Schuman et al., 1997). One possible explanation is logically implausible from the outset, that aging by itself promoted liberalizing change: while each cohort became more liberal as it aged, at any given point age was negatively correlated with racial conservatism. That leaves two other possibilities: that individual attitudes were highly persistent, so prejudiced older cohorts were gradually replaced by more tolerant younger cohorts (a cohort effect); or that widespread liberalizing individual attitude changes occurred (a period effect). Cohort replacement seems to have been the dominant effect as older, more prejudiced cohorts were replaced with younger, less prejudiced ones. But period effects also occurred, as all cohorts showed similar linear liberalizing trends over time (Danigelis & Cutler, 1991; Firebaugh & Davis, 1988). These liberalizing trends within cohorts began to slow by the 1980s, especially on newer racial issues (Steeh & Schuman, 1991; Wilson 1996; for similar results over a broader range of attitudes, see Davis, 1992).

A third approach to persistence is more opportunistic, using natural experiments that test the resistance to change of attitudes presumably acquired early. Changes in social location that place the individual in an altered attitudinal environment might be expected to influence attitudes. For example Miller and Sears (1986) found that adults' levels of racial tolerance were more strongly associated with the level of racial tolerance in their childhood and young adulthood attitudinal environments than by that of their mature adulthood environments (also see Glaser & Gilens, 1997). Migration between congressional districts dominated by opposite parties influenced adults' voting preferences and party identification, though the changes were considerably greater among those who migrated earlier in adulthood (Brown, 1988). Some direct personal experiences in adulthood might also be expected to produce change. One common expectation is that the emergence of economic interests in adulthood will influence individuals' political attitudes. However, extensive research has found surprisingly little evidence of much effect of adults' self-interests, as if sociopolitical attitudes acquired earlier resisted such influences later in adulthood (Sears & Funk, 1991).[1]

The Impressionable Years

The "impressionable years" hypothesis is a variant of the persistence hypothesis, suggesting that adolescents' and young adults' attitudes are weaker and more open to change than they are at later stages (Sears, 1975). At least three psychological propositions lie behind this hypothesis. One is a primacy notion: youths experience political life as a "fresh encounter," in Mannheim's (1952) words, that can seldom be duplicated later. Second, attitudes that are subjected to strong information flows and, regularly practiced, should become stronger with age (Converse, 1969, 1976). Partisanship is a good example, since both election campaigns and the act of voting recur often. Third, the young may be especially open to influence because they are becoming more aware of the social and political world around them just at the life stage when they are seeking a sense of self and identity (Erikson, 1968). These three views agree that the period up to one's late twenties, roughly, should be the most volatile.

Stronger Attitudes with Age

One implication is that young adults will simply have weaker attitudes, such as being less likely to say they are "strong" partisans. Indeed cohort analyses in the United States show that each cohort expresses stronger party identifications as it ages, at least during what Converse (1976) described as the "steady state era" of roughly constant partisan divisions prior to the 1970s (also see Alwin, 1992, 1993, Claggett, 1981). Such aging effects held in the United Kingdom as well (Cassel, 1999).

A second implication is that such attitudes should become more stable with age. Data from two 4-year NES panel studies show that all older cohorts in each study had substantially more stable party identifications than did the youngest cohort (Alwin et al., 1991; Sears, 1983). The youngest cohort in the first study also showed greatly increased stability in the second study, when it was 16 years older, showing that the greater stability is an aging rather than a period effect (Alwin, 1993). The Michigan socialization study cited earlier also showed that high school seniors showed substantially lower levels of attitude stability than did their parents. After the students reached their thirties, though, their attitudes had become as stable as their parents' attitudes, and indeed did not greatly increase in stability as they aged further (Jennings & Stoker, 1999; also see Beck & Jennings, 1991; Jennings & Markus, 1984).

A third implication is that such attitudes ought to become more resistant to influence as the individual ages. Three surveys analyzed by Visser and Krosnick (1998) similarly found increased resistance to influence after early adulthood. Another study assessed attitude change resulting from changes at different life stages in one's social environment, as indexed by demographic location (Miller & Sears, 1986). Changes in the youthful environment seem to have had considerably greater influence on levels of social tolerance than did changes in adult environments. All this represents several kinds of evidence for an "impressionable" period in the life cycle, then.

If indeed attitudes that are well practiced become stronger with age, one might expect that the elderly would show the least change of all. Surprisingly enough, there is some evidence that the relationship of age to attitude stability follows an inverted-U pattern. One early study (Sears, 1981) found that racial prejudice among whites in the 1972–76 NES panel study was least stable over time for the youngest (under 30) and oldest (over 60) age groups. Moreover, it was a period of liberalizing racial attitudes, and the oldest cohort actually changed in a liberal direction the most. These findings held up with education controlled, and apparently could not be explained by greater measurement unreliability in old age. The basic finding was corroborated in a study of the stability of party identification using both NES panels, adding corrections for measurement unreliability (Alwin, 1993; Alwin et al., 1991; also see Visser & Krosnick, 1998). Why these attitudes might become more unstable in old age is unclear, though many of the ways that people are socially embedded in the society often do change after retirement age, in terms of their work, residence, family, and other social networks. That may destabilize their political attitudes.

Political Generations

The impressionable years hypothesis focuses on the particular susceptibility to influence of individuals' attitudes in late adolescence and early adulthood. But if "the times" exert strong pressures to change, they can influence large numbers of people at that stage in common, yielding generational effects. More narrowly, Karl Mannheim (1928/1952) suggested that "generational units," or subsets of a youth cohort, rather than full cohorts, may share powerful experiences that will mark them as distinctive for life. Either way, producing generational effects requires both that individuals have a particular psychological openness at that life stage and evocative political experiences in that historical era.

A number of political generations have been subjected to especially intensive empirical study. One was composed of the women who were politically socialized before 1920, when they were first eligible to vote in national elections. Women only gradually began to turn out to vote, initially producing a substantial gender gap in voting turnout, largest among those socialized prior to women's suffrage; that is, in the cohort born before 1906. No such gender gap held among those socialized well after suffrage; that is, those born after 1925. As the presuffrage cohorts of women were gradually replaced by postsuffrage cohorts, the gender gap in turnout declined, and by the late 1980s it had disappeared (Firebaugh & Chen, 1995). Another was the "New Deal generation" in the United States. Youthful new voters who first entered the electorate during the 1930s remained substantially more Democratic into the 1950s, both in voting behavior and in party identification, than were earlier cohorts at similar ages (Campbell et al., 1960; also see Centers, 1950; Elder, 1974; Butler & Stokes, 1969, for a parallel effect in Great Britain). They also continue to have more knowledge about the New Deal than did younger Americans, even years later (Jennings, 1996).

The young protestors in the United States and Europe in the 1960s were a quite self-conscious generational unit. Most evidence indicates that their left-liberal distinctiveness has persisted since then, especially among those who actively engaged in protest. For example, the students in the Michigan socialization study who had then been active as protestors continued to be considerably more liberal than were college-educated nonprotestors at each of the later three waves of the panel study (Jennings, 1987, 2000; also see Fendrich & Lovoy, 1988; McAdam, 1989; Marwell, Aiken, & Demerath, 1987; Whalen & Flacks, 1984). Interestingly enough, their offspring were also strikingly more liberal than the offspring of nonprotestors (Jennings, 2002). But even "engaged observers"—those who were attentive to the movements but not very active in them—showed lasting political effects years later (Stewart, Settles, & Winter, 1998).

The youth cohort that immediately followed them is another case in point. A number of issues divided both parties internally in the mid-1960s to early 1970s, such as civil rights, conflict over the Vietnam War, and the Watergate scandal. These internal rifts within the parties seem to have much reduced the strength of partisanship in the generation then entering the electorate. Since then the strength of partisan commitment among incoming youthful cohorts has turned back up, and they now more closely resemble those who entered the electorate before that dealigning period (Miller & Shanks, 1996).

But in other respects contemporary young people continue to show unusually low levels of political engagement, in political information, newspaper reading, political interest, and voting turnout. Part of this is a life cycle effect, as young people have historically been less politically engaged than mature adults. But it is partly a generational effect as well, surprisingly so, since education enhances political engagement, and recent generations have received much more education (e.g., Astin, Parrott, Korn, & Sax, 1997; Delli Carpini, 2000; Putnam, 2000; Smith, 1999). Putnam (2000) has suggested that these all reflect a decline in "social capital" in recent generations, paralleling a broad drop in voluntary socializing and organizational membership. He has implicated the rise of television as disruptive of such communal activities, though evidence for its role is necessarily somewhat indirect. The generational decline in turnout, the most extensively analyzed, has otherwise largely resisted extensive efforts at explanation (e.g., Highton & Wolfinger, 2001; Miller & Shanks, 1996).

Finally, a potentially rich line of investigation concerns possible persisting generational effects of political or social traumas. Loewenberg (1971), for example, suggests that the unusually powerful support for the Nazi regime among Germans born from 1900 to 1915 can be ascribed in part to the many traumas they had experienced in early life, including malnutrition and starvation, disease, neglect of children, the disappearance of a generation of fathers, and hyperinflation. Direct exposure to political violence in Israel and South Africa has been shown to increase the likelihood of psychopathology (Slone, Adiri, & Arian, 1998; Slone, Kaminer, & Durrheim, 2000). Even exposure to distal violence, such as the assassination of a popular leader, can have profound emotional effects in the short run (Raviv, Sadeh, Raviv, Silberstein, & Diver, 2000; Wolfenstein & Kliman, 1965), and perhaps long-term political effects as well (Sears, 2002).

Another set of generational effects is reflected in *collective memory*, defined as "memories of a shared past that are retained by members of a group, large or small, that experienced it," especially "shared memories of societal-level events" (Schuman & Scott, 1989, pp. 361–362; also see Halbwachs, 1950/1980). The impressionable years hypothesis would be that people should especially recall events and changes as important if they happened in their adolescence or early adulthood. One method of measuring collective memories asks respondents to cite "national or world changes" that have been "especially important" over the last 50 years or so (Schuman & Scott, 1989). The age cohort most likely to select World War II as especially important had been 20, on average, in 1943, and the cohort most likely to select the Vietnam War averaged age 20 in 1968. Ascribing great importance to the assassination of President John F. Kennedy peaked among those who had been in childhood and adolescence in 1963. When asked in 1990 whether the best analogy for the Gulf War crisis was a "Hitler" metaphor of a voracious dictator or a "Vietnam" metaphor of a Third World quagmire, those over 40 strongly preferred the Hitler analogy, whereas those under 40 were split evenly between the two analogies (Schuman & Rieger, 1992). Even questions about simple pieces of information, such as what was President Roosevelt's party, can reveal marked generational differences (Jennings, 1996).

Robert Jervis (1976) has provided a particularly important application of this notion of collective memory to the question of how foreign policy decision-makers "learn from history." Political leaders who have had dramatic and important firsthand experiences in politics when they are in the "impressionable years" may later apply such experiences to issues they must deal with as mature adults. For example, Harry Truman, confronting the North Korean invasion of South Korea in 1950, and Lyndon Johnson, facing the Vietnam War, both recalled that the buildup to World War II had taught them the danger of not facing up to aggressors at an early stage. Colin Powell and other military leaders who had been young officers in the 1960s later applied the lesson of Vietnam to, among other things, the Persian Gulf War: don't go to war halfheartedly, either stay out or go in with overwhelming force. The danger of those "lessons" learned early, as with any persisting generational effects, is of course that they are long out of date by the time the young person becomes a mature adult, as is expressed in the saying that the military is always "fighting the last war."

Lifelong Openness

The application of developmental approaches to political psychology has undergone considerable cycling in popularity. A generation ago, Greenstein (1970, p. 969) felt that "political socialization is a growth stock," and David Sears (1975, p. 94) opined that "research output has increased at a geometric rate." A reaction then set in, focused especially on two often overly enthusiastic assumptions: of a "primacy principle," that early-acquired predispositions had considerable staying power, and a "structuring principle," that they had some special political power in adulthood, because what is learned early is most important (e.g., Searing et al., 1973, 1976). Some developmentally oriented researchers then called for recognition of more openness to change through the life course than the persistence theory allowed for; for example, that "change during adulthood is normal. . . . [T]he life course should be understood as a more integrated and contingent whole" (Sapiro, 1994, p. 204), and that "learning and development are [not] completed by adulthood; rather they . . . [constitute] a lifelong process." (Sigel, 1989, p. viii). Larger external trends in political science also contributed to greater attention to openness in adulthood, with the growing influence of economic theories emphasizing the rational choices made by adults.

Documenting Change among Mature Adults

The challenges to the persistence view have often provided valuable evidence. Sometimes it too is interpreted overenthusiastically, so some cautionary flags may be in order. One influential line of work argues that adults' partisanship is in fact responsive to "the times," such as economic conditions and judgments of incumbent performance (Fiorina, 1981), and candidate images, issues, or events (Allsop & Weisberg, 1988; Markus, 1983; Niemi & Jennings, 1991). In one study cited for this purpose, candidate evaluations were shown to influence adult party identification, rather than vice versa (Rapoport, 1997). However, the sample comprised only young people newly eligible to vote, not mature adults. The finding would be more consistent with the impressionable years than the openness hypothesis.

An impressive series of studies collected by Sigel (1989) examines the political effects of discontinuities within adulthood, such as entering the workplace, serving in the military, immigrating to a new country, participating in social movements, entering college, getting married, or becoming a parent. Each of these cases, as she notes, incorporates three elements that potentially can affect political attitudes: crystallization of an individual's own unique identity, assumption of new roles, and coping with the novel and unanticipated demands of adulthood. However, all these specific discontinuities also occur most often in late adolescence and early adulthood, again suggesting that these findings may fit the impressionable years hypothesis better than the openness hypothesis. And even the mostly youthful powerful personal experience of military service in Vietnam was found by the Michigan socialization study to have only "modest" effects on political attitudes (Jennings & Markus, 1977).

When mature adults encounter major discontinuities in their attitudinal environments, they sometimes do change their attitudes, as indicated earlier. But relatively few people are exposed to such discontinuities after early adulthood (Miller & Sears, 1986). For example, migration from an area dominated by one party to an area dominated by its opponents is almost three times as likely among young adults as among their elders, and has much more effect among the young (Brown, 1988). Migration between North and South has affected white adults' racial attitudes, but only about 10 percent have engaged in such migration in both directions combined (Glaser & Gilens, 1997). The microenvironments represented by individuals' social networks also tend to be politically supportive, and indeed disagreements are underrecognized (Huckfeldt, Beck, Dalton, & Levine, 1995). Observed changes resulting from environmental changes are not very common, then, and the reason may be both sociological and psychological: environmental continuity is quite great, and when it breaks down change may occur, but both are more common in the "impressionable years."

Political Context as a Moderator

The political context is also critical to how these individual-level processes play out. Two prominent cases involving the normally quite stable party identification and racial attitudes make the point. The polarization of party elites on racial issues led to a substantial shift of Southern whites to the Republican party in the 1980s (Miller & Shanks, 1996). The society-wide elite rejection of the Southern segregation system led to a shift away from Jim Crow racism after the civil rights era (Firebaugh & Davis, 1988).

The strengthening of party identification with age should partly be dependent on the stability of the party system itself. In the United States, intraparty disputes in the period around the early 1970s resulted in *reduced* net strength of partisanship in most cohorts as they aged, contrary to its usual trajectory. In the more polarized and stable party division since, partisan commitment has resumed its normal strengthening with age (Miller & Shanks, 1996). More generally, Converse (1969) found that age was associated with stronger party identifications in the mature democratic systems of the United States and United Kingdom but considerably less so in the interrupted democratic systems in Germany and Italy and in the immature electoral system of Mexico. He found that the strength of individuals' partisanship in those five countries was well predicted by a model including personal partisan experience (years eligible to vote and years voted), inherited partisan experience (communicated partisanship from parents), a forgetting effect when democracy was interrupted, and a socialization effect reflecting the delayed enfranchisement of women. Even Russia, in the aftermath of the demise of the Soviet Union, yields evidence of nascent partisanship that is stable across elections and with meaningful underlying attitudinal cleavages (Brader & Tucker, 2001; Miller & Klobucar, 2000). But later research suggests that the persistence model works well, or at least best, for parties that are large and/or old, consistent with the notion that people need visible and stable attitude objects if they are to learn strong attitudes about them (Converse & Pierce, 1992).

Life Cycle Effects

These questions about the persistence of early learning, as opposed to the continuing openness to new experience, by no means exhaust the possible contributions of a life-span development approach to political psychology. As noted earlier, correlations of attitudes with age can logically reflect either generational or life cycle effects, as in the old French adage that "He who is not a revolutionary at 20 has no heart; he who is a revolutionary at 40 has no head." The two can be distinguished in cohort analyses. These show that people do not seem necessarily to become more conservative with age. In the 1950s, age was positively correlated with Republicanism, when the elderly came from pre–New Deal cohorts, a period of Republican dominance (Crittenden, 1962). In a later era, when the elderly were predominantly from the "New Deal generation," they tilted toward the Democrats. These reflect generational rather than life cycle effects (e.g., Abramson, 1983; Alwin, 1992; Glenn, 1974).

Age was also positively correlated with support for Jim Crow racism among whites after World War II (e.g., Kluegel, 1990; Schuman et al., 1997). However, as noted earlier, cohort analyses actually show waning support for Jim Crow racism within cohorts of white Americans as they aged during that period, reflecting a period rather than a life cycle effect (Danigelis & Cutler, 1991; Firebaugh & Davis, 1988; Sears, 1981). Both examples provide evidence against any universal conservatizing effect of age. Indeed, life cycle effects on attitudes have been especially difficult to pin down (Alwin, 1993, 1994).

An important further distinction is between psychological and sociological interpretations of life cycle effects. A nice behavioral example concerns the low voting turnout of young people. Some of this is generational (Putnam, 2000). But age differences in turnout are of long standing, so life stage is also implicated. A psychological interpretation is that consistent turnout, like strong partisanship, develops through experience with the political system. A common sociological interpretation is that young people are distracted from civic duties by the press of various transitions into adult roles, such as leaving school, leaving home, entering the work force, getting married, home ownership, and, often, geographic mobility. If so, turnout might increase with age merely because young people ultimately evolve past such obstacles to civic duty. Comparing these two views, Highton and Wolfinger (2001) found that successfully transitioning into such adult roles had quite mixed effects on turnout, whereas aging all by itself greatly increased it: having accomplished all six adult tasks increased voting turnout by only 6 percent, a small fraction of the 37 percent turnout gap between the young and those over age 60. The authors prefer the more psychological explanation that "pure learning" may be responsible (p. 208).

◢ The Case of Immigrants

As with many areas of political psychology, the available evidence about childhood and adult development rests heavily on the American political experience. It is only a single case, with a highly stable political system, even compared to other developed democracies such as France, Germany, the former Soviet Union, or South Africa. Examining people only in a stable political context risks overestimating the natural continuities within the individual life history. As one check, we can look at immigrants, who have changed from one political system to another.

Adult Development of National and Ethnic Identity

The persistence hypothesis would suggest that identification with an original nationality group would be stable within immigrants' life spans and would be passed on to their children, generating a strong ethnic group consciousness in politics (Uhlaner, Cain, & Kiewiet, 1989; Wolfinger, 1965). On the other hand, contemporary immigrants might follow the trajectory of the European immigrants of a century ago (Alba, 1990), with their original national identity (e.g., "Mexican") being slowly replaced across generations by an American ethnic identity (e.g., "Latino"), which in turn, with intermarriage, residential and occupational integration, and upward mobility, ultimately might be replaced by identification with the new nation (e.g., "American"), a process more consistent with the impressionable years hypothesis. Another possibility, consistent with the "openness" view, is that this whole process might occur within a single generation. A mixed alternative would be a more "segmented assimilation," in which some immigrant groups follow the trajectory of upward mobility and assimilation while others remain poor and with low levels of education, rebuffed by discrimination, and rejecting core American values, instead developing a strong ethnic identity as an alienated nationality group on American soil (Falcon, de la Garza, Garcia, & Garcia, 1992; Portes & Rumbaut, 2001).

Two recent studies test these alternatives. Surveys of Latino adults in Los Angeles County asked, "How do you primarily think of yourself: just as an American, both as an American and (ethnicity), or only as an (ethnicity)?" They tend to pass through three distinct stages (Citrin & Sears, 2003, ch. 3). Noncitizen immigrants tend to identify themselves primarily as ethnics and feel a strong sense of ethnic identity. Naturalized immigrants overwhelmingly say "both," and also have a fairly strong sense of ethnic identity. Nonimmigrant Latinos are very unlikely to think of themselves primarily as ethnic, their sense of ethnic identity is weaker, and they have a stronger sense of pride in America. Very similar differences between immigrants and nonimmigrants emerged in a large study of Asian and Latino undergraduates in California.

Party Identification

Immigrants also provide a test of the boundaries of the original theory of party identification. They are likely not to be exposed to much family transmission because their nonvoting parents often have no partisan preferences. Yet immigrants, arriving with the traditional attitudes and values of their own culture, appear to gradually assimilate to the norms of the dominant society. Relatively disadvantaged contemporary Latino immigrants gradually come to identify with the Democratic party, just as had those arriving a century earlier from Europe: the most Democratic Latinos tend to be those who are lower in income and unionized (Cain et al., 1991; de la Garza, DeSipio, Garcia, Garcia, & Falcon, 1992; DeSipio & de la Garza, 1992). And current immigrants, like earlier waves of European immigrants, seem to become more Republican as they become more affluent. Whether that change is intergenerational, as the persistence hypothesis would suggest, or intragenerational, as the lifelong openness hypothesis would suggest, is unclear; at least some Latino Republicans have a history of being ex-Democrats (Cain et al., 1991).

But immigrants may also import old loyalties and antagonisms from their native countries. For example, Republicans in the vigorously anticommunist Reagan era commanded majorities among refugees from communism from Cuba, Vietnam, Korea, and Taiwan, especially among those fleeing at the height of communist power. Democrats commanded large majorities among those from Mexico or Puerto Rico, who tend to immigrate for economic reasons (Cain et al., 1991; DeSipio & de la Garza, 1992). There is also some evidence that involvement in a previous political system tends to foster immigrants' politicization. Black (1987; Black, Niemi, & Powell, 1987) found that participation and partisanship in the Canadian political system were higher among the immigrants who had been the most interested in politics and politically active in their home countries.

Immigrants also provide an interesting test case of the hypothesis that partisanship strengthens with political experience, for which age is usually a proxy. Immigrants enter at a variety of different ages, so age does not bear a uniform relationship to the amount of political experience they have had with the new political system of the receiving nation. Rather, the strength of their partisanship should be a function of time since immigration. Indeed the longer immigrants have lived in the United States, and the more generations their families have been in the United States, the more likely they are to develop a party identification and identify as a strong partisan (Cain et al., 1991; Wong, 2000). Their age does not matter much. Of course, time in the new nation is not the only important variable. Naturalized citizens are more likely to acquire a partisan preference, and citizenship explains some of the effects of time, as if time doesn't "count" for as much until citizenship occurs, consistent with the presumed role of practice in the development of a partisan preference.

◣ Conclusions

In our view, continuing research on the problems that originally gave rise to the field have obtained somewhat surprising levels of support for its initial suppositions. The importance of studying the early learning of morality, racial and ethnic attitudes and identity, and partisanship now seems evident. Even proponents of a revisionist view suggest that the findings all "point to much continuity in political-response patterns over the course of an individual's life," notwithstanding the new tasks and roles people later encounter, as well as "considerable change in sociopolitical attitudes and behaviors" in response to new contingencies (Sigel, 1989, p. 458), and "the weight of these studies suggests that we should not usually expect dramatic evidence of change during adulthood" (Sapiro, 1994, p. 204). This recent research nicely documents the conditions under which adult change is most likely to occur. But in our view there has been something of an over-correction against the early claims of a broad and general persistence of political attitudes, and the center of gravity of the debate has swung a bit too far away from recognition of the substantial persistence manifested by some predispositions.

A second point we would make is that in recent years new foci of attention have arisen—such as the importance of distinguishing moral from other domains of reasoning (e.g., social-conventional), the importance of cognitive (in additional to social) factors in racial and ethnic attitudes, the increasing political importance of ethnic and national identity, the contin-uing importance of antagonisms against outgroups, and the increasing con-cern over civic education—that require developmental analyses, even if not to the exclusion of alternative approaches. These foci point to key mediators and moderators of stability and change across the life course. Moreover, long-term persistence is not merely a matter of internal psychology but also of a supportive social and political milieu.

We close with ruminations about two limitations of the literature we have discussed. One is that it has been to an excessive degree generated within North America. No doubt this reflects both where the main body of such research has been done and the limits of our own knowledge. It narrows us particularly in assessing how changing political contexts influ-ence the individual. For example, we present no solid estimate of the extent to which the great experiments at society-molding "took" in Maoist China, the Soviet Union, Nazi Germany or Islamic Iran. Second, we have reviewed a good bit of work on how specifically political events have influenced political development. But these are presumably a subset of the ways that individuals interact with the events of the larger world. Psychologists have not generally been sufficiently attentive to those interactions (though see Stewart & Healy, 1989).

Finally, we noted at the outset that much of the work in this chapter has been motivated, at least in part, by liberal social scientists seeking re-formist solutions to social problems. We should be cautious about normative implications of the research described here. On the matters taken up in this chapter, there is typically no one ideal outcome that all will agree to. The nature of politics—indeed, its primary raison d'être—is to adjudicate dis-putes over competing interests and preferences, not to ratify consensus over political ends. Even ethnocentrism and prejudice are often seen as justified by those who hold them, as harshly as they are condemned by their vic-tims and their sympathizers. Stereotypes have their beneficent uses as sim-plifiers and organizers, as much as they harm their victims and limit the social skills and circles of their holders. The merits of assimilation and separation of contending groups can be and are legitimately debated. And, as often was said in the months after the terrorist attacks on the World Trade Center, one man's "terrorist" is another man's "freedom fighter." If political psychology can teach us anything, it is that we must all constantly struggle to balance the natural tendency to glorify the familiar and those most like us with the need to sympathetically take the perspective of others. Social scientists may engage that struggle in more intellectual terms than the ordinary person, but a struggle it remains.

◣ Notes

We wish to express our thanks for helpful comments to Tom Bradbury, Martin Gilens, Donald Green, M. Kent Jennings, Melanie Killen, Clark McKown, Rodolfo Mendoza-Denton, Virginia Sapiro, Howard Schuman, and Nicholas Valentino.

1. One other early approach used the individual's retrospective judgment to assess persistence: Did they recall ever changing their party identification (Campbell et al., 1960)? Such judgments were later shown to be rather unreliable, usually overestimating stability (Niemi, Katz, & Newman, 1980).

◣ References

Aboud, F. E. (1987). The development of ethnic self-identification and attitudes. In J. S. Phinney & M. J. Rotherham (Eds.), *Children's ethnic socialization* (pp. 32–55). Newbury Park, CA: Sage.

Aboud, F. E. (1988). *Children and prejudice.* New York: Blackwell.

Aboud, F. E., & Amato, M. (2001). Developmental and socialization influences on intergroup bias. In R. Brown & S. Gaertner (Vol. eds.), *Blackwell handbook in social psychology: Vol. 4. Intergroup processes* (pp. 65–85). Oxford: Blackwell.

Aboud, F. E., & Doyle, A. B (1993). The early development of ethnic identity and attitudes. In M. E. Bernal & G. P. Knight (Eds.), *Ethnic identity: Formation and transmission among Hispanics and other minorities* (pp. 47–59). Albany: SUNY Press.

Aboud, F. E., & Doyle, A. B. (1996b). Parental and peer influences on children's racial attitudes. *International Journal of Intercultural Relations, 20,* 371–383.

Aboud, F. E., & Doyle, A. B. (1996a). Does talk of race foster prejudice or tolerance in children? *Canadian Journal of Behavioral Science, 28,* 161–170.

Aboud, F. E., & Fenwick, V. (1999). Evaluating school-based interventions to reduce prejudice in preadolescents. *Journal of Social Issues, 55,* 767–785.

Aboud, F. E., & Levy, S. R. (1999). Are we ready to translate research into programs? *Journal of Social Issues, 55,* 621–626.

Aboud, F. E., & Levy, S. R. (2000). Interventions to reduce prejudice and discrimination in children and adolescents. In S. Oskamp (Ed.), *Reducing prejudice and discrimination* (pp. 269–293). Mahwah, NJ: Erlbaum.

Abramson, P. R. (1983). *Political attitudes in America.* San Francisco: Freeman.

Achen, C. H. (1975). Mass political attitudes and the survey response. *American Political Science Review, 69,* 1218–1231.

Adelson, J. (1972). The political imagination of the young adolescent. In J. Kagan &

R. Coles (Eds.), *Twelve to sixteen: Early adolescence* (pp. 106–143). New York: Norton.

Adelson, J., Green, B., & O'Neil, R. P. (1969). Growth of the idea of law in adolescence. *Developmental Psychology, 1,* 327–332.

Adelson, J., & O'Neil, R. P. (1966). Growth of political ideas in adolescence: The sense of community. *Journal of Personality and Social Psychology, 4,* 295–306.

Adorno, T. W., Frenkel-Brunswick, E., Levinson, D. J., & Sanford, R. N. (1950). *The authoritarian personality.* New York: Harper.

Alba, R. D. (1990). *Ethnic identity: The transformation of white America.* New Haven: Yale University Press.

Alejandro-Wright, M. N. (1985). The child's conception of racial classification: A socio-cognitive model. In M. B. Spencer, G. K. Brookins, & W. R. Allen (Eds.), *Beginnings: Social and affective development of Black children* (pp. 185–200). Hillsdale, NJ: Erlbaum.

Allport, G. W. (1954). *The nature of prejudice.* Reading, MA: Addison-Wesley.

Allsop, D., & Weisberg, H. F. (1988). Measuring change in party identification in an election campaign. *American Journal of Political Science, 32,* 996–1017.

Altemeyer, B. (1998). The other "authoritarian personality." *Advances in Experimental Social Psychology, 30,* 47–92.

Alvarez, R. M., & Brehm, J. (1995). American ambivalence towards abortion policy: Development of a heteroskedastic probit model of competing values. *American Journal of Political Science, 39,* 1055–1082.

Alwin, D. F. (1992). Aging, cohorts, and social change: An examination of the generational replacement model of social change. In H. A. Becker (Ed.), *Dynamics of cohort and generations research* (pp. 93–95). Amsterdam: Thesis.

Alwin, D. F. (1993). Socio-political attitude development in adulthood: The role of generational and life-cycle factors. In Dagmar Krebs & Peter Schmidt (Eds.), *New directions in attitude measurement* (pp. 61–93). Berlin: de Gruyter.

Alwin, D. F. (1994). Aging, personality, and social change: The stability of individual differences over the adult life span. In D. Featherman, R. Lerner, & M. Perlmutter (Eds.), *Life-span development and behavior* (pp. 135–185). Mahwah, NJ: Erlbaum.

Alwin, D. F. (1995). Taking time seriously: Studying social change, social structure, and human lives. In Phyllis Moen, Glen H. Elder, Jr., & Kurt Luscher (Eds.), *Examining lives in context: Perspectives on the ecology of human development* (pp. 211–262). Washington, DC: American Psychological Association.

Alwin, D. F., Cohen, R. L., & Newcomb, T. M. (1991). *Aging, personality and social change: Attitude persistence and change over the life-span.* Madison: University of Wisconsin Press.

Alwin, D. F., & Krosnick, J. A. (1991). Aging, cohorts, and the stability of socio-political orientations over the life span. *American Journal of Sociology, 97,* 169–195.

Ambady, N., Shih, M., Kim, A., & Pittinsky, T. (2001). Stereotype susceptibility in children: Effects of identity activation on quantitative performance. *Psychological Science, 12,* 385–390.

Annis, R. C., & Corenblum, B. (1987). Effect of test language and experimenter race on Canadian Indian children's racial and self-identity. *Journal of Social Psychology, 126,* 761–773.

Arnett, J. J. (1999). Adolescent storm and stress, reconsidered. *American Psychologist,*
    54, 317–326.

Arnett, J. J. (2000). Emerging adulthood: A theory of development from the late
    teens through the twenties. *American Psychologist, 55,* 469–480.

Astin, A. W., Parrott, S. A., Korn, W. S., & Sax, L. J. (1997). *The American freshman:*
    Thirty year trends, 1966–1996. Los Angeles: Higher Education Research Insti-
    tute, Graduate School of Education and Information Studies, University of
    California, Los Angeles.

Banks, J. A. (1995). Multicultural education and the modification of students' racial
    attitudes. In W. D. Hawley & A. W. Jackson (Eds.), *Toward a common destiny*
    (pp. 315–339). San Francisco: Jossey-Bass.

Bar-Tal, D. (1996). Development of social categories and stereotypes in early child-
    hood: The case of "the Arab" concept formation, stereotype and attitudes by
    Jewish children in Israel. *International Journal of Intercultural Relations, 20,* 341–
    370.

Beck, P. A., & Jennings, M. K. (1991). Family traditions, political periods, and the
    development of partisan orientations. *Journal of Politics, 53,* 742–763.

Bernal, M. E., & Knight, G. P. (1993). Introduction. In M. E. Bernal & G. P. Knight
    (Eds.), *Ethnic identity: Formation and transmission among Hispanics and other*
    minorities (pp. 1–7). Albany: SUNY Press.

Bernal, M. E., Knight, G. P., Garza, C. A., Ocampo, K. A., & Cota, M. K. (1990).
    The development of ethnic identity in Mexican-American children. *Hispanic*
    Journal of Behavioral Sciences, 12, 3–24.

Berry, J., Trimble, J., & Olmedo, E. (1986). Assessment of acculturation. In W. Lon-
    ner & J. Berry (Eds.), *Field methods in cross-cultural research* (pp. 292–324).
    Newbury Park, CA: Sage.

Berry, J. W. (1980). Social and cultural change. In H. C. Triandis & R. Brislin (Eds.),
    Handbook of cross-cultural psychology (Vol. 5, pp. 211–279). Boston: Allyn and
    Bacon.

Berry, J. W. (1999). Intercultural relations in plural societies. *Canadian Psychology, 40,*
    12–21.

Bettelheim, B., & Janowitz, M. (1950). *Dynamics of prejudice.* New York: Harper.

Beuf, A. H. (1977). *Red children in white America.* Philadelphia: University of Penn-
    sylvania Press.

Bigler, R. S. (1999). The use of multicultural curricula and materials to counter ra-
    cism in children. *Journal of Social Issues, 55,* 687–705.

Bigler, R. S., & Liben, L. S. (1992). Cognitive mechanisms in children's gender stere-
    otyping: Theoretical and educational implications of a cognitive-based interven-
    tion. *Child Development, 63,* 1351–1363.

Bigler, R. S., & Liben, L. S. (1993). A cognitive-developmental approach to racial
    stereotyping and reconstructive memory in Euro-American children. *Child De-*
    velopment, 64, 1507–1518.

Black, J. H. (1987). The practice of politics in two settings: Political transferability
    among recent immigrants to Canada. *Canadian Journal of Political Science, 20,*
    731–753.

Black, J. H., Niemi, R. G., & Powell, G. B., Jr. (1987). Age, resistance, and political
    learning in a new environment: The case of Canadian immigrants. *Comparative*
    Politics, 73–84.

Black-Gutman, D., & Hickson, F. (1996). The relationship between racial attitudes and social-cognitive development in children: An Australian study. *Developmental Psychology, 32,* 448–456.

Brader, T., & Tucker, J. A. (2001). The emergence of mass partisanship in Russia, 1993–1996. *American Journal of Political Science, 45,* 69–83.

Branch, C. W., & Newcombe, N. (1986). Racial attitude development among Black children as a function of parental attitudes: A longitudinal and cross-sectional study. *Child Development, 57,* 712–721.

Brown, R. (1995). *Prejudice: Its social psychology.* Malden, MA: Blackwell

Brown, T. A. (1988). *Migration and politics: The impact of population mobility on American voting behavior.* Chapel Hill: University of North Carolina Press.

Butler, D., & Stokes, D. (1969). *Political change in Britain.* New York: St. Martin's Press.

Cain, B. E., Kiewiet, D. R., & Uhlaner, C. J. (1991). The acquisition of partisanship by Latinos and Asian Americans. *American Journal of Political Science, 35,* 390–422.

Cameron, J. A., Alvarez, J. M., Ruble, D. N., & Fuligni, A. J. (2001). Children's lay theories about ingroups and outgroups: Reconceptualizing research on prejudice. *Personality and Social Psychology Review, 5,* 118–128.

Campbell, A., Converse, P. E., Miller, W. E., & Stokes, D. E. (1960). *The American voter.* New York: Wiley.

Carlson, J. M., & Iovini, J. (1985). The transmission of racial attitudes from fathers to sons: A study of blacks and whites. *Adolescence, 20,* 233–237.

Carlsson, G., & Karlsson, K. (1970). Age, cohorts, and the generation of generations. *American Sociological Review, 35,* 710–718.

Carmines, E. G., & Stimson, James A. (1989). *Issue evolution: Race and the transformation of American politics.* Princeton: Princeton University Press.

Cassel, C. A. (1999). Testing the Converse party support model in Britain. *Comparative Political Studies, 32,* 626–644.

Centers, R. (1950). Children of the New Deal: Social stratification and adolescent attitudes. *International Journal of Opinion and Attitude Research, 4,* 315–335.

Chaffee, S. H., & Yang, S-M. (1990). Communication and political socialization. In O. Ichilov (Ed.), *Political Socialization, Citizenship Education, and Democracy* (pp. 137–157). New York: Teachers College Press.

Chan, K. S., & Hune, S. (1995). Racialization and panethnicity: From Asians in American to Asian Americans. In W. D. Hawley & A. W. Jackson (Eds.), *Toward a common destiny* (pp. 205–233). San Francisco: Jossey-Bass.

Citrin, J., & Sears, D. O. (2003). The politics of multiculturalism and the crisis of American identity. Unpublished manuscript.

Claggett, W. (1981). Partisan acquisition versus partisan intensity: Life-cycle, generation and period effects, 1952–1976. *American Journal of Political Science, 25,* 193–214.

Clark, K., & Clark, M. (1939)). The development of consciousness of self and the emergence of racial identification of Negro school children. *Journal of Social Psychology, 10,* 591–599.

Clark, K., & Clark, M. (1940). Skin color as a factor in racial identification and preference in Negro children. *Journal of Negro Education, 19,* 341–358.

Colby, A., & Kohlberg, L. (1984). Invariant sequence and internal consistency in moral judgment stages. In W. M. Kurtines & J. L. Gewirtz (Eds.), *Morality, moral behavior, and oral development*. New York: Wiley.

Colby, A., Kohlberg, L., Gibbs, J., & Lieberman, M. (1983). A longitudinal study of moral development. *Monographs of the Society for Research in Child Development, 48* (1–2, Serial No. 200).

Coleman, P. T., & Deutsch, M. (1995). The mediation of interethnic conflict in schools. In W. D. Hawley & A. W. Jackson (Eds.), *Toward a common destiny* (pp. 371–396). San Francisco: Jossey-Bass.

Converse, P. E. (1964). The nature of belief systems in mass publics. In David E. Apter (Ed.), *Ideology and discontent* (pp. 206–261). New York: Free Press of Glencoe.

Converse, P. E. (1969). Of time and partisan stability. *Comparative Political Studies, 2,* 139–171.

Converse, P. E. (1976). *The dynamics of party support: Cohort-analyzing party identification*. Beverly Hills, CA: Sage.

Converse, P. E., & Markus, G. B. (1979). Plus ça change . . . : The new CPS election study panel. *American Political Science Review, 73,* 32–49.

Converse, P. E., & Pierce, R. (1992). Partisanship and the party system. *Political Behavior, 14,* 239–259.

Cook, T. E. (1985). The bear market in political socialization and the costs of misunderstood psychological theories. *American Political Science Review, 79,* 1079–1093.

Crittenden, J. (1962). Aging and party affiliation. *Public Opinion Quarterly, 26,* 648–657.

Cross, W. E., Jr. (1978). The Thomas Cross models of psychological nigrescence: A literature review. *Journal of Black Psychology, 4,* 13–31.

Cross, W. E., Jr. (1991). *Shades of black: Diversity is African-American identity*. Philadelphia: Temple University Press.

Cross, W. E., Jr. (1995). Oppositional identity and African-American youth: Issues and prospects. In W. D. Hawley & A. W. Jackson (Eds.), *Toward a common destiny* (pp. 185–204). San Francisco: Jossey-Bass.

Damon, W. (1975). Early conceptions of positive justice as related to the development of logical operations. *Child Development, 46,* 301–312.

Damon, W. (1977). *The social world of the child*. San Francisco: Jossey-Bass.

Damon, W. (1980). Patterns of change in children's social reasoning: A two-year longitudinal study. *Child Development, 51,* 1010–1017.

Damon, W. (1983). *Social and personality development: Infancy through adolescence*. New York: Norton.

Danigelis, N. L., & Cutler, S. J. (1991). An inter-cohort comparison of changes in racial attitudes. *Research on Aging, 13,* 383–404.

Danowski, J. A., & Ruchinskas, J. E. (1983). Period, cohort, and aging effects: A study of television exposure in presidential election campaigns, 1952–1980. *Communication Research, 10,* 77–96.

Davis, J. A. (1992). Changeable weather in a cooling climate atop the liberal plateau: Conversion and replacement in forty-two general social survey items, 1972–1989. *Public Opinion Quarterly, 56,* 261–306.

de la Garza, R. O., DeSipio, L., Garcia, F. C., Garcia, J. & Falcon, A. (1992). *Latino voices: Mexican, Puerto Rican, & Cuban perspectives on American politics*. Boulder, CO: Westview Press.

Delli Carpini, M. X. (2000). Gen.com: Youth, civic engagement, and the new information environment. *Political Communication, 17,* 341–349.

DeSipio, L., & de la Garza, R. O. (1992, September). Will Latino numbers equal political clout? Core voters, swing voters, and the potential vote. Paper presented at the annual meeting of the American Political Science Association, Chicago.

Deutsch, M. (1993). Educating for a peaceful world. *American Psychologist, 48,* 1–8.

Dovidio, J. F., & Gaertner, S. L. (1986). *Prejudice, discrimination, and racism.* San Diego, CA: Academic Press.

Dovidio, J. F., & Gaertner, S. L. (2000). Aversive racism and selection decisions: 1989 and 1999. *Psychological Science, 11,* 315–319.

Doyle, A. B, & Aboud, F. E. (1995). A longitudinal study of white children's racial prejudice as a social-cognitive development. *Merrill-Palmer Quarterly, 41,* 209–228.

Doyle, A. B., Beaudet, J., & Aboud, F. E. (1988). Developmental patterns in the flexibility of children's ethnic attitudes. *Journal of Cross-Cultural Psychology, 19,* 3–18.

Easton, D., & Dennis, J. (1969). *Children in the political system: Origins of political legitimacy.* New York: McGraw-Hill.

Elder, G. H., Jr. (1974). *Children of the great depression.* Chicago: University of Chicago Press.

Erikson, E. H. (1968). *Identity, youth, and crisis.* New York: Norton.

Espiritu, Y. L. (1992). *Asian American panethnicity: Bridging institutions and identities.* Philadelphia: Temple University Press.

Falcon, A., de la Garza, R. O., Garcia, F. C., & Garcia, J. A. (1992, September). Ethnicity and American political values: A comparison of Puerto Ricans and Anglos. Paper presented at the annual meeting of the American Political Science Association, Chicago.

Fendrich, James M., & Lovoy, Kenneth L. (1988). Back to the future: Adult political behavior of former student activists. *American Sociological Review, 53,* 780–784.

Feuer, L. S. (1969). *The conflict of generations: The character and significance of student movements.* New York: Basic Books.

Fiorina, M. P. (1981). *Retrospective voting in American national elections.* New Haven: Yale University Press.

Firebaugh, G., & Chen, K. (1995). Vote turnout of nineteenth amendment women: The enduring effect of disenfranchisement. *American Journal of Sociology, 100,* 972–996.

Firebaugh, G., & Davis, K. E. (1988). Trends in antiblack prejudice, 1972–1984: Region and cohort effects. *American Journal of Sociology, 94,* 251–272.

Fishbein, H. D. (1996). *Peer prejudice and discrimination: Evolutionary, cultural, and developmental dynamics.* Boulder, CO: Westview Press.

Fordham, S., & Ogbu, J. U. (1986). Black students' school success: Coping with the "burden of 'acting white.' " *Urban Review, 18,* 176–206.

Garcia, E. E., & Hurtado, A. (1995). Becoming American: A review of current research on the development of racial and ethnic identity in children. In W. D. Hawley & A. W. Jackson (Eds.), *Toward a common destiny* (pp. 163–184). San Francisco: Jossey-Bass.

Genesee, F., & Gandura, P. (1999). Bilingual education programs: A cross-national perspective. *Journal of Social Issues, 55,* 627–643.

Genesee, F., Tucker, G. R., & Lambert, W. E. (1978). The development of ethnic identity and ethnic role-taking skills in children from different school settings. *International Journal of Psychology, 13,* 39–57.

Gilligan, C. (1977). In a different voice: Women's conceptions of the self and morality. *Harvard Educational Review, 47,* 481–517.

Gilligan, C. (1982). *In a different voice: Psychological theory and women's development.* Cambridge, MA: Harvard University Press.

Glaser, J. M., & Gilens, M. (1997). Interregional migration and political resocialization: A study of racial attitudes under pressure. *Public Opinion Quarterly, 61,* 72–86.

Glass, J., Bengtson, V. L., & Dunham, C. C. (1986). Attitude similarity in three-generation families: Socialization, status inheritance, or reciprocal influence? *American Sociological Review, 51,* 685–698.

Glenn, N. D. (1974). Aging and conservatism. *Annals of the American Academy of Political and Social Science, 33,* 176–186.

Gonzales, N. A., & Cauce, A. M. (1995). Ethnic identity and multicultural competence: Dilemmas and challenges for minority youth. In W. D. Hawley & A. W. Jackson (Eds.), *Toward a common destiny* (pp. 131–162). San Francisco: Jossey-Bass.

Graves, S. B. (1999). Television and prejudice reduction: When does television as a vicarious experience make a difference? *Journal of Social Issues, 55,* 707–728.

Green, D. P., & Palmquist, B. (1994). How stable is party identification? *Political Behavior, 16,* 437–466.

Green, D. P., & Schickler, E. (1993). A multiple method approach to the measurement of party identification. *Public Opinion Quarterly, 57,* 503–535.

Greene, S. (1999). Understanding party identification: A social identity approach. *Political Psychology, 20,* 393–403.

Greenstein, F. I. (1965). *Children and politics.* New Haven: Yale University Press.

Greenstein, F. I. (1970). A note on the ambiguity of "political socialization": Definitions, criticisms, and strategies of inquiry. *Journal of Politics, 32,* 969–978.

Gregor, J. A., & McPherson, D. A (1966). Racial preference and ego identity among White and Bantu children in the Republic of South Africa. *Genetic Psychology Monographs, 73,* 218–253.

Halbwachs, M. (1950/1980). *The collective memory.* New York: Harper.

Harding, J., Proshansky, H., Kutner, B., & Chein, I. (1969). Prejudice and ethnic relations. In G. Lindzey & E. Aronson (Eds.), *The handbook of social psychology* (Vol. 5, pp. 1–76). Reading, MA: Addison-Wesley.

Hardy, R. J., Carrier, J. J, & Endersby, J. W. (2000, August–September). Family stability and the transmission of partisanship and ideology in one- and two-parent families. Prepared for the annual meeting of the American Political Science Association, Washington, DC.

Hauser, M., & Carey, S. (1998). Building a cognitive creature from a set of primitives: Evolutionary and developmental insights. In D. Cummins Dellarosa & C. Allen (Eds.), *The evolution of mind* (pp. 51–106). New York: Oxford University Press.

Helms, J. E. (Ed.). (1993). *Black and White racial identity: Theory, research and practice.* New York: Greenwood.

Helwig, C. C. (1998). Children's conceptions of fair government and freedom of speech. *Child Development, 69,* 518–531.

Helwig, C. C., & Jasiobedzka, U. (2001). The relation between law and morality: Children's reasoning about socially beneficial and unjust laws. *Child Development, 72,* 1382–1393.

Helwig, C. C., & Prencipe, A. (1999). Children's judgments of flags and flag-burning. *Child Development, 70,* 132–143.

Hess, R. D., & Torney, J. V. (1967). *The development of political attitudes in children.* Chicago: Aldine.

Highton, B., & Wolfinger, R. E. (2001). The first seven years of the political life cycle. *American Journal of Political Science, 45,* 202–209.

Hirschfeld, L. A. (1995). Do children have a theory of race? *Cognition, 54,* 209–252.

Hirschfeld, L. A. (2001). On a folk theory of society: Children, evolution, and mental representations of social groups. *Personality and Social Psychology Review, 5,* 107–117.

Hochschild, J. L. (1981). *What's fair? American beliefs about distributive justice.* Cambridge, MA: Harvard University Press.

Hollins, E. R. (1999). Relating ethnic and racial identity development to teaching. In R. H. Sheets & E. R. Hollins (Eds.), *Racial and ethnic identity in school practices: Aspects of human development* (pp. 183–194). Mahwah, NJ: Erlbaum.

Hraba, J., & Grant, G. (1970). Black is beautiful: A reexamination of racial preference and identification. *Journal of Personality and Social Psychology, 16,* 398–402.

Huckfeldt, R., Beck, P. A., Dalton, R. J., & Levine, J. (1995). Political environments, cohesive social groups, and the communication of public opinion. *American Journal of Political Science, 39,* 1025–1054.

Hyman, H. H. (1959). *Political socialization.* Glencoe, IL: Free Press.

Jennings, M. K. (1987). Residues of a movement: The aging of the American protest generation. *American Political Science Review, 81,* 367–382.

Jennings, M. K. (1996). Political knowledge over time and across generations. *Public Opinion Quarterly, 60,* 228–252.

Jennings, M. K. (2002). The dynamics of student protest behavior: An intra-and intergenerational analysis. *Political Psychology, 23,* 303–324.

Jennings, M. K., & Markus, G. B. (1977). The effect of military service on political attitudes: A panel study. *American Political Science Review, 71,* 131–147.

Jennings, M. K., & Markus, G. B. (1984). Partisan orientations over the long haul: Results from the three-wave political socialization panel study. *American Political Science Review, 78,* 1000–1018.

Jennings, M. K., & Niemi, R. G. (1974). *The political character of adolescence.* Princeton: Princeton University Press.

Jennings, M. K., & Niemi, R. G. (1981). *Generations and politics.* Princeton: Princeton University Press.

Jennings, M. K., & Stoker, L. (1999, April). The persistence of the past: The class of 1965 turns fifty. Prepared for presentation at the Midwest Political Science Association Convention, Chicago.

Jennings, M. K., Stoker, L., & Bowers, J. (1999, September). Politics across generations: Family transmission reexamined. Prepared for presentation at the American Political Science Association convention, Atlanta, GA.

Jervis, R. (1976). *Perception and misperception in international politics.* Princeton: Princeton University Press.

Johnson, D. W., & Johnson, R. T. (2000). The three Cs of reducing prejudice and discrimination. In S. Oskamp (Ed.), *Reducing prejudice and discrimination* (pp. 239–268). Mahwah, NJ: Erlbaum.

Jones, J. M. (1997). *Prejudice and racism.* New York: McGraw-Hill.

Katz, P. A. (1976). The acquisition of racial attitudes. In P. A. Katz (Ed.), *Towards the elimination of racism* (pp. 3–20). New York: Pergamon.

Katz, P. A., Sohn, M., & Zalk, S. R. (1975). Perceptual concomitant of racial attitudes in urban grade-school children. *Developmental Psychology, 11,* 135–144.

Katz, P. A. & Zalk, S. R. (1978). Modification of children's racial attitudes. *Developmental Psychology, 14,* 447–461.

Killen, M., Leviton, M., & Cahill, J. (1991). Adolescent reasoning about drug use. *Journal of Adolescent Research, 6,* 336–356.

Killen, K., McGlothlin, H., & Lee-Kim, J. (2002). Between individuals and culture: Individuals' evaluations of exclusion from social groups. In H. Keller, Y. Poortinga, & A. Schoelmerich (Eds.), *Between biology and culture: Perspectives on the Ontogenetic Development.* (pp. 159–90). Cambridge: Cambridge University Press.

Killen, M., & Stangor, C. (2001). Children's social reasoning about inclusion and exclusion in gender and race peer group contexts. *Child Development, 72,* 174–186.

Kinder, D. R., & Sanders, L. M. (1996). *Divided by color: Racial politics and democratic ideals.* Chicago: University of Chicago Press.

Kluegel, J. R. (1990). Trends in whites' explanations of the black-white gap in socioeconomic status, 1977–1989. *American Sociological Review, 55,* 512–525.

Knight, G. P., Bernal, M. E., Garza, C. A., Cota, M. K., & Ocampo, K. A. (1993). Family socialization and Mexican American identity and behavior. In M. E. Bernal and G. P. Knight (Eds.), *Ethnic identity: Formation and transmission among Hispanics and other minorities.* Albany: SUNY Press.

Kofkin, J. A., Katz, P. A., & Downey, E. P. (1995, April). *Family discourse about race and the development of children's racial attitudes.* Paper presented at meeting of the Society for Research in Child Development, Indianapolis.

Kohlberg, L. (1969). Stage and sequence: The cognitive-developmental approach to socialization. In D. A. Goslin (Ed.), *Handbook of socialization theory and research* (pp. 347–480). Chicago: Rand-McNally.

Kohlberg, L. (1976). Moral stages and moralization: The cognitive-developmental approach to socialization. In D. A. Goslin (Ed.), *Handbook of socialization theory and research.* Chicago: Rand-McNally.

Kohlberg, L. (1984). *Essays on moral development: Vol 2. The psychology of moral development.* San Francisco: Harper & Row.

Kohlberg, L., & Candee, D. (1984). The relationship of moral judgment to moral action. In W. M. Kurtines & J. L. Gewirtz (Eds.), *Morality, moral behavior, and moral development.* (pp. 52–73). New York: Wiley.

Kuhn, D. (1976). Short-term longitudinal evidence for the sequentiality of Kohlberg's early stages of oral development. *Developmental Psychology, 12,* 162–166.

Kurtines, W. M., & Grief, E. B. (1974). The development of moral thought: Review and evaluation of Kohlberg's approach. *Psychological Bulletin, 81,* 453–470.

Lambert, W. E., & Klineberg, O. (1967). *Children's views of foreign peoples.* New York: Appleton-Century-Crofts.

Laupa, M. (1991). Children's reasoning about three authority attributes: Adult status, knowledge, and social position. *Developmental Psychology, 27,* 321–329.

Laupa, M., Turiel, E., & Cowan, P. A. (1995). Obedience to authority in children and adults. In M. Killen, & D. Hart (Eds.), *Morality in everyday life: Developmental perspectives.* (pp. 131–165). Cambridge studies in social and emotional development. New York: Cambridge University Press.

Lawrence, V. W. (1991). Effect of socially ambiguous information on white and black children's behavioral and trait perceptions. *Merrill-Palmer Quarterly, 37,* 619–630.

Lee, S. J. (1999). Are you Chinese or what? Ethnic identity among Asian Americans. In R. H. Sheets & E. R. Hollins (Eds.), *Racial and ethnic identity in school practices: Aspects of human development* (pp. 107–121). Mahwah, NJ: Erlbaum.

Levy, S. R. (1999). Reducing prejudice: Lessons from social-cognitive factors underlying perceiver differences in prejudice. *Journal of Social Issues, 55,* 745–766.

Levy, S. R., & Dweck, C. S. (1999). The impact of children's static vs. dynamic conceptions of people on stereotype formation. *Child Development, 70,* 1163–1180.

Loewenberg, P. (1971). The psychohistorical origins of the Nazi youth cohort. *American Historical Review, 76,* 1457–1502.

Mannheim, K. (1928/1952). The problem of generations. In P. Kecskemeti (Ed.), *Essays on the sociology of knowledge.* London: Routledge and Kegan Paul.

Marchant-Shapiro, T., & Patterson, K. D. (1995). Partisan change in the mountain west. *Political Behavior, 17,* 359–378.

Marcia, J. (1980). Identity in adolescence. In J. Adelson (Ed.), *Handbook of adolescent psychology* (pp. 159–187). New York: Wiley.

Markstrom, C. A., & Hunter, C. L. (1999). The roles of ethnic and ideological identity in predicting fidelity in African American and European American adolescents. *Child Study Journal, 29,* 23–38l.

Markus, G. B. (1983). Dynamic modeling of cohort change: The case of political partisanship. *American Journal of Political Science, 27,* 717–739.

Marsh, D. (1971). Political socialization: The implicit assumptions questioned. *British Journal of Political Science, 1,* 453–465.

Martin, C. L., & Halverson, C. F. (1981). A schematic processing model of sex-typing and stereotyping in children. *Child Development, 52,* 1119–1134.

Marwell, G., Aiken, M. T., & Demerath, N. J., III. (1987). The persistence of political attitudes among 1960s civil rights activists. *Public Opinion Quarterly, 51,* 359–375.

Mason, K. O., Mason, W. M., Winsborough, H. H., & Poole, W. K. (1973). Some methodological issues in cohort analysis of archival data. *American Sociological Review, 38,* 242–258.

Matute-Bianchi, M. (1986). Ethnic identities and patterns of school success and failure among Mexican-descent and Japanese-American students in a California high school: an ethnographic analysis. *American Journal of Education, 95,* 233–255.

McAdam, D. (1989). The biographical consequences of activism. *American Sociological Review, 54,* 744–760.

McKown, C. & Weinstein, R. S. (2002). Modeling the role of child ethnicity and gender in children's differential response to teacher expectations. *Journal of Applied Social Psychology, 32,* 159–184.

Merelman, R. M. (1986). Revitalizing political socialization. In M. G. Hermann (Ed.), *Political Psychology* (pp. 279–319). San Francisco: Jossey-Bass.

Miller, A. H., Gurin, P., Gurin, G., & Malanchuk, O. (1981). Group consciousness and political participation. *American Journal of Political Science, 25*, 494–511.

Miller, A. H., & Klobucar, T. F. (2000). The development of party identification in post-Soviet societies. *American Journal of Political Science, 44*, 667–685.

Miller, S., & Sears, D. O. (1986). Stability and change in social tolerance: A test of the persistence hypothesis. *American Journal of Political Science, 30*, 214–236.

Miller, W. E., & Shanks, J. M. (1996). *The new American voter.* Cambridge, MA: Harvard University Press.

Neville, H. A., Lilly, R. L., Duran, G., Lee, R. M., & Browne, L. (2000). Construction and initial validation of the Color-Blind Racial Attitudes Scale (CoBRAS). *Journal of Counseling Psychology, 47*, 59–70.

Newcombe, N. S., Drummey, A. B., Fox, N. A., Lie, E., & Ottinger-Alberts, W. (2000). Remembering early childhood: How much, how, and why (or why not). *Current Directions in Psychological Science, 9*, 55–58.

Newcomb, T. M. (1943). *Personality and social change.* New York: Dryden Press.

Niemi, R. G. (1973). Political socialization. In J. N. Knutson (Ed.), *Handbook of political psychology* (pp. 117–138) San Francisco: Jossey-Bass.

Niemi, R. G. (1974). *How family members perceive each other.* New Haven: Yale University Press.

Niemi, R. G., & Hepburn, M. A. (1995). The rebirth of political socialization. *Perspectives on Political Science, 24*, 7–16.

Niemi, R. G., & Jennings, M. K. (1991). Issues and inheritance in the formation of party identification. *American Journal of Political Science, 35*, 970–988.

Niemi, R. G., Katz, R. S., & Newman, D. (1980). Reconstructing past partisanship: The failure of the party identification recall questions. *American Journal of Political Science, 24*, 633–651.

Nucci, L. P. (1981). Conceptions of personal issues: A domain distinct from moral and societal concepts. *Child Development, 52*, 114–121.

Nucci, L., & Killen, M. (1991). Social interactions in the preschool and the development of moral and social concepts. In B. Scales & M. Almy (Eds.), *Play and the social context of development in early care and education. Early childhood education series* (pp. 219–233). New York: Teachers College Press.

Nucci, L. P., & Lee, J. Y. (1993). Morality and autonomy. In G. G. Noam & T. E. Wren (Eds.), *The moral self* (pp. 123–148). Cambridge, MA: MIT Press.

Ocampo, K. A., Bernal, M. E., & Knight, G. P. (1993). Gender, race, and ethnicity: The sequencing of social constancies. In M. E. Bernal and G. P. Knight (Eds.), *Ethnic identity: Formation and transmission among Hispanics and other minorities* (pp. 47–59). Albany: SUNY Press.

Oskamp, S. (2000). *Reducing prejudice and discrimination.* Mahwah, NJ: Erlbaum.

Patchen, M. (1983). Students' own racial attitudes and those of peers of both races, as related to interracial behavior. *Sociology and Social Research, 68*, 59–77.

Pew Research Center for the People and the Press. (1998). Teens losing respect for politicians: White House scandal has families talking. Author.

Phelan, P., Davidson, A., & Yu, H. C. (1998). *Adolescents' worlds: Negotiating family, peers, and school.* New York: Teachers College Press.

Phinney, J. (1989). Stages of ethnic identity development in minority group adolescents. *Journal of Early Adolescence, 9*, 34–49.

Phinney, J. S. (1990). Ethnic identity in adolescents and adults: Review of research. *Psychological Bulletin, 108*, 499–514.

Phinney, J. S., & Chavira, V. (1992). Parental ethnic socialization and adolescent coping with problems related to ethnicity. *Journal of Research in Adolescence, 5,* 31–53.

Phinney, J. S., Romero, I., Nava, M., & Huang, D. (2001). The role of language, parents, and peers in ethnic identity among adolescents in immigrant families. *Journal of Youth and Adolescence, 30,* 135–153.

Piaget, J. (1932/1965). *The moral judgment of the child.* New York: Free Press.

Piaget, J. & Weil, A. M. (1951). The development in children of the idea of the homeland and of relations to other countries. *International Social Science Journal, 3,* 561–578.

Portes, A., & Rumbaut, R. G. (2001). *Legacies: The story of the immigrant second generation.* Berkeley: University of California Press.

Powlishta, K. K., Serbin, L. A., Doyle, A., & White, D. (1994). Gender, ethnic, and body type biases: The generality of prejudice in childhood. *Developmental Psychology, 30,* 526–536.

Putnam, R. D. (2000). *Bowling alone: The collapse and revival of American community.* New York: Simon and Schuster.

Quintana, S. M. (1994). A model of ethnic perspective-taking ability applied to Mexican-American children and youth. *International Journal of Intercultural Relations, 18,* 419–448.

Quintana, S. M. (1998). Children's developmental understanding of ethnicity and race. *Applied and Preventive Psychology, 7,* 27–45.

Rapoport, R. B. (1997). Partisanship change in a candidate-centered era. *The Journal of Politics, 59,* 185–199.

Raviv, A., Sadeh, A., Raviv, A., Silberstein, O., & Diver, O. (2000). Young Israelis' reactions to national trauma: The Rabin assassination and terror attacks. *Political Psychology, 21,* 299–322.

Rest, J. R. (1983). Morality. In P. H. Mussen (Ed.), *Handbook of child psychology. Vol. 3. Cognitive development.* New York: Wiley.

Richardson, T. Q., & Silvestri, T. J. (1999). White identity formation: A developmental process. In R. H. Sheets & E. R. Hollins (Eds.), *Racial and ethnic identity in school practices: Aspects of human development* (pp. 183–194). Mahwah, NJ: Erlbaum.

Rogler, L. H., Cortes, D. E., & Malgady, R. G. (1991). Acculturation and mental health status among Hispanics: Convergence and new direction research. *American Psychologist, 46,* 585–597.

Rotheram, M. J., & Phinney, J. S. (1987). Ethnic behavior patterns as an aspect of identity. In J. Phinney & M. J. Rotheram (Eds.), *Children's ethnic socialization: Pluralism and development* (pp. 201–217). Newbury Park, CA: Sage.

Rotheram-Borus, M. J. (1993). Biculturalism among adolescents. In M. E. Bernal & G. P. Knight (Eds.), *Ethnic identity: Formation and transmission among Hispanics and other minorities* (pp. 81–102). Albany: SUNY Press.

Rowe, W., Bennett, S. K., & Atkinson, D. R. (1994). White racial identity models: A critique and alternative proposal. *Counseling Psychologist, 22,* 129–146.

Sagar, H. A., & Schofield, J. W. (1980). Racial and behavioral cues in Black and White children's perceptions of ambiguously aggressive acts. *Journal of Personality and Social Psychology, 39,* 590–598.

Sapiro, V. (1994). Political socialization during adulthood: Clarifying the political time of our lives. *Research in Micropolitics, 4,* 197–223.

Schickler, E., & Green, D. P. (1997). The stability of party identification in western democracies: Results from eight panel surveys. *Comparative Political Studies, 30,* 450–483.

Schofield, J. W. (1986). Causes and consequences of the colorblind perspective. In J. F. Dovidio & S. L. Gaertner (Eds.), *Prejudice, discrimination, and racism* (pp. 231–253). Orlando, FL: Academic Press.

Schuman, H., & Rieger, C. (1992). Historical analogies, generational effects, and attitudes toward war. *American Sociological Review, 57,* 315–326.

Schuman, H., & Scott, J. (1989). Generations and collective memories. *American Sociological Review, 54,* 359–381.

Schuman, H., Steeh, C., Bobo, L., & Krysan, M. (1997). *Racial attitudes in America: Trends and interpretations* (Rev. ed.). Cambridge, MA: Harvard University Press.

Schweder, R. A. (1982). Liberalism as destiny. *Contemporary Psychology, 27,* 421–424.

Searing, D. D., Schwartz, J. J., & Lind, A. E. (1973). The structuring principle: Political socialization and belief systems. *American Political Science Review, 67,* 415–432.

Searing, D. D., Wright, G., & Rabinowitz, G. (1976). The primacy principle: Attitude change and political socialization. *British Journal of Political Science, 6,* 83–113.

Sears, D. O. (1975). Political socialization. In F. I. Greenstein, & N. W. Polsby (Eds.), *Handbook of political science* (Vol. 2, pp. 93–153). Reading, MA: Addison-Wesley.

Sears, D. O. (1981). Life stage effects upon attitude change, especially among the elderly. In S. B. Kiesler, J. N. Morgan, & V. K. Oppenheimer (Eds.), *Aging: Social change* (pp. 183–204). New York: Academic Press.

Sears, D. O. (1983). The persistence of early political predispositions: The roles of attitude object and life stage. In L. Wheeler & P. Shaver (Eds.), *Review of personality and social psychology* (Vol. 4, pp. 79–116). Beverly Hills, CA: Sage.

Sears, D. O. (1990). Whither political socialization research? The question of persistence. In O. Ichilov (Ed.), *Political socialization, citizenship, education, and democracy* (pp. 69–97). New York: Teachers College Press.

Sears, D. O. (2002). Long-term psychological consequences of political events. In K. R. Monroe (Ed.), *Political psychology* (pp. 249–269). Mahwah, NJ: Erlbaum.

Sears, D. O., & Funk, C. L. (1991). The role of self-interest in social and political attitudes. In M. Zanna (Ed.), *Advances in experimental social psychology* (Vol. 24, pp. 1–91). Orlando, FL: Academic Press.

Sears, D. O., & Funk, C. L. (1999). Evidence of the long-term persistence of adults' political predispositions. *Journal of Politics, 61,* 1–28.

Sears, D. O., & Henry, P. J. (2001, July). The origins of symbolic racism: The "blend" of antiblack affect and individualism is more than the sum of its parts. Paper prepared for presentation at the annual meeting of the International Society for Political Psychology, Seattle.

Sears, D. O., & Valentino, N. A. (1997). Politics matters: Political events as catalysts for preadult socialization. *American Political Science Review, 91,* 45–65.

Sears, R. R. (1975). *Your ancients revisited: A history of child development.* Chicago: University of Chicago Press.

Sears, R. R. (1984). The Terman gifted children study (TGC). In S. A. Mednick, M. Harway, & K. M. Finello (Eds.), *Handbook of longitudinal research: Vol. I. Birth and childhood cohorts* (pp. 398–414). New York: Praeger.

Selman, R. (1980). *The growth of interpersonal understanding*. New York: Academic Press.

Sigel, R. S. (Ed.). (1989). *Political learning in adulthood*. Chicago: University of Chicago Press.

Slavin R. E., & Cooper, R. (1999). Improving intergroup relations: Lessons learned from cooperative learning programs. *Journal of Social Issues, 55*, 647–663.

Slone, M., Adiri, M., & Arian, A. (1998). Adverse political events and psychological adjustments: A cross-cultural study of Israeli and Palestinian children. *American Academy of Child and Adolescent Psychiatry, 3*, 1058–1069.

Slone, M., Kaminer, D., & Durrheim, K. (2000). The contribution of political life events to psychological distress among South African adolescents. *Political Psychology, 21*, 465–487.

Smetana, J. G. (1995). Morality in context: Abstractions, ambiguities, and applications. *Annals of Child Development, 10*, 83–130.

Smith, E. S. (1999). The effects of investments in the social capital of youth on political and civic behavior in young adulthood: A longitudinal analysis. *Political Psychology, 20*, 553–580.

Spencer, M. B. (1982). Preschool children's social cognition and cultural cognition: A cognitive developmental interpretation of race dissonance findings. *Journal of Psychology, 112*, 275–286.

Spencer, M. B (1984). Black children's race awareness, racial attitudes and self-concept: A reinterpretation. *Journal of Child Psychology and Psychiatry and Allied Disciplines, 25*, 433–441.

Spencer, M. B. (2001). Identity and school adjustment: Revisiting the "acting white" assumption. *Educational Psychologist, 36*, 21–30.

Spencer, M. B., & Horowitz, F. D. (1973). Effects of systematic social and token reinforcement on the modification of racial and color concept attitudes in black and white preschool children. *Developmental Psychology, 9*, 246–254.

Steeh, C., & Schuman, H. (1991). Changes in racial attitudes among young white adults, 1984–1990. *American Journal of Sociology, 96*, 340–367.

Steele, C. M., & Aronson, J. (1995). Stereotype threat and the intellectual test performance of African Americans. *Journal of Personality and Social Psychology, 69*, 797–811.

Stewart, A. J., & Healy, J. M. (1989). Linking individual development and social changes. *American Psychologist, 44*, 30–42.

Stewart, A. J., Settles, I. H., & Winter, N. J. G. (1998). Women and the social movements of the 1960s: Activists, engaged observers, and nonparticipants. *Political Psychology, 19*, 63–94.

Sullivan, J. L., Piereson, J., & Marcus, G. E. (1982). *Political tolerance and American democracy*. Chicago: University of Chicago Press.

Tapp, J. L., & Kohlberg, L. (1971). Developing senses of law and legal justice. *Journal of Social Issues, 27*, 65–92.

Tapp, J. L., & Levine, F. J (1972). Compliance from kindergarten to college: A speculative research note. *Journal of Youth and Adolescence, 1*, 233–249.

Taylor, R., Casten, R., Flickinger, S., Roberts, D., & Fulmore, C. (1994). Explaining the school performance of African-American adolescents. *Journal of Research in Adolescence, 4*, 21–44.

Tedin, K. L. (1974). The influence of parents on the political attitudes of adolescents. *American Political Science Review, 68*, 1579–1592.

Tedin, K. L. (1980). Assessing peer and parent influence on adolescent political attitudes. *American Journal of Political Science, 24,* 136–154.

Thorkildsen, T. A. (1989). Pluralism in children's moral reasoning about social justice. *Child Development, 60,* 965–972.

Tisak, M. S. (1995). Domains of social reasoning and beyond. *Annals of child development: A research annual, 11,* 95–130.

Turiel, E. (1983). *The development of social knowledge: Morality and convention.* Cambridge: Cambridge University Press.

Turiel, E. (1998). The development of morality. In W. Damon (Ed.), *Handbook of child psychology* (5th ed., vol. 3, pp. 863–932). New York: Wiley.

Turiel, E., & Davidson, P. (1986). Heterogeneity, inconsistency, and asynchrony in the development of cognitive structures. In I. Levin (Ed.), *Stage and structure: Reopening the debate.* Norwood, NJ: Ablex.

Turiel, E., Hildebrandt, C., & Wainryb, C. (1985). Judging social issues: Difficulties, inconsistencies, and consistencies. *Monographs of the Society for Research in Child Development, 56* (Serial No. 224).

Turiel, E., Killen, M., & Helwig, C. C. (1987). Morality: Its structure, functions, and vagaries. In J. Kagan & S. Lamb (Eds.), *The emergence of morality* (pp. 155–243). Chicago: Chicago University Press.

Twenge, J. M. (2000). The age of anxiety? Birth cohort change in anxiety and neuroticism, 1952–1993. *Journal of Personality and Social Psychology, 79,* 1007–1021.

Uhlaner, C. J., Cain, B. E., & Kiewiet, D. R. (1989). Political participation of ethnic minorities in the 1980s. *Political Behavior, 11,* 195–232.

Vaillancourt, P. M. (1973). Stability of children's survey responses. *Public Opinion Quarterly, 37,* 373–387.

Valentino, N. A., & Sears, D. O. (1998). Event-driven political communication and the preadult socialization of partisanship. *Political Behavior, 20,* 127–154.

Verna, G. B. (1982). A study of the nature of children's race preferences using a modified conflict paradigm. *Child Development, 53,* 437–445.

Visser, P. S., & Krosnick, J. A. (1998). Development of attitude strength over the life cycle: Surge and decline. *Journal of Personality and Social Psychology, 75,* 1389–1391.

Watts, M. W. (1999). Are there typical age curves in political behavior? The "age invariance" hypothesis and political socialization. *Political Psychology, 20,* 477–499.

West, C. (1992). *Race matters.* Boston: Beacon.

Westholm, A. (1999). The perceptual pathway: Tracing the mechanisms of political value transfer across generations. *Political Psychology, 20,* 525–551.

Whalen, J., & Flacks, R. (1984). Echoes of rebellion: The liberated generation grows up. *Journal of Political and Military Sociology, 12,* 61–78.

Williams, J. E., & Morland, J. K. (1976). *Race, color and the young child.* Chapel Hill: University of North Carolina Press.

Wilson, T. C. (1996). Cohort and prejudice: Whites' attitudes toward blacks, Hispanics, Jews, and Asians. *Public Opinion Quarterly, 60,* 253–274.

Wolfenstein, M., & Kliman, G. (Eds.) (1965). *Children and the death of a president.* Garden City, NY: Doubleday.

Wolfinger, R. E. (1965). The development and persistence of ethnic voting. *American Political Science Review, 59,* 896–908.

Wong, J. S. (2000). The effects of age and political exposure on the development of party identification among Asian American and Latino immigrants in the United States. *Political Behavior, 22,* 341–371.

Zaller, J., & Feldman, S. (1992). A simple theory of the survey response: Answering questions versus revealing preferences. *American Journal of Political Science, 36,* 579–616.

4 David G. Winter

Personality and Political Behavior

One of the central axioms of political psychology is that political structures and actions are shaped and channeled by people's personalities—that is, by their individually patterned integration of processes of perception, memory, judgment, goal-seeking, and emotional expression and regulation. At the elite level, leaders' styles, choices, and outcomes are affected by their personalities; at the mass level, followers' personalities constitute both affordances (or opportunities) and also limits on what leaders can do. In this chapter, therefore, I will discuss both elite and mass studies.

After a brief discussion of the circumstances in which personality is relevant to politics, this chapter presents a fourfold conception of the elements of personality. It then outlines some of the major methods political psychologists have employed to study the personalities of individual actors and groups. Finally, it reviews some of the major findings relating personality to political outcomes.

◤ A Conception of Personality in Politics

Prologue: When Does Personality Affect Politics?

It seems easy to think of examples of the effect of personality on politics: Woodrow Wilson is said to have lost the peace in 1919 because he negotiated ineptly, confused rhetoric with substance, and refused to compromise. Hitler set Europe aflame with a foreign policy that seemed to be rooted in personal pathology. Bill Clinton's inability to control himself jeopardized his presidential accomplishments. And Osama bin Laden's burning hatred, along with the austere conscientiousness of Mohamed Atta and other airplane hijackers, helped to bring about the deaths of thousands of people on September 11, 2001, setting off a U.S. "war on terrorism" that transformed American domestic society and international relations. In each case, the intrusion of personal appetites, needs, fears, and obsessions gave a quality—irrational, self-defeating, and/or violently aggressive—to many of their highly consequential public actions. Arguing that "the goals, abilities, and foibles of individuals are crucial to the intentions, capabilities, and strategies of a state," Byman and Pollack (2001, p. 109) cite five major cases where the personal characteristics of leaders clearly affected international relations outcomes. Studies of the German kaiser Wilhelm II, by Kennedy (1982), and U.S. president Harry Truman by Hamby (1991) provide further illustrations. Friedlander and Cohen (1975) documented the existence of a "belligerent personality type," that is, leaders who displayed consistent and consequential aggressive behavior that went beyond rational strategic considerations.

Yet we should be cautious about overly simplistic attributions of political outcomes to leaders' personalities, even in these compelling examples, neglecting the importance of constraints and opportunities in the roles and situations in which leaders operate. For example, the American desire to "bring the troops home" in 1918, and reluctance to submit national sovereignty to a supranational League of Nations, made Wilson's weakness a matter of position as much as personality. Whatever the role of Hitler's personal demons in the origins of the Holocaust, it is well to remember that his rise to power was assisted at every step of the way by other persons and institutional forces (Kershaw, 1999), his foreign policy was in many respects little different from that of German professional diplomats (Taylor, 1961, p. 97), and the extermination apparatus depended on the work of thousands of "willing executioners" (Goldhagen, 1996). Similarly, the terrorist successes of Osama bin Laden would not have been possible without assistance, support, and even willingness to die on the part of large numbers of people. Within psychology, this perspective is reflected in the critique of personality concepts and explanations by social psychologists (e.g., Nisbett, 1980) and others who emphasize the controlling power of the situation on people's behavior (e.g. Mischel, 1968; Skinner, 1974).

We find a similar "personality" and "situational" perspectives at the mass or collective level. Thus outcomes as varied as the variable success of imported "Westminster" political institutions in the former British colonies, trajectories of economic development, and occurrences of terrorism are often said to be the result of psychological factors—variously described as mentalities (Geertz, 1973), unspoken assumptions (Joll, 1968), culture (Nisbett & Cohen, 1995; Stille, 2001), national character (Inkeles, 1997), or collective levels of personality variables such as motivation (McClelland, 1961, 1975), traits (Barrett & Eysenck, 1984), attitudes and beliefs, or self-construals (Markus & Kitayma, 1991). Here again, though, an exclusive focus on psychological factors can lead to neglect of situational constraints and opportunities, as well as blaming the victim and sheer stereotyping and prejudice. Moreover, any attempt to assess psychological characteristics of large groups and especially whole nations quickly runs into formidable conceptual and empirical difficulties (see Inkeles & Levinson, 1969; Singer, 1961).

Thus the scholarly terrain of this chapter is defined by two boundaries: on the one hand the naive view of political outcomes as merely the projection of leaders' personalities and on the other the equally simplistic view that individual personalities have no effect. Or, as the former U. S. secretary of state Henry Kissinger put it in an interview with journalists, "as a professor, I tended to think of history as run by impersonal forces. But when you see it in practice, you see the difference personalities make" (Isaacson, 1992, p. 13, quoted by Byman & Pollack, 2001, p. 108). To chart a course between these extremes, we can draw on Greenstein's discussion (1969/ 1987, ch. 2): that personalities of political actors (leaders or groups) are likely to be especially important under four conditions: when a political actor occupies a strategic location; when the situation is ambiguous, unstable, or complex (without clear precedents, expectations, or routine role requirements); when the situation is laden with symbolic and emotional significance; and when spontaneous or especially effortful behavior is required.

More recently, Byman and Pollack (2001) argue that individual personalities become especially important when power is concentrated, when institutions are in conflict, or during times of great change (p. 109). All of these conditions are especially likely to be met in conditions of crisis (especially foreign policy crises involving "enemy" nations), in the organization of a new administration, and also in dealing with emotionally laden events and issues that threaten deeply held values. Thus personality and political behavior studies tend to involve topics such as how leaders act during escalating crises and war, how they structure their advising staff and make decisions, and how public opinion changes under conditions of threat.

While it is easy to think of personality as a static set of fixed "qualities," a more modern conception would view personality as an array of capacities or dispositions that may be engaged, primed, or brought forward depending on the demands of the situation and a person's own "executive apparatus." On this view, personality is like a personal computer: with some relatively fixed "hardware" characteristics and also many "software" applications, each of which can be "opened" or "closed" by the operator—some running in a "window" at the center of the screen, others available in the immediate background "windows," and a few running almost undetected in "deeper" background.

Personality factors affect the arousal and weighting of leaders' goals and preferences, as well as conflicts and fusions among different goals. Personality affects how leaders respond to (or resist) cues, symbols, and signs; how they interpret "stimuli" and transform them into "information." Finally, personality affects leaders' persistence, endurance, and management of emotions. Thus "personality" explanation supplement rather than replace "rational choice" explanations. The conditions favoring the influence of personalities are probably most often present in the arena of foreign policy, so that over the years political psychologists have produced many studies relating various aspects of decision-makers' personalities to foreign policy outcomes (see Winter, 1992a, 1992b, 2003, for a review of these studies, and two edited books, Feldman & Valenty, 2001, and Valenty & Feldman, 2002, for recent studies of political leaders).

How Can We Measure Personality without Direct Access?

Any attempt to study how the personalities of leaders or masses affect political behavior and outcomes quickly runs into the problem of measurement. The important leaders and masses of the past are dead and, to adapt a quotation from Glad (1973), have taken their personality characteristics— Oedipus complexes, authoritarianism, or power motivation—with them. For important living leaders, the difficulty of access is such that it is almost impossible even to imagine administering any of the standard personality tests, questionnaires, surveys, or even interviews. Direct assessment via personality questionnaires seems to be possible up through the level of state legislators in the United States (see Altemeyer, 1996) and members of parliament in Italy (DiRenzo, 1967). Assessment without access sometimes produces little more than undifferentiated and unhelpful cliches. Furthermore, it raises problems of objectivity; for example, the infamous poll of psychiatric opinions published by *Fact* magazine during the 1964 U.S. presidential campaign (see Boroson, 1964; Ginzburg, 1964) bordered on at-a-distance character assassination. The magazine sent questionnaires to more than 12,000 psychiatrist members of the American Psychiatric Association, asking whether they believed Barry Goldwater to be "psychologically fit to be president of the United States." About 20 percent responded; of those, half replied in the negative. While none of the respondents had ever treated (or probably even met) Goldwater, they were not reluctant to offer a wide variety of psychiatric diagnoses.

While it is possible to administer personality tests to random samples of politically significant groups or even nations (Almond & Verba, 1989; Barrett & Eysenck, 1984; Glick et al., 2000; Hofstede, 1980, 2001; Veroff, Depner, Kulka, & Douvan, 1980), it is often prohibitively difficult and expensive. How can we assess in any systematic and objective way, therefore, people's personalities without direct access to them?

Psychobiographers have avoided this problem by making clinical inferences and diagnoses on the basis of a synthesis of known biographical facts and then checking these against further facts (see Elms, 1994; Runyan, 1982, 1988, 1997). Greenstein (1969/1987, ch. 3) provides a useful analysis of the process: after identifying and describing the *phenomenology* (the actions—often surprising and unusual and not explicable by the requirements of role or situation), the psychobiographer then formulates a *dynamic* (psychological mechanisms that "explain" these actions) and may then go on to suggest the *genesis* (origin of the dynamic in the person's childhood experiences). Winter (2003) and Barenbaum and Winter (2003) give a full discussion of the history, methods and issues of psychobiography, as well as extensive references to the literature.

Sometimes psychobiographical judgments are made more systematic by the use of defined dimensions such as organizational capacity, strategic cognitive style, and emotional intelligence (Greenstein, 2000), activity and positive/negative affect (Barber, 1992; see also Henderson, 2001), extent of desired change and breadth of scope (Blondel, 1987; see also Fukai, 2001), standard personality concepts such as extraversion and dominance (Etheredge, 1978), or eclectic sets of personality concepts and variables (Shestopal, 2000). Other researchers have developed a variety of methods for systematic and objective measurement of personality at a distance. For example, Immelman (1993) has developed an elaborate inventory of specific questions and judgments based on Millon's (1986) "prototypes" conception of personality and used it to make assessments of U.S. leaders (Immelman, 1998, 1999). Some researchers ask knowledgeable experts to Q-sort adjectives or statements about the leader on the basis of their knowledge or after reading vignettes with identifying information removed (Historical Figures Assessment Collaborative, 1977; Simonton, 1988). Sometimes they are even asked to fill out standard personality questionnaires for a leader or "as if" they were the leader (Rubenzer, Faschingbauer, & Ones, 2000).

However, political leaders past and present do talk, and so words are a resource that generally exists in great abundance. Thus the most widely used at-a-distance technique is probably content analysis of written text or verbatim transcripts of spoken words (e.g., speeches or interviews) from individual leaders or cultural documents (e.g., government communications, popular fiction, or even children's school readers) taken as reflecting the psychological characteristics or personalities of collectivities or masses (McClelland, 1961).[1] Typically, content analysis measures are carefully designed, with examples and training procedures to enable previously inexperienced scorers to apply them with high reliability (percent agreement and correlation $\geq$ .85). A detailed discussion of issues and methods of psychological content analysis can be found in Holsti (1969), Schafer (2000), Walker (2000), Winter (1992a, 1992b), and Winter and Stewart (1977).

Finally, in the case of collectivities or nations, some researchers (Doty, Peterson, & Winter, 1991; Hofstede, 1980, 2001; Sales, 1973) have made inferences about levels of personality variables (and especially changes in these levels over time) on the basis of social indicators taken to reflect behaviors characteristic of these variables.

A Fourfold Conception of Personality

Some theorists have argued that personality consists only of traits (Allport, 1961; Buss, 1989) or motives (Murray, 1938), but most consider that personality is made up of several fundamentally different kinds of variables (McClelland, 1951; Winter, John, Stewart, Klohnen, & Duncan, 1998). For convenience, I divide personality into four elements, or classes of variables, as illustrated in table 4.1: traits, motives, cognitions, and the social context (see also McClelland, 1951; Winter, 1996; Winter & Barenbaum, 1999). While some writers use the word "trait" to cover different elements—for example, power motivation, cognitive complexity, or authoritarianism—I suggest that scientific precision will be enhanced by using different words for things that are essentially different.

The four elements can be described in terms of two dimensions: (1) whether they are public and observable, or else "inner" and therefore inferential; and (2) whether they are relatively stable across situations and can therefore be described in terms of "typical" levels, or else are highly dependent on situations and contexts. (The difference is relative: probably all aspects of personality are affected to *some* extent by situations.) Table 4.1 lists major theorists and typical personality variables associated with each element.

Traits are the public, observable element of personality, the consistencies of style readily noticed by other people. They reflect the language of "first impressions," the adjectives and adverbs of everyday language that we use

Table 4.1.
The Four Elements of Personality

	Inferential	Observable
	Cognitions	**Temperament, traits**
Trans-situational	*Typical variables:*	*Typical variables:*
	Beliefs	Extraversion
	Attitudes	Energy level
	Values	Neuroticism
	Self-concept(s)	
	Major theorists:	*Major theorists:*
	Gordon Allport	Gordon Allport
	George Kelly	Hans Eysenck
	Carl Rogers	Carl Jung
	Motives	**Social context**
Situation-dependent	*Typical variables:*	*Microcontext:*
	Motives	Immediate situations
	Goals	*Macrocontexts:*
	Regulating mechanisms	Gender
	Defense mechanisms	Social class
		Wealth and resources
		Ethnicity
		Race
		Culture
		Generation
		History
	Major theorists:	*Major theorists:*
	Sigmund Freud	Erik Erikson
	David McClelland	Walter Mischel
	Abraham Maslow	B. F. Skinner
	Henry Murray	Abigail Stewart

to describe other people. For this reason, traits are usually assessed by means of observers' ratings. (Self-reports are also widely used, but they run the danger of confounding people's beliefs about themselves with the impressions that others have of them.)

In contrast, *motives* involve anticipation and pursuit, over time, of goals or desired end states. (This is true of approach motives; avoidance motives involve evasion or escape from undesired states.) Motives are latent dispositions: over time they are activated, satisfied, quiescent, and again activated. When and how any given motive is expressed depends on the perceived opportunities and incentives of the specific situation, the time since previous satisfaction, and the presence of other activated motives that may fuse or conflict. Thus motives do not always involve consistent patterns of action. Moreover, people's motives are often not apparent to others (particularly if they have not observed over time); sometimes they are not even apparent to the persons themselves.

Cognitions include a wide variety of mental representations, schemas, models, categories, beliefs, values, and attitudes: mental representations of the self and its many components of social identity; schemas for representing other people, groups, and social systems; beliefs about the scope and nature of politics; and most broadly, conceptions of the nature of the world, truth, beauty, and goodness. Of course beliefs and values are also studied by social psychologists, sociologists, and mass behavior researchers, because although beliefs do differ across individuals in consistent ways (hence can be considered as part of personality), they also fluctuate over time and can be affected by persuasion campaigns and "electioneering."

The *social context* includes both the immediate situation and broader features of social structure such as gender, class, race and ethnicity, culture, and history. While many features of the social context are internalized as mental representations, the social context also has a separate "reality"; that is, an autonomous existence as a set of channels, opportunities and affordances, limits, and constraints on the expression of all elements of personality. Some readers may find it strange to consider social contexts as an element of personality, since in survey research they are usually considered as demographic variables, while in social psychology they are considered as part of the situation or environment, as opposed to dispositions within the person. In fact, there are grounds for viewing social contexts from all three perspectives: as elements of personality as well as demographic characteristics and situational features. Thus during the period 1930–60, studies of personality were closely linked to analysis of the societal and cultural context (see Kluckhohn, Murray, & Schneider, 1953): personality was seen as being *in*, or *within*, society and culture. In recent years, many personality psychologists have rediscovered the "ecology of personality"—that is, the analysis of social contexts *as an aspect of personality* (see Moen, Elder, & Lüscher, 1995; Winter & Stewart, 1995). From this perspective, we are shaped by external contexts, but these contexts (especially gender, race, social class, nationality, and history) then become part of our personalities. That is, we carry them around within us, as it were, as we select, evoke, and construe new contexts in the present (see Buss, 1987). In fact, personality—apart from genetic inheritance—can be viewed as a series or accumulation of *past* "embodied contexts," resistant to change (or at least harder to change than to acquire), all interacting with the *current* situation.

▲ Research on Personality and Politics

Traits and Political Behavior

Because the essence of traits is consistency of behavior (across situations and over time), factor analysis and other clustering procedures based on correlations are often used—with pools of personality test "items," descriptive statements, or simply adjectives—to identify traits that are "basic" or fundamental. In recent years, some consensus has gathered around the notion that there are five trait factors (often called the Big Five), though there is considerable discussion and variation about the exact content and structure of each factor and even some dispute about the value of the whole factor-analytic approach (see Block, 1995). In Great Britain and the Commonwealth, the three-factor theory of Eysenck (Eysenck & Eysenck, 1985), involving extraversion, neuroticism, and psychoticism, remains popular.[2] While the five factors are fairly robust across Indo-European languages (McCrae & Costa, 1997), some differences do emerge in studies based on languages such as Mandarin, especially when the researchers begin with indigenous adjectives rather than translations of imported words (see, for example, Cheung et al., 2001). Table 4.2 presents the most common labels for these five factors, along with a brief description of politically relevant behaviors of people who score high and low on each factor. While the full five-factor model has only recently been used in political applications (see Rubenzer et al., 2000, discussed later), political psychologists have studied a variety of traits in political actors.

Studies of Political Leaders

In a study of 36 U.S. presidents, secretaries of state, and presidential advisors who served between 1898 and 1968, Etheredge (1978) related scores on two related aspects of trait factor 1 (extraversion and dominance)[3] to foreign policy views and performance. He first measured each leader's extraversion and dominance by having raters read a dossier assembled from disguised passages from scholarly works, insiders' memoirs, biographies, and autobiographies, and then rate the trait on a 10-point scale. Etheredge then fo-

Table 4.2.
Politically Relevant Behaviors for Five trait factors

Trait factor number and names	High scorer	Low scorer
1. Extraversion-surgency	A leader, dominant, aggressive	Loyal follower
2. Warmth, agreeableness	Congenial	Remote, hostile
3. Conscientiousness	Responsible, gets things done, does the "dirty work"	Irresponsible, cuts losses, sociopathic; may discover creative short-cuts
4. Emotional stability, (low) neuroticism	Stable, "unflappable"	Can't make up mind, depressed, neurotic
5. Openness to experience	Curious, learns from experience	Rigid, close-minded

cused on two important kinds of intraelite dyadic disagreements about foreign policy during the period under study: whether threats should be met by coercion, and whether the United States should pursue "inclusionary" policies toward the Soviet Union. As predicted, leaders rated higher in extraversion were more likely to advocate inclusionary policies (that is, favoring negotiation) toward the Soviet Union, while leaders rated higher in dominance were more likely to advocate the use of force in response to a threat.

In the last 15 years, three major attempts have been made to measure objectively the traits of U.S. presidents. Simonton (1986) excerpted personality descriptions from biographical sources (with identifying material removed) and then asked student raters to read each description and then rate that president on 110 adjectives of the Adjective Check List (Simonton, 1986) or a series of phrases (Simonton, 1988). In each case, the major factors extracted and interpreted by Simonton resembled the Big Five trait factors, individually and in combination. In both studies, Simonton used cluster analysis to group the presidents in terms of their trait resemblance. He also identified background characteristics and presidential outcomes associated with each factor. Across both studies, factors resembling two of the Big Five, extraversion (or surgency) and possibly openness, were associated with a variety of measures of presidential performance.

Rubenzer and colleagues (2000) asked 115 "experts" to rate those presidents with whom they had had long-term personal contact or about whom they had published a full-length biography. The experts filled out three instruments specifically designed to measure the five trait factors: the Revised NEO Personality Inventory (Costa & McCrae, 1992), phrases from the California Q-Sort (Block, 1961), and one hundred clusters of ordinary English adjectives (Goldberg, 1990). Relating the resulting scores to historians' ratings presidential greatness, they found mostly nonsignificant results, with the exception of the correlation of greatness with the "openness" factor, which approached significance ($rs = .25$ and $.32$, p of the latter $<.05$). This is consistent with a good deal of previous research attempting to relate traits to successful leadership (see the review by Hollander, 1985). Apparently there is sufficient variation in the situations, problems, and opportunities faced by leaders—both presidents and ordinary leaders—that no single cluster of public, consistent behaviors has much of an effect on performance (in this connection, see Renshon, 2001, especially pp. 242–246).

Trait Portraits of Individual Leaders

Rubenzer and colleagues (2000) also presented information on specific U.S. presidents. For example, George Washington scored high on conscientiousness and surgency but low on agreeableness, while Abraham Lincoln was high on openness but low on emotional stability. On the basis of these results, we might characterize Washington as "conscientious, forceful, and remote"; Lincoln, in contrast, can be seen as a person open to yet tormented by the world and experience. Having done this, however, we might then ask whether the use of elaborate measurement procedures has really told us anything about either president we did not already know. That is, traits, in whatever form they are measured, are really just summary descriptions of a person's consistent public behavior—behavior that is also the source of historians' descriptions and thus popular impressions. Thus invoking "traits" to explain the behavior of George Washington or Abraham Lincoln may simply capitalize on shared method variance, if not on outright tautology.

Traits as Perceived by Leaders

Do the five trait factors identified by factor analyses have anything to do with the actual trait dimensions that political leaders use to describe other leaders? Swede and Tetlock (1986) studied the memoirs of Henry Kissinger, a former U.S. national security advisor and secretary of state under presidents Nixon and Ford. They extracted Kissinger's descriptions of several other leaders and then used clustering procedures to identify the major implicit dimensions of Kissinger's person perception. The results, presented in table 4.3, show that Kissinger did indeed use five clusters or factors to characterize political leaders. However, his clusters seem to involve combinations of the usual five trait factors rather than pure replicas of them. Swede and Tetlock then used their structural analysis to show how Kissinger implicitly *used* personality traits to describe individual leaders, to differentiate among different leaders, and to organize leaders into types.

As a limitation of the five-factor model of traits, it is worth noting that when Kissinger described leaders he knew really well, he used exquisitely subtle and differentiated phrases that go well beyond the Big Five. For

Table 4.3
Henry Kissinger's Implicit Dimensions of Person-Perception

Cluster name	Description	Examples	Possible five-factor "translation"
1. Professional anguish	Insecure, lonely, tough, proud	Indira Gandhi Kissinger himself	III+ IV−
2. Ambitious patriotism	Patriotic, suspicious, ambitious, ungenerous	Richard Nixon Nguyen Van Thieu	I+ II−
3. Revolutionary greatness	Great, ruthless, self-assured, revolutionary, ruthless	Mao Zedong Anwar Sadat	I+
4. Intellectual sophistication	Humorous, knowledgeable, skilled, subtle	Le Duc Tho Zhou Enlai	V+
5. Realistic friendship	Friendly, decisive, ambivalent, close	Nelson Rockefeller Georges Pompidou	II+

example, he described Charles de Gaulle, former president of France as having "the natural haughtiness of a snow-capped Alpine peak," and Lyndon Johnson, former U.S. president, as a "caged eagle" (Swede & Tetlock, 1986, p. 641).

Studies of Collectivities

While no single study has collected mass data on traits across different nations, two articles have brought together results of separate trait studies and norms of groups of people of individual nations. Lynn (1981) collected the results of studies carried out in 22 countries, published between 1958 and 1980, that used Eysenck's measures of extraversion, neuroticism, and psychoticism. Barrett and Eysenck (1984) reported results of somewhat more systematic and parallel studies of the same three traits, published between 1977 and 1984, in people from 25 countries. Barrett and Eysenck were mainly concerned to demonstrate the similarity of factor structure in the different national samples, but political psychologists could also use their results to understand and predict political activity and outcomes in these countries. In the next few years we may expect to see similar compilations of crossnational data for the Big Five traits.

Using Social Indicators

To get around the problems and expense of systematic crossnational surveys and personality testing, some researchers have used social indicators to measure psychological variables. Lynn and Hampson (1975) estimated national "scores" on extraversion and neuroticism for 18 advanced industrial nations, on the basis of variables such as their rates of divorce, suicide, and crime and their per capita consumption of cigarettes and caffeine. Since many of these social indicator measures are also affected by national income, this method may be not be applicable to poorer nations.

Motives and Political Behavior

Motives involve tendencies to approach desired goals or end-states or avoid undesired or feared end-states. While the number of different human goals is potentially without limit, many psychologists have followed Murray (1938) in identifying 20 broad classes of goals as able to account for the major trends or strivings in people's lives. Drawing on theory and a variety of studies Winter (1996, chs. 4, 5) argued that Murray's "catalog" of motives could be represented in spatial terms, organized by three *dimensions of motivated behavior*: achievement, affiliation, and power.

Intelligent pursuit of a goal (or avoidance of a negative goal) depends on selecting an appropriate action or path, given the obstacles and opportunities in the specific situation, from among the many possible ways to reach the end-state. Furthermore, motives wax and wane; even the hungriest person stops eating eventually. Thus motives are usually expressed in a variety of specific actions—depending on the situation and time since previous goal-gratification—rather than with the consistency of traits. Finally, motives often operate at an implicit or even unconscious level—partly because of the operation of defenses and social desirability and partly because people may not attend to or verbalize the long-term trends of their actions. It may be easy for me to answer a question about what I want to get done today, but I may not be aware of the long-term goals toward which my life has been moving over the past several years.

For all these reasons, motives are difficult to measure with the direct questionnaires or even observer ratings that are so useful in the study of traits. (To be sure, there are questionnaires or rating scales that purport to measure motives, but such measures do not correlate with the content analysis measures described hereafter. Regardless of their labels, then, questionnaires and ratings inevitably reflect peoples' traits or else their beliefs or cognitions about their motives.) However, content analysis of verbal behavior has proved to be an effective method of measuring the achievement, affiliation, and power motives—both in people to whom psychologists have direct access, using a "projective" test such as the Thematic Apperception Test (TAT), and in political leaders, historical figures, and other persons studied at a distance.[4]

Studies of Political Leaders

Using content analysis of speeches, interviews, and other texts, researchers have studies the achievement, affiliation, and power motives of U. S. presidents (Winter, 1987), presidential candidates (Winter, 1976, 1988, 1995), and Supreme Court justices (Aliotta, 1988), several different groups of political leaders in southern Africa in the 1970s (Winter, 1980), and candidates in the 1996 Russian presidential election (Valenty & Shiraev, 2001). Hermann included power and affiliation motive measures in her studies of world leaders (Hermann, 1980b), members of the Politburo of the Communist Party of the Soviet Union in the 1970s (Hermann, 1980a), and sub-Saharan Africa leaders (Hermann, 1987a).

Several of these studies suggest that leaders scoring high in power motivation are inclined toward strong, forceful actions: as a result, they may be charismatic to their followers (House, Spangler, & Woycke, 1991) but aggressive and warlike to foreign opponents (Winter, 1980, 1987, 1993). Affiliation-motivated leaders, in contrast, are more peaceable and cooperative—so long as they are surrounded by like-minded others and do not feel threatened. Achievement motivation, which is associated with entrepreneurial success (McClelland, 1961), does not appear to make for success in politics, particularly if it is higher than power motivation (see Winter, 2002), because it leads people to become frustrated with several inherent features of political life.

Motive Portraits of Individual Leaders

Winter and Carlson (1988) used the motive profile of former U.S. president Richard Nixon to resolve several of the apparent paradoxes of his political career, and Winter (1998) related the trend of Bill Clinton's motives to the dramatic turnaround of his political fortunes from the early years of his first term to his overwhelming reelection in 1996. Hermann produced profiles of Ronald Reagan (1983) and the former Syrian president Hafez-al-Assad (1988).

Studies of Collectivities

In his classic study *The Achieving Society,* McClelland (1961) measured national motive levels through content analysis of stories from schoolchildren's readers and found that levels of achievement motivation predicted subsequent economic growth. Using content analysis of several kinds of popular literature, McClelland (1975, chs. 8–9) linked power and affiliation motivation to war and peace, respectively, over the course of two hundred years of United States history. Winter (1993) extended these results to three hundred years of British history, as well as to a comparative study of the outbreak of World War I and the Cuban Missile Crisis of 1962.

Two studies have examined the relationship between motives of a leader (measured through content analysis of speeches) and motives of that leader's society (measured through content analysis of popular literature). Winter (1987) found that the closer the president's motive profile to that of the United States, the higher that president's margin of victory—thus supporting theories of leadership that emphasize psychological congruence between leaders and followers. In a study of short-term fluctuations of candidate speeches and polling data during the 2000 U.S. presidential campaign, Ethington (2001) found a similar relationship. Schmitt and Winter (1998) studied leaders and society in the Soviet Union between 1924 and 1986 and found a different kind of leader-society congruence: the motive profile of Soviet society came to resemble that of the leader during the years after the leader's accession.

Veroff, Depner, Kulka, and Douvan (1980) measured motives of representative samples of American society, tested directly in interviews, in 1957 and 1976. They relate changes for various gender, social class, and age-cohort subgroups to events in trends in U.S. society during that period. For example, during this period American women greatly increased in achievement motivation, while American men increased their power motivation. Perhaps these two trends can illuminate the course of "gender politics" in the United States during the last 40 years of the twentieth century.

Cognitions and Political Behavior

As an element of personality, "cognition" includes both a variety of specific cognitions, such as beliefs and values, and the cognitive structure on the arrangement of these beliefs. One of the most widely used and general set of cognitions is the *operational code* (George, 1969; Holsti, 1977; Walker, 1983, 1990) or set of philosophical beliefs about the nature of political life (harmony or conflict) and the predictability and controllability of political outcomes, and instrumental beliefs about the best way to pursue goals and calculate risks. Walker, Schafer, and Young (1998, 1999) have developed a set of computer-assisted quantitative measures of the operational code concept, in terms of how leaders *diagnose* the political world and how they *choose* and *shift* among different courses of action. Researchers have developed operational codes for a wide variety of political leaders, such as the British prime minister Tony Blair (Schafer & Walker, 2001), the U.S. presidents Woodrow Wilson (Walker, 1995), Lyndon Johnson (Walker & Schafer, 2000), and Jimmy Carter (Walker et al., 1998), and the U. S. secretary of state Henry Kissinger (Walker, 1977), and related them to political (especially foreign policy) behavior (see Walker, Schafer, & Young, 1999, for a review of these studies).

In analyses of particular foreign policy decisions, researchers sometimes use the broader concept of a cognitive map. Walker and Watson (1992), for example, employed several different cognitive measures in a study of the British prime minister Neville Chamberlain in the Munich crisis of 1938 and the Poland crisis of 1939 (see also Walker & Watson, 1994). On some (but not all) measures, scores were higher for the peacefully resolved Munich crisis, while the overall results illustrated the development of "groupthink" under conditions of stress.

Cognitive Structure and Cognitive Style

Cognitive complexity is one of the most widely studied structural or stylistic features of personality. Do leaders process information in simplistic ways, focusing only on a single perspective or black-and-white alternatives, or do they recognize different points of view, perhaps even integrating them into broader complex perspectives? The measure of *integrative complexity*, developed by Suedfeld and his colleagues (Suedfeld, Tetlock, & Streufert, 1992; see also Tetlock, 1993), reflects these two processes of differentiation and integration. Researchers have studied integrative complexity in several different groups of political leaders: U. S. presidents (Tetlock, 1981b), senators (Tetlock, 1981a, 1983), and Supreme Court justices (Tetlock, Bernzweig, & Gallant, 1985); members of the British House of Commons (Tetlock, 1984); Canadian prime ministers (Suedfeld, Conway, & Eichhorn, 2001), successful versus unsuccessful revolutionaries (Suedfeld & Rank, 1976); traditionalist and reformist Soviet politicians during the 1980s (Tetlock & Boettger, 1989), and Soviet and American foreign policy elites during the 1970s and early 1980s (Tetlock, 1985). Specific individuals whose levels of integrative complexity have been assessed include the U.S. president Bill Clinton (Suedfeld, 1994), the Soviet president Mikhail Gorbachev (Wallace, Suedfeld, & Thachuk, 1996), and the British prime minister Winston Churchill (Tetlock & Tyler, 1996).

Content analysis of the rhetoric of advocacy groups suggests that on emotionally charged issues such as slavery (Tetlock, Armor, & Peterson, 1994), abortion (Dillon, 1993), and perhaps "ideological" versus "pragmatic" groups in general (Suedfeld, Bluck, Loewen, & Elkins, 1994), integrative complexity is lower for both extremes than for groups taking a middle position. No doubt this is because groups in the middle may agree with elements of both extreme positions and so experience greater conflict among competing values. In politics, high levels of integrative complexity may not always be a virtue: Shakespeare's Hamlet, for example, was arguably too complex for his own good.

Consistent with these findings, integrative complexity also tends to be higher in conflicts that are peacefully resolved, compared to conflicts that escalate to war (Guttieri, Wallace, & Suedfeld, 1995; Suedfeld & Tetlock, 1977; Suedfeld, Tetlock, & Ramirez, 1977; Suedfeld et al., 1993).

Explanatory Style

A content analysis measure of people's tendency to explain events—especially bad events—in terms of "optimistic" (external, temporary, specific) causes versus "pessimistic" (internal, enduring, global) causes has been developed by Peterson and Seligman and their colleagues (see Peterson, 1992). For U.S. presidential candidates, optimism predicts victory (Zullow & Seligman, 1990); among national leaders, however, it is associated with crisis escalation and aggression (Satterfield & Seligman, 1994; Zullow, Oettingen, Peterson, & Seligman, 1988). Zullow (1991) found that changes in the level of optimism in popular song lyrics predicted subsequent parallel changes in consumer optimism and hence national economic performance.

Specific Cognitive Variables

Authoritarianism, which can be understood as a set of beliefs or belief system—about power, morality, and the social order—is one of the most widely studied personality variables. In studies of groups, authoritarianism is usually measured by Altemeyer's (1981, 1988, 1996) *right-wing authoritarianism* (RWA) questionnaire measure (improving on and replacing the classic but flawed F-scale developed by Adorno et al., 1950). Numerous studies demonstrated that authoritarianism is linked to obedience to "authorities," prejudice against a variety of groups perceived to be "different," and a willingness to accept violence in defense of conventional morality and the status quo (see Meloen, 1983, 1993, and Winter, 1996, ch. 7, for reviews of the political aspects of the authoritarianism literature). Moreover, when an issue is framed in ways that engage the symbolic structures of authoritarianism, the RWA or F-scale scores are often related to their positions (see, for example, Peterson, Doty, & Winter, 1993). In recent years, Sidanius and his colleagues (Sidanius & Pratto, 1999) have developed the related concept of social dominance orientation (SDO) to measure people's belief in the legitimacy of intergroup hierarchies and oppression. Chapter 16 elaborates on both measures.

While there exists no direct at-a-distance measure of authoritarianism, three of the measures Hermann (1980b, 1987b, 1999) has used in her extensive studies of political leaders—ethnocentrism, low cognitive complexity, and distrust—can be used as a proxy measure for authoritarianism. Hermann has also developed content analysis measures of two other cognitive variables, internal control of outcomes and self-confidence.

Cognitions Related to the Self

People's self-concepts are probably their most important cognitive structures, for who and what they think they are affects almost every aspect of their political decision-making and action: setting goals, seeking and using advice and consultation, and responding to positive and negative feedback. Political scientists, especially those studying international relations, also use the term "identity" to refer to self-concept. Indeed, the psychologist Erik Erikson (1963, 1980) first introduced this term to indicate the relationship between "what [people] feel they are" and "what they appear to be in the eyes of others" (Erikson, 1963, p. 228). Following Tajfel (1981), however, many social psychologists use the term "social identity" to highlight those aspects of self-concept that derive from group memberships. Related to self-concept is the notion of "self-esteem," or people's evaluation of their self-concept. Hermann (1987b, 1999) included a measure of self-confidence, a closely related concept, in her system for assessing the personalities of political leaders.

While people have their inner self-concepts, they also present themselves to the external world. Schütz (1993, 2001) developed a content analysis measure of alternative styles of self-presentation (assertive, aggressive, and defensive) and used it in the analysis of German political leaders of the 1990s.

The concept of narcissistic disorder (also the related concept of "malignant narcissism"; see Post, 1991), drawn from psychoanalytic theory and especially the work of Kohut (1985), involves a particular syndrome of "self" cognitions: grandiosity (often alternating with abasement), feelings of being "special" and entitlement, exploiting other people, lack of empathy, and a propensity for rage in the face of frustration. (According to Kohut, the opposite of narcissism is wisdom and a sense of humor.) Narcissism (Post, 1993a, 1997) is clearly relevant to the understanding of many leaders, such as Mao Zedong (Sheng, 2001) and Saddam Hussein (Post, 1991)—perhaps especially as they grow older (Post, 1993b). For example, Mao was a highly successful strategist during his early and middle years. Sheng (2001) used the concept of narcissism to explain the deterioration of Mao's effectiveness in his mid-sixties (especially after 1956). During these years, Mao's grandiosity increased, leading him to overestimate resources and ignore difficulties. The result was a series of ill-thought-out and unrealistic plans, such as the breakneck industrialization of the "Great Leap Forward" of 1958–60 and the Taiwan Straits crisis of 1958. The inevitable failures then increased Mao's paranoia and grandiosity, as displayed in the Cultural Revolution of 1966–76.

The concept of "self," so popular in western psychology and political psychology, derives from the western philosophical tradition of individualism and is closely linked to many features of western industrial society. Drawing on an earlier version of the pioneering work of Hofstede (1980), who formulated individualism-collectivism as a major dimension of cultural difference (see also Triandis, 1995), Markus and Kitayama (1991) have suggested that not all groups construe "self" in the same way. In the west, to be sure, people view the "self" as a bounded, separate, individual entity that actualizes potentials and strives for personal goals. However, in many other cultures there is an alternative conception of self—emphasizing relatedness, harmony, occupying an appropriate place, and group goals.

Even among relatively "individualistic" western leaders and populations, however, conceptions of the self are intimately bound up with the different dimensions of *social identity* (see Brewer & Gardner, 1996): our cultural, social, and institutional memberships are an important component of who we are (see also chapter 15).

Values

As Stanley Feldman points out in chapter 14, values and ideology are an organizing framework for the study of attitudes and opinions. In this chapter I consider values primarily in relation to motives. Both values and motives refer to anticipated end states that people feel are worth pursuing and protecting. Values, however, are consciously articulated conceptions of "intrinsic goods," while motives may not be conscious and—though pursued—may not be endorsed. When values and motives are not consistent, there will be "leaks" (when motives push aside values) and "failures" (when values are not supported by motives). In the words of the Anglican General Confession, the former will be experienced as "doing those things we ought not to have done," while the latter will be felt as "leaving undone those things we ought to have done." Still, conscious values are far from unimportant: for both leaders and groups, values provide emotion-laden cognitive "pegs" on which to hang policies in such vital areas as the economy, pluralism, and war.

Beginning in the 1990s, psychologists and political scientists began to carry out large-scale multinational studies of a variety of cognitions that can be collectively labeled "values." For example, Inglehart (1997) surveyed people in 43 countries to chart the trajectory from modern or "materialist" values to "postmaterialist" values. With the assistance of numerous collaborators, Schwartz (1994; see also Schwartz & Bardi, 2001) has organized a continuing study of values in 63 nations, using a 56-item survey. Schwartz and Bardi (2001) conclude that across nations, some 45 specific values are organized into 10 broad "value types": power, achievement, hedonism, stimulation, self-direction, universalism, benevolence, tradition, conformity, and security. (Several additional values, such as self-respect, true friendship, a spiritual life, and health are not always equivalent in meaning across nations.) They discuss the cases of Singapore, where values of security, conformity, and tradition are rated high, and the United States, in which achievement, hedonism, and power are relatively highly endorsed (pp. 284–287). This is one example of how such a massive data set can be used to understand personality aspects of particular groups or nations. As comparative descriptive statistics for different nations are published, political psychologists will be able to incorporate comparative value profiles into their understanding of politically relevant personality characteristics at the mass level. A country's values, as conscious representations of guiding principles (what is socially considered to be desirable; the "ought"), can be contrasted with its implicit motives (what is actually desired) measured through content analysis of cultural documents (see McClelland, 1961, 1975).

Social Contexts and Political Behavior

All personalities—leaders, followers, cabinet ministers, diplomats, legislators, and the masses—exist in particular social contexts. Most obvious, of course, is the context presented by immediate social situations: the events or "stimuli" (statements, offers, threats) presented by other important political and social actors; the problems, resources, and models that must be considered in formulating responses to these events, and so forth. These can be called the situational microcontext. However, contexts include a much broader range of influences on individual personality: gender, life stage, social class, ethnicity, race, economy, institutions, religion, culture, history, and generation. These can be called the macrocontext. As suggested earlier, people "carry around" their macrocontexts with them, and so they can be considered as an element of personality.

Contexts affect personality in four major ways. First, taken as a whole, they furnish the forces (or "stimuli") that, interacting with genetic endowment, affects the levels of many personality variables. As an example, every religion is a complex of institutional structures and practices, explicit teachings, and shared beliefs. One would therefore expect that different religions might foster different average levels of personality characteristics in their adherents. Thus among United States males in the mid-1950s, levels of achievement motivation were higher for Jews and Catholics than for Protestants (see Veroff, Feld, & Gurin, 1962). Second, contexts provide networks of meanings, customs, and relationships in which personality and behavior are embedded and according to which these are considered "normal" or pathological. For example, many Americans tend to consider extraversion healthy and well-adjusted, while to many Chinese, *introversion* is normal and a high level of extraversion slightly abnormal. Third, certain personality characteristics may be unique to, or at least very common and therefore "typical" of, certain cultures. Examples would include "amok" (a state of destructive, maddened excitement) and "koro" (a man's belief that his penis is retracting into his abdomen) in southeast Asia, or "amae" (a sense of entitled dependency) in Japan (see Berry, Poortinga, Segall, & Dasen, 1992, pp. 89–93). Finally, social contexts channel the expression of all personality characteristics. For example, extraversion is associated with drinking coffee and smoking, but extraverted, devout Mormons are unlikely to do either, because these actions are proscribed by their religion.

As a broader example, consider such personality variables as power motivation, optimistic explanatory style, extraversion, and conscientiousness.

Each is clearly defined. Each has considerable construct validity, which means that it is associated with a recognized and characteristic set of observable behaviors. Yet imagine how differently each would have been expressed on the morning of June 6, 1944, by the following two people, in the following two situations: (1) a 20-year-old white American man storming "Utah Beach" during the World War II invasion of Normandy in France, and (2) a middle-aged Japanese American woman in an internment camp set up in the Utah desert at the beginning of the war by the U. S. government for citizens and residents of Japanese ancestry. While we certainly recognize the enormous effects of the contrasting contexts on the expression of these four personality variables, we probably also could "recognize" each of the variables in the two contexts. The fact that we can do both illustrates the need for considering macrocontexts as an integral element of personality.

Personality and Particular Contexts

Explaining people's politically relevant behavior in terms of their social contexts is usually construed as the task of social psychology (Nisbett, 1980), political sociology (Faulks, 2000), or political anthropology (Lewellen, 1992) rather than political psychology, and of course the effects of different specifically *political* contexts on leader behavior is the province of political psychology itself. As suggested at the beginning of this chapter, however, there are signs that personality psychologists are paying renewed attention to the effects of context. Thus it is appropriate to mention briefly what has been done within political psychology, to survey critical concepts, and thus to suggest domains for future research—because this is relevant to the full understanding of personality and political behavior. In this chapter I merely mention some of these possibilities, citing studies where relevant. In general, there is little difficulty with assessing people's social context, because attributes such as their gender, their culture, the historical background of their culture, and their generation are either known or easily learned: knowing these, implications for the formation of personality and its expression, especially in political contexts, can then be worked out from the different literatures that are specifically concerned with these contexts.

The implications of *gender* for political psychology are discussed at length in chapter 17. Additional sources of modern work on gender that are specifically relevant to political psychology questions can be found in Clinchy and Norem (1995), Duerst-Lahti and Kelly (1995), Vianello and Moore (2000), and especially the series of meta-analytic research reviews of gender and leadership by Eagly and her colleagues (Carli & Eagly, 1999; Eagly & Johnson, 1990; Eagly & Karau, 1991; Eagly, Karau, & Makhijani, 1995; Eagly, Makhijani, & Klonsky, 1992).

The actions and choices of many leaders—from Shakespeare's Lear to Nelson Mandela—can be understood in terms of their *age* or *life cycle stage* (see also chapter 3). Erikson's framework (1963, 1997), along with his stage-related concepts of identity (Erikson, 1959/1980) and *generativity* (Erikson, Erikson, & Kivnick, 1986), provide a useful theoretical framework for understanding the political psychological implications of life stage. Post (1980, 1993b) discussed ways that life stage generally, and the cultural and neurological effects of aging specifically, can affect political leaders.

While the early twentieth-century collaboration between psychology and anthropology known as "culture and personality" studies had run its course by about 1960 on account of conceptual and methodological difficulties (see Inkeles & Levinson, 1969; Singer, 1961), it did set the stage for subsequent more rigorous studies of *cultural and national differences*, conceptualized variously as "national character," "modal personality" (Inkeles, 1997), or "political culture" (Pye, 1991, 1997). Renshon and Duckitt (2000) have recently argued that events of the 1990s—for example, the collapse of communism in eastern Europe, the rise of (often violent) ethnic politics, and globalization of economic life—have refocused scholarly interest on the cultural bases of modernization and democratic politics (see also Renshon & Duckitt, 1997). Studies along the lines of the mass-level studies of traits, motives, and values mentioned earlier could provide ways of describing political culture in operational terms.

Hofstede's (1980, 2001) investigation of the "dimensions of culture," based on survey data from over 88,000 employees of a multinational corporation, is a landmark for the systematic comparative study of cultural contexts. Combining survey results, social indicator data, and the research of many other investigators, Hofstede identified four main dimensions along which cultures or nations differ: high versus low power distance, individualism versus collectivism, tolerance of uncertainty, and high versus low gendering. (Hofstede actually named this fourth factor "masculinity." However, since it comprises variables that involve *differentiation* between women and men—in sex roles, sex-role socialization, occupations and work goals, and higher education—the label "gendering," as I will use it here, seems preferable on grounds of accuracy and precision.) Recently, Hofstede (1999) has suggested that delay of gratification may constitute a fifth dimension of culture. So far, psychologists have paid the most attention to individualism-collectivism, Hofstede's second dimension (see Markus & Kitayama, 1991; Triandis, 1995), but the others are equally important for understanding cultural and national variation in political life and personality expression and dynamics.

Of course cultural variations relevant to the expression of personality go far beyond these overall dimensions. Conceptions of such basic political psychology terms as "power" and "authority" may vary in subtle and obvious ways across nations and cultures. Thus Pye (1985) describes a characteristically "Asian" conception of power that is quite different from that held by most western political actors: power involves consensus rather than competition, the leader is *spared* the chore of decision-making, and power structures are held together by patron/client ties of respect, paternalism, and dependency. Ihanus (2001) traces the ways that contemporary Russian leaders and concepts of authority were shaped by historical and cultural themes such as absolute autocracy (p. 131), the "ecstasy of submission" to a charismatic leader (p. 133), and leader transition by overthrow (p. 134).

In recent years, psychologists and social scientists have developed considerable interest in the concept of *generation* and "generational entelechy" (the distinctive "mindset" of a particular generation), drawing on Mannheim's (1928/1952) classic study (Kertzer, 1983; Schuman & Scott, 1989; see also chapter 3). Writing for the general reader, Strauss and Howe (1991) chronicled United States history in terms of the different perspectives of 13 "generations." The mindset of the so-called Generation X (people born between 1965 and 1978) has been the object of intense analysis in the popular media. Ortner (1998, 2003), however, has made a serious ethnographic study of Generation X and their parents, who are mostly from the "Silent Fifties" generation.

Stewart (see Stewart & Healy, 1989) has elaborated Mannheim's concept into a model for understanding the effects of historical events and social trends in terms of (1) how divergent the event or trend is from the immediate surrounding historical background, and (2) the person's life stage at the time of experiencing the event or trend. Thus the effects of events such as World Wars I and II or the civil rights movement, for example, were quite different for people of different ages.

▲ Toward a Multivariate, Integrative Study of Personality

Personalities are complex. While personality researchers are still looking for the ideal research strategy and statistical algorithms for dealing with such complexity, we can offer a general guideline: if personality is understood as comprising different (and independent) elements, then it follows that the fullest assessments of individual and collective personality, and the most accurate predictions from personality to political behavior, will be made by using *combinations* of variables, preferably variables drawn from different personality elements.

As an example, Hermann (1987b, 1999) has developed a method for constructing integrated, multivariate personality profiles of political leaders from their scores on several different motivational, cognitive, and trait-style component variables, as shown in table 4.4. These particular orientations are focused on leaders' foreign policy orientations and behavior; they may also be useful for characterizing political types generally.[5] Along with her emphasis on combinations and interactions of discrete personality variables, Hermann also suggests a series of other factors, including situational variables, that mediate or "filter" the effects of personality on political behavior. For example, a

Table 4.4
Personality Orientations and Their Component Variables

Orientation	Definition	Component variables
Expansionist	Interest in gaining control over more territory, resources, or people	Power motivation Nationalism Belief in ability to control events Self-confidence Distrust Task orientation
Active independent	Interest in participating in the international community, but on one's own terms and without engendering a dependent relationship with another country	Affiliation motivation Nationalism Belief in ability to control events Cognitive complexity Self-confidence Task orientation
Influential	Interest in having an impact on other nations' foreign policy behavior, in playing a leadership role in regional or international affairs	Power motivation Belief in ability to control events Cognitive complexity Self-confidence Interpersonal orientation
Mediator/ integrator	Concern with reconciling differences between other nations, with resolving problems in the international arena	Affiliation motivation Belief in ability to control events Cognitive complexity Interpersonal orientation
Opportunist	Interest in taking advantage of present circumstances, in dealing effectively with the demands and opportunities of the moment, in being expedient	Cognitive complexity Interpersonal orientation
Developmental	Commitment to the continued improvement of one's own nation with the best help available from other countries or international organizations	Affiliation motivation Nationalism Cognitive complexity Self-confidence Interpersonal orientation

Source: Adapted from Hermann (1987, pp. 170–173)

strong *interest* in foreign policy is likely to amplify the effects of personality on a leader's actions related to foreign policy, while background factors such as training or previous experience, and sensitivity to the environment (probably an aspect of personality), are likely to diminish such effects.

Hermann's system has been used in numerous comparative studies: world leaders (Hermann, 1980a), Soviet Politburo members during the mid-1970s (Hermann, 1980b), and British and German prime ministers (Kaarbo, 2001; Kaarbo & Hermann, 1998). It has also been used to generate personality portraits of individual leaders that could be used to understand historical actions and events (for example, the U.S. president Lyndon Johnson and the Vietnam War; see Preston & t'Hart, 1999) or to predict future actions (for example, the Iranian president Mohammad Khatami; see Taysi & Preston, 2001).

In a unique collaborative assessment enterprise, Winter, Hermann, Weintraub, and Walker (1991b) each applied their own methods of personality measurement to make comparative assessments of the U.S. president George H. W. Bush and the Soviet president Mikhail Gorbachev, with a later followup on predictions made in the original article (Winter, Hermann, Weintraub, & Walker, 1991a).

▲ The Future of At-a-Distance Assessment: A Lesson in Humility

With the growing use of digitally based systems for the analysis of verbal content, we may expect that computerized scoring procedures for many more personality characteristics will be developed in the future, although on account of the incredible subtlety and complexity of human language, such goals may be farther away and more difficult to achieve than cyberoptimists might imagine. At the same time, we must recognize that even with the best measures, predictions of political leaders' behavior must always be phrased in contingent or conditional, "if/then" terms (Wright & Mischel, 1987, 1988). That is, the effects of leaders' personalities will always depend on the situations in which they find themselves—and personality profiling by itself can never predict those exact situations.

For example, in a followup to their earlier analysis of Bush and Gorbachev, Winter and colleagues (1991a) concluded that their earlier predictions should have been "conditionally hedged," to take account of unpredictable changes in the situation. Thus they had described George H. W. Bush as a "peacemaker, concerned with development and not prone to seek political ends through violence and war" (Winter et al., 1991b, p. 237). Yet during the autumn of 1990 Bush threatened military action against Iraq, and in January 1991 this affiliation-motivated president had begun a devastating (if mercifully short) war. Of course the August 1990 Iraqi invasion of Kuwait was the proximate cause of Bush's aggressive policy, and this was certainly not predictable from any knowledge of Bush's personality. That conceded, however, many features of Bush's policy and conduct of the war *can* be derived from the personality portrait sketched by Winter and colleagues (1991b): impulsivity, angry and defensive reactions to perceived threat, demonizing of dissimilar others, and alliance-building with similar others via extensive communication.

Such *contingent or conditional predictions* take the following general form: person X (or people of personality type X, or people scoring high on variable *X*), under particular conditions *Y* is likely to carry out particular action *Z*. In contrast, an *absolute* "personality prediction" would be that person *X* will carry out action *Z*, without any reference to conditions or context, and an absolute "situational prediction" would be that under conditions *Y*, all people will show action *Z*. Wright and Mischel (1987, 1988) have argued that almost all personality variables are really "clusters of if/then propositions"—that is, "predictions about what a person would do under appropriate conditions" (pp. 1159, 1161).[6]

◣ Notes

1. Of course most documents and speeches that bear the name of a major political leader are actually written by one or more speechwriters, and even "spontaneous" press conference responses to questions and "informal" comments may be highly scripted. Thus one may ask whether a content analysis of such materials produces personality estimates of the leader or of the speechwriters. Suedfeld (1994) and Winter (1995) discuss this issue, and conclude that because leaders select speechwriters and review their drafts, and speechwriters "know" their clients, personality "scores" based on content analysis (at least of major speeches) can be taken as a valid indicator of the personality and psychological state of the leader—a claim that has generally been validated by research with such scores.

2. Eysenck's extraversion factor is equivalent to the similarly named Big Five factor 1 and perhaps also factor 2 (agreeableness). His neuroticism factor is equivalent to low emotional stability (factor 4). Eysenck's psychoticism factor has been interpreted by some as low conscientiousness (factor 3) or perhaps low openness (factor 5; see John, 1990; Winter, 1996, ch. 12).

3. Although five-factor trait theorists generally believe that "extraversion" and "dominance" are part of a single factor, in Etheredge's data the two were essentially uncorrelated ($r = .14$). Such a result is not uncommon in trait research and may reflect an irreducible looseness of the trait factors. On the other hand, Etheredge's rating definition of extraversion ("emotionally outgoing . . . leisure time spent with people, warm . . . affable"; see p. 444) sounds more like factor 2, agreeableness.

4. See Smith (1992) for information about these motive scoring systems, as well as several other content analysis systems useful in political psychology research, and for details of measurement, including a discussion of reliability; see Winter (1998) for an account of their development; and see Winter (1994) for a single integrated system for scoring all three motives.

5. Hermann's methodology has become available through Social Science Automation, via its website, http://socialscienceautomation.com, with a detailed description at http://socialscienceautomation.com/Lta.pdf.

6. Actually, the same is true of most scientific constructs, as Wright and Mischel suggest: the adjective "soluble" (i.e., the "trait" of solubility) does not refer to a general behavior of a substance but rather describes a specific set of situation-action tendencies—that is, dissolving when submerged in a liquid (1987, p. 1160).

◣ References

Adorno, T. W., Frenkel-Brunswik, E., Levinson, D. J., & Sanford, R. N. (1950). *The authoritarian personality.* New York: Harper.

Aliotta, J. M. (1988). Social backgrounds, social motives and participation on the U.S. Supreme Court. *Political Behavior, 10,* 267–284.

Allport, G. W. (1961). *Pattern and growth in personality.* New York: Holt, Rinehart, and Winston.

Almond, G. A., & Verba, S. (1989). *The civic culture: Political attitudes and democracy in five nations* (2nd ed.). Newbury Park, CA: Sage.

Altemeyer, B. (1981). *Right-wing authoritarianism.* Winnipeg: University of Manitoba Press.

Altemeyer, B. (1988). *Enemies of freedom: Understanding right-wing authoritarianism.* San Francisco: Jossey-Bass.

Altemeyer, B. (1996). *The authoritarian specter.* Cambridge, MA: Harvard University Press.

Barber, J. D. (1992). *The presidential character: Predicting performance in the White House* (4th ed.). Englewood Cliffs, NJ: Prentice-Hall.

Barenbaum, N. B., & Winter, D. G. (2003). Personality. In I. B. Weiner (Series Ed.) & D. K. Freedheim (Vol. Ed.), *Handbook of psychology: Vol. 1. History of psychology* (pp. 177–203). New York: Wiley.

Barrett, P., & Eysenck, H. J. (1984). The assessment of personality factors across 25 countries. *Personality and Individual Differences, 5,* 615–632.

Berry, J. W., Poortinga, Y. H., Segall, M. H., & Dasen, P. R. (1992). *Cross-cultural psychology: Research and applications.* New York: Cambridge University Press.

Block, J. (1961). *The Q-sort method in personality assessment and psychiatric research.* Springfield, IL: Charles C. Thomas.

Block, J. (1995). A contrarian view of the five-factor approach to personality description. *Psychological Bulletin, 117,* 187–215.

Blondel, J. (1987). *Political leadership: Towards a general analysis.* London: Sage.

Boroson, W. (1964). What psychiatrists say about Goldwater. *Fact, 1*(5), 24–64.

Brewer, M. B., & Gardner, W. (1996). Who is this "we"? Levels of collective identity and self representations. *Journal of Personality and Social Psychology, 71,* 83–93.

Buss, A. H. (1989). Personality as traits. *American Psychologist, 44,* 1378–1388.

Buss, D. M. (1987). Selection, evocation, and manipulation. *Journal of Personality and Social Psychology, 53,* 1214–1221.

Byman, D., & Pollack, K. (2001). Let us now praise great men: Bringing the statesman back in. *International Security, 25* (4), 107–146.

Carli, L. L., & Eagly, A. H. (1999). Gender effects on social influence and emergent leadership. In G. N. Powell (Ed.), *Handbook of gender and work* (pp. 203–222). Thousand Oaks, CA: Sage Publications, Inc.

Cheung, F. M., Leung, K., Zhang, J. X., Sun, H.-F., Gan, Y.-Q., Song, W.-Z., & Xie, D. (2001). Indigenous Chinese personality constructs: Is the five-factor model complete? *Journal of Cross-Cultural Psychology, 32,* 407–433.

Clinchy, B. McV., & Norem, J. K. (Eds.). (1995). *The gender and psychology reader.* New York: New York University Press.

Costa, P. M., & McCrae, R. (1992). *The Revised NEO Personality Inventory professional manual.* Odessa, FL: Psychological Assessment Resources.

Dillon, M. (1993). Argumentative complexity of abortion discourse. *Public Opinion Quarterly, 57,* 305–314.

DiRenzo, G. J. (1967). *Personality, power and politics.* Notre Dame, IN: University of Notre Dame Press.

Doty, R. M., Peterson, B. E., & Winter, D. G. (1991). Threat and authoritarianism in the United States, 1978–1987. *Journal of Personality and Social Psychology, 61,* 629–640.

Duerst-Lahti, G., & Kelly, R. M. (Eds.). (1995). *Gender power, leadership, and governance.* Ann Arbor: University of Michigan Press.

Eagly, A. H., & Johnson, B. T. (1990). Gender and leadership style: A meta-analysis. *Psychological Bulletin, 108,* 233–256.

Eagly, A. H., & Karau, S. J. (1991). Gender and the emergence of leaders: A meta-analysis. *Journal of Personality and Social Psychology, 60,* 685–710.

Eagly, A. H., Karau, S. J., & Makhijani, M. G. (1995). Gender and the effectiveness of leaders: A meta-analysis. *Psychological Bulletin, 117,* 125–145.

Eagly, A. H., Makhijani, M. G., & Klonsky, B. G. (1992). Gender and the evaluation of leaders: A meta-analysis. *Psychological Bulletin, 111,* 3–22.

Elms, A. C. (1994). *Uncovering lives: The uneasy alliance of biography and psychology.* New York: Oxford University Press.

Erikson, E. H. (1963). *Childhood and society* (Rev. ed.). New York: Norton.

Erikson, E. H. (1980). *Identity and the life cycle.* New York: Norton. (Original work published 1959)

Erikson, E. H. (1997). *The life cycle completed.* (Extended version, with new chapters on the ninth stage of development by Joan M. Erikson.) New York: Norton.

Erikson, E. H., Erikson, J. M., & Kivnick, H. Q. (1986). *Vital involvement in old age.* New York: Norton.

Etheredge, L. S. (1978). Personality effects on American foreign policy, 1898–1968: A test of interpersonal generalization theory. *American Political Science Review, 72,* 434–451.

Ethington, L. (2001). *Election 2000: A time-series analysis of motive profiles and other variables in the U.S. presidential campaign.* Unpublished honors thesis, University of Michigan, Ann Arbor.

Eysenck, H. J., & Eysenck, M. W. (1985). *Personality and individual differences: A natural science approach.* New York: Plenum.

Faulks, K. (2000). *Political sociology: A critical introduction.* New York: New York University Press.

Feldman, O., & Valenty, L. O. (Eds.). (2001). *Profiling political leaders: Cross-cultural studies of personality and behavior.* Westport, CT: Praeger.

Friedlander, S., & Cohen, R. (1975). The personality correlates of belligerence in international conflict. *Comparative Politics, 7,* 155–186.

Fukai, S. N. (2001). Building the war economy and rebuilding postwar Japan: A profile of pragmatic nationalist Nobusuke Kishi. In O. Feldman & L. O. Valenty (Eds.), *Profiling political leaders: Cross-cultural studies of personality and political behavior* (pp. 167–184). Westport, CT: Praeger.

Geertz, C. (1973). *The interpretation of cultures.* New York: Basic Books.

George, A. L. (1969). The "operational code:" A neglected approach to the study of political leaders and decision-making. *International Studies Quarterly, 13,* 190–222.

Ginzburg, R. (1964). Goldwater: The man and the menace. *Fact, 1*(5), 3–22.

Glad, B. (1973). Contributions of psychobiography. In J. N. Knutson (Ed.), *Handbook of political psychology* (pp. 296–321). San Francisco: Jossey-Bass.

Glick, P., Fiske, S., Mladinic, A., Saiz, J. L., Abrams, D., Masser, B., Adetoun, B., Osagie, J. E., Akande, A., Alao, A., Annetje, B., Willemsen, T. M., Chipeta, K., Dardenne, B., Dijksterhuis, A., Wigboldus, D., Eckes, T., Six-Materna, I., Exposito, F., Moya, M., Foddy, M., Kim, H.-J., Lameiras, M., Sotelo, M. J., Mucchi-Faina, A., Romani, M., Sakalli, N., Udegbe, B., Yamamoto, M., Ui, M., Ferreira, M. C., & Lopez, W. L. (2000). Beyond prejudice as simple antipathy: Hostile and benevolent sexism across cultures. *Journal of Personality and Social Psychology; 79,* 763–775.

Goldberg, L. R. (1990). An alternative "description of personality": The Big-Five factor structure. *Journal of Personality and Social Psychology, 59,* 1216–1229.

Goldhagen, D. J. (1996). *Hitler's willing executioners: Ordinary Germans and the Holocaust.* New York: Knopf.

Greenstein, F. I. (1987). *Personality and politics: Problems of evidence, inference, and conceptualization.* Princeton: Princeton University Press. (Original work published 1969)

Greenstein, F. I. (2000). *The presidential difference: Leadership style from FDR to Clinton.* New York: Free Press.

Guttieri, K., Wallace, M. D., & Suedfeld, P. (1995). The integrative complexity of American decision makers in the Cuban missile crisis. *Journal of Conflict Resolution, 39,* 595–621.

Hamby, A. L. (1991). An American democrat: A reevaluation of the personality of Harry S. Truman. *Political Science Quarterly, 106,* 33–55.

Henderson, J. (2001). Predicting the performance of leaders in parliamentary systems: New Zealand Prime Minister David Lange. In O. Feldman & L. O. Valenty (Eds.), *Profiling political leaders: Cross-cultural studies of personality and political behavior* (pp. 203–216). Westport, CT: Praeger.

Hermann, M. G. (1980a). Assessing the personalities of Soviet Politburo members. *Personality and Social Psychology Bulletin, 6,* 332–352.

Hermann, M. G. (1980b). Explaining foreign policy behavior using the personal characteristics of political leaders. *International Studies Quarterly, 24,* 7–46.

Hermann, M. G. (1983). Assessing personality at a distance: A profile of Ronald Reagan. *Mershon Center Quarterly Report, 7*(6), 1–8. Columbus: Mershon Center of the Ohio State University.

Hermann, M. G. (1987a). Assessing the foreign policy role orientations of sub-Saharan African leaders. In S. G. Walker (Ed.), *Role theory and foreign policy analysis* (pp. 161–198). Durham, NC: Duke University Press.

Hermann, M. G. (1987b). *Handbook for assessing personal characteristics and foreign policy orientations of political leaders.* Columbus: Ohio State University, Mershon Center.

Hermann, M. G. (1988). Syria's Hafez Al-Assad. In B. Kellerman & J. Z. Rubin (Eds.), *Leadership and negotiation in the Middle East* (pp. 70–95). New York: Praeger.

Hermann, M. G. (1999). *Assessing leadership style: A trait analysis.* Columbus, OH: Social Science Automation.

Historical Figures Assessment Collaborative. (1977). Assessing historical figures: The use of observer-based personality descriptions. *Historical Methods Newsletter 10*(2), 66–76.

Hofstede, G. H. (1980). *Culture's consequences: International differences in work-related values.* Thousand Oaks, CA: Sage.

Hofstede, G. H. (1999, July). *Cultural paradoxes in international politics: Corruption, human rights, and imposed democracy.* Invited address at the annual meeting of the International Society of Political Psychology, Amsterdam.

Hofstede, G. H. (2001). *Culture's consequences: Comparing values, behaviors, institutions, and organizations across nations* (2nd ed.). Thousand Oaks, CA: Sage.

Hollander, E. P. (1985). Leadership and power. In G. Lindzey & E. Aronson (Eds.), *Handbook of social psychology, 3rd ed.* (Vol. 2, pp. 485–537). New York: Random House.

Holsti, O. (1969). *Content analysis for the social sciences and humanities.* Reading, MA: Addison-Wesley.

Holsti, O. (1977). *The "Operational Code" as an approach to the analysis of belief systems.* Final report to the National Science Foundation, Grant No. SOC 75-15368. Duke University.

House, R. J., Spangler, W. D., & Woycke, J. (1991). Personality and charisma in the U.S. presidency: A psychological theory of leader effectiveness. *Administrative Science Quarterly, 36,* 364–396.

Ihanus, J. (2001). Profiling Russian leaders from a psychohistorical and a psychobiographical perspective. In O. Feldman & L. O. Valenty (Eds.), *Profiling political leaders: Cross-cultural studies of personality and political behavior* (pp. 129–147). Westport, CT: Praeger.

Immelman, A. (1993). The assessment of political personality: A psychodiagnostically relevant conceptualization and methodology. *Political Psychology, 14,* 725–741.

Immelman, A. (1998). The political personalities of 1996 U.S. presidential candidates Bill Clinton and Bob Dole. *Leadership Quarterly, 9,* 335–366.

Immelman, A. (1999, July). *The Political Personality of Texas Governor George W. Bush.* Paper presented at the meeting of the International Society of Political Psychology, Amsterdam.

Inglehart, R. (1997). *Modernization and postmodernization: Cultural, economic, and political change in 43 societies.* Princeton: Princeton University Press.

Inkeles, A. (1997). *National character: A psycho-social perspective.* New Brunswick, NJ: Transaction.

Inkeles, A., & Levinson, D. J. (1969). National character. In G. Lindzey & E. Aronson (Eds.), *Handbook of social psychology* (rev. ed., vol. 4, pp. 418–506). Reading, MA: Addison-Wesley.

Isaacson, W. (1992). *Kissinger: A biography.* New York: Simon and Schuster.

John, O. P. (1990). The "Big Five" factor taxonomy: Dimensions of personality in the natural language and in questionnaires. In L. Pervin (Ed.), *Handbook of personality: Theory and research* (pp. 66–100). New York: Guilford.

Joll, J. (1968). *1914: The unspoken assumptions.* London: Weidenfeld and Nicolson.

Kaarbo, J. (2001). Linking leadership style to policy: How prime ministers influence the decision-making process. In O. Feldman & L. O. Valenty (Eds.), *Profiling political leaders: Cross-cultural studies of personality and political behavior* (pp. 81–96). Westport, CT: Praeger.

Kaarbo, J., & Hermann, M. G. (1998). Leadership styles of prime ministers: How individual differences affect the foreign policymaking process. *Leadership Quarterly, 9,* 243–263.

Kennedy, P. (1982). The Kaiser and German Weltpolitik: Reflexions on Wilhelm II's place in the making of German foreign policy. In J. C. G. Röhl & N. Sombart (Eds.), *Kaiser Wilhelm II: New interpretations* (pp. 143–168). New York: Cambridge University Press.

Kershaw, I. (1999). *Hitler, 1889–1936: Hubris.* New York: Norton.

Kertzer, D. I. (1983). Generation as a sociological problem. *Annual Review of Sociology, 9,* 125–149. Palo Alto, CA: Annual Reviews Press.

Kluckhohn, C. K. M., Murray, H. A., & Schneider, D. M. (1953). *Personality in nature, culture and society.* New York: Knopf.

Kohut, H. (1985). *Self psychology and the humanities.* New York: Norton.

Lewellen, T. C. (1992). *Political anthropology: An introduction.* Westport, CT: Bergin & Garvey.

Lynn, R. (1981). Cross-cultural differences in neuroticism, extraversion and psychoticism. In R. Lynn (Ed.), *Dimensions of personality: Essays in honour of H. J. Eysenck* (pp. 263–286). Oxford: Pergamon Press.

Lynn, R., & Hampson, S. L. (1975). National differences in extraversion and neuroticism. *British Journal of Social and Clinical Psychology, 14,* 223–240.

Mannheim, K. (1952). The problem of generations. In *Essays on the sociology of knowledge* (pp. 276–322). New York: Oxford University Press. (Original work published 1928)

Markus, H. R., & Kitayama, S. (1991). Culture and the self: Implications for cognition, emotion, and motivation. *Psychological Review, 98,* 224–253.

McClelland, D. C. (1951). *Personality.* New York: Sloane.

McClelland, D. C. (1961). *The achieving society.* Princeton, NJ: Van Nostrand.

McClelland, D. C. (1975). *Power: The inner experience.* New York: Irvington.

McCrae, R. R., &, Costa, P. T., Jr. (1997). Personality trait structure as a human universal. *American Psychologist, 52,* 509–516.

Meloen, J. (1983). *De autoritaire reaktie in tijden van welvaart en krisis* [The auithoritarian reaction in times of prosperity and crisis]. Unpublished doctoral dissertation, University of Amsterdam.

Meloen, J. (1993). The F scale as a predictor of fascism: An overview of forty years of authoritarianism research. In W. F. Stone, G. Lederer, & R. Christie (Eds.), *Strength and weakness: The authoritarian personality today* (pp. 47–69). New York: Springer-Verlag.

Millon, T. (1986). Personality prototypes and their diagnostic criteria. In T. Millon & G. L. Klerman (Eds.), *Contemporary directions in psychopathology: Toward the DSM-IV* (pp. 671–712). New York: Guilford.

Mischel, W. (1968). *Personality and assessment.* New York: Wiley.

Moen, P., Elder, & Lüscher, K. (Eds.). (1995). *Examining lives in context: Perspectives on the ecology of human development.* Washington, DC: American Psychological Association.

Murray, H. A. (1938). *Explorations in personality.* New York: Oxford University Press.

Nisbett, R. N. (1980). The trait construct in lay and professional psychology. In L. Festinger (Ed.), *Retrospections on social psychology* (pp. 109–130). New York: Oxford University Press.

Nisbett, R., & Cohen, D. (1995). *The culture of honor: The psychology of violence in the South.* Boulder, CO: Westview Press.

Ortner, S. B. (1998). Generation X: Anthropology in a media-saturated world. *Cultural Anthropology, 13,* 414–40.

Ortner, S. B. (2003). *New Jersey dreaming: Capital, culture, and the class of '58.* Durham, NC: Duke University Press.

Peterson, B. E., Doty, R. M., & Winter, D. G. (1993). Authoritarianism and attitudes toward social issues: AIDS, drug use, and the environment. *Personality and Social Psychology Bulletin, 19,* 174–184.

Peterson, C. (1992). Explanatory style. In C. P. Smith (Ed.), *Motivation and personality: Handbook of thematic content analysis* (pp. 376–382). New York: Cambridge University Press.

Post, J. M. (1980). The seasons of a leader's life: Influences of the life cycle on political behavior. *Political Psychology, 2*(3/4), 35–49.

Post, J. M. (1991). Saddam Hussein of Iraq: A political personality profile. *Political Psychology, 12,* 279–289.

Post, J. M. (1993a). Current concepts of the narcissistic personality: Implications for political psychology. *Political Psychology, 14,* 99–121.

Post, J. M. (1993b). Dreams of glory and the life cycle: Reflections on the life course of narcissistic leaders. In Braungart, R. G., & Braungart, M. M. (Eds.), *Life course and generational politics* (pp. 49–60). Lanham, MD: University Press of America.

Post, J. M. (1997). Narcissism and the quest for political power. In C. S. Ellman & J. Reppen (Eds.) *Omnipotent fantasies and the vulnerable self* (pp. 195–232). Northvale, NJ: Jason Aronson, Inc.

Preston, T., & t'Hart, P. (1999). Understanding and evaluating bureaucratic politics: The nexus between political leaders and advisory systems. *Political Psychology, 20,* 49–98.

Pye, L. W. (1985). *Asian power and politics: The cultural dimensions of authority.* Cambridge, MA: Harvard University Press.

Pye, L. W. (1991). Political culture revisited. *Political Psychology, 12,* 487–508.

Pye, L. W. (1997). Introduction: The elusive concept of culture and the vivid reality of personality. *Political Psychology, 18,* 241–254.

Renshon, S. A. (2001). The comparative psychoanalytic study of political leaders: John McCain and the limits of trait psychology. In O. Feldman & L. O. Valenty (Eds.), *Profiling political leaders: Cross-cultural studies of personality and political behavior* (pp. 233–253). Westport, CT: Praeger.

Renshon, S., & Duckitt, J. (Eds.). (1997). Cultural and cross-cultural dimensions of political psychology [special issue]. *Political Psychology, 18*(2).

Renshon, S. A., & Duckitt, J. (Eds.). (2000). *Political psychology: Cultural and cross-cultural foundations.* New York: New York University Press.

Rubenzer, S. J., Faschingbauer, T. R., & Ones, D. S. (2000). Assessing the U.S. presidents using the revised NEO Personality Inventory. *Assessment, 7,* 403–420.

Runyan, W. McK. (1982). *Life histories and psychobiography: Explorations in theory and method.* New York: Oxford University Press.

Runyan, W. McK. (1988). Progress in psychobiography. *Journal of Personality, 56,* 295–326.

Runyan, W. McK. (1997). Studying lives: Psychobiography and the conceptual structure of personality psychology. In R. Hogan, J. Johnson, & S. Briggs (Eds.),

Handbook of personality psychology (pp. 41–69). San Diego, CA: Academic Press.

Sales, S. M. (1973). Threat as a factor in authoritarianism: An analysis of archival data. *Journal of Personality and Social Psychology, 28*, 44–57.

Satterfield, J. M., & Seligman, M. E. P. (1994). Military aggression and risk predicted by explanatory style. *Psychological Science, 5*, 77–82.

Schafer, M. (2000). Issues in assessing psychological characteristics as a distance: An introduction to the symposium. *Political Psychology, 21*, 511–528

Schafer, M., & Walker, S. G. (2001). Political leadership and the democratic peace: The operational code of Prime Minister Tony Blair. In O. Feldman & L. O. Valenty (Eds.), *Profiling political leaders: Cross-cultural studies of personality and political behavior* (pp. 21–35). Westport, CT: Praeger.

Schmitt, D. P., & Winter, D. G. (1998). Measuring the motives of Soviet leadership and Soviet society: Congruence reflected or congruence created? *Leadership Quarterly, 9*, 181–194.

Schuman, H., & Scott, J. (1989). Generations and collective memories. *American Sociological Review, 54*, 359–381.

Schütz, A. (1993). Self-presentational tactics used in a German election campaign. *Political Psychology, 14*, 471–493.

Schütz, A. (2001). Self-presentation of political leaders in Germany: The case of Helmut Kohl. In O. Feldman & L. O. Valenty (Eds.), *Profiling political leaders: Cross-cultural studies of personality and political behavior* (pp. 217–232). Westport, CT: Praeger.

Schwartz, S. H. (1994). Are there universal aspects in the structure and contents of human values? *Journal of Social Issues, 50*(4), 19–45.

Schwartz, S. H., & Bardi, A. (2001). Value hierarchies across cultures: Taking a similarities perspective. *Journal of Cross-Cultural Psychology, 32*, 268–290.

Sheng, M. M. (2001). Mao Zedong's narcissistic personality disorder and China's road to disaster. In O. Feldman & L. O. Valenty (Eds.), *Profiling political leaders: Cross-cultural studies of personality and political behavior* (pp. 111–127). Westport, CT: Praeger.

Shestopal, E. B. (2000). *Psikhologicheskii profil' rossiiskoi politiki 1990-kh: Teoreticheskie i prikladnye problemy politicheskoi psikhologii* [Psychological profiles of Russian politics in the 1990s: Theoretical and applied problems in political psychology]. Moscow: ROSSPEN.

Sidanius, J., & Pratto, F. (1999). *Social dominance: An intergroup theory of social hierarchy and oppression.* New York: Cambridge University Press.

Simonton, D. (1986). Presidential personality: Biographical use of the Gough Adjective Check List. *Journal of Personality and Social Psychology, 51*, 149–160.

Simonton, D. (1988). Presidential style: Personality, biography, and performance. *Journal of Personality and Social Psychology, 55*, 928–936.

Singer, M. (1961). A survey of culture and personality theory and research. In B. Kaplan (Ed.), *Studying personality cross-culturally* (pp. 9–92). New York: Harper and Row.

Skinner, B. F. (1974). *About behaviorism.* New York: Knopf.

Smith, C. P. (Ed.). (1992). *Motivation and personality: Handbook of thematic content analysis.* New York: Cambridge University Press.

Stewart, A. J., & Healy, J. M., Jr. (1989). Linking individual development and social change. *American Psychologist, 44*, 30–42.

Stille, A. (2001, January 13). An old key to why countries get rich. *New York Times*, p. B11.

Strauss, W., & Howe, N. (1991). *Generations: The history of America's future 1584 to 2069*. New York: Morrow.

Suedfeld, P. (1994). President Clinton's policy dilemmas: A cognitive analysis. *Political Psychology, 15*, 337–349.

Suedfeld, P., Bluck, S., Loewen, L. J., & Elkins, D. J. (1994). Sociopolitical values and integrative complexity of members of student political groups. *Canadian Journal of Behavioural Science, 26*, 121–141.

Suedfeld, P., Conway, L. G., & Eichhorn, D. (2001). Studying Canadian leaders at a distance. In O. Feldman & L. O. Valenty (Eds.), *Profiling political leaders: Cross-cultural studies of personality and political behavior* (pp. 3–19). Westport, CT: Praeger.

Suedfeld, P., & Rank, A. D. (1976). Revolutionary leaders: Long-term success as a function of changes in conceptual complexity. *Journal of Personality and Social Psychology, 34*, 169–178.

Suedfeld, P., & Tetlock, P. (1977). Integrative complexity of communications in international crises. *Journal of Conflict Resolution, 21*, 169–184.

Suedfeld, P., Tetlock, P., & Ramirez, C. (1977). War, peace, and integrative complexity. *Journal of Conflict Resolution, 21*, 427–442.

Suedfeld, P., Tetlock, P. E., & Streufert, S. (1992). Conceptual/integrative complexity. In C. P. Smith (Ed.), *Motivation and personality: Handbook of thematic content analysis* (pp. 393–400). New York: Cambridge University Press.

Suedfeld, P., Wallace, M. D., & Thachuk, K. L. (1993). Changes in integrative complexity among Middle East leaders during the Persian Gulf crisis. *Journal of Social Issues, 49*(4),183–199.

Swede, S. W., & Tetlock, P. E. (1986). Henry Kissinger's implicit theory of personality: A quantitative case study. *Journal of Personality, 54*, 617–746.

Tajfel, H. (1981). *Human groups and social categories: Studies in social psychology*. New York: Cambridge University Press.

Taylor, A. J. P. (1961). *The origins of the second world war*. London: Hamish Hamilton.

Taysi, T., & Preston, T. (2001). The personality and leadership style of President Khatami: Implications for the future of Iranian political reform. In O. Feldman & L. O. Valenty (Eds.), *Profiling political leaders: Cross-cultural studies of personality and political behavior* (pp. 57–77). Westport, CT: Praeger.

Tetlock, P. E. (1981a). Personality and isolationism: Content analysis of senatorial speeches. *Journal of Personality and Social Psychology, 41*, 737–743.

Tetlock, P. E. (1981b). Pre- to post-election shifts in presidential rhetoric: Impression management or cognitive adjustment. *Journal of Personality and Social Psychology, 41*, 207–212.

Tetlock, P. E. (1983). Cognitive style and political ideology. *Journal of Personality and Social Psychology, 45*, 118–126.

Tetlock, P. E. (1984). Cognitive style and political belief systems in the British House of Commons. *Journal of Personality and Social Psychology, 46*, 365–375.

Tetlock, P. E. (1985). Integrative complexity of American and Soviet foreign policy rhetoric: A time-series analysis. *Journal of Personality and Social Psychology, 49*, 1565–1585.

Tetlock, P. E. (1993). Cognitive structural analysis of political rhetoric: Methodological and theoretical issues. In S. Iyengar and W. J. McGuire (Eds.), *Explorations in political psychology* (pp. 380–405). Durham, NC: Duke University Press.

Tetlock, P. E., Armor, D., & Peterson, R. S. (1994). The slavery debate in antebellum America: Cognitive style, value conflict, and the limits of compromise. *Journal of Personality and Social Psychology, 66,* 115–126.

Tetlock, P. E., Bernzweig, J., & Gallant, J. L. (1985). Supreme Court decision making: Cognitive style as a predictor of ideological consistency of voting. *Journal of Personality and Social Psychology, 48,* 1227–1239.

Tetlock, P. E., & Boettger, R. (1989). Cognitive and rhetorical styles of traditionalist and reformist Soviet politicians: A content analysis study. *Political Psychology, 10,* 209–232.

Tetlock, P. E., & Tyler, A. (1996). Churchill's cognitive and rhetorical style: The debates over Nazi intentions and self-government for India. *Political Psychology, 17,* 149–170.

Triandis, H. C. (1995). *Individualism and collectivism.* Boulder, CO: Westview Press.

Valenty, L. O., & Feldman, O. (Eds.). (2002). *Political leadership for the new century: Personality and behavior among American leaders.* Westport, CT: Praeger.

Valenty, L. O., & Shiraev, E. (2001). The 1996 Russian presidential candidates: A content analysis of motivational configuration and conceptual/integrative complexity. In O. Feldman & L. O. Valenty (Eds.), *Profiling political leaders: Cross-cultural studies of personality and political behavior* (pp. 37–56). Westport, CT: Praeger.

Veroff, J., Depner, C., Kulka, R., & Douvan, E. (1980). Comparison of American motives: 1957 versus 1976. *Journal of Personality and Social Psychology, 39,* 1249–1262.

Veroff, J., Feld, S., & Gurin, G. (1962). Achievement motivation and religious background. *American Sociological Review, 27,* 205–217.

Vianello, M., & Moore, G. (Eds.). (2000). *Gendering elites: Economic and political leadership in 27 industrialised societies.* New York: St. Martin's Press, 2000.

Walker, S. G. (1977). The interface between beliefs and behavior: Henry Kissinger's operational code and the Vietnam War. *Journal of Conflict Resolution, 21,* 129–168.

Walker, S. G. (1983). The motivational foundations of political belief systems: A reanalysis of the operational code construct. *International Studies Quarterly, 27,* 179–201.

Walker, S. G. (1990). The evolution of operational code analysis. *Political Psychology, 11,* 403–418.

Walker, S. G. (1995). Psychodynamic processes and framing effects in foreign policy decision-making: Woodrow Wilson's operational code. *Political Psychology, 16,* 697–717.

Walker, S. G. (2000). Assessing psychological characteristics at a distance: Symposium lessons and future research directions. *Political Psychology, 21,* 597–602.

Walker, S. G., & Schafer, M. (2000). The political universe of Lyndon Johnson and his advisors: Diagnostic and strategic propensities in their operational codes. *Political Psychology, 21,* 529–543.

Walker, S. G., Schafer, M., & Young, M. D. (1998). Systematic procedures for operational code analysis: Measuring and modeling Jimmy Carter's operational code. *International Studies Quarterly, 42,* 175–190.

Walker, S. G., Schafer, M., & Young, M. D. (1999). Presidential operational codes and the management of foreign policy conflicts in the post–Cold War world. *Journal of Conflict Resolution, 43,* 610–625.

Wallace, M. D., Suedfeld, P., & Thachuk, K. (1993). Political rhetoric of leaders under stress in the Gulf crisis. *Journal of Conflict Resolution, 37,* 94–107.

Wallace, M. D., Suedfeld, P., & Thachuk, K. A. (1996). Failed leader or successful peacemaker? Crisis, behavior, and the cognitive processes of Mikhail Sergeyevitch Gorbachev. *Political Psychology, 17,* 453–472

Walker, S. G., & Watson, G. L. (1992). The cognitive maps of British leaders, 1938–39: The case of Chamberlain-in-cabinet. In E. Singer & V. Hudson (Eds.), *Political psychology and foreign policy* (pp. 31–58). Boulder, CO: Westview Press.

Walker, S. G., & Watson, G. L. (1994). Integrative complexity and British decisions during the Munich and Poland crises. *Journal of Conflict Resolution, 38,* 3–23.

Winter, D. G. (1976, July). What makes the candidates run. *Psychology Today,* pp. 45–49, 92.

Winter, D. G. (1980). An exploratory study of the motives of southern African political leaders measured at a distance. *Political Psychology, 2*(2), 75–85.

Winter, D. G. (1987). Leader appeal, leader performance, and the motive profiles of leaders and followers: A study of American presidents and elections. *Journal of Personality and Social Psychology, 52,* 196–202.

Winter, D. G. (1988, July). What makes Jesse run? *Psychology Today,* pp. 20ff.

Winter, D. G. (1992a). Content analysis of archival data, personal documents, and everyday verbal productions. In C. P. Smith (Ed.), *Motivation and personality: Handbook of thematic content analysis* (pp. 110–125). New York: Cambridge University Press.

Winter, D. G. (1992b). Personality and foreign policy: Historical overview of research. In E. Singer & V. Harper (Eds.), *Political psychology and foreign policy* (pp. 79–101). Boulder, CO: Westview Press.

Winter, D. G. (1993). Power, affiliation and war: Three tests of a motivational model. *Journal of Personality and Social Psychology, 65,* 532–545.

Winter, D. G. (1994). *Manual for scoring motive imagery in running text* (Version 4.2). Ann Arbor: University of Michigan Department of Psychology.

Winter, D. G. (1995). Presidential psychology and governing styles: A comparative psychological analysis of the 1992 presidential candidates. In S. A. Renshon (Ed.), *The Clinton presidency: Campaigning, governing and the psychology of leadership* (pp. 113–134). Boulder, CO: Westview.

Winter, D. G. (1996). *Personality: Analysis and interpretation of lives.* New York: McGraw-Hill.

Winter, D. G. (1998a). A motivational analysis of the Clinton first term and the 1996 presidential campaign. *Leadership Quarterly, 9,* 253–262.

Winter, D. G. (1998b). "Toward a science of personality psychology": David McClelland's development of empirically derived TAT measures. *History of Psychology, 1,* 130–153.

Winter, D. G. (2002). Motivation and political leadership. In L. O. Valenty & O. Feldman (Eds.), *Political leadership for a new century: Personality and behavior among American leaders* (pp. 27–47). New York: Praeger.

Winter, D. G. (2003). Assessing leaders' personalities: A historical survey of academic research studies. In J. Post (Ed.), *The psychological assessment of political leaders* (pp. 11–38). Ann Arbor: University of Michigan Press.

Winter, D. G., & Barenbaum, N. B. (1999). History of modern personality theory and research. In L. Pervin and O. John (Eds.), *Handbook of personality theory and research* (rev. ed., pp. 3–27). New York: Guilford.

Winter, D. G., & Carlson, L. (1988). Using motive scores in the psychobiographical study of an individual: The case of Richard Nixon. *Journal of Personality, 56,* 75–103.

Winter, D. G., Hermann, M. G., Weintraub, W., & Walker, S. G. (1991a). The personalities of Bush and Gorbachev at a distance: Follow-up on predictions. *Political Psychology, 12,* 457–464.

Winter, D. G., Hermann, M. G., Weintraub, W., & Walker, S. G. (1991b). The personalities of Bush and Gorbachev at a distance: Procedures, portraits, and policy. *Political Psychology, 12,* 215–245.

Winter, D. G., John, O. P., Stewart, A. J., Klohnen, E., & Duncan, L. E. (1998). Traits and motives: Toward an integration of two traditions in personality research. *Psychological Review, 105,* 230–250.

Winter, D. G., & Stewart, A. J. (1977). Content analysis as a technique for assessing political leaders. In M. G. Hermann (Ed.), *A psychological examination of political leaders* (pp. 28–61). New York: Free Press.

Winter, D. G., & Stewart, A. J. (1995). Commentary: Tending the garden of personality. *Journal of Personality, 63,* 711–727.

Wright, J. C., & Mischel, W. (1987). A conditional approach to dispositional constructs: The local predictability of social behavior. *Journal of Personality and Social Psychology, 53,* 1159–1177.

Wright, J. C., & Mischel, W. (1988). Conditional hedges and the intuitive psychology of traits. *Journal of Personality and Social Psychology, 55,* 454–469.

Zullow, H. M. (1991). Pessimistic rumination in popular songs and newsmagazines predict economic recession via decreased consumer optimism and spending. *Journal of Economic Psychology, 12,* 501–526.

Zullow, H. M., Oettingen, G. Peterson, C., & Seligman, Martin E. (1988). Pessimistic explanatory style in the historical record: CAVing LBJ, presidential candidates, and East versus West Berlin. *American Psychologist, 43,* 673–682.

Zullow, Harold M., & Seligman, Martin E. (1990). Pessimistic rumination predicts defeat of presidential candidates, 1900 to 1984. *Psychological Inquiry, 1*(1), 52–61.

5 Jim Sidanius and Robert Kurzban

Evolutionary Approaches to Political Psychology

> *He who would fully treat of man must know at least something of biology, of the science that treats of living, breathing things, and especially of that science of evolution which is inseparably connected with the great name of Darwin.*
>
> —*Theodore Roosevelt (1910)*

Roosevelt's admonition notwithstanding, researchers working in the social sciences have historically kept themselves isolated from biology. This is changing, and biological ideas have been used productively in anthropology (Brown, 1991; Symons, 1979), sociology (Dietz, Burns, & Buttel, 1990), psychology (Buss et al., 1998), and economics (Bowles & Gintis, 1998; Hoffman, McCabe, & Smith, 1998). Here we argue that ideas drawn from evolutionary biology can similarly be used to shed light on issues in political psychology and, indeed, that understanding evolution by natural selection is critical for studying one of evolution's products, human beings.

Our approach is as follows. In the first section, we review the basic principles of evolution by natural selection and discuss how these principles apply to understanding human psychology. In the second section we discuss a small number of applications of evolutionary approaches to important issues in political psychology. In particular, we look at ethnocentrism, sex differences in political behavior, the pervasiveness of intergroup bias and conflict, and why discrimination is often directed more extremely toward males rather than females of subordinate groups. Throughout, it will be our position that theory in the social sciences should be consistent with and informed by what is known in the biological sciences in a way that mirrors the multilevel conceptual integration in the natural sciences (Barkow, Cosmides, & Tooby, 1992).

Biological approaches to understanding human behavior are still looked on with skepticism in many circles. In part, this is because early attempts to integrate biological principles into the social sciences were often flawed (see Kitcher, 1985) and sometimes used as a political tool to justify the unpalatable ideas behind doctrines such as social Darwinism. A second reason for skepticism is that those outside the field hold incorrect beliefs about the assumptions and theoretical commitments that underlie evolutionary psychology (Kurzban & Haselton, in press). Because we cannot change the past to redress the first problem, an additional goal we pursue here is to mitigate the effects of the second. In particular, we will emphasize that, contrary to some peoples' misconceptions, *the evolutionary approach is not an endorsement of the "nature" side of the nature/nurture debate*; rather, it rejects this dichotomy as ill-formed. Evolutionary psychology changes the axis of debate to one in which what is at stake is the nature of the cognitive adaptations that characterize the human mind.

▶ Basic Principles of Evolution by Natural Selection

Understanding the evolutionary psychological approach requires a basic understanding of evolutionary theory and, more specifically, theories of the evolution of cooperation. Because many of these ideas are discussed at length elsewhere (Dawkins, 1976; Dugatkin, 1997; Sober & Wilson, 1998; Williams, 1966), we present only a brief sketch here.

We begin at the beginning. At some point in the distant past, the first replicators emerged: entities that made copies of themselves. Some of these copies were not exact, and those new entities that made copies faster than others became plentiful. Over time, replicators (later, genes) that led to improved reproductive outcomes were retained. With some relatively unimportant exceptions, the genes in organisms today are those that were successfully passed on because they produced design features that led to their own propagation (Darwin, 1859).

Genes influence their rate of replication through their effects on the organism's phenotype, its physical structure and behavior. Changes in genes that increase the rate of their own replication, mediated by the design changes they produce in the organism, spread in a population. For this reason, the eloquent biologist Richard Dawkins (1976) has referred to genes as "selfish": the only thing that genes "care" about, that is, that influences whether or not they will persist, is the rate at which they replicate relative to other genes.

More specifically, genes that cause the phenotype to be altered in such a way that the organism is better able to solve a specific *adaptive problem*, a task that influences its rate of reproduction, such as finding food, attracting mates, and so forth, are subject to selection. In short, *natural selection results in the gradual accumulation of design features that improve the functional fit between an organism and its environment*. Because no force other than natural selection is known by which complex functional organization can emerge from chance processes, any complex functional elements of organisms' phenotypes can be attributed to the process of natural selection (Williams, 1966). These features are called adaptations.

An important debate relevant to issues surrounding humans as political creatures is the level at which selection works. In the first half of the twentieth century, some biologists claimed that evolution could shape organisms in such a way that their features functioned to serve the interests of the local group, species, or even entire ecosystem, rather than the individual or the gene (Emerson, 1960; Wynne-Edwards, 1962). The difficulty with this view is that individuals in a group that carry mutations that cause them to benefit themselves at the expense of the group outreproduce more cooperative group members, leading ultimately to the replacement of cooperative types with selfish types (Williams, 1966). Evolutionary biologists now agree that the effect that genes have on their own replication is the critical determinant of selection.

Sexual Selection and Parental Investment Theory

Darwin (1871) argued that an important factor determining the number of offspring an individual left was its ability to obtain matings. This idea explained why certain traits are unique to one sex: intrasexual competition for mates could drive adaptations in one sex but not the other. Similarly, preferences on the part of one sex for particular traits in the other could select for traits designed for being maximally attractive as a mate. For obvious reasons, Darwin referred to this addition to this process as "sexual selection."

This is a specific case of a more general rule about adaptations in species with two sexes. In many domains, the adaptive problems faced by members of both sexes are identical (e.g., finding food), leading to selection for the same adaptations in both sexes. However, in cases in which adaptive problems differ, selection favors adaptations specific to each sex's adaptive problem. For example, in species in which one sex is differentially responsible for, say, hunting, we might expect that individuals of that sex will be better adapted for this particular task.

An important addition to sexual selection theory was Trivers's (1972) theory of parental investment. Trivers began with the idea that species differ in the extent to which they invest in their offspring, expending resources to nurture them during the course of development. Further, in many species, the costs of nurturing young are not evenly divided between the sexes. In species in which one sex invests in offspring more than the other, the investing sex becomes a valuable resource for the less-investing sex. That is, organism A becomes valuable to organism B insofar as organism A expends time and energy contributing to the success of organism B's offspring. Further, the greater the asymmetry in investment between the sexes, the more intense competition for sexual access to the greater-investing sex is likely to be. Usually, in sexually reproducing species, the male (defined as the sex with the smaller gamete) invests less time and effort than the female, though this is not true for all species.

A consequence of differential parental investment is that the sex that invests less will tend to have greater variance in reproductive success. If one sex invests minimally in offspring, this sex can, if able to obtain a large number of matings, produce a large number of offspring. In contrast, for the greater-investing sex, because resources are always limited, the maximum reproductive output will tend to be constrained not by matings but rather by factors such as resource acquisition. Thus, the lesser-investing sex should be expected to have adaptations designed to obtain many matings, while the greater-investing sex should be expected to have adaptations designed to secure resources.

Sex differences in reproductive strategies have important behavioral consequences for sex differences in humans (Symons, 1979; see hereafter). It is worth noting that unlike the case of gender (see chapter 17), sex, in biology, is a clear-cut, discrete variable. Many species have two morphs, a male and a female, and these morphs are reliably reproduced from generation to generation. Adaptations unique to each morph can evolve because of this consistency.

The Evolution of Altruism and Cooperation

This "selfish" view of the gene does not entail the idea that altruism and cooperation, issues central to many questions in political psychology, will never be observed. There are a number of ways, either by design or by accident, that organisms benefit one another. For example, a buzzard might fly toward a carcass for the straightforward reason that it is looking for a meal. The fact that other scavengers can follow the first one and so similarly feed themselves does not mean that the genes that produce the buzzard's behaviors persisted *because* they helped other organisms—this is merely a byproduct. However, some features of organisms are indeed designed to deliver benefits to others at a cost to themselves (where costs and benefits should always be understood to be denominated in the currency of reproductive fitness). Hamilton's (1964) theory of kin selection, Trivers's (1971) theory of reciprocal altruism, and Sober and Wilson's (1998) theory of multilevel selection are three models that can explain the evolution of altruistic design.

Kin Selection

Hamilton (1964) pointed out that a gene could increase in frequency both by replicating itself and by replicating identical copies of itself. Further, he noted that identical copies of genes were differentially likely to be found in organisms related by descent. Hamilton's ideas suggested calculating a gene's fitness (rather than an individual's) by including relatives' reproduction in addition to the individual's own, and is therefore also known as inclusive fitness theory. The crucial insight of the theory was that selection could favor genes that generated altruistic behavior toward relatives.

There are important restrictions on the operation of this process. The relevant ones are: (1) the probability that an identical copy of the gene in question is found in the recipient of the benefit of altruism, and (2) the magnitude of the costs incurred and the benefits delivered. Consider a gene that coded for the delivery of minuscule benefits to a distantly related other at a large cost to the self. This gene would compare unfavorably to alternative designs that were more discriminating in altruistic practices (i.e., delivered large benefits to more closely related others at small cost to self) and would soon vanish from the gene pool.

More precisely, Hamilton quantified the restrictions on the evolution of kin altruism with his inequality, known as Hamilton's rule:

$$C < rB$$

where C and B are the magnitudes of the costs incurred and benefits delivered and r is the coefficient of relatedness, the probability that an exact copy of the gene is present in the target of altruism by virtue of descent. Thus, as genealogical distance increases, the ratio of the benefit to the cost must correspondingly increase for selection to favor the altruistic gene.

It is important to bear in mind that this analysis only makes sense at the level of the gene. From the standpoint of one gene, it makes no difference which other genes reside in the target organism, or how many genes the target organism shares with the organism in which the altruistic gene is found. "Genetic similarity," therefore, in the sense of proportion of shared genome, is not a useful concept in understanding kin selection (Tooby & Cosmides, 1989).

Reciprocal Altruism

A second theory explaining the evolution of cooperation, reciprocal altruism theory, used the prisoner's dilemma (PD) as a model (Axelrod & Hamilton, 1981). In the PD, two organisms engage in an interaction such that each has two options, a cooperative one (C), and a noncooperative one (D, for "defect). If both cooperate, both are better off than if both defect. However, the payoffs are structured such that regardless of what the other organism does, each organism is itself better off if it defects (see fig. 5.1).

	C	D
C	5, 5	0, 8
D	8, 0	3, 3

Figure 5.1. Payoff structure for the Prisoner's Dilemma. Each player can choose to Cooperate (C) or Defect (D). Payoffs to the players are listed Row, Column.

Trivers (1971) argued that this structure characterized many potential interactions among organisms of the same species, and was a useful model for understanding how cooperation could emerge. In particular, he showed that if organisms interacted repeatedly, cooperative strategies could be selected for if organisms conditioned their moves on their partner's previous moves. Thus, if one organism had a strategy such that it cooperated if and only if its partner cooperated on previous moves, and the benefits to cooperation were sufficiently large, a strategy that conditionally cooperated could do better than one that always defected (see also Axelrod & Hamilton, 1981).

Natural selection, unlike the individual organism, "sees" the results of strategies embodied by different genotypes and "chooses" the one that fares better than the others in terms of replication, or fitness.[1] The evolutionary process is thus rational in the sense that it obeys the game theoretical calculus, with strategies persisting solely on the basis of the number of offspring that they leave. The strategies that are selected, in contrast, will not necessarily appear rational at all (Cosmides & Tooby, 1994a; Kurzban, in press). Strategies, to persist, must simply be the best decision rule available among the existing possibilities. While the process of evolution is algorithmic, the adaptations, the cognitive information-processing circuits that this process builds, are necessarily heuristic, shaped by their performance in the environmental circumstances of the organism (Symons, 1992).

Multilevel Group Selection

Group selection, a model once condemned to theoretical oblivion, has recently been revived and shown to be viable (Hamilton, 1975; Price, 1972; Wilson, 1975; Sober & Wilson, 1998). The argument is as follows. Consider a "group" to be any set of individuals that have a fitness impact on one another. Assume that groups consist of two types of individuals, "altruistic" and "selfish" types. In all groups, altruists are at a disadvantage (being altruistic), and leave fewer descendants than selfish types. However, critically, groups that have more altruistic types leave more descendants, in aggregate, than groups with fewer altruistic types. Now, even though altruists are at a disadvantage within all groups, if the reproductive advantage that accrues to individuals in groups that consist of a larger fraction of altruistic types is sufficiently great, the frequency of altruistic types in the whole population (i.e., across both groups combined) can increase from one generation to the next (see Sober & Wilson, 1998, pp. 23–26, for a clear mathematical demonstration of this counterintuitive result). The extent to which having altruistic types in a group increases reproductive success for members of that particular group compared with the fitness advantage that selfish types have over altruists within individual groups determines whether or not genes for altruistic trait will increase in frequency in the whole population.

This version of group selection, also called multilevel selection, should not be understood as an alternative to the genic view of evolution by natural selection. Rather, these models are simply another way to do the "book-keeping," keeping track of genes' success by looking at their relative replication rates within and between groups (Reeve, 2000). No matter how the score is kept, the critical factor is the proportion of genes of one type relative to genes of the alternative type in the total population in successive generations. The effects that a gene has on its own replication rate determines whether or not it will spread in a population. The multilevel selection model illustrates that considering genes' effects at different levels of analysis can clarify the level at which adaptations evolve.

Evolutionary Psychology

Having outlined the major features of the theory of evolution by natural selection, we now discuss how these general ideas inform our understanding of human psychology. The evolutionary view helps to guide hypotheses about the mind in a number of ways. First, the focus on adaptive problems helps carve nature at its joints—it tells us the kinds of tasks our minds might be designed to perform. Second, it constrains the potential hypothesis space to be explored: the only design features the mind is likely to have are those that would have served functions associated with the lifestyle of our hunter-gatherer ancestors (see hereafter). Similarly, the models of cooperation discussed earlier generate game-theoretical constraints on the nature of cooperative psychology—we should be skeptical of models of psychology that appear to be unevolvable. Finally, the evolutionary view makes clear that organisms are composed of numerous, functionally specialized, integrated components. We should expect the same to be true of the human mind. This insight leads to a core component of the evolutionary approach: domain specificity.

Domain Specificity

Adaptive problems that organisms face, such as finding food, avoiding predation, attracting a mate, and so on depend on their lifestyles. Further, these challenges cannot all be solved with the same structures, or mechanisms. This is why organisms have different parts, each one designed for a particular function. The variety of human organs reflects this principle: lungs are for the exchange of gasses, hearts are for pumping blood, and so forth.

Problems associated with information processing, the function of the brain, are no different. The brain, and the nervous system more generally, is designed to take in information from the world, process it, and generate adaptive behavior. However, because different adaptive problems require different kinds of information-processing systems to solve them, the brain consists of specialized machinery to solve these problems. This is obvious in the context of neural circuits associated with the senses, such as vision and hearing, but should be expected to be true of circuits designed to solve other kinds of problems—recognizing faces, selecting food, finding mates, maintaining friendships, and so forth (Tooby & Cosmides, 1992).

This conclusion represents the single most important conceptual element of the evolutionary psychological approach. The principle of domain specificity suggests that we should expect brains to consist of a large number of functionally specialized circuits designed by natural selection to solve the adaptive problems faced by our ancestors. This contrasts with other views prevalent in the social sciences that construe the brain as a very general learning machine (see Tooby & Cosmides, 1992; Plotkin, 1997 for a discussion).

Learning and Culture

A second critical element of the evolutionary approach is the rejection of the nature/nurture distinction. For any trait of any organism, it must be true that changes to its genes or its developmental environment could alter the trait—the construction of the phenotype is inherently an interaction. So, as Tooby and Cosmides (1992) put it, "*everything,* from the most delicate nuance of Richard Strauss's last performance of Beethoven's Fifth Symphony to the presence of calcium salts in his bones at birth, is totally and to exactly the same extent genetically and environmentally codetermined (pp. 83–84, italics original).

On this view, it is senseless to counter a claim that a given behavior is the product of an interaction between the environment and genes with the claim that the behavior is "cultural" or "learned."[2] Every behavior "is" *both* "cultural" and "biological" in the sense that every behavior has both environmental and genetic causes, labeling behaviors as either carries no meaning. What is at stake is the nature of human developmental programs and the information acquisition mechanisms they build: the cognitive systems that construct knowledge from interaction with the environment. The reproductive outcomes produced by different developmental programs over evolutionary time led to the retention of the programs that regulated development, including learning in its many forms, in adaptive ways (Tooby & Cosmides, 1992).

Different developmental programs respond to different aspects of the environment. For example, the language one learns depends exquisitely on the auditory inputs one receives during childhood. Some developmental programs, however, produce outcomes that are consistent across the multitude of environments that humans normally develop in. These traits have therefore been referred to as "reliably developing" traits (see Cosmides & Tooby, 1994b). Language per se is a reliably developing trait, occurring whenever and wherever a child develops in a normal social world, even though the specific language learned depends on the linguistic environment.

To put it another way, humans' beliefs, traits, behaviors, and artifacts are what Dawkins (1982) would call humans' "extended phenotype," all the things in the world that are produced as a downstream result of human gene–environment interaction. Beaver dams come into being because of the behavior produced from beaver brains, themselves built from an interaction between the environment and beavers' genetic programs. This causal pathway is no different for bones, symphonies, or political institutions.

This is not to say that every trait or behavior is an example of an adaptation. Humans drive cars, do calculus, and write novels, none of which could have been the phenotypic traits that led to selection for the developmental programs that ultimately make these things possible. Byproducts, side effects of adaptations, are plentiful. The argument is not that everything humans do is adaptive, or that every feature of humans is an example of adaptation. The argument is that considering the adaptations humans are likely to possess, the functions of the mechanisms designed by selection over our species' evolutionary history, can guide theory by drawing attention to what features the human evolved psychological architecture is likely to have.

Minds Are Adapted to Ancestral Environments

The specialized neural circuits that humans possess should be expected to be well designed to solve the adaptive problems faced by our hunter-gatherer ancestors (Tooby & Cosmides, 1990b). Natural selection is a gradual process, requiring a large number of generations for the accumulation of complex design. Further, natural selection can only act relative to stable features of organisms' environment. That is, for evolution to result in a trait that guides adaptive behavior in response to particular environmental conditions, these conditions must be present with sufficient frequency over a sufficiently long period for the slow accretion of incrementally more adaptive design modifications.

Because anthropological evidence suggests that our ancestors lived in small hunter-gatherer bands, human cognitive adaptations are likely to be designed to solve adaptive problems associated with this lifestyle. In contrast, because agriculture and high population densities are recent phenomena (evolutionarily speaking), we should not expect human cognitive adaptations to be designed specifically to solve the unique problems associated with these elements of modern life (Tooby & Cosmides, 1990b).

A very brief example will illustrate the general idea. Because food resources were considerably less plentiful over evolutionary time than they are now, natural selection seems to have equipped the human aesthetic system with a taste for animal fat. This probably represented a useful design feature because it motivated the consumption of calorie-rich food items. In the modern world, where animal fat is available in enormous quantities, this appetite leads to unhealthful consequences for many. Thus brains with ancestral appetites can generate disastrous consequences within modern environments.

Universal Psychology, Unique Individuals

Evolutionary psychology is sometimes construed as having difficulty accounting for differences among individuals. This is possibly because biological explanations are often understood to be arguments for genetic determinism (see hereafter). However, the evolutionary view is not deterministic in this sense.

Very generally, differences among individuals come from two sources: genetic differences and environmental differences. The degree to which differences between individuals can be traced to genetic causes is measured by the *heritability* statistic. Heritability refers to the proportion of variation in a trait that is due to genetic differences between individuals. Heritability, as a measure of variance, cannot be applied sensibly to a single individual. As discussed earlier, the traits of any given individual are all the result of complex interactions between that individuals' genes and the environment in which it develops.

Because humans are a sexually reproducing species, two complete, successful sets of genes are broken apart each time a new individual's genetic complement is generated. Genes in these new sets must nonetheless work in concert to create the species-typical elements of the human phenotype. If each set of genes did not code for functionally identical phenotypic elements, then genetic recombination would fail to produce viable new genomes because combining parts of two complex but functionally different machines is unlikely to yield a functional result. This implies that at the level of complex functional phenotypes, such as cognitive mechanisms, individuals must be virtually identical.

Genetic differences between individuals, therefore, are unlikely to code for complex design features but instead tend to be restricted to nonfunctional elements of organismic design (Tooby & Cosmides, 1990a; but see Miller, 2000). Traits such as hair color, eye color, and so forth, can, however, have relatively high heritability—the pressure for homogeneity does not exert a powerful selective force on nonfunctional traits. Note that finding high heritability for a trait in one particular environment does not necessarily indicate how hard it is to change a trait. Visual acuity is highly heritable but can easily be changed because of optical technology. Similarly, heritability depends exquisitely on the environment in which differences are being measured.

There are, of course, nonheritable individual differences. A trivial example is that people living in a more physically dangerous environment are likely to have more cuts, abrasions, and so forth. More interestingly, whereas every child is born with the same mechanism for acquiring language, the specific language the child learns depends on the environment (Chomsky,

1981). Here heritability is (essentially) zero—all differences among individuals are due to environmental differences that "calibrate" open parameters (Pinker, 1994).

More generally, differences among individuals often exist because evolution selects for mechanisms that cause organisms to develop contingently on their environments. A well-designed organism does not behave identically across all situational contexts but rather responds adaptively to environmental circumstances. A well-known physical example is the mechanism that creates calluses. Continual friction against the skin leads to improved protection for those areas.

A similar example in the psychological domain is Gangestad and Buss's (1993) work in cultural differences in mating psychology. Because perceived physical attractiveness is one index of how resistant one is to parasitic infection, Gangestad and Buss reasoned that in regions with relatively large numbers of parasites, it might make adaptive sense to be particularly attuned to physical attractiveness because this would correlate with the presence of genes that are pathogen resistant. They analyzed a large crosscultural data set and found supporting evidence, suggesting that mate choice mechanisms are designed to change as a function of certain environmental parameters.

Individual differences and crosscultural differences are therefore not a particular problem for evolutionary approaches. Very generally, many evolutionary psychologists focus on those differences that have low heritability because they are interested in humans' universal psychological architecture. For these, the key question is the nature of the mechanism that is responding to features of the environment. Some mechanisms, like language acquisition, are responsive to elements of the local human phenotype (e.g., Boyd & Richerson, 1985; Boyer, 1994) while others are responsive to physical environmental factors (Gangestad & Buss, 1993).

Finally, changes over time are similarly not problematic for evolutionary views. Changes in language, ideology, tool design, and so forth occur for a variety of reasons and hinge on the nature of the cognitive mechanisms involved in acquiring and transmitting information in these domains. Random changes in word usage are adopted, new religious ideas are accepted by converts, and inventions that improve functions of artifacts are imitated. Anthropologists continue to make progress understanding the rules that govern the transmission of ideas in various domains (Boyd & Richerson, 1987; Boyer, 1994).

Merits of Adaptationism

Adaptationism, the idea that organisms are designed by natural selection to solve adaptive problems faced during their evolutionary history, has been applied to every species that biologists study. Indeed, most biologists would not consider an analysis of any species possible without reference to evolutionary theory. This is simply because an organism's selective history has shaped and sculpted the species-typical design embodied by the organism.

Humans, as biological entities, are no different. All of their design features, including their cognitive mechanisms of learning, reasoning, emotion, planning, and so on, are products of the process of evolution by natural selection. A great deal is now known about the way the process of natural selection operates and about humans' ancestral past, allowing biologically informed researchers to apply this knowledge to generate new and useful predictions about a multitude of domains of human psychology (see Buss et al., 1998, for a review).

Trying to understand humans and their interactions with other humans without the benefits of adaptationist thinking is an unnecessary handicap. In the natural sciences, research in chemistry is informed by physics, and hypotheses are restricted to ones that are compatible with "lower" or more basic theoretical levels (Barkow, Cosmides, & Tooby, 1992). The social sciences ought to be similarly continuous with what is known about evolutionary biology. In what follows we attempt to show some of the ways the evolutionary view can be profitably exploited in understanding human social life and used to make new and novel predictions that can be subjected to additional testing. It is important to note in this regard that hypotheses about human psychology and behavior derived from an evolutionary viewpoint are no less falsifiable than hypotheses derived from any perspective (see Ketelaar and Ellis, 2000, for a discussion).

A Political Note on Evolutionary Political Psychology

The "naturalistic fallacy" (a term coined by Moore, 1903) is to infer what should be from what is thought to be true. Evolutionary psychologists tend to bend over backward to reject this fallacy and make clear and explicit their view that the normative domain of policy is distinct from the positive domain of scientific inquiry (e.g., Thornhill & Palmer, 2000; see pp. 5–6). Nevertheless, evolutionary claims are often construed politically.

One possible reason for this is that evolutionary approaches are perceived as deterministic and therefore pessimistic about the possibility of change effected through policy. Those who have argued against various kinds of interventions in education or business have sometimes invoked an "evolutionary" justification—if peoples' destinies were written in their genes, it has been argued, then government assistance would be wasted on trying to stop the inexorable force of genetic heritage. As discussed earlier, however, a hallmark of the (modern) evolutionary view is adaptive flexibility, rather than fixity—no aspect of the phenotype is immune from environmental influence.

In short, an evolutionary view neither entails particular views on the desirability of particular policies nor implies that any particular kinds of political changes are impossible. In this regard, evolutionary psychology is no different from other scientific approaches.

The Relevance of Evolutionary Perspectives to Political Psychology

In the remainder of this chapter we will suggest that an evolutionary perspective helps us to understand certain political phenomena with a depth and breath that has not been possible in the past. It is worth beginning with a question that seems so obvious it rarely gets asked. Why do humans have politics at all? This question becomes more compelling when it is pointed out that politics in a recognizable form does not seem to characterize behavior in most other species. Politics, being fundamentally about social relationships, is important in social species. Orangutans, largely solitary creatures, seem to have little political sophistication. Bee social life, on the other hand, is so complex that their behavior evokes political metaphors ("queens" and "citizens"; Dugatkin, 1999).

Adaptations for political cognition are likely to the extent that there are fitness consequences to political maneuvering. More specifically, we would like to suggest that *adaptations for political psychology are driven by the possibility of fitness gains through coordinated, cooperative activity with conspecifics.*

Why Elephant Seals Don't Have Politics

Elephant seals are highly polygynous. Each mating season, one male elephant seal bests its competitors and mates with a harem of scores of females. Imagine a pair of elephant seals that broke the tradition of one-on-one combat and combined forces against competitors. Given that across taxa, coalitions with more members almost always emerge victorious (Harcourt, 1992), it is reasonable to expect that any such pair, even one consisting of relatively smaller seals, would easily outmatch any single challenger. Subsequent to vanquishing their foes, the victorious pair could divide the harem.

This behavior is not, however, observed. Two possible reasons for this are (1) coordinating in combat is a complex computational problem, and these animals do not have the requisite cognitive mechanisms, and (2) once a pair is victorious, the larger seal has no incentive not to turn on its former ally. A mutation that caused a small seal to pair with a larger one, only to subsequently be denied matings, would not spread. Hence the inability to enforce contracts might prevent alliances from forming. These are speculations, and the reason elephant seals don't form coalitions is debatable. Potential for gains from forming alliances does not, in itself, appear to be sufficient to drive adaptations for forming them.

Why Chimpanzees Do Have Politics

Frans de Waal (1982) recounted the political machinations of three male chimpanzees, Yeroen, Nikkie, and Luit, engaged in the kind of coalition formation absent in elephant seals. In the Arnhem zoo in 1976, Luit and Nikkie joined forces to overthrow the previously dominant male, Yeroen, with Luit winding up in the position of dominance. From this position, Luit instituted what de Waal unapologetically labels "policies," including intervening in disputes between members of the troop, enforcing a kind of peace. Subsequently, Luit was the victim of a coalition formed by the other two legs of the triangle, resulting in Nikkie's ascension to power. Chimpanzees, which have been observed to hunt in groups, seem to have the ability to coordinate to cooperate, as well as to sustain, for at least some period of time, an alliance without defection.

Similarly, Packer's (1977) classic work with baboons indicated that animals that paired up for agonistic encounters enjoyed success against single opponents, occasionally separating an estrous female from her consort. Cheating seems to be overcome among these and other nonhuman primates by a system of reciprocal altruism (see earlier). Joining with a partner today seems to elicit help from that partner tomorrow (Bercovitch, 1988; Packer, 1977). Kin selection mechanisms might also be contributing to the problem of cheating in other organisms that cooperate in groups, such as lions (Packer et al., 1991)—cheating becomes less of an obstacle to the extent that genetic interests are aligned.

Why Humans Have Politics

What was it about human evolutionary history that led to features that characterize human political psychology: within- and between-group hierarchy, xenophobia, coalitional psychology, and so on? Harcourt (1992), in his discussion of nonhuman primate coalitions, suggests that there are ecological preconditions for coalitions, namely stability in group membership, variation in members' abilities, and a "rich, divisible resource, compactly distributed" (p. 466). He also suggests there are information-processing requirements—choosing partners and manipulating alliances is a complex endeavor.

In terms of ecological conditions, it is likely that human bands were at least relatively stable over our evolutionary history, and, importantly, hunted large game (Lee & DeVore, 1968). Successful big game hunting hints at the presence of mechanisms that allow complex, interindividual coordination, allowing humans to overcome a hurdle that elephant seals perhaps cannot. It also produces a "rich, divisible" resource that makes gains in trade possible—hunters who are successful on a given day have meat to spare, while those who are not are hungry. If this situation is possibly reversed in the future, there is the potential for consumption smoothing, trading meat for a reciprocal obligation.

Indeed, there is evidence that humans have adaptations designed for social exchange and, more specifically, detecting and punishing violators of social exchanges (Cosmides & Tooby, 1992). These adaptations might not have evolved specifically for the political arena but, once in place, might have been critical to the evolution of adaptations more specific to political domains. In addition, the evolution of punishment psychology, though still poorly understood, has been shown to be potentially important for the generation of group-based cooperation (Boyd & Richerson, 1992).

Taken together, the ability to coordinate and the ability to punish cheaters might have laid the groundwork for adaptations designed to form factions within groups. To the extent that factions could appropriate resources, those best able to form and maintain dominant factions would have been at a profound reproductive advantage. In a species in which multiple factions are forming, it is not hard to imagine increasingly sophisticated mechanisms for detecting alliances (Kurzban, Tooby, & Cosmides, 2001) and manipulating the alignments of those in one's social world (Byrne & Whiten, 1988).

Like elephant seals, humans are known to be polygynous to at least some extent (e.g., Low, 1988). So there might have been large potential fitness gains if males in groups could exploit the reproductive females of other groups. The ability to coordinate activities, coupled with adaptations to punish defectors against the group, could have led to cognitive adaptations designed to exploit other groups' resources, especially reproductive females (Kurzban & Leary, 2001; Tooby & Cosmides, 1988).

Finally, the presence of adaptations designed for within-group power, as well as adaptations designed for between-group conflict and exploitation, sets up an intriguing dynamic. While an individual's interests might lie in exploiting as many other members of one's own group as possible to maximize appropriation of the group's resources, divided and conflict-ridden groups might have been at a severe disadvantage if between-group conflict were relatively common. This creates a tension between within-group and between-group success that mirrors the tension in Sober and Wilson's group selection model described earlier.

This tension might help explain what appears to be "leadership" and "followership" psychology, the desire for power (see hereafter) and peoples' preferences for strong leaders, even if leadership comes at the price of sacrificing rights or freedoms (Boehm, 1999; Fromm, 1941). In a world with between-group conflict, in which victors obtains sizable fitness gains, selection might favor mechanisms designed to support a leader, increasing the chance of victory, even though one's share of the gains might be less than proportionate. If between-group pressures were sufficiently strong, individuals who created within-group tension by contesting power might have been at a selective disadvantage. Once cognitive mechanisms were in place for coalitions to work effectively, selection might have favored mechanisms that motivated the individual to seek subordinate positions in existing coalitions rather than superordinate positions in weaker groups.

Human political psychology, we would argue, is the bundle of adaptations designed for seeking within-group power and influence, combined with the adaptations designed for between-group conflict and exploitation. The complexities of human political relations are an outcome of this dynamic.

Here we look at four domains of political behavior from an evolutionary perspective: ethnocentrism and intergroup conflict, patriarchy and sex differences in political behavior, group-based social hierarchies, and the distinction between patriarchy and racial/ethnic discrimination.

Ethnocentrism and Intergroup Conflict

Ethnocentrism, the belief in the superiority of one's own ethnic group, had been known to be a widespread feature of human sociality even before Sumner coined the term in 1906. Since Sumner's time, continued ethnographic and experimental research has further confirmed the essentially ubiquitous preference for "us" versus "them" (e.g., Eibl-Eibesfeldt, 1979). The well-known "minimal groups experiments" conducted by Tajfel and his colleagues (1978) have demonstrated the ease with which ingroup favoritism is elicited. Not only has the tendency toward ingroup favoritism been found to hold across several different nations and cultures, but there has not been a single culture in which these results have failed to replicate (for a review, see Mullen, Brown, & Smith, 1992). Numerous theorists have spent the last thirty years trying to make sense of these basic findings, the dominant interpretation being that ingroup bias is an effort to enhance one's positive social distinctiveness and/or reduce subjective uncertainty (see Huddy this volume; see also Grieve & Hogg, 1999; Turner, 1999).

However, these proximal explanations seem unlikely from a functional perspective (see Leary & Downs, 1995), and we suggest that a richer understanding of ethnocentrism can be found by considering its ultimate (evolutionary) roots. From the standpoint of evolutionary theory, explaining cooperation in groups is a vexing problem. The difficulty is to explain how a gene that leads to altruism toward multiple other group members can outcompete a gene that is selfish, accepting the benefits of altruism without incurring the costs of generating benefits to others. In dyads, this problem has been solved by reciprocal altruism theory and kin selection theory, discussed earlier. In social insects, the problem is solved because colonies consist of closely related individuals. In human groups, however, in which average degree of relatedness is very small (see hereafter,), group cooperation cannot be explained in this way. Group-level cooperation in humans therefore remains the subject of debate.

Early attempts at developing an evolutionary theory of ethnocentrism used Hamilton's (1964) kin-selection theory of inclusive fitness, generalizing from dyadic interactions to group-level interactions. These models began with the idea that human evolution occurred in the context of small groups of genetically related individuals (e.g., brothers, sisters, nephews, cousins, etc.). In such groups, the average degree of interindividual relatedness within groups was assumed to be higher than the average degree of interindividual relatedness between groups. Thus ethnocentrism was regarded as a form of extended kin selection and nepotism (see Jones, 2000; van den Berghe, 1981).

This model, however, can be criticized on a number of grounds. First, these arguments require very specific population structures in order to work. For example, if within-group mating was low while migration rates between groups were sufficiently large, kin selection forces would be insufficient to select for group-level altruistic behavior (Boyd & Richerson, 1985). Jones (2000) reported average coefficients of relatedness within groups for a number of modern tribal societies in the .05 to .1 range. Jones suggests that for kin selection to operate, this range would require "substantial" benefits to be conferred on fellow group members over time scales of tens of thousands of years.

An additional problem is that these kin selection processes are strongest in the context of one's closest relatives, which necessarily also means the smallest number of other individuals. The problem for getting cooperation to remain stable in larger kin networks, therefore, is that the relatively stronger forces of the smaller component kin groups are very likely to destabilize the larger level of organization (Richerson & Boyd, 1998). A related problem is that because of the nature of inheritance, kin selection forces fall off exponentially with the distance between relations. The coefficient of relatedness for first cousins, for example, is .125, meaning that kin selection will only operate when the benefits conferred are eight times as great as the costs to the altruistic individual (see Hamilton's rule, earlier).

An alternative to kin selection is the possibility that human cooperation in groups can be explained by a process of cultural group selection (Boyd & Richerson, 1985). Assume that different groups have adopted different social norms to govern their behavior, and these norms are followed by everyone in the group. Some groups will, by chance, have norms that are beneficial to the group as a whole, and some will have norms that are, groupwise, detrimental. Over time, the norms of the groups that are groupwise beneficial will tend to spread because of the greater relative success enjoyed by groups with cooperative norms. This structure can be understood as a cultural selection process that favored groups that were cooperative in their interactions within groups and competitive in between-group interactions.

This argument turns critically on groups consisting of individuals who share the same values and norms. As with the genetic version, cultural group selection models require that cooperative individuals be grouped differentially with other cooperative individuals. To the extent that migration (of norms rather than genes) between groups or other processes mix selfish and cooperative individuals together, the group selection process is inhibited. Conversely, to the extent that groups are homogenous with respect to these norms, the cultural group selection process is facilitated.

Boyd and Richerson (1985) argued that a distinctive feature of humans is that they tend to adopt the ideas and practices that are common within their group. This conformist tendency, they believe, is an adaptation designed to acquire ideas or information that others in the population have found to be good ones. Gil-White (2001) has recently extended this idea, arguing that the conformist tendency in the context of interpersonal interactions was driven by the fact that coordinating one's actions to achieve mutually beneficial outcomes is easier when individuals share the same norms. In the modern cultural environment, for example, each individual is best off stopping on red and going on green. Deviating from local customs can have seriously detrimental effects. The process of conformism facilitates cultural group selection by homogenizing groups with respect to norms, avoiding the barrier to group selection posed by migration.

The advantages of sharing norms and acquiring the cultural practices of those around you might also explain why it is that people everywhere use markers of group identity, cultural "badges" such as social customs, traditions, scarification, styles of dress, haircuts, language, and dialect (see Alexander, 1979; Dawkins, 1976; Eibl-Eibesfeldt, 1998; Reynolds, Falger, & Vine, 1987; Symons, 1979; van den Berghe, 1978; 1981). Boyd and Richerson (1987), for example, have suggested that ethnic markings might have emerged to allow individuals to identify precisely which other people individuals ought to be imitating.

Whatever the reason for the practice, cultural marking might provide another explanation for human large-scale cooperation. Some have argued that adaptations originally designed to confer benefits on genetic kin were co-opted to include individuals who share these cultural badges. Altruism, nepotism, and cooperation, originally bestowed on close relatives, were extended to members of "fictive kinship" groups. Wiessner (1998) suggested that the evolution of socially defined kinship was "a critical adaptation of *Homo sapiens.* It permitted the construction of broad social security networks for risk reduction by granting access to human and natural resources lying outside the group. Losses due to fluctuations in natural resources, inability to find mates, conflict, and so on, could then be absorbed by a broader population" (p. 134). Thus, because of the human ability for symbol construction and abstraction, what began as a form of ingroup cooperation and ethnocentrism based on the degree of genetic relatedness (kin selection) was transformed into the potential for ingroup cooperation and ethnocentrism on a much broader scale and encompassing an almost infinitely large number of socially defined "kin."

The strength of the relationship between ethnocentrism and socially constructed kinship is illustrated by the fact that political appeals to ethnocentric, patriotic, and xenophobic identity are very often framed by the use of familial and kinship terms (e.g., motherland, fatherland, "brothers in arms") and by the invocation of "myths of blood" and common descent (e.g., "the founding fathers"; see, e.g., Johnson, 1986; Johnson, Ratwik, &

Sawyer, 1987; Patterson, 1983). However, it is not yet clear exactly how such a system can be resistant to a mutant that declined to deliver benefits to fictive kin; such a mutation would appear to be at a selective advantage relative to genes that caused the delivery of costly benefits to nonkin.

Although the definitional characteristics and boundaries of ingroups and outgroups show remarkable plasticity over different social and political contexts, certain types of ingroup/outgroup boundaries seem to recur. Recent work in developmental psychology and cognitive anthropology suggests that humans possess specialized mechanisms designed to parse the social world into particular kinds of human groups (Gil-White, 2001). These systems seem to be sensitive to visual cues (Hirschfeld, 1996), and track those cues that correlate with coalitional alliance structures. The sensitivity to visual information might explain in part why "race" is one persistent group boundary. However, racial cues appear to be no different from other kinds of visual markings. Consistent with an earlier conception of "race" as an "arbitrary-set" (i.e., Pratto, 1999; Sidanius, 1993), Kurzban, Tooby, and Cosmides (2001) have recently provided evidence supporting the view that, rather than racial categorization being an automatic process, "racial" classification might be an eradicable construct that persists only so long as it is actively maintained through being linked to parallel systems of social alliance.

In sum, while an evolutionary perspective might lead us to expect ethnocentrism to be the default condition among human populations, it is also clear that the precise form, intensity, and breadth of this ethnocentric response depends on a host of situational and contextual factors. Thus, everything else being equal, ethnocentrism might be related to factors such as economic uncertainty and scarcity, population density, idiosyncratic aggressive psychological proclivities of particular political elites, and the nature of political ideologies.

There are two primary lessons to be taken from the evolutionary approach to ethnocentrism. The first is that any discussion of cooperation in groups must begin with biologically sound assumptions about what could, in principle, evolve. Models of the evolution of cooperation must always show what prevents less cooperative strategies from invading populations of cooperative individuals. Second, the evolutionary view binds the issues of cooperation and competition. Models of the evolution of cooperation at the group level are always implicitly and often explicitly also models of intergroup competition. Evolutionarily speaking, the world of genetic fitness is zero sum. There are no genetic winners without genetic losers.

Patriarchy and Sex Differences in Political Behavior

We argue that the differential reproductive constraints and opportunities faced by males and females have led to the evolution of subtle differences in cognitive adaptations that that have profound implications for political behavior and social structure. The reasoning behind these expectations is generated by the implications of Darwin's sexual selection theory and Trivers's (1972) parental investment theory, discussed earlier. Trivers argued that in sexually reproducing organisms, reproductive effort will be some combination of two basic activities: (1) mating effort—the time and effort devoted to finding and attracting mates, and (2) parental effort—the time and effort devoted to the care of offspring. Any sex difference in the potential variance in the rate of reproduction can create a sex difference in the relative effort devoted to one reproductive strategy versus the other. Because there is no monotonic relationship between the number of mates human females have sexual access to and their reproductive success, they will maximize fitness by devoting relatively more effort into parental than mating activities. In contrast, because human males are potentially able to produce a large number of offspring, their fitness will be maximized by devoting relatively more effort into mating than parenting activities (see Clutton-Brock, 1991). Thus, over evolutionary time, for males there will be a strong positive relationship between the number of mates they have sexual access to and their reproductive success.

These differential reproductive constraints confronting the two sexes have additional important consequences. Females, for example, should be expected to be substantially choosier in their selection of mates. Among social primates (e.g., baboons, chimpanzees, and humans) as well as several other species, females are attracted to males with demonstrably good health and vigor, high social status, control over valued economic resources, and an apparent willingness to deploy these resources to her and her offspring (Buss, 1989; Pratto, 1996). In general, males will be substantially less choosy in their mate choice, exploiting whatever mating opportunities present themselves because additional copulations with low-quality mates can be a benefit for males, while constituting a cost for females.

Because of their substantially higher levels of investment in offspring, human females are a limited reproductive resource for males, leading to higher levels of intrasexual competition. This expresses itself not only in direct competition over sexual access to females but also in male-male competition for social status, power, and economic resources (see hereafter). For males, resources often led to high levels of reproductive success, typically because successful males have had sexual access to multiple and more fertile mates. For example, powerful male rulers of the world's first major empires (e.g., the Aztec, Inca, and Chinese empires) had exclusive access to harems including as many as ten thousand wives (see e.g., Betzig, 1993). In contrast, while females also need resources in order to raise healthy children, and will engage in competition to get these resources, it will not benefit them to accumulate *very* large resources because they will generally be unable to convert these resources into reproductive success. In fact, not only will the marginal reproductive utility of additional resources generally be lower for females than for males, but intense striving after resources might even lower their reproductive success (see Hawkes, O'Connell, & Rogers, 1997; Packer, Gilbert, Pusey, & O'Brien, 1995).

The different selection pressures acting on males and females over evolutionary time are likely to have produced cognitive mechanisms with different design features. Preferences in mating is one area in which these differences are clear: men and women put different weight on the traits that are most important in their long-term mates (Buss, 1989). The political implications of these male/female differences in mating preferences are then fairly straightforward. If it is true that over evolutionary time the fitness returns of obtaining control over other people and their resources were greater for males than for females, it is reasonable to expect that selection would have led to greater tastes for acquiring and exerting political power and dominance in males than in females.

A good deal of empirical evidence is consistent with these expectations. For example, patriarchy, or the disproportionate exercise of political and military power by males, appears to be a human universal (e.g., Goldberg, 1994; Harris, 1993; Rosaldo, 1974; Sanday, 1974). Approximately 70 percent of human societies have only male political leaders, while in the remaining societies, the more powerful the political position is, the more likely it is to be occupied by a male (Whyte, 1978, 1979). Although there are a number of *matrilineal* societies (i.e., societies in which ancestral descent is traced through the female line) and societies in which individual rulers have been women (e.g., Queen Elizabeth of England), there have been no recorded societies in human history in which women have held a disproportionate amount of elite political power.[3] While it is clear that the *degree* of patriarchy shows meaningful variation across cultures, social contexts and time periods, patriarchy itself appears to be a constant. Furthermore, patriarchy is not only characteristic of human societies but, with a few exceptions, is also characteristic of most other species of social mammals.[4]

There are also consistent male/female differences in power-relevant sociopolitical attitudes. While men and women do share overlapping distributions in sociopolitical attitudes (as in just about all other characteristics, such as psychical size and strength), mean differences between the sexes show males consistently to be more militaristic, ethnocentric, xenophobic, antiegalitarian, punitive, and positively disposed to the predatory exploitation of outgroups than women (e.g., Ekehammar, 1985; Ekehammar & Sidanius, 1982; Furnham, 1985; Marjoribanks, 1981; Sapiro & Mahajan, 1986; Sidanius and Ekehammar, 1980, 1983; Smith, 1984; see also Everitt, 1998; Montoya, 1996).

Given the precise nature of the politically relevant attitudinal differences between men and women, some theorists have described the sociopolitical attitudes of men as being more "hierarchy-enhancing" and those of women as being more "hierarchy-attenuating" (see Pratto, 1999; Sidanius & Pratto, 1999; see also Eisler & Loye, 1983).[5] While there is good reason to expect fairly stable male/female differences with respect to this continuum, these differences do not *necessarily* have to express themselves as differences in partisanship or political party preference. Rather, male/female differences in basic sociopolitical orientation should only be expected to manifest themselves as differences in partisanship to the extent that political parties take differing, visible, and stable positions along this "hierarchy-enhancing versus hierarchy-attenuating" continuum.

Therefore, given our evolutionary assumptions discussed earlier, there is reason to believe that, everything else being equal, males should have a greater generalized predisposition to compete against, extract resources from, and subordinate the generalized "other" than females. The desire to establish and maintain systems of socioeconomic exploitation of and dominance over other groups has recently been captured by the construct of *social dominance orientation* (SDO; Pratto, Sidanius, Stallworth, & Malle, 1994; Sidanius & Pratto, 1999; see also Altemeyer, 1998; Jackson & Esses, 2000; Whitley, 1999); SDO is conceptually and empirically distinct from more familiar constructs such as individual dominance, racism, authoritarianism, and political conservatism yet shows strong and consistent relationships with a number of politically relevant attitudes and behaviors such as generalized ethnic prejudice, sexism, militarism, patriotism, nationalism, political conservatism, ideologies of political legitimacy (e.g., just-world beliefs), racial and social welfare policy attitudes, criminal justice and immigration attitudes, and partisanship and voting behavior.[6]

Thus evolutionary theory would lead us to expect men to have significantly higher average levels of social dominance orientation than women. That this is, in fact, the case is one of the most well-documented findings within the social dominance literature and has been documented across a broad range of cultures and social situations (see especially Sidanius & Pratto, 1999; see also Heaven & Bucci, 2001; Pratto, Stallworth, & Sidanius, 1997; Sidanius, Cling, & Pratto, 1991; Sidanius, Levin, Liu, & Pratto, 2000; Sidanius, Pratto, & Bobo, 1994; Sidanius, Pratto, & Brief, 1995).

This gender difference in SDO implies that one of the fundamental reasons for the broadly observed "gender gap" in sociopolitical attitudes[7] has to do with male/female differences in the willingness to exercise dominance over others. To test this idea, Sidanius and Pratto (1999) examined the relationships between sex and a wide range of political attitudes (e.g., racism) and political policy preferences (e.g., aid to the poor) using several independent samples and across three nations (Israel, Sweden, and the United States). Consistent with expectations, social dominance orientation was found to mediate the relationship between gender and these attitudes in 98 percent of the cases and account for more than 50 percent of the covariation between sex, on the one hand, and political attitudes and policy preferences on the other.

The Emergence of Group-Based Social Hierarchy

Recall that males can improve reproductive success by acquiring additional mates, whereas females generally cannot. One of the primary means by which males can acquire reproductively desirable females is by the accumulation of power, status, and dominance—goals leading to relatively intense intrasexual competition. As part of this enterprise, human males form *expropriative coalitions* (e.g., gangs, raiding parties, armies), engaging in intergroup warfare and extracting social, economic, and sexual resources from other groups of males (Tooby & Cosmides, 1988). Consistent with the observation of greater levels of attitudinal militarism among males, discussed earlier, Tooby and Cosmides (1988) argue that the differential reproductive benefits to males and females of coordinated conflict has led to a domain-specific cognitive adaptation in human males for "coalitional psychology" (see also Kurzban & Leary, 2001), designed in part to motivate intergroup competitive behavior.

This reasoning is consistent with the observation that warfare has been and remains essentially an all-male activity. For example, in Murdock and White's (1969) ethnographic study of 224 known human societies around the world, the waging of war was found to be an *exclusively* male activity. While women have certainly participated in warfare and have been known to defend themselves, their homes, and their children, there is not a single recorded event in human history of women organizing and constituting armies for the purposes of conquest or intergroup predation (e.g., Keegan, 1993; Rodseth, Wrangham, Harrigen, & Smuts, 1991). Consistent with our evolutionary perspective, the forming of expropriative and predatory male coalitions are not just restricted to humans but also tend to be the case among other social mammals such as baboons, chimpanzees, and dolphins (see Low, 2000).

Because males have a greater tendency to strive toward political power, status, the accumulation of social resources, and the formation of predatory coalitions against other groups, not only should we expect to observe patriarchy and male-driven intergroup conflict, but also within complex and large human social systems we should observe hierarchically structured sets of relations between "groups" or coalitions of males. Male coalitions with more efficient and powerful political, organizational, and/or military capabilities are able to extract economic and social resources from less powerful male coalitions. Because of the great human flexibility in constructing and defining these ingroup/outgroup or coalitional boundaries, these hierarchically structured social groups manifest themselves in any number of different ways, including conceptualization in terms of castes, estates, clans, lineages, nationalities, tribes, ethnic groups, "races," regions, or social classes. Because of this definitional plasticity, social dominance theorists refer to such groups as *arbitrary sets* and the hierarchical arrangement of these groups within a given social system as an *arbitrary-set hierarchy* (Sidanius & Pratto,

1999). Thus, as both Chagnon (1979) and Betzig (1993) suggest, the net result of this more expropriative and power-oriented male reproductive strategy is not only the patriarchic control of women but also the development and maintenance of systematic economic inequality among arbitrary sets in general.

The Distinction between Patriarchy and Arbitrary-Set Hierarchy

A number of feminist thinkers and many social scientists have tended to assume that patriarchy/sexism and racism are almost functionally and psychologically equivalent (e.g., Fernandez, Castro, & Torrejon, 2001; Marti, Bobier,& Baron, 2000). They are both regarded as forms of prejudice against stigmatized outgroups and thus both assumed to be subject to the same psychological principles and constraints[8]. In contrast, Sidanius and Pratto (1999) have argued that while both patriarchy and arbitrary-set hierarchy share some of the same causative roots (i.e., the relative male predisposition toward social power) and the two forms of social hierarchy tend to be correlated across societies, these two systems of social organization are qualitatively different. Of the several distinctions that can be drawn between patriarchic and arbitrary-set forms of social organization (see Sidanius & Veniegas, 2000), three are critically important here.

First, unlike different "races," members of the two sexes are objects of the other sex's desire. Each sex has a stake in the continued existence of the other. This is not true of groups such as black Americans and white Americans. In broad strokes, members of each sexual category have an evolved psychology designed to be attracted to members of the other for various types of social interactions. The same cannot be said of "racial," ethnic, or religious categories. While violence against women by men is of course not unknown, sexual genocide would represent the destruction of a scarce resource desired by men.

Second, there has been a tendency to regard sexism and patriarchy as essentially misogynist projects driven by male hatred of and contempt for women (e.g., Dworkin, 1974; Mies, Bennholdt-Thomsen, & von Werlhof, 1988).[9] In contrast, the evolutionary perspective suggests that patriarchy should be primarily seen as a project of *control* rather than a project of *aggression* (i.e., aggression defined as a desire to harm). Because males were critically dependent on females for reproductive success, they should be inclined toward the restriction and control of female sexuality and of the resources on which females depend. Among other things, this implies that patriarchy is substantially more *paternalistic* than *misogynist* in nature.[10] Thus, rather than being a group against whom males must compete for precious reproductive resources, females have historically been the precious reproductive resource over which males competed with each other. While it is certainly true that females compete against one another for desired mates, they will generally not compete against one another for simultaneous sexual access to multiple mates, nor does this competition reach the ferocity of organized violence and warfare.

Third, by definition, while patriarchy is an intersexual phenomenon and subject to all of the constraints just described, because most arbitrary-sets are patriarchically structured groups (e.g., tribes, nations, races), arbitrary-set confrontations are also essentially male-on-male phenomena. Not only are arbitrary sets most often patriarchically structured but they are also often psychologically conceived of in male-gendered terms. For example, Eagly and Kite (1987) found that stereotypes of national groups were more strongly correlated with peoples' stereotypes of men than with their stereotypes of women. Similarly, Zarate & Smith (1990) found that men are more readily perceived in terms of their race than are women.

The Subordinate Male Target Hypothesis

These distinctions between patriarchy and arbitrary-set hierarchy lead us to counterintuitive expectations regarding intergroup discrimination. Because patriarchy is a project of intersexual social control, while arbitrary-set confrontation is essentially a project of intrasexual competition, the primary targets of arbitrary-set aggressive discrimination are therefore more likely to be outgroup males rather than outgroup females. So, while females (regardless of arbitrary-set group membership) will be the targets of patriarchic control, one should expect that males will be the primary targets of aggressive arbitrary-set discrimination. Furthermore, the primary agents of this active discrimination against arbitrary-set outgroup males should be ingroup males rather than ingroup females. Social dominance theorists have referred to this as the *subordinate male target hypothesis* and have recently amassed a good deal of empirical evidence across a wide range of domains consistent with these expectations (see Sidanius & Pratto, 1999; Sidanius & Veniegas, 2000; see also Davis, Cheng, & Strube, 1996). Not only is there experimental evidence showing that outgroup males are more likely to be the targets of arbitrary-set discrimination than females (e.g., Eckel & Wilson, 2002; Fershtman & Gneezy, 2001; Sidanius & Pratto, 1999) but there is also evidence suggesting that males are the most likely perpetrators of arbitrary-set discrimination (see Fershtman & Gneezy, 2001; Sidanius, 2001).

◣ Conclusions

This chapter has been devoted to discussing how an evolutionary perspective can inform and deepen our understanding of human political behavior. In doing this, we have tried to make three major points. First, we have presented the basic principles of modern evolutionary thinking and tried to correct the ways it has been misinterpreted and misunderstood. Among the most deeply rooted misapprehension is the idea that evolutionary thinking is necessarily an exercise in genetic determinism. While some nineteenth-century evolutionary approaches to human behavior were indeed deeply infected with a simplistic and highly deterministic view of human action (e.g., Galton, 1892; Kidd, 1898; Spencer, 1862), contemporary evolutionary psychology emphasizes the deep and complex interaction between evolved cognitive mechanisms and environmental contexts, rejecting the "nature versus nurture" distinction as ill formed.

Second, we suggested that some of the most straightforward applications of evolutionary theory to an understanding of political behavior can be found in the domains of ethnocentrism and intergroup conflict, the political psychology of sex, and the stubborn resilience of patriarchic and arbitrary-set social hierarchies. Thus for example, while there has been a distinct tendency to regard both sexism and racism as very similar, if not identical, psychosocial phenomena, an evolutionary approach allows us to understand both why and how these two forms of social prejudice should differ one from the other. While the domains of ethnocentrism, group conflict, the political psychology of sex, and social hierarchy are the most obvious areas in which one might fruitfully apply an evolutionary approach to political behavior, these are certainly not the only domains possible. We look forward to additional applications of these ideas in the future.

Third and finally, it bears emphasizing that the evolutionary view does not replace psychological, sociological, or historical approaches, nor does it deny the existence of learning or socialization. Rather, the evolutionary perspective suggests that proposed learning mechanisms ought to be consistent with what is known about natural selection and cognition. Information that is "cultural," in the sense of information that is localized in a spatially and temporally contiguous set of human minds, is nonetheless acquired by evolved learning systems (see e.g., Boyer, 1994; Boyd & Richerson, 1985). In short, rather than regard socialization and evolutionary explanations as mutually hostile and competing cosmologies, we are suggesting the necessity of integrating the two sets of explanations into an internally consistent and congruent paradigm. Thus we could regard socialization processes as the more proximal yet nonetheless evolved sources of human action. We suggest that major and continued progress in our understanding of human political behavior will be greatly facilitated by the achievement of vertical integration across the social sciences, including an appreciation of the evolved character of the human mind. We will not be able to successfully confront the challenges to our continued existence (e.g., war), or the affronts to our democratic values (e.g., racism, sexism) until we achieve a much better understanding of the complex and multileveled manner in which the psychological mechanisms that underlie human political behavior have been shaped by evolutionary processes.

Notes

We thank Shana Levin, Hillary Haley, Francisco Gil-White, and Brian Lowery for their extremely helpful comments on preliminary drafts of this chapter.

1. The intentional language here is of course metaphorical, used only for clarity of exposition. See Dawkins (1976) for a lucid discussion of paying out this kind of language rigorously.

2. "Culture" and "learning" are also not *alternative* explanations for claims that a given behavior, such as voting, is caused by the operation of an evolved psychological mechanism. To object to such a claim requires either (1) an alternative to evolution as an explanation for organized functional complexity (of which none are currently on offer), or (2) dualism (i.e., that mechanisms are not required for generating behavior). Of course, all events are multiply caused. The claim here is a weak one: that evolution must be one of the many causal agents in functionally organized biological systems.

3. Goldberg's (1994, pp. 231–247) careful ethnographic analysis has debunked the alleged exceptions to this rule (e.g., the Iroquois, the Hopi, the Jivaro).

4. For a description of patriarchy among other, nonhuman primate species, see de Waal (1993) and Eibl-Eibesfeldt (1989). Among the few exceptions to patriarchic rule among primates are bonobos, rhesus macaques, and muriqui monkeys (see Castillo, 1997).

5. By the term "hierarchy-enhancing," social dominance theorists mean the generalized desire to established a hierarchical system of power relations between dominant and subordinate groups.

6. See e.g., Altemeyer, 1998; Bates & Heaven, 2001; Danso & Esses, 2001; Heaven, 1999; Heaven & Bucci, 2001; Heaven Greene, Stones, & Caputi, 2000; Jackson & Esses, 2000; Jost & Thompson, 2000; Martinez Paterna, Rosa, & Angosto, 2000; Nelson & Milburn, 1999; Roccato Gattino, & Patris, 2000; Pratto et al., 1994; Schwarzwald & Tur-Kaspa, 1997; Sidanius & Pratto, 1999; Strunk & Chang, 1999; Walter Thorpe, & Kingery, 2001; Whitley, 1999; Whitley & Aesgisdottir, 2000.

7. See, e.g., Norrander, 1997, 1999; Studlar, McAllister, & Hayes, 1998; Trevor, 1999; Wirls, 1986.

8. For a synthetic and individual difference approach to the nature of prejudice, see chapter 16.

9. For a recent exception to this tendency, see Glick and Fiske (2001).

10. See Jackman (1994) for an empirical demonstration of this distinction.

References

Alexander, R. D. (1979). *Darwinism and human affairs.* Seattle: University of Washington Press.

Altemeyer, B. (1998). The "other authoritarian personality." In M. P. Zanna (Ed.), *Advances in experimental social psychology* (Vol. 30, pp. 46–92). San Diego: Academic Press.

Axelrod, R., & Hamilton, W. D. (1981). The evolution of cooperation. *Science, 211,* 1390–1396.

Barkow, J., Cosmides, L. & Tooby, J. (Eds.). (1992). *The adapted mind.* New York: Oxford University Press.

Bates, Cathy, & Heaven, Patrick C. L. (2001). Attitudes to women in society: The role of social dominance orientation and social values. *Journal of Community and Applied Social Psychology, 11,* 43–49.

Bercovitch, F. B. (1988). Coalitions, cooperation and reproductive tactics among adult male baboons. *Animal Behaviour, 36,* 1198–1209.

Betzig, L. (1986). *Despotism and differential reproduction: A Darwinian view of history.* New York: de Gruyter.

Betzig, L. (1993). Sex, succession, and stratification in the first six civilizations: How powerful men reproduced, passed power on to their sons, and used power to defend their wealth, women and children. In L. Ellis (Ed.), *Social stratification and socioeconomic inequality: A comparative biosocial analysis* (pp. 37–74). New York: Praeger.

Boehm, C. (1999). *Hierarchy in the forest: The evolution of egalitarian behavior.* Cambridge, MA: Harvard University Press.

Bowles, S., & Gintis, H. (1998). Is equality passé? Homo reciprocans and the future of egalitarian politics. *Boston Review, 23,* 4–35.

Bowles, S., & Gintis, H. (1998). The moral economy of community: Structured populations and the evolution of prosocial norms. *Evolution and Human Behavior 19,* 3–25.

Boyd, R., & Richerson, P. J. (1985). *Culture and the evolutionary process.* Chicago: University of Chicago Press.

Boyd, R., & Richerson, P. J. (1987). Evolution of ethnic markers. *Cultural Anthropology 2,* 65–79.

Boyd, R., & Richerson, P. J. (1992). Punishment allows the evolution of cooperation (or anything else) in sizable groups. *Ethology and Sociobiology, 13,* 171–195.

Boyer, P. (1994). Cognitive constraints on cultural representations: Natural ontologies and religious ideas. In L. Hirschfeld & S. Gelman (Eds.), *Mapping the mind: Domain specificity in culture and cognition* (pp. 391–411). New York: Cambridge University Press.

Brown, D. E. (1991). Human universals. New York: McGraw-Hill.

Buss, D. M. (1989). Sex differences in human mate preferences: Evolutionary hypotheses tested in thirty-seven cultures. *Behavioral and Brain Sciences, 12,* 1–49.

Buss, D. M, Haselton, M. G., Shackelford, T. K., Bleske, A. L., Wakefield, J. C. (1998). Adaptations, exaptations, and spandrels. *American Psychologist, 53,* pp. 533–548.

Byrne, R. W., & Whiten, A., (Eds). (1988). *Machiavellian intelligence: Social expertise and the evolution of intellect in monkeys, apes, and humans.* Oxford: Clarendon Press.

Castillo, R. (1997). *Culture and mental illness.* New York: Brooks-Cole.

Chagnon, N. A. (1979). Is reproductive success equal in egalitarian societies? In N. Chagnon & W. Irons (Eds.), *Evolutionary biology and human social behavior: An anthropological perspective* (pp. 374–402). North Scituate, MA: Duxbury.

Chomsky, N. (1981). Principles and parameters in syntactic theory. In N. Hornstein & D. Lightfoot (Eds.), *Explanation in linguistics: The logical problem of language acquisition* (pp. 32–75). London: Longman.

Clutton-Brock, T. H. (1991). *The evolution of parental care.* Princeton: Princeton University Press.

Cosmides, L., & Tooby, J. (1992). Cognitive adaptations for social exchange. In J. Barkow, L. Cosmides, & J. Tooby (Eds.), *The adapted mind* (pp. 163–228). New York: Oxford University Press.

Cosmides, L., & Tooby, J. (1994a). Better than rational: Evolutionary psychology and the invisible hand. *American Economic Review, 84,* 327–332.

Cosmides, L., & Tooby, J. (1994b). Origins of domain specificity: The evolution of functional organization. In L. A. Hirschfeld & S. A. Gelman (Eds.), *Mapping the mind: Domain specificity in cognition and culture* (pp. 85–116). New York: Cambridge University Press.

Cosmides, L., Tooby, J., & Barkow, J. H. (1992). Introduction: Evolutionary psychology and conceptual integration. In J. H. Barkow, L. Cosmides, & J. Tooby (Eds.), *The adapted mind* (pp. 3–15). New York: Oxford University Press.

Danso, H. A., & Esses, V. M. (2001). Black experimenters and the intellectual test performance of White participants: The tables are turned. *Journal of Experimental Social Psychology, 37,* 158–165.

Darwin, C. (1859). *On the origin of species by means of natural selection.* London: Murray.

Darwin, C. (1871). *The descent of man and selection in relation to sex.* London: Murray.

Davis, L. E., Cheng, L. C., & Strube, M. J. (1996). Differential effects of racial composition on male and female groups: Implications for group work practice. *Social Work Research, 20,* 157–166.

Dawkins, R. (1976). *The selfish gene.* New York: Oxford University Press.

Dawkins, R. (1982). *The extended phenotype: The long reach of the gene.* New York: Oxford University Press.

de Waal, F. (1988). *Chimpanzee politics: Power and sex among apes.* Baltimore: Johns Hopkins University Press.

de Waal, F. B. M. (1993). Sex differences in chimpanzee (and human) behavior: A matter of social values? In M. Hechter, L. Nadel, & R. E. Michod (Eds.), *The origin of values* (pp. 285–303). New York: de Gruyter.

Dietz, T., Burns, T. T., & Buttel, F. H. (1990). Evolutionary thinking in sociology: An examination of current thinking. *Sociological Forum, 5,* 155–171.

Dugatkin, L. (1997). *Cooperation among animals: An evolutionary perspective.* New York: Oxford University Press.

Dugatkin, L. (1999). *Cheating monkeys and citizen bees: The nature of cooperation in animals and humans.* New York: Free Press.

Dworkin, A. (1974). *Woman hating.* New York: Dutton.

Eagly, A. H., & Kite, M. (1987). Are stereotypes of nationalities applied to both women and men? *Journal of Personality and Social Psychology, 53,* 451–462.

Eckel, C., & Wilson, R. (2002, January). Is Trust a risky decision? Paper presented at the annual meeting of the American Economic Association/Allied Social Science Associations, Atlanta, Georgia.

Eibl-Eibesfeldt, I. (1979). *The biology of war, men, animals and aggression.* London: Thames and Hudson.

Eibl-Eibesfeldt, I. (1989). *Human ethology.* New York: de Gruyter.

Eibl-Eibesfeldt, I. (1998). *Ethnic conflict and indoctrination: Altruism ands identity in evolutionary perspective.* New York: Berghahn Books.

Eisler, R. & Loye, D. (1983). The "failure" of liberalism: A reassessment of ideology from a new feminine-masculine perspective. *Political Psychology, 4,* 469–475.

Ekehammar, B. (1985). Sex differences in socio-political attitudes revisited. *Educational Studies, 11,* 3–9.

Ekehammar, B., & Sidanius, J. (1982). Sex differences in socio-political ideology:

A replication and extension. *British Journal of Social Psychology, 21,* 249–257.

Emerson, A. E. (1960). The evolution of adaptation in population systems. In S.Tax (Ed.), *Evolution after Darwin* (pp. 307–348). Chicago: University of Chicago Press.

Everitt, J. (1998). The gender gap in Canada: Now you see it, now you don't. *Canadian Review of Sociology and Anthropology, 35,* 191–219.

Fernandez, M. L., Castro, Y., & Torrejon, M. J. S. (2001). Sexism and racism in a Spanish sample of secondary school students. *Social Indicators Research, 54,* 309–328.

Fersthtman, C., & Gneezy, U. (2001, February). Discrimination in a segmented society: An experimental approach. *Quarterly Journal of Economics,* 351–372.

Fromm, E. (1941). *Escape from freedom.* New York: Holt.

Furnham, A. (1985). Adolescents' sociopolitical attitudes: A study of sex and national differences. *Political Psychology, 6,* 621–636.

Galton, F. (1892). Hereditary genius: an inquiry into its laws and consequences. 2nd edition. New York: Macmillian.

Gangestad, S. W., & Buss, D. M. (1993). Pathogen prevalence and human mate preferences. *Ethology and Sociobiology, 14,* 89–96

Geary, D. C. (1999). *Male, female: The evolution of human sex differences.* Washington, DC: American Psychological Association.

Gil-White, F. J. (2001). Are ethnic groups biological "species" to the human brain?: Essentialism in our cognition of some social categories. *Current Anthropology 42,* 515–554.

Gil-White, F. J. (in press). Sorting is not categorization: A critique of the claim that Brazilians have fuzzy racial categories. *Cognition and Culture.*

Glick, P., & Fiske, S. T. (2001). Ambivalent sexism. In Zanna, Mark P. (Ed). (2001). Advances in experimental social psychology, Vol. 33 (pp. 115–188). San Diego, CA: Academic Press.

Goldberg, S. (1994). *Why men rule: A theory of male dominance.* Chicago: Open Court.

Grieve, P. G., & Hogg, M. A. (1999). Subjective uncertainty and intergroup discrimination in the minimal group situation. *Personality and Social Psychology, 25,* 926–940.

Hamilton, W. D. (1964). The genetical evolution of social behavior. *Journal of Theoretical Biology, 7,* 1–52.

Hamilton, W. D. (1975). Innate social aptitudes of man: An approach from evolutionary genetics. In R. Fox (Ed.), *Biosocial anthropology* (pp. 133–155). New York: Wiley.

Harcourt, A. H. (1992). Coalitions and alliances: Are primates more complex than non-primates. In A. H. Harcourt & F. B. B. de Waal (Eds)., *Coalitions and alliances in humans and other animals* (pp. 445–471). Oxford: Oxford University Press.

Harris, M. (1993). The evolution of gender hierarchies: A trial formulation. In D. Miller (Ed.), *Sex and gender hierarchies* (pp. 57–79. Cambridge: Cambridge University Press.

Haselton, M. G., & Buss, D. M. (2000). Error management theory: A new perspective on biases in cross-sex mind reading. *Journal of Personality & Social Psychology, 78,* 81–91.

Hawkes, K., O'Connell, J. F., & Rogers, L. (1997). The behavioral ecology of modern hunter-gathers, and human evolution. *Trends in Ecology and Evolution, 12,* 29–31.

Heaven, P. C. L. (1999). Attitudes toward women's rights: Relationships with social dominance orientation and political group identities. *Sex Roles, 41,* 605–614.

Heaven, P. C. L., & Bucci, S. (2001). Right-wing authoritarianism, social dominance orientation and personality: An analysis using the IPIP measure. *European Journal of Personality, 15,* 49–56.

Heaven, P. C. L., Greene, R. L., Stones, C. R., & Caputi, P. (2000). Levels of social dominance orientation in three societies. *Journal of Social Psychology, 140,* 530–532.

Hirschfeld, L. (1996). *Race in the making: Cognition, culture, and the child's construction of human kinds.* Cambridge, MA: MIT Press.

Hoffman, E., McCabe, K., & Smith, V. (1998). Behavioral foundations of reciprocity: Experimental economics and evolutionary psychology. *Economic Inquiry, 36,* 335–352.

Jackman, M. R. (1994). *The velvet glove: Paternalism and conflict in gender, class, and race relations.* Los Angeles: University of California Press.

Jackson, L. M., & Esses, V. M. (2000). Effects of perceived economic competition on people's willingness to help empower immigrants. *Group Processes and Intergroup Relations, 3,* 419–435.

Johnson, G. R. (1986). Kin selection, socialization, and patriotism: An integrating theory. *Politics and Life Sciences, 4,* 127–154.

Johnson, G. R., Ratwik, S. H., & Sawyer, T. J. (1987). The evocative significance of kin terms in patriotic speech. In V., Reynolds, V., Falger, & I. Vine (Eds.), *The sociobiology of ethnocentrism: Evolutionary dimensions of xenophobia, discrimination, racism and nationalism* (pp. 157–174). Beckenham, Kent, England: Croom Helm.

Jones, D. 2000 Group Nepotism and Human Kinship. *Current Anthropology 41:* 779–809.

Jost, J. T., & Thompson, E. P. (2000). Group-based dominance and opposition to equality as independent predictors of self-esteem, ethnocentrism, and social policy attitudes among African Americans and European Americans. *Journal of Experimental Social Psychology, 36,* 209–232.

Keegan, J. (1993). *A history of warfare.* New York: Alfred A. Knopf.

Ketelaar, T., & Ellis, B. J. (2000). Are evolutionary explanations unfalsifiable? Evolutionary psychology and the Lakatosian philosophy of science. *Psychological Inquiry, 11,* 1–21.

Kidd, B. (1898). *The control of the tropics.* New York: Macmillan.

Kitcher, P. (1985). *Vaulting ambition: Sociology and the quest for human nature.* Cambridge, MA: MIT Press.

Kurzban, R. (in press). *Biological foundations of reciprocity.* E. Ostrom & J. Walker (Eds.), *Trust reciprocity, and gains from association: Interdisciplinary lessons from experimental research* (pp. 105–127). New York: Sage.

Kurzban, R., & Haselton, M. G. (in press). Making hay out of straw: Real and imagined controversies in evolutionary psychology. In J. H. Barkow (Ed.), *Missing the revolution: Darwinism for social scientists.* New York: Oxford University Press.

Kurzban, R., & Leary, M. R. (2001). Evolutionary origins of stigmatization: The functions of social exclusion. *Psychological Bulletin, 127,* 187–208.

Kurzban, R., Tooby, J., & Cosmides, L. (2001). Can race be erased? Coalitional computation and social categorization. *Proceedings of the National Academy of Sciences, 98,* 15387–15392.

Leary, M. R., & Downs, D. L. (1995). Interpersonal functions of the self-esteem motive: The self-esteem system as a sociometer. In M. Kernis (Ed.), *Efficacy, agency, and self-esteem* (pp. 123–144). New York: Plenum.

Lee, R., & DeVore, I. (Eds.). (1968). *Man the hunter.* Chicago: Aldine.

Low, B. S. (1988). Pathogen stress and polygyny in humans. In L. Betzig, M. Borgerhoff Mulder, & P. Turke (Eds.), *Human reproductive behavior: A Darwinian perspective* (pp. 115–127). Cambridge: Cambridge University Press.

Low, B. S. (2000). *Why sex matters: A Darwinian look at human behavior.* Princeton: Princeton University Press.

Marjoribanks, K. (1981). Sex-related differences in socio-political attitudes: A replication. *Educational Studies, 7,* 1–6.

Marti, M. W., Bobier, D. M., & Baron, R. S. (2001). Right before our eyes: The failure to recognize non-prototypical forms of prejudice. *Group Processes and Intergroup Relations, 3,* 403–418.

Martinez, C., Paterna, C., Rosa, A. I., & Angosto, J. (2000). The principle of social hierarchy as explanation: From prejudice and rejection to positive action. *Psicologia Politica, 21,* 55–71.

Mies, M., Bennholdt-Thomsen, V. & von Werlhof, C. (1988). *Women: The last colony.* London: Zed Books.

Miller, G. F. (2000). Mental traits as fitness indicators: Expanding evolutionary psychology's adaptationism. In D. LeCroy & P. Moller (Eds.), *Evolutionary perspectives on human reproductive behavior, Annals of the New York Academy of Sciences* (Vol. 907, pp. 62–74). New York: New York Academy of Sciences.

Montoya, L. J. (1996). Latino gender differences in public opinion: Results from the Latino National Political Survey. *Hispanic Journal of Behavioral Sciences, 18,* 255–276

Moore, G. E. (1903). *Principia ethica.* Cambridge: Cambridge University Press.

Mullen, B., Brown, R., & Smith, C. (1992). Ingroup bias as a function of salience, relevance, and status: An integration. *European Journal of Social Psychology, 22,* 103–122.

Murdock, G. P., & White, D. R. (1969). Standard cross-cultural sample. *Ethnology, 8,* 329–369.

Nelson, L., & Milburn, T. W. (1999). Relationships between problem-solving competencies and militaristic attitudes: Implications for peace education. *Peace and Conflict: Journal of Peace Psychology, 5,* 149–168.

Norrander, B. (1997). The independence gap and the gender gap. *Public Opinion Quarterly, 61,* 464–476

Norrander, B. (1999). The evolution of the gender gap. *Public Opinion Quarterly, 63,* 566–576.

Packer, C. (1977). Reciprocal altruism in Papio anubis. *Nature, 265,* 441–443.

Packer, C., Collins, D. A., Sindimwe, A., & Goodall, J. (1995). Reproductive constraints on aggressive competition in female baboons. *Nature, 373,* 60–63.

Packer, C., Gilbert, D. A., Pusey, A. E., & O'Brien, S. J. (1991). A molecular genetic analysis of kinship and cooperation in African lions. *Nature, 351,* 562–565.

Patterson, D. (1983). The nature, causes and implications of ethnic identification. In C. Fired (ed.), *Minorities: Community and identity.* Berlin: Springer.

Pinker, S. 1994. *The language instinct.* New York: Morrow.

Plotkin, H. (1997). *Evolution in mind: An introduction to evolutionary psychology.* Cambridge, MA: Harvard University Press.

Pratto, F. (1996). Sexual politics: The gender gap in the bedroom, the cupboard, and the cabinet. In D. M. Buss & N. M. Malamuth (Eds), *Sex, power, conflict: Evolutionary and feminist perspectives* (pp. 179–230). New York: Oxford University Press.

Pratto, F. (1999). The puzzle of continuing group inequality: Piecing together psychological, social and cultural forces in social dominance theory. In M. P. Zanna (Ed.), *Advances in experimental social psychology,* (Vol. 31, pp. 191–263). New York: Academic Press.

Pratto, F., Sidanius, J., Stallworth, L. M., & Malle, B. F. (1994). Social dominance orientation: A personality variable predicting social and political attitudes. *Journal of Personality and Social Psychology, 67,* 741–763.

Pratto, F., Stallworth, L. M., & Sidanius, J. (1997). The gender gap: Differences in political attitudes and social dominance orientation. *British Journal of Social Psychology, 36,* 49–68.

Price, G. R. (1972). Extension of covariance selection mathematics. *Annals of Human Genetics, 35,* 485–490.

Reeve, H. K. (2000). [Review of the book *Unto Others: The Evolution and Psychology of Unselfish Behavior*]. *Evolution and Human Behavior, 21,* 65–72.

Reynolds, V., Falger, V., & Vine, I. (1987). *The sociobiology of ethnocentrism: Evolutionary dimensions of xenophobia, discrimination, racism and nationalism.* Beckenham, Kent, England: Croom Helm.

Richerson, P. J., & Boyd, R. (1998). The Evolution of human ultra-sociality. In I. Eibl-Eibisfeldt & F. Salter (Eds.), *Ideology, Warfare, and Indoctrinability* (pp. 71–95). Berghan Books.

Roccato, M., Gattino, S., & Patris, E. (2000). Personality, values, and political orientation. *Psicologia Politica, 21,* 73–97.

Rodseth, L., Wrangham, R. W., Harrigen, A. M., & Smuts, B. B. (1991). The human community as a primate society. *Current Anthropology, 32,* 221–254.

Rogers, L. (1997). The behavioral ecology of modern hunter-gathers, and human evolution. *Trends in Ecology and Evolution, 12,* 29–31.

Rosaldo, M. Z. (1974). Woman, culture, and society: A theoretical overview. In M. Z. Rosaldo & L. Lamphere (Eds.), *Women, culture and society* (pp. 17–42). Stanford, CA: Stanford University Press.

Sanday, P. R. (1974). Female status in the public domain. In M. Z. Rosaldo & L. Lamphere (Eds.), *Women, culture and society* (pp. 189–206). Stanford, CA: Stanford University Press.

Sapiro, V., & Mahajan, H. (1986). Gender differences in policy preferences: A summary of trends from the 1960s to the 1980s. *Public Opinion Quarterly, 50,* 42–61.

Schwarzwald, J., & Tur-Kaspa, M. (1997). Perceived threat and social dominance as determinants of prejudice toward Russian and Ethiopian immigrants in Israel. *Megamot, 38,* 504–527.

Sidanius, J. (2001, May). The interactive interface between gender and ethnic discrimination: A social dominance and evolutionary perspective. Invited address to the Western Psychological Association, Maui, Hawaii.

Sidanius, J. (1993). The psychology of group conflict and the dynamics of oppression:

A social dominance perspective (pp. 183–219). In S. Iyengar & W. McGuire (Eds.), *Explorations in political psychology*. Durham, NC: Duke University Press.

Sidanius, J., Cling, B. J., & Pratto, F. (1991). Ranking and linking as a function of sex and gender role attitudes. *Journal of Social Issues, 47,* 131–149.

Sidanius, J., & Ekehammar, B. (1980). Sex-related differences in socio-political ideology. *Scandinavian Journal of Psychology, 21,.* 17–26.

Sidanius, J., & Ekehammar, B. (1983). Sex, political party preference and higher-order dimensions of socio-political ideology. *Journal of Psychology, 115,* 233–239.

Sidanius, J., Levin, S., Liu, J. H., & Pratto, F. (2000). Social dominance orientation and the political psychology of gender: An extension and cross-cultural replication. *European Journal of Social Psychology, 30,* 41–67.

Sidanius, J., & Pratto, F. (1999). *Social dominance: An intergroup theory of social hierarchy and oppression.* New York: Cambridge University Press.

Sidanius, J., Pratto, F., & Bobo, L. (1994). Social dominance orientation and the political psychology of gender: A case of invariance? *Journal of Personality and Social Psychology, 67,* 998–1011.

Sidanius, J., Pratto, F., & Brief, D. (1995). Group dominance and the political psychology of gender: A cross-cultural comparison. *Political Psychology, 16,* 381–396.

Sidanius, J., & Veniegas, R. C. (2000). Gender and Race Discrimination: The Interactive Nature of Disadvantage. In S. Oskamp (Ed.), *Reducing prejudice and discrimination: The Claremont Symposium on Applied Social Psychology* (pp. 47–69). Mahwah, NJ: Erlbaum.

Smith, T. W. (1984). Gender and attitudes toward violence. *Public Opinion Quarterly, 48,* 384–396.

Sober, E., & Wilson, D. S. (1998) *Unto others: The evolution and psychology of unselfish behavior.* Cambridge MA: Harvard University Press.

Spencer, H. (1862). *First principles.* London: Williams and Norgate.

Springer, K., & Keil, F. (1989). On the development of biologically specific beliefs: The case of inheritance. *Child Development, 60,* 637–648.

Studlar, D. T., McAllister, I., & Hayes, B. C. (1998). Explaining the gender gap in voting: A cross-national analysis. *Social Science Quarterly, 79,* 779–798.

Sumner, W. G. (1906). *Folkways: A study of the sociological importance of usages, manners, customs, mores and morals.* Boston: Ginn.

Symons, D. (1979). *The evolution of human sexuality.* New York: Oxford University Press.

Symons, D. (1992). On the use and misuse of Darwinism in the study of human behavior. In J. Barkow, L. Cosmides, & J. Tooby (Eds.), *The adapted mind* (137–159). New York: Oxford University Press.

Tajfel, H. (1978). *Differentiation between social groups* (pp. 61–76). London: Academic Press.

Thornhill, R., & Palmer, C. T. (2000). *A natural history of rape: Biological bases of sexual coercion.* Cambridge, MA: MIT Press.

Tooby, J., & Cosmides, L. (1988). *The evolution of war and its cognitive foundations.* Institute for Evolutionary Studies Technical Report 88–1. Palo Alto, CA.

Tooby, J. & Cosmides, L. (1989). Kin selection, genic selection, and information-dependent strategies. *Behavioral and Brain Sciences, 12,* 542–544.

Tooby, J. & Cosmides, L. (1990a). On the universality of human nature and the uniqueness of the individual: The role of genetics and adaptation. *Journal of Personality, 48,* 17–67.

Tooby, J., & Cosmides, L. (1990b). The past explains the present: Emotional adaptations and the structure of ancestral environments. *Ethology and Sociobiology, 11,* 375–424.

Tooby, J., & Cosmides, L. (1992). The psychological foundations of culture. In J. H. Barkow, L. Cosmides, & J. Tooby (Eds.). *The adapted mind: Evolutionary psychology and the generation of culture* (pp. 19–136). New York: Oxford University Press

Tooby, J., & Cosmides, L. (1996). Friendship and the banker's paradox: Other pathways to the evolution of adaptations for altruism. *Proceedings of the British Academy, 88,* 119–143.

Trevor, M. C. (1999). Political socialization, party identification, and the gender gap. *Public Opinion Quarterly, 63,* 62–89.

Trivers, R. L. (1971). The evolution of reciprocal altruism. *Quarterly Review of Biology, 46,* 35–57.

Trivers, R. L. (1972). Parental investment and sexual selection. In B. Campbell (Ed.), *Sexual selection and the descent of man, 1871–1971.* Chicago: Aldine.

Turner, J. C. (1999). Some current issues in research on social identity and self-categorization theories. In N. Ellemers, R. Spears, & B. Doosje (Eds.), *Social identity* (pp. 6–34). Oxford: Blackwell.

van den Berghe, P. L. (1978). Race and ethnicity: A sociobiological perspective. *Ethnic and Racial Studies, 1,* 401–411.

van den Berghe, P. L. (1981). *The ethnic phenomenon.* New York: Elsevier.

de Waal, F. B. M. (1982). *Chimpanzee politics: Power and sex among apes.* London: Jonathan Cape.

Walter, M. I., Thorpe, G. L., & Kingery, L. R. (2001). The Common Beliefs Survey-III, the Situational Self-Statement, and Affective State Inventory and their relationship to authoritarianism and social dominance orientation. *Journal of Rational-Emotive and Cognitive Behavior Therapy, 19,* 105–118.

Whitley, B. E., Jr. (1999). Right-wing authoritarianism, social dominance orientation, and prejudice. *Journal of Personality and Social Psychology, 77,* 126–134.

Whitley, B. E., Jr., & Aegisdottir, S. (2000). The gender belief system, authoritarianism, social dominance orientation, and heterosexuals' attitudes toward lesbians and gay men. *Sex Roles, 42,* 947–967.

Whyte, M. K. (1978). Cross-cultural codes dealing with the relative status of women. *Ethnology, 17,* 211–237.

Whyte, M. K. (1979). *The status of women in pre-industrial society.* Princeton: Princeton University Press.

Wiessner, P. (1998). Indoctrinability and the evolution of socially defined kinship. In I. Eibl-Eibesfeldt, (Ed.), *Ethnic conflict and indoctrination: Altruism ands identity in evolutionary perspective* (pp. 133–150). New York: Berghahn Books.

Williams, G. C. (1966). *Adaptation and natural selection.* Princeton: Princeton University Press.

Wilson, D. S. (1975). A theory of group selection. *Proceedings of the National Academy of Sciences, 72,* 143–146.

Wilson, D. S., & Sober, E. (1994). Reintroducing group selection to the human behavioral sciences. *Behavioral and Brain Sciences, 17,* 585–654.

Wilson, E. O. (1975). *Sociobiology: The new synthesis*. Cambridge, MA: Belknap.

Wirls, D. (1986). Reinterpreting the gender gap. *Public Opinion Quarterly, 50*, 316–330.

Wynne-Edwards, V. C. (1962). *Animal dispersion in relation to social behavior*. Edinburgh: Oliver and Boyd.

Zarate, M. A., & Smith, E. R. (1990). Person categorization and stereotyping. *Social Cognition, 8*, 161–185.

6 George E. Marcus

The Psychology of Emotion and Politics

Understanding emotion has for a very long time been central to the ongoing attempt to understand human nature. And this understanding has also been central in the debate about the proper political regime that human nature can sustain. Indeed some have argued that it was concern about the noxious impact of emotion that gave rise to philosophy in ancient Greece (Nussbaum, 1994). Most share with many ancient Greek philosophers the presumption that emotions are a problem, indeed *the* problem that hinders our ability to sustain individual and collective just rule. Consider the following quote from John Locke's Second Treatise (1993): "The freedom then of man and liberty of acting according to his own will, is grounded on his having reason, which is able to instruct him in that law he is to govern himself by, and make him to know how far he is left to the freedom of his own will" (p. 45). That view is representative of dominant tradition: rationality is the mental faculty that makes us free and that gives us the capacity to establish political regimes that are democratic and just. With this claim comes the companion view that emotion, a powerful enigmatic force, too often intrudes and undermines our capacity to reason. The tradition has it that if reason cannot be autonomous we must abandon not only this ennobling ideal but also the political programs of democracy and justice that rest on reason's foundation.[1]

But perhaps there are other possibilities; perhaps emotion is not as we have long imagined it, mysterious and detrimental.[2] Perhaps a reexamination of emotion will offer an escape from the following conundrum: if people are emotional creatures, they cannot thereby also be rational creatures—leaving us with little prospect for achieving democratic rule and justice. We have placed collective rule founded on reason's sovereign nobility beyond the reach of humans. Whether emotion is a help, or hindrance, in achieving democratic and just regimes is perhaps the highest-stakes issue current in political psychology.

I have three goals for this chapter. First, I illuminate the normative presumptions that have shaped the study of emotions and politics. Second, I review how the predominant approaches in political psychology attempt to deal with the scientific study of emotions and politics, with special attention to each of their strengths and weaknesses. I argue for neuroscience as the preferred scientific literature to derive insights as to how emotions impact on politics. Finally, further progress requires resolving an ongoing dispute over the structure of emotion. I offer some suggestions as to the research necessary to resolve the dispute. Notably absent in this list is a comprehensive discussion of the research literature. I have recently published such a review (Marcus, 2000). Other recent reviews on emotion in the psychology literature are also readily available (Bradley, 2000; Cacioppo & Gardner, 1999; Zajonc, 1998). Also available is an excellent history of the treatment of emotions in psychology from William James onward (Cornelius, 1996). What is most needed at this juncture is theoretical clarity to direct the future course of research on emotions, thinking, and their various roles in politics.

▶ Foundations for Inquiry

Perhaps the oldest presumption regarding the psychology of emotion is the separation of emotion from the mind. We are familiar with common metaphors to depict this formulation; among the most widely used is that emotion and cognition reside in separate locations; passions arise from the "heart" and reason from the "mind." Emotion is one kind of force, reason another. Moreover, it is perhaps most common to view reason as existing within a container (the "mind") and emotion existing "outside" but forcefully attempting to intrude. Since Epicurus it has often been thought that emotions are "deep" and "hidden."[3] Again, emotion exists outside the mind, the seat of reason, buried deeply "beneath." This familiar conception lives in current psychological conceptions, with "cognition" being a surface phenomenon of the neocortex and "affect" being located deep within in the "older" regions of the brain (MacLean, 1990).[4]

This view is reflected in the presumption that emotions *undermine* the capacity to reason, a view shared with Plato, especially in the simile of the Cave (Plato, 1974) where he places human beings deep within the bowels of the earth, entrapped by their desires, self-indulgently preventing themselves from moving up and out into the light of reason. This view is today well represented in contemporary political psychology by the program of research of David Sears (Sears, 1993, 2000; Sears, Hensler, & Speer, 1979; Sears, Lau, Tyler, & Allen, 1980). As in Plato's cave, emotion in the symbolic politics view ties people to their ancient desires and blinds them so that they do not engage in accurate and rational assessment of their condition. As I will show, this is not the only instance wherein contemporary research programs on emotion are congruent with ancient conceptions.

The qualities assigned to reason and emotion have a long-established genealogy. Before I move to these familiar qualities, I note the equally familiar normative imperatives that loom over the tradition of exploring the emotions. The primary reason we, and the ancients, have given so much attention to the emotions is that it is believed that they have the capacity to undermine the sovereign dignity of reason. Emotion has been and remains largely understood as a force that invades and cripples reason's otherwise autonomous capacity to rule and do so publicly, justly, and wisely. Hence emotion continues to be thought of as a detrimental force that must be controlled, if not extirpated. These conceptions not only were largely at play throughout the classic Greek period (with variations to be discussed later) but remain influential in modern psychology. Thus, as Martha Nussbaum (1994) has argued, the passions were significant because they played such a detrimental role in "undermining" reason.

Emotion has been conceived as separate from reason and forceful not only with respect to the misuse of reason but also because it is able to wrest control of behavior away from reason. Hence the presumptive claim that we can too often act out of "blind" passion. We are thus "blinded" by passion because only reason properly grasps the world as it is and guides our behavior in a rational fashion. Implicit is the presumption that only the conscious mind has provides a veridical portrait of the world given by the senses and displayed solely within conscious awareness. Reason can be autonomous if and only if it is a faculty of the mind that requires nothing other than the mind for its realization. And if this presumption is accurate, then of course it follows that emotion located elsewhere can have at best a neutral and more likely a negative relationship to reason. This pivotal presumption remains potent today in much of the traditional literature on decision-making (Irving L. Janis & Mann, 1977) as well as political philosophy (Steinberger, 1993). This has led, of course, to considerable interest in how emotions intrude and impact decision-making (Abele & Petzold, 1994; Baron, 1994; Bodenhausen, Sheppard, & Kramer, 1994; Forgas, 1994, 1995; Isen, 1993; Johnson & Tversky, 1983; Loewenstein, Weber, Hsee, & Welch, 2001; Mayer, Gaschke, Braverman, & Evans, 1992; Ottati, 1988; Ottati & Isbell, 1996; Ottati & Wyer, 1993; Petty, Gleicher, & Baker, 1991; Schwarz & Bless, 1991; Schwarz & Clore, 1983, 1996). Much of the relevant work holds that people can either rely on heuristics, of which feeling states are held to be an example, or they can engage in explicit deliberation.[5] In the modern era the thinking is much the same as in ancient times: feeling and thought are alternative and often antagonistic foundations for decision-making.

We can organize our understanding of the resulting possibilities by setting them in a simple taxonomy based on these two questions: First, can reason be shielded from the influence of emotion? and second, Should reason rule by itself or only in conjunction with emotion?

The first and most stringent normative perspective is that offered by Plato and developed by the Stoic school of philosophy. Because it was held that passion is so detrimental to rationality and clarity of vision and judgment, it followed that people must learn sole reliance on reason and exclude emotion from any part of their lives. Plato drew the conclusion that the necessary discipline to realize this radical eschewing of passion would be plausible only for the specially trained philosopher-kings; only they would be able to rule wisely and justly.

Epicurus and the Stoic school developed and taught a discipline, for this was a therapeutic application of philosophy, that could be more widely applied. Thus this normative view of emotion is not necessarily aristocratic in its relationship to politics. But the presumption that feeling must be removed from political judgment as a precondition to just political rule is one that continues through Descartes and Kant.[6] And, as noted earlier, studies of decision-making retained this presumption as it was applied to rationality, that is, efficient and prudent linkage of means to ends (Janis, 1982; Janis & Mann, 1977). But problems began to arise. The influential work of Daniel Kahneman, Richard Nisbett, and so many others, which demonstrated how substantially humans depart from the rational decision-making judgments, has serious and far-reaching consequences, inasmuch as it confirmed these ancient presumptions about the limitations of human nature (Kahneman, Slovic, & Tversky, 1982; Nisbett & Ross, 1982). Humans do not normally weigh the evidence fairly and accurately, consider all points of view, or accurately evaluate the outcomes under consideration. This conclusion has troubling implications, as it is widely believed that only reason can validate public judgment in matters political. Hence evidence that people will not, or cannot, reason has had grave consequences for the normative status of popular rule (Kornhauser, 1959; Sartori, 1987).

The second formulation is no less stringent in its normative attitude to emotion. But holding that emotion cannot be extirpated from human psychology means that an accommodation must be established to control and limit the impact of emotion. Perhaps the most widely known and honored of the accounts of how and why this can and should be achieved is that offered in the *Federalist* papers (Madison, Hamilton, & Jay, 1961). While emotion's impact is serious and largely detrimental, a wisely drawn constitution can mitigate the most severe impacts of passion and make positive use of the energizing force of emotion to drive politics through the refining institutions that will yield justice and the public good (Marcus, 2002; Scanlan, 1959; White, 1987). Thus, according to this formulation, emotion need not and cannot be removed, but reason can remain sovereign and in control.

The most influential modern formulation of this view, offered by Freud (1961, 1962), holds that civilization cannot aspire to replace the passions with reason. But in Freud's view, at least for properly socialized individuals, reason can be generally, if not exclusively, in executive control. Thus an accommodation can be found: emotions drive us to action, but reason retains its status as sovereign master. Emotions do not disappear, and not just because that would be impossible, given human nature. A wise regime can make use of emotion in engendering action while at the same time ameliorating emotion's detrimental impacts by shielding passion from civic decisions. Civilization is precisely the achievement that results when humans find the institutional means of removing the passions and their power. This is so even if, as Hobbes so famously proposed, the most potent of emotions, fear of death, is used to achieve that end (Hobbes, 1968). For in Hobbes, fear leads us to seek and accept a sovereign who will ensure public peace and mutual compliance with freely made agreements and their resulting obligations.

The third formulation also accepts the fundamental distinction between reason and emotion but understands their relationship to be harmonious and productive for the most part rather than antagonistic and destructive. Only erroneous beliefs are likely to generate problematic passions. Accurate beliefs and just beliefs can be bolstered by appropriate emotions, yielding a productive alliance between thought and feeling. So care must be given to avoid the destructive consequences of passion: we must undertake a critical consideration of the merit of our beliefs. Furthermore, if we take appropriate care to match valid belief with suitable feeling, both emotion and reason are fortified in the bargain. This perspective is generally associated with Aristotle and has its contemporary expression in political philosophers who, as did Aristotle, see a constructive integrity between emotion as a motivational force and as a cognitively rich tool for evaluation and communication. In this view, emotion offers a unified group of faculties necessary to individual and collective action (Aristotle, 1954; Bickford, 2000; Koziak, 2000; Leighton, 1996; Nussbaum, 1996; Rorty, 1996; Stiker, 1996). The integration of belief, context, and feeling generates a beneficial capacity for appropriate action and response to the fluid experience of civic life (Ben-Ze'ev, 2000; Nussbaum, 2001).

The fourth formulation reaches its fullest expression in the Scotch enlightenment (Hume, 1975, 1984; Smith, 1959, 1986). Unlike the British and French versions of the Enlightenment, the major figures of the Scotch enlightenment saw that reason could not be sundered from its emotional roots. The privileged position of reason as the sovereign judge is turned topsy-turvy. Reason becomes a faculty of the mind that is called into service by emotion, which now holds the commanding role. Rather than accepting the elevation and normative superiority of reason, emotion is now understood to be the foundation of human action, with reason placed in a subordinate role as useful for critical calculation and public deliberation.

This formulation holds that reason is given its force and vitality from its dependence on emotion and has been well supported by recent work in philosophy and neuroscience. The philosopher Bernard Williams (1983) noted that Kant's categorical imperative had no motivational engine to drive people to implement its conclusions, an insight also corroborated by experiments on how people respond when they have no emotional cues (Bechara, Damasio, Tranel, & Damasio, 1997). Reason yields analysis, but absent some motivation, reason cannot itself impel us to act. As we gain greater insight into how the brain is organized, we may well learn more about how humans function as social and reasoning creatures (Damasio, 1994; Goleman, 1995). Even in the task of moral judgment, recent research in neuroscience establishes the central role of emotions in the resolution of moral dilemmas (Greene, Sommerville, Nystrom, Darley, & Cohen, 2001). Taken as a whole, this and other work simplifies the schema of possibilities. We can discard the normative and empirical combinations that seek to preclude emotion from human experience, for humans cannot function without their emotional capacities.

Before I turn to a more careful consideration of how these formulations are displayed in contemporary political psychology, I should consider the first issue of any science: conceptual clarity. Implicit in the foregoing discussion is that categories of emotion and reason are clear and agreed on, yet careful examination of emotion finds it to be a category in which many perhaps different qualities are often included (Rorty, 1985). Are appetites and drives forms of emotion? Are motives? What about feelings, passions, and moods? Are they all fully within the domain of emotion? Resolving these definitional and taxonomic questions is perhaps the most immediate barrier to progress in the scientific study of emotion. I shall devote the principal section of this chapter to describe the current state of affairs, as well as to suggest where research is most required to address current shortcomings.

Defining emotions: The difficulty of clearly categorizing emotion is not a new problem. For example, in the seventeenth and eighteenth centuries a major rethinking led to new formulations, giving rise to new taxonomic categories. "Interests" and "sentiments" emerged as a new category of emotion, a calculating version of emotion. This formulation was useful to explain the newly emergent forms of economic activity then taking place (Hirschman, 1977; Rorty, 1982, 1993; Rothschild, 2001). These new taxonomic creations—the interests and sentiments—were initially created as variants of emotion. Over time, interest and sentiments increasingly become thought of as independent categories of psychological activity. Thus the original clarity of two distinct psychological categories—reason (thinking or cognizing) on one hand, and feeling (emotions and passion) on the other—becomes a triumvirate, with "interests" and "sentiments" not just a compound of thinking and feeling but independent constructs in their own right. These new constructs are neither fully rational nor fully emotion, having some of the qualities of each, adapted to explain human actions political, economic, and civic (Burke, 1973; Madison et al., 1961).[7] Since it is common now to treat interest as an entity distinct and separate from emotion, emotion then becomes, in the modern period, a narrower category more closely associated with the passions and zeal—the dangerous variants of emotion.

But even with this complication, the terms "emotion" and "reason" remain notoriously confused, even in contemporary psychology, notwithstanding the application of "scientific" terms to replace lay terminology. The terms "cognition" and "affect" are no more clearly defined even in formal texts than are the ancient antecedents "reason" and "emotion." Perhaps the most serious taxonomic issue is the treatment of emotion as distinct from reason. The treatment of emotion as a distinct property results in the casual presumption that being "emotional" has uniform results, principally those already mentioned. The more emotional a person, the greater the likelihood that obsession, delusion, and demagoguery will hold sway (Hatfield, Cacioppo, & Rapson, 1994). And the more intense the emotion, the less the mind is in command. Nor is this conclusion restricted to some emotions, such as anger or rage; it is equally applicable to the "positive" emotions such as love. The problems of obsession, delusion, and demagoguery are no less problematic when experiencing "positive" emotions, for love or desire can cause one to "lose one's mind" no less so than anger or rage.

Central to the long tradition of the opposition between emotion and reason is the too often unexamined presumption that emotion is a singular and homogenous state. If emotion is not a coherent phenomenon but rather a class of disparate elements, it naturally follows that the presumption of its unity is deeply flawed (Ben-Ze'ev, 2000). Similarly, the conscious mind is taken to be the autonomous seat of reason. Thus it is not surprising that emotion and reason have been seen as two autonomous agents wresting for sovereign control. And given the lauded position of reason, political psychologists are often led to approach "affect," the "scientific" term for emotion, with the presumption that affect is not only unnecessary but also detrimental to "cognition," the "scientific" term for reasoning. A representative example of this view in political psychology is that constructed by Jim Kuklinski and his colleagues (Kuklinski, Riggle, Ottati, Schwarz, & Wyer, 1991): "In a democratic society, reasonable decisions are preferable to unreasoned ones: considered thought leads to the former, emotions to the latter; therefore deliberation is preferable to visceral reaction as a basis for democratic decision making" (p. 1) Here we see the presumption of autonomous reason fully at play. It is not only possible to be reasonable and thoughtful without being emotional, it is necessary that emotion be excluded from judgment.

The newly emergent findings derived from neuroscience challenge much we had thought we knew about emotion and reason. And neuroscience challenges not only these traditional understandings but also the established approaches to emotion in political psychology. In the section that follows I explore what the established approaches hold with respect to emotion and how research in neuroscience modifies these understandings. I will now turn to each of the major approaches to emotion in political psychology, beginning first with the psychoanalytic perspective.

◤ The Psychoanalytic Perspective on Emotion

While Freud introduces a rich set of metaphoric understandings, at heart his approach is a hydraulic model that shares many features with Galen's theory of the humors. But instead of four factors (one for each of the humors), each driving a temperamental quality, Freud envisioned a simpler system in which there are only two dynamic forces at play. On the one hand, the pleasure principle, libidinal energy, strives for immediate gratification, a process in which an eroticized conception of passion is fully displayed. On the other hand, the reality principle is articulated in the dispassionate mind attempting to resist, control, and manage the subterranean pressures applied by the passions arising from the "unconscious," the site of eros (the *id*). The war between emotion and reason is central to the Freudian conception, and in this respect it is largely in accord with the Hellenistic schools of ancient Greece in its empirical and normative presumptions.

I will not discuss the principal feature of psychoanalytic orientation to personality and temperament. There is a considerable literature on this application (George & George, 1998; Post, 1993; Renshon, 1998; Rogow, 1963; Volkan & Itkowitz, 1984; Volkan, Itkowitz, & Dod, 1997). Suffice it to say that there is considerable agreement with the Stoic and Skeptical schools of philosophy that passions are often early formed in life, deeply buried, and, unless set aside by heroic action, have enduring effects throughout the life of a person.

Emotion is attached to the salient features of experience (*cathexis*), and emotions, once formed, control our reactions, orientations, dispositions, and behavior toward these objects—to persons, events, and circumstances— whether favorably or unfavorably. The emotional bond, once formed, fixes these objects in memory, where they remain unless through strenuous and sustained effort this connection is broken (*decathexis*). The conscious ego, through introspection, can descend into the unconscious by its own autonomous efforts to reconstruct this subterranean territory. This feat is often supported by a trained therapeutic guide. Emotion is understood as a unified if inchoate force existing outside the realm of reason but intruding when and where it can.

But apart from this general conception, the psychoanalytic has no specific theory of emotion, (Davies, 1980) apart from its claim that emotion is the force by which the id overwhelms the ego (hence the presence of "defense mechanisms," which operate both internally, in that war between the two antagonistic principles, each with its separate domain, and externally, against the assaults of reality, which can frustrate, or reward, both principles). And while emotion is taken as unitary in its opposition to reason, the *expression* of emotion takes on a multifaceted quality. Each of the passions—understood by Freud as discrete entities: the "basic" emotions, emotion now becoming plural—are articulated in different ways in different circumstances. The structure of the passions is held to be discrete—each "basic" emotion supposedly results from the intersection of one of the two principles and fundamental beliefs. Thus when the pleasure principle is at play and some desired object is secured, we experience pleasure. When the object is lost, we experience sorrow; when it is taken by someone else, anger; when its acquisition is blocked, frustration, and so on. However, among psychoanalytic theorists, there is no agreement as to what these "basic" emotions are, each nominates a different set in number and content (Marcus, 1991), and there is no biological account to provide a neurological foundation for these "basic" emotions.

Discrete theories of the structure of emotion were formulated by the Greeks, principal among them Aristotle, Galen, and others in the Hellene schools of philosophy (Nussbaum, 1994; Plutchik, 1980a). In discrete theories of emotion, belief is the organizing imperative by which an otherwise inchoate generalized emotion is made definite. Something bad happens to generate a "negative" or "bad" emotion, but which emotion is generated depends on the associated belief. If I perceive that I am the cause, then "blame" or "guilt" might be the experience (or "shame" if the action is public or widely known). On the other hand, if I am not the cause but perceive others to be the cause of my loss, then "annoyance," "resentment," "anger," or "rage" might be the designation of the consequential emotional experience. The number of discrete emotions thus derives from the variety of beliefs thought to be salient to the construction of emotion (hence the method by which cultural factors are thought to become significant (Lutz, 1988)). But psychoanalytic accounts are not alone in accepting some variant of discrete formulations. Social psychologists have also subscribed to the discrete theory of emotion (Frijda, Kuipers, & Schure, 1989; Kinder, 1994; Parkinson, 1997, Roseman, 1979, 1984, 1991; Roseman, Antoniou, & Jose, 1996; Smith, 1989). Rather than review these in any detail, I shall instead consider the principal structural alternative, dimensional theories of emotion, in the next section.

◣ Social Psychological Perspectives on Emotion

As I have elsewhere provided a useful history of the treatment of emotion in political psychology (Marcus, 2000; Marcus, Neuman, & MacKuen, 2000, app. A and B), and an excellent history of the research on emotion in academic psychology is also readily available (Cornelius, 1996), I will here review in an abbreviated fashion the three primary structural approaches to emotion: the valence, discrete, and dimensional theories of emotion.[8] The problem begins, as does all science, with description. The lexicon of emotion is rich in providing different nominal categories; by one estimate over seven hundred different terms exist (Storm & Storm, 1987). But are these each distinct or are some equivalent (i.e., synonymous)? Does this richness of emotion language clarify or confuse us with what are nothing more than an abundance of synonymous terms?

For poets, from Homer onward and for sculptors, painters, and other artists—the task is how to depict both the particular and the general. This person (specific) is angry (universal). How emotion can be depicted has long intrigued artists and philosophers. What general rules apply so that we can recognize the particular emotion? The face as the palette on which humans, and other creatures, display emotion has been a particular subject of inquiry. In the seventeenth century Charles Le Brun, a French academician, developed and presented a lecture on the emotions and their representation that proved to be very popular and influential (Montagu, 1994). His work derived from Descartes's work on the psychology of emotion (Descartes, 1989). Charles Darwin (1998) and, more recently, Paul Ekman (1982, 1984, 1992; Ekman & Davidson, 1994; Ekman & Friesen, 1982; Ekman & Oster 1979; Ekman & Rosenberg, 1997), have continued the project to discover the rules and display characteristics that differentiate one facial display of emotion from another.

The effort to find "pure" or "basic" emotions seems analogous to the task of discerning the structure of colors. Mixing different proportions of basic colors can create millions of different colors. Different emotions might similarly arise from some smaller set of emotions. Alternatively, differently named emotions may really be equivalent, reflecting synonymous experiences. When one person says he is happy while another says she is elated, are they in agreement or disagreement? There are many variations in emotional experience; hundreds have been named (Storm & Storm, 1987). In the interest of parsimony we resist the impulse to generate thousands of emotion names to apply to each and every observable and distinguishable variant.

Faced with the task of reducing the many variants of feeling to a much smaller set of categories, social psychologists have advanced three different solutions. The greatest reduction is offered by "valence" theories of emotion. Here the solution is straightforward: emotions are the means by which living creatures solve the problem of "approach" and "avoidance" (Tooby & Cosmides, 1990a, 1990b). Initial investigations suggested that humans apply a single bipolar valence dimension of evaluation to all objects in their ken (Osgood, Suci, & Tannenbaum, 1957). However, while it is certainly the case that we all can readily respond to instructions to classify our perceptions into binary oppositions, such as good or bad, that does not mean that emotional experiences are fully and adequately captured by such a severe reduction in presumptive structure, even though the methodology of binary oppositions, as in semantic differentials and feeling thermometers, is widely practiced.[9]

Discrete theories of emotion reject the valence extreme reduction of all emotional experience to a single liking-disliking dimension. Discrete theories of emotion attribute emotion to the application of multiple concurrent cognitive evaluations. The theory of the psychologist Ira Roseman (1984) is representative. He argues (Roseman, 1984) that *it is interpretation of events rather than the events per se that determine which emotions will be felt* (p. 14, italics in the original). This produces a "structural model" that results from applying a hierarchy of considerations. He begins with whether the events are perceived as positive or negative and then differentiates further according to whether reward is present or punishment absent for positive assessment and reward is absent or punishment present for a negative assessment. Then circumstances are either deserved or undeserved and, within that, certain or uncertain. Finally, the scheme incorporates whether the object of evaluation is the self or someone else. The number of discrete emotions results from the number of applicable considerations and their subcategories within each consideration (normally these are binary oppositions, e.g., rewarding *or* punishing). Different discrete theories reduce the hundreds of discernable emotional states, whether observed in others or felt, to some manageable set of 8, 10, 12 or 16 "basic" emotions. There is a substantial literature of such cognitive accounts of emotion (Ekman, 1992; Ellsworth, 1991; Forgas, 1995; Frijda et al., 1989; Mauro, Sato, & Tucker, 1992; Ortony, Clore, & Collins, 1989; Parkinson & Manstead, 1992; Smith, Haynes, Lazarus, & Pope, 1993). And the body of work demonstrates that people do distinguish one emotion from another by its suitability to the circumstances in which they are placed.

Central to discrete theories is the presumption that these emotional states are by definition discrete, that is, mutually exclusive.[10] Perhaps the most important study in political psychology of that claim is that done by Robert Ableson and his colleagues (Abelson, Kinder, Peters, & Fiske, 1982). Abelson and his colleagues were interested in the emotions citizens experienced when confronted with the major presidential candidates during elections.[11] Using a list of discrete theory–based emotional reactions to presidential candidates, derived from Roseman, they asked, in the American National Elections pilot study of 1979, how people rated the presidential candidates on the discrete terms: hope, pride, sympathy, disgust, anger, fear, and uneasy (Kinder, Abelson, & Fiske, 1979).

The two theoretical structural accounts, valence and discrete, discussed up to this point would predict quite different results. The former would find that these terms are all readily arrayed from most negative, most likely disgust, to the most positive, perhaps pride, with all other terms arrayed intermediately on a single bipolar dimension. The latter would find that each candidate would probably provoke only one discrete emotion, that most aptly resulting from the germane cognitive considerations (hence we would find very low correlations among the various terms that subjects used to evaluate each candidate). Since each of these arises from a distinct set of cognitive considerations, the general expectation was that people who felt fear when thinking of a particular candidate would not also report feeling hope, pride, sympathy, anger, disgust, or unease (and so on).

As is well known, neither theoretical account provided an acceptable description of the empirical results. Instead of either the discrete pattern of mutually exclusive states or one valence dimension, the results required two orthogonal dimensions. This gives rise to the third alternative, dimensional theories of emotion. Unhappily, as I will show, they chose to name the two dimensions "positive" and "negative," which produced two unfortunate consequences. To anticipate a fuller discussion hereafter, there are two problems with these labels. First, the terms *positive* and *negative* imply a binary opposition (comparable to the semantic differential oppositions, such as good-bad, strong-weak, etc.), when the results showed that people often experience, concurrently, both varieties of emotional reactions. That is, for most people a single candidate elicited both positive and negative feelings. Second, the terms *positive* and *negative* reinforce the premise that approach-avoidance lie at the heart of these emotional evaluations, again suggesting a singular consideration that the data contravene.

By now it has become well established that when a diverse array of stimuli is used—faces, words, objects such as those used in Peter Lang's Universal Affective Picture System (Bradley, Greenwald, Petry, & Lang, 1992; Cuthbert, Bradley, & Lang, 1996; Lang, 1994; Lang, Greenwald, Bradley, & Hamm, 1993)—a two-dimensional array is necessary to account for the emotional responses experienced. That is to say, objects elicit not one emotional response arrayed along a bipolar dimension, from negative (disliked, avoidance) to positive (liked, approach) but two simultaneous dimensions of emotions (Almagor & Ben-Porath, 1989; Clark & Watson, 1988; Feldman, 1995; Kern, 1989; Larsen & Diener, 1992; Mayer & Gaschke, 1988; McCrae & Costa, 1989; Meyer & Shack, 1989; Plutchik, 1980a, 1980b; Plutchik & Kellerman, 1989; Remington, Fabrigrar, & Visser, 2000; Russell, 1980, 1983; Watson, 1988a; Watson & Clark, 1992b; Watson, Clark, & Tellegen, 1984; Watson & Tellegen, 1985).[12] These findings, of which the foregoing citations are only a sample, had consequences for the valence view of emotion (Zajonc, 1998) and also for the other competing account, the aforementioned discrete theory of emotion. More important, these findings fueled interest in dimensional theories of emotion that hold that specific emotion terms are place markers that identify values along underlying continuous dimensions of appraisal.

A representative example is displayed in figure 6.1. This example is drawn from a study in which subjects were asked how often they experienced each of 48 feelings during the course of a day. If the valence model is valid, then the 48 words used to label different emotions would array on a single line going from the most positive (e.g., enthusiastic, delighted, elated, etc.) to the most negative (e.g., sad, unhappy, miserable, etc.). If the discrete model were the valid solution, then feelings would be grouped into 8, 10, or 12 clusters (the number depends on the specific discrete theory and the number of synonymous terms included in any given study). However, neither result obtained (Rusting & Larsen, 1995). Instead, as with other similar studies, whether as in this instance self-report of feeling states or emotional reactions to politicians, or various objects, or faces, a two-

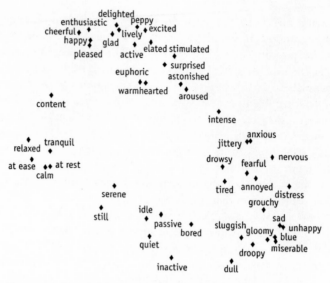

Figure 6.1. Emotions experienced during a day. Adapted from Rusting & Larsen, 1995

dimensional array is generally required to summarize the variance, because the 48 terms neither fit along one dimension nor cluster into synonymous groups. Instead, the 48 terms are distributed in a two-dimensional space.[13]

When even more emotion terms are used, and when other objects are used to generate emotional reactions, as in Peter Lang's work on pictures (Cuthbert et al., 1996; Ito, Cacioppo, & Lang, 1998; Lang et al., 1993), the two-dimensional space becomes even more densely filled. This led psychologists to surmise that the variation from one feeling to another reflected more than one underlying appraisal. Feelings, though many and varied, might then be expressions of some analytic appraisals or evaluations (Scherer, Schorr, & Johnstone, 2001). Appraisals produced by one system would probably yield variations along a single axis. As the space is two-dimensional, psychologists have surmised that two different appraisal systems are continuously active. The resulting variations in feelings, though many and varied, might then reflect just two ongoing assessments, much as variations in just three base colors, red, green, and blue, can generate millions of shades of color. But what underlying appraisals might generate this two-dimensional space?

The "circumplex," as these emotion spaces have been labeled (Almagor & Ben-Porath, 1989; Larsen & Diener, 1992; Plutchik, 1980a; Remington et al., 2000; Russell, 1980; Russell, Lewicka, & Niit, 1989; Watson et al., 1984), suggests that the many different feelings are distributed in a two-dimensional dense space. At about the same time, the psychologist Robert Zajonc published a series of articles that argued that emotions can arise prior to and independent of explicit conscious awareness, hence independent of cognitive appraisal (Kunst-Wilson & Zajonc, 1980; Moreland & Zajonc, 1979; Zajonc, 1980, 1982). This suggests that preconscious and nonconscious appraisals other than cognition are at play.[14] For if conscious considerations follow rather than precede the expression of feelings, the central premise of discrete or cognitive appraisal theories fails. Zajonc's account suggests that preconscious emotional evaluations arise before as well as outside of consciousness.[15] Hence we may understand our anger and come to know its source, but this understanding derives from reflection on our feelings and is not the basis for the feelings themselves.

Hence discrete and dimensional theories differ not only in their depiction of the structure of emotion; they also differ on their view of the temporal relationship of emotion (affect) and reason (cognition). The former argues that emotions are subordinate to and derivative of cognitive activity. The latter, informed by work in neuroscience, argues that emotions arise prior to and independent of cognitive activity (Adolphs, Tranel, Damasio, & Damasio, 1995; Armony & LeDoux, 1997; Damasio, 1999, 1994; Davis, 1992, 1997; Gray, 1987a, 1987b; LeDoux, 1991, 1992, 1993a, 1993b, 1995, 1996; Rolls, 1999). These two views need not be mutually contradictory. That is to say, emotional systems may produce emotional states that subsequently, when sufficiently strong and enduring as to enter into conscious awareness, give rise to conscious assessment that then yields explicit and more differentiated semantic labels. It is of course of interest whether the subsequent cognitive processing alters the effects of preconscious emotional appraisal. But there are other differences between discrete and dimensional views of emotion.

The most important difference is that the discrete view suggests that emotion is generated by just one process: the cognitive appraisal of a situation. On the other hand, the dimensional view suggests that there may be multiple sources for the expression of emotion, hence the multiple dimensions needed to describe emotional experience. Perhaps there are emotion-generating systems, each with different properties and hence consequences. With at least two dimensions comes a challenge to the longstanding presumption that emotion has uniform and coherent effects (contrasting emotion, and its effects, with reason, and its effects).[16] Hence preconscious emotional appraisals may generate feelings that, when consciously apparent, may be further elaborated by cognitive appraisal.

It has long been argued that humans have two different modes of information, feelings that have long seemed mysterious in their origins and the seemingly veridical representation of reality that arises through conscious awareness. Each of the three theories of emotion argues that feelings are not very mysterious. Each of the three models offers an account of the underlying appraisal that gives rise to emotional expression. However they arise, the coexistence of feelings and thoughts generates the likelihood that people can rely either on their thoughts and/or their feelings. Psychologists have been exploring this vein of thought assiduously. Gerald Clore and his colleagues (Clore, Schwarz, & Conway, 1994; Schwarz, 1990) have developed the suggestion that people use feelings as information, presuming an assimilation relationship (e.g., I feel happy, so I like these new people I have just met), though others have found counterassimilation effects (Ottati & Isbell, 1996). Indeed the search for "affective" and "cognitive" influences is now a rich industry (Crites, Fabrigar, & Petty, 1994; Erdley & D'Agostino, 1988; Fabrigar & Petty, 1999; Greene, 1998; Ingram, 1989; Kuklinski et al., 1991; Marcus, Sullivan, Theiss-Morse, Flathman, & Healy, 1990; Millar & Tesser, 1986; Mischel & Shoda, 1995; Ottati, 1988; Ottati, Riggle, Wyer, Schwarz, & Kuklinski, 1989; Ottati, Steenbergen, & Riggle, 1992; Stangor, Sullivan, & Ford, 1991). And feelings resulting from preconscious emotional appraisals may have unique impacts, apart from working with cognitive components (Loewenstein et al., 2001).[17]

The idea that affective reactions, feelings, can have powerful effects as "heuristics" used in lieu of serious deliberation in decision-making circumstances (Forgas, 1994, 1995) returns us to the basic presumptions of the Hellene schools of philosophy. Some argue that use of such affective heuristics is acceptable, by virtue of being a "reasonable" if not reasoned method of making decisions (Baron, 1994). But others find reliance on heuristics, whether affectively based or not, is not an acceptable alternative to thoughtful explicit consideration (Arkes, 1993). Such disputes replicate the disagreements among the Stoic, Skeptic, and other schools of philosophy. Contemporary theoretical accounts such as the elaboration likelihood model (Petty & Cacioppo, 1986) argue that people can either be thoughtful and deliberate or thoughtlessly receptive to heuristics and persuasive messages, again reflecting the attraction of binary oppositions such as emotion versus reason (Chaiken & Trope, 1999). When contrasting reason and emotion, we ignore the possibility that there are multiple systems of emotion, suggesting a more complex set of relationships, with different emotion systems having different impacts not only on the expression of feeling but on various aspects of "cognition" and behavior. Recent work in neuroscience gives us a preliminary and provisional understanding of the multiple systems of emotional appraisal.

◥ The Neuroscience Perspective on Emotion

The literature on emotion and neuroscience is large and growing ever larger. (For a useful set of readings consider Adolphs, Damasio, Tranel, & Damasio, 1996; Adolphs, Tranel, & Damasio, 1998; Adolphs, Tranel, Damasio, & Damasio, 1994; Adolphs et al., 1995; Bechara et al., 1995, 1997; Borod, 2000; Cacioppo, Berntson, Crites, & Stephen 1996; Damasio, 1994, 1999; Davidson, 2000; Davidson, Jackson, & Kalin, 2000; Davis, 1992, 1997; Etcoff, 1986; George et al., 1993; Gray, 1985a, 1987a, 1987b,

1990; Jeannerod, 1997; Lane, Nadel, & Ahern, 2000; LeDoux, 1991, 1996; LeDoux, Romanski, & Xagoraris, 1989; Panksepp, 1991; Tomarken, Davidson, Wheeler, & Doss, 1992; Tranel, Damasio, & Damasio, 1995; Zuckerman, 1991.) Before I turn to the currently recognized multiple emotion systems, I should mention that it is now agreed that there are some common features to all of these emotion systems. First, emotion systems have access to the sensory stream well before the brain systems that generate conscious awareness can complete their work and, further, the emotion systems produce appraisals that then initiate emotional, cognitive, and behavioral actions (Libet, 1985; Libet, Gleason, Wright, & Pearl, 1983; Libet et al., 1991; Libet, Wright, Feinstein, & Pearl, 1979).[18] Moreover, these appraisal systems attend to the full sensory stream, while consciousness only attends to a very small and preselected sample (Zimmermann, 1989). Indeed, one of the functions of the preconscious emotion systems is to focus and direct conscious attention.

Neuroscience offers another crucial insight into the multiple systems of memory (Mishkin & Appenzeller, 1987; Schacter, 1996; Squire, 1987). Memory had previously been conventionally thought of as unitary or, more recently, divided into "short-term" and "long-term" (Forgas, Burnham, & Trimboli, 1988; Lau & Sears, 1986; Lodge, McGraw, & Stroh, 1989). Perhaps the two most important systems of memory, one labeled associative (or sometimes procedural) and the other declarative (or semantic), demonstrate how much rethinking is required in exploring the role of emotion in political psychology. Associative memory, generally accepted to be active in the prefrontal cortex, is not only the realm of emotional predispositions (i.e., our "likes" and "dislikes") but also where our learned actions are located. A simple task, such as reaching for and lifting a cup of water from a table to one's mouth, is actually a very complex set of integrated and learned skills (linking sensory and somatosensory streams with prior experience). How firmly we will grip and how much effort we will apply to lift that cup depends on how full it appears to be (sensory data), how far away it is, and whether it is made of paper, plastic, or glass. Each circumstance will probably be somewhat different from a prior occasion (perhaps the table is lower or higher, nearer or farther, the cup less full, smaller, larger, slipperier, etc.). Associative memory is where all these variations, and how to enact and manage such familiar actions, are stored. And emotion plays a crucial role in these actions, as well as resolving conflicting concurrent goals (Gray & McNaughton, 2000).

Declarative memory manages the recall of "facts" such as: what I had for breakfast, what color shirt I wore yesterday, my birthday, and so on. The amygdala and the hippocampus, two regions in the limbic area of the brain, are specifically engaged in these memory systems.[19] Political psychologists have attended almost exclusively to declarative memory, yet much of what we now know about political judgments, such as in deciding whom to vote for, reflects the powerful impact of associative memory, for example ideology and partisan identification, both of which are influential, because of the affective component, on political judgment (MacKuen, Neuman, & Marcus, 2000; Marcus et al., 2000).

Studies of patients who have suffered bilateral damage to their amygdala exhibit complete impairment of their capacity to experience an emotional response to the world in which they exist. It is interesting to note that not only is the capacity to experience preconscious emotional reactions eliminated but also the capacity to experience "discrete" emotions. But perhaps most interesting is that these patients have no cognitive impairment (Bechara et al., 1995 1997). That is to say, these patients can do all the things that a bright, fully reasoning subject can do, except for their one crucial inability to experience emotion. They cannot enact the behavior recommended by their contemporary reasoning—even when they know what the best course of action to take is. They are unable to initiate the behavior recommended by their own analysis. Thus the ancient dream of obliterating the impact of emotion on reason can now be actually realized, but its full consequences are quite different from those long thought. For with emotion comes the capacity to enact behavior, something of which reason alone is not capable. All of which suggests that Aristotle had it more right than his philosophic competitors, emotion and reason are both cooperatively necessary to fully realize all that emotion and reason enable.

But what do we know about the emotional systems and how they work? The identification of emotion systems has been explored through the issue of where to locate the axes, or dimensions of appraisal, using data resulting from subjects' emotional reactions to various stimuli. And these studies, as noted earlier, report that two dimensions are the minimum necessary to adequately represent the resulting variance. Although there is an infinite set of possibilities, two competing dimensional theories of emotion emerged in social psychology.[20] One, most associated with the work of David Watson and his colleagues (Watson, 1988b; Watson et al., 1984; Watson, Clark, & Tellegen, 1988; Watson & Tellegen, 1985) describes the two dimensions as "positive" and "negative." In this account, the axes would be located, in figure 6.1, vertically and horizontally, identifying on the vertical dimension variation from depressed to elated and enthusiastic (the dimension of positive affect). The horizontal dimension reveals the expression of variation from calm to anxious that has been generally labeled negative affect, adopting the same problematic labels used by Abelson and his colleagues (1982). The other account, most associated with James Russell (Russell, 1980; Russell, Lewicka, & Niit, 1989; Russell, Weiss, & Mendelsohn, 1989) argued for a different location of the dimensions, a rotation of 45 degrees, yielding axes that describe emotions as varying on valence, low to high, and arousal, low to high.

Unfortunately, the terminology used in these two structural models has lent considerable confusion as to what the terms "positive emotion" and "negative emotion" mean. This can best be shown by example. Consider

figure 6.2. It shows the data from figure 6.1 superimposed on a representative idealization of the "circumplex" of emotional response. Below are schematic representations of the two-dimensions solutions with their axes locations. As you can see, the valence model identifies two regions where positive and negative emotions are located, but these regions are different from the regions that the positive-negative model identically labels. Thus,

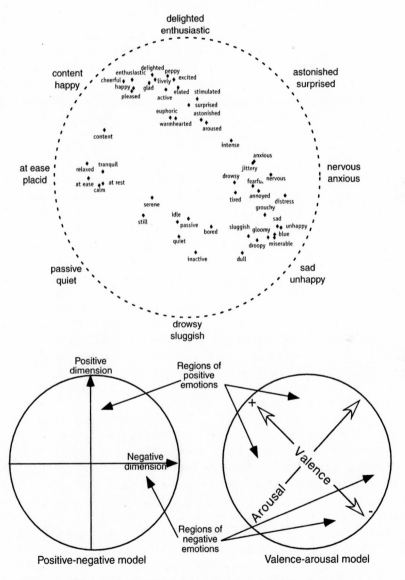

Figure 6.2. The circumplex and competing structural models of emotion

for example, sad is characteristically a "negative" feeling state according to the valence model but not for the positive-negative model (rather it is a feeling state that arises from the absence of positive feeling). Anxiety is the characteristic negative feeling state of the positive-negative model, but that feeling state is located as close to the arousal dimension of the valence model as to the negative region in the valence model, leaving its status rather ambiguous. Since both models use the same terms, *positive* and *negative,* but identify quite different feeling states, considerable confusion arises, unless great care is taken in reading research reporting on the effects of "positive" or "negative" feeling states on judgment and behavior.[21] Many articles report, for example, that "positive" emotion induces people to rely on what they already know, but these reports are really derived not from studying all variants of positive emotion but rather only "happiness" (Bless et al., 1996; Bless & Fiedler, 1995; Schwarz & Bless, 1991). Similarly, studies of negative emotion making categorical claims about what "negative affect" does conflates what are really quite different negative emotion states (more on this shortly).

The bulk of the research reported on the structure of emotional responses focuses on data reduction in isolation from any substantive theory. Each of the two models account for the variety of feeling states excepting emotion terms of animus (Barrett & Russell, 1998). But there are serious problems evident in these studies.

If the two alternative models were not 45 degree rotations, one to the other, the evidence collected to date on the effects of "positive" and "negative" emotion might be more useful. Dimensions that are orthogonal one to the other (i.e., 90 degrees) are uncorrelated (so their distinct relationships to third factors are not confounded). Dimensions that are located 45 degrees apart (as are the two proposed "negative" emotions and the two "positive" emotions (see fig. 6.2) means that findings purporting to show the effects of sadness may fit one of three alternative accounts, as follows. First, sadness or *any other* negative emotion has this effect (i.e., all negative emotions are equivalent in their effects on human judgment and behavior). We could use any "negative" emotion. It matters not which is selected for use in research; any would generate the same findings.

Second, the relationship is actually due to another negative emotion, say anxiety, not sadness, but because the dimensions are positively correlated this effect is falsely attributed to sadness. This would be revealed had separate measures of the two negative responses, sadness and anxiety, been included so that multivariate controls could establish their distinctive effects, if any, and control for this possibility. Few studies have done this, and therefore conclusions about the effects of "happiness" and "sadness" (as in Bless & Fielder, 1995) do not support their principal conclusions. Third, sadness, but only sadness, has this effect. The vast array of research on *the* impact of "negative" and "positive" emotions has not been conducted so as to effectively distinguish among these three alternatives.[22]

Yet another article that compares yet another factor solution on yet another data series will not determine which model is superior (not surprising, as fitting factor axes to *any* arbitrary location is going to fit this kind of data as well as any other location of factor axes). It is apparent then that neither of these structural models actually accounts for the full range of feeling states that people experience. There are other issues that neither the valence-arousal nor the positive-negative views explain. These structural investigations share an unstated premise that the dimensions identify independent qualities of emotional response (though they do not agree on the nature of these primary characteristics). Hence each model fits orthogonal solutions, implicitly requiring the two dimensions to be uncorrelated. But Abelson and colleagues (1982) have found, as have others since, that the relationship between "positive" and "negative" dimensions is dynamic, moving from more to less orthogonality as the stimulus becomes more familiar to the subject. Neither structural model attempts to depict this dynamic pattern. Imposing uncorrelated factor solutions obscures this feature of emotional response and prevents further research as to when and why such dynamic shifts arise.

Accounting for Aversion

But there is an additional issue that directly challenges the presumption that these models provide comprehensive descriptions of all forms of emotional response. Neither structural model accounts for the emotions of aversion (e.g., disgust, contempt, hatred, anger, and so on). Studies of emotional reactions to candidates, to issues, and to other political stimuli often show that people experience this third variant of emotion (Conover & Feldman, 1986; Marcus et al., 2000; Mikula, Scherer, & Athenstaedt, 1998). And, studies have shown that forms of aversion (e.g., contempt, disgust, hatred, etc.) have quite different effects on people from the other primary negative affects of anxiety and depression (Ax, 1953; Bodenhausen, Kramer, & Süsser, 1994; MacKuen, Marcus, Neuman, Keele, & Wolak, 2001). When these mood terms are included, and when aversive stimuli are present, a third dimension of emotional response is required to account for the variance in subject responses (MacKuen et al., 2001; Marcus et al., 2000). Watson, and Clark (1992a) have offered one effort to integrate these emotions in the positive-negative model, but the scholars advocating the valence-arousal model has not attempted any such integration. The valence-arousal model is especially inattentive to the third dimension of emotional response—aversion—and the dynamic character of emotional responses. Given the frequent and powerful role of anger, hatred, and the like, in politics, it seems unlikely that either of these models offers much promise for political psychology.

How then to resolve this dilemma? Since data fitting will not be identify the superior model, perhaps it is best to turn to more relevant and determinative criteria. A theory of political affect requires not just a measurement model but, even more, a substantive theory. A substantive theory generates testable propositions about how emotion arises and the consequences for judgment and behavior. Producing the research that resolves which measurement model is more promising, on substantive criteria, will have the additional benefit of offering real and new insights into how emotion influences political behavior.

So what are the substantive theories that lurk behind the two structural models? The valence-arousal model is a return to the old idea that the primary function of emotion is to identify and mark approach-avoidance circumstances with "arousal" dimension measuring the strength of the response. Why such a system would equally apply to the emotions experienced when the self is the object of assessment (as in fig. 6.1) is not well explained. The positive-negative model is problematic, as the term "negative" is applied to one region (nervous, anxious, etc, the section to the right in fig. 6.1) but could equally be applied to the bottom region of the display (i.e., terms such as *sluggish, blue,* and *gloomy*), which identify feelings of depression, a subjective state that would appear to most to be "negative."[23] Since neither measurement model offers discriminating predictions as to the behavioral and cognitive effects, as well as the specifying predictions regarding emotional expression, I turn to a theory that has explicit measurement and substantive elements: the theory of affective intelligence (Marcus et al., 2000). Unlike either measurement models, this theory begins with a biological account of the emotions. The theory evolved from a program of research begun by Jeffrey Gray (Corr, Pickering, & Gray, 1997; Corr et al., 1995; Gray, 1970, 1973, 1981, 1985b, 1987a, 1987b, 1990; Pickering & Gray, 1999; Wilson, Kumari, Gray, & Corr, 2000), largely in animal studies. It has been translated into political psychology by Marcus and colleagues (Marcus, 1988; Marcus & MacKuen, 1993; Marcus & Rahn, 1990; Marcus, Wood, & Theiss-Morse, 1998; Marcus et al., 1995, 2000). It elaborates the fundamental insight of Aristotle that emotion and reason are cooperatively interrelated and mutually advantageous to the challenge of achieving a full life.[24]

Space precludes a full exposition of Gray's work (Carver & Scheier, 1990; Carver, Sutton, & Scheier, 2000) here. Suffice it to say that one system of emotion—Gray calls it the behavioral activation system and my colleagues and I have renamed it the disposition system, functions to manage learned behavior, what we have called habits and predispositions in all their variety (Marcus et al., 2000). Many habits are thoughtless; their execution requires considerable mental resources though not much in the way of conscious attention.[25] Thus this system is deeply implicated in the power of previously learned attachments, often attributed to "symbols," to control political judgments (Marcus, 1988; Sears et al., 1979, 1980). This system gives rise to emotions that fall along the continuous ranges of happiness-sadness and those that depict aversion (e.g., contempt, bitterness, anger, and hatred).

The second system, Gray's behavioral inhibition system (we have renamed it the surveillance system), functions to warn us of unusual and/or threatening circumstances. The system gives rise to the emotions that vary along the continuous range of anxious to calm. The first system is efficient in storing strategically successful behaviors in associative memory, enabling them to be reused whenever their specific goals are salient. This function is crucial, as most learned behaviors are not well executed by reliance on conscious attention.[26] Yet this efficiency becomes highly vulnerable when displayed in environments that may not display the same features as those experienced previously. The task of this system is to swiftly scan the contemporary environment, comparing its features to those expected, when executing the current ongoing plans. As long as the comparison is favorable—I am at a rally hosted by my political party, and all that is taking place is congruent with prior experience, speeches, people, and red, white, and blue balloons and bunting—then this system remains unobtrusive, apart from generating feelings of calm reassurance. However, if there is a mismatch—perhaps the new candidate of my party gives a terrible speech, inept and clumsy—then in addition to intruding with feelings of anxiety, this system causes people to give heightened attention to the moment, disinhibits people from reliance on the ongoing behavior, habit, and invokes conscious considerations, including not only attention but also learning (Marcus & MacKuen, 1993).

Both of Gray's systems, along with a third, the fight/flight system (Gray & McNaughton, 2000), depend on multiple concurrent appraisals of ongoing plans, via somatosensory and sensory streams executed well before conscious awareness. One appraisal is strategically devoted to the habitual execution of plans for obtaining familiar rewarding goals and avoiding familiar punishments (hence the deployment of emotions of happiness in the case of the former and aversion in the case of the latter). When habits fail, we feel frustration and sadness. The other appraisal is strategically devoted to quickly identifying the unexpected novel change in our familiar environment or unexpected challenges to our plans, hence the deployment of the emotions of anxiety.[27]

One clear implication of this theory is that we respond to the familiar quite differently from how we respond to the unfamiliar. Furthermore, the theory offers a substantive account of the three different "negative" affects: anxiety, sadness, and anger. Anxiety is the output of the surveillance system, identifying the unexpected appearance of unfamiliar and or threatening circumstances. Sadness arises when exhaustion and failure accompany the execution of our otherwise rewarding habits. Anger arises when familiar threats impede our way. This offers a theoretical account of the dynamic pattern between anxiety and enthusiasm in campaigns found by (Abelson et al.,

1982). Early in campaigns candidates evoke both anxiety and enthusiasm, while latter in the campaign the same candidates evoke generally just one or the other. This pattern arises because many things begin as unfamiliar, for example presidential candidates early in the campaign period. But repeated exposure enables citizen to familiarize themselves with these aspirants, turning them into familiar objects of hope, for those who identify with them, or danger, for those who oppose them.

This account matches Watson's interpretation of emotional experience discussed earlier, that is to say, the Gray account argues that the "positive" dimension of affect is the emotion generated by the disposition system and that the "negative" dimension of affect is the emotion generated by the behavioral, or surveillance, system. Thus we have a merger between biological and psychological accounts with amply substantive hypotheses to explore.[28] On the other hand, the valence-arousal interpretation does not have a biological account, and its substantive account, describing little more than approach-avoidance, is rather meager.

The principal claim of Gray's multiple systems of emotion theory holds that different emotion systems operate to subserve behavioral learning as well as control attention. These systems enable attention to be shifted from one thing to another but also sustain the ability to focus attention more deeply and ignore distraction. Further, these systems inhibit or strengthen reliance on habits (of action and of thought) as circumstances warrant. Emotions thus enhance the ways politics can be engaged, sometimes casually, sometimes with great seriousness of purpose, sometimes thoughtfully, sometimes deliberatively, sometimes committed to existing loyalties, sometimes open to new possibilities, sometimes focused on self-interest, sometimes setting aside parochial commitments and loyalties for the needs of strangers. Emotions generated by the disposition system motivate our capacity to rely on our habits, eschewing explicit consideration of alternative courses of action. But emotions generated by the surveillance system motivate reliance on reason. Thus emotion is intimately involved not only in habits, prejudices, and other instances of reliance of learned behavior but in the recruitment of reason and the full display of cognitive activities (Marcus, 2002).[29] Thus the theory of affective intelligence provides a measurement model for each of the three negative emotions: depression, anxiety, and aversion.[30] It also provides a substantive theory on the sources, the biology, and the impact of these emotions on judgment and behavior.

How does the theory of affective intelligence differ from the two alternative structural models, valence-arousal and positive-negative? In depicting the strategic dimensions of emotional response, the theory of affective intelligence aligns with the positive-negative view of the structure of emotion, but with an important codicil. When familiar and strategically salient stimuli associated with punishment appear, then the theory of affective intelligence holds that the distinct emotional dimension of aversion will be apparent, and, further, that the dimension of aversion will function much as the dimension of enthusiasm functions for familiar strategic stimuli associated with reward; that is, it is controlled by the disposition system. More important, what does each model offer in the way of generating insights of interest to political psychology?

It is important to reiterate that the valence dimension of the approach-avoidance view of emotion identifies different emotions from those identified by either the positive-negative model or the theory of affective intelligence. The former identifies as "positive" and "negative" different emotions from those so labeled by the latter. For example, anxiety is not identified as a crucial emotion in the valence-arousal view of the structure of emotion. Rather, valence identifies liking and disliking and arousal, which, as can be seen in figure 6.2, locates the salient emotions as happy versus sad (valence) and quiet versus astonished (aroused). Affective intelligence, on the other hand, argues that the salient emotions are variations along the enthusiastic and anxious axes (labeled "positive" and "negative" in figure 6.2). It is important that in that research the emotions specific to each model are measured when testing their respective hypotheses (hence when testing the claim that negative stimuli generate greater scrutiny, the valence-arousal model would test different "negative" emotions from those either of the other two models would). Moreover, the theory of affective intelligence identifies aversion as a significant emotion, while this emotion is essentially ignored by the two alternative structural models. More important, neither of the two-dimensional models have much to say about when and why people are motivated to learn, or when and why people are likely to abandon habits for new plans of action and belief or when they are likely to strongly hold to established belief and actions. Resolving which theory is the more productive requires research that tests the competing claims of these three accounts.

◤ Conclusion

The primary thrust of this chapter is to call for two major changes in the way research is conducted on the role of emotion in political judgment and behavior. First, conceptual clarity on the alternative theoretical models is imperative, for without such clarity we cannot expect to collect the date necessary to properly compare the competing claims. Second, we need to collect rich arrays of data on emotional response that can differentiate between hypothesized factors enabling competing theories to be properly tested. It is only in this way that political psychology can fully explore the ways that emotion impacts on learning, persuasion, attention, and action.

It is useful to point out that this or other biologically based research has the capacity to add new evidence on old arguments about the capacities for reason and emotion and what roles both capacities sustain, individually and collectively. Much of political psychology has unreflectively accepted the millennia-old conception of two diametrically opposed forces, reason (recast as "cognition") and emotion (recast as "affect"). It has also, in the main, accepted the presumptive features of each that were first depicted in Hellenic schools of philosophy. Thus the normative imperative to strengthen reason and, necessarily, weaken or control emotion has been adopted as well. I believe that the most important contribution of neuroscience to the study of emotion is that it has provided new perspectives that offer a way out of the conundrum that was posed by the ancients and largely accepted since then: that humans are emotional, yet because emotion is so detrimental to reason, our capacity to rule ourselves, individually and collectively, is suspect. It is my hope that continued work will suggest, contrary to our long tradition, that emotion enhances our capacity to reason and indeed that to reason requires emotion not just to recruit its abilities but also to execute its conclusions.

◣ Notes

Eugene Borgida and Leonie Huddy offered very useful suggestions during the drafting of various iterations of this chapter. I would also like to thank three of my political psychology class, Elizabeth Chase, Heather Foran, and Nick Hiza, who gave excellent suggestions to improve the exposition.

1. It is hard to argue with the presumption that in democracies policies and the choice of leaders should be a matter of deliberate reasoning rather than fervent loyalty or dogmatic belief.

2. I offer one possibility (Marcus, 2002).

3. The discovery of the "unconscious" thus predates Freud by at least two millennia (Nussbaum, 1994).

4. It is of course familiar to presume that reason is the newer, as well as "higher," faculty while passion is designated the older and "lower" force.

5. I postpone to a later section a fuller discussion of this work, as it embodies a theoretical confusion that requires a lengthier discussion than is germane here.

6. One might think it appropriate to add Rawls (1971) here, but as Okin (1989) has noted, Rawls requires citizens behind the veil of ignorance to bring beneficence with them to mobilize their conclusions into action.

7. This new triumvirate is a precursor to the concept of "attitude" in psychology. Attitudes are defined in psychology as having three components: conation, what we believe about the object; affect, what we feel about the object; and behavioral, what we normally do to or with the object (Breckler, 1984).

8. It remains equally the case that emotion in social psychology is a rather mysterious entity. Though clearly a mental phenomenon, emotion is a subjective experience that is better described than explained in social psychological theories (Cornelius, 1996).

9. It did not help that the semantic differential methodology imposes a binary opposition. Still, this has been a popular approach to emotional assessment, most often seen in survey research, where "feeling thermometers" are efficient if nonetheless problematic means of discerning what people feel about some candidates, group, or policy (see Marcus, 1988, app.).

10. I feel anger when hurt by another's duplicity. But I will not feel guilty unless my incautiously placed trust in a false friend was my fault.

11. A line of work more extensively studied by Roger Masters and Denis Sullivan (Masters & Sullivan, 1993; Masters, 1991; Masters, Frey, & Bente, 1991; Masters & Sullivan, 1989; Masters & Way, 1996; McHugo, Lanzetta, Sullivan, Masters, & Englis, 1985; Sullivan & Masters, 1988).

12. I will set aside discussing a recent controversy sparked by a 1993 article (Green, Goldman, & Salovey, 1993) that seemed to suggest that only one dimension was required once measurement error was considered. This provoked a spate of exchanges (Cacioppo, Gardner, & Berntson, 1999; Green & Salovey, 1999; Green, Salovey, & Truax, 1999; Russell & Barrett, 1999a, b, Russell & Carroll, 1999; Tellegen, Watson, & Clark, 1999a, 1999b; Watson & Tellegen, 1999; Watson, Wiese, Vaidya, & Tellegen, 1999). All parties now agree that two dimensions are necessary, not one (Marcus, 2000).

13. There is an occasional third dimension, best described as aversion, which is occasionally present. For a fuller discussion of this third dimension see, Marcus, 2002, Marcus et al., 2000, and the discussion following.

14. A good deal of sloppy thinking has been at play in psychology. The term "implicit cognition" is one of a number of similarly phrased terms that has been used to cover such nonconscious information processing. But if the term "cognition" is used in this fashion, then, as I have noted previously, it is no longer apt as a synonym for thinking (in its various forms). Further, such usage stretches the meaning of "cognition" to include all information processing in the brain, thereby making the term so imperial in its application as to render it useless (Marcus, 1991).

15. For a brief period this view was controversial and resisted (Lazarus, 1982, 1984).

16. Though it is possible that the different effects of emotion are comparable even if differently sourced.

17. My colleagues and I have explored this approach with some success as applied to political tolerance judgments (Marcus, Sullivan, Theiss-Morse, & Wood, 1995).

18. A useful introduction is provided in Nørretranders (1998).

19. Bilateral damage to the amygdala prevents emotional response to new stimuli, while bilateral damage to the hippocampus has the same impact but on declarative memory (Bechara et al., 1995; Scott et al., 1997; Stanton, 2000; Zola-Morgan, Squire, Alvarez-Royo, & Clower, 1991).

20. I have placed the discussion of these social psychological accounts here rather than in the previous section because the discussion in the social psychological literature there is largely restricted to the question of which model better fits emotion data.

21. In reviewing studies that describe the effects of "positive" and or "negative" affect it is best to ignore these terms and pay particular attention to the exact stimuli used in a given study, as otherwise contrary effects may be not so contrary.

22. It is not uncommon for such studies to include emotional self-report measures of only, for example, happiness and sadness. Absent measures of other positive and negative emotion, such studies cannot test the three aforementioned possibilities. For example, Rahn (2001) has created a single valence conception of "public mood," holding that "positive moods" have one effect and "negative" moods another, yet this measure is based on emotion self-report items that clearly require a two-dimensional solution (Marcus, Neuman, & MacKuen, 2000), so it is not clear whether the effects of negative public mood she reports are due to sadness or anxiety or anger, all three, or some pair of the three.

23. And, as I noted earlier, the occasional appearance of feelings of aversion further muddies the waters, making the term "negative" apply to three quite different emotional states (anxiety, depression, and aversion). For more on this see Marcus et al., 2000, apps. A, B.

24. A view also argued by feminist and Aristotelian political theorists (Bickford, 1996, 2000; Rorty, 1985, 1996; Young, 1990).

25. Many habits do have elements of thought, as when dogmatic and cliched responses are familiarly elicited to manage recurring tasks (e.g., when engaged in familiar banter with a friend over which political party has a better record on crime, the economy, or leadership).

26. If you doubt this then you can attempt the following experiment. Take something you "know" how to do, writing your signature. Put the pen or pencil in your nondominant hand, and unless you are one of the rare ambidextrous individuals, you will find that you cannot consciously "will" that hand to replicate the deft skill you normally display.

27. I refer the interested reader to the work of Gray for the biological details. See also the work of LeDoux, Davis, Panksepp, and Damasio.

28. The work of John Cacioppo (Cacioppo, Gardner, & Berntson, 1997; Ito, Larsen, Smith, & Cacioppo, 1998) is important here as well. He finds that the response of each emotion system has distinguishing characteristics. The "negative" appraisal has a steeper response curve, i.e., we respond more intensely with increasing mismatch, which is to say people are generally risk-averse. On the other hand, we respond to neutral stimuli positively, a "positivity offset", i.e., we are curious (both features are general depictions, there being important individual differences across subjects).

29. It is also worth reconsidering the traditional assignment of women as the more emotional gender, implying their unsuitability for politics and leadership role, now challenged and even reversed. We might well conclude that women are better, not ill, suited for these roles.

30. *Depression* is a better term for this affect than *sadness*, as sadness may arise from either internal or external sources while depression results from inadequate psychic and physical resources to meet the demands of the action that is underway or contemplated.

▶ References

Abele, A., & Petzold, P. (1994). How does mood operate in an impression formation task? An information integration approach. *European Journal of Social Psychology, 24,* 173–187.

Abelson, R. P., Kinder, D. R., Peters, M. D., & Fiske, S. T. (1982). Affective and semantic components in political personal perception. *Journal of Personality and Social Psychology, 42,* 619–630.

Adolphs, R., Damasio, H., Tranel, D., & Damasio, A. R. (1996). Cortical systems for the recognition of emotion in facial expressions. *Journal of Neuroscience, 16,* 7678–7687.

Adolphs, R., Tranel, D., & Damasio, A. R. (1998). The human amygdala in social judgment. *Nature, 393,* 470–474.

Adolphs, R., Tranel, D., Damasio, H., & Damasio, A. (1994). Impaired recognition of emotion and facial expressions following bilateral damage to the human amygdala. *Nature, 372,* 669–672.

Adolphs, R., Tranel, D., Damasio, H., & Damasio, A. R. (1995). Fear and the human amygdala. *Journal of Neuroscience, 15,* 5879–5891.

Almagor, M., & Ben-Porath, Y. S. (1989). The two-factor model of self-reported mood: A cross-cultural replication. *Journal of Personality Assessment, 53,* 10–21.

Aristotle. (1954). *Rhetoric* (W. R. Roberts, Trans.). New York: Modern Library.

Arkes, H. (1993). Can emotion supply the place of reason? In G. E. Marcus & R. L. Hanson (Eds.), *Reconsidering the democratic public* (pp. 287–305). University Park: Pennsylvania State University Press.

Armony, J. L., & LeDoux, J. E. (1997). How the brain processes emotional information. *Annals of the New York Academy of Sciences, 821,* 259–270.

Ax, A. (1953). The physiological differentiation between fear and anger in humans. *Psychosomatic Medicine, 15,* 433–422.

Baron, J. (1994). *Thinking and deciding* (2nd ed.). New York: Cambridge University Press.

Barrett, L. F., & Russell, J. A. (1998). Independence and bipolarity in the structure of current affect. *Journal of Personality and Social Psychology, 74,* 967–984.

Bechara, A., Damasio, H., Tranel, D., & Damasio, A. R. (1997). Deciding advantageously before knowing the advantageous strategy. *Science, 175,* 1293–1295.

Bechara, A., Tranel, D., Damasio, H., Adolphs, R., Rockland, C., & Damasio, A. R. (1995). Double dissociation of conditioning and declarative knowledge relative to the amygdala and hippocampus in humans. *Science, 269,* 1115–1118.

Ben-Ze'ev, Aaron. *The subtlety of emotions.* Cambridge, Mass.: MIT Press, 2000.

Bickford, S. (1996). *The dissonance of democracy: listening, conflict, and citizenship.* Ithaca, NY: Cornell University Press.

Bickford, S. (2000, April). *Cultivating citizens: Political perception and the practice of emotion talk.* Paper presented at the annual meeting of the Midwest Political Science Association, Chicago.

Bless, H., Clore, G. L., Schwarz, N., Golisano, V., Rabe, C., & Wölk, M. (1996). Mood and the use of scripts: Does happy mood really lead to mindlessness? *Journal of Personality and Social Psychology, 71,* 665–679.

Bless, H., & Fiedler, K. (1995). Affective states and the influence of activated general knowledge. *Personality and Social Psychology Bulletin, 21,* 766–778.

Bodenhausen, G. V., Kramer, G. P., & Süsser, K. (1994). Happiness and stereotypic thinking in social judgment. *Journal of Personality and Social Psychology, 66,* 621–632.

Bodenhausen, G. V., Sheppard, L. A., & Kramer, G. P. (1994). Negative affect and social judgment: The differential impact of anger and sadness. *European Journal of Social Psychology, 24,* 45–62.

Borod, J. C. (2000). *The neuropsychology of emotion.* New York: Oxford University Press.

Bradley, M. M. (2000). Motivation and emotion. In J. T. Cacioppo, L. G. Tassinary & G. G. Berntson (Eds.), *Handbook of psychophysiology* (pp. 602–642). New York: Cambridge University Press.

Bradley, M. M., Greenwald, M. K., Petry, M. C., & Lang, P. J. (1992). Remembering pictures: Pleasure and arousal in memory. *Journal of Experimental Psychology: Learning, Memory and Cognition, 18,* 379–390.

Breckler, S. J. (1984). Empirical validation of affect, behavior, and cognition as distinct components of attitude. *Journal of Personality and Social Psychology, 47,* 1191–1205.

Burke, E. (1973). *Reflections on the revolution in France.* Garden City, NY: Anchor Books.

Cacioppo, J. T., Berntson, G. G., & Crites, Stephen L. (1996). Social neuroscience: Principles of psychophysiological arousal and response. In T. E. Higgins & A. W. Kruglanski (Eds.), *Social psychology: Handbook of basic principles* (pp. 72–101). New York: Guilford Press.

Cacioppo, J. T., & Gardner, W. L. (1999). Emotion. *Annual Review of Psychology, 50,* 191–214.

Cacioppo, J. T., Gardner, W. L., & Berntson, G. G. (1997). Beyond bipolar conceptualizations and measures: The case of attitudes and evaluative space. *Personality and Social Psychology Review, 1,* 3–25.

Cacioppo, J. T., Gardner, W. L., & Berntson, G. G. (1999). The affect system has parallel and integrative processing components: Form follows function. *Journal of Personality and Social Psychology, 76,* 839–855.

Carver, C. S., & Scheier, M. F. (1990). Origins and functions of positive and negative affect: A control-process view. *Psychological Review, 97,* 19–35.

Carver, C. S., Sutton, S. K., & Scheier, M. F. (2000). Action, emotion, and personality: Emerging conceptual integration. *Personality and Social Psychology Bulletin, 26,* 741–751.

Chaiken, S., & Trope, Y. (Eds.). (1999). *Dual process models in social psychology.* New York: Guilford Press.

Clark, L. A., & Watson, D. (1988). Mood and the mundane: Relations between daily life events and self-reported mood. *Journal of Personality and Social Psychology, 52,* 296–308.

Clore, G. L., Schwarz, N., & Conway, M. (1994). Affective causes and consequences of social information processing. In R. S. Wyer, Jr. & T. K. Srull (Eds.), *Handbook of social cognition* (2nd ed., vol. 1, pp. 323–417). Hillsdale, NJ: Erlbaum.

Conover, P., & Feldman, S. (1986). Emotional reactions to the economy: I'm mad as Hell and I'm not going to take it any more. *American Journal of Political Science, 30,* 30–78.

Cornelius, R. R. (1996). *The science of emotion: Research and tradition in the psychology of emotions.* Upper Saddle River, NJ: Prentice-Hall.

Corr, P. J., Pickering, A. D., & Gray, J. A. (1997). Personality, punishment, and procedural learning: A test of J. A. Gray's anxiety theory. *Journal of Personality and Social Psychology, 73,* 337–344.

Corr, P. J., Wilson, G. D., Fotiadou, M., Kumari, V., Gray, N. S., Checkley, S., Gray, J. A. (1995). Personality and affective modulation of the startle reflex. *Personality and Individual Differences, 19,* 543–553.

Crites, S. L., Fabrigar, L. R., & Petty, R. E. (1994). Measuring the affective and cognitive properties of attitudes: Conceptual and methodological issues. *Personality and Social Psychology Bulletin, 20,* 619–634.

Cuthbert, B. N., Bradley, M. B., & Lang, P. J. (1996). Probing picture perception: Activation and emotion. *Psychophysiology, 33,* 103–111.

Damasio, A. (1994). *Descartes' error: Emotion, reason and the human brain.* New York: Putnam's.

Damasio, A. (1999). *The feeling of what happens: Body and emotion in the making of consciousness.* New York: Harcourt Brace.

Darwin, C. (1998). *The expression of the emotions in man and animals* (3rd ed.). New York: Oxford University Press.

Davidson, R. J. (2000). Affective style, psychopathology, and resilience, brain mechanisms and plasticity. *American Psychologist, 55,* 1196–1214.

Davidson, R. J., Jackson, D. C., & Kalin, N. H. (2000). Emotion, plasticity, context, and regulation: Perspectives from affective neuroscience. *Psychological Bulletin, 126,* 890–909.

Davies, A. F. (1980). *Skills, outlooks and passions: A psychoanalytic contribution to the study of politics.* Cambridge: Cambridge University Press.

Davis, M. (1992). The role of the amygdala in fear and anxiety. *Annual Review of Neuroscience, 15,* 353–375.

Davis, M. (1997). Neurobiology of fear and anxiety. *Annals of the New York Academy of Sciences, 821,* 221–235.

Descartes, R. (1989). *The passions of the soul* (S. H. Voss, Trans.). Indianapolis: Hackett.

Ekman, P. (Ed.). (1982). *Emotion in the human face* (2nd ed.). Cambridge: Cambridge University Press.

Ekman, P. (1984). Expression and the nature of emotion. In P. Ekman & K. Scherer (Eds.), *Approaches to emotion* (pp. 319–343). Hillsdale, NJ: Erlbaum.

Ekman, P. (1992). An argument for basic emotions. *Cognition and Emotion, 6,* 169–200.

Ekman, P., & Davidson, R. J. (Eds.). (1994). *The nature of emotion.* New York: Oxford University Press.

Ekman, P., & Friesen, W. V. (1982). Felt, false, and miserable smiles. *Journal of Personality and Social Psychology, 39,* 1124–1134.

Ekman, P., & Oster, H. (1979). Facial expression of emotion. *Annual Review of Psychology, 30,* 527–554.

Ekman, P., & Rosenberg, E. (Eds.). (1997). *What the face reveals: Basic and applied studies of spontaneous expression using the facial action coding systems (FACS).* New York: Oxford University Press.

Ellsworth, P. (1991). Some implications of cognitive appraisal theories of emotion. In K. T. Strongman (Ed.), *International Review on Studies of Emotion* (pp. 143–161). Cambridge: Cambridge University Press.

Erdley, C. A., & D'Agostino, P. R. (1988). Cognitive and affective components of automatic priming effects. *Journal of Personality and Social Psychology, 54,* 741–747.

Etcoff, N. L. (1986). The neuropsychology of emotional expression. In G. Goldstein & R. E. Tarter (Eds.), *Advances in clinical neuropsychology* (Vol. 3). New York: Plenum.

Fabrigar, L. R., & Petty, R. E. (1999). The role of affective and cognitive bases of attitudes in susceptibility to affectively and cognitively based persuasion. *Personality and Social Psychology Bulletin, 25,* 363–381.

Feldman, L. A. (1995). Valence focus and arousal focus: Individual differences in the structure of affective experience. *Journal of Personality and Social Psychology, 69,* 153–166.

Forgas, J. P. (1994). The role of emotion in social judgments. *European Journal of Social Psychology, 24,* 1–24.

Forgas, J. P. (1995). Mood and judgment: The affect infusion model (AIM). *Psychological Bulletin, 117,* 39–66.

Forgas, J. P., Burnham, D. K., & Trimboli, C. (1988). Mood, memory, and social judgments in children. *Journal of Personality and Social Psychology, 54,* 687–703.

Freud, S. (1961). *Civilization and its discontents* (J. Strachey, Trans.). New York: Norton.

Freud, S. (1962). *Totem and taboo: Some points of agreement between the mental lives of savages and neurotics.* New York: Norton.

Frijda, N. H., Kuipers, P., & Schure, E. T. (1989). Relations among emotion, appraisal, and emotional action readiness. *Journal of Personality and Social Psychology, 57,* 212–228.

George, A. L., & George, J. L. (1998). *Presidential personality and performance.* Boulder, CO: Westview.

George, M. S., Ketter, T. A., Gill, D. S., Haxby, J. V., Ungerleider, L. G., Herscovitch, P., Post, R. M. (1993). Brain regions involved in recognizing facial emotion or identity: An Oxygen-15 PET Study. *Journal of Neuropsychiatric Clinical Neuroscience, 5,* 384–394.

Goleman, D. (1995). *Emotional intelligence: Why it can matter more than IQ.* New York: Bantam Books.

Gray, J. A. (1970). The psychophysiological basis of introversion-extroversion. *Behaviour Research and Therapy, 8,* 249–266.

Gray, J. A. (1973). Causal theories of personality and how to test them. In J. R. Joyce (Ed.), *Multivariate analysis and psychological theory* (pp. 409–463). New York.: Academic Press.

Gray, J. A. (1981). The psychophysiology of anxiety. In R. Lynn (Ed.), *Dimensions of personality: Papers in honour of H. J. Eysenck* (pp. 233–252). New York: Pergamon Press.

Gray, J. A. (1985a). The neuropsychology of anxiety. In C. D. Spielberger (Ed.), *Stress and anxiety* (Vol. 10, pp. 201–227). Washington, DC: Hemisphere.

Gray, J. A. (1985b). A whole and its parts: Behaviour, the brain, cognition, and emotion. *Bulletin of the British Psychological Society, 38,* 99–112.

Gray, J. A. (1987a). The neuropsychology of emotion and personality. In S. M. Stahl, S. D. Iversen & E. C. Goodman (Eds.), *Cognitive neurochemistry* (pp. 171–190). Oxford: Oxford University Press.

Gray, J. A. (1987b). *The psychology of fear and stress* (2nd ed.). Cambridge: Cambridge University Press.

Gray, J. A. (1990). Brain systems that mediate both emotion and cognition. *Cognition and Emotion, 4,* 269–288.

Gray, J. A., & McNaughton, N. (2000). *The neuropsychology of anxiety: An enquiry into the functions of the septo-hippocampal system* (2nd ed.). New York: Oxford University Press.

Green, D. P., Goldman, S. L., & Salovey, P. (1993). Measurement error masks bipolarity in affect ratings. *Journal of Personality and Social Psychology, 64,* 1029–1041.

Green, D. P., & Salovey, P. (1999). In what sense are positive and negative affect independent? *Psychological Science, 10,* 304–306.

Green, D. P., Salovey, P., & Truax, K. M. (1999). Static, dynamic, and causative bipolarity of affect. *Journal of Personality and Social Psychology, 76,* 856–867.

Greene, J. D., Sommerville, R. B., Nystrom, L. E., Darley, J. M., & Cohen, J. D. (2001). An fMRI investigation of emotional engagement in moral judgment. *Science, 293*(5537), 2105–2108.

Greene, S. (1998, April). Affective and cognitive components of partisanship: A new approach. Paper presented to the annual meeting of the Midwest Political Science Association, Chicago.

Hatfield, E., Cacioppo, J. T., & Rapson, R. L. (1994). *Emotional contagion*. Cambridge: Cambridge University Press.

Hirschman, A. O. (1977). *The passions and the interests: Political arguments for capitalism before its triumph*. Princeton: Princeton University Press.

Hobbes, T. (1968). *Leviathan*. London: Penguin Books.

Hume, D. (1975). *Enquiries concerning human understanding and concerning the principles of morals* (3rd ed.). Oxford: Clarendon Press.

Hume, D. (1984). *A treatise of human nature*. London: Penguin Books.

Ingram, R. E. (1989). Affective confounds in social-cognitive research. *Journal of Personality and Social Psychology, 57,* 715–722.

Isen, A. M. (1993). Positive affect and decision making. In M. Lewis & J. E. Haviland (Eds.), *Handbook of emotions* (pp. 261–277). New York: Guilford Press.

Ito, T. A., Cacioppo, J. T., & Lang, P. J. (1998). Eliciting affect using the international affective picture system: Trajectories through evaluative space. *Personality and Social Psychology Bulletin, 24,* 855–879.

Ito, T. A., Larsen, J. T., Smith, N. K., & Cacioppo, J. T. (1998). Negative information weighs more heavily on the brain: The negativity bias in evaluative categorizations. *Journal of Personality and Social Psychology, 75,* 887–900.

Janis, I. L. (1982). *Groupthink* (2nd ed.). Boston: Houghton Mifflin.

Janis, I. L., & Mann, L. (1977). *Decision making*. New York: Free Press.

Jeannerod, M. (1997). *The cognitive neuroscience of action*. Cambridge, MA: Blackwell.

Johnson, E. J., & Tversky, A. (1983). Affect, generalization, and the perception of risk. *Journal of Personality and Social Psychology, 45,* 20–31.

Kahneman, D., Slovic, P., & Tversky, A. (1982). *Judgment under uncertainty: Heuristics and biases*. Cambridge: Cambridge University Press.

Kern, M. (1989). *30-second politics: Political advertising in the eighties*. New York: Westport.

Kinder, D. R. (1994). Reason and emotion in American political life. In R. Schank & E. Langer (Eds.), *Beliefs, reasoning, and decision-making: Psycho-logic in honor of Bob Abelson* (pp. 277–314). Hillsdale, NJ: Erlbaum.

Kinder, D. R., Abelson, R. P., & Fiske, S. T. (1979). *Developmental research on candidate instrumentation: Results and recommendations*. Technical Report submitted to the Board of Overseers, National Election Studies, Ann Arbor, MI.

Kornhauser, W. (1959). *The politics of mass society*. Glencoe, IL: Free Press.

Koziak, B. (2000). *Retrieving political emotion: Thumos, Aristotle, and gender*. University Park: Pennsylvania State University Press.

Kuklinski, J. H., Riggle, E., Ottati, V., Schwarz, N., & Wyer, R. S., Jr. (1991). The cognitive and affective bases of political tolerance judgments. *American Journal of Political Science, 35,* 1–27.

Kunst-Wilson, W. R., & Zajonc, R. B. (1980). Affect discrimination of stimuli cannot be recognized. *Science, 207,* 557–558.

Lane, R. D., Nadel, L., & Ahern, G. (2000). *Cognitive neuroscience of emotion*. New York: Oxford University Press.

Lang, A. (Ed.). (1994). *Measuring psychological responses to media*. Hillsdale, NJ: Lawrence Erlbaum.

Lang, P. J., Greenwald, M. K., Bradley, M. M., & Hamm, A. O. (1993). Looking at pictures: Affective, facial, visceral and behavioral reactions. *Psychophysiology, 30,* 261–273.

Larsen, R. J., & Diener, E. (1992). Promises and problems with the circumplex model of emotion. In M. S. Clark (Ed.), *Emotion* (pp. 25–59). Newbury Park, CA: Sage.

Lau, R. R., & Sears, D. O. (1986). An introduction to political cognition. In R. R. Lau & D. O. Sears (Eds.), *Political cognition* (pp. 3–8). Hillsdale, NJ: Erlbaum.

Lazarus, R. (1982). Thoughts on the relations of emotion and cognition. *American Psychologist, 37,* 1019–1024.

Lazarus, R. (1984). On the primacy of cognition. *American Psychologist, 39,* 124–129.

LeDoux, J. E. (1991). Emotion and the limbic system concept. *Concepts in Neuroscience, 2,* 169–199.

LeDoux, J. E. (1992). Brain mechanisms of emotion and emotional learning. *Current Opinion in Neurobiology, 2,* 191–198.

LeDoux, J. E. (1993b). Emotional networks in the brain. In M. Lewis & J. M. Haviland (Eds.), *Handbook of emotions* (pp. 109–118). New York: Guilford Press.

LeDoux, J. E. (1993a). Emotional memory systems in the brain. *Behavioural Brain Research, 58,* 68–79.

LeDoux, J. E. (1995). Emotion: Clues from the brain. *Annual Review of Psychology, 46,* 209–235.

LeDoux, J. E. (1996). *The emotional brain: The mysterious underpinnings of emotional life.* New York: Simon and Schuster.

LeDoux, J. E., Romanski, L., & Xagoraris, A. (1989). Indelibility of subcortical emotional memories. *Journal of Cognitive Neuroscience, 1,* 238–243.

Leighton, S. R. (1996). Aristotle and the emotions. In A. O. Rorty (Ed.), *Aristotle's Rhetoric* (pp. 206–237). Berkeley, CA: University of California Press.

Libet, B. (1985). Unconscious cerebral initiative and the role of conscious will in voluntary action. *Behavioral and Brain Sciences, 8,* 529–566.

Libet, B., Gleason, C. A., Wright, E. W., & Pearl, D. K. (1983). Time of conscious intention to act in relation to onset of cerebral activity (readiness-potential). *Brain, 106,* 623–642.

Libet, B., Pearl, D. K., Morledge, D., Gleason, C. A., Morledge, Y., & Barbaro, N. (1991). Control of the transition from sensory detection to sensory awareness in man by the duration of a thalamic stimulus. *Brain, 114,* 1731–1757.

Libet, B., Wright, J., Elwood W., Feinstein, B., & Pearl, D. K. (1979). Subjective referral of the timing for a conscious sensory experience. *Brain, 102,* 1597–1600.

Locke, J. (1993). *Two treatises of government.* London: Everyman.

Lodge, M. G., McGraw, K. M., & Stroh, P. (1989). An impression-driven model of candidate evaluation. *American Political Science Review, 83,* 399–420.

Loewenstein, G. F., Weber, E. U., Hsee, C. K., & Welch, N. (2001). Risk as feelings. *Psychological Bulletin, 127,* 267–286.

Lutz, C. (1988). *Unnatural emotions: Everyday sentiments on a Micronesian atoll and their challenge to Western theory.* Chicago: University of Chicago Press.

MacKuen, M., Marcus, G. E., Neuman, W. R., Keele, L., & Wolak, J. (2001, August). *Emotions, information, and political cooperation.* Paper presented to the annual meeting of the American Political Science Association, San Francisco.

MacKuen, M., Neuman, W. R., & Marcus, G. E. (2000, August). *Affective intelli-*

gence, voting, and matters of public policy. Paper presented to the annual meeting of the American Political Science Association, Washington, DC.

MacLean, P. D. (1990). *The Triune brain in evolution.* New York: Plenum Press.

Madison, J., Hamilton, A., & Jay, J. (1961). *The Federalist papers.* Cleveland: World.

Marcus, G. E. (1988). The structure of emotional response: 1984 Presidential candidates. *American Political Science Review, 82,* 735–761.

Marcus, G. E. (1991). Emotions and politics: Hot cognitions and the rediscovery of passion. *Social Science Information, 30,* 195–232.

Marcus, G. E. (2000). Emotions in politics. In N. W. Polsby (Ed.), *Annual Review in Political Science* (Vol. 3, pp. 221–250). Palo Alto, CA: Annual Reviews.

Marcus, G. E. (2002). *The sentimental citizen: Emotion in democratic politics.* University Park: Pennsylvania State University Press.

Marcus, G. E., & MacKuen, M. (1993). Anxiety, enthusiasm and the vote: The emotional underpinnings of learning and involvement during presidential campaigns. *American Political Science Review, 87,* 688–701.

Marcus, G. E., Neuman, W. R., & MacKuen, M. B. (2000). *Affective intelligence and political judgment.* Chicago: University of Chicago Press.

Marcus, G. E., & Rahn, W. (1990). Emotions and democratic politics. In S. Long (Ed.), *Research in micropolitics* (pp. 29–57). Greenwich, CT: JAI Press.

Marcus, G. E., Sullivan, J. L., Theiss-Morse, E., Flathman, M., & Healy, S. (1990, April). *Political tolerance and threat: Affective and cognitive influences.* Paper presented to the Annual Meetings of the Midwest Political Science Association. Chicago.

Marcus, G. E., Sullivan, J. L., Theiss-Morse, E., & Wood, S. (1995). *With malice toward some: How people make civil liberties judgments.* New York: Cambridge University Press.

Marcus, G. E., Wood, S. L., & Theiss-Morse, E. (1998). Linking neuroscience to political intolerance and political judgment. *Politics and the Life Science, 17,* 165–178.

Masters, R. D. (1991). Individual and cultural differences in response to leaders' nonverbal displays. *Journal of Social Issues, 47,* 151–165.

Masters, R. D., Frey, S., & Bente, G. (1991). Dominance & attention: Images of leaders in German, French, and American TV news. *Polity, 23,* 373–394.

Masters, R. D., & Sullivan, D. G. (1989). Facial displays and political leadership in France. *Behavioral Processes, 19,* 1–30.

Masters, R. D., & Sullivan, D. (1993). Nonverbal behavior and leadership: Emotion and cognition in political attitudes. In S. Iyengar & W. McGuire (Eds.), *Explorations in political psychology.* Durham, NC: Duke University Press.

Masters, R. D., & Way, B. (1996). Experimental methods and attitudes toward leaders: Nonverbal displays, emotion, and cognition. In S. Peterson & A. Somit (Eds.), *Research in biopolitics* (Vol. 4, pp. 61–98). Greenwich, CT: JAI Press.

Mauro, R., Sato, K., & Tucker, J. (1992). The role of appraisal in human emotions: A cross-cultural study. *Journal of Personality and Social Psychology, 62,* 301–317.

Mayer, J. D., & Gaschke, Y. N. (1988). The experience and meta-experience of mood. *Journal of Personality and Social Psychology, 55,* 102–111.

Mayer, J. D., Gaschke, Y., Braverman, D., & Evans, T. (1992). Mood congruent judgment is a general effect. *Journal of Personality and Social Psychology, 63,* 119–132.

McCrae, R. R., & Costa, P. T., Jr. (1989). The structure of interpersonal traits: Wiggin's circumplex and the five-factor model. *Journal of Personality and Social Psychology, 56,* 586–595.

McHugo, G. J., Lanzetta, J. T., Sullivan, D. G., Masters, R. D., & Englis, B. (1985). Emotional reactions to expressive displays of a political leader. *Journal of Personality and Social Psychology, 49,* 1512–1529.

Meyer, G. J., & Shack, J. R. (1989). Structural convergence of mood and personality: Evidence for old and new directions. *Journal of Personality and Social Psychology, 57,* 691–706.

Mikula, G., Scherer, K. R., & Athenstaedt, U. (1998). The role of injustice in the elicitation of differential emotional reactions. *Personality and Social Psychology Bulletin, 24,* 769–783.

Millar, M. G., & Tesser, A. (1986). Effects of affective and cognitive focus on the attitude-behavior relation. *Journal of Personality and Social Psychology, 51,* 270–276.

Mischel, W., & Shoda, Y. (1995). A cognitive-affective system theory of personality: Reconceptualizing situations, dispositions, dynamics, and invariance in personality structure. *Psychological Review, 102,* 246–268.

Mishkin, M., & Appenzeller, T. (1987). The anatomy of memory. *Scientific American, 256,* 80–89.

Montagu, J. (1994). *The expression of the passions: The origin and influence of Charles Le Brun's conference Sur L'Expression Generale Et Particuliere.* New Haven: Yale University Press.

Moreland, R. L., & Zajonc, R. B. (1979). Exposure effects may not depend on stimulus recognition. *Journal of Personality and Social Psychology, 37,* 1085–1089.

Nisbett, R., & Ross, L. (1982). *Human inference: Strategies and shortcomings of social judgment.* Englewood Cliffs, NJ: Prentice-Hall.

Nørretranders, T. (1998). *The user illusion* (J. Sydenham, Trans.). New York: Viking.

Nussbaum, M. C. (1994). *The therapy of desire: Theory and practice in Hellenistic ethics.* Princeton: Princeton University Press.

Nussbaum, M. C. (1996). Aristotle on emotions and rational persuasion. In A. O. Rorty (Ed.), *Aristotle's Rhetoric* (pp. 303–323). Berkeley: University of California Press.

Nussbaum, M. C. (2001). *Upheavals of thought: The intelligence of emotions.* Cambridge: Cambridge University Press.

Okin, S. (1989). Reason and feelings in thinking about justice. *Ethics, 99,* 229–249.

Ortony, A., Clore, G. L., & Collins, A. (1989). *The cognitive structure of emotions.* New York: Cambridge University Press.

Osgood, C. E., Suci, G. J., & Tannenbaum, P. H. (1957). *The measurement of meaning.* Urbana: University of Illinois Press.

Ottati, V. C. (1988, August). The cognitive and affective determinants of political judgments. Paper presented to the *American Political Science Association Annual Meeting.* Washington, DC.

Ottati, V. C., & Isbell, L. M. (1996). Effects of mood during exposure to target information on subsequently reported judgments: An on-line model of misattribution and correction. *Journal of Personality and Social Psychology, 71,* 39–53.

Ottati, V. C., Riggle, E. J., Wyer, R. S., Jr., Schwarz, N., & Kuklinski, J. (1989). Cognitive and affective bases of opinion survey responses. *Journal of Personality and Social Psychology, 57,* 404–415.

Ottati, V. C., Steenbergen, M. R., & Riggle, E. (1992). The cognitive and affective components of political attitudes: Measuring the determinants of candidate evaluations. *Political Behavior, 14,* 423–442.

Ottati, V. C., & Wyer, R. S., Jr. (1993). Affect and political judgment. In S. Iyengar & W. McGuire (Eds.), *Explorations in political judgment* (pp. 296–320). Durham, NC: Duke University Press.

Panksepp, J. (1991). Affective neuroscience: A conceptual framework for the neurobiological study of emotions. In K. T. Strongman (Ed.), *International review of studies on emotion* (Vol. 1, pp. 59–99). New York: Wiley.

Parkinson, B. (1997). Untangling the appraisal-emotion connection. *Personality and Social Psychology Review, 1,* 62–79.

Parkinson, B., & Manstead, A. S. R. (1992). Appraisal as a cause of emotion. In M. S. Clark (Ed.), *Emotion* (pp. 122–149). Newbury Park, CA: Sage.

Petty, R. E., & Cacioppo, J. T. (1986). *Communication and persuasion: Central and peripheral routes to attitude change.* New York: Springer-Verlag.

Petty, R. E., Gleicher, F., & Baker, S. M. (1991). Multiple roles for affect in persuasion. In J. P. Forgas (Ed.), *Emotion and social judgments* (pp. 181–199). Oxford: Pergamon Press.

Pickering, A. D., & Gray, J. A. (1999). The neuroscience of personality. In L. A. Pervin & O. P. John (Eds.), *Handbook of personality: Theory and research* (2nd ed., pp. 277–299). New York: Guilford Press.

Plato. (1974). *The republic* (D. Lee, Trans.). (2nd ed.). New York: Penquin.

Plutchik, R. (1980a). *Emotion: A psychoevolutionary synthesis.* New York: Harper and Row.

Plutchik, R. (1980b). A general psychoevolutionary theory of emotion. In R. Plutchik & H. Kellerman (Eds.), *Emotion: Theory, research and experience: Theories of emotion* (Vol. 1, pp. 3–34). San Diego, CA: Academic Press.

Plutchik, R., & Kellerman, H. (Eds.). (1989). *Emotion theory, research, and experience: The measurement of emotions* (Vol. 4). San Diego, CA: Academic Press.

Post, J. M. (1993). Current concepts of the narcissistic personality: Implications for political psychology. *Political Psychology, 14,* 99–121.

Rahn, W. (2001). Affect as information: The role of public mood in political reasoning. In A. Lupia, M. McCubbins, & S. Popkin (Eds.), *Elements of reason: Cognition, choice, and the bounds of rationality* (pp. 130–150). New York: Cambridge University Press.

Rawls, J. (1971). *A theory of justice.* Cambridge, MA: Harvard University Press.

Remington, N. A., Fabrigrar, L. R., & Visser, P. S. (2000). Reexamining the circumplex model of affect. *Journal of Social Psychology, 79,* 286–300.

Renshon, S. A. (1998). *The psychological assessment of presidential candidates.* New York: Routledge.

Rogow, A. A. (1963). *James Forrestal, a study of personality, politics, and policy.* New York: Macmillan.

Rolls, E. T. (1999). *The brain and emotion.* New York: Oxford University Press.

Rorty, A. O. (1982). From passions to emotions to sentiments. *Philosophy, 57,* 159–172.

Rorty, A. O. (1985). Varieties of rationality, varieties of emotion. *Social Science Information, 24,* 343–353.

Rorty, A. O. (1993). From passions to sentiments: The structure of Hume's "Treatise." *History of Philosophy Quarterly, 10,* 165–179.

Rorty, A. O. (Ed.). (1996). *Aristotle's Rhetoric*. Berkeley: University of California Press.

Roseman, I. J. (1979, August). *Cognitive aspects of emotion and emotional behavior*. Paper presented at the Eighty-seventh Annual Convention of the American Psychological Association, New York.

Roseman, I. J. (1984). Cognitive determinants of emotions: A structural theory. In P. Shaver (Ed.), *Review of personality and social psychology* (Vol. 5), pp. 11–36, Beverly Hills, CA: Sage.

Roseman, I. J. (1991). Appraisal determinants of discrete emotions. *Cognition and Emotion, 5*, 161–200.

Roseman, I. J., Antoniou, A. A., & Jose, P. E. (1996). Appraisal determinants of emotions: Constructing a more accurate and comprehensive theory. *Cognition and Emotion, 10*, 241–277.

Rothschild, E. (2001). *Economic sentiments: Adam Smith, Condorcet, and the Enlightenment*. Cambridge, MA: Harvard University Press.

Russell, J. A. (1980). A circumplex model of affect. *Journal of Personality and Social Psychology, 39*, 1161–1178.

Russell, J. A. (1983). Pancultural aspects of human conceptual organization of emotions. *Journal of Personality and Social Psychology, 45*, 1281–1288.

Russell, J. A., & Barrett, L. F. (1999). Core affect, prototypical emotional episodes, and other things called *emotion*: Dissecting the elephant. *Journal of Personality and Social Psychology, 76*, 805–819.

Russell, J. A., & Carroll, J. M. (1999a). On the bipolarity of positive and negative affect. *Psychological Bulletin, 125*, 3–30.

Russell, J. A., & Carroll, J. M. (1999b). The Phoenix of bipolarity: Reply to Watson and Tellegen (1999). *Psychological Bulletin, 125*, 611–617.

Russell, J. A., Lewicka, M., & Niit, T. (1989). A cross-cultural study of a circumplex model of affect. *Journal of Personality and Social Psychology, 57*, 848–856.

Russell, J. A., Weiss, A., & Mendelsohn, G. A. (1989). Affect grid: A single-item scale of pleasure and arousal. *Journal of Personality and Social Psychology, 57*, 493–502.

Rusting, C. L., & Larsen, R. L. (1995). Moods as sources of stimulation: Relationships between personality and desired mood states. *Personality and Individual Differences, 18*, 321–329.

Sartori, G. (1987). *The theory of democracy revisited*. Chatham, NJ: Chatham House.

Scanlan, J. P. (1959). The *Federalist* and human nature. *Review of Politics, 21*, 657–677.

Schacter, D. L. (1996). *Searching for memory*. New York: Basic Books.

Scherer, K. R., Schorr, A., & Johnstone, T. (2001). *Appraisal processes in emotion: Theory, methods, research*. New York: Oxford University Press.

Schwarz, N. (1990). Feelings as information: Informational and motivational functions of affective states. In R. Sorrentino & E. T. Higgins (Eds.), *Handbook of motivation and cognition: Foundations of social behavior* (Vol. 2, pp. 527–561). New York: Guilford.

Schwarz, N., & Bless, H. (1991). Happy and mindless, but sad and smart? The impact of affective states on analytic reasoning. In J. Forgas (Ed.), *Emotion and social judgments* (pp. 55–71). New York: Pergamon Press.

Schwarz, N., & Clore, G. L. (1983). Mood, misattribution, and judgments of well-being: Informative and directive functions of affective states. *Journal of Personality and Social Psychology, 45*, 513–523.

Schwarz, N., & Clore, G. L. (1996). Feelings and phenomenal experiences. In E. T. Higgins & A. W. Kruglanski (Eds.), *Social psychology: Handbook of basic principles* (pp. 433–464). New York: Guilford.

Scott, S. K., Young, A. W., Calder, A. J., Hellawell, D. J., Aggleton, J. P., & Johnson, M. (1997). Impaired auditory recognition of fear and anger following bilateral amgydala lesions. *Nature, 385,* 254–257.

Sears, D. O. (1993). Symbolic politics: A socio-psychological theory. In S. Iyengar & W. J. McGuire (Eds.), *Explorations in political psychology* (pp. 113–149). Durham, NC: Duke University Press.

Sears, D. O. (2000). The role of affect in symbolic politics. In J. Kuklinski (Ed.), *Citizens and politics: Perspective from political psychology.* New York: Cambridge University Press.

Sears, D. O., Hensler, C., & Speer, L. (1979). Whites' opposition to "busing": Self-interest or symbolic politics? *American Political Science Review, 73,* 369–385.

Sears, D. O., Lau, R. R., Tyler, T. R., & Allen, H. M., Jr. (1980). Self-interest vs. symbolic politics in policy attitudes and presidential voting. *American Political Science Review, 74,* 670–684.

Smith, A. (1959). *The theory of moral sentiments.* Indianapolis: Liberty Fund.

Smith, A. (1986). *The wealth of nations: Books 1–3.* New York: Viking.

Smith, C. A. (1989). Dimensions of appraisal and physiological response in emotion. *Journal of Personality and Social Psychology, 56,* 339–353.

Smith, C. A., Haynes, K. N., Lazarus, R. S., & Pope, L. K. (1993). In search of the "hot" cognitions: Attributions, appraisals, and their relation to emotion. *Journal of Personality and Social Psychology, 65,* 916–929.

Squire, L. R. (1987). *Memory and brain.* New York: Oxford University Press.

Stangor, C., Sullivan, L. A., & Ford, T. E. (1991). Affective and cognitive determinants of prejudice. *Social Cognition, 9,* 359–391.

Stanton, M. E. (2000). Multiple memory systems, development and conditioning. *Behavioral Brain Research, 110,* 25–37.

Steinberger, P. J. (1993). *The concept of political judgment.* Chicago: University of Chicago Press.

Stiker, G. (1996). Emotions in context: Aristotle's treatment of the passions in the *Rhetoric* and his moral psychology. In A. O. Rorty (Ed.), *Aristotle's Rhetoric* (pp. 286–302). Berkeley: University of California Press.

Storm, C., & Storm, T. (1987). A taxonomic study of the vocabulary of emotions. *Journal of Personality and Social Psychology, 53,* 805–816.

Sullivan, D., & Masters, R. (1988). Happy warriors: Leaders' facial displays, viewers emotions, and political support. *American Journal of Political Science, 32,* 345–368.

Tellegen, A., Watson, D., & Clark, L. A. (1999a). Further support for a hierarchical model of affect. *Psychological Science, 10,* 307–309.

Tellegen, A., Watson, D., & Clark, L. A. (1999b). On the dimensional and hierarchical structure of affect. *Psychological Science, 10,* 297–303.

Tomarken, A. J., Davidson, R. J., Wheeler, R. E., & Doss, R. C. (1992). Individual differences in anterior brain asymmetry and fundamental dimensions of emotion. *Journal of Personality and Social Psychology, 62,* 676–687.

Tooby, J., & Cosmides, L. (1990a). On the universality of human nature and the uniqueness of the individual: The role of genetics and adaptation. *Journal of Personality, 58,* 17–67.

Tooby, J., & Cosmides, L. (1990b). The past explains the present: Emotional adaptations and the structure of ancestral environments. *Ethology and Sociobiology, 11,* 375–424.

Tranel, D., Damasio, H., & Damasio, A. R. (1995). Double dissociation between overt and covert face recognition. *Journal of Cognitive Neuroscience, 7,* 425–432.

Volkan, V. D., & Itkowitz, N. (1984). *The immortal Ataturk: A psychobiography.* Chicago: University of Chicago Press.

Volkan, V. D., Itkowitz, N., & Dod, A. W. (1997). *Richard Nixon: A psychobiography.* New York: Cambridge University Press.

Watson, D. (1988a). Intraindividual and interindividual analyses of positive and negative affect: Their relation to health complaints, perceived stress, and daily activities. *Journal of Personality and Social Psychology, 54,* 1020–1030.

Watson, D. (1988b). The vicissitudes of mood measurement: Effects of varying descriptors, time frames, and response formats on measures of positive and negative affect. *Journal of Personality and Social Psychology, 55,* 128–141.

Watson, D., & Clark, L. A. (1992a). Affects separable and inseparable: On the hierarchical arrangement of the negative affects. *Journal of Personality and Social Psychology, 62,* 489–505.

Watson, D., & Clark, L. A. (1992b). On traits and temperament: General and specific factors of emotional experience and their relation to the five-factor model. *Journal of Personality, 60,* 441–476.

Watson, D., Clark, L. A., & Tellegen, A. (1984). Cross-cultural convergence in the structure of mood: A Japanese replication and a comparison with U. S. findings. *Journal of Personality and Social Psychology, 47,* 127–144.

Watson, D., Clark, L. A., & Tellegen, A. (1988). Development and validation of brief measures of positive and negative affect: The PANAS scales. *Journal of Personality and Social Psychology, 54,* 1063–1070.

Watson, D., & Tellegen, A. (1985). Toward a consensual structure of mood. *Psychological Bulletin, 98,* 219–235.

Watson, D., & Tellegen, A. (1999). Issues in the dimensional structure of affect—effects of descriptors, measurement error, and response formats: Comment on Russell and Carroll (1999). *Psychological Bulletin, 125,* 601–610.

Watson, D., Wiese, D., Vaidya, J., & Tellegen, A. (1999). The two general activation systems of affect: Structural findings, evolutionary considerations, and psychobiological evidence. *Journal of Personality and Social Psychology, 76,* 820–838.

White, M. (1987). *Philosophy, the Federalist, and the Constitution.* New York: Oxford University Press.

Williams, B. A. O. (1983). *Moral luck: Philosophical papers, 1973–1980.* Cambridge; Cambridge University Press.

Wilson, G. D., Kumari, V., Gray, J. A., & Corr, P. J. (2000). The role of neuroticism in startle reactions to fearful and disgusting stimuli. *Personality and Individual Differences, 29,* 1077–1082.

Young, I. M. (1990). *Justice and the politics of difference.* Princeton, NJ: Princeton University Press.

Zajonc, R. B. (1980). Feeling and thinking: Preferences need no inferences. *American Psychologist, 35,* 151–175.

Zajonc, R. B. (1982). On the primacy of affect. *American Psychologist, 39,* 117–123.

Zajonc, R. B. (1998). Emotions. In D. Gilbert, S. Fiske & G. Lindzey (Eds.), *Hand-*

book of social psychology (4th ed., Vol. 1, pp. 591–632). New York: McGraw Hill.

Zimmermann, M. (1989). The nervous system in the context of information theory. In R. F. Schmidt & G. Thews (Eds.), *Human physiology* (2nd ed., pp. 166–173). Berlin: Springler-Verlag.

Zola-Morgan, S. M., Squire, L. R., Alvarez-Royo, P., & Clower, R. P. (1991). Independent of memory functions and emotional behavior: Separate contributions of the hippocampal formation and the amygdala. *Hippocampus, 1,* 207–270.

Zuckerman, M. (1991). *Psychobiology of personality*. Cambridge: Cambridge University Press.

7 Michael Billig

Political Rhetoric

The term "rhetoric" has a dual meaning in that it can refer both to the ways that speakers try to persuade audiences and to the academic study of oratorical persuasion. Consequently, "political rhetoric" can denote both the oratory that politicians might use and the study of such oratory. This duality is nothing new but dates from the earliest times of rhetoric's long history. In ancient Greece, the Sophists taught rhetoric as a practical discipline, claiming that their courses of instruction would equip pupils with the skills of persuasion. By contrast, Aristotle (1909) approached the topic of rhetoric in an analytic spirit, claiming in *Rhetorica* that the function of rhetoric was "not to persuade, but to discover the available means of persuasion in each case" (p. 5). Aristotle laid the foundations for the study of rhetoric that was to be a vital part of European education from Roman times until the nineteenth century and was to be profoundly influential in the Islamic world during the Middle Ages (Vickers, 1988). Aristotle distinguished between three forms of oratory: deliberative or political oratory; forensic oratory, as practiced in the law courts; and epideictic oratory, which comprised the speeches of praise delivered at the funerals of notable figures. According to Aristotle, different forms of persuasive strategy would be required for these different types of oratory. In particular Aristotle emphasized three factors to which the orator needed to pay attention: *ethos*, *pathos*, and *logos*. Ethos referred to the character the speaker wished to present; pathos was the mood or tone of the speech; and logos was the argument the speaker was advancing.

Over the past 150 years, rhetoric has ceased to be a central discipline in Western education. Much of its subject matter as an academic inquiry was taken over by new emerging disciplines such as linguistics, sociology, and psychology. For a while it seemed as if rhetoric as a discipline might entirely disappear. Nevertheless, in the mid–twentieth century there was a revival of rhetoric, notably in the writings of Kenneth Burke and Chaim Perelman (see Burke, 1969; Perelman & Olbrechts-Tyteca, 1971). More recently, this revival has been continued in a number of directions, for example, the rhetoric of inquiry movement and the construction of a new discursive/rhetorical psychology; also the traditions of American and European rhetorical study have continued to develop (for the rhetoric of inquiry, see Nelson, Megill, & McCloskey, 1987; McCloskey, 1986; more generally, see Simons, 1989, 1990; Mailloux, 1996; Meyer, 1994; Myerson, 1994; Plett, 1995). The history of rhetoric, and particularly its recent revival, is mentioned because this chapter will not merely treat political rhetoric as a topic to be studied by the discipline of social psychology. It will suggest that the topic of political persuasion calls for a psychological approach that is itself rooted within the study of rhetoric. Consequently, this chapter will discuss the discursive or rhetorical approach to psychology that has been developed in the past 15 or so years. This way of doing psychology poses a challenge to more traditional approaches but has, it will be argued, particular advantages for understanding the nature of political rhetoric.

▶ *The Yale Studies of Persuasion*

Experimental social psychology offered the promise that the great questions of traditional rhetoric might be finally settled. Scientific evidence might be produced to determine when, for instance, pathos might be effective or to estimate how important a speaker's ethos might be. This was the thinking behind the pathbreaking studies of attitude change, known as the Yale studies, that Brewster Smith has described as constituting the new rhetoric (Smith, 1981, p. xii). This research owed its origins to a practical, political question. During World War II, Carl Hovland was commissioned by the Information and Education Division of the United States War Department to conduct research into the effectiveness of propaganda films. The War Department wanted to prepare propaganda films to persuade the troops that the war still might continue for a long time. However, the Department was unsure whether the films should only present the point of view to be communicated or whether the films should present and then refute counterarguments. Hovland produced both types of film and tested the attitudes of viewers before and after watching the films. His results suggested that two-sided messages were more effective with better-educated audiences. He and his coworkers then tested the relative effects of several rhetorical variables relating to pathos and ethos, examining, for instance, fear messages and the effects of communicator credibility. The research program was continued after the war at Yale University (Hovland, Janis, & Kelley, 1953; Hovland, Lumsdaine, & Sheffield, 1949; Hovland & Weiss, 1951). In the later studies, many of the stimuli were not political, although some of the studies remained rooted in issues of political rhetoric (Sherif & Hovland, 1961).

The Yale research program had aimed to discover general laws of persuasion. In the event, the program produced a mass of unintegrated findings (see, for instance, critical summaries by Fisbein & Azjen, 1981; Jaspars, 1978). The problem had been that each general statement seemed to demand a qualification, as exceptions were found for each finding (Billig, 1987, pp. 69–72). For instance, Hovland and Weiss (1951) had hoped to show that high credibility (or good "ethos") increased persuasion. Their results showed that on some topics with certain audiences, the low-credibility source could be more effective. Part of the problem was that the research was not based on a psychological theory of thinking that could be used to make sense of the disparate findings. The strategy had been to treat the rhetorical variables as independent variables and to discover their effect on the dependent variable of attitude-change. The intervening psychological processes tended not to be investigated. As such, the Yale research tended to assume a separation between the independent or rhetorical variables and the psychology of the recipients.

Two important lines of experimental attitude research suggested that the relationship between political message and audience can be seen as a form of rhetorical dialogue in which the nature of argumentation is crucial. William McGuire's (1964) "inoculation theory," like the Yale studies, stemmed from a practical issue. In McGuire's case the problem was the potential brainwashing of American soldiers taken prisoner by communist troops in the Far East. There had been persistent rumors that captured soldiers could be turned into communist supporters by techniques of intensive propaganda. The American military were keen to develop psychological techniques to counter the effects of such propaganda. McGuire hypothesized that those most at risk from political propaganda were those whose basic ideological beliefs had never been challenged, just as those who lived in "germ-free" environments never built up antibodies against future infection. McGuire's experiments demonstrated that subjects will be more resistant to propaganda challenges if they are previously exposed to small "doses" of propaganda that provoke them to create or look for counterarguments. Armed with counterarguments, recipients are better equipped to resist the appeals of propaganda. In effect, McGuire's research was pointing to the importance of the Aristotelian notion of logos or rhetorical argument: argumentation was a property not merely of the message but also of the recipients' thought processes. Thus McGuire's research depicted the relationship between message and recipient as being deeply rhetorical, based on the clash of argument and counterargument, or, to use the terminology of classical rhetoric, logos and anti-logos (Billig, 1987).

The second line of research that was implicitly moving the tradition of the Yale studies toward a more rhetorical psychology was Petty and Cacioppo's elaboration likelihood model (e.g., Petty & Cacioppo, 1981, 1984). The model suggested that there are two routes to persuasion—the peripheral and the central. Basically the two routes matched classical rhetoric's distinction between persuasion by content and persuasion by form. Petty and Cacioppo postulated that when recipients are interested in a topic they will be influenced by the strength of an argument, or what in classical rhetoric was known as logos. In this central route to persuasion, recipients are likely to elaborate on the arguments of a message, developing counterarguments if the message is weak. When uninterested in the topic, recipients will be more likely to be influenced by the "peripheral route." This latter type of influence, according to Petty and Cacioppo's model, was shallower and less enduring. The peripheral route concerned matters of presentation, such as celebrity endorsement or use of humor. Such variables reflect the traditional concepts of ethos and pathos, for they relate to the character of the presenter or the form of delivery rather than the content of the message. The model has been primarily applied to commercial advertising but is equally applicable to political advertising. Not only are political advertisements produced by the same commercial agencies, but similar techniques, including celebrity endorsements, are employed (Devlin, 1995; Scammell & Semetko, 1995), although, as Pardo (2001) has shown in an analysis of political advertising in Venezuela, much political advertising can be directed toward discrediting opponents. In common with McGuire's inoculation model, the elaboration likelihood model assumes that recipients, at least when interested in a topic, will respond to a message with argumentation. Moreover, it assumes that the thinking of respondents will develop through argumentation. Again the assumption is that thinking can be intrinsically rhetorical (Billig, 1987).

▲ The Nature of Contemporary Political Oratory

It is arguable that the traditional distinctions between the form and the content of a message are hard to maintain in contemporary politics, and this would affect the direct applicability of Petty and Cacioppo's model to contemporary political oratory. Kathleen Jamieson (1988) suggests that the electronic media have changed the nature of political oratory. The old style, which required a loud voice and formal gestures, as orators spoke in person to mass audiences, is no longer required. Instead there is a more informal, conversational style. Indeed political interview is a form of conversation where there is turn-taking (Bull et al., 1996), although the editing of interviews on television news may present politicians' answers as if they are not responses to questioning (Ekström, 2001). In parliamentary debates there is also turn-taking, which can be regulated by both formal and informal codes of practice (Carbó, 1992; Shaw, 2000). Moreover, there has been a blurring of the distinction between front stage and back stage, or between public and private life (Meyrowitz, 1986). In these circumstances, according to Jamieson, political figures are expected to present their personal selves to their public audiences, although there are cultural differences (Obeng, 1997). Castells (1999) had called this trend a "personalization of politics."

Some analysts might see this as a trivialization of politics, as viewers treat political figures as show-business stars and are more influenced by peripheral characteristics than their actual arguments (Postman, 1984). These criticisms, in effect, are claiming that audiences in the age of personalized politics put form over content, valuing the peripheral factor of ethos more than the central factors of logos. However, another interpretation is possible, and it is one that raises doubt about the direct applicability of Petty and Cacioppo's basic distinction to the world of contemporary politics. It has been argued that politics in the western democracies today is marked by a lack of sharp ideological division (e.g., Giddens, 1998; Fukuyama, 1992; see Weltman & Billig, 2001, for an analysis of the way that this might affect the discourse of local politicians in England). Because the ideological differences between political parties are often small and because many of the issues are highly complex, personalization can be expected. Voters are looking for leaders whom they feel they can trust and who will have the character to react well to unforeseen crises. Simons (1996), analyzing the Gore-Perot debates in the 1992 American presidential campaign, suggests that it was crucial for the speakers to appear reasoned and knowledgeable on an issue like the North American Free Trade Agreement, where few if any of the audience would have read the 12,000 page proposal before Congress. In the event Perot was reckoned to have come out of the debate badly because of his shrill tone and ad hominem attacks on Gore. In these circumstances of complex political issues and closely observed candidate, ethos, far from being a peripheral matter, would, in fact, be a central issue for attentive viewers.

Furthermore, it could be argued that the visual image "is the semantic and technical unit of the modern mass media at the heart of the postwar popular culture" (Evans & Hall, 1999, p. 2). As Jamieson suggests, electors have become skilled at judging character from televised closeup shots of politicians. This points to the growing importance of what Roland Barthes (1977) called the "rhetoric of the image" that was not envisaged by the purely verbal logic of traditional rhetoric (see, for instance, Barthes's classic analysis of the political candidates photograph in *Mythologies*; and more generally see Beloff, 1986, and Burgin, 1976, for analyses of photography, including political photography). Where the visual images of politicians carry as much semantic meaning, if not more, than their spoken words, then the credibility of the communicator is not a peripheral matter that might only influence those uninterested in politics. Instead it might be something that voters attend to closely, with the politicians knowing that they do. If this is so, then the traditional distinction between form and content that lies at the heart of Petty and Cacioppo's model may not map easily onto the rhetoric of contemporary politics and its underlying psychology in the electronic age. The point is not that Petty and Cacioppo tended to ignore visual rhetoric—in fact, psychological theories that explicitly concentrate on rhetoric tend to confine themselves to verbal rhetoric. The point is that their distinction between the central and peripheral routes of persuasion may not work easily when dealing with the complex visual and verbal rhetoric of contemporary politics.

▶ Discursive Approaches

Social psychological research that has continued in the tradition of the Yale studies has not been particularly concerned to examine the details of verbal rhetoric, let alone visual rhetoric. Such research has been primarily concerned with the effects of particular types of message rather than with examining the rhetorical properties of the messages themselves. For rhetorical studies, one has to look toward the methodologies of conversation and discourse analysis. The techniques of conversation analysis have been most notably applied to political communication in order to solve the riddle of applause. Atkinson (1984a, 1984b) and Heritage and Greatbach (1986) noted that when politicians address live audiences, the applause seems to be instantly coordinated. For this to happen, speakers must be using what Atkinson (1984a) calls rhetorical "clap-traps." In some way speakers must communicate to audiences that they have come to a completion point at which applause can be expected. In order to show exactly how such "clap-traps" operate, Heritage and Greatbach (1986) analyzed the speeches of British politicians addressing party members at annual party conferences. As Ghiglione (1994) has suggested, speeches at party congresses are organized liturgically, with the emphasis on the mode of enunciation rather than content as the speakers seek to elicit outward signs of validation.[1] Heritage and Greatbach (1986) demonstrated that rhetorical formatting is crucial for obtaining coordinated applause. They identified seven key rhetorical devices, including contrasts, three-part lists, and puzzle solutions. Experienced speakers use these devices with appropriate timing and intonation, and the large audiences respond with immediate, coordinated applause. Coordinated applause rarely occurred during a speech without such rhetorical formatting, and if the device was poorly delivered or only partially accomplished then the applause would typically be weaker, less instantaneous, and less coordinated (see also Bull & Noordhuizen, 2000).

Heritage and Greatbach's analysis makes no assumptions about the psychological states of the recipients or of the intentions of the speechmakers. In this regard, it resembles the cause-effect research of the Yale studies, except that it is uses naturalistic, nonexperimental occurrences and it analyzes the detailed rhetorical properties of the speeches. By the same token, technical rhetorical analyses of political speeches, concentrating on demonstrating the use of metaphors and rhetorical tropes, also do not have the aim of exploring the psychology of speakers and hearers, although they typically make assumptions about speakers' strategies and the effects of rhetorical patterns on recipients (i.e., Condit, 1987; Condit & Lucaites, 1991; Smith & Windes, 2000; see also the comparison of apology speeches in American and Israeli politics in Neuman, Libershohn, & Beckerman, 2001). Particularly of note are analyses of discourse that have been using the techniques of critical discourse analysis, combining linguistics with critical social theory (e.g., Chouliaraki & Fairclough, 1999; Fairclough, 1992, 1995;

Fowler, Hodge, Kress, & Trew, 1979; van Dijk, 1993b, 1998). Such work has developed some of the traditional concerns of rhetoricians with figures of speech. For instance, Fairclough (1992) discussed the use of metaphors in political discourse. He noted how the metaphor of "politics as war" in British general election discourse "naturalizes" the way people think about politics as conflict. De Cillia, Reisigl, and Wodak (1999) have looked at figures of speech in Austrian political discourse, pointing out that the use of metonyms (such as "the foreigner" or "the Austrian") can dissolve indi-vidualities, thereby permitting nationalist generalizations. However, not all metaphors in political discourse have such conservative effects. Chilton and Ilyin (1993) examined the origins and spread of the metaphor of Europe as a "common house," showing how it operated in the discourse of western and Russian politicians. They suggest that new metaphors "can break up the rigid conceptual frames of an existing political order" (Chilton & Ilyin, 1993, p. 10).

The most concerted attempt to bring together psychology and rhetoric is to be found in the development of discursive psychology, which has been developed in British social psychology over the past 15 years (for general accounts of discursive psychology see: Antaki, 1994; Billig, 1987, 1991; Edwards, 1997; Edwards & Potter, 1992; Harré & Gillett, 1994; Parker, 1991; Potter, 1996a,b; Potter & Wetherell, 1987). Discursive psychologists often use methodologies derived from conversation analysis and critical dis-course analysis as well as from rhetorical theory. What distinguishes discur-sive psychology is not so much its methodology as its underlying presup-positions about the nature of mentality. According to discursive psychologists, many of the phenomena that psychologists traditionally treat as internal mental processes are actually formed within discourse (see Potter, 1996a,b; Shotter, 1993a, 1993b; Shotter & Billig, 1998, for discussions of the philosophical basis of this assumption). This implies both a theoretical and methodological shift of focus. Instead of searching for inner psycho-logical processes, or looking for the outward manifestations of such inner processes, discursive psychologists directly examine the use of language in interaction. In doing this, discursive psychologists argue that social psy-chologists, who have studied topics such as attitudes or attribution, have actually being looking at language-based phenomena but have lacked the theoretical and methodological tools for examining how language is actually used in practice; for this reason, discursive psychologists argue that the results of attribution studies are difficult to incorporate into a discursive perspective (Edwards & Potter, 1992, 1993). Discursive psychology also assumes that it is possible to study people's thinking directly by examining the ways people talk. In the course of discussions, turns and counterturns can occur so quickly that it makes little sense to assume that the uttered words are merely a reflection of inner, unobservable thinking (Billig, 1991, 1999; Edwards, 1997; Potter, 1996a). Thus people's political thinking can be analyzed directly by examining political talk, noting the outward discursive and rhetorical functions performed by such talk.

This has an important consequence in relation to the study of rhetoric. Human thinking is assumed to be inherently rhetorical in itself, with internal thinking as a form of self-deliberation and self-persuasion (Billig, 1987). The discursive position can be illustrated in relation to the topic of attitudes, especially political attitudes. Social psychologists have tended to view attitudes as internal structures that organize the responses of individuals toward particular stimuli. The rhetorical position sees attitudes as stances that persons may make in matters of public controversy (Billig, 1987, 1991). Thus one's attitudinal opinion is a stance that is directed against counterstances or anti-logoi. This is because attitudes are positions that are taken on issues that are known to be controversial. For instance, to declare oneself to be pro–capital punishment means to take a stance against the abolition of the death penalty and against those who advocate its abolition. This has consequences for understanding the meaning of attitudes. The meaning of opinion-statements is not derived from their supposed psychological function for the individual but from their use within the context of controversy. Therefore, to understand the meaning of opinions, one needs to examine opinion-giving and stance-taking within the context of controversy and argumentation. Discursive psychologists, then, recommend studying how people give their opinions in talk.

Potter (1996a) draws particular attention to three factors that have a particular bearing on the discursive reinterpretation of attitude theory: (1) when people talk they construct versions of the world; (2) speakers perform actions with their talk; and (3) speakers use rhetoric. Potter illustrated this point with a close examination of a political episode in which the British chancellor of the exchequer tendered his resignation (see Edwards & Potter, 1992; Potter & Edwards, 1990). The chancellor, the prime minister of the time, and opposition politicians all gave different versions of the events leading up to the resignation. These versions cannot be understood to be the reflection of "inner attitudes" or as simple descriptions of events in the world. The accounts were rhetorical in that they were constructed to explain, and above all to justify, the self and to assign blame to others. Speakers, in constructing their own versions, were implicitly or explicitly discrediting the versions of others. Thus the meaning of such blamings and explanations depended on the context of controversy in which rival accounts were being produced. In this regard, the speakers were being rhetorical, using justification and criticism, which Perelman and Olbrechts-Tyteca (1971) identify as the two key features of rhetorical argument.

Potter and Edwards (1990) showed how the politicians involved in the resignation episode had a "stake" in their accounts. However, the idea of "stake" itself often becomes a matter of controversy in political debate. Politicians would portray themselves as having no ulterior motive, thereby suggesting that their versions of events are unbiased. By contrast, they suggested that rivals had particular "stakes" in their counterversions of the events, thereby implying that these rival versions could not be trusted as unbiased accounts. Potter and Edwards (1990) refer to this rhetorical tactic as "stake-inoculation." One way of attempting to achieve stake-inoculation is to cite apparently neutral sources to validate one's own position. Abell (2000) analyzed the way that British politicians, speaking in the House of Commons on a controversy about the government's handling of agricultural disease, cited "independent scientists" to warrant their particular political claims. Dickerson (1997), analyzing British political interviews, noted how often politicians dismissed rivals as being politically motivated and claimed "neutral" observers as supporting their own position: "It's not just me who's saying this" was an often-used rhetorical gambit. It is not just neutral sources who can be recruited rhetorically to support a speaker's own position. Antaki and Leudar (2001) examine how members of the British House of Commons quote the past words of opponents from the official parliamentary record in order to bolster their own rhetorical arguments.

The notions of "stake" and "stake-inoculation" are also used by Le-Couteur, Rapley, and Augoustinos (2001) in their analysis of the political controversy in Australia about Aboriginal land rights. They suggest that the use of reported speech is particularly useful when discussing racially sensitive issues. It allows the speaker to claim that his position is based on "facts" rather than a particular "stake" or even prejudice (see also van Dijk, 1993a, for an analysis of European politicians' discourse about immigration). Of course, stake-inoculation, like any rhetorical tactic, cannot guarantee persuasive success, for there are always countermoves that can be made (Billig, 1987). In this case, the character or ethos of the so-called independent source can be attacked, as Simons (2000) shows in his examination of the apology speech of the U.S. president Bill Clinton following a sex scandal.

The ways that politicians account for their actions do not intrinsically differ from the ways that ordinary people give versions of events. When people give their opinions, they rarely merely state preferences, except when explicitly asked to do so by opinion pollsters. Instead, attitudinal talk typically has a twofold nature. People give their views as their own "subjective" opinions while at the same time offering justifications for such views. These justifications are offered as being more than merely subjective preferences (Billig, 1991). Moreover, as Potter and Wetherell (1987) emphasize, such talk tends to be flexible: people do not merely have a set attitudinal position that they trot out identically on each occasion the topic arises. Instead, they address their remarks to the rhetorical context in which they are talking, just as the politicians studied by Potter and Edwards (1990) did. Even those with supposedly strong political views show such flexibility (Billig, 1991). In a study of views about the British monarchy, Billig (1991, 1992) analyzed the way English families talked about the royal family. In one family, everyone agreed that the father had strong views against the monarchy. He constantly argued with his wife and children on the topic. In his arguments, he did not merely repeat the same statements but flexibly managed his arguments to counter those of the other members. Moreover, he alternated between using a radical and a conservative rhetoric as he counterposed his logoi to the anti-logoi of his family, presenting himself at one moment as a radical opposing the establishment and at other times as the defender of British values. At one moment in the argument, when he was accused by the other family members of being a communist, he launched himself into a passionate declaration of his traditional patriotism. In doing so he was not doing anything extraordinary, for egalitarian and traditionalist values are both commonly shared values in contemporary British common sense.

The example illustrates a wider point about the rhetorical nature of shared patterns of belief. Common sense or ideology is not unitary but dilemmatic, in that it contains contrary values (Billig et al., 1988). Without such contrary themes there could be no rhetoric of debate. The point can be illustrated in relation to classical rhetoricians who advised speakers to advance their cases by using "commonplaces" or moral values that would be shared by audiences (Billig, 1987). Prosecutors in the law courts were advised to employ the commonplaces of "justice" and defending lawyers to counter by employing the maxims of "mercy." It would be assumed that the juries would value both justice and mercy. Only because both justice and mercy are both valued is debate about their relative merits in particular issues possible. Political discourse is typically marked by the use of commonplaces, or what McGee (1980) has called "ideographs." Such political commonplaces frequently express basic ideological values, such as those of "freedom" or "responsibility." Just as juries can be expected to value both justice and mercy, so the shared patterns of ideological discourse contain contrary commonplaces that are both valued. As such, there are ideological dilemmas as speakers and public manage these contrary themes (Billig et al., 1988).

In his pioneering work, Murray Edelman (1977) showed the complex character of the political language of poverty. Politicians regularly use both the discourses of blame and sympathy, or modern political equivalents of "justice" and "mercy." As Edelman showed, politicians habitually express sympathy for the poor, while at the same time criticizing those who fail to exert effort to better themselves. The result is, according to Edelman, that poverty is simultaneously both deplored and tolerated. One might say that the conventional political discourse employs both conservative and liberal commonplaces, with parties giving emphasis to one or other sets of commonplace without abandoning the other. The contrary character that Edelman (1977) noted about the language of poverty is to be found in other topics. For example, Augoustinos, Tuffin, and Rapley (1999) found that white Australian speakers simultaneously symphasized with the plight of Aboriginal peoples while also criticizing them for supposed lack of effort.

In talk on particularly sensitive issues, the dilemmatic quality of ideology is often expressed in the common rhetorical strategy of prefacing views with a denial of prejudice. "I'm not racist but . . ." has been found commonly in discourses by politicians and members of majority groups when discriminatory legislation, such as immigration controls, are defended and immigrants are criticized (Billig, 1991; Bonilla-Silva & Forman, 2000; van Dijk, 1991, 1992; Wetherell & Potter, 1992). The rhetorical device is not confined to race. "I'm not sexist but . . ." can also be heard as an expression of an ideological dilemma where sexism is both deplored and perpetuated (Edley & Wetherell, 1999; Wetherell, Stiven, & Potter, 1987; see Condor, 2000, for analyses of the denials of being "nationalist" among English speakers). In uttering such formulas, speakers are asserting their own ethos, denying that they should be seen as prejudiced. Nevertheless, the prefatory denial rhetorically recognizes that what follows the "but" might be heard as being prejudiced. As such, the preface seeks to disarm countercriticism, using the strategy that classical rhetoricians called "prolepsis" (Billig, 1987). In this way, the speaker simultaneously appears to deplore prejudice, while uttering views that might conventionally be judged to be prejudiced. Such utterances, therefore, attempt to accomplish several rhetorical tasks simultaneously: they purport to describe critically the actions of others (whether the poor, minority groups, or whatever); they often mobilize unflattering stereotypes to do so; they also assert the cultural value against prejudice; they seek to neutralize potential criticisms; and they defend the ethos of the speaker. In this regard, such utterances and, indeed, political discourse generally, possess a rhetorical complexity that cannot be reduced to a single, simple function.

▶ Political Discourse and Rhetorical Identification

Discursive psychologists have tended to reconceptualize variables that psychologists have conventionally treated as internal processes as external rhetorical actions. When applied to political materials, this approach not only provides a detailed way of examining the rhetorical nature of political speech but also shows how social psychological theory can be transformed in the course of such examination. This can be seen in relation to the notion of identification, which can be treated as a rhetorical process rather than an internal psychological state that produces a sense of identity. In discussing this here, the focus will be on studies analyzing the talk of politicians or those who are often described as "elite actors." The discursive approach is by no means confined to the analysis of formal speechmaking or of elite actors. Identification by ordinary actors can be analyzed discursively. For example, Billig (1991) examined how ordinary English people expressed their national identification through talk about the British royal family; Wetherell and Potter (1992) examined national identification in New Zealand expressed in talk about culture, minorities, and immigration. It is probably fair to say that at present discursive analysts have not sought to link the study of elite speakers with the studies of mass publics in order to study effects of messages in the way that the Yale studies developed. The discursive approach would, however, caution against the search for simple one-way effects, for, as will be suggested, the presumed audience affects the ways that elite speakers present themselves discursively.

Kenneth Burke (1969), in his book *A Rhetoric of Motives*, presented a rhetorical view of identification. In the book's introduction, Burke wrote that identification was a key rhetorical concept and could be used to show "how a rhetorical motive is often present where it is not usually recognised, or thought to belong" (p. xiii). According to Burke, identification lies at the heart of persuasion, for "you persuade a man [*sic*] only insofar as you can talk his language by speech, gesture, tonality, order, image, attitude, idea, *identifying* your ways with his" (p. 55). Thus identification is a rhetorical project—something to be accomplished rhetorically by the speaker. Burke quotes the maxim that Aristotle cited in *Rhetorica*: "it is not hard to praise Athenians to Athenians" (p. 55; Aristotle, 1909, p. 39). Speakers, by praising what their audiences value, suggest a commonality, as if they and their audiences possess what Burke calls "consubstantiality," or a common substance. This is most easily achieved by citing shared commonplaces (Billig, 1987). In contemporary politics, politicians will employ cliches about freedom and democracy, secure in the knowledge that their audiences will support such values. As Burke suggested, speakers may wish to persuade audiences of a particular point, but they can only do that if they yield "to that audience's opinions in other respects" (p. 56). Consequently, political orators should argue that the particular policy, which they are advocating, would enhance the general morality that they all share. In doing this, the politicians will be rhetorically identifying with the audience and will also be promoting their own ethos as someone who values what the audience values.

Kenneth Burke outlined his theory of rhetorical identification in general terms, but it points the way toward a detailed discursive analysis of the ways that speakers address their audiences. Reicher and Hopkins (1996a) analyzed how a particular political speaker categorized himself in order to suggest a commonality with the audience. The example concerned a British member of parliament who was speaking against abortion to an audience of doctors. In the course of his speech the politician suggested that doctors had lost their freedom of choice and were being forced to conduct abortions. In so doing, according to Reicher and Hopkins, the speaker was attempting to "present himself as a member of a common ingroup with medics, to include all medics in an antiabortion category and to present the relationship between medical identity and abortion as one of dissonance" (p. 307).

This particular speech was conducted in the traditional setting of oratory: the speaker was addressing an audience who were physically present. In the electronic age, multiple audiences hear speeches through television and newsprint. The skilled political speaker can address what Myers (1999) calls the "composite audience." As Myers illustrates with the speech of a former British foreign minister, the speaker can formulate incompatible messages simultaneously with different components of the audience in mind. Indeed, the party conference speeches analyzed by Heritage and Greatbach (1986) did not have a simple audience. Heritage and Greatbach examined the reactions of the audience who were physically present in the hall and who seemed to be being overtly addressed by speakers. However, many of the speakers were aware that the high spots of their speeches would be carried by television to a wider audience. In this regard, the elicitation of applause would have been part of the message to convey to the wider audience, as the speakers wished to project the message of a party united in its applause for its leaders. The appearance of identification of speaker with the physically present audience was itself a message for another audience outside the auditorium.

Reicher and Hopkins (1996a), in their analysis of the rhetoric used by the antiabortion politician, did not specifically address the theoretical questions posed by Kenneth Burke. Their theoretical focus was on social psychology and particularly on Henri Tajfel's influential social identity theory (Tajfel, 1981, 1984) and its offshoot, self-categorization theory (Turner, 1984; Turner, Hogg, Oakes, Reicher, & Wetherell, 1987; for recent evaluations of both theories, see Capozza & Brown, 2000; Ellemers, Spears, & Doosje, 1999; Robinson, 1996). Social identity theory (SIT) provides a sophisticated framework for understanding intergroup relations. At its core lies a series of propositions about social categorization, social identity, and social comparison. The theory says that social identity depends on social categorization and that the act of categorizing the social world involves the positing of ingroups and outgroups. The theory makes a number of predictions about the ways that ingroups compare themselves with outgroups and what happens if such social comparisons lead to an unsatisfactory evaluations of the ingroup's social identity. There is not space here to do justice to the subtlety of SIT or to document its importance, especially in the development of European social psychology. Self-categorization theory points to the importance of categorizing the self, which, according to Turner (1999), provides the basis for social psychological phenomena such as group identity, identification, stereotyping, and so on. The theory asserts that once the social actor has categorized the self as belonging to a particular social group, then the actor will accept the norms, values, and stereotypes associated with the group. In this respect, the theory ambitiously attempts to make self-categorization the key social psychological concept in understanding social relations (see Billig, 2002, for a critical discussion of the way self-categorization theory departs from social identity theory and for its limitations in dealing with the topic of prejudice).

Reicher and Hopkins (1996a), in analyzing the rhetoric of the antiabortion speaker, make the point that the key variables of the social identity and self-categorisation theories are discursive or rhetorical variables. In referring to social categorizations and social comparisons, SIT theorists are, in effect, talking about actions that must be accomplished in rhetoric. As Edwards (1991) noted, categories are for talking, and their use should be understood in terms of the rhetorical business they are accomplishing. Consequently, theories like SIT, when applied to politics, should include a detailed analysis of the ways political actors actually use categories, for social identities are created through talk (Antaki, Condor, & Levine, 1996; Antaki & Widdicombe,1998). Talk is flexible, and political speakers will often declare their identities to achieve specific rhetorical ends, thereby attempting to create rhetorical consubstantiality with their audiences. In effect, this is what the British antiabortion politician was doing when rhetorically constructing a common identity with doctors.

Reicher and Hopkins (1996b) looked at the use of ingroup and outgroup categories in the speeches of the British Conservative prime minister Margaret Thatcher and of Neil Kinnock, the leader of the Labour opposition, during the 1984–85 miners' strike in Britain (for a general rhetorical analysis of Thatcherism, see Phillips, 1996). Both Thatcher and Kinnock tried to make their ingroup categories as wide as possible, thereby depicting the outgroup in a way that was "as restricted as possible" (p. 369). The Labour leader, Kinnock, referred to "the erosion of our economic standards, standards of liberty, of compassion, of care and of opportunity" (p. 364). In speaking thus, Kinnock was using shared commonplaces: no one in the audience was likely to declare themselves against "compassion," "care," and "liberty." In identifying his party with the audience and with those who supported the values, Kinnock was implying that the outgroup, which was the Conservative government, represented a minority of unfeeling persons. By contrast, Thatcher represented the miners and their supporters as "the antithesis of all that is British," thereby identifying herself with the nation and implying that her opponents were national enemies or traitors and thus a small minority group. As Reicher and Hopkins (1996b) emphasize, the self-categories that the speakers employed to depict themselves and their parties were not fixed but were rhetorically constructed and used in argument. As such, self-categorization cannot be the prior social psychological variable from which identity, position and attitude follow but is a rhetorical action that is flexibly managed within rhetorical contexts.

In the political context, the management of stake and the way that audiences are addressed can be complex. Rapley (1998) has analyzed the maiden speech in the Australian parliament of Pauline Hanson, the independent member of parliament who had been elected on an antiimmigration stance. Hanson explicitly did not try to suggest a commonality with her immediate audience, her fellow members of parliament. Instead she depicted herself in ways that distanced her from other members yet stressed commonality with the broader public, whom, as she knew, would hear reports of the speech. In this respect, the immediate audience was rhetorically addressed as if it were the minority outgroup. Hanson claimed to speak "just as an ordinary Australian" and not as "a polished politician," thereby working up an identity for herself as part of her ethos. This identity was being used to validate her political claims and to discredit the counterpositions of opponents. She claimed, for instance, that "my view on issues is based on commonsense, and my experience as a mother of four children, as a sole parent, and as a business-woman running a fish and chip shop" (quoted in Rapley, 1998, p. 331). As Rapley notes, Hanson was distancing herself from politicians, who largely opposed her direct antiimmigrant rhetoric. In presenting herself as a single mother and a businesswoman, she was suggesting a commonality of interests amongst "ordinary people," or "ordinary Australians," as opposed to the minority of interests of politicians and immigrants. In this way, subtle political alignment and criticism were being managed by the presentation of the self and the depiction of the composite audience of both proximal or distant hearers.

This type of analysis has been used to argue that a psychological theory of identification such as self-categorization theory should be understood in terms of rhetorical action rather than internal cognitive processing. In political debate, the very categories used to describe one's own group and that of political opponents can themselves be matters of contention. Leudar and Nekvapil (2000) have illustrated this in their detailed analysis of debates in the Czech media between leaders of the Romanies and the non-Romany Czechs. Of the two terms in Czech whose English equivalents are "gypsy" and "Romany," the former carries a derogatory tone, being associated with unfavorable stereotypes. Critics of Romanies would insist on using the term "gypsy," while disclaiming their own prejudices. The leaders of the Romanies were particularly concerned to insist on the term "Romany," and to associate this category with new, more favorable predicates. In this respect, the Romany leaders were acting in ways that conform to the predictions of social identity theory, which suggests that groups will attempt to change negative ingroup categories and will do so by searching for new dimensions of comparison with the outgroup. So instead of wishing to be compared with non-Romany Czechs in terms of criminality, the Romanies were making comparisons in terms of creativity. What Leudar and Nekvapil (2000) show is that such actions must be accomplished discursively. Making comparisons with the outgroup, proposing new dimensions of comparison, and categorizing the ingroup are all rhetorical actions whose accomplishment depends on subtle details of rhetoric that are worked out in the context of argumentation and addressed to specific audiences. In this regard, a psychological approach such as social identity theory should rest on detailed discursive analyses of rhetorical actions when applied to political speakers. The point can be extended to cover ordinary members of publics speaking about political issues and asserting their own identities through such talk. The discursive approach, it can be argued, has much to offer for the study of what is being called "identity politics," for identity in general is discursively constructed as the categories of identity are conventionally used and contested in political discourse.

▲ The Rhetoric of "Us" and "Them"

Social identity theory emphasizes the importance of social categorization in the creation of social identity. In a series of laboratory experiments, Tajfel showed how the imposition of a meaningless social category was sufficient to create a minimal social identity that led to participants favoring their own group and discriminating against members of the outgroup (Tajfel, Billig, Bundy, & Flament, 1971). In the laboratory, these intergroup divisions were created rhetorically by the experimenters' words, which were received and acted on by the participators. Tajfel (1981) emphasized that social categorization segmented the social world: it was impossible to have an ingroup without an outgroup. In this respect, the "we" of an ingroup identity implied a contrastive "them" who did not belong to the ingroup. Sacks (1992) from a very different theoretical perspective was implying something similar with his concept of a "membership category." If social categorization depends on acts of language, then it is important to examine the use of "us" and "them" in the details of political rhetoric. The processes of constituting political and national ingroup loyalty, as well as the processes of what Riggins (1997) calls the language of "othering," will be located within such rhetoric.

In some contexts the discourses of "us" and "them" will appear in a relatively straightforward manner. This can occur as the communicator is explicitly taking sides in an intergroup conflict. The communicator will be contrasting the ingroup favourably with the outgroup, while identifying the self and imagined audience with the ingroup. Chouliaraki (2000) shows linguistically how the media in Greece, when reporting on the issue of Cyprus, positioned "us" Greeks as western and defensive, while "they," the Turks, were depicted as aggressive and alien. Oktar (2001) examined the discourse of "us" and "them" in the Turkish press in relation to religion and secularism. Both secularist and religious papers emphasized the positive features of "us" and the negative features of "them" while suppressing "our" negative and "their" positive features (see also Thetela, 2001, for an analysis of the linguistics of "us" and "them," as well as national and political stereotypes, in press reports of the South African intervention in Lesotho).

Some linguists have noted that the political use of pronouns can be ambiguous in political discourse (Seidel, 1975; Wilson, 1990). In English, as in many other European languages, the first person plural is ambiguous, for "we" can be used both inclusively and exclusively (Mühlhäusler & Harré, 1990). A politician can use "we" both to include and exclude the audience addressed. In totalitarian discourse "we" is often used exclusively. Ilie (1998), in a rhetorical analysis of Ceausescu's government in Romania, comments that the exclusive use of "we" can be alienating. For instance, the statement "we are building socialism and communism with the people and for the people" is likely to be interpreted as if the "we" of the government excludes the "people," who are the recipients of the communication (Ilie, 1998, p. 68; for other recent analyses of the linguistics of totalitarian discourse, see Galasinski & Jaworski, 1997; Xing Lu, 1999).

Typically in political discourse the use of "we" is ambivalent, its scope of reference left unclear. Wilson (1990) and Maitland and Wilson (1987) have specifically looked at the ambivalence of "we" in politicians' speeches, particularly in relation to the speeches of Margaret Thatcher while she was prime minister of the United Kingdom. Within the same speech, indeed within the same sentence, she would switch between different uses of "we" without giving rise to confusion. There was a widening circle of "us." For instance, "we" might denote "we the Conservative party," "we, the government," and "we, the speaker and immediate audience" but also "we, the nation," and, most important, "we, all right-thinking people." The last-named "we" conveys what Perelman called "the universal audience" (Perelman & Olbrechts-Tyteca, 1968; Perelman, 1979). Among rhetorical analysts, the idea of a universal audience has been controversial; nevertheless, it can be understood to be an intrinsic feature of rhetorical argumentation. Speakers, whether professional politicians or ordinary people, do not generally offer opinions as if the opinions were purely personal. When stating their opinions, they typically give reasons for their stance (Billig, 1991; Schiffrin, 1985). Utterances along the lines of "I believe in x because of y" convey a duality. They imply that the stance is subjective but at the same time they convey that the reasons for the stance are universally valid and thus not merely subjective.

This duality can be found in political speeches, especially in relation to the ambiguity of "we." The speaker addresses a particular audience, although the limits of "we, the audience" can be left vague. In giving reasons and justifications, the speaker will convey that his or her position is universally justified and, by implication, will be appealing to a "universal audience." Thus a speaker might use an undefined "we" with the rhetoric of commonplaces, asserting, for example, "We must stand against the enemies of democracy." Such a statement will combine the particular and the universal "we" without specifying who "we" denotes. This lack of specification, far from being confusing, has its own rhetorical force: it suggests an "identity of identities," as if all those in the potential audience comprise a unity (Billig, 1995; Wilson, 1990). In this way, the outgroup of opponents can be rhetorically contracted (Reicher & Hopkins, 1996b). The outgroup—the implied "they" who oppose "us"—are rhetorically depicted not merely as the opponents of "us" but also as the opponents of universal principles with which "we" have identified ourselves and our audience. All this is accomplished rhetorically by the routine, ambiguous use of small words such as "we" and the banal use of political cliches.

The use of "we" plays an important rhetorical role in the discourses of nationalism. Nations are not objective categories but, as Benedict Anderson (1983) has argued, "imagined communities." Their histories, sense of collectivity, sense of destiny, and so on have to be constructed or "imagined." Such imaginative construction of "us" typically occurs as nationalist movements develop during the struggle for independence or the creation of the nation-state (Hroch, 1985; Reicher & Hopkins, 2001). Carbó (1997) has shown how pronouns, especially "we" and "them," have been used to construct the image of the united national community in the history of Mexico (see also de Cillia, Reisigl, & Wodak, 1999, for an account of the use of pronouns in discourses of national identity in Austria). Billig (1995) argues that researchers into nationalism have typically concentrated on the "hot" nationalism of actual nationalist movements, whose politics are constructed around a desire to create new nation-states or at least alter existing national boundaries. In so doing, they tend to ignore the "banal," or routine, nationalism of established nation-states (see also Condor, 2000, 2001, for discussions of the specificities of nationalism in relation to social identity theory). Once the nation-state has been established, a more routine or banal form of nationalism may become evident: flags are hung outside public buildings rather than being waved as overt political symbols. In political speech, which will be transmitted daily by the media, politicians will routinely address a national audience, a national "we." United States presidents will often begin televised addresses with terms such as "my fellow Americans." In this way, an imagined national audience is hailed. The audience is often praised as the speaker mentions the supposed good points of an assumed national character (Billig, 1995; for analyses of banal nationalism in Turkish politics, see Yumal & Özkirimli, 2000, and more generally Özkirimli, 2000).

More generally, the nation-state is often taken to be the frame of reference for political discourse. This frame of reference will be conveyed by small words that are not the rhetorical focus of attention. Indeed, "we" is not necessary to evoke the imagined community, for the nation will frequently be presumed to constitute the context for the discourse. Listeners will hear about *the* prime minister or *the* president: *the* will convey the national frame, as any other prime minister or president will not be *the* prime minister or *the* president (Billig, 1995). Similarly, in such discourse, *the* economy will be presumed to be the economy of the nation of the speaker and audience (Rae & Drury, 1993). In addition, politicians, in denying that they have a personal stake in an issue, will routinely say that they are working for the country (Dickerson, 1998). Achard (1993) analyzed the following sentence in a British newspaper: "Government pressure has forced colleges to increase dramatically the number of students." Achard points out that the frame of the text is the nation, without being designated as such. He comments that "Britain is the universe of the ongoing discourse," despite the fact that "the term "we" is not used, and no external point relative to this universe is designated" (p. 108; for extended analyses of the discourse of nationalism in a variety of political discourses, see Reicher & Hopkins, 2001). In this way, the citizenry of established nation-states are reminded routinely and banally of their national identity. Moreover, the world of nation-states appears as the rhetorical background of much contemporary political discourse. In this way, such discourse routinely "naturalizes" the world of nation-states (Billig, 1995).

In the "new world order discourse" of American presidents since the fall of communism, a further widening of the third person plural can be detected. "We" not only can signify the nation-state of the United States but it can signify in foreign policy statements the "we" of the world order, which, as Der Derian (1993) points out, is used "to describe an American-led, United Nations–backed system of collective security" (p. 117). In the discourse of the new world order, "our" (national) interests are presumed to be equated with those of the world order: an elision of "we, the nation" with "we, the world" rhetorically accomplishes this sense of identity, in what has been called the "syntax of hegemony" (Billig, 1995). Moreover, the "we" of the political alliance also conveys through its use of argumentation the universal "we," to suggest that the specific alliance is defending universal morality. These rhetorical elisions, for example, were common in the speeches George Bush Senior gave during the Gulf War but can be found much more generally in U.S. foreign policy discourse (Billig, 1995). Again, the rhetoric conveys simultaneously an address to unspecified political audiences as well as the imagined universal audience.

◤ Projection and Language

The exclusive use of "we" in political discourse provides the basis for discourse about "them," who are supposedly different from "us". As Tajfel (1981) stressed, the mere act of social categorisation implies both an ingroup and outgroup. Consequently, social identity depends on a sense of otherness as much as on a sense of commonality. This raises the issue of psychodynamic factors that have been explored in the psychology of bigotry (i.e., Adorno, Frenkel-Brunswik, Levinson, & Sanford, 1951; Frosh, 1997, 2002; Kristeva, 1991; Kovel, 1995). The image of the "Other" may not be based on the characteristics that the outgroup actually possesses but may represent an imagined Other who embodies the very characteristics that the ingroup itself denies possessing. According to psychoanalytic theory, such a denial can be a means of repressing the possibility that the self possesses such unwanted characteristics. In this regard the Other can become the projection of denied wishes, with the result that the force of feeling against the Other reflects such a denial.

There is a strong rhetorical dimension in any such projection, which is based on judgments about the self (or self's group) and the other. In fact, discursive psychology has specifically been extended to embrace psychodynamic factors (Billig, 1999, 2002; see also Parker, 1998). According to this perspective, language is seen as both expressive and repressive, for it is suggested that speakers must acquire the skills of repression as they acquire the skills of language. Moreover, the skills of repression are based on the rhetorical skills of changing topics and blaming (see Billig, 1999, for more details). This means that if one wishes to examine projection or other ego defenses in political discourse, then one should see projection as a rhetorical feature rather than a discursive manifestation of deeper and essentially nonrhetorical mental processes.

Othering plays an important role in prejudiced and outwardly nationalist discourse, for the "we" of the rhetorically imagined ingroup implies others who are outside the ingroup. In mainstream political discourse against immigration in the United States and Europe, politicians are careful to deny their own racism while at the same time they mobilize images of immigrants that are counterposed to "us" (see van Dijk, 1991, 1992, 1993a, for analyses of the strategies of denial and mitigation that characterize this discourse). In such discourse, the other is "abnormalized," or treated as being problematically different (Verkuyten, 2001). In themselves denials are not necessarily indicators of projection. The possibility of projection arises when it can be suspected that the characteristics assigned to the other are characteristics that reflect unacknowledged wishes related to the self. As Adorno (1951) suggested, the anti-Semitism of fascist propagandists had a force that could not be explained in rational terms, as the images of Jews reflected the psyche of the bigots rather than the actual characteristics of Jews. This assumption lay behind *The Authoritarian Personality* (Adorno et al., 1950) as well as Fromm's (1942) earlier examination of anti-Semitism and Norman Cohn's (1967) classic examination of the myth of the world Jewish conspiracy in Nazi propaganda. Current prejudice in eastern Europe against Romanies might well fit the pattern. The "gypsy" has become the hated image of dirt and of freedom from the restraints of contemporary life (Helleiner & Szuchewycz, 1997; Leudar & Nevkapil, 2000; see Mac Laughlin, 1999, for a historical account of anti-Gypsy hatred). Such is the strength of the hatred in some cases that one might suspect that the utterance of such stereotypes has become a means for the hater to deny the attractions of dirt and freedom and to reassert his or her own commitment to the demanding constraints of contemporary life. In this way, the hated other represents the features that haters wish to deny being attracted to.

Other psychodynamic themes may be interpreted within the discourses of political hatred. In Freudian theory, jokes are said to express wishes that cannot be expressed directly because of social taboos (Freud, 1905/1991; Legman, 1969). The assumption can be used to interpret political jokes (Benton, 1988; Speier, 1998; for a general discussion of role of humor in social life, see Billig, 2001a). Where there are taboos against racism, the racist joke can be told as a means of uttering racist sentiments under the guise of nonseriousness, thereby validating the stereotypes underlying the humor (Husband, 1988; de Sousa, 1987; see Lockyer & Pickering, 2001, for a discussion of the way that complaints against offensive humor are rhetorically phrased). In the circles of the extreme racist right, there are no such taboos against the expression of racist views, but racist jokes continue to circulate. In parties of the extreme right, there is often a tension between an outward politics of democratic respectability and an inner ideology that cannot be too openly expressed (Blee, 2002; Billig, 1978). As Billig (2001b) suggests on the basis of an examination of Ku Klux Klan humor, the jokes mock the constraints of reasonableness and express a direct violence that also has to be denied in other settings. In this respect, the violent racist joke reveals the pleasures and fantasies of racist violence within a politics of unreasonable hatred that often for the sake of public presentation proclaims its own reasonableness.

On a less intense level, patterns of belief, described as "the third person effect," may indicate a discursively based and socially shared mechanism of ego defense. The third person effect describes the belief that other people are more influenced by negative political propaganda than one is oneself. By contrast, people tend not to believe that others will be more influenced by positive, prosocial messages than themselves. The effect has been found widely in contemporary publics, especially in relation to political propaganda (e.g., Davison, 1983; Duck, Hogg, & Terry, 1995; Duck & Mullin, 1995; Hoorens & Ruiter, 1996). Qualitative studies also reveal how people claim that it is other members of the public who are politically gullible (Dickerson, 2000). Billig (1991) found an analogous set of beliefs in talk about the British royal family. Speakers often criticized the press reporting of royal scandals and claimed that the papers only printed royal gossip because others, but not themselves, were interested in such details. Moreover, they claimed that others were influenced by the inaccuracies of the press but they themselves had learned how to "read between the lines."

The third person effect is interesting for a number of reasons. First, it shows that mass communication is not to be studied merely by searching for elite effects on mass publics. Members of the public have views about the communication process itself and its effect on themselves and on others. These views are themselves part of the processes of mass communication and need to be studied in their own right. Second, the research exemplifies how psychodynamic factors can be tied to ideological and rhetorical ones. One might presume that the conditions of contemporary social life create a potentially threatening dilemma. Individuals today are primarily reliant on the mass media for political information. However, distrust of the media, particularly newsprint, is widespread. If this distrust were taken to logical and psychological conclusions, then individuals would distrust their own beliefs: a collective lack of confidence in one's own opinions would result. However, a shared social defensive reaction is possible: it can be claimed that "others" are gullible whereas the self is capable of assessing the information of the media. If this is so, then not only are defensive reactions built into the conditions of mass publics today but also is the divisiveness of "othering", for the effect depends upon a distinction between the sense-making of the self and the gullibility of others. Consequently, a discursive pattern of interpretation is shared as an ideological view that has psycho-dynamic ego-defensive features. The implication is that "othering" is not merely a feature of extreme prejudice but it is a component of mainstream political reactions.

All this demonstrates the importance of rhetorical factors in political discourse. Traditionally rhetorical analysts have often concentrated on figures of speech such as metaphors or on the "big" symbolism of political discourse. However, it is arguable that the little words of political discourse—such as "we" and "they"—play crucial, complex, and easily overlooked roles. Moreover, such little words are vital for the rhetorical constitution of psychological and psychodynamic factors such as identification and projection. The study of the little words demands detailed discursive analyses of the type that discursive psychologists are now pursuing. The project for discursive psychologists is to show how ideological, rhetorical, and psychological factors are contained and reproduced within the details of political talk.

▲ Note

1. Robert Jervis (personal communication, 2002) points to an episode when the communication following a party speech had a direct effect on political action. When a speaker nominating Woodrow Wilson for reelection in 1916 used the phrase "he kept us out of war," the convention delegates spontaneously broke into prolonged applause, shouting out the phrase later in the convention. The result was that Wilson and his supporters adopted the phrase as one of their main campaign slogans.

▲ References

Abell, J. (2000). *Politics and the rhetoric of identities: A discursive analysis of the BSE debate.* Unpublished doctoral dissertation, University of Loughborough, Loughborough UK.

Achard, P. (1993). Discourse and social praxis in the construction of nation and state. *Discourse and Society, 4,* 75–98.

Adorno, T. W. (1951). Freudian theory and the pattern of fascist propaganda. In G. Roheim (Ed.), *Psychoanalysis and the social sciences* (pp. 118–137). New York: International Universities Press.

Adorno, T. W., Frenkel-Brunswik, E., Levinson, D. J. & Sanford, R. N. (1950). *The authoritarian personality.* New York: Harper and Row.

Anderson, B. (1983). *Imagined communities.* London: Verso.

Antaki, C. (1994). *Explaining and arguing.* London: Sage.

Antaki, C. Condor, S., & Levine, M. (1996). Social identities in talk: Speakers' own orientations. *British Journal of Social Psychology, 35,* 473–492.

Antaki, C., & Leudar, I. (2001). Recruiting the record: Using opponents' exact words in parliamentary argumentation. *Text, 21,* 467–488.

Antaki, C., & Widdicombe, S. (Eds.) (1998). *Identities in talk.* London: Sage.

Aristotle. (1909). *Rhetorica.* Cambridge: Cambridge University Press.

Atkinson, J. M. (1984a). *Our masters' voices.* London: Methuen.

Atkinson, J. M. (1984b). Public speaking and audience responses: Some techniques for inviting applause. In J. M. Atkinson & J. Heritage (Eds.), *Structures of social action* (pp. 370–409). Cambridge: Cambridge University Press.

Augoustinos, M., Tuffin, K., & Rapley, M. (1999). Genocide or a failure to gel? Racism, history and nationalism in Australian talk. *Discourse and Society, 10,* 351–378.

Barthes, R. (1972). *Mythologies.* London: Jonathan Cape.

Barthes, R. (1977). *Image-music-text.* London: Fontana.

Beloff, H. (1986). *Camera culture.* Oxford: Blackwell.

Benton, G. (1988). The origins of the political joke. In C. Powell & G. E. C.Paton (Eds.), *Humour in society* (pp. 33–55). Basingstoke, England: Macmillan.

Billig, M. (1978). *Fascists: A social psychological view of the National Front.* London: Academic Press.

Billig, M. (1987). *Arguing and thinking.* Cambridge: Cambridge University Press.

Billig, M. (1991). *Ideology and opinions.* London: Sage.

Billig, M. (1992). *Talking of the royal family.* London: Routledge.

Billig, M. (1995). *Banal nationalism.* London: Sage.

Billig, M. (1999). *Freudian repression.* Cambridge: Cambridge University Press.

Billig, M. (2001a). Humour and embarrassment: The limits of nice guy theories of social life. *Theory, Culture and Society, 18(5),* 23–43.

Billig, M. (2001b). Humour and hatred: The racist jokes of the Ku Klux Klan. *Discourse and Society, 12,* 267–289.

Billig, M. (2002). Henri Tajfel's "Cognitive aspects of prejudice" and the psychology of bigotry. *British Journal of Social Psychology, 41,* 171–188.

Billig, M., Condor, S., Edwards, D., Gane, M., Middleton, D., & Radley, A. R. (1988). *Ideological dilemmas: A social psychology of everyday thinking,* London: Sage.

Blee, K. M. (2002). *Inside organized racism: Women in the hate movement.* Berkeley: University of California Press.

Bonilla-Silva, E., & Forman, T. A. (2000). "I am not a racist but . . .".: Mapping white college students' racial ideology in the USA. *Discourse and Society, 11,* 50–85.

Bull, P., Elliott, J., Palmer, D., & Walker, L. (1996). Why politicians are three-faced: The face model of political interviewees. *British Journal of Social Psychology, 35,* 267–284.

Bull, P., & Noordhuizen, M. (2000). The mistiming of applause in political speeches. *Journal of Language and Social Psychology, 19,* 275–294.

Burgin, V. (1976). *The camerawork essays.* London: Rivers Oram Press.

Burke, K. (1969) *A rhetoric of motives.* Berkeley: University of California Press.

Capozza, D., & Brown, R. (Eds.) (2000), *Social identity processes.* London: Sage.

Carbó, T. (1992). Towards an interpretation of interruptions in Mexican parliamentary discourse (1920–1960). *Discourse and Society, 3,* 25–45.

Carbó, T. (1997). Who are they? The rhetoric of instututional policies toward the indigenous populations of postrevolutionary Mexico. In S. H. Riggins (Ed.)., *The language and politics of exclusion* (pp. 88–108). Thousand Oaks, CA: Sage.

Castells, M. (1999). An introduction to the media age. In H. Mackay & T. O'Sullivan (Eds.), *The media reader* (pp. 398–410). London: Sage.

Chilton, R., & Ilyin, M. (1993). Metaphor in political discourse. *Discourse and Society, 4*, 7–31.

Chouliaraki, L. (2000). Political discourse in the news: Democratizing responsibility or aestheticizing politics? *Discourse and Society, 11*, 293–314.

Chouliaraki, L., & Fairclough, N. (1999). *Discourse in late modernity*. Edinburgh: Edinburgh University Press.

Cohn, N. (1967). *Warrant for genocide*. London: Chatto Heinemann.

Condit, C. M. (1987). Crafting virtue: The rhetorical construction of public morality. *Quarterly Journal of Speech, 73*, 79–97.

Condit, C. M., & Lucaites, J. L. (1991). The rhetoric of equality and the expatriation of African-Americans. *Communication Studies, 42*, 1–21.

Condor, S. (2000). Pride and prejudice: Identity management in English people's talk about "this country." *Discourse and Society, 11*, 175–205.

Condor, S. (2001). Nations and nationalisms: Particular cases and impossible myths. *British Journal of Social Psychology, 40*, 177–181.

Davison, W. P. (1983). The 3rd person effect in communication. *Public Opinion Quarterly, 47*, 1–15.

De Cillia, R. Reisigl, M., & Wodak, R. (1999). The discursive construction of national identities. *Discourse and Society, 10*, 149–163.

de Sousa, R. (1987). When is it wrong to laugh? In J. Morreall (Ed.), *The philosophy of laughter and humor* (pp. 226–249). Albany: SUNY Press.

Der Derian, J. (1993). S/N: International theory, Balkanization and the new world order. In M. Ringrose & A. J. Lerner (Eds.), *Reimagining the nation* (pp. 98–124). Buckingham: Open University Press.

Devlin, L. P (1995). Political commercials in American presidential elections. In L. L Kaid & C. Holtz-Bacha (Eds.), *Political advertising in western democracies* (pp. 186–205). Thousand Oaks, CA: Sage.

Dickerson, P. (1997). "It's not just me who's saying this . . ." The deployment of cited others in televised political discourse. *British Journal of Social Psychology, 36*, 33–48.

Dickerson, P. (1998). "I did it for the nation": Repertoires of intent in televised political discourse. *British Journal of Social Psychology, 37*, 477–494.

Dickerson, P. (2000). "But I'm different to them": Constructing constrasts between self and others in talk-in-interaction. *British Journal of Social Psychology, 39*, 381–398.

Duck, J. M., Hogg, M. A., & Terry, D. J (1995). Me, us and them: Political identification and the third person effect in the 1993 Australian Federal Election. *European Journal of Social Psychology, 25*, 195–215.

Duck, J. M., & Mullin, B. A. (1995) The perceived impact of the mass media: Reconsidering the 3rd person effect. *European Journal of Social Psychology, 25*, 77–93.

Edelman, M. (1977). *Political language: Words that succeed and policies that fail*. New York: Academic Press.

Edley, N., & Wetherell, M. (1999). Imagined futures: Young men's talk about father-hood and domestic life. *British Journal of Social Psychology, 38,* 181–195.

Edwards, D. (1991). Categories are for talking. *Theory and Psychology, 1,* 515–542.

Edwards, D. (1997). *Discourse and cognition.* London: Sage.

Edwards, D., & Potter, J. (1992). *Discursive psychology.* London: Sage.

Edwards, D., & Potter, J. (1993). Language and causation: A discursive action model of description and attribution. *Psychological Review, 100,* 23–41.

Ekström, M. (2001). Politicians interviewed on television news. *Discourse and Society, 12,* 563–584.

Ellemers, N. Spears, R., & Doosje, B. (Eds.), (1999). *Social identity: Context, commitment, content.* Oxford: Blackwell.

Evans, J., & Hall, S. (1999). What is visual culture? In J. Evans & S. Hall (Eds.), *Visual culture* (pp. 1–7). London: Sage.

Fairclough, N. (1992). *Discourse and social change.* Cambridge, UK: Polity.

Fairclough, N. (1995). *Critical discourse analysis.* London: Longman.

Fishbein, M., & Azjen, I. (1981). Acceptance, yielding and impact: Cognitive processes in persuasion. In R. E. Petty, T. M. Ostrom, & T. C. Brock (Eds.), *Cognitive responses in persuasion.* Hillsdale: Erlbaum.

Fowler, R., Hodge, B., Kress, G., & Trew, T. (1979). *Language and control.* London: Routledge.

Freud, S. (1905/1991). *Jokes and their relation to the unconscious.* Harmondsworth, England: Penguin.

Fromm, E. (1942) *Fear of freedom.* London: Routledge and Kegan Paul.

Frosh, S. (1997). *For and against psychoanalysis.* London: Routledge.

Frosh, S. (2002). Enjoyment, bigotry, discourse and cognition. *British Journal of Social Psychology, 41,* 189–193.

Fukuyama, F. (1992). *The end of history and the last man.* Harmondsworth, England: Penguin.

Galasinski, D., & Jaworski, A. (1997). The linguistic construction of reality in the "Black Book of Polish Censorship." *Discourse and Society, 8,* 341–357.

Ghiglione, R. (1994). Paroles de meetings. In A. Trognon & J. Larrue (Eds.), *Pragmatique du discours politique* (pp. 17–53). Paris: Armand Colin.

Giddens, A. (1998). *The third way: The renewal of social democracy.* Cambridge UK: Polity Press.

Harré, R., & Gillett, G. (1994). *The discursive mind.* London: Sage.

Helleiner, J., & Szuchewycz, B. (1997). Discourses of exclusion: The Irish press and travelling people. In S. H. Riggins (Ed.), *The language and politics of exclusion* (pp. 109–130). Thousand Oaks, CA: Sage.

Heritage, J., & Greatbach, D. (1986). Generating applause: A study of rhetoric and response at party political conferences. *American Journal of Sociology, 92,* 110–157.

Hoorens, V., & Ruiter, S. (1996). The optimal impact effect: Beyond the third person effect. *European Journal of Social Psychology, 26,* 599–610.

Hovland, C. I., Janis, I. L., & Kelley, H. H. (1953). *Communication and persuasion.* New Haven: Yale University Press.

Hovland, C. I., Lumsdaine, A. A., & Sheffield, F. D. (1949). *Experiments on mass communication.* Princeton: Princeton University Press.

Hovland, C. I., & Weiss, W. (1951). The influence of source credibility on communication effectiveness. *Public Opinion Quarterly, 15,* 635–650.

Hroch, M. (1985). *Social preconditions for national revival in Europe.* Cambridge: Cambridge University Press.

Husband, C. (1988). Racist humour and racist ideology in British television or I laughed till you cried. In C. Powell & G. E. C. Paton (Eds.), *Humour in society* (pp. 149–178). Basingstoke, England: Macmillan.

Ilie, C. (1998). The ideological remapping of semantic roles in totalitarian discourse, or how to paint white roses red. *Discourse and Society, 9,* 57–80.

Jamieson, K. H. (1988). *Eloquence in an electronic age.* New York: Oxford University Press.

Jaspars, J. M. F. (1978). Determinants of attitudes and attitude change. In H. Tajfel & C. Fraser (Eds.), *Introducing social psychology* (pp. 277–301). Harmondsworth, England: Penguin.

Kovel, J. (1995). On racism and psychoanalysis. In A. Elliott & S. Frosh (Eds.), *Psychoanalysis in contexts* (pp. 205–222). London: Routledge.

Kristeva, J. (1991). *Strangers to ourselves.* Hemel Hempstead, England: Harvester/Wheatsheaf.

Le Couteur, A., Rapley, M., & Augoustinos, M. (2001). "This very difficult debate about Wik": Stake, voice and the management of category membership in race politics. *British Journal of Social Psychology, 40,* 35–57.

Legman, G. (1969). *The rationale of the dirty joke.* London: Cape.

Leudar, I., & Nekvapil, J. (2000). Presentations of Romanies in Czech media: On category work in television debates. *Discourse and Society, 11,* 487–513.

Lockyer, S., & Pickering M. (2001). Dear shit-shovellers: Humour, censure and the discourse of complaint. *Discourse and Society, 12,* 633–651.

Mac Laughlin, J. (1999). European gypsies and the historical geography of loathing. *Review: Fernand Braudel Center, 22,* 31–59.

Mailloux, S. (Ed.) (1996). *Rhetoric, sophistry, pragmatism.* Cambridge: Cambridge University Press.

Maitland, K., & Wilson, J. (1987). Pronominal selection and ideological conflict. *Journal of Pragmatics, 11,* 495–512.

McCloskey, D. (1986). *The rhetoric of economics.* Brighton Sussex, England: Harvester Wheatsheaf.

McGee M. C. (1980). The "ideograph": A link between rhetoric and ideology. *Quarterly Journal of Speech, 66,* 1–16.

McGuire, W. J. (1964). Inducing resistance to persuasion: Some contemporary approaches. In L. Berkowitz (Ed.), *Advances in experimental social psychology* (Vol. 1, (pp. 191–229). New York: Academic Press.

Meyer, M. (1994). *Rhetoric, language and reason.* University Park: University of Pennsylvania.

Meyrowitz, J. (1986). *No sense of place.* Oxford: Oxford University Press.

Mühlhäusler, P., & Harré, R. (1990). *Pronouns and people.* Oxford: Blackwell.

Myers, F. (1999). Political argumentation and the composite audience: A case study. *Quarterly Journal of Speech, 85,* 55–71.

Myerson, G. (1994). *Rhetoric, reason and society.* London: Sage.

Nelson, J., Megill, A., & McCloskey, D. N. (Eds.) (1987). *The rhetoric of the human sciences.* Madison: University of Wisconsin Press.

Neuman, Y., Libershohn, Y., & Beckerman, Z. (2001). *Oh baby, it's hard for me to say I'm sorry: Public apologetic speech and cultural rhetorical resources.* Unpublished manuscript, University of Ben-Gurion, Beersheba, Israel.

Obeng, S. G. (1997). Language and politics: Indirectness in political discourse. *Discourse and Society, 8,* 49–83.

Oktar, L. (2001). The ideological organization of representational processes in the presentation of *us* and *them. Discourse and Society, 12,* 313–346.

Özkirimli, U. (2000). *Theories of nationalism.* London: Macmillan.

Pardo, M. L. (2001). Linguistic persuasion as an essential political factor in current democracies: Critical analysis of the globalization discourse in Argentina at the turn and at the end of the century. *Discourse and Society, 12,* 91–118.

Parker, I. (1991). *Discourse dynamics.* London: Routledge.

Parker, I. (1998). Discourse and psycho-analysis. *British Journal of Social Psychology, 36,* 479–495.

Perelman, C., & Olbrechts-Tyteca, L. (1971). *The new rhetoric.* Notre Dame, Indiana: University of Notre Dame Press.

Perelman, C. (1979). *The new rhetoric and the humanities.* Dordrecht: Reidel.

Petty, R. E., & Cacioppo, J. T. (1981). *Attitudes and persuasion.* Iowa City, IA: Brown.

Petty, R. E., & Cacioppo, J. T. (1984). The effects of involvement on responses to argument quantity and quality: Central and peripheral routes to persuasion. *Journal of Personality and Social Psychology, 46,* 69–81.

Phillips, L. (1996). Rhetoric and the spread of Thatcherism. *Discourse and Society, 7,* 209–241.

Plett, H. F. (ed.) (1995). *Die Aktualität der Rhetorik.* Munich: Wilhelm Fink.

Postman, N. (1984). *Amusing ourselves to death.* London: Methuen.

Potter, J. (1996a). Attitudes, social representations and discursive psychology. In M. Wetherell (Ed.), *Identities, groups and social issues* (pp. 119–174). London: Sage.

Potter, J. (1996b). *Representing reality.* London: Sage.

Potter, J., & Edwards, D. (1990). Nigel Lawson's tent: Discourse analysis, attribution theory and the social psychology of fact. *European Journal of Social Psychology, 20,* 405–424.

Potter, J., & Wetherell, M. (1987). *Discourse and social psychology.* London: Sage.

Rae, J., & Drury, J. (1993). Reification and evidence in rhetoric on economic recession: Some methods used in the UK press, final quarter 1990. *Discourse and Society, 4,* 357–394.

Rapley, M. (1998). "Just an ordinary Australian": Self-categorization and the discursive construction of facticity in 'new racist' political rhetoric. *British Journal of Social Psychology, 37,* 325–344.

Reicher, S., & Hopkins, N. (1996a). Seeking influence through characterising self-categories: An analysis of anti-abortionist rhetoric. *British Journal of Social Psychology, 35,* 297–311.

Reicher, S., & Hopkins, N. (1996b). Self-category constructions in political rhetoric: An analysis of Thatcher's and Kinnock's speeches concerning the British Miners strike (1984–5). *European Journal of Social Psychology, 26,* 353–371.

Reicher, S., & Hopkins, N. (2001). *Self and nation.* London: Sage.

Riggins, S. T. (1997) The rhetoric of othering. In S. H. Riggins (Ed.), *The language and politics of exclusion* (pp. 1–30). Thousand Oaks, CA: Sage.

Robinson, W. P. (ed.) (1996). *Social groups and identities: Developing the legacy of Henri Tajfel.* London: Butterworth-Heinemann.

Sacks, H. (1992). *Lectures on conversation.* Oxford: Blackwell.

Scammell, M., & Semetko, H. A. (1995). Political advertising on television: The British experience. In L. L. Kaid & C. Holtz-Bacha (Eds.), *Political advertising in western democracies* (pp. 19–43). Thousand Oaks, CA: Sage.

Schiffrin, D. (1985). Everyday argument: The organization of diversity in talk. In T. A. van Dijk (Ed.), *Handbook of discourse analysis*. London: Academic Press.

Seidel, G. (1975). Ambiguity in political discourse. In M. Bloch (Ed.), *Political language and oratory in traditional society*. London: Academic Press.

Shaw, S. (2000). Language, gender and floor apportionment in political debates. *Discourse and Society, 11,* 401–418.

Sherif, M., & Hovland, C. I. (1961). *Social judgement*. New Haven: Yale University Press.

Shotter, J. (1993a). *Conversational realities*. London: Sage.

Shotter, J. (1993b). *Cultural politics of everyday life*. Buckingham, England: Open University Press.

Shotter, J., & Billig, M. (1998). A Bakhtinian psychology: From out of the heads of individuals into the dialogues between them. In M. Gardiner & M. M. Bell (Eds.), *Bakhtin and the human sciences* (pp. 13–29). London: Sage.

Simons, H. (Ed.). (1989). *Rhetoric in the human sciences*. London: Sage.

Simons, H. (Ed.). (1990). *The rhetorical turn*. Chicago: University of Chicago Press.

Simons, H. (1996). Judging a policy proposal by the company it keeps: The Gore-Perot NAFTA debate. *Quarterly Journal of Speech, 82,* 274–287.

Simons, H. (2000). A dilemma-centered analysis of Clinton's August 17th apologia: Implications for rhetorical theory and method. *Quarterly Journal of Speech, 86,* 438–453.

Smith, M. B. (1981). Foreword to R. E. Petty, T. M. Ostrom, & T. C. Brock (Eds.), *Cognitive responses in persuasion* (pp. xi–xii). Hillsdale: Erlbaum.

Smith, R. R., & Windes, R. R. (2000). *Progay/antigay: The rhetorical war over sexuality*. Thousand Oaks, CA: Sage.

Speier, H. (1998). Wit and politics: An essay on laughter and power. *American Journal of Sociology, 103,* 1352–1401.

Tajfel, H. (1981). *Human groups and social categories*. Cambridge: Cambridge University Press.

Tajfel, H. (1984). Intergroup relations, social myths and social justice in social psychology. In H. Tajfel (Ed.), *The social dimension* (pp. 695–715). Cambridge: Cambridge University Press.

Tajfel, H., Billig, M., Bundy, R. P., & Flament, C. (1971). Social categorization and intergroup behaviour. *European Journal of Social Psychology, 1,* 149–78.

Thetela, P. (2001). Critique discourses and ideology in newspaper reports: A discourse analysis of the South African press reports on the 1998 SADC's military intervention in Lesotho. *Discourse and Society, 12,* 347–370.

Turner, J. C. (1984). Social identification and psychological group formation. In H. Tajfel (Ed.), *The social dimension* (pp. 518–538). Cambridge: Cambridge University Press.

Turner, J. C. (1999). Some current issues in research on social identity and self-categorization theories. In N. Ellemers, R. Spears, & B. Doosje (Eds.), *Social identity: Context, commitment, content* (pp. 6–34). Oxford: Blackwell.

Turner, J. C., Hogg, M. A., Oakes, P. J., Reicher, S. D., & Wetherell, M. (1987). *Rediscovering the social group*. Oxford: Blackwell.

van Dijk, T. A. (1991). *Racism and the press.* London: Routledge.

van Dijk, T. A. (1992). Discourse and the denial of racism. *Discourse and Society, 3,* 87–118.

van Dijk, T. A. (1993a). *Elite discourse and racism.* London: Newbury Park, CA: Sage.

van Dijk, T. A. (1993b). Principles of critical discourse analysis. *Discourse and Society, 4,* 249–283.

van Dijk, T. A. (1998). *Ideology.* London: Sage.

Verkuyten, M. (2001). "Abnormalization" of ethnic minorities in conversation. *British Journal of Social Psychology, 40,* 257–278.

Vickers, B. (1988). *In defence of rhetoric.* Oxford: Clarendon Press.

Weltman, D., & Billig, M. (2001). The political psychology of contemporary anti-politics: A discursive approach to the end-of-ideology era. *Political Psychology, 22,* 367–382.

Wetherell, M., & Potter, J. (1992). *Mapping the language of racism.* London: Sage.

Wetherell, M., Stiven, H., & Potter, J.(1987). Unequal egalitarianism: A preliminary study of discourses concerning gender and employment opportunities. *British Journal of Social Psychology, 26,* 59–71.

Wilson, J. (1990). *Politically speaking.* Oxford: Blackwell.

Xing Lu, (1999). An ideological/cultural analysis of political slogans in Communist China. *Discourse and Society, 10,* 487–508.

Yumal, A., & Özkirimli, U. (2000). Reproducing the nation: "Banal nationalism" in the Turkish press. *Media, Culture and Society, 22,* 787–804.

International Relations

8 Jack S. Levy

Political Psychology and Foreign Policy

Scholars have developed a number of alternative frameworks to organize explanations of foreign policy behavior.[1] Perhaps the most influential is the levels-of-analysis framework, which emerged from Waltz's (1959) distinction between three different images of war in international politics: individual, nation-state, and system. Some scholars disaggregate the national level into separate societal and governmental levels (Rosenau, 1966), and others suggest a small group level (Janis, 1982; 't Hart, 1990). Psychological variables, which are the focus of this essay, originate at the individual level of analysis but interact with causal variables at several other levels in explaining foreign policy decisions and actions.

Psychological variables are also useful for the analysis of behavior at other levels of the dependent variable, or other "units of analysis."[2] They are central to the explanation of individual beliefs, preferences, and decisions, and to decision-making in small groups and organizations as well as states. By shaping foreign policy, psychological variables affect outcomes at the dyadic and systemic levels. They also affect public opinion, nationalism, identity formation, and other variables operating at the societal level. My primary focus in this essay is on the impact of psychological factors on judgment and decision-making by political leaders. The influence of psychological variables on identity formation and intergroup conflict is discussed elsewhere in this book, particularly in chapters 15, 16, 19, and 20.

I begin this essay with some general conceptual issues confronting the application of psychological variables to foreign policy and international relations. After a brief survey of the historical evolution of applications of social psychology to the study of foreign policy, I examine the role of psychological variables in some of the leading paradigms of foreign policy analysis during the last half-century. I argue that psychology had little direct influence on early decision-making models in international relations, and that the turning point in the systematic development of a cognitive paradigm of foreign policy analysis came with Jervis's (1976) seminal study of perceptions and misperceptions in international politics. Jervis's emphasis on the cognitive biases that distort judgment and decision-making have particularly important implications for the study of threat perception, which I discuss in some detail. I examine the concept of misperception and describe common psychological biases and the cognitive heuristics and emotional factors that give rise to them. I then look at the impact of framing effects and loss aversion on decision-makers' evaluation of outcomes and on risk propensities. I conclude with a brief discussion of some other areas of foreign policy analysis that would benefit from greater attention to political psychology.

◣ Preliminary Conceptual Issues

It would be useful to start with some general limitations on the utility of political psychology for foreign policy analysis. First, psychological variables, which originate at the individual level, cannot by themselves provide a logically complete explanation of foreign policy, which is a state-level dependent variable. Psychological variables must be integrated into a broader theory of foreign policy that incorporates state-level causal variables and that explains how the preferences, beliefs, and judgments of key individual actors get aggregated into a foreign policy decision for the state. True, in a highly centralized state the preferences of the dominant decision-maker may determine state foreign policy, but in that case the centralized nature of the state itself is part of the explanation. This does not preclude the possibility of psychological variables having the most powerful influence on foreign policy, in terms of explaining most of the variance in foreign policy outcomes, but it does require that psychological variables operate in conjunction with variables at the state level of analysis.

Similarly, because war and other forms of strategic interaction are the joint product of the actions of two or more states at the dyadic or systemic levels, psychological variables (or domestic or government-level variables, for that matter) cannot by themselves provide a logically complete explanation for war or for other international patterns. Such explanations require the inclusion of dyadic or system-level causal variables. This is what Waltz (1979) meant when he argued that a theory of foreign policy is not a theory of international politics.

While psychological variables cannot by themselves provide a *sufficient* explanation for state foreign policy behavior, the question of whether they are *necessary* for such an explanation raises a different set of issues. Some argue that because state actions require decisions by political leaders, it is necessary to include decision-makers' preferences and perceptions in foreign policy explanations. Snyder, Bruck, and Sapin (1962, p. 33; quoted in Jervis, 1976, p. 13), for example, argue that if one wishes to probe the *why* questions underlying the events, conditions, and interaction patterns that rest on state action, then decision-making analysis is necessary. The implicit argument is that international structures and domestic forces influence foreign policy only insofar as they are perceived, interpreted, and evaluated by foreign policy decision-makers, and that a theory of foreign policy must explain each link in the causal chain leading to foreign policy decisions and international interactions. The problem with this argument is that it is reductionist, because not all links in the chain necessarily carry causal weight. It also posits an impossible standard, because there is a potentially infinite number of links in any causal chain. As Jervis (1976) notes, "One can always ask for the links between the links" (p. 14).

Our aim as social scientists is not to explain all the links but to explain variations in outcomes, and to do so with theory that abstracts from a "complete" description of reality and identifies the key causal variables and relationships. It is conceivable in principle that international and domestic structures could explain all or almost all of the variation in foreign policy outcomes. Most neorealists, for example, argue that system-level distributions of power and associated variables explain most of the relevant variation in foreign policy and international politics (Mearsheimer, 2001), though Waltz (1979) argues that international structures explain only systemic patterns and not particular state foreign policies.[3]

If it were true that systemic structures explained most of the variance in foreign policy behavior, the question is whether a complete explanation of foreign policy decisions would still require the specification of the intervening causal mechanisms, including the beliefs and perceptions of individual decision-makers. Specifying a complete causal chain, and incorporating the place of individuals in that chain is not the same as saying that individual-level variables have a causal impact on the outcome. If different individuals responded in the same way to similar situations, then individual beliefs and perceptions would be endogenous to (explained by) the situation and have no autonomous causal impact.

Other than neorealists, most foreign policy analysts reject this structuralist claim and argue instead that structural systemic variables cannot by themselves provide a satisfactory explanation of the foreign policy behavior of states. In terms of the psychological variables of interest here, the working assumption is that variations in the beliefs, psychological processes, and personalities of individual decision-makers explain a significant amount of the variation in foreign policy behavior of states in the international system, and that these variables are not endogenous to systemic structures or domestic interests. The contribution of psychological variables to foreign policy analysis rests on their ability to explain significant additional variation in outcomes and not just on their ability to explain more of the "links between the links."

▲ The Evolution of the Study of Psychology and Foreign Policy

The study of foreign policy has evolved in significant ways over the last half-century. Prior to the 1950s, foreign policy analysis was more descriptive, policy driven, and interpretive than theoretical. It typically involved single case studies that were bounded in space and time and that did little to facilitate theoretical generalizations that might be valid for other times and situations. Foreign policy analysis was also more outcome oriented than process oriented. Scholars were more interested in describing the foreign policies of states and providing general interpretations based on different conceptions of policy goals and strategies for advancing them than in looking inside the "black box" of decision-making and analyzing the processes through which foreign policy is actually made.

To the extent that the study of foreign policy gave much attention to the foreign policy–making process, there was no well-developed, systematic paradigm of foreign policy analysis before the 1960s. Some scholars implicitly adopted a rationalist framework, in which states had certain 'national interests' that political leaders attempted to maximize through a careful weighing of costs and benefits. This framework, which was not fully systematized until Allison (1971) constructed his "rational actor model," allowed no role for political leaders' personalities, emotional states, flawed information processing, or other psychological variables.[4] Other scholars implicitly assumed that there were significant departures from rationality in the formulation of foreign policy, but they made little effort to draw on the literature in social psychology to categorize these deviations or to explain them.

Interest in the psychological dimensions of foreign policy and international relations goes back at least to the 1930s, but most of this work was by personality and social psychologists rather than political scientists.[5] Much of the focus, after the experiences of World War I and then World War II, was on the psychology of war and war prevention. The growing interest in the study of attitudes (Thurstone & Chave, 1929) led to the examination of attitudes toward war, nationalism, and aggression (Droba, 1931; Stagner, 1942). Following Freud's emphasis on aggressive instincts as the root cause of war (Einstein & Freud, 1932),[6] there was considerable interest in applying psychoanalytic perspectives to the study of war (Durbin & Bowlby, 1939). Others adopted general learning frameworks (May, 1943), and there were more specific studies of the sources of tensions and possible means of alleviating them (Cantril, 1950; Klineberg, 1950).

Most of this work had little impact on the study of war and peace in political science.[7] One reason was that psychoanalytic and social learning perspectives focused more on the question of what made war possible, or what explained the general proclivity toward war, rather than on the more social scientific and policy relevant question of the conditions or processes under which war was most likely to occur. Another reason for the lack of influence of the social-psychological literature on war and peace was that it generally extrapolated hypotheses of individual behavior to the international level without attention to the specific causal mechanisms leading to war or the distinctive political and international contexts for cognition and choices about war and peace. As Kelman (1965) concluded in his useful review of the evolution of psychological approaches to the study of international relations, "any attempt . . . to conceptualize the causes of war and the conditions of peace that starts from individual psychology rather than from an analysis of the relations between nation-states is of questionable relevance" (p. 5). As I will show, the study of psychology and foreign policy has not fully transcended this limitation.

By the 1950s and 1960s social psychologists had begun to devote more attention to the study of attitudes toward foreign affairs and the social, demographic, and personality correlates of foreign policy attitudes (Larson, 1985). This was one area in which social psychology had some influence on the political science literature on foreign policy, as illustrated by Almond's (1950) incorporation of social psychological research on attitudes into his classic study of changing "moods" in American foreign policy. Scholars analyzed the psychology of nationalism and of national ideologies more generally and conducted crossnational studies of images and stereotypes of other nations (Campbell & LeVine, 1961). Most of this work focused on the mass level, however, and gave relatively little attention to the mechanisms through which shifting public moods were translated into state foreign policy actions.[8]

The study of personality was another field in psychology that had a clear impact on the analysis of foreign policy in political science in the 1950s and 1960s. One example was the work by political scientists and historians on psychobiography or psychohistory, which relied heavily on psychoanalytic theory and attempted to explain political behavior in terms of early childhood experiences or development crises later in adulthood (Erikson, 1962; George & George, 1956). Psychoanalytic perspectives also influenced some of the early "operational code" analyses of political belief systems (Leites, 1953), a topic I examine later. While scholars continued to show an interest in more general models of personality and foreign policy (Etheridge, 1978; Hermann, 1978; Winter, 2002), interest in personality and especially psychobiographical approaches began to wane by the 1970s, with the development of alternative psychological frameworks and a shift in orientation toward more parsimonious and empirically testable theories.[9]

The 1960s also witnessed new research in social psychology on individual perception and choice, with some applications to foreign policy at both the elite and mass levels (DeRivera, 1968; White, 1968), but most of this research had little impact on decision-making studies in international relations. This research was generally based on laboratory experiments designed to examine typical individuals' responses to relatively simple problems, with little attention to the question of whether experimental findings could be generalized to real-world settings.

One problem is that the kinds of individuals selected into political leadership roles differ from the typical subjects in many experiments, namely college students. In the absence of explicit controls there is a possibility that it is these selection-based differences, not the hypothesized causal variables, that account for observed causal effects in the laboratory. Foreign policy–making also differs from the laboratory in terms of the stakes involved. The higher stakes facing political leaders as compared to experimental subjects give leaders greater incentives to expend the mental energy to make rational decisions and to learn from their mistakes, but those stakes also create higher levels of stress and (after a certain point) suboptimal performance (Holsti, 1989).

Another limitation on the generalizability of typical experiments in social psychology to foreign policy behavior is that most of these experiments ignore the political or strategic context of decisions. This includes the institutional context within which decisions are made, the accountability of decision-makers to political constituencies (Tetlock, 1992), and the international context and the conflicts of interests between states. The neglect of the strategic context of foreign policy decisions, along with a strong policy interest in reducing international conflict, has often led to a bias toward emphasizing actors' flawed judgments and choices and minimizing the impact of genuine conflicts of interests (Jervis, 1976, pp. 3–4).

The first systematic analysis of decision-making in foreign policy emerged in the mid-1950s with the "decision-making approach" associated with Richard Snyder and his colleagues (Snyder, Bruck, & Sapin, 1954).[10] By this time there was growing dissatisfaction with the rational, unitary, apolitical, and outcome-oriented focus of many existing studies of foreign policy. Snyder and his colleagues acknowledged that states were the major actors in international politics but argued that in order to understand the behavior of states it was necessary to focus on the individuals who make the key decisions in foreign policy and on the intellectual and political processes leading to those decisions.

The decision-making approach focused on political elites, their conception of the national interest, their "definition of the situation," the domestic political contexts in which they operated, and the role of communication and information in those processes. Subsequent elaborations of the decision-making approach gave added emphasis to bargaining among different actors and different interests within the government and generally concluded that foreign policy was driven as much by the aim of gaining agreement among key decision-makers and by the "pulling and hauling" of competing internal interests as by the merits of policy (Huntington 1961; Neustadt, 1960; Schilling, Hammond, & Snyder, 1962).

While the focus on political leaders' definition of the situation and the importance of information and communication in the 'first-wave' decision-making approach (Art, 1973) clearly allowed a substantial role for psychological factors, there was little explicit theorizing about the influence of psychological variables in the foreign policy process. Scholars emphasized political leaders' assumptions about the world but generally treated those assumptions as exogenous and made little attempt to explain the specific social, intellectual, and psychological processes that generated them. As a result, the potential for incorporating psychological processes was only partially fulfilled in early decision-making analyses.

There was even less room for psychological variables in the "second wave" of decision-making studies, which emerged with Allison's (1971) elaboration of the organizational process and governmental politics models of foreign policy. The organizational process model involves organizations implementing preplanned routines or standard operating procedures and provides little room for variations in behavior based on differences in individual belief systems, biased information processing, personalities, or other individual-level attributes.[11] The governmental politics model is based on interest maximization by the heads of different bureaucratic organizations. The preferences of each of the leading bureaucratic actors are determined primarily by those individuals' organizational roles—hence the aphorism "Where you stand is where you sit"—and these preferences are aggregated by bureaucratic bargaining.

It is certainly possible to construct a bureaucratic politics model in which individual or group psychology plays a central role—through political leaders' belief systems, definitions of their interests, conceptions of their roles, or unique skills or styles in bargaining over policy among different bureaucratic actors—but few of the "second wave" bureaucratic models did this.[12] Although Allison's labeling model I the "rational actor model" created some confusion by leading many to infer that his other two models were not rational models, there is little doubt that Allison's (1971) governmental politics model, and most subsequent elaborations on it as well, are rationalist, interest-maximization models (Bendor & Hammond, 1992). The difference is that Allison's model I is a rational unitary model of decision-making, while the governmental politics model is rational but not unitary.[13]

Dissatisfaction with the neglect of psychological variables in the leading paradigms of foreign policy analysis led to a number of more focused, middle-range research projects in which political psychology was central. One particularly influential study was Wohlstetter's (1962) analysis, based on an explicit information-processing framework, of the American intelligence failure at Pearl Harbor. Wohlstetter argued that the problem was not so much too little information but rather the inability to distinguish signals from noise and the compartmentalization of information in different bureaucratic agencies. This study was particularly influential on subsequent research programs on the perception and misperception of threat, and the potential generalizability of its key findings has been enhanced by the identification (in preliminary assessments) of similar patterns in the American intelligence failure of 9/11, sixty years later.

Another major line of inquiry, which originated in Leites (1951, 1953) analysis of Bolshevik ideology, focused on the "operational codes" of political leaders. The operational code concept was subsequently reformulated and simplified by George (1969), who eliminated the psychoanalytic component that was prominent in Leites's (1953) work, focused on the cognitive dimensions of the operational code concept, and generally tried to frame the analysis in terms of the cognitive revolution and contemporary social science analysis.[14] George (1969) argued that an individual's beliefs are interdependent, consistent, hierarchically organized around a small set of "master beliefs," and resistant to change. The anchors of belief systems include philosophical beliefs about the nature of politics and conflict and instrumental beliefs about the efficacy of alternative strategies for advancing one's interests. Images of the enemy are a particularly important component of operational code belief systems.[15]

George's (1969) revised formulation was the basis for studies of the operational codes of a number of political leaders, including John Foster Dulles (Holsti, 1970) and Henry Kissinger (Walker, 1977). Others developed new typologies for operational codes (Holsti, 1977), further grounded the concept in terms of the emerging literature on cognitive schemas and scripts (George, 1979),[16] and, in some cases, began to reincorporate personality elements into the operational code (Walker, 1995). There are debates, however, as to whether the increasing complexity of the operational code concept has significantly enhanced its explanatory power (Walker, 2003), and operational code analysis continues to be confined to a relatively small research community in the field.

Another subject that had begun to attract increasing interest by the mid-1960s, undoubtedly in response to Soviet-American crises in Berlin and Cuba, was crisis decision-making. Researchers gave particular attention to the impact of stress induced by the high stakes, short decision time, and surprise associated with acute international crises (Hermann, 1972; Holsti, 1972, 1989; Holsti & George, 1975). One influential research program on crisis decision-making was the Stanford Project on International Conflict and Integration, known as the 1914 Project, which was novel both in its application of mediated stimulus-response models to international politics and in its use of formal content analyses of diplomatic documents to examine decision-makers' perceptions and the discrepancy between perceptions and reality (Holsti, 1972; North, 1967). Other scholars provided more detailed historical case studies of crisis decision-making (Brecher & Geist, 1980; Stein & Tanter, 1980).

While the 1914 studies demonstrated that political leaders systematically misperceived the capabilities and intentions of their adversaries, these studies were less thorough in specifying the causal mechanisms that drove misperceptions, the conditions under which misperceptions were most likely to occur, the kinds of individuals most likely to be affected, and the actual causal impact of misperceptions on foreign policy choices and international outcomes. These were among the many contributions of Jervis's (1976) classic study *Perception and Misperception in International Politics*. This was, and still is, the most influential study of the role of misperception in foreign policy and international politics, and indeed it marks the beginning of a systematic "cognitive paradigm" of foreign policy analysis.

Jervis (1976) provided a comprehensive synthesis of theory and experimental evidence from many of the leading approaches in social psychology, illustrated by a wide range of historical examples. He also recognized, in a way that earlier social-psychological analysts did not, that many outcomes predicted by psychological models could also be explained by systemic or domestic political models. Jervis (1976) identified these alternative explanations and discussed the types of evidence and research designs that would be appropriate to empirically differentiate among these competing explanations. This attention to alternative explanations, threats to valid inference, and to research designs for dealing with these inferential problems was a major methodological contribution and a significant step forward in the application of psychological models to foreign policy behavior.

Besides generating general interest in the role of psychology in foreign policy and international relations, Jervis's (1976) study helped initiate or accelerate several more specific research programs in this area. One of the most important was the study of threat perception. The evolving study of threat perception (Jervis, 1985; Lebow, 1981; Stein, 1985, 1993) incorporated new research in social psychology on cognitive heuristics and biases (Nisbett & Ross, 1980; Tversky & Kahneman, 1974),[17] while at the same time giving renewed emphasis to emotional factors that had been downplayed as a result of the cognitive revolution in social psychology. I now examine this research program in more detail.

◤ Psychology and Threat Perception

The perception and misperception of threat take many forms and have many sources at all levels of causation—systemic uncertainty, organizational structures and processes, culture and ideology at the organizational and societal levels, small group dynamics, and individual cognition and affect. Here I focus primarily on individual-level psychological variables. First, however, it will be useful to examine some of the analytic problems that complicate the analysis of the role of misperception in foreign policy decisions and strategic interaction between states.

Analytic Problems in the Study of Misperception

Although misperceptions are often associated with "bad" outcomes, that is misleading. Misperceptions can contribute to peace as well as to war. Overestimation of adversary capabilities, for example, may lead a state to refrain from initiating a war that it might otherwise want. In the longer term, the overestimation of adversary capabilities may lead a state to build up its arms, which can trigger an arms race and conflict spiral that increases the likelihood of war. The multiple consequences of misperceptions make it imperative to identify different kinds of misperceptions, the distinct causal paths through which they affect decisions for war or peace, and the conditions and types of states and leaders for which each is most likely to occur. The most important forms of misperception are misperceptions of the capabilities and intentions of adversaries and third parties (Levy, 1983).[18]

One methodological problem in the empirical literature on misperception and international conflict is that analysts have looked at wars, intelligence failures, or other undesirable outcomes and then sought to identify the misperceptions and decision-making pathologies leading to those outcomes, while neglecting nonwar outcomes. It is conceivable, however, that misperceptions are just as common and egregious in nonwar outcomes, and the exclusion of this comparison group makes it difficult to demonstrate whether misperceptions have a causal impact or whether their effects are dominated by those of other variables. The study of misperception should include cases that involve "positive" as well as "negative" outcomes (Jervis, 1988, p. 680).

A more basic problem is that misperception is an enormously slippery concept that is difficult to define, identify, and measure. There are two general approaches to the definition of misperception; one treats it as an outcome and the other treats it as a process (Jervis, 1976). In the first a misperception is a discrepancy between perceptions and reality, and in the second a misperception is associated with a decision-making process that deviates from a standard rational model of information processing.

In some cases we might have reliable evidence to determine both an actor's intentions and his adversary's perceptions of those intentions and thus have the information to make a judgment about the accuracy of perceptions. These situations are rare, however, because it is remarkably difficult to determine an actor's intentions (Jervis, 1976). Historians, even with the benefit of hindsight and far more complete information than was available to decision-makers at the time, are often unable to agree on an actor's intentions.[19] Decision-makers have diplomatic, bureaucratic, and domestic political incentives to misrepresent their true perceptions in order to influence others' perceptions and behavior, and their concern for their image in history as well as memory lapses and hindsight biases must be considered in using later autobiographies as evidence. The documentary record itself may be distorted for political reasons (Herwig, 1987).

These and related methodological problems (Holsti, 1976) led Jervis (1976) to set aside the question of the accuracy of perceptions and to focus instead on variations in perceptions across different actors with different backgrounds, roles, and interests. The aim was to use comparative analysis as leverage to get at causation and deal with the problem of alternative explanations without relying on the problematic concept of accuracy.[20]

There are other analytic problems with the concept of intentions. That concept implies that behavior is purposeful and that the actor plans to act in certain ways under various future contingencies. But individuals are not always aware of their preferences; preferences may not be stable over time; and preferences may be influenced by irrelevant options or information, as Kahneman and Tversky (1979) argue in their analysis of framing effects.

These problems are compounded for collective decision-making bodies, where preferences may be cyclical and unstable and where decisions are often determined by bureaucratic bargaining, small-group dynamics, and domestic political pressures (Allison, 1971; Janis, 1982), each of which is inherently difficult to predict.

In the context of uncertainty, rational actors rarely make point predictions about the capabilities and intentions of adversaries or third states. Rather, they anticipate a range of possible outcomes with approximate probabilities attached to each, and thus actors have subjective probability distributions over likely outcomes. Low probability outcomes occasionally occur, and when they do we should not necessarily conclude that the actor misperceived reality because she believed that another outcome was more likely.

The more appropriate question is whether the actor's subjective probability distribution of outcomes was reasonable in the first place. We can often answer this question where we have a larger number of comparable observations and where we can compare the distribution of actual outcomes with the actor's subjective probability distribution,[21] but many issues of security policy involve relatively small numbers of cases of a given class of events. "The tape of history runs only once," as Tetlock (1998, p. 870) argues, so it is not really possible to compare the accuracy of some expected distribution of outcomes with the distribution of actual outcomes. Thus if we treat perceptions of adversary capabilities and intentions as subjective probability judgments, and if we have a small number of observations, then a single observation does not necessarily invalidate one's expectations, and the concept of misperception becomes very problematic.[22]

Intractable problems such as these lead many scholars back to a process-oriented conceptualization of misperceptions. As Jervis (1976) argues, we may ask not "Was this perception correct?" but "How was it derived from the information available?" (p. 7). The standard for evaluation is how closely the actual decision-making process conforms to a "rational model" of information processing. There is no single accepted conception of rationality, of course, and attempts to define the concept are complicated by the fine line between rationality and "bounded rationality" (Jones, 1999; March, 1978; Simon, 1957) and by strategic behavior that can produce counterintuitive incentives (Wagner, 1992). Many decision-making pathologies produce such substantial deviations from rationalist expectations, however, as to leave little doubt about their deviation from most conceptions of a rational decision-making process.

Common Errors and Biases

The basic premises of what Tetlock (1998) calls the "cognitive research program" in world politics are that the world is extraordinarily complex, incoherent, and changing, while people are limited in their capacities to process information and fully satisfy standards of ideal rationality in their attempts to maximize their interests. People adopt a number of cognitive shortcuts or heuristics that help to impose some degree of simplicity and orderliness on a complex and uncertain world in order to make that world more comprehensible. These heuristics may serve people very well in a wide variety of situations, but they are also the source of significant errors and biases. In this model of "cognitive economy," people may try to act rationally, but they do so within their simplified mental representations of reality (Jervis, 1976; Nisbett & Ross, 1980; Tversky & Kahneman, 1974). The resulting biases are "unmotivated" because they are the result of "cold cognitions" and not influenced by affective or motivational considerations.

The other main class of biases is "motivated biases," which focus on individuals' psychological needs, fears, guilt, and desires (Janis & Mann, 1977). Motivated biases are most likely to manifest themselves in decisions involving high stakes and consequential actions that might affect important values or tradeoffs among important values, and the resulting stress from threats to basic values often leads decision-makers to deny those threats or the need to make tradeoffs between values (Holsti & George, 1975). Resulting judgments are often rationalizations for political interests or unacknowledged psychological needs and for the policies that serve those interests and needs (Jervis, 1985, p. 25).

Cognitive biases and motivated errors generate some of the same pathologies of judgment and decision, and they often work to reinforce each other. Often the same behavior can be explained either in terms of unmotivated or motivated biases, and it is often difficult to empirically differentiate between the two.[23] These different sources of biases have yet to be integrated into a single analytic framework, and for that reason I organize them separately hereafter. The literature over the last quarter-century has given greater attention to cognitive biases, and I follow that emphasis here, though by the 1990s scholars had renewed their attention to motivated biases and emotions (Crawford, 2000; Hermann, 2002; Marcus, 2000).

Cognitive Biases

The most basic unmotivated bias is the impact of an individual's prior belief system on the observation and interpretation of information. While beliefs simplify reality and make that reality more comprehensible, they also create a set of cognitive predispositions that shape the way new information is processed. The central proposition is that people have a strong tendency to see what they expect to see on the basis of their prior beliefs. They are systematically more receptive to information that is consistent with their prior beliefs than to information that runs contrary to those beliefs. This "selective attention" to information contributes to the perseverance of beliefs (George, 1980). There is a related tendency toward "premature cognitive closure." Rather than engage in a complete search for information relevant to the problem at hand, people tend to terminate their information search when they get enough information to support their existing views. In various ways, information processing is more theory driven than data driven (Jervis, 1976).[24]

This "selective attention" to information and the perseverance of beliefs raise questions about rational models of learning. In particular, individuals update their beliefs more slowly than a rational Bayesian model would predict, and initial judgments (or "priors"), because they are slow to change, serve as a conceptual anchor on beliefs. Whereas in Bayesian models beliefs quickly converge in response to new information, regardless of initial prior beliefs, there is considerable evidence that in reality the adjustment process is inefficient, and that different starting points often result in different outcomes. This is the "anchoring and adjustment" heuristic (Tversky & Kahneman, 1974). I return to this point later.

These biases have important implications for foreign policy and international relations. If you believe that the adversary is fundamentally hostile yet at the same time responsive to external threats and opportunities, you may perceive the adversary's aggressive actions as reflecting its innate hostility and its conciliatory actions as reflecting its response to your own resolute actions. This "inherent bad faith model" (Holsti, 1970) of the adversary is difficult for actors to disconfirm by the evidence and can lead to missed opportunities for conflict resolution (Tetlock, 1998).[25]

Alternatively, erroneous beliefs that the adversary's intentions are benign can render decision-makers insensitive to signals of an impending military attack. A major cause of the Israeli intelligence failure in 1973, for example, was Israeli leaders' strong beliefs that Egypt would not go to war unless it was able to mount air strikes deep into Israel in order to neutralize Israel's air force. This assumption, along with others, came to be known as "the conception." Israeli leaders did not correctly evaluate evidence of an impending Arab attack because of their doctrinaire adherence to "the conception" (Shlaim, 1976, pp. 352–353) and because of their proclivity to discount the unprecedented magnitude of Syrian and Egyptian deployments at the front lines as evidence merely of routine Egyptian military exercises and Syrian defensive moves (Stein, 1985).

While there is a bias toward the perseverance of beliefs, individuals do change their beliefs if the discrepant information is sufficiently strong and salient, if it arrives all at once, if there are bottom-line indicators of successful outcomes that provide an objective baseline for the evaluation of the accuracy of beliefs, and if decision-makers are self-critical in their styles of thinking or when they operate in "multiple advocacy" decision-making units (George, 1980; Jervis, 1976; Tetlock, 1998, p. 880).

When belief change occurs, it generally follows the cognitive-consistency principle of least resistance (McGuire, 1985; Tetlock, 1998, p. 880). When people are faced with repeated inconsistencies between their belief systems and the world they observe, they first change tactical beliefs about the best means to particular ends. They change their strategic assumptions and orientation only after the failure of tactical solutions, and they reconsider their basic goals or objectives only after repeated strategic failures. Change in fundamental beliefs is often so psychologically difficult that it is likely to occur only in conjunction with a major change in personnel or regime (Tetlock, 1991, pp. 27–31).

Another source of erroneous threat assessment relates to the fundamental attribution error, the tendency for people to interpret others' undesirable behavior in terms of internal dispositional factors, as opposed to external environmental constraints (Nisbett & Ross, 1980). This often leads to significant overestimations of threat in international politics. Actors discount the extent to which their adversary's security policies might be driven by external threats to the adversary's interests and instead attribute those actions to the adversary's hostile intentions. As a result, actors tend to underestimate the security dilemma in international politics—the fact that actions taken to increase one's security often result in the decrease in the security of others, who respond with actions to enhance their own security. As a result, all states are less secure.

The overestimation of adversary threat is compounded by actors' tendencies to explain their own behavior in terms of situational factors rather than dispositional factors (the actor-observer discrepancy). The logic is that if we take security measures because we have no choice, presumably others recognize this and understand that we are no threat to them, so that if they buy arms or mobilize forces it must be because they have hostile intentions, which leads to conflict spirals. One consequence of the fundamental attribution error is the tendency to perceive the adversary's regime as more centralized than it actually is and to underestimate the impact of domestic political and bureaucratic constraints on adversary leaders (Jervis, 1976). Actions intended to pacify domestic constituencies may be misinterpreted as the first steps in a deliberate policy of aggression and lead to a conflict spiral.[26]

Several of these processes are fueled by a lack of empathy, an inability to understand others' worldviews, definitions of their interests, threats to those interests, and possible strategies for neutralizing those threats. The inability to empathize and see the world as the adversary sees it is compounded if the two actors have different cultural, ideological, or religious orientations. The Chinese-American war in Korea in 1950 was driven in part by the failure of the United States to understand how threatening a United States–backed regime in North Korea would be to China. The Israeli intelligence failure in 1973 was influenced in part by their failure to imagine that Egypt might anticipate political gains from an unsuccessful war (Jervis, 1985; Stein, 1985). Israeli leaders also failed to recognize that the Egyptians might have an intermediate strategy between doing nothing and launching an all-out war, and that the Israeli strategic "conception" of the necessary conditions for war was inappropriate for a less ambitious Egyptian military action involving a limited crossing of the Suez Canal.

Another reason for Israeli leaders' intelligence failure in 1973 was their belief that war could easily arise from a conflict spiral driven by fears and misperceptions (Stein, 1985). This view was influenced in part by a re-evaluation of the lessons of the 1967 war and by the growing belief that the Israeli preemptive attack that initiated the earlier war had not been absolutely necessary. In 1973, Israeli leaders worried that preparatory measures to counter Arab military activities would fuel a conflict spiral, raise the risk of a preemptive first strike by Egypt, and risk undercutting American diplomatic support (and military resupply). These concerns led Israeli decision-makers to avoid potentially provocative actions and refrain from measures that might have reinforced deterrence (Jervis, 1985; Stein, 1985).

The reliance on the "lessons of the past" and on particular historical analogies to help shape judgments of current situations is commonplace and has attracted considerable attention in the literature (Jervis, 1976; Khong, 1992; Levy, 1994; May, 1973; Vertzberger, 1990). Analogical reasoning is often used as a cognitive shortcut by actors who face a complex and uncertain world and who lack a good theory to simplify that complexity. This is often linked to the "availability" heuristic, in which judgments of probability are shaped by events that are familiar and salient and come easily to mind (Tversky & Kahneman, 1974). The problem, of course, is that these events do not constitute a scientific sample for the purpose of drawing inferences, and consequently judgments based on availability are often quite misleading.

With respect to learning from history, the basic questions are what lessons people learn, the processes by which they learn, and the impact of those lessons on subsequent policy preferences and decisions. There are countless historical analogies from which individuals might learn, but there is a tendency to learn from events that have a major impact, affect the individual or his society directly, occur recently in time, and are observed firsthand and at a formative period in a person's life (Jervis, 1976).[27] Most analysts conclude that learning is oversimplified and insensitive to the context of the historical analogy, the impact of that context (as opposed to the causal hypothesis being learned) on the outcome, and how that context might differ from the current situation. As Jervis (1976) argues, "People pay more attention to *what* has happened than to *why* it has happened. Thus learning is superficial, overgeneralized. . . . As a result, lessons learned will be applied to a wide variety of situations without a careful effort to determine whether the cases are similar on crucial dimensions" (p. 228).

While hypotheses on learning provide potentially powerful explanations of political leaders' beliefs and judgments, empirical research on learning must be sensitive to the possibility that the causal arrows are reversed or spurious (Jervis, 1976; Levy, 1994; Tetlock, 1998, p. 879). Current policy preferences might lead decision-makers to select those analogies that support their positions, either subconsciously because of cognitive consistency or motivated biases, or deliberately for leverage in political debates. Alternatively, an individual's beliefs may simultaneously shape her selection and interpretation of a particular historical analogy and her preferences on a current issue, leaving no causal connection between analogy and preference. Researchers are increasingly aware of these threats to valid inference and have tried to construct research designs to deal with these potential problems (Khong, 1992; Snyder, 1991).

Motivated Biases

Whereas unmotivated biases result from the use of cognitive shortcuts in an attempt to make a complex and ambiguous world more comprehensible, motivated biases refer to individuals' psychological needs to maintain their own emotional well-being and to avoid fear, shame, guilt, and stress. Whereas unmotivated biases generate perceptions based on expectations, motivated biases generate perceptions based on needs, desires, or interests (Janis & Mann, 1977; Lebow, 1981). Unmotivated biases are pervasive, while motivated biases are most likely to arise in highly consequential decisions.

One key proposition arising from motivated biases is "wishful thinking." Whereas rational models of decision-making assume that the probability and utility of an outcome are analytically distinct, in wishful thinking probabilities are influenced by values: desirable outcomes are seen as more likely to occur while undesirable outcomes are seen as less likely.[28] If the success of a particular strategy is seen as necessary for highly valued goals to be attained, wishful thinking can lead to an exaggeration of the probability of success of that strategy. In his study of offensive military doctrines in World War I, Snyder (1984) found a tendency for military organizations "to see the necessary as possible" despite objective circumstances that might have induced more caution about the efficacy of offensive war plans. The tendency to exaggerate the probability of success of aggressive diplomatic or military policies may also result from political leaders' domestic political interests and the motivated biases generated by those interests (Lebow, 1981). These processes are reinforced by a tendency for preferences for a particular strategy to influence judgments of enemy intentions and capabilities. British estimates of Germany's capabilities in the 1930s went up as Chamberlain pursued his appeasement policies, but once Britain recognized the seriousness of the threat and began to prepare for war, their estimates of Germany's capabilities began to decline (Stein, 1993, p. 379). In this case, perceptions of threats served to rationalize existing policy rather than inform and shape that policy.

Because actors with different interests have different policy-motivated biases, we can sometimes test for the presence of these biases through a comparative study of different actors in different roles with different policy preferences and consequently different motivated biases. This is sometimes referred to as the "third party criterion" (Lebow, 1981). It is often argued, for example, that German misperceptions of British intentions in World War I (Fischer, 1988) were due to German motivated biases: German leaders' *hopes* that Britain would not intervene led them to *expect* that Britain would not intervene. The motivated bias interpretation of German misperceptions is weakened, however, by the fact that the opposite motivated biases of French and Russian leaders did not lead them to expect British intervention; instead they were also highly uncertain about how Britain would respond.

The third party criterion can be misleading if the different observers have access to different information, because differences in assessments might be based on informational asymmetries rather than motivated biases. This has important consequences for research design. While it is possible for the experimenter in the laboratory to control for information and for different conditions likely to lead to certain biases, it is much more difficult to do this in empirical studies of foreign policy behavior. It requires a sensitivity to alternative explanations, a carefully constructed research design to discriminate empirically among these explanations, and intensive data collection to conduct empirical tests.

A good example of such an effort is Kaufman's (1994) analysis of alternative explanations of how political actors update their belief systems in response to new information.[29] Kaufman included models of motivated defensive avoidance based on psychological commitment, information salience based on the availability heuristic, and belief system defense based on the resistance of core beliefs to change. Kaufman (1994) applied these models to German decision-making in the 1905–6 Moroccan crisis, carefully controlled for interests and information, and tested these models against a competing model of rational Bayesian updating. He concluded that variations in rates of belief change were hard to reconcile with rational Bayesian updating but were consistent with the predictions of the three psychological models, especially the motivated defensive avoidance hypothesis.

Heuristics and biases help to explain how political leaders judge their adversary's intentions and relative capabilities, which help shape the expected probabilities of various outcomes. Psychological variables also help to explain how leaders respond to probabilistic outcomes by influencing the values that individuals attach to outcomes and their willingness to take risks. I shall now consider recent work on loss aversion, framing, and risk propensity and their implications for foreign policy.

▲ Loss Aversion, Framing, and Risk Propensity

Whereas expected-utility theory posits that individuals act to maximize their expected utility, there is growing evidence that people systematically depart from the predictions of this core theory of rational decision making. Many of these anomalies are incorporated into prospect theory (Kahneman &

Tversky, 1979), an alternative theory of choice under conditions of risk that scholars have begun to apply to foreign policy and international relations (Davis, 2000; Farnham, 1994; Jervis, 1992; Levy, 1997, 2000; McDermott, 1998; Stein & Pauly, 1992).

Prospect theory posits that people are more sensitive to changes in assets than to net asset levels, in contrast to expected-utility theory's definition of value in terms of net assets or levels of wealth. People "frame" choice problems around a reference point (reference dependence), give more weight to losses from that reference point than to comparable gains (loss aversion), and engage in risk-averse behavior with respect to gains and risk-acceptant behavior with respect to losses.[30] Individuals' strong aversion to losses, particularly to "dead" losses that are perceived as certain (as opposed to those that are perceived as probabilistic), induces them to take significant risks in the hope of avoiding loss, even though the result may be an even greater loss and even though the expected value of the gamble may be considerably lower than the value of the certain loss. In addition, people value what they have more than comparable things not in their possession (the endowment effect), which in turn makes actual losses hurt more than foregone gains (Kahneman & Tversky, 1979).

As a result of the sensitivity to changes in assets, how people identify their reference points and hence frame a choice problem is critical, because gains and losses are measured with respect to deviations from the reference point. A change in reference point can lead to a change in preference (preference reversal) even if the values and probabilities associated with possible outcomes remain unchanged. People facing decisions over medical treatments, for example, respond differently to the idea of a 90 percent survival rate than to a 10 percent mortality rate, although the two are logically equivalent.

Most experimental work on framing and almost all of its applications to international relations focus on the effects of framing on choice rather than on the sources of framing and gives little attention to the question of why individuals select one reference point rather than another. While people often frame choice problems around the status quo, they are sometimes influenced by expectation levels, aspiration levels, and social comparisons to select a different reference point. There is substantial evidence, for example, that people "renormalize" their reference points after making gains faster than they do after incurring losses (Jervis, 1992; Kahneman, Knetsch, & Thaler, 1990, p. 1342).

These basic principles lead to a number of important propositions about foreign policy and international relations (Levy, 2000). (1) When states define their reference points around the status quo, there is a "status quo bias," which is stabilizing. If actors frame their choices around a reference point that is preferred to the status quo, there is a "reference point bias," a tendency to move away from the status quo toward the reference point, that is destabilizing. (2) State leaders take more risks to maintain their international positions, reputations, and domestic political support against potential losses than they do to enhance their positions. (3) Domestic publics punish their leaders more for losses than for the failure to make gains. (4) After suffering losses, political leaders have a tendency not to adjust to the new status quo but instead to take excessive risks to recover those losses. After making gains, political leaders tend to renormalize their reference points and to take excessive risks to defend the new status quo against subsequent losses. As a result, both sides engage in more risk-seeking behavior than expected-utility theory predicts. (5) Because people are slow to accept losses, sunk costs frequently influence decision-makers' calculations and state behavior, contrary to microeconomic theory. (6) Deterring an adversary from making gains is easier than deterring that adversary from recovering losses or compelling him to accept losses. (7) It is easier for states to cooperate in the distribution of gains than in the distribution of losses; political leaders will take more risks and bargain harder to minimize their share of the costs than to maximize their share of the gains.

While many of these hypotheses resonate well with common understandings of international politics, they reflect the generalization of robust findings for individual behavior in simple choice problems in the laboratory. Much more research is necessary to apply these hypotheses to collective decision-making bodies and to strategic interaction between states, and to construct convincing empirical tests of these hypotheses against competing explanations in settings where controlling for other sources of risk propensity and choice is extraordinarily difficult. One particularly critical task is to construct better research designs to determine how actors identify their reference points. While process tracing through case studies might be very useful for this task (Davis, 2000; McDermott, 1998), we should also explore the potential utility of more formal content analysis (Levi & Whyte, 1997) or other methodological approaches. More fundamental, however, is the need to reconceptualize risk orientation for situations in which the key variables of interest (power, reputation, security, and identity, for example) cannot easily be measured on an interval-level scale (O'Neill, 2001).

◤ Conclusions

By any standard, the analysis of the role of psychological variables in foreign policy and international relations has progressed enormously over the last half-century. Fifty years ago much of the research on the psychology of foreign policy and war was conducted by psychologists who gave little attention to the political and strategic contexts in which foreign policy decisions were made or to the methodological problems of generalizing from experimental findings in the laboratory to the more ill-defined contexts of foreign policy and international relations. While early decision-making frameworks in foreign policy analysis allowed for a potentially important role for psychological variables, researchers did not explore the origins and impact of these variables in any great detail.

Since the mid-1970s, however, we have witnessed the emergence of an increasingly influential cognitive research program. It has built on new developments in social psychology, including theories of attribution, schemas, and heuristics and biases, and it has begun to emphasize affective as well as strictly cognitive variables in response to a revival of interest in the importance of emotions, first in social psychology and then in political science. The literatures on cognition and affect are still basically distinct, however, and we know more about the separate effects of unmotivated and motivated biases than about how cognitive and affective factors interact to shape judgment and decision. We know that errors and biases are pervasive, but we do not understand the specific conditions under which they are most likely to arise.

While scholars have taken some steps to make applications of social psychology to foreign policy more sensitive to the political and strategic contexts in which foreign policy decisions are made, this is more advanced in some areas—learning and deterrence, for example—than in others (Herrmann & Fischerkeller, 1995), and we still have a long way to go. Social psychologists have not generally incorporated controls for key political variables into their experimental work, and few foreign policy analysts have been willing to test their more integrated hypotheses through experimental designs.[31] We have many historical case studies of threat perception that emphasize the political and strategic context of judgments and decision, but controlling for the relevant variables and ruling out alternative explanations remains a difficult and data-intensive task. The growing use of carefully matched comparative case studies have made important contributions in this direction, but more multimethod studies would provide greater confidence in the validity of our hypotheses.

One particularly important area for future research on threat perception lies at the intersection of political psychology and game theory. My discussion of threat perception, like nearly all such studies in the literature, has been one-sided, in that it has focused on how one state perceives adversary intentions and/or capabilities while ignoring how the adversary attempts to influence the way it is perceived by others by strategically manipulating the images it projects.[32] There is a substantial literature on "signaling" (Banks, 1991; Fearon, 1994), but this literature is almost exclusively rationalist and ignores the literature on the psychology of threat perception.[33] This is a serious limitation, because neither is really complete without the other (Jervis, 2002).

Game-theoretic "signaling models" incorporate the behavior of both sender and receiver, but they assume that signals are perceived and interpreted as the sender intends.[34] The theoretical and empirical literature on threat perception suggests, however, that the receiver's prior belief system, emotional needs, political interests, and organizational culture often lead to significant distortions in the way she interprets those signals.[35] The manipulation of images will be most effective if the sender understands the psychology of threat perception and shapes his projection of images to exploit the proclivities of the receiver. At the same time, threat assessment will be more accurate if it incorporates the adversary's incentives to influence the way others perceive them. An integrated theory of signaling and threat perception—which includes the manipulation of images, the psychology of threat perception, and the strategic interaction between them—and which is tested against the evidence through multiple methodologies—is a potentially fruitful area for future research.

The potential utility of integrating psychological theories of threat perception and game-theoretic models of signaling can be generalized. With the increasing emphasis in applied game theory on information, beliefs, and learning (Fudenberg & Levine, 1998; Hirshleifer & Riley, 1992), there are expanding possibilities for using game theoretic concepts and propositions to inform the psychology of strategic interaction, and perhaps also for the incorporation of "psychological" variables into game-theoretic models. One innovative example is O'Neill's (1999) game-theoretic analysis of honor, symbols, and war.

Although I have focused on the political psychology of threat perception, there are many other questions of foreign policy and international relations that could be much better understood by incorporating political psychology. Consider liberal international theory and in particular the common argument that ideas have an important impact on outcomes. Many of those interested in the effects of ideas express no interest in the sources of those ideas and make no effort to explore the role of learning or psychological variables more generally (Goldstein & Keohane, 1993, p. 7). It is difficult to assess the impact of ideas, however, without understanding their origins. If ideas change in response to changing international structures or shifting domestic or bureaucratic interests, those ideas do not have an autonomous causal impact on policy outcomes. Hypotheses on the causal influence of ideas would be more convincing if they were linked theoretically to a model of how ideas originate and change and were tested empirically against the evidence.

The social constructivist literature on international politics (Wendt, 1999) could also benefit from greater attention to the literature on political psychology. The emphasis on the *social* construction of identities and worldviews tends to give priority to the social and cultural sources of identity formation but to downplay the individual psychological needs that are satisfied by those identities and that systematically shape the social construction of identities (Kowert & Legro, 1996). As Goldgeier (1997) argues, "social psychological needs . . . constrain the construction of identities in a way which the analysis of cultural or institutional variables does not capture" (p. 142). The incorporation of psychological variables and their interaction effects into social and cultural explanations of identity would create a better balance between social structures and individual agency in constructivist research.

The literature on the diversionary theory of war (Levy, 1989) is another area in which greater attention to political psychology would be quite beneficial. Diversionary theory is based on the idea that conflict with the outgroup enhances cohesion within the ingroup and that the anticipation of this effect often tempts political leaders to initiate military conflict with external adversaries in order to benefit from a domestic "rally 'round the flag" effect. The literature on diversionary theory incorporates no theory of the enemy, however, and says little about which outgroups make optimal targets or generate the strongest and most long-lasting rally effects for political leaders. More fundamentally, diversionary theory does not incorporate a theory of the formation of identity groups. This may have been a modest limitation for traditional applications of diversionary theory to well-defined territorial states, but it is a glaring weakness for applications of diversionary theory to contemporary ethnonational conflicts, where identity is a key variable. Studies of diversionary behavior could benefit enormously by building on theories of identity formation and the role of the "other" in studies of ethnonationalism and in constructivist theory more generally.

Still another area in which greater attention to political psychology could enhance our understanding of foreign policy and international relations is foreign economic policy and international political economy. This field has been dominated by structural approaches that basically ignore individual-level sources of behavior and indeed the decision-making process itself (Caporaso & Levine, 1992; Gilpin, 2001). There is good reason to believe, however, that there is substantial variation in political and economic leaders' belief systems, the lessons they draw from history, their priorities among different economic values, their perception of threats to those values, their time horizons and the kinds of tradeoffs they are willing to make between current and future costs and benefits, and consequently in their economic policy preferences. Some might argue that structural theories of economic policy generate stronger predictions than do structural theories of security policy, leaving a smaller role for psychological variables, but this is an empirical question that needs to be investigated rather than assumed a priori.

This leaves a broad agenda for future research on the political psychology of foreign policy. We need to pay more attention to the interaction effects between psychological variables and the political and strategic conditions under which they have the greatest impact on foreign policy decisions and international interactions. Although some applications of social psychology attempt to contrast analytically distinct psychological models of foreign policy and international relations with alternative realist or domestic political models, this is probably not the most useful way to proceed in the long term. Psychological models alone do not provide complete explanations for foreign policy because they fail to explain how international and domestic conditions shape preferences and beliefs, or how the policy process aggregates individual preferences and beliefs into policy outputs for the state. Cognition and affect mediate between international and domestic structures and processes and the foreign policy decisions of political leaders, and we need to explain the nature of those reciprocal linkages by integrating psychological variables into more comprehensive theories of foreign policy and strategic interaction.

◣ Notes

I am grateful to Robert Jervis and David Sears for helpful comments on an earlier draft of this essay.

1. International relations theorists have traditionally distinguished between the actions and interactions of states in the world system. The study of foreign policy concerns the actions of states and the primary influences on those actions, while the study of international relations concerns the structural characteristics of the international system and the patterns of interactions between states. These two approaches basically focus on different dependent variables, or different units of analysis. In terms of Waltz's (1979) distinction, foreign policy analysis attempts to explain unit level behavior, while international politics attempts to explain system-level patterns.

2. The fact that the levels-of-analysis framework can be applied to both independent variables and dependent variables (to the former as a system for the classification of causal variables and to the latter as a description of the units of analysis whose behavior is to be explained—individual, organization, state, dyad, system) has created some confusion, and scholars are not always explicit about how they are using the concept.

3. Waltz (1979) is not always consistent on this matter, and one can find unambiguous statements about foreign policy behavior in his work (Elman, 1996, pp. 10–11).

4. Steinbrunner's (1974) "analytic paradigm" was another useful, though perhaps less influential, effort to systematize a rational model of decision-making.

5. An important exception was Lasswell's (1930) study *Psychopathology and Politics.*

6. By the mid-1940s many scholars, reacting against Freud, argued that there was little evidence in psychology or anthropology to support the argument that war was rooted in human nature and consequently inevitable (Allport, 1945).

7. In his comprehensive *Study of War,* for example, Quincy Wright (1942) gave far less attention to the psychology of war than to the military, technological, economic, or political dimensions of war. One important exception was Osgood's (1962) influential model of the graduated reduction in international tensions (GRIT).

8. For reviews of early social-psychological studies relating to foreign policy and international relations see Klineberg (1950, 1965), Osgood (1962), Kelman (1965), and DeRivera (1968).

9. For a general discussion of the psychobiographical approach see Lowenberg (1969). For a critique see Tetlock, Crosby, and Crosby (1981). For a more general treatment of the impact of personality on politics see Greenstein (1975).

10. For a useful review of the decision-making approach see Rosenau (1967).

11. The organizational process model rarely stands alone, and its key features are usually incorporated into an expanded governmental or bureaucratic politics model (Halperin, 1974).

12. For a combination of a political model of bureaucratic politics with a social psychological model of small group dynamics, see 't Hart (1990).

13. Model II raises a difficult set of questions with regard to classification. The emphasis on following routines or rules rather than maximizing interests based on a careful cost-benefit calculation may differ from the consequentialist logic of rationalist models and may fit some aspects of a constructivist paradigm, particularly the logic of rule-following based on social identity and social norms (Goldgeier & Tetlock, 2001, pp. 82–83; March & Olson, 1989). Rational choice theorists respond that the development of these rules and routines in the first place is a rational response to the uncertainty and complexity facing organizational actors.

14. George (1969, p. 195) urged analysts to focus on those beliefs that "can be inferred or postulated by the investigator on the basis of the kinds of data, observational opportunities, and methods generally available to political scientists." Note that some of George's earlier work was more psychodynamic in orientation (George & George, 1956) and that some scholars emphasize George's willingness to incorporate links between cognitive and personality elements of the operational code (Walker, 2002).

15. Images of the enemy are also central in scholarship outside of the operational code research program (Boulding, 1959; Finlay, Holsti, & Fagen, 1967; Holsti, 1967; White, 1968), including constructivist analyses of "self" and "other." For a summary and evaluation of research on images see chapter 9.

16. On schemas and scripts see Fiske and Taylor (1991) and Lau and Sears (1986).

17. See the discussion in chapter 2 of decisional heuristics that individuals use in their voting decisions.

18. While much of the literature on misperceptions suggests that political leaders have a bias toward the overestimation of external threats, which leads to the escalation of conflict spirals, another important line of research focuses on the underestimation of threats and the sources of intelligence failure (Bar-Joseph & Kruglanski, forthcoming, Betts, 1978; Handel, 1977; Shlaim 1976; Wohlstetter, 1962).

19. A good example is the origins of World War I, where the release of most of the relevant diplomatic documents has fueled rather than settled ongoing debates.

20. Rational choice theories of conflict also emphasize the importance of perceptions but sidestep the question of the accuracy of perceptions. While *differences* in perceptions have profound consequences (two unitary actors with complete information cannot rationally go to war; Fearon, 1995), the question of which set of perceptions is most accurate is basically irrelevant.

21. We can judge the accuracy of weather forecasts, for example, by examining the frequency of rain as a function of various forecasts of the likelihood of rain. If it rains about 70 percent of the time a forecast calls for a 70 percent chance of rain (and similarly for other estimates), we can conclude that forecasts are accurate.

22. Whether political decision-makers do in fact treat their perceptions of adversary capabilities and intentions as something comparable to a subjective probability distribution over possible outcomes is an interesting research question. There is some evidence that people downplay or deny the probabilistic nature of their estimates of adversary capabilities and intentions, because of tendencies toward overconfidence, bolstering to avoid value-tradeoffs, and other psychological mechanisms (Kahneman, Slovic, & Tversky, 1982; Nisbett and Ross, 1980).

23. For an integrated model of "motivated reasoning" that includes both cognition and affect, see Redlawsk (2002).

24. While most scholars interpret these various manifestations of theory-driven observation as nonmotivated, it is also possible to incorporate them into a framework of motivated biases. In cognitive dissonance theory (Festinger, 1957), for example, the discomfort of maintaining a belief system composed of inconsistent elements motivates people to reduce or eliminate those inconsistencies or to prevent them from arising. Selective attention, belief perseverance, and the principle of least resistance are each useful in this regard (Janis & Mann, 1977). I thank David Sears for raising this issue.

25. See the discussion in chapter 9 of enemy stereotypes.

26. For an application of attribution theory to the role of reputation in international politics, see Mercer (1996).

27. It is sometimes said that people learn more from failure than from success (Stein, 1994, p. 173). This may be true, but this pattern may reflect a bias toward emphasizing lessons that lead to policy change and hence are more observable and salient than lessons of success that reinforce existing policy.

28. The wishful thinking effect is exacerbated if decision-makers have an "illusion of control" (Langer, 1975) and exaggerate the degree of influence they have over the course of events. Students of crisis escalation and crisis management have explored beliefs and feelings about the "loss of control" and their often self-fulfilling character (George, 1991, pp. 545–566; Lebow, 1987, chs. 2–3).

29. For an alternative research design for studying perceptions see Herrmann (1988).

30. See O'Neill (2001) for a critique of common conceptions of risk propensity in international relations.

31. One of the more interesting exceptions is a study of the dynamics of foreign policy strategy selection that uses a computer-based "process tracer" (Mintz, Geva, Redd, & Carnes, 1997). For a study of the dynamics of voter decision-making in election campaigns using a similar methodology, see Lau and Redlawsk (1997).

32. The literature on intelligence failure includes some discussion of the role of strategic deception (Shlaim, 1976; Whaley, 1962).

33. Jervis's (1970) study of how states project images gave some attention to the symbolic and psychological dimensions of signaling but was primarily rationalist in orientation. It anticipated the logic of signaling games before the analytic tools for specifying and solving those games had been developed, and it preceded the emerging literature on heuristics and biases (Tversky & Kahneman, 1974) and on the psychology of threat perception (Jervis, 1976).

34. Signaling models are sequential games in which an uninformed player A, who is uncertain about her adversary B's "type" (hawk or dove, for example), makes inferences about B by observing B's behavior and then updating her prior probabilities about B's type. B understands this and behaves in such a way as to influence A's perceptions of B. Each understands that the other is behaving strategically to maximize its utility. Each understands also that the only behavior that is informative is that which is costly to the sender ("costly signals," as opposed to "cheap talk"), so that there are certain behaviors that one type but not the other would be willing to adopt. For a conceptually useful application of a signaling game model to an important historical case, see Wagner's (1989) analysis of the Cuban missile crisis.

35. See the discussion in chapter 9 of the limitations of rational models of signaling and deterrence.

▶ References

Allison, G. T. (1971). *Essence of decision: Explaining the Cuban missile crisis.* Boston: Little, Brown.

Allport, G. W. (1945) Human nature and the peace. *Psychological Bulletin, 42,* 376–78.

Almond, G. A. (1950). *The American people and foreign policy.* New York: Harcourt Brace.

Art, R. J. (1973). Bureaucratic politics and American foreign policy: A critique. *Policy Sciences, 4,* 467–90.

Banks, J. S. (1991) *Signaling games in political science.* New York: Routledge.

Bar-Joseph, U. & Kruglanski, A. W. (forthcoming). Intelligence failure and the need for cognitive closure: On the psychology of the Yom Kippur surprise. *Political Psychology.*

Bendor, J. & Hammond, T. H. (1992). Rethinking Allison's models. *American Political Science Review, 86,* 301–22.

Betts, R. K. (1978). Analysis, war and decision: Why intelligence failures are inevitable. *World Politics, 31,* 61–89.

Boulding, K. (1959). National images and international systems. *Journal of Conflict Resolution, 3,* 120–131.

Brecher, M. & Geist, B. (1980). *Decisions in crises: Israel, 1967 and 1973.* Berkeley: University of California Press.

Campbell, D. T., & LeVine, R. A. (1961). A proposal for cooperative cross-cultural research on ethnocentrism. *Journal of Conflict Resolution,* 5, 82–108.

Cantril, H. (1950). *Tensions that cause wars.* Urbana: University of Illinois Press.

Caporaso, J. A., & Levine, D. P. (1992). *Theories of political economy.* New York: Cambridge University Press.

Crawford, N. C. (2000). The passion of world politics: Propositions on emotion and emotional relationships. *International Security, 24,* 116–56.

Davis, J. W., Jr. (2000). *Threats and promises.* Baltimore: Johns Hopkins University Press.

DeRivera, J. H. (1968). *Psychological dimension of foreign policy.* Columbus, OH: Merrill.

Droba, D. D. (1931) Effect of various factors on militarism-pacifism. *Journal of Abnormal and Social Psychology, 26,* 141–53.

Durbin, E. F. M., & Bowlby, J. (1939) *Personal aggressiveness and war.* London: Kegan Paul.

Einstein, A., & Freud, S. (1932) *Why war?* Paris: International Institute of Intellectual Cooperation.

Elman, C. (1996). Why *not* neorealist theories of foreign policy? *Security Studies, 6,* 7–53.

Erikson, E. H. (1958). *Young man Luther: A study in psychoanalysis and history.* New York: Norton.

Etheridge, L. (1978). *A world of men: The private sources of American foreign policy.* Cambridge, MA: MIT Press.

Farnham, B. (1994). *Taking risks/avoiding losses.* Ann Arbor: University of Michigan Press.

Fearon, J. D. (1994). Signaling versus the balance of power and interests: An empirical test of a crisis bargaining model. *Journal of Conflict Resolution, 38,* 236–69.

Fearon, J. D. (1995). Rationalist explanations for war. *International Organization. 49,* 379–414.

Festinger, L. (1957). *A theory of cognitive dissonance.* Stanford, CA: Stanford University Press.

Finlay, D., Holsti, O. R., & Fagen, R. (1967). *Enemies in politics.* Chicago: Rand McNally.

Fischer, F. (1988). The miscalculation of English neutrality. In S. Wank, (Eds.), *The mirror of history* (pp. 364–393) Santa Barbara, CA: ABC-Clio.

Fiske, S. T., & Taylor, S. E. (1991). *Social cognition.* 2nd ed. New York: McGraw-Hill.

Fudenberg, D., & Levine, D. K. (1998). *The theory of learning in games.* Cambridge: MIT Press.

George, A. L. (1969). The "operational code": A neglected approach to the study of political leaders and decisionmaking. *International Studies Quarterly, 13,* 190–222.

George, A. L. (1979). The causal nexus between cognitive beliefs and decision-making behavior: The "operational code belief system." In L. S. Falkowski (Ed.), *Psychological models in international politics* (pp. 95–124). Boulder, CO: Westview.

George, A. L. (1980). *Presidential decisionmaking in foreign policy: The effective use of information and advice.* Boulder, CO: Westview.

George, A. L. (Ed.). (1991). *Avoiding inadvertent war: Problems of crisis management.* Boulder, CO: Westview.

George, A. L., & George, J. L. (1956). *Woodrow Wilson and Colonel House: A personality study.* New York: John Day.

Gilpin, R. (2001). *Global political economy.* Princeton: Princeton University Press.

Goldgeier, J. M. (1997). Psychology and security. *Security Studies, 6,* 137–66.

Goldgeier, J. M., & Tetlock, P. E. (2001). Psychology and international relations theory. *Annual Review of Political Science, 4,* 67–92.

Goldstein, J. & Keohane, R. O. (Eds.). (1993). *Ideas and foreign policy: Beliefs, institutions, and political change.* Ithaca, NY: Cornell University Press.

Greenstein, F. I. (1975). *Personality and politics.* New York: Norton.

Halperin, M. (1974). *Bureaucratic politics and foreign policy.* Washington, DC: Brookings.

Handel, M. I. (1977). The Yom Kippur War and the inevitability of surprise. *International Studies Quarterly, 21,* 461–502.

Hermann, C. F. (Ed.). (1972). *International crises: Insights from behavioral research.* New York: Free Press.

Hermann, M. G. (1978). Effects of personal characteristics of political leaders on foreign policy. In M. A. East, S. A. Salmore, & C. F. Hermann (Eds.), *Why nations act* (pp. 49–68). Beverly Hills, CA: Sage.

Hermann, M. G. (2002). Political psychology as a perspective on the study of politics. In K. R. Monroe (Ed.), *Political psychology* (pp. 43–63). Mahwah, NJ: Erlbaum.

Herrmann, R. K. (1988). The empirical challenge of the cognitive revolution: A strategy for drawing inferences about perceptions. *International Studies Quarterly, 32,* 175–203.

Herrmann, R. K., & Fischerkeller, M. (1995). Beyond the enemy image and spiral model: Cognitive-strategic research after the Cold War. *International Organization, 49,* 415–50.

Herwig, H. (1987). Clio deceived: Patriotic self-censorship in Germany after the Great War. *International Security, 12,* 5–44.

Hirshleifer, J., & Riley, J. G. (1992). *The analytics of uncertainty and information.* New York: Cambridge University Press.

Holsti, O. R. (1967). Cognitive dynamics and images of the enemy. *Journal of International Affairs, 21,* 16–29.

Holsti, O. R. (1970). The "operational code" approach to the study of political leaders: John Foster Dulles' philosophical and instrumental beliefs. *Canadian Journal of Political Science, 3,* 123–57.

Holsti, O. R. (1972). *Crisis, escalation, war.* Montreal: McGill-Queens University Press.

Holsti, O. R. (1976). Foreign policy formation viewed cognitively. In R. Axelrod (Ed.), *The structure of decision: The cognitive maps of political elites* (pp. 18–54). Princeton: Princeton University Press.

Holsti, O. R. (1977). *The "operational code" as an approach to the analysis of belief systems.* Final Report to the National Science Foundation, Grant No. SOC 75-15368. Duke University.

Holsti, O. R. (1989). Crisis decision making. In P. E. Tetlock, J. L. Husbands, R. Jervis, P. C. Stern, & C. Tilly, (Eds.), *Behavior, society, and nuclear war* (Vol. 1, pp. 8–84). New York: Oxford University Press.

Holsti, O. R., & George, A. L. (1975). The effects of stress on the performance of foreign policy-makers. In C. P. Cotter (Ed.), *Political Science Annual* (pp. 255–319). Indianapolis: Bobbs-Merrill.

Huntington, S. P. (1961). *The common defense.* New York: Columbia University Press.

Janis, I. L. (1982). *Groupthink.* (2nd rev. ed.) Boston: Houghton Mifflin.

Janis, I. L., & Mann, L. (1977). *Decision making: A psychological analysis of conflict, choice, and commitment.* New York: Free Press.

Jervis, R. (1970). *The logic of images in international relations.* Princeton: Princeton University Press.

Jervis, R. (1976). *Perception and misperception in international politics.* Princeton: Princeton University Press.

Jervis, R. (1985). Perceiving and coping with threat. In R. Jervis, R. N. Lebow, & J. G. Stein, *Psychology and deterrence* (pp. 13–33). Baltimore: Johns Hopkins University Press.

Jervis, R. (1988). War and misperception. *Journal of Interdisciplinary History, 18,* 675–700.

Jervis, R. (1992). Political implications of loss aversion. *Political Psychology, 13,* 87–204.

Jervis, R. (2002). Signaling and perception: Drawing inferences and projecting images. In K. R. Monroe (Ed.), *Political psychology* (pp. 293–312). Mahwah, NJ: Erlbaum.

Jones, B. D. (1999). Bounded rationality. *Annual Review of Political Science, 2,* 297–321.

Kahneman, D., Knetsch, J. L, & Thaler, R. H. (1990). Experimental tests of the endowment effect and the Coase theorem. *Journal of Political Economy, 98,* 1325–48.

Kahneman, D., Slovic, P., & Tversky, A. (Eds.). (1982). *Judgment under uncertainty: Heuristics and biases.* Cambridge: Cambridge University Press.

Kahneman, D., & Tversky, A. (1979). Prospect theory: An analysis of decision under risk. *Econometrica, 47,* 263–91.

Kaufman, C. D. (1994). Out of the lab and into the archives: A method for testing psychological explanations of political decision making. *International Studies Quarterly, 38,* 557–86.

Kelman, H. C. (1965). Social-psychological approaches to the study of international relations: Definition of scope. In H. C. Kelman (Ed.), *International behavior: A social-psychological analysis* (pp. 3–39). New York: Holt, Rinehart and Winston.

Khong, Y. F. (1992). *Analogies at war.* Princeton: Princeton University Press.

Klineberg, O. (1950). *Tensions affecting international understanding.* New York: Social Science Research Council.

Klineberg, O. (1965). *The human dimension in international relations.* New York: Holt, Rinehart and Winston.

Kowert, P., & Legro, J. (1996). Norms, identity, and their limits: a theoretical reprise. In P. J. Katzenstein (Ed.), *The culture of national security: Norms and identity in world politics* (pp. 451–497). New York: Columbia University Press.

Langer, E. J. (1975). The illusion of control. *Journal of Personality and Social Psychology, 32,* 311–28.

Larson, D. W. (1985). *Origins of containment: A psychological explanation.* Princeton: Princeton University Press.

Lasswell, H. D. (1930). *Psychopathology and politics.* Chicago: University of Chicago Press.

Lau, R. R., & Redlawsk, D. P. (1997). Voting correctly. *American Political Science Review, 91,* 585–98.

Lau, R. R., & Sears, D. O. (Eds.). (1986). *Political cognition.* Hillsdale, NJ: Erlbaum.

Lebow, R. N. (1981). *Between peace and war.* Baltimore: Johns Hopkins University Press.

Lebow, R. N. (1987). *Nuclear crisis management.* Ithaca, NY: Cornell University Press.

Leites, N. (1951). *The operational code of the Politburo.* New York: McGraw-Hill.

Leites, N. (1953). *A study of Bolshevism.* New York: Free Press.

Levi, A. S., & Whyte, G. (1997). A cross-cultural exploration of the reference dependence of crucial group decisions under risk. *Journal of Conflict Resolution, 41,* 792–813.

LeVine, R. A., & Campbell, D. T. (1972). *Ethnocentrism: Theories of conflict, ethnic attitudes, and behavior.* New York: Wiley.

Levy, J. S. (1983). Misperception and the causes of war. *World Politics, 36,* 76–99.

Levy, J. S. (1989). The diversionary theory of war: A critique. In M. I. Midlarsky, (Ed.), *Handbook of war studies* (pp. 259–288). London: Unwin-Hyman.

Levy, J. S. (1994). Learning and foreign policy: Sweeping a conceptual minefield. *International Organization, 48,* 279–312.

Levy, J. S. (1997). Prospect theory, rational choice, and international relations. *International Studies Quarterly, 41,* 87–112.

Levy, J. S. (2000). Loss aversion, framing effects, and international conflict. In M. I. Midlarsky (Ed.), *Handbook of war studies* II (pp. 193–221). Ann Arbor: University of Michigan Press.

Lowenberg, P. (1969). *Decoding the past: The psychohistorical approach.* Berkeley: University of California Press.

March, J. G. (1978). Bounded rationality, ambiguity, and the engineering of choice. *Bell Journal of Economic Management Science, 9,* 587–608.

March, J. G. & Olson, J. P. (1989). *Rediscovering institutions: The organizational basis of politics.* New York: Free Press.

Marcus, G. E. (2000). Emotions in politics. *Annual Review of Political Science, 3,* 221–50.

May, E. R. (1973). *Lessons of the past.* London: Oxford University Press.

May, M. A. (1943). *A social psychology of war and peace.* New Haven: Yale University Press

McDermott, R. (1998). *Risk-taking in international politics: Prospect theory in American foreign policy.* Ann Arbor: University of Michigan Press.

McGuire, W. J. (1985). Attitudes and attitude change. In G. Lindzey & E. Aronson (Eds.), *The handbook of social psychology* (Vol. 2, pp. 233–346). New York: McGraw-Hill.

Mearsheimer, J. (2001). *The tragedy of great power politics.* New York: Norton.

Mercer, J. (1996). *Reputation and international politics.* Ithaca, NY: Cornell University Press.

Mintz, A., Geva, N., Redd, S. B., & Carnes, A. (1997). The effect of dynamic and static choice sets on political decision making: An analysis using the decision board platform. *American Political Science Review, 91,* 553–66.

Neustadt, R. (1960). *Presidential power.* New York: Wiley.

Nisbett, R., & Ross, L. (1980). *Human inference: Strategies and shortcomings of social judgment.* Englewood Cliffs, NJ: Prentice-Hall.

North, R., C. (1967). Perception and action in the 1914 crisis. *Journal of International Affairs, 21,* 103–22.

O'Neill, B. (1999). *Honor, symbols, and war.* Ann Arbor: University of Michigan Press.

O'Neill, B. (2001). Risk aversion in international relations theory. *International Studies Quarterly, 45,* 617–40.

Osgood, C. E. (1962). *Alternative to war or surrender.* Urbana: University of Illinois Press.

Redlawsk, D. P. (2002). Hot cognition or cool consideration: Testing the role of motivated reasoning in political decision making. *Journal of Politics, 64,* 1021–1044.

Rosenau, J. N. (1966). Pre-theories and theories of foreign policy. In R. B. Farrell (Ed.), *Approaches to comparative and international politics* (pp. 27–92). Evanston, IL: Northwestern University Press.

Rosenau, J. N. (1967). The premises and promises of decision-making analysis. In J. C. Charlesworth (Ed.), *Contemporary political analysis* (pp. 189–211). New York: Free Press.

Schilling, W., Hammond, P., & Snyder, G. (Eds.). (1962). *Strategy, politics and defense budgets.* New York: Columbia University Press.

Shlaim, A. (1976). Failures in national intelligence estimates: The case of the Yom Kippur War. *World Politics, 28,* 348–80.

Simon, H. A. (1957). *Models of man.* New York: Wiley.

Snyder, J. (1984). *The ideology of the offensive: Military decision-making and the disasters of 1914.* Ithaca, NY: Cornell University Press.

Snyder, J. (1991). *Myths of empire: Domestic politics and international ambition.* Ithaca, NY: Cornell University Press.

Snyder, R. C., Bruck, H. W., & Sapin, B. (Eds.). (1962). *Decision-making as an approach to the study of international politics*. New York: Free Press.

Stagner, R. (1942). Some factors related to attitude toward war, 1938. *Journal of Social Psychology, 16*, 131–42.

Stein, J. G. (1985). Calculation, miscalculation, and conventional deterrence, II: The view from Jerusalem. In R. Jervis, R. N. Lebow, & J. G. Stein (Eds.), *Psychology and deterrence* (pp. 60–88). Baltimore: Johns Hopkins University Press.

Stein, J. G. (1993). Building politics into psychology: The misperception of threat. In N. J. Kressel (Ed.), *Political psychology* (pp. 367–392). New York: Paragon.

Stein, J. G. (1994). Political learning by doing: Gorbachev as uncommitted thinker and motivated learner. *International Organization, 48*, 155–84.

Stein, J. G., & Pauly, L. (Eds.). (1992). *Choosing to cooperate: How states avoid loss*. Baltimore: Johns Hopkins University Press.

Stein, J. G., & Tanter, R. (1980). *Rational decision-making: Israel's security choices, 1967*. Columbus: Ohio State University Press.

Steinbrunner, J. D. (1974). *The cybernetic theory of decision*. Princeton: Princeton University Press.

Tetlock, P. E. (1991). Learning in U.S. and Soviet foreign policy. In G. W. Breslauer & P. E. Tetlock (Eds.), *Learning in U.S. and Soviet foreign policy* (pp. 20–61). Boulder: Westview.

Tetlock, P. E. (1992). The impact of accountability on judgment and choice: Toward a social contingency model. In M. P. Zanna (Ed.), *Advances in experimental social psychology* (Vol. 25, pp. 331–76). New York: Academic Press.

Tetlock, P. E. (1998). Social psychology and world politics. In D. Gilbert, S. Fiske, & G. Lindzey (Eds.), *Handbook of social psychology* (4th ed., pp. 868–912). New York: McGraw-Hill.

Tetlock, P. E., Crosby, F., & Crosby, T. L. (1981). Political psychobiography. *Micropolitics, 1*, 191–213

't Hart, P. (1990). *Groupthink in government: A study of small groups and policy failure*. Amsterdam: Swets and Zeitlinger.

Thurstone, L. L., & Chave, E. J. (1929). *The measurement of attitude*. Chicago: University of Chicago Press.

Tversky, A., & Kahneman, D. (1974). Judgment under uncertainty: Heuristics and biases. *Science, 185*, 1124–31.

Vertzberger, Y. Y. I. (1990). *The world in their minds*. Stanford, CA: Stanford University Press.

Wagner, R. H. (1989). Uncertainty, rational learning, and bargaining in the Cuban missile crisis. In P. C. Ordeshook (Ed.), *Models of strategic choice in politics* (pp. 177–205). Ann Arbor: University of Michigan Press.

Wagner, R. H. (1992). Rationality and misperception in deterrence theory. *Journal of Theoretical Politics, 42*, 115–141.

Walker, S. G. (1977). The interface between beliefs and behavior: Henry Kissinger's operational code and the Vietnam War. *Journal of Conflict Resolution, 21*, 129–68.

Walker, S. G. (1995). Psychodynamic processes and framing effects in foreign policy decision-making: Woodrow Wilson's operational code. *Political Psychology, 16*, 697–717.

Walker, S. G. (2003). A cautionary tale: Operational code analysis as a scientific research program. In C. Elman & M. F. Elman (Eds.), *Progress in international relations theory*. Cambridge, MA: MIT Press.

Waltz, K. N. (1959). *Man, the state, and war*. New York: Columbia University Press.

Waltz, K. N. (1979). *Theory of international politics*. Reading, MA: Addison-Wesley.

Wendt, A. E. (1999). *Social theory of international politics*. New York: Cambridge University Press.

Whaley, B. (1962). *Codeword Barbarossa*. Cambridge, MA: MIT Press.

White, R. (1968). *Nobody wanted war*. New York: Doubleday.

Winter, D. G. (2002). An intellectual agenda for political psychology. In K. R. Monroe (Ed.), *Political psychology* (pp. 385–398). Mahwah, NJ: Erlbaum.

Wohlstetter, R. (1962). *Pearl Harbor: Warning and decision*. Stanford, CA: Stanford University Press.

Wright, Q. (1942). *A study of war*. Chicago: University of Chicago Press.

9 Richard K. Herrmann

Image Theory and Strategic Interaction in International Relations

Lee J. Cronbach (1957) described social psychology as divided into two disciplines, one that explained an actor's behavior from the outside, relying on the notion of the environment (Skinner, 1960), and the other explaining behavior from the inside, relying on the concept of personality. In international relations theory a similar division was evident in the 1950s. One school sought to explain state behavior from the outside, looking primarily at the distribution of power in the system and the external constraints and incentives it represented for any particular state. Another school sought to explain state behavior by examining the various motives and perceptions that prevailed in each state (Sprout & Sprout, 1965). Both schools of thought employed the basic methods of positivist research, defining concepts, laying out deductive models, and pursuing empirical tests (Riker, 1962; Snyder, Bruck, & Sapin, 1962). Where they differed was with regard to their assumptions about the nature of decision-making.

Do people respond to the external environment as if they were rationally maximizing the payoffs available given the objective situation? That was the question that lay at the center of the dispute between the two perspectives. The first school of thought argued that it made sense to assume that actors do perceive the environment correctly and do decide rationally. Scholars in this school assumed that actors would make mistakes but learn from these and over time act as if they were rational players responding to objective incentive structures. The second school of thought assumed that people do not make decisions or learn as effectively as a rational model assumed. This school also doubted that the external environment looked the same to the actors as it did to the scholarly observers (Brecher, 1972, 1973; Rummel, 1975). For instance, people may disagree over how compelling the forces in the environment are and not share scholarly judgments on these matters, especially not scholarly judgment employing twenty-twenty hindsight. Scholars in this school also felt it was a mistake to assume that prescriptions for how people ought to make decisions were good descriptions of how people did make decisions (Steinbruner, 1974). They argued that more empirical attention needed to be paid to both the substance of people's beliefs and the procedures of their decision-making (Axelrod, 1976; Holsti, 1970; Simon, 1985). This perspective has often concentrated on the importance of leaders and the differences among them (Byman and Pollack, 2001).

Deciding to explain action as a product of an actor's beliefs rather than as a result of an objective external environment has important implications for research. It suggests that the identification of an actor's beliefs, including beliefs about other actors, the environmental situation, and how relationships work in the system need to be the substance of empirical investigation (Herrmann, 1988). In the laboratory, this means the inclusion of manipulation checks. In the natural setting of international relations, the task is complicated because it means both identifying the beliefs of leaders who have many reasons not to reveal these—and who in fact have many reasons to manipulate other people's understanding of what they believe—and moving from an individual level of a leader, who may have beliefs, to the level of a collective actor, granting to that collective actor anthropomorphic qualities. It was in the effort to meet the challenges posed by the phenomenological perspective that the image concept was refined and theories of images developed.

This chapter begins with a discussion of the concept of image. It defines the concept and explains how it has been used to study substantive beliefs that actors have about the world, and especially the other actors they interact with. This initial discussion concentrates on both the substantive dimensions scholars have used to organize their conception of images and the cognitive processes that images are associated with. The second part of the chapter turns to various theories regarding the origins of images and the functions they serve. This includes a discussion of both the factors that motivate images and the relationship between images and emotions. It also involves the uses that stereotypical images are put to in efforts to infer underlying motives. The third part of the chapter explores the implications of using an image-based approach when theorizing about the interaction between states, nations, and other groups. The implications for understanding processes of communication and interpretation receive special attention, as do the implications for rational deterrence theory. The final part of the chapter also discusses the implications of an image-based approach for theories of learning and conflict resolution, although this later topic is left mostly for chapter 10.

◤ Images as Conceptual Constructs

The Components of an Image

To describe an actor's view of the world or perception of another actor is a complicated task. A person may have many beliefs about another actor, including, among other things, what the actor values, what role it plays in a particular region, and how its economy works or political system functions. Images also can include information about the self as well as the other, this is especially true when key components of an image refer to relational attributes like the compatibility of goals or relative power. In a study of statements made by top leaders in 71 governments, K. J. Holsti (1970) identified 17 role conceptions. Each role conception included a package of information about the self, others, and expectations for behavior. More recently, constructivists studying international relations have concentrated on the notion of an actor's identity, defining the concept in terms reminiscent of previous notions of role.

Like Holsti, recent constructivists often rely on inductive methods to identify the role conceptions (identities) that actors may have and share. For the most part, these constructivist efforts have not tried to develop a taxonomy of roles (identities) as Holsti did but have instead sought to describe identities in specific cases. They have also sought to establish identities as shared—meaning around which there is intersubjective agreement among actors. Hoslti also discussed the shared aspects of roles and explored both the possibility that role conceptions are shared and the possibility that actors do not agree on the role of a particular actor. In sociology, meanwhile, Alan Page Fiske (1991) has developed a theory of social relations that rests heavily on the idea that incompatible role conceptions lead to contradictory behavioral expectations and to conflict.

The effort to describe role conceptions and identities from a process that is believed to be mostly inductive can lead to the reification of conceptual categories that the researcher brings to the task and to the implicit imposition of the researcher's views. Of course, deductive strategies also impose categories and ideas but do so in an explicit fashion. Robert Axelrod (1976) sought to employ a minimal deductive frame built around the idea that policy-relevant beliefs are composed of mostly causal claims and inferences. These cognitive maps that Axelrod and others drew, however, like role conceptions and idiosyncratic constructed identities, quickly became extremely complicated. Because they are induced from the cases they sought to explain, they also were potentially tautological and typically nontransferable to other cases. In an effort to provide parsimony and explanatory power, Holsti (1970), offered preliminary theoretical speculations about the sources and underlying causes of national role conceptions. He identified such factors as perceptions of threat, economic needs, ideological principles, and superior capabilities. Other scholars moved in a parallel direction, at least in the sense that they focused on what were thought to be a smaller set of basic perceptions that defined the underlying architecture of relationships.

Kenneth Boulding (1959), for example, posited a theory of national images. He argued that "the images which are important in international systems" are "those which a nation has of itself and of those other bodies in the system which constitute its international environment" (pp. 120–121). In his conception, the perceived hostility or friendliness and the perceived strength or weakness of a unit were the central features of a subject's image of that unit (pp. 124–125). These two core dimensions of both self-image and images of others were thought to shape strategic decisions and thus provide a parsimonious focus for the study of an actor's beliefs (Boulding, 1956).

In addition to these two architectural dimensions identified by Boulding, a number of scholars have subsequently argued that images of a unit's culture as more or less sophisticated, democratic, and advanced or crude, nondemocratic, and backward are also a basic underlying cognitive component that is central to foreign policy decision-making (M. Cottam, 1994; R. Cottam, 1977; Herrmann, 1985). John Owen (1997) has argued that perceptions of another state's intentions as hostile or friendly may derive from prior images of the state's culture as liberal and democratic or illiberal and nondemocratic.

Karl Deutsch and Richard Merritt (1965) defined images as "combinatorial constructs" that represented the integration of multiple dimensions. Richard Cottam (1977), drawing on the work of Solomon Asch (1952), defined images as gestalts or descriptive constructs employed to describe the integrative combination of judgments about a unit regarding the threat or opportunity it represented, its relative power, and its relative culture. Cottam, like William Scott (1965) earlier, also argued that images included an emotional component that gave rise to behavioral inclinations vis-à-vis the perceived actor.

The dimensions thought to be important in image theories are not arbitrarily selected. Relative power, of course, is the central explanatory concept in traditional realism (Morgenthau, 1973). Perceived threat is also important in realism and is a foundational concept in neorealism (Waltz, 1979) and, as Jack Levy recounts (chapter 8), has been central to psychological approaches to foreign policy. Perceived opportunity has received less attention than perceived threat but is central to any theory of foreign policy motivation that distinguishes between imperial and status quo or offensive and defensive actors. Cultural status is central to anthropological and sociological notions of intergroup relations (Horowitz, 1985).

As an analytic construct, the image concept is designed to capture the understandings of relationships. That is, each dimension is defined in relational terms. A perception of another actor as stronger or weaker than the perceiving actor defines both the view of the other and the view of the self. This is also true for perceived relative cultural status. Identifying threat and opportunity defines the understanding of the interdependent relationship between the goals of the perceiving actor and the goals of the perceived actor.

Herrmann and colleagues (1997, p. 409) outlined the range of possible three-dimensional combinational gestalts that could be used to describe actors' beliefs about the relationships they are in. Of course, developing the conceptual construct is a necessary step in the research task, but it does not solve the problem of identifying what any particular actor's images are. Studies of what leaders believe found a number of empirical patterns. For instance, Robert Jervis (1976, pp. 319–329) concluded thát leaders were prone to believe that other actors had highly centralized decision-making structures and were able to plan and execute unified operations. He also found that leaders often overestimated their own importance as the target of other actors and as the cause of other actors' behavior (Jervis, 1976, pp. 343–349). Ralph K. White (1968) had previously (white, 1965) argued that several substantive stereotypes were very common in international relations. He described the "diabolical enemy-image," the "virile self-image," and the "moral self-image" as three of these. Finlay, Holsti, and Fagen (1967) studied the enemy image in detail. Richard Cottam (1977) proposed a general theory of images that connected the possible combinational analytic gestalts serving as analytic constructs and the substantive patterns described by Jervis and White.

Ideal-Type Images and Stereotypes

Cottam (1977) argued that the substantive patterns found in stereotypes were associated with ideal-typical gestalts. In other words, certain ideal-typical understandings of a relationship were associated with stereotypical substantive beliefs about the self and the other. These stereotypes provide a degree of simplicity and orderliness that make the world more easily comprehensible and represent what Levy (chapter 8) refers to as common cognitive shortcuts. The enemy image was the best-known example of this pattern. Perceptions of threat when combined with perceptions of relatively similar capability and cultural status were in the ideal-typical case associated with the diabolical enemy-stereotype. This stereotype was characterized by the claim that the enemy had aggressive and evil intentions and was led by a centralized and monolithic leadership that was capable of carrying out intricate conspiracies. Moreover, in the stereotype, the enemy is seen as responsive to the perceiver's influence and as acting with the perceiver as the primary target. Typically, the enemy is presumed to take advantage of opportunities presented by the perceiver's weakness and to retreat in the face of the perceiver's strength and resolution.

Although the enemy-image has received a lot of attention (Holsti, 1967; Silverstein, 1989), it is not the only image that is important in world affairs. Other combinatorial constructs describing other perceived relationships also associate in ideal-typical fashion with stereotypes. For example, perceived opportunity to exploit combined with a perception that the perceiver's state is superior in capability and culture has associated with stereotypes of colonies and dependents (M. Cottam, 1994; R. Cottam, 1977; Herrmann & Fischerkeller, 1995). In this stereotype, the colony is described as torn between progressive, moderate, and responsible leaders and irresponsible agitators. The population is assumed to be apolitical and not yet aware of mass politics, while the progressive leaders are thought to be well-meaning but somewhat incompetent and in need of tutelage. The flip-side self-image is that the perceiver is helping the moderate, responsible leadership to fend off the agitators and to help the community develop in positive directions.

Another relationship that has been studied is characterized by perceptions of opportunity to exploit another actor combined with perceptions of superior power and comparable culture. The stereotype associated with this perceived relationship is the degenerate (Herrmann, 1985). It is characterized by a picture of the other as weak of will and currently consumed by hedonistic desires. The degenerate is seen as having a glorious past but currently suffering from decadence and corruption. The related self-image is that the perceiver is providing moral discipline and helping the degenerate to pull itself out of the gutter and return to civilized status. When perceptions of opportunities feature mutual gain and not exploitation and are combined with perceptions of comparable power and culture, an allied stereotype is thought to form that is different from the degenerate. In the allied stereotype, the ally is seen as already morally upright and driven by benign and altruistic motives. Its government is seen as enjoying widespread respect and popularity along with gifted and intelligent leaders.

Stereotypes as Schemata

The stereotypes associated with each ideal-typical combinatorial gestalt operate as integrated mental models or schemata (Fiske & Taylor, 1991; Northway, 1940; Sherman, Judd & Park, 1989). That is, these stereotypical clusters of knowledge define templates that, when evoked, provide a picture of the situation that fills in missing information and facilitates decision-making (Abelson, Dasgupta, Park, and Banaji 1998; Campbell 1967). In other words, if a person believes he is in a particular type of relationship, then he may define the self and the other in stereotypic schematic terms and construct a picture of the self and other that draws as much on prior knowledge about the general stereotype as on information specific to the other actor in question. When the schema is well learned, if a perceiver receives one piece of information about another actor and classifies the relationship, he is likely to fill in the rest of the picture of the other actor with schema-consistent features. In the process, the perceiver is likely to lose track of which pieces information about the other actor emanate from empirical evidence and which pieces are schematic fill-ins.

Several studies have investigated the schematic quality of foreign policy stereotypes. Martha Cottam (1986, pp. 61–109) surveyed decision-makers in Washington to see how they categorized countries. She found that they used categories that they labeled ally, enemy, dependent of enemy, dependent of United States, and neutral. She also examined the use of hegemonist and puppet as categories. In a series of experiments Herrmann, Voss, Schooler, and Ciarrochi (1997) examined the enemy, ally, degenerate, and colony stereotypes. They provided participants with information about one feature of another country, describing, for example, the country's motives, capability, or decision-making process. After receiving the one piece of information, participants were asked to identify the other features of the country to see if they indeed would fill in schemata-consistent information. Participants did this for the enemy, ally, and colony stereotypes. Alexander, Brewer, and Herrmann (1999) conducted a subsequent experiment with similar results for the enemy, ally, dependent, and barbarian stereotypes.

Schemata, of course, do more than organize information about other actors and the self into a coherent picture. They also affect the memory of information, the reception of new information, and the process of learning (Alba & Hasher, 1983). Once a perceiver constructs a picture of a relationship in stereotypic terms, she is likely to remember old information and interpret new information in a fashion consistent with the stereotype. Learning, therefore, is more likely to involve increasing confidence in one's prior view and less likely to involve changing the substance of that view. This is made only more likely in the international realm by the ambiguous nature of many actions and sources of information and the analytic escape hatches that protect the most common stereotypes from disconfirming evidence.

The stereotypes that have received attention as prevalent in foreign policy include features that make them difficult to disconfirm (Scott, 1965). The enemy stereotype, for example, includes several features that immunize it from disconfirmation and allow it to function as an "inherent bad faith" model (Holsti, 1970; Stuart & Starr, 1982). The stereotype pictures the other actor as motivated by evil and unlimited motives yet responsive to the perceiver's actions. Consequently, when the target country behaves aggressively, this confirms the initial premise; when it does not, the restraint is typically attributed to the resolute and strong act of the perceiver's country. The enemy may be pictured as a "paper tiger," meaning that it seeks easy and unopposed opportunities but when met with firm resistance is shown to be hollow. In the political realm this hollowness is often attributed to the unpopular nature of the stereotyped government and its inability to motivate its people by any means other than coercion. When it is simply impossible to construct a picture of a strong and resolute act on the part of the perceiver's country to which the other side's nonaggressive behavior can be attributed, then the belief that the other actor is highly unified and able to carry out conspiracy protects the prior view. The perceiver explains the apparent nonaggressive restraint as a trick, perhaps even a conspiracy, designed to lull the perceiver's state into a condition of relaxed vulnerability.

The enemy stereotype is the best-studied inherent bad faith model. It is not unique, however, in its immunization from falsification. The stereotype of a dependent colony also has features that protect it from empirical contradiction (M. Cottam, 1994; R. Cottam, 1977; Herrmann et al., 1997). Central to this stereotype, for example, is the belief that the leaders in the target country are inept and unable to manage complicated matters without tutelage. Also integral to the stereotype is the belief that the agitators in the country have secret links to foreign agents who are advising them. Consequently, if native leaders behave in surprisingly intelligent and farsighted manner, this can be attributed to the foreign agents and the enemy's conspiracy.

The imperialist stereotype that leaders in former colonies often have of the former metropole likewise includes features that protect it from such falsification. For instance, in this stereotype of an imperialist, the empire is pictured as working through a conspiratorial "hidden hand." Consequently, decisions that appear on the surface to be made locally can be attributed to unseen foreign advisers. Meanwhile, acts that have no obvious exploitative purpose can be seen as clever tricks and conspiracies designed to mislead.

Ally images depend less on conspiracy beliefs and more on constructions of the situation to resist contradictory information. In this case, beliefs about the ally's benign intentions can be sustained by attributing aggressive and violent behavior to situational provocation, preemptive self-defense, and other justificatory accounts (Scott & Lyman, 1968).

Ideal-Type Images as Referents

Stereotypical images may operate as schemata, but this does not mean they are useful descriptors of any particular person's beliefs. Advocates of image theory (Cottam, 1977; Herrmann, 1985) do not argue that most people's views are stereotypic. Rather, they argue that understandings of a relationship can be represented with a three-dimensional combinatorial construct. In the ideal-typical case, the values on each of these three dimensions (goal interdependence, relative capability, and relative cultural status) may be defined as reaching an end-point on a scale (Alexander, Brewer & Herrmann, 1999). This creates a referent that is an extreme version of the belief. The views of actual people can be measured as more or less like the ideal-typical. Because the ideal-typical images are associated with recognizable stereotypes, the resemblance between a particular person's views and the substance of the stereotypes can be taken as a measure of the similarity between the person's beliefs and the ideal-typical combinatorial construct.

As Levy explains in chapter 8, defining, identifying and measuring misperception is very difficult. It is for that reason that comparing actual views to stereotypical images is valuable. It provides a way to measure and identify perceptions without necessarily treating them as misperceptions. Rather than comparing a person's views to a presumed reality, this strategy compares a person's views to well-known stereotypes. It is not necessary to establish the accuracy of the stereotype, although, as will be explained later, their role in balancing emotional and cognitive inclinations may suggest bias in a person's perception.

The creation of conceptual constructs and measurement strategies is necessary to empirically investigate beliefs. Important puzzles, however, remain. Perhaps the most vexing of these is what explains the individual variation in the stereotypic character of beliefs. In other words, why are some people inclined to stereotypic beliefs and other people not? Is this a personality disposition that leads a person to hold stereotypic images across all actors, or is it specific to certain actors and situations? Related to the question of why there are individual differences is the broader theoretical question of where images come from and what drives the shape they take. These questions attract substantial attention because they are at the center of discussions regarding how to change images and thus engineer political relationships. Before I turn to a further discussion of theories that use images to explain the dynamics of interaction in intergroup relations, I examine briefly theories that purport to explain images.

▶ Theories of Images

Of course the question of what causes beliefs and drives images was at the center of the debate between the two disciplines of social psychology identified by Cronbach (1957, 1975). It is also at the center of the dispute between material and ideational approaches to international relations theory. In materialist perspectives, beliefs are caused by the objective environment and the person's goals. Bureaucratic politics models, for example, expect a person's beliefs to follow from his role and the organizational incentives that role involves. Models with a more economic flavor assume that beliefs about world politics are shaped by the economic self-interest evident in material circumstances (Snyder, 1991; Solingen, 1998). Beliefs might also be motivated by emotional affinities (favorable or hostile) with outgroups or by a desire to protect self-images and self-esteem (Kunda, 1990).

A theory that claims that beliefs follow from specific material factors is difficult to test because it is difficult to control for the possible effects of many other factors such as personality, prior ideology, and family experience. It has proved extremely difficult, even in the laboratory, to determine if a belief is motivated by some ulterior interest (Tetlock & Levi, 1982). To determine this in the natural setting is perhaps impossible, although Chaim Kaufmann (1994) argues in favor of one strategy for accomplishing this. He searches for cases in which he feels it is possible to assume that leaders all had access to the same information and then attributes differences in judgments to motivated reasoning. Because it is so difficult to determine how the myriad of factors that might affect reasoning will combine to produce beliefs, the cognitive revolution has focused attention on the substance and consequences of beliefs rather than the prior question of their causes (Gardner, 1985). This skepticism regarding the ability to demonstrate with empirical rigor the predictive and explanatory accuracy of theories purporting to explain the origins of images has not deterred scholars from exploring the functions images serve. These include both cognitive functions and emotional functions.

Images as Cognitive Shortcuts

Images and stereotypes serve a necessary cognitive function. They provide categories that allow people to sort and make sense of the political environment and their relationships in it. As cognitive simplifications, they manage inevitable information overload and facilitate decision-making. They also give rise to heuristic shortcuts that fit with a picture of people as cognitive misers trying to make sense of the world in a parsimonious fashion. Social psychologists typically argue that this sort of simplification and categorization is required because of inherent limitations in people's information-processing abilities. Robert Jervis described the processes of perception, about which social psychologists were fairly confident, as they pertain to international politics. He illustrated how cognitive shortcuts and heuristic rules could be used to explain biased patterns in foreign policy thinking. He argued that patterns that were often attributed to self-serving motives could be explained in these cognitive terms without evoking theories of motivated and wishful thinking (1976, pp. 117–216, 356–381). At the time, other scholars working on international relations who shared Jervis's interests in cognition argued that the emotional aspect of particularly stereotypical images was hard to deny and that the association between images and suspected motives was quite important.

Images as Motivated Reasoning

Richard Ned Lebow (1981), for example, in his study of war initiation, argued that one route to war included motivated misperceptions. He found that when leaders faced strong domestic challenges and needed a foreign policy victory, they often came to believe such a victory was possible even though it was not. This led these leaders to challenge adversaries and initiate military campaigns in the expectation of success. These initiatives, rather than proving successful, led to conflict and war. Robert Jervis (1985) argued that both unmotivated and motivated biases influenced threat perceptions and discussed at some length the effects of both affect and the subconscious need to see the world in certain ways. Although neither Lebow nor Jervis evoked psychodynamic theories, earlier scholars had argued that underlying personal needs, such as that for power, shaped perception and thinking, often leading to pathologies (Lasswell, 1930, 1948).

Ralph K. White (1968) argued that stereotypes, like that of the diabolical enemy, and what he called "black-and-white" thinking in general, followed from a number of unconscious motives, including desires for power and prestige. Lloyd Etheredge (1978) examined career foreign service officers at the U.S. Department of State and built on Lasswell's previous work. He argued that personality affected perception and concentrated on what he called projective intuition and emotion-based syndromes. Robert

Robins and Jerrold Post (1997) also developed theory in this direction and explored in detail the phenomenon of paranoia. They suggested that a need for enemies might also be a subconscious motive affecting cognitive understandings and developed a multidimensional picture of the mind of the paranoid and conspiracy theorist. Robins and Post explored both subconscious and conscious aspects of hate and analyzed in this regard Pol Pot, Idi Amin, Joseph Stalin, and Adolf Hitler, as well as religious extremists and terrorists.

Richard Cottam (1977) also emphasized the role of emotion and developed a theory that emphasized motivated reasoning. Cottam, however, did not draw on psychodynamic foundations; rather, he built on the balance theory of Fritz Heider (1958). This theory proposed one way that cognitive and affective factors interact to shape judgment and decision, a subject that Levy (chapter 8) acknowledges has not been explored often enough. Cottam suspected that images were motivated, but he separated the identification of the specific motives and the general cognitive processes. Cottam argued that many different specific motives could serve as the basis for seeing threats and opportunities and argued that as feelings of threat and opportunity became more intense the inclination to stereotypes would increase. Cottam borrowed from Fritz Heider (1958) the idea that people seek a harmonious balance between their sentiments about another actor and the attributes they attach to that actor in their cognitive representation of that actor. In other words, when a foreign actor provoked a high degree of felt threat in a perceiver, the perceiver would be inclined to believe in a cognitive picture of that target actor that balanced with this felt threat. Balance, in this case, would mean that the cognitive picture of the other actor would include attributes that allowed the perceiver to act to reduce the threat without moral inhibition. For example, intense perceived threat would generate the diabolic enemy stereotype, which, given its emphasis on evil intentions and centralized monolithic decision-making, justifies using force to destroy the enemy.

The idea that people are motivated to balance their affect toward and their cognitive beliefs about another actor is somewhat different from the idea that people seek consistency in the cognitive attributes they attach to another actor. In many of the stereotypes that balance affect and cognition, there are contradictory cognitive beliefs. For example, in the enemy-image there is the belief that the enemy is very strong and dangerous and at the same time the belief that the enemy is a paper tiger and hollow adversary. The Reagan administration described the Soviet Union as an evil empire and warned that its military had grown so strong that the United States needed to take urgent measures to catch up, at the same time describing that country as a spent force ready to be thrust on the ash bin of history. The contradiction in the assessment of Soviet capability can be understood as a balancing of the sentiment generated by felt threat. This balancing process provides a picture that calls for action against the enemy and justifies the use of extraordinary means, and at the same time this picture holds out the promise of success if strength and resolution is demonstrated.

The enemy stereotype is not the only stereotype that balances emotional sentiments and cognitive beliefs. Cottam (1977) and later Herrmann (1985, 1988) deduced stereotypes that they argued balanced the sentiments generated in a series of ideal-typical relationships. This included stereotypes that balanced opportunity as well as threat. The degenerate stereotype, for example, was said to facilitate the seizing of an opportunity to exploit another actor. It did this by providing a picture that defined the exercise of control over the other actor as an act of benevolence, even moral duty, lifting the decadent actor out of its moral decay. The colony stereotype did the same thing by providing a picture that presented the exercise of control over the other actor as an altruistic act, providing needed tutelage and modernizing assistance to backward and dependent people. The colony stereotype balances moral concerns regarding the violation of sovereignty and self-determination by picturing the target society as too undeveloped to have masspolitics of any meaningful type. The picture also balances concerns regarding the violation of human rights or democratic practice. By picturing the population and culture as backward and uncivilized, the stereotype dismisses the appropriateness and practicality of these sorts of political concerns.

A balance theory approach to images assumes that the process of balancing is unconscious. To the degree that the production of a self-serving stereotype of the other actor is a post hoc rationalization, the stereotype does not serve the psychological balance function. If soldiers, for instance, come to doubt the stereotypes that justify the killing of the enemy, the expectation is that they will suffer psychological distress. This assumes, of course, that they are motivated to retain a positive self-image. In Heider's (1958) theory, it is possible to balance a negative self-image by attaching all negative attributes to self and characterizing one's actions as evil. Theorists applying balance theory to explain international relations assume this self-hating case would be very unusual when the subject in question is a national leader. Presumably, to be a leader of a large community, a person must invest an important part of her self-identity in the community and persuade followers that she has deep positive affect for the community. Leaders who provide pictures of the contemporary behavior of their community in a very negative moral light are unlikely to remain popular. Of course, it is possible that leaders simply use stereotypical pictures to justify actions and to mobilize public support. In this case, the stereotypes would serve the balance function for the followers but not the leaders.

It is difficult to test whether a leader's images motivate balance processes. Jack Snyder (1991) treats stereotypes as myths that are manipulated by leaders to mobilize masses, which of course is critical in an era of mass armies and mass politics. This assumes that leaders do not need the psychological relief that balancing provides and need only the rationalizing justification that stereotypes provide for mass mobilization. Hans Morgenthau (1973, pp. 88–91), on the other hand, argued that leaders more than followers need the relief from moral stress that balanced images provide. Morgenthau felt that the closer a person came to having authority and decision-making responsibility, the more he needed a cognitive disguise, what he called an ideology, to shelter his self-image from the realities of politics. He assumed that leaders would act on their sentiments and willingly believe in their own propaganda so as to sleep comfortably at night.

Robert Jervis (1976, pp. 128–142) argued that the stress of decision-making can lead top leaders to engage in irrational consistency. That is, in order to feel more comfortable about a decision, leaders often are motivated not to see a tradeoff and to instead believe that multiple, if not all, considerations point to the same policy conclusion. Irrational consistency, in other words, eliminates the stress of the decision by providing a cognitive picture in which nothing needs to be sacrificed. Jervis argues that leaders often decide which policy they prefer and then come to believe that all considerations, moral, material, and otherwise point in that direction. His analysis suggests that the psychological failure to acknowledge tradeoffs is likely to increase with the responsibility and stress of decision-making, implying that leaders are as likely to fall prey to this pathology as followers. Jervis illustrates the argument with cases of prominent U.S. leaders who he claims suffered from irrational consistency and belief system "overkill."

Cottam (1977) and Herrmann (1985, 1988) make arguments parallel to Morgenthau's and Jervis's, treating the inclination to balance as likely to vary across individuals and circumstances. They used the study of a leader's inclination to stereotype another country to infer what underlying sentiments were at work. In other words, they used the stereotypes as operational indicators of felt threats and felt opportunities. They hoped this would partly address the problem of differentiating between offensively minded revisionist actors and defensively minded status quo actors. For example, enemy stereotypes would indicate felt threat, and colony and degenerate stereotypes would indicate felt opportunities. Of course, if a leader was not balancing but was rationalizing her choices in a conscious post hoc way, then the imagery would reveal the mass mobilization strategy she was employing. In this case, it may serve as an early warning indicator of forthcoming behavior but not as a valid indicator of underlying sentiments and motives. This assumes, of course, that images and stereotypes are associated with predictable behaviors.

Images and Strategic Behavior

Philip Converse (1964, 1975), among other scholars, found that cognitive beliefs do not always lead to predictable policy choices and that there can be a substantial gap between professed attitude and observed behavior. To investigate whether images are related to strategic policy choices, Keith Shimko (1991) examined the relationship between images and arms control policy preferences within the Reagan administration. He found substantial individual differences in the administration and that the more fully and completely a person's image of the Soviet Union resembled the enemy stereotype, the more hostile he or she was to arms control. Shimko did not explain why persons held the views they did, but he argued that studying their imagery did provide some understanding of the choices they made.

Martha Cottam (1994) studied the relationship between images and policy choices in U.S. policy toward Latin America. She found that the enemy image and the dependent image were associated with identified policy preferences. The dependent image was associated with interventionist policies and the enemy image with containment and the use of force. When the two images were combined and U.S. leaders saw countries in Latin America in dependent terms and, at the same time, saw the Soviet Union in enemy terms, Martha Cottam found that there was a special sense of urgency and purpose that led to especially violent and determined intervention.

Beyond finding an association between stereotypic images and strategic choices, Martha Cottam made a case for the causal significance of images. She argued that the material and structural conditions in Latin America could not explain the variation in U.S. intervention. Washington intervened, for instance, in Guatemala in 1954 and Cuba in 1960 but not in Bolivia in 1952, even though the material conditions in all three cases were similar. By contrasting U.S. policy toward Chile, between 1970 and 1973, where the United States did intervene and toward Peru, between 1968 and 1971, where it did not, she made a similar argument. That is, she contended that the political and structural geopolitical conditions were similar and would have predicted intervention in both cases, while the study of prevailing imagery would predict intervention only in the cases where it in fact happened. Cottam provided a speculative interpretation of why stereotypic images formed in some cases and not in others. Her argument revolved around the influence of specific leaders and the process of domestic political contest. She emphasized, regardless of why certain views prevailed in Washington, the prevalence of these images associated with specific behavior.

Herrmann and Fischerkeller (1995) developed strategic scripts that they argued were associated with five stereotypic images. They argued that although stereotypic images may not associate strongly with individual actions, they would associate with sets of actions. Using Robert Abelson's (1976) notion of a script to describe a set of interrelated actions, they constructed five strategic scripts that were constituted of multiple objectives and policy tracks. They linked theoretically the enemy image to a containment script, the ally image to an institutional cooperation script, the degenerate image to a revisionism script, the imperialist image to an independent fortress script, and the colony image to an intervention script. They explored the empirical strength of the association in a preliminary way by treating the Persian Gulf as a microcosm of international politics and examining the multiple relationships among the United States, the Soviet Union, Iran, and Iraq.

Experimental Tests

Of course, the patterns found in the natural setting cannot establish clear correlation, much less causation. They serve as only preliminary evidence for balance and other theories of motivated reasoning. In social psychology, a much stronger case for motivated reasoning has been made in experimental studies (Kunda, 1990). In the foreign policy context, Herrmann and colleagues (1997) sought to provide experiment-based evidence for the core balance assumptions underlying various stereotypic images. They did this by manipulating affect. They predicted that higher levels of affect should associate with more stereotypical pictures and more script-like policy preferences. They found this to be in the case of negative affect and enemy imagery. Alexander, Brewer, and Herrmann (1999), in a different set of experiments, found for the ally, enemy, dependent, and barbarian images the expected relationships between affective arousal and stereotyping and, in turn, policy choices. Affective arousal was particularly important in stimulating barbarian stereotypes of outgroups.

Although experimental evidence is consistent with the idea that stereotypes serve a motivated functional purpose, the role that emotion plays in the process is still unclear (Jost & Banaji, 1994; Fiske, 1998; Sande, Goethals, Ferrari, & Worth, 1989). One possibility is that an appraisal process involving feelings about threats and opportunities along with relative capabilities and cultural status gives rise to specific emotions that promote stereotyping. These stereotypes, in turn, lead to script-consistent behavior. As actions are taken, they may intensify emotion and the need to balance these sentiments with stereotypic pictures. Cottam and Cottam (2001, pp. 105–122) identify a number of emotions that may associate with ideal-typical images. For instance, they argue that anger, envy, and fear are associated with enemy images and that disgust, contempt, and anger associate with degenerate images. Imperial images are thought to relate to fear and respect, while colonial images are thought to relate to pity, contempt, and disgust.

Understanding the emotional and possible motivated dynamics of imagery is important for psychological reasons (Bodenhausen, 1993; Vanman & Miller, 1993). It also is important because images are associated with strategic choices. This means that the factors that affect images also affect policy choice and the process of interaction in relationships. When images are seen as being affected by more than simply the external objective reality, it is necessary to develop models of strategic interaction that are more complicated than those that assume perfect communication and rational effective learning. Images that are serving a cognitive simplifying role may produce predictable learning patterns, but these are not likely to be the same patterns as those anticipated in a perfect Bayesian updating model. Images that are fueled by emotion and that serve balancing and functional motives may persevere or change independently of change in the objective situation. Moreover, different people can see the same situation very differently and draw very different inferences from it. Although this is a commonly recognized point, it is often overlooked in models of strategic interaction. It is in the analysis of interaction that image-based models have had their largest impact on international relations theory.

◤ Strategic Interaction

Simple models of intergroup or interstate relations assume that there are only two actors in the system and each one constitutes the environment for the other. The two actors are said to be strategic to the extent that they each plan their moves in light of their expectations regarding the other actor's moves, with attention paid to how current moves will affect the future moves of the other actor (Lake & Powell, 1999). In other words, strategic actors operate with some anticipation of the future, which presumably is affected by their understanding of the past. One way to represent this situation is to assume that an actor forms an image of the other actor by reading the signals that other actor sends and updates this image over time as new information is received. To simplify the modeling process, we might assume that both actors understand the meaning of signals in the same way and update their images in a rational way, perhaps drawing inferences from new information along the lines advised by Bayes.

Modeling interaction as a process of accurate and rational communication provides useful tools for analyzing economic bargaining. Phenomenologically oriented scholars and image theorists argue, however, that it is important to incorporate the implications of the cognitive revolution and that these stylized rational game-theoretic models fail to do this. Because these models are used to draw prescriptive conclusions that affect financial decisions and public policy, the discussions about how to understand strategic interaction often takes on special urgency.

This was particularly clear in debates about using rational game-theoretic models to guide U.S. nuclear deterrence policy, where the stakes were seen as extraordinarily high. The rational models were seen as deficient in at least two ways. First, they failed to take into account the importance of the starting assumptions about existing worldviews and values (George & Smoke, 1974, 1989; Jervis, 1989b). Second, they made unrealistic assumptions about the process of updating and learning (Lebow & Stein, 1989). A closer look at the fundamental concerns is warranted.

Initial Values

Models of interaction need to establish a starting point. Rational deterrence theories, for instance, need as a basic input estimates of what the actors value. They also require estimates of what expectations actors have regarding the consequences of certain actions. Sometimes these models require the identification of an initiator and a defender. Of course, these inputs are not facts that are simply known. As Alexander George and Richard Smoke (1974), along with Robert Jervis (1985), pointed out, they are core features of the images that actors have of themselves and others. Assuming that these images are affected by the cognitive and motivated processes already discussed, they are likely to be very different from one actor to the next. In other words, the actors in the game-theoretic model will start from different initial images, which are likely to be self-serving and biased. Fred Greenstein and Richard Immerman (1992) illustrate, in the context of John F. Kennedy's meetings with Dwight D. Eisenhower in which they discussed Indochina policy, how participants in a single meeting can hear and later recall very different things depending on the interests and expectations they bring into the meeting.

It is possible to create hypergame models that assume that actors begin with different initial images (Bennett, 1977; Bennett & Dando, 1979). To the extent that image theory helps to identify the beliefs that should be taken as these inputs, it is complementary and not contradictory to rational game-theoretic models. Of course, as Herbert Simon (1985) argued, once these inputs are estimated empirically, much of the explanatory work is done. Just the same, the logic of a rational game-theoretic model might still contribute to the understanding of the iterated process of interaction, assuming that the model captures the process of change and updating. It is in the understanding of this learning process that rational and image-based perspectives diverge the most.

Learning Processes

Because the image one country has of another plays a role in decision-making, manipulating that image becomes a strategic objective. This means that actors might not only enter into an interaction with different initial beliefs but also may draw very different inferences from what transpires during the interaction. The meaning of an act or a signal can be interpreted differently by different actors even if we assume that all actors are trying to send clear and straightforward messages (Lebow, 1985; Stein, 1985a, 1985b). After all, the meaning attached to an act derives partly from the context or background against which it is set. If actors define the context in different ways, then the act will take on different meanings. In politics, of course, actors typically see the context differently. Palestinians, for instance, see a legacy of imperialism and occupation where Israelis see a field of rejection and hostility. The same act against the different backgrounds takes on different meanings and leads to different inferences regarding how to update prior beliefs (Heradstveit, 1981).

The possible impact of contextual assumptions makes predicting the meaning that an actor will attach to a signal and the inferences he will draw from it very difficult. Knowing that actors may be trying to deceive one another and may be acting to manipulate other actors' images of them makes the predictive task nearly impossible. Actors may reason that a message is meant to be clear and designed to convince but at the same time understand the message as part of a deception strategy (Jervis, 1970). Rather than believing the message, the perceiver may infer that because the other actor wants us to believe X, the real situation must be Y. Of course, this type of reasoning could be extended across another mental iteration of the logic. In other words, the perceiving actor could reason that the other actor is signaling X, thinking that we will assume that this means the situation must really be Y, and therefore the situation must really be X, or maybe something altogether different like C. As the logic of deception is integrated, modeling the potential interaction becomes extremely complicated. This is true not because various potential logic chains cannot be imagined but because it is easy to imagine so many potential inferential possibilities.

Image-based theories assume that prior images will affect the interpretation of signals and events and guide the updating process in a theory-driven fashion. Consequently, the process of learning will not resemble a rational Bayesian formula. Actors are not expected to compare outcomes to prior expectations, accurately recognize hits and misses, and then update according to a prior diagnostic weight attached to identified predictions. Instead, actors are expected to engage in selective and biased search for information, recognize mostly confirmatory information, either not see or discount information that runs counter to their preexisting image, and remain mostly prisoners of their preconceptions (Jervis, 1976, pp. 217–282; Tetlock, 1999). If prior images affect the meaning attached to observed acts and events, and if these prior images differ across actors, then the process of interaction may follow a pattern very different from the pattern expected in a rational game-theoretic scheme. The signals one actor sent may never be received or not received with the meaning intended. Meanwhile, other events that were not signals at all may be read as signals and attributed to actors who had nothing to do with them.

The stereotypical images discussed earlier all produce expectations about an actor's behavior. The enemy image, for instance, draws attention to the evil and authoritarian character of the enemy and anticipates aggressive behavior. It also expects deception and can evoke conspiracy theory to explain apparent unanticipated positive moves on the other side's part. The colony image anticipates that the moderate responsible leaders in the colony will face subversive challenges fostered surreptitiously by agents of another great power enemy. It also can trigger conspiratorial logic, if needed—as can the imperial image, which forecasts efforts to exercise control through hidden agents. Different images by drawing attention to different things evoke different theory-driven inferential processes. Consequently, different inferences can be drawn from the same event. Rather than modeling the interaction between two actors as a tit-for-tat system of agents responding rationally to signals that have clear, intersubjectively agreed-on meaning, image-based perspectives conceive of the interactive process as constituted by actors who are only partly responding to the actions of others and perhaps more often following their preconceived notions and visions of the environment in a partially autistic fashion.

Image and Reputations

In rational deterrence theory, signaling and the establishment of reputation for resolve are important. Substantial effort has been devoted in both formal theoretical and empirical efforts to the task of identifying what acts send clear deterrent signals and promote credibility (George & Smoke, 1974). Unfortunately, the logical deductions are easier to generate than the empirical tests. For instance, in the Cold War, logical arguments about how nuclear deterrence might work were easier to construct than tests of whether they did work (Jervis, 1984; Lebow & Stein, 1990, 1994). In the early 1980s, the argument was made by the Reagan administration that Soviet leaders might doubt the U.S. deterrent. The Administration reasoned that Soviet leaders would see a window of opportunity because the United States deployed most of its retaliatory force in sea-based and air-based systems that could not retaliate quickly against Soviet land-based missiles. Soviet leaders, the Reagan logic contended, could believe that after a Soviet first strike on U.S. land-based intercontinental ballistic missiles, the American president would have a choice between (1) retaliating with residual land-based systems that were not sufficient in accuracy or numbers to do anything but destroy Soviet cities and invite the destruction of U.S. cities; (2) retaliating with sea-based forces that were not accurate enough to hit land-based silos, or air forces that were too slow and would hit only empty silos as the Soviet Union launched on warning, and (3) not retaliating. According to this logic chain, Soviet leaders might question the credibility of U.S. deterrence, seeing in foresight that they could disarm a portion of the U.S. land-based force and confront the U.S. president with an agonizing choice.

My purpose in recounting the argument surrounding the deployment of the MX missile in the United States is not to enter that substantive issue but to draw attention to the complexity of the possible logical deductions regarding what acts and developments might or might not send credible signals of resolve. The complexity of the potential logics mean that a host of possible factors and events or acts can be thought to affect another actor's image. Actors in the real world, along with scholarly observers, therefore, can come to believe all sorts of possible deterrent scenarios and act accordingly. Which of these are rational would be extremely difficult to say. It might, however, be possible to predict the type of logics that people will accept as plausible if we know their prior image of the actor they are trying to influence. Hawks, for instance, who saw the communist leadership in Moscow in nearly stereotypical enemy terms, found the Reagan logic compelling, while doves who rejected this picture of the Soviet Union found the logic unpersuasive. At the center of the logic itself, of course, was an image-based assumption regarding the civilian casualties the communist regime would risk, with those operating with an enemy image estimating it in the millions and up to 50 percent of the Soviet population and those with a different image of Moscow assuming that far less would successfully deter.

Enemy images may drive a preoccupation with maintaining an effective deterrent. At the same time, the image the other actor has of the actor that is worried about projecting deterrence needs to be taken into account. Leaders often assume that they are seen as benign and underestimate how concerned other actors are about them (Jervis, 1976, pp. 354–355). This leads them to worry that they will be seen as soft and their resolve doubted, when, in fact, they are seen as tough and threatening. Jon Mercer (1996), following up on the basic pattern described by Jervis, explored this possibility in depth. At the same time, Mercer explored the effect that other preexisting images had on the interpretation of actions and the development of reputations. He found that actors who saw another actor as an enemy typically saw the acts of that enemy as signaling resolve and aggressive intent. To the extent that observers even saw an enemy's nonaggressive acts, they were attributed to situational constraints. This left the primary judgments about the offensiveness and determination of the enemy unchanged. Mercer (1996, p. 213) concluded that enemies typically get reputations for having resolve and rarely get reputations for lacking it.

Mercer found a very different pattern among allies. When an actor saw another actor as an ally, it did not interpret that ally's actions as indicative of resolve and commitment. To the contrary, the ally's apparently resolute acts of support were attributed to situational factors. Mercer (1996, p. 214) concluded that although allies can get reputations for lacking resolve, they rarely get reputations for being resolved or loyal. By working through the implications of the fundamental attribution error in the context of different types of perceived relationships, Mercer illustrated one way to deal with interaction that is sensitive to the effect of preexisting images and the diverse inferences that are likely to the be drawn from the same experience.

Images and Third Parties

In a simple model of interaction, the number of actors in the system might be limited to two and the number of different things any actor could do would also be kept small. In more complex circumstances, however, there will be other players and substantial uncertainty about the relationship between the actions of these third parties and the principle actors. One actor, for instance, might see the action of a third player as a move orchestrated by the principle rival when in fact the principle rival had nothing to do with the third party's decision. This sort of complexity was a key part of the Cold War. In the 1950s, actions taken by China were often read in Washington as moves made by Moscow. In the 1980s, Moscow, at times, attributed Chinese moves to Washington. Of course, many U.S. leaders believed that Moscow exercised influence over several Third World clients (e.g., Cuba) while Soviet leaders attributed the opposition mujahideen in Afghanistan to Pakistan's Interservices Intelligence Directorate, which they assumed took orders from the Central Intelligence Agency in Washington (Herrmann, 1988).

Preexisting images affect the presumed relationship between principle actors and third parties. The enemy and the dependent or colony images, for example, work together to create a tight linkage between the enemy and negative developments in the colony (Cottam, 1994). The enemy is presumed to seek opportunities to expand its influence in the colony, and disturbances in the colony that threaten the colony's dependence on the perceiver are attributed to the enemy's hidden agents (Cottam, 1977, pp. 67–70). For instance, U.S. leaders who saw Moscow in enemy-image terms and the shah's Iran in mostly colony-image terms suspected that Ayatollah Khomeini was either a KGB tool or serving its interests (Huyser, 1986, pp. 176, 227, 233; Sick, 1985, p. 106). When enemy and colony images combine in this fashion, the interaction between the two principle actors can be especially complicated. Developments in a third place (in this case Iran) will be attributed by Washington to Moscow. In Moscow, leaders will know they did not cause this development and will draw negative inferences about the United States's intention from Washington's accusation. Washington, in turn, will affirm its suspicions, fueled by the preexisting enemy image when Moscow professes its innocence. Developments that are, in fact, unrelated to decisions taken in either of the principle actors can thus provoke negative interaction in the principle bilateral relationship.

Preexisting images are likely to attach meaning to unfolding events. This means that events that in one perspective are benign in geostrategic terms can be seen as dangerous in another perspective. That is, otherwise intrinsically unimportant events take on substantial symbolic importance in the logic of strategic interaction (Jervis, 1989a, pp. 174–225). For instance, in the mid-1970s, if the scene in Angola was understood in local intertribal and postcolonial independence terms, then the civil war erupting with the granting of interdependence might be seen as a local dilemma with few geostrategic consequences. If on the other hand the scene was perceived in enemy and colony stereotypes, then it would be understood as a United States–Soviet contest with each superpower acting through its pawns. Without knowing how the scene is understood in both Washington and Moscow, it is difficult to imagine how the bilateral U.S.-Soviet interaction will unfold. If both sides see it in regional terms, as was the case in the 1990s, then both will attribute little significance to the bilateral relation even if the local fighting is horrific. If both see it in enemy-colony terms, even if the local fighting is less intense, they will intervene to battle the other superpower's supposed expansionist probe. If one superpower sees the scene in local terms and the other superpower sees it in enemy and colony terms, then the bilateral interaction can be complicated and hard to predict, as discussed earlier.

When images have emotional and motivated origins, the construction of the picture of regional and peripheral matters can also be influenced by these emotions and motives. In other words, the same motives that drive stereotypical simplification also drive the search for information in the environment that reaffirms the stereotypical beliefs. In this case, constructions of the local scene and its relation to the principle actors may not be amenable to disconfirmation by any empirical means. The perceiver is not really interested in investigating or thinking hard about the relationship between the third party and the principle actor, the perceiver wants to find evidence consistent with the preexisting image of the principle actor and is constructing the picture of the regional scene to fit. When these types of factors affect the imagery, the interaction is likely to take the asymmetric form noted at the end of the previous paragraph.

Images and Domino Beliefs

Enemy and colony images not only construct pictures that tightly link together principle actors and third parties but also establish expectations that retreat in one domain will signal weakness and undermine images of an actor's general resoluteness. In bilateral terms, the expectation that the enemy, in the face of retreat on our part, will press for still greater advantage, leads to the sort of concerns about reputation that are discussed by Mercer. In the more complex three-way and multiple-player situations, these concerns can produce images of falling dominoes (Jervis & Snyder, 1991). Revolution or change in one peripheral actor is seen as leading to change in another, and perhaps another after that. The process is fueled by the belief that the enemy's image of your resolve in the next case is a function of your resolve and success in the last case. In concrete terms, for instance, it was thought that lack of success in Vietnam would lead Soviet leaders to believe that Washington would retreat from commitments to allies in the Middle East, and anti-American revolutions in the Middle East would undermine Soviet images of the United States as determined to defend western Europe.

The domino metaphor, which is common when enemy and colony images are active, has generated an interesting line of research. Robert Jervis outlined the basic logic of the psychological inferences being drawn and called for empirical research on the question of how much an actor's more general image of its adversary is affected by the outcomes of peripheral conflicts (Jervis, 1991). Ted Hopf (1994) explored this question in the context of U.S.-Soviet relations. He studied the inferences and lessons Soviet leaders drew from both U.S. behavior and the eventual outcome in regional conflicts. He began with the observation that in the United States many people believed that U.S. setbacks in the Third World led Soviet leaders to modify their image of the United States by reducing their estimates of U.S. willpower. Hopf engaged in a detailed study of multiple Soviet sources and found that this modification in image of the United States did not take place. Soviet leaders after U.S. setbacks did not draw general inferences regarding U.S. willpower and did not change their images of the United States in fundamental ways. To the contrary, the preexisting image of the United States as an aggressively imperial enemy led to theory-consistent interpretations of the events and reinforced confidence in the initial image.

▶ Image Change

It has long been recognized that mirror enemy images can lead to spirals of escalating hostility (Broffenbrenner, 1961). As both sides attempts to deter each other and persuade each other of their will and resolve, they ratchet upward the competition. The dynamic interaction between two parties when one sees the other in stereotypic imperial terms and the other sees the first in stereotypic colony terms does not necessarily escalate in military fashion but remains locked in a cycle of frustration and resentment. How to break out of these interactive cycles that are partially powered by stereotypic images is the question that has been at the center of research on conflict resolution. Deborah Larson (1997), for instance, has analyzed how mistrust led Soviet and American leaders to miss what Larson argues were opportunities for deescalating the Cold War. She finds that a "tit-for-tat" strategy was not enough to shake leaders free from their enemy stereotypes. It is clear that images, once formed, are hard to change and do not change in the rational fashion that Bayesian models might expect. At the same time, images can be affected and cycles of confrontation can be broken. Several strategies for accomplishing this have been explored.

The best-known strategy for defusing an escalating mirror enemy image interactive relationship is to promote gradual reciprocal reduction in tension (GRIT), as Charles Osgood (1962) labeled it. A GRIT strategy tests the possibility that the other side's aggressive moves are motivated by its fears of us. Because the initiating side remains uncertain as to the other side's intentions, it protects its basic security but takes an initial deescalatory move in a peripheral area. Expecting the other side to be suspicious, the first side may make several moves of this type in hopes of inducing reciprocation.

By analyzing the diplomacy surrounding the Austrian State Treaty, Deborah Larson (1987) argues that when mistrust is high and neither party is willing to make multiple positive initiative, GRIT may fail.

GRIT can be pursued in a more forgiving or more strict tit-for-tat fashion. Robert Axelrod (1984) explored in computer simulations what the effect of various strategies of play might be, given certain assumptions about the rigidity of preexisting beliefs. Secretary of State James Baker (1995, pp. 71–74) explains that such a logic led the Bush administration to test Gorbachev's "new thinking" by exploring the possibilities in peripheral regional conflicts rather than in the arena of strategic nuclear weapons. The arms control arena involved issues too close to core national security concerns, and disputes in places like Angola and Namibia did not; in addition, the domestic interests that motivated positions toward arms control were much stronger than those related to most regional conflicts.

The Cold War case illustrates two important points regarding image change. The first is that repeated acts, in this case by the Soviet Union, that are inconsistent with the expectations that a preexisting image generates can lead to the rethinking of the existing image. Initial acts are likely to be interpreted as consistent with the preexisting image; for example, Gorbachev's initial moves were interpreted by U.S. leaders as pubic relations stunts and tricks. However, these sorts of interpretations are more difficult to sustain in the face of repeated moves and moves that involve significant physical changes that are inconsistent with enemy image interpretations, for instance, arms control agreements that reduced Moscow's ability to strike. For the strategy to work, of course, the other side must truly be operating with an enemy image and not a different image—for instance, one that pictures the first party as degenerate. In addition, the other side must not be so motivated by auxiliary interests that it needs to produce an enemy image to justify other policies.

The relationship between underlying interests and imagery is the second point the Cold War case draws attention to. Existing images that lead to broad strategic programs create institutionalized constituencies that have large vested interests in the continuation of the policies consistent with the image. These interests, as seen in the arms control case, can include large stakes beyond the immediate national security concerns. They can involve career, financial, and bureaucratic interests, to say nothing of personal authority and political popularity. To change images, therefore, at the level of interacting collective political actors, as distinct from interacting individuals, it is important to address the alignment of political interests and possible domestic coalitions. Creating an environment that is conducive to open-mindedness and generating acts that challenge expectations may be enough to affect the cognitive anchors of an image but will not necessarily be sufficient to loosen the motivated and emotional anchors. To generate change in these dimensions, it may be necessary to think in terms of revising the distribution of interests among leaders in the community (Solingen,

1998). This is precisely the sort of logic that underpins strategies of engagement that aim to create new personal interests among leaders in cooperative relations with foreign outgroups.

Conflict resolution strategies are taken up in more detail in the next chapter. Like deterrence strategies, they aim to affect the images that define for the actors the character of the relationship. To study these constructions of the situation in a parsimonious way, scholars have conceived of images as a three-dimensional combinatorial construct. Ideal-typical appraisals of a relationship have been conceptually distinguished according to the judgments regarding the interdependence of goals, relative capabilities, and relative cultural status. These gestalts can lead people to see other actors in terms consistent with stereotypic schemata. This can happen for both cognitive reasons, as people attempt to make sense and categorize their environment in a parsimonious way, and for motivated reasons, as people balance their emotional sentiments and cognitive constructions. Because images are expected to affect policy choices as well as the reception and interpretation of new information, they also affect the interaction between actors.

Questions related to conflict resolution and deterrence—that is, to interaction in general—highlight some of the most important questions that image theorists need to explore further. First, it is necessary to see if these ideal-typical gestalts and images operate at a generic level across different cultural communities. Second, image theorists, to engineer change, need to understand more about the emotional and motivated origins of imagery. More experimental work is needed to examine the functional utility of stereotypes and especially the relationship between different emotions and cognitive constructs. In the same vein, more research is needed to identify the relationship between emotions and behavior. Finally, the focus on interaction draws attention to the possible interactive patterns that may exist in relationships that are not characterized by enemy-to-enemy images. These spiral models of mirror enemy images have received far more attention than the more asymmetric relationships, for example, such as those between imperial and colonial images (Herrmann and Fischerkeller, 1995). As the usefulness of image theory is explored in ethnic and racial relations, these other possible interactive possibilities need to be examined. So too must the relationship between social identity and imagery; I leave the further discussion of that subject as well to a later chapter.

◣ References

Abelson, R. (1976). Script processing in attitude formation and decision making. In J. Carroll & J. Payne (Eds.), *Cognition and social behavior*. Hillsdale: Erlbaum.

Abelson, R., Dasgupta, N., Park, J., & Banaji, M. (1998). Perceptions of the collective other. *Personality and Social Psychology Review, 2,* 243–250.

Alba, J. W., & Hasher, L. (1983). Is memory schematic? *Psychological Bulletin, 93*, 203–231.

Alexander, M., Brewer, M., & Herrmann, R. (1999). Images and affect: A functional analysis of out-group stereotypes. *Journal of Personality and Social Psychology, 77*, 78–93.

Asch, S. (1952). *Social psychology.* Englewood Cliffs, NJ: Prentice-Hall.

Axelrod, R. (1976). *The structure of decision: The cognitive maps of political elites.* Princeton: Princeton University Press.

Axelrod, R. (1984). *The evolution of cooperation.* New York: Basic Books.

Baker, J., & DeFrank, T. (1995). *The politics of diplomacy: Revolution, war and peace, 1989–1992.* New York: Putnam.

Bennett, P. G. (1977). Toward a theory of hypergames. *OMEGA, 5*, 749–751.

Bennett, P. G., & Dando, M. (1979). Complex hypergame analysis: A hypergame perspective of the fall of France. *Journal of Operational Research Society, 30*, 23–32.

Bodenhausen, G. V. (1993). Emotions, arousal, and stereotypic judgments: A heuristic model of affect and stereotyping. In D. M. Mackie & D. L. Hamilton (Eds.), *Affect, cognition, and stereotyping: Interactive processes in group perception* (pp. 13–37). San Diego, CA.: Academic Press.

Boulding, K. (1956). *The image.* Ann Arbor: University of Michigan Press.

Boulding, K. (1959). National images and international systems. *Journal of Conflict Resolution, 3*, 120–131.

Brecher, M. (1972). *The foreign policy system of Israel: Setting, image, process.* New Haven: Yale University Press.

Brecher, M. (1973). Images, process and feedback in foreign policy: Israel's decision on German reparations. *American Political Science Review, 67*, 73–102.

Broffenbrenner, U. (1961). The mirror image in Soviet-American relations: A social psychologist's report. *Journal of Social Issues, 17*, 45–56.

Byman, D. & Pollack, K. (2001). Let us now praise great men: Bringing the statesman back in. *International Security, 25*, 107–146.

Campbell, D. T. (1967). Stereotypes and the perception of out-group differences. *American Psychologist, 22*, 812–829.

Converse, P. E. (1964). The nature of belief systems in mass publics. In David Apter (Ed.), *Ideology and discontent,* (pp. 206–261). New York: Wiley.

Converse, P. E. (1975). Public opinion and voting behavior. In F. Greenstein & N. Polsby (Eds.), *Handbook of political science* (Vol. 4, pp. 75–169). Reading, MA: Addison-Wesley.

Cottam, M. (1986). *Foreign policy decision making: The influence of cognition.* Boulder, CO: Westview.

Cottam, M. (1994). *Images & intervention: U.S. policies in Latin America.* Pittsburgh, PA: University of Pittsburgh Press.

Cottam, M., & Cottam, R. (2001). *Nationalism and politics: The political behavior of nation states.* Boulder, CO: Lynne Rienner.

Cottam, R. (1977). *Foreign policy motivation: A general theory and a case study.* Pittsburgh: University of Pittsburgh Press.

Cronbach, L. J. (1957). The two disciplines of scientific psychology. *American Psychologist, 12*, 671–684.

Cronbach, L. J. (1975). Beyond the two disciplines of scientific psychology. *American Psychologist, 30*, 116–127.

Deutsch, K. & Merritt, R. (1965). Effects of events on national and international images. In H. Kelman (Ed.), *International behavior: A social-psychological analysis* (pp. 130–187). New York: Holt, Rinehart and Winston.

Etheredge, L. (1978). *A world of men: The private sources of American foreign policy.* Cambridge, MA: MIT Press.

Finlay, D., Holsti, O., & Fagen, R. (1967). *Enemies in politics.* Chicago: Rand McNally.

Fiske, A. P. (1991). *Structures of social life: The four elementary forms of human relations.* New York: Free Press.

Fiske, S., & Taylor, S. (1991). *Social cognition.* New York: Random House.

Fiske, S. T. (1998). *Stereotyping, prejudice, and discrimination.* In D. T. Gilbert, S. T. Fiske, & G. Lindzey (Eds.), *The handbook of social psychology* (4th ed., pp. 357–411). New York: McGraw-Hill.

Gardner, H. (1985). *The mind's new science: A history of the cognitive revolution.* New York: Basic Books.

George, A., & Smoke, R. (1974). *Deterrence in American foreign policy: Theory and practice.* New York: Columbia University Press.

George, A., & Smoke, R. (1989). Deterrence and foreign policy. *World Politics, 41*(2), 170–182.

Greenstein, F. & Immerman, R. (1992). What did Eisenhower tell Kennedy about Indochina? The politics of misperception. *Journal of American History, 79,* 568–587.

Heider, F. (1958). *The psychology of interpersonal relations.* New York: Wiley.

Heradstveit, D. (1981). *The Arab-Israeli conflict: Psychological obstacles to peace.* Oslo: Universitetsforlaget.

Herrmann, R. (1985). *Perceptions and behavior in Soviet foreign policy.* Pittsburgh: University of Pittsburgh Press.

Herrmann, R. (1988). The empirical challenge of the cognitive revolution: A strategy for drawing inferences about perceptions. *International Studies Quarterly, 32,* 175–203.

Herrmann R., & Fischerkeller, M. (1995). Beyond the enemy image and spiral model: Cognitive-strategic research after the Cold War. *International Organization, 49,* 415–450.

Herrmann, R., Voss, J., Schooler, T., & Ciarrochi, J. (1997). Images in international relations: An experimental test of cognitive schemata. *International Studies Quarterly, 41,* 403–433.

Holsti, K. J. (1970). National role conceptions in the study of foreign policy. *International Studies Quarterly, 14,* 233–309.

Holsti, O. (1967). Cognitive dynamics and images of the enemy. In D. Finlay, O. Holsti, & R. Fagen (Eds.), *Enemies in politics* (pp. 25–96). Chicago: Rand McNally.

Holsti, O. (1970). The 'operational code' approach to the study of political leaders: John Foster Dulles' philosophical and instrumental beliefs. *Canadian Journal of Political Science, 3,* 123–157.

Hopf, T. (1994). *Peripheral visions: Deterrence theory and American foreign policy in the third world, 1965–1990.* Ann Arbor: University of Michigan Press.

Horowitz, D. (1985). *Ethnic groups in conflict.* Berkeley: University of California Press.

Huyser, R. (1986). *Mission to Tehran*. New York: Harper and Row.

Jervis, R. (1970). *The logic of images in international relations*. Princeton: Princeton University Press.

Jervis, R. (1976). *Perception and misperception in international politics*. Princeton: Princeton University Press.

Jervis, R. (1984). *The illogic of American nuclear strategy*. Ithaca, NY: Cornell University Press.

Jervis, R. (1985). Perceiving and coping with threat. In R. Jervis, R. N. Lebow, & J. G. Stein (Eds.), *Psychology and deterrence* (pp. 13–33). Baltimore: Johns Hopkins University Press.

Jervis, R. (1989a). *The meaning of the nuclear revolution: Statecraft and the prospect of Armageddon*. Ithaca, NY: Cornell University Press.

Jervis, R. (1989b). Rational deterrence: Theory and evidence. *World Politics, 41*(2), 183–207.

Jervis, R. (1991). Domino beliefs and strategic behavior. In R. Jervis & J. Snyder (Eds.), *Dominoes and bandwagons: Strategic beliefs and great power competition in the Eurasian rimland* (pp. 20–50). New York: Oxford University Press.

Jervis, R., & Snyder, J. (Eds.). (1991). *Dominoes and bandwagons: Strategic beliefs and great power competition in the Eurasian rimland*. New York: Oxford University Press.

Jost, J. T., & Banaji, M. R. (1994). The role of stereotyping in system-justification and the production of false consciousness. *British Journal of Social Psychology, 33*, 1–27.

Kaufman, C. (1994). Out of the lab and into the archives: A method for testing psychological explanations of political decision making. *International Studies Quarterly, 38*, 557–586.

Kunda, Z. (1990). The case for motivated reasoning. *Psychology Bulletin, 108*, 480–498.

Lake, D., & Powell, R. (1999). *Strategic choice and international relations*. Princeton: Princeton University Press.

Larson, D. W. (1997). *Anatomy of mistrust: U.S.-Soviet relations during the Cold War*. Ithaca, NY: Cornell University Press.

Larson, D. W. (1987). Crisis prevention and the Austrian state treaty. *International Organization, 41*, 27–60.

Lasswell, H. (1930). *Psychopathology and politics*. Chicago: University of Chicago Press.

Lasswell, H. (1948). *Power and personality*. New York: Norton.

Lebow, R. N. (1981). *Between peace and war: The nature of international crisis*. Baltimore: Johns Hopkins University Press.

Lebow, R. N. (1985). Miscalculation in the South Atlantic: The origins of the Falklands war. In R. Jervis, R. N. Lebow, & J. G. Stein (Eds.), *Psychology and deterrence* (pp. 89–124). Baltimore: Johns Hopkins University Press.

Lebow, R. N., & Stein, J. G. (1989). Rational deterrence theory: I think, therefore I deter. *World Politics, 41*(2), 208–224.

Lebow, R. N., & Stein, J. G. (1990). Deterrence: The elusive dependent variable, *World Politics, 42* (3), 336–369.

Lebow, R. N., & Stein, J. G. (1994). *We all lost the Cold War*. Princeton: Princeton University Press.

Mercer, J. (1996). *Reputation and international politics*. Ithaca, N.Y.: Cornell University Press.

Morgenthau, H. (1973). *Politics among nations: The struggle for power and peace* (5th ed.). New York: Knopf.

Northway, M. L. (1940). The concept of the "schema." *British Journal of Psychology, 31,* 22–36.

Osgood, C. (1962). *An alternative to war or surrender*. Urbana: University of Illinois Press.

Owen, J. (1997). *Liberal peace liberal war: American politics and international security*. Ithaca, NY: Cornell University Press.

Riker, W. (1962). *The theory of political coalitions*. New Haven: Yale University Press.

Robins, R. & Post, J. (1997). *Political paranoia: The psychopolitics of hatred*. New Haven: Yale University Press.

Rummel, R. J. (1975). *Understanding conflict and war: The dynamic psychological field*. New York: Wiley.

Sande, G. N., Goethals, G. R, Ferrari, L., & Worth, L. T. (1989). Value-guided attributions: Maintaining the moral self-image and the diabolical enemy-image. *Journal of Social Issues, 45,* 91–118.

Scott, M., & Lyman, S. (1968). Accounts. *American Sociological Review, 33,* 46–62.

Scott, W. (1965). Psychological and social correlates of international images. In H. Kelman (Ed.), *International behavior: A social-psychological analysis* (pp. 70–103). New York: Holt, Rinehart and Winston.

Sherman, S., Judd, C., & Park, B. (1989). Social cognition. *Annual Review of Psychology, 40,* 281–326.

Shimko, K. (1991). *Images and arms control: Perceptions of the Soviet Union in the Reagan administration*. Ann Arbor: University of Michigan Press.

Sick, G. (1985). *All fall down: America's tragic encounter with Iran*. New York: Random House.

Silverstein, B. (1989). Enemy images: The psychology of U.S. attitudes and cognition regarding the Soviet Union. *American Psychologist, 44,* 903–913.

Simon, H. (1985). Human nature in politics: The dialogue of psychology with political science. *American Political Science Review, 79,* 293–304.

Skinner, B. F. (1960). *Behavior theory and conditioning*. New Haven: Yale University Press.

Snyder, J. (1991). *Myths of empire: Domestic politics and international ambition*. Ithaca, NY: Cornell University Press.

Snyder, R., Bruck, H., & Sapin, B. (1962). *Foreign policy decision-making: An approach to the study of international politics*. New York: Free Press.

Solingen, E. (1998). *Regional orders at century's dawn: Global and domestic influences on grand strategy*. Princeton: Princeton University Press.

Sprout, H., & Sprout, M. (1965). *The ecological perspective on human affairs with special reference to international relations*. Princeton: Princeton University Press.

Stein, J. G. (1985a). Calculation, miscalculation, and conventional deterrence I: The view from Cairo. In R. Jervis, R. N. Lebow, & J. G. Stein (Eds.), *Psychology and deterrence* (pp. 34–59). Baltimore: Johns Hopkins University Press.

Stein, J. G. (1985b). Calculation, miscalculation, and conventional deterrence II: The view from Jerusalem. In R. Jervis, R. N. Lebow, & J. G. Stein (Eds.), *Psychology and deterrence* (pp. 60–88). Baltimore: Johns Hopkins University Press.

Stuart, D., & Starr, H. (1982). Inherent bad faith reconsidered: Dulles, Kennedy, and Kissinger. *Political Psychology, 3,* 1–33.

Steinbruner, J. (1974). *The cybernetic theory of decision.* Princeton: Princeton University Press.

Tetlock, P. (1999). Theory-driven reasoning about plausible pasts and probable futures in world politics: Are we prisoners of our preconceptions? *American Journal of Political Science, 43,* 335–366.

Tetlock, P., & Levi, A. (1982). Attribution bias: On the inconclusiveness of the cognition-motivation debate. *Journal of Experimental Social Psychology, 18,* 68–88.

Vanman, E. J., & Miller, N. (1993). Applications of emotion theory and research to stereotyping and intergroup relations. In D. M. Mackie & D. L. Hamilton (Eds.), *Affect, cognition, and stereotyping: Interactive processes in group perception* (pp. 151–78). San Diego, CA: Academic Press.

Waltz, K. (1979). *Theory of international politics.* Reading, MA: Addison-Wesley.

White, R. K. (1965). Images in the context of international conflict: Soviet perceptions of the U.S. and the U.S.S.R. In H. C. Kelman (Ed.), *International behavior: A social-psychological analysis* (pp. 236–276). New York: Holt, Rinehart, and Winston.

White, R. K. (1968). *Nobody wanted war: Misperception in Vietnam and other wars.* Garden City, NY: Doubleday.

10   Herbert C. Kelman and Ronald J. Fisher

Conflict Analysis and Resolution

This chapter presents a social-psychological approach to the analysis and resolution of international and intercommunal conflicts. Its central focus is on interactive conflict resolution (see Fisher, 1997), a family of models for intervening in deep-rooted, protracted conflicts between identity groups, which is anchored in psychological principles.

International conflict resolution can be placed in the context of a larger, growing field of practice, applied at different levels and in different domains, and anchored in different disciplines, theoretical traditions, and fields of practice. Despite this diversity, certain common threads run through most of the work in this field. Thus these approaches to conflict resolution generally call for a nonadversarial framework for addressing the conflict, an analytic point of departure, a problem-solving orientation, direct participation of the conflicting parties in joint efforts to shape a solution, and facilitation by a third party trained in the process of conflict resolution. Crosslevel exchanges are very valuable for developing general principles, but the application of these principles requires sensitivity to the unique features of the context in which they are applied.

In this spirit, this chapter begins with presentation of a social-psychological perspective on the nature of international conflict and the normative and perceptual processes that contribute to its escalation and perpetuation. This analysis of international conflict has clear implications for our approach to conflict resolution. The chapter then turns to a brief discussion of negotiation and mediation, the most common diplomatic approaches to conflict, which have been subjects of extensive research in political psychology. This review provides a useful reference point for our discussion of interactive conflict resolution itself. To illustrate the family of approaches subsumed under this rubric, we proceed to a more detailed description of the assumptions and procedures of interactive problem solving, as applied in particular to the Israeli-Palestinian conflict (Kelman, 1997a, 1998b). The chapter concludes with an identification of some of the challenges confronting scholar-practitioners in the field of conflict analysis and resolution.

◤ The Nature of International Conflict

A social-psychological perspective can expand on the view of international conflict provided by the realist or neorealist schools of international relations

315

or other, more traditional approaches focusing on structural or strategic factors (Kelman, 1997b). Without denying the importance of objectively anchored national interests, the primacy of the state in the international system, the role of power in international relations, and the effect of structural factors in determining the course of an international conflict, it enriches the analysis in a variety of ways: by exploring the subjective factors that set constraints on rationality; by opening the black box of the state as unitary actor and analyzing processes within and between the societies that underlie state action; by broadening the range of influence processes (and, indeed, of definitions of power) that play a role in international politics; and by conceiving international conflict as a dynamic process, shaped by changing realities, interests, and relationships between the conflicting parties.

Social-psychological analysis suggests four propositions about international conflict. These propositions are particularly relevant to existential conflicts between identity groups—conflicts in which the collective identities of the parties are engaged and in which the continued existence of the group is seen to be at stake. Thus the propositions apply most directly to ethnic or ideological conflicts but also to more mundane interstate conflicts, insofar as issues of national identity and existence come into play—as they often do.

The first proposition says that *international conflict is a process driven by collective needs and fears* rather than entirely a product of rational calculation of objective national interests on the part of political decision-makers. Human needs are often articulated and fulfilled through important collectivities, such as the ethnic group, the national group, and the state. Conflict arises when a group is faced with nonfulfillment or threat to the fulfillment of basic needs: not only such obvious material needs as food, shelter, physical safety, and physical well-being but also, and very centrally, such psychological needs as identity, security, recognition, autonomy, self-esteem, and a sense of justice (Burton, 1990). Moreover, needs for identity and security and similarly powerful collective needs, and the fears and concerns about survival associated with them, contribute heavily to the escalation and perpetuation of conflict once it has started. Even when the conflicting parties have come to the conclusion that it is in their best interest to put an end to the conflict, they resist going to the negotiating table or making the accommodations necessary for the negotiations to move forward, for fear that they will be propelled into concessions that in the end will leave their very existence compromised. The fears that drive existential conflicts lie at the heart of the relationship between the conflicting parties, going beyond the cycle of fears resulting from the dynamics of the security dilemma (Jervis, 1976).

Collective fears and needs, though more pronounced in ethnic conflicts, play a part in all international conflicts. They combine with objective factors—for example, a state's resources, the ethnic composition of its population, or its access or lack of access to the sea—in determining how different segments of a society perceive state interests and what ultimately becomes the national interest as defined by the dominant elites. Similarly, all conflicts—interstate no less than ethnic—represent a combination of rational and irrational factors, and in each type of conflict the mix may vary from case to case. Some ethnic conflicts may be preponderantly rational, just as some interstate conflicts may be preponderantly irrational. Furthermore, in all international conflicts, the needs and fears of populations are mobilized and often manipulated by the leadership, with varying degrees of demagoguery and cynicism. Even when manipulated, collective needs and fears represent authentic reactions within the population and become the focus of societal action. They may be linked to individual needs and fears. For example, in highly violent ethnic conflicts, the fear of annihilation of one's group is often (and for good reason) tied to a fear of personal annihilation.

The conception of conflict as a process driven by collective needs and fears implies, first and foremost, that conflict resolution—if it is to lead to a stable peace that both sides consider just and to a new relationship that enhances the welfare and development of the two societies—must address the fundamental needs and deepest fears of the populations. From a normative point of view, such a solution can be viewed as the operationalization of justice within a problem-solving approach to conflict resolution (Kelman, 1996b). Another implication of a human-needs orientation is that the psychological needs on which it focuses—security, identity, recognition—are not inherently zero sum (Burton, 1990), although they are usually seen as such in deep-rooted conflicts. Thus it may well be possible to shape an integrative solution that satisfies both sets of needs, which may then make it easier to settle issues like territory or resources through distributive bargaining. Finally, the view of conflict as a process driven by collective needs and fears suggests that conflict resolution must, at some stage, provide for certain processes that take place at the level of individuals and interactions between individuals, such as taking the other's perspective or realistic empathy (White, 1984), creative problem solving, insight, and learning.

Focusing on the needs and fears of the populations in conflict readily brings to mind a second social-psychological proposition: that *international conflict is an intersocietal process*, not merely an intergovernmental or interstate phenomenon. The conflict, particularly in the case of protracted ethnic struggles, becomes an inescapable part of daily life for each society and its component elements. Thus analysis of conflict requires attention not only to its strategic, military, and diplomatic dimensions but also to its economic, psychological, cultural, and social-structural dimensions. Interactions on these dimensions, both within and between the conflicting societies, shape the political environment in which governments function and define the political constraints under which they operate.

An intersocietal view of conflict alerts us to the role of internal divisions *within* each society, which often play a major part in exacerbating or even creating conflicts *between* societies. Such divisions impose constraints on political leaders pursuing a policy of accommodation, in the form of accusations by opposition elements that they are jeopardizing national existence and of anxieties and doubts within the general population that the opposition elements both foster and exploit. The internal divisions, however, may also provide potential levers for change in the direction of conflict resolution, by challenging the monolithic image of the enemy that parties in conflict tend to hold and enabling them to deal with each other in a more differentiated way. Internal divisions point to the presence on the other side of potential partners for negotiation and thus provide the opportunity for forming pronegotiation coalitions across the conflict lines (Kelman, 1993). To contribute to conflict resolution, any such coalition must of necessity remain an "uneasy coalition," lest its members lose their credibility and political effectiveness within their respective communities.

Another implication of an intersocietal view of conflict is that negotiations and third-party efforts should ideally be directed not merely to a political *settlement* of the conflict, in the form of a brokered political agreement, but to its *resolution*. A political agreement may be adequate for terminating relatively specific, containable interstate disputes, but conflicts that engage the collective identities and existential concerns of the adversaries require a process that is conducive to structural and attitude change, to reconciliation, and to the transformation of the relationship between the two societies. Finally, an intersocietal analysis of conflict suggests a view of diplomacy as a complex mix of official and unofficial efforts with complementary contributions. The peaceful termination or management of conflict requires binding agreements that can only be achieved at the official level, but many different sectors of the two societies have to be involved in creating a favorable environment for negotiating and implementing such agreements.

Our third proposition says that *international conflict is a multifaceted process of mutual influence* and not only a contest in the exercise of coercive power. Much of international politics entails a process of mutual influence, in which each party seeks to protect and promote its own interests by shaping the behavior of the other. Conflict occurs when these interests clash: when attainment of one party's interests (and fulfillment of the needs that underlie them) threatens, or is perceived to threaten, the interests (and needs) of the other. In pursuing the conflict, therefore, the parties engage in mutual influence, designed to advance their own positions and to block the adversary. Similarly, in conflict resolution—by negotiation or other means—the parties exercise influence to induce the adversary to come to the table, to make concessions, to accept an agreement that meets their interests and needs, and to live up to that agreement. Third parties also exercise influence in conflict situations by backing one or the other party, by mediating between them, or by maneuvering to protect their own interests.

Influence in international conflict typically relies on a mixture of threats and inducements, with the balance often on the side of force and the threat of force. Thus, the U.S.-Soviet relationship in the Cold War was predominantly framed in terms of an elaborate theory of deterrence—a form of influence designed to keep the other side from doing what you do not want it to do (George & Smoke, 1974; Jervis, Lebow, & Stein, 1985; Schelling, 1963; Stein, 1991). In other conflict relationships, the emphasis may be on compellence—a form of influence designed to make the other side do what you want it to do. Such coercive strategies entail serious costs and risks, and their effects may be severely limited. For example, they are likely to be reciprocated by the other side and thus lead to escalation of the conflict, and they are unlikely to change behavior to which the other is committed. Thus the effective exercise of influence in international conflict requires a broadening of the repertoire of influence strategies, at least to the extent of combining "carrots and sticks"—of supplementing the negative incentives that typically dominate international conflict relationships with positive incentives (see Baldwin, 1971; Kriesberg, 1982) such as economic benefits, international approval, or a general reduction in the level of tension. An example of an approach based on the systematic use of positive incentives is Osgood's (1962) graduated and reciprocated initiatives in tension reduction (GRIT) strategy. President Anwar Sadat of Egypt, in his 1977 trip to Jerusalem, undertook a unilateral initiative, with the expectation (partly prenegotiated) of Israeli reciprocation, but—unlike GRIT—he started with a large, fundamental concession in the anticipation that negotiations would fill in the intervening steps (Kelman, 1985).

Effective use of positive incentives requires more than offering the other whatever rewards, promises, or confidence-building measures seem most readily available. It requires actions that address the fundamental needs and fears of the other party. Thus the key to an effective influence strategy based on the exchange of positive incentives is *responsiveness* to the other's concerns: actively exploring ways that each can help meet the other's needs and allay the other's fears and ways to help each other overcome the constraints within their respective societies against taking the actions that each wants the other to take. The advantage of a strategy of responsiveness is that it allows parties to exert influence on each other through positive steps (not threats) that are within their own capacity to take. The process is greatly facilitated by communication between the parties in order to identify actions that are politically feasible for each party yet likely to have an impact on the other.

A key element in an influence strategy based on responsiveness is *mutual reassurance*, which is particularly critical in any effort to resolve an existential conflict. The negotiation literature suggests that parties are often driven to the table by a mutually hurting stalemate, which makes negotiations more attractive than continuing the conflict (Touval & Zartman, 1985, p. 16; Zartman & Berman, 1982). But parties in existential conflicts are afraid of negotiations, even when the status quo has become increasingly painful and they recognize that a negotiated agreement is in their interest. To advance the negotiating process under such circumstances, it is at least as important to reduce the parties' fears as to increase their pain.

Mutual reassurance can take the form of acknowledgments, symbolic gestures, or confidence-building measures. To be maximally effective, such steps need to address the other's central needs and fears as directly as possible. When President Sadat of Egypt spoke to the Israeli Knesset during his dramatic visit to Jerusalem in November 1977, he clearly acknowledged Egypt's past hostility toward Israel and thus validated Israelis' own experiences. In so doing, he greatly enhanced the credibility of the change in course that he was announcing. At the opening of this visit, Sadat's symbolic gesture of engaging in a round of cordial handshakes with the Israeli officials who had come to greet him broke a longstanding taboo. By signaling the beginning of a new relationship, it had an electrifying effect on the Israeli public. In deep-rooted conflicts, acknowledgement of what was heretofore denied—in the form of recognition of the other's humanity, nationhood, rights, grievances, and interpretation of history—is an important source of reassurance that the other may indeed be ready to negotiate an agreement that addresses your fundamental concerns. By signaling acceptance of the other's legitimacy, each party reassures the other that negotiations and concessions no longer constitute mortal threats to its security and national existence. By confirming the other's narrative, each reassures the other that a compromise does not represent an abandonment of its identity.

An influence strategy based on responsiveness to each other's needs and fears and the resulting search for ways of reassuring and benefiting each other has important advantages from a long-term point of view. It does not merely elicit specific desired behaviors from the other party but also can contribute to a creative redefinition of the conflict, joint discovery of mutually satisfactory solutions, and transformation of the relationship between the parties.

The influence strategies employed in a conflict relationship take on special significance in light of the fourth proposition: *international conflict is an interactive process with an escalatory, self-perpetuating dynamic*, not merely a sequence of action and reaction by stable actors. In intense conflict relationships, the natural course of interaction between the parties tends to reinforce and deepen the conflict rather than reduce and resolve it. The interaction is governed by a set of norms and guided by a set of images that create an escalatory, self-perpetuating dynamic. This dynamic can be reversed through skillful diplomacy, imaginative leadership, third-party intervention, and institutionalized mechanisms for managing and resolving conflict. But in the absence of such deliberate efforts, the spontaneous interaction between the parties is more likely than not to increase distrust, hostility, and the sense of grievance.

The needs and fears of parties engaged in intense conflict impose perceptual and cognitive constraints on their processing of new information, with a resulting tendency to underestimate the occurrence and the possibility of change. The ability to take the role of the other is severely impaired. Dehumanization of the enemy makes it even more difficult to acknowledge and access the perspective of the other. The inaccessibility of the other's perspective contributes significantly to some of the psychological barriers to conflict resolution described by Ross and Ward (1995). The dynamics of conflict interaction tend to entrench the parties in their own perspectives on history and justice. Conflicting parties display particularly strong tendencies to find evidence that confirms their negative images of each other and to resist evidence that would seem to disconfirm these images (see chapter 9 for a fuller discussion of the image concept). Thus interaction not only fails to contribute to a revision of the enemy image but actually helps to reinforce and perpetuate it. Interaction guided by mirror images of a demonic enemy and a virtuous self (see Bronfenbrenner, 1961; White, 1965) creates self-fulfilling prophecies by inducing the parties to engage in the hostile actions they expect from one another.

Self-fulfilling prophecies are also generated by the conflict norms that typically govern the interaction between parties engaged in an intense conflict. Expressions of hostility and distrust toward the enemy are not just spontaneous manifestations of the conflict but are normatively prescribed behaviors. Political leaders' assumption that the public's evaluation of them depends on their adherence to these norms influences their tactical and strategic decisions, their approach to negotiations, their public pronouncements, and, ultimately, the way they educate their own publics. For the publics, in turn, adherence to these norms is often taken as an indicator of group loyalty. Thus the discourse in deep-rooted conflicts is marked by mutual delegitimization and dehumanization. Interaction governed by this set of norms—at the micro and macro levels—contributes to escalation and perpetuation of the conflict. Parties that systematically treat each other with hostility and distrust are likely to become increasingly hostile and untrustworthy.

The dynamics of conflict interaction create a high probability that opportunities for conflict resolution will be missed. Parties whose interaction is shaped by the norms and images rooted in the history of the conflict are systematically constrained in their capacity to respond to the occurrence and possibility of change. They find it difficult to communicate the changes that have occurred on their own side or to notice the changes on the other side, and to explore the possibilities for change that would serve both sides' interests. Conflict resolution efforts, therefore, require promotion of a different kind of interaction, capable of reversing the escalatory and self-perpetuating dynamics of conflict: an interaction that is conducive to sharing perspectives, differentiating the enemy image, and developing a language of mutual reassurance and a new discourse based on the norms of responsiveness and reciprocity.

▲ Normative and Perceptual Processes Promoting Conflict

Social-psychological analysis can be particularly helpful in explaining why and how, once a conflict has started, normative and perceptual processes are set into motion that promote its escalation and perpetuation and create or intensify barriers to conflict resolution. By the same token, social-psychological analysis, in helping to identify and understand these barriers, can also suggest ways of overcoming them.

Normative Processes

A variety of interaction processes at the mass and elite levels within conflicting societies that influence the evolving course of the conflict are governed by a set of powerful social norms that encourage actions and attitudes conducive to the generation, escalation, and perpetuation of conflict and that inhibit the perception and occurrence of change in the direction of tension reduction and conflict resolution (Kelman, 1997b, pp. 212–222).

One such process is the *formation of collective moods*. With periodic shifts in collective mood, public opinion can act as both a resource and a constraint for political leaders in the foreign policy process. In principle, it can provide support for either aggressive or conciliatory policies, but under the prevailing norms in an intense, protracted conflict, leaders are more likely to expect—and to mobilize—public support for the former than for the latter. Apart from transitory moods, certain pervasive states of consciousness underlie public opinion in a society engulfed in a deep-rooted conflict, reflecting the existential concerns and the central national narratives widely shared within the population. In many cases—such as Serbia, Northern Ireland, and the Middle East—historical traumas serve as the points of reference for current events. Though these memories may be manipulated by demagogic leaders, they—and the associated sense of injustice, abandonment, and vulnerability—are part of the people's consciousness and available for manipulation. The effect of such collective moods is to bring to the fore powerful social norms that support escalatory actions and inhibit moves toward compromise and accommodation. When fundamental concerns about survival and identity are tapped, national leaders, with full expectation of public support, are far more ready to risk war than to take risks for peace—in line with the proposition derived from prospect theory that people are more reluctant to take risks to achieve gains than to avoid losses (see Levy, 1992). Any change in the established view of the enemy and of the imperatives of national defense comes to be seen as a threat to the nation's very existence.

Public support is an essential resource for political leaders engaged in a conflict relationship, both in assuring the public's readiness to accept the costs that their policies may entail and in enhancing the credibility of their threats and promises to the other side. The primary means of gaining public support is *the mobilization of group loyalties*. Arousal of nationalist and patriotic sentiments, particularly in a context of national security and survival, is a powerful tool in mobilizing public support. It may evoke automatic endorsement of the policies the leadership defines as necessary and a willingness to make sacrifices that cannot be entirely understood in terms of rational calculations of costs and benefits. The nation generates such powerful identifications and loyalties because it brings together two central psychological dispositions: the needs for self-protection and self-transcendence (Kelman 1969, 1997c).

Group loyalties can potentially be mobilized in support of conciliatory policies. Political leaders may promote painful compromises and concessions to the adversary on the grounds that the security, well-being, integrity, and survival of the nation require such actions. Indeed, leaders with impeccable nationalist credentials—such as Charles de Gaulle, Yitzhak Rabin, or F. W. de Klerk—are often most effective in leading their populations toward peaceful resolution of conflicts, once they have decided that this approach best serves the national interest. In general, however, group loyalties are more readily available to mobilize support for aggressive policies than for conciliatory ones. Proposals for aggressive actions can more easily rely on the vocabulary of nationalism, which characteristically marks off the ingroup from the outgroup to the detriment of the latter. An appeal to defend the nation against an imminent attack, in particular, is more compelling than an appeal to seize a promising opportunity—as prospect theory might predict (Farnham, 1992; Levy, 1992). Such an appeal also elicits almost unanimous response among members of the population, whereas an appeal to take advantage of an opportunity for peace holds no attraction to that segment of the population that equates peace with surrender.

Processes of group loyalty create barriers to change in a conflict relationship. Group loyalty requires adherence to the group's norms—which, in an intense conflict, call for a militant, unyielding, and suspicious attitude toward the enemy. Militancy and intransigence thus become the measures of loyalty. Hence, particularly in situations of perceived national crisis, the militants exercise disproportionate power and often a veto over official actions and policies. They impose severe constraints on the ability of leaders to explore peaceful options. Dissent from the dominant conflict norms becomes defined as an act of disloyalty and is suppressed, thus further undermining the exploration of peaceful alternatives.

Decision-making processes in a conflict situation tend to inhibit the search for alternatives and the exploration of new possibilities, particularly when decision-makers are operating in an atmosphere of crisis. These tendencies are by no means inevitable, and there are historical instances—such as the Cuban missile crisis—of creative decision-making in dangerous crisis situations (Allison, 1971; Lebow, 1981). Conflict norms do, however, impose serious burdens on the decision-making process.

A major source of reluctance to explore new options are the domestic constraints under which decision-makers labor. In an intense conflict situation, adherence to the conflict norms tends to be seen as the safest course of action. Cautious decision-makers assume that they are less vulnerable domestically if they stay with the conflict's status quo, adhere to a discourse of hostility and distrust vis-à-vis the other side, or threaten escalatory actions than if they take steps toward accommodation and compromise. The search for alternatives in response to changing realities is also inhibited by institutionalized rigidities in the decision-making apparatus. Decision-makers and their bureaucracies operate within a framework of assumptions about available choices, effective strategies, and constituency expectations, shaped by the prevailing conflict norms, which may make them unaware of the occurrence and possibility of change. Furthermore, they often rely on established procedures and technologies, which are more likely to be geared toward pursuing the conflict—by military and other means—than toward resolving it.

The microprocesses of action and interaction in crisis decision-making further inhibit the exploration of new options. At the level of individual decision-makers, the stress they experience in situations of crisis—when consequential decisions have to be made under severe time pressures—limits the number of alternatives they consider and impels them to settle quickly on the dominant response, which, in intense conflicts, is likely to be aggressive and escalatory (Holsti, 1972; Lebow, 1987). At the level of decision-making groups, crisis decision-making often leads to "groupthink" (Janis, 1982), a concurrence-seeking tendency that is designed to maintain the cohesiveness of the group. Decision-making under these circumstances is much more likely to produce policies and actions that perpetuate and escalate the conflict than innovative ideas for conflict resolution.

The norms governing *negotiation and bargaining processeses* between parties involved in longstanding conflict strongly encourage zero-sum thinking, which equates the enemy's loss with one's own gain. Negotiation—even distributive bargaining in its narrowest form—is possible only when both parties define the situation, at least at some level, as a win-win, mixed-motive game in which they have both competitive and cooperative goals. While pursuing its own interests, each party must actively seek out ways the adversary can also win and appear to be winning. But this is precisely the kind of effort that is discouraged by the conflict norms.

At the micro level, negotiators in an intense conflict tend to evaluate their performance by the forcefulness with which they present their own case and by their effectiveness in resisting compromise. To listen to what the other side needs and to help the other side achieve its goals would violate the conflict norms and might subject the negotiators to criticism from their own constituencies and particularly from their hard-line domestic opposition. At the macro level, the parties—even when they recognize their common interest in negotiating certain specific issues—tend to pursue an overall outcome that strengthens their own strategic position and weakens the adversary's. Such a strategy reduces the other's incentive for concluding an agreement and ability to mobilize public support for whatever agreement is negotiated. Zero-sum thinking at both levels undermines the negotiating process, causing delays, setbacks, and repeated failures.

Finally, conflict creates certain *structural and psychological commitments*, which then take on a life of their own (see Pruitt & Gahagan, 1974; Rubin, Pruitt, & Kim, 1994). Most obviously, in a conflict of long standing, various individuals, groups, and organizations—military, political, industrial, scholarly—develop a vested interest in maintaining the conflict as a source of profit, power, status, or raison d'être. Others, though not benefiting from the conflict as such, may have a strong interest in forestalling a compromise solution because it would not address their particular grievances or fulfill their particular aspirations. Vested interests do not necessarily manifest themselves in deliberate attempts to undermine efforts at conflict resolution. They may take indirect and subtle forms, such as interpreting ambiguous realities and choosing between uncertain policy alternatives in ways that favor continuation of the conflict.

Vested interests and similar structural commitments to the conflict are bolstered by psychological commitments. People involved in a longstanding and deep-rooted conflict tend to develop a worldview that is built around the conflict and would be threatened by an end to the conflict. Resistance to change is likely to be more pronounced the more elaborate the cognitive structure or ideology in which the view of the conflict is embedded, since changing this view would have wider ramifications. In an intense conflict, the image of the enemy is often a particularly important part of people's worldview, with implications for their national identity, view of their own society, and interpretation of history. This is one reason why images of the enemy, to which we turn next, are highly resistant to change and contribute to the escalatory and self-perpetuating dynamic of conflict.

Perceptual Processes

Perceptual and cognitive processes—the ways we interpret and organize conflict-related information—play a major role in the escalation and perpetuation of conflict and create barriers to redefining and resolving the conflict despite changing realities and interests. Two perceptual processes that characterize mutual images of parties in conflict can account for this effect: the formation of mirror images and the resistance of images to contradictory information (Kelman, 1997b, pp. 222–231; see also chapter 9).

Social psychologists writing about U.S.-Soviet relations (Bronfenbrenner, 1961; White, 1965) first noted the phenomenon of *mirror image formation* as a characteristic of many conflict relationships. Both parties tend to develop parallel images of self and other, except with the value reversed. The core content of mirror images is captured by the good-bad dimension: each side sees itself as virtuous and peaceful, arming only for defensive reasons and prepared to compromise. The enemy, by contrast, is seen as evil and hostile, arming for aggressive reasons and responsive only to the language of force.

A typical corollary of the good-bad images in protracted conflicts is the view that the other's aggressiveness is inherent in its nature (its ideology, religion, national character, or political system), whereas any signs of aggressiveness on one's own part are entirely reactive and defensive. In the language of attribution theory (see hereafter), the enemy's aggression is explained in dispositional terms and one's own aggression in situational terms. John Foster Dulles's "inherent bad faith" model of the Soviet Union (Holsti, 1962), with its counterpart in Soviet views of the west, illustrates this feature of mirror images. Another common corollary of the good-bad image—one that derives from the virtuous self-image—is the assumption on each side that the enemy knows very well that we are not threatening them. Our own basic decency and peacefulness, and the provocation to which we have been subjected, are so obvious to us that they must also be obvious to the other side (see the discussion of naive realism in Ross & Ward, 1995). Apart from such generic features of mirror images, which arise from the dynamics of intergroup conflict across the board, mirror images in any given case may reflect the dynamics of the specific conflict. Thus ethnic conflicts may be characterized by mutual denial of the other's national identity, accompanied by efforts to delegitimize the other's national movement and claim to nationhood (see Kelman 1978, 1987); mutual fear of national and personal annihilation; a mutual sense of victimization by the other side; or a mutual view of the other as a source of one's own humiliation and vulnerability.

The mirror image concept implies that certain symmetries in the parties' reactions arise from the very nature of conflict interaction and that they play an important role in escalating the conflict. There is no assumption that *all* images of self and enemy are mirror images; that images on the two sides are equally inaccurate; or that there is empirical symmetry in the two sides' historical experiences and current situation or moral equivalence in their positions. The dynamics of the conflict relationship, however, produce a degree of parallelism in some of the images developed by both participants in that relationship, arising out of the motivational and cognitive contexts in which they operate. Motivationally, each side is concerned with "looking good" when blame for the conflict events is being apportioned; political leaders, therefore, feel a strong need to persuade themselves, their own people, the rest of the world, and future historians that the blame rests with the enemy. Cognitively, each side views the conflict from its own perspective and—painfully aware of its own needs, fears, historical traumas, grievances, suspicions, and political constraints—is convinced that it is acting defensively and with the best intentions and that this is so self-evident that it must be equally clear to the enemy.

Mirror images produce a spiraling effect (exemplified by the classical pattern of an arms race) because each side interprets any hostile action by the other as an indication of aggressive intent against which it must defend itself, yet its own reactions—whose defensive nature, it assumes, should be obvious to the enemy—are taken by the other as signs of aggressive intent. The effect of mirror images is accentuated insofar as the enemy's ideology or national character is perceived to be inherently aggressive and expansionist. In addition to their escalatory effect, mirror images tend to make conflicts more intractable because the sharp contrast between the innocent self and the aggressive other makes it difficult to break out of a zero-sum conception of the conflict. However, the concept of mirror images may be a useful tool in conflict resolution. In problem-solving workshops, for example, the parties' discovery that their own actions are perceived differently by the other side than by themselves may open them up to the possibility that the reverse may be true. Thus they may gain access to each other's perspective, insight into the escalatory effects of such two-directional differences in perception, and awareness of the need for mutual reassurance in order to set a deescalatory process in motion.

The second feature of conflict images, their high degree of *resistance to contradictory information,* inhibits the perception of change and the expectation of future change. A great deal of social-psychological theorizing and research has addressed the general phenomenon of the persistence of attitudes and beliefs in the face of new information that, from an outside point of view, challenges their validity but is somehow neutralized or ignored. Research has focused on several types of mechanisms that account for resistance to contradictory information: selectivity, consistency, attribution, and the self-fulfilling prophecy. The concepts of selective exposure, selective perception, and selective recall all point to the fact that our attitudes help determine the kind of information that is available to us. We are more likely to seek out and be exposed to information that confirms our existing attitudes and to perceive and remember new information in ways that fit into our preexisting cognitive framework. The various models of cognitive consistency—such as Heider's (1958) theory of cognitive balance and Festinger's (1957) theory of cognitive dissonance—suggest that, in the interest of maintaining consistency, people tend to screen out information that is incongruent with their existing beliefs and attitudes. Though inconsistent information may also instigate attitude change, it is more likely to be resisted when the existing attitudes are strongly held and have wide ramifications— as is the case with enemy images. Attribution mechanisms (Jones & Nisbett, 1971) promote confirmation of the original enemy image, because hostile actions by the enemy tend to be attributed dispositionally, thus providing further evidence of the enemy's inherently aggressive, implacable character, while conciliatory actions are explained away as reactions to situational forces, thus requiring no revision of the original image (for research in support of this proposition, see Heradstveit, 1981; Rosenberg & Wolfsfeld, 1977; Rouhana, 1997). Finally, interactions between conflicting parties tend to create self-fulfilling prophecies by causing our adversaries to behave in line with our expectations—to take on the roles in which we have cast them (Weinstein & Deutschberger, 1963)—thus confirming our original attitudes.

The mechanisms that account for resistance to disconfirming information are particularly powerful in a conflict relationship, for several reasons. First, images of the enemy and conflict-related self-images are central aspects of the national consensus, and resistance to disconfirming information is therefore reinforced by strong normative pressures. Second, in a conflict relationship, the opportunities and capacity for taking the perspective of the other side are limited, which reduces the impact of potentially new information about the varieties, changes, and signs of flexibility in the other side's views. Third, the resistance of enemy images to disconfirmation is magnified by strong beliefs about the unchangeability of the enemy, reinforced by the view that it is dangerous or even treasonous to propose that the enemy has changed or will change.

Despite all the reasons why conflict images are particularly resistant to contradictory information, they are not immutable. Social-psychological evidence suggests that they can change, and historical evidence shows that they do change. The challenge for scholars and practitioners of international conflict resolution is to devise the means to overcome their resistance to change. Interactive conflict resolution is specifically designed to address these kinds of resistances, along with the other social-psychological processes that contribute to the escalation and perpetuation of conflict. Before turning to interactive conflict resolution, however, we present a brief review of negotiation and mediation—the more traditional approaches to dealing with international conflict—and some of the social-psychological literature that addresses them.

▶ Negotiation

The most common approach to addressing international conflict within the domain of diplomacy is that of negotiation, an interactive process that appears to have a semblance of universality at a generic level, even though cultural differences in approaches and styles are a current focus of study (e.g., Cohen, 1997). Negotiation is typically defined as a discussion among parties aimed at resolving incompatible goals (Pruitt & Carnevale, 1993), although a broader definition sees negotiation as a process by which parties

develop agreements to guide and regulate their future behavior (Sawyer &
Guetzkow, 1965). The broader definition alerts us to the fact that all manner of issues at the international level are approached through negotiation,
from trade disputes to financial arrangements to environmental problems,
while the more focused definition places negotiation at the center of conflict
resolution over territory, governance, and identity, with other methods and
interventions playing a supplementary and supportive role. It is therefore
essential to understand the processes, outcomes, and context of international
negotiation, so that a range of efforts can be directed toward achieving
mutually acceptable settlements that contribute to sustainable and largely
cooperative relationships.

There are two important distinctions in considering expressions of international negotiation: bilateral versus multilateral and competitive versus
integrative. The former distinction has gained importance since the end of
the Cold War, with the shift away from a bipolar power struggle to a field
of multiple actors attempting to forge a new world order. A concise treatment of multilateral negotiation by Touval (1989) covered the phases, impediments, facilitating factors, and the challenge of building consensus, all
in comparison to bilateral negotiation. Efforts to understand the complexity
of multiparty, multiissue negotiations seeking unanimity of agreement must
go beyond the common concepts applied to bilateral negotiations (bargaining, information processing) to include additional concepts (coalition formation, role differentiation) in the context of a system perspective. Treatments of multilateral negotiation, it is hoped, will enable us to understand
more deeply this increasingly common way of dealing with international
issues (e.g., Hampson, 1995).

The second distinction has been central to the negotiation literature for
some time, stemming from the differences between domination, compromise, and integration identified by Mary Parker Follett (1924), with the
latter approach seeking to find expression of all parties' interests without
sacrificing any essential ones. The distinction was crystallized in the organizational literature through Walton and McKersie's (1965) differentiation
of distributive versus integrative bargaining, the former involving competing
interests over resources in short supply and the latter engaging cooperative
moves to increase the resource domain so that all primary interests can be
satisfied. This duality has been represented in numerous treatments of negotiation to the point where we can speak of competing theories of negotiation (Murray, 1986), one concerned with hard bargaining and resistance
to concession making in order to maximize one's gains, the other geared to
joint analysis and problem solving yielding mutually high outcomes. This
distinction is applied to the international level by Hopmann (1995), who
contends empirically that bargaining is more frequent in international negotiations, even though problem solving produces greater flexibility and
superior agreements. Part of the reason for this discrepancy between practice
and effectiveness is that the more traditional, competitive bargaining style

finds support in the dominant paradigm of realism in international relations, whereas problem solving is more compatible with the assumptions and orientations of liberalism, and as such is only more recently gaining consideration by international diplomats and other negotiators. The primary thrust of theory and research on negotiation in social and political psychology has been to support the shift from a distributive, zero-sum mentality to an integrative, non-zero-sum perspective, the latter being expressed through a firm and cooperative orientation.

A number of approaches to the study of international negotiation have been taken. Fisher (1990) identifies general descriptions based on diplomatic experience, studies that draw on mathematical models and game theory, and comparative case analyses of a systematic nature. Carnevale and Pruitt (1992) note books of advice to negotiators that are largely prescriptive (e.g., Fisher & Ury, 1981), mathematical treatments of rational negotiation that are mainly descriptive (e.g., Raiffa, 1982), and behavioral studies in both the field and laboratory that are descriptive yet yield prescriptions that can be useful to negotiators (e.g., Pruitt, 1981). Druckman (1997) provides the broadest sweep of perspectives that have been taken to understanding negotiation, seeing it as puzzle solving directed toward making optimal choices, as a bargaining game in which concessions are exchanged, as organizational management requiring consensus building both within and between parties, or as diplomatic politics in which negotiation is one strand of multifaceted international relations. Social and political psychologists have made contributions to both the descriptive and prescriptive treatments of negotiation.

An early and influential model by Sawyer and Guetzkow (1965) cast the negotiation process as a temporal flow affected by antecedent, concurrent, and consequent conditions. Druckman (1973, 1983) has utilized their model to organize research in the field and as a base for elaborating the process of negotiation into a series of stages, turning points, and crises in which momentum can be built toward the final agreement. He also makes a strong case for expanding negotiation research to consider a range of contextual factors, a direction that later studies at the international level are taking seriously (e.g., Hopmann, 1996). Carnevale and Pruitt (1992) review behavioral studies of negotiation in terms of a motivational orientation, which predicts outcomes based on strategic choices rooted in negotiator motives, and a cognitive orientation, which predicts outcomes based on negotiator perceptions and information processing. The descriptive stance of the behavioral orientation shifts in the prescriptive direction in the theory and research on problem solving by Pruitt (1986), which identifies methods for attaining integrative agreements. In addition to the time-honored technique of logrolling to transform distributive situations involving multiple issues into integrative outcomes, Pruitt identifies expanding the pie, nonspecific compensation, cost cutting, and bridging, wherein a new option is created to satisfy underlying interests. Such outcomes are achievable if it is possible to inject sufficient flexibility into the negotiation process along with the essential amount of firmness (Druckman & Mitchell, 1995).

A common question in negotiation research is how elements of the negotiating situation (e.g., prenegotiation experience, constituent pressure) affect process and outcomes. Druckman (2001) adds the more challenging question of how the processes and outcomes affect the long-term, postsettlement relations among the parties, which has significance for conflict resolution. At the same time, we must also ask how other methods in the domain of conflict resolution can be directed toward achieving and implementing integrative agreements that work to improve relations among former adversaries and thus help to build a lasting peace.

▶ Mediation

When negotiation is nonexistent or unsuccessful in situations of destructive and protracted conflict, a common response is for a neutral third party to enter the arena, either by invitation from the parties or on its own initiative. There are a wide variety of activities that intermediaries can undertake, or more generally, a number of different roles they can enact in conflicts. Kriesberg (1996, 1998) identifies activities that range from providing a space for communication to saving face, helping invent new options, and adding resources and generating pressures to reach an agreement. Fisher and Keashly (1990) provide a taxonomy of third-party intervention, which describes roles approximately in line with traditional terminology found in the literature at both the domestic and international levels. Six roles are identified in terms of their primary functions and along a continuum of the control that the third party possesses over both the process and the outcome of the interaction between or among the parties. *Conciliation* and *consultation* are at the low power end of the continuum and are essentially defined as providing an informal communication link and facilitating creative problem solving respectively. At the high end of the control continuum, *peacekeeping* is seen as maintaining a cease fire supplemented by humanitarian and political activities, while *arbitration* provides a binding third-party settlement on the substantive issues in dispute.

At the intermediate level of control is the third-party role of mediation, which, like conciliation and consultation, is a noncoercive and nonbinding approach to managing conflict with the consent of the parties. Specifically, mediation is defined as the intervention of an impartial third party designed to create a mutually acceptable negotiated settlement on the substantive issues of the conflict. In addition, Fisher and Keashly (1990) follow the lead of other theorists in the field by distinguishing *pure mediation* from *power mediation*. The former works toward agreement through the use of reasoning, persuasion, the control of information, and the suggestion of alternatives. The latter goes beyond these facilitative functions to include the use of leverage in the form of rewards and punishments and often involves the third party as a powerful guarantor of the settlement. This distinction can be connected to the primary functions of mediators identified by Touval and Zartman (1985) in that pure mediation involves the functions of *communication* and *formulation*, whereas power mediation goes beyond that to include *manipulation*. While this function can be seen as compatible with the world of power politics in which it operates, it does raise both ethical concerns over the use of coercion by powerful third parties and strategic concerns about the garnering of agreements that involve settlement but do not result in lasting resolution.

In the past 20 years, the method of mediation has witnessed a significant growth in theory, research, and practice at both the domestic and international levels (e.g., Kressel, Pruitt, & Associates, 1989). Moore (1996) provides a comprehensive coverage of the history and expression of mediation, which is found in almost all cultures in the world, practiced by a variety of individuals and institutions in both informal and formal roles. In Western societies, the last three decades have seen a profusion of mediator roles to address various types of conflict, often as an alternative to formal, legal processes of litigation or adjudication. At the international level, mediation has a history as long as that of diplomacy itself and has also received increased scholarly attention in recent times (e.g., Bercovitch & Rubin, 1992). Bercovitch (1997) provides a concise overview of this domain of study, indicating the unique characteristics of mediation as the continuation of negotiations by other means. He garners empirical evidence that attests to the frequent use of mediation in international relations by a variety of individuals, states, and institutions, and he identifies a number of variables that have been related to mediation effectiveness (e.g., Bercovitch & Houston, 1996). It is clear that intermediary activities need to be a central component of conflict management and resolution, as the world searches for alternative mechanisms to deterrence, compellence, and warfare.

With the growth of mediation, attention is being given to the many difficult issues that arise through third-party interventions in the conflicts of others. Fisher (2001) identifies a number of these in relation to the identity, motives, qualities, and competencies of the intervenor and the timing, ethics, and effectiveness of intervention. The issue of cultural generalizability is especially salient when the third party enters from a different and dominant culture in relation to those of the parties in conflict. Power asymmetry between the parties and the entry of a powerful third party both raise questions about the limits of applicability of intervention methods. The traditional view of an impartial third party is being challenged by the proclaimed effectiveness of biased mediators whose interests may help deliver a settlement. The question of timing asks whether conflicts must reach a level of destruction and a point of impasse before parties are willing to abandon their unilateral, coercive measures to seek a mediated compromise. The effectiveness of mediation is an issue of considerable import, with studies of domestic interventions generally showing higher success rates than those at the international level, especially in protracted ethnopolitical conflicts over identity and governance. Finally, the ethics of intervention is a continuing concern, which can be addressed through the development of mediation as a form of professional practice, regardless of the forum in which it is practiced. All of these issues must be addressed for mediation and other types of third-party intervention to achieve their potential for reducing human destructiveness and facilitating social transformation toward greater harmony, equity, and justice.

▶ Interactive Conflict Resolution

Frustrations in achieving negotiated settlements and failures at mediation, particularly in intractable ethnopolitical conflicts, were part of the impetus for exploring alternative methods of conflict resolution that did not arise from a base in realist assumptions about international relations. John Burton is credited not only with challenging the dominant paradigm of realism but also with the creation of a problem-solving approach to international conflict analysis and resolution, which he initially termed *controlled communication* (Burton, 1969). Following Burton's method, high-level representatives of parties in destructive conflict are brought together in unofficial discussions with a third-party panel of social scientists, who work to build an open and supportive climate in which the antagonists can analyze their situation, examine their perceptions and evaluations, and create mutually acceptable options for conflict resolution. Herbert Kelman was a panel member in one of Burton's early workshops on the Cyprus conflict and went on to develop his own method of *interactive problem solving*, which is described hereafter with reference to the Israeli-Palestinian conflict. Leonard Doob experimented with the application of human-relations training methods to destructive conflicts in the Horn of Africa and Northern Ireland (Doob, 1970; Doob & Foltz, 1973). A variety of interventions and studies applying these types of methods to intergroup and international conflict are reviewed by Fisher (1972, 1983), who also developed a generic model of *third party consultation* to represent the essential components of the approach.

Fisher (1997) has recently captured the work of Burton, Kelman, and others under the rubric of *interactive conflict resolution*, which is defined as "small-group, problem-solving discussions between unofficial representatives of identity groups or states engaged in destructive conflict that are facilitated by an impartial third party of social scientist-practitioners" (p. 8). Given the proliferation of interactive methods over the past decade, Fisher (1997) also provides a broader view of interactive conflict resolution as involving facilitated, face-to-face activities in communication, training, education, or consultation that promote collaborative conflict analysis and problem solving among antagonists. In either case, the method is based in social-psychological assumptions about intergroup and international conflict that see the importance of subjective factors (attitudes, perceptions, emotions) alongside objective elements and that propose that meaningful interaction among conflicting parties is as necessary to deescalate the conflict as it was to escalate it. However, the method also takes a system perspective, knowing that any changes in individuals that take place in problem-solving workshops or other interactive fora must be transferred successfully to the level of political discourse and policy-making for any positive effects to occur. Interactive conflict resolution is therefore a form of unofficial or *track two diplomacy* (Montville, 1987), which initially gained its currency through complementary contributions that it can make to official peacemaking efforts. At the same time, interactive methods are becoming increasingly important in postconflict peace-building; to help implement settlements and rebuild war-torn relationships so that reescalating cycles of violence are prevented.

There are a variety of different forms of interactive conflict resolution, in addition to the classic problem-solving workshop model articulated by Burton (1987), Mitchell (1981), Kelman (1986), Azar (1990), Fisher (1986), and others. Vamik Volkan and his colleagues have developed a psychodynamic approach to both understanding and ameliorating ethnopolitical conflict among contesting communal groups. Volkan (1991) contends that deeper psychological processes, such as projection and victimization, need to be addressed along with political and economic issues, and he has developed a workshop methodology for bringing together influential members of conflicting groups to establish workable relationships and develop mutually acceptable options. The approach has been successfully applied to the Arab-Israeli conflict (Julius, 1991) and to conflicts in the post-Soviet Baltic republics between majority populations and Russian minorities (Volkan & Harris, 1993). Although the psychodynamic underpinnings of Volkan's method are different from those of the social-psychological model, the design of the workshops and role of the third-party facilitators are remarkably similar.

Another form of interactive conflict resolution has been developed by Harold Saunders, a former U.S. diplomat and policy-maker, who has worked as a member of the third-party team in workshops organized by both Volkan and Kelman. For many years, Saunders was involved in the Dartmouth Conference, bringing together Soviet (now Russian) and American influentials to engage in citizen-to-citizen dialogue. He served as the American cochair of the regional conflict task force that examined superpower interaction in Cold War hot spots as a means of understanding the relationship between the two countries. Based on this experience, Chufrin and Saunders (1993) articulated a public peace process involving five stages of unofficial dialogue between conflicting groups. Following the end of the Cold War, Saunders and Randa Slim worked with American and Russian colleagues to apply the dialogue model with considerable success to the civil war in the former Soviet republic of Tajikistan (Saunders, 1995). Based on this and other experiences, including a dialogue on race relations in the United States, Saunders (1998) has articulated a broadly applicable model of facilitating sustained dialogue between members of conflicting groups.

A number of scholar-practitioners have contributed to the development of methods for intercommunal dialogue that have useful application to ethnopolitical conflicts at the international level. These forms of interactive conflict resolution tend to involve ordinary members of conflicting groups or their diasporas, who are concerned if not influential in policy-making but who represent the modal sentiments of the conflicting parties. Such dialogue also tends to focus more on developing mutual understanding through conflict analysis rather than creating alternative solutions to the conflict. However, it may result in policy options that call for useful de-escalatory moves by involved or interested parties. Louis Kriesberg and his colleagues initiated the Syracuse Area Middle East Dialogue in the early 1980s to bring Jewish-American and Arab-American citizens together to increase mutual understanding and develop policy ideas for the U.S. government to improve Israeli-Palestinian relations. Richard Schwartz (1989) provides a useful description of the very challenging dialogue process and a valuable exposition of the rationale and procedures of the methodology that was developed. Another example of the creation of structured dialogue processes comes from the work of Richard Chasin and his colleagues, formerly at the Center for Psychology and Social Change and now at the Public Conversations Project. Based in family systems therapy, this approach follows a systematic process for increasing understanding between hostile parties and creating cooperation across lines of the conflict. The approach was initially applied to Soviet and American relations during the Cold War and has been further developed through application to a variety of other conflicts, including the abortion issue in the United States (Chasin & Herzig, 1993; Chasin et al., 1996). These and other examples of dialogue projects provide a rich source for developing a generic methodology of dialogue that is highly contributive to the field of interactive conflict resolution (Fisher, 1997).

▶ Problem-Solving Workshops

To illustrate the microprocess of interactive conflict resolution, we shall describe the problem-solving workshops carried out by Herbert Kelman and his colleagues with politically influential Israelis and Palestinians, starting in the early 1970s (Kelman, 1992, 1998b; Kelman & Cohen, 1976; Rouhana & Kelman, 1994). Kelman's approach, *interactive problem solving* (Kelman, 1986, 1998a), derives from the work of John Burton (1969, 1979, 1984, 1987; see also Kelman, 1972). It is an academically based, unofficial, third-party approach to conflict resolution, anchored in social-psychological principles. It brings together politically involved and often politically influential members of conflicting parties for direct communication, facilitated by a panel of social scientists with expertise in group process, international conflict, and the particular region in which the conflict takes place.

The ultimate goal of interactive problem solving is to promote change in individuals—through face-to-face interaction in small groups (Kelman, 1997a)—as a vehicle for change in national policies and in the larger conflict system. The core of the work is a particular microprocess, best exemplified by problem-solving workshops, that is intended to contribute to the macroprocess of conflict resolution.

Relationship to Negotiations

Problem-solving workshops and related activities are not negotiating sessions. Negotiations can be carried out only by officials authorized to conclude binding agreements, and workshops—by definition—are completely nonbinding. Their nonbinding character, in fact, represents their special strength and is the source of their unique contribution to the larger process. They provide an opportunity for sharing perspectives, exploring options, and joint thinking. Such exploratory interaction is essential to negotiation at all of its stages, but it is usually difficult to arrange in an official context, especially around the negotiating table.

Even though workshops must be clearly distinguished from official negotiations, they can be viewed as an integral part of the larger negotiating process, relevant at all stages of that process. At the prenegotiation stage, they can help the parties move toward the negotiating table by contributing to the creation of a political environment that is conducive to negotiation. At the negotiation stage itself they can perform useful paranegotiation functions: they can contribute to overcoming obstacles to the negotiations, to creating momentum and reviving the sense of possibility, and to identifying options and reframing issues so that they can be negotiated more effectively once they get to the table. Finally, at the postnegotiation stage, workshops can contribute to resolving problems in the implementation of negotiated agreements, as well as to the process of peacebuilding and reconciliation in the aftermath of an agreement and to the transformation of the relationship between the former enemies.

Israeli-Palestinian Experiences

Kelman's and his colleagues' Israeli-Palestinian work has sought to contribute to all three of these stages of the negotiating process over the course of the years. All of the workshops in the 1970s and 1980s took place, of course, in the prenegotiation stage and were designed to explore the possibilities for movement toward the negotiating table. A variety of workshops were carried out during that period—in different contexts and with different types of participants. All of the participants, however, were members (or were soon to be members) of the political elite. They included political actors, such as parliamentarians and leaders or activists of political parties or political movements; political influentials, such as journalists, editors, directors of think tanks, politically involved academicians, and former diplomats or military officers; and preinfluentials, such as advanced graduate students who seemed headed for politically important careers (some of whom did indeed become political influentials as their careers progressed). Moreover, all of the workshops during this period were "one-time" events: the particular group of Israelis and Palestinians who took part in a given workshop convened only for this one occasion—usually over an extended weekend. Some of the individuals participated in more than one such workshop, and the one-time workshops held over the years had a cumulative effect within the two societies and helped to inject new ideas into the two political cultures. But until 1990 no attempt was made to reconvene the same *group* of participants for another occasion.

In 1990, for the first time in this program, Kelman and Nadim Rouhana organized a continuing workshop: a group of highly influential Israelis and Palestinians—six on each side—who agreed to participate in a series of three meetings over the course of a year, and in the end continued to meet (with some changes in personnel) until August 1993 (Rouhana & Kelman, 1994). As it happened, with the onset of official negotiations in 1991, first in Madrid and then in Washington, this continuing workshop also provided the organizers' first experience with interactive problem solving as a paranegotiation process. The political relevance of this work was enhanced by the appointment, in 1991, of four of the six initial Palestinian participants in the group to key positions in the official negotiating teams and, in 1992, of several Israeli participants to ambassadorial and cabinet positions in the new Rabin government. Some participants left the group at this point because they saw a conflict of interests between their roles in the official and unofficial process (Kelman, 1998b, pp. 19–20).

These workshops from the 1970s to the early 1990s, along with other unofficial activities, helped to lay the groundwork for the Oslo agreement of September 1993 (Kelman, 1995, 1997d). Such efforts contributed by developing cadres prepared to carry out productive negotiations; by sharing information and formulating new ideas that provided substantive inputs into the negotiations; and by fostering a political atmosphere that made the parties open to a new relationship.

After the Oslo agreement, Kelman and Rouhana initiated a new project: the Joint Working Group on Israeli-Palestinian Relations, which met regularly between 1994 and 1999. For the first time in this program, the group set itself the goal of producing written documents: joint concept papers on the issues in the final-status negotiations, viewed in the context of what would be required to establish a long-term peaceful and mutually enhancing relationship between the two societies. The group thus intended to contribute both to the negotiations themselves and to the postnegotiation process of peace-building and reconciliation. Three papers, on general principles for the final-status negotiations (Joint Working Group on Israeli-Palestinian Relations, 1998), the problem of Palestinian refugees and the right of return (Alpher & Shikaki, 1998), and the future Israeli-Palestinian relationship (Joint Working Group, 1999), have been published. A fourth, on Israeli settlements, was close to completion but remains unpublished.

Dual Purpose

Problem-solving workshops can best be viewed as "workshops" in the literal sense of the term: as providing a specially constructed space in which the parties can engage in the process of exploration, observation, and analysis and fashion new products that can be exported into the political arena. Workshops thus have a dual purpose. They are designed, first, to produce change—new learning, in the form of new understandings, new insights, and new ideas for resolving the conflict—in the particular individuals who participate in the workshop and, second, to transfer these changes into the political debate and the decision-making process in the two societies. Depending on their particular positions in the society, individual participants can communicate their new insights and ideas through their writing, lecturing, and political activities, or the advice they give to political decision-makers. The participants in the Joint Working Group took a further step by shaping these insights and ideas into concept papers, which were made available to decision-makers, political elites, and the wider public as the two sides moved into the final-status negotiations.

An important theoretical and practical consequence of the dual purpose of workshops is that the two purposes may create contradictory requirements. The best example of these dialectics of interactive problem solving is provided by the selection of participants. *Transfer* into the political process would be maximized by officials who are close to the decision-making apparatus and thus in a position to apply immediately what they have learned. *Change*, however, would be maximized by participants who are removed from the decision-making process and therefore less constrained in their interactions and freer to play with ideas and explore hypothetical scenarios. To balance these contradictory requirements, selection has focused on participants who are not officials but are politically influential. They are thus relatively free to engage in the process, but, at the same time, any new ideas they develop in the course of a workshop can have an impact on the thinking of decision-makers and the society at large.

Ground Rules for Interaction

Problem-solving workshops follow a set of ground rules that are presented to the participants in great detail. The central ground rule is the principle of privacy and confidentiality. In the early Israeli-Palestinian workshops, confidentiality was particularly important for the protection of the participants, because the mere fact of meeting with the enemy was controversial and exposed them to political, legal, and even physical risks. Confidentiality is equally important, however, for protection of the process that workshops seek to promote. The ground rules are designed to encourage the participants to talk and listen to each other, rather than focus on their constituencies, an audience, third parties, or the record. They are asked to think out loud, to experiment with ideas, and explore different options, without having to worry about how others would react if their words were quoted outside. This is why there is no audience, no publicity, no record, and no attribution. Focusing on each other enables and encourages the participants to enter into a type of interaction that is generally not feasible among parties engaged in a bitter conflict—a type of interaction, indeed, that deviates from the conflict norms that usually govern their behavior: an interaction that is *analytic* rather than polemical, that is, in which the parties seek to explore each other's perspective and gain insight into the causes and dynamics of the conflict; and an interaction that is *problem solving* rather than adversarial, that is, in which the parties sidestep the usual attempt to allocate blame and instead take the conflict as a shared problem that requires joint effort to find a mutually satisfactory solution.

Another ground rule is that in a workshop—unlike a negotiating session—there is no expectation that the parties will reach an agreement. As in any conflict resolution effort, there is an interest in finding common ground, but the amount of agreement achieved in the discussions is not necessarily a measure of the success of the enterprise. If participants come away with a better understanding of the other's perspective, their own priorities, and the dynamics of the conflict, the workshop will have fulfilled its purpose, even if it has not produced an outline of a peace treaty. The Joint Working Group was an exception in this respect, in that its purpose was to produce joint concept papers, although even these papers—while they explore different options and seek to reframe issues—do not necessarily come up with a single agreed-on solution. The Joint Working Group also differs from the earlier work in that the participants eventually went public with the issuance of the completed concept papers; up to the point of publication, however, the principle of confidentiality was strictly observed.

Yet another ground rule calls for the equality of the two parties within the workshop setting. Asymmetries in power, moral position, or reputation clearly play an important role in the conflict and must be taken into account in the workshop discussions. But the two parties are equals in the workshop setting in the sense that each party has the same right to serious consideration of its needs, fears, and concerns. Within the rules of the workshop, Israeli participants cannot dismiss Palestinian concerns on the grounds that the Palestinians are the weaker party and, therefore, in a poor bargaining position, nor can Palestinian participants dismiss Israeli concerns on the grounds that the Israelis are the oppressors and, therefore, not entitled to sympathy. Each side has the right to be heard in the workshop and each side's needs and fears must be given equal attention in the search for a mutually satisfactory solution.

A final ground rule concerns the facilitative role of the third party. The third party in this model does not take part in the substantive discussion; it does not give advice or offer its own proposals, nor does it take sides, evaluate the ideas presented, or arbitrate between different interpretations of historical facts or international law. Its task is to create the conditions that allow ideas for resolving the conflict to emerge out of the interaction between the parties themselves. The facilitation of the third party, however, is an important part of the process. The third party sets the ground rules and monitors adherence to them; it helps to keep the discussion moving in constructive directions, tries to stimulate movement, and intervenes as relevant with questions, observations, and even challenges, relating both to the content and the process of the interaction. It also serves as a repository of trust for parties who, by definition, do not trust each other. They feel safe to participate because they trust the third party and its ability to maintain confidentiality and protect their interests.

Workshop Agenda

In the typical one-time, free-standing workshop, the agenda is relatively open and unstructured with respect to the substantive issues under discussion. The way these issues are approached, however, and the order of discussion are structured so as to facilitate the kind of discourse that the ground rules are designed to encourage. A similar structure, with some necessary modifications, characterizes the agenda within and across the meetings of a continuing workshop.

The first discussion session of any workshop is usually devoted to an exchange of information between the two sides, which serves to break the ice and set the tone for the kind of exchange the workshop hopes to generate. Each party is asked to talk about the situation on the ground and the current mood in its own community, about the issues in the conflict as seen in that community, about the spectrum of views on the conflict and its solution, and about participants' own positions within that spectrum. This exchange provides a shared base of information and sets a precedent for the two sides to deal with each other as mutual resources rather than solely as combatants.

Following the opening discussion, the core agenda of the workshop consists of four parts. It begins with a needs analysis, in which members on each side are asked to discuss their central concerns in the conflict—the fundamental needs that would have to be addressed and the existential fears that would have to be allayed if a solution is to be satisfactory to them. The parties are asked not to debate the issues raised, although they may ask for clarification of what the other says. The purpose is for each side to gain an adequate understanding of the other's needs, fears, and concerns, from the perspective of the other. Once they have demonstrated that they understand each other's needs to a substantial degree, the workshop moves to the second phase of the agenda: joint thinking about possible solutions. The difficult assignment that participants are given in this phase is to develop, through an interactive process, ideas about the overall shape of a solution for the conflict as a whole or, perhaps, a particular issue in the conflict, that would address the needs and fears of *both* sides.

As participants develop some common ground in this process of joint thinking, they turn to the next phase of the workshop: discussion of the political and psychological constraints within the two societies that would create barriers to carrying out the ideas for solution that have been developed in the group. This is a very important part of the discussion, because parties in conflict usually find it extremely difficult to understand the constraints on the other side—or even to recognize that the other, like themselves, has constraints. But it is best to leave the discussion of constraints to this later phase, so that it does not hamper the creative process of jointly generating new ideas. Finally, depending on how much progress has been made and how much time is left, the parties are asked to engage in another round of joint thinking—this time about ways of overcoming the constraints that have been presented. The participants are asked to come up with ideas about what their governments, their societies, and they themselves might do—separately or jointly—that would help to overcome the barriers to negotiating mutually satisfactory solutions to the conflict.

◣ Challenges Facing the Field

Conflict analysis and resolution from a social-scientific base with a professional practice orientation is a relatively new field of endeavor, which, in addition to the fundamental complexity and intractability of the phenomenon that it addresses, must also confront and overcome many difficult issues. This brief section will only be able to identify a number of the most important of these.

Culture and Gender

Scholars and practitioners of conflict resolution need to take the questions of cultural and gender influences seriously (Avruch, 1998; Taylor & Miller, 1994). It is not appropriate to assume the universality of concepts and methods, regardless of the societal environment to which they are applied. Each society has its "culture of conflict," which incorporates the beliefs, practices, and institutions relevant to managing differences and which affects what is defined as conflict and how it is addressed (Ross, 1993a). Culture is important in how it affects negotiating styles and third-party roles, and representatives and intermediaries who work across cultural boundaries require sensitivity to their own culture and crosscultural understanding in order to interact appropriately and effectively. A first step is to carry out a cultural analysis of the situation, so that the effects of cultural differences on the etiology and expression of the conflict are clearly understood (Avruch & Black, 1993). Similar points can be made about gender differences as they are expressed in conflict, especially given the patriarchal and hierarchical nature of most societies, which incorporates significant differences in status and power. An analysis based on gender differences created by traditional socialization contrasts the dominant male, competitive, adversarial, rights-based approach with a relationship-oriented, cooperative, and caring female style. However, research in North America tends not to support these differences clearly in studies of either negotiation or mediation (Keashly, 1994; Stamato, 1992), possibly because the variable of biological sex is often confused with that of gender, which is socially constructed. Nonetheless, there are indications that the manner in which women versus men enter into conflict analysis and resolution may be different, with important implications for the focus and outcomes of the activity. For example, based on an analysis of interactive problem-solving workshops, d'Estrée and Babbitt (1998) conclude that women tend to engage in deeper self-disclosure, leading to empathy for the enemy, and a reciprocal acknowledgment of concerns, coupled with an orientation to build relationships and a capacity to surface emotional as well as strategic issues. This implies that women may be better equipped to build relationships in the pre-negotiation phase and to craft more integrative agreements that have increased sustainability following settlement. Continuing attention to both gender and cultural issues is thus warranted.

Professionalization, Training, and Ethics

Most people who come to the work of conflict analysis and resolution are professionals from a related field, such as international relations, law, psychology, human relations, diplomacy, or psychiatry, which enables them to analyze social problems and provide some form of service. Only recently have a small number of interdisciplinary graduate programs been established to train scholar-practitioners in the many intricacies of conflict and its resolution, a daunting task that involves the application of a variety of concepts and models from social science and the acquisition of a range of strategies and skills from various domains of social practice. Many practitioners begin their practice with only a modicum of the analytical tools and social skills they need and must learn through experience from more seasoned professionals. Thus there is a challenge to develop training programs, both at the graduate and midcareer levels, that will provide practitioners with the knowledge and capacities they require to engage successfully as negotiators, mediators, third-party consultants, dialogue facilitators, or trainers of conflict resolution. There is also a need to provide continuing professional development opportunities for scholar-practitioners to broaden their conceptual knowledge and to enhance their strategic and tactical repertoire. Such offerings now exist, but there is no understanding of their quality or depth, or how some collection of them might coalesce toward an adequate level of professional competence. Thus it would be valuable to initiate activities that would assist in the professionalization of the field at the international level, so that knowledge bases and best practices could be shared toward the improvement of human welfare. Currently, many scholar-practitioners connect through existing associations, such as the International Society of Political Psychology, and have engaged in some useful networking activities in these fora. Such interactions need to be enhanced in order to provide an ongoing arena for the discussion of developmental issues, such as training and the ethics of practice, that affect the character and effectiveness of the field.

Evaluation

One of the key challenges confronting the field of interactive conflict resolution is evaluation of the effectiveness of its efforts in achieving the goals it sets out to achieve. As a field that proposes to introduce innovative, academically based forms of intervention in conflict into the larger diplomatic process, interactive conflict resolution has a special obligation to demonstrate its utility and success by way of systematic, empirical evidence that is consistent with scholarly standards. Writers in the field have increasingly moved to respond to this challenge (e.g., Ross & Rothman, 1999; Rouhana, 2000; Saunders, 2000; Chataway, in press; d'Estrée, Fast, Weiss, & Jacobsen, 2001). The ultimate goal of interactive conflict resolution is to *contribute* to the achievement of a negotiated agreement that is mutually satisfactory and lasting and that transforms the relationship between the conflicting parties. Since interactive problem solving—which is not in the business of negotiating agreements—cannot *produce* such an outcome but only *contribute* to it, the most relevant criteria for evaluating it refer to its success in achieving its intermediate goals rather than its ultimate goal. The intermediate goals constitute changes in the political cultures of the conflicting parties that would make them more receptive to negotiation with each other (Kelman, 1996a). Standard models of evaluation—such as the experimental field test—are not applicable to this problem. Furthermore, the use of obtrusive observations and experimental manipulations is often ethically or methodologically unacceptable in research on ongoing interventions. The challenge, therefore, is to develop evaluation models and research methods that are appropriate to the nature and purpose of the enterprise. Appropriate models have to be based on the gradual accumulation of pieces of evidence in support of the underlying assumptions of the approach. These may involve identifying and testing the individual steps in the process of interactive conflict resolution that are hypothesized to account for its effectiveness, or testing some of the theoretical assumptions of the approach in other settings, including experimental analogs and laboratory simulations.

Complementarity of Interventions

There is a challenge to understand how variations in third-party roles contribute differentially and uniquely to negotiation success and sustainable resolution. The early proponents of interactive conflict resolution were clear on its potential as a useful prenegotiation activity (e.g., Burton, 1969, Kelman & Cohen, 1976), in line with a rationale more fully articulated by Fisher (1989) but it is now evident that it can make contributions at all stages of the negotiation and resolution process (Kelman, 1992, 1998b). Given that conflict, especially of an ethnopolitical nature between identity groups, is a potent mix of objective and subjective factors, interventions are required to address the latter, in terms of the misperceptions, misattributions, hostile attitudes, mistrust, hatred, and vengeance that fuel escalation and intractability. In fact, it is difficult to see how identity-based conflicts can be addressed without methods that focus on the human and psychological side of the equation (Ross, 1993b; Rothman, 1997). The question is how these methods can be related to and sequenced with the more traditional forms of conflict management. Fisher and Keashly (1991) developed a contingency approach to third-party intervention, proposing that different methods be matched to the stage of conflict escalation for maximum utility. They also propose that methods need to be sequenced in a complementary fashion, so that a lead intervention gives way to others designed to deescalate and resolve the conflict. There are two points of complementarity between interactive conflict resolution (represented by third-party consultation) and mediation, in both its pure and power forms. The first occurs where consultation serves as a premediation activity that improves understanding and builds trust in the relationship so that pure mediation can deal more effectively with objective issues. The second sees consultation as following power mediation, which has achieved a cease-fire or initial settlement on substantive issues, in order to rebuild the torn relationship toward a comprehensive agreement and a sustainable peace. While a limited amount of experimental and empirical research supports the contingency approach (Keashly & Fisher, 1996), it remains a skeletal representation of a complex set of relationships that may not play out as diagramed in the complexity of real-world dynamics. Nonetheless, the contingency model and similar attempts (e.g., Kriesberg, 1996) challenge theorists and practitioners to think more seriously about the coordination and complementarity of interventions that may well be required to adequately address intractable ethnopolitical conflicts.

A Comprehensive Approach to Diplomacy

An intersocietal view of conflict, as we have proposed, calls for a complex mix of official and unofficial processes, complementing each other in the achievement of the overall diplomatic goal. While binding agreements can be signed only through official negotiations, other tracks—public diplomacy, people-to-people projects, media programs, curricular changes, nonviolent action campaigns, along with interactive conflict resolution—can each make their own unique contributions to the larger enterprise. Interactive conflict resolution is particularly useful in providing opportunities for the parties to engage in the processes of exploring ideas, sharing perspectives, analytic thinking, and joint problem solving that are essential to the search for a mutually satisfactory solution to the conflict but that are often inhibited by the constraints that characterize interactions around the negotiating table. The microprocess of interactive conflict resolution thus helps to promote four components of conflict resolution that must take place somewhere in an effective macroprocess of conflict resolution: identification and analysis of the problem in the relationship that the conflict represents; joint shaping of ideas for a mutually acceptable solution; mutual influence through reassurance and other positive incentives; and creation of a supportive political environment (Kelman, 2000). The challenge is to make effective use of the potential contributions of interactive conflict resolution and other unofficial tracks in the official diplomatic process. Ideally, the products of problem-solving workshops and related activities can be used for exploring possibilities, formulating options, and framing issues in ways that can advance negotiations at its various stages. This has indeed happened on occasion, but it needs to be done systematically, while making sure that track two efforts maintain their integrity and independence and do not become—or come to be seen as—merely another component of the track one process. Official negotiations can also benefit from adopting some of the exploratory, analytical, and problem-solving methods of interactive conflict resolution in their own proceedings, insofar as they can be accommodated within the constraints of the official process. Practitioners of interactive conflict resolution, on their part, need to be well informed of the issues, problems, and progress of the official process so that they can provide input that will be most directly relevant to the status of ongoing negotiations.

Institutionalization

At the level of a particular conflict, it might be useful to institutionalize interactive conflict resolution as part of the peace-building process that must accompany and follow the negotiation of a peace agreement. An ongoing mechanism for conflict resolution is generally an essential component of the civil society institutions across the national lines that must be built to ensure a stable peace and cooperative relationship between former enemies who must coexist in close proximity to one another. At the global level, the persistence and proliferation of deadly conflicts between ethnic groups around the world suggest the urgent need for a large, well-endowed, mostly nongovernmental organization devoted to monitoring such conflicts as they evolve and ready to intervene with efforts to help prevent and resolve them (Burton, 1983). The purpose of such an institution would be to supplement the work of existing governmental, intergovernmental, and nongovernmental organizations devoted to peacemaking, peacekeeping, and postconflict humanitarian aid by bringing together politically influential representatives of the opposing sides in an active or impending conflict for joint exploration, within a problem-solving framework, of steps toward preventing, de-escalating, or resolving the conflict. The institution might include a permanent staff to monitor conflict regions and provide the infrastructure for workshops as the need arises; a cadre of regional and conflict resolution specialists available to organize and lead workshops; and a cadre of local representatives to recommend appropriate actions or evaluate proposals from the staff and to assist by organizing and participating in workshops as needed. There is no direct evidence of how much a global institution organized along these lines and dedicated to the systematic application of interactive conflict resolution techniques to ethnic conflicts around the world could contribute to preventing such conflicts, defusing them once they have turned violent, and rebuilding the societies torn apart by violence. But research and observation suggest that the assumptions behind interactive conflict resolution are sound, and experience suggests that it has the potential for transforming conflict relationships. If the resources needed for a large-scale effort of this kind can be generated, there is at least the hope that it can begin to tackle the problem of ethnic violence that has been plaguing the international community.

◣ Note

This chapter represents a joint effort to which the two authors made equal contributions. Herbert Kelman gratefully acknowledges the William and Flora Hewlett Foundation's support for the Program on International Conflict Analysis and Resolution (PICAR) that he directs at the Weatherhead Center for International Affairs, Harvard University.

◣ References

Allison, G. T. (1971). *Essence of decision: Explaining the Cuban missile crisis.* Boston: Little, Brown.

Alpher, J., & Shikaki, K., with the participation of the additional members of the Joint Working Group on Israeli-Palestinian Relations (1998). *The Palestinian refugee problem and the right of return.* Weatherhead Center for International Affairs Working Paper No. 98–7. Cambridge, MA: Weatherhead Center for International Affairs, Harvard University. (Reprinted in *Middle East Policy,* February 1999, *6*[3], 167–189).

Avruch, K. (1998). *Culture and conflict resolution.* Washington, DC: United States Institute of Peace.

Avruch, K., & Black, P. (1993). Conflict resolution in intercultural settings: Problems and prospects. In D. J. D. Sandole & H. van der Merwe (Eds.), *Conflict resolution theory and practice: Integration and application* (pp. 131–145). Manchester, England: Manchester University Press.

Azar, E. E. (1990). *The management of protracted social conflict.* Hampshire, England: Dartmouth.

Baldwin, D. (1971). The power of positive sanctions. *World Politics, 24,* 19–38.

Bercovitch, J. (1997). Mediation in international conflict. In I. W. Zartman & J. L. Rasmussen (Eds.), *Peacemaking in international conflict: Methods and techniques* (pp. 125–153). Washington, DC: United States Institute of Peace.

Bercovitch, J., & Houston, A. (1996). The study of international mediation: Theoretical issues and empirical evidence. In J. Bercovitch (Ed.), *Resolving international conflicts: The theory and practice of mediation* (pp. 11–35). Boulder, CO: Lynne Rienner.

Bercovitch, J., & Rubin, J. Z. (Eds.). (1992). *Mediation in international relations: Multiple approaches to conflict management.* New York: St. Martin's Press.

Bronfenbrenner, U. (1961). The mirror image in Soviet-American relations: A social psychologist's report. *Journal of Social Issues, 17*(3), 45–56.

Burton, J. W. (1969). *Conflict and communication: The use of controlled communication in international relations.* London: Macmillan.

Burton, J. W. (1979). *Deviance, terrorism and war: The process of solving unsolved social and political problems.* New York: St. Martin's Press.

Burton, J. W. (1983, April). *A continuing seminar and an international facilitating service.* A proposal by members of the Centre for the Analysis of Conflict (University of Kent, Canterbury, England) presented at the annual meeting of the International Studies Association, Mexico City.

Burton, J. W. (1984). *Global conflict: The domestic sources of international crisis.* Brighton, England: Wheatsheaf.

Burton, J. W. (1987). *Resolving deep-rooted conflict: A handbook.* Lanham, MD: University Press of America.

Burton, J. W. (Ed.). (1990). *Conflict: Human needs theory.* New York: St. Martin's Press.

Carnevale, P. J., & Pruitt, D. G. (1992). Negotiation and mediation. *Annual Review of Psychology, 43,* 531–582.

Chasin, R., & Herzig, M. (1993). Creating systemic interventions for the sociopolitical arena. In D. Berger Gould & D. Hilleboe DeMuth (Eds.), *The global family therapist: Integrating the personal, professional, and political* (pp. 149–192). Boston: Allyn and Bacon.

Chasin, R., Herzig, M., Roth, S., Chasin, L., Becker, C., & Stains, R., Jr. (1996). From diatribe to dialogue on divisive public issues: Approaches drawn from family therapy. *Mediation Quarterly, 13,* 323–344.

Chataway, C. (in press). Assessing the social-psychological support for Kelman's interactive problem-solving workshops. In A. Eagly, R. M. Baron, & V. L. Hamilton

(Eds.), *The social psychology of group identity and social conflict: Theory, application, and practice.* Washington, DC: American Psychological Association.

Chufrin, G. I., & Saunders, H. H. (1993). A public peace process. *Negotiation Journal, 9,* 155–177.

Cohen, R. (1997). *Negotiating across cultures* (2nd ed.). Washington, DC: United States Institute of Peace.

d'Estrée, T. P., & Babbitt, E. F. (1998). Women and the art of peacemaking: Data from Israeli-Palestinian interactive problem-solving workshops. *Political Psychology, 19,* 185–209.

d'Estrée, T. P., Fast, L. A., Weiss, J. N., & Jacobsen, M. S. (2001). Changing the debate about "success" in conflict resolution efforts. *Negotiation Journal, 17,* 101–113.

Doob, L. W. (Ed.). (1970). *Resolving conflict in Africa: The Fermeda workshop.* New Haven: Yale University Press.

Doob, L. W., & Foltz, W. J. (1973). The Belfast workshop: An application of group techniques to a destructive conflict. *Journal of Conflict Resolution, 17,* 489–512.

Druckman, D. (1973). *Human factors in international negotiations: Social-psychological aspects of international conflict.* Sage Professional Paper in International Studies 02–020.

Druckman, D. (1983). Social psychology in international negotiations. In R. F. Kidd & M. J. Saks (Eds.), *Advances in applied social psychology* (Vol. 2, pp. 51–81). Hillsdale, NJ: Erlbaum.

Druckman, D. (1997). Negotiating in the international context. In I. W. Zartman & J. L. Rasmussen (Eds.), *Peacemaking in international conflict: Methods and techniques* (pp. 81–123). Washington, DC: United States Institute of Peace.

Druckman, D. (2001, June). *New advances in negotiation theory and research.* Paper presented at the annual conference of the International Association for Conflict Management, Paris.

Druckman, D., & Mitchell, C. (Eds.). (1995, November). Flexibility in international negotiation and mediation. *Annals of the American Academy of Political and Social Science, 542.*

Farnham, B. (Ed.). (1992). Special issue: Prospect theory and political psychology. *Political Psychology, 13,* 167–329.

Festinger, L. (1957). *A theory of cognitive dissonance.* Stanford, CA: Stanford University Press.

Fisher, R., & Ury, W. (1981). *Getting to "yes": Negotiating agreement without giving in.* Boston: Houghton Mifflin.

Fisher, R. J. (1972). Third party consultation: A method for the study and resolution of conflict. *Journal of Conflict Resolution, 16,* 67–94.

Fisher, R. J. (1983). Third party consultation as a method of intergroup conflict resolution: A review of studies. *Journal of Conflict Resolution, 27,* 301–334.

Fisher, R. J. (1986). Third party consultation: A problem-solving approach for de-escalating international conflict. In J. P. Maas & R. A. C. Stewart (Eds.), *Toward a world of peace: People create alternatives* (pp. 18–32). Suva, Fiji: University of the South Pacific Press.

Fisher, R. J. (1989). Prenegotiation problem-solving discussions: Enhancing the potential for successful negotiation. In J. G. Stein (Ed.), *Getting to the table: The process of international prenegotiation* (pp. 206–238). Baltimore: Johns Hopkins University Press.

Fisher, R. J. (1990). *The social psychology of intergroup and international conflict resolution*. New York: Springer-Verlag.

Fisher, R. J. (1997). *Interactive conflict resolution*. Syracuse, NY: Syracuse University Press.

Fisher, R. J. (2001). Methods of third party intervention. In N. Ropers, M. Fischer, & E. Manton (Eds.), *The Berghof handbook of conflict transformation* (pp. 1–27). Berlin: The Berghof Centre for Conflict Management.

Fisher, R. J., & Keashly, L. (1990). Third party consultation as a method of intergroup and international conflict resolution. In R. J. Fisher, *The social psychology of intergroup and international conflict resolution* (pp. 211–238). New York: Springer-Verlag.

Fisher, R. J., & Keashly, L. (1991). The potential complementarity of mediation and consultation within a contingency model of third party intervention. *Journal of Peace Research, 28,* 29–42.

Follett, M. P. (1924). *Creative experience*. Boston: Longmans Green.

George, A. L., & Smoke, R. (1974). *Deterrence in American foreign policy: Theory and practice*. New York: Columbia University Press.

Hampson, F. O. (1995). *Multi-lateral negotiations*. Baltimore: Johns Hopkins University Press.

Heider, F. (1958). *The psychology of interpersonal relations*. New York: Wiley.

Heradstveit, D. (1981). *The Arab-Israeli conflict: Psychological obstacles to peace* (2nd ed.). Oslo: Universitetsforlaget.

Holsti, O. R. (1962). The belief system and national images: A case study. *Journal of Conflict Resolution, 6,* 244–252.

Holsti, O. R. (1972). *Crisis, escalation, war*. Montreal: McGill-Queen's University Press.

Hopmann, P. T. (1995, November). Two paradigms of negotiation: Bargaining and problem solving. *The Annals of the American Academy of Political and Social Science, 542,* 24–47.

Hopmann, P. T. (1996). *The negotiation process and the resolution of international conflicts*. Columbia: University of South Carolina Press.

Janis, I. L. (1982). *Groupthink* (2nd ed.). Boston: Houghton Mifflin.

Jervis, R. (1976). *Perceptions and misperceptions in international politics*. Princeton: Princeton University Press.

Jervis, R., Lebow, R. N., & Stein, J. G. (1985). *Psychology and deterrence*. Baltimore: Johns Hopkins University Press.

Joint Working Group on Israeli-Palestinian Relations (1998). *General principles for the final Israeli-Palestinian agreement*. PICAR Working Paper. Cambridge, MA: Program on International Conflict Analysis and Resolution, Weatherhead Center for International Affairs, Harvard University. (Reprinted in *Middle East Journal,* February 1999, *53*[1], 120–175).

Joint Working Group on Israeli-Palestinian Relations (1999). *The future Israeli-Palestinian relationship*. Weatherhead Center for International Affairs Working paper No. 99–12. Cambridge, MA: Weatherhead Center for International Affairs, Harvard University. (Reprinted in *Middle East Policy,* February 2000, *7*[2], 90–112).

Jones, E. E., & Nisbett, R. E. (1971). The actor and the observer: Divergent perceptions of the causes of behavior. In E. E. Jones, D. E. Kanouse, H. H. Kelley, R. E. Nisbett, S. Valins, & B. Weiner (Eds.), *Attribution: Perceiving the causes of behavior* (pp. 79–94). Morristown, NJ: General Learning Press.

Julius, D. A. (1991). The practice of track two diplomacy in the Arab-Israeli conferences. In V. D. Volkan, J. V. Montville, & D. A. Julius (Eds.), *The psychodynamics of international relationships*. Vol. 2: *Unofficial diplomacy at work* (pp. 193–205). Lexington, MA: Lexington Books.

Keashly, L. (1994). Gender and conflict: What does psychological research tell us? In A. Taylor & J. B. Miller (Eds.), *Conflict and gender* (pp. 217–235). Cresskill, NJ: Hampton Press.

Keashly, L., & Fisher, R. J. (1996). A contingency perspective on conflict interventions: Theoretical and practical considerations. In J. Bercovitch (Ed.), *Resolving international conflicts: The theory and practice of mediation* (pp. 235–261). Boulder, CO: Lynne Rienner.

Kelman, H. C. (1969). Patterns of personal involvement in the national system: A social-psychological analysis of political legitimacy. In J. N. Rosenau (Ed.), *International politics and foreign policy: A reader in research and theory* (Rev. ed., pp. 276–288). New York: Free Press.

Kelman, H. C. (1972). The problem-solving workshop in conflict resolution. In R. L. Merritt (Ed.), *Communication in international politics* (pp. 168–204). Urbana: University of Illinois Press.

Kelman, H. C. (1978). Israelis and Palestinians: Psychological prerequisites for mutual acceptance. *International Security, 3,* 162–186.

Kelman, H. C. (1985). Overcoming the psychological barrier: An analysis of the Egyptian-Israeli peace process. *Negotiation Journal, 1,* 213–234.

Kelman, H. C. (1986). Interactive problem solving: A social-psychological approach to conflict resolution. In W. Klassen (Ed.), *Dialogue: Toward interfaith understanding* (pp. 293–314). Tantur, Jerusalem: Ecumenical Institute for Theological Research.

Kelman, H. C. (1987). The political psychology of the Israeli-Palestinian conflict: How can we overcome the barriers to a negotiated solution? *Political Psychology, 8,* 347–363.

Kelman, H. C. (1992). Informal mediation by the scholar/practitioner. In J. Bercovitch & J. Z. Rubin (Eds.), *Mediation in international relations: Multiple approaches to conflict management* (pp. 64–96). New York: St. Martin's Press.

Kelman, H. C. (1993). Coalitions across conflict lines: The interplay of conflicts within and between the Israeli and Palestinian communities. In S. Worchel & J. Simpson (Eds.), *Conflict between people and groups* (pp. 236–258). Chicago: Nelson-Hall.

Kelman, H. C. (1995). Contributions of an unofficial conflict resolution effort to the Israeli-Palestinian breakthrough. *Negotiation Journal, 11,* 19–27.

Kelman, H. C. (1996a, November). *An approach to evaluation of NGO contributions to the resolution of ethnonational conflicts.* Paper presented at the Carnegie Corporation Conference on the Role of International NGOs in Ethnic and National Conflicts, New York.

Kelman, H. C. (1996b) Negotiation as interactive problem solving. *International Negotiation: A Journal of Theory and Practice, 1*(1), 99–123.

Kelman, H. C. (1997a). Group processes in the resolution of international conflicts: Experiences from the Israeli-Palestinian case. *American Psychologist, 52,* 212–220.

Kelman, H. C. (1997b). Social-psychological dimensions of international conflict. In I. W. Zartman & J. L. Rasmussen (Eds.), *Peacemaking in international conflict:*

Methods and techniques (pp. 191–237). Washington, DC: United States Institute of Peace.

Kelman, H. C. (1997c). Nationalism, patriotism, and national identity: Social-psychological dimensions. In D. Bar-Tal & E. Staub (Eds.), *Patriotism in the lives of individuals and nations* (pp. 165–189). Chicago: Nelson-Hall.

Kelman, H. C. (1997d). Some determinants of the Oslo breakthrough. *International Negotiation, 2,* 183–194.

Kelman, H. C. (1998a). Interactive problem solving: An approach to conflict resolution and its application in the Middle East. *PS: Political Science & Politics, 31*(2), 190–198.

Kelman, H. C. (1998b). Social-psychological contributions to peacemaking and peace-building in the Middle East. *Applied Psychology: An International Review, 47,* 5–28.

Kelman, H. C. (2000). The role of the scholar-practitioner in international conflict resolution. *International Studies Perspectives, 1,* 273–287.

Kelman, H. C., & Cohen, S. P. (1976). The problem-solving workshop: A social-psychological contribution to the resolution of international conflict. *Journal of Peace Research, 13,* 79–90.

Kressel, K., Pruitt, D., & Associates. (Eds.). (1989). *Mediation research: The process and effectiveness of third-party intervention.* San Francisco: Jossey-Bass.

Kriesberg, L. (1982). Non-coercive inducements in international conflict. In C. M. Stephenson (Ed.), *Alternative methods for international security* (pp. 105–120). Washington, DC: University Press of America.

Kriesberg, L. (1996). Varieties of mediating activities and mediators in international relations. In J. Bercovitch (Ed.), *Resolving international conflicts: The theory and practice of mediation* (pp. 219–233). Boulder, CO: Lynne Rienner.

Kriesberg, L. (1998). *Constructive conflicts.* Lanham, MD: Rowman and Littlefield.

Lebow, R. N. (1981). *Between peace and war.* Baltimore: Johns Hopkins University Press.

Lebow, R. N. (1987). *Nuclear crisis management: A dangerous illusion.* Ithaca, NY: Cornell University Press.

Levy, J. S. (1992). Prospect theory and international relations: Theoretical applications and analytical problems. *Political Psychology, 13,* 283–310.

Mitchell, C. R. (1981). *Peacemaking and the consultant's role.* Westmead, England: Gower.

Montville, J. V. (1987). The arrow and the olive branch: The case for track two diplomacy. In J. W. McDonald & D. B. Bendahmane (Eds.), *Conflict resolution: Track two diplomacy* (pp. 5–20). Washington, DC: Foreign Service Institute, Department of State.

Moore, C. W. (1996). *The mediation process: Practical strategies for resolving conflict* (2nd ed.). San Francisco: Jossey-Bass.

Murray, J. S. (1986). Understanding competing theories of negotiation. *Negotiation Journal, 1,* 23–29.

Osgood, C. E. (1962). *An alternative to war or surrender.* Urbana: University of Illinois Press.

Pruitt, D. G. (1981). *Negotiation behavior.* New York: Academic Press.

Pruitt, D. G. (1986). Achieving integrative agreements in negotiation. In R. K. White (Ed.), *Psychology and the prevention of nuclear war* (pp. 463–478). New York: New York University Press.

Pruitt, D. G., & Carnevale, P. J. (1993). *Negotiation in social conflict.* Pacific Grove: Brooks/Cole.

Pruitt, D. G., & Gahagan, J. P. (1974). Campus crisis: The search for power. In J. T. Tedeschi (Ed.), *Perspectives on social power* (pp. 349–392). Chicago: Aldine.

Raiffa, H. (1982). *The art and science of negotiation.* Cambridge, MA: Harvard University Press.

Rosenberg, S. W., & Wolfsfeld, G. (1977). International conflict and the problem of attribution. *Journal of Conflict Resolution, 21,* 75–103.

Ross, L., & Ward, A. (1995). Psychological barriers to dispute resolution. In M. P. Zanna (Ed.), *Advances in experimental social psychology* (Vol. 27, pp. 255–304). New York: Academic Press.

Ross, M. H. (1993a). *The culture of conflict: Interpretations and interests in comparative perspective.* New Haven: Yale University Press.

Ross, M. H. (1993b). *The management of conflict.* New Haven: Yale University Press.

Ross, M. H., & Rothman, J. (1999). *Theory and practice in ethnic conflict management: Theorizing success and failure.* London: Macmillan.

Rothman, J. (1997). *Resolving identity-based conflict.* San Francisco: Jossey-Bass.

Rouhana, N. N. (1997). *Palestinian citizens in an ethnic Jewish state: Identities in conflict.* New Haven: Yale University Press.

Rouhana, N. N. (2000). Interactive conflict resolution: Issues in theory, methodology, and evaluation. In P. C. Stern & D. Druckman (Eds.), *International conflict resolution after the Cold War* (pp. 294–337). Washington, DC: National Academy Press.

Rouhana, N. N., & Kelman, H. C. (1994). Promoting joint thinking in international conflicts: An Israeli-Palestinian continuing workshop. *Journal of Social Issues, 50* (1), 157–178.

Rubin, J. Z., Pruitt, D. G., & Kim, S. H. (1994). *Social conflict: Escalation, stalemate, and settlement* (2nd ed.). New York: McGraw-Hill.

Saunders, H. H. (1995). Sustained dialogue on Tajikistan. *Mind and Human Interaction, 6(3),* 123–135.

Saunders, H. H. (1998). *A public peace process.* New York: St. Martin's Press.

Saunders, H. H. (2000). Interactive conflict resolution: A view for policy makers on making and building peace. In P. C. Stern & D. Druckman (Eds.), *International conflict resolution after the Cold War* (pp. 251–293). Washington, DC: National Academy Press.

Sawyer, J., & Guetzkow, H. (1965). Bargaining and negotiation in international relations. In H. C. Kelman (Ed.), *International behavior: A social-psychological analysis* (pp. 466–520). New York: Holt, Rinehart and Winston.

Schelling, T. C. (1963). *The strategy of conflict.* Cambridge, MA: Harvard University Press.

Schwartz, R. D. (1989). Arab-Jewish dialogue in the United States: Toward track two tractability. In L. Kriesberg, T. A. Northrup, & S. J. Thorsen (Eds.), *Intractable conflicts and their transformation* (pp. 180–209). Syracuse, NY: Syracuse University Press.

Stamato, L. (1992). Voice, place and process: Research on gender, negotiation and conflict resolution. *Mediation Quarterly, 9,* 375–386.

Stein, J. G. (1991). Deterrence and reassurance. In P. E. Tetlock, J. L. Husbands, R.

Jervis, P. C. Stern, & C. Tilly (Eds.), *Behavior, society, and nuclear war* (Vol. 2, pp. 8–72). New York: Oxford University Press.

Taylor, A., & Miller, J. B. (Eds.) (1994). *Conflict and gender*. Cresskill, NJ: Hampton Press.

Touval, S. (1989). Multilateral negotiation: An analytic approach. *Negotiation Journal, 5,* 159–173.

Touval, S., & Zartman, I. W. (Eds.). (1985). *International mediation in theory and practice*. Boulder, CO: Westview Press.

Volkan, V. D. (1991). Psychological processes in unofficial diplomacy meetings. In V. D. Volkan, J. V. Montville, & D. A. Julius (Eds.), *The psychodynamics of international relationships. Vol. 2: Unofficial diplomacy at work* (pp. 207–222). Lexington, MA: Lexington Books.

Volkan, V. D., & Harris, M. (1993). Vaccinating the political process: A second psychopolitical analysis of relationships between Russia and the Baltic States. *Mind and Human Interaction, 4*(4), 169–190.

Walton, R. E., & McKersie, R. B. (1965). *A behavioral theory of labor negotiations*. New York: McGraw-Hill.

Weinstein, E. A., & Deutschberger, P. (1963). Some dimensions of altercasting. *Sociometry, 26,* 455–466.

White, R. K. (1965). Images in the context of international conflict: Soviet perceptions of the U.S. and the U.S.S.R. In H. C. Kelman (Ed.), *International behavior: A social-psychological analysis* (pp. 238–276). New York: Holt, Rinehart and Winston.

White, R. K. (1984). *Fearful warriors: A psychological profile of U.S.-Soviet relations*. New York: Free Press.

Zartman, I. W., & Berman, M. R. (1982). *The practical negotiator*. New Haven: Yale University Press.

Mass Political Behavior

11 Donald R. Kinder

Communication and Politics in the Age of Information

Over the latter half of the twentieth century, mass communications have transformed the landscape of American politics, vastly increasing the information about public affairs that is available to ordinary citizens. Through multiple channels—network, cable, and satellite television, radio, newspapers and magazines, regular, overnight and electronic mail, and the Internet and World Wide Web—the volume of information relevant to politics circulating through American society is massive and increasing (Lindblom, 1977; Mutz, 1998; Pool, 1983). Today we Americans are virtually bombarded with news and propaganda about public affairs: inundated with suggestions about how issues should be understood; instructed on which problems are worth our attention; informed as to how our institutions and officials are performing; told when our opinions are sensible and when they should be altered; and advised what actions, if any, we should take. With what effect?

Not much, was Joseph Klapper's (1960) famous and surprising answer. In *The Effects of Mass Communication*, Klapper presented a careful and thorough review of the available findings. Sifting through the evidence, Klapper concluded that "mass communication functions far more frequently as an agent of reinforcement than as an agent of change" (p. 15).

My purpose here is to survey the same terrain of communications and politics that Klapper reviewed 40 years ago. Like Klapper, I take my subject to be the effects of *mass* communication: that is, communication that takes place predominantly one-way, from a small number of professional communicators to a vast number of amateur "receivers" (Pool, 1973). My review concentrates on the contemporary and near contemporary United States, as Klapper's did, and so takes for granted the presence of liberal democratic institutions (fair and frequent elections, the right to vote widely extended, citizens free to express their views; Dahl, 1989) on the one hand and mass communication enterprises driven by commercial imperatives and governed by professional norms of objectivity and balance (Neuman, 1991; Schudson, 1978), on the other. Whether different findings might obtain in other societies, arranged in systematically different ways, is an open question.

Taking up essentially the same subject Klapper did, I come to a very different conclusion. Klapper's ruling of "minimal effects" was faithful to the evidence available to him at the time, but now, some four decades and

357

a substantial research effort later, the findings lead in quite a different direction, or so I will try to show here. I present this "new look" in communications research in three parts. Each organizes and reviews evidence around a single broad claim to mass communication influence: the first has to do with *attention*, the second with *persuasion*, and the third with *action*. I conclude with a few thoughts on how far the science of communication has come, and how far we have yet to go.

▲ Attention

In nations the size and complexity of the United States, the command and control of public attention is accomplished—if it is accomplished at all—primarily through mass communication. Conceivably at stake in this process is influence of three kinds. Mass communication could influence how citizens make sense of politics (what I will call *framing*); how citizens decide what is important in politics (*agenda setting*); and how citizens evaluate the alternatives that politics puts before them (*priming*). In my review, I treat framing, agenda setting, and priming as though they were separate and distinct processes. In the literature, however, the distinctions are not so clearly drawn, and particular empirical examples may prove difficult to classify. I proceed nevertheless on the idea that it is analytically useful to organize communication findings not around attention in general but around framing, agenda setting, and priming in particular.

Framing

How might Americans go about making sense of what Walter Lippmann (1925, p. 24) once called the "mystery off there," the "swarming confusion of problems" that populate public life? Lippmann understood that a good answer to this question should begin by recognizing that in modern society, ordinary citizens must rely on others for their news of national and world affairs. Such reports inevitably and inescapably privilege and promote particular points of view. Reporters and editors but also presidents, members of Congress, corporate publicists, activists, and policy analysts are all engaged in a more or less continuous conversation over the meaning of current events. In one common vocabulary, this conversation takes place through an exchange of "frames" (Gamson, Croteau, Hoynes, & Sasson, 1992). Frames, it is said, "make the world beyond direct experience look natural" (Gitlin, 1980, p. 6); they "bring order to events by making them something that can be told about; they have power because they make the world make sense" (Manoff, 1986, p. 228); they supply "a central organizing idea or story line that provides meaning to an unfolding strip of events, weaving a connection among them" (Gamson & Modigliani, 1987, p. 143). Frames come in all sizes: "master frames" that coordinate particular accounts of grievance (Snow & Benford, 1992) or that spell out what politics is about (Capella & Jamieson, 1997; Weaver, 1972) as well as "issue frames" applied to a single controversy, as in the argument that affirmative action for blacks should be understood as reverse discrimination against whites (Gamson & Modigliani, 1987; Kinder & Sanders, 1990). Frames include both the rhetorical tools fashioned by political elites to advance their ideas and the often unarticulated rules of selection, emphasis, and presentation that govern the work of journalism. Frames take on significance because politics is complex. The issues taken up by government and the events that animate political life are subject to alternative interpretation; they can always be read in more than one way. Framing arises "whenever there is more than one way to think about a subject" (Popkin, 1993, p. 83). It might be said that in pure form, frames supply no new information. Rather, by offering a particular perspective, frames *organize*—or better, *reorganize*—information that citizens already have in mind.[1] Frames suggest how politics should be thought about, encouraging citizens to understand events and issues in particular ways.[2] To say that frames supply no new information, that they merely supply a framework for organizing information, is not to say that frames are innocuous or neutral. By defining what the essential issue is and suggesting how to think about it, frames imply what, if anything, should be done. Elites spend as much time and money as they do crafting and disseminating frames on the assumption that the frames that prevail will shape how the public sees politics and therefore influence what the public is prepared to support. Is this assumption correct?

So it seems. One empirical test for framing arises out of longstanding concerns about the capacity of ordinary people to govern themselves. Many perceptive analysts of politics have questioned whether citizens really know what they want and need; whether opinions on matters of public policy are actually, in one powerful formulation, "nonattitudes" (Converse, 1970, 2000). Nonattitudes are usually taken as a sign of the average citizens' indifference to politics, but they may also point to the absence of a serious debate among elites. Put the other way around, when elites provide useful frames, citizens may be more likely to see a connection between what they care about and what politics offers, and so may be more likely to develop real opinions. This hypothesis has been tested in a series of question-wording experiments embedded in national surveys. These experiments compare public opinion elicited in one of two ways: either by questions that refer explicitly to the rival frames that dominate elite discourse (the "framed" condition) or by questions that do not (the "stripped" condition). Here the framed treatment is intended to mimic the political situation in which citizens witness a debate between opposing elites, each pushing an alternative definition of the issue. Meanwhile, the stripped treatment is intended to simulate the situation where there is no elite debate, where citizens are on their own in formulating what the issue is about. As predicted, for a variety of issues, when provided helpful frames, citizens are more likely to express opinions, and such opinions are often more stable over time and better anchored in the political considerations that the frames appear to highlight (e.g., Kinder & Nelson, 1990; Kinder & Sanders, 1996; Zaller, 1990).

Other experiments compare one frame against another. Because alternative frames highlight different features of an issue, they should alter the relative weight given to the interests, group sentiments, and political values that potentially go into making up an opinion—and so they do (e.g., Capella & Jamieson, 1997; Jacoby, 2000; Kinder & Sanders, 1990, 1996; Nelson, Clawson, & Oxley, 1997; Nelson & Kinder, 1996; Price, 1989). In this respect, frames are like recipes, advice from experts on how citizens should cook up their opinions (Kinder & Sanders, 1996).

Shifting the underlying foundations of opinion is one thing, moving opinion itself is another. That framing may accomplish the first is no guarantee that it can pull off the second. For to move opinion, a frame must not only be compelling (that is, fit its subject well), though it must be that, and it must not only induce large numbers of people to think about the subject in a new way, though it must do that as well. To move opinion, a frame must also induce large numbers of people to think about the subject in a way that pushes them in a new direction.

Suppose, to borrow an example from Nelson and his colleagues, the Ku Klux Klan plans to hold a rally in your community. The local press could frame this news to highlight the constitutional protection of assembly and speech or to highlight the government's obligation to preserve order. The two frames are compelling, they induce large numbers of people to think about the subject in a way they otherwise would not, and they push hard in opposite directions. Because Americans believe both in protecting free speech and in preserving social order, when presented with frames that highlight the one as against the other, they end up expressing different positions on whether the rally should be held at all (Nelson, Clawson, & Oxley, 1997; for other examples and discussions of opinion change through framing, see Chong, 1993; Kinder & Sanders, 1996).

Virtually all the framing results I have cited so far come from experiments. Experiments have real advantages (Kinder & Palfrey, 1993; Sniderman & Grob, 1996), and these experiments in particular have some very desirable features. For one thing, most of them deliberately mimic actual elite debates and everyday journalistic conventions. For another, many are inserted into representative sample surveys, so the common complaint about experiments—that they exploit convenient but unrepresentative populations (compare Sears, 1986, and Anderson, Lindsay, & Bushman 1999)—does not apply here.

Nevertheless, experimental results can always be questioned on their generalizability, and framing effects are no exception. The major worry in this respect is that framing experiments—like experiments in mass communication generally—typically erase the distinction between the supply of information on the one hand and its consumption on the other. That is, experiments are normally carried out in such a way that virtually everyone in the audience is hand-delivered the message. The typical experiment thereby avoids a major obstacle standing in the way of communication effects: namely, an inattentive audience, lost in the affairs of private life (more on this point later). By ensuring that frames reach their intended audiences, experiments may exaggerate their power. A more balanced reading of frame effects requires methodological diversification, experiments *and* studies oriented to the world outside.[3]

A second problem is that while the experimental literature I've just reviewed makes a good case that frames can affect how (and even whether) people evaluate various matters of politics, it actually skips over the focal concern I began with: how people make sense of these matters in the first place. In all the studies of frames and framing, understanding itself is never directly addressed or measured. This is unfortunate, since democratic institutions often presume that ordinary citizens understand the matters that come before them. It is actually doubly unfortunate, because over the past decade, cognitive psychology has been developing conceptual and methodological tools that are well suited to analyzing the problem of political sense-making. Here I have in mind Pennington's and Hastie's analysis of jurors transforming the jumble of evidence presented to them during a trial into a compelling narrative (Pennington & Hastie, 1992, 1993); Holyoak's and Thagard's (1995) account of reasoning by analogy; and Kintsch's (1998) theorizing and research on how people are able to understand text. In short, the conceptual and methodological tools to undertake a serious examination of how ordinary Americans make sense of the mysteries of politics now appear to be available (for a first and small step in this direction, see Berinsky & Kinder, 2000). To pin down more precisely what frames are and how they shape understanding seems a worthwhile project, since, as Gitlin (1980) once put it, frames appear to "organize the world both for journalists who report it and, in some important degree, for us who rely on their reports" (p. 7).[4]

Agenda Setting

Among the most important decisions in any society are those that determine which issues become part of politics (Bachrach & Baratz, 1970). In Schattschneider's crisp formulation, "some issues are organized into politics while others are organized out" (1960, p. 71). The public is somehow implicated in this process: citizens develop ideas about what is and what is not important, which problems are and which are not proper subjects for government action, and these ideas, in turn, shape and constrain what government attempts to do (Burstein, 1985; Verba & Nie, 1972). How does the public come to believe that crime is an urgent problem and acid rain is not?

More than 50 years ago, Lazarsfeld and Merton (1948) suggested that the answer to such a question might lie in the agenda setting power of the news media. While expressing considerable skepticism about the influence of mass communications in general—they regarded the automobile as vastly more consequential than the radio and thought that much of what passed for contemporary analysis was infected by "magical" thinking—Lazarsfeld and Merton nevertheless proceeded to sketch out several mechanisms through which mass communications might have real effects. Prominent among these was agenda setting: "mass media *confer* status on public issues, persons, organizations, and social movements" (p. 101). Lazarsfeld and Merton thought that mere attention was enough, that "enhanced status accrues to those who merely receive attention in the media, quite apart from any editorial support. . . . Recognition by the press or radio or magazines or newsreels testifies that one has arrived, that one is important enough to have been singled out from the large anonymous masses, that one's behavior and opinions are significant enough to require public notice" (pp. 101–102).

Good idea—but an idea only. Lazarsfeld and Merton offered no evidence for their conjecture, and a dozen years later, neither could Klapper. Agenda-setting's first and rather oblique brush with evidence did not come until Cohen's (1963) perceptive analysis of newspapers and U.S. foreign policy. On the basis of interviews with journalists and government officials, Cohen concluded that the press "may not be successful much of the time in telling people what to think, but it is stunningly successful in telling its readers what to think about" (p. 13). Cohen had in mind policy experts and the attentive public, however, so his strong conclusion doesn't necessarily speak to agenda setting among the general public, what Riker (1993) once called the "misty swamp" (p. 2) of everyday politics.

More immediately relevant is the evidence supplied by McCombs and Shaw (1972), who, toward the end of the 1968 presidential campaign, interviewed a small sample of uncommitted voters living in and around Chapel Hill, North Carolina. McCombs and Shaw found an almost perfect correlation between the problems that voters believed were the country's most serious and those problems given great prominence in the news they were reading and watching at the time. McCombs and Shaw concluded that "in choosing and displaying news, editors, newsroom staff, and broadcasters play an important part in shaping political reality" (p. 176).

McCombs's and Shaw's successful demonstration inspired numerous replications and, for a time, considerable confusion. The best studies turned up modest and often mysteriously contingent support for agenda setting (e.g., Erbring, Goldenberg, & Miller 1979). "Stunningly successful" (Cohen, 1963, p. 13) overstates these results considerably.

The problem, looking back on it, was a failure of design. Cross-sectional comparisons miss the real variation in agenda setting, which is temporal rather than spatial. Agenda setting is dynamic—problems emerge, move for a while to the center of the stage, and then gradually drift back to the wings—and so should be investigated over time. Consistent with this, Funkhouser (1973) found in a simple analysis a close correspondence between the amount of attention paid to various problems in the national press over the 1960s on the one hand and the importance subsequently accorded such problems by the American public, on the other.

This basic finding has stood up well to further and more sophisticated testing. Subsequent studies have controlled on the possibility that news organizations are responding to the public's priorities (and not just the other way around); have taken into account the independent effects due to real-world conditions (e.g., changes in prices or interest rates); and have simultaneously considered the possibility that presidents can alter what the public takes to be important through major addresses to the nation. Under these quite stringent conditions, strong empirical support for agenda setting repeatedly emerges. Rising prices, unemployment, energy shortages, arms control: all these (and more) become high-priority issues for the public after they first become high priority for newspapers and networks. For a wide variety of problems, the American public's concern for political problems closely and rapidly tracks changes over time in the attention paid them by media (e.g., Behr & Iyengar, 1985; Fan, 1992; MacKuen, 1981, 1984; McCombs & Zhu, 1995; Neuman, 1990; Protess et al., 1991).

These results are nicely complemented by the findings from experimental research (Iyengar & Kinder, 1987; Miller & Krosnick, 2000). In effect, these experiments convert the variation in news coverage that occurs naturally over time to contemporaneous variation across experimental conditions. People shown network broadcasts unobtrusively edited to highlight a particular problem subsequently assigned greater importance to that problem—greater importance than they themselves did before the experiment began and greater importance than did people randomly assigned to control conditions that emphasized different problems. These effects are apparent immediately after the conclusions of the broadcasts as well as one week later, are enhanced when the edited stories lead off the broadcasts, and emerge for a wide array of problems.[5]

If agenda-setting effects are robust and powerful, they also seem to be quite specific. Thus news about energy affects beliefs about the importance of energy and energy alone; news about national defense affects beliefs about national defense and national defense alone; and so on. Stories about one problem don't seem to spill over onto others, even when the problems are related. Such specificity may reflect the way news is typically presented, in tight, self-contained bundles (Weaver, 1972). More important may be the way most Americans approach politics, innocent of broad ideological frameworks that might link one national problem with another (Converse, 1964; Kinder, 1998).

Priming

Every now and again Americans are called on to evaluate alternatives put before them by their political system: they decide whether to support or reject a candidate; they find policy proposals wise or terrible; they take the consequences of government action to be successful or disastrous; they judge their president's performance in office to be inspiring or deplorable; and so on. These various alternatives that citizens are asked to evaluate are inevitably complex, and such complexity makes it difficult in any particular case to know what standards should be applied. The intuition behind priming is that these standards are supplied or at least encouraged by the preoccupations of mass communications. How political alternatives are evaluated depends in part on which stories news media choose to cover and, consequently, which standards are made salient. The more attention the news media pay to a particular aspect of political life—the more frequently that aspect is *primed*—the more people will incorporate what they know about it into their political evaluations.

Defined this way, priming has received strong and consistent support in a series of television news experiments (Iyengar & Kinder, 1987). After being primed by stories that focus on national defense, for example, viewers judge the president largely by how well he has provided, as they see it, for the nation's defense; after being primed by stories about inflation, viewers evaluate the president by how he has managed, in their view, to keep prices down; and so on. Priming shows up across a variety of problems, for Democratic and Republican presidents alike, for good news as well as bad, for opinion and for choice, and at the peak of campaigns as in the quieter moments in between.

These results and the various experiments that followed (e.g., Gross, 2001; Iyengar, 1991; Miller & Krosnick, 2000; Valentino, 1999; Valentino, Hutchings, & White, 2002) demonstrate convincingly that priming can be detected under controlled circumstances, but not whether priming is important in the world of politics. For that we need evidence of another kind, "natural experiments" that take analytic advantage of sudden shifts in the news stream. Priming shows up in these circumstances as well. For example, following revelations in November 1986 that funds from secret arm sales to Iran were being illegally channeled to the Nicaraguan Contras, the public's evaluations of President Reagan suddenly became preoccupied with matters of foreign policy (Krosnick & Kinder, 1990). In similar fashion, immediately after public disclosure of Gary Hart's sexual escapades in the spring of 1987, moral conservatism, which was utterly unconnected to the public's evaluations of Hart prior to the revelations, suddenly became very connected (Stoker, 1993; for other positive cases, see Bartels, 1997; Krosnick & Brannon, 1993; Mutz, 1998; Pollock, 1994; and for an interesting analysis of an apparent priming failure, see Zaller, 1998).

As defined here, priming is provoked by mere attention. Drawing attention to a particular problem means that the audience will be more likely to draw on what they know about that problem when it comes to offering an evaluation—the more so the more recent and frequent the priming (Higgins, Bargh, & Lombardi, 1985; Higgins, Rholes, & Jones 1977; Srull & Wyer, 1979). But of course news does more than simply draw attention to some problems while ignoring others: it also frames problems in particular ways. Especially important in this respect is the extent to which problems are framed in such a way as to suggest that they have political causes or political remedies. Priming effects are augmented when television news coverage implies that the president is responsible either for causing a problem or for failing to solve it, and are diminished when coverage implies that a problem's causes and remedies are to be found elsewhere (Iyengar & Kinder, 1987; Iyengar, 1991).

Given the empirical support for priming, we might expect that political campaigns would be organized with priming at least partly in mind. And so they seem to be. Here we are moving from inadvertent to deliberate priming; from priming as an unintentional consequence of news organizations trying to tell good stories and attract large audiences to priming as an intentional effect of campaigns trying to build political support.

Petrocik (1996) places priming at the center of campaigns. In Petrocik's vocabulary, candidates and parties attempt to make elections be about issues they "own." Ownership is rooted in history, a reflection of each party's long-term pattern of "attention, initiative, and innovation" toward particular problems and certain constituencies. When a party owns an issue, voters are inclined to believe that the party and its candidates are more sincerely committed to doing something about it. Following this logic out, rival candidates should "argue along lines that play to the issue strength of their party, and sidestep their opponent's issue assets" (p. 829). It turns out that in recent presidential campaigns, both Democratic and Republican candidates do in fact emphasize issues they own: Democrats talk about education and health care, Republicans talk about defense and tax cuts.

In short, campaigns are not so much debates over a common set of issues as they are struggles to define what the election is about. So campaigns are today, and so, it seems, they have been. In an examination of the debate over ratification of the Constitution, Riker (1993) found ample support for what he called the dominance principle: "when one side successfully wins an argument on an issue, the other side ceases to discuss it, while the winner continues to exploit it" (pp. 81–82). Campaigns are "mostly about salience, not confrontation" (p. 4; Budge, 1993; Gelman & King, 1993; Jacobs & Shapiro, 1994, 2000).

I suggested earlier that agenda-setting effects are characterized by considerable specificity. The same appears to be true, for the most part, for priming (e.g., Iyengar & Kinder, 1987; Krosnick & Brannon, 1993; Krosnick & Kinder 1990). There are exceptions, however, and they show up (so far at least) primarily in a single realm: race. In that realm, communications that have nothing ostensibly to do with blacks and whites nevertheless appear to prime the audience's racial predispositions. Flagrantly racist speech is now out of bounds in the United States, and most white Americans subscribe to racial equality as a matter of principle. At the same time, many whites feel resentful toward blacks and uncomfortable in their presence. These conditions have given rise to euphemistic discourse—appeals to racism that traffic in code words (Kinder & Sanders, 1996). Mendelberg (2001) refers to this as "implicit communication." Drawing on a recent stream of research in psychology (e.g., Banaji & Greenwald, 1995; Bargh & Pietromomaco, 1982; Devine, 1989), Mendelberg argues that carefully calibrated messages can prime racial predispositions automatically, outside the recipient's awareness. A covert appeal to racism is successful precisely because it evades the self-censorship that whites would exercise if they were to notice that the incoming message violated the norm of equality.

A typical if demoralizing example of covert communication is provided by the 1988 American presidential campaign and the carefully crafted and well-coordinated initiative to portray the Democratic nominee, Governor Dukakis, as soft on crime. In some ways 1988 can be read as a clear example of Petrocik's (1996) issue ownership theory in action: the Republicans stressing their issue (controlling crime) while the Democrats tried to change the subject.[6] The 1988 campaign thus appears straightforward—except that the Republicans' effort, though ostensibly about crime, was really about race, featuring the story of one Willie Horton. Horton, a black man convicted of murder and sentenced to life imprisonment, was granted a weekend leave by the Massachusetts prison furlough program while Dukakis was governor. Horton fled the state and terrorized a white couple in Maryland, beating the man and raping the woman before being recaptured and returned to prison. In the local uproar that followed, Dukakis defended the furlough program and appeared indifferent to Horton's victims. Horton's story became a fixture in Bush's speeches, in Republican campaign fliers, and in a set of memorable television advertisements. This was covert communication about race. On the surface, the message was about crime and crime only, and race words were scrupulously avoided. But Horton's name and story and picture were ever-present. The effort was deliberate (Jamieson, 1992; Kinder & Sanders, 1996; Mendelberg, 2001), and it succeeded: the campaign primed predispositions on race (not crime), moving racially conservative Democrats and Independents into the Republican column (Kinder & Sanders, 1996; Mendelberg, 1997, 2001). In the 1988 campaign, and in a variety of other cases (Mendelberg, 2001; Valentino, Hutchings, & White, 2002; Winter, 2001), communications that appear to be about one subject—crime, welfare reform, government spending, privatization of Social Security—turn out, in their consequences, to be about another, namely, race.

▶ Persuasion

By *persuasion* I mean "changing people's attitudes [and behavior] through the spoken and written word" (McGuire, 1973, p. 216). Political persuasion entails the supply of arguments and evidence through which people are induced to change their minds about some aspect of politics: in light of new information, people come to think that the president is smarter than he first seemed, or that school desegregation is ineffective and should be abandoned, or that more effort and money must now be invested in national defense.

On the question of what role mass communication plays in political persuasion, Klapper's answer of course was not to worry: mass communications seldom persuade, and minimal effects are the rule (others who say this are Hovland, 1959; Key, 1961; McGuire, 1986, 2001; Mueller, 1994; Schudson, 1984). Zaller (1996) disagrees, insisting that the right answer to the question of persuasion is not minimal effects, but, to paraphrase lightly, massive effects, all the time. The truth, as I will try to show, lies somewhere in between.

Klapper was influenced heavily by *The People's Choice*, the landmark examination of the 1940 presidential contest in Erie County, Ohio, that was carried out by a team headed by Paul Lazarsfeld (Lazarsfeld, Berelson, & Gaudet, 1948). To their surprise, Lazarsfeld's team discovered that relatively few voters altered their intentions over the course of the year. Indeed, by the time of the summer conventions, before the formal campaign even began, roughly 80 percent of voters had become permanently committed to one candidate or the other. From spring to fall, only a handful of voters—some 5 percent—actually changed sides. What little change that did occur, moreover, apparently had less to do with the campaign than with the personal influence of family and friends. Lazarsfeld, Berelson, and Gaudet concluded that presidential campaigns are generally ineffective at persuasion. Rather than converting voters from one side to the other, presidential campaigns *reinforce* the early deciders and *activate* the latent predispositions of the initially uncommitted.

So it was in 1940, and so it was, evidently, in 1948. In *The Voter Decides*, Berelson, Lazarsfeld, and McPhee (1954) report the results of a similar investigation, situated this time in Elmira, New York, and focusing on the famous Dewey-Truman presidential contest. Once again, or so it seemed, mass communication "crystallizes and reinforces more than it converts" (p. 248).

Klapper took the results from these two exemplary studies seriously, and he was wise to do so, for their main conclusions have stood up very well. Despite dramatic changes over the last half-century in politics and society, American presidential campaigns still fail as exercises in political persuasion.[7] We know this from panel studies patterned after the original Lazarsfeld design (e.g., Bartels, 1997; Finkel, 1993; Markus, 1982; Patterson, 1980) and from aggregate forecasting models that accurately predict the outcome of American presidential elections from information available before the campaign gets underway (e.g., Bartels, 1992; Gelman & King, 1993; Rosenstone, 1983). Klapper was right about presidential campaigns: not much persuasion, mostly reinforcement and activation.[8]

Conceding this point—that little persuasion takes place from Labor Day to Election Day—should not, however, lead us to conclude that presidential campaigns are therefore dispensable. To the contrary, activation and reinforcement are vital political processes, as Lazarsfeld and his colleagues knew. Campaigns activate voters by arousing their interest and providing them with information, thereby allowing them to choose wisely—or in any case, more wisely than they would have in the absence of a campaign (Bartels, 1988; Gelman & King, 1993; Johnston, Blais, Brady, & Crete, 1992; Shanks & Miller, 1992). And campaigns reinforce voters by providing good reasons for their choices, reminding them why they are Democrats or Republicans, thereby keeping partisans in line and defections to a minimum (Bartels, 1993; Katz & Feldman, 1962; Sears & Chaffee, 1979).

Acknowledging the importance of activation and reinforcement, the main and arresting lesson of more than a half-century of empirical research on presidential campaigns is the failure of persuasion. In the next section I sketch out three reasons why this might be so—three principle obstacles to persuasion: neutralization, resistance, and indifference.

Neutralization

One reason why presidential campaigns are ineffective as instruments of persuasion is that the campaign mounted by one side is "neutralized" by the campaign mounted by the other (Lazarsfeld & Merton, 1948; Bartels, 1992; Gelman & King, 1993). Under current arrangements—electoral competition dominated by two well-established parties and presidential campaigns funded primarily by public sources—both sides assemble roughly equally capable teams, of roughly equal experience and intelligence, who set about spending roughly the same (large) amount of money in roughly the same ways.[9] Whatever persuasive effect is accomplished by the one is offset by the other.

Imagine a different world. What would we see if one of the political parties managed somehow to monopolize mass communications?

> European experience with totalitarian control of communications suggests that under some conditions the opposition may be whittled down until only the firmly convinced die-hards remain. In many parts of this country, there are probably relatively few people who would tenaciously maintain their political views in the face of a continuous flow of hostile arguments. Most people want—and need—to be told that they are right and to know that other people agree with them. Thus, the parties could

forego their propagandizing only at considerable risk, and never on a unilateral basis. (Lazarsfeld, Berelson, & Gaudet 1948, p. 87)

It seems unimaginable that either party will unilaterally disarm, for the reasons that Lazarsfeld, Berelson, and Gaudet suggest, and so neutralization—a stalemate of roughly equal and opposing forces—is likely to be with us indefinitely in presidential campaigns. But campaigns need not be as two-sided as presidential contests normally are. Consider, as a contrary and real example, campaigns for the U.S. House, which these days are famously lopsided. House incumbents typically raise vast sums of money, much more than their challengers, and this enables them to run virtually continuous campaigns for reelection (Jacobson, 1980, 2001). As a consequence, incumbents entice significant numbers of voters who ought to be voting for their challengers to vote for them instead, and these "defections" turn out to be concentrated among moderately attentive voters: just those who are most likely to notice the incumbent's campaign but miss the weaker campaign mounted by the challenger (Zaller, 1992).

A similar point is suggested by the remarkable success enjoyed by Ross Perot in 1992. Third-party candidates are a regular though usually invisible feature of American presidential elections, but in 1992 Perot won nearly 20 percent of the popular vote, surpassing the record of any third-party candidate since Teddy Roosevelt. Perot did so well at least in part because of his ability to mount a serious campaign. Perot outspent both Clinton and Bush in 1992, shelling out some 73 million dollars, nearly all of it drawn against his own personal fortune. And he apparently spent it well, building and maintaining a national and professional organization and mounting a memorable advertising campaign and spending 45 million dollars on television alone. Most third-party campaigns are underfinanced, ragged affairs; Perot's quite difference experience shows the potential persuasive power of campaigns (Alvarez & Nagler, 1995; Rosenstone, Behr, & Lazarus 1996; Zaller & Hunt, 1994, 1995).

Resistance

Klapper (1960) thought that a principal cause of stability in voters' partisan preferences over the course of presidential campaigns was selective exposure: "by and large, people tend to expose themselves to those mass communications which are in accord with their existing attitudes and interests. Consciously or unconsciously, they avoid communications of opposite hue" (p. 19). Klapper was sure that this was so, and he was not alone (Behavioral Sciences Subpanel, 1962; Berelson & Steiner, 1964; Festinger, 1957, 1964; Hyman & Sheatsley, 1947; Lazarsfeld, Berelson, & Gaudet, 1948).

Despite all the early confidence, the evidence for selective exposure turns out to be thin. We now know that people do not, for the most part, seek out mass communications that reinforce their political predispositions, nor do they choose to seal themselves off from communications that threaten them (e.g., Eagly & Chaiken, 1998; Freedman & Sears, 1965; Iyengar et al., 2001; Milburn, 1979; Mutz & Martin, 2001; Sears & Freedman, 1967). All things considered, this may be a good thing, since selective exposure assumes that people are "living autistically in a fool's paradise, endeavoring to remain blissfully ignorant of belief-threatening material, even though in actual environments it is often adaptive to acquaint oneself with the opposition arguments (McGuire, 1985, p. 275). Maladaptive or not, selective exposure cannot account for persuasion's failure.[10]

People are adept at defending their views, not by hiding from threatening messages but by rejecting them (Abelson, 1959, 1968; Sears & Freedman, 1967). That is, persuasion fails not through selectivity in exposure but through selectivity in acceptance. In scores of studies of presidential debates, for example, voters' evaluations of debate performance polarize sharply along partisan lines (Katz & Feldman, 1962; Sears & Chaffee, 1979). More generally, people assess communications that challenge their attitudes as weakly argued, unconvincing, and laced with error (e.g., Lord, Ross, & Lepper, 1979; Pomerantz, Chaiken, & Tordesillas, 1995), and they subject such communications to more active counterarguing and greater scrutiny than they do communications that confirm their attitudes (e.g., Cacioppo & Petty, 1979; Edwards & Smith, 1996; Feather, 1963).

From this point of view, presidential campaigns enjoy such limited success in converting voters from one side to the other partly because they run up against heavy resistance. Resistance is especially heavy because presidential campaigns play directly on the voters' primary political predisposition, their attachment to party. For many partisans, the details brought forward by any particular campaign are simply further corroboration of their party's comparative virtuosity (Bartels, 1993; Campbell et al., 1960; Converse, 1966; on the decline and revival of strong partisanship in the American electorate, see Bartels, 2000).[11]

Resistance is a serious obstacle to political persuasion, but if it cannot be avoided altogether, it can be reduced. For example, persuasion should be more common during the presidential nomination process, where the strong predisposition of partisanship is less relevant (Bartels, 1988). Likewise, emerging issues or topics that elicit relatively weak attitudes should be opportunities for persuasion as well (Bassili, 1993, 1996; Krosnick & Abelson, 1992). More generally, resistance will diminish when people lack the contextual information that would otherwise enable them to notice that an incoming message is inconsistent with their predispositions (Zaller, 1992).

Indifference

If strong partisans are essentially unmovable because they are so deeply committed, other potential voters are difficult to persuade because they're not paying attention. In the midst of analyzing the flood of political propaganda unleashed by the 1940 presidential campaign, Lazarsfeld, Berelson, and Gaudet (1948) noticed that far from being drowned in information, most voters "did not even get their feet wet" (p. 121).

Lazarsfeld and his associates were referring to presidential campaigns, but their point is a very general one. "Perhaps the principal incontestable moral of the data about politics and mass communications," V. O. Key once wrote, "is that many of the political messages carried by the communications networks do not reach many people. The limits of the audience fix the area of direct influence of the mass media: a message unheard is a message unheeded" (1961, p. 345). A major obstacle in the way of persuasion is a habitually inattentive and often distracted audience (Converse, 1975; Delli Carpini & Keeter, 1996; Hyman & Sheatsley, 1947).[12] That said, there remain two general openings for persuasion.

First is what I will call *low-information persuasion*. The major claim here is that generally uninterested citizens might still be susceptible to persuasion when elite sources supply simple and decisive cues; simple so that the cue can be easily communicated and decisive so that the cue can make a difference. An excellent demonstration of this point is provided by Lupia (1994), who showed that California voters who knew little about the details of various complicated proposals to reform the automobile insurance industry in their state nevertheless made choices that were indistinguishable from those made by well-informed voters. All the generally ill-informed voters needed to know was which proposals were backed by which interest groups. When Californians knew, for example, that the insurance industry itself was behind a particular proposal, they knew enough to vote against it. In terms of Petty and Cacioppo's elaboration likelihood model of attitude change, Lupia is tracing out a peripheral route to persuasion (Petty & Cacioppo, 1986; for a related formulation, see Chaiken, Liberman, & Eagly, 1989).[13] By taking cues from those who are well informed (e.g., Brody, 1991; Katz & Lazarsfeld, 1955; Huckfeldt & Sprague, 1995; Lupia & McCubbins, 1998), common citizens can "be knowledgeable in their reasoning about political choices without necessarily possessing a large body of knowledge about politics" (Sniderman, Brody, & Tetlock, 1991, p. 19).[14]

The second opportunity is *persuasion over the long haul*. An excellent case in point is supplied by Page and Shapiro (1992), who find in a wide-ranging study that in those instances when American public opinion on matters of policy has changed, "it has not done so wildly or capriciously or randomly; it has generally shifted in comprehensible ways, in response to new information and changing conditions" (p. 321). The changing conditions that Page and Shapiro have in mind are for the most part historic events—World War II, riots that raced through American cities in the 1960s, the skyrocketing inflation of the late 1970s, Chernobyl—and the new information that they say moves opinion comes notably from presidents, commentators, and experts, supplied to the general public through mass communication.

Page and Shapiro's result turns out to be quite representative of the empirical returns from a wide range of recent inquiry into the dynamics of public opinion (e.g., Fan, 1988; Haller & Norpoth, 1994; Haynes & Jacobs, 1994; Hibbs, Rivers, & Vasilatos, 1982; Kellstadt, 2000; MacKuen, 1983; MacKuen, Erikson, & Stimson, 1989, 1992; Mueller, 1971, 1991, 1994; Ostrom & Simon, 1985; Stimson, 1991/1998). In these various investigations, public opinion *in the aggregate* seems quite responsive to social, economic, and political change, indeed sometimes exquisitely so. The role of the media in these dynamics is not always explicit, but it is always at least implied. In short, if we ask not about the short term but the longer haul, and not about individuals but about the public as a whole, then persuasion seems to be the rule, not the exception.

How can this be? How, especially, can this result be reconciled with the supposedly imposing obstacle to persuasion posed by the low exposure and low interest of the average citizen? One answer is that the engine of opinion change pointed to in these studies is history in capital letters—not humdrum politics but historic turning points, like World War II or the civil rights movement, that are exceptional in the attention they command and the interest they arouse.

A second answer is that the movement in collective opinion that these studies uncover may be due primarily to change among the most attentive members of the public. In aggregating to the public as a whole, the random error contributed by individual ignorance, indifference, and confusion may be canceled out (though not always and never completely; see, for example, Althaus, 1998; Bartels, 1996a; Berinsky, 1999). Given a sufficient number of cases, clear signals can emerge from even a "sea of noise" (Converse, 1990, p. 382). The implication here is that the systematic and sensible movement of public opinion in the aggregate may be determined disproportionately by a mere handful of citizens who are paying close attention (Converse, 1990; Stimson, 1991/1998; Zaller, 1992).[15]

To sum up my discussion so far: political persuasion is contingent on circumstance. Persuasion grows more likely when campaigns face little opposition, when resistance is diminished, when well-placed sources provide simple and decisive cues, and when history intrudes on attentive citizens. Neutralization, resistance, and indifference are formidable but not insuperable obstacles to persuasion. If Klapper was right to say that presidential campaigns in particular seldom persuade, we seem nevertheless to have come quite far from his general conclusion of "minimal effects."

Zaller (1996) wants to take us farther still, arguing that the correct conclusion is massive persuasion, almost all the time. We've failed to see this, Zaller says, for three reasons. First, we have measured exposure to mass communication poorly (here echoing Bartels's [1993] complaint). Second, we have looked for evidence of opinion change where there is no change in mass communication content.[16] And third (the heart of the matter), we have failed to model persuasion properly. In particular, Zaller contends that standard assessments of persuasion overlook the crucial fact that citizens are often exposed to countervailing messages and so are pushed simultaneously in opposite directions. What appear in standard analysis to be minimal effects are actually, in Zaller's telling, massive but offsetting effects.

Trying to do better, Zaller begins by drawing on the same set of psychological ideas that inform much recent research on communications generally. Zaller presumes that people arrive at their opinions by averaging across the considerations that happen to be accessible at the moment. Accessibility, in turn, depends on memory retrieval that is probabilistic and incomplete. Considerations that have been "in thought" recently are more likely to be sampled. To make this model of opinion come alive for understanding political persuasion, Zaller (1992) introduces two additional assumptions, building on insights offered by Hovland (1959; Hovland, Lumsdaine, & Sheffield, 1949), Converse (1962), and McGuire (1968). The first is that people will be more likely to receive a communication as a direct function of their level of general information about politics, where reception involves both exposure to and comprehension of the given communication. Second, people will resist communications that are inconsistent with their political predispositions only insofar as they possess sufficient information to detect such inconsistency. Zaller's model recognizes that citizens differ sharply from one another in their partisan and ideological predispositions and that they differ enormously from one another in the care and attention they invest in politics.

So specified, Zaller's model can account for a variety of empirical cases: the electoral advantages enjoyed by congressional incumbents, shifts in American opinion on school desegregation, variations in popular support for Ross Perot during his 73 million-dollar presidential campaign adventure of 1992, and changes in American opinion on the Vietnam War, among others (Zaller, 1989, 1991, 1992; Zaller & Hunt, 1994, 1995). In all these instances, public opinion appears to move in response to alterations in the supply of information provided by elites. The story is complicated because it takes into account differences in the motivation and skill that citizens bring to politics, and because it recognizes that overall shifts in public opinion typically conceal underlying combinations of changes that move in opposite and partially offsetting directions.

Zaller offered his model as an attempt to provide a general account of public opinion. On the first page of *The Nature and Origins of Mass Opinion* (1992), Zaller announced his aim to "to integrate as much as possible of the dynamics of public opinion within a cohesive theoretical system." In fact, the model does very well, even judged against that audacious aspiration. But Zaller's is not the only way to represent and understand political persuasion. The strongest alternative psychological model currently in play is supplied by Milton Lodge (1995) and his associates, who hope to specify "the main architectural and procedural features of a psychologically realistic model of the candidate-evaluation process" (p. 111). In this pursuit, Lodge takes inspiration from the information-processing approach to human cognition generally, drawing heavily on the "on-line" model of information processing developed by Hastie in particular (Hastie & Park, 1986; Hastie & Pennington, 1989). Lodge argues that over the course of a campaign, most citizens most of the time develop their impressions of the candidates on-line: that is, "each piece of campaign information is immediately evaluated and linked to the candidate node in working memory at the time of exposure, when the information is in the senses, so to speak, and not typically computed at a later date from memory traces" (p. 119). Campaigns deliver messages; citizens sometimes notice them; when they do, they (somehow) detect the implications of the messages for their evaluations of a candidate; thereupon they immediately integrate these implications into their summary evaluation (or "running tally") of the candidate; transfer their now updated overall evaluation to long-term memory; and quickly forget the details that prompted the updating in the first place (for corroborating evidence for this account, all supplied by experiments, see Lodge, McGraw, & Stroh, 1989; Lodge & Steenbergen, 1995; Lodge & Stroh, 1993; Rahn, Aldrich, & Borgida, 1994).

We need both on-line and accessibility (or memory-based) models. How can we reconcile their differences? One possibility is to dissolve or at least soften the differences between the two, by specifying intermediate or hybrid modes of opinion formation and change, partly on-line and partly memory-based (Hastie & Pennington, 1989). Another possibility is that people differ systematically and persistently in their reliance on one process or the other (Jarvis & Petty, 1996). Still another is to say that the two models cover different domains. Perhaps on-line processing applies primarily to the evaluation of candidates. Citizens understand that when the campaign comes to a close they will be asked to make a decision, which should encourage on-line processing. In contrast, perhaps memory-based models apply when people are surprised by a request for a judgment on matters that they had previously regarded as insignificant (Hastie & Park, 1986). Just such a surprise occurs, Zaller (1992) suggests, when people are accosted by an interviewer wanting to know what they think about health care or the war in Afghanistan.

▲ Action

Up to now, I have been concerned with mass communication as an instrument for directing attention and changing attitudes. I will now turn briefly to the role that communication might play in influencing action.

Participation in politics can take a variety of forms, but the most common is turning out to vote (Rosenstone & Hansen, 1993; Tilly, 1978; Verba, Schlozman, & Brady, 1995; Verba & Nie, 1972). And on the question of mobilizing turnout, the evidence suggests that mass communication is less important than personal influence. Both surveys and experiments show that people who are contacted by a party representative during the campaign are more likely to vote (e.g., Caldeira, Clausen, & Patterson, 1990; Eldersveld, 1956; Gosnell, 1927; Kramer, 1970; Rosenstone & Hansen, 1993; Wielhouwer & Lockerbie, 1994). In a field experiment carried out recently in New Haven, Connecticut, for example, Gerber and Green (2000) found that turnout was increased substantially by personal canvassing but only slightly by direct mail and not at all by appeals over telephone.

These results suggest an explanation for the disappearing American voter. That turnout in American national elections is down sharply from the high-water marks of the early part of the twentieth century (Burnham, 1970; Converse, 1972; McDonald & Popkin, 2001) may have to do in part with the transformations that have come to political campaigns over this period. Where mobilization once relied on face-to-face contact between prospective voters and party activists (Gosnell, 1937; Wolfinger, 1974), mobilization belongs now to "professional campaign consultants, direct mail vendors, and commercial phone banks" (Gerber & Green, 2000, p. 653). As the political parties substituted telephone calls and direct mailings for personal canvassing, more and more potential voters remained home (Rosenstone & Hansen, 1993; Gerber & Green, 2000).

While candidates and parties have been spending less of their resources on personal canvassing, they have been spending more on mass communications, especially television. And as campaigns are waged increasingly over the airwaves, they are turning more and more negative. So at least is the contention of Ansolobehere and Iyengar. In the television age, they say, campaigns have become "hostile and ugly. More often than not, candidates criticize, discredit, or belittle their opponents rather than promoting their own ideas and programs" (Ansolobehere, Iyengar, Simon, & Valentino, 1994). This development is not just unseemly, again according to Ansolobehere and Iyengar, but is real trouble for the American political system. For negative campaigns are demobilizing: they sour citizens on politics and drive them away from the polls. Ansolobehere and Iyengar reach this conclusion primarily on the basis of a series of well-crafted experiments in which negative advertisements are embedded within actual campaigns. They find essentially the same result—negative campaigns turn voters off—when they examine voting rates in Senate elections that vary in campaign negativity, and when they analyze turnout among Americans questioned in a pair of National Election Study surveys, some of whom were witness to negative advertisements and some of whom were not (Ansolobehere et al., 1994; Ansolobehere & Iyengar, 1995; Ansolobehere, Iyengar, & Simon, 1999).

This is an impressive line of research, but it seems to me that settled conclusions on the effects of negative campaigns are not yet possible. Negative campaigns do not always lead to demobilization (Lau, Sigelman, Heldman, & Babbitt, 1999), and some forms of negative advertising, by clarifying that important differences separate the candidates, may actually enhance turnout (Kahn & Kenney, 1999; West, 1993). Nor, finally, is it obvious that recent campaigns are all that negative (Jamieson, 1992; West, 1993). To Herbert Hoover, the New Deal was "Fascism," "despotism," and "the poisoning of Americanism" (Sundquist, 1983, p. 301). Bryce characterized American campaigns of the late nineteenth century as "thick with charges, defences, recriminations, till the voter knows not what to believe" (1888/1995, p. 879, quoted in Lau et al., 1999, p. 851). And Riker (1996) turned up plenty of criticism and hostility in the campaign for ratification of the U.S. Constitution.[17]

◤ Conclusions and Implications

If, as Bartels maintains (perhaps mischievously), the minimal effects verdict should be regarded as "one of the most notable embarrassments of modern social science" (1993, p. 267), I am happy to announce that we are now relieved of at least that burden. Better yet, we have replaced a sweeping generalization with a set of reasonably refined and contingent conclusions.

When Klapper was writing his review, television was not yet a settled part of political life; the digital revolution, personal computers, the Internet, and the Web were still decades off. Dramatic changes have certainly come to the technology of mass communications. This system is evolving rapidly, and it would be foolish to claim that these developments will prove irrelevant to politics (Mutz & Martin, 2001; Neuman, 1991). Nevertheless, change in our thinking about mass communications and politics over the last 40 years has had to do with alterations in social science more than in communications technology. Such alterations are partly methodological: stronger designs, more sensitive instruments, and better analysis. Still more important, or so it seems to me, are theoretical and conceptual advances, an infusion of good ideas. While Klapper was putting the finishing touches on *The Effects of Mass Communication*, a revolution was brewing in psychology, one that placed cognition at the center of study. Much of the "new look" in communication research is indebted to and inspired by this turn to cognition (e.g., Anderson, 1983; Collins & Loftus, 1975; Simon, 1955; Tversky & Kahneman, 1973, 1981). In possession of a more sophisticated understanding of human judgment and choice, research has begun to develop a dependable, complex, and detailed account of how mass communications influence the politics of everyday citizens.

Such influence proceeds in a variety of ways, as I have tried to show here. Mass communications frame and organize information and facts, thereby encouraging citizens to see and understand politics in certain ways. By singling out some aspects of politics for special attention, media influence what problems citizens see as urgent (and which candidates they take as serious). By dwelling on some problems and issues and neglecting others, media prime certain memories and not others, thereby altering the standards citizens apply when they evaluate the wisdom of a policy, the virtue of a candidacy, or the performance of their government. By providing compelling arguments and decisive cues, mass communications persuade citizens to replace one opinion with another. And by trafficking in certain kinds of negative advertising, media (perhaps) discourage participation in politics.

All in all, in these various ways, the media's power seems quite impressive—but it is not without limits. For one thing, framing, agenda setting, priming, and persuasion are all constrained by the anticipated reaction of the audience or, to use a different language, by what the American political culture finds permissible. If communications wander too far afield, they will be rejected (e.g., Gamson & Modigliani, 1987; Sherif & Hovland, 1961; Petty, Cacioppo, & Haugtvedt, 1992). Likewise, agenda setting seems limited to altering the priorities that citizens attach to such *plausible* problems as unemployment or drug abuse, problems that are reasonably regarded as relevant to the national interest and widely understood as potentially affecting the lives of millions of Americans. In the same way, priming appears to be restricted to elevating the importance of *reasonable* standards: to privilege national security or health care above other pressing problems. Media determine which accounts, problems, and standards predominate in public discourse, but these selections are taken from a short list of predominantly serious possibilities contending for attention.

And of course not everyone is influenced. The standard currency of average effects that I have adopted here overlooks the near certainty that Americans differ from one another in ways that are relevant to their susceptibility to media influence. The one variable that has drawn the most research attention so far in this regard is engagement in politics. That some Americans are deeply interested in politics while others couldn't care less is widely appreciated, but how this difference is implicated in citizen's vulnerability to media influence is unclear (e.g., Iyengar & Kinder, 1987; Kinder & Sanders, 1990; Krosnick & Brannon, 1993; Krosnick & Kinder, 1990; Miller & Krosnick, 2000; MacKuen, 1981, 1984; Weaver, Graber, McCombs, & Eyal, 1981).[18] Much clearer are the results on credibility. Those who mistrust media organizations are less subject to their influence: less taken by their frames (Druckman, 2001); less shaped by their agendas (Iyengar & Kinder, 1985); less thoroughly primed (Miller & Krosnick, 2000); and less persuaded by their arguments (Lupia & McCubbins, 1998). This result is corroborated by scores of attitude change experiments in social psychology, which show that the credibility of the source is a vital ingredient in persuasion (McGuire, 1969, 1985; Petty & Duane 1998).

Taken all around, we now seem quite a way further along toward the "science of communication" that Klapper (1960), Hovland (1954) and other founders of the field originally hoped for. Of course, there is still quite a bit left to do. For one thing, given all the evidence about how mass communications matter, we need to get smarter about how information is created and disseminated. For this we need theories of campaigns and journalism, and we need systematic empirical work that connects the "information system" on the one hand with the judgments made and actions taken by individual citizens on the other (for promising steps in this direction, see Armstrong, Carpenter, & Hojnacki, 2000; Bartels, 1996b; Bovitz, Druckman, & Lupia, 2000; Freedman, 1999; Gamson & Modigliani, 1987, 1989; Glaser, 1996; Hilgartner & Bosk, 1988; Jones, 1994; Page, 1996; Petrocik, 1996; Schudson, 1978).

For another, we need clarification of the psychological mechanisms that mediate mass communication influence. The standard interpretation for framing, agenda setting, and priming builds directly on basic research in cognition and gives center stage to automatic processing (Cappella & Jamieson, 1997; Price & Tewksbury, 1997). The story runs roughly this way: communications highlight some aspects of politics at the expense of others; when citizens notice such communications, relevant parts of their memory are automatically activated; those bits and pieces of activated memory are thereby rendered accessible; and accessible constructs and information exercise disproportionate influence over the opinions and evaluations that citizens express. Under this account, mental processes are set into motion by environmental provocations and operate outside of conscious awareness.

Whether framing, agenda setting, and priming effects can actually be explained in this way is a matter of current contention. The evidence for accessibility and automatic processing is either mixed (e.g., Valentino, Hutchings, & White, 2002, find evidence that priming is mediated by accessibility, while Miller & Krosnick, 2000, do not) or indirect (e.g., Mendelberg, 2001). The major alternative to accessibility entails a more thoughtful, self-conscious, and effortful process. In the case of framing, for example, the argument is that by singling out certain features of an issue or event, frames imply which considerations to take into account, but the final arbiter is the citizen, who *chooses* which of the available considerations are relevant and who *decides* how important each consideration should be (Gross, 2001; Nelson, Clawson, & Oxley, 1997; Nelson, Oxley, & Clawson, 1997; Chong, 1996). This debate about the psychological underpinnings of framing recapitulates a broader conversation in psychology over the extent to which everyday judgments, decisions, and behavior are under conscious control (see, for example, Posner & Snyder, 1975; Bargh & Ferguson, 2000). My point here is simply that a deep understanding of communication and politics in our age of information requires specification of psychological mechanism.

Finally, there remains the task of explicating the downstream consequences of mass communication influence, of spelling out the political differences that framing and persuading and such actually make. The obligation here is to integrate communication results into the larger story of politics. It might be thought that this work is someone else's business, that it belongs to mainstream political science, not to political psychology. Perhaps. But it seems to me that a truly successful science of mass communications cannot be just a wing of cognitive psychology, as important as psychology has been to the development of the field. The full story must at least be informed by the ways—partial, incomplete, intermittent and halting as they may be—that the worries and aspirations and sentiments of ordinary citizens give shape and direction to government.[19]

▶ Notes

I thank the editors for their patience, and Skip Lupia, David Sears, and Nick Valentino for their valuable comments on an earlier version of the chapter.

1. In this regard, framing effects in political communication resemble Tversky and Kahneman's (1981) famous experimental demonstrations of the difference that alternative frames make to decision-making.

2. No one should imagine that every analyst who makes use of the idea of frame means just the same thing by it (Entman, 1993). The conceptual diversity on display in this area of scholarship is impressive and perhaps regrettable, but probably not fatal. Consider as a conceivably comparable and instructive case the idea of "paradigm". By Masterman's (1970) count, Thomas Kuhn's book *The Structure of Scientific Revolution* (1964) used "paradigm" in 21 distinct ways. We might wish that Kuhn had been more precise, but his idea, we should remember, changed the way everyone thinks about science.

3. One might expect to find such demonstrations in the literature on social movements. To explain the emergence and occasional successes of social movements, researchers (by now a bit of a movement themselves) point to various contributing conditions: precipitating grievances, material resources, political constraints and opportunities, pre-existing organizational structures (e.g., McAdam, 1982; McCarthy & Zald, 1977; Tarrow, 1994; Tilly, 1978), and, increasingly in recent years, compelling frames (e.g., Gamson, 1992; McAdam, McCarthy, & Zald, 1996; Snow & Benford, 1992). But while there now exists considerable evidence that movement leaders spend a fair amount of time formulating frames and strategizing about their dissemination (e.g., Branch, 1988; Ellingson, 1995; Freedman, 1999; Garrow, 1978; Gerhards & Rucht, 1992), this is not the same as demonstrating that such frame work matters, and empirical studies in natural settings with this object in mind are in short supply (McAdam, 1996).

4. For a thoughtful and fascinating essay on the normative difficulties that framing makes for democratic politics, see Bartels, 2002.

5. In Lazarsfeld and Merton's (1948) original formulation, agenda setting should apply not only to issues and problems but to persons as well. A splendid venue for examining this process is provided by the contemporary American presidential nomination system, which features multiple challengers competing in a sequence of closely bunched contests. Under this system, an unexpectedly strong showing can bring a barrage of media attention. Picked out of the crowd of presidential hopefuls, a lucky candidate can become, almost overnight, a serious contender, as Gary Hart showed in 1984 and as John McCain demonstrated again in 2000. What most voters learn in such circumstances, at least in the short run, has very little to do with the candidate's policy proposals or personal background or general philosophy. The lesson is more rudimentary:

it is that *this* candidate has arrived, that *this* candidate is to be taken seriously. Showered with attention, such candidates are handed an opportunity to make their case to the public (Bartels, 1988).

6. Indeed at the time, it was seen this way by the national press (Mendelberg, 2001).

7. As do presidential debates, which might be thought of as campaigns in miniature: here too, there is little persuasion and lots of activation and reinforcement (Katz & Feldman, 1962; Sears & Chaffee, 1979).

8. In reaching his conclusion of minimal effects, Klapper also drew quite heavily on the results from a series of studies carried out by Carl Hovland and his colleagues for the Information and Education Division of the War Department during World War II, presented in *Experiments on Mass Communication* (1949). Hovland's team carried out randomized experiments on large and representative samples of American recruits to assess the effects of War Department propaganda films. They discovered that the films were generally quite successful in conveying salient facts but almost entirely ineffective in changing attitudes (Hovland, Lumsdaine, & Sheffield, 1949, p. 65). This result— information gain without corresponding attitude change (see also Robinson, 1976)— would seem to be a sign of *resistance*, discussed later in this section.

9. Not to mention the candidates themselves, also roughly equally matched and battle tested. Were nominees selected by lottery, we no doubt would see more evidence of campaign persuasion, as the candidates staggered from one disaster to the next.

10. Without deliberately choosing to do so, people typically find themselves in informational environments that are on balance reinforcing, more so in the selection of friends and mates than in the selection of communication sources (Mutz & Martin, 2001). Sears and Freedman (1967) refer to this as "de facto selectivity."

11. Conceptions of partisan identification differ over this point of immunity to the campaign (see, for instance, Fiorina, 1981; Jennings & Markus, 1984; Markus & Converse, 1979).

12. The best predictor of exposure to new information is a person's preexisting fund of information (Delli Carpini & Keeter, 1996; Gilens, 2001; Graber, 1984; Price & Zaller, 1993). This gives rise to a kind of virtuous cycle, where information breeds interest and interest breeds an appetite for more information and where the costs of assimilating new information decline steeply among those already in the know. This means that the audience for political communications consists disproportionately of the relatively well informed, and this fact has a crisscrossing implication for persuasion. On the one hand the audience that actually shows up for any media campaign is comparatively well equipped to comprehend, absorb, and retain the message; but on the other the audience is also comparatively well equipped to defend against and ultimately reject messages that challenge preexisting views.

13. In some ways this example is reminiscent of the claim of *The American Voter* (Campbell et al., 1960) that citizens much prefer simple constructions of group interest to ideological abstraction when it comes to evaluating parties and candidates ("ideology by proxy").

14. Research on cue-taking is flourishing, as it should, but it is unlikely in the end, to provide a completely satisfying solution to the problem of ignorance, for reasons I spell out elsewhere (Kinder 1998).

15. Whether the public as a whole really deserves the attribution of rationality that some analysts wish to bestow on it is therefore open to serious question (Converse, 1975, 1990; Kinder, 1998).

16. Zaller (1996) claims that "the flow of political communication in the United States on many (and perhaps most) important matters is relatively stable over time—locked into fixed patterns that reflect underlying divisions of power, partisanship, and social inertia" (p. 19).

17. On the possibility that voters might also be turned off by news coverage that emphasizes the strategic side of campaigns at the expense of issues, see Capella and Jamieson (1997) and Valentino, Beckmann, and Buhr (2001).

18. Part of the problem is that engagement is likely to have offsetting consequences at different stages of the influence process. Part of the problem is that different aspects of engagement have distinctive or even opposite implications for influence (Krosnick & Brannon, 1993). And, finally, whether engagement in politics makes people more or less susceptible to media influence may also depend on the magnitude of the "story." The terrorist attack on New York and Washington on September 11, 2001, was such big news that it probably washed away much of the normal variation in exposure. More often, news commands far less attention, and in this routine world, many less-engaged citizens may miss the message altogether. Bold claims notwithstanding (Miller & Krosnick, 2000), it seems premature at this stage to say anything conclusive about the relationship between engagement and influence.

19. As in, for example, Key (1961); Bartels (1991); and Stimson, MacKuen, and Erickson (1995).

▲ References

Abelson, R. P. (1959). Modes of resolution in belief dilemmas. *Journal of Conflict Resolution, 3,* 343–352.

Abelson, R. P. (1968). Psychological implication. In R. P. Abelson, E. Aronson, W. J. McGuire, T. M. Newcomb, M. J. Rosenberg, & R. H. Tannenbaum (Eds.), *Theories of cognitive consistency: A sourcebook* (pp. 112–139). Chicago: Rand McNally.

Althaus, S. L. (1998). Information effects in collective preferences. *American Political Science Review, 92,* 545–558.

Alvarez, R. M., & Nagler, J. (1995). Economics, issues and the Perot candidacy: Voter choice in the 1992 presidential election. *American Journal of Political Science, 39,* 714–744.

Anderson, C. A., Lindsay, J. J., & Bushman, B. (1999). Research in the psychological laboratory: Truth or triviality? *Current Directions in Psychological Science, 8,* 3–9.

Anderson, J. R. (1983). *The architecture of cognition.* Cambridge, MA: Harvard University Press.

Ansolabehere, S. D., & Iyengar, S. (1995). *Going negative: How political advertising shrinks and polarizes the electorate.* New York: Free Press.

Ansolabehere, S. D., Iyengar, S., Simon, A., & Valentino, N. (1994). Does attack advertising demobilize the electorate? *American Political Science Review, 88,* 829–838.

Ansolabehere, S. D., Iyengar, S., & Simon, A. (1999). Replicating experiments using aggregate and survey data: The case of negative advertising and turnout. *American Political Science Review, 93,* 901–909.

Armstrong, E. M., Carpenter, D. P., & Hojnacki, M. (2000, August). *The dynamics of media and congressional attention to disease.* Paper prepared for the annual meeting of the American Political Science Association.

Bachrach, P., & Baratz, M. S. (1970). *Power and poverty.* New York: Oxford University Press.

Banaji, M. R., & Greenwald, A. G. (1995). Implicit gender stereotyping in judgments of fame. *Journal of Personality and Social Psychology, 68*(2), 181–198.

Bargh, J. A., & Ferguson, M. J. (2000). Beyond behaviorism: On the automaticity of higher mental processes. *Psychological Bulletin, 126,* 925–945.

Bargh, J. A., & Pietromonaco, P. (1982). Automatic information processing and social perception: The influence of trait information presented outside of conscious awareness on impression formation. *Journal of Personality and Social Psychology, 55,* 1173–1182.

Bartels, L. M. (1988). *Presidential primaries and the dynamics of public choice.* Princeton: Princeton University Press.

Bartels, L. M. (1991). Constituency opinion and congressional policy making: the Reagan defense build-up. *American Political Science Review, 85,* 457–474.

Bartels, L. M. (1992). The impact of electioneering in the United States. In D. Butler & A. Ranney (Eds.), *Electioneering* (pp. 244–277). New York: Oxford University Press.

Bartels, L. M. (1993). Messages received: the political impact of media exposure. *American Political Science Review, 87,* 267–285.

Bartels, L. M. (1996a, August). Politicians and the press: Who leads, who follows? Presented at the annual meeting, of the American Political Science Association, San Francisco.

Bartels, L. M. (1996b). Uninformed votes: Information effects in presidential elections. *American Journal of Political Science, 40,* 194–230.

Bartels, L. M. (1997). *How campaigns matter.* Unpublished paper. Department of Politics, Princeton University.

Bartels, L. M. (2000). Partisanship and voting behavior, 1952–1996. *American Journal of Political Science 44,* 35–50.

Bartels, L. M. (2002). Democracy with attitudes. In M. MacKuen & G. Rabinowitz (Eds.), *Essays in honor of Philip Converse.* Ann Arbor: University of Michigan Press.

Bassili, J. N. (1993). Response latency versus certainty as indices of the strength of voting intentions in a CATI survey. *Public Opinion Quarterly, 57,* 54–61.

Bassili, J. N. (1996). Meta-judgemental versus operative indexes of psychological attributes: The case of measures of attitude strength. *Journal of Personality and Social Psychology, 71,* 637–653.

Behavioral Sciences Subpanel, President's Science Advisory Committee. (1962). Report to the President. *Behavioral Science, 7,* 277.

Behr, R. L., & Iyengar, S. (1985). Television news, real-world cues, and changes in the public agenda. *Public Opinion Quarterly, 49,* 38–57.

Berelson, B., Lazarsfeld, P., & McPhee, W. N. (1954). *Voting: A study of opinion formation in a presidential election.* Chicago: University of Chicago Press.

Berelson, B., & Steiner, G. A. (1964). *Human behavior.* New York: Harcourt Brace and World.

Berinsky, A. J. (1999). The two faces of political opinion. *American Journal of Political Science, 43,* 1209–1230.

Berinsky, A. J., & Kinder, D. R. (2000, August). *Making sense of issues through frames: Understanding the Kosovo crisis.* Paper prepared for annual meeting of the American Political Science Association.

Blumer, H. (1971). Social problems as collective behavior. *Social Problems, 18,* 298–306.

Bobo, L., & Kleugel, J. R. (1993). Opposition to race targeting: Self-interest, stratification ideology, or racial attitudes? *American Sociological Review, 58,* 443–464.

Bovitz, G. L., Druckman, J. N., & Lupia, A. (2000). *When can a news organization lead public opinion? Ideology versus market forces in decisions to make news.* Unpublished paper.

Branch, T. (1988). *Parting the waters.* New York: Simon and Schuster.

Brody, R. A. (1991). *Assessing the president.* Stanford, CA: Stanford University Press.

Bryce, J. (1888/1995). *The American commonwealth.* London: Macmillan.

Budge, I. (1993). Issues, dimensions, and agenda change in post-war democracies: Longterm trends in party election programs and newspaper reports in twenty-three democracies. In W. H. Riker (Ed.), *Agenda formation* (pp. 41–79). Ann Arbor: University of Michigan Press.

Burnham, W. D. (1970). *Critical elections and the mainsprings of American politics.* New York: Norton.

Burstein, P. (1985). *Discrimination, jobs, and politics.* Chicago: University of Chicago Press.

Cacioppo, J. T., & Petty, R. E. (1979). Attitudes and cognitive response: An electrophysiological approach. *Journal of Personality and Social Psychology, 37,* 2181–2199.

Caldiera, G. A., Clausen, A. R., & Patterson, S. C. (1990). Partisan mobilization and electoral participation. *Electoral Studies, 9*(3), 191–204.

Campbell, A., Converse, P. E., Miller, W. E., & Stokes, D. E. (1960). *The American voter.* New York: Wiley.

Cappella, J. N., & Jamieson, K. H. (1997). *Spiral of cynicism: The press and the public good.* New York: Oxford University Press.

Chaiken, S., Liberman, A., & Eagly, A. H. (1989). Heuristic and systematic processing within and beyond the persuasion context. In J. S. Uleman & J. A. Bargh (Eds.), *Unintended thought* (pp. 212–252). New York: Guilford Press.

Chong, D. (1993). How people think, reason, and feel about rights and liberties. *American Journal of Political Science, 37,* 867–899.

Chong, D. (1996). Creating common frames of reference on political issues. In D. C. Mutz, P. M. Sniderman, & R. A. Brady (Eds.), *Political persuasion and attitude change* (pp. 195–224). Ann Arbor: University of Michigan Press.

Cohen, B. (1963). *The press and foreign policy.* Princeton: Princeton University Press.

Collins, A., & Loftus, E. (1975). A spreading-activation theory of semantic memory. *Psychological Review, 82,* 407–428.

Converse, P. E. (1962). Information flow and the stability of partisan attitudes. *Public Opinion Quarterly, 26,* 578–599.

Converse, P. E. (1966). The concept of a normal vote. In A. Campbell, P. E. Converse, W. E. Miller, & D. E. Stokes (Eds.), *Elections and the political order* (pp. 9–39). New York: Wiley.

Converse, P. E. (1964). The nature of belief systems in mass publics. In D. E. Apter (Ed.), *Ideology and discontent* (pp. 206–261). New York: Free Press.

Converse, P. E. (1970). Attitudes and non-attitudes: Continuation of a dialogue. In

Edward R. Tufte (Ed.), *Analysis of social problems* (pp. 168–189). Reading, MA: Addison-Wesley.

Converse, P. E. (1972). Change in the American electorate. In A. Campbell & P. E. Converse, *Human meaning of social change* (pp. 307–317). New York: Russell Sage Foundation.

Converse, P. E. (1975). Public opinion and voting behavior. In F. I. Greenstein & N. W. Polsby (Eds.), *Handbook of political science* (pp. 75–168). Reading, PA: Addison-Wesley.

Converse, P. E. (1990). Popular representation and the distribution of information. In J. A. Ferejohn & J. H. Kuklinski (Eds.), *Information and democratic processes* (pp. 369–388). Urbana: University of Illinois Press.

Converse, P. E. (2000). Assessing the capacity of mass electorates. *Annual Review of Political Science, 3,* 331–354.

Dahl, R. A. (1989). *Democracy and its critics.* New Haven: Yale University Press.

Delli Carpini, M. X., & Keeter, S. (1996). *What Americans know about politics and why it matters.* New Haven: Yale University Press.

Devine, P. (1989). Stereotypes and prejudice: Their automatic and controlled components. *Journal of Personality and Social Psychology, 56,* 5–18.

Druckman, J. N. (2001). On the limits of framing effects. *Journal of Politics, 63,* 1041–1066.

Eagly, A., & Chaiken, S. (1998). Attitude structure and function. In D. Gilbert, S. Fiske, & G. Lindzey (Eds.), *Handbook of social psychology* (4th ed., vol. 1, pp. 269–322). New York: McGraw-Hill.

Edwards, K., & Smith, E. E. (1996). A disconfirmation bias in the evaluation of arguments. *Journal of Personality and Social Psychology, 71,* 5–24.

Eldersveld, S. J. (1956). Experimental propaganda techniques and voting behavior. *American Political Science Review, 50,* 154–165.

Ellingson, S. (1995). Understanding the dialectic of discourse and collective action: Public debates and rioting in antebellum Cincinnati. *American Journal of Sociology, 101,* 100–144.

Entman, R. M. (1993). Framing: Toward clarification of a fractured paradigm. *Journal of Communication, 43,* 51–58.

Erbring, L., Goldenberg, E. & Miller, A. H. (1980). Front-page news and real-world cues: Another look at agenda-setting by the media. *American Journal of Political Science, 24,* 16–49.

Fan, D. P. (1988). *Predictions of public opinion from the mass media: Computer content analysis and mathematical modeling.* Westport, CT: Greenwood.

Feather, N. T. (1963). Cognitive dissonance, sensitivity, and evaluation. *Journal of Abnormal and Social Psychology, 66,* 157–163.

Festinger, L. (1957). *A theory of cognitive dissonance.* Evanston, IL: Row, Peterson.

Festinger, L. (1964). *Conflict, decision, and dissonance.* Stanford, CA: Stanford University Press.

Finkel, S. E. (1993). Reexamining the "minimal effects" model in recent presidential campaigns. *Journal of Politics, 55,* 1–21.

Fiorina, M. P. (1981). *Retrospective voting in American national elections.* New Haven: Yale University Press.

Freedman, J. L., & Sears, D. O. (1965). Selective exposure. In L. Berkowitz (Ed.), *Advances in experimental social psychology* (Vol. 2, pp. 58–97). New York: Academic Press.

Freedman, P. (1999). *Framing the abortion debate: Public opinion and the manipulation of ambivalence.* Unpublished doctoral dissertation, University of Michigan, Ann Arbor.

Funkhouser, G. R. (1973). The issues of the sixties: An exploratory study in the dynamics of public opinion. *Public Opinion Quarterly 37,* 62–75.

Gamson, W. A. (1992). *Talking politics.* Cambridge, UK: Cambridge University Press.

Gamson, W. A., Croteau, D., Hoynes, W., & Sasson, T. (1992). Media images and the social construction. *Annual Review of Sociology, 18,* 373–393.

Gamson, W. A., & Modigliani, A. (1987). The changing culture of affirmative action. In R. A. Braumgart (Ed.), *Research in political sociology* (Vol. 3, pp. 137–177). Greenwich, CT: JAI Press.

Gamson, W. A., & Modigliani, A. (1989). Media discourse and public opinion on nuclear power: A constructionist approach. *American Journal of Sociology, 95,* 1–37.

Garrow, D. J. (1978). *Protest at Selma: Martin Luther King, Jr., and the Voting Rights Act of 1965.* New Haven: Yale University Press.

Gelman, A., & King, G. (1993). Why are American presidential election campaign polls so variable when votes are so predictable? *British Journal of Political Science, 23,* 409–451.

Gerber, A. S., & Green, D. P. (2000). The effects of personal canvassing, telephone calls, and direct mail on voter turnout: A field experiment. *American Political Science Review, 94,* 653–664.

Gerhards, J., & Rucht, D. (1992). Mesomobilization: Organizing and framing in two protest campaigns in West Germany. *American Journal of Sociology, 98,* 555–596.

Gilens, M. (2001). Political ignorance and collective policy preferences. *American Political Science Review, 95,* 379–396.

Gitlin, T. (1980). *The whole world is watching: Mass media in the making and unmaking of the new left.* Berkeley: University of California Press.

Glaser, J. M. (1996). *Race, campaign politics, and the realignment in the South.* New Haven: Yale University Press.

Gosnell, H. F. (1927). *Getting-out-the-vote: An experiment in the stimulation of voting.* Chicago: University of Chicago Press.

Gosnell, H. F. (1937). *Machine politics: Chicago model.* Chicago: Chicago University Press.

Graber, D. (1984). *Processing the news: How people tame the information tide.* New York: Longman.

Gross, K. A. (2001). *Images of "others": The effects of media coverage of racial unrest on public opinion.* Unpublished dissertation, University of Michigan, Ann Arbor.

Haller, H. B., & Norpoth, H. (1994). Let the good times roll: The economic expectations of U.S. voters. *American Journal of Political Science, 38,* 625–650.

Hastie, R., & Park, B. (1986). The relationship between memory and judgment depends on whether the task is memory-based or on-line. *Psychology Review, 93,* 258–268.

Hastie, R., & Pennington, N. (1989). Notes on the distinction between memory-based versus on-line judgments. In J. Bassili (Ed.), *On-line cognition in person perception* (pp. 1–18). Hillsdale, NJ: Erlbaum.

Haynes, S. E., & Jacobs, D. (1994). Macroeconomics, economic stratification, and partisanship: A longitudinal analysis of contingent shifts in political identification. *American Journal of Sociology, 100,* 70–103.

Hibbs, D. A., Jr., Rivers, R. D., & Vasilatos, N. (1982). The dynamics of political support for American presidents among occupational and partisan groups. *American Journal of Political Science, 26,* 312–332.

Higgins, E. T., Bargh, J. A., & Lombardi, W. (1985). The nature of priming effects on categorization: learning, memory, and cognition. *Journal of Experimental Psychology, 11,* 59–69.

Higgins, E. T., Rholes, W. S., & Jones, C. R. (1977). Category accessibility and impression formation. *Journal of Experimental Social Psychology, 13* (2), 141–154.

Hilgartner, S., & Bosk, C. L. (1988). The rise and fall of social problems: A public arenas model. *American Journal of Sociology, 94,* 53–78.

Holyoak, K. J., & Thagard, P. (1995). *Mental leaps: Analogy in creative thought.* Cambridge, MA: MIT Press.

Hovland, C. I. (1954). Effects of the mass media of communication. In G. Lindzey (Ed.), *Handbook of social psychology: Special fields and applications* (pp. 1062–1103). Cambridge, MA: Addison-Wesley.

Hovland, C. I. (1959). Reconciling conflicting results derived from experimental and survey studies of attitude change. *American Psychologist, 14,* 8–17.

Hovland, C. I., Janis, I. L., & Kelley, H. H. (1953). *Communication and persuasion.* New Haven: Yale University Press.

Hovland, C. I., Lumsdaine, A. A., & Sheffield, F. D. (1949). *Experiments on mass communication.* Princeton: Princeton University Press.

Huckfeldt, R., & Sprague, J. (1993). Citizens, contexts, and politics. In A. Finifter (Ed.), *Political science: The state of the discipline II* (pp. 281–303). Washington, DC: American Political Science Association.

Huckfeldt, R., & Sprague, J. (1995). *Citizens, politics, and social communication: Information and influence in an election campaign.* Cambridge: Cambridge University Press.

Hyman, H. H., & Sheatsley P. B. (1947). Some reasons why information campaigns fail. *Public Opinion Quarterly, 11,* 413–423.

Iyengar, (1991). *Is anyone responsible?: How television frames political issues.* Chicago: University of Chicago Press.

Iyengar, S., Hahn, K., & Prior, M. (2001, August). *Has technology made attention to political campaigns more selective? An experimental study of the 2000 presidential campaign.* Paper prepared for the annual meeting of the American Political Science Association.

Iyengar, S., & Kinder, D. (1985) Psychological accounts of agenda-setting. In S. Kraus & R. Perloff (Eds.), *Mass media and political thought.* Beverly Hills, CA: Sage.

Iyengar, S., & Kinder, D. (1987). *News that matters: Television and American opinion.* Chicago: University of Chicago Press.

Jacobs, L. R., & Shapiro, R. Y. (1994). Issues, candidate image, and priming: The use of private polls in Kennedy's 1960 presidential campaign. *American Political Science Review, 88,* 527–540.

Jacobs, L. R., & Shapiro, R. Y. (2000). *Politicians don't pander: Political manipulation and the loss of democratic responsiveness.* Chicago: University of Chicago Press.

Jacobson, G. C. (1980). *Money in Congressional elections.* New Haven: Yale University Press.

Jacobson, G. C. (2001). *The politics of Congressional elections* (5th edition). New York: Longman.

Jacoby, W. G. (2000). Issue framing and public opinion on government spending. *American Journal of Political Science, 44*(4), 750–767.

Jamieson, K. H. (1992). *Dirty politics: Deception, distraction, and democracy.* New York: Oxford University Press.

Jarvis, W. B. G., & Petty, R. E. (1996). The need to evaluate. *Journal of Personality and Social Psychology, 70,* 172–194.

Jennings, M. K., & Markus, G. B. (1984). Partisan orientations over the long haul: Results from the three-wave political socialization panel study. *American Political Science Review, 78,* 1000–1018.

Johnston, R., Blais, A., Brady, H. E., & Crete, J. (1992*). Letting the people decide: Dynamics of a Canadian election.* Stanford, CA: Stanford University Press.

Jones, B. D. (1994). *Reconceiving decision-making in democratic politics.* Chicago: University of Chicago Press.

Kahn, K. F., & Kenney, P. J. (1999). Do negative campaigns mobilize or suppress turnout? Clarifying the relationship between negativity and participation. *American Political Science Review, 93,* 877–890.

Katz, E., & Feldman, J. J. (1962). The debates in the light of research: A survey of surveys. In S. Kraus (Ed.), *The great debates* (pp. 173–223). Bloomington: Indiana University Press.

Katz, E., & Lazarsfeld, P. F. (1955). *Personal influence: The part played by people in the flow of mass communication.* New York: Free Press.

Kellstedt, P. M. (2000). Media framing and the dynamics of racial policy preferences. *American Journal of Political Science, 44,* 245–260.

Key, V. O., Jr. (1961). *Public opinion and American democracy.* New York: Knopf.

Kinder, D. R. (1998). Opinion and action in the realm of politics. In D. Gilbert, S. Fiske, & G. Lindsey (Eds.), *Handbook of social psychology* (4th ed., pp. 778–867). Boston: McGraw-Hill.

Kinder, D. R., & Nelson, T. E. (1990). *Experimental investigations of opinion frames and survey responses.* A report to the National Election Studies Board. Institute for Social Research, University of Michigan, Ann Arbor.

Kinder, D. R., & Palfrey, T. R. (Eds.). (1993). *Experimental foundations of political science.* Ann Arbor: University of Michigan Press.

Kinder, D. R., & Sanders, L. M. (1990). Mimicking political debate with survey questions: The case of white opinion on affirmative action for blacks. *Social Cognition, 8,* 73–103.

Kinder, D. R., & Sanders, L. M. (1996). *Divided by color: Racial politics and democratic ideals.* Chicago: University of Chicago Press.

Kintsch, W. (1998). *Comprehension: A paradigm for cognition.* Cambridge: Cambridge Press.

Klapper, J. T. (1960). *The effects of mass communications.* Glencoe, IL: Free Press.

Kramer, G. H. (1970). The effects of precinct-level canvassing on voting behavior. *Public Opinion Quarterly, 34,* 560–72.

Krosnick, J. A., & Abelson, R. P. (1992). The case for measuring attitude strength in surveys. In J. Tanur (Ed.), *Questions about questions: Inquiries into the cognitive bases of surveys* (pp. 177–203). New York: Russell Sage Foundation.

Krosnick, J. A., & Brannon, L. A. (1993). The impact of the Gulf War on the ingredients of presidential evaluations: Multidimensional effects of political involvement. *American Political Science Review, 87,* 963–75.

Krosnick, J. A., & Kinder, D. R. (1990). Altering the foundations of popular support for the president through priming: Reagan and the Iran-Contra affair. *American Political Science Review, 84,* 495–512.

Kuhn, T. S. (1962). *The structure of scientific revolutions.* Chicago: University of Chicago Press.

Lau, R. R., Sigelman, L., Heldman, C., & Babbitt, P. (1999). The effects of negative political advertisements: A meta-analytic assessment. *American Political Science Review, 93,* 851–876.

Lazarsfeld, P., Berelson, B., & Gaudet, H. (1948). *The people's choice* (2nd ed.). New York: Columbia University Press.

Lazarsfeld, P. F., & Merton, R. K. (1948). Mass communication, popular taste, and organized social action. In L. Bryson (Ed.), *The communication of ideas* (pp. 95–118). New York: Harper.

Lindblom, C. E. (1977). *Politics and markets.* New York: Basic Books.

Lippmann, W. (1922/1965). *Public opinion.* New York: Macmillan.

Lippmann, W. (1925). *The phantom public.* New York: Harcourt, Brace and Company.

Lodge, M. (1995). Toward a procedural model of candidate evaluation. In M. Lodge & K. M. McGraw (Eds.), *Political judgment: Structure and process* (pp. 11–140). Ann Arbor: University of Michigan Press.

Lodge, M., McGraw, K. M., & Stroh, P. (1989). An impression-driven model of candidate evaluation. *American Political Science Review, 83,* 399–419.

Lodge, M., & Steenbergen, M. (1995). The responsive voter: Campaign information and the dynamics of candidate evaluation. *American Political Science Review, 89,* 309–326.

Lodge, M., & Stroh, P. (1993). Inside the mental voting booth. In S. Iyengar & W. McGuire (Eds.), *Explorations in political psychology* (pp. 225–263). Durham, NC: Duke University Press.

Lord, C. G., Ross, L., & Lepper, M. R. (1979). Biased assimilation and attitude polarization: The effects of prior theories on subsequently considered evidence. *Journal of Personality and Social Psychology, 37,* 2098–2109.

Lupia, A. (1994). Shortcuts versus encyclopedias: Information and voting behavior in California insurance reform elections. *American Political Science Review, 88,* 63–76.

Lupia, A., & McCubbins, M. (1998). *The democratic dilemma: Can citizens learn what they need to know?* Cambridge, UK: Cambridge University Press.

MacKuen, M. (1981). Social communication and the mass policy agenda. In M. B. MacKuen & S. L. Coombs (Eds.), *More than news: Media power in public affairs* (pp. 19–144). Beverly Hills, CA: Sage.

MacKuen, M. (1983). Political drama, economic conditions, and the dynamics of presidential popularity. *American Journal of Political Science, 27,* 165–192.

MacKuen, M. (1984). Exposure to information, belief integration and individual responsiveness to agenda change. *American Political Science Review, 78,* 372–391.

MacKuen, M., Erikson, R. S., & Stimson JA. (1989). Macropartisanship. *American Political Science Review, 83,* 1125–1142.

MacKuen, M., Erikson, R. S., & Stimson, J. S. (1992). Question wording and macro-partisanship. *American Political Science Review, 86,* 475–481.

Manoff, R. K. (1986). Writing the news (by telling the "story"). In R. K. Manoff & M. Schudson (Eds.), *Reading the new: A pantheon guide to popular culture* (pp. 197–229). New York: Pantheon Books.

Markus, G. B. (1982). Political attitudes during an election year: A report of the 1980 NES Panel Study. *American Political Science Review, 76,* 538–560.

Markus, G. B., & Converse, P. E. (1979). A dynamic simultaneous equation model of electoral choice. *American Political Science Review, 73,* 1055–1070.

Masterman, M. (1970). The nature of a paradigm. In I. Lakatos & A. Musgrave (Eds.), *Criticism and the growth of knowledge* (pp. 59–90). Cambridge, UK: Cambridge University Press.

McAdam, D. (1982). *Political process and the development of black insurgency, 1930–1970.* Chicago: University of Chicago Press.

McAdam, D. (1996). The framing function of movement tactics: Strategic drama-turgy in the American civil rights movement. In D. McAdam, J. D. McCarthy, & M. N. Zald (Eds.), *Comparative perspectives on social movements: Cambridge Studies in Comparative Politics* (pp. 338–355). Cambridge, UK.: Cambridge University Press.

McAdam, D., McCarthy, J. D., & Zald, M. N. (Eds.). (1996). *Comparative perspectives on social movements.* Cambridge Studies in Comparative Politics. Cambridge, U.K.: Cambridge University Press.

McCarthy, J. D., & Zald, M. N. (1973). *The trend of social movements in America: Professionalization and resource mobilization.* Morristown, NJ: General Learning Press.

McCombs, M., & Zhu, J. H. (1995). Capacity, diversity, and volatility of the public agenda: Trends from 1954 to 1994. *Public Opinion Quarterly, 59,* 495–525.

McCombs, M. E., & Shaw, D. L. (1972). The agenda-setting function of the media. *Public Opinion Quarterly, 36,* 176–187.

McDonald, M. P., & Popkin, S. L. (2001). The myth of the vanishing voter. *American Political Science Review, 95,* 963–974.

McGuire, W. J. (1968). Personality and susceptibility to social influence. In E. F. Borgatta & W. W. Lambert (Eds.), *Handbook of personality theory and research* (pp. 1130–1187). Chicago: Rand McNally.

McGuire, W. J. (1969). The nature of attitudes and attitude change. In G. Lindzey & E. Aronson (Eds.), *Handbook of social psychology* (2nd ed., vol. 3, pp. 136–314). Reading, MA: Addison-Wesley.

McGuire, W. J. (1973). Persuasion, resistance, and attitude change. In I. De Sola Pool and Wilbur Schramm (Eds.), *Handbook of communication* (pp. 216–252). Chicago: Rand McNally.

McGuire, W. J. (1985). Attitudes and attitude change. In G. Lindzey & E. Aronson (Eds.), *Handbook of social psychology* (3rd ed., vol. 2, pp. 233–246). New York: Random House.

McGuire, W. J. (1986). The myth of massive media impact: Savagings and salvagings. *Public Communication and Behavior, 1,* 175–259.

McGuire, W. J. (2001). After a half century of election studies: Whence, where, and whither? In E. Katz & Y. Warshel (Eds.), *Election studies: What's their use?* (pp. 15–57). New York: Westview.

Mendelberg, T. (1997). Executing Hortons: Racial crime in the 1988 presidential campaign. *Public Opinion Quarterly, 61,* 134–57.

Mendelberg, T. (2001). *The race card.* Princeton: Princeton University Press.

Milburn, M. A. (1979). A longitudinal test of the selective exposure hypothesis. *Public Opinion Quarterly, 43,* 507–517.

Miller, J. M., & Krosnick, J. A. (2000). News media impact on the ingredients of presidential evaluations: Politically knowledgeable citizens are guided by a trusted source. *American Journal of Political Science, 44*(2), 301–315.

Mueller, J. E. (1971). Trends in popular support for the wars in Korea and Vietnam. *American Political Science Review, 65,* 358–375.

Mueller, J. E. (1991). Changing attitudes toward war: The impact of the First World War. *British Journal of Political Science, 21,* 1–28.

Mueller, J. E. (1994). *Policy and opinion in the Gulf War.* Chicago: University of Chicago Press.

Mutz, D. C. (1998). *Impersonal influence.* Cambridge, UK: Cambridge University Press.

Mutz, D. C., & Martin, P. S. (2001). Facilitating communication across lines of political difference: The role of mass media. *American Political Science Review, 95* (1), 97–114.

Nelson, T. E., & Kinder, D. R. (1996). Issue frames and group-centrism in American public opinion. *Journal of Politics, 58,* 1055–1078.

Nelson, T. H., Clawson, R. A., & Oxley, Z. M. (1997). Media framing of a civil liberties conflict and its effect on tolerance. *American Political Science Review, 91,* 567–583.

Nelson, T. H., Oxley, Z. M., & Clawson, R. A. (1997). Toward a psychology of framing effects. *Political Behavior, 19,* 221–246.

Neuman, W. R. (1990). The threshold of public attention. *Public Opinion Quarterly, 54,* 159–176.

Neuman, W. R. (1991). *The future of the mass audience.* New York: Cambridge University Press.

Ostrom, C. W., & Simon, D. M. (1985). Promise and performance: A dynamic model of presidential popularity. *American Political Science Review, 79,* 334–358.

Page, B. I. (1996). *Who deliberates? Mass media in modern democracy.* Chicago: University of Chicago Press.

Page, B. I., & Shapiro, R. Y. (1992). *The rational public.* Chicago: University of Chicago Press.

Patterson, T. E. (1980). *The mass media election: How Americans choose their president.* New York: Praeger.

Patterson, T. E. (1993). *Out of order.* New York: Knopf.

Pennington, N., & Hastie, R. (1992). Examining the evidence: Tests of the story model for juror decision making. *Journal of Personality and Social Psychology, 62* (2), 189–206.

Pennington, N., & Hastie, R. (1993). Reasoning in explanation-based decision-making. *Cognition, 49,* 123–163.

Petrocik, J. R. (1996). Issue ownership in presidential elections, with a 1980 case study. *American Journal of Political Science, 40,* 825–850.

Petty, R. E., & Cacioppo, J. T. (1986). *Communication and persuasion: Central and peripheral routes to attitude change.* New York: Springer-Verlag.

Petty, R. E., Cacioppo, J. T., & Haugtvedt, C. (1992). Involvement and persuasion: An appreciative look at the Sherifs' contribution to the study of self-relevance and attitude change. In D. Granberg & G. Sarup (Eds.), *Social judgment and intergroup relations: Essays in honor of Muzafer Sherif* (pp. 147–175). New York: Springer-Verlag.

Petty, R. E., & Duane, T. (1998). Attitude change: Multiple roles for persuasion variables. In D. Gilbert, S. Fiske, & G. Lindzey (Eds.), *Handbook of social psychology* (4th ed., vol. 1, pp. 323–390). New York: McGraw Hill.

Pollock, P. H., III. (1994). Issues, values, and critical moments: Did "Magic" Johnson transform public opinion on AIDS? *American Journal of Political Science, 38,* 426–446.

Pomerantz, E. M., Chaiken, S., & Tordesillas, R. S. (1995). Attitude strength and resistance processes. *Journal of Personality and Social Psychology, 69,* 408–419.

Pool, I. de S. (1973). Communication systems. In I. de S. Pool, W. Schramm, F. W. Frey, N. Maccoby, & E. B. Parker (Eds.), *Handbook of communication* (pp. 3–26). Chicago: Rand McNally.

Pool, I. de S. (1983). Tracking the flow of information. *Science, 221,* 609–613.

Popkin, S. L. (1991). *The reasoning voter.* Chicago: University of Chicago Press.

Popkin, S. L. (1993). Information shortcuts and the reasoning voter. In B. Grofman (Ed.), *Information, participation, and choice: An economic theory of democracy in perspective* (pp. 17–36). Ann Arbor: University of Michigan Press.

Posner, M. I., & Snyder, C. R. R. (1975). Attention and cognitive control. In R. L. Solso (Ed.), *Information processing and cognition: The Loyola Symposium* (pp. 55–85). Hillsdale, NJ: Erlbaum.

Price, V. (1989). Social identification and public opinion: Effects of communicating group conflict. *Public Opinion Quarterly, 53,* 197–224.

Price, V., & Tewksbury, D. (1997). News values and public opinion: A theoretical account of media priming and framing. In G. A. Barnett & F. J. Boster (Eds.), *Progress in the communications sciences* (vol. 13). Greenwich, CT: Ablex.

Price, V., & Zaller, J. (1993). Who gets the news? Alternative measures of news reception and their implications for research. *Public Opinion Quarterly, 57,* 133–164.

Protess, D. L., Cook, F. L., Doppelt, J. C., Ettema, J. S., Gordon, M. T., Leff, D. R., & Miller, P. (1991). *The journalism of outrage: Investigative reporting and agenda building in America.* New York: Guilford.

Rahn, W. M., Aldrich, J. H., & Borgida, E. (1994). Individual and contextual variations in political candidate appraisal. *American Political Science Review, 88,* 193–199.

Riker, W. H. (1982). *Liberalism against populism: A confrontation between the theory of democracy and the theory of social choice.* San Francisco, CA: Freeman.

Riker, W. H. (1993). *Agenda formation.* Ann Arbor: University of Michigan Press.

Riker, W. H. (1996). *The strategy of rhetoric: Campaigning for the American Constitution.* New Haven: Yale University Press.

Robinson, M. J. (1976). Public affairs television and the growth of political malaise: The case of "the selling of the Pentagon." *American Political Science Review, 70,* 409–432.

Rosenstone, S. J. (1983). *Forecasting presidential elections.* New Haven: Yale University Press.

Rosenstone, S. J., Behr, R. L., & Lazarus, E. H. (1996). *Third parties in America: Cit-*

izen response to major party failure (Rev. ed.). Princeton: Princeton University Press.

Rosenstone, S. J., & Hansen, J. M. (1993). *Mobilization, participation and democracy in America.* New York: Macmillan Press.

Schattschneider, E. E. (1960). *The semisovereign people.* New York: Holt, Rinehart, and Winston.

Schudson, M. (1978). *Discovering the news.* New York: Basic Books.

Schudson, M. (1984). *Advertising, the uneasy persuasion.* New York: Basic Books.

Sears, D. O. (1986). College sophomores in the laboratory: influence of a narrow data base on social psychology's view of human nature. *Journal of Personality and Social Psychology, 51,* 515–530.

Sears, D. O., & Chaffee, S. H. (1979). Uses and effects of the 1976 debates: An overview of empirical studies. In S. Kraus (Ed.), *The great debates, 1976: Ford vs. Carter* (pp. 223–261). Bloomington, IN: Indiana University Press.

Sears, D. O., & Freedman, J. L. (1967). Selective exposure to information: A critical review. *Public Opinion Quarterly, 31,* 195–213.

Sears, D. O., Whitney, R. E. (1973). Political persuasion. In I. de S. Pool & W. Schramm, F. W. Frey, N. Macroby, & E. B. Parker (Eds.), *Handbook of communication* (pp. 253–63). Chicago: Rand McNally.

Sherif, M., & Hovland, C. I. (1961). *Social judgment: Assimilation and contrast effects in communication and attitude change.* New Haven: Yale University Press.

Simon, H. A. (1955). A behavioral model of rational choice. *Quarterly Journal of Economics, 69,* 99–118.

Sniderman, P. M., Brody, R. A., & Tetlock, P. E. (1991). *Reasoning and choice: Explorations in political psychology.* Cambridge, UK: Cambridge University Press.

Sniderman, P. M., & Grob, D. (1996). Innovations in experimental design in general population attitude surveys. *Annual Review of Sociology, 22,* 377–399.

Snow, D. E., & Benford, R. D. (1992). Master frames and cycles of protest. In A. Morris & C. M. Mueller (Eds.), *Frontiers in social movement theory* (pp. 133–55). New Haven: Yale University Press.

Srull, T. K., & Wyer, R. S., Jr. (1979). The role of category accessibility in the interpretation of information about persons: Some determinants and implications. *Journal of Personality and Social Psychology, 37*(10), 1660–1172.

Stimson, J. A. (1991/1998). *Public opinion in America: Moods, cycles, and swings.* Boulder, CO: Westview Press.

Stimson, J. A., MacKuen, M. B., & Erikson, R. S. (1995). Dynamic representation. *American Political Science Review, 89,* 543–565.

Stoker, L. (1993). Judging presidential character: The demise of Gary Hart. *Political Behavior, 15,* 193–223.

Sundquist, J. L. (1983). *Dynamics of the party system: Alignment and realignment of political parties in the United States* (Rev. ed.). Washington, DC: Brookings Institution.

Tarrow, S. (1994). *Power in movement: Social movements, collective action and politics.* Cambridge, MA: Cambridge University Press.

Tilly, C. (1978). *From mobilization to revolution.* Reading, MA: Addison and Wesley.

Tversky, A., & Kahneman, D. (1973). Availability: A heuristic for judging frequency and probability. *Cognitive Psychology, 5,* 207–232.

Tversky, A., & Kahneman, D. (1981). The framing of decisions and the psychology of choice. *Science, 211,* 453–458.

Valentino, N. A. (1999). Crime news and the priming of racial attitudes during evaluations of the president. *Public Opinion Quarterly, 63,* 293–320.

Valentino, N. A., Beckmann, M. N., & Buhr, T. A. (2001). A spiral of cynicism for some: The contingent effects of campaign news frames on participation and confidence in government. *Political Communication, 18,* 347–367.

Valentino, N. A., Hutchings, V. L., & White, I. (2002). Cues that matter: How political ads prime racial attitudes during campaigns. *American Political Science Review.*

Verba, S., & Nie, N. H. (1972). *Participation in America: Political democracy and social equality.* New York: Harper and Row.

Verba, S., Schlozman, K. L., & Brady, H. E. (1995). *Voice and equality: Civic voluntarism in American politics.* Cambridge, MA: Harvard University Press.

Weaver, P. (1972). Is television news biased? *Public Interest, 26,* 57–74.

Weaver, D. H., Graber, D. A., McCombs, M. E., & Eyal, C. E. (1981). *Media agenda-setting in a presidential election: Issues, images, and interest.* New York: Praeger.

West, D. (1993). *Airwars, TV advertising, and election campaigns, 1952–1992.* Washington: CQ Press.

Wielhouwer, P. W., & Lockerbie, B. (1994). Party contacting and political participation. *American Journal of Political Science, 38,* 211–229.

Winter, N. J. G. (2001). *Mental images and political stories: Tracing the implicit effects of race and gender rhetoric on public opinion.* Unpublished doctoral dissertation, University of Michigan, Ann Arbor.

Wolfinger, R. E. (1974). *The politics of progress.* Englewood Cliffs, NJ: Prentice-Hall.

Zaller, J. (1989). Bringing Converse back in: Modeling information flow in political campaigns. In J. A. Stimson (Ed.), *Political analysis: an annual publication of the methodology section of the American Political Science Association* (vol. 1, pp. 181–234). Ann Arbor, MI: University of Michigan Press.

Zaller, J. (1990). Political awareness, elite opinion leadership, and the mass survey response. *Social Cognition, 8,* 125–153.

Zaller, J. (1991). Information, values, and opinion. *American Political Science Review, 85,* 1215–1237.

Zaller, J. (1992). *The nature and origin of mass opinion.* Cambridge, UK: Cambridge University Press.

Zaller, J. (1996). The myth of massive media impact revived: New support for a discredited idea. In D. C. Mutz, P. M. Sniderman, & R. A. Brody (Eds.), *Political persuasion and attitude change* (pp. 17–78). Ann Arbor: University of Michigan Press.

Zaller, J. (1998) Monica Lewinsky's contribution to political science. *PS: Political Science and Politics,* 182–189.

Zaller, J., & Hunt, M. (1994). The rise and fall of candidate Perot: Unmediated versus mediated politics, Part 1. *Political Communication, 11,* 357–390.

Zaller, J., & Hunt, M. (1995). The rise and fall of candidate Perot: The outsider versus the political system, Part II. *Political Communication, 12,* 97–123.

12 Kathleen M. McGraw

Political Impressions

Formation and Management

> *Whenever men are discussed (and especially princes, who are more exposed to view), they are noted for various qualities which earn them either praise or condemnation. Some, for example, are held to be generous and others miserly. Some are held to be benefactors, others are called grasping; some cruel, others compassionate; one man faithless, another faithful; one man effeminate and cowardly, another fierce and courageous . . . So a prince has of necessity to be so prudent that he knows how to escape the evil reputation attached to those vices that could lose him his state, and how to avoid those vices which are not so dangerous, if he possibly can. . . . A prince need not necessarily have all of the good qualities I mentioned above, but he should certainly appear to have them.*
>
> —Niccolo Machiavelli, The Prince

In these famous passages, describing "the things for which men, and especially princes, are praised and blamed" (chapter 15), Machiavelli notes that princes, like ordinary men, have reputations that "of necessity" they must know how to manipulate. Moreover, when it comes to reputations, appearance is more important than reality. So conceived, political reputations are perceptions that are the end result of a dynamic process linking citizens and politicians. The holding (in the minds of individual citizens) and shaping (via the strategies of politicians) of reputations are principal elements of democratic politics, and political psychologists have much to contribute to understanding these dynamics.

To recast this in contemporary social science parlance, political reputations are a function of two interrelated processes, *impression formation* and *impression management*.[1] The former refers to an individual's construction of a mental representation—a cognitive structure stored in memory—consisting of knowledge and beliefs about another person. In the political realm, citizens' impressions of politicians consist of inferences about not only the types of traits Machiavelli was concerned with but also personal and political attributes, appearance, behaviors, and so on. Impression management, on the other hand, refers to the activities people engage in to regulate and to control the information about themselves that they present to other people. In his classic book *Home Style* (1978), Fenno emphasized that self-presentation is central to engendering political support: "politicians believe that a great deal of their support is won by the kind of individual self they present to others, i.e., to their constituents. More than most other people, they consciously try to manipulate it" (p. 55).

My goal in this chapter is to survey what political psychologists know, and have yet to discover, about impression formation and impression management. The processes are two sides of the same coin, and my starting presumption is a simple one: a complete understanding of what ordinary citizens think about politicians will be out of reach until political psychologists take into account the strategic interplay between elites and the mass public. Although this presumption is simple and perhaps obvious, a word of warning is in order at the outset: empirical research rarely grapples with the explicit connections between the two processes. Jervis (2002) makes exactly this point in his recent call for unifying the study of "signaling and perception" in international politics, when he contends that "what we need are studies that are two-sided in looking at both the actor and the perceiver" (p. 308). Unfortunately, the two topics—how citizens think about politicians and the strategic attempts by politicians to influence those perceptions—occupy separate shelves in our offices and separate chapters in scholarly treatments. Crossfertilization between the two literatures is rare. As a consequence, the manifest empirical links between the two processes are few and far between. I will try to make some limited steps in linking the two, but my ultimate goal is to challenge the next generation of scholars in political psychology to develop research agendas that more fully integrate these perspectives.

There are three psychological processes that are critical to understanding both impression formation and impression management: cognition, affect, and motivation. This tripartite distinction can be traced at least back to Plato, who conceived of the human soul as comprising three distinct components: the rational soul (thinking and reason), the spirited soul (volition or will), and the appetitive soul (emotion and desire). Plato's tripartite division of the self has exerted tremendous influence on western thinking, and nearly all social scientists recognize the importance of the three as explanatory elements of human behavior.[2] As the pages that follow will illustrate, cognition, affect, and motivation all play an important role in our theorizing and understanding of the complex links between citizens' impressions and politicians' attempts to influence those impressions. Having made this claim, I immediately want to back off and note that few, if any, scholars have rigorously pursued documenting these multiple determinants within a given program of research. Rather, their role is gleaned from disparate sources. A second goal of this chapter is to urge political psychologists to develop and test ever more rigorous theories that elaborate simultaneously on these three mechanisms.

I use these terms in their most generic sense, with no commitment to specific theoretical frameworks or operational definitions. By *cognition* I simply mean the mental processes involved in making sense of the political world—how people perceive other people, groups, policies, and events. For both sides of the coin, these mental processes—perceptions—are fundamental. That may seem obvious when we talk about impression formation among everyday people but perhaps less obvious when we talk about elite strategies of manipulation. But elite perceptions of the public are also critical to understanding how elites select among different self-presentation strategies, although we have less empirical evidence about those processes (Fenno, 1978; Jervis, 2002). *Affect* is a generic term for a range of phenomena—preferences, evaluations, moods, and emotions (Fiske & Taylor, 1991). Politics is rarely a dispassionate exercise, so affect and cognition must be intrinsically intertwined in political perception and in our theories describing those processes.

Finally, *motivation* refers to the psychological mechanisms that guide thought and behavior toward some goal; motives are the reasons (conscious or unconscious) behind the choices we make (see Lane, 1986, and Lau, 1990, for political psychology discussions). In theorizing about social and political perception among everyday people, two motives are central. *Accuracy goals* motivate the perceiver to reach as accurate or correct a judgment as possible under the circumstances. In contrast, *directional goals* motivate the perceiver to reach a judgment that is consistent with a preferred, or existing, conclusion; this process is often referred to as *motivated reasoning* (Kunda, 1990; Lodge & Taber, 2000). The perceptual trick for citizens is to achieve a balance, to "believe both what accounts satisfactorily for the sensory evidence and what suits their purposes" (Fiske, 1992).

As human beings, politicians presumably possess the same motivational mechanisms as ordinary people, but those are not what are emphasized in the scholarly literature that informs my analysis. Rather, the emphasis has been on *political motivations.*[3] Analyses of politicians in democratic polities have concluded that two motives predominate: first, enacting policies that they personally prefer and/or are preferred by party loyalists; and, second, seeking reelection (Fenno, 1973; Smith & Deering, 1990). Most scholars acknowledge that both motivations are important (an exception is Mayhew (1974), who treated members of Congress as "single-minded reelection seekers," (p. 17), and so the tactical problem facing politicians is balancing policy and reelection goals in the face of often competing considerations. The prominence of the reelection goal is fundamental to this chapter's central themes. That is, it is precisely because politicians need to cultivate and sustain public support that their actions are key to understanding the impressions that citizens hold about them.

A few words about intellectual history. It is undeniably the case that political psychology scholarship on impressions has been strongly informed by social psychological theories and methods. This is particularly true for the first side of the coin, impression formation. Political psychologists have, to some extent, moved beyond direct applications of the tenets from the study of "ordinary personology" (Gilbert, 1998), but we could go further.

In particular, most investigations of political impression formation adopt the paradigmatic social psychology laboratory experiment, where information about a politician is provided in a neat and tidy package, and various measures are taken that allow us to make inferences about the underlying structure and content of the resulting impression. This paradigm has a number of commendable features, but researchers should be aware that it is rooted in social psychology's historic preference for clear and static intrapsychic snapshots of individual representations over more dynamic and interpersonal representations (Gilbert, 1998). In fact, it is the rare study in social cognition that considers the development of impressions over an extended period of real time (see Park, 1986, for an exception) or considers strategic attempts on the part of some actor to influence the perceiver's cognitive processes. But it is axiomatic in politics that politicians take an active role in trying to shape and manipulate citizens' perceptions (McGraw, 1991). Successful attempts in building theories that combine both strategic elite interactions and citizens' cognitive processes provide an avenue for political psychologists to contribute to the development of more general psychological theory (Krosnick & McGraw, 2002).

A final caveat: much of the political psychological literature on forming impressions of politicians focuses on those politicians as individuals, outside of the context of electoral choice. This follows from the social psychological models of impression formation that have informed much of this tradition, as they are fundamentally concerned with thinking about individuals, not choosing between alternatives (this is a focus of the quite distinct decision-making literature, where specifying mental processes is of secondary concern). Just as the social psychological tradition neglects the dynamics of impression formation, it also has virtually nothing to say about forming impressions of individuals in the context of making a choice. For the most part, I conform to this convention and focus on impressions of politicians as individuals, having relatively little to say about the context of choice, particularly voting (see chapter 2, for an extended discussion). I would also add that investigating impression formation mechanisms in the choice context is an important avenue for empirical inquiry (McGraw, 2000; see Lau, 1995; Lau and Redlawsk, 1997, 2001; Rahn, 1995; Rahn, Aldrich, Borgida, & Sullivan, 1990; Redlawsk, 2001, for examples).

Now that preliminary matters are out of the way, the remainder of this chapter is organized into three sections. The first considers the research evidence on impression formation: how impressions of politicians are formed and the content of those impressions. Second, I take up the issue of political impression management, considering scholarly research that has informed our understanding of how politicians strategically influence citizens' views of them. Finally, I grapple with the question of how citizens react to these strategies of impression management, and in particular their susceptibility to manipulation and deception.

▶ Impression Formation

The phrase "impression formation" suggests that impressions are the result of a dynamic *process* involving the building of some mental *structure*. Thus impressions are more than just summary evaluative judgments about other people but rather are mental structures stored in memory that have two properties. First, impressions consist of what we know and believe about another person, the information we have learned and the inferences we have drawn. Second, these structures are not random collections of disconnected attributes but rather are more or less organized into conceptually similar clusters. Impression formation is also a dynamic, constructive process, evolving over time. New information is incorporated, and impressions are systematically, and sometimes not so systematically, revised. These revisions can occur at a slow, imperceptible pace, or they can be dramatic and palpable (left-leaning readers might consider their impressions of President Bush or Mayor Giuliani before and after September 11, 2001). It is because impressions are dynamic entities that politicians can effectively shape them.

Although there are a number of research topics that might be considered in a discussion of political impression formation, I concentrate on two: (1) the content of political impressions (in particular, traits, stereotypes, and affect) and (2) the processes by which impressions, particularly summary opinions, are formed (Lodge & McGraw, 1995).

Content: The Raw Materials of Political Impressions

Traits Are Central

What are the basic categories or building blocks of our impressions of politicians? Miller, Wattenberg, and Malanchuk's (1986) analysis of National Election Survey (NES) responses to open-ended questions asking for 'likes and dislikes' about presidential candidates revealed four general categories: issue positions, partisanship, group-related beliefs, and personal attributes (consisting of traits, appearance, and background information).[4] It is worth noting that this list is different from the "big three" categories evident from studies of ordinary personology, namely appearance, behavior, and traits (Fiske & Taylor, 1991; Park, 1986). The presence of issues and partisan and group concerns in political impressions demonstrates, reassuringly, that there are unique aspects of political impression formation that reflect the roles and responsibilities of the political context. Despite the contextual differences, it is also the case that traits are the central components of ordinary and political impressions, and it is traits that have received the lion's share of theoretical and empirical attention (for seminal theoretical treatments, see Asch, 1946; Heider, 1958; Jones & Davis, 1965; for a recent review, Gilbert, 1998). Trait inferences dominate impressions, and theorizing about impressions, because they are functional, and so motivation is central. That is, trait inferences are rooted in the perceiver's need to understand the root causes of human behavior, to be able to predict the future, and to control events. In Heider's view, an observer "grasps reality, and can predict and control it only by referring transient and variable behavior and events to relatively unchanging underlying conditions" (1958, p. 79), and "we need to perceive things and people with invariant properties" (p. 53). A number of scholars have argued that traits perform this instrumental role in political impressions, namely, the ability to predict how a given leader will perform in elected office (Barber, 1972; Kinder, 1986; Page, 1978).

Traits are unobservables. Unlike the color "green" or the taste "sweet," none of us has ever directly sensed "competence" or "honesty." Rather, these traits are inferred from observable qualities of the politician. The most fully developed psychological model of the trait inference process posits three sequential operations: (1) categorization of an observed behavior; (2) trait inference; and (3) adjustment (maybe) for situational constraints (Gilbert, 1998). The first two stages are relatively automatic, whereas the latter stage of adjustment requires more cognitive effort. Consider, for example, Senator Edmund Muskie's apparent public display of tears in New Hampshire during his 1972 presidential campaign, during a speech in defense of his wife. An observer of this behavior could have drawn a number of different trait inferences: Muskie is emotional, devoted to his wife, compassionate, weak, unstable. In fact, the attribution that dominated in subsequent press coverage was that the incident was indicative of Muskie's weakness, and it was seen as the event that led to the collapse of his campaign. What about the third step, adjusting for the situation? The Muskie speech was given outside during a windy snowstorm, and so it is possible that his wet cheeks were due to the snow (a situational attribution, which was put forth as an explanation by the Muskie campaign after the event) rather than representative of any enduring personality trait. An observer who was willing to invest the cognitive resources to consider and accept this situational constraint might be hard-pressed to draw any inference about Muskie's character from this particular behavior.

The Muskie example illustrates additional principles about trait inferencing. Behavior is often ambiguous, so there is rarely an inevitable correspondence between a behavioral episode and the resulting trait inference. The behavior itself must be interpreted and then the trait inference follows. In line with motivated reasoning arguments, impressions tend to be evaluatively consistent, so that people with preexisting positive views about Muskie might have made very different inferences (compassionate) from those with negative opinions (weak). Moreover, in the world of politics, trait inferences are subject to manipulation and "spin" by elites with a stake in the outcome; in the Muskie example, both sides vigorously attempted to manipulate the public's interpretation the behavior.

A substantial amount of research has been directed toward understanding the role of traits in evaluations of politicians (see Funk, 1996, for a review). Three general areas of inquiry have received attention. First, although there are a seemingly infinite number of traits available in the ordinary language lexicon, the traits used to characterize politicians tend to fall into a limited number of broad categories. There is some disagreement about the exact number of categories, and these conclusions are surely dependent on both the specific techniques used to measure the traits and the statistical method used to extract the underlying dimensions. In general, competence, leadership, integrity, and empathy appear as empirically separable dimensions (Kinder, 1986). As dimensions of political personality, *competence* refers to the extent to which a leader is a qualified, intelligent manager (terms such as "intelligent" and "hard-working" are used to assess this dimension), whereas *leadership* is the "heroic, mythical" dimension (p. 236), captured by such trait terms as "inspiring" and "(not) weak." *Integrity* is the extent to which a leader is ethical and moral ("honest," "moral") whereas *empathy* is the extent to which the leader is understanding and connected to the "common man" ("compassionate," "cares about people").

Second, the specific traits used to articulate these higher order dimensions are subject to systematic motivated bias. Traits vary in their breadth, such that broad traits (such as "good") encompass a large number of distinct behaviors, whereas narrower traits (such as "charitable") apply to a more limited number of behaviors. If I have a positive impression of a politician, the use of broad positive traits implies that she will exhibit that trait (e.g., "intelligent") in a wide range of circumstances. If I have to grudgingly admit she has negative qualities, the choice of a narrow trait (e.g., "sly") constrains the circumstances in which that trait will be applicable and so does minimal damage to my overall positive impression. Consistent with this logic, people tend to select broad positive traits (e.g., "kind") and narrower negative traits ("gullible") to describe politicians that they like; conversely, people tend to select broad negative traits ("unintelligent") and narrower positive traits ("softhearted") to describe politicians that they dislike (McGraw, Fischle, Stenner, & Lodge, 1996). This is an illustration of how the balancing act between accuracy and directional goals is accomplished, as people are willing to acknowledge that a favored politician has faults but do so in a way that manages to sustain the overall opinion.

Finally, trait inferences are consequential for evaluations of political candidates and vote choice in the United States (see Funk, 1996 and Kinder, 1998, for detailed references). Of the various dimensions, competence seems to be the most influential, at least in terms of evaluations of presidential candidates (Kinder, 1986; Markus, 1982). Much of the available data are cross-sectional, raising the real possibility that trait inferences are rationalizations rather than causes of evaluations. However, experimental research (e.g., Funk, 1996; Huddy & Terkildsen, 1993) verifies that traits can play a causal role in shaping evaluations of politicians.

Stereotyping

Having established the nature and consequences of traits for political impressions, the question of the sources of trait inferences becomes important. Kinder (1986) concluded that "judgments of presidential character reflect both (default) assumptions people make about political leaders in general as well as particular and often distinctive things they know about particular leaders" (p. 253). In other words, trait inferences can be rooted in both stereotypes and evidence about the specific case. Recall that trait inferencing is initiated by a process of categorization. Contemporary accounts of stereotyping view it as an inevitable byproduct of normal cognitive processes, in particular categorization of individuals into different types or "groups" (Allport, 1954; Fiske, 1998). As a type of cognitive structure, stereotypes contain mental elements, including traits, that are then applied by default to individual category members, particularly if no specific information about the applicability of the trait is available. (See chapters 3 and 16 for further perspectives on stereotyping.)

Political psychologists have investigated the stereotypic basis of political trait inferences by focusing on four categories: physical appearance, gender, race, and partisanship. The first three promote stereotyping because they are physically manifest and so activated by visual cues. There is good reason to think that membership in these categories has powerful consequences, as trait inferences drawn from physical or nonverbal cues tend to be even *more* automatic than those drawn from verbal sources (Gilbert, 1989). Gender and race, as well as partisanship, may also promote stereotyping because they are politically meaningful categories that play a prominent role in contemporary politics. In the discussion that follows, I emphasize the extent to which these stereotypic categories shape trait inferences. However, stereotypes also include information about other attributes of group members, and I briefly note examples of scholarship that have provided evidence about these other attributes (in particular, policy positions).

Physical appearance. Despite the admonition "Don't judge a book by its cover," it is clear that people have a strong tendency to rely on physical appearance when reaching first impressions. Absent any other information about a candidate's qualities (and holding race and gender constant), attractive facial appearances produce more positive trait inferences than unattractive appearances for male (Rosenberg, Bohan, McCafferty, & Harris, 1986) and female political candidates (Sigelman, Sigelman, & Fowler, 1987). However, when information about partisanship and issue positions is available, physical attractiveness has no effect, suggesting a limit to the effects of attractiveness on trait inferences (Riggle, Ottati, Wyer, Kuklinksi, & Schwarz, 1992).

In addition to attractiveness, other physical cues have been linked to political trait perceptions. For example, height has been found to be positively correlated with perceptions of leadership (Chaiken, 1986; Stogdill, 1948). Facial maturity also has been implicated. People attribute greater warmth, honesty, and submissiveness to "baby-faced" adults (those with relatively large eyes, round chins, and thick lips) than to those with more "mature" facial features (like small eyes, square jaws, and thinner lips), which elicit attributions of dominance and strength; Zebrowitz, 1994). In a creative demonstration of the impact of facial maturity cues on political trait inferences, Keating, Randall, and Kendrick (1999) manipulated the facial images of well-known contemporary presidents through digital techniques, creating a "baby-faced" and (more) mature version of each. These subtle changes in facial cues affected perceivers' trait ratings of these well-known leaders. For example, both Clinton supporters and nonsupporters saw him as more honest, attractive, and compassionate when the baby-faced features (thick lips and large eyes) were substituted for his normal ones. Before political consultants rush to order collagen and belladonna treatments for their clients because of these results, it should be noted that baby-faced features also have negative trait consequences, such as decreased power.

Gender. Of the four stereotype categories, gender has received the most scholarly attention, and the results from a variety of methodological perspectives converge nicely (see Huddy, 1994, and Huddy & Capelos, forthcoming, for reviews). All else equal, female candidates are ascribed stereotypic female traits (e.g., sensitive, warm, emotional) whereas male candidates are described in stereotypic male terms (e.g., assertive, tough, competent; Kahn, 1992; Rosenwasser & Seale, 1988; Sapiro, 1983). In addition to these trait ascriptions, the stereotypes of male and female candidates extend to other political attributes (ideology and partisanship) as well as competency in different policy domains (Huddy & Terkildsen, 1993; Koch, 2000; Sanbonmatsu, 2002; Sapiro, 1983). Huddy and Terkildsen (1993) have provided the most sophisticated analysis of the complex links among candidate gender, traits, beliefs, and issue competency, concluding that gender trait stereotypes play an independent causal role in shaping beliefs about policy competencies. Although gender stereotypes can be potent, they do not necessarily disadvantage female candidates. For example, although perceived competence is a critical determinant of candidate evaluations and male candidates typically have the advantage in terms of general trait competence as well as competence in some policy domains (such as economics and foreign policy), female candidates have the advantage in competence for social welfare issues and also typically receive higher scores on empathy and integrity. In some electoral circumstances, then, women may be disadvantaged (e.g., in times of foreign conflict) and in others they may be advantaged (e.g., when social welfare issues are at the forefront). As a result, although the existence of gender stereotypes in politics has been well documented in both laboratory and "real-world" studies, there is no compelling theoretical reason to expect that gender stereotyping should uniformly translate into voter bias against female candidates. Moreover, it is clear that individual differences exist in the propensity to stereotype political candidates on the basis of gender (Huddy, 1994). In line with this argument, Sanbonmatsu (2002) has argued that many voters have a predisposition to support male or female candidates and that this predisposition (which benefits candidates of both genders) can be linked to gender-stereotypic beliefs.

Race. It is abundantly clear that racial considerations are consequential for public opinion, although their influence depends on a number of contingency factors (Citrin, Green, & Sears, 1990; Peffley, Hurwitz, & Sniderman, 1997). On the specific question of racial stereotypes about politicians and their consequences, however, there is surprisingly little evidence, and that which exists points to contradictory conclusions (see Callaghan and Terkildsen, forthcoming, for a review). Given that white Americans historically have held negative stereotypes about Blacks (Devine, 1989; Katz & Braly, 1933; but see Judd, Park, Ryan, Brauer, & Krauss, 1995), one might expect a negative impact of racial stereotypes on judgments about black candidates. However, the empirical evidence is decidedly mixed, with black candidates described in more negative trait terms than white candidates in some studies (Williams, 1990) but attributed more positive traits in others (Colleau et al., 1990; Sigelman, Sigelman, Walkosz, & Nitz, 1995). Racial prejudice (i.e., holding a negative attitude toward blacks in general) appears to moderate these effects, as racist whites attribute more negative personality traits to a black candidate, whereas nonracist whites attribute marginally more positive traits to the same candidate (Moskowitz & Stroh, 1994). As with the gender stereotype literature, there is no evidence that racial stereotypes per se (in contrast to the larger question of racial prejudice) contribute to voter bias at the polls, in large part because this is a question that has not been subject to careful scrutiny. Careful attention to measurement will be necessary, as it will be difficult to disentangle the impact of stereotypes and prejudice in order to estimate their independent effects on evaluations and vote choice.

Partisanship. Partisanship is a central cue in political judgment and decision-making (Rahn, 1993), but to my knowledge there is no evidence demonstrating that partisan stereotypes influence trait attributions. Not surprisingly, citizens of different partisan stripes vary in their willingness to attribute traits to specific politicians (e.g., Republicans described Reagan more positively than Democrats; Kinder, 1986), but that is a different phenomenon than a generalized propensity to assign different traits to Republican and Democratic officials. It is clear that party stereotypes exist in the realm of policy, with people holding clear and consensual beliefs about the policy positions (and competencies) that "go with" partisan affiliation (Feldman & Conover, 1983; Hamill, Lodge, & Blake, 1985; Lodge & Hamill, 1986). Given evidence from the gender stereotype literature demonstrating links among perceived policy competencies, traits, and partisan beliefs

(Huddy & Terkildsen, 1993), a reasonable expectation is that a candidate's partisan label has implications for trait attributions in some, probably low-information, conditions, but this intuition awaits empirical verification.

In summary, the empirical evidence implicates stereotyping processes in shaping judgments about the trait characteristics of politicians. The evidence is certainly better for some types of stereotypic categories than others, and there are many gaps in our knowledge. To date, we know little about the impact of multiple stereotypes in a single context and how citizens cope with inconsistent implications within and across stereotypic categories (see Huddy & Capelos, forthcoming, for evidence that candidate partisanship dominates over candidate gender, and Sigelman et al., 1995, for evidence of interactions between candidate ideology and race). We also know too little about how individual characteristics of citizens, such as sophistication and personality characteristics, influence the use of political stereotypes.

Individuating Processes

The use of stereotypes depends on a number of limiting conditions, in particular the "fit" between the particular target of judgment and the broader stereotype (e.g., Hurwitz & Peffley, 1997; Peffley, Hurwitz, & Sniderman, 1997; Rahn, 1993; Terkildsen, 1993). Citizens are flexible information processors, capable of engaging in both "theory-driven" (stereotypic) and "data-driven" (individuating) processing when making political judgments, in line with the theoretical predictions drawn from dual processing models (Fiske, 1986; Fiske & Neuberg, 1990). By *individuation*, I mean judgment processes reliant on the specific information that is available, without reference to category-based knowledge. Briefly, three types of individuating information have been linked to political trait inferences. First, and hopefully this comes as no surprise, candidate-specific differences are evident in trait ratings of real politicians among experts (Simonton, 1986) and ordinary people (Kinder, 1986), corresponding to actual variations in the politicians' histories and reputations. To illustrate by negative example for contemporary American presidents (see Weisberg & Hill, 2001, for the data): Jimmy Carter received the lowest trait ratings among recent presidents on the leadership dimension, prompted perhaps by his folksy, informal demeanor and the unfortunate "rabid rabbit" canoeing incident; Bill Clinton was viewed as having the least integrity—understandable, given the constant stream of scandals that plagued his administration; George Bush (senior) received low ratings on empathy and was seen as "out of touch," a perception no doubt fueled by incidents such as his infamous unfamiliarity with grocery scanner technology; and Ronald Reagan was viewed as least competent and intelligent, in keeping with his public persona of running a hands-off administration, taking daily naps, and pleading ignorance about the sale of arms to Iran. Moreover, the impact of trait judgments on overall evaluations varies across candidates (for example, perceptions of integrity were significant determinants of evaluations of Clinton in 1992 and 1996 but not of Bush in 1988 and 1992; Funk, 1999).

Second, inferences about trait characteristics follow from information about a candidate's issue positions, as found by Rapoport, Metcalf, and Hartman (1989). Interestingly, the resulting trait inferences in that study were often idiosyncratic, suggesting that is not the operation of consensual stereotypes about specific issue positions but rather inferences drawn from the individual's unique set of beliefs and predispositions. This causal link between issue positions and traits is central to Fenno's (1974) analysis, when he noted: "issues have little autonomous effect . . . Rather, issues are vehicles that some House members use to convey their qualifications, their sense of identification, and their sense of empathy" (p. 134).

Finally, and most important for my purposes, trait perceptions are under the control of politicians themselves, who can structure communication strategies to emphasize or deemphasize different personality characteristics. For example, Kahn (1996) has documented the strategies that female senatorial and gubernatorial candidates use in their political ads to stress their "male" qualities such as competence and to avoid the negative effects of gender stereotypes. In addition, the explanatory strategies that politicians make use of to contain or minimize political damage influence judgments about their personality traits (McGraw, 2001). Jacobs and Shapiro's (1994) analysis of John F. Kennedy's 1960 presidential campaign suggests that manipulation of his perceived personality attributes was a central objective. (I return to this important theme later). Reflecting the lack of crossfertilization between the two topics, however, there has been little systematic consideration of the relative impact of stereotypes and elite strategic behaviors on citizens' impressions of political candidates.

Affect

Investigations of the impact of traits, stereotypes, and individuating information are concerned, to varying degrees, with the development, mental representation, and consequences of different types of information content for political impressions. Quite independent from the content of information is its affective valence. I have in mind not emotional responses to candidates (see chapter 6) but rather more simple positive and negative reactions, or evaluations. So, for example, the category "Republican" not only conveys information about probable policy preferences (stereotypic content) but also is likely to generate an affective reaction that varies in direction and intensity, and we can theorize about the implications of that affective reaction per se. A number of questions have motivated investigations of the role of affect in political impressions. One question is: What matters more, positive or negative information? An asymmetry in impact is evident, as a number of studies of political impression formation indicate that negative information has a greater influence on impressions than positive information (e.g., Holbrook, Krosnick, Visser, Gardner, & Cacioppo, 2001; Klein, 1991, 1996; Lau, 1982, 1985). This so-called negativity bias exists for both cognitive (perceptual) and motivational reasons.[5] That is, negative information tends to be more diagnostic as to underlying traits and abilities (Skowronski & Carlston, 1989), and it draws more attention because negative acts and attributes are less common than positive ones (Lau, 1985); the motivational component is linked to the tendency to avoid costs rather than to seek gains (Lau, 1985). The analysis of Holbrook and colleagues (2001) demonstrates that the marginal utility of negative information decelerates less quickly than the marginal utility of positive information, suggesting that negative information about politicians has a longer "half-life."

Second, there has been some consideration of the extent to which impressions of politicians are characterized by *ambivalence*, that is, the simultaneous holding of both positive and negative beliefs about the politician. Although most of the work on ambivalence in political psychology has been concerned with policy preferences (Alvarez & Brehm, 1995, 1997, 1998; Huckfeldt & Sprague, 1998; Steenbergen & Brewer, 2000; Zaller, 1992; Zaller & Feldman, 1992), a handful of recent studies have examined the consequences of ambivalence for opinions about politicians. Increasing ambivalence about politicians has been linked to more moderate and less confident evaluations (Meffert, Guge, & Lodge, 2000), as well as more negative evaluations (McGraw, Hasecke, & Conger, forthcoming). In addition, ambivalence has been linked to less stable and predictable evaluations, and a delay in the formation of voting intentions (Lavine, 2001).

The third question concerns the extent to which impressions of political figures are primarily organized along the affective dimension, a proposition that essentially posits that positive beliefs and information will be stored in one part of the mental structure and negative beliefs and information in another. My investigations of this possibility, using recall clustering measures, have led me to conclude that the evaluative organization does not predominate; rather, people appear to organize their impressions of political actors along the basic "stuff" (i.e., issues and personal characteristics) of politics (McGraw, Pinney, & Neumann, 1991; McGraw & Steenbergen, 1995). To the extent that evaluative memory organization did occur in those studies, it was most evident among individuals with less interest and knowledge about politics; such people's political judgments are generally more likely to be shaped by affective considerations (Rahn, 2000; Sniderman, Brody, & Tetlock, 1991).[6]

Impression Formation Processes

Quite separate, in terms of scholarly practice, from investigations of the content of political impressions is the issue of process, or "how citizens assemble their views, how they put the various ingredients together"

(Kinder, 1998, p. 812). Two models have been put forth to describe the processes underlying the formation of opinions about politicians, distinguished in large part by the temporal parameter of *when* opinions are formed (Hastie & Park, 1986; Lodge, McGraw, & Stroh, 1989). The first posits that opinions about politicians are formed *on-line*, at the time of initial exposure to information. Under on-line processing, people integrate the evaluative implications of new information about political actors by continuously updating an "on-line running tally" of the summary evaluation when information is first encountered. When it is necessary to express an opinion, the summary tally (part of the impression structure) is retrieved from memory, not the specific pieces of information that contributed to it. In contrast, under what has been designated *memory-based processing*, opinions are constructed at the time the judgment is expressed, by retrieving specific pieces of information from long-term memory and combining the evaluative implications of the retrieved information to compute the judgment (Zaller, 1992; Zaller & Feldman, 1992). In evaluating the operation of the two models in any given context, researchers have made use of either correlations between information retrieved from memory and the summary evaluative judgment, or response latency measures (on-line processing is supported by negligible memory-judgment correlations and rapid response latencies, whereas memory-based processing is characterized by substantial memory-judgment correlations and slower response latencies).

Both models are primarily concerned with cognitive processes (how information that is encoded and stored in memory is used to construct summary opinions), but affect is also fundamental. That is, both models presume that it is the overall direction (pro or con) of the affective implications of information or "considerations" that is the basis of opinions. Note that, in practice, political psychological investigations of on-line and memory-based processing have focused on a global net (positive-negative) tally, constructed either as information is encountered (in the case of on-line processing) or at the time of judgment (in the case of memory-based). This focus on the summary evaluation may appear to be inconsistent with, and even contradict, the prior discussion about the importance of traits, and in particular the differentiation of trait judgments about politicians into meaningful, separate categories. In fact, the disparity is a function of the restricted emphasis of the extant research and does not point to any fundamental incompatibility between the theoretical frameworks. It is possible, and I would argue even desirable, to conceptualize impressions as having both global, or superordinate, on-line tallies and subcategory on-line tallies for different trait and other domains. Information may be relevant to one subtally but not another, and the subtallies themselves are the component pieces of the larger global evaluation. Social psychological investigations have demonstrated that specific trait inferences occur on-line (e.g., Park, 1989; Uleman, Hon, Roman, & Moskowitz, 1996); unfortunately, studies in this tradition have not considered the global evaluative implications of these trait-specific inferences. The political psychology research, in contrast, focuses on the global summary tally but has not considered the links to the lower order components. What is needed is a more comprehensive research strategy aimed at linking our understanding of on-line processing across multiple dimensions during impression formation.

The literature has evolved by specifying the contingent nature of the two types of processing models, and several moderating variables have been identified.[7] The key condition regulating on-line processing is motivational: the prior existence or activation of the goal to form a summary evaluative judgment about the target (Hastie & Park, 1986; Lodge, et al., 1989). This goal is critical because the activation and continual updating of the on-line tally requires some investment of cognitive resources to attend to relevant information as it is encountered and to update the judgment. Relatedly, more sophisticated individuals are more likely to engage in on-line processing than those less sophisticated, presumably because sophisticates are habitually motivated to be informed and opinionated about politics and so are motivated to form impressions about prominent politicians (McGraw, Lodge, & Stroh, 1990).

A second set of contingency principles points to situational parameters. A complex learning environment, such as learning about multiple (four or six) candidates simultaneously (Redlawsk, 2001), as well as receiving information in a debate-like format (alternating between two candidates; Rahn, Aldrich, & Borgida, 1994), results in more memory-based processing, arguably because the complexity of those situations disrupts "normal" processing routines. Third, individual differences have been implicated in nonpolitical applications, with individuals high in the need to evaluate (Tormala & Petty, 2001) and those described as "entity theorists" (i.e., who tend to believe other people's personalities are static and fixed rather than dynamic and malleable; McConnell, 2001) more likely to manifest on-line processing. Both of these characteristics can be linked to the impression formation goal, with those chronically high in the need to evaluate being habitually motivated to form summary evaluative judgments and "entity theorists" being habitually inclined to believe there is a coherent impression to be formed.

In summary, the evidence points to a set of theoretically meaningful parameters that regulate the propensity to engage in on-line and memory-based processing, with motivation to form an impression as the critical determinant of which processing route is adopted. A limitation of the research to date is that scholars have adopted an either-or approach to the two models, even though there is good reason to suspect that a hybrid approach, incorporating both *time-of-exposure* and *time-of-judgment* information effects on evaluative judgments may provide a more psychologically realistic model (Hastie & Pennington, 1989; Lavine, 2002). Under a hybrid model, a citizen may process information about a candidate on-line and also be influenced by considerations that are accessible at the time when asked to express an opinion about the candidate. Recent evidence from my laboratory provides preliminary support for this hybrid approach (McGraw, Hasecke, & Conger, forthcoming). In that study, candidate evaluations were strongly shaped by on-line processing mechanisms but also influenced by the mental state (ambivalence and uncertainty) at the time of judgment.

The substantive implications of the memory-based and on-line processing models are important, as the research has informed our understanding of how impressions of politicians are formed and the conditions under which the different processing models apply. But the normative implications are also considerable, as the two models paint very different portraits of the ability of citizens to live up to democratic standards. As Lodge and Steenbergen (1995; Lodge, 1995) have forcefully argued, the on-line model paints a fairly rosy picture because it suggests that citizens are responsive to—take into account—information that they encounter, even if that information eventually fades from memory. "Responsiveness" may seem like a low bar of accomplishment, but it is a more positive characterization of democratic citizens than those that dominate the public opinion literature. Memory-based accounts, on the other hand, suggest a more ephemeral and random basis to political judgments, where citizens are "making it up as they go along" and are largely influenced by whatever information, from whatever sources, is available at the time of judgment (Zaller, 1992). I concur with Kinder (1998) that conclusions about the normative superiority of the two models are premature until scholars have evaluated more systematically the nature of the information, and the information sources, that contribute to opinion formation in each model.

▲ Strategies of Impression Management

The general topic of "political impression management" is potentially a very large one, encompassing the literatures on campaigns, advertising, fundraising, lobbying, media control, and more (see chapter 11 for an appraisal of the media and public opinion literature). I have chosen to narrow the focus considerably, in order to describe specific research topics that illustrate the impact of various strategic behaviors on citizens' impressions and that suggest the potential for extending this line of inquiry within political psychology. In particular, I focus on three topics at the intersection of political psychology and legislative politics, as it is here that we see and understand representative democracy at work: Fenno's (1978) analysis of "home style"; position-taking (in particular, ambiguity and pandering); and political explanations.

Home Style

Richard Fenno (1978) coined the phrase "home style" to refer to three sets of activities that elected representatives engage in in their home districts (as opposed to Washington) to cultivate their constituents' support (thus the electoral goal is fundamental to this analysis). These activities are the allocation of resources to the district (time and staff), explanation of Washington activity to constituents, and presentation of self. I consider the topic of explanations separately later; here just a few words will suffice about Fenno's insights on self-presentation, which are both politically and psychologically astute. Fenno viewed self-presentation as the "centerpiece" (p. 60) of home style. The ultimate objective in self-presentation is not high approval ratings but rather the more nebulous and fragile construct of *trust*, conceptualized as a willingness on the part of citizens to let the representative adopt the trustee role, or to use his or her own judgment in making decisions (Bianco, 1994, provides an extensive analysis of trust between legislators and constituents). Fenno's analysis outlines three components of self-presentation styles: conveying qualifications (competence and honesty), a sense of identification with constituents ("I am one of you"), and empathy.[8] Note that these components dovetail nicely with the trait ascriptions that predominate in surveys of citizens' impressions of candidates, although we have no direct empirical evidence as to how citizens perceive the self-presentation strategies Fenno describes, or whether and how these perceptions contribute to citizen trust. In addition, the advent of the Internet as a primary medium of communication between representatives and their constituents (Davis, 1999) has produced new self-presentation strategies and has obscured the distinction between "in Washington" and "in the district," suggesting that an extension of Fenno's analysis is long overdue.

Ironically, the answer to the central question Fenno poses at the outset of *Home Style*—"What does an elected representative see when he or she sees a constituency?" (p. xiii)—remains elusive. So phrased, the problem is one of impression formation on the part of elected representatives. Fenno's analysis points to four concentric circles of constituents (geographic, reelection, primary, and personal), a "complicated context" (p. 27) that requires a considerable amount of strategic skill on the part of the representative and analytic nuance on the part of scholars interested in the links between representatives and citizens. Fenno is quick to admit that there are other ways that House members might "see" their constituencies, so further theoretical and empirical development on this question is warranted.

Position-Taking

One of the attractive properties of Fenno's analysis is that he conceives of representation in terms of dynamics and process, as a series of two-way communications between representative and constituents. This procedural conceptualization of representation is counter to the traditional, and still dominant, structural view that emphasizes policy congruence. In normative theory and in empirical analyses, representation has traditionally been treated as the congruence between the policy preferences of constituents in the geographic district and the policy decisions (roll call votes) of the representative; "representation" occurs when this congruence is high. Mayhew's (1974) analysis has been influential, wherein he points to "position-taking" as one of the key activities that "congressman find it electorally useful to engage in" (p. 49). That is, adopting and articulating positions that are congruent with constituents' preferences not only satisfies the public's demand for representation but also is the central means of satisfying the elected official's electoral goals. Ultimately, in Mayhew's analysis, position-taking is strategic—not motivated, for example, by a principled commitment to a "delegate" model of representation. Two questions are particularly relevant to understanding the link between position-taking and citizens' impressions, namely the extent to which "pandering" and ambiguous position-taking occur.

Pandering

One of the most widely accepted principles of elite behavior, held by journalists and scholars alike, is that politicians, motivated by electoral concerns, strategically ingratiate themselves to constituents by modifying their issue positions to be consistent with public opinion (e.g., Barone, 1997; Dowd, 1998; Geer, 1996; Graber, 1976; Lippmann, 1955; Page, 1978). This argument is made recently and forcefully by Stimson, MacKuen, and Erikson (1995), claiming that "like antelopes in an open field . . . when politicians perceive public opinion change, they adapt their behavior to please their constituency" (p. 545, 559). This strategic behavior can be described positively as "democratic responsiveness" (Jacobs & Shapiro, 2000; Page & Shapiro, 1992) but is more frequently viewed pejoratively as "pandering." Larry Jacobs and Bob Shapiro provide a provocative challenge to the conventional wisdom, arguing against it in their book *Politicians Don't Pander* (2000). Jacobs and Shapiro contend that politicians are motivated by both electoral and "good policy" objectives and simultaneously pursue both through a strategy of "crafted talk" that is aimed at changing public opinion in order to minimize the risk of electoral retribution as a consequence of appearing to be unresponsive to voters' preferences. The starting assumption is critical, as it places the politician's policy preferences as the anchor for subsequent strategies and so paints a picture of political strategy that is antithetical to pandering. Three techniques contribute to the process of crafted talk. First, politicians make use of polls and focus groups to determine the arguments and symbols about specific policies that the public finds most appealing. Second, they influence media coverage by "staying on message" with simple, carefully crafted messages. Third, rather than adopting a strategy of direct persuasion or education of the public, politicians make use of a "priming" strategy that is aimed not at changing the public's fundamental values or preferences but rather at influencing the weight the public assigns to relevant considerations in the policy realm.

Particularly relevant to the concerns of this chapter is Jacobs's and Shapiro's (1994) illustration of these processes at work in John F. Kennedy's 1960 presidential campaign. The Kennedy campaign relied heavily on private polls to develop specific policy proposals. Moreover, the campaign viewed position-taking on salient issues as the "means by which to project the candidate's 'move-ahead' image . . . as 'caring' and willing to offer new approaches" (p. 535). In other words, the strategy of crafted talk was used to stake out issue positions that ultimately would shape the voters' impressions of Kennedy's personality traits (a strategy that is upheld by the Fenno, 1978, and Rapoport, Metcalf, & Hartman, 1989, analyses described earlier), thus underscoring the interdependence of issues and traits in political impressions.

The Jacobs and Shapiro model of "simulated responsiveness" awaits additional systematic verification. The model may be a more valid characterization of prominent national politicians, such as presidents and high-profile members of Congress, who have the power of "going public" through the media to secure support for their policies (Kernell, 1997). Politicians at the state and local level are less adept at manipulating media coverage and so may be more likely to pander. However, to the extent that it accurately describes politicians' behavior, the Jacobs and Shapiro framework provides a more sophisticated picture of the interrelationships among public opinion, elites, and the media than those that assume a simple unidirectional causal flow (i.e., public opinion determining elites' positions or vice versa).

Ambiguity

Both Downs (1957) and Key (1958) noted that candidates often have an incentive to adopt ambiguous, or unclear, issue positions, Key going so far as to suggest that politicians "become addicted to equivocation and ambiguity" (p. 241). The motivation for this, like pandering, is electoral: "by shunning clear stands, they avoid offending constituents who hold contrary opinions; ambiguity maximizes support" (Page, 1976, p. 742). So, for example, in their classic analysis Page and Brody (1972) argued that both Richard Nixon and Hubert Humphrey projected ambiguous positions on Vietnam in the 1972 campaign in order to avoid alienating voters. Scholars have formalized the incentives for taking ambiguous positions, as well as the circumstances under which they should be avoided (Enelow & Hinich, 1984; Page, 1976; Shepsle, 1972). Surprisingly, there has been no systematic analysis of how politicians project ambiguity or clarity, the prevalence of the practice, or the conditions under which it is more or less likely to occur.

From the perspective of political psychology, taking ambiguous issue positions has three potential drawbacks. When information is ambiguous, people are more likely to rely on preexisting beliefs, including stereotypes, to draw inferences about a target (Darley & Gross, 1983; Devine, 1989).

The stereotypes act as a lens through which the ambiguous situation is interpreted. As a result, ambiguity about a candidate's position on a given policy should increase the reliance on stereotypes, a consequence that may be antithetical to the candidate's goals. Second, ambiguity is likely to create uncertainty about the candidate's position, uncertainty having been linked to more negative evaluations of political leaders (Alvarez, 1997; Glasgow & Alvarez, 2000; McGraw, Lodge, & Jones, 2002). Third, to the extent that citizens prefer a delegate style of representation, where politicians adopt positions that are consistent with public preferences, than the failure to conform to this expectation may also be politically damaging (evidence suggests that citizens want elected officials to act as delegates rather than trustees; Patterson, Hedlund, & Boynton, 1975; Sigelman, Sigelman, & Walkosz, 1992).

Explanations

A significant form of political communication is *explanations*, or *accounts* (I used the terms interchangeably), in terms of both normative theory and their impact on public opinion. Normatively, explanation is a fundamental manifestation of accountability in a representative democracy. According to Pitkin (1967), representation implies "acting in the interest of the represented, in a manner responsive to them. . . . The representative must act in such a way that there is no conflict, or if it occurs, an explanation is called for (pp. 209–210). Fenno (1978) also emphasized the centrality of explanation to theories of representation: "theories of representation will always be incomplete without theories that explain explaining" (p. 162).

Congressional scholars have long recognized the importance of "explaining the vote" (Bianco, 1994; Fenno, 1978; Kingdon, 1973; Mayhew, 1974). One of the important insights from this literature is that explanations loom large in the calculus of legislators. They anticipate the potential need to explain their voting decisions to constituents, and this *anticipation* of accountability results in a variety of *blame-avoidance* behaviors directed toward evading a negative situation altogether (e.g., through adjustment of voting decisions; Austen-Smith, 1992; Kingdon, 1973; as well as for a host of strategic behaviors such as agenda setting and automatic indexation; Weaver, 1986, 1988). Beyond the question of avoiding explanations, the evidence on the antecedents of political explanation—that is, who explains?— is "mostly impressionistic" (Rivers & Fiorina, 1991, p. 17) rather than being based on systematic empirical evidence, and advances in this direction are overdue (Bianco, 1994; McGraw, Anderson, & Willey, 2000; Willey, 2002). The congressional wisdom suggests that representatives from safe districts, and those with more seniority, are less likely to explain their voting decisions than those who have less electoral security (Kingdon, 1973). Representatives from more heterogeneous districts may explain more often those from homogenous districts, because the former are more likely to cast votes with which sizable segments of their constituency disagree (Fenno, 1978; Kingdon, 1973).

A central theme in the literature is reflected by the adage "If you have to explain, you're in trouble" (Fenno, 1978, p. 145). In other words, explanation occurs when the politician's actions have negative implications, be it personal misconduct or an unpopular policy decision. Pitkin's discussion (earlier) also assumes that explanation follows "conflict" or unpopular actions, as do prominent social psychological treatments (Goffman, 1971; Schlenker, 1980). There is no doubt that when politicians violate their constituents' expectations, they respond with explanations, or *blame-management strategies* (McGraw, 1991, 2001), to contain the political fallout and damage to their reputations. However, explanations can also be provided in the context of positive actions. Bianco (1994) has argued that explanations can be used to strengthen perceptions of accessibility and as a mechanism for position-taking; more generally, explanations can be a key component of the "electorally useful" activities identified by Mayhew (i.e., advertising, credit-claiming, and position-taking; 1974). Although there has been little systematic research on the antecedents of political explanation, a recent study sheds some light on this question of explanation as blame management or credit claiming (McGraw, Anderson, & Willey, 2000). We examined explanations posted to House members' personal webpages for their votes on the articles of impeachment against President Clinton in 1998. Members were more likely to post an explanation of their impeachment votes when those votes were compatible with district preferences, rather than in violation of district preferences, consistent with the argument that explanations can be motivated by self-promotion.

Explanations are not simply "empty rhetoric" but rather have systematic consequences for a wide range of public opinion phenomena (see McGraw, 2001, 2002, for extended discussions). For example, excuses (a category of accounts that entail a denial of full or partial responsibility for an outcome) influence attributions of responsibility, with satisfactory excuses resulting in more credit and unsatisfactory excuses resulting in more blame. Justifications (a category of accounts that attempt to redefine evaluations of the act and its consequences) influence opinions about the controversial act or policy. Third, political explanations shape inferences about specific trait characteristics. For example, a "trustee-like" justification ("in the end, I used my own judgment as to what is in your best interests") increases perceptions of leadership, whereas a "delegate-like" justification ("I owe it to my constituents to vote according to their wishes, and that is what I did") increases perceptions of empathy (McGraw, 2001).

Finally, satisfactory explanations boost evaluations of politicians, whereas unsatisfactory explanations have damaging evaluative consequences. This begs the question of what makes for a satisfactory political explanation, and some broad generalizations exist. First, explanations that are perceived to be more common in political rhetoric are generally more satisfactory (Bennett, 1980; McGraw, 1991), in line with the general argument that the public responds more favorably to political rhetoric that is familiar (Edelman, 1988). A second principle points to the individual characteristics: all else equal, more trusting and less sophisticated citizens are more satisfied with political accounts (McGraw & Hubbard, 1996). Third, existing attitudes about the politician (Gonzalez, Kovera, Sullivan, & Chanley, 1995) or the decision to be explained (McGraw, Best, & Timpone, 1995) serve as an anchor: simply, citizens are more satisfied with explanations that are provided by politicians whom they like or for decisions that they feel positively toward. Fenno pointed to the importance of consistency between established reputations and explanatory style (1978), and laboratory evidence provides support for this intuition (McGraw, Timpone, & Bruck, 1993). Finally, at least in the political realm,[9] justifications appealing to normative principles (particularly ethical standards like fairness, moral conscience, and collective social benefits) are consistently among the most positively evaluated explanations, whereas excuses involving a diffusion of responsibility are consistently unacceptable (Chanley, Sullivan, Gonzales, & Kovera, 1994; McGraw, et al., 1995; McGraw, et al., 1993).

Political explanations are both normatively and substantively important, and there are many gaps in our understanding of their dynamics. Much of the work has focused on "explaining the vote," whereas scandal and corruption have been relatively neglected, despite the wealth of examples provided by contemporary politicians (Chanley et al., 1994, and Gonzales et al., 1995, are exceptions). There has been little attention to how explanations evolve over time, that is, how, when, and why politicians select multiple, often contradictory accounts, to explain their actions and how citizens respond to these extended explanatory chains. Virtually nothing is known about the consequences of political accounts outside the experimental laboratory. It is clear that being charged with misconduct has negative consequences for electoral support (although the decline in vote share may not be sufficient to produce defeat; Alford, Teeters, Ward, & Wilson, 1994; Jacobson & Dimock, 1994; Welch & Hibbing, 1997), but the extent to which the accompanying explanatory rhetoric mitigates these consequences is unknown. Finally, whereas we have a fair understanding of the impact of excuses and justifications, we understand much less about other types of accounts, such as denials and concessions (which often include apologies). The latter should be of particular interest, given the profusion of apologies for personal, institutional, and national wrongdoing in contemporary political discourse. Apologies in interpersonal conflicts are generally regarded as the most effective accounts, in terms of minimizing negative repercussions for the transgressing actor (Schlenker & Weigold, 1992), but the extent to which those positive benefits are manifested in the political context is very much an open question.

▶ Deception, Manipulation, and Citizens' Responses to Elites' Communications

The elite strategies just considered—self-presentation, position-taking, and explanatory rhetoric—illustrate the steps that politicians can take to effectively shape public opinion, including the impressions citizens have of them. The potency of these strategies pose few normative questions if we can safely assume that the communications put forth by politicians are truthful, that is, accurate and sincere articulations of their true selves, positions, and reasons for acting. However, for most people, politics seems almost unimaginable without some deception, and most scholars take it as a given that politicians on occasion mislead, manipulate, and deceive the public (Bok, 1989; Jamieson, 1992; Page, 1996; Page & Shapiro, 1992).

I am going to sidestep most of the very important questions surrounding the problem of manipulation and deception in politics (How much occurs? When, if ever, is it justified? Do some political situations and certain individual characteristics promote more political deception than others?) and instead focus on the one that is really the linchpin between the two topics addressed in this chapter. Namely, how do citizens respond to strategic elite communications that are potentially untrue? An assumption underlying this question is that not all political information is created equal. All information is perceived and so has potential consequences for impressions. But I am not faced with having to mull over the truthfulness of some information—the president is a white male Republican from Texas, and those facts are incontrovertible (postmodern critiques aside). In contrast, information, or signals (Jervis, 2002), that are under the control of the actor can and often do raise questions about meaning and authenticity. Signals include not only explicit persuasive communication attempts but also more subtle self-presentational strategies (e.g., clothing and other aspects of personal appearance, public behaviors, linkages to symbols). I focus on explicit communication strategies here, but the principles may be applied more generally to these broader categories of signals. Citizens might respond to an elite communication in a variety of ways: by accepting the message, suspending judgment, or systematic distortion. I briefly consider each in turn.

Passive Acceptance

Machiavelli, the high priest of political manipulation, firmly believed that the dominant response of cititzens to strategic appeals is passive acceptance. He argued in *The Prince* that the practice of hypocrisy and manipulation not only is necessary but also is easily sustained because citizens are "so simple, and so subject to present necessities, that he who seeks to deceive will always find someone who will allow himself to be deceived" (chapter 18). This characterization is echoed in understandings of contemporary citizenship: people are so distracted by "present necessities" that politics is just a "sideshow" to which they devote few resources; to the extent they do think about politics, it is done a simplistic and unprincipled manner (Converse, 1964; Dahl, 1961; Kinder, 1998; Lippmann, 1922). However, there is no necessary link between political "simple-mindedness" and acceptance of strategic communications; for this we turn to psychology. Gilbert (1991), drawing on Spinoza, has put forth the provocative argument that the first instinct of human mental systems is to believe and accept what is perceived; rejection requires a subsequent second step that takes cognitive effort that we may not be disposed to invest. Note that the point here is not that acceptance is inevitable but rather that it is the natural first reaction that is likely to persist, absent any more effortful attempt on the part of the perceiver (self-instigated or prompted by outsider sources) to subject the communication to more scrutiny.

The powerful psychological forces that contribute to acceptance of strategic messages are bolstered by liabilities in detecting deception, even when people are motivated to scrutinize for veracity. In regard to people's ability to detect deception, the literature is quite clear: we aren't very good at it, rarely demonstrating accuracy rates beyond chance levels (Friedman & Tucker, 1990). Professional "lie detectors" (for example, police officers, journalists, and college professors) have strategies that they believe are more effective in detecting deception, but all of these strategies require direct interaction between the detector and the deceiver (Kalfbleisch, 1994), which is rarely the case in political communication. Nonverbal indicators can provide modestly reliable cues to deception, but the mediated nature of much political communication renders these cues less useful, particularly if the visual medium is stripped away.

If citizens are disinclined to detect and reject deceptive communications if left to their own psychological devices, it is possible that political forces may prompt skepticism and scrutiny. Politics is adversarial, and opponents or the media may challenge the veracity or legitimacy of statements. We do not have a very good understanding of the role that these adversarial dynamics play in impression formation and the rejection of elite communications, but there are good reasons to expect that counphrcharges of "liar" and its synonyms do not occur very frequently (McGraw, 1998). Public officials recognize that political rhetoric is "heavily ritualized" (Graber, 1976, p. 12), and they share a mutual respect for that ritual, even it if means bending, shading, and distorting the truth. In addition, to declare someone a "liar" is often a no-win situation for the accuser: "conventionally, it appears that it is the challenger and not the alleged liar who has broken the stronger rule" (Robinson, 1993, p. 364). Finally, Jamieson's (2001) analysis of rhetoric on the floor of the House of Representatives indicates that explicit use of the word "liar" and its synonyms is rare, and when it does occur it is more likely to be directed toward foreign nationals, not American politicians.

Suspicion and the Suspension of Judgment

Readers may be skeptical about an argument positing blind acceptance for a citizenry increasingly characterized by deep distrust of politicians and the system. Affective reactions to political communications are an important determinant of whether blind acceptance or a more effortful cognitive reaction—specifically, suspicion—results (McGraw, Lodge, & Jones, 2002). In that study, a politician took a policy stand in circumstances strongly suggestive of pandering. Only those people who disagreed with the policy exhibited reactions indicative of more effortful cognitive processing (suspicion, heightened scrutiny of the message, and better recall) and as a consequence expressed greater uncertainty about the politician's attributes. The heightened attention and suspicion when the message was disagreeable is an instance of the more generalized tendency for increased monitoring of the political information environment under negative affective states (Marcus, Neuman, & MacKuen, 2000). In contrast to when the message was disagreeable, a favorable response to the message resulted in less scrutiny, suspicion, and uncertainty about the politician, even in a situation suggestive of pandering. These results suggest that people take things that they are prone to agree with at face value and in a totally uncritical way, even in a suspect situation. Finally, note that this tendency of people to be uncritical consumers of what they want to believe plays right into the hands of the strategically self-interested and rational politician, who is unlikely to project qualities or take issue positions that are disagreeable to large segments of their constituency.

Rejection through Systematic Distortion

Suspicion and the willingness to entertain the possibility that a message is deceptive involve a suspension of judgment, a netherworld between message acceptance and rejection. An account of the mechanisms of rejection is provided by theories of motivated reasoning—updated versions of cognitive consistency theories (Kunda, 1990, 1999; Lodge & Taber, 2000; Steenbergen, 2001; Taber & Lodge, 2000). In those accounts, the directional goal—to reach judgments that are consistent with preferred or preexisting opinions—dominates over the accuracy goal in political information processing. Accordingly, people work hard to hold on to their existing views (Festinger, 1957). One manifestation of this is the *confirmation bias*, where information that contradicts established opinions is discounted.[10] Much of the relevant empirical work has focused on the rejection of persuasive messages about policies, but Fischle (2000) provides an insightful demonstration of the mechanisms of motivated bias in evaluations of a political figure, namely, Bill Clinton during the Lewinsky scandal. It should come as absolutely no surprise to anyone who was politically sentient during that period that Clinton supporters and detractors had different reactions to the scandal. The strength of the Fischle analysis is the demonstration of the mechanisms by which Clinton loyalists maintained their support, namely by expressing uncertainty about the truth of the allegations, downplaying the importance of the scandal, and attributing the scandal to the "vast right-wing conspiracy." Other research points to active counterarguing and the construction of justifications (Kunda, 1999).

These mechanisms of motivated reasoning are important because they suggest that when people are faced with undesirable evidence, they work hard—invest cognitive resources—to undermine it. It is through this hard cognitive work that rejection of an politician's attempts at impression management is most likely to occur, but primarily among those who are predisposed to reject it. These systematic distortions of evidence contribute to "double standards" in political judgment, where people apply one set of standards for political actors they like and another set of standards for actors they dislike (recall the charges against feminists, in the late 1990s, for different reactions to the allegations of sexual harassment against Clarence Thomas [by Anita Hill] and Bill Clinton [by Paula Jones]). What is ironic is that the application of double standards is apparently most likely to occur when people invest cognitive resources to think about the problem, and particularly among those citizens who are sophisticated, involved, and interested in politics (Lodge & Taber, 2000).

I say apparently because the jury is still out. We still do not have a lot of good evidence on the extent of such motivated reasoning in political, or for that matter, social impression formation. There is a long tradition of research in social psychology that leads to the conclusion that observers have "excellent trait accuracy" (Fiske, 1992), thus working against the view that impressions are substantially biased by directional goals. However, work in that tradition has not considered the accuracy of trait perceptions in a context where strategic self-presentation may be occurring, and it is here that political psychological perspectives might be especially informative. It is possible that political trait perceptions are relatively accurate, but perceptions of other qualities, such as issue or other political positions, are subject to either blind acceptance or systematic distortion.

However, based on the extant theorizing and evidence, my conclusions about the ability of citizens to carefully scrutinize and detect deceptive signals are bleak. Two dominant pathways are suggested. In the first, people are passive receptors of information, and blind acceptance is the automatic first response (Gilbert, 1991), particularly if the communication or self-presentation is agreeable (McGraw, Lodge, and Jones, 2002). Given the assumption that rationally self-interested politicians are unlikely to project qualities or take issue positions that a majority of the public will find to be disagreeable, as well as the strategic use of "crafted talk" to bring the public in line with desired images and policy stances (Jacobs & Shapiro, 2000), this route may well prevail. According to the motivated reasoning account, people are willing and able to invest cognitive resources to scrutinize communications as to truthfulness. However, this scrutiny does not yield an evenhanded inspection of information but rather systematic distortions based on prior opinions.

◣ Concluding Comments

I suspect that readers will have mixed reactions to the literatures surveyed and arguments made in this chapter. Political psychologists and political scientists have made considerable advances within each separate topic, but our understanding of the links between impression formation and impression management strategies are very much at a fledgling stage. The "half-empty" appraisal is that we have neglected taking seriously these obviously interlinked processes for too long, and as a result reaching even the most tentative conclusions is frustrating; the "half-full" appraisal is that some of the important groundwork has been laid and there are tremendous opportunities for future research to expand on and clarify these processes. It is clear that understanding the dynamics of impression formation and impression management requires integrating affect, cognition, and motivation. Political impressions are cognitive structures consisting of a beliefs and inferences that also include overall affective evaluations that are differentially responsive to positive and negative information and that are heavily shaped by motivational considerations in their formation and modification. The impression management strategies adopted by politicians are rooted in strategic calculations linked to two motives (to sustain support and to enact good policy), both of which are largely affective in their function (that is, to be liked and to promote preferred policies); the politician's cognitive perceptions of his or her constituents, and their preferences, certainly must play a role in how impression management strategies are selected and presented. Finally, citizens' responses to potentially manipulative and deceptive communications from political elites are shaped by the three processes, as evidenced by patterns of blind acceptance of positive, agreeable communications; the investment of cognitive resources to scrutinize under some limited conditions; and systematic distortion attributable to directional goals, or motivated reasoning. There is every reason to believe that future theorizing about these phenomena will be ever more sophisticated and facile in incorporating these three processes.

If the next generation of political psychologists take seriously what is happening at the intersection of individual citizens' processes of impression formation and elite strategies of impression management, they will be well poised to contribute to the parent disciplines of political science and psychology. The issues are fundamental to both disciplines, yet neither has advanced very far in developing theories about these mechanisms. In related discussions, scholars have recently argued for integrating "internalist" accounts of individual cognitive processes with "externalist" accounts that take seriously the constraints imposed by the political context, including elite strategies and institutional mechanisms (Jackman & Sniderman, 2002; Lupia, McCubbins, & Popkin, 2000). The challenge I am putting forth here fits squarely within this emerging tradition (see also Jervis, 2002).

Finally, in addition to opportunities to contribute to theoretical understandings of the links between elites and the mass public, pursuing these questions has tremendous normative implications, most of which I have only been able to touch briefly on in this chapter. It seems clear that the behaviors and strategies of political leaders have consequences for public opinion, and "downstream" (see chapter 11) for the larger political system. The conclusions we reach about these strategies and consequences have fundamental implications for theories of politics writ large. What is the extent of deceit and manipulation in politics, how is it practiced, and how effective is it? What is the true nature of representation? How do elected officials strive to "be representative," and how do citizens respond to these attempts? More generally, how do citizens' judgments about political elites and their responses to strategic communications shape our understanding about the qualities of democratic citizenship? How are citizens' impressions about their elected officials linked to their more general feelings of trust in the political system? These are fundamental theoretical questions to which political psychologists are poised to contribute answers.

◤ Notes

1. *Impression management* is also referred to as *self-presentation*. Although often used interchangeably, these two terms can be used to characterize different processes (Schlenker & Weigold, 1992). In this chapter, I do not make a distinction between the two.

2. Although there is an implicit recognition that all three are meaningful explanatory constructs, debates have also raged in social psychology about the primacy of one of the three (e.g., cognition versus affect [Lazarus, 1999; Zajonc, 1980], and cognition versus motivation [Miller & Ross, 1975; Tetlock & Levi, 1982]. Once the dust settled, the consensus emerged that in many, if not most, applications, the three concepts are not empirically distinguishable and so the question of primacy is often unanswerable (e.g., Eagly & Chaiken, 1993; Tetlock & Levi, 1982). As Gilbert (1998) recounts in his review of one aspect of this history, "the motivation-cognition debate was never resolved in anyone's favor because no one could produce the crucial experiment that would instantly bring the other side to its knees. So after a while, the game was called on account of boredom—as well it should have been, as this was less a contest of facts than of definitions" (p. 124). In other words, one scholar's measure of "cognition" is all too often another's measure of "motivation" or "affect." Hopefully, political psychologists will learn from this futile history and not invest too much (or any) energy in trying to prove "affect/cognition/motivation" is primary.

3. Accordingly, I do not take into account the types of motivations linked to more basic personality mechanisms that have informed some political psychological investigations of political leaders (e.g., Lasswell, 1948; see chapter 4 for a discussion).

4. Of course, these are comparable to the categories evident from the analyses of Converse (1964) and *The American Voter* (Campbell, Converse, Miller, & Stokes, 1960). The use of the open-ended "like/dislike" NES questions represents just one technique for measuring the content of political memory, and these questions can be problematic for making these inferences. However, the basic categories identified by Miller, Wattenberg, and Malanchuk (1986) are also evident using other methods to elicit the content of political impressions, although the relative prevalence of the various categories is contingent on how memory is "probed" (McGraw, Fischle, & Stenner, 2000).

5. The existence of a negativity bias in impression formation does not preclude the existence of a *positivity bias*, as the two biases refer to distinct phenomena. Whereas the negativity bias refers to the greater impact of negative rather than positive information on opinions, the "positivity bias" refers to the persistent finding that politicians are evaluated favorably (e.g., above the midpoint of evaluative scales; Lau, Sears, & Centers, 1979; Sears, 1983), even when the individual knows nothing about the politician (Holbrook et al., 2001; although see Blais, Nevitte, Gidengil, & Nadeau, 2000, for contradictory findings).

6. This conclusion may appear to contradict the well-known finding that the public policy opinions of more sophisticated citizens exhibit more constraint (Converse, 1964; Judd, Krosnick, & Milburn, 1981), but the conclusions diverge across the two judgment domains and are characterized by very different methodologies. In the realm of impressions of political candidates, evaluative organization (as indexed by separate clusters for positively and negatively evaluated attributes in recall) occurs more frequently among less sophisticated individuals; the more sophisticated organize their impressions instead along substantive content domains. In contrast, in the domain of policy preferences, constraint is indexed by correlations in policy agreement among policies that logically go together (i.e., from the perspective of ideology); these policy agreement correlations are more substantial for more sophisticated individuals.

7. On-line and memory-based processing models have been applied to the formation of opinions about policy preferences and candidates. I limit this discussion of moderators to the latter.

8. The specific mechanisms by which these attributes are conveyed varies as a function of contextual (district), personal, and strategic considerations; the core of *Home Style* is concerned with understanding how these factors shape individual representatives' self-presentation styles.

9. This conclusion is limited to the political realm, because the evidence as to which general types of accounts are more or less effective outside of politics varies by context (e.g., interpersonal, legal, organizational; Cody & McLaughlin, 1990).

10. A second possibility is what Steenbergen (2001) has labeled a *conservatism bias*, where prior beliefs are modified, but insufficiently, in the light of new information. Both the confirmation bias and the conservatism bias have implications for the descriptive accuracy of Bayesian models of political decision making (Gerber & Green, 1999; see Steenbergen, 2001, for a particularly enlightening discussion).

◤ References

Alford, J., Teeters, H., Ward, D. S., & Wilson, R. K. (1994). Overdraft: The political cost of congressional malfeasance. *Journal of Politics, 56,* 788–801.

Allport, G. (1954). *The nature of prejudice*. Reading, MA: Addison-Wesley.

Alvarez, R. M. (1997). *Information and elections*. Ann Arbor: University of Michigan Press.

Alvarez, R. M. & Brehm, J. (1995). American ambivalence towards abortion policy: Development of a heteroskedastic probit model of competing values. *American Journal of Political Science, 39*, 1055–1082.

Alvarez, R. M. & Brehm, J. (1997). Are Americans ambivalent towards racial policies? *American Journal of Political Science, 41*, 345–374.

Alvarez, R. M., & Brehm, J. (1998). Speaking in two voices: American equivocation about the Internal Revenue Service. *American Journal of Political Science, 42*, 418–452.

Asch, S. E. (1946). Forming impressions of personality. *Journal of Abnormal and Social Psychology, 41*, 1230–1240.

Austen-Smith, D. (1992). Explaining the vote: Constituency constraints on sophisticated voting. *American Journal of Political Science, 31*, 68–95.

Barone, M. (1997). Polls are part of the air politicians breathe. *The Public Perspective, 8*, 1–2.

Barber, J. D. (1972). *The presidential character*. Englewood Cliffs, NJ: Prentice-Hall.

Bennett, W. L. (1980). The paradox of public discourse: A framework for the analysis of political accounts. *Journal of Politics, 42*, 792–817.

Bianco, W. T. (1994). *Trust: Representatives and constituents*. Ann Arbor: University of Michigan Press.

Blais, A., Nevitte, N., Gidengil, E., & Nadeau, R. (2000). Do people have feelings toward leaders about whom they say they know nothing? *Public Opinion Quarterly, 64*, 452–463.

Bok, S. (1989). *Lying: Moral choice in public and private life*. New York: Vintage Books.

Campbell, A., Converse, P., Miller, W., & Stokes, D. (1960). *The American voter*. New York: Wiley.

Chaiken, S. (1986). Physical appearance and social influence. In C. P. Herman, M. P. Zanna, & E. T. Higgins (Eds.), *Physical appearance, stigma, and social behavior: The Ontario symposium* (Vol. 3, pp. 143–177). Hillsdale, NJ: Erlbaum.

Chanley, V., Sullivan, J. L., Gonzales, M. H., & Kovera, M. B. (1994). Lust and avarice in politics: Damage control by four politicians accused of wrongdoing (or, politics as usual). *American Politics Quarterly, 22*, 297–333.

Citrin, J., Green, D. P., & Sears, D. O. 1990. White reactions to black candidates: When does race matter? *Public Opinion Quarterly, 54*, 74–96.

Cody, J. J., & McLaughlin, M. L. (1990). Interpersonal accounting. In H. Giles & W. P. Robinson (Eds.), *Handbook of language and social psychology*. New York: Wiley.

Colleau, S. M., Glynn, K., Lybrand, S., Merelman, R. M., Mohan, P., & Wall, J. E. (1990). Symbolic racism in candidate evaluation: An experiment. *Political Behavior, 12*, 385–402.

Converse, P. E. (1964). The nature of belief systems in mass publics. In D. E Apter (Ed.), *Ideology and discontent*. London: Collier-Macmillan.

Dahl, R. A. (1961). *Who governs? Democracy and power in an American city*. New Haven: Yale University Press.

Darley, J. M., & Gross, P. H. (1983). A hypothesis-confirming bias in labeling effects. *Journal of Personality and Social Psychology, 44*, 20–33.

Davis, R. (1999). *The web of politics: The Internet's impact on the American political system.* New York: Oxford University Press.

Devine, P. (1989). Stereotypes and prejudice: Their automatic and controlled components. *Journal of Personality and Social Psychology, 56,* 5–18.

Dowd, M. (1997, January 12). Leaders as followers. *New York Times.* Section 4, p. 17.

Downs, A. (1957). *An economic theory of democracy.* New York: Harper and Row.

Eagly, A, H., & Chaiken, S. (1993). *The psychology of attitudes.* Fort Worth, TX: Harcourt Brace Jovanovich.

Edelman, M. (1988). *Political language: Words that succeed and policies that fail.* New York: Academic Press.

Enelow, J. & Hinich, M. J. (1984). *The spatial theory of voting.* New York: Cambridge University Press.

Feldman, S., & Conover, P. J. (1983). Candidates, issues and voters: The role of inference in political perception. *Journal of Politics, 45,* 810–839.

Fenno, R. E. (1973). *Congressmen in committees.* Boston: Little, Brown.

Fenno, R. E. (1977). U.S. House members in their constituencies: An exploration. *American Political Science Review, 71,* 883–917.

Fenno, R. E. (1978). *Home style: House members in their districts.* Boston, MA: Little, Brown.

Festinger, L. (1957). *A theory of cognitive dissonance.* Stanford, CA: Stanford University Press.

Fischle, M. (2000). Mass response to the Lewinsky scandal: Motivated reasoning or Bayesian updating? *Political Psychology, 21,* 135–159.

Fiske, S. T. (1986). Schema-based versus piecemeal politics: A patchwork quilt, but not a blanket, of evidence. In R. R. Lau & D. O. Sears (Eds.), *Political cognition: The nineteenth Annual Carnegie Symposium on Cognition.* Hillsdale, NJ: Erlbaum.

Fiske, S. T. (1992). Thinking is for doing: Portraits of social cognition from daguerreotype to laserphoto. *Journal of Personality and Social Psychology, 63,* 877–889.

Fiske, S. T. (1998). Stereotyping, prejudice, and discrimination. In D. T. Gilbert, S. T. Fiske, & G. Lindzey (Eds.), *The handbook of social psychology* (4th ed., vol. 2, pp. 357–411). New York: McGraw-Hill.

Fiske, S. T., & Neuberg, S. L. (1990). A continuum model of impression formation: From category-based to individuating processes as a function of information, motivation, and attention. In M. P. Zanna (Ed.), *Advances in experimental psychology* (Vol. 23, pp. 1–108). San Diego, CA: Academic Press.

Fiske, S. T., & Taylor, S. E. (1991). *Social cognition* (2nd ed.). New York: McGraw-Hill.

Franklin, C. (1991). Eschewing obfuscation? Campaigns and the perception of U.S. Senate incumbents. *American Political Science Review, 85,* 1193–1214.

Friedman, H. S., & Tucker, J. S. (1990). Language and deception. In H. Giles & W. P. Robinson (Eds.), *Handbook of language and social psychology.* New York: Wiley.

Funk, C. L. (1996, a). Understanding trait inferences in candidate images. In M. X. Delli Carpini, L. Huddy, & R. Y. Shapiro (Eds.), *Research in micropolitics* (Vol. 5, pp. 97–123). Greenwich, CT: JAI Press.

Funk, C. L. (1996, b). The impact of scandal on candidate evaluations: An experimental test of the role of candidate traits. *Political Behavior, 18,* 1–24.

Funk, C. (1999). Bringing the candidate into models of candidate evaluation. *Journal of Politics, 61,* 700–720.

Geer, J. G. (1996). *From tea leaves to opinion polls.* New York: Columbia University Press.

Gerber, A., & Green, D. R. (1999). Misperceptions about perceptual bias. *Annual Review of Political Science, 2,* 189–210.

Gilbert, D. T. (1989). Thinking lightly about others: Automatic components of the social inference process. In J. S. Uleman & J. A. Bargh (Eds.), *Unintended thought.* New York: The Guilford Press.

Gilbert, D. T. (1991). How ordinary mental systems behave. *American Psychologist, 46,* 107–119.

Gilbert, D. T. (1998). Ordinary personology. In D. T. Gilbert, S. T. Fiske, & G. Lindzey (Eds.), *The handbook of social psychology* (4th ed., Vol. 2, pp. 89–150). New York: McGraw-Hill.

Glasgow, G., & Alvarez, R. M. (2000). Uncertainty and candidate personality traits. *American Politics Quarterly, 28,* 26–49.

Goffman, E. (1971). *Relations in public: microstudies of the public order.* New York: Basic Books.

Gonzales, M. H., Kovera, M. B., Sullivan, J. L., & Chanley, V. (1995). Private reactions to public transgressions: Predictors of evaluative responses to allegations of political misconduct. *Personality and Social Psychology Bulletin, 21,* 136–148.

Graber, D. A. (1976). *Verbal behavior and politics.* Urbana: University of Illinois Press.

Hamill, R., Lodge, M., & Blake, F. (1985). The breadth, depth, and utility of class, partisan, and ideological schemata. *American Journal of Political Science, 29,* 850–870.

Hastie, R., & Park, B. (1986). The relationship between memory and judgment depneds on whether the task is memory-based or on-line. *Psychological Review, 93,* 258–268.

Hastie, R., & Pennington, N. (1989). Notes on the distinction between memory-based versus on-line judgments. In J. M. Bassili (Ed.), *On-line cognition in person perception.* Hillsdale, NJ: Erlbaum.

Heider, F. (1958). *The psychology of interpersonal relations.* New York: Wiley.

Holbrook, A. L., Krosnick, J. A., Visser, P. S., Gardner, W. L., & Cacioppo, J. T. (2001). Attitudes toward presidential candidates and political parties: Initial optimism, inertial first impressions, and a focus on flaws. *American Journal of Political Science, 45,* 930–950.

Huckfeldt, R., & Sprague, J. (1998, July). Sources of ambivalence in public opinion: The certainty and accessibility of abortion attitudes. Paper presented at the annual meeting of the International Society of Political Psychology. Montreal, Canada.

Huddy, L. (1994). The political significance of voters' gender stereotypes. In M. X. Delli Carpini, L. Huddy, & R. Y. Shapiro (Eds.), *Research in micropolitics* (Vol. 4, pp. 169–196). Greenwich, CT: JAI Press.

Huddy, L., & Capelos, T. (2002). Gender stereotyping and candidate evaluation: Good news and bad news for women politicians. In V. C. Ottati, R. S. Tindale, J. Edwards, F. B. Bryant, L. Heath, D. C. O'Connell, Y. Suarez-Balcazar, & E. J. Posavac (Eds.), *The social psychology of politics* (pp. 29–53). New York: Kluwer Academic/Plenum Publishers.

Huddy, L., & Terkildsen, N. (1993). Gender stereotypes and the perception of male and female candidates. *American Journal of Political Science, 37,* 119–147.

Hurwitz, J., & Peffley, M. (1997). Public perceptions of race and crime: The role of racial stereotypes. *American Journal of Political Science, 41,* 375–401.

Jackman, S., & Sniderman, P. M. (2002). Institutional organization of choice spaces: A political conception of political psychology. In K. M. Monroe (Ed.), *Political psychology* (pp. 209–224). Mahwah, NJ: Erlbaum.

Jacobs, J. R., & Shapiro, R. Y. (1994). Issues, candidate image, and priming: The use of private polls in Kennedy's 1960 presidential campaign. *American Political Science Review, 88,* 527–540.

Jacobs, L. R., & Shapiro, R. Y. (2000). *Politicians don't pander: Political manipulation and the loss of democratic responsiveness.* Chicago: University of Chicago Press.

Jacobson, G., & Dimock, M. A. (1994). Checking out: The effects of bank overdrafts on the 1992 House elections. *American Journal of Political Science, 38,* 601–624.

Jamieson, K. H. (1992). *Dirty politics: Deception, distraction, and democracy.* New York: Oxford University Press.

Jamieson, K. H. (2001). *Civility in the House of Representatives: The 106th Congress.* Annenberg Public Policy Center of the University of Pennsylvania. Philadelphia, PA.

Jervis, R. (2002). Signaling and perception: Drawing inferences and projecting images. In K. R. Monroe (Ed.), *Political psychology* (pp. 293–312). Mahwah, NJ: Erlbaum.

Jones, E. E., & Davis, K. E. (1965). From acts to dispositions: The attribution process in person perception. In L. Berkowitz (Ed.), *Advances in experimental social psychology* (Vol. 2, pp. 219–266). New York: Academic Press.

Judd, C. M., Krosnick, J. A., & Milburn, M. A. (1981). Political involvement and attitude structure in the general public. *American Sociological Review, 46,* 660–669.

Judd, C. M., Park, B., Ryan, C. S., Brauer, M., & Kraus, S. (1995). Stereotypes and ethnocentrism: Diverging interethnic perceptions of African-American and white urban youth. *Journal of Personality and Social Psychology, 69,* 460–481.

Kahn, K. F. (1992). Does being male help? An investigation of the effects of candidate gender and campaign coverage on evaluations of U.S. Senate candidates. *Journal of Politics, 54,* 497–517.

Kahn, K. F. (1996). *The political consequences of being a woman: How stereotypes influence the conduct and consequences of political campaigns.* New York: Columbia University Press.

Kalfbleisch, P. J. (1994). The language of detecting deceit. *Journal of Language and Social Psychology, 13,* 469–496.

Katz, D., & Braly, K. W. (1933). Racial stereotypes of 100 college students. *Journal of Abnormal and Social Psychology, 28,* 180–290.

Keating, C. F., Randall, D., & Kendrick, T. (1999). Presidential physiognomies: Altered images, altered perceptions. *Political Psychology, 20,* 593–610.

Kernell, S. (1997). *Going public: New strategies of presidential leadership.* Washington, DC: CQ Press.

Key, V. O. 1958. *Politics, parties, and pressure groups* (4th ed.) New York: Crowell.

Kinder, D. R. (1986). Presidential character revisited. In R. R. Lau and D. O. Sears

(Eds.), *Political cognition: The nineteenth Annual Carnegie Symposium on Cognition.* Hillsdale, NJ: Lawrence Erlbaum.

Kinder, D. R. (1998). Opinion and action in the realm of politics. In D. T. Gilbert, S. T. Fiske, & G. Lindzey (Eds.), *The handbook of social psychology* (4th ed., vol. 2, pp. 778–867). New York: McGraw-Hill.

Kingdon, J. W. (1973). *Congressmen's voting decisions.* New York: Harper and Row.

Klein, J. G. (1991). Negativity effects in impression formation: A test in the political arena. *Personality and Social Psychology Bulletin, 17,* 412–418.

Klein, J. G. (1996). Negativity in impressions of presidential candidates revisited: The 1992 election. *Personality and Social Psychology Bulletin, 22,* 288–295.

Koch, J. W. (2000). Do citizens' apply gender stereotypes to infer candidates' ideological orientations? *Journal of Politics, 62,* 414–429.

Krosnick, J. A., & McGraw, K. M. (2002). Psychological political science v. political psychology 'true to its name:' A plea for balance. In K. R. Monroe (Ed.), *Political psychology* (pp. 79–94). Mahwah, NJ: Erlbaum.

Kunda, Z. (1990). The case for motivated reasoning. *Psychological Bulletin, 108,* 480–498.

Kunda, Z. (1999). *Social cognition: Making sense of people.* Cambridge, MA: MIT Press.

Lane, R. E. (1986). What are people trying to do with their schemata? The question of purpose. In R. R. Lau & D. O. Sears (Eds.), *Political cognition: The nineteenth Annual Carnegie Symposium on Cognition.* Hillsdale, NJ: Erlbaum.

Lasswell, H. D. (1948). *Power and personality.* New York: Norton.

Lau, R. R. (1982). Negativity in political perception. *Political Behavior, 4,* 353–377.

Lau, R. R. (1985). Two explanations for negativity effects in political behavior. *American Journal of Political Science, 29,* 119–138.

Lau, R. R. (1990). Political motivation and political cognition. In E. T. Higgins & R. M. Sorrentino (Eds.), *Handbook of motivation and cognition: Foundations of social behavior.* (Vol. 2). New York: Guilford Press.

Lau, R. R. (1995). Information search during an election campaign: Introducing a process-tracing methodology for political scientists. In M. Lodge & K. M. McGraw (Eds.), *Political judgment: Structure and process.* Ann Arbor: University of Michigan Press.

Lau, R. R., & Redlawsk, D. P. (1997). Voting correctly. *American Political Science Review, 91,* 585–598.

Lau, R. R., & Redlawsk, D. P. (2001). Advantages and disadvantages in using cognitive heuristics in political decision making. *American Journal of Political Science, 45,* 951–971.

Lau, R. R., Sears, D. O., & Centers, R. (1979). The "positivity bias" in evaluations of public figures: Evidence against instrument artifacts. *Public Opinion Quarterly, 43,* 347–358.

Lavine, H. (2001). The electoral consequences of ambivalence toward presidential candidates. *American Journal of Political Science, 45,* 915–929.

Lavine, H. (2002). On-line versus memory-based process models of candidate evaluation. In K. R. Monroe (Ed.), *Political psychology* (pp. 225–247). Mahwah, NJ: Erlbaum.

Lazarus, R. S. (1999). *Stress and emotion: A new synthesis.* New York: Springer.

Lippmann, W. (1922). *Public opinion.* New York: Macmillan.

Lippmann, W. (1955). *Essays in the public philosophy*. Boston: Little, Brown.

Lodge, M. (1995). Towards a procedural theory of candidate evaluation. In M. Lodge & K. M. McGraw (Eds.), *Political judgment: Structure and process* (pp. 111–140). Ann Arbor: University of Michigan Press.

Lodge, M., & Hamill, R. (1986). A partisan schema for political information processing. *American Political Science Review, 80*, 505–519.

Lodge, M., & McGraw, K. M. (Eds.) (1995). *Political judgment: Structure and process*. Ann Arbor: University of Michigan Press.

Lodge, M., McGraw, K. M., & Stroh. P. (1989). An impression-driven model of candidate evaluation. *American Political Science Review, 83*, 399–420.

Lodge, M., & Steenbergen, M., with Brau, S. (1995). The responsive voter: Campaign information and the dynamics of candidate evaluation. *American Political Science Review, 89*, 309–326.

Lodge, M., & Taber, C. (2000). Three steps toward a theory of motivated reasoning. In A. Lupia, M. D. McCubbins, & S. L. Popkin (Eds.), *Elements of reason: Cognition, choice, and the bounds of rationality* (pp. 183–213). New York: Cambridge University Press.

Lupia, A., McCubbins, M. D., & Popkin, S. L. (2000). *Elements of reason: Cognition, choice, and the bounds of rationality*. New York: Cambridge University Press.

Marcus, G. E., Neuman, W. R., & MacKuen, M. (2000). *Affective intelligence and political judgment*. Chicago: University of Chicago Press.

Markus, G. B. (1982). Political attitudes during an election year: A report on the 1980 NES Panel Study. *American Political Science Review, 76*, 538–560.

Mayhew, D. (1974). *Congress: The electoral connection*. New Haven: Yale University Press.

McConnell, A. R. (2001). Implicit theories: Consequences for social judgments of individuals. *Journal of Experimental Social Psychology, 37*, 215–227.

McGraw, K. M. (1991). Managing blame: An experimental investigation into the effectiveness of political accounts. *American Political Science Review, 85*,1133–1158.

McGraw, K. M. (1998). Manipulating public opinion with moral justification. *Annals, AAPSS, 560*, 129–142.

McGraw, K. M. (2000). Contributions of the cognitive approach to political psychology. *Political Psychology, 21*, 805–832.

McGraw, K. M. (2001). Political accounts and attribution processes. In J. H. Kuklinski (Ed.), *Citizens and politics: Perspectives from political psychology* (pp. 160–197). New York: Cambridge University Press.

McGraw, K. M. (2002). Manipulating public opinion. In B. Norrander & C. Wilcox (Eds.), *Understanding public opinion*. Washington, DC: CQ Press.

McGraw, K. M., Anderson, W., & Willey, E. (2000, April). *The E-Connection: House members' use of the internet to explain impeachment votes*. Paper presented at the annual meeting of the Midwest Political Science Association. Chicago, IL.

McGraw, K. M., Best, S., & Timpone. R. (1995). What they say or what they do? The impact of elite explanation and policy outcomes on public opinion. *American Journal of Political Science, 39*, 53–74.

McGraw, K. M., Fischle, M., & Stenner, K. (2000). *What citizens "know" depends on how they are asked*. Unpublished manuscript.

McGraw, K. M., Fischle, M., Stenner, K., & Lodge, M. (1996). What's in a word? Bias in trait attributions of political leaders. *Political Behavior, 18,* 263–281.

McGraw, K. M., Hasecke, E., & Conger, K. (In press). Ambivalence, uncertainty and processes of candidate evaluation. *Political Psychology.*

McGraw, K. M., & Hubbard, C. (1996). Some of the people some of the time: Individual differences in acceptance of political accounts. In D. C. Mutz, P. M. Sniderman, & R. Brody (Eds.), *Political persuasion and attitude change.* Ann Arbor: University of Michigan Press.

McGraw, K. M., Lodge, M., & Jones, J. (2002). The pandering politicians of suspicious minds. *Journal of Politics, 64,* 362–383.

McGraw, K. M., Lodge, M., & Stroh, P. (1990). On-line processing in candidate evaluation: The effects of issue order, issue salience and sophistication. *Political Behavior, 12,* 41–58.

McGraw, K. M., Pinney, N., & Neumann, D. (1991). Memory for political actors: Contrasting the use of semantic and evaluative organizational strategies. *Political Behavior, 13,* 165–189.

McGraw, K. M., & Steenbergen, M. (1995). Pictures in the head: Memory representations of political actors. In M. Lodge & K. M. McGraw (Eds.), *Political judgment: Structure and process.* Ann Arbor: University of Michigan Press.

McGraw, K. M., Timpone, R., & Bruck, G. (1993). Justifying controversial political decisions: *Home Style* in the laboratory. *Political Behavior, 15,* 289–308.

Meffert, M., Guge, M., & Lodge, M. (in press). Good, bad, indifferent, and ambivalent: The consequences of multidimensional political attitudes. In P. Neijens & W. Saris (Eds.), *Real opinions, real change.* Princeton: Princeton University Press.

Miller, A. H., Wattenberg, M. P., & Malanchuk, O. (1986). Schematic assessments of presidential candidates. *American Political Science Review, 79,* 359–372.

Miller, D. T., & Ross, M. (1975). Self-serving biases in the attribution of causality: Fact or fiction. *Psychological Bulletin, 82,* 213–225.

Moskowitz, D., & Stroh, P. (1994). Psychological sources of electoral racism. *Political Psychology, 15,* 307–329.

Page, B. I. (1976). The theory of political ambiguity. *American Political Science Review, 70,* 742–752.

Page, B. I. (1978). *Choices and echoes in presidential elections.* Chicago: University of Chicago Press.

Page, B. I. (1996). *Who deliberates? Mass media in modern democracy.* Chicago: University of Chicago Press.

Page, B. & Brody, R. (1972). Policy voting and the electoral process: The Vietnam War issue. *American Political Science Review, 66,* 979–995.

Page, B. I., & Shapiro, R. Y. (1992). *The rational public: Fifty years of trends in Americans' policy preferences.* Chicago: University of Chicago Press.

Park, B. (1986). A method for studying the development of impressions of real people. *Journal of Personality and Social Psychology, 51,* 907–917.

Park, B. (1989). Trait attributes as on-line organizers in person impressions. In J. N. Bassili (Ed.), *On-line cognition in person perception* (pp. 39–59). Hillsdale, NJ: Erlbaum.

Patterson, S. C., Hedlund, R. D., & Boynton, G. R. (1975). *Representatives and represented: Bases of public support for the American legislature.* New York: Wiley.

Peffley, M., Hurwitz, J., & Sniderman, P. M. (1997). Racial stereotypes and whites' political views of blacks in the context of welfare and crime. *American Journal of Political Science, 41,* 30–60.

Pitkin, H. F. (1967). *The concept of representation.* Berkeley: University of California Press.

Rahn, W. M. (1993). The role of partisan stereotypes in information processing about political candidates. *American Journal of Political Science, 37,* 472–496.

Rahn, W. M. (1995). Candidate evaluation in complex information environments: Cognitive organization and comparison processes. In M. Lodge & K. M. McGraw (Eds.), *Political judgment: Structure and process* (pp. 43–64). Ann Arbor: University of Michigan Press.

Rahn, W. M. (2000). Affect as information: The role of public mood in political reasoning. In A. Lupia, M. McCubbins, & S. Popkin (Eds.), *Elements of reason* (pp. 130–150). New York: Cambridge University Press.

Rahn, W. M., Aldrich, J. H., & Borgida, E. (1994). Individual and contextual variations in political candidate appraisal. *American Political Science Review, 88,* 193–199.

Rahn, W. M., Aldrich, J. H., Borgida, E., & Sullivan J. L. (1990). A social cognitive model of candidate appraisal. In J. A. Ferejohn & J. H. Kuklinski (Eds.), *Information and democratic processes* (pp. 136–159). Urbana: University of Illinois Press.

Rapoport, R. B., Metcalf, K. L., & Hartman, J. A. (1989). Candidate traits and voter inferences: An experimental study. *Journal of Politics, 51,* 917–932.

Redlawsk, D. (2001). You must remember this: A test of the on-line model of voting. *Journal of Politics, 63,* 29–58.

Riggle, E. D., Ottati, V. C., Wyer, R. S., Kuklinski, J. H., & Schwarz, N. (1992). Bases of political judgments: The role of stereotypic and nonstereotypic judgment. *Political Behavior, 14,* 67–87.

Rivers, D., & Fiorina, M. P. (1991). Constituency service, reputation, and the incumbency advantage. In M. P. Fiorina & D. W. Rohde (Eds.), *Home style and Washington work: Studies of congressional politics* (pp. 17–46). Ann Arbor: University of Michigan Press.

Robinson, W. P. (1993). Lying in the public domain. *American Behavioral Scientist, 36,* 359–382.

Rosenberg, S. W., Bohan, L., McCafferty, P., & Harris, K. (1986). The image and the vote: The effect of candidate presentation on voter preference. *American Journal of Political Science, 30,* 108–127.

Rosenwasser, S. M., & Seale, J. (1988). Attitudes toward a hypothetical male or female presidential candidate: A research note. *Political Psychology, 9,* 591–598.

Sanbonmatsu, K. (2002). Gender stereotypes and vote choice. *American Journal of Political Science, 46,* 20–34.

Sapiro, V. 1983. *The political integration of women: Roles, socialization and politics.* Urbana: University of Illinois Press.

Schlenker, B. R. 1980. *Impression management.* Monterey, CA: Brooks/Cole.

Schlenker, B. R., & Weigold, M. F. (1992). Interpersonal processes involving impression regulation and impression management. *Annual Review of Psychology 43,* 133–168.

Sears, D. O. (1983). The person-positivity bias. *Journal of Personality and Social Psychology, 44,* 233–240.

Shepsle, K. (1972). The strategy of ambiguity: Uncertainty and electoral competition. *American Political Science Review, 66,* 555–68.

Sigelman, L., Sigelman, C. K., & Fowler, C. (1987). A bird of a different feather? An experimental investigation of physical attractiveness and the electability of female candidates. *Social Psychological Quarterly, 50,* 32–43.

Sigelman, L., Sigelman, C. K., & Walkosz, B. (1992). The public and the paradox of leadership: An experimental analysis. *American Journal of Political Science, 36,* 366–385.

Sigelman, L., Sigelman, C. K., Walkosz, N., & Nitz, M. (1995). Black candidates, white voters: Understanding racial bias in political perceptions. *American Journal of Political Science, 39,* 243–265.

Simonton, D. K. (1986). Presidential personality: Biographical use of the Gough Adjective Check List. *Journal of Personality and Social Psychology, 51,* 149–160.

Skowronski, J. J., & Carlston, D. E. (1989). Negativity and extremity biases in impression formation: A review of explanations. *Psychological Bulletin, 105,* 131–142.

Smith, S. S., & Deering, C. J. (1990). *Committees in Congress.* Washington, DC: CQ Press.

Sniderman, P. M., Brody, R. A., & Tetlock, P. E. (1991). *Reasoning and choice: Explorations in political psychology.* New York: Cambridge University Press.

Steenbergen, M. (2001, July). *The Reverend Bayes meets John Q. Public: Patterns of belief updating in citizens.* Paper presented at the annual meeting of the International Society of Political Psychology. Cuernavaca, MX

Steenbergen, M., & Brewer, P. (in press). The not-so-ambivalent public. In P. Neijens & W. Saris (Eds.), *Real opinions, real change.* Princeton: Princeton University Press.

Steenbergen, M., Wolak, J., & Kilburn, W. (2001, April). Affective moderators of on-line and memory-based processing in candidate evaluation. Paper presented at the annual meeting of the midwest Political Science Association. Chicago, IL

Stimson, J. A., MacKuen, M. B., & Erikson, R. S. (1995). Dynamic representation. *American Political Science Review, 89,* 543–565.

Stogdill, R. (1948). Personal factors associated with leadership. *Journal of Psychology, 25,* 35–71.

Taber, C., & Lodge, M. (2000). *Motivated skepticism in the evaluation of political beliefs.* Manuscript submitted for publication.

Terkildsen, N. (1993). When white voters evaluate black candidates: The processing implications of candidate skin color, prejudice, and self-monitoring. *American Journal of Political Science, 37,* 1032–1053.

Tetlock, P., & Levi, A. (1982). Attribution bias: On the inconclusiveness of the cognition-motivation debate. *Journal of Experimental Social Psychology, 18,* 68–88.

Tormala, Z., & Petty, R. E. (2001). On-line versus memory-based processing: The role of "need to evaluate" in person perception. *Personality and Social Psychology Bulletin, 27,* 1599–1612.

Uleman, J. S., Hon, A., Roman, R. J., & Moskowitz, G. B. (1996). On-line evidence for spontaneous trait inferences at encoding. *Personality & Social Psychology Bulletin, 22,* 377–394.

Weaver, R. K. (1986). The politics of blame avoidance. *Journal of Public Policy, 6,* 371–398.

Weaver, R. K. (1988). *Automatic government: The politics of indexation.* Washington, DC: Brookings Institution.

Weisberg, H., & Hill, T. (2001). *The succession presidential election of 2000: The battle of legacies.* Paper presented at the Conference on the 2000 Elections, The Ohio State University, Columbus, OH.

Welch, S., & Hibbing, J. R. (1997). The effects of charges in corruption on voting behavior in Congressional elections, 1982–1990. *Journal of Politics, 59,* 226–239.

Willey, E. (2002). *Explaining the vote: Claiming credit and managing blame in the United States Senate.* Unpublished doctoral dissertation, Ohio State University. Columbus, OH.

Williams, L. F. (1990). White/black perceptions of the electability of black political candidates. *National Political Science Review, 2,* 145–164.

Zajonc, R. (1980). Feeling and thinking: Preferences need no inferences. *American Psychologist, 35,* 151–175.

Zaller, J. R. (1992). *The nature and origins of mass opinion.* New York: Cambridge University Press.

Zaller, J. R., & Feldman, S. (1992). A simple theory of the survey response: Answering questions versus revealing preferences. *American Journal of Political Science, 36,* 579–616.

Zebrowitz, L. A. (1994). Facial maturity and political prospects: Persuasive, culpable, and powerful faces. In R. C. Schank & E. Langer (Eds.), *Beliefs, reasoning, and decision making: Psych-logic in honor of Bob Abelson* (pp. 315–345). Hillsdale, NJ: Erlbaum.

13 Charles S. Taber

Information Processing and Public Opinion

I have opinions of my own—strong opinions—but I don't always agree with them.

—George Herbert Walker Bush

"Democracy," quipped H. L. Mencken a half-century ago (1949), "is the art and science of running the circus from the monkey-cage" (p. 622). Elephants and donkeys may be only marginally better prepared to govern, as the epigraph might suggest, but a central question of political theorists, commentators, and scholars has been whether the monkeys are up to the task. Most often, the answer has been no. One may lament the lack of interest in politics, the ignorance, the undemocratic values, and the unsophistication of average citizens, but these defects seem difficult to deny, at least in the American public. Yet, two and a quarter centuries later, the American experiment with democracy persists. Tyranny has not replaced republicanism, and democracy has not committed suicide, as John Adams feared it would. Moreover, the monkeys still run the circus, and that circus, despite its many problems, is now the envy of carnivals around the world! This paradox—apparently dysfunctional citizens who compose an apparently functional public—comes into sharp relief when one examines the empirical findings and theoretical debates of public opinion research over the past half-century.

My task in this chapter is to review modern public opinion research from an information-processing perspective. The tour will be neither comprehensive nor particularly representative of the public opinion field as a whole. I will adopt a quite microscopic focus, which I recognize may disconcert those who prefer a more panoramic lens. Of course, there is nothing new in viewing public opinion from an individualistic perspective; the influence of social psychology on the development of the field is readily apparent. What may be new, however, is the intimacy of the affair with psychology and the growing concern with mental process (see Kinder, 1998; Kuklinski & Quirk, 2000; Lavine, 2002; Lodge & McGraw, 1995; McGraw, 2000; Sniderman, 1993; Steenbergen & Lodge, n.d.; Sullivan & Rahn, 2002). To an increasing extent, political psychologists and social psychologists use a common language to address an overlapping set of research questions. Citations to Philip Converse run seven lines in the index of the recent *Handbook of Social Psychology* (Gilbert, Fiske, & Lindzey, 1998), and one can find reference to such social psychologists as Susan Fiske or Russell

Fazio in the *American Political Science Review*.[1] A surprising number of social psychologists now affiliate with and even draw paychecks from political science departments (McGraw, 2000), leading to an even more intimate exchange of ideas. Social psychology, moreover, has changed substantially over the period in question. Much of the recent work in public opinion that I will discuss draws theoretical inspiration at least partly from *social cognition* research, a relatively new development in social psychology that itself has borrowed its theoretical framework from cognitive psychology.

Several important areas of research on public opinion and information processing are taken up in other chapters of this book: Kathleen McGraw discusses impression formation and candidate evaluation; Richard Lau looks at decision-making more generally; Donald Kinder considers the elite management of the information environment, including the influence of the mass media; Stanley Feldman reviews the structure and stability of values and political culture; Leonie Huddy social identity; John Duckitt stereotypes and prejudice; George Markus emotion. I will strive not to trespass too much on these topics, but the world we analyze into conceptual categories is in fact seamless, and occasional poaching will be unavoidable. On the other hand, any overlap that does occur will surely be useful in offering positive contact among our individual efforts.

The chapter will proceed as follows. In the next section, I attempt to come to grips with the role of "citizen in a democracy" and the importance of "public opinion" in understanding that role. I then embark on a theoretical and historical discussion of "the information-processing perspective" and the influence of the cognitive revolution on public opinion research. Finally, at the end of the chapter I return to the normative and empirical questions raised in the opening paragraph concerning the "paradox of the dysfunctional citizen" and consider a number of solutions that have been proposed. Indeed, given the overwhelming inertia of decades of research supporting the notion of minimalism—"that ordinary citizens [tend] to be muddle-headed (lacking constraint), or empty-headed (lacking genuine attitudes)—or both" (Sniderman, 1993, p. 219)—it may seem strange that current fashion holds that the "monkeys" may be up to the task of running the circus after all.

▲ The Democratic Citizen and Public Opinion

Public opinion, one might say without exaggeration, is the very lifeblood of democracy. In his marvelous review of the public opinion literature, Donald Kinder (1998) describes the "democratic imperative" as the "translating of opinion into action" (p. 823), which of course presupposes the existence of opinion as the fundamental guide to political action. But how do citizens come to know what they want, and how might their opinions affect the broader political process?

Opinion Formation

I want to assert rather dogmatically that the engines of public opinion are individual citizens as information processors. However humble their location in the political process, people form their opinions—*when* they form opinions—in response to political discourse, public and private. At times they may actively seek out information about candidates, parties, or issues; more frequently, citizens receive political information unsolicited. When they attend to it, this information is interpreted and evaluated by citizens and integrated into their existing political attitudes and beliefs. These "private opinions" become public when they are converted into some form of political action—voting, answering a public opinion survey, talking about politics with friends and family. Admittedly, individual citizens may all too infrequently participate in, or even attend to, political discourse. Politics may be a "sideshow" for most people (Dahl, 1961, p. 305) and democracy in America may have grown "pale" (Kinder, 1998, p. 826) since Tocqueville (1848/1945) observed that political discussion was the "biggest concern" and "only pleasure" (p. 260) of American citizens, but that does not change the fact that in principle democracy invests the responsibility for public opinion in individual citizens. Democracy, at least in its Enlightenment form, is inherently individualistic.

I hear objections. *Public* opinion, I am told, is a collective phenomenon that has political meaning (not to mention coherence) only in the aggregate. Democracy is majoritarian, pluralist, group-based. Public opinion gathers momentum, changes course, runs roughshod over those who stand in its way. In the sociological tradition, it is an emergent property of a collective that cannot be traced in any simple way to the individual members of the body politic. Public opinion, in an organic sense, is *real*. Without claiming that these notions are without value, I want to insist that they are at best analytic constructions of public opinion that will be most useful as one views the *effects* of public opinion on the larger political process but will be of more limited utility as one considers the *causes* of opinion. They are a sort of useful shorthand that allows us to sweep away the daunting complexity of individuality when theorizing about how events and environmental forces translate into policy responses in the political system. For some, of course, public opinion in this "organic" sense is much more than a convenient simplification (Blumer, 1946; MacKuen, Erikson, & Stimson, 1989; Stimson, 1991). "Spokesperson for the herd" is James Stimson's (1991, p. 2) pithy characterization of the individual.[2] Since my primary concern here is the opinion formation process, I will give only cursory response to these more serious challenges to individualistic democracy.[3]

First, at a normative level, it seems to me that some of these notions— those that go beyond majoritarian, or populist, views of public opinion— are not compatible with ideals long cherished in democratic theory. If the aggregate is thought to be significantly more than—and *different* from—

the aggregation of individual preferences, more than some tally of yeas and nays on a given issue, so that we deny the critical link between individual preferences and public action formed by more individualistic conceptions of public opinion, then we have raised a potentially fatal challenge to the basic fairness, equity, and individualism of democracy not unlike that posed by Condorcet's voting paradox. Fortunately for democratic theory, I suspect that most of the rhetoric of aggregation stems from a very specific failure to think clearly about our basic theoretical conceptualization of public opinion.

At least some critics of individualism may really mean that citizens are not fully independent actors, that their behavior seems to be driven by collective or environmental forces. Sometimes, we are creatures of the crowd and fail to resist the forces of conformity. John Ruskin (2001/1864) said of the common man, "he thinks by infection, catching an opinion like a cold" (p. 48). Here we fail to be independent of our perceptions of aggregated public opinion, a problem that may be aggravated by the widespread publication of polling data. Or we may be collectively driven by some powerful event or other force in our environment. As I write one week after the terrorist attacks on New York and Washington of September 11, 2001, for example, it seems quite clear that Americans are unusually unified in their opinions—and *affects*. Or we may be heavily influenced by the information we receive through social networks, which may homogenize experience at the local level. Or we may be collectively manipulated by the media, the government, business interests. All of these positions—and I certainly have not exhausted the variations—assert some external force or combination of forces that appears to explain public opinion without recourse to individual citizens.

To the extent that they erase individuals from our explanations of public opinion, however, these arguments fall prey to a basic logical fallacy. When causal forces are not independent *because they form a chain or sequence*, we cannot eliminate intermediate processes without breaking the explanatory chain (Greenstein, 1969; Hyman, 1955). In the various cases just sketched, external factors do not directly cause aggregate public opinion but rather pass through the perceptions and information processing of individual citizens, whose responses may then be aggregated.[4] Moreover, there are certainly times when collective responses to external forces *cannot* easily be predicted without considering individual variation. The public does not often speak with one voice. Thus, at a theoretical level, it seems difficult to conceptualize public opinion apart from the information processing of individual human beings.

Opinion Aggregation

Although it is possible for individual citizens as singular agents to have direct impact on the political process (e.g., casting the deciding vote in an election), they are much more likely to affect public policy collectively. This raises the difficult question of how individual opinions combine together.

Majoritarian Aggregation

One possibility—the dominant view in public opinion research since at least *The American Voter* (Campbell, Converse, Miller, & Stokes, 1960)—is that opinions are *counted*. Collective opinion—in direct analogy with electoral aggregation—is the result of the simple summation of individual opinions on a given topic. This is the collective public opinion that underlies the normative individualism of Enlightenment democracy and the descriptive individualism of the modern public opinion poll (J. Converse, 1987; P. Converse, 1987). The early view of survey instruments, in particular, was essentially psychometric: how to quantify the strength and valence of individual opinions in order to report the marginal frequencies for the sample in meaningful response categories (Thurstone, 1927). Given such a report, one would be in a position to make some claims about the variety and distribution of individual opinions within the collective. As I will show, however, this view—still influential in public opinion research today—is questionable both politically and psychologically.

Weighted Aggregation

Despite the seductive simplicity of the majoritarian view, there may be good reason to doubt the empirical validity of a "one person, one vote" account of opinion aggregation. For one thing, such a view—at least in simple-minded form—seems painfully naive when confronted with what we know of "real politics." It has been 40 years since Robert Dahl (1961) punctured the myth of individual equality in American politics, opening *Who Governs?* with the question: "In a political system where nearly every adult may vote but where knowledge, wealth, social position, access to officials, and other resources are unequally distributed, who actually governs?" (p. 1). His answer, reminiscent of George Orwell's *Animal Farm* (1946), was that a variety of creatures participate in running the circus, but not equally so. For political cynics and those familiar with the workings of actual politics (overlapping categories, surely), the "power of the people" is frequently little more than symbolic. Power elites and *opinion elites* exert disproportionate influence. In short, the political process of aggregation may *weight* individual opinions differently before adding them, something that has all too rarely been considered in empirical studies of public opinion, and this weighting may need to vary by issue (Converse, 1964; Lavine & Gschwend, n.d.).

Compositional Aggregation

In their influential book *The Rational Public* (1992), Benjamin Page and Robert Shapiro offer an account of opinion aggregation based on the deliberative process inherent in public discourse. *Collective deliberation*, in their conceptualization, rests on the public "conversations" among officials, opinion elites, the media, and citizens. Individual citizens need not master the arguments and issues at play; they need only contribute bits and pieces to the discussion, perhaps in the form of questions, criticisms, or partial ideas. This "division of political labor," to use Kinder's description (1998, p. 800), views opinion aggregation as a compositional process in which individually unformed opinions are assembled into coherent aggregate opinion through the process of collective "discussion." Individual citizens need not possess complete opinions to be counted, as would be required in the majoritarian view.

Perhaps the most interesting form of the compositional aggregation approach focuses on the social networks within which individual citizens interact (Huckfeldt & Sprague, 1987; Page & Shapiro, 1992). Robert Huckfeldt and John Sprague (1995) put it thus: "If citizens are seen as individually disconnected information processors, we are unlikely to make significant progress toward relating the study of individual voters to the larger study of politics and electorates. Alternatively, to the extent that citizens are seen as being interdependent, then electorates become more than the simple summation of individual citizens" (pp. 290–291). This view of citizens embedded within social networks may appear at first glance to be particularly unfriendly to the individualistic perspective adopted earlier, but I think that such an interpretation would seriously misread both the individualistic view—which does not claim that citizens are *autonomous* information processors—and Huckfeldt and Sprague's notion of social networks of interdependent citizens who construct their preferences out of the complex interplay among *local* information environments (e.g., conversations over the water cooler), institutional and organizational contexts, and individual goals and motivations.

By focusing on informational interdependence as their theoretical core, Huckfeldt and Sprague give us unique leverage on the nature of compositional aggregation. This is aggregation formed on the *input* side of individual information processing rather than on the *output* side. Just as is suggested in Page and Shapiro's notion of collective deliberation, this is aggregation arising out of individual information processing within the social context of public discourse. It is not majoritarian aggregation, yet the information processing is still individualistic.

Summary

To recap, democratic citizens may fruitfully be thought of as information processors. Immersed in a complex information environment, ideal citizens are expected to attend to (or actively seek out) both formal (e.g., media) and informal (e.g., conversational) sources of information, and form opinions (or at least "bits" of opinions) about politically relevant issues, candidates, or groups. They are then expected to convert their private opinions into public participation, including simply expressing their opinions or asking questions as part of the ongoing political discourse. Their now *public* opinions may have greatest impact on public policy and broader political action when combined with the opinions of others, but this does not invalidate the individualistic nature of the opinion formation process.

▶ Information Processing

One may, of course, talk of public opinion at the individual level without taking account of the *information processing* of individual citizens. Without suggesting a false temporal construction of public opinion research as following distinct developmental phases, it is possible to divide the field into three categories. Figure 13.1a represents *behaviorism*, in which the individual is only present as an unspecified package of responses; which responses are evoked depend *only* on the nature of the environmental stimulus; citizens are not truly individual since the model gives us no way to account for individual variation. Figure 13.1b shows a relatively simple *perceptual model*, in which individuals' subjective perceptions of environmental stimuli trigger a set of response potentials from which an actual behavioral response is selected. Figure 13.1c represents a much more complex view of the individual's *cognitive architecture and processing;* mental activity and subsequent behavior in this cognitive model is interactive between environmental stimuli and stored knowledge. Figure 13.1b and c are both forms of information-processing models, in the sense that *some account is attempted of the actual mechanisms that intervene between stimulus and response.* These mechanisms presumably are geographically located between the citizen's left and right ears; they may only be observed, short of some neurophysiological methods (Morris, Squires, Taber, & Lodge, forthcoming; Schreiber & Zaller, 2001), indirectly. My focus will be on work that resembles panels (b) and especially (c) in its theoretical orientation.

To be precise, the information-processing perspective rests on the following set of basic assumptions (adapted from Eysenck & Keane, 1990; Hastie, 1986).

- Citizens are viewed as individual information processors embedded within an information environment, and their mental processing is interactive between environmental and internally stored information.
- This information is perceived, changed, and stored in symbolic form by the mind, which is viewed as a general symbol processor.
- Mental processes take time and effort, which may be measured through timing or interference experiments.

· The symbol processing of the mind rests on an underlying physical system (the nervous system), but one need not theorize at the physical level to understand mental events.

To be sure, very few scholars of public opinion have felt it necessary to confront these assumptions explicitly, being largely content to think of mental processing in simpler terms. But even the dominant "attitudinal model" of public opinion (fig. 13.1b) does rest implicitly on at least some of these assumptions, and more recent work on the organization of attitudes, on framing effects, and on memory retrieval has found it useful to take a closer look at the information-processing underpinnings of public opinion. In a moment, we will consider the most influential model of cognitive structure and processing—the associative network model of memory—but a brief historical detour may help provide some context.

(a) Black Box Models of the Individual

$$S \rightarrow R$$

(b) Stimulus/Organism/Response Models of the Individual

$$S \rightarrow O \rightarrow R$$

(c) Cognitive Models of the Individual

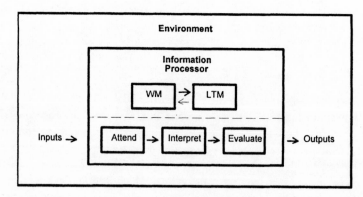

Figure 13.1.

Historical Overview

A number of different influences, themselves not fully independent, may be identified when one considers the intellectual heritage of the information-processing approach to human psychology. First, the general context set by the Enlightenment view of man should not be overlooked. Man as "rational calculator"—taken to its zenith in Charles Babbage's attempt to design a general analytical machine—asserted an intellect capable of rising above both human nature and Mother Nature; moreover, this intellect, like all processes found in nature, was mechanistic in form and process. Sigmund Freud's mentalism, though less often acknowledged in cognitive psychology, was a second important influence in establishing the principle that one must take account of mental events if one is to understand human behavior. In addition, the interest of early social psychologists in the organization of memory (Bartlett, 1932; James, 1890), higher cognitive learning (Tolman, 1932), cognitive motivation (Festinger, 1957; Heider, 1946, 1958), and especially attitudes (Allport, 1935) had a profound and lasting impact on what later became known as the cognitive revolution.

By the 1950s, behaviorism and its rejection of internal mental states and processes was under sustained attack from several directions. Edward Tolman (1932), himself a card-carrying behaviorist, demonstrated persuasively that "shallow learning" theories (e.g., Hull, 1930) could not explain the learning behavior of rats in mazes. In a classic study, Tolman found that rats who had learned to run a maze were able to swim it when flooded, showing rather definitively that their learned knowledge ("cognitive maps" was Tolman's phrase) went well beyond mere motor responses. The acquisition of language and the ability to solve complex problems seemed also to be beyond behaviorism, requiring theories about mental states and processes (Broadbent, 1958; Bruner, Goodnow, & Austin, 1956; Chomsky, 1957; Miller, 1957; Newell, Shaw, & Simon, 1958).

The most important development in the gestation of the information-processing perspective was the advent of the digital computer.[5] Keeping in mind that analogies between computing machines and human reasoning long predated the invention of computers, it is nonetheless true that the computer provided a powerful model (and *tool!*) for theorizing about thinking (Broadbent, 1958). "It might have been necessary a decade ago," wrote Herbert Simon in 1980 (p. 45), "to argue for the commonality of the information processes that are employed by such disparate systems as computers and human nervous systems. The evidence for that commonality is now overwhelming." Though many psychologists might cringe at this extreme claim, the *computational philosophy of mind* represented in this quotation nevertheless did carry the flag for the cognitive revolution and led to the creation of a wholly new cognitive science at the intersection of psychology, computer science, and philosophy (Boden, 1988; Feigenbaum & Feldman, 1963/1995; Luger, 1995).

At much the same time that the cognitive perspective was gathering momentum in psychology and spilling over into related disciplines, a parallel movement was afoot in economics. Rational choice—roughly, the view that human behavior is fully explained by the maximization of utility, defined in terms of individual preferences over possible outcomes—rapidly colonized much of political science and profoundly influenced psychology as well (e.g., behavioral decision theory, reviewed in chapter 2). Though current thought is far more enlightened (e.g., Lupia, McCubbins, & Popkin, 2000), *homo economicus* and *homo psychologicus* seemed to many social scientists to be utterly incompatible. Herbert Simon—appropriately recognized as a seminal thinker in political science, economics, psychology, and computer science—went a very great way toward bridging this gap by distinguishing bounded from substantive rationality (Simon, 1978, 1985). The bounded rationality model of human behavior, which was rapidly embraced by many political economists, was also acceptable to many political psychologists—indeed, some found a suspicious resemblance to *homo psychologicus*. In any event, the notions of satisficing, rather than maximizing, behavior and limited information-processing capacity provided the common ground needed for constructive discussion between political economists and political psychologists.

Cognitive Architecture and Process

At least two general theories of human cognition have gained acceptance within cognitive science (Hastie, 1986). One of these—the parallel distributed processing (PDP) approach of David Rumelhart and his colleagues (Rumelheart, McClelland, and the PDP Research Group, 1986)—has had relatively little influence in social and political psychology. The associative network model of memory (Anderson, 1983; Collins & Quillian, 1969), by contrast, has become the central conceptual framework for the architecture of social cognition, and though its application in public opinion research has most often been more metaphorical than explicitly theoretical, its influence has nevertheless been profound.[6]

The Associative Network Model of Memory

Human memory is most remarkable for its contrasts: a nearly unlimited storage capacity but relatively inefficient retrieval processes; the ability to vividly recall events from early childhood coupled with an inability to keep in mind the lunch menu at McDonald's; the capacity to process staggering amounts of information automatically (that is, out of awareness) along with an attentional focus for conscious processing so narrow as to almost debilitate complex thought. There is room, one could say, in what we know of human information processing for both delusions of grandeur (*homo economicus*) and humility (*homo psychologicus*). The dominant structural model of the mind for social and political cognitivists, based on the classic architectural distinction between long-term memory (LTM) and working memory (WM), developed in cognitive psychology out of the effort to reconcile these contrasts (Anderson, 1983; Atkinson & Shiffrin, 1968; Broadbent, 1958; James, 1890; Miller, 1957).

Human long-term memory is organized associatively in networks of meaning. When people are asked to freely recall what they know on some topic—say terrorism—what they say seems often to be remarkably structured, as though each memory triggers additional thoughts in a cognitive chain reaction. Moreover, subsequent cues on the topic—say *domestic* terrorism—may trigger another set of thoughts that also seems to cluster in meaningful ways. Precisely *how* memory is organized remains controversial; that it is organized associatively is not. The associative network model represents this central feature of human LTM by adopting the formal structure of linked nodes, as illustrated in figure 13.2 (adapted from Lodge & Taber, 2000). Objects of memory are represented as nodes (circles in fig. 13.2) and beliefs or "implicational relations" (Judd & Krosnick, 1989) are shown

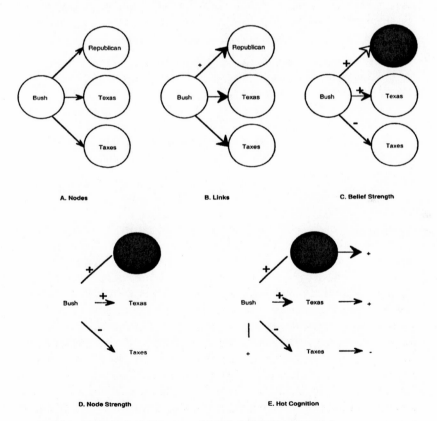

Figure 13.2. Node-Link Architecture of Political Beliefs and Attitudes

as directional links (arrows in fig. 13.2). Beliefs and concepts vary in strength (the thickness of link arrows and node circles in fig. 13.2c and d). And in this recent version of the model, objects in memory carry affective tags (fig. 13.2e). We might translate the fragment of individual knowledge in fig. 13.2 as follows: (1) there is a strong belief that Bush is Republican, a moderate belief that he is from Texas, and a weak belief that he opposes taxes; (2) the concepts *Bush* and *Republican* are stronger (i.e., more accessible, more practiced) in memory than the concepts *Texas* and *taxes*; and (3) Bush and Republicans are strongly liked, Texas is weakly liked, and taxes are weakly disliked.[7]

Long-term memory provides primary storage for information processing, for recording experience and mental activity. Imagine a giant, tangled network of concept nodes and links chalked on an enormous blackboard in a dark cellar. You have in one hand a tiny penlight called "conscious awareness" and in the other a piece of chalk.[8] This brings us to the second structural component of the associative network model. Working memory corresponds to the portion of LTM that you are able to illuminate in the focus of attention at any given moment. Quite literally, the processing limitations that led Simon to his notion of bounded rationality derive from the inefficiencies of WM (that is, from the feebleness of your penlight). There are three primary bottlenecks in WM:

- A very limited capacity—we are able to hold only 7 ± 2 chunks of information in awareness at the same time (Miller, 1957)
- Attention is serial—in order for new information to enter WM from LTM or from sensory experience, old information must be displaced (Payne, 1982)
- The fixation rate for recording (encoding) information from WM to LTM is very slow—it takes on the order of 8–10 seconds to organize new information and "write" it to LTM (Simon, 1978)

To this point, my discussion of the associative network model has been largely static, but given this bicameral structure of memory, how might we represent the fundamental processes of memory retrieval?[9] Briefly, the primary mechanism for recall is *spreading activation* in LTM. At any moment, all objects in memory (i.e., nodes) have some activation or arousal level that can go up or down as a result of conscious or unconscious processing. Since the probability that a node will pop into conscious WM (i.e., be recalled) is a monotonically increasing function of its level of activation, these activation processes are critically important (for a more technical discussion, see Taber & Timpone, 1996). First, conscious thought increases the activation level of implicated memory objects; reading about George W. Bush activates the corresponding node(s) in LTM. Second, activation spreads automatically through LTM from highly aroused nodes to all directly linked nodes, and from there to second-order nodes, and so on, in what is known as the fan effect (see Thomsen, Lavine, & Kounios, 1996).[10] Third, activation decays rapidly and with it accessibility to conscious processing, though some memory objects may be chronically more accessible than other objects (Bargh, Chaiken, Govender, & Pratto, 1992; Fazio, Sanbonmatsu, Powell, & Kardes, 1986; Neely, 1977).

A Stage Model of Information Processing

Many models of information processing have been built upon the structural foundation of the associational network model of memory. Figure 13.1c leaves much unspecified about how an individual might convert the myriad informational inputs from the environment and from LTM into the outputs of public opinion and political action. One common approach that has found some application in political psychology divides information processing into broad stages (Lodge, 1995; Lodge & Taber, 2000; Ottati & Wyer, 1990; Steenbergen & Lodge, n.d.; Taber, 1998; Taber, Lodge, & Glathar, 2001; Wyer & Ottati, 1993), as follows.

- Attention and exposure: information must capture attention (i.e., enter WM) before it can influence subsequent processing and behavioral outputs.
- Interpretation: new information must be mapped onto existing knowledge from LTM to be meaningful, and it is these internal representations of information that may influence subsequent processing.
- Evaluation: some of the most important judgments that must be rendered on information concern the evaluative implications of that information for the individual; attitudes are formed, like-dislike "ratings" generated, perhaps summary impressions are formed or updated for the relevant candidates, groups, or issues.
- Storage: if they are to guide subsequent information processing and action, interpreted and evaluated information (now knowledge) must be linked back into the associative network of LTM.

Delineating general stages of information processing may be very useful in guiding research or organizing literature reviews, but there are also drawbacks. First, identifying stages may imply iron sequence, in which mental processing goosesteps through an assembly line from raw materials to finished product. Moreover, separating processing into stages may suggest sharp empirical distinctions that only exist roughly in nature. Mental processing is simply not this orderly, and steps often are out of sequence or mixed. Second, there may be too much emphasis on conscious processing in the stage model, on controlled activity in WM. This may understate the importance of automaticity in information processing. Finally, it is not always recognized that the general stage model does not rise to the status of a "working" process model of cognition.[11] Though there has been considerable empirical and theoretical work on the various stages of processing, actual mechanisms—the so-called elementary information processes (Payne,

Bettman, & Johnson, 1992; Taber & Steenbergen, 1995)—remain under-specified and controversial.

Summary

The information-processing approach to human intelligence has a long and distinguished pedigree. Its view of *homo symbolicus* forms the theoretical core of modern cognitive science and motivates the "cognitive revolution" throughout the social sciences. Individual humans are portrayed as symbol processors within a complex information environment, their thinking the result of both controlled and automatic manipulations of external information and internally stored knowledge (including beliefs and attitudes). Memory processes—divided into the structures of LTM and WM and most often represented as an associative network—play a central role. A stage model provides a useful framework for theorizing about the key processes of attention, interpretation, evaluation, and storage. Indeed, my discussion of modern public opinion research will be organized around the first three of these stages.

▶ Information Processing and Public Opinion Research

Perhaps because of the early psychological sophistication of the attitudinal model of *The American Voter* (Campbell et al., 1960), the development of the cognitive movement in public opinion research has really been more evolutionary than revolutionary.[12] A deeper interest in cognitive processing in the formation of public opinion seemed natural, given longstanding questions concerning the structure of beliefs and ideology, the stability and constraint of attitudes and values, and the informational ingredients of opinion.

Informational Inputs

When does political discourse rise enough above the informational din of modern life for citizens to take notice? What types of political information provoke more thought than others? Can the infinite variations in information environments and citizens that define the input side of political cognition be simmered down to a manageable set of dimensions? In his recent commentary on the field, Donald Kinder (1998; see also Sears & Funk, 1991) identifies three broad types of information that may be of special concern to citizens as they form opinions about political persons, groups, and issues: "(1) the material interests that citizens see at stake, (2) the sympathies and resentments that citizens feel toward social groupings, and (3) commitment to the political principles that become entangled in public issues" (p. 800). I shall consider each of these broad categories in terms of how they provide "motivational orientations" for citizens in their political information processing. I will conclude the section with a brief discussion of selective attention and exposure.

Material Self-Interest

Political theorists from Marx to Mosca, from Dahl to Downs, have built their diverse understandings of political systems on the seemingly solid foundation of self-interest. No organ has been more central to the anatomy of *homo economicus*. Even psychologists accept the potency of egoism in motivating human thought and behavior. The principle is so firmly embedded in political science explanations of the vote and public opinion that in some circles it approaches dogma.[13] And, not surprisingly, cynical realism permeates standard explanations of political action in the media and in popular culture. Despite the ubiquity of self-interest explanations of public opinion, however, there are powerful reasons to question its empirical importance (Citrin & Green, 1990; Sears & Funk, 1991).

Unfortunately for those who wish to test its potency in explaining public opinion, self-interest has been nearly as slippery a concept as rationality, and for related reasons. To almost any restriction on the definition, it is possible to respond that somehow the "essence" of egoism has been lost. David Sears and his colleagues, who have mounted the most sustained empirical exploration of the role of self-interest in public opinion, suggest three criteria: first, the interests involved must be tangible or material; second, the self involved is the individual (or perhaps the individual's family); and third, self-interest concerns imminent outcomes (Sears & Funk, 1991). Psychic gratification, concern for others, and future consideration are all excluded, reasonably it seems to me, because they tend to stretch self-interest beyond recognition and render it theoretically tautological and empirically unmeasurable.

Short-term, material self-interest, it turns out in study after study, has remarkably little to do with public opinion on a wide range of political issues. Kinder (1998) provides a long list of examples:

> When faced with affirmative action, white and black Americans come to their views without calculating personal harms or benefits (Kinder & Sanders, 1996; Kluegel & Smith, 1986). The unemployed do not line up behind policies designed to alleviate economic distress (Schlozman & Verba, 1979). The medically indigent are no more likely to favor government health insurance than are the fully insured (Sears et al., 1980). Parents of children enrolled in public schools are generally no more supportive of government aid to education than are other citizens (Jennings, 1979). Americans who are subject to the draft are not especially opposed to military intervention or to the escalation of conflicts already under way (Lau, Brown, & Sears, 1978; Mueller, 1973, 1994). Women employed outside the home do not differ from homemakers in their sup-

port for policies intended to benefit women at work (Sears & Huddy, 1990). (p. 801)

Moreover, personal economic considerations have been found to be far less important in presidential voting than are general concerns about the national economy (Kiewiet, 1983). One must conclude, looking at the litany of negative findings, that citizens do not seem especially sensitive to their own material interests when making political decisions. Unless the material outcomes from a public policy or issue are very clear, very large, and very imminent (Sears & Funk, 1991), self-interest does not determine opinion or action.[14]

Can we conclude from its puny impact on political attitudes and actions that self-interest is unimportant to political information processing? Surprisingly, given the emphatic rejection of self-interest as a determinant of opinion, it turns out that material self-interest *does* influence attention to political information. Citizens whose interests are implicated in an issue tend to consider that issue important. Presumably, they are also more attentive to information concerning that issue, though the evidence here remains sketchy (Krosnick, 1988, 1990). The elderly, the unemployed, African Americans, those who would benefit or suffer from tax relief—all place a higher priority on the issues that affect them most personally (Boninger, Krosnick, Barent, & Fabrigar, 1995; Iyengar & Kinder, 1987; Sears & Citrin, 1982; Thomsen, Borgida, & Lavine, 1995). In determining what information they will pay attention to, self-interest provides some guidance for ordinary citizens.

Group Orientations

If narrow self-interest is not a central guide to public opinion, perhaps basic orientations to social and political groups will prove more potent. After all, we have long understood the importance of social identity to the development of social and political attitudes (Brewer & Brown, 1998; Converse, 1964; Deaux, Reid, Mizrahi, & Ethier, 1995; Fiske, 1998; Kinder, 1998). Affiliations with social, religious, historical, cultural, national, and political groups surely are powerful orienting forces in guiding public opinion and political action. Just as likely to be consequential are our negative identifications, our feelings and cognitions toward groups to which we do not belong.[15] "Conflict between groups," wrote Roger Brown in his classic social psychology textbook (1986), "is like a sturdy three-legged stool. It is sturdy because two legs are universal ineradicable psychological processes, ethnocentrism and stereotyping, and the third leg is a state of society, unfair distribution of resources, which has always existed everywhere" (p. 533).

For these same reasons, social group cleavages, from gender to generation, socioeconomic class to regionalism, have been found to be important determinants of public opinion on a wide range of issues (Kinder, 1998).

One of the most firmly established findings in this literature, for example, is that black and white Americans differ in their positions on many political issues, sometimes quite markedly. Important debates remain concerning the degree to which racial prejudice has declined in recent decades, the theoretical interpretation of "modern racism" (Kinder, 1986; Sniderman & Tetlock, 1986b, 1986a), and the role of "realistic group conflict" in explaining discrimination (Bobo, 1988; Coser, 1956), but race clearly remains a potent orienting force for many Americans (Black & Black, 1987; Bobo & Kluegel, 1993; Dawson, 1994; Kinder & Mendelberg, 1995; Kinder & Sanders, 1996). Similarly, attitudes on welfare (Gilens, 1999), immigration (Pettigrew & Meertens, 1995), and AIDs policy (Price & Hsu, 1992) all turn on hostility toward the outgroup.

Under what conditions will group identifications exert maximal pull on public opinion? Theory and data suggest three factors, corresponding neatly to Brown's three-legged stool. First, a great deal of research—most famously, *The Authoritarian Personality* (Adorno, Frankel-Brunswick, Levinson, & Sanford, 1950)—has emphasized individual differences. Some people are simply more ethnocentric or more personally invested in group identifications than others. A second argument has focused on the information environment and widely shared group stereotypes. Group orientations cannot affect opinions on a political issue, for example, if these orientations are not understood to be relevant to the issue, and this "relevance" may be supplied by elite manipulations of information concerning stereotypes (e.g., Kinder & Sanders, 1996; chapter 11). Third, group conflict—and reliance on social identity for information processing—is surely responsive to genuine conflicts of interest (Bobo, 1988; Coser, 1956; Sumner, 1906; chapter 5). Periods of greater intergroup conflict or issues that highlight conflicting group interests should also raise the salience of group identifications in individual information processing.

Political Values

For many people, politics is all about principles. Public debates on abortion, national health care, gun control, capital punishment, welfare, and funding for the arts revolve on the central axes of the American ethos: individualism, equality, suspicion of power (Kinder, 1998). Politics is contentious in part because it brings values into conflict, certainly on a societal scale (Feldman & Zaller, 1992; Kinder & Sanders, 1996; Stoker, 1992) but also within individual citizens (Feldman & Zaller, 1992; Tetlock, 1986). Values, moreover, may be key elements in the *structure* of political knowledge (i.e., memory), providing constraint across issues and response stability across time for at least some citizens (Feldman, 1988; chapter 14). Given their centrality in political discourse and in democratic theory, one might expect that values would powerfully determine individual opinion on a wide range of political issues. It may be surprising, then, that the impacts of individualism, egalitarianism, tolerance, and opposition to government power have generally been muted, contingent, and complex. To illustrate this point, I will briefly consider research on individualism.

Hardy individualism—the notion that people are responsible for their own lot in life—clearly does help to explain opposition to government assistance programs (Feldman, 1988; Feldman & Zaller, 1992; Kinder & Sanders, 1996) and normative beliefs that the poor are to blame for their condition (Feldman, 1983; Sniderman & Brody, 1977). But things become murky when we consider white Americans' attitudes toward blacks. On the one hand, opposition to government programs designed to alleviate the economic hardships of black Americans may be understood as a simple extension of this same principled logic: blacks are poor because they do not work hard enough (Sniderman, 1985; Sniderman & Tetlock, 1986b, 1986c). On the other hand, I have already shown that racial group identifications provide a powerful explanation for the same policy attitudes, especially so when we take into account the role of egalitarianism (Kinder, 1986; Kinder & Mendelberg, 2000; Kinder & Sanders, 1996; Kinder & Winter, 2001).

Selective Exposure

Self-interest, political values, and especially group identifications create a powerful field of motivational forces, which orients citizens within their information environments. Traditionally, public opinion research has viewed the citizen as a relatively passive pawn of larger, sometimes sinister forces, with neither the inclination nor the capacity to control the information environment. By contrast, a flurry of recent work pictures the citizen as more actively involved, if not actually standing at the helm of information processing (Kuklinski & Quirk, 2000; Lavine, 2002; Lodge & Taber, 2000, 2001; Rahn, Aldrich, & Borgida, 1994; Taber & Lodge, 2000; Taber, Lodge, & Glathar, 2001; Zaller & Feldman, 1992). The critical point for current purposes is that citizens, if motivated, may selectively attend to or seek out particular information from the environment; they need not be passive recipients.

Surprisingly, the large literature on selective exposure that came out of the cognitive dissonance tradition in social psychology does not provide straightforward support for the hypothesis (Eagly & Chaiken, 1993; Frey, 1986; Kunda, 1990; Sears & Freedman, 1967). Perhaps the clearest evidence of selective exposure in processing political information comes from a series of experiments I have conducted with Milton Lodge (Taber & Lodge, 2000). Subjects in these studies, using a computerized information board paradigm,[16] actively sought out information that they knew would support their prior beliefs on affirmative action and gun control and avoided information that they knew would challenge those beliefs. Selective exposure was greatest among knowledgeable subjects and for those with the strongest beliefs, precisely those whom we might expect to be most motivated to control information.

The Structure of Memory and Interpretation Processes

A central principle of information-processing theory is that people do not respond directly to external stimuli but rather must first construct internal representations of that information, what Walter Lippman (1922) called "pictures in the head." This section takes up the question of how knowledge is structured and the impact of that structure on the interpretation of new information. Rather than attempting a comprehensive review (see Eagly & Chaiken, 1993; McGraw & Steenbergen, 1995), I will focus on several themes that are of special importance for public opinion.

One contentious debate was sparked by the publication in 1964 of Philip Converse's seminal article on mass belief systems. Ordinary citizens, Converse declared, were "remarkably innocent" (p. 255) of the "familiar belief systems that, in view of their historical importance, tend most to attract the sophisticated observer" (1964, p. 256). Western ideology, and in particular its left-right, liberal-conservative dimensionality, seemed not to constrain the political beliefs of American citizens. Lacking hierarchical structure, mass beliefs had little coherence and less stability. Research on ideology and public opinion since Converse can be read as an extended controversy over this central thesis (Kinder, 1998; Sniderman, 1993; Sniderman & Tetlock, 1986ca; chapter 14). Converse himself suggested one reply: "we do not disclaim the existence of entities that might best be called 'folk ideologies,' nor do we deny for a moment that strong differentiations in a variety of narrower values may be found within subcultures of less educated people" (pp. 255–256). Citizens, in other words, might organize their political beliefs hierarchically, but in terms of core values rather than the liberal-conservative dimension (Feldman, 1988; Hurwitz & Peffley, 1987; but see Abramowitz & Saunders, 1998).

A related controversy concerns schemas (see Conover & Feldman, 1991; Kuklinski, Luskin, & Bolland, 1991; Lodge & McGraw, 1991): Is memory organized in discrete attitudes and beliefs (singular nodes and links), or is it "chunky" (tightly knit subnetworks for a given memory object)? When people encounter "Hillary Rodham Clinton" in a newspaper story, for example, how much and how structured is the knowledge they bring to bear from LTM? It turns out that people who have thought a bit about Senator Clinton in the past—political sophisticates, for example, or those who have taken a special interest in the Clinton saga—are quite likely to possess a schema in LTM that organizes their knowledge, attitudes, and inferences about her. And subjectively important attitudes are more likely than unimportant ones to "grow" elaborate structures in memory (Barent & Krosnick, 1995). Two implications of the schematic organization of memory deserve some comment. First, to the degree that schemas in LTM have become "unitized," they may expand significantly the capacity of working memory and therefore the amount of knowledge that may be held in conscious awareness. Second, schemas enrich "pictures in the head" by filling in many of the details about an object of thought from inferential knowledge. This provides another gain in efficiency for information processing, but at the risk of inferential error.

The role of affect in the organization of memory has gotten surprisingly little play in public opinion research (but see chapter 6), and when it has been considered, evaluative affect has generally not been found to structure political knowledge (McGraw & Steenbergen, 1995). Milton Lodge and I (2000) have recently offered a theory of motivated political reasoning that builds on the tight integration of evaluative affect (likes and dislikes) within associative memory (recall fig. 13.2). We claim that all political concepts that have been evaluated in the past carry an affective tag in LTM; these evaluations come *automatically* and inescapably to mind whenever the concept node enters awareness, with important implications for subsequent reasoning (discussed hereafter). This approach has the benefit of marrying a rather simple view of affect with the standard information-processing model that has guided research in political cognition for several decades. Its primary disadvantage, however, is that it may be *too* simple. In particular, its view of affect in terms of like-dislike evaluations may seem too tepid for those interested in true emotions (Marcus & MacKuen, 1993). Moreover, the mechanisms for updating affective tags remain controversial, and the model as it stands cannot easily account for ambivalence in political attitudes (Lavine, 2001).

Evaluation

The fundamental task of the citizen in forming public opinions is evaluative. In conversation, in the voting booth, on opinion surveys, citizens are asked to report their considered evaluations of candidates, groups, or issues, and there is in this a presumption that citizens *have* opinions to report. Converse (1964) thought not. The second of his twin indictments of the American citizen was that most did not hold political attitudes worthy of the name. If anything, this produced an even hotter fire than did his "innocence of ideology" thesis.

I will limit my commentary on the "nonattitudes" debate to two key replies to Converse. First, it may be that inadequate measurement was more to blame for response instability than inadequate citizens (Achen, 1975). Remarkably, in a reanalysis of Converse's own panel data, Christopher Achen was able to account for virtually all of the over-time change in responses as measurement error; underlying attitudes were almost perfectly stable! But how is one to interpret this measurement error? Is it unsystematic, as implied by Achen, or might there be good information-processing explanations for question wording, order, or context effects that could be included in models of public opinion? This question takes us to a second response to Converse, which suggests that people do not *hold* attitudes that they simply retrieve and report; rather, they *construct* attitudes out of the particular sample of considerations that they recall from LTM at the time they respond to a survey question (Martin & Tesser, 1992; Tourangeau, Rips, & Rasinski, 2000; Zaller & Feldman, 1992). Since memory recall in the associative network model is probabilistic and cued by the specific context of the moment, the sample of considerations retrieved into working memory in response to a survey question will be mightily affected by the wording of the question, the nature of preceding questions, and a host of contextual factors. Far from being empty-headed, say John Zaller and Stanley Feldman (1992), many citizens possess multiple, conflicting considerations relevant to a given topic; their unstable responses to survey questions simply reflect this ambivalence.

The Zaller and Feldman model is memory-based, in the sense that evaluations are formed from the likes and dislikes that citizens can recall at the time a judgment is needed. One might imagine the citizen in the voting booth dutifully weighing pros and cons before pulling the lever. By contrast, on-line models of political evaluation (Lodge, McGraw, & Stroh, 1989; Lodge, Steenbergen, & Brau, 1995) claim that "citizens spontaneously extract the evaluative implications of political information as soon as they are exposed to it, integrate these implications into an ongoing summary counter or running tally, and then proceed to forget the nongist descriptive details of the information" (Lavine, 2002, p. 227). The citizen in the voting booth need not reconsider pros and cons, for an evaluation has already been made.

These models are commonly presented as competing or even incompatible—with memory-based processes being seen as more applicable to complex, ambivalent attitude objects (issues) and on-line processes as more applicable to simpler, univalent objects, especially when citizens expect to be asked for a judgment (candidates). To my mind, however, this has not been a particularly productive debate, in part because it has been driven by extreme interpretations that nobody really believes. The on-line model cannot mean that all details are forgotten; such an organism would not have in LTM the ingredients necessary to discern the evaluative implications of new information on exposure. Conversely, the memory-based approach cannot mean that people refrain from all evaluation of information at the time of exposure; such an organism would have no ability to resist persuasion or otherwise maintain beliefs through time. A far more plausible account of impression formation, in my view, builds on hybrid models (Hastie & Pennington, 1989; Scherpenzeel & Saris, 1997). For example, evaluative tags created through an on-line process may become activated and enter working memory along with other considerations; a strong evaluative tag might heavily constrain the construction of a judgment (and in the extreme, may determine it), while a weak tag might act as one among many considerations (Lavine, 2002).

There has been a resurgence in recent years in motivational models of information processing, including selective exposure, described earlier, and a variety of motivated evaluation processes (Kunda, 1990; Lodge & Taber, 2000; Taber & Lodge, 2000; Taber, Lodge, & Glathar, 2001). As in earlier cognitive consistency theories (Festinger, 1957; Heider, 1958), these frameworks assert that the pressure for evaluative consistency in attitudes is a powerful motivational force in information processing. Milton Lodge and I, for example, build a theory of motivated political reasoning on three principles: first, evaluative affect is inseparably linked into the structures of LTM in what Robert Abelson (1963) called "hot cognition"; second, these evaluations are updated on-line, as one encounters relevant political information; and third, recall of these evaluations is automatic, according to the same memory retrieval processes used for "cold cognitions." Using an affective priming task (Bargh, Chaiken, Govender, & Pratto, 1992; Fazio, Sanbonmatsu, Powell, & Kardes, 1986), we find clear experimental evidence for the hot cognition and automaticity hypotheses in processing information about a variety of political objects (Lodge & Taber, 2000, 2001).[17] That is, our experimental subjects clearly possess automatic affect toward many political candidates, groups, and issues; their evaluations come to mind mere milliseconds after exposure to a political prime, far too quickly for them to be constructed in WM. This tripartite theory has important implications for political reasoning. For example, we might expect the evaluative affect that comes automatically to mind for many citizens when they encounter information about political candidates, groups, or issues to substantially color their processing of that information. Experiments have strongly supported this "disconfirmation bias" (Edwards & Smith, 1996; Taber & Lodge, 2000): subjects with strong prior affect on affirmative action, gun control, and public support for the arts, for example, showed evidence of bias in their processing of counterattitudinal arguments and evidence, and their attitudes grew more extreme from this counterarguing.

My discussion of political evaluation thus far has focused exclusively on processes internal to the citizen. By contrast, research on *framing* and *priming* in the formation of political attitudes offers a splendid example of the theoretical benefits that accrue when we take seriously the citizen's interaction with the information environment and the broader political context (Gamson, 1992; Iyengar, 1991; Iyengar & Kinder, 1987; Lau, Smith, & Fiske, 1991; Nelson, Clawson, & Oxley, 1997; chapter 11). I will limit my discussion to what I see as the theoretical core and point interested readers to chapter 11. Most fundamentally, this work asserts the critical role of knowledge structures (schemas, frames, scripts), which allow elites to penetrate and possibly manipulate the evaluation and inference processes of ordinary citizens. Simplifying considerably, framing—generally assumed to be strategic on the part of elites, but which need not be—can occur in at least two ways: elites may articulate a novel frame for understanding some political object, with the expectation that many citizens will come to view the candidate, issue, or group through that lens; or elites may increase the accessibility or perceived relevance of some commonly shared frame. For an example of the latter, a Ku Klux Klan rally might be framed by the media in terms of free speech or in terms of public order, with predictable effects on citizen attitudes toward the rally (Nelson, Clawson, & Oxley, 1997).

Summary

Philip Converse (1964) worried that studies of belief systems "have often served as primary exhibits for the doctrine that what is important to study cannot be measured and that what can be measured is not important to study" (p. 206). The research reported in this section, in part catalyzed by Converse's own seminal work, shows just how far we have come. The topics are empirically, theoretically, and normatively important; the information-processing approach gives us methods and theory that allow us to peer into the minds of citizens. Moreover, the stage model of information process-ing—attention, interpretation, evaluation—that I use to roughly organize my review does not, I think, fundamentally distort the underlying reality; to adapt Kristin Monroe's (1994) memorable metaphor, the public opinion literature when clothed in the information-processing perspective does not resemble "a fat lady in a corset."

▶ The Paradox of the Dysfunctional Citizen

The American voter, as revealed in public opinion research over the past half-century, is a wretched caricature of the noble citizen of normative dem-ocratic theory. Uninterested in politics, poorly informed on public matters, intolerant of diversity, ideologically unsophisticated—it seems a miracle that any system dependent on such a creature could have survived, let alone prospered.

The Dysfunctional Citizen

Democratic theorists and critics alike have wondered whether average citi-zens would have any genuine interest in public affairs, given the more per-sonal and more immediate relevance of private concerns. Echoing the ghost of Walter Lippman, Robert Dahl (1961) famously asserted that "politics is a sideshow in the great circus of life" (p. 305). And survey data emphatically agree: citizens care relatively little about politics (Bennett, 1986; Bennett & Resnick, 1990). Of course, we may be naive to expect anything else. Citizen apathy may well be a rational allocation of limited resources in either the economic (Downs, 1957) or psychological senses (Fiske & Taylor, 1991).

Given the cost of information and the paltry expected payoff of political engagement, rational citizens may well be "cognitive misers" in their processing of political information.

Lack of interest, one might expect, will motivate political ignorance, and such seems to be the result in America (Delli Carpini & Keeter, 1996). Indeed, "the depth of ignorance demonstrated by modern mass publics can be quite breathtaking" (Kinder, 1998, p. 785). Large numbers of citizens do not understand the basic structures of their government, the issue positions or even identities of their representatives, or the basic geographical or political facts surrounding current international crises. Certainly they know very little about what their government actually does (e.g., a majority of Americans regularly report that they think we spend less on Medicare than on aid to foreign countries).

Moreover, as I have shown, there is some reason to worry about the ideological sophistication of American citizens. What little citizens do know seems not to be structured as democratic theorists normatively expect. That is, the left-right ideological dimension so important to theorists of politics seems largely irrelevant to the average citizen. By one way of thinking, this means at least that citizens are ill prepared to comprehend public discourse presented in left-right terms and at most that citizens lack the fundamental points of reference necessary for stable and internally coherent political beliefs. Of course, this lack of ideological constraint may be less debilitating if citizens find and use other standards to organize their beliefs.

Among the principles thought to be central to democracy is tolerance of diversity (Mill, 1861/1951). Freedom of speech and of the press were included in the Bill of Rights as fundamental values, necessary to the very survival of democracy. What then should we make of the long line of public opinion research that documents widespread intolerance in America? There appears to be a distressing disjuncture between support for tolerance (and other principles, for that matter) in the abstract and lack of tolerance in specific cases (McClosky, 1964; Prothro & Grigg, 1960). Citizens might agree, for example, that freedom of expression is a bedrock of American democracy, yet blithely deny the rights of communists, socialists, or atheists to speak in public or teach in our schools (Stouffer, 1955). And the optimism among those who saw a sea change in tolerance by the 1970s (Davis, 1975; Nunn, Crockett, & Williams, 1978) evaporated when it was discovered that Americans remained generally intolerant, though less unified in their target groups (Sullivan, Pierson, & Marcus, 1982; but see Wilson, 1994). Indeed, there is good reason to believe that feelings toward ingroups and outgroups remain among the most potent sources of motivational orientation for American citizens in their information processing. And quite possibly, these group identifications become especially important under conditions of threat; the enthusiasm in the aftermath of the September 11 terrorist attacks for curtailments of the civil liberties of immigrants, and especially Arabs or Muslims, seems a clear case in point.

Yet, as I have already observed, obituaries for democracy seem premature.

Dehorning the Dilemma

Three types of solution to the paradox of the dysfunctional citizen have been discussed in the public opinion literature: aggregation processes, individual information processes, and external constraints on individuals.

Aggregation

Perhaps the mechanisms that compose a public out of individual citizens "miraculously" compensate for their individual inadequacies (Kinder, 1998). Earlier, I identified majoritarian, weighted, and compositional principles of aggregation, and for each we can identify an answer to the dysfunctional citizen.

Majoritarian aggregation, it will be recalled, is the notion that opinions on any political issue can be simply tallied into response categories; collective public opinion is found in the distribution of responses. How might such a process discover a rational public when many of the individuals are indifferent, ignorant, unsophisticated, and intolerant? Simple. The law of large numbers from statistical theory gives formal justification for the belief that "the inadequacies of individual citizens, when combined, are more likely to cancel than to multiply" (Kinder, 1998, p. 797). Moreover, when we consider that indifferent citizens may be less inclined to participate, we might expect the "active public" to be considerably more rational than their inert brethren. Unfortunately, and apart from its normative deficiencies (Converse, 1990), this account of aggregation is unsatisfying as a mechanism for collective rationality. The central rub is that "error" in individual information processing is frequently not random, as is assumed in the statistical account, but rather is systematically distributed, so that it will accumulate through aggregation rather than cancel out (Page & Shapiro, 1992). If poorly informed citizens, for example, are disproportionately driven to one side in a given debate or election—perhaps because they more easily fall prey to elite manipulations of information—their uninformed opinions will certainly not cancel (Bartels, 1996).

Weighted aggregation seeks to account for motivational and informational asymmetries in the electorate. Elites—citizens who are motivated and positioned to influence real politics—matter more, so their opinions must be weighted more (Stimson, 1991). Here too there are both normative and empirical objections. First, I should point out, the wide adoption of the majoritarian view in public opinion polling gives the simple tally of individual opinions considerable self-fulfilling power. To put it less obscurely, it is not always clear whether elites drive majoritarian opinion or are driven by it. If they believe that polls reflect genuine sentiment, they may be inclined to adjust their own positions rather than try to mold mass opinion. Second, the weighted position assumes that elites are significantly wiser than citizens, that they have a firm grasp of the relevant information and will make more informed decisions. Certainly, there is some truth here; by definition elites know and care more, at least in their areas of special interest. But there is no guarantee that elites have *any* knowledge about the critical dimensions for a given decision, and one can easily find examples in hindsight where a majority of citizens held wiser opinions than did elites.

Compositional aggregation, and the social network variant in particular, provides what I find to be the most intellectually satisfying answer from the aggregation perspective (Huckfeldt & Sprague, 1987, 1995; Page & Shapiro, 1992). Collective deliberation, distributed across a complex information environment of local social networks, institutional constraints, and elite/mass interactions, assembles rational collective opinion even when most individuals involved do not possess whole opinions. Ordinary citizens contribute bits and pieces of information, preferences, and questions to the public discourse; the complex system puts things together. I like this story, and it becomes more intriguing as one examines theoretical accounts of how the system might put things together (especially Huckfeldt & Sprague, 1995), but Kinder (1998) is generally right that "so far, it is only a story" (p. 800). Empirical analyses have been limited to (1) rather general manifestations of public opinion like "national mood" (Stimson, 1991) or "macropartisanship" (MacKuen, Erikson, & Stimson, 1989) and (2) local analyses of the impact of social networks on individual information processing and preferences (Huckfeldt, 2001; Huckfeldt & Sprague, 1987, 1995). Moreover, the processes of compositional aggregation need considerably more theoretical development; for this, the theories and methods developed for complex, nonlinear systems analysis—adaptive agent modeling, for example (see Kollman, Miller, & Page, 1992)—might be particularly useful.

Individual Information Processes

One of the most influential ideas of recent years concerning citizen rationality "is that individuals use heuristics—mental shortcuts that require hardly any information to make fairly reliable political judgments" (Kuklinski & Quirk, 2000, p. 153). Party identification (Campbell et al., 1960), candidate traits (Popkin, 1991), trusted elites (Mondak, 1993), interest groups (Lupia, 1994), public mood (Rahn, 2000), and liberals or conservatives (Sniderman, Brody, & Tetlock, 1991) all provide useful cues to citizens in their information processing. Such heuristics may allow "low information rationality" (Popkin, 1991); that is, apparently inadequate citizens may be able to behave quite rationally. The strong claims are that ill-informed citizens behave just as they would if fully informed and that such a process saves democracy from the ignorance of its citizens.

Without denying the prevalence of heuristic reasoning, there is some cause for skepticism on both counts. First, it may be instructive to note that work on heuristics in social psychology emphasizes not only the utility of shortcuts to information processing but also the inferential shortcomings (Nisbett & Ross, 1980). Heuristic reasoning may mislead citizens, sometimes quite seriously (Kuklinski & Quirk, 2000; Lau & Redlawsk, 2001). Poorly informed citizens, for example, do not distribute their votes in presidential elections as do their well-informed counterparts (Bartels, 1996; see also Gilens, 2001). Assuming that these are the folks most reliant on heuristics, it does not appear to be an entirely happy bargain. At least two sources of error intervene: the information provided by cue sources may not be accurate, and it may not be perceived accurately. Indeed, a variety of systematic biases stand in the way of the straightforward use of political heuristics (Kuklinski & Quirk, 2000). The bottom line, it seems to me, is this: there is little question that citizens use heuristics to simplify their information processing; there is considerable question whether such shortcuts allow them to behave competently.

Milton Lodge and his colleagues at Stony Brook (Lodge, McGraw, & Stroh, 1989; Lodge, Steenbergen, & Brau, 1995; Lodge & Taber, 2000) suggest a somewhat different answer to the problem of the dysfunctional citizen based on the on-line model of information processing. Citizens, it seems, may possess far more "knowledge" than they can articulate. Their impressions of political objects—candidates, groups, perhaps issues—may incorporate a very great deal of prior political information processing, even though they can recall very little of that information. Ask a customer in a Manhattan cafe about Governor Pataki of New York, and she may be quite certain that she dislikes him, but she may be much less sure why. Most important, this strong impression of Pataki, which she can only support with a few recollections (and probably a few more rationalizations), may be *perfectly responsive* to the considerable information she has processed concerning Pataki.

I have already made clear my own views regarding the several debates surrounding this model. Perhaps the most critical concern for my purposes here is the degree to which "hot cognition" and the on-line (OL) model for updating impressions enable rational action by citizens in a democracy. In early work, Lodge and colleagues argued quite forcefully in the affirmative, and indeed much of cachet of the OL model stems from the belief that it may provide the *most* powerful individual-level answer for the problem of the dysfunctional citizen (Kinder, 1998). Quite simply, OL processing, unlike its heuristic brethren, holds out the tantalizing prospect of *high* information rationality.

But all is not rosy in Stony Brook land. First, there is good reason to think that the OL tally may be a *heavily biased* summary of the information that has been processed. Normative models of belief updating require a degree of independence between one's prior beliefs and new information (Green & Shapiro, 1994) that may not be possible when cognition is hot. Exactly contrary to early "learning" models of elite or media influence, some citizens may hold onto their beliefs beyond reason and resist persuasion even when the evidence clearly warrants a change of heart (Lazersfeld, Berelson, & Gaudet, 1948). Second, attitudes frequently become even more extreme when citizens process counter attitudinal evidence. Third, citizens actively seek out congenial information and avoid evidence that they expect might question their beliefs. Fourth, sophisticated citizens—presumably those on whom we most rely—are most subject to these "disconfirmation" and "confirmation" biases in motivated reasoning (Taber & Lodge, 2000). On the other hand, it may be perfectly rational under some circumstances to protect one's prior beliefs, and what I have called bias might be reinterpreted as a healthy skepticism. In my view at least, the jury is still out on the question of the high information rationality of on-line processing.

External Constraints

Political institutions, and their role in structuring individual choices and preferences, have recently been offered as a solution to the problem of the dysfunctional citizen (Lupia & McCubbins, 1998; Sniderman, 2000). For example, Arthur Lupia and Mathew McCubbins argue that institutions simplify the application of political heuristics by answering questions like "Who can we trust?" Citizens do not need much information to be competent. They can rely on experts, elites, media sources—a host of others whom they may reasonably expect to be better informed than they are. Institutions "regulate" the reliability of these information sources by imposing penalties for lying, by probabilistic threat of verification, and by making clear the costs that elites bear in publicizing their views. To the degree that talk is not cheap for potential sources of information, they are more credible. Paul Sniderman (2000) makes a similar argument, but focuses on the simplification of "choice sets" by political institutions, in particular by political parties.

This approach alleviates at least one of the complaints against the heuristic processing perspective. Institutions may raise confidence in the competence and truthfulness of information sources. On the other hand, despite some suggestive experimental evidence (Kuklinski, Quirk, Jerit, & Rich, 2001), this basic point still awaits empirical corroboration. In particular, I would be interested in how effectively institutions in fact do regulate elite behavior. Other criticisms of the heuristic approach still apply, it seems to me. Finally, proponents of institutional constraints need to more explicitly address normative questions of rationality for individuals. To the extent that these mechanisms foster elite manipulation of individual choice, they may not solve the democratic dilemma we face.

Summary

Given the apathy, ignorance, unsophistication, and intolerance of many American citizens, public opinion scholars have long wondered how democracy has managed to persist. One set of answers focuses on collective rationality; aggregation processes may somehow correct for the deficiencies of individual citizens. Others have argued that individual citizens actually are sufficiently competent, either because they use heuristic cues to compensate for their lack of knowledge or because they possess "knowledge" that they cannot articulate. Most recently, scholars have noted that political institutions may simplify the use of heuristics. These are not, in my mind, competing mechanisms. Each offers important insights that surely do help to explain the paradox of dysfunctional citizens in a functional public, and their deficiencies are sufficiently different that one might hope that a theoretical integration would offer a much more satisfactory solution. Notably, however, none addresses the problem of intolerance, though there is "good" news here: citizens, it seems, may not generally act on their undemocratic beliefs or values (Kinder, 1998). All in all, I believe that optimism is warranted: citizens are less dysfunctional and their deficiencies are less important than we have long thought.

◤ Foxes in the Henhouse

As I have worked through this chapter, my own ardor for public opinion research has been substantially rekindled. I am more convinced than ever that information processing is the most natural analytic approach to public opinion. But there are also foxes in this henhouse.

One common complaint has been the meager standing of emotion and affect in information-processing theory. The traditional Enlightenment view of emotion as pathological for decision-making clearly needs revision; research from many quarters now places affect at the center of human cognition (see Marcus, this *Handbook*). For example, it is quite well established that affect can cue attention, motivate deeper and less heuristic processing, and promote more efficient knowledge structures in memory. Empirically, evaluative processes may be inseparable from cognition (e.g., Damasio, 1994). In truth, however, the complaint of "too little affect" is overdrawn. Political psychologists have long been interested in affect (e.g., David Sears and John Sullivan), and over the past decade evaluative affect has become one of the hot "new" topics in political cognition (Judd & Krosnick, 1989; Lodge & Taber, 2000; Marcus & MacKuen, 1993; McGraw & Steenbergen, 1995; Ottati, Steenbergen, & Riggle, 1992; Rahn, 2000; Sniderman, Brody, & Tetlock, 1991).

A more genuine limitation of the work reviewed here may be its unrelenting individualism. With several notable exceptions—for example, work on social networks and work that explicitly accounts for elite and media manipulations of information—this literature pays scant attention to the information context; my own work on motivated reasoning, for example, concentrates on internal information processes to the virtual exclusion of how these might interact with external behavior. On the other hand, I worry that highly contextualized research may pay too little attention to internal cognitive processes, leaving us with a new generation of black box models at the individual level.

The most pressing challenge for the literature on political cognition and public opinion, in my estimation, may also seem the most obscure.[18] One can read the cognitive revolution in psychology as a symphony in three movements: first, the basic themes of information processing and models of the mind; second, variations on those themes designed to account for affect; and third, a slow crescendo of interest in automaticity. Social psychologists today consider the distinction between automatic and controlled processes to be absolutely vital to an understanding of human cognition (e.g., Banaji, Lemm, & Carpenter, 2001; Bargh, 1997; Bargh & Chartrand, 1999; Bargh & Ferguson, 2000; Gardner & Cacioppo, 1997; Logan, 1992). The most fertile models of persuasion, for example, distinguish between deep, systematic, controlled processing and peripheral, heuristic, automatic processing (Eagly & Chaiken, 1993; Petty & Wegener, 1998). And the use of stereotypes, surely central to political cognition, has long been conceived in terms of uncontrolled categorization processes (Banaji & Dasgupta, 1998; Bargh, Chen, & Burrows, 1996; Devine, 1989; Fiske & Taylor, 1991). Even power abuse and corruption have been linked to individual differences in automaticity; that is, some people are more likely to selfishly abuse power than others, not because they choose to do so but rather because power goals are chronically accessible for them in LTM (Lee-Chai & Bargh, 2001). Some of these ideas have influenced political psychology—note the heuristics movement[19]—but with some recent exceptions (Bassili, 1995; Huckfeldt, Levine, Morgan, & Sprague, 1999; Krosnick, 1989; Lodge & Taber, 2000; Miller & Krosnick, 2000), one rarely sees explicit mention of automaticity (for a notable exception, see Sears's work on symbolic predispositions, summarized in Sears, 1993). Political science, long under the spell of the Enlightenment view of rationality, has not been particularly friendly ground for the germination of either affective or automatic models of information processing, and I think this biases research in public opinion today.

The ramifications of automaticity are, I believe, very serious, and especially so for public opinion research. Mental processing that occurs outside of awareness and differs from conscious thought will be invisible to the empirical technologies of survey research (and to much experimental research as well). The evidence has been growing for several decades that a great deal of the work of thinking is in fact submerged in automatic processes (Bargh & Chartrand, 1999; Neely, 1977; Uleman & Bargh, 1989), and studies that directly compare conscious responses to nonreactive measures (measures outside of conscious control) have found big differences (Crosby, Bromley, & Saxe, 1980; Devine, 1989). For example, one recent study found that physiological (fMRI) measures of racial attitudes correlated strongly with unconscious measures (Implicit Association Test and startle response) but were unrelated to conscious expression of race attitudes, as measured in the Modern Racism Scale (Phelps, et al., 2000). These and a large number of similar findings go beyond simple social desirability explanations of the divergence between expressed and "real" attitudes because subjects in these studies are *genuinely unaware* of their automatic stereotyping. In the next decade, I believe we will have to come to grips with what John Bargh (1999) has called "the cognitive monster": the unconscious and automatic underpinnings of thought. I will not be surprised if much of what we know about attention, knowledge structures and interpretation, and evaluation in political information processing will require substantial revision as a result.

A part of me is happy that we have foxes to battle. Certainly some hens will be eaten, and more will be chased from their roosts, but the henhouse as a whole will be better for it. Mass public opinion has grown into the most productive and mature field of political psychology with a remarkable history of controversy and success. One cannot help but be impressed with the achievements of the past half-century. But we need a few foxes to keep the henhouse from becoming a dull and complacent place.

◣ Notes

1. It would be mulish, however, to deny that theoretical influence still runs predominantly from social psychology into political science. Note that two of the three editors of this book are psychologists by training. On the other hand, I do not think it would be accurate to say that political psychologists are simply sampling the soup *du jour* of social psychology, as some have charged (see debate in Kuklinski, 2002). Political psychologists, it seems to me, have been increasingly concerned with mental process as part of the larger influence of the cognitive revolution throughout the social sciences, and it is those common theoretical concerns that make the new social cognition attractive.

2. Stimson (1991) goes on to point out that the individual is also an abstraction: "except perhaps for hermits, there exist no atomistic individuals whose ideas or context of ideas are wholly their own" (p. 2). Agreed. Individual citizens exist within social networks (Huckfeldt & Sprague, 1995), which heavily influence the informational inputs they receive and thus their perspectives and habitual processes (including favored heuristics) over time. The locus of information processing is, however, within individual heads. The more "natural" abstraction when one speaks of public opinion, it seems to me, is the individual. The self-awareness and reality of experience of individual humans (they *bleed!*) sets them apart from groups. Though aggregation processes are known to have nontrivial effects on decisions, groups do not have preferences over outcomes apart

from the preferences of their individual members. We evaluate the rationality of a collective body (recall Page & Shapiro, *The Rational Public*, 1992) in terms that are meaningful only for individuals. The bottom line is that groups do not experience policy outcomes; individuals do.

3. It is worth noting that similar debates have raged in the small groups literature in social psychology (Levine & Moreland, 1998). There is another perspective from evolutionary biology that will probably influence public opinion research in the coming decade. This work falls under several labels—morphogenesis, emergence theory, self-organization theory—but the common thrust is the relatively old idea that systems of individual agents have important characteristics that may not be traced to those agents. Biosystems of very simple (demonstrably unintelligent) agents sometimes display apparently intelligent collective behavior (e.g., Edward Wilson's mold spores or ants that "learn" to traverse a maze). I would caution that it is not entirely clear that the collective behavior of intelligent agents (even democratic citizens) will follow the same aggregation principles as in the self-organization of non-sentient agents.

4. Even if all individuals responded to an external event in exactly the same way, so that there was no variation in the causal links from external force to citizen and from citizen to public opinion—surely an extremely rare occurrence—we would still need to account for the individual in an explanatory analysis. Note that this fallacy is quite common in regression-type analyses in which we may seek to control away nonindependent factors, forgetting that they may form part of a causal chain.

5. It may be worth reminding the reader that the computers developed during World War II came about precisely to address deficiencies in our information processing and computational capabilities—to break codes or to simulate subatomic processes, for example.

6. Taber and Timpone (1996) explain PDP and semantic network models in much more detail.

7. I have not discussed balance theory at all, but it is worth noting that all attitudinal elements in figure 13.2e are in balance. That need not be the case, of course.

8. Among the several limitations of this analogy is that it ignores inputs from the world (sensory experience). Working memory (in this case, you with your flashlight) stands between LTM and experience, and to the degree that attention is captured by either, awareness of the other diminishes.

9. For more information on these and other memory processes (e.g., forgetting), see Collins and Smith (1988), Conway (1997), and Eysenck and Keane (1990). Taber and Timpone (1996) offer a treatment for social scientists.

10. Saying "and so on" here is rather unsatisfactory, since how far activation spreads and how much it diminishes as it spreads are unresolved questions.

11. A primary goal of cognitive science is the creation and formalization of process theories of human cognition. Computational models (i.e., working computer representations) of these theories are the primary tool for determining the completeness and generating the implications of these cognitive theories (see Anderson, 1983; Boynton & Lodge, 1998; Taber, 1992; Taber & Steenbergen, 1995; Taber & Timpone, 1996).

12. One can certainly see this movement, however, by comparing the portrayals of the field in the 1981 (Kinder & Sears) and 1998 (Kinder) chapters in the *Handbook of Social Psychology*. Steenbergen and Lodge (mimeo) trace the inception of the field of political cognition to several seminal publications in the early 1980s (Fiske & Kinder, 1981; Graber, 1984; Herstein, 1981), but they hasten to point out the foreshadowing

work of Lippman (1922), McPhee (1963), and Axelrod (1973). I would add to this list a series of publications focused on elite foreign policy decision-making (Carbonell, 1978; Jervis, 1970; Snyder, Bruck, & Sapin, 1962).

13. Recent definitions of rationality from political economists (representative examples can be found in Lupia, McCubbins, & Popkin, 2000) consciously dissociate the principle of rationality from selfish goals. Simon's (1985) challenge, it seems, has been taken to heart.

14. Hotly contested campaigns over easily understood material interests, as in some tax relief referenda, have been found to trigger much greater self-interested action (Courant, Gramlich, & Rubinfield, 1980; Hawthorne & Jackson, 1987).

15. Recognizing that modern pluralist society locates the individual within a field of complex, and sometimes crosscutting, group identifications, and that identity itself changes with social and political circumstance, the simple language of ingroups and outgroups nevertheless provides a powerful framework for discussing the effect of intergroup relations on public opinion.

16. An information board is a matrix of hidden information; subjects must click on a cell of the matrix to reveal the information from that cell. In this variant, the hidden information consisted of pro and con arguments on affirmative action or gun control, and the rows were labeled with the source of the arguments (e.g., NRA or Committee Against Handguns).

17. We have additional evidence in support of hot cognition and automaticity in the processing of political objects from Event Related Potential studies that track brain activity using a physiological (EEG) method. The OL hypothesis has been well supported in a variety of prior studies (e.g., Lodge, Steenbergen, & Brau, 1995).

18. I realize that some readers will see in my concern for automaticity yet another step away from the stuff of politics, but I make no apology. I have always believed that critiques of political cognition as too psychological and apolitical miss the basic point of this research, which is to understand in process terms the formation of political attitudes and beliefs. Surely understanding political opinions is central to politics!

19. However, political heuristics are commonly discussed as if they are consciously chosen.

▶ References

Abelson, R. (1963). Computer simulation of "hot" cognition. In S. S. Tomkins & S. Messick (Eds.), *Computer simulation of personality* (pp. 277–298). New York: Wiley.

Abramowitz, A. I., & Saunders, K. L. (1998). Ideological realignment in the U.S. electorate. *Journal of Politics, 60,* 634–652.

Achen, C. H. (1975). Mass political attitudes and the survey response. *American Political Science Review, 69,* 1218–1231.

Adorno, T. W., Frankel-Brunswick, E., Levinson, D. J., & Sanford, N. (1950). *The authoritarian personality.* New York: Harper and Row.

Allport, G. W. (1935). Attitudes. In C. Murchison (Ed.), *Handbook of social psychology.* Worcester, MA: Clark University Press.

Anderson, J. R. (1983). *The Architecture of Cognition.* Cambridge, MA: Harvard University Press.

Atkinson, R. C., & Shiffrin, R. M. (1968). Human memory: A proposed system and its control processes. In K. W. Spence & J. T. Spence (Eds.), *The psychology of learning and motivation* (Vol. 2, pp. 90–195). London: Academic Press.

Axelrod, R. (1973). Schema theory: An information processing model of perception and cognition, *American Political Science Review, 67,* 1248–1266.

Barent, M. K., & Krosnick, J. K. (1995). The relation between political attitude importance and knowledge structure. In M. Lodge & K. McGraw (Eds.), *Political judgment: Structure and process.* Ann Arbor, MI: University of Michigan Press.

Banaji, M. R., & Dasgupta, N. (1998). The consciousness of social beliefs: A program of research on stereotyping and prejudice. In V. Y. Yzerbyt, G. Lories, & B. Dardenne (Eds.), *Metacognition: Cognitive and social dimensions* (pp. 157–170). London: Sage.

Banaji, M. R., Lemm, K. M., & Carpenter, S. J. (2001). Automatic and implicit processes in social cognition. In A. Tesser & N. Schwartz (Eds.), *Blackwell handbook of social psychology: Intraindividual processes* (pp. 134–158). London: Blackwell.

Bargh, J. A. (1997). The automaticity of everyday life. In R. S. Wyer (Ed.), *The automaticity of everyday life, advances in social cognition* (Vol. 10, pp. 1–61). Mahwah, NJ: Erlbaum.

Bargh, J. A. (1999). The cognitive monster: The case against controllability of automatic stereotype effects. In S. Chaiken & Y. Trope (Eds.), *Dual process theories in social psychology* (pp. 361–382). New York: Guilford.

Bargh, J. A., Chaiken, S., Govender, R., & Pratto, F. (1992). The generality of the automatic attitude activation effect. *Journal of Personality and Social Psychology, 62,* 893–912.

Bargh, J. A., & Chartrand, T. L. (1999). The unbearable automaticity of being. *American Psychologist, 54,* 462–479.

Bargh, J. A., Chen, M., & Burrows, L. (1996). Automaticity of social behavior: Direct effects of trait construct and stereotype priming on action. *Journal of Personality and Social Psychology, 71,* 230–244.

Bargh, J. A., & Ferguson, M. L. (2000). Beyond behaviorism: On the automaticity of higher mental processes. *Psychological Bulletin, 126,* 925–945.

Bartels, L. M. (1996). Uninformed votes: Information effects in presidential elections. *American Journal of Political Science, 40,* 194–230.

Bartlett, F. C. (1932). *Remembering: A study in experimental and social psychology.* Cambridge: Cambridge University Press.

Bassili, J. N. (1995). Response latency and the accessibility of voting intentions: What contributes to accessibility and how it affects vote choice. *Personality and Social Psychology Bulletin, 21,* 686–695.

Bennett, S. E. (1986). *Apathy in America.* Dobbs Ferry, NY: Transnational.

Bennett, S. E., & Resnick, D. (1990). The implications of non-voting for democracy in the United States. *American Journal of Political Science, 34,* 771–802.

Black, E., & Black, M. (1987). *Politics and society in the south.* Cambridge, MA: Harvard University Press.

Blumer, H. (1946). Collective behavior. In A. M. Lee (Ed.), *New outlines of the principles of sociology* (pp. 167–22). New York: Barnes & Noble.

Bobo, L. (1988). Attitudes toward the black political movement: Trends, meaning, and effects on racial policy preferences, *Social Psychology Quarterly, 51,* 287–302.

Bobo, L., & Kluegel, J. R. (1993). Opposition to race targeting: Self-interest, stratification ideology, or racial attitudes? *American Sociological Review, 58,* 443–464.

Boden, M. A. (1988). *Computer models of mind.* Cambridge: Cambridge University Press.

Boninger, D. S., Krosnick, J. A., Barent, M. K., & Fabrigar, L. R. (1995). The causes and consequences of attitude importance. In R. E. Petty & J. A. Krosnick (Eds.), *Attitude strength: Antecedents and consequences* (pp. 159–189). Mahwah, NJ: Erlbaum.

Boynton, G. R., & Lodge, M. (1998). J. Q. Public: A computational model of a survey respondent. *Political Communication,* CD-ROM insert.

Brewer, M. B., & Brown, R. J. (1998). Intergroup relations. In D. T. Gilbert, S. T. Fiske, & G. Lindzey (Eds.), *Handbook of social psychology* (4th ed., pp. 554–594). London: Oxford University Press.

Brown, R. (1986). *Social psychology: The second edition.* New York: Free Press.

Broadbent, D. E. (1958). *Perception and communication.* Oxford: Pergamon.

Bruner, J. S., Goodnow, J. J., & Austin, G. A. (1956). *A study of thinking.* New York: Wiley.

Campbell, A., Converse, P., Miller, W., & Stokes, D. (1960). *The American voter.* New York: Wiley.

Carbonell, J. G., Jr. (1978). Politics: Automated ideological reasoning. *Cognitive Science, 2,* 27–51.

Chomsky, N. (1957). *Syntactic structures.* The Hague: Mouton.

Citrin, J., & Green, D. (1990). The self-interest motive in American public opinion. *Research in Micropolitics, 3,* 1–27.

Collins, A. M., & Quillian, M. R. (1969). Retrieval time from semantic memory. *Journal of Verbal Learning and Verbal Behavior, 8,* 240–248.

Collins, A., & Smith, E. E. (Eds.). (1988). *Readings in cognitive science: A perspective from psychology and artificial intelligence.* San Mateo, CA: Morgan Kaufmann.

Conover, P. J., & Feldman, S. (1991). Where is the schema? Critiques. *American Political Science Review, 85,* 1364–1369.

Converse, J. M. (1987). *Survey research in the United States.* Los Angeles: University of California Press.

Converse, P. E. (1964). The nature of belief systems in mass publics. In D. E. Apter (Ed.), *Ideology and discontent* (pp. 206–261). New York: Free Press.

Converse, P. E. (1987). Changing conceptions of public opinion in the political process. *Public Opinion Quarterly, 51,* 12–24.

Converse, P. E. (1990). Popular representation and the distribution of information. In J. A. Ferejohn & J. H. Kuklinski (Eds.)., *Information and democratic processes.* Urbana: University of Illinois Press.

Conway, M. A. (Ed.). (1997). *Cognitive models of memory.* Cambridge, MA: MIT Press.

Coser, L. A. (1956). *The functions of social conflict.* Glencoe, IL: Free Press.

Courant, P. N., Gramlich, E. M., & Rubinfield, D. L. (1980). Why voters support tax limitation amendments: The Michigan case. *National Tax Journal, 32,* 147–158.

Crosby, F., Bromley, S., & Saxe, L. (1980). Recent unobtrusive studies of black and white discrimination and prejudice: A literature review. *Psychological Bulletin, 87,* 546–563.

Dahl, R. A. (1961). *Who governs?* New Haven: Yale University Press.

Damasio, A. R. (1994). *Descartes' error: Emotion, reason, and the human brain.* New York: Putnam.

Davis, J. A. (1975). Communism, conformity, cohorts and categories: American tolerance in 1954 and 1972–1973. *American Journal of Sociology, 81,* 491–513.

Dawson, M. (1994). *Behind the mule.* Princeton: Princeton University Press.

Deaux, K., Reid, A., Mizrahi, K., & Ethier, K. A. (1995). Parameters of social identity. *Journal of Personality and Social Psychology, 68,* 280–291.

Delli Carpini, M. X., & Keeter, S. (1996). *What Americans know about politics and why it matters.* New Haven: Yale University Press.

Devine, P. G. (1989). Stereotypes and prejudice: Their automatic and controlled components. *Journal of Personality and Social Psychology, 56,* 5–18.

Downs, A. (1957). *An economic theory of democracy.* New York: Harper and Row.

Eagly, A. H., & Chaiken, S. (1993). *The psychology of attitudes.* Fort Worth, TX: Harcourt Brace Jovanovich.

Edwards, K., & Smith, E. E. (1996). A disconfirmation bias in the evaluations of arguments. *Journal of Personality and Social Psychology, 71,* 5–24.

Eysenck, M. W., & Keane, M. T. (1990). *Cognitive psychology: A student's handbook.* London: Erlbaum.

Fazio, R. H., Sonbonmatsu, D. M., Powell, M. C., & Kardes, F. R. (1986). On the automatic activation of attitudes. *Journal of Personality and Social Psychology, 50,* 229–238.

Feigenbaum, E. A., & Feldman, J. (Eds.). (1963/1995). *Computers and thought.* Menlo Park, CA: AAAI Press.

Feldman, S. (1983). Economic individualism and American public opinion. *American Politics Quarterly, 11,* 3–29.

Feldman, S. (1988). Structure and consistency in public opinion: The role of core beliefs and values. *American Journal of Political Science, 32,* 416–440.

Feldman, S., & Zaller, J. (1992). The political culture of ambivalence: Ideological responses to the welfare state. *American Journal of Political Science, 36,* 268–307.

Festinger, L. (1957). *A theory of cognitive dissonance.* Palo Alto, CA: Stanford University Press.

Fiske, S. T. (1998). Stereotyping, prejudice, and discrimination. In D. T. Gilbert, S. T. Fiske, & G. Lindzey (Eds.), *Handbook of social psychology* (4th ed., pp. 357–419). London: Oxford University Press.

Fiske, S. T. & Kinder, D. R. (1981). Involvement, expertise, and schema use: Evidence from political cognition. In N. Cantor & J. F. Kihlstrom (Eds.), *Personality, cognition, and social interaction.* Hillsdale, NJ: Erlbaum.

Fiske, S. T., & Taylor, S. E. (1991). *Social cognition* (2nd ed.). New York: McGraw-Hill.

Frey, D. (1986). Recent research on selective exposure to information. In L. Berkowitz (Ed.), *Advances in experimental social psychology* (Vol. 19, pp. 91–80). New York: Academic.

Gamson, W. A. (1992). *Talking politics.* New York: Cambridge University Press.

Gardner, W. L., & Cacioppo, J. T. (1997). Automaticity and social behavior: A model, a marriage, and a merger. In R. S. Wyer, Jr. (Ed.), *Advances in social cognition* (Vol. 10, pp. 133–141). Mahwah, NJ: Erlbaum.

Gilbert, D. T., Fiske, S. T., & Lindzey, G. (Eds.). (1998). *Handbook of social psychology* (4th ed.). London: Oxford University Press.

Gilens, M. (1999). *Why Americans hate welfare: Race, media, and the politics of anti-poverty policy.* Chicago: University of Chicago Press.

Gilens, M. (2001). Political ignorance and collective policy preferences. *American Political Science Review, 95,* 379–396.

Graber, D. (1984). *Processing the news: How people tame the information tide.* New York: Longman.

Green, D. P., & Shapiro, I. (1994). *Pathologies of rational choice theory.* New Haven: Yale University Press.

Greenstein, F. 1969. *Personality and politics.* Princeton: Princeton University Press.

Hastie, R. (1986). A primer of information-processing theory for the political scientist. In R. R. Lau & D. O. Sears (Eds.). *Political cognition* (pp. 11–39). Hillsdale: Erlbaum.

Hastie, R., & Pennington, N. (1989). Notes on the distinction between memory-based and on-line judgment. In J. Bassili (Ed.), *On-line cognition in person perception* (pp. 1–17). Hillsdale, NJ: Lawrence Erlbaum.

Hawthorne, M. R., & Jackson, J. E. (1987). The individual political economy of tax policy. *American Political Science Review, 81,* 757–774.

Heider, F. (1946). Attitudes and cognitive organization. *Journal of Psychology, 21,* 107–112.

Heider, F. (1958). *The psychology of interpersonal relations.* New York: Wiley.

Herstein, J. (1981). Keeping the voter's limits in mind: A cognitive process analysis of decision making and voting. *Journal of Personality and Social Psychology, 40,* 843–861.

Huckfeldt, R. (2001). The social communication of political expertise. *American Journal of Political Science, 45,* 425–438.

Huckfeldt, R., Levine, J., Morgan, W., & Sprague, J. (1999). Accessibility and the political utility of partisan and ideological orientations. *American Journal of Political Science, 43,* 888–911.

Huckfeldt, R., & Sprague, J. (1987). Networks in context: The social flow of political information. *American Political Science Review, 81,* 1197–1216.

Huckfeldt, R., & Sprague, J. (1995). *Citizens, politics, and social communication.* New York: Cambridge University Press.

Hull, C. L. (1930). Knowledge and purpose as habit mechanisms. *Psychological Review, 37,* 511–525.

Hurwitz, J., & Peffley, M. (1987). How are foreign policy attitudes structured? A hierarchical model. *American Political Science Review, 81,* 1099–1110.

Hyman, H. H. (1955). *Survey design and analysis: Principles, cases, and procedures.* Glencoe, IL: Free Press.

Iyengar, S. (1991). *Is anyone responsible? How television frames political issues.* Chicago: University of Chicago Press.

Iyengar, S., & Kinder, D. (1987). *News that matters: Television and American opinion.* Chicago: University of Chicago Press.

James, W. (1890). *Principles of psychology.* New York: Holt.

Jennings, M. K. (1979). Another look at the life cycle and political participation. *American Journal of Political Science, 23,* 755–771.

Jervis, R. (1970). *The logic of images in international relations.* Princeton: Princeton University Press.

Judd, C., & Krosnick, J. (1989). The structural basis of consistency among political attitudes: Effects of political expertise and attitude importance. In A. Pratkanis, S. Becker, & A. Greenwald (Eds.), *Attitude structure and function* (pp. 99–128). Mahwah, NJ: Erlbaum.

Kiewiet, D. R. (1983). *Macroeconomics and micropolitics*. Chicago: University of Chicago Press.

Kinder, D. R. (1986). The continuing American dilemma: White resistance to racial change forty years after Myrdal. *Journal of Social Issues, 42,* 151–172.

Kinder, D. R. (1998). Opinion and action in the realm of politics. In D. T. Gilbert, S. T. Fiske, & G. Lindzey (Eds.), *Handbook of social psychology* (4th ed., pp. 778–867). London: Oxford University Press.

Kinder, D. R., & Mendelberg, T. (1995). Cracks in American apartheid: The political impact of prejudice among desegregated whites. *Journal of Politics, 57,* 401–424.

Kinder, D. R., & Mendelberg, T. (2000). Individualism reconsidered: Principles and prejudice in contemporary American opinion. In D. O. Sears, J. Sidanius, & L. Bobo (Eds.), *Racialized politics* (pp. 44–74). Chicago: University of Chicago.

Kinder, D. R., & L. M. Sanders. (1996). *Divided by color: Racial politics and democratic ideals.* Chicago: University of Chicago Press.

Kinder, D. R., & Sears, D. O. (1981). Public opinion and political action. In G. Lindzey & E. Aronson (Eds.), *Handbook of Social Psychology* (3rd ed., Vol. 2, pp. 659–741). New York: Random House.

Kinder, D. R., & N. Winter. (2001). Exploring the racial divide: Blacks, whites, and opinion on national policy. *American Journal of Political Science, 45,* 439–453.

Kluegel, J. R., & Smith, E. R. (1986). *Beliefs about inequality: Americans' views about what is and what ought to be.* New York: de Gruyter.

Kollman, K., Miller, J. H., & Page, S. E. (1992). Adaptive parties in spatial elections. *American Political Science Review, 86,* 929–937.

Krosnick, J. A. (1988). Attitude importance and attitude change. *Journal of Experimental Social Psychology, 24,* 240–255.

Krosnick, J. A. (1989). Attitude importance and attitude accessibility. *Personality and Social Psychology Bulletin, 15,* 297–308.

Krosnick, J. A. (1990). Government policy and citizen passion: A study of issue publics in contemporary America. *Political Behavior, 12,* 59–92.

Kuklinski, J. (Ed.). (2002). *Thinking about political psychology.* Cambridge: Cambridge University Press.

Kuklinski, J. H., Luskin, R., & Bolland, J. (1991). Where is the schema? Going beyond the "S" word in political psychology. *American Political Science Review, 85,* 1341–1356.

Kuklinski, J. H., & Quirk, P. J. (2000). Reconsidering the rational public: Cognition, Heuristics, and Mass Opinion. In A. Lupia, M. D. McCubbins, & S. L. Popkin (Eds.), *Elements of reason: Cognition, choice, and the bounds of rationality* (pp. 153–182). Cambridge,: Cambridge University Press.

Kuklinski, J. H., Quirk, P. J., Jerit, J., & Rich, R. F. (2001). The political environment and citizen competence. *American Journal of Political Science, 45,* 410–424.

Kunda, Z. (1990). The case for motivated reasoning. *Psychological Bulletin, 1083,* 480–498.

Lau, R. R., Brown, T. A., & Sears, D. O. (1978). Self-interest and civilians' attitudes toward the Vietnam War. *Public Opinion Quarterly, 42,* 464–483.

Lau, R. R., & Redlawsk, D. P. (2001). Advantages and disadvantages of cognitive heuristics in political decision making. *American Journal of Political Science, 45,* 951–971.

Lau, R. R., Smith, R. A., & Fiske, S. T. (1991). Political beliefs, policy interpretations, and political persuasion. *Journal of Politics, 53,* 644–675.

Lavine, H. (2001). The electoral consequences of ambivalence toward presidential candidates. *American Journal of Political Science, 45,* 915–929.

Lavine, H. (2002). On-line vs. memory-based process models of political evaluation. In K. Monroe (Ed.), *Political psychology* (pp. 225–248). Mahwah, NJ: Erlbaum.

Lavine, H., & Gschwend, T. (n.d.). *Ideology and rationality: The role of issue constraint in electoral decision-making.* Mimeograph. Department of Political Science, State University of New York at Stony Brook.

Lazersfeld, P. F., Berelson, B. R., & Gaudet, H. (1948). *The people's choice.* New York: Columbia University.

Lee-Chai, A. Y., & Bargh, J. A. (Eds.). (2001). *The use and abuse of power.* Philadelphia: Psychology Press.

Levine, J. M., & Moreland, R. L. (1998). Small groups. In D. T. Gilbert, S. T. Fiske, & G. Lindzey (Eds.), *Handbook of social psychology* (4th ed., pp. 415–469). London: Oxford University Press.

Lippman, W. (1922). *Public opinion.* New York: Macmillan.

Lodge, M. (1995). Toward a procedural model of candidate evaluation. In M. Lodge & K. McGraw (Eds.), *Political judgment: Structure and process* (pp. 111–139). Ann Arbor: University of Michigan Press.

Lodge, M., & McGraw, K. (1991). Where is the schema? Critiques. *American Political Science Review, 85,* 1357–1364.

Lodge, M., & McGraw, K. (Eds.). (1995). *Political judgment: Structure and process.* Ann Arbor: University of Michigan Press.

Lodge, M., McGraw, K., & Stroh, P. (1989). An impression-driven model of candidate evaluation. *American Political Science Review, 83,* 399–419.

Lodge, M., Steenbergen, M., & Brau, S. (1995). The responsive voter: Campaign information and the dynamics of candidate evaluation. *American Political Science Review, 89,* 309–326.

Lodge, M., & Taber, C. (2000). Three steps toward a theory of motivated political reasoning. In A. Lupia, M. D. McCubbins, & S. L. Popkin (Eds.), *Elements of reason: Cognition, choice, and the bounds of rationality* (pp. 183–213). Cambridge: Cambridge University Press.

Lodge, M., & Taber, C. S. (2001, April). *Automatic affect: A test of hot cognition for candidates, groups, and issues.* Paper presented at the annual meeting of the Midwest Political Science Association, Chicago.

Logan, G. D. (1992). Attention and preattention in theories of automaticity. *American Journal of Psychology, 105,* 317–339.

Luger, G. F. (Ed.). (1995). *Computation and intelligence.* Menlo Park, CA: AAAI Press.

Lupia, A. (1994). Shortcuts versus encyclopedias: Information and voting behavior in California insurance reform elections. *American Political Science Review, 88,* 63–76.

Lupia, A., & McCubbins, M. D. (1998). *The democratic dilemma: Can citizens learn what they need to know?* Cambridge: Cambridge University Press.

Lupia, A., McCubbins, M. D., & Popkin, S. L. (Eds.). (2000). *Elements of reason:*

Cognition, choice, and the bounds of rationality. Cambridge: Cambridge University Press.

MacKuen, M., Erikson, R. S., & Stimson, J. A. (1989). Macropartisanship. *American Political Science Review, 83,* 1125–1142.

Marcus, G. E., & MacKuen, M. B. (1993). Anxiety, enthusiasm and the vote: On the emotional underpinnings of learning and involvement during presidential campaigns. *American Political Science Review, 87,* 672–685.

Martin, L. L., & Tesser, A. (Eds.). (1992). *The construction of social judgments.* Hillsdale, NJ: Erlbaum.

McClosky, H. (1964). Consensus and ideology in American politics. *American Political Science Review, 58,* 316–382.

McGraw, K. (2000). Contributions of the cognitive approach to political psychology. *Political Psychology, 21,* 805–832.

McGraw, K., & Steenbergen, M. (1995). Pictures in the head: Memory representations of political candidates. In M. Lodge & K. McGraw (Eds.), *Political judgment: Structure and process* (pp. 15–42). Ann Arbor: University of Michigan Press.

McPhee, W. N. (1963). *Formal theories of mass behavior.* New York: Free Press.

Mencken, H. L. (1949). *A Mencken chrestomathy.* New York: Knopf.

Mill, J. S. (1861/1951). *Three essays.* Oxford: Oxford University Press.

Miller, G. A. (1957). The magic number seven, plus or minus two: Some limits on our capacity for processing information. *Psychological Review, 63,* 81–93.

Miller, J. M. & Krosnick, J. A. (2000). News media impact on the ingredients of presidential evaluations: Politically knowledgeable citizens are guided by a trusted source. *American Journal of Political Science, 44,* 295–309.

Mondak, J. (1993.) Source cues and policy approval: The cognitive dynamics of public support for the Reagan agenda. *American Journal of Political Science, 37,* 186–212.

Monroe, K. R. (1994). A fat lady in a corset: Altruism and social theory. *American Journal of Political Science, 38,* 861–893.

Morris, J. P., Squires, N. K., Taber, C. S., & Lodge, M. (forthcoming). The automatic activation of political attitudes: A psychophysiological examination of the hot cognition hypothesis. *Political Psychology.*

Mueller, J. E. (1973). *War, presidents, and public opinion.* New York: Wiley.

Mueller, J. E. (1994). *Policy and opinion in the Gulf War.* Chicago: University of Chicago Press.

Neely, J. H. (1977). Semantic priming and retrieval from lexical memory: Roles of inhibitionless spreading activation and limited capacity attention. *Journal of Experimental Psychology: General, 106,* 226–254.

Nelson, T. E., Clawson, R. A., & Oxley, Z. M. (1997). Media framing of a civil liberties conflict and its effect on tolerance. *American Political Science Review, 91,* 567–583.

Newell, A., Shaw, J. C., & Simon, H. A. (1958). Elements of a theory of human problem solving. *Psychological Review, 65,* 151–166.

Nisbett, R. E., & Ross, L. (1980). *Human inference: Strategies and shortcomings of social judgment.* Englewood Cliffs, NJ: Prentice-Hall.

Nunn, C. Z., Crockett, Jr., H. J., & Williams, J. A., Jr. (1978). *Tolerance for noncomformity.* San Francisco: Jossey-Bass.

Orwell, G. (1946). *Animal farm.* New York: Harcourt Brace.

Ottati, V. C., Steenbergen, M. R., & Riggle, E. (1992). The cognitive and affective components of political attitudes: Measuring the determinants of candidate evaluations. *Political Behavior, 14,* 4223–4442.

Ottati, V. C., & Wyer, R. S. (1990). The cognitive mediators of political choice: Toward a comprehensive model of political information processing. In J. A. Ferejohn & J. H. Kuklinski (Eds.), *Information and democratic processes* (pp. 186–216). Urbana: University of Illinois Press.

Page, B. I., & Shapiro, R. Y. (1992). *The rational public: Fifty years of trends in Americans' policy preferences.* Chicago: University of Chicago Press.

Payne, J. W. (1982) Contingent decision behavior. *Psychology Bulletin, 92,* 382–402.

Payne, J. W., Bettman, J. R., & Johnson, E. J. (1992). Behavioral decision research: A constructive processing perspective. *Annual Review of Psychology, 43,* 87–131.

Pettigrew, T. F., & Meertens, R. W. (1995). Subtle and blatant prejudice in western Europe. *European Journal of Social Psychology, 25,* 57–75.

Petty, R. E., & Wegener, D. T. (1998). Attitude change: Multiple roles for persuasion variables. In D. T. Gilbert, S. T. Fiske, & G. Lindzey (Eds.), *Handbook of social psychology* (4th ed., pp. 323–390). London: Oxford University Press.

Phelps, E. A., O'Connor, K. J., Cunningham, W. A., Funayama, E. S., Gatenby, J. C., Gore, J. C., & Banaji, M. R. (2000). Performance on indirect measures of race evaluation predicts amygdala activation. *Journal of Cognitive Neuroscience, 12,* 729–738.

Popkin, S. L. (1991). *The reasoning voter: Communication and persuasion in presidential campaigns.* Chicago: University of Chicago Press.

Price, V., & Hsu, M. L. (1992). Public opinion about AIDS: The role of misinformation and attitudes toward homosexuals. *Public Opinion Quarterly, 57,* 133–164.

Prothro, J. W., & Grigg, C. W. (1960). Fundamental principles of democracy: Biases of agreement and disagreement. *Journal of Politics, 22,* 276–294.

Rahn, W. M. (2000). Affect as information: The role of public mood in political reasoning. In A. Lupia, M. D. McCubbins, & S. L. Popkin (Eds.), *Elements of reason: Cognition, choice, and the bounds of rationality* (pp. 130–152). Cambridge: Cambridge University Press.

Rahn, W. M., Aldrich, J., & Borgida, E. (1994). Individual and contextual variations in political candidate appraisal. *American Political Science Review, 88,* 193–199.

Rumelhart, D. E., McClelland, J. L., & the Parallel Distributed Processing Research Group (Eds.). (1986). *Parallel distributed processing: Vol. 1. Foundations.* Cambridge, MA: MIT Press.

Ruskin, J. (1864/2002). *Sesame and lilies.* New Haven: Yale University Press.

Scherpenzeel, A. C., & Saris, W. E. (1997). The validity and reliability of survey questions: A meta-analysis of MTMM studies. *Sociologocal Methods and Research, 23,* 341–383.

Schreiber, D., & Zaller, J. 2001. *Thinking about politics: A functional magnetic resonance imaging study.* Unpublished paper presented at the American Political Science Association Annual Meeting, San Francisco.

Schlozman, K. L., & Verba, S. (1979). *Injury to insult.* Cambridge, MA: Harvard University Press.

Sears, D. O. (1993). Symbolic politics: A socio-psychological theory. In S. Iyengar & W. J. McGuire (Eds.), *Explorations in political psychology*. Durham, NC: Duke University.

Sears, D. O., & Citrin, J. (1982). *Tax revolt: Something for nothing in California*. Cambridge, MA: Harvard University Press.

Sears, D. O., & Freedman, J. L. (1967). Selective exposure to information: A critical review. *Public Opinion Quarterly, 31,* 194–213.

Sears, D. O., & Funk, C. L. (1991). The role of self-interest in social and political attitudes. *Advances in Experimental Social Psychology, 24,* 1–91.

Sears, D. O., & Huddy, L. (1990). On the origins of political disunity among women. In L. A. Tilly & P. Gurin (Eds.), *Women, politics, and change* (pp. 249–280). New York: Russell Sage Foundation.

Sears, D. O., Lau, R. R., Tyler, T., & Allen, A. M., Jr. (1980). Self-interest versus symbolic politics in policy attitudes and presidential voting. *American Political Science Review, 74,* 670–684.

Simon, H. A. (1978). Rationality as process and as product of thought. *American Economic Review, 68,* 1–16.

Simon, H. A. (1980). Cognitive science: The newest science of the artificial. *Cognitive Science, 4,* 33–46.

Simon, H. A. (1985). Human nature in politics: The dialogue of psychology and political science. *American Political Science Review, 79,* 293–304.

Sniderman, P. M. (1985). *Race and inequality: A study in American values*. Chatham, NJ: Chatham House.

Sniderman, P. M. (1993). The new look in public opinion research. In A. Finifter (Ed.), *Political science: The state of the discipline II* (pp. 219–245). Washington, DC: American Political Science Association.

Sniderman, P. M. (2000). Taking sides: A fixed choice theory of political reasoning. In A. Lupia, M. D. McCubbins, & S. L. Popkin (Eds.), *Elements of reason: Cognition, choice, and the bounds of rationality* (pp. 67–84). Cambridge: Cambridge University Press.

Sniderman, P. M., & Brody, R. A. (1977). Coping: The ethic of self-reliance. *American Journal of Political Science, 21,* 501–522.

Sniderman, P. M., Brody, R. A., & Tetlock, P. E. (1991). *Reasoning and choice: Explorations in political psychology*. New York: Cambridge University Press.

Sniderman, P. M., & Tetlock, P. E. (1986a). Interrelationship of political ideology and public opinion. In M. G. Hermann (Ed.), *Political psychology* (pp. 62–96). San Franciso: Jossey-Bass.

Sniderman, P. M., & Tetlock, P. E. (1986b). Reflections on American racism. *Journal of Social Issues, 42,* 173–187.

Sniderman, P. M., & Tetlock, P. E. (1986c). Symbolic racism: Problems of motive attribution in political analysis. *Journal of Social Issues, 42,* 129–150.

Snyder, R. C., Bruck, H. W., & Sapin, B. (1962). *Foreign policy decision making: An approach to the study of international politics*. New York: Free Press.

Steenbergen, M. R., & Lodge, M. (n.d.). *Process matters: Cognitive models of candidate evaluation*. Mimeograph. Department of Political Science, State University of New York at Stony Brook.

Stimson, J. A. (1991). *Public opinion in America: Moods, cycles, and swings*. Boulder, CO: Westview.

Stoker, L. (1992). Interests and ethics in politics. *American Political Science Review,* *86,* 369–380.

Stouffer, S. (1955). *Communism, conformity, and civil liberties.* New York: Doubleday.

Sullivan, J. L., Pierson, J. E., & Marcus, G. E. (1982). *Political tolerance and American democracy.* Chicago: University of Chicago Press.

Sullivan, J. L., Rahn, W. M., & Rudolph, T. J. (2002). The contours of political psychology: Situating research on political information processing. In J. H. Kuklinski (Ed.), *Thinking about political psychology* (pp. 23–51). Cambridge: Cambridge University Press.

Sumner, W. G. (1906). *Folkways.* Boston: Ginn.

Taber, C. S. (1992). POLI: An expert system model of U.S. foreign policy belief systems. *American Political Science Review, 86,* 423–428.

Taber, C. S. (1998). The interpretation of foreign policy events: A cognitive process theory. In D. A. Sylvan & J. F. Voss (Eds.), *Problem representation in political decision making* (pp. 29–52). London: Cambridge University Press.

Taber, C. S., & Lodge, M. (2000, August). *Motivated skepticism in the evaluation of political beliefs.* Paper presented at the annual meeting of the American Political Science Association, Washington, DC.

Taber, C. S., Lodge, M., & Glathar, J. (2001). The motivated construction of political judgments. In J. H. Kuklinski (Ed.), *Citizens and politics: Perspectives from political psychology* (pp. 198–226). Cambridge: Cambridge University Press.

Taber, C. S., & Steenbergen, M. R. (1995). Computational experiments in electoral behavior. In M. Lodge & K. McGraw (Eds.), *Political judgment: Structure and process.* Ann Arbor: University of Michigan Press.

Taber, C. S., & Timpone, R. J. (1996). *Computational modeling.* Sage University Paper Series on Quantitative Applications in the Social Sciences, No. 07-113. Newbury Park, CA: Sage.

Tetlock, P. E. (1986). A value pluralism model of ideological reasoning. *Journal of Personality and Social Psychology, 50,* 819–827.

Thomsen, C. J., Borgida, E., & Lavine, H. (1995). The causes and consequences of personal involvement. In R. E. Petty & J. A. Krosnick (Eds.), *Attitude strength: Antecedents and consequences.* Mahwah, NJ: Erlbaum.

Thomsen, C. J., Lavine, H., & Kounios, J. (1996). Social value and attitudinal concepts in semantic memory: Relational structure, concept strength, and the fan effect. *Social Cognition, 14,* 191–225.

Thurstone, L. (1927). A law of comparative judgment. *Psychological Review, 34,* 273–286.

Tocqueville, A. de. (1848/1945). *Democracy in America.* New York: Appleton-Century-Crofts.

Tolman, E. C. (1932). *Purposive behavior in animals and men.* New York: Appleton-Century-Crofts.

Tourangeau, R., Rips, L. J., & Rasinski, K. (2000). *The psychology of the survey response.* Cambridge: Cambridge University Press.

Uleman, J. S., & Bargh, J. A. (Eds.). (1989). *Unintended thought.* New York: Guilford.

Wilson, T. C. (1994). Trends in tolerance toward rightist and leftist groups, 1976–1988: Effects of attitude change and cohort succession. *Public Opinion Quarterly, 58,* 539–556.

Wyer, R. S., Jr., & Ottati, V. C. 1993. Political information processing. In S. Iyengar & W. J. McGuire (Eds.), *Explorations in political psychology* (pp. 264–295). Durham, NC: Duke University Press.

Zaller, J. R. (1992). *The nature and origins of mass opinion*. Cambridge: Cambridge University Press.

Zaller, J. R., & Feldman, S. (1992). A simple theory of the survey response. *American Journal of Political Science, 36*, 579–616.

14 Stanley Feldman

Values, Ideology, and the Structure of Political Attitudes

▶ Political Attitudes, Values, and Ideology

It would be difficult, if not impossible, to count the number of political attitudes that a person develops throughout his lifetime. Political figures, groups, government policies, and policy proposals are just some of the potential elements of the political landscape that people may come to evaluate. While many of these attitudes might be interesting to study on their own, a great deal of research in political psychology has been devoted to finding the sources of structure for political attitudes. Given the complexity of politics, the ambiguity of much political information, and relatively low levels of political knowledge among members of the public, it would be easy to believe that these attitudes are unstructured and relatively unpredictable. Although there is still considerable debate about the typical magnitude of political attitude structure, it is clear that people's political evaluations are at least somewhat predictable and the relationships among them far exceed chance. There are many potential sources of structure that probably interact in complex ways. Partisanship, for example, provides many with a baseline for evaluating candidates for political office and the policies they propose. Similarly, social group identities may allow people to determine what is in the best interest of their group.

A focus on the structure of political attitudes naturally raises the question of the role of ideology. References to ideology have abounded in discussions of politics over the past three hundred years. The language and rhetoric of politicians and journalists often suggests that evaluations of politics should be organized along a left-right or liberal-conservative dimension. Many models of voting behavior and partisan competition have assumed that parties and voters can be located in some simple ideological space (Downs, 1957).

Although politicians, philosophers, and social scientists often discuss politics as if it were organized on a single left-right dimension, 50 years of research on public opinion shows that a unidimensional model of ideology is a poor description of political attitudes for the overwhelming proportion of people virtually everywhere (Kinder, 1998). This conclusion is not simply a result of research based on attitude surveys (see, for example, Converse, 1964). Even in-depth interview studies show that people rarely use any simple, overarching standard for evaluating politics (Hochschild, 1981; Lane, 1960).

Evidence for the existence of ideological structure among political attitudes depends in part on the research approach. When correlations among political attitudes—typically issue preferences—are computed, there is virtually always some evidence of ideological consistency. While the magnitude of these correlations varies considerably from study to study and country to country (see Knutsen, 1995a, for a good summary), the pattern of relationships among issue preferences is generally consistent with a traditional left-right dimension. However, even when correlations reach the .5 level (as they sometimes do in Europe but rarely in the U.S.), less than 25 percent of the variance in issue positions is being explained by a left-right factor.

While correlations among attitudes may be consistent with an ideological dimension, they do not demonstrate that people are actively using ideology to structure those attitudes. In a classic article, Converse (1964) forcefully argued that the liberal-conservative dimension was not a major source of attitude constraint for most Americans. Large majorities of people could not adequately define the terms *liberal* and *conservative,* and only a small group of people appeared to use the liberal-conservative continuum in their evaluations of political candidates and parties. Analysis of data from other countries supports the same conclusion. For example, Dalton (2002) reports that in data collected in 1974–75 only 21 percent of people in the United States and Great Britain used ideological concepts to evaluate the political parties while 34 percent of West Germans did so.

When asked to, many people are willing to place themselves on scales representing the left-right or liberal-conservative continuum. And these self-placements do help to predict policy preferences (Jacoby, 1991). However, evidence suggests that ideological self-placements do not necessarily reflect the use of ideological concepts. Conover and Feldman (1981) found that liberal-conservative self-placements in the United States were largely a function of attitudes toward salient social and political groups. It is therefore possible for people to utilize ideological labels without a working knowledge of the logic of a political ideology.

While it is easy enough to imagine, from a psychological perspective, how individuals could get along without using ideology to understand politics, this does create significant difficulties for politics. If political attitudes are not generally structured by any common ideology, how do political leaders communicate with the public? Absent ideology, it is difficult for candidates to judge what positions will appeal to the majority of the electorate. It is even more difficult to see how political parties can be organized without some consistent basis for distinguishing themselves from each other. Politics doesn't seem to "work" without some structure that allows broad sets of policies to somehow go together. And democratic representation may depend on people having some understanding of that structure. If a simple ideological continuum is not a good model for understanding how people organize their political attitudes, is there some alternative that can provide the basis for political communications and competition?

One potentially valuable approach to the attitude organization problem that has not received sufficient attention in the political psychology literature is based on the values construct. Theorists and researchers in philosophy, anthropology, sociology, and psychology have long discussed the role of values in human life (see Rohan, 2000, for a review). As generalized standards, values are assumed to be "the criteria people use to select and justify actions and to evaluate people (including the self) and events" (Schwartz, 1992, p. 1). Rokeach (1973) began his major study of values by asserting that "it is difficult for me to conceive of any problem social scientists might be interested in that would not deeply implicate human values" (p. ix).

Many researchers have argued that values are the ultimate underpinnings of attitudes. Bem (1970) described how attitudes emerge from syllogistic-like reasoning that leads, finally, to some value. Tetlock's (2000) value pluralism model assumes that "underlying all political belief systems are ultimate or terminal values that specify the end-states of public policy. These values—which may take such diverse forms as economic efficiency, social equality, individual freedom, crime control, national security, and racial purity—function as the back stops of belief systems" (p. 247).

Values have characteristics that appear to lend themselves to the analysis of political attitudes and behavior. Values are assumed to be relatively few in number, certainly far fewer than the number of attitudes that a person may hold. Thus they could provide a basis for reducing the complexity of political judgments and for creating consistency among attitudes. On the other hand, all discussions of values suggest that they are more numerous than the single ideological dimension that is typically used to understand political conflict. Political attitudes that are structured by values may not exhibit any simple unidimensional structure. In addition, many theorists argue that values exist not in isolation but as systems. If there is indeed an organization to the values people hold, this may provide an even simpler structure for political attitudes—and an underlying basis for political ideology. Finally, values are also assumed to be relatively stable, a property necessary for them to act as ongoing standards of evaluation. Value priorities may change slowly over time, as may be necessary for people adapting to a nonconstant environment. They should be inertial enough, however, to lend stability to evaluations and behavior.

The structure of values, the overall relationships among them, may be critical for the development of theories of political attitudes. This possibility also highlights a major difference in the approaches typically used by political scientists and psychologists. Much of the research that uses values as predictors of political attitudes commonly includes one or more values that are considered to be most relevant to the attitudes being studied. This is particularly true in political science. Psychologists have been much more concerned with identifying the entire range of human values and the relationships among those values. The piecemeal approach to values, while having produced a large body of interesting research, leaves open the possibility that important effects of values on political attitudes are missed. Perhaps more important, an understanding of the overall structure of values and value systems may yield insights into the nature of attitudinal structure and ideology.

Another way values can be useful in understanding political processes is by providing a link between the societal and individual levels. Researchers have not only attempted to study the values that people hold but also to map differing patterns of values across societies. In addition to variation in values across individuals in a society, there appears to be mean differences in value priorities across people living in different societies. An interesting question is whether value differences across societies are simply a function of other identifiable characteristics, or if societal values themselves exert an ongoing influence on individual values. The existence of societal values also has implications for the sources of structure underlying political attitudes.

◤ Definitions of Values

Despite decades of research using values, the definition and operationalization of the construct continues to be one of the major problems facing researchers. And for values to be useful in explanations of other political cognitions, it is necessary to clearly distinguish them from constructs like attitudes and beliefs. This is not an easy task in public opinion research since all cognitions—including values—must be inferred from responses to stimuli, typically verbal responses.

How do we distinguish values from other cognitions, like beliefs and attitudes? As Bem (1970) notes, values are, like attitudes, fundamentally evaluative and, in contrast to attitudes, are relatively few and more central. Two definitions from prominent values researchers give a good sense of the contemporary use of the construct. According to Rokeach (1973), a *"value* is an enduring belief that a specific mode of conduct or end-state of existence is personally or socially preferable to an opposite or converse mode of conduct or end-state of existence. A *value system* is an enduring organization of beliefs concerning preferable modes of conduct or end-states of existence along a continuum of relative importance" (p. 5). For Schwartz (1992), "values (1) are concepts or beliefs, (2) pertain to desirable end states or behaviors, (3) transcend specific situations, (4) guide selection or evaluation of behavior and events, and (5) are ordered by relative importance. Values, understood this way, differ from attitudes primarily in their generality or abstractness (feature 3) and in their hierarchical ordering by importance (feature 5)" (p. 4).

In principle, then, the distinction between attitudes and values is clear.

Attitudes refer to evaluations of specific objects while values are much more general standards used as a basis for numerous specific evaluations across situations. As Rohan (2000) argues: "when the values construct is viewed in terms of an abstract meaning-producing cognitive structure, the divide between value priorities and evaluations of specific entities seems wide indeed" (p. 258). Still, if that divide is potentially wide enough to create a clear distinction, it is not necessarily true that the gap will always be so wide in every instance. At what level of generality does an attitude become a value?

Since values refer to a preferable mode of conduct or desirable end-state, it is likely that an individual will positively evaluate a sizable number of values, perhaps giving no value an unambiguously negative assessment. It is therefore common to speak of value *priorities*: the relative endorsement of values with respect to each other. People may think that, taken individually, ambition, success, responsibility, and social justice are all desirable values. Yet one person may attach a higher priority to ambition and success while another person may see responsibility and social justice as more important.

The idea that values are ordered in terms of priorities raises two important issues. First, if most values are positively evaluated, it is likely that many specific assessments require the resolution of conflicts between values (see Tetlock, Peterson, & Lerner, 1996). Specific "attitudes and behaviors are guided not by the priority given to a single value but by tradeoffs among competing values that are implicated simultaneously in a behavior or attitudes" (Schwartz, 1996, p. 2). Second, if people must prioritize a number of values, it suggests that it may be best to think in terms of value systems. Values may not exist in isolation from each other but, owing to the potential conflicts among them, may be linked in some sort of general configuration. If values do exist within overall systems and often are in conflict with each other, research that focuses on a small number of values may miss the conflicts and tension that Tetlock and Schwartz have argued are central to the dynamics of values.

▲ Early Approaches to Values

Theory and research on values developed in the twentieth century at the intersection of philosophy, anthropology, sociology, and psychology. The absence of any agreement about the identification of human values led to measurement instruments (and research) that were generally noncomparable. Investigators used very different approaches in their study of values. While much interesting research was produced, each contribution remained relatively isolated.

For example, on the basis of the work of Spranger, *Types of Men* (1928), Allport, Vernon, and Lindzey (1960) developed the Study of Values instrument (the first version was published in 1931). Their measure attempted to tap six broad value orientations based on ideal types of people: the theoretical person, the economic person, the aesthetic person, the social person, the political person, and the religious person. Prior to the 1970s, this was probably the most widely used values measure.

Starting from a very different perspective, Morris (1956) developed a measure based on 13 "ways to live" presented as paragraph-long descriptions that were rated on the basis of how much each subject liked or disliked each description. The wide range of value types allowed the measure to be used across diverse cultures (Braithwaite & Scott, 1991). On the basis of from student samples in the United States, Morris was able to reduce the information in the 13 ratings to five basic factors: social restraint and self-control, enjoyment and progress in action, withdrawal and self-sufficiency, receptivity and sympathetic concern, and self-indulgence.

A third example, from sociology, is the study *Variations in Value Orientations* by F. Kluckhohn and Strodtbeck (1961). This research explored differences in values across "cultures" in the U.S. Southwest. The researchers administered structured interviews to samples of American Indians, Spanish Americans, Mormons, and Texas and Oklahoma farmers. The measures were designed to tap five broad value orientations defined by the questions: (1) What is the character of innate human nature? (2) What is the relationship of man to nature? (3) What is the temporal focus of human life? (4) What is the modality of human activity? and (5) What is the modality of man's relationship to other men? (Kluckhohn & Strodtbeck 1961, p 11). Their research focused on finding characteristic value orientations within each community and exploring differences across the communities.

▲ Milton Rokeach

There is no question that research on values over the past 30 years has been influenced tremendously by the work of Milton Rokeach, especially in psychology. His 1973 book *The Nature of Human Values* provided a huge impetuous to the empirical study of values. Rokeach devoted the first chapter of his book to a careful conceptual discussion of values and value systems. His measure of values helped standardize empirical research. It became widely used in psychology and has served as the basis for subsequent value instruments. He also conducted a number of studies demonstrating the properties of his measure of values, the impact of values on attitudes and behavior, and processes of value change. As any review of the literature on values since 1973 will easily demonstrate, Rokeach's conceptualization and measurement of values has been a major inspiration for researchers.

One of Rokeach's major contributions was to highlight the overall structure of value systems. Values don't exist in isolation, and rarely will any single attitude or behavior be a function of just one value. Rokeach was not simply trying to study *some* values, his goal was to identify *all* of the major values that exist across human cultures. He approached this problem by assuming that values were relatively few in number. How few? Rokeach never gives a precise answer to this question, nor does he provide a clear mechanism for obtaining the answer. Rokeach did suggest that the number of human values should be related to basic biological and social needs, although he did not really follow through with this line of reasoning.

Rokeach's identification of the number of values was, in the end, intimately bound up with his development of a measure of values. In fact, while Rokeach devoted a great deal of attention to the conceptualization of values and value systems, it was his measure of values that ultimately had the greatest impact. The Rokeach value measure was actually two measures, constructed to distinguish between instrumental and terminal values.[1] Each measure included a list of 18 values with each value given a short one- or two-word label with a further clarification in parentheses, for example: freedom (independence, free choice). Consistent with the idea that all (or almost all) values are positively evaluated, subjects are asked to "arrange them in order of importance to YOU, as guiding principles in YOUR life" (Rokeach, 1973, p. 27). This is an attempt to avoid the problem of having subjects rate all the values as highly important to them, thus yielding little variance. Later research has begun to evaluate the benefits and drawbacks of using ranking procedures like this to measure value priorities (see Alwin & Krosnick, 1985).

It seems odd in retrospect that Rokeach used such ad hoc procedures to develop his value measures, since he was concerned about tapping the entire range of values that might be found among all people everywhere. Given the substantial amount of work that Rokeach put into the measurement and study of values, the "intuitive" development of the list of values in his final measure must be considered a major limitation. It clearly leaves open the possibility that his values measure is not complete, and researchers soon suggested omissions that would significantly increase the number of values that a respondent would have to rank (see Braithwaite & Law, 1985).

Although it was probably deficient in many ways, it is difficult to overestimate Rokeach's contribution. He provided a clear conceptualization of values and value systems. His measure was widely used in psychology and became the basis for other value measures. His research demonstrated the usefulness of examining the effects of large systems of values on attitudes and behaviors. Other researchers have used the foundation he constructed to improve on the study of values.

▶ Shalom Schwartz

If Rokeach motivated much of the recent psychological research on values, the work of Shalom Schwartz seems to be becoming the new standard for researchers in psychology. While I will focus on his theory and measurement of values, Schwartz is interested more generally in the effects of values on attitudes and behaviors, the origins of values in people's shared and unique experiences, and crosscultural differences in value priorities.

Given Schwartz's interest in crosscultural differences in values, the first task he set himself was to specify and test a universal structure of values. While this was one of Rokeach's original goals as well, the absence of a working theory of value structure in his research prevented him from knowing whether he had accomplished it.[2] Schwartz begins by developing a theory that specifies the *types of values* that should be found in all human societies (see Schwartz & Bilsky 1987, 1990). To do this he goes back to Rokeach's observation that values should emerge out of basic biological and social needs. Schwartz reasons that underlying specific values are a smaller number of goals or motivations. In particular, he argues (1992) that "values represent, in the form of conscious goals, three universal requirements of human existence to which all individuals and societies must be responsive: needs of individuals as biological organisms, requisites of coordinated social interaction, and survival and welfare needs of groups" (p. 4). While many people have suggested that values are based on a set of universal human needs or motivations, Schwartz has attempted to build a comprehensive theory of values by specifying these needs.

Using this framework, and samples drawn from 20 countries, a set of 10 motivational types of values was derived.[3] These value types are intended to represent basic human motivations or goals. Individual value items (freedom, equality) derive their meaning from the motivation they represent. To identify these value types, Schwartz used 21 of the Rokeach value items and added a number of others drawn from studies of values outside the United States. The set of 10 value types and individual values contained within each type are shown in Table 14.1. The value types are more general than the individual values in Rokeach's measure. In fact, the single value items that Rokeach used become indicators of the value type for Schwartz. For example, while Rokeach considered freedom and independence to be distinct values, for Schwartz these are both indicators of the self-direction value type.

Schwartz's model simultaneously reduces the number of fundamental value types to 10 and increases the number of individual values. Rokeach's value measure included 18 terminal and 18 instrumental values. Schwartz's measure includes 54 (or more) individual value items. While the increase in the number of value items seems inconsistent with the idea that there should be a relatively small number of values, Schwartz focuses on the 10 value types and is less concerned with the number of individual items. Since having subjects rank a list of 54 values would be extremely difficult, if not impossible, subjects are asked to rate each value individually on a scale ranging from 7, "of supreme importance," through 0, "not important," to −1, "opposed to my values."

Table 14.1
Schwartz Value Types and Items

1. Self-direction: independent thought and action (creativity, freedom, choosing own goals, curious, independent)
2. Stimulation: variety, novelty, challenge (a varied life, an exciting life, daring)
3. Hedonism: pleasure, gratification (pleasure, enjoying life)
4. Achievement: personal success through demonstrating competence (ambitious, successful, capable, influential)
5. Power: social status, prestige, dominance and control (authority, wealth, social power, preserving my public image, social recognition)
6. Security: safety, harmony, stability of society (social order, family security, national security, reciprocation of favors, clean, sense of belonging, healthy)
7. Conformity: restraint of actions, inclinations, and impulses likely to harm others and violate social expectations or norms (obedient, self-discipline, politeness, honoring parents and elders)
8. Tradition: respect, commitment, and acceptance of the customs and ideas that one's culture or religion impose on the individual (respect for tradition, humble, devout, accepting my portion in life, moderate)
9. Benevolence: concern for the welfare of close others in everyday interaction (helpful, loyal, forgiving, honest, responsible, true friendship, mature love)
10. Universalism: understanding, appreciation, tolerance, and protection for the welfare of *all* people and for nature (broadminded, social justice, equality, world at peace, world of beauty, unity with nature, wisdom, protecting the environment)

Schwartz's conceptualization of values is interesting because it seems to suggest how value *systems* are organized. By understanding value types in terms of basic human and social needs, he is able to specify relationships among the 10 value types: which values types are most compatible and which are most opposed. For example, benevolence and universalism should be compatible since they both reflect (different aspects of) prosocial orientations. On the other hand, universalism and power should stand in opposition to each other, since power involves the accumulation of individual dominance and control of resources, while universalism is concerned with protecting the welfare of all people. These relationships suggest that the individual value items should be arrayed in two-dimensional space, with the 10 value types emerging as areas in that space with compatible values next to each other and opposing values opposite.

To test this model of value structure, Schwartz took the correlations among ratings of each value and analyzed them using a multidimensional scaling algorithm. As shown in figure 14.1, a two-dimensional configuration of the 54 values from 40 samples taken from 20 countries shows the (largely) expected pattern. The individual value items are distributed across the space, which is then divided as a pie cut into 9 pieces, with one of those pieces further divided into two—the tradition and conformity value types.

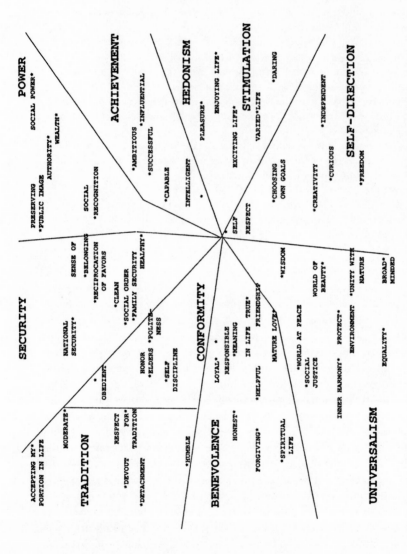

Figure 14.1. Analysis based on a multidimensional scaling algorithm. (I would like to thank Shalom Schwartz for permission to reprint Figure 2 from Schwartz, 1994.)

It is important to recognize that the lines dividing the space into the value types are not a function of the analysis but rather an interpretation of the multidimensional scaling solution. This means that, empirically, the value types are a inference from the clustering of the individual values in the two-dimensional space. While the location of the individual items in the space is a function of the observed correlations among the ratings of each, the division of the space into the value types is conceptual and other researchers could divide up the space differently. For example, the angles defining the hedonism and stimulation types are relatively small compared with the angles defining the universalism and benevolence types. Are hedonism and stimulation distinct value types, or should the clusters of values in this space represent a single type? As Schwartz (1992) notes,

> what this means is that the partition lines in the SSAs [Smallest Space Analyses] represent conceptually convenient decisions about where one type of motivation ends and another begins. Because the array of values represents a continuum of motivations, the precise locations of the partition lines are arbitrary. Values found near a partition line express a combination of the related motivational goals associated with the value types on both sides of that partition line. (p. 45)

A two-dimensional space can also be defined by two axes crossing at the center of the space. Schwartz proposes two such dimensions that suggest an even simpler understanding of overall value structure. One dimension, running from self-direction and stimulation at one end through security, conformity, and tradition is labeled openness to change versus conservation. The second, self-transcendence versus self-enhancement, is located at an approximately 90 degree angle to the first and has the universalism and benevolence value types at one end and achievement and power at the other. As I will discuss in more detail shortly, this two-dimensional solution provides an interesting way to view the structure of values and the possible relationship between values and fundamental social and political processes.

Much more research is clearly necessary to validate Schwartz's conceptualization of value structure and to determine whether this is, in fact, a universal model of values. Schwartz presents some results that suggest that the 10 value types may not be quite universal. The model only partly replicates in several samples from China, and some other value types do appear in those samples. It is too soon to know, however, whether these are just sampling issues or whether they will replicate with other Chinese samples and in other populations. It is also difficult to know whether any variations across cultures are the result of true cultural variations in the structure of values or of problems in translating the values instrument into different languages.

Schwartz's conceptualization has the advantage of being based on an analysis of the motivations underlying values so that the resulting conceptualization is less ad hoc than previous ones. The hypothesized motivational basis of the value types should also make it easier to generate hypotheses relating value types with specific attitudes and behaviors. The relatively small number of value types also means that models of political attitudes based on values can reduce the complexity of such explanations down to 10 or fewer value types or even two underlying dimensions.

On the other hand, it is less clear what the status of individual values is in this conceptualization. Consider, for example, the universalism value type. It includes the individual values of *equality, unity with nature, world at peace,* and others. Their proximity in the two-dimensional space is a result of their being rated similarly by people. Thus it is likely that if someone rates *equality* highly she will also give a high rating to *world at peace.* A measure of the universalism value type would be based on the sum of a person's ratings of these different values. However, it is possible that specific attitudes would be better predicted by one or the other of these individual values rather than the overall universalism value type. For example, attitudes toward social welfare spending might be strongly predicted by *equality* but not by *world at peace.* To what extent should political psychologists be interested in the relationship between political attitudes and very precisely defined values like equality or more general motivational types like universalism?

▲ Values, Political Attitudes, and Political Reasoning

Numerous research studies have found evidence of relationships between values and political attitudes. It would take many pages just to list the published studies that have presented data on this issue. The quality of this evidence varies considerably. In some cases it is no more than bivariate correlations between a value and an attitude, with no statistical controls for other variables. In other cases, complex multivariate models are estimated that control for many other variables and take into account measurement error. Since values are likely to be correlated with many other factors that could predict political attitudes, it is difficult to have confidence in results based only on correlations.

Even if only multivariate studies are considered, it is clear that there is abundant evidence that values and attitudes are related. Research has demonstrated consistent effects of values on policy preferences (Feldman 1988; Peffley & Hurwitz, 1985; Pollock, Lilie, & Vittes, 1993; Zaller, 1992), attitudes toward social groups (Biernat, Vescio, Theno, & Crandall, 1996; Kinder & Sanders, 1996; Sagiv & Schwartz, 1995), political action (Borg, 1995; Gundelach, 1995), and politicians and parties (Knutsen, 1995b; Miller & Shanks, 1996).

Despite the collective empirical evidence, we still have little systematic evidence of the relationships among many of the values that theorists like Rokeach and Schwartz have proposed and political attitudes. Most studies examining the effects of values typically choose a small number (perhaps only one) and estimate their effects on political attitudes. A study of attitudes toward social welfare attitudes might include values like equality and individualism while an examination of attitudes toward abortion might focus on religious values and tradition. Specifications of values and their measurement often vary considerably from study to study. Rarely are a full battery of values (or value types) like those of Schwartz included. Evidence on the relationship of values and political attitudes thus accumulates in a piecemeal fashion, shedding little light on the broader effects of values.

Schwartz (1996) has argued that his two-dimensional structure of 10 value types predicts that attitudes should be related to the entire set of value types in a clearly identifiable pattern. Correlations of attitudes with the values should increase and decrease uniformly across adjacent values. Schwartz provides evidence of this pattern with data on cooperation, vote choice, and intergroup contact. For example, the reported willingness of Israeli (Jewish) public school teachers to have contact with Israeli Arabs is most positively correlated with the universalism value type ($r = .40$) and the adjacent self-direction values ($r = .32$). The correlations decline to the maximum negative correlation of $-.41$ with the traditional value type, and correlations of $-.31$ and $-.19$ with the adjacent security and conformity values. Although this analysis again presents only simple correlations between the values and the dependent variables without any statistical controls, it suggests that the prediction of attitudes from a system of values is likely to be better and more informative than predictions from one or several individual values.

Unfortunately, there is still little theory that specifies how values or value structures should be related to political attitudes. Schwartz's model provides predictions about the patterns of correlations of attitudes with his 10 value types, once he identifies the value types that should have the most positive and most negative correlations with each particular attitude. While there may be a strong intuition about these relationships, there is no theory that generates such predictions. As Rokeach (1973) noted, "the values that people hold are conceived to be the explanations of the attitudes they hold (and the behaviors they engage in), but which values underlie which attitudes (and behaviors), and why? At this stage of theory and research, we simply do not know enough about the nature of values and how they determine attitudes and behavior to answer questions of this kind satisfactorily" (pp. 120–121).

Researchers also have not devoted enough attention to the conditions under which values will be strongly related to political attitudes. Most studies examine simple relationships without testing any contingencies that would influence the magnitude of the relationship. One factor for which there is some evidence is political sophistication. Although it may be plausible to assume that the value-attitude connection should be simple enough to require little sophistication, Zaller (1991, 1992) has argued that the relationship between values and political attitudes will depend on levels of political sophistication. Those who are less sophisticated will be unable to connect the cues in the political messages they receive with their values and thus will fail to form strong relationships between their values and attitudes.

While Zaller provides evidence showing that relationships between values and attitudes grow stronger with increasing political sophistication, Pollock, Lilie, and Vittes (1993) suggest that the moderating effect of sophistication may depend on the nature of the attitudes. Following Carmines and Stimson (1980), they distinguish between "hard" and "easy" issues. Easy issues have "literal referents that directly evoke moralistic or economic values" (Pollock, Lilie, & Vittes, 1993, p. 30). These are "symbolic" issues that are likely to be familiar to most people. As a result they are easily understood and connected with major values.

Hard issues, those that are more technical and less familiar, require that political elites frame them in terms of values and that people to have sufficiently high levels of political sophistication to understand those frames. We should therefore find robust relationships between easy issues and values that are not moderated by sophistication and more tenuous connections for hard issues that emerge only for those who are politically sophisticated.

Pollock, Lilie, and Vittes provide some evidence for these hypotheses, on the basis of a analysis of attitudes toward nuclear energy (a hard issue) and the "easy issues" of abortion, flag burning, and homosexuality. They find that the relationship between values and attitudes toward nuclear energy is substantially larger for those who score high on political involvement than those score low. However, the effects of values are still generally statistically significant even among those who are low in involvement. In contrast, there is little evidence that the relationship between values and attitudes toward the easy issues is affected by levels of involvement. This study suggests that the role of sophistication in the relationship between values and attitudes is somewhat complex. Analyses of influence of values need to consider attributes of the political attitudes under study, as well as the nature of elite discourse and media presentation of the issues involved.

Another factor that may play a role in the relationship of values and attitudes is the motivational basis of the attitudes. Some attitude theorists have proposed models of the psychological functions of attitudes (Katz, 1960; Smith, Bruner, & White, 1956). Katz's model suggests that there are four main attitude functions: utilitarian, ego-defensive, knowledge, and value-expressive. The *utilitarian* function involves the maximization of rewards and minimization of negative reinforcements; the *ego-defensive* function serves to protect the ego from threats and impulses; the *knowledge* function serves to give meaning and understanding of the environment; and the *value-expressive* function helps to express basic values and self-concept. Recent research suggests that the functions that attitudes serve may influence the relationship between values and attitudes (Kristiansen & Zanna, 1998; Maio & Olsen, 1994, 1995). In particular, value-expressive attitudes should exhibit much stronger connections to values than attitudes serving other functions.

Two studies by Maio and Olson provide evidence of the importance of attitude function. In the first study, of attitudes toward smoking (Maio & Olson, 1994), they measured attitude function using a thought-listing approach (see Shavitt, 1990). They found significant relationships between several values and attitudes among people with value-expressive attitudes but no relationship among those with utilitarian attitudes. In the second study they manipulated the functions of attitudes toward cancer by making salient either value expressive or utilitarian reasons for donating to cancer research. As expected, Maio and Olson found substantial differences in the predictors of attitudes in the two conditions, with one of Schwartz's value dimensions—self-enhancement versus self-transcendence—correlating with attitudes in the value-expressive condition but not at all in the utilitarian condition.

The functional approach to attitudes could make a potentially important contribution to a better understanding of the role of values in politics. We need to know when political attitudes will serve a primary function of expressing core values and the self-concept. Certain attitudes may be more likely to function in this way, and there may be conditions under which the value-expressive function becomes more important. The distinction between value-expressive and utilitarian functions seems particularly critical for politics, since one of the major controversies in the political behavior and public opinion literature has been the relative influence of self-interest versus "symbolism" in political attitudes. Self-interest should be associated with attitudes that serve a utilitarian function. Although it is somewhat less clear, symbolic attitudes are likely to be more value expressive in nature. To the extent to which this distinction is meaningful, symbolic attitudes should be strongly predicted by values. And, given the difficulties of linking self-interest and political attitudes (Sears & Funk, 1991), political attitudes may be especially likely to serve a value-expressive function for many people.

▶ Values and Political ideology

The preceding section reviewed evidence on the relationship between values and specific political attitudes. If most people do not think about politics in ideological terms, values may allow people to organize their political evaluations in a relatively consistent manner. But it is also necessary to consider how the structure of these attitudes relates to political conflict in the society. If people were to draw on a large number of values or if people varied significantly in their use of values, the resulting complexity would make the relationships among the public, parties, and politicians tenuous. Indeed, this is the attractiveness of the ideology construct: it allows easy communication between politicians and the public and provides a basis for the organization of political parties. It is therefore important to look beyond simple relationships between values and attitudes to see if values can provide this more general level of structure for political attitudes.

Several researchers have attempted to create connections between values and political ideology by arguing that certain values may form the very basis for differences among ideologies. Rokeach presented a simple model of value-based ideology in *The Nature of Human Values*. He began by arguing that the four major twentieth-century ideologies—socialism, communism, fascism, and capitalism—are best understood from a two-dimensional perspective. According to Rokeach, the unequal distribution of power in every society will lead to competing proposals to deal with social and economic problems. The nature of these conflicts will be expressed in terms of differing levels of satisfaction with the amount of freedom and inequity in society. Thus the major differences between ideologies should be defined by the priorities placed on the key values of freedom and equality.

On the basis of this logic, Rokeach argued that the two dimensions underlying modern ideologies are formed by these two values. This two-dimensional model yields four cells created by high and low priorities attached to each value. Socialism is located in the high-equality, high-freedom cell while fascism is in the low-equality, low-freedom cell. Communism occupies the high-equality, low-freedom cell and capitalism is in the low-equality, high-freedom cell.

To test this model, Rokeach (1973) conducted a content analysis of samples of the writings of key representatives of these four ideological positions. The content analysis counted positive and negative mentions of all terminal and instrumental values including, freedom and equality. This analysis provided considerable support for Rokeach's model, with the ranking of the values in the selected writings matching the predictions in each case.

In addition to the content analysis of political leaders, Rokeach also measured the value priorities of samples of Americans and their presidential preferences in 1968. As opposed to the content analyses of the values of major ideological figures, the value priorities of the supporters of the various presidential candidates could easily be arrayed on a single left-right dimension. This was possible because all of the groups ranked freedom highly (between 1 and 4 among all 18 terminal values). What distinguished them was the priority they placed on equality. Supporters of liberal candidates like Robert Kennedy, Eugene McCarthy, and Hubert Humphrey ranked equality near the top of the list while supporters of the conservative candidates, Richard Nixon, Ronald Reagan, and George Wallace, ranked equality much lower. On the basis of these findings, Rokeach argued that the two-dimensional ideological space could reduce to one dimension when there is little variance on one of the values (in this case, freedom).

Rokeach's findings on the impact of equality on candidate choice anticipated a great deal of research that demonstrates the importance of this value for political attitudes. Studies in the United States have shown that equality is a major predictor of social welfare attitudes (Feldman, 1988; Feldman & Steenbergen, 2001; Kluegel & Smith, 1986), racial attitudes (Kinder & Sanders, 1996; Sears, Henry, & Kosterman, 2000), and candidate evaluation (Miller & Shanks, 1996). Verba and his colleagues (1987) demonstrated the centrality of equality to politics in the United States, Sweden, and Japan. Research in Europe finds substantial effects of the traditional left-right dimension, which is frequently interpreted (at least in part) as reflecting the value of equality (see Knutsen, 1995a).

Although Rokeach's two-value model is a parsimonious way of explaining modern political ideologies, there are significant problems with it. First, the meaning of values like freedom and equality can shift from one setting to another. Freedom in particular is a difficult value to pin down in the abstract. For a capitalist, freedom is the absence of coercion, particularly from the government. For a socialist, freedom is being able to accomplish your goals, and this may require government efforts to remove barriers like poverty and racism. Subscribers to all ideologies can therefore value freedom as long as it is interpreted to their liking.

Second, while Rokeach obtained evidence consistent with his model from an analysis of the writings of major political figures and theorist, value rankings from supporters of these ideologies are not consistent with the major predictions. Rokeach's finding that, in the United States, only the priority attached to equality is related to the variations in ideology may be sensible: without a history of significant support for either communism or fascism, ideological debate reduces to a single dimension opposing socialism (or, in the U.S., liberalism) with capitalism (conservatism). The role of freedom should, however, emerge in a context in which communist and fascist ideologies were represented. This was the goal of a study in England conducted by Cochrane, Billig, and Hogg (1979). From samples of local activists and supporters of the Labour, Conservative, Communist, and National Front parties, these researchers obtained rankings of values using Rokeach's measure of 18 terminal values. Consistent with Rokeach's findings, equality discriminated most strongly among both activists and supporters. However, freedom did not discriminate at all in the sample of supporters, and the differences in the sample of activists were inconsistent with Rokeach's predictions.

Braithwaite (1982, 1994, 1997) has proposed another approach to the relationship between values and ideology. She began by attempting to correct the limitations of the Rokeach two-value model but has produced a quite different account. After modifying Rokeach's value measure to include more social/political values, Braithwaite factor analyzed responses to those values and obtained two relatively uncorrelated dimensions. The first, labeled *international harmony and equality*, includes the values "a good life for others," "rule by the people," "international cooperation," "social progress and social reform," "a world at peace," "a world of beauty," "human dignity," "equal opportunity," "greater economic equality," and "preserving the natural environment." The second factor, *national strength and order*, is measured by "national greatness," "national economic development," "the rule of law," "and national security." These two social value factors were then combined with more personal values to create two somewhat broader dimensions, "harmony" and "security" (Braithwaite, 1997).

Braithwaite shows that these two factors are related to different personal values and are relatively uncorrelated (actually somewhat positively correlated). However, as Schwartz (1994) points out, the lack of correlation between the factors may be a methodological artifact. Since almost all values tend to receive positive ratings, there very few observed negative correlations among any pairs of value items. Therefore, all scales based on ratings of value items will have some induced positive correlation among them. They may appear to be uncorrelated or even positively correlated when the "true" correlation among the constructs could be quite negative.

There are other problems with the evidence that Braithwaite presents for these value factors. One of Rokeach's most interesting arguments was that the very structure of ideology required a two-dimensional model: ideologies cannot be properly arrayed on a single dimension. Yet virtually all of the evidence that Braithwaite reports shows both value dimensions correlated with political attitudes and vote choice. The international harmony and equality dimension is always negatively correlated with conservative attitudes and behavior, and the national strength and order factor is positively correlated. In effect, these two dimensions of values always reduce to a single ideological dimension.

Schwartz's two-dimensional representation provides another perspective on political ideology that appears to have real promise. Recall that in addition to the 10 value types that Schwartz identified, he also showed that two axes seem to fit the overall value configuration: openness to change versus conservation and self-transcendence versus self-enhancement. Schwartz (1994) notes that these two dimensions correspond to two dimensions of ideology. The first, which he labels classical liberalism, "refers to whether government should devote more to guarding and cultivating individual freedoms and civil rights or to protecting the societal status quo by controlling deviance from within or enemies from without" (p. 39). This ideological dimension should be most closely related to the openness to change versus conservation value dimension. The second ideological dimension, economic egalitarianism, "refers to whether government should devote itself more to promoting equality by redistributing resources or to protecting citizens' ability to retain the wealth they generate in order to foster economic growth and efficiency" (p. 40). The self-transcendence versus self-enhancement value dimension should be most closely linked to economic egalitarianism.

There is some evidence that these two value dimensions are associated with other constructs that are strongly linked to political attitudes. Several researchers (Altemeyer, 1998; Rohan & Zanna, 1996) have found that right-wing authoritarianism is strongly related to the openness to change versus conservation dimension. Its strongest positive correlations are with the conformity and tradition value types, and it is most negatively correlated with the self-direction and stimulation values. Altemeyer also reports evidence suggesting that social dominance orientation (Sidanius & Pratto, 1999) is related to the self-enhancement versus self-transcendence dimension.

Schwartz's two-dimensional model of values also suggests some interesting variations on these two dimensions. For example, self-transcendence is represented by values from the universalism and benevolence value types. While similar in many respects, universalism has a broader scope compared to the more ingroup focus of benevolence. Similarly, Schwartz finds that at the other end of this dimension power values typically conflict more with benevolence and universalism than achievement values. Thus slight changes in orientation in this two-dimensional space may give rise to different political orientations and ideological preferences. The underlying two-dimensional structure of Schwartz's conceptualization may provide a useful basis for thinking about political and social conflict in society.

▶ The Stability and Primacy of Values

For values to help structure political attitudes, it is necessary for them to be more stable than attitudes and for causality to run from values to attitudes. If values were found to be temporally or situationally unstable, or if there were evidence that values were significantly influenced *by* attitudes, it would be difficult to argue that values play a central role in political attitude organization. At a minimum, our understanding of the values-attitude relationship would be substantially complicated. Unfortunately, there is too little empirical evidence to provide firm answers to these critical questions.

All value theorists have assumed that values are *relatively* stable. Completely stable values would be dysfunctional for people, leaving them unable to deal with changes in the world around them. The critical question is how much temporal instability should be observed before values lose their status as enduring standards that shape attitudes and behavior.

Rokeach (1973) presented measures of stability for his values measures by computing rank-order correlations for each instrument over periods of several weeks (and over a year in one case). A perfect rank-order correlation would indicate that an individual ordered the 18 values exactly the same way at the two measurement points. The median correlations were generally in the .7 to .8 range for terminal values. Since these rank-order correlations are computed for each individual, it is possible to examine the distribution of stability, across individuals. While most of the subjects in these studies exhibited fairly high levels of stability, others were significantly more unstable. It is of course possible (even likely) that some of this instability is due to measurement error. However, Rokeach noted that some of the variation in stability was related to characteristics of the subjects: sex, age, intellectual ability, and liberalism.

These results suggest that there is a substantial degree of stability in the overall configuration of values. What about the individual value items? Rokeach reported test-retest correlations for each value by computing Pearson correlation coefficients for two administrations of the values measures. These correlations varied substantially, from .45 for "responsible" and .51 for "a sense of accomplishment" to .71 for "equality" and .88 for "salvation." The only correlation above .71 was for salvation, and the majority of the correlations were in the .6 range. The individual values thus show greater instability than the entire set of rankings. There should be more measurement error for single value items than for the relative rankings of many values, so these results are not completely surprising. What then do we conclude about the stability of values from results like this? We could be pleased with rank-order correlations for value systems around .8. Should we be concerned to find correlations for individual values of only .6?

Evidence about the stability of other measures of individual values is limited, especially for representative national samples. Such evidence requires that measures of values be included in panel studies. Even when such data is available, conclusions seem to vary substantially. For example, using a four-item Likert-type measure of support for equality of opportunity in the American National Election Studies (NES), McCann (1997) reports a surprisingly low (standardized) stability coefficient of .41 for a two-year interval (1990–92). The stability coefficient for a four-item measure of "moral traditionalism" is much higher, .84. Sheng (1995), using the same data but adding two additional indicators of equality of opportunity, reports a unstandardized stability of .81.[4] His estimate of the stability of moral traditionalism is 1.00. Both of these estimates take measurement error (random and systematic) into account.

It is clear that we need considerably more empirical evidence on the stability of values. We also need to think more about how stable values should be and what type of measures are being used. Rokeach's results show substantial differences between the stability of (ranked) value systems and individual values. Each of the measures is a single item with very short phrase. The questions used in the NES are statements that respondents agree or disagree with (for example: "It is not really that big a problem if some people have more of a chance in life than others."). Should value measures constructed from multiple statements like this be more reliable than single items? Or does the content of the statements make them *more* susceptible to short-term changes?

Do values change systematically in the long term? Rokeach (1973) devoted a great deal of attention to this question. Using a method that provided feedback to subjects about discrepancies between their reported value priorities and their self-concept (the value confrontation method), Rokeach was able to observe systematic changes in value priorities and attitudes. Others (e.g., Kristiansen & Hotte, 1996) have noted that this manipulation seems to produce fairly small changes in values.

It is difficult to find good evidence on long-term value change, since this requires reinterviews with people over a substantial time interval. It is much easier to compare value priorities over time using independent samples, but the interpretation of observed changes in data like this is unclear. For example, Rokeach and Ball-Rokeach (1988) found that the ranking of equality on U.S. national samples decreased significantly from the late 1960s to the early 1980s. While they argued that this was the result of changes in the political environment and elite discourse, there is no way to empirically test such a hypothesis with data like these.

Some evidence of systematic change in values comes from McCann (1997). Using the 1990–92 NES panel data, he showed that people who voted for Bill Clinton in 1992 increased their support for equality of opportunity and decreased their support for moral traditionalism. Those who voted for George Bush shifted their value priorities in the opposite direction. In the absence of other studies like this, it is difficult to know how generalizable these results are.

In addition to stability, values should also be exogenous to attitudes. If values were significantly influenced by attitudes, it would be difficult to view values as a basis for attitude organization. And since most studies of the effects of values on attitudes begin by *assuming* that values are causally prior to attitudes, significant evidence of the endogeneity of values casts doubt on the conclusions of those studies. As with the stability of values, the best way to examine the causal relationship between values and attitudes is with panel data.

McCann's (1997) examination of the NES panel data provides some support for the exogeneity of values. Despite finding that support for equality of opportunity and moral traditionalism were significantly affected by presidential vote preferences, McCann showed that voters' issue preferences had no significant effect on these two values. On the other hand, there were significant effects of the values on a number of issue preferences in 1992, even holding constant the values two years prior. Thus while these values appear to be influenced by preferences for presidential candidates (or some aspect of the election campaign), there is no evidence that values are endogenous to policy preferences—in this one study.

Other researchers are more concerned about the exogeneity of values. Seligman and Katz (1996) present evidence in a series of studies that value systems may not be as stable as many assume. Subjects first completed a Rokeach-like values ranking. Then, after attitudes toward an issue (abortion, the environment) were assessed (along with some filler material), the subjects rank-ordered the values a second time. Half of the subjects were given the same general instructions to rank the values, while the other half were asked to do the ranking in terms of their feelings about the issue. Seligman and Katz found that the correlation between these two rankings was substantially lower when subjects were asked to express their values in terms of the issue than in the general condition. The correlations between several of the values and issue preferences were also higher in the issue condition.

This study suggests that value priorities may be influenced by contextual factors rather than being stable structures. However, it is difficult to know from these manipulations whether we are observing true changes in value priorities or changes in reported values that are due to the demand characteristics of the studies. Since the subjects are asked to rank the values on the basis of their feelings toward the issue, there are strong pressures to be consistent. In addition, Seligman and Katz added two or three values closely related to the issue to Rokeach's terminal value list. These additional values are most likely to be affected by consistency pressures, and there is some suggestion that a significant amount of the reported value change is due to these additional items.

There are reasons to be concerned about the causal relationships between values and attitudes. As Kristiansen and Zanna (1994) suggest, in the functional approach, attitudes may serve not only a value-expressive function but also an ego-defensive function. Values may be an important way that people justify their attitudes and behaviors. From this perspective, values may be as much a function of attitudes as their cause. This is clearly an area in which more research is needed. Most work on values begins with the assumption that values influence attitudes but not the reverse. At this point, there is little hard evidence to support this assumption.

▶ Societal and Individual Values

In an effort to account for the structure of political attitudes, political psychologists have naturally focused on the value priorities of individuals. Indeed, psychologically, values exist as mental constructs. However, there is a long tradition in the social sciences that has attempted to account for certain characteristics of societies on the basis of shared social values. Much of the early work on this topic was based on simple observation of social behaviors and attitudes (see Lipset, 1979, for a good summary of this approach in the case of the U.S.). More recently, a growing body of quantitative research has examined differences in cultural values and their effects on psychological processes and behavior. For political psychologists, this research raises the interesting possibility of using values to link the micro and macro levels of analysis. To the extent that the value priorities of individuals are shaped by societal values (or by social, economic, and political conditions more generally), the relationships between individual political behavior and social conditions would become clearer. Shared social values would also help us understand how individual values and political attitudes become organized.

To be fully successful, this enterprise requires a clear conceptualization of societal values and the ways they are shaped and maintained. Unfortunately, this is currently a major gap in the literature. Societal values are either taken as a given in order to examine their consequences[5] or are measured by mean levels of value priorities in (typically) small samples. And while researchers have used a variety of means to explore crosscultural differences in values, they have not really systematically explored how those differences emerge. As a result, much of the research in this area tends to be more descriptive than theoretical. Despite this, it is important to consider whether and how peoples' value priorities may vary across cultures. Given the large number of studies on this topic, it is impossible to even attempt to review this literature in the space available in this chapter. My goal is to raise some key issues and to suggest how this research may help understand the way political attitudes are structured.

Without a doubt, the central value dimension in the crosscultural values literature has been individualism-collectivism. Interest in the nature and consequences of individualism dates from at least the French Revolution. Arguments that politics and society in the United States has been dominated by individualism began to emerge soon after the founding of the nation (see Lipset, 1979; Tocqueville, 1954). Empirical evidence that seemed to support this observation came in 1980 from the research of Geert Hofstede. Using self-completed interviews with workers from 40 countries who were employees of a large multinational corporation, Hofstede extracted four dimensions of societal values: power distance, uncertainty avoidance, masculinity, and individualism. According to Hofstede (1980) individualism "describes the relationship between the individual and the collectivity which prevails in a given society" (p. 213). As defined by Oyserman, Coon, & Kemmelmeier (2002), "the core element of individualism is the assumption that individuals are independent of one another," while "the core element of collectivism is the assumption that groups bind and mutually obligate individuals." (pp. 4–5).

Hofstede's analysis of the workplace data produced a ranking of the 40 nations on his individualism measure. As expected, the United States was the highest in individualism, although Australia and Great Britain scored barely lower. The three next-highest countries were Canada, the Netherlands, and New Zealand. The most collectivist countries were Venezuela, Colombia, Pakistan, Peru, and Taiwan. In general, western, industrialized countries were highest in individualism, especially those with a British heritage. The most collectivist countries were those in South America and Asia. Hofstede's analysis provided researchers with a guide to highly individualist and collectivist nations that could serve as the basis for research into the consequences of individualism.

Whether or not societies differ most prominently in individualism, it is a value with particular importance to political psychology. Ever since the industrial revolution, individualism has been linked to the desire for social mobility and support for a market economy. Individualism should also help shape the way that people respond to poverty and inequality. Individualists believe that people are ultimately responsible for themselves, and thus society should not have to come the aid of the needy. Collectivists, on the other hand, see the individual as, first and foremost, a member of the social group and someone whose welfare depends on the well-being and actions of the group.

The assumptions that nations differ in levels of individualism and that the ranking of countries in individualism/collectivism can be clearly identified have been crucial to much of the crosscultural values literature. These assumptions were recently put to a rigorous test by Oyserman, Coon, and Kemmelmeier (2002), who conducted an extensive meta-analysis of studies that involved comparisons of measures of individualism/collectivism for the United States and at least one other country. Their findings generally supported these assumptions but with significant qualifications. In many cases the differences across countries were smaller than anticipated. And there was considerable diversity across Asian nations: Chinese samples were quite low in individualism, while Japanese and Korean samples were significantly higher.

The relationship between societal values and individual values also requires close attention. It is not clear that there will always be a one-to-one relationship between the cultural values that characterize a society and the value priorities of people in that society. To make the distinction clear, Triandis et al. (1985) introduced the terms *idiocentrism* and *allocentrism* to describe the person-level values corresponding to individualism and collectivism. Triandis and colleagues find that, at the individual level, idiocentrism and allocentrism are not necessarily strongly negatively correlated, even though individualism and collectivism are considered to be opposite ends of a single continuum at the societal level.

The difficulty in moving from the cultural to individual levels may the reason why measures of individualism in studies of political attitudes in the United States often have weaker-than-expected explanatory power (see Feldman, 1988; Feldman & Steenbergen, 2001, Sears, Henry & Kosterman, 2000; but compare Kinder & Mendelberg, 2000). In these studies it is the value of equality that has a stronger impact on Americans' attitudes toward social welfare policy and race. Although these findings may appear to be inconsistent with the claim that the United States, as a society, is particularly high in individualism, it is possible that these two conclusions are quite compatible: if individualism is a widely shared value in the United States, there may be little real variance to explain differences in political attitudes. Indeed, Feldman and Zaller (1992) found that references to individualism were widespread in open-ended comments about social welfare policies, even among people who supported those policies. We may learn more about the influence of individualism on political attitudes from crossnational research than from studies within any one nation (particularly one very high in individualism). There is some evidence that differences in mean levels of support for individualism are associated with variations in social welfare spending in western, industrialized societies (Smith, 1987).

A different attempt to link social conditions and values comes from the extensive work of Ronald Inglehart. Beginning with simple assumptions about the socialization of value priorities, Inglehart (1977, 1990) developed a model of value change that is associated with the transition from economic scarcity to relative affluence. Inglehart based his model on two assumptions: the *scarcity hypothesis*, that values develop in response to conditions that are in short supply, and the *socialization hypotheses*, that values form during the preadult years and are relatively resistant to change after that. The structure of his model was further elaborated through Abraham Maslow's (1952) hierarchical value theory, which posited that people pursue basic goals in order, from subsistence needs to the need for order, belonging and sociability, self-esteem, and finally postactualization needs. Only as lower order needs become satisfied do individuals turn to succeeding higher order needs. In Inglehart's framework, economic deprivation in the preadult years produces a focus on sustenance and security needs that leads to the development of bourgeois or materialist values. The absence of economic deprivation allows for attention to higher order needs, which results in postbourgeois or postmaterialist values. As economic security in a society increases, more and more young people should develop postmaterialist values and generational turnover should make these values, increasingly prevalent in society.

Inglehart has measured these values by having people (partially) rank-order groups of four value items. His first measure was based on a single group of four: maintain order in the nation, give people more say in the decisions of the government, fight rising prices, and protect freedom of speech. The first and third items are assumed to tap materialist values, the second and fourth postmaterialist values. In subsequent studies up to 12 items were employed. The use of items that referred directly to economic conditions (fight rising prices, maintain a high level of economic growth, maintain a stable economy) has led some (Clarke & Dutt, 1991; Duch & Taylor, 1993) to argue that the proportion of materialist values in a society is a function of short-term economic conditions rather than stable value priorities. While this debate has not yet been put to rest, it seems clear that measures of postmaterialist values are at least somewhat (and perhaps substantially) responsive to short-term forces.

Even among those who agree that value change is proceeding, the nature of that change is in some dispute. Flanagan (1982, 1987) has argued that Inglehart's model obscures two different patterns of change: one involving a shift from economic to noneconomic values and another from authoritarian to libertarian values. Braithwaite, Makkai, and Pittelkow (1996), using Braithwaite's reinterpretation of Rokeach's freedom/equality model, argue that value change is better interpreted as a shift from security to harmony values.

What are the consequences of this value change? Inglehart's original research (1977) focused on student protests and challenges to political authority. Subsequent research has dealt with issues like the environment and support for "green" parties, nuclear energy, and women's role in society. Correlations between postmaterialist values and these issues are almost always positive, although their magnitude varies substantially. For example, Dalton (2002) reports correlations between postmaterialist values and support for antinuclear groups ranging from .09 to .26 in the United States, Great Britain, France, and western Germany, with a correlation of .01 in eastern Germany. The results are very similar for support for women's rights groups in those countries. These are relatively low correlations, and there is no control for other political or social factors that may be correlated with both values and issue preferences. Postmaterialist values do predict vote choice in western European nations, although the relationship is usually weaker than for the traditional left-right dimension (Knutsen, 1995b). Unfortunately, in many of these studies only percentage differences or simple correlations are presented, making it difficult to determine how strong the effects of these values would be in well-specified multivariate models.

While Inglehart's theory and research has received its share of criticism, it has been extremely influential in political science, particularly in studies of European political attitudes, participation, and voting. And Inglehart has worked, perhaps harder than any other value theorist, to develop a theory of value change that can help understand the dynamics of politics in industrialized nations. An empirical comparison of Inglehart's materialist/ postmaterialist value dimension with Schwartz's structural model could help to integrate two major lines of research on the crossnational dynamics of value systems (one in political science and one in psychology).

I conclude this section with an interesting example of how the study of social values can shed light on social and political processes. Utilizing data on values that he has collected in many nations, Schwartz (1997) explored the potential effects of communism on societal values. Specifically, he compared samples of public school teachers and college students in 9 eastern European countries with comparable samples from 11 western Europe nations. All of the samples were obtained between 1989 and 1993.

Schwartz found substantively large differences in values in several important domains. The eastern Europe samples were all higher in conservatism values (his conformity, tradition, and security value types) than the every one of the western Europe samples. The eastern Europe sample were also higher on average in hierarchy (power) values than the western Europe samples, though the differences were not quite as pronounced. Conversely, the eastern Europe samples were lower in affective autonomy (stimulation) and intellectual autonomy (self-direction) values and, interestingly, egalitarian (universalism and benevolence) values. As with the conservatism values, all nine eastern Europe nations had lower means on egalitarian values than each of the western Europe nations. These differences appear to withstand simple controls for variables like religion and economic development. The eastern European value patterns certainly don't fit expectations about "socialist" societies, although, as Schwartz argues, they may be the consequences of authoritarian regimes.

As Schwartz notes, the best design to examine the effects of different political systems on societal values would be to have repeated samples over time in countries that experience changes in political systems. In the absence of such studies, data like this can provide important evidence of the consequences of sociopolitical structures on values and, ultimately, on the attitudes necessary to foster democracy. Since it is likely that younger people will be most affected by changes in political systems, even samples from after political change should be useful, as the values of younger people should be increasingly different from older people in the society in predictable ways.

► Conclusion: Values, Politics, and Political Ideology

Even a review of this length must be quite selective, and there is a great deal of research on values that I have not been able to discuss. My goal has been to suggest how values can help political psychologists understand the structure of political attitudes. The search for attitude organization has been one of the major concerns of research in political science and psychology. While no single approach to this problem will suffice, there is now a substantial amount of evidence that values are a major source of structure for political attitudes. I have reviewed some of this evidence, but I have also tried to show how recent theories and research can advance our understanding much further. Psychologists have made substantial contributions to the study of values since Rokeach's book was published in 1973. Yet political psychologists often ignore this work and incorporate values into their research in a piecemeal fashion. For many purposes this may suffice. Discoveries that equality is a major predictor of social welfare attitudes (Feldman, 1988) or that individualism is not a major predictor of racial attitudes (Kinder & Mendelberg, 2000) are important findings in their own right. But there is reason to believe that attention to broader value structures may be even more fruitful.

The relationship among values is especially important as we move from understanding specific attitudes to attitude organization and ideology. Finding an underlying, simple structure to values may provide a basis for linking individual and societal value priorities to fundamental social and political conflicts. This is one of the promising aspects of Schwartz's value theory. By linking values to basic human needs and motivations, Schwartz sets out a systematic way of thinking about the relationship among values. The two-dimensional structure apparent in the associations among the values may provide the foundation for a value-based model of ideology. Greater attention to a theory of value structure and a more comprehensive measure of values may have considerable value for political psychology.

As I have emphasized throughout, there are still many questions surrounding the use of values in political psychology research. We know too little about the stability of values and the extent to which they are exogenous to political attitudes. We need to learn more about the conditions under which values are most strongly related to attitudes. Theories of values give us too little guidance to predict which values will structure particular political attitudes. Much more work is necessary to determine the ultimate value of values for political psychology.

◤ Notes

1. Instrumental values refer to "modes of conduct" while terminal values involve "end-states of existence." Subsequent research has generally failed to support this distinction (see Schwartz, 1992).

2. In addition, virtually all of Rokeach's analysis was with samples from the United States. This obviously prevented him from assessing any cultural variation in value content and structure.

3. The list began originally as eight types, was expanded to 11, and then reduced to 10 when one type—spirituality—failed to emerge from the analysis.

4. McCann reports an unstandardized stability coefficient of .49.

5. A priori differences in societal values are sometimes derived from general observations of societal characteristics (based perhaps on anthropological studies) or from one of the handful of quantitative studies of cross-national value differences, primarily the work of Hofstede (1980).

◤ References

Allport, G. W., Vernon, P. E., & Lindsey, G. (1960). *Study of values* (3rd ed.). Boston: Houghton Mifflin.

Altemeyer, B. (1998). The other "authoritarian personality." In M. P. Zanna (Ed.), *Advances in experimental social psychology* (Vol. 30, pp. 47–92). San Diego, CA: Academic Press.

Alwin, D. F., & Krosnick, J. A. (1985). The measurement of values in surveys: A comparison of ratings and rankings. *Public Opinion Quarterly, 49,* 535–552.

Bem, D. J. (1970). *Beliefs, attitudes, and human affairs.* Belmont, CA: Wadsworth.

Biernat, M., Vescio, T. K., Theno, S. A., & Crandall, C. S. (1996). Values and prejudice: toward understanding the impact of American values on outgroup attitudes. In C. Seligman, J. M. Olson, & M. P. Zanna (Eds.), *The psychology of values* (pp. 153–190). Mahwah, NJ: Erlbaum.

Borg, S. (1995). Electoral participation. In J. W. van Deth & E. Scarbrough (Eds.), *The impact of values* (pp. 441–460). New York: Oxford University Press.

Braithwaite, V. (1982). The structure of social values: Validation of Rokeach's two-value model. *British Journal of Social Psychology, 21,* 203–211.

Braithwaite, V. (1994). Beyond Rokeach's equality-freedom model: Two-dimensional values in a one-dimensional world. *Journal of Social Issues, 50,* 67–94.

Braithwaite, V. (1997). Harmony and security value orientations in political evaluation. *Personality and Social Psychology Bulletin, 23,* 401–414.

Braithwaite, V. A., & Law, H. G. (1985). Structure of human values: Testing the adequacy of the Rokeach Value Survey. *Journal of Personality and Social Psychology, 49,* 250–263.

Braithwaite, V., Makkai, T., & Pittelkow, Y. (1996). Inglehart's materialism-postmaterialism concept: Clarifying the dimensionality debate through Rokeach's model of social values. *Journal of Applied Social Psychology, 26,* 1536–1555.

Braithwaite, V. A., & Scott, W. A. (1991). Values. In J. P. Robinson, P. R. Shaver, & L. S. Wrightsman (Eds.), *Measure of personality and social psychological attitudes* (pp. 661–753). San Diego CA: Academic Press.

Carmines, E. G., & Stimson, J. A. (1980). The two faces of issue voting. *American Political Science Review, 74,* 78–91.

Clarke, H., & Dutt, N. (1991). Measuring value change in western industrialized societies. *American Political Science Review, 85,* 905–920.

Cochrane, R., Billig, M., & Hogg, M. (1979). Politics and values in Britain: A test of Rokeach's two-value model. *British Journal of Social and Clinical Psychology, 18,* 159–167.

Conover, P. J., & Feldman, S. (1981). The origins and meaning of liberal/conservative self-identification. *American Journal of Political Science, 25,* 617–645.

Converse, P. E. (1964). The nature of belief systems in mass publics. In D. E. Apter (Ed.), *Ideology and discontent* (pp. 206–261). New York: Free Press.

Dalton, R. J. (2002). *Citizen politics.* New York: Chatham House.

Downs, A. (1957). *An economic theory of democracy.* New York: Harper and Row.

Duch, R., & Taylor, M. (1993). Postmaterialism and the economic condition. *American Journal of Political Science, 37,* 747–779.

Feldman, S. (1988). Structure and consistency in public opinion: The role of core beliefs and values. *American Journal of Political Science, 32,* 416–440.

Feldman, S. (1983). Economic individualism and American public opinion. *American Politics Quarterly, 11,* 3–29.

Feldman, S., & Steenbergen, M. R. (2001). The humanitarian foundation of public support for social welfare. *American Journal of Political Science, 45,* 658–677.

Feldman, S., & Zaller, J. (1992). The political culture of ambiguity: Ideological responses to the welfare state. *American Journal of Political Science, 36,* 268–307.

Flanagan, S. (1982). Changing values in advanced industrial society. *Comparative Political Studies, 14,* 403–444.

Flanagan, S. (1987). Value change in industrial society. *American Political Science Review, 81,* 1303–1319.

Gundelach, P. (1995). Grass-roots activity. In J. W. van Deth & E. Scarbrough (Eds.), *The impact of values.* New York: Oxford University Press.

Hochschild, J. (1981). *What's fair?* Princeton: Princeton University Press.

Hofstede, G. (1980). *Culture's consequences: International differences in work-related values.* Beverly Hills, CA: Sage.

Inglehart, R. (1977). *The silent revolution.* Princeton: Princeton University Press.

Inglehart, R. (1990). *Cultural shift in advanced industrial society.* Princeton: Princeton University Press.

Jacoby, W. (1991). Ideological identification and issue attitudes. *American Journal of Political Science, 35,* 178–205.

Katz, D. (1960). The functional approach to the study of attitudes. *Public Opinion Quarterly, 24,* 163–204.

Kinder, D. R. (1998). Opinion and action in the realm of politics. In D. T. Gilbert, S. T. Fiske, & G. Lindzey (Eds.), *Handbook of social psychology* (Vol. 1, pp. 778–867). New York: Oxford University Press.

Kinder, D. R., & Mendelberg, T. (2000). Individualism reconsidered. In D. O. Sears, J. Sidanius, & L. Bobo (Eds.), *Racialized politics* (pp. 44–74). Chicago: University of Chicago Press.

Kinder, D. R., & Sanders, L. M. (1996). *Divided by color.* Chicago: University of Chicago Press.

Kluckhohn, F. R., & Stodtbeck, F. (1961). *Variations in value orientations.* Evanston, IL: Row, Peterson.

Kluegel, J. R., & Smith, E. R. (1986). *Beliefs about inequality.* Hawthorne, NY: de Gruyter.

Knutsen, O. (1995a). Left-right materialist value orientations. In J. W. van Deth & E. Scarbrough (Eds.), *The impact of values* (pp. 160–196). New York: Oxford University Press.

Knutsen. O. (1995b). Party choice. In J. W. van Deth & E. Scarbrough (Eds.), *The impact of values* (pp. 460–491). New York: Oxford University Press.

Kristiansen, C. M., & Hotte, A. M. (1996). Morality and the self: Implications for the when and how of value-attitude-behavior relations. In C. Seligman, J. M. Olson, & M. P. Zanna, (Eds.), *The psychology of values* (pp. 77–106). Mahwah, NJ: Erlbaum.

Kristiansen, C. M., & Zanna, M. P. (1988). Justifying attitudes by appealing to values: A functional perspective. *British Journal of Social Psychology, 27,* 247–256.

Kristiansen, C. M., & Zanna, M. P. (1994). The rhetorical use of values to justify social and intergroup attitudes. *Journal of Social Issues, 50,* 47–65.

Lane, R. (1960). *Political ideology.* New York: Basic Books.

Lipset, S. M. (1979). *The first new nation.* New York: Norton.

Maio, G. R., & Olson, J. M. (1994). Value-attitude-behavior relations: The moderating role of attitude functions. *British Journal of Social Psychology, 33,* 301–312.

Maio, G. R., & Olson, J. M. (1995). Relations between values, attitudes, and behavioral intentions: The moderating role of attitude function. *Journal of Experimental Social Psychology, 31,* 266–285.

Maslow, A. (1952). *Toward a psychology of being.* New York: Nostrand.

Maslow, A. (1954). *Motivation and personality.* New York: Harper and Row.

McCann, J. A. (1997). Electoral choices and core value change: The 1992 presidential campaign. *American Journal of Political Science, 41,* 564–583.

Miller, W., & Shanks, J. M. (1996). *The new American voter.* Cambridge, MA: Harvard University Press.

Morris, C. (1956). *Varieties of human value.* Chicago: University of Chicago Press.

Oyserman, D., Coon, H. M., & Kemmelmeier, M. (2002). Rethinking individualism and collectivism: Evaluation of theoretical assumptions and meta-analyses. *Psychological Bulletin, 128,* 3–72.

Peffley, M. A., & Hurwitz, J. (1985). A hierarchical model of attitude constraint. *American Journal of Political Science, 29,* 871–890.

Pollock, P. H., Lilie, S. A., & Vittes, M. E. (1993). Hard issues, core values and vertical constraint: The case of nuclear power. *British Journal of Political Science, 23,* 29–50.

Rohan, M. J. (2000). A rose by any name? The values construct. *Personality and Social Psychology Review, 4,* 255–277.

Rohan, M. J., & Zanna, M. P. (1996). Value transmission in families. In C. Seligman, J. M. Olson, & M. P. Zanna, (Eds.), *The psychology of values* (pp. 253–276). Mahwah, NJ: Erlbaum.

Rokeach, M. (1960). *The open and closed mind.* New York: Basic Books.

Rokeach, M. (1968). *Beliefs, attitudes, and values.* New York: Free Press.

Rokeach, M. (1973). *The nature of human values.* New York: Free Press.

Rokeach, M., & Ball-Rokeach, S. J. (1988). Stability and change in American value priorities, 1968–1981. *American Psychologist, 44,* 775–784.

Sagiv, L., & Schwartz, S. H. (1995). Value priorities and readiness for out-group social contact. *Journal of Personality and Social Psychology, 69,* 437–448.

Schwartz, S. H. (1992). Universals in the content and structure of values. In M. P. Zanna (Ed.), *Advances in experimental social psychology* (Vol. 25, pp. 1–65). New York: Academic Press.

Schwartz, S. H. (1994). Are their universal aspects in the structure and content of human values? *Journal of Social Issues, 50,* 19–46.

Schwartz, S. H. (1996). Value priorties and behavior: Applying a theory of integrated value systems. In C. Seligman, J. M. Olson, & M. P. Zanna (Eds.), *The psychology of values* (pp. 1–24). Mahwah, NJ: Erlbaum.

Schwartz, S. H. (1997). Influences of adaptation to communist rule on value priorities in eastern Europe. *Political Psychology, 18,* 385–410.

Schwartz, S. H., & Bilsky, W. (1987). Toward a psychological structure of human values. *Journal of Personality and Social Psychology, 53,* 550–562.

Schwartz, S. H., & Bilsky, W. (1990). Toward a theory of the universal content and structure of values: Extensions and cross-cultural replications. *Journal of Personality and Social Psychology, 58,* 878–891.

Sears, D. O., & Funk, C. L. (1991). The role of self-interest in social and political attitudes. *Advances in Experimental Social Psychology, 24,* 1–91.

Sears, D. O., Henry, P. J., & Kosterman, R. (2000). Egalitarian values and contemporary racial politics. In D. O. Sears, J. Sidanius, & L. Bobo (Eds.), *Racialized politics* (pp. 75–117). Chicago: University of Chicago Press.

Seligman, C., & Katz, A. N. (1996). The dynamics of value systems. In C. Seligman, J. M. Olson, & M. P. Zanna, (Eds.), *The psychology of values* (pp. 53–76). Mahwah, NJ: Erlbaum.

Shavitt, S. (1990). The role of attitude objects in attitude functions. *Journal of Experimental Social Psychology, 26,* 124–148.

Sheng, S. Y. (1995). *NES measurement of values and predispositions, 1984–1992.* National Election Studies, Technical Report No. 50.

Sidanius, J., & Pratto, F. (1999). *Social dominance: An intergroup theory of social hierarchy and oppression.* New York: Cambridge University Press.

Smith, M. B., Bruner, J. S., & White, R. W. (1956). *Opinions and personality.* New York: Wiley.

Smith, T. W. (1987). Report: The welfare state in cross-national perspective. *Public Opinion Quarterly, 51,* 404–421.

Spranger, E. (1928). *Types of men: The psychology and ethics of personality.* Halle, Germany: Max Niemeyer Verlag.

Tetlock, P. E. (2000). Coping with trade-offs: Psychological constraints and political implications. In S. Lupia, M. McCubbins, & S. Popkin (Eds.), *Political reasoning and choice* (pp. 239–263). Berkeley: University of California Press.

Tetlock, P. E., Peterson, R. S., & Lerner, J. S. (1996). Revising the value pluralism model: Incorporating social content and context postulates. In C. Seligman, J. M. Olson, & M. P. Zanna, (Eds.), *The psychology of values* (pp. 25–52). Mahwah, NJ: Erlbaum.

Tocqueville, A. de. (1975). *Democracy in American*. Garden City, NY: Doubleday.

Triandis, H. C., Leung, K., Villareal, M. J., & Clark, F. L. (1985). Allocentric versus idiocentric tendencies. *Journal of Research in Personality, 19,* 395–415.

Verba, S., Kelman, S., Orren, G. R., Miyake, I., Watanuki, J., Kabashima, I., & Ferree, G. D. (1987). *Elites and the idea of equality*. Cambridge, MA: Harvard University Press.

Zaller, J. (1992). *The nature and origins of mass opinion*. New York: Cambridge University Press.

Zaller, J. R. (1991). Information, values, and opinion. *American Political Science Review, 85,* 1215–1237.

Intergroup Relations

15 Leonie Huddy

Group Identity and Political Cohesion

Political psychologists have a longstanding interest in the impact of group membership on political behavior, an interest that is heightened in the current era of identity politics, and ethnic separatist and emergent nationalist movements. Group allegiances have been blamed in the modern era for civil strife and violent conflict. But this is only one, and perhaps the least common, political consequence of group loyalties. Most group memberships have no political consequences, as is seen in the meager political impact of various sociodemographic characteristics such as class, age, and marital status in the United States and other western countries. In some groups, membership produces a common set of political preferences, resulting in a gender gap in vote choice, for example, without generating intergroup violence. Occasionally, group membership diminishes conflict by promoting crossgroup alliances, as is manifested in panracial and panethnic political movements, such as Jesse Jackson's rainbow coalition in the United States, or international alliances that cross national boundaries. And in a few salient instances, group membership results in extreme intergroup hostility, as is exemplified by the fervent actions of suicide bombers. The diverse political consequences of group membership are the subject of this review.

The political consequences of group membership played a central role in the earliest political behavior research. Lazarsfeld and his colleagues uncovered the impact of ethnic and religious affiliation on vote choice, (Berelson, Lazarsfield, & McPhee, 1954; Lazarsfeld, Berelson, & Gaudet, 1944); Stouffer demonstrated the powerful effects of reference groups in shaping expectations about individual outcomes (1949); and Campbell, Converse, Miller, and Stokes (1960) examined the origins of partisan loyalties in union membership, religion, and socioeconomic status. But interest in the social origins of political behavior has waxed and waned in the intervening decades. It was a key focus of political behavior research in the 1950s and early 1960s, a period of considerable political cohesion characterized by the pervasive influence of traditional ethnic, religious, and occupational groups in the United States and elsewhere. There was renewed interest in the political impact of groups in the late 1970s and early 1980s, sparked by the emergence of new social movements centered among blacks, college students, and women (Miller, Gurin, Gurin, & Malanchuk, 1981; Gurin, Miller, & Gurin, 1980). And the end of communism in eastern Europe, large-scale international immigration, and the eruption of ethnic independence movements and breakaway nationalism reignited interest in the concept of group-based politics, especially identity, in the 1990s and 2000s (Breakwell & Lyons, 1996; Huddy, 2001).

As interest in the political fallout of group membership has shifted with changes in social and political reality, the central question motivating research on groups has also changed quite radically. In the 1970s, researchers asked why members of low-status groups did not engage in collective action to rectify their social standing, in line with new social movements agitating for the rights of the disenfranchised (Miller et al., 1981); in the 1990s and 2000s researchers reversed this question to ask instead how groups could be prevented from engaging in collective action in a context dominated by genocide and violent intergroup conflicts (see also Duckitt, 1994).

◣ A Central Focus on Subjective Identification

One of the enduring findings of research on groups is the greater political power of subjective group loyalties than objective group membership. This notion—that subjective loyalties overwhelm the role of objective group membership—was central to early work on reference groups (Hyman & Singer, 1968; Merton & Kitt, 1950). Centers's (1949) research on class identification provides a good example of the reference group approach and its key findings. When respondents were asked whether they identified with the middle, lower, working, or upper class, their sense of subjective identification was a far more powerful indicator of their conservative-radical orientation, position on socioeconomic issues, and voting preference than objectively determined membership in a socioeconomic class based on factors such as income and occupation.

Reference group theory placed a distinctive emphasis on the power of identification with groups to which individuals did not belong—a working-class person who identified with the middle class or a black who identified as white, for example (Hyman & Singer, 1968). Subjective group loyalties were seen as more powerful than actual group memberships. But a central focus on nonmembership groups was also the undoing of reference group theory, to some degree, because of the difficulty faced by researchers in explaining the conditions under which someone would choose to identify with a nonmembership group over a group to which they belonged, or explaining the choice of one nonmembership group over another (Deutsch & Krauss, 1965).

Social identity theory emerged more recently as a powerful psychological alternative to reference group theory that provides a more detailed account of the adoption of group identification and its consequences. But one of the crucial insights of reference group theory got lost in this transition. In the minimal intergroup situation, social identity theory's basic research paradigm, group membership is effectively treated as an objective assignment rather than a subjective identification. I believe that subjective identification remains critical to understanding the political ramifications of group membership (Huddy, 2001; 2002)—a view that is shared by many political scientists and has gained growing acceptance among social psychologists (Branscombe, Schmitt, & Harvey, 1999; Conover, 1984; Ethier & Deaux, 1994; Lau, 1989). A central emphasis is placed on subjective identification in this review in an effort to resurrect the earlier insights of reference group theory while drawing on a diversity of theoretical approaches, including social identity theory, to better understand the development of political identity and account for its political consequences.

The focus throughout this review is on the *political* effects of group membership, although I pay greater attention to political attitudes and electoral behavior than collective action, which is discussed in chapter 19. I also stress the consequences of group membership for ingroup solidarity but spend less time discussing its implications for outgroup antipathy, a topic covered in chapter 16. In reviewing a very large literature in both psychology and political science, I cannot hope to comprehensively cover psychological research on intergroup relations or its major theoretical approaches, which are well reviewed elsewhere (Brewer & Brown, 1998; Brown 1995, 2000; Duckitt, 1994; Taylor & Moghaddam, 1996).

▶ Group Membership and Group Identification

Group membership does not always lead to a distinct political outlook or result in political action, and I draw several distinctions and define a terminology to make sense of extant research findings. *Group membership* is based on objective inclusion in a group and does not require an internalized sense of membership. This fits with Newcomb's (1952) definition of a membership group as "one in which a person is recognized by others as belonging," although the current definition extends beyond what is visible to others to include covert but undisputed indicators of membership (e.g., Latino origins or war veteran status). But not all group memberships fit this pattern neatly, especially those that are based on unclear, ambiguous, or vague criteria. Social class is a classic example. In the United States, relatively few individuals call themselves working-class, even though their incomes and occupations might qualify them on an objective basis. The criteria for class membership are not well defined among members of the public, and it is difficult to know where to draw the lines that distinguish between socioeconomic classes.

The ambiguous nature of some group memberships and the fact that not all objective members feel a sense of attachment to others belonging to the same group heightens the importance of *group identification*, a more restrictive, subjective, or internalized sense of belonging to the group. I confine a sense of group identification to a subset of objective group members. This is at odds with reference group theory, which placed an emphasis on identification with nonmembership groups (Hyman & Singer, 1968). The difference may be more illusory than real, however, because membership criteria are vague or ambiguous for a sizeable number of sociodemographic and political groups. Within reference group theory, for example, class was treated as externally identifiable. But the objective criteria for class inclusion are less clear-cut in contemporary thinking, making it difficult to know what level of household income signifies a shift from working to middle-class, or from middle-class to upper middle-class. Some men feel perfectly comfortable identifying as feminist, while others worry that they cannot legitimately call themselves feminists because they believe the category excludes men. There are some groups for whom objective membership criteria are clear-cut, however. It is almost impossible for a man to identify as a woman, given that membership in the two groups is mutually exclusive. It is possible for men to sympathize with women, but this affiliation is likely to be less powerful and central than women's subjective sense of gender identity. Thus in this review I emphasize the importance of membership as a precursor to identification, even though membership is not always easy to determine objectively.

Group identification involves a subjective sense of membership and can be divided into two kinds of attachments—*social identity* and a sense of realistic *interdependence* or common fate. Social identity involves the incorporation of group membership into the self-concept. According to Tajfel (1981), a social identity involves an individual's "knowledge of his membership in a social group (or groups) together with the value and emotional significance attached to the membership" (p. 255). In other words, social identity is a "self awareness of one's objective membership in the group *and* a psychological sense of attachment to the group" (Conover, 1984, p. 761). This also fits Campbell and colleagues' (1960) definition of partisan identification in *The American Voter* as not only a set of beliefs but also feelings that culminate in a sense of "psychological attachment" to a political group—in this instance, Democrats or Republicans. But not all forms of group attachment are necessarily predicated on identity. A sense of subjective interdependence or shared common fate with other group members simply depends on the recognition that group members share similar interests or face a similar threat but does not require group members to subjectively identify as group members.

The emphasis on subjective sense of belonging or identification helps to explain why groups do not always engage in intergroup conflict or cohere into a potent political force even when their members are highly visible within a given society. Political behavior researchers are often struck by the absence of group conflict or the weakness of political identities among members of distinct and salient groups such as the Chinese in Indonesia, indigenous peoples in Argentina, or northern Africans in Italy. Subjective identification plays a key role in determining when group members will coalesce politically.

▶ The Nature of Political Groups

The distinction between group membership and group loyalties prompts further inquiry into the types of groups likely to mobilize their members or to promote a coherent political outlook. Identity researchers often distinguish between group memberships that help to define who we are as individuals, based on age or marital status for example, from those that define us as part of a collective, such as race and ethnicity. Jenkins (1996), for instance, differentiates a category in which individuals are "united by some common characteristic" apparent to outsiders (e.g., gender) from a group in which members "are aware of their similarities" and define themselves on that basis (e.g., feminists; p. 23). Along similar lines, Young (1990) describes the difference between a superficial association in which individuals retain their sense of individual identity and a group that constitutes part of the individual self. In her view, membership in an association is equivalent to adding another adjective to one's self-description but conveys little more about shared experiences or a common outlook.

This distinction also emerges within political psychology. Brewer, along with others (Brewer, 2001; Hogg, Hardie, & Reynolds, 1995; Thoits & Virshup, 1997), argues that there is a difference between social identities based on membership in racial, ethnic, or other demographic groups and role identities based on familial or work-related roles. She suggests that role identities constitute part of the self but have more of a "me" than a "we" orientation because they describe one's attributes as an individual but do not connote commonality with a collective. In her view, role identities are not the stuff of collective action because they constitute an individual, not a group identity.

But even role identities can be translated into political action, as is demonstrated by groups such as Mothers Against Drunk Driving (MADD), organizations representing the families of people with AIDS, or unions representing a specific occupation. In reality, the line between individualistic and collective group-based identity is blurred. It is extremely difficult to exclude a specific class of groups from consideration as a potential source of collective political beliefs, since membership in any collective has the potential, whether realized or not, to mobilize group members. Consider political groups such as environmentalists, feminists, political partisans, and white supremacists (Abrams, 1994; Duck, Hogg, & Terry, 1995; Duck, Terry, & Hogg, 1998; Greene, 1999; Huddy, 2001; Kelly, 1989). On the one hand, membership in these groups is based on individual support for a specific political outlook. Yet when citizens talk about what they like and dislike about the political parties, for example, they comment on the shared beliefs, common traits, and the specific individuals who typify group members. The existence of these clear partisan stereotypes suggests that political groups are seen as cohesive social entities with shared beliefs and common social characteristics (Rahn, 1993). Indeed, when Deaux, Reid, Mizrahi, &

Ethier (1995) investigated the individual and collective nature of various identities among college students, they expected "predictions from social identity theory to be most applicable to ethnic, religious, [and] political" identities, since they are more "collective in nature" than other individual aspects of identity (p. 286). For these reasons, I consider any group and its members a candidate for the development of a cohesive political outlook and concerted political action.

◤ Theoretical Approaches

Four broad classes of theory that purportedly account for the development of group-based cohesion are considered in this review (for a similar distinction see Rothbart, 1993; for a more exhaustive list, see Brewer & Brown, 1998).[1] Each theory highlights a somewhat different set of active ingredients in the development of political cohesion. My goal is not to evaluate how well each approach accounts for the emergence of group solidarity but rather to derive a set of factors linked to the emergence and development of group loyalties and political cohesion. Before proceeding, I need to clarify the meaning of the term *political cohesion*, which I use somewhat differently from earlier psychological theorists. Cohesion was originally defined within research on small group decision-making as "the degree to which the members of a group desire to remain in the group" (Cartwright, 1968, p. 91). Converse and Campbell (1968) used it in a similar sense to refer to the degree of positive attraction among group members. I deviate somewhat from this usage and define *political cohesion* as the existence of shared attitudes, beliefs, and behavior among group members that can be directly attributed to group membership. In this sense, political cohesion connotes a form of political unity or solidarity that does not necessarily derive from any personal attraction among group members.

The Cognitive Approach

This approach emphasizes the role of self-categorization in the development of group cohesion (Turner, Hogg, Oakes, Reicher, & Wetherell, 1987). Within self-categorization theory, the shift from a personal to a collective identity is accompanied by a desire to emulate the attitudes and behavior of typical group members, which, in turn, produces group cohesion (Turner et al., 1987). The perception of ingroup and outgroup boundaries produces self-classification as members of the ingroup and promotes conformity to the attributes of typical group members (Hogg, Hardie, & Reynolds, 1995). Conformity heightens cohesion among group members and is most pronounced when group identity is highly salient. Researchers have considerable evidence that group members stereotype themselves, expect to agree with each other, and strive for consensus (Abrams, Wetherell, Cochrane,

Hogg, & Turner, 1990; Haslam, Oakes, Turner, McGarty, & Reynolds, 1998; for an overview see Spears, Oakes, Ellemers, & Haslam, 1997). From this perspective, conformity is cognitive in nature and driven by a heightened sense of group membership, not a desire for group acceptance (one of the motives underlying conformity within reference group theory; Kelley, 1952).

Self-categorization theorists draw extensively on developments in categorization research to move away from a "classical" view of category membership as defined by a set of clear rules or a set of common features to view categories instead as a fuzzy set with unclear boundaries and a "graded" or probabilistic structure in which some members are rated as more typical or better members of the category than others (Lakoff, 1987; Neisser, 1987). Turner and his colleagues borrow Lakoff's (1987) "prototype theory" to argue that perceived similarity to the prototypic group member plays a key role in the formation and development of social identity and the emergence of group conformity (Hogg, 1996; Hogg & Hains, 1996; McGarty, Turner, Hogg, David, & Wetherell, 1992; Turner et al., 1987).

Self-categorization researchers also hold an extremely labile view of social identity as driven almost completely by one's immediate perceptual context. In an article on Australian stereotypes of Americans, Turner and his colleagues write that "salient self-categories are . . . intrinsically variable and fluid, not merely being passively 'activated' but actively constructed 'on the spot' to reflect the contemporary properties of self and others" (Haslam, Turner, Oakes, McGarty, & Hayes, 1992, p. 5). From their perspective, identities vary, in part, because social categories such as age or gender vary in salience across situations. Indeed, one of the key tenets of self-categorization theory is that individuals constantly shift back and forth between an individual and a social identity (Brewer & Weber, 1994; Simon, 1997; Turner et al., 1987). Thus, within a cognitive approach, group cohesion and conformity rest heavily on the salience of group membership.

Realistic Interest Approaches

These approaches include realistic group conflict, relative deprivation, and social dominance theories and Blumer's sense of group position (Blumer, 1958; Bobo, 1983; Bobo & Hutchings, 1996; Campbell, 1965; Coser 1956; LeVine & Campbell, 1972; Sidanius & Pratto, 1999; see Brown, 1995, for an overview). They suggest collectively that group membership is politically consequential to the extent that political decisions drive group members' tangible gains and losses. In other words, group membership translates into political cohesion when group members have tangible interests in common. Realistic interest theories include the protection of self- and group interests that might indicate long-term or future interests that are objective or subjective, direct or indirect (Bobo, 1983). Thus the unemployed might cohere politically around their mutual reliance on monthly unemployment benefits; the elderly could unite over threats to cut Social Security benefits; and African Americans could unify in opposition to the death penalty, which disproportionately affects members of their group.

In most studies of Americans' policy preferences, self-interest has had very circumscribed and limited effects on a range of policies, including support for unemployment policies, taxation, busing, women's issues, and bilingual education (Huddy & Sears, 1995; Sears & Citrin, 1985; Sears & Funk, 1991; Sears & Huddy, 1990). Self-interest has its most pronounced political effects when it is large, clear, and certain (Sears & Funk, 1991). At times, self-interest may even motivate political action (Begley & Alker, 1982; Green & Cowden, 1992). But the political effects of self-interest need to be disentangled from those of group interests, which could be more powerful. For example, upper-income blacks may not benefit directly from low-income housing projects (self-interest) but may see the projects as beneficial to blacks as a group with whom they feel interdependent (group interest). Bobo (1983) helped to rekindle interest in research on group interests in the early 1980s by suggesting that they motivate opposition among whites to racial policies that assist blacks; he went on to develop this approach as an elaboration of Blumer's group position model (Bobo, 1999; Bobo & Hutchings, 1996; for an alternative interpretation of the data, see Sears & Kinder, 1985).

Some theorists argue that additional beliefs are needed to create political cohesion even when group members share a sense of common fate (Simon & Klandermans, 2001). A sense of subjective deprivation is critical to *relative deprivation theory*—the perception that one's group's finances are deteriorating relative to those of others. Relative deprivation theorists refer to this as a sense of fraternal deprivation and contrast it with egoistic deprivation, which arises when an individual feels relatively deprived compared to an individual or group with whom he compares himself (Gurr, 1970; Merton & Kitt, 1950).[2]

Symbolic Approaches: Social Identity Theory

Status politics provides one of the earliest explorations of the symbolic impact of group standing on support for political issues and action. This approach was developed, in part, to account for right-wing political movements, the political impact of declining group status, and the prospect of rising group status (Bell, 1963; Gusfield, 1963; Lipset & Raab, 1973) and has been extended to account for opposition to the Equal Rights Amendment (Scott, 1985). Within this framework, movements such as temperance are viewed as an attempt to renew the prestige of a formerly admired lifestyle and its adherents (Gusfield, 1963). In essence, status politics emphasizes the political power of group members' declining status.

Social identity theory also emphasizes the political importance of symbolic concerns surrounding group status, although it is less focused on the actions of groups with formerly high but declining status. There are two distinct branches of social identity theory: the version developed by Tajfel (1981) and Tajfel and Turner (1979), known as social identity theory, and the cognitive offshoot known as self-categorization theory (Turner et al., 1987). Both theories acknowledge the origins of social identity in cognitive and motivational factors, although they place differing emphasis on them (Hogg, 1996, p. 67). The earliest versions of social identity theory developed by Tajfel (1981) and Tajfel and Turner (1979) placed key emphasis on the psychological motivations that lead a group member to endorse or disavow an existing group membership. Turner and colleagues (1987) have described this motive as a need among group members "to differentiate their own groups positively from others to achieve a positive social identity" (p. 42).

In contrast, self-categorization theory, developed by Turner and colleagues (1987), has concentrated on the cognitive underpinnings of social identity. This approach builds on Tajfel's (1981) early research and theorizing, which began from a purely cognitive perspective, attempting to explain the perceptual distortions that accompanied categorization (Tajfel, 1981; Tajfel & Wilkes, 1963; see Eiser, 1996, for a lengthier review of this early work). But at some point, Tajfel concluded that cognitive factors—the perceptual distortions that arise from the accentuation of intergroup differences—could not on their own explain the emergence of intergroup discrimination and, in response, modified social identity theory to include additional motivational factors (Wilder, 1986).

According to Tajfel, the effects of social identity are driven by a need for positive distinctiveness in which one's own group is positively distinguished from an outgroup. This means that group identity is likely to emerge among members of a high-status group because membership positively distinguishes group members from outsiders; in contrast, the development of group identity is less certain among members of low-status groups who need to additionally develop an identity around alternative, positively valued group attributes (social creativity) or fight to change the group's negative image (social change) before membership can enhance their status (Tajfel & Turner, 1979).[3]

Social Constructivism and the Meaning of Group Membership

The reach of social constructivism extends well beyond the dynamics of identity, but I include it here to address the nagging concern that other approaches fail to consider the subjective meaning of an identity and its ability to shape group members' political outlook and actions (Duveen, 2001; Erikson, 1993; Huddy, 2001; 2002). Social constructivism—the notion that concepts derive their meaning through social processes—underlies a good deal of thinking across the contemporary social sciences and humanities. It is certainly central to social identity and self-categorization theory—the major cognitive and symbolic approaches to identity just discussed. Both theories stress the ease with which social groups and social identities form even among groups of strangers with almost nothing in common except membership in an arbitrarily designated group. As a number of critics have noted, however, social identity theorists have explored the socially fluid nature of identities but have not closely examined or analyzed the meaning of identities (Duveen, 2001; Forbes, 1997; Huddy, 2001). From a social constructivist perspective, it is difficult to understand the consequences of group identification without understanding its subjective meaning to group members (Billig, 1995; Bruner, 1990; Gergen, 1989). This may be especially true for politically relevant identities, which are often the target of political manipulation—efforts by politicians and group entrepreneurs to create, define, and redefine identities to serve their political ends (Erikson, 1993).

Sociologists, especially those working within a symbolic interactionist framework, and anthropologists have paid greater attention than political scientists or social psychologists to the processes by which individuals and group members negotiate and construct the meaning of identity (Barth, 1969, 1981; Erikson, 1993; Jenkins, 1996; Mead, 1934). Erikson discusses in detail how Indians transported by the British in the nineteenth century to work on plantations throughout the empire developed an identity as good at politics but bad at business in Mauritius, while Indians in Trinidad came to see themselves in exactly opposite terms. Erikson goes on to document how the Indians of Trinidad forged a self-conscious culture and identity over the last several decades that rests more on an upper-caste version of Indian life than their former lifestyle in India as members of lower castes.

From a social constructivist perspective, the emphasis on trivial or newly formed groups that lack meaning in research on social identity and self-categorization theory may seriously hamper an understanding of both identity acquisition and its consequences (Huddy, 2001). For example, members of diverse groups may attach different meanings to the same identity in different regions of a country or within distinct national subgroups (Cohen, 1986; Jenkins, 1996). Group membership can also take on diverse connotations when its meaning is contested, perhaps for political reasons. To complicate matters further, the internal meaning of a group can be quite different from its meaning to outsiders (Cohen, 1986). Group members' attempts to elevate their group's standing and redefine negative identities plays a role in this discrepancy. Group members may even choose to internalize a group identity because they hold a different conception of what group membership means than potential members who fail to adopt the identity. The meaning of group membership has received increasing attention from social psychologists over the last decade (Breakwell, 2001; Deaux, 1993, 2001).

Contrasting the Four Approaches

The four theoretical approaches just discussed highlight differing sources of commonality among members, place differing emphasis on the importance of conflicting interests with an outgroup, emphasize different types of groups as candidates for political mobilization, and stress different issues around which members are likely to mobilize. The cognitive approach predicts cohesion among the members of any salient group; realistic interest theory confines cohesion to groups whose members share a common fate; social identity theory points to unity among widely stigmatized groups, such as low-status ethnic or racial groups, religious sects, women, and gays and lesbians, whose members cannot easily pass as belonging to a higher status group; and a social constructivist perspective predicts cohesion among members who share a common understanding of group membership.

◣ Sources of Political Cohesion

One of the central goals of this review is to identify the conditions under which group membership is translated into political cohesion. Experimental social psychological research in the social identity tradition suggests that political cohesion is an automatic consequence of salient group membership. The experimental situation popularized by Tajfel and his followers, in which groups were designated by nothing other than a common label, became known as the *minimal intergroup situation* (see Diehl, 1990, for a review). In these studies "the subjects believed they had been assigned to groups simply for administrative convenience"; they had no contact with each other and no reason to believe that they held shared interests (Turner et al., 1987, p. 27). Tajfel's work documenting the astonishing effects of simple social categorization are now quite well known. Blue eyes, a preference for the painter Kadinsky over Klee, calling some people over estimators and others underestimators is sufficient to produce a preference for fellow group members and elicit discrimination against outsiders (Allen & Wilder, 1975; Billig & Tajfel, 1973; Brewer & Silver, 1978; Doise & Sinclair, 1973; Tajfel, Billig, & Bundy, 1971; see Brewer, 1979, for a summary). As Brown (1995) notes, study participants do not simply reward their group but attempt to balance ingroup preference against intergroup fairness. In the usual group allocation task, the most common strategy is one of "maximizing difference" in which one's own group is rewarded to a greater degree than the outgroup, even if the difference between the two groups is not large.

Political behavior researchers working outside the lab have had less success in documenting the simple effects of group membership, however. In many nonlab studies, group membership does not automatically produce a common political or social outlook among group members, suggesting that additional factors beyond simple group membership are needed to explain the emergence of political cohesion in real-world groups.

Identity Measurement

Before examining the evidence on the conditions under which identity leads to political cohesion, I briefly review the measurement of subjective identifications, a research area that has been troubled by a lack of consistent measurement, divergent measurement approaches between psychologists and political scientists, and relatively few studies that have attempted to crossvalidate measures.

Felt group closeness was one of the earliest measures of subjective group attachments to appear in political behavior research and still dominates measures of group loyalty in political science, especially in the American National Election Studies (NES). The closeness question is asked after the respondent has been given a list of groups. The wording in the recent NES is as follows: "Here is a list of groups. Please read over the list and tell me the letter for those groups you feel particularly close to—people who are most like you in their ideas and interests and feelings about things." If respondents mention more than one group, they are then asked the group to which they feel closest. This allows the assessment of some differences in the strength of group identification, but it is a relatively weak measurement approach because it involves a crude distinction between close and closest and is not assessed for all group members but only those individuals who choose the group. The closeness measure grew out of reference group theory, but it is no longer adequate to test theoretical refinements that have emerged since then. For example, it does not separate identification from common fate, it does not distinguish between identification and sympathy for a group that one does not belong to, and it does not distinguish between ingroup belonging and a liking for other group members (Conover, 1984; Herring, Jankowski, & Brown, 1999).

In contrast, partisan identification is almost always measured with a single direct question that simply taps subjective identification. Respondents are typically asked whether, and the degree to which, they think of themselves as Democrats, Republicans or independents (for further discussion see chapter 3). This approach has been adopted for other political identities such as feminist, liberal, and conservative. Unlike the group closeness question, this approach better captures the important dimension of identity strength and allows each respondent to indicate his or her identification with a specific group. Degrees of identification captured by this question prove to be very important in understanding the political consequences of identity. For example, women are more likely to call themselves feminists if they can qualify feminist identity by indicating that they are not especially strong feminists (Huddy, Neely, & LaFay, 2000).

Sears and colleagues pursued an open-ended measure (along with other closed-ended items) of ethnic identity, reminiscent of an early approach to identity measurement embodied in the original 20-statement test developed by Kuhn and McPartland. They asked incoming UCLA freshmen in the summer of 1996 "Which ethnic/racial group do you most closely identify with?" and used 131 different categories to code 2,080 responses. These were further collapsed into broad panethnic and more specific national identifications (Sears, Henry, Fu, & Bui, 2001; see also Gibson & Gouws, 2000).

Social identity researchers have taken a very different approach to the measurement of identity. They have typically assumed the emergence of identity in the minimal group situation in which participants are assigned to groups on the basis of nothing more than a common label. When members of a minimal group demonstrated a preference for ingroup over outgroup members, researchers typically assumed that group members had temporarily adopted a common social identity. The major difficulty with this approach is that it does not allow for the measurement of identity strength; nor is it easily transported to a survey setting.[4]

More recently, psychologists and a few political scientists have moved toward a multiitem approach that provides a stronger measure of identity strength than does a single item (for examples of question wording see Brown, Maras, Masser, Vivian, & Hewstone, 1986; Cadinu & Cerchioni, 2001; Herring et al., 1999; Hornsey & Hogg, 2000; Sears, Henry, Fu, & Bui, 2001; Verkuyten & Nekuee 1999). Luhtanen and Crocker's (1992; Crocker, Luhtanen, Blaine, & Broadnax, 1994) collective self-esteem (CSE) scale is one of the most widely used of these measures. In the CSE, collective self-esteem is broken into four subscales: interdependence of esteem with other members (membership), private collective self-esteem, public collective self-esteem, and the importance of identity to one's self-image. The identity subscale has the most relevance for the assessment of subjective identification as it is defined here—as a subjective attachment uncontaminated by concerns about group status or common fate. The CSE items were originally worded to refer generically to my group but have since been modified for specific groups such as race and ethnicity (Crocker, Luhtanen, Broadnax, & Blaine, 1999).

Jackson and Smith (1999) sort through a very broad group of items linked to social identity and identify a central dimension that is similar to that of the CSE's identity subscale. They refer to this as group attraction and find that it encompasses the notion of group cohesion or attraction to the group and its members and a sense of subjective identification. Moreover, the combined measure of group attraction (which encompasses the CSE identity and membership subscale) was strongly linked to a sense of ingroup pride and ingroup bias in this study. Karasawa (1991) distinguished further among items that tap a sense of group attachment or identity and found that identification with one's group more powerfully predicted ingroup evaluations than did identification with fellow group members.

Implicit attitudes provide yet another approach to the measurement of subjective identification. On the basis of work by Aron (Aron, Aron, Tudor, & Nelson, 1991; Aron, Aron, & Smalden, 1992), Smith and colleagues (Smith & Henry, 1996; Coats, Smith, Claypool, & Banner, 2000) have developed a method to assess the extent to which automatic attitudes about a group's attributes are incorporated into the self-concept. Group members who respond more rapidly to traits that are characteristic of both themselves and an ingroup are assumed to have internalized their group identity more completely. This approach may prove to be an important tool for examining individual differences in identity strength.

Unfortunately, very few studies have examined how these multiitem or implicit attitude scales perform in predicting political cohesion. Much more is needed on that score. Greene (1999) found that a multiitem measure of partisan identity helped to explain the divergent political views of Democrats, Republicans, and party leaders. Sears and colleagues found that stronger identities among UCLA freshmen, assessed by a three-item scale, predicted support for ethnic activism and ingroup bias and, among Latinos, support for more immigration and opposition to official English language policies (Sears et al., 2001). Both studies suggest that multiitem measures of group identity hold considerable promise for political psychologists.

Strong, Subjective Group Identity

Political cohesion rests on the development of strong, subjective identities. But even weak subjective identities have a more powerful influence on political membership than objective group membership—a fact that was astutely observed by the first political behavior researchers (Centers, 1949; Hyman & Singer, 1968; Merton & Kitt, 1950). Voting studies conducted in the 1940s and 1950s confirmed and extended these findings, providing evidence of greater support for the Democratic party among Jews, union leaders, and blacks who felt close to their respective membership groups, regardless of identity strength (Berelson et al., 1954; Campbell et al., 1960). Several contemporary studies also have found that subjective group identification promotes political cohesion independently of identity strength (Conover, 1988; Granberg, Jefferson, Brent, & King, 1981; Lau, 1989).

Reference group researchers did not just champion the role of subjective identification; they also understood the importance of identification strength, observing that individuals who highly valued their group membership were more likely to internalize normative group beliefs (see Hyman & Singer, 1968, for a review). This finding was reinforced in later work by Conover (1984), who uncovered evidence of a distinctive political outlook among group members, but only among those who identified strongly with their sociodemographic group. Not only did highly identified group members share similar political positions in Conover's research, they were also more likely to pay attention to group-related issues and vote on that basis. This research makes clear that it is strong identification, not identification per se, that is most likely to promote political cohesion among group members.

The view that strong, subjective identities predict political cohesion has been amplified in a number of subsequent studies in both psychology and political science, with data from a diverse set of groups. In the United States, African Americans have an especially pronounced sense of group identification that makes them an ideal group in which to examine more closely the political effects of subjective identification. Tate (1993) used the 1984 and 1988 National Black Elections Studies to examine the political effects of subjective group identification among African Americans (see also Dawson, 1994). She found a strong sense of racial identity among American blacks, with 56 percent feeling very close and 38 percent feeling fairly close to members of their race in 1984; in addition, 75 percent felt economically interdependent with other blacks. Bobo and Johnson (2000) confirm that this pervasive sense of race-linked common fate among African-Americans is stronger than that observed among whites, Latinos, or Asians.

Tate (1993) goes on to demonstrate that African Americans who identified strongly with their race were more likely to adopt a progroup position on racial issues such as affirmative action, government aid to minorities, and South Africa than less-identified blacks. In addition, highly identified blacks were more supportive of government spending on social services such as food stamps and government-guaranteed work. But the impact of black racial identity does not extend to issues with little racial relevance such as defense spending or U.S. government policy in Central America. Tate's evidence suggests that strong group identifiers are especially likely to support policies that benefit their group. This finding has been verified in other studies involving African Americans and members of other minority groups in the United States. African Americans who identify with their race are more likely to stress the importance of voting for black political candidates (Reese & Brown, 1995). Sears and colleagues (2001) found that UCLA students who were strongly identified with their ethnic group (white, African American, Latino, Asian) were more inclined to vote for a group member and to demonstrate and sign a petition on behalf of a group-related cause.

Strong group ties not only influence members' political outlook but also flavor the tone of intergroup relations (a topic explored in greater detail in chapter 16). Negative attitudes toward an outgroup are often most pronounced among those who strongly identity with the ingroup. Gibson and Gouws (2000) amassed supportive evidence in South Africa. They found that strong racial and ethnic identities among blacks, whites, coloreds, and Asians increased their perceived need for group solidarity. This, in turn, produced greater antipathy toward outgroups, increased the perception that such outgroups posed a threat, and promoted intolerance. Perreault and Bourhis (1999) found that strong group identifiers were more likely to discriminate against an outgroup in a resource allocation task.

Sidanius, Feshbach, Levin, and Pratto (1997) present intriguing evidence that the stronger sense of group loyalty experienced by members of oppressed minority groups not only drives support for group-beneficial policies but may also dampen support for policies designed to benefit the majority outgroup. The researchers draw a parallel between African Americans and Palestinian Israelis and find that minority individuals who identified strongly with their respective racial or ethnic group were less patriotic than other nationals.

Strong group identifiers are also more positive toward their ingroup. Consider the following supportive evidence. Germans with stronger regional identity feel more positively about their region than about the nation and demonstrate greater regional homogeneity (Simon, Kulla, & Zobel, 1995). Purdue students who identify strongly with their school exhibit higher levels of ingroup bias and ingroup pride (Jackson & Smith, 1999). Individuals with a strong identity as a member of a marginalized group (e.g., sexual and political) are more likely than those with a weak identity to accept their identity, share it with friends and family, and feel less estranged from society when they participate in a group-related electronic news group (McKenna & Bargh, 1998). German and British students who identified most strongly with their country rated it most positively (Mummendey, Klink, & Brown 2001). And Japanese students who identified strongly with their vocational school were less likely than weak identifiers to denigrate their fellow ingroup members after reading negative information about their group (Karasawa, 1991).

There are links between strong group identity and political action. Simon and colleagues (1998) provide evidence that older people who identify strongly with the Gray Panthers and gay men who strongly identify with the gay movement were more likely than others to express willingness to participate in group-related political action, although the direction of causality remains untested in this research.

Finally, the strongest forms of group identity may also be the least affected by context, helping to maintain identity strength over time. Kinket and Verkuyten (1997) differentiated strength of ethnic identity among Turkish and Dutch school children aged between 10 and 13 who attended primary school in the Netherlands. They distinguished ethnic self-identification and self-description from ethnic self-esteem and the internalization of negative group comments (introjection) and found that the highest (or strongest) level of identity (as measured by introjection) was unaffected by classroom context (e.g., percentage of Dutch and Turkish students), whereas the lowest (or weakest) level was most affected. Overall, strong subjective identities have a pervasive influence on political cohesion. Strong group identifiers are more likely than weak identifiers to support policies that favor their group, hold positive attitudes toward their ingroup, disparage an outgroup, and engage in political action (Huddy, 2002).

Common Subjective Meaning of Group Membership

Not all strong, subjective identities translate readily into group-based solidarity, however, and other factors are needed to understand the development of political cohesion (Sears & Jessor, 1996). The second factor considered here as a precursor to political cohesion is the shared meaning of group membership (Deaux, 1993; Sellers, Smith, Shelton, Rowley, & Chavous, 1998). The studies reviewed in this section emphasize the importance of meaning to the emergence of political cohesion, placing special emphasis on an identity's *political* meaning. An identity can attain meaning in different ways; two of the most common ways in which this develops is via the social characteristics of typical group members—image, lifestyle choices, and personal characteristics—and through the common values shared among group members that become synonymous with group membership. Both types of meaning are touched on in the studies reviewed here.

The consequences of group meaning emerge from Citrin and his colleagues' investigation of American identity. They explore the subjective meaning of being American and uncover widespread consensus that it depends on support for the fundamental American values of equality and individualism. Nonetheless, they also discover contested aspects of American identity that concern the need to believe in God or speak up for one's country in order to be considered a "true American" (Citrin, Reingold, & Green, 1990; Citrin, Wong, & Duff, 2001). And it is these contentious aspects of American identity that mediate the political consequences of national identity. Individuals who support the less consensual, nativist aspects of American identity such as being Christian are more likely to oppose policies designed to benefit new immigrants, view negatively the impact of immigration, and believe it is difficult to become American without adopting American customs (Citrin et al., 1990; Citrin et al., 2001). Other researchers have also found that the political effects of patriotism depend on its subjective meaning (Schatz, Staub, & Lavine, 1999).

Research on pangroup identities highlights the importance of meaning in both shaping identities and determining their political consequences. Breakwell (2000) documents differences among Europeans in the extent to which they see European identity as compatible with their existing national identity. In Eurobarometer data from 1992, as few as 13 percent of Italians but as many as 32 percent of Irish and 38 percent of those in the United Kingdom felt they would lose their national identity if all European countries came together in a European union. Clearly, a greater number of individuals living in the British Isles see European identity as incompatible with their existing national identity than members of other European nations. This is generally consistent with the tendency to see Europeans as individuals who live on the continent. Moreover, in the same data, the potential loss of national identity was one of the top three reasons for why individuals opposed the development of a single European market economy. The differing meanings of European identity, thus, shape reactions to policies designed to create a single community, affecting levels of national cohesion on this issue.

The political consequences of an identity may depend even more centrally on its political content and meaning. As noted earlier, Simon and colleagues (1998) found that a willingness to engage in collective action depended on having a politicized identity (e.g., with the gay movement), not a general allegiance to the group (e.g., gays) as a whole. Brady and Kaplan (2002) contend that political content continues to define the meaning of Estonian and Slav identity in Estonia. They argue that Estonian identity rests on the pre-Soviet history of Estonia as an independent republic and its subsequent treatment by the Soviets. This produces an identity tied to homeland and shared history that is linked to a common rejection of strong ties with Russia, the denial of domestic civil rights abuses in Estonia, and a denial of Estonian privilege. In contrast, Slavs in Estonia have a less clearly politicized identity and less uniform political views on these issues.

In other groups, the meaning of an identity may not be expressly political but can have very clear political consequences. This is true of Sellers and colleagues' (1998) distinction between an African-American identity that embraces the uniqueness of being black and an identity that is based on commonality among blacks and members of other oppressed minorities. These two identities hold quite different implications for the preferred political solution to racial and ethnic inequality in the United States. African Americans whose identity encompasses members of other minority groups will more readily support programs designed to improve the situation of Latinos; African Americans who view their situation as unique will be less willing to support programs targeted at members of other minority groups. Moreover, group members can differ among themselves on the meaning of an identity, undermining group-based political cohesion. This difference is found among Mexicans in the United States; United States–born Mexicans equate the terms *Hispanic* and *Latino* with a politicized, pan-Hispanic identity, but for Mexican-born individuals, neither term is viewed as political (Gurin et al., 1994). This hints at the difficulty of mobilizing Mexican immigrants under either panethnic label.

In summary, the meaning of an identity, especially political meaning, affects its political impact. In Europe, individuals who believe their national identity is at odds with being European—a feeling that is more pronounced in the British Isles, for historical reasons—are less likely to support a single European economic market. Nonnaturalized Mexican immigrants to the United States who view the term *Latino* as apolitical are unlikely to take political action on behalf of other Latinos. Americans are unlikely to support expanded immigration from Latin America if they believe that a true American needs to speak English.

Common Fate: Realistic versus Symbolic Concerns

Realistic interest theory has emphasized that a sense of subjective identity is insufficient to motivate group-based political action. Group members need to share common interests or perceive that they do. From this perspective, affluent whites might band together against affirmative action to protect what they see as threatened privileges, or women might cohere around issues linked to gender discrimination. In the first instance, common group interests are at risk and need to be defended, in the second, group members feel aggrieved and wish to improve their position. The existence or perception of common fate is the third factor considered here as a basis for political cohesion.

Researchers typically equate common fate with the existence of shared realistic interests. But I extend this discussion to include both shared *realistic* interests, such as income and employment, and shared *symbolic* concerns, such as the esteem and respect that group members receive from non–group members. A sense of realistic common fate is derived from realistic interest theory and includes a sense that group members share similar economic outcomes. A sense of symbolic common fate touches on shared concerns about the status and esteem accorded to group members and arises from social identity theory and related approaches. The distinction between the two types of common fate matters, because they hint at the emergence of political cohesion in different types of groups—stigmatized groups are more likely to cohere according to social identity theory, whereas realistic interest approaches suggest political cohesion among members who share a similar economic fate.

Realistic Interests

Realistic shared interests have been assessed in two ways. First, researchers have assessed the political consequences of a sense of perceived common fate and deteriorating group finances without any explicit comparison to the outcomes of other groups. Drawing on data from the 1984 NES, Kinder, Adams, and Gronke (1989) examined the impact of perceived common economic interests on vote choice. Americans who felt a sense of economic interdependence with other group members such as the elderly, farmers, or the middle class and who saw their group situation as deteriorating were more likely to rate the national economy negatively and vote on that basis. In this research, a sense of common fate worked in conjunction with a sense of economic grievance to promote political cohesion. In other cases, a simple sense of common fate promotes political cohesion in the absence of grievances (Gurin & Townsend, 1986).

More commonly, however, shared economic interests have been examined in a second form—as a function of fraternal deprivation, the sense that one's group is doing worse than another. This research provides consistent evidence that fraternal deprivation drives political cohesion. Whites who felt they were doing worse than blacks were more inclined to supported George Wallace's candidacy in 1968 (Vanneman & Pettigrew, 1972) and become involved in the Boston antibusing movement (Begley & Alker, 1982). Guimond and Dubé-Simard (1983) observed that Quebecois who felt deprived compared to Anglo Canadians were more likely to support Quebec nationalism. Tripathi and Srivastava (1981) found in a study of Muslims and Hindus in India that those who felt their group was relatively deprived held more negative attitudes toward their religious outgroup.[5]

It would be tempting to conclude from these studies that a sense of fraternal deprivation drives political cohesion. But in some research the impact of fraternal deprivation is confined to individuals who strongly identify with their group, revealing an interaction between identity and perceived deprivation. Supportive evidence comes from a study by Struch and Schwarz (1989) in which hostility toward orthodox Israelis was most pronounced among nonorthodox who viewed the interests of the two groups as in conflict *and* who identified strongly as nonorthodox Jews. Brown and colleagues (2001) found that English passengers who were blocked from traveling to the continent by French fishermen were less positive toward the French than those whose trip took place, and that this negativity was most pronounced among those with a strong English identity. A sense of relative deprivation better predicted activists' degree of involvement in the women's and prochoice movement among those who also identified with their group (Hinkle, Fox-Cardamone, Haseleu, Brown, & Irwin, 1996). Kramer and Brewer (1984) observed higher levels of cooperation in a commons dilemma in which members shared collective interests and a common ingroup membership. And Sears and McConahay (1973) found that a sense of racial grievance had its most pronounced impact on participation in the Watts riots among those who identified as black.

Group consciousness models complicate this picture even further by suggesting that political cohesion depends on three factors working interactively: the two factors discussed so far—identification and fraternal deprivation—and blaming the system for group disparities. Miller and colleagues (1981) examined the impact of group consciousness on voter turnout among members of different sociodemographic groups in the United States using data from the 1972 and 1976 NES. They examined self-reported voter turnout as a function of subjective group closeness (identification), feelings of polar power analogous to fraternal deprivation (that one's group has less access to power than a competing group), polar affect (feeling more positive about one's own than a competing group), and blaming the system for group-based disparities. They examined the confluence of these forces among groups based on class, race, age, and gender. In their analyses, electoral participation was highest among businessmen, the poor, blacks, and women who identified with their group, saw the group as relatively deprived in terms of power, and blamed the system for this situation. In other words, political participation was enhanced among subjectively identified group members who felt fraternally deprived and viewed this as the result of unfair discrimination.

It thus appears that shared interests (perceived or actual) and related grievances play a role in producing political cohesion, either directly or in combination with group identification. But some caution is needed in interpreting these results. Typically fraternal deprivation is assessed subjectively. But there is reason to believe that subjective grievances are intensified among strong group identifiers, raising questions about the origins of perceived common fate. Evidence that ingroup identification heightens a sense of ingroup grievances, resulting in perceived fraternal deprivation, comes from two distinct sources: experimental studies in which group identity is made salient and that provide a direct test of causal order (Kawakami & Dion, 1993; Smith, Spears, & Oyen, 1994) and weaker correlational studies in which strong group identification is linked to grievances (Gurin & Townsend, 1986; Petta & Walker, 1992; Reese & Brown, 1995; Tropp & Wright, 1999). Findings such as these have prompted Simon and Klandermans (2001, p. 325) to conclude that the "relationship between collective identity and awareness of shared grievances is therefore bi-directional."

These findings raise a number of important questions. Is fraternal deprivation a simple function of objective realistic interests and threat? Or does it derive from group identification and possibly related symbolic concerns over group esteem and respect? And if it is the latter, and perceived common realistic fate reflects symbolic concerns, it becomes more difficult to disentangle the impact of the two motives for political cohesion.

Symbolic Concerns

Concerns about group standing and status (actual or perceived), central factors within social identity theory, also play a role in shaping political cohesion. After examining a large number of ethnic conflicts in postcolonial countries, Horowitz (1985) concluded that conflict over tangible resources was an insufficient explanation for ethnic violence because members of different ethnic groups are not frequently in direct economic competition, and when groups do engage in conflict it often has disastrous economic consequences for group members. As an example of the latter, Horowitz points to Sinhalese opposition to the demands of the Tamils for decentralization in Sri Lanka, a situation that would have furthered, not opposed, Sinhalese economic interests. He goes on to compile impressive anecdotal evidence that ethnic conflicts are often fueled by disputes over noneconomic factors concerning status and respect.

Horowitz's data is based on an objective determination of group interests, ingroup commonality, and intergroup conflict. Several additional studies provide evidence that symbolic concerns motivate political cohesion when they are assessed subjectively. Huddy (1989) found that status considerations had a greater impact than economic concerns on older people's support for U.S. government old-age policies such as Social Security and Medicare. Older respondents (aged 60 and older) in the 1985 NES pilot study who felt their status was generally affected by the status accorded older people were more supportive of old-age policies designed to assist the elderly than were others. And this was a far more powerful influence on policy attitudes than feeling economically interdependent with age peers.

Research by Huddy and Feldman (2001) on attitudes toward the status of the English language in Puerto Rico provides further evidence of the relatively greater power of symbolic than economic considerations. Puerto Ricans who reside on the island and are least threatened economically by the introduction of English into everyday life—better educated individuals who speak English fluently—are most opposed to making English the island's sole official language. Their opposition stems more from a concern for the preservation of traditional Spanish-Puerto Rican culture and the status of Puerto Ricans compared to other Americans than any realistic economic threat or advantage that would accrue to themselves or the island from adopting English as its official language.

Tajfel and Turner (1979) take a position similar to that of group consciousness researchers by arguing that grievances are necessary but not sufficient to motivate group-based action, although they place greater stress on symbolic grievances concerning status than realistic grievances over access to power. According to Tajfel and Turner, group members need to identify with their group, perceive intergroup status differences, and view status differences as illegitimate before action is likely. This model has not been tested on the development of political cohesion, but Ellemers, Wilke, and van Knippenberg (1993) find related evidence in an experimental setting. In their study, subjects were randomly allocated to a high-status management role or a low-status worker role, told that their assignment was either arbitrary or meritorious, and that they could or could not work their way out of the lower status group. In accordance with the predictions of social identity theory, those allocated to their group in an arbitrary fashion were the most angry about their group's position. And the highest levels of identification were observed among individuals in low-status groups whose low status seemed illegitimate because it was not based on performance. It remains to be seen whether all three factors—low status, illegitimacy, and closed membership—are needed to generate political cohesion.

As noted earlier, very few studies have directly contrasted the role of realistic and symbolic concerns. But Tate (1993) provides some evidence that economic interdependence and symbolic considerations may affect differing types of political outcomes. She found that perceived economic common fate had a greater impact on black support for the Democratic presidential candidate in 1984 and 1988 than did racial identity. But racial identity, which is equated within social identity theory with symbolic, not realistic, concerns, played a significant role in shaping support for Jesse Jackson in the 1984 Democratic presidential primaries and the presidential election. In other words, Jesse Jackson's candidacy raised symbolic questions for blacks concerning their identity as African American and their need to support a black candidate, whereas overall electoral choice was more a function of concerns about black finances.

In summary, realistic threats and fraternal deprivation can act as a powerful stimulus to political cohesion. But it remains unclear whether this effect is confined to those who identify strongly with their group or is even further restricted to those who additionally feel that fraternal deprivation is unjust. There are also additional concerns about the degree to which subjective fraternal deprivation derives from symbolic concerns linked to group identification. In the few studies that have contrasted them directly, status considerations and group identity eclipse the effects of economic concerns. More work is needed to contrast these two forces directly, but the wealth of evidence from minimal intergroup studies suggests that economic competition is not necessary for the development of group cohesion (Brewer, 1979; Brewer & Brown, 1998).

► Development of Group Identity

One of the crucial ingredients in the development of political cohesion is the existence of a strong, internalized subjective identity. This finding raises an additional challenge for political psychologists: How do we explain an individual group member's decision to identify as a group member? Research on this question has moved well beyond the notion of Campbell and colleagues (1960) that subjective identification is simply a function of the percentage of one's life spent as a group member. Recent research, influenced in part by social identity theory, has investigated several possible factors that promote the development of strong social identities.

Salient Identity

One of the key insights of social-identity theory, developed most fully in self-categorization theory, is that individuals constantly shift back and forth between an individual and a social identity, and among social identities (Brewer & Weber, 1994; Simon, 1997; Turner et al., 1987). Thus, if a national figure contrasts the valor of one ethnic group of citizens against the sloth of another, ethnic identities rise to the fore. But if, in contrast, the politician rails against the evils of an opposing nation, national identity is transcendent. Social identity researchers consider group salience an essential ingredient in the development of identity and group political cohesion. According to Oakes (in Turner et al., 1987) salience is heightened by any factor that increases the "separateness" and "clarity" of a category, and one of the factors most likely to increase a category's clarity is minority status, when a group's members are outnumbered by members of an outgroup (see also Brewer & Brown, 1998).

Category salience plays a clear role in shaping identity. For instance, McGuire and his colleagues report evidence that children in an ethnic minority in their classroom (and whose ethnicity is therefore salient) are more likely to describe themselves in terms of their ethnicity; children in families where there are more members of the opposite gender are more likely to mention their gender when describing themselves (McGuire, McGuire, Child, & Fujioka, 1978; McGuire & Padawer-Singer, 1976). In a similar vein, Hogg and Turner (1985) found that increasing the salience of study participants' gender increased the likelihood that they thought of themselves in gender-stereotypic terms. The importance of group salience is confirmed in a meta-analysis conducted by Mullen, Brown, and Smith (1992) in which group salience promoted the development of ingroup bias across a large number of studies.

Findings also extend to politicized groups. Abrams (1994) found, for example, that support of a minority political party in the United Kingdom (e.g., the Liberals or Greens) is more central to young people's identity than support for one of the two major parties (Labour or Tory). This is in line with expectations that minor parties are more salient and provide their supporters with a more distinctive social identity than do large political parties. A salient political group can have an even greater impact on identity development among outsiders. Huddy (1997) found that male and female nonfeminists were even less likely to call themselves feminists after reading a story about the women's movement that made explicit references to feminists, although doing so did not heighten feminist identity among supporters.

But political behavior research also suggests that there are clear limits to the impact of category salience on the development of social identity. Sears and Citrin uncover substantial evidence that members of diverse ethnic and racial groups in the United States identify primarily as American and only secondarily as members of their ethnic or racial group, despite the greater salience of minority group status in the United States (Citrin et al., 2001; Sears, Citrin, Cheleden, & Van Laar, 1999; Sears & Henry, 1999). In contrast, Sidanius and colleagues (1997) report that black students who identify with their race are less patriotic than black students who do not. This finding contradicts Citrin and colleagues' (2001) results and is more consistent with the predictions of social identity theory. The limited ability of simple group salience to account for ethnic identity is reinforced in a study by Gurin, Hurtado, & Peng (1994) on national and ethnic identity among Mexican Americans. Mexican Americans who regularly came into contact with Anglos, and for whom Mexican ethnicity was therefore highly salient, were no more likely to hold national (Mexican) or ethnic identities (e.g., Chicano) than are other Mexican Americans. Hispanic students who attended a high school with relatively few other Hispanics, and whose ethnic group membership was highly salient, were less likely to identify as Hispanic than Hispanic students attending schools in heavily Hispanic areas (Eschbach & Gomez, 1998). This raises important questions for social identity theory, and particularly self-categorization theory, about the extent to which the salience of one's ethnic or racial group—the key ingredient in identity development for many social identity researchers—explains the emergence of ethnic and racial identities.

Meaning and Valence of Identity

If salience has an important but limited impact on the development of group identity, we need to identify other factors that account for the emergence of politically potent identities. The meaning of group membership is a crucial additional ingredient that is particularly important for groups with vague or ambiguous membership criteria, a description that fits political groups quite well (Huddy, 2001). As an example, Huddy (1998,) finds in a series of experimental studies that feminist identity among women and men depends on sharing the gender-linked traits and role orientation of women depicted as feminists, especially leaders of the women's movement. This suggests that *social characteristics* such as the personality traits and lifestyle choices of typical group members may be used to define the meaning of political groups when the definition of membership is murky or contested. But even the meaning of national identity can be vague. Erikson (1993) highlights ambiguity surrounding the meaning of a German identity. Does it include all German speakers? Those of German ancestry? Germans living in another country? The fluidity of German identity is demonstrated by a change in the definition of German citizenship in the late 1990s from a purely ethnic definition to one that awarded citizenship to the children of immigrants born in Germany. Gibson and Gouws (2000) find that black South Africans were more likely to call themselves African, whereas whites, colored, and Asians were more likely to identify as South African, suggesting that blacks equate South Africa with its racist past and consequently eschew the national label.

In addition to social characteristics of group members, another possible source of meaning for politicized groups is provided by the *values* with which they are associated. In early work inspired by reference group theory, Hartley (1960) documented that holding beliefs similar to those endorsed by group members increased the adoption of group identity. Research by

Schwartz, Struch, and Biesky (1990) illustrates one way to assess the values underlying group membership. In their study of German and Israeli students, students ranked 19 terminal and 18 instrumental values on the basis of their own preference order and that of their national group. Not surprisingly, one's own views and that of one's group are related, although this link is stronger for Israeli than for German students. This suggests that an important source of national identity—shared values—is stronger among Israeli than among German students and hints at an important source of weakened national identity among Germans.

Valence is a third aspect of identity that plays a crucial role in affecting identity development and is in essence the affective counterpart to the cognitive meaning conveyed by the characteristics of group members and their shared values. There is evidence that ethnic identity is more strongly developed among members of objectively identified, higher status groups and among individuals who perceive their group as having higher status. For example, national identity is more strongly developed among Cubans in the United States than among other Latinos because they believe their social status far exceeds that of Mexican Americans or Puerto Ricans (Huddy & Virtanen, 1995). Ethier and Deaux (1994) demonstrated that freshmen Hispanic students at an Ivy League university who found the university environment threatening to their Hispanic identity viewed their group as having lower status, which in turn weakened their identification as Hispanic. In a similar vein, Swann and Wyer (1997) found that men were more likely to think of themselves in gender-stereotypic terms—and thus identify with their gender—when in the minority, but women, members of a lower status group, were not as likely to stereotype themselves as typical women when outnumbered by men. Condor (1996) found that English university students preferred to call themselves "English" rather than "British" because the English label carries fewer negative connotations of colonialism and aggression.

There is more specific evidence that members of lower status groups who perceive an outgroup as prejudiced against them have a heightened sense of group identification. Branscombe and colleagues (1999) found that African-American students who were more likely to attribute a personal negative outcome to racial prejudice and had some past experience with discrimination were more likely to identify with their racial group. Moreover, their findings suggested that a willingness to perceive racism had greater influence on group identification than vice versa.

Acquired versus Ascribed Identities

Identity strength is also related to identity choice. I distinguish here between ascribed identities, which are quite difficult to change, and acquired identities, which are adopted by choice. A far greater number of modern identities are subject to choice than in the past. Such choice extends to religion, class, occupation, domestic roles, and even the adoption of ethnic designations such as Irish or Latino. Turner, Hogg, Turner, and Smith (1984) report a study in which subjects were either ascribed or could choose to belong to one of two teams competing in a problem-solving exercise. Members of winning teams indicated higher self-esteem and cohesion when they had been ascribed to the team. But members who voluntarily chose their team were more likely to report high self-esteem and group cohesion when they had lost, suggesting a stronger sense of group commitment when identity is acquired than when ascribed. Perreault and Bourhis (1999) extend this research to include the effects of identity acquisition on the development of outgroup discrimination. They found that group identification increased in strength with the sense that lab group membership was voluntary. In addition, strong ingroup identification in this study increased discriminatory behavior against an outgroup in a resource allocation task.

Permeable Group Boundaries

One of the most important implications of identity choice is that it can result in permeable group boundaries.[6] Tajfel and Turner (1979) suggest that one option available to members of a low-status group with permeable boundaries is to deny one's group membership or identify with an alternative higher status group. They refer to this strategy as social mobility, and several researchers provide evidence of its existence among members of low-status groups (Jackson, Sullivan, Harnish, & Hodge, 1996; Taylor, Moghaddam, Gamble, & Zellerer, 1987; Wright, Taylor, & Mogghaddam, 1990).[7] Research by Wright (1997) suggests that boundary permeability does not have to be very extensive for group members to contemplate individual rather than collective solutions to problems of low ingroup status, hinting at the existence of weak group identities among members of permeable groups. Permeability is not just a feature of highly fluid groups but can also characterize membership in relatively fixed groups based on ethnic and regional boundaries. Mummendey, Kessler, Klink, and Mielke (1999) found that East Germans differed in how easy they thought it was to be considered West German, and that individuals who thought that passing as West German was quite difficult hold stronger East German identities. In contrast, East Germans who viewed regional boundaries as relatively more permeable were more likely to adopt West German identity and were, in turn, more likely to think of themselves as simply German.

In contrast, when group boundaries are impermeable, there is evidence that members of low-status groups bolster their identity and enhance their group's standing through the strategies of social creativity and social change (Tajfel & Turner, 1979). Jackson and colleagues (1996) found that members of a low-status group attempted to change their group's status by rating an undesirable attribute more positively or rating the group more favorably on other dimensions that were less central to the group's negative image.

Overall, questions of group permeability raise concomitant questions about the influence of *external labeling* on identity acquisition. If group membership is obvious to others, it will be more difficult for a group members to avoid external identification. It may be relatively easy for an East German to pass as someone from the West but much more difficult for an African American to escape the label "black." Less permeable group boundaries and a higher incidence of external labeling should increase the likelihood that a group member will internalize group identity. Relevant external cues include skin color, gender, group-specific physical features, language, and cultural practices, although the latter two are obviously easier to change than overt physical characteristics. Conversely, attributes that can be hidden or disguised enhance the role of choice in identity acquisition (see McKenna & Bargh, 1998).

Individual Differences

The notion that social identities are more often acquired than ascribed suggests the importance of individual differences in the process of identity acquisition, an issue that has been largely ignored by social identity researchers. Is there, for instance, individual variation in the general proclivity to identify with social groups? Duckitt (1989) suggests that authoritarian behavior can be explained, in part, by the stronger tendency of some individuals to identify with dominant social groups (e.g., whites in the United States or Christians in western Europe). Can this tendency be accounted for by basic personality traits such as an intolerance of ambiguity, a need for coherence, or the absence of an openness to experience? Perhaps individuals who are less open to experience or intolerant of ambiguity prefer ascribed to acquired identities and feel uncomfortable with the myriad identity choices that confront individuals in contemporary society.

In one of the few studies to directly examine individual differences in identity acquisition, Perreault and Bourhis (1999) explored the effects of ethnocentrism, authoritarianism, and personal need for structure on strength of ingroup identification in an experimentally created lab group. They found that all three personality measures were correlated with strength of group identification but that these relationships with identification appeared to be driven by ethnocentrism. In other words, individuals who expressed antipathy toward outsiders were more likely to adopt an ingroup identity in the lab. But in some ways, Perreault and Bourhis's findings raise more questions than they answer. What are the origins of a general dislike of outsiders? Does this drive the desire for an ingroup identity? Or are there additional underlying personality attributes that explain both ethnocentrism and the adoption of in-group identity? Obviously, more research is needed to untangle the personality traits most likely to influence the adoption of group identity.

There is some evidence, reviewed by Brewer and Brown (1998), that group identification is more pronounced among members of minority than majority groups (see also Mullen et al., 1992). Brewer suggests that ingroup identity depends on a balance between the need to belong and the need for uniqueness, countervailing motives that she combines within optimal distinctiveness theory (Brewer 1991, 1993). According to Brewer, identities need to confer the optimal mix of distinctive and common attributes, thus explaining why members of large, majority groups evince weaker ingroup identities than do members of smaller, minority groups. It would be worthwhile to follow Brewer's lead and examine the impact of individual differences in the need to belong and the need for uniqueness as possible influences on identity development.

Mullin and Hogg (1998) introduced an additional motive to account for ingroup bias, which Hogg and his colleagues describe as people's "need to feel certain that their perceptions, attitudes, and behaviors are correct" (Grieve & Hogg, 1999, p. 927). They argue that ingroup bias emerges in the minimal intergroup situation because group members feel uncertain about their views and identify with other group members, especially typical group members, to dispel this unpleasant feeling. The role of certainty was hinted at by Tajfel (1969), who suggested that the search for coherence may underlie the development of stereotyping and prejudice. Intellectually, reference group theory provides an even more obvious origin for this motive. Kelley (1952) described the need to accurately assess one's opinions as one of the two key motives for adopting a reference group (the other motive is to gain acceptance). Festinger (1954) built on this notion to develop a broader theory of social comparison. The need for certainty is linked to cognitive complexity, a quality that varies across individuals, and it may be fruitful to investigate the impact of cognitive or attibutional complexity on identity adoption and development (Neuberg & Newsom, 1993; Levy, 1999).

► *The Impact of Threat on Group Identification*

In this review, I have focused so far on ingroup cohesion and, for the most part, put aside discussion of intergroup hostilities. But the notion of threat—which typically involves an external threat from a known outgroup—is relevant here because it can strengthen ingroup unity, in addition to inflaming outgroup hostilities (a topic discussed in greater detail in chapter 16). There is a longstanding assertion and some supportive evidence that an external threat enhances ingroup solidarity and tightens ingroup boundaries and that ingroup solidarity increases in relation to the degree of threat (Coser, 1956; Levine & Campbell, 1972). As evidence, Giles and Evans (1985) found that white respondents in the 1972 NES who perceived blacks as more threatening (too influential and the civil rights movement as moving too quickly) rated whites more positively as a group. This effect was more pronounced in the South than in the North, though significant in both regions. Attraction to the ingroup was heightened after a defeat and failure, in research by Turner and colleagues (1984), who observed that this process was most pronounced for those who were highly committed to the group.

Threat is not a unitary concept, however, and encompasses both symbolic and realistic threats, in line with the earlier distinction between symbolic and realistic interests as differing sources of political cohesion. Symbolic threats concern threats to group identity or group esteem, whereas realistic threats pose a challenge to group power, influence, and wealth. There is some ambiguous evidence that fraternal deprivation and group-based grievances strengthen identity. As noted earlier, a number of cross-sectional studies report an association between identity and fraternal deprivation or grievances. I discussed this earlier as possible evidence that grievances may derive from identity (Bobo & Johnson, 2000; Gurin & Townsend, 1986; Petta & Walker, 1992; Reese & Brown, 1995; Tropp & Wright, 1999). But findings could also be interpreted as evidence that a threat to realistic group interests intensifies identity. Ideally, future panel studies will resolve the direction of causality.

Researchers have also investigated whether symbolic threats increase ingroup identification; the evidence here is somewhat more convincing. Grant and Brown (1995) define a threat to social identity as "some action or communication that directly or indirectly seems to undermine the value of being a group member" (p. 198), although several other researchers have extended the concept to include not only an attack on the group's value and beliefs but also a challenge to individual group member's membership (Schmitt & Branscombe, 2001). Grant and Brown manipulate identity threat in a complex experiment involving small groups of female students, selected on the basis of their support for gender equality, who draft a joint statement about gender-based wage inequities. Identity is threatened by the other group in two manipulations: a negative evaluation of the ingroup's statement and opposition to the values expressed in the group statement. Grant and Brown do not indicate whether threat intensifies group identification, but they do find greater ingroup bias among group members whose work has been negatively evaluated by the outgroup. Similar effects are observed in other groups. Rothgerber (1997) found that Texas A & M students who were told that students from the University of Texas were biased against them rated students at Texas A & M as more similar and rated themselves as more like Texas A & M students than students who were not given this information. Jetten, Branscombe, Schmitt, and Spears (2001) found that experimentally heightened levels of perceived discrimination against people with body piercings increased group identification among students who actually had body piercings.

Duckitt and Mphuthing (2002) report that black South African students in South Africa who were upset or angry about differences between the socioeconomic status of black Africans and Afrikaans-speaking whites identified more strongly as African. They interpret this as consistent with the effects of symbolic, not economic, threat by comparing the reactions of black Africans to English- and Afrikaans-speaking whites. As evidence they point to the greater perceived economic differences between blacks and English-speaking whites than between blacks and white Afrikaans and note that these perceived economic differences with English whites had no impact on African identity. Duckitt and Mphuthing go on to suggest that the greater sense of outrage at disparities with Afrikaans-speaking whites is driven by the belief that they are more prejudiced toward blacks than English-speaking whites, who played a greater role in the opposition to apartheid. The researchers argue, in essence, that white Afrikaans pose an identity threat to black Africans, which, in turn, strengthens a sense of black African identity and fuels a greater dislike of Afrikaans than of English whites.

In the studies just discussed, identity threat is often documented among members of lower status groups, limiting more general conclusions about the effects of identity threat. A study by Schmitt, Brancombe, Kobrynowicz, and Owen (2002) suggests further caution in generalizing the effects of identity threat too broadly from members of low-status to members of higher status groups. They found that women reacted to perceived gender discrimination by increasing their identification with other women but perceived gender discrimination had no effect on gender identity among men, members of a higher status group.

One way that identity threats increase group members' cohesion is through the process of social creativity—elevating the importance of positive ingroup characteristics that confer superiority over an outgroup (Jackson et al., 1996; Lalonde, 1992; Mummendey & Schrieber, 1984; Tajfel & Turner, 1979; van Knippenberg, 1978; van Knippenberg & van Oers, 1984). Cadinu and Cerchoni (2001) observed this process at work among emergency medical service volunteers in Italy. Workers were told that their organization had responded more slowly to an emergency than rival organizations; those who identified strongly with their unit rated their group more highly on personality and other dimensions unrelated to work performance. Crocker and Major (1989) found that members of a stigmatized group were more likely to attribute negative feedback to prejudice than members of nonstigmatized groups. They conclude that such attributions serve to protect the self-esteem of members of low-status groups in the face of external criticism by essentially denigrating the motives of outgroup members.

There is additional data to support this conclusion, including evidence that threat can further diminish group attachments among weak group identifiers. This was observed among Hispanic students attending Ivy League schools in the study by Ethier and Deaux (1994) described earlier. Hispanic students who perceived more extensive anti-Hispanic discrimination in their school environment when they started college were most negative about being Hispanic at a later point in time. Verkuyten and Nekuee (1999) observed a similar process among Iranian immigrants to the Netherlands. Iranians who identified strongly with their nationality group and who perceived the Dutch as discriminatory toward their group (in jobs and housing, and on the streets) were more likely to self-stereotype themselves as typically Iranian. The impact of perceived anti-Iranian discrimination on self-stereotyping was less pronounced among Iranians who identified less strongly with their group.

In the research examples just cited, threat is construed as threat from an outgroup. But research within the paradigm of terror management demonstrates heightened ingroup cohesion when one's mortality is made salient—a personally threatening situation. Greenberg, Pyszczynski, Solomon, Rosenblatt, Veeded, and Kirkland (1990) found that Christians who were asked to form an impression of a Jewish and Christian individual evaluated the Christian more positively and the Jew more negatively when their mortality had been made salient. In other studies, terror management researchers find that mortality salience also heightens stereotyping of outgroup individuals (Schimel et al., 1999).

◤ Political Context

Early political behavior researchers were well aware that group-based political cohesion develops within a specific political context (Berelson et al., 1944; Campbell et al., 1960). All of the three major psychological factors that I have pointed to as determinants of political cohesion—salient identities, a common political meaning associated with membership, and the types of interests held in common by group members (symbolic vs. realistic)—can be influenced by the political environment and manipulated by political rhetoric, to constitute an additional powerful ingredient in the development of group loyalties and their political manifestation. I review the impact of political context on each of these three factors, in turn.

Political Salience

The political salience of a group is a key ingredient in understanding the origins of political cohesion. Salience can work by either intensifying an identity or by heightening the link between an identity and politics. Lau (1989) provides intriguing empirical evidence of the former, demonstrating one way that salience heightens group identity. He identified liberals and conservatives in the 1972 and 1976 NES (based on their strong opposed feelings for the two ideological groups and a consistent set of issue positions). He then scored the ideology of each candidate running in an individual's district for the U.S. House of Representatives. He found that liberal and conservative citizens living in a district contested by a congressional candidate who shared their political ideology felt much closer to their ideological group than citizens living in areas without such a candidate. Reese and Brown (1995) went further to demonstrate the influence of church messages on black racial identity among black respondents in the 1984 National Black Election Study. Black respondents who attended politically active churches where politics was discussed regularly had a stronger sense of racial identity (as assessed by a sense of interdependence with other blacks) than members of other congregations. These two studies provide direct evidence that political context can intensify group identity.

The second way that salience enhances political cohesion is through a tightened link between a group and politics. Campbell and colleagues (1960) referred to this link as *political proximity* and argued that it increased, in part, whenever a group member ran for political office by heightening the group's political salience. This process is at work in contemporary U.S. politics. Paolino (1995) found, for example, that the presence of women U.S. Senate candidates in 1992 increased the likelihood that women would translate their support for women's issues, such as affirmative action, into electoral support for women candidates. In other words, the presence of women candidates increased the salience of women's issues, although it is difficult to rule out the prospect that the heightened salience of women's issues encouraged women to run for Senate seats in certain states.

Shamir and Arian (1999) provide another clear example of how the relationship between group membership and electoral outcomes varies over time. They draw on data from Israel to document a growing division in vote choice between religious and secular Jews over the last several decades. The two groups hold differing national/religious identities—secular individuals identify as Israelis, while the religious think of themselves as Jews. And the two groups are politically distinctive, differing in their support for return of the territories and security issues more generally. As these issues have come to the fore in Israeli politics, religious and national identities have had a growing impact on vote choice in Israeli elections. In this instance, political events have elevated the political significance of religious affiliations in Israel.

Contested Meaning

The meaning of an identity and the prospects for political cohesion also vary with political rhetoric. Hopkins and Reicher (1996) highlighted the contested nature of national identities and illustrated the role of politics in the process of identity definition. They examined speeches from the 1992 Scotland elections and documented the salience and meaning given to the respective identities of Scottish and British. The Scottish National Party, which favored independent statehood in 1992, emphasized during the election that Scottish identity was incompatible with English identity and denied the existence of a true British identity that spanned both groups. In contrast, the conservatives, who supported continued ties with Britain, emphasized Britishness and the commonalities between the Scots and English while downplaying the distinctiveness of the Scots. In this election, political leaders were in competition over the salience of British and Scottish identity; they were also involved in defining the meaning of these respective identities.

Disputes over the meaning of group membership can foster battles over who draws and defines group boundaries. The adoption of the term *African American,* championed by Jesse Jackson, carries with it notions of African ancestry that alter the meaning of black identity and may not appeal to all or even many black Americans (Martin 1991). Feminists in the United States battled among themselves in the late 1960s and early 1970s over who could and who could not be rightfully considered a feminist, with conflicts erupting over one's political ideology, sexual preference, and the gender of one's children (Ryan 1992). Along similar lines, there has been an attempt to forge a "rainbow" coalition among racial and ethnic minority groups in the United States by fashioning a minority identity based on common experiences with discrimination (Sears et al., 2001).

At the same time, it is important to acknowledge that political rhetoric has its limits, as any politician who has tried and failed to coin a new political slogan or associate with a populist symbol can attest. Huddy 1997, documents the difficulty in reversing accepted cultural definitions of a typical feminist. Altering feminists in a news story from the leaders of a women's rights groups—the typical feminist—to ordinary women such as homemakers and clerical workers proved unconvincing to study participants. Women who held similar views to those expressed in the story by feminists only adopted feminist identity when such views were expressed by the leader of a women's rights group. Moreover, social identities such as partisan and ethnic identity demonstrate remarkable stability over time when assessed in surveys on social and political topics and are much more stable than a range of other social and political attitudes, suggesting some immunity to immediate context (Alwin, Cohen, & Newcombe; 1990; Converse & Markus, 1979; Ethier & Deaux, 1994; Sears & Henry, 1999; Sears, 1983; see also chapter 3).

Politicized Interests

Increasing the salience or altering the meaning of group identities is not the only way that political context affects the emergence of political group cohesion. Resource mobilization theorists argue that group members' grievances are manufactured or brought to the fore by social movement organizations and their leaders in an effort to mobilize potential members (Jenkins, 1983; McCarthy & Zald, 1976; Snow, Rochford, Worden, & Benford, 1986). Thus, a very visible incident of sexual harassment, such as Anita Hill's claims against Supreme Court Justice Clarence Thomas, is likely to increase the number of women who report having been the victim of sexual harassment. Or the politicization of a hate crime targeted at someone of a specific race, ethnicity, or sexual orientation is likely to increase group members' perception of societal discrimination against their group. Group members' awareness of grievances can thus be strengthened by events, their political interpretation, and the rhetoric of politicians and group leaders. These tactics are commonly employed in the world of politics and deserve much closer scrutiny from political psychologists than they have received to date.

◣ Conclusion

One thing is resoundingly clear from this review. Group membership may be a necessary condition for the development of political cohesion, but it is certainly not sufficient. This analysis has focused on several additional factors that are pivotal to the development of a cohesive political outlook and a strong group identity. But research on many of these mediating factors is still quite rudimentary, and a multitude of questions remain unanswered, suggesting a fertile area for future research. Are there limits, for example, to politicians' ability to redefine the meaning of group membership? And are these efforts least fruitful among individuals who identify strongly with their group? Are there certain kinds of people who develop a sense of group identification more readily and more permanently than others? What are the cognitive and motivational mechanisms by which strong group identifiers maintain positive feelings for their group and fellow group members? And are symbolic concerns such as identity threat sufficient to account for the development of ingroup cohesion and intergroup antipathies? Answers to these and other questions will propel research forward on the political effects of group membership at a time when real-world international and civil conflicts have amplified interest in group identification across the social sciences.

◣ Notes

1. This is a selective account of the major theoretical approaches to ingroup cohesion. Other approaches not covered here include evolutionary psychology and the concept of inclusive fitness (see chapter 5), a psychodynamic approach, and social comparison theory (Brewer and Brown 1998).

2. For a more complete account of realistic interest and relative deprivation theory, see Brown (1995) and Taylor and Mogghadam (1996).

3. For a more detailed overview of social identity theory see Brown (1995) and Brewer and Brown (1998).

4. Social identity researchers counter that direct questions tend to emphasize individual over social identity and ignore the contextually fluid nature of all identities (Brown 2000).

5. Other beliefs, such as blaming inequality on an external enemy or the perceived efficacy of protest, may be additionally needed to translate realistic grievances into political action (Klandermans 1984; chapter 19).

6. Boundary permeability is often manipulated in an experimental setting in a way that is analogous to external permeability as it is perceived by outsiders. But the subjective perception of permeability is more important than reality in influencing identity acquisition among group members. External permeability places limits on the perception of subjective permeability, but the two can diverge.

7. There is some tension between the influence of low group status and group salience on identity acquisition. To the extent that low group status heightens group salience, it may actually enhance identity acquisition. But this effect needs to be distinguished from the effects of low group status independent of group salience, whose effects are quite opposite and serve to hinder the development of group identity.

▲ References

Abrams, D. (1994). Political distinctiveness: An identity optimising approach. *European Journal of Social Psychology, 24,* 357–365.

Abrams, D., Wetherell, M., Cochrane, S., Hogg, M., & Turner, J. C. (1990). Knowing what to think by knowing who you are: Self-categorization and the nature of norm formation, conformity and group polarization. *British Journal of Social Psychology, 29,* 97–119.

Allen, V. L., & Wilder, D. A. (1975). Categorization, belief similarity, and group discrimination. *Journal of Personality and Social Psychology, 32,* 971–977.

Alwin, D. F., Cohen, R. L., &. Newcomb, T. M. (1992). *Political attitudes over the life span: The Bennington women after fifty years.* Madison: University of Wisconsin Press.

Aron, A., Aron, E. N., & Smollan, D. (1992). Inclusion of other in the self scale and the structure of interpersonal closeness. *Journal of Personality and Social Psychology, 63,* 596–612.

Aron, A., Aron, E. N., Tudor, M., & Nelson, G. (1991). Close relationships as including other in the self. *Journal of Personality and Social Psychology, 60,* 241–253.

Barth, F. (1969). Introduction to F. Barth (Ed.), *Ethnic groups and boundaries* (pp. 9–38). Boston: Little, Brown, and Co.

Barth, F. (1981). *Process and form in social life.* London: Routledge and Kegan Paul.

Begley, T. M., & H. Alker. (1982). Anti-busing protest: Attitudes and actions. *Social Psychology Quarterly, 45,* 187–197

Bell, D. (1963). *The new American right.* New York: Doubleday.

Berelson, B. R., Lazarsfeld, P. F., & McPhee, W. N. (1954). *Voting: A study of opinion formation in a presidential campaign* (pp. 54–76). Chicago: University of Chicago Press.

Billig, M. (1995). Rhetorical psychology, ideological thinking, and imagining nationhood. In H. Johnston & B. Klandermans (Eds.), *Social movements and culture* (pp. 64–81). Minneapolis: University of Minnesota Press.

Billig, M., & Tajfel, H. (1973). Social categorization and similarity in inter-group behavior. *European Journal of Social Psychology, 3,* 27–52.

Blumer, H. (1958). Race and prejudice as a sense of group position. *Pacific Sociological Review, 1,* 3–7.

Bobo, L. D. (1999). Prejudice as group position: Micro-foundations of a sociological approach to racism and race relations. *Journal of Social Issues, 55,* 445–472.

Bobo, L. D. (1983). Whites' opposition to busing: Symbolic racism or realistic group conflict? *Journal of Personality and Social Psychology, 45,* 1196–1210.

Bobo, L. D., & Hutchings, V. L. (1996). Perceptions of racial group competition: Extending Blumer's theory of group position to a multiracial context. *American Sociological Review, 61,* 951–972.

Bobo, L. D., & Johnson, D. (2000). Racial attitudes in a prismatic metropolis: Mapping identity, stereotypes, competition, and views on affirmative action. In L. D. Bobo, O. L. Melvin, J. H. Johnson, Jr., & A. Valenzeula, Jr. (Eds.), *Prismatic metropolis: Inequality in Los Angeles.* New York: Russell Sage Foundation.

Bobo, L. D., & Kluegel, J. R. (1993). Opposition to race-targeting: Self-interest, stratification ideology, or racial attitudes? *American Sociological Review, 58,* 443–464.

Boninger, D. S., J. A. Krosnick, & Berent, M. K. (1995). Origins of attitude importance: Self-interest, social identification, and value relevance. *Journal of Personality and Social Psychology, 68,* 61–80.

Brady, H. E., & Kaplan, C. S. (2000). Categorically wrong: Nominal versus graded measures of ethnic identity. *Studies in Comparative International Development, 35,* 56–91.

Branscombe, N. R., Schmitt, M. T., & Harvey, R. D. (1999). Perceiving pervasive discrimination among African-Americans: Implications of group identification and well-being. *Journal of Personality and Social Psychology, 77,* 135–149.

Breakwell, G. M. (1996). Identity Processes and Social Change. In Breakwell, G. M., & Lyons, E. (Eds.), *Changing European identities: Social psychological analyses of social change* (pp. 13–30) Oxford: Butterworth-Heinemann.

Breakwell, G. M. (2001). Social representational constraints upon identity. In K. Deaux & G. Philogene (Eds.) *Representations of the social* (pp. 271–284). Malden, MA: Blackwell.

Breakwell, G. M., & Lyons, E. (1996). *Changing European identities: Social psychological analyses of social change.* Oxford: Butterworth-Heinemann.

Brewer, M. B. (1979). In-group bias in the minimal inter-group situation: A cognitive motivational analysis. *Psychological Bulletin, 86,* 307–324.

Brewer, M. B. (1991). The social self: On being the same and different at the same time. *Personality and Social Psychology Bulletin, 17,* 475–482.

Brewer, M. B. (1993). Social identity, distinctiveness, and in-group homogeneity. *Social Cognition, 11,* 150–164.

Brewer, M. B. (2001). The many faces of social identity: Implications for political psychology. *Political Psychology, 22,* 115–126.

Brewer, M. B., & Brown, R. (1998). Intergroup relations In D. Gilbert, S. Fiske, &

G. Lindzey (Eds.), *Handbook of social psychology* (4th ed., vol. 2, pp. 554–594). New York: McGraw Hill.

Brewer, M. B., & Silver, M. (1978). In-group bias as a function of task characteristics. *European Journal of Social Psychology, 8,* 393–400.

Brewer, M. B., & Weber, J. G. (1994). Self-evaluation effects of interpersonal versus intergroup social comparison. *Journal of Personality and Social Psychology, 66,* 268–275.

Brown, R. (1995). *Prejudice: Its social psychology.* Oxford: Blackwell.

Brown, R. (2000). Social identity theory: Past achievements, current problems and future challenges. *European Journal of Social Psychology, 30,* 745–778.

Brown, R., Condor, S., Mathews, A., Wade, G., & Williams, J. (1986). Explaining intergroup differentiation in an industrial organization. *Journal of Occupational Psychology, 58,* 273–286.

Brown, R., Maras, P., Masser, B., Vivian, J., & Hewstone, M. (2001). Life on the ocean wave: Testing some intergroup hypotheses in a naturalistic setting. *Group Processes and Intergroup Relations, 4,* 81–97.

Bruner, J. (1990). *Acts of meaning.* Cambridge, MA: Harvard University Press.

Cadinu, M. R., & Cerchioni, M. (2001). Compensatory biases after ingroup threat: "Yeah, but we have a good personality." *European Journal of Social Psychology, 31,* 353–367.

Campbell, A., Converse, P., Miller, W. E., & Stokes, D. E. (1960). *The American voter.* New York: Wiley.

Campbell, D. T. (1965). Ethnocentric and other altruistic motives. In D. Levine (Ed.), *Nebraska Symposium on Motivation.* Lincoln: Nebraska University Press.

Cartwright, D. (1968). The nature of group cohesiveness. In D. Cartwright, and A. Zander (Eds.) *Group Dynamics: Research and theory* (3rd ed., pp. 91–109). New York: Harper and Row.

Centers, R. (1949). *The psychology of social classes.* Princeton: Princeton University Press.

Citrin, J., Reingold, B., & Green, D. P. (1990). American identity and the politics of ethnic change. *Journal of Politics, 52,* 1124–1154.

Citrin, J., Wong, C., & Duff, B. (2001). The meaning of American national identity: Patterns of ethnic conflict and consensus. In R. D. Ashmore & L. Jussim (Eds.), *Social identity, intergroup conflict, and conflict reduction* (pp. 71–100). New York: Oxford University Press.

Coats, S., Smith, E. R., Claypool, H. M., & Banner, M. J. (2000). Overlapping mental representations of self and in-group: Reaction time evidence and its relationship with explicit measures of group identification. *Journal of Experimental Social Psychology, 36,* 304–314.

Cohen, A. P. 1986. Belonging: The experience of culture. In A. P. Cohen (Ed.), *Symbolising boundaries: Identity and diversity in British cultures* (pp. 1–17). Manchester: Manchester University Press.

Condor, S. (1996). Unimagined community? Some social psychological issues concerning English national identity. In G. M. Breakwell & E. Lyons (Eds.), *Changing European identities: Social psychological analyses of social change* (pp. 41–68). Oxford: Butterworth-Heinemann.

Conover, P. J. (1984). The influence of group identification on political perception and evaluation. *Journal of Politics, 46,* 760–785.

Conover, P. J. (1988). The role of social groups in political thinking. *British Journal of Political Science, 18,* 51–76.

Converse, P. & Campbell, A. (1968). Political standards in secondary groups. In D. Cartwright & A. Zander (Eds.), *Group dynamics: Research and theory* (3rd ed., pp. 199–211). New York: Harper and Row.

Converse, P. E., & Markus, G. B. (1979). Plus ca change . . . : The new CPS election study panel. *American Political Science Review, 73,* 2–49.

Coser, L. (1956). *The functions of social conflict.* New York: Free Press.

Crocker, J., Luhtanen, R., Blaine, B, and Broadnax, S. (1994). Collective self-esteem and psychological well-being among White, Black, and Asian college students. *Personality and Social Psychology Bulletin, 20,* 503–513.

Crocker, J., Luhtanen, R., Broadnax, S., & Blaine, B. E. (1999). Belief in U.S. government conspiracies against blacks among black and white college students: Powerlessness or system blame? *Personality and Social Psychology Bulletin, 25,* 941–953.

Crocker, J., & Major, B. (1989). Social stigma and self-esteem: The self-protective properties of stigma. *Psychological Review, 96,* 608–630.

Dawson, M. C. (1994). *Behind the mule: Race and class in African-American politics.* Princeton: Princeton University Press.

Deaux, K. (1993). Reconstructing social identity. *Personality and Social Psychology Bulletin, 19,* 4–12.

Deaux, K. (2001). Meaning and making: Some comments on content and process. In K. Deaux & G. Philogene (Eds.) *Representations of the social* (pp. 312–317). Malden, MA: Blackwell.

Deaux, K., Reid, A., Mizrahi, K.,& Ethier, K. A. (1995). Parameters of social identity. *Journal of Personality and Social Psychology, 68,* 280–291.

Deutsch, M., & Krauss, R. M. (1965). *Theories in social psychology.* New York: Basic Books.

Diehl, M. (1990). The minimal group paradigm: Theoretical explanations and empirical findings. *European Review of Social Psychology, 1,* 263–292.

Doise, W., & Sinclair, A. (1973). The categorization process in intergroup relations. *European Journal of Social Psychology, 3,* 145–157.

Duck, J. M., Hogg, M. A., & Terry, D. J. (1995). Me, us and them: Political identification and the third-person effect in the 1993 Australian federal election. *European Journal of Social Psychology, 25,* 195–215.

Duck, J. M., Terry, D. J., & Hogg, M. A. (1998). Perceptions of a media campaign: The role of social identity and the changing intergroup context. *Personality and Social Psychology Bulletin, 24,* 3–16.

Duckitt, J. (1989). Authoritarianism and group identification: A new view of an old construct. *Political Psychology, 10,* 63–84.

Duckitt, J. (1994). *The social psychology of prejudice.* Westport, CT: Praeger.

Duckitt, J., & Mphuthing, T. (2002). Relative deprivation and intergroup attitudes. In I. Walker & H. J. Smith (Eds.), *Relative deprivation: Specification, development, and integration.* (pp. 69–90). Cambridge: Cambridge University Press.

Duveen, G. (2001). Representations, identities, resistance. In K. Deaux & G. Philogene (Eds.), *Representations of the social* (pp. 257–270). Malden, MA: Blackwell.

Eiser, J. R. (1996). Accentuation revisited. In W. P. Robinson, (Ed.), *Social groups and identities: Developing the legacy of Henri Tajfel* (pp. 121–142). Oxford: Butterworth-Heinemann.

Ellemers, N., Wilke, H., & Van Knippenberg, A. (1993). Effects of the legitimacy of low group or individual status as individual and collective status-enhancing strategies. *Journal of Personality and Social Psychology, 64*, 766–778.

Eschbach, K., & Gomez, C. (1998). Choosing Hispanic identity: Ethnic identity switching among respondents to High School and Beyond. *Social Science Quarterly, 79*, 74–90.

Erikson, T. H. (1993). *Ethnicity and nationalism: Anthropological perspectives.* Boulder, CO: Pluto Press.

Ethier, K. A., & Deaux, K. (1994). Negotiating social identity when contexts change: Maintaining identification and responding to threat. *Journal of Personality and Social Psychology, 67*, 243–251.

Festinger, L. (1954). A theory of social comparison processes. *Human Relations, 7*, 117–40.

Forbes, H. D. (1997). *Ethnic conflict: Commerce, culture, and the contact hypothesis.* New Haven: Yale University Press

Gergen, K. (1989). Social psychology and the wrong revolution. *European Journal of Social Psychology, 19*, 463–84.

Gibson, J. L., & Gouws, A. (2000). Social identities and political intolerance: Linkages within the South African mass public. *American Journal of Political Science, 44*, 272–286.

Giles, M. W., & Evans, A. S. (1985). External threat, perceived threat, and group identity. *Social Science Quarterly, 66*, 50–66.

Granberg, D., Jefferson, N. L., Brent, E. B., Jr., & King, M. (1981). Membership group, reference group, and the attribution of attitudes to groups. *Journal of Personality and Social Psychology, 40*, 833–842.

Grant, P. R., & Brown, R. (1995). From ethnocentrism, to collective protest: Responses to relative deprivation and threats to social identity. *Social Psychology Quarterly, 58*, 195–211.

Green, D. P., & Cowden, J. A. (1992). Who protests: Self-interest and white opposition to busing. *Journal of Politics, 54*, 471–496.

Greenberg, J., Pyszczynski, T., Solomon, S., Rosenblatt, A., Veeded, M., & Kirkland, S. (1990). Evidence for terror management theory II: The effects of mortality salience on reactions to those who threaten or bolster the cultural world view. *Journal of Personality and Social Psychology, 58*, 308–318.

Greene, S. (1999). Understanding party identification: A social identity approach. *Political Psychology, 20*, 393–403.

Grieve, P. G., Hogg, M. A. (1999). Subjective uncertainty and intergroup discrimination in the minimal intergroup situation. *Personality and Social Psychology Bulletin, 25*, 926–940.

Guimond, S., & Dubé-Simard, L. (1983). Relative deprivation theory and the Quebec nationalist movement: The cognition-emotion distinction and the personal-group deprivation issue. *Journal of Personality and Social Psychology, 44*, 526–535.

Gurin, P., Hurtado, A., & Peng, T. (1994). Group contacts and ethnicity in the social identities of Mexicanos and Chicanos. *Personality & Social Psychology Bulletin, 20*, 521–532.

Gurin, P., Miller, A. H., & Gurin, G. (1980). Stratum identification and consciousness. *Social Psychology Quarterly, 43*, 30–47.

Gurin, P., & Townsend, A. (1986). Properties of gender identity and their implications for consciousness. *British Journal of Social Psychology, 25*, 139–148.

Gurr, T. R. (1970). *Why men rebel.* Princeton: Princeton University Press.

Gurr, T. R., & Moore, W. H. (1997). Ethnopolitical rebellion: A cross-sectional analysis of the 1980s with risk assessments for the 1990s. *American Journal of Political Science, 41,* 1079–1103.

Gusfield, J. (1963). *Symbolic crusade, status politics, and the American temperance movement.* Urbana: University of Illinois Press.

Hartley, R. E. (1960). Norm compatibility, norm preference, and the acceptance of reference group norms. *Journal of Social Psychology, 52,* 87–95.

Haslam, S. A., Turner, J. C., Oakes, P. J., McGarty, C., & Reynolds, K. J. (1998). The group as a basis for emergent stereotype consensus. *European Review of Social Psychology, 9,* 203–239.

Haslam S. A., Oakes, P. J., Turner, J. C., McGarty, C., & Hayes, B. K. (1992). Context-dependent variation in social stereotyping 1: The effects of intergroup relations as mediated by social change and frame of reference. *European Journal of Social Psychology, 22,* 3–20.

Herring, M., Jankowski, T. B., & Brown, R. E. (1999). Pro-black doesn't mean anti-white: The structure of African-American group identity. *Journal of Politics, 61,* 363–386.

Hinkle S, Fox-Cardamone, L., Haseleu, J. A., Brown, R., & Irwin, L. M. (1996). Grassroots political action as an intergroup phenomenon. *Journal of Social Issues 52,* 39–51.

Hogg, M. A. (1996). Intragroup processes, group structure, and social identity. In W. P. Robinson, (Ed.), *Social groups and identities: Developing the legacy of Henri Tajfel* (pp. 65–93). Oxford: Butterworth-Heinemann.

Hogg, M. A., & Hains, S. C. (1996). Friendship and group identification: A new look at the role of cohesiveness in groupthink. *European Journal of Social Psychology, 28,* 323–41.

Hogg, M. A., Hardie, E. A., & Reynolds, K. J. (1995). Prototypical similarity, self-categorization, and depersonalized attraction: A perspective on group cohesiveness. *European Journal of Social Psychology, 25,* 159–177.

Hogg, M. A., Terry, D. J., & White, K. M. (1995). A tale of two theories: A critical comparison of identity theory with social learning theory. *Social Psychology Quarterly, 58,* 255–269.

Hogg, M. A., & Turner, J. C. (1985). Interpersonal attraction, social identification, and psychological group formation. *European Journal of Social Psychology, 15,* 51–66.

Hopkins, N., & Reicher, S. (1996). The construction of social categories and processes of social change: Arguing about national identities. In G. M. Breakwell, & E. Lyons (Eds.), *Changing European identities: Social psychological analyses of social change* (pp. 69–94). Oxford: Butterworth-Heinemann.

Horowitz, D. L. (1985). *Ethnic groups in conflict.* Berkeley: University of California Press.

Hornsey, M. J., & Hogg, M. A. (2000). Intergroup similarity and subgroup relations: Some implications for assimilation. *Personality and Social Psychology Bulletin, 26,* 948–958.

Huddy, L. (1997, September). *Political identification as social identity.* Paper presented at the annual meeting of the American Political Science Association, Washington, DC.

Huddy, L. (1998, September). *The social nature of political identity: Feminist image and feminist identity.* Paper presented at the annual meeting of the American Political Science Association, Boston.

Huddy, L. (1989). *Generational agreement on old-age policies: Explanations based on realistic interests, symbolic political attitudes, and age identities.* Unpublished doctoral dissertation, University of California at Los Angeles.

Huddy, L. (2001). From social to political identity: A critical examination of social identity theory. *Political Psychology, 22,* 127–156.

Huddy, L. (2002). The role of context within social identity theory: A response to Oakes. *Political Psychology, 23,* 825–838.

Huddy, L., & Feldman, S. (2001). *Puerto Rican nationalism: Language policies and the protection of culture.* Unpublished manuscript. State University of New York at Stony Brook.

Huddy, L., Neely, F., & LaFay, M. (2000). Attitudes towards the women's movement. *Public Opinion Quarterly, 64,* 309–350.

Huddy, L., & Sears, D. O. (1995). Opposition to bilingual education: Prejudice or the defense of realistic interests? *Social Psychology Quarterly, 58,* 133–143.

Huddy, L., & Virtanen, S. (1995). Subgroup differentiation and subgroup bias among Latinos as a function of familiarity and positive distinctiveness. *Journal of Personality and Social Psychology* 68, 97–108.

Hyman, H. H., & Singer, E. (1968). Introduction. In *Readings in reference group theory and research* (pp. 3–21). New York: Free Press.

Jackson, J. W., & Smith, E. R. (1999). Conceptualizing social identity: A new framework and evidence for the impact of different dimensions. *Personality and Social Psychology Bulletin, 25,* 120–135.

Jackman, M. (1994). *The velvet glove: Paternalism and conflict in gender, class, and race relations.* Berkeley: University of California Press.

Jackson, L. A., Sullivan, L. A., Harnish, R., & Hodge, C. N. (1996). Achieving positive social identity: Social mobility, social creativity, and permeability of group boundaries. *Journal of Personality and Social Psychology, 70,* 241–254.

Jenkins, C. J. (1983). Resource mobilization theory and the study of social movements. *Annual Review of Sociology, 9,* 527–53.

Jenkins, R. (1996). *Social identity.* London: Routledge.

Jetten, J., Branscombe, N. R., Schmitt, M. T., & Spears, R. (2001). Rebels with a cause: Group identification as a response to perceived discrimination from the mainstream. *Personality and Social Psychology Bulletin, 27,* 1204–1213.

Karasawa, M. (1991). Toward an assessment of social identity: The structure of group identification and its effects on in-group evaluations. *British Journal of Social Psychology, 30,* 293–307.

Kawakami, K., & Dion, K. (1993). The impact of salient self-identities on relative deprivation and action intentions. *European Journal of Social Psychology, 23,* 525–540.

Kelley, H. H. (1952). Two functions of reference groups. In G. E. Swanson, T. M. Newcomb, & E. L. Hartley (Eds.), *Readings in Social Psychology* (2nd ed., pp. 410–414). New York: Holt.

Kelly, C. (1989). Political identity and perceived intragroup homogeneity. *British Journal of Social Psychology, 28,* 239–250.

Kinder, D. R., Adams, G. S., & Gronke, P. W. (1989). Economics and politics in the 1984 American presidential election. *American Journal of Political Science, 33,* 491–515.

Kinder, D. R., & Sanders, L. M. (1996). *Divided by color: Racial politics and democratic ideals.* Chicago: University of Chicago Press.

Kinder, D. R., & Winter, N. (2001). Exploring the racial divide: Blacks, whites, and opinion on national policy. *American Journal of Political Science, 45,* 439–456.

Kinket, B., & Verkuyten, M. (1997). Levels of ethnic self-identification and social context. *Social Psychology Quarterly, 60,* 338–354.

Klandermans, B. (1984). Mobilization and participation: Social-psychological expansions of resource mobilization theory. *American Sociological Review, 49,* 583–600.

Kramer, R. M., & Brewer, M. B. (1984). Effects of group identity on resource use in a simulated commons dilemma. *Journal of Personality and Social Psychology, 46,* 1044–1057.

Lakoff, G. (1987). *Women, fire, and dangerous things: What categories reveal about the mind.* Chicago: University of Chicago Press.

Lalonde, R. N. (1992). The dynamics of group differentiation in the face of defeat. *Personality and Social Psychology Bulletin, 18,* 336–342.

Lau, R. R. (1989). Individual and contextual influences on group identification. *Social Psychology Quarterly, 52,* 220–231.

Lazarsfeld, P. F., Berelson, B., & Gaudet, H. (1944). *The people's choice* (pp. 16–27). New York: Columbia University Press.

Levine, R. A., & Campbell, D. T. (1972). *Ethnocentrism: Theories of conflict, ethnic attitudes and behavior.* New York: Wiley.

Levy, S. R. (1999). Reducing prejudice: Lessons from social-cognitive factors underlying perceiver differences in prejudice. *Journal of Social Issues, 55,* 745–766.

Lipset, S., & Raab, E. (1973). *The politics of unreason.* New York: Harper and Row.

Luhtanen, R., & Crocker, J. (1992). A collective self-esteem scale: Self-evaluation of one's social identity. *Personality & Social Psychology Bulletin, 18,* 302–318.

Martin, B. L. (1991). From Negro to Black to African American: The power of names and naming. *Political Science Quarterly, 106,* 83–107.

McCarthy, J. D., & Zald, M. N. (1976). Resource mobilization and social movements: A partial theory. *American Journal of Sociology, 82,* 1212–1241.

McGarty, C., Turner, J. C., Hogg, M. A., David, B., & Wetherell, M. S. (1992). Group polarization as conformity to the prototypical group member. *British Journal of Social Psychology, 31,* 1–20.

McGuire, W. J., McGuire, C. V., Child, P., & Fujioka, T. (1978). Salience of ethnicity in the spontaneous self-concept as a function of one's ethnic distinctiveness in the social environment. *Journal of Personality and Social Psychology, 36,* 511–520.

McGuire, W. J., & Padawer-Singer, A. (1976). Trait salience in the spontaneous self-concept. *Journal of Personality and Social Psychology, 33,* 743–754.

McKenna, K. Y. A., &. Bargh, J. A. (1998). Coming out in the age of the Internet: Identity demarginalization through virtual group participation. *Journal of Personality and Social Psychology, 75*(3), 681–694.

Mead, G. H. (1934). *Mind, self, and society.* Chicago: University of Chicago Press.

Merton, R. K., & Kitt, A. S. (1950). Contributions to the theory of reference group behavior. In R. K. Merton & P. F. Lazarsfeld (Eds.), *Continuities in social research: Studies in the scope and method of the "The American Soldier"* (pp. 40–105). Glencoe, IL: Free Press.

Miller, A. H., Gurin, P., Gurin, G., & Malanchuk, O. (1981). Group consciousness and political participation. *American Journal of Political Science, 25,* 494–511.

Mullen, B., Brown, R., & Smith, C. (1992). Ingroup bias as a function of salience, relevance, and status: An integration. *European Journal of Social Psychology, 22,* 103–122.

Mullin, B. A., & M. A. Hogg. (1998). Dimensions of subjective uncertainty in social identification and minimal intergroup discrimination. *British Journal of Social Psychology, 37,* 345–65.

Mummendey, A., Kessler, T., Klink, A., & Mielke, R. (1999). Strategies to cope with negative social identity: Predictions by social identity theory and relative deprivation theory. *Journal of Personality & Social Psychology, 76*(2), 229–45.

Mummendey, A., Klink, A., & Brown, R. (2001). Nationalism and patriotism: National identification and out-group rejection. *British Journals of Social Psychology, 40,* 159–172.

Mummendey, A., & Schrieber, H. J. (1984). "Different" just means "better": Some obvious and hidden pathways to ingroup favoritism. *British Journal of Social Psychology, 23,* 363–367.

National Opinion Research Council (NORC). General Social Survey, 1966. On-line; available at: www.icpsv.umich.edu/ass.

Neisser, U. (1987). From direct perception to conceptual structure. In U. Neisser, (Ed.), *Concepts and conceptual development: Ecological and intellectual factors in categorization.* Cambridge: Cambridge University Press.

Neuberg, S. L., & Newsom, J. T. (1993). Personal need for structure: Individual differences in the desire for simple structure. *Journal of Personality and Social Psychology, 65,* 113–131.

Newcomb, T. M. (1952). Attitude development as a function of reference groups: The Bennington Study. In G. E. Swanson, T. M. Newcomb, & E. L. Hartley (Eds.), *Readings in social psychology* (Rev. ed., pp. 420–30). New York: Holt.

Opp, K., & Gern, C. (1993). Dissident groups, personal networks, and spontaneous cooperation: The East German revolution of 1989. *American Sociological Review, 58,* 659–680.

Paolino, P. (1995). Group-salient issues and group representation: Support for women candidates in the 1992 Senate elections. *American Journal of Political Science, 39,* 294–313.

Perreault, S., & Bourhis, R. Y. (1999). Ethnocentrism, social identification, and discrimination. *Personality and Social Psychology Bulletin, 25*(1), 92–103.

Petta, G., & Walker, I. (1992). Relative deprivation and ethnic identity. *British Journal of Social Psychology, 31,* 285–293.

Rahn, W. M. (1993). The role of partisan stereotypes in information processing about political candidates. *American Journal of Political Science, 37,* 472–496.

Reese, L., & Brown, R. E. (1995). The effects of religious messages on racial identity and system blame among African Americans. *Journal of Politics, 57,* 24–43.

Reicher, S. (1982). The determination of collective behavior. In H. Tajfel (Ed.), *Social identity and intergroup relations* (pp. 41–83). Cambridge: Cambridge University Press.

Rothbart, M. (1993). Intergroup Perception and Social Conflict. In S. Worchel & J. A. Simpson (Eds.)., *Conflict between people and groups* (pp. 93–109). Chicago: Nelson-Hall.

Rothgerber, H. (1997). External intergroup threat as an antecedent to perceptions of in-group and out-group homogeneity. *Journal of Personality and Social Psychology, 73,* 1206–1212.

Ryan, B. (1992). *Feminism and the women's movement: Dynamics of change in social movement ideology and activism.* New York: Routledge.

Schatz, R. T., Staub, E., & Lavine, H. (1999). On the varieties of national attachment: Blind versus constructive patriotism. *Political Psychology, 20,* 151–174.

Schimel, J., Simon, L., Greenberg, J., Pyszczynski, T., Solomon, S., Waxmonsky, J., & Arndt, J. (1999). Stereotypes and terror management: Evidence that mortality salience enhances stereotoypic thinking and preferences. *Journal of Personality and Social Psychology, 77,* 905–26.

Schmitt, M. T., & Branscombe, N. R.. (2001). The good, the bad, and the manly: Threats to one's prototypicality and evaluations of fellow in-group members. *Journal of Experimental Social Psychology, 37,* 510–517.

Schmitt, M. T., Branscombe, N. R., Kobrynowicz, D., & Owen, S. (2002). Perceiving discrimination against one's gender group has different implications for well-being in women and men. *Personality and Social Psychology Bulletin, 28,* 197–210.

Schuman, H., Steeh, C., Bobo, L. D., & Krysan, M. (1997). *Racial attitudes in America: Trends and interpretations.* Cambridge, MA: Harvard University Press.

Schwartz, S. H., Struch, N., & Bilsky, W. (1990). Values and intergroup social motives: A study of Israeli and German students. *Social Psychology Quarterly, 53,* 185–198.

Scott, W. J. (1985). The Equal Rights Amendment as status politics. *Social Forces, 64,* 499–506.

Sears, D. O. (1983). The persistence of early political predispositions: The roles of attitude object and life stage. In L. Wheeler & P. Shaver (Eds.), *Review of personality and social psychology* (Vol. 4, pp. 79–116). Beverly Hills, CA: Sage.

Sears, D. O., & Citrin, J. (1985). *The tax revolt: Something for nothing in California.* Cambridge, MA: Harvard University Press.

Sears, D. O., Citrin, J., Cheleden, S. V., & Van Laar, C. (1999). Cultural diversity and multicultural politics: Is ethnic balkanization psychologically inevitable? In D. Prentice & D. Miller (Eds.), *Cultural divides: The social psychology of cultural contact.* New York: Russell Sage Foundation.

Sears, D. O., Citrin, J., Vidanage, S., & Valentino, N. (1994, September). *What ordinary Americans think about multiculturalism.* Paper presented at the annual meeting of the American Political Science Association, New York.

Sears, D. O., & Funk, C. (1991). The role of self-interest in social and political attitudes. *Advances in Experimental Psychology, 24,* 1–91.

Sears, D. O., & Henry, P. J. (1999). Ethnic identity and group threat in American politics. *Political Psychologist, 4*(1), 12–17.

Sears, D. O., Henry, P. J., Fu, M., & Bui, K. (2001, July). *The origins and persistence of ethnic identity among contemporary American university students.* Paper presented at the annual meeting of the International Society for Political Psychology. Cuernavaca, Mexico.

Sears, D. O., & Huddy, L. (1990). On the origins of the political disunity of women. In P. Gurin & L. Tilly (Eds.), *Women, politics, and change* (pp. 249–277). New York: Russell Sage.

Sears, D. O., & Jessor, T. (1996). Whites' racial policy attitudes: The role of white racism. *Social Science Quarterly, 77,* 751–759.

Sears, D. O. & Kinder D. R. (1985). Whites' opposition to busing: On conceptualizing and operationalizing group conflict. *Journal of Personality and Social Psychology, 48,* 1141–1147.

Sears, D. O., & McConahay, J. (1973). *The politics of violence: The new urban blacks and the Watts riots.* Boston: Houghton Mifflin.

Sellers, R. M., Smith, M. A., Shelton, J. N., Rowley, S. A. J., & Chavous, T. M. (1998). Multidimensional model of racial identity: A reconceptualization of African American racial identity. *Personality and Social Psychology Bulletin, 2,* 18–39.

Shamir, M., & Arian, A. (1992). Collective identity and electoral competition in Israel. *American Political Science Review, 93,* 265–277.

Sidanius, J., Feshbach, S., Levin, S., & Pratto, F. (1997). The interface between ethnic and national attachment: Ethnic pluralism or ethnic dominance? *Public Opinion Quarterly, 61,* 102–133.

Sidanius, J., & Pratto, F. (1999). *Social dominance: An intergroup theory of social hierarchy and oppression.* New York: Cambridge University Press.

Simon, B. (1997). Self and group in modern society: Ten theses on the individual self and the collective self. In R. Spears, P. J. Oakes, N. Ellemers & S. A. Haslam (Eds.), *The social psychology of stereotyping and group life* (pp. 318–335). Oxford: Blackwell.

Simon, B., & Klandermans, B. (2001). Politicized collective identity: A social psychological analysis. *American Psychologist, 56,* 319–331.

Simon, B., Kulla, C., & Zobel, M. (1995). On being more than just a part of the whole: Regional identity and social distinctiveness. *European Journal of Social Psychology, 25,* 325–340.

Simon, B., Loewy, M., Sturmer, S., Weber, U., Freytag, P., Habig, C., Kampmeier, C., & Spahlinger, P. (1998). Collective identification and social movement participation. *Journal of Personality and Social Psychology, 74,* 646–658.

Smith, E. R., & Henry, S. (1996). An in-group becomes part of the self: Response time evidence. *Personality and Social Psychology Bulletin, 22*(6), 635–642.

Smith, H. J., Spears, R., & Oyen, M. (1994). People like us: The influence of personal deprivation and group membership salience on justice evaluations. *Journal of Experimental Social Psychology, 30,* 277–299.

Snow, D. A., Rochford, E. B. Jr., Worden, S. K., & Benford, R. D. (1986). Frame alignment processes, micromobilization and movement participation. *American Sociological Review, 51,* 456–481.

Spears, R., Oakes, P. J., Ellemers, N., & Haslam, S. A. (1997). *The social psychology of stereotyping and group life.* Oxford: Blackwell.

Stouffer, S. A. (1949). *The American soldier.* Princeton: Princeton University Press.

Struch, N., & Schwartz, S. H. (1989). Intergroup aggression: Its predictors and distinctness from in-group bias. *Journal of Personality and Social Psychology, 56,* 364–373.

Swan, S., & Wyer, R. S., Jr. (1997). Gender stereotypes and social identity: How being in the minority affects judgments of self and others. *Personality and Social Psychology Bulletin, 23*(12), 1265–1276.

Tajfel, H. 1969. Cognitive aspects of prejudice. *Journal of Social Issues, 25,* 75–97.

Tajfel, H. C., Billig, M. G., and Bundy, R. P. (1971). Social categorization and intergroup behavior. *European Journal of Social Psychology, 1,* 149–178.

Tajfel, H. (1981). *Human groups and social categories*. Cambridge: Cambridge University Press.

Tajfel, H., & Turner, J. C. (1979). An integrative theory of intergroup conflict. In W. G. Austin & S. Worchel (Eds.), *The social psychology of intergroup relations* (pp. 33–48). Monterey, CA: Brooks/Cole.

Tajfel, H., & Wilkes, A. L. (1963). Classification and quantitative judgement. *British Journal of Psychology, 54,* 101–114.

Tate, K. (1993). *From protest to politics: The new black voters in American elections.* New York: Russell Sage.

Taylor, D., & Moghaddam, F. M. (1996). *Theories of intergroup relations*. Westport, CT: Praeger.

Taylor, D. M., Moghaddam, F. M., Gamble, I., & Zellerer, E. (1987). Disadvantaged group responses to perceived inequality: From passive acceptance to collective action. *Journal of Social Psychology, 127,* 259–272.

Thoits, P. A., & Virshup, L. V. (1997). Me's and we's: Forms and functions of social identities. In R. Ashmore & L. Jussim (Eds.), *Self and identity: Fundamental issues* (Vol 1, pp. 106–133). New York: Oxford University Press.

Tripathi, R. C., & Srivastava, R. (1981). Relative deprivation and intergroup attitudes. *European Journal of Social Psychology, 11,* 313–318.

Tropp, L. R., & Wright, S. C. (1999). Ingroup identification and relative deprivation: An examination across multiple social comparisons. *European Journal of Social Psychology, 29,* 707–724.

Turner, J. C. (1996). Henri Tajfel: An introduction. In W. P. Robinson (Ed.), *Social groups and identities: Developing the legacy of Henri Tajfel* (pp. 1–23). Oxford: Butterworth-Heinemann.

Turner, J. C., Hogg, M. A., Oakes, P. J., Reicher, S. D., & Wetherell, M. S. (1987). *Rediscovering the social group: A self-categorization theory*. Oxford: Blackwell.

Turner, J. C., Hogg, M. A., Turner, P. J., & Smith, P. M. (1984). Failure and defeat as determinants of group cohesiveness. *British Journal of Social Psychology, 23,* 97–111.

Van Knippenberg, A. (1978). Status differences, comparative relevance and intergoup differentiation. In H. Tajfel (Ed.), *Differentiation between social groups: Studies in the social psychology of intergroup relations,* London: Academic Press.

Van Knippenberg, A., & van Oers, H. (1984). Social identity and equity concerns in intergroup perceptions. *British Journal of Social Psychology, 23,* 351–361.

Vanneman, R. D., & Pettigrew, T. F. (1972). Race and relative deprivation in the urban United States. *Race, 13,* 461–486.

Verba, S., & Nie, N. H. (1972). *Particiaption in America: Political democracy and social equality*. New York: Harper.

Verkuyten, M., & Nekuee, S. (1999). Ingroup bias: The effect self-stereotyping, identification, and group threat. *Euorepan Journal of Social Psychology, 29,* 411–418.

Wilder, D. A. (1986). Social categorization: Implications for creation and reduction of intergroup bias. In L. Berkowitz (Ed.), *Advances in experimental psychology*. Orlando, FL: Academic Press.

Wright, S. C. (1997). Ambiguity, social influence, and collective action: Generating collective protest in response to tokenism. *Personality and Social Psychology Bulletin, 23,* 1277–1290.

Wright, S. C., Taylor, D. T., & Moghaddam, F. M. (1990). Responding to membership in a disadvantaged group: From acceptance to collective protest. *Journal of Personality and Social Psychology, 58,* 994–1003.

Young, I. M. (1990). *Justice and the politics of difference.* Princeton: Princeton University Press.

Young, I. M. (1997). *Intersecting voices: Dilemmas of gender, political philosophy, and policy.* Princeton: Princeton University Press.

16 John Duckitt

Prejudice and Intergroup Hostility

Social scientists have used a number of concepts to describe and understand intergroup hostility and conflict. The concept of prejudice, which has been typically defined as a negative intergroup attitude (Allport, 1954; Ashmore & DelBoca, 1981; Brown, 1995), has probably been the broadest and most influential of these.

The conceptualization of prejudice as a negative intergroup attitude involves two fundamental issues. The first is that of social categorization. It is only when others are not seen as individuals but are categorized as members of social groups or categories that negative intergroup attitudes can be activated toward them. The second issue is that of the structure and dimensionality of these negative intergroup attitudes. Social psychologists have distinguished three distinct components of prejudice, or ways in which negative intergroup attitudes can be expressed. These are negative stereotypes (cognitive component), negative feelings (affective component), and negative behavioral inclinations (behavioral component) toward outgroups. These three components have traditionally been seen as three expressions or components of a single basic attitudinal dimension of intergroup evaluation. Recently, however, evidence has accumulated suggesting that there may be two different dimensions of intergroup evaluation, disliking versus liking and disrespecting versus respecting, with each manifest across these three ways of expressing prejudice.

The issue of social categorization as providing the fundamental social-cognitive basis of or precondition for prejudice will be considered in the next section, followed by a consideration of the nature, the dimensionality, and the varieties of prejudice. Finally, the chapter will examine the causes of prejudice, as both an individual and intergroup phenomenon.

▲ Groups and Categories: The Social-Cognitive Basis of Prejudice

The fundamental prerequisite for prejudice as a negative intergroup attitude is the division of human society into groups or social categories. While ubiquitous in human affairs, groups and social categories are not formed by nature but are socially constructed and created by human cognitive activity. Social categorization, or the perceptual classification of individuals into discrete categories or groups, is a basic cognitive process that simplifies, structures, and gives meaning to the social environment. It is a fundamental precondition for intergroup behavior of any kind, and its role in prejudice and stereotyping has been long acknowledged (Allport, 1954; Lippman, 1922; Tajfel, 1969). The tendency to perceive others as group or as category members rather than as individuals occurs pervasively, rapidly, and in apparently automatic fashion in many situations. It has a number of effects germane to prejudice on perception, information processing, and behavior, which, as Fiske (1998, 2000) has noted, often occur automatically and outside conscious awareness or control.

One effect of social categorization is the accentuation of intracategory similarities and intercategory differences, which Tajfel (1969) argued was fundamental to stereotyping. Numerous studies have shown when individuals are categorized into groups their similarity to their fellow ingroup members and the dissimilarity of ingroup members to outgroup members will be exaggerated (Allen & Wilder, 1975; Wilder, 1986). Another consequence of individuals being categorized into ingroup and outgroup is a general tendency for ingroup members to view outgroups as relatively less complex, less variable, and less individuated than their ingroups (Hamilton & Trolier, 1986; Judd & Park, 1988; Wilder, 1986).

The most dramatic effects of categorization have been demonstrated using the minimal intergroup paradigm pioneered by Tajfel and his co-workers (Tajfel, 1970; Tajfel, Flament, Billig, & Bundy, 1971). Here participants are simply informed that they have been divided into groups, often on a relatively arbitrary basis. These groups are truly minimal, involving no group activity or contact between members. Yet when these participants are asked to evaluate anonymous ingroup and outgroup members or apportion rewards between them, they do so in a biased and discriminatory fashion, favoring ingroup over outgroup members (Brewer, 1979; Tajfel, 1981). Moreover, the more salient the intergroup categorization is, the greater the intergroup bias and discrimination that is shown (Mullen, Brown, & Smith, 1992).

This intergroup discrimination and bias triggered by mere categorization into groups has often been viewed as "a rudimentary form of behavioral prejudice" (Brown, 1995, p. 45). However, prejudice is generally conceptualized as involving negativity to an outgroup, and the evidence from minimal intergroup studies has indicated that this bias and discrimination derives primarily from enhanced ingroup evaluations and not outgroup deprecation (Brewer, 1979; Brown, 2000). Moreover, when negative outcomes are being allocated between ingroup and outgroup members in minimal intergroup situations, the bias and discrimination typically shown for positive outcomes disappears (Otten & Mummendey, 2000). This suggests that categorization does not generate negativity or prejudice to the outgroup but an identification with and enhancement of the ingroup, which might be more appropriately viewed as a precondition or precursor of prejudice rather than as a form of prejudice (see Brown, 2000).

If salient social categorization is a necessary but not sufficient condition for prejudice, then it should consistently accompany prejudice. In support of this, research indicates that when people are prejudiced against a particular group, that group categorization will be highly accessible for them. Thus, anti-Semitic people were found to be more ready to classify others as Jewish (Allport & Kramer, 1946; Quanty, Keats, & Harkins, 1975), and when targets were race-ambiguous, racially prejudiced persons took more time trying to classify them (Blascovitch, Wyer, Swart, & Kibler, 1997). Persons prejudiced against particular groups are thus especially ready to shift from what Brewer (1998) has termed person-based processing of social information to category-based processing when responding to individuals from those groups. In societies characterized by high levels of prejudice, those particular intergroup categorizations would tend to be highly salient across situations (Brewer & Miller, 1984).

Overall, therefore, categorization is implicated in prejudice and intergroup behavior in several ways. First, categorization into groups is a precondition for intergroup behavior. Second, the salience of categorization influences the amount of intergroup bias and discrimination generated, in the form of ingroup enhancement, which, while not equating to prejudice, seems to be a precursor for prejudice (see chapter 15 for a more extensive review of the effects of categorization on ingroup bias, group identity, and political cohesion). And third, prejudice against particular groups tends to be associated with those group categorizations being highly accessible for prejudiced persons and highly salient in social situations where prejudice exists.

◤ The Tripartite Nature of Prejudiced Intergroup Attitudes

Intergroup attitudes have typically been conceptualized as encompassing three different components or ways in which intergroup attraction or hostility can be expressed. These have invariably included a cognitive component, in the form of negative or positive group stereotypes, an affective component, in the form of negative or positive feelings toward groups; and a behavioral component, expressed in inclinations to behave negatively to outgroup members, for example, through discriminatory actions and maintaining social distance (Allport, 1954; Rosenfeld & Stephan, 1981).

Stereotypes and Prejudice

Contemporary social scientists typically define *stereotypes* as beliefs about the personal characteristics of a group or category of people (see Ashmore & DelBoca, 1981). In contrast to more traditional approaches that saw stereotypes as necessarily incorrect, irrational, rigid, or faulty in some way, this approach sees stereotypes as arising basically out of essentially normal and adaptive cognitive processes, such as categorization, that function to reduce the complexity of social information processing (Brewer & Kramer, 1985; Messick & Mackie, 1989).

A great deal of contemporary social psychological research has derived from this view of stereotyping as a purely cognitive process and the concept of stereotype as a cognitive structure organizing and representing information about social categories (see Fiske, 1998, 2000; Hilton & von Hippel, 1996; Maccrae, Stangor & Hewstone, 1996). An important and well-established conclusion from this research has been that stereotypes function as generalized expectancies about categories or groups that bias the perception of and behavior to individual members of those groups so as to maintain the stereotype and generate behavioral confirmation of it.

Stereotyping per se, however, does not necessarily involve prejudice. Outgroup stereotypes can be evaluatively positive, neutral, or negative. Only evaluatively negative stereotypes are usually viewed as expressive of prejudiced attitudes. This raises two important questions about stereotyping and prejudice. First, how strongly are negative stereotypes of particular groups related to other expressions of prejudice against those groups? Second, are negative outgroup stereotypes organized on just one evaluative dimension, or, as recent research suggests, are there two distinct evaluative dimensions of negative stereotypes?

In the first instance it was traditionally assumed that negative stereotypes should be strongly associated with other expressions of prejudice, such as affective dislike or discriminatory behavior (Allport, 1954). The evidence thus far, however, does not support this. Brigham's (1971) review of research on stereotyping concluded that negative stereotypes and prejudice were only weakly and inconsistently related. Later research has come to similar conclusions (Gardner, 1973, 1993; Lalonde & Gardner, 1989; Stephan, Ageyev, Coates-Shrider, Stephan, & Abalakina, 1994). A meta-analysis of 30 hypothesis tests from 12 different studies indicated that American whites' evaluative stereotypes of blacks correlated only .25 with whites' overall racial attitudes and .16 with indices of discriminatory behavior to blacks (Dovidio, Brigham, Johnson, & Gaertner, 1996).

A problem with this research is that these studies examined the relationship between prejudice and stereotypes, with the latter assessed as a single overall dimension of positive to negative evaluation. However, a number of studies have indicated that intergroup stereotypes involve two clearly distinct evaluative dimensions. One dimension is typically labeled competence and involves trait attributes indicative of achievement, ability, prestige, strength, and power versus incompetence, inferiority, and weakness, whereas the second, usually labeled beneficence, warmth, or morality involves trait attributes indicating niceness, likeability, generosity, and moral goodness versus badness, malevolence, meanness, insincerity, and immorality. These two evaluative stereotype dimensions emerged in Brewer and Campbell's

(1976) research on East African tribal groups and in studies of ethnic stereotypes (Giles & Ryan, 1982; Singh, Choo, & Poh, 1998), national stereotypes (Phalet & Poppe, 1997; Poppe & Linnssen, 1999), and stereotypes
of social groups (Fiske, Xu, Cuddy, & Glick, 1999).

In addition, these two dimensions of evaluative stereotypes seem to have
quite different correlates. Evaluation on the competence dimension has been
associated with groups' status (Fiske et al., 1999), power (Phalet & Poppe,
1997), or technological advancement (Brewer & Campbell, 1976), while
evaluation on the beneficence dimension has been associated with the degree
of conflict with or competitive threat from the group (Fiske et al., 1999;
Phalet & Poppe, 1997). While these two dimensions of evaluative stereotypes have not been directly explored in relation to racial stereotypes, it will
later be argued that they appear to have important implications for understanding racism and developing an adequate typology of racisms.

Overall, therefore, modern approaches view stereotyping not as a pathological process but as arising out of universal and adaptive cognitive processes, such as categorization, that simplify social complexity and operate as
self-perpetuating expectancies about others. Contrary to expectation, empirical studies have found relatively weak relationships between overall measures of outgroup prejudice and the evaluative stereotypes held of those
groups. However, these findings might be misleading, since recent evidence
seems to indicate that stereotypes involve two quite distinct dimensions of
intergroup evaluation: the dimensions of competence and beneficence.

Intergroup Affect and Prejudice

Stangor, Sullivan, and Ford (1991) have noted that while psychologists
traditionally believed that negative affect or feelings of dislike for outgroups
were the central core of prejudice, during the past 2 decades their emphasis
has largely shifted to cognitive aspects, such as categorization and stereotyping. However, several influential commentaries have suggested a possible
shift back to an emphasis on affect as central to intergroup attitudes, behavior, and relations. For example, Fiske (1998) has suggested that prejudice
should be conceptualized specifically as negative intergroup affect. Smith
(1993) has also proposed a theory suggesting that when group identity is
salient, the way people appraise intergroup contexts or relationships generates particular feelings about outgroups, and it is these "social emotions"
that constitute prejudice and determine intergroup behavior.

Research has also suggested that affect toward outgroups may be the
most critical component of prejudiced attitudes. Stangor and colleagues
(1991) found that affective responses to national, ethnic, and religious
groups were clearly better predictors of general favorability and social distance to these groups than the stereotypes held about those groups. Haddock, Zanna, and Esses (1994) also found that affective responses were
better predictors than stereotypes of people's overall evaluations of ethnic

groups. A meta-analysis by Dovidio and colleagues (1996) of 30 hypothesis tests from 12 different studies found that affective prejudice to blacks correlated more strongly with discriminatory behavior to blacks ($r = .32$) than did the stereotypes held of blacks ($r = .16$).

There is evidence, however, that prejudiced affect or feelings to outgroups might also be not unidimensional but organized along two dimensions directly paralleling those noted for evaluative stereotypes (see chapter 6 for further evidence on the two-dimensional nature of affect). Research by Dijker (1987) examined the emotions that three immigrant groups elicited from his Dutch participants. Factor analysis revealed two relatively independent affective dimensions of prejudice. One was characterized by three closely related negative affects of anger or irritation, worry or concern, and anxiety, while the other was characterized by positive affect, so that prejudice could be indicated by either high negative affect or low positive affect toward outgroups. Djiker found that both negative and positive affect predicted the overall evaluation of minority groups but that the positive affect dimension was a better predictor. Stangor and colleagues (1991) later also found that low positive emotion was a better predictor than negative emotion of overall prejudice to a number of minority groups in the United States.

Two other important investigations have obtained findings closely paralleling Dijker's. Fiske and colleagues' (1999) research on stereotype content for social groups in the United States also suggested two dimensions of intergroup attitudes, one characterized by liking versus disliking (paralleling beneficence stereotypes) and the other by respecting versus disrespecting (paralleling competence stereotypes). Brewer and Campbell (1976) in their earlier research on East African tribal groups had also suggested that intergroup liking or attraction and intergroup respect emerged as two distinct dimensions of intergroup attitudes. Disliking would clearly involve negative affects toward outgroups, while disrespecting would seem to involve a lack of positive affects.

Thus the findings from three different investigations converge in suggesting two distinct dimensions of intergroup feelings or affect, which directly parallel the two dimensions of evaluative stereotypes already noted. Negative affects to outgroups or disliking them would accompany stereotyping them as bad, evil, immoral, and malevolent, while a lack of positive affect (disrespecting) would accompany stereotyping them as incompetent, weak, backward, and unsuccessful.

Behavioral Expressions of Prejudice: Social Distance, Discrimination, and Violence

While social psychologists have primarily studied the cognitive, perceptual, and affective aspects of prejudice, sociologists have devoted more attention to its behavioral expressions, in the form of peoples' intentions and dispositions to behave negatively to outgroup members. The most studied behavioral expressions of prejudice have probably been social distance preferences (behavioral avoidance) and discriminatory behavior. Interestingly, intentional acts of serious violence against individuals because of their group or category membership, or "hate crimes," have been much less studied.

Social distance is typically measured using variants of Bogardus's (1925) original questionnaire, which asked about people's willingness to have personal contact of varying degrees of intimacy ("close kinship by marriage," "in my street as neighbors," "employment in my occupation," citizenship in my country") with members of particular social groups. An important finding from social distance research has been of the relatively consensual or normative nature of prejudice within societies. Numerous studies have documented a hierarchy of social distance preferences in the United States that is widely accepted and has remained remarkably stable over much of the twentieth century (Dovidio et al., 1996; Owen, Eisner, & McFaul, 1981). At the top of this hierarchy are fair-skinned northern European peoples, followed by eastern and southern Europeans, then Asian peoples, and finally African peoples at the bottom. Even low-ranking minorities accept the hierarchy, except for their own group, which they rank high (Simpson & Yinger, 1985).

Hagendoorn's (1995) comparative research on the social distance hierarchies within a number of western and eastern European societies confirmed that these hierarchies were highly consensual within social groups. They also tended to be consensual across groups within particular societies, except when there were sharp ideological or cultural cleavages within the society, in which case the conflicting groups might disagree on the hierarchy. This was the case, for example, for Islamic versus non-Islamic groups in several countries from the former Soviet Union.

The existence of pervasive discrimination against groups that are the targets of prejudice has been extensively documented. For example, Pettigrew (1998b) has reviewed the substantial body of research on high levels of prejudice against and discrimination to the new immigrant minorities of western Europe. Numerous studies have shown the existence of pervasive discrimination against blacks in the United States, despite apparent declines in overt prejudice (e.g., Crosby, Bromley, & Saxe, 1980).

It is interesting that at the group level there seems to be a strong tendency for those groups who are negatively stereotyped and the targets of prejudiced affect to be most discriminated against (see Hagendoorn, 1995). This contrasts with the weak relationship obtained between discriminatory behavior and negative stereotypes and the moderate one between discriminatory behavior and intergroup affect at the individual difference level (Dovidio et al., 1996). However, as noted already, the weakness of the latter findings might be because individual differences in intergroup attitudes seem to be organized along two dimensions, which have usually not been measured separately.

Aggression and violence toward outgroup members constitute more extreme behavioral expressions of prejudice. Numerous studies have documented the long history of violence against blacks in the United States (Simpson & Yinger, 1985), and Pettigrew (1998b) has described the recent upsurge in antiimmigrant violence in western Europe. Much attention has therefore focused on the conditions that lead to prejudice being expressed in violence.

Early findings suggesting a correlation between lynching of blacks in the American South and economic hardship (Hovland & Sears, 1940; Raper, 1933) have not been supported by more recent reanalysis and new data (Green, Glaser, & Rich, 1998). Nor has clear evidence emerged of a relationship between unemployment and hate crimes against either blacks in the United States (Green & Rich, 1998) or "foreigners" in Germany (Krueger & Pischke, 1997). Instead, ecological studies have suggested that xenophobic reactions might be particularly likely in situations where "established groups confront outsiders whose growing numbers and social practices challenge the preexisting hierarchy in which they occupied a favorable position" (Green, Abelson, & Garnett, 1999, p. 430).

Finally, there are also indications that two different dimensions of discriminatory intergroup behavior might be identifiable that parallel those identified for evaluative stereotypes and intergroup affect. For example, Kovel (1970) suggested a distinction between aversive racism, characterized by dislike of blacks and avoidance of them, and dominative racism, characterized by belief in their inferiority and support for their social subordination. This distinction is similar to the more recent difference proposed by Fiske (1998) between "hot" discrimination, associated with negative affects such as anger and hostility (and presumably stereotypes reflecting low beneficence such as bad, immoral, evil), and "cold" discrimination, associated with negative stereotypes about an outgroup indicating its inferiority (and presumably low positive affect, or disrespecting). These distinctions suggest that dislike of and negative affect to outgroups who are seen as bad, immoral, and threatening would be accompanied by and expressed in certain kinds of intergroup discrimination and particularly by avoidance, while disrespect for and low positive affect to groups seen as incompetent and inferior would be accompanied by and expressed in other kinds of intergroup avoidance and particularly by discriminatory treatment. The most serious kinds of negative intergroup behavior, such as hate crimes, might then be directed against groups that are both disliked and disrespected.

◤ The Varieties of Prejudice

Prejudiced intergroup attitudes invariably involve the three components of unfavorable stereotypes, feelings of dislike or disrespect, and some behavioral expressions of prejudice, even if the latter are relatively subtle. These are therefore relatively universal aspects of prejudice. A somewhat different issue is that of whether different kinds of prejudice exist. One approach has emerged from research in the United States and suggests the existence of different kinds of racism. A second approach has distinguished between prejudice and stereotypes that are implicit or automatic as opposed to explicit or controlled. A third approach derives from the identification of the two distinct dimensions of prejudice that have been noted here and uses them to construct broader typologies of prejudice.

Traditional Racism and the New Racisms

Several closely related theories have proposed that a new kind of racism has emerged in the United States in the decades following the desegregation of the South that has partially supplanted an older, more traditional form of racism. These theories emerged in response to findings showing that despite survey evidence of sharp and continued declines in whites' racial prejudice after the early 1960s (Schuman, Steeh, & Bobo, 1985), antiblack discrimination and racial inequality did not show corresponding decreases (Crosby, Bromley, & Saxe, 1980). Moreover, many ostensibly nonprejudiced whites have powerfully opposed policies designed to reduce these inequalities (see Huddy & Sears, 1995). Research also indicated that whites' overtly friendly behavior to blacks or apparently nonprejudiced questionnaire responses could be accompanied by covert negative affect revealed by subtle indicators such as voice tone (Weitz, 1972) and seating distance (Hendricks & Bootzin, 1976), or detected using the bogus pipeline, a frequently used technique to increase the honesty of self-reports. (Allen, 1975; Sigall & Page, 1971). Overall, these findings suggested that the traditional or old-fashioned American racism, characterized by beliefs in black biological inferiority, white supremacy, and the desirability of segregation, and formal discrimination, had been at least partially supplanted by a new, more subtle, and socially acceptable form of racism.

There have been four main approaches to describing this new racism: as symbolic or modern racism, subtle versus blatant prejudice, ambivalent racism, and aversive racism. These four approaches have varied in their conceptualization of this new racism, but their essential features seem similar. The most important of these approaches is that termed symbolic (McConahay & Hough, 1976; Sears & Kinder, 1971) or modern racism (McConahay, 1983) or, more recently, racial resentment (Kinder & Sanders, 1996). It has been described as a blending of antiblack affect with the traditional Protestant ethic and conservative values. Thus blacks are disliked because they are seen as violating basic moral values such as self-reliance, individual responsibility, and the work ethic (Kinder & Sears, 1981). The modern racism scale (McConahay & Hough, 1976) was developed to measure this dimension and has tended to be highly correlated with measures of traditional racism yet factorially distinct from them (McConahay, 1986;

Sears, van Laar, Carillo, & Kosterman, 1997). Numerous studies have found that the modern racism scale is a markedly more powerful predictor of whites' racial policy preferences and candidate preferences in racialized election campaigns than measures of traditional racism, political preference, or conservative ideology (Kinder & Sanders, 1996; Kinder & Sears, 1981; Sears et al., 1997).

The second approach to the new racism was subsequently developed by Pettigrew and Meertens (1995), who constructed a set of scales to measure constructs very similar to symbolic and traditional racism, which they have used extensively in European countries to measure prejudice against local minorities and outgroups. Their first component, "blatant prejudice," was assessed by subscales of "threat" and "rejection" and seems essentially equivalent to traditional racism. Their second component, "subtle prejudice," was assessed by three subscales of "defense of traditional values," "exaggeration of cultural differences," and "lack of positive affect" and is clearly similar to symbolic racism.

Third, Katz and Hass (1988) took the new-versus-old racism distinction a step further by suggesting that white Americans' racial attitudes could involve not just a new symbolic or subtle racism but also racial ambivalence. Their findings suggested that many whites could simultaneously hold antiblack and problack attitudes, and the resulting ambivalence could account for highly polarized responses to blacks, with "desirable" behavior by blacks eliciting particularly positive responses and "undesirable" behavior eliciting particularly negative and discriminatory responses (see Katz, Cohen, & Glass, 1975).

The fourth approach, which has been termed that of aversive racism, also emphasizes ambivalence in American whites' attitudes to blacks, though in a somewhat different form (Dovidio et al., 1996; Gaertner & Dovidio, 1986). It proposes that most whites acquire egalitarian beliefs and a nonprejudiced self-image at a conscious level. At the same time, however, their exposure to a society characterized by black-white differentiation and inequality generates underlying covert negative feelings to blacks. This ambivalence results in whites generally behaving in an overtly nondiscriminatory manner towards blacks in order to preserve their nonprejudiced self-images, while also behaving in a discriminatory manner in more ambiguous situations where the discrimination can be rationalized away or excused.

The concept of new racisms has not been without controversy. Critics have asserted that symbolic racism has been conceptualized and measured inconsistently over time and that the varying themes identified with it have not yet been coherently articulated or adequately measured (Sniderman & Tetlock, 1986; Stoker, 1998). The various facets associated with subtle prejudice (Pettigrew & Meertens, 1995), modern and symbolic racism (Kinder & Sears, 1981), and the racial resentments identified by Kinder and Sanders (1996) do indeed suggest that the construct may be more complex and multifaceted than is represented by existing measures and conceptualizations. It will be suggested later that this complexity can be more adequately captured by a two-dimensional typology of prejudices.

Implicit and Explicit Prejudice

The findings showing that avowedly nonracist persons would readily discriminate against blacks whenever the discriminatory behavior could be excused (Gaertner & Dovidio, 1986) have also led to research distinguishing implicit and explicit stereotyping and prejudice (Greenwald & Banaji, 1995). Explicit measures of prejudice and stereotyping, such as measures of modern or traditional racism, operate at a conscious level, while implicit measures are assumed to operate in an unconscious and automatic fashion.

A variety of implicit measures have been used. Some are indirect or covert behavioral indices of prejudice, such as linguistic biases (Maass, 1999), eye contact (Weitz, 1972), or nonverbal behaviors (Brown, Dovidio, & Ellyson, 1990), which could be subject to intentional control but typically would not be. Others are truly implicit measures of automatic cognitive or physiological responses that cannot readily be intentionally controlled. The most common have been measures of response latency for the activation of positive or negative stereotypes following category priming (Blair & Banaji, 1996; Dovidio, Evans, & Tylor, 1986; Gilbert & Hixon, 1991) and variations of that procedure, such as the Implicit Association Test (IAT; Greenwald, McGhee, & Schwartz, 1998).

While it has often been assumed that implicit measures might provide more accurate information about peoples' real attitudes, the findings have suggested a more complex picture, which is still not well understood. Generally whites have shown markedly greater negativity to blacks on implicit measures of racism than they do on explicit measures (Dovidio & Gaertner, 1993). However, the problem has been that different measures of implicit stereotyping and prejudice have typically been only weakly or not at all associated with each other and explicit measures of prejudice or behavioral indices of discrimination (Dovidio et al., 1996; Greenwald et al., 1998; Karpinski & Hilton, 2001; Maass et al., 2000). Intriguingly, physiological indices of negative or positive affect, which are the most implicit measures of all, have shown virtually no association with other indices of prejudice or discrimination (Maass et al., 2000).

One possible reason for the discrepancies between implicit and explicit measures is that they might reflect different response systems. Dovidio and colleagues (1996) have shown that automatically activated implicit evaluative stereotypes do predict people's spontaneous interracial reactions (such as eye contact and rate of blinking) but not more deliberative, controlled interracial judgments or behaviors (interview evaluations or judgments of guilt). Explicit prejudice measures such as the modern racism scale, on the other hand, predicted deliberative responses but not spontaneous reactions.

Dovidio and colleagues' (1996) findings were obtained using a priming task to measure implicit prejudice. Studies with the more widely used IAT seem to have been less successful in predicting any kind of behavioral outcomes (see, e.g., Karpinski & Hilton, 2001), suggesting that its validity might need further investigation (Devine, 2001).

A second possible reason for discrepancies between implicit and explicit attitude measures is that social norms prohibiting prejudice against particular groups might be responsible for the discrepancies between explicit and implicit racism measures. In support of this, Franco and Maass (1999) found that measures of implicit and explicit prejudice were uncorrelated when the target group was one for which prejudice was not socially acceptable (Jews) but significantly correlated when the target group was Islamic fundamentalists, against whom prejudice seemed more socially acceptable. However, the effects in this study were relatively weak, and social norms concerning prejudice were not measured but merely inferred. Moreover, Karpinski and Hilton (2001) have shown that implicit and explicit attitudes to a variety of targets were uncorrelated when social desirability was clearly not an issue.

Two theories suggest that discrepancies between explicit and implicit prejudice could arise not from external norms but from internal value-based motives to control automatically activated prejudices, though the values and motives proposed are somewhat different. Aversive racism theory suggests that many whites do have underlying, covert racist attitudes but adopt and express egalitarian attitudes at an overt level in order to maintain a self-image of themselves as nonprejudiced and egalitarian (Gaertner & Dovidio, 1986). Because of their covert racism, they will act in discriminatory ways in situations in which they can rationalize or excuse it, and will do so without guilt. Devine's (1989) theory suggests that all whites acquire negative stereotypes and affect toward blacks during socialization. Later some whites come to internalize explicitly antiracist values and nonprejudiced attitudes, which are genuine and deeply held. As a result, their underlying and automatically activated prejudiced reactions engender guilt and are therefore inhibited whenever they are under conscious control.

These theories have assumed that implicit prejudice and stereotypes are relatively stable evaluative orientations that are automatically activated in the presence of stigmatized group members (Devine, 2001). However, a good deal of evidence has now accumulated that challenges this. It has been shown that implicit prejudices, particularly as measured by the IAT, seem to be highly malleable and fluid and vary markedly in response to situational cues and motivational influences (e.g., Blair, Ma, & Lenton, 2001; Dasgupta & Greenwald, 2001; Karpinski & Hilton, 2001; Rudman, Ashmore, & Gary, 2001). Karpinski and Hilton (2001) have therefore suggested that implicit attitudes reflect the evaluative associations with outgroups that people have been exposed to in their environment, and not the degree to which they endorse these associations. Implicit racism would thus indicate exposure to an environment in which positive information was associated with whites and less positive information with blacks. One extrapolation from this is that because these "implicit" associations have not been consciously articulated, organized, and anchored in "explicit" form, the actual pattern of evaluative outgroup associations that are elicited may be markedly influenced by the nature of the activating cues, procedures, and situation. This could account for the malleability of implicit prejudice across situations and measuring techniques, and the weak or effectively zero correlations between different implicit measures, and between them and explicit measures of prejudice.

In general, the significance of implicit prejudice and stereotypes in understanding prejudice still has to be clearly demonstrated. Current theory (e.g., Devine, 1989) and research (e.g., Dovidio et al., 1996) suggest that these implicit responses may well be significant determinants of people's spontaneous reactions to outgroup persons in interpersonal situations, and that these may be quite inconsistent with their more considered and explicit emotional, cognitive, and behavioral responses to outgroups. It seems possible that these implicit attitudes might largely reflect the kind of evaluative associations with outgroups that people have been exposed to in their social environments in the past that are being cued in a particular situation.

Typologies of Prejudices

In addition to the symbolic-traditional racism distinction, several other kinds of explicit prejudice or racism have been proposed. For example, van den Berghe (1967) differentiated paternalistic from traditional racism. In paternalistic racism, whites do not dislike blacks and may even have positive feelings toward them but stereotype them as inferior, dependent, and childlike. Glick and Fiske (2001) have shown that the concept of paternalistic prejudice is also useful for understanding gender relations and sexism (see also Jackman, 1994). Second, Bettelheim and Janowitz (1964) suggested that the prejudice directed at high-status groups such as Jews would be colored by superego concerns such as resentment and envy deriving from one's own failure to succeed. This envious and resentful prejudice would differ from the "traditional racism" directed at low-status groups, such as American blacks, which would derive from id projections and be colored by contempt and disgust.

Several more comprehensive and systematic typologies have been based on the observation by Fiske and colleagues (1999) that there seem to be two distinct dimensions of prejudiced attitudes: one dimension of disliking versus liking and another of disrespecting versus respecting. This distinction is consistent with the evidence already noted that these two dimensions are expressed in stereotype evaluation (beneficence or warmth stereotypes for liking, and competence stereotypes for respecting), intergroup affect (negative affect for disliking and low positive affect for disrespecting), and intergroup discriminatory behavior (aversive racism for disliking and dominative racism for disrespecting).

It has also been suggested that these two intergroup attitude dimensions can be seen as expressions of two basic kinds of intergroup categorization schemas, that is, ways of differentiating "us" from "them," that are intrinsically associated with prejudice (Duckitt, 2001). In one case the social world is categorized into "us" who are good, decent, moral people versus "them" who are bad, disruptive, and immoral. In the second, the social world is categorized into "us" who are superior, competent, strong, and dominant (or should rightfully be dominant) and "them" who are inferior, incompetent, and weak. These two intergroup categorization schema dimensions and their corresponding stereotype, affective, behavioral, and overall attitudinal expressions are summarized in table 16.1.

Glick and Fiske (2001) have shown how crossing the two stereotype dimensions of high versus low warmth (also termed beneficence or morality) and high versus low competence produces a fourfold typology of outgroup attitudes. These four kinds of outgroup attitude are outgroup admiration (outgroup seen as competent and warm), envious prejudice (outgroup seen as competent but not warm), contemptuous prejudice (outgroup seen as not warm and incompetent), and paternalistic prejudice (outgroup seen as warm but incompetent).

It has been proposed that this typology could also be based on the two categorization schema dimensions (good versus bad and superior versus inferior) corresponding to these two stereotype dimensions (Duckitt, 2001). This would suggest an important addition to the typology. While two levels seem adequate to model the "good" versus "bad" groups' categorization schema dimension, the second categorization schema dimension of "supe-

Table 16.1
Two Intergroup Categorization Schema Dimensions and Their Corresponding Stereotype, Affective, Behavioral, and Overall Attitudinal Expressions

Intergroup categorization schema dimensions	Evaluative stereotypes	Intergroup affect or feelings	Intergroup behavior	Overall intergroup orientation
Good (supportive) versus bad (threatening)	High versus low beneficence (morality) traits	Low versus high negative affect (anger, fear, anxiety)	Aversive, "hot" discrimination and racism	Intergroup liking versus disliking
Superior (dominant) versus inferior (subordinate)	High versus low competence traits	High versus low positive affect (admiration, respect versus disdain)	Dominative, "cold" discrimination and racism	Intergroup respecting versus disrespecting

rior" versus "inferior" groups seems to require a third intermediate category of groups as "equal."

This expanded typology, which is shown in table 16.2, therefore adds two important kinds of intergroup attitude to those suggested by Glick and Fiske. First, the combination of categorizing outgroups as equal and good would define an outgroup attitude of tolerance, or genuine nonprejudice. Second, the combination of categorizing outgroups as equal but bad (threatening) would define hostile prejudice, which would be the typical pattern for threat-driven outgroup hostility against competing outgroups that are relatively equal in status and power (see Sherif & Sherif, 1953).

The two kinds of intergroup attitude derived from crossing the level of "superior" with "good" and "bad" groups would most typically involve the attitudes of subordinate to dominant groups. Glick and Fiske (2001) in their typology described these outgroup attitudes as "outgroup admiration" and "envious prejudice," respectively. Outgroup admiration would be directed toward groups that are seen as higher status, more powerful, and legitimately advantaged compared to one's own group, which would typically be expressed in outgroup favoritism.

The kind of prejudice directed against groups categorized as "bad" (threatening) and "superior" would seem better described as resentful prejudice than Glick and Fiske's envious prejudice, for several reasons. Since such groups are seen as "bad," their "superiority" would typically be seen as illegitimate, violating norms and values of equity and justice, for which resentment seems a more typical reaction than envy. This resentful prejudice would be associated with relative deprivation and could be experienced by

Table 16.2
Two Intergroup Categorization Schemas as Dual Dimensions Defining a Sixfold Typology of Outgroup Attitudes

Superior versus inferior group categorization	Good versus bad group categorization	
	Good (supportive)	**Bad** (threatening)
Superior (dominant)		
Outgroup attitude	Outgroup preference	Resentful prejudice
Outgroup image	Advanced	Unfairly privileged
Behavior to outgroup	Deferential	Antagonistic
Equal		
Outgroup attitude	Tolerance	Hostile prejudice
Outgroup image	Friendly (ally)	Threatening (enemy)
Behavior to outgroup	Accepting	Conflict/avoidance
Inferior (subordinate)		
Outgroup attitude	Paternalistic prejudice	Contemptuous prejudice
Outgroup image	Dependent	Inferior and threatening
Behavior to outgroup	Patronising	Domination/exclusion

subordinate groups against dominant groups, or by insecure dominant groups against powerful subordinate groups making gains at their expense.

Finally, the two categories of "inferior and good" and "inferior and bad" will be seen as characteristic of groups that are socially subordinate and low in status and power. Contemptuous prejudice is directed against groups classified as "inferior and bad" who are disliked and derogated, which seems equivalent to the American pattern of traditional racism. Groups seen as "inferior and good" are disrespected but liked, with the pattern being one of paternalistic prejudice.

This sixfold typology would seem to accommodate most of the kinds of prejudice that have been distinguished, though symbolic or modern racism seems likely to encompass several different kinds of prejudice, each of which might characterize different white subgroups. Thus hostile prejudice might be most characteristic of conservative middle-class whites and would derive from the perception of blacks not as inferior (i.e., therefore as being "equal") but as threatening and violating important conservative and Protestant ethic values and therefore as "bad." Resentful prejudice might be more characteristic of working-class and southern whites and involve resentment of advantages or gains by blacks that are seen as unfair and unjust (i.e., blacks seen as advantaged and therefore "superior" in that sense, but "bad"). And finally, paternalistic prejudice might be characteristic of liberal middle-class whites. This could involve feelings that blacks have been discriminated against and unjustly treated and are therefore deserving ("good" and "liked") but are low in social status and achievement and just can't seem to make it without help and supportive policies (therefore "inferior" and "disrespected").

▲ Two Approaches to Explaining Prejudice and Intergroup Conflict

Two broad approaches have dominated inquiry into the causes of prejudice and intergroup hostility. One approach has viewed intergroup hostility as an attitude held by individuals, while the other has seen it as a group or intergroup phenomenon. Both have important empirical bases.

Numerous studies have shown that persons who are relatively unfavorable to one outgroup or minority tend to be relatively less favorable to others as well, irrespective of the characteristics of these outgroups or their relationship to the ingroup. As a result, attitudes toward completely different outgroups and even fictitious ones tend to be strongly positively correlated (Altemeyer, 1988; Bierly, 1985; Duckitt, 1992; Hartley, 1946). This "generality of prejudice" suggests that there are stable characteristics of individuals that make them more or less prone to adopt and hold prejudiced intergroup attitudes in general. This approach has generated theories focusing on individual differences in prejudice and explaining prejudice as an attitude acquired and held by individuals.

On the other hand, group and intergroup approaches to prejudice are supported by the socially consensual and patterned nature of prejudice within sociocultural groups. This suggests that intergroup hostility derives from the nature of the relationships between social groups, causing particular groups to hold widely shared negative attitudes to particular outgroups or minorities but not to others.

These two approaches to explaining prejudice, the individual and the intergroup, will be considered in the next two sections. This will be followed by discussion of a model that attempts to integrate the two approaches into a more comprehensive explanation of prejudice.

▲ Individual Explanations of Prejudice

One approach to how individuals acquire and adopt prejudiced intergroup attitudes simply assumes that these attitudes are learned like other attitudes during socialization, and then modified through contact experiences with outgroup members. Two other prominent theories, the authoritarian personality and social dominance orientation approaches, focus on characteristics that are presumed to make individuals particularly disposed to prejudice and intergroup hostility.

Socialization and the Learning of Prejudice

It is widely assumed that during socialization, individuals' intergroup attitudes are learned and modified by their exposure to the attitudes held to these groups by significant others in their milieu, their exposure to positive and negative information about these groups, and the nature of their personal contact experiences with outgroup members (see Ashmore & DelBoca, 1976; Harding, Proshansky, Kutner, & Chein, 1969; Simpson & Yinger, 1985). Allport (1954) suggested that this learning would be mainly indirect, through observation, inference, and experience rather than through direct instruction and reinforcement. Thus prejudice would be "caught" rather than "taught." This seems similar to the more recent suggestion by Karpinski and Hilton (2001) that implicit intergroup attitudes would reflect the kind of intergroup associations people would have been exposed to in their social environments.

Contact theory has focused on the kind of personal contact with outgroup members that would reduce prejudice, that is, contact that was equal status, cooperative, rewarding, and individuating with institutional support and that led to friendship with outgroup members (Allport, 1954; Pettigrew, 1998a). The converse also holds. Prejudice would be caused or increased by contact experiences that were competitive, unrewarding, and institution-ally discouraged, that made intergroup distinctions more salient, that inhib-ited friendship formation with outgroup members, and where the outgroups were of lower status.

Devine's (1989) theory of automatic and controlled stereotypes pro-poses that indirect learning during socialization can result in the acquisition of negative outgroup stereotypes that will then be automatically elicited when the particular group categorization becomes salient. Wilson, Lindzey, and Schooler's (2000) theory of dual attitudes also suggests that indirect learning through observation and experience would be the basis of implicit and automatically activated intergroup attitudes that might be quite differ-ent from, and even contrary to, explicit and more consciously formed and held intergroup attitudes. These explicit intergroup attitudes seem likely to be derived from the later conscious learning of values and ideological beliefs that might contradict implicit intergroup attitudes formed during earlier socialization. Both the authoritarian personality and social dominance ori-entation perspectives, which involve consciously held ideological attitudes and values, seem relevant to the formation of these explicit intergroup at-titudes.

The Authoritarian "Personality" and Prejudice

Adorno, Frenkel-Brunswick, Levinson, and Sanford's (1950) theory of the authoritarian personality originated from their finding that anti-Semitic at-titudes were not held in isolation but formed part of a broader syndrome of social attitudes involving generalized prejudice against outgroups and minorities, ethnocentric ingroup glorification, politicoeconomic conserva-tism, and profascist attitudes. They viewed this attitudinal syndrome as an expression of a basic personality dimension, consisting of nine covarying traits, which they termed the authoritarian personality. Their F scale, with items such "Obedience and respect for authority are the most important virtues children should learn," was developed to measure this personality dimension. The theory proposed that authoritarian personalities were char-acterized by repressed feelings of resentment and hostility originating from punitive parental socialization that were displaced onto outgroups and mi-norities whose dislike seemed sanctioned by conventional authority.

This theory and the F scale attracted enormous interest initially. By the early 1960s, however, interest in the approach had waned. First, empirical evidence had not supported the psychoanalytic mechanisms proposed to underlie authoritarian personalities and their social attitudes (Altemeyer, 1981; Duckitt, 1992). Second, the F scale was shown to have serious psy-chometric flaws, which largely derived from its lack of reliability and uni-dimensionality when acquiescent bias due to the all-positive formulation of its items was controlled. As Altemeyer (1981) later showed, it appeared to be measuring several poorly related factors.

Several decades later, however, the idea of an authoritarian personality was revived. On the basis of extensive research, Altemeyer (1981) found that three of the original nine facets of authoritarianism described by Adorno and colleagues (1950), that is, conventionalism, authoritarian aggression, and authoritarian submission, did covary strongly to form a unitary dimension. He therefore developed his Right-Wing Authoritarianism (RWA) Scale to measure this dimension.

Subsequent research by Altemeyer (1981, 1988, 1998) and others (see Stone, Lederer, & Christie, 1993) has shown that the RWA scale is a unidimensional and reliable psychometric measure. It powerfully predicts a wide range of political, social, ideological, and intergroup phenomena, as well as generalized prejudice and chauvinistic ethnocentrism. Later research by Altemeyer (1988, 1998) suggested that authoritarian personalities' hostile and punitive attitudes to outgroups and minorities might be due to their having been socialized to see the social world as a dangerous and threatening place. In support of this, other investigations have also shown significant associations between authoritarianism and threat (e.g., Doty, Peterson, & Winter, 1991; Feldman & Stenner, 1997; Sales, 1973; Sales & Friend, 1973).

Social Dominance Orientation and Prejudice

During the 1990s an important new perspective on group conflict and ethnocentrism emerged. Social dominance theory suggested that societies minimize group conflict by promoting consensual ideologies that legitimize social and intergroup inequality and discrimination (Pratto, Sidanius, Stallworth, & Malle, 1994; Sidanius & Pratto, 1993, 1999). The theory proposed an individual difference dimension, social dominance orientation (SDO), measured by the SDO scale, which would cause individuals to adopt and hold prejudiced and ethnocentric attitudes toward minorities and stigmatised outgroups. Pratto and colleagues (1994) described SDO as a "general attitudinal orientation toward intergroup relations, reflecting whether one generally prefers such relations to be equal, versus hierarchical" and the "extent to which one desires that one's ingroup dominate and be superior to outgroups" (p. 742).

Research with the SDO scale has shown that it powerfully predicts a range of sociopolitical and intergroup phenomena very similar to that predicted by the RWA scale. Despite this, the two scales seem relatively independent, often being nonsignificantly or only weakly correlated with each other (Altemeyer, 1998; McFarland, 1998; McFarland & Adelson, 1996). Thus both scales powerfully predict prejudice and ethnocentrism independently of each other and together account for a substantial proportion of the variance in generalized prejudice (Altemeyer, 1998; Pratto et al., 1994; Sidanius, Pratto, & Bobo, 1994).

The predominant role of RWA and SDO as individual difference predictors of prejudice was confirmed in a series of studies that found no other psychological individual difference variables added notably to the proportion of variance in generalized prejudice explained by RWA and SDO (Altemeyer, 1998; McFarland, 1998; McFarland & Adelson, 1996). Altemeyer (1998) has noted that the RWA and SDO scales seem to relate to different sets of the original nine "trait" clusters listed by Adorno and colleagues (1950) and therefore concluded that these two scales measure two different kinds of authoritarian personality (the "submissive" and the "dominant"), with both determining basic dispositions to generalized prejudice and ethnocentrism.

RWA and SDO as Personality or Social Attitudes

Altemeyer's conclusion has been criticized, however, and it has been pointed out that both the RWA and SDO scales seem more appropriately viewed as measuring social attitude or ideological belief dimensions rather than personality (Duckitt, 2001). Thus commentators have frequently pointed out that the items of the RWA scale, and its predecessor, the F scale, pertain not to personality traits and behavior but to social attitudes and beliefs of a broadly ideological nature (Feldman & Stenner, 1997; Goertzel, 1987; Saucier, 2000; Stone, Lederer, & Christie, 1993, p. 232). The items of the SDO scale also consist of statements of social attitude and belief, and Pratto (1994) have usually described the SDO scale as a measure of enduring beliefs.

The view of the RWA and SDO scales as measuring social or ideological attitudes was supported by a review of research showing that investigations of the structure of sociopolitical attitudes and sociocultural values have typically revealed two roughly orthogonal dimensions, with one corresponding closely to RWA and the other to SDO (Duckitt, 2001, see table 3). Investigators have usually labeled the RWA-like dimension as social conservatism, traditionalism, or collectivism versus personal freedom, openness, or individualism, and the SDO-like dimension as economic conservatism, belief in inequality, or power distance versus social welfare, egalitarianism, or humanitarianism. Moreover, the social conservatism dimension of social attitudes, when reliably measured, has correlated powerfully with the RWA scale and scaled with it as a single general factor or dimension (Forsyth, 1980; Raden, 1999; Saucier, 2000). For example, Saucier (2000), in a large-scale study of social attitudes, obtained a correlation of .77 between the RWA scale and a well-established attitudinal measure of social conservatism. The RWA scale and its predecessor, the F scale, have also been shown to be highly reactive to situational threat manipulations (Altemeyer, 1988; Duckitt & Fisher, in press; Sales & Friend, 1973), which again suggests that these scales are measures of social attitudes rather than personality.

If RWA and SDO are measures of two social or ideological attitude and value dimensions, this raises the questions of what the personality or psychological bases of these two dimensions are, and why and how these two dimensions influence generalized prejudice.

A Cognitive-Motivational Model of Personality, Ideology, and Prejudice

A model has been suggested in which the two basic dimensions of social or ideological attitudes measured by the RWA and SDO scales are viewed as expressing motivational goals that have been made salient or activated for individuals, both by their social worldviews, that is, their beliefs about the nature of their social environments, and by their personalities (Duckitt, 2000, 2001). According to this model, high RWA would express the motivational goal of social cohesion (as a way of establishing stability, control, and security), activated by a view of the social world as dangerous and threatening (measured by agreement with items such as: "We live in a dangerous society, in which good, decent, and moral people's values and way of life are threatened and disrupted by bad people"). The causal personality dimension would be that of social conformity versus autonomy (i.e., traits such as "obedient" and "respectful" versus "nonconforming" and "rebellious"). Being higher in dispositional social conformity would create a greater readiness for individuals to perceive threats to the existing social order and see the social world as dangerous and threatening. High social conformity would also have a direct impact on authoritarian attitudes by making the motivational goal of social control, security, and stability more salient for the individual.

In the case of SDO, the model proposes that the underlying personality dimension is that of tough versus tendermindedness, characterized by the opposing traits of being hard, tough, ruthless, and unfeeling to others, as opposed to compassionate, generous, caring, and altruistic. Toughminded personalities would tend to adopt a view of the world as a ruthlessly competitive jungle in which the strong win and the weak lose (measured by agreement with items such as: "It's a dog-eat-dog world where you have to be ruthless at times"). This view of the world would activate the motivational goals of power, dominance, and superiority over others, which would be expressed in high SDO.

These two worldviews, one of a dangerous threatening world and the other of a competitive-jungle world, would also be powerfully influenced by individuals' real social situations, as well as by their personalities. Thus dangerous, threatening social situations would increase authoritarianism through influencing individuals to adopt a corresponding worldview, while social situations that really are competitive jungles will impact on social dominance ideological attitudes through influencing individuals to adopt a competitive-jungle worldview. The causal model of personality, social situation, worldview, ideological attitudes and prejudice is summarized in figure 16.1 (see also Duckitt, 2001). As the model indicates, the influence of

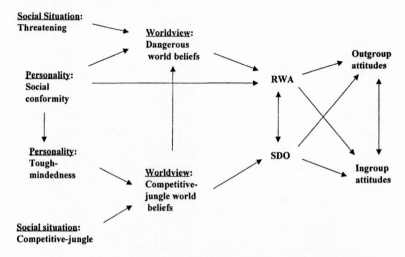

Figure 16.1. A causal model of the impact of personality, social situation, and worldview on the two ideological attitude dimensions of right-wing authoritarianism (RWA) and social dominance orientation (SDO) and their impact on intergroup attitudes

personality, the social situation, and individuals' worldviews on prejudice are indirect being entirely mediated through their impact on the two ideological attitude dimensions of RWA and SDO.

Recent research has supported the model. Three studies showed that the personality dimensions of social conformity and toughmindedness could be reliably measured and related as expected to ideological attitudes (Duckitt, 2001, study 1). Social conformity was strongly correlated with RWA but not with SDO, while toughmindedness was correlated with SDO but not with RWA. Second, four studies using structural equation modeling with latent variables showed excellent overall fit for the model of the causal relationships proposed between the two personality, two worldview, two ideological attitude dimensions with each other and with intergroup attitudes for large samples in New Zealand, South Africa, and the United States (Duckitt, 2001; Duckitt, Wagner, du Plessis, & Birum, in press). These studies confirmed all the causal paths proposed by the model, except for an originally suggested direct path from toughmindedness to SDO, which was then dropped from the model and is therefore not shown in figure 16.1.

This model has several implications. One is that these two ideological attitude dimensions concern conscious beliefs and values and would therefore influence explicit prejudice primarily. A second is that RWA and SDO express two motivational goals that have been made salient for individuals, that is, threat-driven cohesion-security and competitively driven dominance-superiority, respectively. This suggests that the impact of RWA on prejudice would be driven by group cohesion-security motivation, and directed primarily at groups seen as threatening or disrupting the stability, survival, and cohesion of the ingroup or society. The perception of outgroups as threatening seems likely to activate the intergroup categorization schema of "them" as bad, dangerous, and immoral versus "us" as good, decent, and moral and therefore evaluation on the disliking-liking intergroup attitude dimensions specifically. Thus threatening outgroups would be seen primarily as bad or evil and therefore disliked but would not necessarily be seen as less competent or inferior and disrespected.

The impact of SDO on prejudice would be driven by competitive desires to maintain or establish dominance and superiority over outgroups, and directed primarily to outgroups who it is believed are or should be inferior to the ingroup in power and status. Since it is believed that these groups are or should legitimately be inferior to the ingroup in power and status, this seems likely to activate the intergroup categorization schema of "them" as less worthy, less deserving, and less competent than "us" and therefore evaluation on the disrespecting-respecting intergroup attitude dimension specifically. Thus the competitively motivated desire to establish or maintain justified dominance over an outgroup that is seen as legitimately inferior to the ingroup should be primarily associated with that outgroup being disrespected, though not necessarily disliked.

These implications suggest it might be possible to integrate individual difference and intergroup dynamic approaches to explaining prejudice into a common motivational framework. This will be considered when intergroup approaches to explaining prejudice have been discussed.

◣ Intergroup Explanations of Prejudice

Four major approaches seem able to explain what kind of intergroup relationships or conditions of contact and interaction between groups generate widely shared negative attitudes to certain outgroups and not to others within particular societies. One focuses on social and intergroup conditions that make particular intergroup categorizations or differentiations highly and pervasively salient, a second on intergroup competition, a third on intergroup threat, and a fourth on intergroup inequalities in power and status.

Salient Intergroup Distinctions

Salient group or intergroup categorizations are a prerequisite for the activation and expression of group or intergroup attitudes. This raises two questions. First, what social and intergroup conditions make group or intergroup differentiation salient and pervasive in social situations? Second, do highly salient and pervasive group differentiations in themselves generate outgroup prejudice, or do they merely create social circumstances that facilitate the emergence of prejudice?

Social psychologists have given relatively little attention to the issue of what social conditions make particular social categorizations highly and pervasively salient across a wide range of settings. Brewer and Miller (1984), in one of the few discussions of the issue, note several factors that would accentuate group differentiations, such as convergent group boundaries, differential group treatment, intergroup conflict and competition, and group inequality in power and status.

When groups are characterized by convergent boundaries—the coincidence of many possible distinctions, such as language, religion, social class, urban or rural residence, political affiliation, and so forth—and social category membership is therefore multiply determined, it makes the probability high that at least one cue to category identity would be salient in any given situation. When group boundaries are not convergent, individuals should find themselves belonging to different groups on some criteria but the same group on other criteria. LeVine and Campbell (1972) have noted how the crosscutting of category memberships and group loyalties reduced internal conflict in tribal societies, while experimentally created crosscutting categorizations have been shown to reduce intergroup bias and discrimination (Deschamps & Doise, 1978; Vanbeselaere, 1987). Experimental studies have also shown how creating superordinate identities and recategorizing intergroup into intragroup distinctions can reduce intergroup biases (Dovidio, Gaertner, & Validzic, 1998).

The extent to which different categories or groups of persons are subject to differential treatment, particularly by social or institutional agencies, seems to be highly significant in creating and reinforcing group identities and accentuating intergroup differentiation. This has been shown in experimental studies using artificial and real groups (Brewer & Brown, 1998; Rabbie & Horwitz, 1969) and documented in naturalistic situations. For example, Chirot (2001) has noted how differential treatment by the colonial power in Rwanda transformed Hutu and Tutsi from two thoroughly intertwined groups sharing the same language, culture, and institutions, who rarely differentiated between each other, into two highly differentiated and virtually segregated ethnicities, with ultimately catastrophic consequences.

And finally, Brewer and Miller (1984) noted two factors that markedly accentuate the salience of intergroup distinctions: direct competition and conflict between groups and intergroup inequality in power and status. However, these two factors not only make group distinctions more salient but also seem to be direct determinants of intergroup prejudice and hostility. A discussion of their role will therefore be deferred while it is considered whether highly salient and pervasive group distinctions in themselves generate outgroup prejudice or merely create circumstances facilitating the emergence of prejudice.

The idea that salient group distinctions may themselves generate prejudice would be consistent with Sumner's (1906) classic concept of ethnocentrism, which proposed that group differentiation inevitably generates ingroup attachment and outgroup hostility, and with more recent findings by social identity theorists showing that any kind of salient group categorization generates bias and discrimination in favor of the ingroup and against the outgroup (Brewer, 1979; Wilder, 1986). Subsequent research has indicated, however, that the bias and discrimination triggered by mere categorization in minimal group situations seems to involve enhanced evaluation of and identification with the ingroup and not outgroup negativity or derogation (Brewer, 1979; Brown, 2000).

Moreover, measures of ingroup identification in either minimal or naturalistic groups have shown relatively weak and inconsistent associations with outgroup negativity (Brown, 2000; Hinkle & Brown, 1990). Several studies indicate that group identification seems to be associated with outgroup prejudice only when other conditions are present, such as intergroup threat and competition (Brown, Hinkle, Ely, Fox-Cardamone, Maras, & Taylor, 1992; Duckitt & Mphuthing, 1998; Struch & Schwartz, 1989). Naturalistic examples are also readily available of intergroup situations where group distinctions are convergent and salient but intergroup attitudes are tolerant, as seems to be the case for the Italian, French, and German minorities in Switzerland (Willemsen & van Oudenhoven, 1989).

These findings suggest that highly salient intergroup differentiations might not cause prejudice themselves but might create particularly fertile conditions for more direct causes of prejudice to generate hostility and conflict. Thus, when intergroup distinctions are highly salient and pervasive, relatively trivial intergroup threats and apparently minor inequalities in power and status may readily become infused with significance and hostility. On the other hand, when intergroup distinctions are not salient, as is often the case for social class distinctions, potentially threatening intergroup circumstances and quite substantial intergroup inequalities may simply be disregarded or viewed as unimportant.

Intergroup Competition

A great deal of evidence shows that direct competition between groups over almost any issue rapidly elicits markedly hostile intergroup perceptions and attitudes. Realistic conflict theory has focused on intergroup competition over "real" issues of power or resources (Sherif & Sherif, 1953), while social identity theory has focused on "social" competition over relative prestige and status (Tajfel & Turner, 1979).

The role of real competition was demonstrated in a series of dramatic field experiments by Sherif and Sherif (1953) using boys' summer camps. When two boys' camps began competing with each other in a sporting tournament, intergroup hostility rapidly developed between them and at times escalated into open conflict. When the two groups were given a common superordinate goal that they had to cooperate to achieve, this hostility was largely defused. These findings have been extensively replicated over a variety of settings and groups (Blake & Mouton, 1979; Brown, Maras, Masser, Vivian, & Hewstone, 2001; Diab, 1970). Simpson and Yinger (1985) also provide many examples of how the emergence of direct conflict or competition between nations over political or economic issues was rapidly followed by hostile intergroup attitudes and perceptions.

Social identity theory proposes that when an intergroup distinction becomes salient, it activates a motivated tendency to positively differentiate ingroup from outgroup or to establish a positive group identity (Tajfel & Turner, 1979). In minimal groups this desire to achieve a positive social identity for ingroup relative to outgroup seems to produce ingroup bias and discrimination that involves only ingroup enhancement and not outgroup derogation or dislike. However, the underlying competitive orientation that this involves seems to easily escalate into open and direct competition over relative status and prestige between groups, particularly when group distinctions are highly salient. Such direct competition over status and prestige seems able to generate outgroup negativity in the absence of any "realistic" bases for competition. Sherif's own experiments appear to support this. First, it has been noted that even before a sporting tournament had been organized between the two camps, the boys "eagerly challenged each other to competitive sports, each confident of their own victory" (Sherif & Sherif, 1969, p. 239). Second, the competition between the boys' camps was not about power or resources but purely over the prestige of winning and not losing—yet was capable of generating intense intergroup hostility.

A question that has not received much attention is that of exactly how intergroup competition generates outgroup negativity. One possibility, which is discussed in the next section, is that competition typically involves the outgroup threatening the ingroups' likelihood of gaining a contested objective. Competition, however, can also involve the hope of gain rather than the fear of loss, or the desire to win and not to lose, as seems to have been the case at least initially for the boys in Sherif's experiments. Competition aims at establishing one group's superiority or dominance over the other, and this invariably generates the belief that the ingroup is indeed entitled to that superiority or dominance and the outgroup is inferior in comparison. Thus intergroup competition or conflict may elicit prejudice in two ways: first through the perception of the outgroup as threatening the ingroup, and second by eliciting a competitive desire to establish the ingroup's superiority that tends to generate an evaluation of the outgroup as relatively inferior, less worthy, less competent, or less deserving than the ingroup.

Intergroup Threat

There is a great deal of evidence to support the view that intergroup threat, or at least the perception of intergroup threat, is a powerful determinant of intergroup prejudice and hostility. Three kinds of intergroup threat have received particular attention in the literature: real threats to a group's resources, power, and well-being; symbolic threats to an ingroup's values, beliefs, and worldview; and threats to valued group identities.

LeVine and Campbell (1972) have noted that realistic conflict or competition between groups will generally involve each group posing a real threat to the resources and well-being of the other. This real threat, they suggest, will elicit hostility to the source of threat that should be proportional to its magnitude. The role of perceived threat from outgroups to a group's power, resources, and well-being has been extensively documented in numerous empirical studies (Blake & Mouton, 1979; Brown et al., 2001; Huddy & Sears, 1995; Struch & Schwartz, 1989).

Symbolic threats arise from intergroup differences in basic values, norms, and beliefs that seem to undermine or challenge a group's worldview. Two important theories have emphasized the role of symbolic threats in generating prejudice against outgroups with different basic beliefs and values. Rokeach's theory of belief congruence suggested that prejudice is fundamentally caused by real or assumed dissimilarity in beliefs (Rokeach, Smith, & Evans, 1960). Terror management theory proposes that peoples' cultural worldviews give them a sense of meaning and worth that protects and buffers them from the paralyzing existential anxiety that an awareness of human insignificance and mortality would otherwise create (Solomon, Greenberg, & Pyszczynski, 1991). When confronted by others who have different values, beliefs, and norms that threaten this worldview, people respond by derogating and rejecting these others.

There is a great deal of research showing that group dissimilarities are associated with prejudice. Rokeach and his colleagues demonstrated that dissimilarities in beliefs were more important than racial dissimilarity in generating rejection of others (Rokeach et al., 1960). De Ridder and Tripathi (1992) have shown that others who violate ingroup norms are disliked and rejected, and Esses, Haddock, and Zanna (1993) have shown that dissimilarities in basic values and symbolic beliefs generate outgroup dislike. Crosscultural and anthropological research has also shown strong associations between cultural dissimilarity and intergroup dislike (Brewer & Campbell, 1976; LeVine & Campbell 1972).

Social identity theorists have suggested that when a group's maintenance or establishment of a positive social identity is threatened by an outgroup, animosity or prejudice will be generated to that outgroup (Brown, 1995; Reynolds & Turner, 2001). For example, Brown (1995, see pp. 173–176) describes several studies in which hostile feelings were aroused to an outgroup when group members heard that the outgroup had disparaged their group's status or accomplishments. In naturalistic social situations, many commentators have noted that affronts to the prestige, status, and pride of national and ethnic groups have seemed more important in causing intergroup hostility than conflicts over realistic economic, political, and military interests (Chirot, 2001; see also chapter 15). Obvious examples have been the conflict between India and Pakistan over Kashmir and between Britain and Argentina over the Falklands. Social identity theorists have also focused particular attention on identity threats arising from intergroup status differentials or inequalities in group status and prestige (Tajfel & Turner, 1979), which will be discussed in the next section.

Overall, therefore, three kinds of intergroup threat seem powerfully associated with outgroup hostility and prejudice: "realistic" threat to groups' power, resources, and well-being, symbolic threats to groups' basic values and beliefs, and threats to groups' social identity. Threat not only seems to cause hostility to the outgroup that is viewed as the source of threat but also tends to make intergroup distinctions highly salient, and may be a critical factor in transforming "open" identities into "barricaded" or ethnocentric identities (Jowitt, 2001).

Intergroup Inequality

In naturalistic social groups, intergroup inequality in power and status seems to be consistently associated with negative intergroup attitudes, most commonly in the form of negative evaluations of and heightened social distance to the lower ranked group, but sometimes also in resentful hostility to a higher ranked group (Brewer & Campbell, 1976; Fiske et al., 1999; Hagendoorn, 1995; Poppe & Linssen, 1999). Intergroup inequality may generate conflicts of interests between higher and lower ranked groups, so that intergroup threat could account for some of the negative attitudes. However, negative evaluations of lower power or status group are common, even where no conflict of interests or threat exist, and seem to accompany any apparent group differences on socially valued dimensions, such as sophistication, education, living circumstances, appearance, skill, and achievement.

Several important theories have seen intergroup inequality as a fundamental cause of prejudice, either by causing prejudice directly or by generating intergroup threats that cause prejudice. In the former case, social dominance theory has focused on the role of system or inequality justification in causing prejudice, while in the latter case group position theory and social identity theory have focused on inequality generating intergroup threat.

Social dominance theory proposes that human beings have a basic disposition to establish and maintain group-based social hierarchies (Sidanius & Pratto, 1993, 1999). These group-based inequalities need to be legitimized to minimize social conflict, and this is done through creating consensual ideologies that justify the superiority of dominant over subordinate groups. Negative stereotypes and prejudiced attitudes to subordinate groups and more positive stereotypes and attitudes to dominant groups function as such "legitimizing myths" that explain and rationalize group inequality.

Sidanius and Pratto (1999) have extensively documented the ubiquity of group-based inequality and discrimination against socially subordinate groups in human societies. They and others have also shown that beliefs legitimizing these inequalities and favoring dominant group advantages are widely accepted by members of socially subordinate groups ("false consciousness"; see Jost & Banaji, 1994) as well as by dominants.

System or inequality justification can also be expressed in just-world beliefs, that is, the belief that the world is a just and predictable place where people generally get what they deserve and deserve what they get (Lerner, 1980). Thus people who have been victims of misfortune or groups that are disadvantaged, exploited, or oppressed may be derogated and seen as deserving their suffering. Crandall (1994), for example, has shown that just-world beliefs were associated with negative attitudes to fat people and blaming them for their situation.

Group position theory and social identity theory see intergroup inequality causing prejudice through either generating intergroup threat or in association with threat. Group position theory (Blumer, 1958; Bobo, 1999) was originally formulated to explain white American racial prejudice but clearly has broader applicability. This theory sees prejudice arising out of the relative status positions of groups in the social order. Members of dominant groups will have a sense of superiority toward subordinate groups, and adopt a belief that their superior group position entitles them to a relatively greater share of social goods and resources.

This sense of group position is transformed into prejudice against a subordinate group when dominant group members begin to perceive that members of the subordinate group are threatening and encroaching on their special entitlements and prerogatives. Little research has directly tested this theory, but there is evidence consistent with it indicating that violence against blacks in the United States and foreigners in Europe tends to be closely associated with lower status minorities or "outsiders" beginning to cross previously prohibited group boundaries or encroaching on the entitlements of a group higher in the social hierarchy (Green et al., 1999).

Social identity theory proposes that the existence of intergroup status differentials will tend to create social identity threat and therefore elicit antagonistic intergroup behavior and attitudes (Bettencourt, Dorr, Charlton, & Hume, 2001; Tajfel & Turner, 1979). Two sets of factors are assumed to influence the effect of status differentials on social identity threat. These are: first, the permeability of group boundaries, that is, how easy or difficult it is for individuals to leave the ingroup and become a member of the outgroup, and second, the legitimacy and stability of the intergroup status differential (Tajfel & Turner, 1979).

If intergroup boundaries are permeable, members of low-status groups should react to the threat of negative social identity by adopting a social mobility orientation rather than engaging in social competition with the higher status group. Thus, with permeable group boundaries, low-status group members would show little intergroup bias and discrimination against the higher status outgroup and instead would identify with it and aspire to move into it. Experimental studies by Ellemeers and her colleagues (Ellemers, van Knippenberg, de Vries, & Wilkie, 1988; Ellemers, van Knippenberg, & Wilkie, 1990) have shown that low-status groups do indeed show less outgroup bias and identify less with their ingroup when group boundaries are permeable as opposed to when they are impermeable.

When intergroup boundaries are relatively impermeable and social mobility is not an option, the stability and legitimacy of the intergroup status differential is expected to become significant. If the intergroup status differential is perceived to be stable and legitimate ("secure"), both higher and lower status groups should show little bias and discrimination against each other. The high-status group's advantage will not be threatened in any way, and the low-status group will not be able to conceive of "cognitive alternatives" to the existing status relationship. On the other hand, when the status differential is perceived to be unstable and illegitimate ("insecure"), both groups are expected to show much more bias and discrimination, with the high-status group trying to defend its threatened positive identity and the lower status group trying to enhance its illegitimately negative social identity by improving its relative status position.

An experiment by Turner and Brown (1978) manipulated the degree to which status differences between groups were seen as legitimate and stable. The effects for stability were weak, but the overall findings were as predicted by the theory. Both the high- and low-status groups showed high levels of intergroup bias and discrimination when status differentials were insecure but not when they were secure.

More recently, Bettencourt and colleagues (2001) conducted a meta-analysis of studies examining the impact of intergroup status differentials on intergroup bias and attitudes under varying conditions of group boundary permeability, status legitimacy, and status stability. The meta-analysis showed a pattern of effects that was consistent with that predicted for social identity threat in the various conditions of permeability, stability, and legitimacy, but only for status irrelevant measures of intergroup bias. These included measures of general liking and seem to fit the "liking-disliking" dimension of intergroup attitudes (see table 16.1). On these measures, high-status groups showed markedly more intergroup bias than low-status groups when group boundaries were permeable. When group boundaries were impermeable, high-status groups showed reduced bias when status differentials were secure (legitimate and stable), presumably because their positive social identity was not threatened. On the other hand, when group boundaries were impermeable and status differentials were unstable and illegitimate (insecure), low-status groups showed as much intergroup bias as high-status groups.

The pattern of findings was quite different, however, for status-relevant measures of intergroup bias, which seem to fit the respecting-disrespecting or competence intergroup attitude dimension (table 16.1). High-status groups showed consistently higher levels of intergroup bias than low-status groups across all conditions of intergroup permeability, stability, and legitimacy. This intriguing discrepancy for the two kinds of measures seems to suggest that social identity threat appears to produce effects on the liking-disliking intergroup attitude dimension, while status differentials themselves also produce an effect independent of social identity threat on the respecting-disrespecting (competence) dimension.

Overall, therefore, intergroup inequality seems to produce powerful and pervasive effects on intergroup attitudes. There seems to be a general tendency for groups higher in power and status to evaluate lower status and power groups negatively, and the lower status and power groups may share this evaluation as well. Bettencourt and collegues' (2001) meta-analysis suggests that this effect may occur primarily on the disrespecting attitudinal dimension. However, inequality also seems to generate threat, which elicits negative attitudes to the threatening outgroup or groups, and this effect may occur primarily on the disliking dimension of intergroup attitudes.

▶ Integrating Individual and Intergroup Explanations of Prejudice

At the intergroup level, it seems likely that while salient intergroup distinctions may not directly cause prejudice, they will be important preconditions for the emergence of prejudice. The more pervasively salient these intergroup distinctions and identities are, the more conducive to prejudice the situation will be. Intergroup competition or conflict, threat from outgroups, and intergroup inequality seem to play more direct causal roles in generating prejudice. Exactly how they do this has not yet been definitively established. However, the most important theories focus on motivation: either the motivated rationalization and justification of the dominance or superiority of high power and status groups over subordinate groups in the social hierarchy, or the competitively motivated desire to establish group superiority or dominance over outgroups seen as less worthy, or group defensive hostility to perceived outgroup threat.

This suggests that these group dynamic factors can be integrated with the motivational model of individual difference determinants of prejudice described earlier (Duckitt, 2001). This integrated motivational model proposes that when intergroup distinctions and identities are salient, intergroup inequality, competition, or threat will activate one or both of the two basic motivational goals, which in individuals would be expressed in authoritarian-conservative or social dominance ideological beliefs, and through them generate outgroup hostility.

Thus intergroup or social threat from an outgroup or minority activates social cohesion, control, and group defense motivation, which in individuals would be indexed by their level of authoritarian attitudes, and elicits hostility to the threatening group. Authoritarian attitudes, being threat driven, would determine individuals' reactivity to outgroup threat and therefore their readiness to be hostile to outgroups perceived as threatening. As suggested earlier, perceived threat from outgroups would tend to activate an intergroup categorization schema of the threatening outgroup as bad, evil, dangerous, and immoral versus "us" as good, decent, moral people (see figure 16.2). Thus threatening outgroups seem likely to be disliked but not necessarily disrespected, and will be particularly disliked by persons with authoritarian attitudes.

Intergroup power and status differentials and intergroup competition would activate competitively driven group power and superiority motivation (indexed in individuals by their level of SDO) to establish or maintain dominance and superiority over outgroups believed to be legitimately inferior. Higher SDO persons would therefore feel more competitive with subordinate or competing outgroups, and this would generate the intergroup categorization schema of "them" as less worthy, less competent, and less deserving than "us," who are more worthy, more competent, and more deserving and therefore should be superior. This categorization schema will be associated with the attitudinal dimension of disrespecting versus respect-

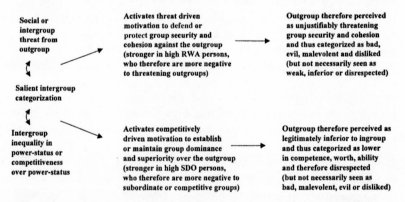

Figure 16.2. The two kinds of situational intergroup dynamics that in the presence of a salient intergroup categorization activate two corresponding group motivational goals (the chronic accessibility of which in individuals will be indexed by the ideological beliefs of RWA and SDO) for ingroup members against the outgroup to generate the adoption of two corresponding prejudiced intergroup categorization schemas and negative attitudinal evaluations

ing. The higher individuals are in SDO, the more reactive they should be to intergroup competition and relations of dominance-subordination, and the greater should be their tendency to disrespect socially subordinate or competing outgroups, thereby legitimizing their actual or desired dominance.

Evidence supporting this integrative motivational model comes from research indicating that these intergroup and individual difference factors do seem to interact in predicting prejudice and do seem to predict these two intergroup attitude dimensions differentially. For example, the effect of RWA on antigay prejudice was mediated by perceived threat (Esses, Haddock, & Zanna, 1993), while the effect of SDO on antiimmigrant attitudes was mediated by perceived economic competition (Esses, Jackson, & Armstrong, 1998). This has also been supported by research using arbitrarily selected social categories varying in threat or social subordination (Duckitt, 2002). Thus RWA was found to predict negative attitudes to social categories that were socially threatening but not socially subordinate (e.g., "rock stars," "drug dealers") while SDO did not, with the effect of RWA mediated by perceived threat from these groups. The SDO predicted negative attitudes to social categories that were socially subordinate but not threatening (e.g., "housewives") while the RWA did not, with the effect of SDO being mediated by competitiveness to these groups. Moreover, RWA was more strongly related to disliking these threatening social categories than to disrespecting them, while SDO was more strongly related to disrespecting these subordinate social categories than to disliking them.

Fiske and colleagues (1999) also found that the status of social groups predicted their evaluation on the competence stereotype dimension, while perceived threat from these groups predicted how they were evaluated on the warmth dimension. Poppe and Linssen (1999) similarly found that the power of national and ethnic groups predicted how they were evaluated on the competence stereotype dimension, while the degree of threat from or conflict with these groups predicted how they were evaluated on the warmth dimension.

This model therefore seems to integrate both individual difference and intergroup factors into a single motivational model explaining prejudice. However, it focuses on salient motivational goals and their expression in explicitly held ideological beliefs and values, such as RWA and SDO. As such, it can explain explicit intergroup attitudes but does not seem likely to account for implicit intergroup attitudes, particularly when these are inconsistent with explicit attitudes. In support of this, McFarland and Mattern (2001) have shown that RWA and SDO were powerfully correlated with explicit prejudices against particular groups but uncorrelated with implicit prejudice against those groups (see also, Karpinski & Hilton, 2001). It may be, as Devine's (1989) theory suggests, that implicit prejudices are acquired during socialization through indirect learning and inferences about intergroup relations of a primarily nonmotivational nature, what Allport

(1954) described as prejudice being "caught not taught." Such implicit "caught" prejudices would therefore, as Karpinski and Hilton (2001) have suggested, reflect individuals' exposure to social environments characterized by predominantly negative associations with stigmatized outgroups, which might be quite different from the degree to which these individuals endorsed these associations. The degree to which they actually endorsed these associations would then be expressed in more consciously acquired and held explicit intergroup attitudes based on and buttressed by overtly held ideological beliefs and values.

Thus, while important advances have occurred in the understanding of the nature and causes of explicitly held prejudiced attitudes and overt intergroup hostility, understanding the nature and causes of underlying implicit prejudices and covert intergroup hostility poses major new challenges for social scientists. The more ultimate challenge will be use the knowledge acquired to develop programs and policies to alleviate intergroup tensions and conflict and reduce the destructive role of prejudice in human affairs.

▲ References

Adorno, T., Frenkel-Brunswick, E., Levinson, D., & Sanford, N. (1950). *The authoritarian personality*. New York: Harper.

Allen, B. (1975). Social distance and admiration reactions of unprejudiced whites. *Journal of Personality, 43*, 709–726.

Allen, V., & Wilder, D. (1975). Categorization, belief similarity, and intergroup discrimination. *Journal of Personality and Social Psychology, 32*, 971–977.

Allport, G. (1954). *The nature of prejudice*. Reading, MA: Addison-Wesley.

Allport, G., & Kramer, B. M. (1946). Some roots of prejudice. *Journal of Psychology, 22*, 9–39.

Altemeyer, B. (1981). *Right-wing authoritarianism*. Winnipeg, Canada: University of Manitoba Press.

Altemeyer, B. (1988). *Enemies of freedom: Understanding right-wing authoritarianism*. San Francisco: Jossey-Bass.

Altemeyer, B. (1998). *The other "authoritarian personality."* In M. P. Zanna (Ed.), *Advances in experimental social psychology* (Vol. 30, pp. 47–92). San Diego, CA: Academic Press.

Ashmore, R., & DelBoca, F. (1976). Psychological approaches to understanding intergroup conflict. In P. Katz (Ed.), *Towards the elimination of racism* (pp. 73–123). New York: Pergamon.

Ashmore, R., & DelBoca, F. (1981). Conceptual approaches to stereotypes and stereotyping. In D. Hamilton (Ed.), *Cognitive processes in stereotyping and intergroup behavior* (pp. 1–36). Hillsdale, NJ: Erlbaum.

Berkowitz, L., & Green, J. A. (1962). The stimulus qualities of the scapegoat. *Journal of Abnormal and Social Psychology, 64*, 293–301.

Bettelheim, B., & Janowitz, M. (1964). *Social change and prejudice*. London: Collier-Macmillan.

Bettencourt, B., Dorr, N., Charlton, K., & Hume, D. (2001). Status differences and in-group bias: A meta-analytic examination of the effects of status stability, status legitimacy, and group permeability. *Journal of Personality and Social Psychology, 127,* 520–542.

Bierly, M. M. (1985). Prejudice toward contemporary outgroups as a generalized attitude. *Journal of Applied Social Psychology, 15,* 189–199.

Blair, I., & Banaji, M. (1996). Automatic and controlled processes in stereotype priming. *Journal of Personality and Social Psychology, 70,* 1142–1163.

Blair, I., Ma, J., & Lenton, A. (2001). Imagining stereotypes away: The moderation of implicit stereotypes through mental imagery. *Journal of Personality and Social Psychology, 81,* 828–841.

Blake, R. R., & Mouton, J. S. (1979). Intergroup problem solving in organizations: From theory to practice. W. G. Austin & S. Worchel (Eds.), *The social psychology of intergroup relations* (pp. 19–32). Monterey, CA: Brooks/Cole.

Blascovitch, J., Wyer, N., Swart, L., & Kibler, J. (1997). Racism and racial categorization. *Journal of Personality and Social Psychology, 72,* 1364–1372.

Blumer, H. (1958). Race prejudice as a sense of group position. *Pacific Sociological Review, 1,* 3–7.

Bobo, L. (1999). Prejudice as group position: Microfoundations of a sociological approach to racism and race relations. *Journal of Social Issues, 55,* 445–472.

Bogardus, E. (1925). Measuring social distance. *Journal of Applied Sociology, 9,* 299–308.

Brewer, M. (1979). In-group bias in the minimal intergroup situation: A cognitive-motivational analysis. *Psychological Bulletin, 86,* 307–324.

Brewer, M. (1998). Category-based versus person-based perception in intergroup contexts. In W. Stroebe & M. Hewstone (Eds.), *European review of social psychology* (Vol. 9, pp. 77–106). New York: Wiley.

Brewer, M., & Brown, R. (1998). Fiske, S. (1998). Intergroup relations. In D. Gilbert, S. Fiske, & G. Lindzey (Eds.), *The handbook of social psychology* (4th ed., vol. 2, pp. 554–594). New York: McGraw-Hill.

Brewer, M., & Kramer, R. (1985). The psychology of intergroup attitudes and behavior. *Annual Review of Psychology, 36,* 219–243.

Brewer, M. B., & Campbell, D. T. (1976). *Ethnocentrism and intergroup attitudes: East African evidence.* New York: Sage.

Brewer, M. B., & Miller, N. (1984). Beyond the contact hypothesis: Theoretical perspectives on desegregation. In N. Miller & M. B. Brewer (Eds.), *Groups in contact: The psychology of desegregation* (pp. 281–302). San Diego, CA: Academic.

Brigham, J. (1971). Ethnic stereotypes. *Psychological Bulletin, 76,* 15–38.

Brown, C., Dovidio, J., & Ellyson, S. (1990). Reducing sex differences in visual displays of dominance: knowledge is power. *Personality and Social Psychology Bulletin, 16,* 358–368.

Brown, R. (1995). *Prejudice: It's social psychology.* Oxford: Blackwell.

Brown, R. (2000). Social identity theory: Past achievements, current problems and future challenges. *European Journal of Social Psychology, 30,* 745–778.

Brown, R., Hinkle, S., Ely, P., Fox-Cardamone, L., Maras, P., & Taylor, L. (1992). Recognizing group diversity: Individualist-collectivist and autonomous-relational social orientations and their implications for intergroup processes. *British Journal of Social Psychology, 31,* 327–342.

Brown, R., Maras, P., Masser, B., Vivian, J., & Hewstone, M. (2001). Life on the ocean wave: Testing some intergroup hypotheses in a naturalistic setting. *Group Processes and Intergroup Relations, 4,* 81–97.

Chirot, D. (2001). Introduction. In D. Chirot & M. Seligman (Eds.), *Ethnopolitical warfare: Causes, consequences, and possible solutions* (pp. 3–26). Washington, DC: American Psychological Association.

Crandall, C. (1994). Prejudice against fat people: Ideology and self-interest. *Journal of Personality and Social Psychology, 66,* 882–894.

Crosby, F., Bromley, S., & Saxe, L. (1980). Recent unobtrusive studies of Black and White discrimination and prejudice: A literature review. *Psychological Bulletin, 87,* 546–563.

Dasgupta, N., & Greenwald, A. (2001). On the malleability of automatic attitudes: Combating automatic prejudice with images of admired and disliked individuals. *Journal of Personality and Social Psychology, 81,* 800–814.

De Ridder, R., & Tripathi, R. (1992). *Norm violation and intergroup relations.* Oxford: Clarendon Press.

Deschamps, J-C., & Doise, W. (1978). Crossed category memberships in intergroup relations. In H. Tajfel (Ed.), *Differentiation in social groups: Studies in the social psychology of intergroup relations* (pp. 141–158). London: Academic.

Devine, P. (1989). Stereotypes and prejudice: Their automatic and controlled components. *Journal of Personality and Social Psychology, 56,* 5–18.

Devine, P. (2001). Implicit prejudice and stereotyping: How automatic are they? *Journal of Personality and Social Psychology, 81,* 757–759.

Diab, L. (1970). A study of intragroup and intergroup relations among experimentally produced small groups. *Genetic Psychology Monographs, 82,* 49–82.

Dijker, A. (1987). Emotional reactions to ethnic minorities. *European Journal of Social Psychology, 17,* 305–325.

Doty, R., Peterson, B., & Winter, D. (1991). Threat and authoritarianism in the United States, 1978–1987. *Journal of Personality and Social Psychology, 61,* 629–640.

Dovidio, J., Brigham, J., Johnson, B., & Gaertner, S. (1996). Stereotyping, prejudice, and discrimination: Another look. In N. Macrae, C. Stangor, & M. Hewstone (Eds.), *Stereotypes and stereotyping* (pp. 276–319). New York: Guilford.

Dovidio, J., Evans, N., & Tylor, R. (1986). Racial stereotypes: The contents of their cognitive representations. *Journal of Experimental Social Psychology, 22,* 22–37.

Dovidio, J., & Gaertner, S. (1993). Stereotypes and evaluative intergroup bias. In D. Mackie & D. Hamilton (Eds.), *Affect, cognition, and stereotyping* (pp. 167–193). San Diego, CA: Academic Press.

Dovidio, J., Gaertner, S., & Validzic, A. (1998). Ingroup bias: status, differentiation, and a common ingroup identity. *Journal of Personality and Social Psychology, 75,* 109–120.

Duckitt, J. (1992). *The social psychology of prejudice.* New York: Praeger.

Duckitt, J. (2000). Culture, personality, and prejudice. In S. Renshon & J. Duckitt, (Eds.), *Political psychology: Cultural and crosscultural foundations* (pp. 89–107). New York: New York University Press.

Duckitt, J. (2001). A dual process cognitive-motivational theory of ideology and prejudice. In M. P. Zanna (Ed.), *Advances in experimental social psychology* (Vol. 33, pp. 41–113). San Diego, CA: Academic Press.

Duckitt, J. (2002). Intergroup threat and competitiveness mediate the relationships between dual dimensions of ideological attitudes and prejudice. Manuscript submitted for publication.

Duckitt, J., & Fisher, K. (in press). The impact of social threat on worldview and ideological attitudes. *Political Psychology*.

Duckitt, J., & Mphuthing, T. (1998). Group identification and intergroup attitudes: A longitudinal analysis in South Africa. *Journal of Personality and Social Psychology, 74*, 80–85.

Duckitt, J., Wagner, C., du Plessis, I., & Birum, I. (2002). The psychological bases of ideology and prejudice: Testing a dual process model. *Journal of Personality and Social Psychology, 83*, 75–93.

Ellemers, N., van Knippenberg, A., de Vries, N., & Wilkie, H. (1988). Social identification and permeability of group boundaries. *European Journal of Social Psychology, 18*, 479–513.

Ellemers, N., van Knippenberg, A., & Wilkie, H. (1990). The influence of the permeability of group boundaries and stability of group status on strategies of individual mobility and social change. *British Journal of Social Psychology, 29*, 233–246.

Esses, V., Haddock, G., & Zanna, M. (1993). Values, stereotypes, and emotions as determinants of intergroup attitudes. In D. Mackie & D. Hamilton (Eds.), *Affect, cognition, and stereotyping* (Vol. 17, pp. 137–166). San Diego, CA: Academic.

Esses, V., Jackson, L., & Armstrong, T. (1998). Intergroup competition and attitudes toward immigrants and immigration: An instrumental model of group conflict. *Journal of Social Issues, 54*, 699–724.

Feldman, S., & Stenner, K. (1997). Perceived threat and authoritarianism. *Political Psychology, 18*, 741–770.

Fiske, S. (1998). Stereotyping, prejudice, and discrimination. In D. Gilbert, S. Fiske, & G. Lindzey (Eds.), *The handbook of social psychology* (4th ed., vol. 2, pp. 357–411). New York: McGraw-Hill.

Fiske, S. (2000). Stereotyping, prejudice, and discrimination at the seam between the centuries: evolution, culture, mind, and brain. *European Journal of Social Psychology, 30*, 299–322.

Fiske, S., Xu, J., Cuddy, A., & Glick, P. (1999). (Dis)respecting versus (dis)liking: Status and interdependence predict ambivalent stereotypes of competence and warmth. *Journal of Social Issues, 55*, 473–489.

Forsyth, D. (1980). A taxonomy of ethical ideologies. *Journal of Personality and Social Psychology, 39*, 175–184.

Franco, F., & Maass, A. (1999). Intentional control over prejudice: When the choice of the measure matters. *European Journal of Social Psychology, 29*, 469–477.

Gaertner, S., & Dovidio, J. (1986). The aversive form of racism. In J. Dovidio & S. Gaertner (Eds.), *Prejudice, discrimination, and racism* (pp. 61–89). Orlando, FL.: Academic.

Gardner, R. (1973). Ethnic stereotypes: The traditional approach, a new look. *Canadian Psychologist, 14*, 133–148.

Gardner, R. (1993). Stereotypes as consensual beliefs. In M. Zanna & J. Olson (Eds.), *The psychology of prejudice: The Ontario symposium* (Vol. 7, pp. 1–32). Hillsdale, NJ: Erlbaum.

Gilbert, D., & Hixon, J. (1991). The trouble of thinking: activation and application of stereotypic beliefs. *Journal of Personality and Social Psychology, 60*, 509–517.

Giles, H., & Ryan, E. (1982). Prolegomena for developing a social psychological theory of language attitudes. In E. Ryan & H. Giles (Eds.), *Attitudes toward language variation* (pp. 208–223). London: Edward Arnold.

Glick, P., & Fiske, S. (2001). Ambivalent sexism. In M. P. Zanna (Ed.), *Advances in experimental social psychology* (Vol. 33, pp. 115–188). San Diego, CA: Academic Press.

Goertzel, T. (1987). Authoritarianism of personality and political attitudes. *Journal of Social Psychology, 127*, 7–18.

Green, D., Abelson, R., & Garnett, M. (1999). The distinctive political views of hate-crime perpetrators and White supremacists. In D. Prentice & D. Miller (Eds.), *Cultural divides: Understanding and overcoming group conflict* (pp. 429–464). New York: Russell Sage.

Green, D., Glaser, J., & Rich, A. (1998). From lynching to gay-bashing: The elusive connection between economic conditions and hate crime. *Journal of Personality and Social Psychology, 75*, 82–92.

Green, D., & Rich, A. (1998). White supremacist activity and cross-burnings in North Carolina. Journal of Quantitative Criminology, 14, 263–282.

Greenwald, A., & Banaji, M. (1995). Implicit social cognition: Attitudes, self-esteem, and stereotypes. *Psychological Review, 102*, 4–27.

Greenwald, A., McGhee, D., & Schwartz, J. (1998). Measuring individual differences in implicit cognition: The Implicit Association Test. *Journal of Personality and Social Psychology, 74*, 1464–1480.

Haddock, G., Zanna, M., & Esses, V. (1994). The (limited) role of trait-laden stereotypes in predicting attitudes toward native peoples. *British Journal of Social Psychology, 33*, 83–106.

Hagendoorn, L. (1995). Intergroup biases in multiple group systems: The perception of ethnic hierarchies. In W. Stroebe & M. Hewstone (Eds.), *European review of social psychology* (Vol. 6, pp. 199–228). Chichester, UK: Wiley.

Hamilton, D. L., & Trolier, T. K. (1986). Stereotypes and stereotyping: An overview of the cognitive approach. In J. F. Dovidio & S. L. Gaertner (Eds.), *Prejudice, discrimination, and racism* (pp. 127–164). Orlando, FL: Academic.

Harding, J., Proshansky, H., Kutner, B., & Chein, I. (1969). Prejudice and ethnic relations. In G. Lindzey & E. Aronson (Eds.), *The handbook of social psychology,* Vol. 5 (pp. 1–76). Reading, MA: Addison-Wesley.

Hartley, E. L. (1946). *Problems in prejudice.* New York: King's Crown Press.

Hendricks, M., & Bootzin, R. (1976). Race and sex as stimuli for negative affect and physical avoidance. *Journal of Social Psychology, 98*, 111–120.

Hilton, J., & von Hippel, W. (1996). Stereotypes. *Annual Review of Psychology, 47*, 237–271.

Hinkle, S., & Brown, R. (1990). Intergroup comparisons and social identity: Some links and lacunae. In D. Abrams & M. Hogg (Eds.), *Social identity theory: Constructive and critical advances* (pp. 48–70). New York: Springer.

Hovland, C., & Sears, R. (1940). Minor studies of aggression. Vol. 1. Correlation of lynchings with economic indices. *Journal of Psychology, 9*, 301–310.

Huddy, L., & Sears, D. (1995). Opposition to bilingual education: Prejudice or the defense of realistic interests. *Social Psychology Quarterly, 58*, 133–143.

Jackman, M. (1994). *The velvet glove: Paternalism and conflict in gender, class, and race relations.* Berkeley: University of California Press.

Jost, J., & Banaji, M. (1994). The role of stereotyping in system justification and the production of false consciousness. *British Journal of Social Psychology, 33,* 1–27.

Jowitt, K. (2001). Ethnicity, nice, nasty, and nihilistic. In D. Chirot & M. Seligman (Eds.), *Ethnopolitical warfare: Causes, consequences, and possible solutions* (pp. 27–36). Washington, DC: American Psychological Association.

Judd, C. M., & Park, B. (1988). Out-group homogeneity: Judgments of variability at the individual and group levels. *Journal of Personality and Social Psychology, 54,* 778–788.

Karpinski, A., & Hilton, J. (2001). Attitudes and the Implicit Association Test. *Journal of Personality and Social Psychology, 81,* 744–788.

Katz, I., Cohen, S., & Glass, D. (1975). Some determinants of cross-racial helping behaviors. *Journal of Personality and Social Psychology, 32,* 964–970.

Katz, I., & Hass, R. (1988). Racial ambivalence and American value conflict: Correlational and priming studies of dual cognitive structures. *Journal of Personality and Social Psychology 59,* 692–704.

Kinder, D., & Sanders, L. (1996). *Divided by color: Racial politics and democratic ideals.* Chicago: University of Chicago Press.

Kinder, D., & Sears, D. (1981). Prejudice and politics: Symbolic racism versus racial threats to the good life. *Journal of Personality and Social Psychology, 40,* 414–431.

Kovel, J. (1970). *White racism: A psychological history.* New York: Pantheon.

Krueger, A., & Pischke, J. (1997). A statistical analysis of crime against foreigners in unified Germany. *Journal of Human Resources, 32,* 182–209.

Lalonde, R., & Gardner, R. (1989). An intergroup perspective on stereotype organization and processing. *British Journal of Social Psychology, 28,* 289–303.

Lerner, M. J. (1980). *The belief in a just world: A fundamental delusion.* New York: Plenum.

LeVine, R., & Campbell, D. (1972). *Ethnocentrism: Theories of conflict, ethnic attitudes, and group behavior.* New York: Wiley.

Lippman, W. (1922). *Public opinion.* New York: Harcourt Brace Jovanovich.

Maass, A. (1999). Linguistic intergroup bias: stereotype-perpetuation through language. In M. P. Zanna (Ed.), *Advances in experimental social psychology* (Vol. 31, pp. 79–190). San Diego, CA: Academic Press.

Maass, A., Castelli, L., & Arcuri, L. (2000). Measuring prejudice: Implicit versus explicit techniques. In D. Capozza & R. Brown (Eds.), *Social identity processes: Trends in theory and research* (pp. 96–116). London: Sage.

MacCrae, C., Stangor, C., & Hewstone, M. (Eds.). (1996). *Stereotypes and stereotyping.* New York: Guilford.

McConahay, J. (1983). Modern racism and modern discrimination: The effects of race, racial attitudes, and context on simulated hiring decisions. *Personality and Social Psychology Bulletin, 9,* 551–558.

McConahay, J. (1986). Modern racism, ambivalence, and the modern racism scale. In J. Dovidio & S. L. Gaertner (Eds.), *Prejudice, discrimination, and racism: Theory and research* (pp. 91–125). New York: Academic.

McConahay, J., & Hough, J. C. (1976). Symbolic racism. *Journal of Social Issues, 32,* 23–45.

McFarland, S. (1998, July). *Toward a typology of prejudiced persons.* Paper presented at the annual meeting of the International Society of Political Psychology, Montreal.

McFarland, S., & Adelson, S. (1996, July). *An omnibus study of personality, values, and prejudice*. Paper presented at the annual meeting of the International Society of Political Psychology, Vancouver.

McFarland, S., & Mattern, K. (2001). *Generalized explicit and implicit prejudice*. Unpublished manuscript.

Messick, D. M., & Mackie, D. (1989). Intergroup relations. *Annual Review of Psychology, 40*, 45–81.

Mullen, B., Brown, R., & Smith, C. (1992). Ingroup bias as a function of salience, relevance and status: An integration. *European Journal of Social Psychology, 22*, 103–122.

Otten, S., & Mummendey, A. (2000). Valence-dependent probability of ingroup favouritism between minimal groups: An integrative view of the positive-negative asymmetry in social discrimination. In D. Capozza & R. Brown (Eds.), *Social identity processes: Trends in theory and research* (pp. 33–48). London: Sage.

Owen, C., Eisner, H., & McFaul, T. (1981). A half-century of social distance research: National replication of the Bogardus studies. *Sociology and Social Research, 66*, 80–98.

Pettigrew, T. (1998a). Intergroup contact theory. *Annual Review of Psychology, 49*, 65–85.

Pettigrew, T. (1998b). Reactions toward the new minorities of western Europe. *Annual Review of Sociology, 24*, 77–103.

Pettigrew, T., & Meertens, R. (1995). Subtle and blatant prejudice in western Europe. *European Journal of Social Psychology, 25*, 57–75.

Phalet, K., & Poppe, E. (1997). Competence and morality dimensions of national and ethnic stereotypes: A study in six eastern-European countries. *European Journal of Social Psychology, 27*, 703–723.

Poppe, E., & Linssen, H. (1999). Ingroup favouritism and the reflection of realistic dimensions of difference between national states in Central and Eastern European nationality stereotypes. *British Journal of Social Psychology, 38*, 85–102.

Pratto, F., Sidanius, J., Stallworth, L., & Malle, B. (1994). Social dominance orientation: A personality variable predicting social and political attitudes. *Journal of Personality and Social Psychology, 67*, 741–763.

Quanty, M., Keats, J., & Harkins, S. (1975). Prejudice and criteria for identification of ethnic photographs. *Journal of Personality and Social Psychology, 32*, 449–454.

Rabbie, J. M. & Horwitz, M. (1969). Arousal of ingroup-outgroup bias by a chance win or loss. *Journal of Personality and Social Psychology, 13*, 269–277.

Raden, D. (1999). Is anti-Semitism currently part of an authoritarian attitude syndrome. *Political Psychology, 20*, 323–244.

Raper, A. (1933). *The tragedy of lynching*. Chapel Hill: University of North Carolina Press.

Reynolds, K., & Turner, J. (2001). Prejudice as a group process: The role of social identity. In M. Augoustinos & K. Reynolds (Eds.), *Understanding prejudice, racism, and social conflict* (pp. 159–178). London: Sage.

Richards, G. (1997). *"Race," racism, and psychology*. London: Routledge.

Rokeach, M., Smith, P., & Evans, R. (1960). Two kinds of prejudice or one? In M. Rokeach (Ed.), *The open and the closed mind* (pp. 132–168). New York: Basic Books.

Rosenfield, D., & Stephan, W. (1981). Intergroup relations among children. In S.

Brehm, S. Kassim, & F. Gibbons (Eds.), *Developmental social psychology* (pp. 271–297). New York: Oxford University Press.

Rudman, L., Ashmore, R., & Gary, M. (2001). "Unlearning" automatic biases: The malleability of implicit prejudice and stereotypes. *Journal of Personality and Social Psychology, 81,* 856–868.

Sales, S. (1973). Threat as a factor in authoritarianism. *Journal of Personality and Social Psychology, 28,* 44–57.

Sales, S., & Friend, K. (1973). Success and failure as determinants of level of authoritarianism. *Behavioral Science, 18,* 163–172.

Samelson, F. (1978). From "race psychology" to "studies in prejudice": Some observations on the thematic reversal in social psychology. *Journal of the History of the Behavioral Sciences, 14,* 265–278.

Saucier, G. (2000). Isms and the structure of social attitudes. *Journal of Personality and Social Psychology, 78,* 366–385.

Schuman, H., Steeh, C., & Bobo, L. (1985). *Racial attitudes in America.* Cambridge, MA: Harvard University Press.

Sears, D., & Kinder, D. (1971). Racial tensions and voting in Los Angeles. In W. Z. Hirsch (Ed.), *Los Angeles: Viability and prospects for metropolitan leadership* (pp. 135–170). Cambridge, MA: Harvard University Press.

Sears, D., van Laar, C., Carillo, M., & Kosterman, R. (1997). Is it really racism? The origins of White Americans opposition to race-targeted policies. *Public Opinion Quarterly, 61,* 16–53.

Sherif, M., & Sherif, C. (1953). *Groups in harmony and tension.* New York: Harper.

Sherif, M., & Sherif, C. (1969). *Social psychology.* New York: Harper.

Sidanius, J., & Pratto, F. (1993). The dynamics of social dominance and the inevitability of oppression. In P. Sniderman & P. Tetlock (Eds), *Prejudice, politics, and race in America today* (pp. 173–211). Stanford, CA: Stanford University Press.

Sidanius, J., & Pratto, F. (1999). *Social dominance: An intergroup theory of social hierarchy and oppression.* Cambridge: Cambridge University Press.

Sidanius, J., Pratto, F., & Bobo, L. (1994). Social dominance orientation and the political psychology of gender: A case of invariance? *Journal of Personality and Social Psychology, 67,* 998–1011.

Sigall, H., & Page, R. (1971). Current stereotypes: A little fading, a little faking. *Journal of Personality and Social Psychology, 18,* 247–255.

Simpson, G., & Yinger, J. (1985). *Racial and cultural minorities: An analysis of prejudice and discrimination* (5th ed.). New York: Plenum Press.

Singh, R., Choo, W., & Poh, L. (1998). Ingroup bias and fair-mindedness as strategies of self-presentation in intergroup perception. *Personality and Social Psychology Bulletin, 24,* 147–162

Smith, E. (1993). Social identity and social emotions: Toward new conceptualizations of prejudice. In D. Mackie & D. Hamilton (Eds.), *Affect, cognition, and stereotyping: Interactive processes in group perception* (pp. 297–315). San Diego, CA: Academic.

Sniderman, P., & Tetlock, P. (1986). Symbolic racism: Problems of motive attribution in political analysis. *Journal of Social Issues, 42,* 129–150.

Solomon, S., Greenberg, J., & Pyszczynski, T. (1991). A terror management theory of social behavior: The psychological function of self-esteem and cultural worldviews. *Advances in Experimental Social Psychology, 24,* 93–159.

Stangor, C., Sullivan, L., & Ford, T. (1991). Affective and cognitive determinants of prejudice. *Social Cognition, 9,* 59–80.

Stephan, W., Ageyev, V., Coates-Shrider, L., Stephan, C., & Abalakina, M. (1994). On the relationship between stereotypes and prejudice: An international study. *Personality and Social Psychology Bulletin, 20,* 277–284.

Stoker, L. (1998). Understanding Whites' resistance to affirmative action: The role of principled commitments and racial prejudice. In J. Hurwitz & M. Peffley (Eds.), *Perception and prejudice: Race and politics in the United States* (pp. 51–88). New Haven, CT: Yale University Press.

Stone, W., Lederer, G., & Christie, R. (1993). The status of authoritarianism. In W. Stone, G. Lederer, & R. Christie (Eds.), *Strength and weakness: The authoritarian personality today* (pp. 229–245). New York: Springer.

Struch, N., & Schwartz, S. (1989). Intergroup aggression: Its predictors and distinctness from in-group bias. *Journal of Personality and Social Psychology, 62,* 564–576.

Sumner, W. G. (1906). *Folkways.* New York: Ginn.

Tajfel, H. (1969). Cognitive aspects of prejudice. *Journal of Social Issues, 25,* 79–97.

Tajfel, H. (1970). Experiments in intergroup discrimination. *Scientific American, 223*(2), 6–102.

Tajfel, H. (1981). *Human groups and social categories.* Cambridge: Cambridge University Press.

Tajfel, H., Flament, C., Billig, M., & Bundy, R. (1971). Social categorization and intergroup behaviour. *European Journal of Social Psychology, 1,* 149–177.

Tajfel, H., & Turner, J. (1979). An integrative theory of intergroup conflict. In W. Austin & S. Worchel (Eds.), *The social psychology of intergroup relations* (pp. 33–47). Monterey, CA: Brooks/Cole.

Turner, J. C., & Brown, R. J. (1978). Social status, cognitive alternatives and intergroup relations. In H. Tajfel (Ed.), *Differentiation between social groups* (pp. 201–234). London: Academic.

Vanbeselaere, N. (1987). The effects of dichotomous and crossed social categorizations upon intergroup discrimination. *European Journal of Social Psychology, 17,* 143–156.

Van den Berghe, P. L. (1967). *Race and racism.* New York: Wiley.

Weitz, S. (1972). Attitude, voice and behavior: A repressed affect model of interracial interaction. *Journal of Personality and Social Psychology, 24,* 14–21.

Wilder, D. (1986). Social categorization: Implications for creation and reduction of intergroup bias. In L. Berkowitz (Ed.), *Advances in experimental social psychology* (Vol. 19, pp. 291–355). New York: Academic.

Willemsen, T., & van Oudenhoven, J. (1989). Social psychological perspectives on ethnic minorities: An introduction. In J. van Oudenhoven & T. Willemsen (Eds.), *Ethnic minorities: Social psychological perspectives* (pp. 11–21). Amsterdam: Swets & Zeitlinger.

Wilson, T., Lindzey, S., & Schooler, T. (2000). A model of dual attitudes. *Psychological Review, 107,* 101–126.

17 Virginia Sapiro

Theorizing Gender in Political Psychology Research

> *Let tyrants fear, I have always so behaved myself that, under God, I have placed my chiefest strength and safeguard in the loyal hearts and good-will of my subjects; and therefore I am come amongst you, as you see, at this time, not for my recreation and disport, but being resolved, in the midst and heat of the battle, to live and die amongst you all; to lay down for my God, and for my kingdom, and my people, my honour and my blood, even in the dust. I know I have the body but of a weak and feeble woman; but I have the heart and stomach of a king, and of a king of England too, and think foul scorn that Parma or Spain, or any prince of Europe, should dare to invade the borders of my realm; to which rather than any dishonour shall grow by me, I myself will take up arms, I myself will be your general, judge, and rewarder of every one of your virtues in the field. I know already, for your forwardness you have deserved rewards and crowns; and We do assure you in the word of a prince, they shall be duly paid you.*
>
> —Elizabeth I of England to the troops at Tilbury (1588)

In 1588 England and her monarch prepared to meet the Spanish Armada, the most fearsome force in Europe. But that was not all. Internal forces had placed both England and Elizabeth I in precarious positions. Britain had an official religion, as her neighboring countries did, but this one was different. The new church—a *national* church—was founded but not consolidated in the reign of Henry VIII. Given the draw of her kinswoman, Mary, Queen of Scots, for those who preferred the Roman church, and the fragility of her governing institutions and coalitions, Elizabeth knew she had insufficient power to assert her will by mere force.

Elizabeth I must be recognized as a brilliant strategist and tactician who can be given considerable credit for nation-building in England. That success rested in part on her understanding of the relationship of gender to political psychology, and on finely honed skills of political communication and symbolic politics that used this understanding to advantage. The character of women, thought to reside in the nature of their bodily differences from men, was generally regarded as antithetical to that of a prince and a warrior, and thus all the problems England and Elizabeth faced were compounded by her womanhood. Repeatedly, she transformed her female "weakness" into a political asset through rhetoric and symbolic representation. At Tilbury, for example, she spoke of a different kind of power, derived from the "loyal hearts and goodwill of [her] subjects," that contrasted favorably with the coercion of the "tyrants" who ruled the other great kingdoms. She appeared for no mere feminine "recreation and disport" but to stand among these men and join with them in common defense.

Elizabeth was no Joan of Arc; she did not cut her hair or wear suits of armor. To the contrary. She transformed one of her chief liabilities—her refusal to provide the throne with an heir or king consort—by favoring resplendent white gowns and developing the persona of the Virgin Queen. She called attention to her woman's body by her dress and words and, with suitable double-entendre, she framed her troops' view by declaring that rather than allowing any foreign prince to "dare to invade the borders of my realm" and to avoid "dishonor," she herself would take up arms to defend herself and her realm. She challenged them to defend the honor of their nation and queen, two symbols merged in "Gloriana."[1]

Many elements of this speech are foci of contemporary research on gender and political psychology, including the nature of the relationship of gender, sex, and sexuality to political character and action; the linkages between gender and leadership; the differing political strategies of action, decision-making, and communication that might be required of men and women, especially in light of stereotype-based expectations; the implications of gender for the nature and incidence of politically based violence; linkages between gender and other group-based politics; and the role of gender in political communication and symbolism.

Despite the existence of a lively research field, in political psychology more broadly gender remains only vaguely conceptualized and remarkably undertheorized. Given how central gender is to human conceptions of self and their social organization, its relevance to political psychology is rarely explored outside noting the gender differences in the vote and some questions of public opinion that occur in some countries (most notably the United States) in some historical periods (especially since the 1970s). This chapter, therefore, offers not a compendium of research findings but a research-driven guide to theorizing about the relationship of gender to political psychology, with research agenda elements noted throughout. It begins with an introduction to gender in public opinion and political behavior research organized around exploring four approaches to defining gender empirically. Second, I examine how people understand politics in a gendered world through research on political and social cognition. Finally, we turn to the potential of political psychology for understanding gender systems of stigma, coercion, and inequality in politics.

Social research on gender at this point in its history tends to be framed by four widely accepted observations, each of which has important implications for theory and design construction in political psychology.[2] First, *gender is a socially constructed, historically shaped phenomenon.* Definitions of male and female, masculinity and femininity have varied in substantial ways over history and across different cultures. Researchers should not assume that the definitions of masculinity and femininity hold in other times and places. Second, in all known societies, *some socially constructed norms about gender—for example, that women cannot lead men—are naturalized;* that is, they are treated as fundamental facts of life. The history of justifications of the social and legal restrictions placed on women underscores the degree to which claims about the "natural" differences between sexes have undergirded the imposition of these restrictions. Researchers must be careful about their assumptions of "natural" differences between the sexes.

Third, in all known societies, *gender has been the basis for differentiation* of many people into different tasks, activities, and institutional positions. Women have often faced outright exclusion from conventional politics or specific aspects of it, while men as such[3] have rarely encountered exclusion from political activities and spaces. Although the degree of differentiation and the domains it covers vary crossculturally and over time, scholars have not identified a historical or contemporary society in which gender is irrelevant to dividing up social, cultural, economic, and political tasks.

Finally, in all known societies, *gender has been the basis not just of differentiation but of inequality,* especially in politics, largely because of women's historical exclusion. Although the degree of inequality and the domains it covers vary crossculturally and over time, and despite scholarly searches for the gender-egalitarian society, research has yet to find a society in which gender is irrelevant to the division of power and authority. Men have been generally been accorded higher status and more authority and power, including over the lives of women, than women have over themselves or certainly, over men. Men have always held the majority of seats in every national legislature in the world. In 2001, in only six countries did women hold even one-third of the national legislative seats, including Sweden (43 percent), Denmark and Finland (37 percent), Norway, the Netherlands, and Iceland (36 percent). Women in some of these countries are aided by vigorous public or party quota systems. In only 19 countries did women hold at least 25 percent of the national legislative seats. In the majority of countries, women constitute no more than 20 percent of the national legislators. These patterns would not appear if gender were irrelevant to divisions of power and authority.

If gender serves so ubiquitously as a socially and historically constructed element of structures of political differentiation and stratification, it would seem important to understand the ways it is integrated into political psychology, especially given that self-defined democracies have rarely perceived this exclusion of women from governance as problematic (Sapiro, 1998). This itself is an interesting problem for political psychology.

▶ *Alternative Conceptions of Gender in Research on Public Opinion and Political Behavior*

When scholars use gender as a variable in political research, what concept stands behind the indicator? At the simplest level, of course, gender stands for a social label that most 3-year-olds can grasp: Is a person commonly identified as a male or female? But for scholarly purposes, processes of social categorization are analytically more complex than novice 3-year-olds know.

The central, and fascinating, point of complexity in defining gender is the interaction of its biological and social construction. Scholars have long used the contrasting terms *sex* and *gender* to underscore the theoretical distinction between specifically *biological* phenomena implicated in "female" and "male" on the one hand and *sociocultural* phenomena on the other (Eagly 1987, 1995; Eagly & Wood, 1999). The utility of this distinction is largely theoretical, not dependent on being able to sort out empirically what elements of human thought and action are caused by biology or social forces. Many common concepts used by social and natural scientists, of course, are theoretical constructs that may not, themselves, be directly observable (Matheson & Kline, 1998, Maxwell, 1998).

Manifest gender (what the 3-year-old or survey coder sees) is variably associated with physiological sex, especially depending on which aspect of human biology is taken as the determinant of sex differentiation, and how society, culture, and individual differences further "dress up" gender differentiation. Sex, as suggested by secondary sex characteristics, does not necessarily even correspond to the "XX/XY" dichotomy of genetic sex indication, let alone any of the other defining aspects of gender people use, such as clothes, hair, and demeanor (Hyde 1996; Sloan 2001). Thus researchers attempting to attribute gender differences in political attitudes or behavior to "natural" or biological phenomena must theorize with care which specific aspect(s) of sex differentiation—genomic structure, brain physiology, the hormonal system, reproductive capacity and functioning, or anatomy—drives the political consequences. They should also take account of both the considerable degree of *overlap between men and women* and *within-sex* variation in "sex differentiating" characteristics that might have sociopolitical consequences (Hyde 1996; Sloan 2001). Relatively little research explores the impact of physiological variation associated with sex on politically relevant phenomena. Some is directly and systematically empirical (Dabbs, Alford, & Fielden, 1998; Dabbs, Bernieri, Strong, Campo, & Milun, 2001; Peterson, 1978). But more common is theorizing on the basis of ethology, disparate studies of human physiology and behavior, and evolutionary theory (Masters, 1989, Mesquida & Wiener, 1999). Most political psychology research involving gender focuses on sociocultural sources, and this chapter will deal exclusively with that.

Thus, despite the sense that ordinary classification of people into males and females makes to most people, it is not the only theoretically or empirically interesting conception of gender; indeed, researchers often use ordinary classification to stand for very different conceptions of gender. Among these, discussed hereafter, are subjective content of gender; personality, personal styles, and practices; and social roles and resources. These are not competing conceptions of the same thing but different elements within the complex that is gender (Eagly, 1995; Deaux & Lafrance, 1998, Ridgeway & Smith-Lovin, 1999).

Ordinary Categorization and "Gender Differences"

Most people most of the time find ordinary classification of people as male or female on the basis of outward appearances meaningful. This categorization further serves as a basis for intentional and unintentional socialization that both reproduces and alters the meaning of gender in new generations. It is a sorting mechanism used by law, policy, institutional processes, and social custom to differentiate among people and place them in different positions, which, in turn, may create different political interests, preferences, responses, and styles.[4]

Although a large body of research extending back to the 1920s (Merriam & Gosnell, 1924; Ogburn & Goltra, 1919; Willey & Rice, 1924) examines gender difference and similarity[5] in public opinion and political participation in the United States and, to a lesser degree, elsewhere, it is remarkably difficult to summarize it accurately, for three reasons. First, literature reviews of gender politics tend to offer an unrepresentative view of the state of research by cherry-picking findings of difference and ignoring findings of similarity, often by relying on a now-classic but out-of-date report on public opinion findings (Shapiro & Mahajan, 1986). Second, as in most of the empirical social sciences, "findings" are more likely to be published than "nonfindings", thus scholarly articles on gender are disproportionately likely to reveal gender differences. Third, the majority of reports of gender effects—especially the lack of them—are embedded in research reports in which gender is not noted as a main theme in the title or abstract; rather, the findings are noted in passing (or appear unremarked in a table) when gender is merely one of the "background" or "control" variables. These findings pass largely unnoted in the gender politics literature. In the 1995–2000 volumes of the *American Political Science Review* and the *American Journal of Political Science*—two premier journals for public opinion and political behavior research—the titles or abstracts of seven articles indicated that gender was a variable (Burns, Schlozman, & Verba, 1997; Dolan, 1998; Kaufmann, & Petrocik, 1999; McDermott, 1997; Paolino, 1995; Schlozman, Burns, Verba, & Donahue, 1995; Stoker & Jennings, 1995). In these, gender makes a difference. Close reading of these volumes shows that at least another 40 used gender as a variable, usually as an untheorized "control" variable, with either unreported or no significant effects.[6]

The large body of research on gender difference and similarity in public opinion, when viewed as a whole, leads to six important conclusions about gender differences in public opinion.

First, the *range of public opinion phenomena on which research finds consistent gender differences is limited*. Table 17.1, for example, shows the appearance of gender differences in the basic spending battery of the General Social Survey (GSS) from the 1970s to 2000.[7] Of the 15 areas that receive regular attention, only in 4 of them do gender differences appear more often than not. Leaving aside policy questions formulated as spending issues, the most consistent gender differences in public opinion in the United States involve attitudes toward legitimized use of violence, including attitudes toward war and militarism, capital punishment, gun control, and some aspects of social welfare policy. Since the late 1970s, U.S. women have been more Democratic than men. Other gender difference findings tend to be more dependent on the precise nature of the question and the historical context. There are remarkably few gender differences, for example, in attitudes toward the women's movement (Huddy, Neely, & Lafay, 2000). No research has uncovered gender differences in public opinion that emerge consistently crossnationally, although in many countries there is insufficient longitudinal analysis to reach judgment.

Second, the *gender differences that emerge in public opinion tend to be modest in size*. In table 17.1, for example, even where there are relatively consistent gender differences, the overall correlation with gender is small and often statistically significant only because of massive case number. By far the largest public opinion differences occur in attitudes toward gun control and capital punishment. In the 20 year history of GSS polling on these questions, the largest gender difference in gun control support was 20 percentage points, and the largest difference in capital punishment support was 13 percentage points (Sapiro, 2001). Gender differences in partisan vote have loomed large in recent U.S. presidential election news, gender differences remained at or below 5 percentage points in six elections between 1952 and 2000 and surpassed 10 percentage points only in the 1990s and 2000. In the majority of cases in which a gender difference appeared, a plurality of men and women actually supported the same candidate, but to different degrees. These are substantively interesting differences, but the large overlap in male and female opinion overrules attributing the differences to wholesale bifurcation in the male and female persona that writing on the subject often implies.

Third, the *size and very existence of gender differences depends on the formulation of the question and the specific aspect of political issues and subjects are under consideration*. Table 17.1 shows the distribution of gender difference across issues in GSS questions. The GSS offered slightly modified wording of these questions in some years; using the responses to those questions slightly alters the distribution of gender difference across issue areas and years.[8] Within the broad area of "women's issues," the existence

Table 17.1
Gender Differences in the General Social Survey "Spending" Series, 1973–2000

Policy area	Women more supportive	No difference	Men more supportive	Summary all years
Big cities	75, 76, 77, 78, 80, 82, 83, 85, 86, 89, 91, 94, 96, 98, 00	73, 74, 84, 87, 88, 89, 90, 93		r=−.08, SE=.007 N= 22,577
Condition of blacks	76, 77, 80, 82, 83, 85, 86, 88, 94, 96, 98, 00	73, 74, 75, 78, 84, 87, 89, 90, 91, 93		r=−06, SE=.006 N= 23,769
Crime	73, 77, 80, 82, 83, 84, 85, 86, 89, 91, 92, 93, 94, 96, 98, 00	74, 75, 76, 78, 87, 88, 90		r=−.07, SE=.006 N= 24,749
Defense	91	73, 74, 75, 76, 77, 78, 82, 83, 84, 85, 86, 87, 89, 90, 93, 94, 96	80, 88, 00	r=.01, SE=.006 24,378
Drugs	90, 91, 93, 94, 98, 00	73, 74, 75, 76, 77, 78, 80, 82, 83, 84, 85, 87, 88, 89, 96		r=−.04, SE=.006 N= 24,458
Education	75, 82, 94, 96, 98	73, 74, 76, 77, 78, 80, 83, 84, 85, 86, 87, 88, 89, 90, 91, 93, 00		r=−.05, SE=.006 N= 25,089
Environment	75, 78, 80, 82	73, 74, 76, 77, 83, 84, 85, 86, 87, 88, 89, 90, 91, 93, 94, 96, 98, 00		r=−.03, SE=.006 N= 24,561
Foreign aid	80, 86, 89, 93, 96, 98, 00	73, 74, 75, 76, 77, 78, 82, 83, 84, 85, 87, 88, 90, 91, 94		r=−.03, SE=.006 N= 24,583
Health	80, 86, 91, 93, 96, 98, 00	73, 74, 75, 76, 77, 78, 82, 83, 84, 85, 87, 88, 89, 90		r=−.05, SE=.006 N= 24,982
Highways & bridges		85, 86, 88, 89	84, 87, 90, 91, 93, 94, 96, 98, 00	r=.07, SE=.007 N= 23,333
Mass transit		84, 85, 86, 87, 88, 89, 90, 93, 94, 96, 98, 00	91	r=.01, SE=.007 N= 21,981

(continued)

Table 17.1
Gender Differences in the General Social Survey "Spending" Series, 1973–2000
(continued)

Policy area	Women more supportive	No difference	Men more supportive	Summary all years
Parks and recreation		84, 85, 86, 87, 88, 89, 91, 93, 94, 96, 98, 00	90	$r = .02$, SE = .007 N = 23,480
Social security	84, 85, 86, 87, 88, 89, 90, 91, 93, 94, 96, 98, 00			$r = -.10$, SE = .006 N = 23,382
Space exploration			73, 74, 75, 76, 77, 78, 80, 82, 83, 84, 85, 86, 87, 88, 89, 90, 91, 93, 94, 96, 98, 00	$r = .21$, SE = .006 N = 24,452
Welfare	78, 82, 84, 85, 91	73, 74, 75, 76, 77, 80, 83, 86, 87, 88, 89, 90, 93, 94, 96, 98, 00		$r = -.04$, SE = .007 N = 24,758

Note: Entries show the years in which there was a statistically significant correlation between gender and support for budgetary investment in each policy area.
Source: General Social Survey, analyzed and available on-line at: www.icpsr.umich.edu/GSS/.

of gender differences depends on what aspect is under consideration; for example, research generally finds gender differences in beliefs and attitudes respecting rape and sexual harassment, but not abortion (Anderson, Cooper, & Okamura, 1997; Welsh, 1999). Although women tend to be more antimilitarist than men, research shows that the existence and size of gender differences depends on whether the question concerns beliefs, attitudes, or emotions; general attitudes or views of a particular war; assessments of a war as it has been conducted or the possibility of escalation (Bendyna, Finucane, & Kirby, 1996; Conover & Sapiro, 1993; Schlesinger & Heldman, 2001). The National Election Studies (NES) "Guide to Public Opinion" shows that on the question of whether to cut or increase government services and spending, there is a gender difference of nine to fifteen percentage points on cutting services and spending, but the gap ranges from 3 to 15 percentage points on the side of increasing services and spending. With respect to whether the government should guarantee a job and good standard of living, the gender differences on the side of government assistance once reach 10 percentage points between 1972 and 2000, but most often, there was no significant gender difference. In contrast, on the side of leaving people to their own devices, the difference ranged from 8 to 17 percentage points.[9] Theorizing about gender difference and similarity must recognize these subtleties.

Fourth, the *existence and magnitude of gender differences on the same political issues or objects depend on the historical moment.* Most obviously, gender differences in candidate and party support differ from election to election in different countries (Domínguez & McCann, 1995; Kaufmann & Petrocik, 1999; Norris, 1999, Shamir & Arian, 1999). In the United States, gender differences in partisan vote in presidential elections have varied from 0 to 14 percentage points. In the 1950s, men leaned more toward the Democratic party than women did, and since the 1980s women have leaned more toward the Democrats, sometimes substantially. As table 17.1, as well as the patterns cited from the NES "Guide to Public Opinion" show, the existence of gender differences varies over time in ways that should be at least partly explicable. In fact, beyond a few issues such as gun control and capital punishment in the United States, differences do not show up consistently over time, and even when the *existence* of gender differences seems consistent, their magnitude does not (Sapiro, 2001). Some historical periods may be marked by more concern or worry over issues relating to gender and sexuality. Social movements and interest groups can highlight the importance of gender-related questions to their constituents at certain times, as can electoral campaigns. Unfortunately, because even scholars have tended to rely on broad, quasi-naturalistic explanations of gender differences (e.g. women's greater compassion or men's aggression), very little research has focused carefully on explaining change in gender differences over time. A good example to the contrary is Kaufmann and Petrocik's (1999) exploration of the growth in the "gender gap" in the United States, in which they locate the major source of change in men's responses to major political issues.

Fifth, the *size and magnitude of gender differences vary across countries and subpopulations.* Gender differences found in one country do not appear in another, or appear to a much greater or lesser degree (Christy, 1987; Banaszak & Plutzer, 1993; Claibourn & Sapiro, 2001; Prince-Gibson & Schwartz, 1998). Consider the fact that although research in the United States consistently finds that women are less militaristic than men, gender differences on these questions are variable generally crossnationally and, notably, are absent in most research in Israel and the Middle East (Jelen, Thomas, & Wilcox 1994; Tessler & Nachtwey, 1999; Tessler & Warriner, 1997; Togeby, 1994; Wilcox, Hewitt, & Allsop, 1996). Unfortunately, there is little truly comparative research on gender difference and similarity in public opinion, and even less that attempts to explain crossnational variation in the amount of gender difference (Claibourn & Sapiro 2001). Even within

one country, gender differences vary across different subpopulations, defined, for example, by class, race, or age (Everitt, 1998; Lien, 1998; Montoya, 1996; Welch & Sigelman, 1989); and across geographic areas in which
variation in the political context can drive variation in gender differences
in public opinion. Research on the 1992 U.S. presidential elections, for
example, showed that whether voters lived in an area in which there was a
woman running for major office—House, Senate, or governor—had an
impact on the existence and size of gender differences in response to the
presidential candidates; in other words, the context created by exposure to
some electoral contests in which gender was highlighted had an effect on
people's responses to other contests going on at the same time (Sapiro &
Conover, 1997). Campaign organizers in the United States are well aware
of the existence of these gender differences, and, depending on the matrix
of their partisan and electoral interests, they work to take advantage of these
forces or suppress them (Sapiro & Canon, 1999).

Even having pointed out the utility of ordinary categorization for certain aspects of political psychology, I have already, in fact, demonstrated
why ordinary categorization is an excessively limited conception of gender
for purposes of political psychology. The fact that gender emerges variably
in the context of specific interactions and situations and social conditions
also shows the limitations of simple ordinary classifications of gender for
research on gender and political psychology. Thus ordinary categorization
of gender is only one dimension of gender as it is relevant to political
psychology.

The Subjective Content of Gender

Once children learn to labels themselves *boy* or *girl* they begin the lifelong
process of filling out the meaning and structure of that identity. Although
there are important dominant expectations that define the basic shape of
cultural gender norms, even these dominant expectations vary across time,
culture, and subculture, and their implications for human behavior and
social interaction are contextually driven (Deaux & Lafrance, 1998; Frable,
1997; Howard, 2000; Kane, 2000). The degree and exclusivity to which
women "belong" to the home or the private realm varies, and should have
important implications for their relationship to politics. An early study of
adult political socialization demonstrated that the degree to which women
held a gender ideology of privatization—whether they believed that
"women's place was in the home" or that women should play equal roles
with men in business, industry, and government—affected their political
attitudes and orientations, such as political efficacy and political engagement, among others (Sapiro, 1983). Here, gender role attitudes are understood not just as political attitudes like any others but as a subjective component of gender itself.[10] Unfortunately, as rare as investigation of the

subjective components of gender is in political psychology research on women, there is even less regarding men. Adequate measures of subjective aspects of men's gender are rare, thus we know little about the impact of its variation on their political orientation and behavior.

Scholars across the social sciences have used a variety of concepts such as identity, self-definition, self-concept, and self-schemas to identify and explore the implications of gender in people's understanding of who they are and how they relate to other people.[11] Most of these involve the structure of expectations and perceptions of men and women as men and women more generally and thus are related to stereotypes but involve the application of these expectations to oneself (Biernat & Kobrynowicz, 1999; Deaux & Kite, 1993; Signorella, 1999). Unfortunately, there is as yet little research that applies these concepts specifically to political psychology.

One rich seam of empirical research on the political implications of the subjective content of gender emphasizes the impact of gender or feminist *consciousness* (Cole, Zucker, & Ostrov, 1998; Conover & Sapiro, 1993; Cook, 1989; Dean, 1997; Gurin, 1985; Gurin, & Townsend, 1986; Henderson-King & Stewart, 1994; Klein, 1984; Miller, Gurin, Gurin & Malanchuk, 1981; Reingold & Foust, 1998; Rinehart, 1992; Wilcox, 1991; 1997). Gender consciousness (defined somewhat differently by different scholars) is a politicized form of self-identity that specifically incorporates recognition of the role of gender in determining social differentiation and stratification, and a sense of collective fate.

Most research has focused on *feminist* gender consciousness; that is, gender consciousness incorporating the idea that women's options have been limited by gender differentiation and stratification and that these limitations should be overcome. Some research suggests that this kind of gender consciousness stimulates women's political involvement (Miller, et al., 1981) generally, but certainly in feminist politics (Klein, 1984, Rinehart, 1992). Some research suggests that women's feminism also shapes other political attitudes and orientations (Conover, 1988).

Two core problems remain in the study of the impact of feminist gender consciousness or feminism. First, there is considerable debate over the conceptual meaning of *feminist* and *feminist consciousness*, as well as over appropriate operationalization (Berryman-Fink & Verderber, 1985; Conover & Sapiro, 1993; Cook, 1989; Frieze & McHugh, 1998; Henley, Meng, O'Brien, McCarthy, & Sockloskie, 1998; Hyde, 1998; Spence, 1998). Moreover, although there is widespread support for the women's movement in the United States, feminism is viewed less positively (Huddy, Neely, & Lafay, 2000). A second question is whether survey questions used to measure feminist consciousness or feminism function the same way for men and women; that is, whether *feminism* is the same phenomenon for men and women or whether, for example, feminism is rooted more directly in women's experience, is more closely tied to identity, while it functions more like an attitude—like any other—among men (Crosby & Herrek, 1986; Davis & Robinson, 1991; Goldman, 1992; Klein, 1984; Rhodebeck, 1996; Rinehart, 1992; Sapiro, 1990).

Gender consciousness need not be associated with left-wing or liberal politics in order to encourage political engagement; it can also be important in stimulating political engagement on the right, as in the case of those who are mobilized in defense of traditional gender values (Ginsburg, 1989; MacLean, 1994). Moreover, gender consciousness affects both men and women. Many nationalist and ethnic movements, for example, have concerned themselves very directly with constructions of masculinity and what it means to "be a man" (Nagel, 1998, 2000; Sapiro, 1993a), and conceptions of masculinity often appear prominently in the politics of domestic and foreign defense (Cohn, 1987; Cuordileone, 2000). It is widely accepted in the field of gender studies that identity and consciousness mediate and are mediated by other social bases of identity such as race and nationality, but too few studies empirically investigate the interrelationships of these different characteristics in people's identity, consciousness, and the significance of these for politics (Gay & Tate, 1998; Thompson, 1999; Wade & Brittan-Powell, 2001).

The subject content of gender is most often conceptualized as an independent variable in research on political orientations and behavior, but another subject for research is the impact of public policy and political organizations such as social movements on individual and collective conceptions of gender (Lewin & Tragos, 1987; Lovejoy, 1998; Rosenthal, 1984; Sapiro, 1990). Consider the efforts aimed at changing gender stereotypes and attitudes and men's and women's understanding of their gendered selves, as when women are encouraged to strive for success in previously male-dominated areas, when men and women are told "there is no excuse" for gender-based violence against women,[12] or when conservative religious regimes attempt to institute more gender segregation and privatization of women. More research in these areas is needed.

Personality, Personal Styles, and Practices

Research on gender and political psychology often theorizes that conventional wisdom about men's and women's personality traits, their emotions and cognitive skills, their communication and interaction shape their political orientations, behavior, and interaction. Explanations of gender differences in attitudes toward violence are often grounded in supposed gender differences in nurturance; differences in social policy attitudes reference women's special nurturance or compassion. Other discussions of political gender difference assume that gender differences in aggression, competitiveness, or emotionality are givens that explain political differences even when these personality characteristics remain unmeasured, leaving ordinary gender characterization as a surrogate for personality variation between the stereo-

typic masculine and feminine, complexes that vary historically, crossculturally, and contextually (Kashima, Yamaguchi, & Kim, 1995; Swann, Langlois, & Gilbert, 1999). Gender studies scholars generally agree that the
complex that is gender includes personality characteristics, styles, and practices that are culturally identified with a masculinity-femininity continuum
(Deaux & Lafrance, 1998). Ordinary gender classifications, however, cannot
stand as surrogates for this variation in political psychology research.

The search for explanations for findings of gender differences in attitudes toward social welfare, violence issues, environmental policy, and even
certain race questions leads many researchers to refer to women's "different
voice," citing Carol Gilligan's classic work on the structure of women's
moral thinking, often cited as though it offered strong evidence of a tendency for women to use a framework of an "ethic of care" while men use
an "ethic of justice"or abstract individual rights (Gilligan, 1982). The large
body of empirical research following up on Gilligan's original hypotheses
suggest that women's and men's reputation for moral difference far outstrips
their actual differences (Jaffee & Hyde, 2000). Research that explicitly looks
for the "justice" and "connection" frames tend to show little difference in
use of the "justice" standard, but a tendency toward the expected gender
differences in the "connection" standard (Ford & Lowery, 1986; Lifton,
1985; Walker, 1984, Gump & Baker, 2000; Humphries & Parker, 2000).

Although these findings do not close the field of gender and moral
reasoning, they do suggest that it is time to stop referring automatically to
women's "different voice" as a means of explaining the gender basis of
political judgment. Rather, if these or other underlying structures of reasoning are implicated in structures of the relationship between gender and
political thinking, they should be examined directly, to see both how they
vary within and across gender categories and, crucially, whether there are
gender differences in the application of these reasoning principles to politics.
A good example is the work by Felicia Pratto, Jim Sidanius, and their
colleagues, in their crosscultural investigations of social dominance orientations (i.e. preferences for group-based inequalities), in which they find
men generally score higher, and this difference has implications for the
gender, race, and ethnonationalist politics (Pratto, Liu, & Levin, 2000;
Pratto, Sidanius, Stallworth, & Malle, 1994; Pratto, Stallworth, & Sidanius,
1997; Sidanius, Levin, Liu, & Pratto, 2000).

Gender-Based Divisions of Roles and Resources

The psychologist Kay Deaux has been quoted as saying, in the context of
trying to understand gender, masculinity, and femininity, that "a strictly
psychological approach is—well—too psychological" (Spence, 1999,
p. 284). Gender is often theorized as a matrix of social and economic roles
and divisions of labor, especially in the family and workplace. Although
gender norms and stereotypes help sort people into social roles and orga-

nizational positions, these divisions of labor and institutionalization of social practices determine the expectations that are applied to people, and gender stereotypes revolve around these roles (Eagly 1987; Eagly & Steffen, 1984). The stereotype of women as especially nurturant (a personality trait) is linked to the stereotype that their most central life mission is motherhood (a social and institutional role), but these are not the same thing.

Ordinary classification of gender is often taken to "stand for" particular social roles. As Feldberg and Glenn (1979; revised in Sapiro, 2002, ch. 14) argue, sociologists (and, we can add, other social scientists) tend to use different models to explain men's and women's behavior and orientations. For men, there is the *job model*, assuming that men's primary connection to the social world, and the main source of their sociopolitical attitudes, interests, and activities is their occupational roles and status and their connection to the economy. For women, there is the *family model*, assuming that women's primary connection to the social world, and the main source of their sociopolitical attitudes, interests, and activities is their familial roles and their connection to families and family members.

Should we expect gender differentiation in attitudes toward the welfare state or war because of gender-based divisions of labor in caring for dependents? Empirical evidence thus far has refused to cooperate with this common hypothesis; having children does not seem to affect men's or women's defense and foreign policy attitudes (Conover & Sapiro, 1993; Bendyna, et al., 1996). Are women less likely than men to have a strong sense of political efficacy because they are more generally excluded from public life? Is women's political engagement limited because of their family roles? Does gender segregation of men and women into different kinds of occupations have implications for the relationship of gender to political interests, attitudes, and activities? These are good empirical questions, deserving of specific research; the answers cannot be derived directly from ordinary gender categorization.

Adequate theorizing about the connections among gender, socioeconomic roles, and political psychology requires recognizing three basic facts about gender roles. First, although all known societies have divisions of familial and economic labor, the exact structure of these divisions, and the status accorded to them, vary over time, crossculturally, and even across different social subgroups. Second, conventional wisdom about gender-based divisions of labor is often wrong or out of date. In the United States, for example, even scholars often seem to miss the fact that the majority of adult women have long been in the workforce; since 1980, this includes the majority of women with babies under 1 year of age. Although the total amount of housework women do has declined in recent decades as they have become integrated into the labor force, their *share* of it has not changed much, because men's share has not increased as much as conventional wisdom suggests (Coltrane, 2000).

Third, particular roles and resources (for example, education, employment) might *or might not* affect women and men similarly. Gender differences in political involvement, for example, might be due to gender differences in education, but it is also possible that because of the constraints placed on women, a degree of education cannot "buy" as much involvement for women as for men. This appears to be the case in some countries (Claibourn & Sapiro, 2001). Likewise, women's domestic labor may seclude them from the public world more in one country than another, or more in one time than another.

The most and comprehensive treatment of roles, institutions, and gender is Burns, Schlozman, and Verba's (2001) study of political participation in the United States. They transform the many findings, suggestions, and bits of conventional wisdom found in the scholarly literature and public commentary into a set of hypotheses focusing on how the major participatory factors of resources, political orientations, and recruitment are transformed into political participation in the context of familial, educational, occupational, and social institutions that are themselves gender-differentiated and gender-stratified. Their results only sometimes confirm conventional wisdom. Although they found that "women are, on average, disadvantaged with respect to education, income, and occupational status" (p. 359), they found no evidence that the time constraints imposed on women by employment and domestic roles inhibited their participation, nor did they find that women with young children lacked the psychic space for politics. Their investigation of the impact of family structures yields an interesting and complicated set of findings, suggesting, for example, that the impact of family patriarchy may be more on boosting men's participation than inhibiting women's. Their work shows the benefits of researching the specific and distinct impacts of different roles and resources in terms of both actual activity and subjective attitudes and interpretations, in relation to each other and their institutional contexts, and in a manner that judges their indirect and direct effects on women and men distinctly. Both employment and employment in traditionally male-dominated positions, for further example, tend to increase feminism and feminist gender consciousness among women in a way that we would not expect for men (Banaszak & Leighley, 1991; Gruber & Bjorn, 1988; Plutzer, 1988; Sapiro, 1983), although married men's attitudes are shaped by the employment status of their wives (Sapiro & Conover, 2001; Smith, 1985). Having children draws people into political participation revolving around children, but this effect is greater for women than men (Schlozman, Burns, Verba, & Donahue, 1995). Relatively little research, unfortunately, attempts to understand the *process* by which these personal roles translate into political phenomena. Among the key exceptions are Burns, Schlozman, and Verba (2001), who focus on gender differentiation of roles, and the resources provided by these roles that can be transformed into political engagement; and Stoker and Jennings (1995), identify the life disruption of the early stages of marriage as a cause of temporary decreases in political engagement.

◤ Responding to a Gendered Political World

Thus far I have considered some of the ways that people's gender affects the way they think about and respond to politics. Another problem for political psychology is how the gender of political persons and objects shapes the way people respond to them. There are two major approaches to research in this area. Many branches of cultural studies contain lively research communities specializing in analysis of text, discourse, and symbolic representations of gender in politics. This chapter focuses on the other branch, based on empirical study of cognition and affect in politics.

The Politics of Perceiving the Gender of Political People

When Elizabeth I went to Tilbury, she knew she would have been regarded as a wholly different monarch if she were a man, and her leadership would have been determined by different opportunities and constraints. Imagine the strategic options of her predecessor had that monarch been Henrietta, not Henry VIII. Gender stereotypes may have changed substantially, and loosened some of their grip in some societies over the centuries, but they remain a substantial force in even the most "modern" societies, such as the United States (Swann, Langlois, & Gilbert, 1999). Even in Sweden, the country most reputed for gender egalitarianism, domestic labor continues to be divided in traditional ways (Nyman, 1999).

This field of gender stereotyping has been very lively in recent years.[13] Some research has followed the lead set in the study of race stereotyping and has considered whether a "new" form of sexism, based on symbolic politics, has replaced an older, more direct form of sexism (Masser & Abrams, 1999; Swim, Aikin, Hall, & Hunter, 1995; Swim & Cohen, 1997). Indeed, current research abandons the idea that prejudice and stereotype are necessarily formed around "bad" statements about the target group, turning instead to the implications of two different forms: "hostile" (women are overemotional) and "benevolent" (women are more compassionate) stereotypes. Crossnational research shows that both forms are connected with inequality, but they operate differently; one through exclusion and antagonism, the other through protective paternalism and chivalry. There tend to be more gender differences in hostile than benevolent sexism (Glick & Fiske, 2001). Given the strongly intertwined relationship of gender and sexuality stereotyping, recent work on stereotypes revolving around sexuality, including, especially, homophobia, also could be investigated more for their links to person perception in politics (Herek, 2000; Plummer, 2001; Wong, McCreary, & Carpenter, 1999). Some of the more interesting issues revolve around the question of the conditions under which culturally derived stereotypes are activated (Kray, Thompson, & Galinsky, 2001).

The most common political application found in research on prejudice and stereotype in person perception concerns response to male and female candidates and political leaders. Often researchers present subjects with a speech, advertisement, or other document giving information about a "candidate" and experimentally manipulate the gender of the candidate to assess the impact of gender stereotypes on perceptions of candidate competence or other aspects of evaluation (Alexander & Andersen, 1993; Bernstein 2000; Huddy & Terkildson, 1993; Iyengar, Valentino, Ansolabehere, & Simon, 1997; McDermott, 1997, 1998; Riggle, Miller, Shields, & Johnson, 1997; Rosenwasser & Seale, 1988; Rosenwasser, Rogers, Fling, Silvers-Pickens, & Butemeyer, 1987; Sapiro, 1982). These studies vary the stimulus, circumstances, or questions, but their conclusions converge: the public uses common gender stereotypes to fill in information about candidates, especially in low-information elections. Survey research on citizens during actual electoral contests also shows that stereotypes can frame candidate perception (Koch, 2000).

Other applications of gender-based prejudice and stereotype research focus on power, influence, and leadership, most of it flowing from Paula Johnson's (1976) argument that because gender-based stereotypes create different expectations of men and women, they must rely on different styles and strategies to exert power and influence or be effective leaders. Among the major bases of power that may have gendered implications are *expertise* or competence, *legitimacy* or authority, and *likability* or other aspects of social relationships. Linda's Carli's (1999) review of the literature finds evidence that gender-based perceptions yield greater expert and legitimate power to men than women (also Foschi, 2000) unless the task at hand is traditionally associated with women. Women leaders may be regarded as warmer, more caring, and likeable, but the characteristics people associate with effective leadership tend to be the ones stereotypically regarded as male, thus undercutting women's leadership (Carli, 1999; Kawakami, White, & Langer, 2000).

Because emotions are gender-typed (Plant, Hyde, & Keltner, 2000),[14] people react to male and female leaders differently when they display the same emotions. In a study of CEOs, Lewis (2000) found that women leaders were rated higher when they showed no emotion than when they showed sadness or anger, while men were rated higher when they showed no emotion or showed anger than when they showed sadness. Men were rated similarly when they displayed either no emotion or anger. Women, in other words, are generally regarded as overly emotional and thus have to be careful about showing any negative emotion. A study of the development of policy to deal with victims of breast cancer showed that opponents of "informed consent" legislation dismissed women activists' competence on the grounds that they are too emotional (Montini, 1996).

The application of stereotypes depends on the circumstances. Reliance on stereotypes is an information strategy; thus candidate perception literature suggests that stereotypes are used when other information cues are absent. Stereotyping can also be motivated by self-defense. Sinclair and

Kunda's (2000) experimental research shows that when people evaluate someone who is in a position to evaluate them, assessments of the competence of the female evaluators depend more on the positivity of their evaluations than do assessments of men's competence. Sinclair and Kunda suggest that unless gender stereotyping diminishes, as more women hold positions of authority, that is, are in the position of giving negative feedback, they will increasingly encounter skepticism about their competence.

The Politics of Perceiving the Gender of Issues

Political issues may be also be gendered, and in at least three ways. First, some policy questions are manifestly *about gender*; their subjects are women as women and/or men as men, as in the case of "women's rights," "men's rights," and gender equality, among others. A large literature investigates the nature of public opinion on these kinds of questions—its sources and structure as well as distribution—at the mass level (Banaszak & Leighley, 1991; Banaszak & Plutzer, 1993; Crosby & Herek, 1986; Davis & Robinson, 1991; Sapiro & Conover, 2001; Sigel, 1996; Sigelman & Wilcox, 2001; Wilcox, 1991, 1992, 1997) and elite and activist level (Dolan, 1997; Montini, 1996; Reingold, 2000).

Second, policy questions can be gendered in that they *relate to situations in which men and women tend to play different roles or have different experiences, needs, or problems or tend to be treated differently*. Examples include reproduction and child care, employment, poverty, domestic and sexual violence, criminal justice, education, aging, health care, military issues, consumer policy, among many others. Some of them—such as domestic violence, child care policy, or parental leave—are conventionally understood as "women's issues," but this itself is an interesting problem for analysis, because they are social phenomena (gender-based violence, parenthood) that involve both men and women, even though they stand in different relationships to these phenomena and perhaps have different interests in them. Child care policy is a "women's" issue only in societies in which women, not parents, bear primary responsibility for caring for their children. As recent policies of *gender mainstreaming* suggest, given the large amount of gender differentiation across much of human society, a much wider range of social issues and policies can be understood in gendered terms than most policy-makers have realized. Gender mainstreaming, a policy concept endorsed by many international agencies, such as the UN, and national governments, argues that rather than having separate ministries to focus on "women's" issues, policy-makers and administrators in all areas should consider the gendered implications of their domains of focus (Sen, 2000, True, 2001).

A large literature on attitudes toward abortion shows that gender is not a predictor of them (Alvarez & Brehm, 1995; Dillon, 1993; Hildreth & Dran, 1994; Wattier, Daynes, & Totovitch, 1997). A long stream of research on sexual and domestic violence and sexual harassment shows, among other things, disturbing patterns indicating that female victims tend to be held accountable for the violence perpetrated against them, especially by people with more conservative gender ideology, and in organizations with conservative norms (Welsh, 1999; Williams, Giuffre, & Dellinger, 1999). Questions remain that merit systematic empirical treatment. Most notably, do citizens and political leaders react to policy issues differently if one sex or the other is more at the center of the problem, and a potential beneficiary of policy?

A third way that policy and political questions can be gendered is that *extant policies not originally designed with gender in mind can have different effects on men and women.* Controlling the size of government by cutting social services has gendered effects because women are more likely to use many of those services and are more likely to have to take up the slack with their own labor when those services disappear. The United States's unusually small public health system, compared with other advanced industrial countries, means that the apparently "gender-neutral" problem of health care costs in fact affects men and women differently, especially because of women's health care needs during their reproductively active years and as caretakers of children. Many policy analyses have studied the intended and unintended consequences of public policy and the design of state institutions (Corcoran, Danziger, Kalil, & Seefeldt, 2000; Glass & Estes, 1997; Haney, 2000).

Research on framing shows that any given policy area may be represented and interpreted in a variety of ways and that these representations draw people to different solutions (Iyengar, 1994; Stone, 1989). Different groups of people systematically understand the same event or issue in very different terms, not just because they have been exposed to different media frames but because of their own experiences, orientations, and styles of cognitive processing. The degree to which people are gender schematic, for example, has an impact on the way they see the world around them (Frable & Bem, 1985). By the same token, gender consciousness, especially as mobilized by social movements, should also affect people's interpretation of political information through gender terms. So might the degree to which the context of a policy discussion threatens people's sense of gender or sexual identity (chapter 15).

Single events or issues may have a wide range of possible meanings, some of which are gendered. Sapiro and Soss (1999) argue, for example, that one of the reasons the 1991 Clarence Thomas confirmation hearings were so controversial was that members of the public didn't just disagree over whether they thought Anita Hill's charges held up; they disagreed over what these events were really about. For some people, this whole spectacle revolved around questions of gender and related issues such as sexual harassment of women. For others, gender was much less relevant compared to racial questions or, simply, the conflict between liberals and conservatives,

Democrats and Republicans. Thus an important agenda for research is investigating the conditions under which culturally derived stereotypes and frames are activated (Kray, Thompson, & Galinsky, 2001).

◤ Gender, Power, and Political Psychology: Problems of Inequality and Stigma

The analysis of power is an essential part of the study of politics, and one too often ignored in dominant approaches to political psychology. This field has a lot to offer those who seek to understand power dynamics, including those that undergird and change gender systems. It can provide handles on understanding how cultural norms become integrated into the actions of human beings, how people act and interact within different systems of rules and social expectations, why and how systems of stigma (Crocker, Major, & Steel, 1998) operate in everyday life, how people cope with being victims of inequality and stigma, and what is the effect on them. These are questions that should be investigated both at a general and comparative level, across the social categorizations that form the basis of inequality and stigma and in terms of the specificity of specific categorizations, such as gender.

Stigma and political subordination function through the dynamics of stereotype and prejudice, already discussed, and within patterns of communication and social interaction. Verbal and nonverbal communication and social interaction all have "rules of the road" that are often followed nonconsciously but reflect the social dominance of those involved; they indicate the communications "rights of way" (Sapiro, 2002, ch. 10). Higher status people occupy and control more space (including personal space proportional to their body size), including others' space; they can initiate touch with others more; stare more while not being required to look as attentive; make more noise; interrupt others; control the duration and timing of communications; initiate and change topics; and control the level of familiarity. Lower status people are perceived as rude or insubordinate when they assert equality with a higher status person in these matters; these communication rules-of-the-road are encoded in the principles of politeness.

Research shows that gender inequality invokes these principles (Cameron, 1998; Deaux & Lafrance, 1998, pp. 801–807). Men can initiate conversation, topics, physical approach, touch, and gaze with women that would be regarded, variously, as rude, "dominating," masculine, or specifically sexual if a woman acted similarly to a man. Of course, these principles do not float fully free of institutions and specific social roles; as long as gender differentiates institutional positions, these positions shape communication and interaction. Cathryn Johnson's (1994) experimental research shows that the *position* of a person (in this case, as manager or subordinate) is much more important than gender itself in determining communication patters, but the gender composition of the group, and in interaction with the gender of the leader, also has some effects. But as the discussion of social expectations pointed out, the expectations placed on incumbents of role positions spills over to the general social categories. Other research shows broader gender differences even within status positions (Hall & Friedman, 1999). Lyn Kathlene's (1994) study of transcripts of state legislative committee hearings showed that men actually became more verbally aggressive as the percentage of women increased and as women took positions of power. Thus it should not be surprising that even when they occupy leadership positions, women's communication and interaction patterns are regarded differently from men's and can undercut their leadership and reputations, as already discussed. Research shows that there are ways for women who are aware of these tendencies to mitigate them (for example, by enhancing their likeability), but this requires places extra burdens on women leaders to be aware of their social interactions and their effects (Carli, 1999; Kawakami, White, & Langer, 2000).

It is common to find psychological and physical threat and coercion involved in maintaining systems of power inequality and stigma. This is certainly true of gender relations, with the added dimension that the primary forms of gender-based threat, coercion, and even violence involved in gender inequality are imbued with sexual character and occur in the context of working, familial, and other regular social relationships, including sexual assault, sexual harassment, and domestic violence. *Gender-based violence* or *coercion* is defined as violence or coercion that is understood, explained, or justified in terms of gender difference or roles. In the common forms of gender-based violence or coercion, the assaults and threats are generally understood as based in male aggression or sexual needs (when provoked, their antisocial behavior is widely regarded as understandable if not justifiable), justified in terms of victim precipitation and women's irrationality (she asked for it). Women and men tend to use different standards and definitions for identifying these forms of sexual coercion and violence. For example, many men tend to read more sexuality into women's behavior than they intend to be displaying; men who are especially likely to do this are more likely to engage in sexual harassment (Koukounas & Letch, 2001). This gender difference in perception is especially important if men dominate the positions that determine how victims and perpetrators will be treated.

Gender-based harassment occurs not just in organizations but on the street and in other public places, just as does racial harassment and harassment of sexual minorities, and with the same implications for the structure of power and inequality (Gardner, 1995). These everyday acts are mechanisms of larger stigma systems that grant permission to higher status people to harass those of subordinate and stigmatized groups. Unlike racial harassment, harassment of women is widely regarded as a frivolous part of human nature, perhaps even romantic. Placing this "naturalized" framing in a distinctly political context, Sapiro has pursued the question of why gender-based violence has been so widely tolerated within democratic theory and, indeed, treated as a form of violence that is irrelevant to democratic theory (Sapiro 1993b).

Gender-based violence and coercion is grounded in relationships defined by inequality and in turn perpetuates inequality. Leaders and even peers in a workplace create climates in which potential perpetrators understand that harassment is tolerated, and in which targets understand that their perceptions of the problem would not be taken seriously (Deaux & Lafrance, 1998). Consider the issue of sexist jokes. People who are not inclined to be sympathetic to concerns about sexual harassment find the preoccupation with sexist jokes unjustified and perhaps an interference with the right to speech. But research shows that for people who are high in hostile sexism, exposure to sexist jokes leads to greater tolerance of sexist events. Those high in hostile sexism also found the jokes funnier in the first place (Ford 2000).

An increasing amount of research focuses on how targets of sexual harassment and gender-based discrimination respond to this situation (Welsh, 1999). The first question is whether someone views the experience she is having as harassing; the second is what she will do about it. The status of the perpetrator can have contradictory effects on targets. If the perpetrator is a supervisor or in a high-level organizational position, that can enhance a target's view that she has experienced harassment; on the other hand, the higher social dominance of someone in a high-level position inhibits this perception (Sheets & Braver, 1999). This second effect turns on the "communication right of way" discussed earlier.

As far as taking action is concerned, reactions vary, depending especially on women's perceptions of whether there are viable options for recourse. A very small percentage of women who believe they have been harassed actually report their experiences to a superior or other "intake" person. Those in more vulnerable positions or in organizations in which they believe they cannot attract much sympathy are relatively unlikely to have any options but to try to ignore the situation. A study of black women firefighters, however, suggests that some women may feel so marginalized that they believe they have nothing to lose in fighting (Yoder & Aniakudo, 1995).

A study in which women were treated to either harassing or nonharassing interviews provides good insight into the experience of harassment and how it differs from what people expect it might be like. In this study, no one refused to answer the objectionable questions, and very few confronted the perpetrator. Those who responded tended to do so indirectly; a little over one third asked why the offending question was asked, and the vast majority of those asked only after the interview was over. Interestingly, although a majority of subjects thought they would respond actively to harassment, often quite bluntly, most in the end did not respond, and no one did so bluntly. A record of the subjects' *nonverbal* behavior showed that the harassed subjects displayed "non-Duchenne" smiles (a smile that does not show positive emotion) longer during the interview than did nonharassed subjects—a sign of accommodation—as well as other facial signs of stress. One possible explanation lies in the emotional experience of harassment; while subjects expected to feel angry in response to harassment, most in fact felt fear. Fear was inversely related to actively confronting the perpetrator, while anger was not correlated with confrontation (Woodzicka & LaFrance, 2001). These results are consistent with another study, in which only a small minority of women confronted a harasser directly (and only a minority did at all), although most women thought they would respond directly to a perpetrator. Normative pressures, such as the pressure to "be polite," and fear of retaliation silenced the women or attenuated their protest. The responses people make to harassment and discrimination make a difference for their own well-being. The more people respond by using social support rather than avoidance, the lower their feelings of helplessness and the more collective action they take (Foster, 2000).

Indeed, responding to discrimination, stigma, and harassment can be costly. Women do not tend to expect to gain much from charging perpetrators with harassment or discrimination, and many expect retaliation. The problem is especially great if the victim expects to have to work or interact with the perpetrator in the future, and especially if that person is more powerful than the victim. Experimental research shows that even under conditions of near certainty that an African-American student got a low grade because of discrimination, if he attributed his poor grade to discrimination rather than his own ability, subjects viewed him more as a "complainer" and had a less favorable view of him (Kaiser & Miller, 2001). There is no reason to believe that a woman attributing failure to gender discrimination would fare any better.[15]

Conclusion: Gender and Political Psychology

Thinking back to Elizabeth, standing at Tilbury, women shouldn't have to be terribly clever in order to manage both being a woman and gaining respect in the political world. Or at least no more clever than men need to be. Elizabeth's knowledge that she was regarded by others as a "weak and feeble" woman, having to pretend she accepted that view, while ruling with strength masked in flowing, frilly, virginal white, cannot be an incomprehensible situation to women of this very different era, even if fashion has changed dramatically. Political systems encompass structures of power and inequality, and the means to redress the problems of power and inequality, and they create a means to share in collective self-governance. Political psychology offers means to help understand these systems and changes in them.

▶ Notes

1. For an excellent book elaborating on this view of Elizabeth I, see Weir, 1999.

2. The following assertions are derived from 30 years of reading masses of literature in the field without uncovering exceptions to these generalizations; there is no single study that can be cited for its research on "all known societies." Should anyone find exceptions, please contact the author.

3. In discussing men or women "as such" I mean to say that while men and women may be treated or perceived on the basis of any characteristics they might possess (or be presumed to possess), in this case I am focusing on how men (or women) are treated or perceived *because, aside from anything else, they are men* (or women). As I shall point out shortly, the social construction of gender means that the treatment of men as men or women as women can be mitigated and moderated by other social characteristics and classifications such as race or age.

4. In terms of its political relevance, gender classification has historically been more crosscut by other social classifications for men than for women. Because women as such have tended to be excluded from many aspects of politics, and even basic "rights of citizenship," their age, race, or religion, for example, has often made much less difference for their political standing than for that of men.

5. I use the term *gender difference* and not *gender gap*. The latter was a rhetorical device based on the concept of gender differences in politics that was originally meant to help empower women in electoral politics (Bonk, 1988). The term became popularized so that even scholars began to use the term to express any concept of gender difference. As I shall argue, *gap* is exactly the wrong concept to express the phenomenon as research has revealed it. In addition, there is no reason to use a terminology that is different from the one we use for other forms of social differentiation, such as class, race, or crossnational *differences*.

6. The list is available from the author.

7. In this series, respondents are asked whether they think too much, too little, or the right amount is being spent by the U.S. national government in a wide range of policy areas.

8. Analysis by author.

9. The NES "Guide to Public Opinion" can be found on-line at www.umich.edu/~nes/nesguide/nesguide.htm.

10. The same *variables* may serve as indicators of different theoretical concepts. The variable used to measure women's ideology of privatization of their own gender—most widely recognized as the standard seven-point scale on women's roles that has appeared in the NES since 1972—is more often used simply as a political attitude.

11. The terms listed in this sentence refer to overlapping concepts and theories that are embedded, variously, in personality, cognitive, and social psychology. For an introduction to these concepts and theories, see Deaux & Lafrance, 1998; Hyde, 1996; Spence, 1985. For more discussion specifically of identity and political psychology, see chapter 15.

12. In 1994, the Family Violence Prevention Fund (U.S.A.) launched a national campaign against domestic violence in partnership with the Advertising Council, called "There's No Excuse for Domestic Violence." See Klein, Campbell, Soler, & Ghez, 1997, and www.fvpf.org/publiced/.

13. Good reviews of the literature on stereotype and prejudice are available elsewhere in Deaux & Kite, 1993; Fiske, 1998; Hamilton & Sherman, 1994; Hilton von Hippel,

1996; Macrae & Bodenhausen, 2000; Macrae, Stangor, & Hewstone, 1996; Swann, Langlois, & Gilbert, 1999.

14. *Gender-typed* means that they are stereotypically understood as gender differentiated, not that they are in actuality gender differentiated.

15. For more on credibility of accused and accuser, see Dunn & Cody, 2000.

▶ References

Alexander, D., & Andersen, K. (1993). Gender as a factor in the attribution of leadership traits. *Political Research Quarterly, 46,* 527–545.

Alvarez, R. M., & Brehm, J. (1995). American ambivalence towards abortion policy: Development of a heteroskedastic probit model of competing values. *American Journal of Political Science, 39,* 1055–82.

Anderson, K. B., Cooper, H., & Okamura, L. (1997). Individual differences and attitudes toward rape: A meta-analytic review. *Personality and Social Psychology Bulletin, 23,* 295–315.

Banaszak, L. A., & Leighley, J. E. (1991). How employment affects women's gender attitudes: The workplace as a locus of contextual effects. *Political Geography Quarterly, 10,* 174–185.

Banaszak, L. A., & Plutzer, E. (1993). Contextual determinants of feminist attitudes: National and subnational influences in Western Europe. *American Political Science Review, 87,* 147–157.

Bendyna, M. E., Finucane, T., & Kirby, L. (1996). Gender differences in public attitudes toward the Gulf War: A test of competing hypotheses. *The Social Science Journal, 33,* 1–22.

Bernstein, A. G. (2000). The effects of message theme, policy explicitness, and candidate gender. *Communication Quarterly, 48,* 159–173.

Berryman-Fink, C., & Verderber, K. S. (1985). Attributions of the term feminist: A factor analytic development of a measuring instrument. *Psychology of Women Quarterly, 9,* 51–64.

Biernat, M., & Kobrynowicz, D. (1999). A shifting standards perspective on the complexity of gender stereotypes and gender stereotyping. In W. B. Swann, J. H. Langlois, & L. A. Gilbert (Eds.), *Sexism and stereotypes in modern society: The gender science of Janet Taylor Spence* (pp. 75–98). Washington, DC: APA Press.

Bonk, K. (1988). The selling of the "gender gap": The role of organized feminism. In C. M. Mueller (Ed.), *The politics of the gender gap: The social construction of political influence* (pp. 82–101). Newbury Park, CA: Sage.

Burns, N., Schlozman, K. L., & Verba, S. (1997). The public consequences of private inequality: Family life and citizen participation. *American Political Science Review, 91,* 373–89.

Burns, N., Schlozman, K. L., & Verba, S. (2001). *The private roots of public action: Gender, equality, and political participation.* Cambridge, MA: Harvard University Press.

Cameron, D. (1998). Gender, language, and discourse: A review essay. *Signs, 23,* 945–974.

Carli, L. L. (1999). Gender, interpersonal power, and social influence. *Journal of Social Issues, 55,* 81–99.

Chaney, C. K., Alvarez, R. M., & Nagler, J. (1998). Explaining the gender gap in U.S. presidential elections. *Political Research Quarterly, 51,* 311–370.

Christy, C. A. (1987). *Sex differences in political participation: Processes of change in fourteen nations.* New York: Praeger.

Claibourn, M., & Sapiro, V. (2001, April). *Gender differences in citizen-level democratic citizenship: Evidence from the comparative study of electoral systems.* Paper prepared for delivery to the annual meeting of the Midwest Political Science Association, Chicago.

Cohn, C. (1987). Sex and death in the rational world of defense intellectuals. *Signs, 12,* 687–718.

Cole, E. R., Zucker, A. N., & Ostrove, J. M. (1998). Political participation and feminist consciousness among women activists of the 1960s. *Political Psychology, 19,* 349–371.

Coltrane, S. (2000). Research on household labor: Modeling and measuring the social embeddedness of routine family work. *Journal of Marriage & the Family, 62,* 1208–1234.

Conover, P. J. (1988). Feminists and the gender gap. *Journal of Politics, 50,* 985–1010.

Conover, P. J., & Sapiro, V. (1993). Gender, feminist consciousness, and war. *American Journal of Political Science, 37,* 1079–1099.

Cook, E. A. (1989). Measuring feminist consciousness. *Women and Politics, 9,* 71–88.

Corcoran, M., Danziger, S. K., Kalil, A., & Seefeldt, K. S. (2000). How welfare reform is affecting women's work. *Annual Review of Sociology, 26,* 241–269.

Crocker, J., Major, B., & Steele, C. (1998). Social stigma. In D. T. Gilbert, S. T. Fiske, & G. Lindzey (Eds.), *The handbook of social psychology* (4th ed., pp. 504–553). Boston: McGraw-Hill.

Crosby, F., & Herek, G. M. (1986). Male sympathy with the situation of women: Does personal experience make a difference? *Journal of Social Issues, 42,* 55–66.

Cuordileone, K. A. (2000). Politics in an age of anxiety: Cold War political culture and the crisis in American masculinity, 1949–1960. *Journal of American History, 87,* 515–46.

Dabbs, J. M., Jr., Alford, E. C., & Fielden, J. A. (1998). Trial lawyers: Blue collar talent in a white collar world. *Journal of Applied Social Psychology, 28,* 84–94.

Dabbs, J. M., Jr., Bernieri, F. J., Strong, R. K., Campo, R., & Milun, R. (2001). Going on stage: Testosterone in greetings and meetings. *Journal of Research in Personality, 35,* 27–40.

Davis, N. J., & Robinson, R. V. (1991). Men's and women's consciousness of gender inequality: Austria, West Germany, Great Britain, and the United States. *American Sociological Review, 56,* 72–84.

Dean, J. (1997). Feminist solidarity, reflective solidarity: Theorizing connections after identity politics. *Women and Politics, 18,* 1–26.

Deaux, K., & Kite, M. (1993). Gender stereotypes. In F. L. Denmark & M. A. Paludi (Eds.), *Psychology of women: A handbook of issues and theories* (pp. 107–139). Westport, CT: Greenwood Press.

Deaux, K., & Lafrance, M. (1998). Gender. In D. T. Gilbert, S. T. Fiske, & G. Lindzey (Eds.), *The handbook of social psychology* (4th ed., pp. 788–827). New York: McGraw-Hill.

Dillon, M. (1993). Argumentative complexity of abortion discourse. *Public Opinion Quarterly, 57,* 305–314.

Dolan, J. (1997). Support for women's interests in the 103rd Congress: The distinct impact of congressional women. *Women and Politics, 18,* 81–94.

Dolan, K. (1998). Voting for women in the "year of the woman." *American Journal of Political Science, 42,* 272–293.

Domínguez, J. I., & McCann, J. A. (1995). Shaping Mexico's electoral arena: The construction of partisan cleavages in the 1988 band 1991 national elections. *APSR, 89,* 34–48.

Dunn, D., & Cody, M. J. (2000). Account credibility and public image: Excuses, Justifications, denials, and sexual harassment. *Communication Monographs, 67,* 372–392.

Eagly, A. H. (1987). *Sex differences in social behavior: A social role interpretation.* Hillsdale, NJ: Erlbaum.

Eagly, A. H. (1995). The science and politics of comparing women and men. *American Psychologist, 50,* 145–158.

Eagly, A. H., & Steffen, V. J. (1984). Gender stereotypes stem from the distribution of women and men into social roles. *Journal of Personality and Social Psychology, 46,* 735–754.

Eagly, A. H., & Wood, W. (1999). The origins of sex differences in human behavior: Evolved dispositions versus social roles. *American Psychologist, 54,* 408–423.

Everitt, J. (1998). The gender gap in Canada: Now you see it, now you don't. *Canadian Review of Sociology and Anthropology, 35,* 191–219.

Feldberg, R. K., & Glenn, E. N. (1979). Male and female: Job versus gender models in the sociology of work. *Social Problems, 26,* 524–538.

Fiske, S. T. (1998). Stereotyping, prejudice, and discrimination. In D. T. Gilbert, S. T. Fiske, & G. Lindzey (Eds.), *The handbook of social psychology* (4th ed., pp. 357–411). New York: McGraw-Hill.

Ford, M. R., & Lowery, C. R. (1986). Gender differences in moral reasoning: A comparison of the justice and care orientations. *Journal of Personality and Social Psychology, 50,* 777–783.

Ford, T. E. (2000). Effects of sexist humor on tolerance of sexist events. *Personality and Social Psychology Bulletin, 26,* 1094–1107.

Foschi, M. (2000). Double standards for competence: Theory and research. *Annual Review of Sociology, 26,* 21–42.

Foster, M. D. (2000). Positive and negative responses to personal discrimination: Does coping make a difference? *The Journal of Social Psychology, 140,* 93–106.

Frable, D. E. S. (1997). Gender, racial, ethnic, sexual, and class identities. *Annual Review of Psychology, 48,* 139–162.

Frable, D. E. S., & Bem, S. L. (1985). If you are gender schematic, all members of the opposite sex look alike. *Journal of Personality and Social Psychology, 49,* 459–468.

Frieze, I. H., & McHugh, M. C. (1998). Measuring feminism and gender role attitudes. (Response to Henley et al., 1998). *Psychology of Women Quarterly, 22,* 349–352.

Gardner, C. B. (1995). *Passing by: Gender and public harassment.* Berkeley: University of California Press.

Gay, C., & Tate, K. (1998). Doubly bound: The impact of gender and race on the politics of Black women. *Political Psychology, 19,* 169–184.

Gilligan, C. (1982). *In a different voice: Psychological theory and women's development.* Cambridge, MA: Harvard University Press.

Ginsburg, F. D. (1989). *Contested lives: The abortion debate in an American community.* Berkeley: University of California Press.

Glass, J. L., & Estes, S. B. (1997). The family responsive workplace. *Annual Review of Sociology, 23,* 289–313.

Glick, P., & Fiske, S. T. (2001). An ambivalent alliance: Hostile and benevolent sexism as complementary justifications for gender inequality. *American Psychologist, 56,* 109–118.

Goldman, J. G. (1992). Discursive autobiography as a path to feminist consciousness. *Journal of Feminist Family Therapy, 4,* 69–78.

Gruber, J. E., & Bjorn, L. (1988). Routes to a feminist orientation among women's autoworkers. *Gender and Society, 2,* 496–509.

Gump, L. S., & Baker, R. C. (2000). Cultural and gender differences in moral judgment: A study of Mexican Americans and Anglo-Americans. *Hispanic Journal of Behavioral Sciences, 22,* 78–94.

Gurin, P. (1985). Women's gender consciousness, *Public Opinion Quarterly, 49,* 143–163.

Gurin, P., & Townsend, A. (1986). Properties of gender identity and their implications for gender consciousness. *British Journal of Social Psychology, 25,* 139–48.

Hall, J. A., & Friedman, G. B. (1999). Status, gender, and nonverbal behavior: A study of structured interactions between employees of a company. *Personality and Social Psychology Bulletin, 25,* 1082–1091.

Hamilton, D. L., & Sherman, J. W. (1994). Stereotypes. In R. S. Wyer & T. K. Srull (Eds.), *Handbook of social cognition* (2nd ed., pp. 1–68). Hillsdale, NJ: Erlbaum.

Haney, Lynne A. 2000. Feminist state theory: Applications to jurisprudence, criminology, and the welfare state. *Annual Review of Sociology* 26:641–666.

Henderson-King, D. H., & Stewart, A. J. (1994). Women or feminists? Assessing women's group consciousness. *Sex Roles, 31,* 505–516.

Herek, G. M. (2000). Sexual prejudice and gender: Do heterosexuals' attitudes toward lesbians and gay men differ? *Journal of Social Issues, 56,* 251–266.

Henley, N. M., Meng, K., O'Brien, D., McCarthy, W. J., & Sockloskie, R. (1998). Developing a scale to measure the diversity of feminist attitudes. *Psychology of Women's Quarterly, 22,* 317–48.

Hildreth, A., & Dran, E. M. (1994). Explaining women's differences in abortion opinion: The role of gender consciousness. *Women and Politics, 14,* 35–52.

Hilton, J. L., & von Hippel, W. (1996). Stereotypes. *Annual Review of Psychology, 47,* 237–271.

Howard, J. A. (2000). Social psychology of identities. *Annual Review of Sociology, 26,* 367–393.

Huddy, L., Neely, F. K., & Lafay, M. R. (2000). The polls-trends: Support for the women's movement. *Public Opinion Quarterly, 64,* 309–350.

Huddy, L., & Terkildsen, N. (1993). Gender stereotypes and the perception of male and female candidates. *American Journal of Political Science, 37,* 119–147.

Humphries, M. L., & Parker, B. L. (2000). Predictors of moral reasoning among African American children: A preliminary study. *Journal of Black Psychology, 26,* 51–65.

Hyde, J. S. (1998). Measuring feminist attitudes: A possible rapprochement between feminist theory and empirical data? (Response to Henley, et al. 1998). *Psychology of Women Quarterly, 22,* 361–62.

Hyde, J. S. (1996). *Half the human experience: The psychology of women* (5th ed.). Boston: Houghton-Mifflin.

Iyengar, S. (1994). *Is anyone responsible? How television frames political issues.* Chicago: University of Chicago Press.

Iyengar, S., Valentino, N. A., Ansolabehere, S., & Simon, A. F. (1997). Running as a woman: Gender stereotyping in political campaigns. In P. Norris (Ed.), *Women, media, and politics* (pp. 77–98). New York: Oxford University Press.

Jaffee, S., & Hyde, J. S. (2000). Gender differences in moral orientation: A meta-analysis. *Psychological Bulletin, 126,* 703–726.

Jelen, T. G., Thomas, S., & Wilcox, C. (1994). The gender gap in comparative perspective. *European Journal of Political Research, 25,* 171–186.

Johnson, C. (1994). Gender, legitimate authority, and leader-subordinate conversations. *American Sociological Review, 59,* 122–135.

Johnson, P. (1976). Women and power: Toward a theory of effectiveness. *Journal of Social Issues, 32,* 99–109.

Kaiser, C. R., & Miller, C. T. (2001). Stop complaining! The social costs of making attributions to discrimination. *Personality and Social Psychology Bulletin, 27,* 254–263.

Kane, E. W. (2000). Racial and ethnic variations in gender-related attitudes. *Annual Review of Sociology, 26,* 419–439.

Kashima, Y., Yamaguchi, S., & Kim, U. (1995). Culture, gender, and self: A perspective from individualism-collectivism research. *Journal of Personality and Social Psychology, 69,* 925–937.

Kathlene, L. (1994). Power and influence in state legislative policymaking: The interaction of gender and position in committee hearing debates. *American Political Science Review, 88,* 560–576.

Kaufmann, K. M., & Petrocik, J. R. (1999). The changing politics of American men: Understanding the sources of the gender gap. *American Journal of Political Science, 43,* 864–887.

Kawakami, C., White, J., & Langer, E. J. (2000). Mindful and masculine: Freeing women leaders from the constraints of gender roles. *Journal of Social Issues, 56,* 49–63.

Klein, E. (1984). *Gender politics: From consciousness to mass politics.* Cambridge, MA: Harvard University Press.

Koukounas, E., & Letch, N. M. (2001). Psychological correlates of perception of sexual intent in women. *The Journal of Social Psychology, 141,* 443–456.

Koch, J. W. (2000). Do citizens apply gender stereotypes to infer candidates' ideological orientations? *Journal of Politics, 62,* 414–429.

Kray, L. J., Thompson, L., & Galinsky, A. (2001). Battle of the sexes: Gender stereotype confirmation and reactance in negotiations. *Journal of Personality and Social Psychology, 80,* 942–958.

Leeper, M. S. (1990). The impact of prejudice of female candidates: An experimental look at voter inference. *American Politics Quarterly, 19,* 248–261.

Lewin, M., & Tragos, L. M. (1987). Has the feminist movement influenced adolescent sex role attitudes? A reassessment after a quarter century. *Sex Roles, 16,* 125–136.

Lewis, K. M. (2000). When leaders display emotion: How followers respond to negative emotional expression of male and female leaders. *Journal of Organizational Behavior, 21,* 221–234.

Lien, Pei-Te. (1998). Does the gender gap in political attitudes and behavior vary across racial groups? *Political Research Quarterly, 51,* 869–894.

Lifton, P. D. (1985). Individual differences in moral development: The relation of sex, gender, and personality to morality. *Journal of Personality, 53,* 306–334.

Lovejoy, M. (1998). "You can't go home again": The impact of women's studies on intellectual and personal development. *NWSA Journal, 10,* 119–138.

Maclean, N. K. (1994). *Behind the mask of chivalry: The making of the second Ku Klux Klan.* New York: Oxford University Press.

Macrae, C. N., & Bodenhausen, G. V. (2000). Social cognition: Thinking categorically about others. *Annual Review of Psychology, 51,* 93–120.

Macrae, C. N., Stangor, C., & Hewstone, M. (Eds.) (1996). *Stereotypes and stereotyping.* New York: Guilford.

Masser, B., & Abrams, D. (1999). Contemporary sexism: The relationships among hostility, benevolence, and neosexism. *Psychology of Women Quarterly, 23,* 503–517.

Masters, R. D. (1989). Gender and political cognition: Integrating evolutionary biology and political science. With commentary and author's response. *Politics and the Life Sciences, 8,* 3–26.

Matheson, C., & Kline, A. D. (1998). Is there a significant observational-theoretical distinction? In E. D. Klemke, R. Hollinger, & D. W. Rudge (Eds.), *Introductory readings in the philosophy of science* (3rd ed., pp. 374–390). New York: Prometheus Books.

Maxwell, G. (1998). The ontological status of theoretical entities. In E. D. Klemke, R. Hollinger, & D. W. Rudge (Eds.), *Introductory readings in the philosophy of science* (3rd ed., pp. 363–373). New York: Prometheus Books.

McDermott, M. (1997). Voting cues in low-information elections: Candidate gender as a social information variable in contemporary United States elections. *American Journal of Political Science, 41,* 270–283.

McDermott, M. L. (1998). Race and gender cues in low-information elections. *Political Research Quarterly, 51,* 895–918.

Merriam, C., & Gosnell, H. (1924). *Nonvoting.* Chicago: University of Chicago Press.

Mesquida, C. G., & Wiener, N. I. (1999). Male age composition and severity of conflicts. *Politics and the Life Sciences, 18,* 113–117.

Miller, A. H., Gurin, P., Gurin, G., & Malanchuk, O. (1981). Group consciousness and political participation. *American Journal of Political Science, 25,* 494–511.

Montini, T. (1996). Gender and emotion in the advocacy for breast cancer informed consent legislation. *Gender and Society, 10,* 9–23.

Montoya, L. (1996). Latino gender differences in public opinion: Results from the Latino national political survey *Hispanic Journal of Behavioral Sciences, 18,* 255–276.

Nagel, J. (1998). Masculinity and nationalism: Gender and sexuality in the making of nations. *Ethnic and Racial Studies, 21,* 242–270.

Nagel, J. (2000). Ethnicity and sexuality. *Annual Review of Sociology, 26,* 107–133.

Norris, P. (1999). Gender: A gender-generation gap? In G. Evans & P. Norris (Ed.), *Critical elections: British parties and voters in long-term perspective* (pp. 148–163). London: Sage.

Nyman, C. (1999). Gender equality in "the most equal country in the world"? Money and marriage in Sweden. *Sociological Review, 47,* 766–793.

Ogburn, W. F., & Goltra, I. (1919). How women vote: A study of an election in Portland, Oregon. *Political Science Quarterly, 34,* 413–433.

Paolino, P. (1995). Group-salient issues and group representation: Support for women candidates in the 1992 Senate elections. *American Journal of Political Science, 39,* 294–311.

Peterson, S. A. (1978). The menstrual cycle and politics: A preliminary exploration. *Social Science Information, 17,* 993–1001.

Plant, E. A., Hyde, J. S., & Keltner, D. (2000). The gender stereotyping of emotions. *Psychology of Women Quarterly, 24,* 81–92.

Plummer, D. C. (2001). The quest for modern manhood: Masculine stereotypes, peer culture and the social significance of homophobia. *Journal of Adolescence, 24,* 15–23.

Plutzer, E. (1988). Work life, family life, and women's support for feminism. *American Sociological Review, 53,* 640–649.

Pratto, F., Liu, J. H., & Levin, S. (2000). Social dominance orientation and the legitimization of inequality across cultures. *Journal of Cross Cultural Psychology, 31,* 369–409.

Pratto, F., Sidanius, J., Stallworth, L. M., & Malle, B. F. (1994). Social dominance orientation: A personality variable predicting social and political attitudes. *Journal of Personality and Social Psychology, 67,* 741–763.

Pratto, F., Stallworth, L. M., & Sidanius, J. (1997). The gender gap: Differences in political attitudes and social dominance orientation. *British Journal of Social Psychology, 36,* 49–68.

Prince-Gibson, E., & Schwartz, S. H. (1998). Value priorities and gender. *Social Psychology Quarterly, 61,* 49–68.

Reingold, B. (2000). *Representing women: Sex, gender, and legislative behavior in Arizona and California.* Chapel Hill: University of North Carolina Press.

Reingold, B., & Foust, H. (1998). Exploring the determinants of feminist consciousness in the United States. *Women and Politics, 19,* 19–48.

Rhodebeck, L. A. (1996). The structure of men's and women's feminist orientations: Feminist identity and feminist opinion. *Gender and Society, 10,* 386–403.

Ridgeway, C. L., & Smith-Lovin, L. (1999). The gender system and interaction. *Annual Review of Sociology, 25,* 191–216.

Riggle, E., Miller, P., Shields, T., & Johnson, M. (1997). Gender stereotypes and decision context in the evaluation of political candidates. *Women and Politics, 17,* 69–88.

Rinehart, S. T. (1992). *Gender consciousness and politics.* New York: Routledge.

Rosenthal, N. B. (1984). Consciousness-raising: From revolution to re-evaluation. *Psychology of Women Quarterly, 8,* 309–326.

Rosenwasser, S. M., Rogers, R. R., Fling, S., Silvers-Pickens, K., & Butemeyer, J. (1987). Attitudes toward women and men in politics: Perceived male and female candidate competencies and participant personality characteristics. *Political Psychology, 8,* 91–200.

Rosenwasser, S. M., & Seale, J. (1988). Attitudes toward a hypothetical male or female candidate: A research note. *Political Psychology, 9,* 591–599.

Sapiro, V. (1982). If U.S. Senator Baker were a woman: An experimental study of candidate images. *Political Psychology, 3,* 161–183.

Sapiro, V. (1983). *The political integration of women: Roles, socialization, and politics.* Urbana: University of Illinois Press.

Sapiro, V. (1990). The women's movement and the creation of gender consciousness: Social movements as social agents. In O. Ichilov (Ed.), *Political socialization for democracy* (pp. 266–280). New York: Teachers' College Press.

Sapiro, V. (1993a). Engendering cultural differences. In M. Crawford Young (Ed.), *The rising tide of cultural pluralism: The nation state at bay?* (pp. 36–54). Madison: University of Wisconsin Press.

Sapiro, V. (1993b). "Private" coercion and democratic theory. In G. E. Marcus & R. Hansen (Eds.), *Reconsidering the democratic public* (pp. 427–450). University Park: Pennsylvania State University Press.

Sapiro, V. (1998). Democracy minus women is not democracy: Gender and world changes in citizenship. In O. Ichilov (Ed.), *Citizenship and citizenship education in a changing world* (pp. 174–190). London: Woburn Press.

Sapiro, V. (2001). It's the context, situation, and question, stupid: The gender basis of public opinion. In B. Norrander & C. Wilcox (Eds.), *Understanding public opinion* (2nd Ed.). Washington, DC: CQ Press.

Sapiro, V. (2002). *Women in American society: An introduction to women's studies* (5th ed.). Mountain View, CA: Mayfield.

Sapiro, V., & Canon, D. (1999). Race, gender, and the Clinton presidency. In C. Campbell & B. Rockman (Eds.), *The Clinton legacy* (pp. 207–241). Chatham, NJ: Chatham House.

Sapiro, V., & Conover, P. J. (1997). The variable gender basis of electoral politics: Gender and context in the 1992 U.S. election. *British Journal of Political Science, 27,* 497–523.

Sapiro, V., & Conover, P. J. (2001). Gender equality in the public mind. *Women and Politics, 22,* 1–35.

Sapiro, V., & Soss, J. (1999). Spectacular politics, dramatic interpretations: Multiple meanings in the Thomas/Hill Hearings. *Political Communication, 16,* 285–314.

Schlesinger, M., & Heldman, C. (2001). Gender gap or gender gaps? New perspectives on support for government action and policies. *Journal of Politics, 63,* 59–92.

Schlozman, K. L., Burns, N., Verba, S., & Donahue, J. (1995). Gender and citizen participation: Is there a different voice? *American Journal of Political Science, 39,* 267–293.

Sen, G. (2000). Gender mainstreaming in finance ministries. *World Development, 28,* 1379–1390.

Shamir, M., & Arian, A. (1999). Collective identity and electoral competition in Israel. *American Political Science Review, 93,* 265–278.

Shapiro, R. Y., & Mahajan, H. (1986). Gender differences in policy preferences: A summary of trends from the 1960's to the 1980's. *Public Opinion Quarterly, 50,* 42–61.

Sheets, V. L., & Braver, S. L. (1999). Organizational status and perceived sexual harassment: Detecting the mediators of a null effect. *Personality and Social Psychology Bulletin, 25,* 1159–1171.

Sidanius, J., Levin, S., Liu, J., & Pratto, F. (2000). Social dominance orientation, antiegalitarianism and the political psychology of gender: An extension and cross-cultural replication. *European Journal of Social Psychology, 30,* 41–67.

Sigel, R. (1996). *Ambition and accommodation: How women view gender relations.* Chicago: University of Chicago Press.

Sigelman, L., & Wilcox, C. (1991). Public support for gender equality in athletics programs. *Women and Politics, 22,* 85–96.

Signorella, M. (1999). Multidimensionality of gender schemas: Implications for the development of gender-related characteristics. In W. B. Swann, J. H. Langlois, & L. A. Gilbert (Eds.), *Sexism and stereotypes in modern society: The gender science of Janet Taylor Spence.* Washington, DC: American Psychological Association Press.

Sinclair, L., & Kunda, Z. (2000). Motivated stereotyping of women: She's fine if she praised me but incompetent if she criticized me. *Personality and Social Psychology Bulletin, 26,* 1329–1342.

Sloan, E. (2001). *Biology of women* (4th ed.). New York: Delmar.

Smith, T. W. (1985). Working wives and women's rights: The connection between the employment status of wives and feminist attitudes of husbands. *Sex Roles, 12,* 501–508.

Spence, J. T. (1985). Gender identity and implications for concepts of masculinity and femininity. In T. B. Sondereggr (Ed.), *Nebraska symposium on motivation: Psychology and gender* (pp. 59–96). Lincoln: University of Nebraska Press.

Spence, J. T. (1998). Developing a scale to measure the diversity of feminist attitudes: A work in progress. *Psychology of Women Quarterly, 22,* 353–360.

Spence, J. T. (1999). Thirty years of gender research: A personal chronicle. In W. B. Swann, Jr., J. H. Langlois, & L. A. Gilbert (Eds.), *Sexism and stereotypes in modern society: The gender science of Janet Taylor Spence* (pp. 255–289). Washington, DC: American Psychological Association.

Stoker, L., & Jennings, M. K. (1995). Life-cycle transitions and political participation: The case of marriage. *American Political Science Review, 89,* 421–436.

Stone, D. A. (1989). Causal stories and the formation of policy agendas. *Political Science Quarterly, 104,* 281–301.

Swann, W. B., Jr., Langlois, J. H., & Gilbert, L. A. (Eds.). 1999. *Sexism and stereotypes in modern society: The gender science of Janet Taylor Spence.* Washington, DC: American Psychological Association.

Swim, J. K., Aikin, K. J., Hall, W. S., & Hunter, B. A. (1995). Sexism and racism: Old-fashioned and modern prejudices. *Journal of Personality and Social Psychology, 68,* 199–214.

Swim, J. K., & Cohen, L. L. (1997). Overt, covert, and subtle sexism: A comparison between the Attitudes Toward Women and Modern Sexism scales. *Psychology of Women Quarterly, 21,* 103–118.

Swim, J. K., & Hyers, L. L. (1999). Excuse me—what did you just say?! Women's public and private responses to sexist remarks. *Journal of Experimental Social Psychology, 35,* 68–88.

Swim, J. K, Hyers, L. L., Cohen, L. L., & Ferguson, M. J. (2001). Everyday sexism: Evidence for its incidence, nature, and psychological impact from three daily diary studies. *Journal of Social Issues, 57,* 31–53.

Tessler, M., & Nachtwey, J. (1999). Further tests of the women and peace hypothesis: Evidence from cross-national survey research in the Middle East. *International Studies Quarterly, 43,* 519–533.

Tessler, M., & Warriner, I. (1997). Gender, feminism, and attitudes toward international conflict: Exploring relationships with survey data from the Middle East. *World Politics, 49,* 250–281.

Thompson, V. L. S. (1999). Variables affecting racial-identity salience among African Americans. *Journal of Social Psychology, 139,* 748–776.

Togeby, L. (1994). The gender gap in foreign policy attitudes. *Journal of Peace Research, 31,* 375–392.

True, J. (2001). Transnational networks and policy diffusion: The case of gender mainstreaming. *International Studies Quarterly, 45,* 27–58.

Verba, S., Schlozman, K., & Brady, H. (1995). *Voice and equality: Civic voluntarism in American politics.* Cambridge, MA: Harvard University Press.

Wade, J. C., & Brittan-Powell, C. (2001). Men's attitudes toward race and gender equity: The importance of masculinity ideology, gender-related traits, and reference group identity dependence. *Psychology of Men & Masculinity, 2,* 42–50.

Walker, L. (1984). Sex differences in the development of moral reasoning: A critical review. *Child Development, 55,* 667–691.

Wattier, M., Daynes, B. W., & Tatovich, R. (1997). Abortion attitudes, gender, and candidate choice in presidential elections: 1972 and 1992. *Women and Politics, 17,* 55–72.

Weir, A. (1999). *The life of Elizabeth I.* New York: Ballantine Books.

Welch, S., & Sigelman, L. (1989). A black gender gap? *Social Science Quarterly, 70,* 120–133.

Welsh, S. (1999). Gender and sexual harassment. *Annual Review of Sociology, 25,* 169–190.

West, C., & Zimmerman, D. H. (1987). Doing gender. *Gender and Society, 1,* 125–151.

Wilcox, C. (1991). The causes and consequences of feminist consciousness among western European women. *Comparative Political Studies, 23,* 519–545.

Wilcox, C. (1992). Race, sex, and support for women in the military. *Social Science Quarterly, 73,* 310–323.

Wilcox, C. (1997). Racial and gender consciousness among African-American women: Sources and consequences. *Women and Politics, 17,* 73–94.

Wilcox, C., Hewitt, L., & Allsop, D. (1996). The gender gap in attitudes toward the Gulf War: A cross-national perspective. *Journal of Peace Research, 33,* 67–82.

Willey, M. M., & Rice, S. A. (1924). A sex cleavage in the presidential election of 1920. *Journal of the American Statistical Association, 19,* 519–520.

Williams, C. L, Giuffre, P. A, & Dellinger, K. (1999). Sexuality in the workplace: Organizational control, sexual harassment, and the pursuit of pleasure. *Annual Review of Sociology, 25,* 73–93.

Wong, F. Y., McCreary, D. R., & Carpenter, K. M. (1999). Gender-related factors influencing perceptions of homosexuality. *Journal of Homosexuality, 37,* 19–31.

Woodzicka, J. A., & LaFrance, M. (2001). Real versus imagined gender harassment. *Journal of Social Issues, 57,* 15–20.

Yoder, J. D., & Aniakudo, P. (1995). When pranks become harassment: The case of African American women firefighters. *Sex Roles, 35,* 253–270.

Political Change

18 Orit Ichilov

Education and Democratic Citizenship in a Changing World

In recent years, there has been burgeoning academic and public interest in citizenship education all over the globe. Citizenship education has become a central issue on the public agenda of many countries and of regional and international organizations. Several leading examples ought to be mentioned. The Council of Europe, an intergovernmental organization with 41 member states, started its Democratic Education project (EDC) in 1997. The central aims of the project include the heightening of public understanding and awareness of the many aspects of democratic citizenship, particularly in the context of social change, as well as making citizens aware of various threats for democracy such as extremist movements, violence, racism, xenophobia, and social exclusion. The project gained great visibility and support at the fiftieth anniversary of the Council of Europe in 1997. A document entitled "Declaration and Programme on Education for Democratic Citizenship, Based on the Rights and Responsibilities of Citizens" was adopted by the Committee of Ministers and the Parliamentary Assembly of the European Council. Citizenship education is a flagship of the European Council, which is deeply involved in supporting educational projects, conferences, research, and the production of instructional materials (Audigier, 2000; Bîrzèa, 2000; Carey & Forrester, 2000; Duerr, Spajic-Vrkaš, & Martins, 2000).

In 1994 UNESCO organized a conference to deliberate on issues related to the role of education in nurturing values conducive to peace, human rights, and democracy (International Bureau of Education, 1994); UNESCO is also involved in revision of textbooks to make them more suitable for learning about democracy (Pingel, 1999).

In the United States there have been calls for greater attention to civic education (National Commission on Civic Renewal, 1998). The American Political Science Association formed a task force on civic education, and a series of White House conferences culminated in recommendations to improve civic education in the United States (Branson, 1998).

In the United Kingdom, citizenship education became part of the National Curriculum. Attainment targets for citizenship were set, describing the types and range of performance that the majority of pupils should characteristically demonstrate by the end of each stage of schooling, having been taught the relevant program of study (Department for Education and Employment, Qualifications and Curriculum Authority, 1999).

The International Association for the Evaluation of Educational Achievement (IEA), an organization that regularly conducts comparative studies of educational policies and practices in various countries, undertook a study on civic education in which 28 countries participated (Torney-Purta, Schwille, & Amadeo, 1999; Torney-Purta, Lehmann, Oswald, & Schulz, 2001). The participating countries included countries with disparate political cultures and democratic traditions. Included, for example, were England and the United States, former Soviet bloc countries such as Estonia, Hungary, and the Russian federation, and Mediterranean countries such as Greece and Cyprus, as well as Hong Kong, Chile, and Columbia.

This high tide of interest in my view is, undoubtedly, related to paramount political, economic, social, and cultural changes that have taken place around the globe in recent years, changes that potentially may have transformed the meanings of both citizenship and citizenship education (Ichilov, 1998).

In order to provide a comprehensive overview of citizenship education in democracy, we must draw on several intellectual traditions and areas of inquiry. As I am a sociologist, my analysis will necessarily address issues using mainly a sociological perspective. One must recall, however, that political psychology is a pluralistic universe (Greenstein, 1973), described by Knutson (1973) as "an interdisciplinary effort: knowledge gained by behavioral scientists is focused on critical human needs, so that the good life—which is the ancient promise of the polity—can be better realized" (p. vii). I hope that this chapter will make a modest contribution to our understanding of issues related to citizenship and citizenship education and the potential that education has for developing and sustaining democratic regimes in a changing world.

In view of the fact that "citizenship" is the purpose of citizenship education, I'll start by examining the impact of changes such as globalization and postmodernism on the citizenship role. I'll demonstrate that citizenship has taken on new dimensions and meanings and that the traditional bonds between citizens and their polity, as well as the affinity among citizens, may have eroded.

Concerning citizenship education, I'll proceed to make a distinction between education in general and more specialized forms of education that are specifically designed to promote citizenship education. The concept of democratic education will be explored next, focusing on its components: the democratic rationale for education, the nature of democratic control of schools, and the contents of democratic education. The contribution that sociological theory and research concerning schooling may have for resolving the enigma of how schooling affects so profoundly the development of citizenship orientations will be explored next. Sociologists attribute schooling effects to two distinct yet interrelated processes: socialization and allocation. The allocation tradition has been greatly overlooked by scholars who have studied the effects of schooling on the development of citizenship. My view is that the allocative perspective provides important insights and clues about schooling effects and democracy. For one thing, it demonstrates that citizenship education is not as universal as had been suggested and that differentiated educational experiences produce dissimilar citizenship roles: leadership versus followership. In conclusion, some suggestions will be offered concerning citizenship education in a changing world.

▲ Citizenship in a Changing World

Citizenship is a complex and multidimensional concept. It consists of legal, cultural, social, and political elements, and provides citizens with defined rights and obligations, a sense of identity, and social bonds. Citizenship vests bonded populations with a specific set of rights and duties and excludes others, usually on the grounds of nationality (Ichilov, 1990, 1998). Citizenship thus controls the access of individuals and groups to scarce resources such as housing, health, income, employment, and education (Turner, 1997).

My argument is that the bonding power of citizenship may be eroding as a result of immense political, social, and cultural changes that transform the relationships both between citizens and the polity and among citizens.

Concerns about the future of traditional forms of citizenship predominate the literature that will be discussed. Much of the anticipated changes, however, remain speculative, and in many instances there is little empirical evidence to support the proclaimed trends of development. One must also take into account that unexpected events, such as the terrorist assault on the United States on September 11, 2001, may serve as a galvanizing force, reinforcing (at least temporarily) both national identification and support for the government.

I'll begin by discussing some of the developments that could enfeeble the bond between citizens and their government. According to Walzer (1989), a citizen is primarily a member of a political community, and citizenship is an expression of the political relationships between the individual and a polity. Classical definitions of citizenship typically identify the "political community" as a state or a nation-state. Political communities, however, are changing and diversifying in many ways. The powerful pressures toward the fragmentation of large political units, regional autonomy, localism, and nationalism may reinforce traditional concepts of a political community, while the striving for globalism and unification may foster a vision of citizenship that entails membership in more than one political community. Take, for example, the disintegration of the Soviet bloc into nation-states on the one hand and the formation of the European Community on the other. In the Soviet bloc, communist rule kept a lid on nationalist passions. The breakup of multinational communist regimes created successor states that are much more ethnically homogeneous (Rose, 1999). Recent studies by Sovietologists illustrate how national issues came to permeate all aspects of the formerly Soviet polity, economy, and society (Motyl, 1992). Nodia (1994) claims that this revival of nationalism reflects a drive to recover one's own identity, and an attempt of postcommunist nations to resume their history from the point where it was interrupted by communism.

In western Europe, a study of values was carried out in two waves: 1981 and 1990 (Ester, Halman, de Moor, 1994). One of the issues that was addressed was the effect that the disappearance of internal borders between European Community countries might have on national cultures. One prediction was that national values would be fostered, because citizens of the member states might fear losing their distinct national identities. The findings showed no evidence of reinforced collective identities, national or European, but rather that economic and cultural individualism were on the rise. The recent introduction of the euro as the official common currency in 12 European countries, replacing national currencies, may come to symbolize European unity and heighten the salience of a European identity. Citizenship may, thus, come to represent multiple political allegiances rather than a single political identity. This, in turn, may raise issues concerning the centrality and salience for citizens of the various political identities, and the possibility that allegiances may be incongruent and even conflict with one another.

The bond between citizens and a polity is grounded to a large extent in an understanding that the government is in control of the conditions that assure citizens a good life. However, traditional political communities have lost much of their ability to guarantee citizens a good life. Globalization, the emergence of new supranational structures, and the shift from an economy based on material, energy, and labor to one grounded on information and communication reduce the importance of the state as a critical player in guaranteeing the fortunes of the marketplace. Klein (1999) claims that some corporations have grown so big that their budget supersedes that of some governments. For example, the advertising budget of Nike in 1997 was 500 million U.S. dollars (Klein, 1999, p. 19). Unlike governments, however, corporations are accountable only to their shareholders. Heying (1997) demonstrates that as company interests shift from a local and national to a transnational focus, so do their commitments. This, he argues, may have grave consequences for the capacity of civil society: decreasing support for local community organizations and community betterment and a growing sense of crisis in the nonprofit sector. Rifkin (1995) considers global corporations to be quasi-political institutions that exercise great power over people and places by reason of control over information and communication. The use of military force, a primary function of the modern polity, is considered by him to be of little service—it cannot stop or slow down the flow of information and communication across national frontiers. In Barber's view (1995), cosmopolitan companies tend to undermine the autonomy of individuals and nations alike, primarily by creating global classes of haves and have-nots with no sense of local community. Consequently, democratic governments may lose their ability to balance the interests of economic utility and social justice. Kiernan (1997) emphasizes that globalization and loss of national control endanger the fulfillment of all citizenship rights, because such rights have not become institutionalized in supranational institutions.

The introduction of transnational and global organizations dedicated to social causes may reinforce among citizens the recognition that economic well-being, preservation of the environment, and security from nuclear war can be better promoted through international corporations than through unilateral national actions (Ichilov, 1998). During the past few years, and especially since the much-publicized demonstrations against the World Trade Organization in Seattle in 1999, the term "global civil society" has been much in vogue (Scholte, 2000). However, while citizens from different countries are certainly speaking on global issues, the rights and responsibilities of citizens at the global level are ill defined (Edwards, 2001; Edwards & Gaventa, 2001). Currently, "global civil society" tends to operate through networks of interest groups, especially nongovernmental organizations (NGOs), rather than through formal representative structures (Keck & Sikkink, 1998; Higgott & Bieler, 1999). Therefore, NGOs are perceived as self-selected and unaccountable by those who question their legitimacy as participants in global debates (Edwards, 2001). There is also a concern that citizenship engagement may be distorted in favor of NGOs that are perceived as having great resources and access to decision-makers in capital cities. For example, by 1990, Greenpeace UK had more members than the British Labour party (Clark, 1991).

With the erosion of the welfare state, governments no longer are the major provider of social services such as health care and education. The traditional tradeoff between polity and citizens, that is, provision of services in exchange for legitimization and support, is being replaced by a new deal. Liberal political theory tends to resist conceptions of citizenship that entail rights of assistance from the state. Rights to welfare are more readily conceived as charitable acts toward those members of a society unable to care for themselves (Dodds, 1998; Kymlicka, 1995). Privatized services and charity organizations increasingly come to replace governmental welfare and social services. New right arguments suggest that economic deregulation of social services endorse freedom of choice and consumer accountability (Saunders, 1993). For many critics, however, the contemporary reliance on the market to solve political and social problems is an attack on the principles of democratic citizenship (Marshall, 1977, 1981; Turner, 1993). Schild (2000) argues that a shift in conceptions of citizens as clients of public goods to empowered clients applies to most governmental services and not solely to welfare services. "Market citizens," as Schild (2000) designates this pattern of citizenship, may express limited commitment to the polity. Overall, then, the diminishing power of governments to guarantee a good life may weaken the bond between citizens and their polity. This contention is supported, for example, by data indicating that in recent years many countries have witnessed a sharp and consistent erosion of political support for governmental institutions (Norris, 1999; Ester, Halman, & de Moor, 1994).

Consider the consequences of change for the bonds among citizens in a democracy. According to Heater (1990), citizenship is one among many identities of an individual and "helps to tame the divisive passions of other identities" (p. 184). It does so by conveying to each individual citizen a society's collective memory, cultural togetherness and nationality, and the collaborative sense of purpose in fraternity. These elements bind people together with a common identity of citizenship. My argument is that the traditional foundations needed to form a social bond and to transform a random collection of consumers, or an aggregation of political, ethnic, and economic interests, into citizens striving for the common good are also eroding.

Postmodernity, which declared obsolete all the grand narratives of western society, may be one of the forces that shake the foundations of citizenship. The pattern of postmodern change is in the direction of fragmentation of old cultures and the frenzied proliferation of new values, attitudes, and lifestyles in their place (Lyotard, 1984). Wexler (1990) argues that postmodernism marks the end of citizenship as an emblem of modernity by replacing rationality and solidarity with "semiosis, the structural law of value, the free play of signifiers without reference" (p. 165). Some believe that by their very plurality, these new cultural forms may come to constitute a preventive force against all forms of total political ideology. However, much radical thought, particularly Marxism and feminism, rejects postmodernity, arguing that indiscriminate pluralism may lead not to sharpened awareness of and increased respect for differences but to uncritical sponge-headedness (Boyne & Rattansi, 1990; Gibbins, 1989; Lovibond, 1990). The fragmentary and nihilist tendencies of postmodern society may threaten the commonness on which the concept of citizenship is founded. Are society, politics, and morality possible when partiality, relativity, uncertainty, and the absence of common foundations are the rule (Gilbert, 1992; Heater, 1990)? Sartori (1997) argues that "the ongoing vitality of pluralism rests on the tension between conviction and toleration, not on the still waters of indifference and relativism" (p. 65), that postmodernity may advance. Wood (1996) argues that postmodernity in the arts and scholarship in the United States is related to what he calls postintellectualism, namely, "loss of effectual personal knowledge, decline in analytic thinking" (p. 20). He brings up the falling Scholastic Aptitude Test (SAT) scores and other standardized assessments as evidence for declining verbal literacy in the United States and argues that American citizens have lost their sense of purpose and system of cultural values and can no longer comprehend their own affairs or direct their own destinies (pp. 69–70, 113).

Multiculturalism represents a new way of thinking about minority rights. It is true that most organized political communities throughout recorded history have been multiethnic, and the growing cultural heterogeneity within contemporary societies is not a novel phenomenon (Kymlicka, 1995). However, such pluralism has been handled using different philosophies and practices. After World War II it was hoped that minority rights would be best resolved not by group-specific rights but via the new emphasis on human rights as they were articulated in the UN Universal Declaration of Human Rights. Affirmative action for disadvantaged ethnic groups was acknowledged as a justified temporary and remedial measure, but the idea that specific ethnic or national groups should be given a permanent political identity or constitutional status was generally opposed. Minorities too generally strived for integration. Martin Luther King, Jr., the leader of the civil rights movement of African Americans in the 1960s, struggled for the integration of African Americans into all social spheres of mainstream American society.

It has become, however, increasingly clear over time that some of the most controversial questions relating to cultural minorities cannot be resolved by human rights endeavors alone. Current multiculturalism can be perceived as "politics of recognition" (Taylor, 1994). As Taylor puts it, "the demand for recognition . . . is given urgency by the supposed link between recognition and identity . . . [That is,] our identity is partly shaped by recognition or its absence, often by the misrecognition of others . . . nonrecognition or misrecognition can inflict harm, can be a form of oppression" (p. 25). Minorities and majorities increasingly clash over a variety of issues, including language rights, education and curriculum. For example, should minority languages be recognized as official languages used in parliaments and courts? Should each ethnic or national group have a right to publicly funded education in its mother tongue?

Minority issues and minority rights have also returned to prominence in international relations, to a large extent because of a recent resurgence of nationalism and ethnic conflicts in various parts of the world (Diamond & Plattner, 1994, p. ix). For example, the Conference on Security and Cooperation in Europe (CSCE) adopted a declaration on the rights of national minorities in 1991 and established a High Commissioner on National Minorities in 1993. The United Nations has been debating both a Declaration on the Rights of Persons Belonging to National or Ethnic, Religious and Linguistic Minorities (1993), and a Draft Universal Declaration on Indigenous Rights (1988). The Council of Europe adopted a declaration on minority language rights in 1992: the European Charter for Regional Minority Languages (Hannum, 1993; Kymlicka, 1995; Lerner, 1991; Thornberry, 1991).

While some contemporary political philosophers stress the need for recognizing the specific identity of minority groups and the need to supplement human rights with some special collective rights (Kymlicka, 1991, 1995; Taylor, 1994), others dread such fragmentation within democratic societies. Sartori (1997), for example, argues that "in practice, to the large extent to which current multicultural demands are aggressive, intolerant, and divisive, to the same extent multiculturalism is the very negation of pluralism" (p. 62). Furthermore, some ethnic and religious traditions notably attitudes toward women and their role in society, may be incongruent with liberal democracy. What degree of cultural integration can be required of immigrants and refugees before they acquire citizenship? Should democracies allow for various forms of religious fundamentalism to be represented in the educational system?

Etzioni (1992) emphasizes the need for the shared virtues of communitarian values to bind a democratic society together. In his view, pluralism must fit within some kind of overarching unity, and some ultimate values must be shared if the diversity in a democratic society is to be contained democratically. For Janowitz (1983), the rise of "hyphenated Americans" (e.g., Mexican Americans, African Americans) in the United States is considered to be eroding the foundations of civic obligation. In addition, there are in the United States millions of inhabitants who enjoy citizenship benefits and rights without becoming full-fledged citizens. They limit their citizenship to social and economic participation in a capitalist welfare state, enjoy civil liberties, and neglect to become political participants with a right to share in the exercise of power (Schneider, 2000). In Europe concerns have been raised about citizen status, not only for minorities but also for all forms of transient and migrant labor, stateless people, and refugees. These concerns brought to the fore the perception that human rights should complement citizenship rights and an anticipation that as politics become more global, human rights will have an expanded role in the normative regulation of politics (Turner, 1993).

The great diversity of citizenship patterns raises also the issue of what are the common obligations that bind citizens. Some argue that, given the absence of a universal draft in many industrialized nations, paying taxes is almost the only nearly universal obligation of citizenship (Dahrendorf, 1994, 1996; Mead, 1996). Essentially, then, citizens today may no longer share collective memory, cultural togetherness, and nationality. This situation may reinforce the tendency to shift from public goals to private ones and may nurture the decline in political participation and associational life (McDonnell, 2000; Putman, 1995, Verba, Schlozman, & Brady, 1995). Under these circumstances, how can a collaborative sense of purpose in fraternity be achieved?

The infusion of citizenship with market metaphors could act as another divisive force among citizens. Schild (2000) argues that citizens are transformed into what he calls "market citizens" whose relationships are governed by the liberal norms of the marketplace. However, processes of economic bargaining and processes of civil deliberation are at odds with one another. Bargaining encourages participants to act strategically with respect to one another, even lie to one another about their preferences and beliefs when it serves their purpose, and to assume that others will do likewise. Deliberation, in contrast, is founded on trust, sharing of knowledge, and citizens' recognition of their joint involvement in a common fate (March & Olsen, 2000).

According to Walzer (1989), "a citizen is, most simply, a member of a political community, entitled to whatever prerogatives and encumbered with whatever responsibilities that are attached to membership" (p. 211). My analysis suggests that citizenship today is much more complex and multidimensional. Given that "citizenship" is the purpose of citizenship education, some scholars suggest that a revised concept of citizenship must develop and must embrace both the globalization of social relations and the increased social differentiation of social systems. Citizenship can no longer be conceived as exclusively related to the local and national spheres but should be more broadly envisaged as encompassing a wide array of social concerns that may be international in scope, a citizenship concept that is adequate for multiethnic and multicultural societies (Habermas, 1995; Ichilov, 1990, 1998); Mouffe, 1992). The implications of these existing and anticipated changes for citizenship education are considered later in this chapter.

▲ Democratic Education

Gutmann (1987) makes a distinction between political socialization that tends to focus on what she calls "unconscious social reproduction" and education as "conscious social reproduction." In this respect, schooling is perhaps the most deliberate form of human instruction (p. 15). The term "citizenship education" commonly refers to institutionalized forms of political knowledge acquisition that take place within formal educational frameworks (such as schools and universities) and informal frameworks (such as youth movements) (Ichilov, 1994). A distinction should also be made between specific and diffuse citizenship education. Specific citizenship education proceeds through curricular and extracurricular school activities (such as civics classes or service learning programs) that are specifically designed to prepare youngsters for citizenship, as well as through the "hidden curriculum" of the school (this includes, for example, instructional styles and patterns of authority relationships), better known as the school climate. "Diffuse citizenship education" refers to educational attainment in general. It is based on the assumption that "schooling provides civic education even when its content is not explicitly civic" (Bricker, 1989, p. 2).

The following issues that predominate in modern democratic political thought will be addressed concerning education and democracy. What is the democratic rationale for a universal provision of education? What makes education an indispensable asset for democracy? Whose responsibility it is to control the schools in democracy? What is the role that the state, parents, and children should assume in this respect? What are the characteristics of democratic education in terms of its explicit contents and its "hidden curriculum"?

The Democratic Rationale for Education

Political thought has assigned education a prominent role for the stability and good functioning of any type of regime. Aristotle, for example, said: "that which contributes most to the permanence of constitutions is the adaptation of education to the form of government. The best laws will be of no avail unless the young are trained by habit and example in the spirit of the constitution" (1943, pp. 249–250). Citizenship education is an imperative in modern democratic political thought (for example: Dewey, [1916/1966]; Gutmann, 1987). Democratic citizenship is perceived as consisting of habits and competences that require cultivation without which they will not sprout, or will sprout but wither quickly. Barber (1992) considers the empowerment of the ignorant to represent a mob rule but not a democracy. Volunteerism is also a central idea in democratic political thought. In this respect, citizens' behavior should be controlled internally rather than by external coercion, and this end should be achieved through rationality and education rather than through emotional propaganda (Lybarger, 1991).

In the United States there has been a concern in recent years that the role of public education in the making of citizens has become marginalized and that civic education has receded in the face of increased emphasis on preparation for work (McDonnell, Timpane, & Benjamin, 2000). It has been suggested that the democratic purpose of education should be rediscovered and reinvigorated and include, among other things, the teaching of tolerance, mutual respect, skills essential for deliberation, a common core of knowledge, a common set of values, and democratic practices (Conover & Searing, 2000; Gutmann, 2000; Hochschild & Scovronick, 2000).

The democratic rationale for education has been globalized to apply to all humankind. Education was recognized as a basic human right, as empowerment that is a key to establishing and reinforcing democracy, and as means for the realization of human progress that is both sustainable and humane and for a peace that is founded on mutual respect and social justice. The major milestones in the acknowledgment of the right to education as a human right were article 26 of the 1948 Universal Declaration of Human Rights, article 28 of the 1989 Convention on the Rights of the Child, and declarations made in a series of UNESCO world conferences on education for all (Brownlie, 1992; UNESCO, 2000a, 2000b, 2000c; Spring, 2000).

It follows that equality of educational opportunities is crucial for democracy. To quote Dewey (1916/1966), a democratic society "must see to it that intellectual opportunities are accessible to all on equitable and easy terms . . . [and] must see to it that its members are educated to personal initiative and adaptability" (pp. 7–8). This issue will be discussed in more detail later.

Democratic Control of Education

It is generally agreed that the three major parties to education in democracy are the state, parents, and children. The interest of the state is to ensure that schools turn youngsters into able, participating citizens. This is the basic justification for setting up publicly funded common schools that bring citizens of all sects under one roof, and for passing compulsory attendance laws (Reich, 1995, Pangle & Pangle, 2000). Spring (2000) emphasizes that governments should not misuse their authority in the provision of education for all by advancing nationalistic or particularistic political ends through the use of indoctrination and propaganda, and Gutmann (1987) asserts that democratic control in education should secure nonrepression and nondiscrimination.

According to Gutmann (1987), one of the hallmarks of democratic education is the empowerment of citizens "to influence the education that in turn shapes the political values, attitudes, and modes of behavior of future citizens" (p. 14). Her view is that because in democracy political authority is ultimately vested in every citizen, it follows that "when citizens rule in a democracy, they should determine, among other things, how future citizens will be educated" (p. 3). The authority of citizens should, thus, prevail over the authority of the state in education.

In the 1989 Convention on the Rights of the Child, children are viewed not merely as prospective citizens or solely as minors who are under adult benevolent care and supervision. Children bear inherent rights that should be respected and implemented within various social frameworks, including schools. These rights clearly include citizenship rights, such as freedom of thought, conscience, and religion (article 14), freedom of association, and freedom of peaceful assembly (article 15). Each child should have the right "to freedom of expression: this right should include freedom to seek, receive and impart information and ideas of all kinds, regardless of frontiers, either orally or in print, in the form of art, or through any other media of the child's choice" (article 13, clause 1; Brownlie, 1992). The Convention may advance the outlook that in a democracy education should not be decided by the state and by adult members of society alone. The implementation of these rights in schools means that children should participate in the shaping of their own education and that their voice should be heard when decisions concerning schooling are made.

It is generally agreed that to serve the best interest of society, democratic control of the schools must ensure an education that is based on freedom of ideas and nondiscrimination in relation to race, gender, religion, ethnic origin, political affiliation, and disabilities. Democratic education should be nonrepressive and based on free access to information and freedom of thought, allowing students to consider different concepts of the good life (Gutmann, 1987; Spring, 2000). Gutmann (1987) assigns educators a prominent role in democratic education. "Democratic professionalism" on part of educators implies that "their professional responsibility is to uphold the principle of nonrepression by cultivating the capacity for democratic deliberation" (p. 76). Spring (2000) adds to these professional responsibilities the moral duty to protect human rights (p. 92).

The plausibility of the idea of democratic control of education was challenged on several grounds. First, it has been suggested that the reality of democratic control of public schools is that those who have more political power determine what the democratic purposes of schooling will be. Thus the democratic missions of schools are not necessarily fashioned in the best interest of society but are simply reflections of the specific interests of powerful political actors (Moe, 2000). Interest groups, for example, may attempt to promote the inclusion of their children in schools but on terms distinctive of and specified by the group; may desire to use public resources to educate outside the mainstream; may desire to change the mainstream to accommodate the group; or may desire to be left alone or to remove their children from the mainstream (Hochschild & Scovronick, 2000).

Under democratic control, tensions may also arise between professional norms and democratic accountability. Democratic control assumes that as governmental institutions, schools derive their legitimacy from the consent of the electorate and should thus be held publicly accountable. It further assumes that as public employees educators' behavior should be monitored through externally imposed controls (Dahl, 1982; Gruber, 1987). In contrast, professionalism assumes that the application of a specialized body of knowledge by educators should be regulated by a code of ethics internal to their profession (Barber, 1965). Thus the credibility of a democratic control of education as means for securing the interest of society may be seriously questioned. In reality it seems that schooling and educational decisions are shaped by political, bureaucratic, and professional elites and organizations and not by empowered citizens. Students rarely participate in decisions concerning their own education (Kymlicka, 1995).

The Contents of Democratic Education

Niemi and Junn (1998) claim that "there is no 'canon' that defines what students (or adults) should know" about citizenship in democracy (p. 11). However, ideas concerning the contents of democratic education do exist; some are old, and others have been introduced more recently. A major issue in this respect is: What are the responsibilities of publicly funded schools in terms of the provision of contents that would nurture a democratic citizenry? What are the contents that should be imparted to students in schools that are conducive for democratic citizenship? It is generally agreed that democratic education consists of the inculcation of knowledge, virtues, and skills that should be cultivated across all school subjects and educational activities, as well as through specially designed programs for the development of various aspects of democratic citizenship. Such programs have been proliferating in recent years, as will be demonstrated later.

Literacy has long been recognized as a basic skill that is vital for democracy. The founding fathers of American democracy believed that by becoming adept in speaking, writing, and reading young people are equipped to function as economically independent and politically sophisticated citizens (Pangle & Pangle, 2000). Reading in particular has been recognized as an essential civic competence—so much so that Rod Paige, America's education secretary, was quoted as saying that "reading is the new civil right" and that no modern society can function without a literate population, and no one can function well in a modern society without being literate (*Economist*, February 24, 2001, p. 91). Stotsky (1991) considers inability to read basic civic documents and general public information a serious obstacle for taking advantage of one's rights and for understanding and fulfilling one's civic responsibilities. Reading is also part of a critical social literacy that entails the analysis and evaluation of textual ideologies and cultural messages and an understanding of the linguistic and discursive technique with which texts represent social reality, relations, and identity (Luke & Walton, 1994).

It is believed that schools should be called on to cultivate skills and virtues that are needed for dealing with disagreements in democracy, notably skills essential for deliberation (Gutmann, 2000; Conover & Searing, 2000). Citizens in democracy are required to practice the civilized conduct of civic discourse. Stotsky (1991) demonstrates how teachers of language can help students acquire that ability, that is, the ability to present their views in informed and responsible discourse, with voices that are at once forceful and considerate.

Critical thinking is another important civic virtue. Dewey (1916/1966) asserts that "no one doubts, theoretically, the importance of fostering in school good habits of thinking" (p. 152). "Education for critical thinking" is a generation-old movement of philosophers and educators who seek to transform education in general and turn educational institutions into "smart schools" that develop critical thinking in their students (Barnes, 1992; Lipman, 1988; Lo & Si-wai, 1996; McPeck, 1981, Paul, 1993).

It is generally believed that "moral persons" constitute the foundation of a just society, although no consensus exists concerning the makeup of a moral person. Moral education is associated most closely with the names of the French sociologist Emil Durkheim and with the name of Lawrence Kohlberg, who articulated a cognitive developmental theory of moralization (Weinreich-Haste, 1986). Durkheim considered discipline, attachment to social groups, and autonomy as key elements of morality that should be inculcated through education (Durkheim, 1961). Kohlberg advocated the "just society approach" to moral education in schools, focusing on "the moral issues arising in day-to-day concerns of staff and students, governed by democracy, and motivated by an altruistic commitment to community" (Power, Higgins, & Kohlberg, 1989, p. 2). Moral citizens should be aware that citizenship entails the protection of citizens against the arbitrary exercise of state power. They should, therefore, be able to make independent judgments, express dissent, not just consent, and develop civic courage to sometimes resist the authorities (Etzioni, 1970; Giroux, 1983; Ichilov, 1990; Lo and Si-Wai, 1996; Turner, 1997). Crick (2000) argues that if it is to be internalized in behavior, moral education must arise from experiencing conflicts of values. He emphasizes that moral education should not consist of rote learning of moral precepts, or solely of a philosophical inquiry of the different meanings of such terms.

With globalization and deregulation, consumer education is increasingly being linked to citizenship education (Ichilov, 1998). Value considerations are gaining in importance with regard to the consumption of goods. Conscious consumers check product labels and consumer information sites, and prefer to even pay more for goods whose production does not involve experimentation with animals, damage to the environment, and exploitation of workers inside one's country or abroad. Advertising is a pervasive feature of the culture of consumption. Commercials are not simply informative messages about goods and services; they are social and cultural texts that manipulate customers into specific choices of consumer goods as well as of public elected officials. Teaching students to decode commercials instead of taking them at face value is a way of empowerment that would encourage people to make rational decisions instead of being unconsciously maneuvered into specific choices (Frith, 1997; Solomon, 1988). Educating for rational and critical media consumption is also an essential part of democratic education. Hepburn (1998) expresses concern that the mass communication media, dominated by television, are not generally serving democracy well. She is also concerned about schools in the United States that receive expensive video equipment from television channels in return for presenting their news programs and advertising to a national captive audience of millions of students. Students should learn to understand how programs are produced and funded, what is selected as news of the day, and should become aware of the fact that what they see with their own eyes on television may not represent "the truth" (Hepburn, 1998; Postman & Powers, 1992).

Other traditions that are linked to citizenship education address issues that are of global concern and issues within democratic societies that are increasingly witnessing the growing of cultural and ethnic diversity. To name just a few: "human rights education," "peace education," "environmental education," "education for conflict resolution," and "multicultural education."

Overall, then, it seems that the contents associated with citizenship education represent a patchwork more than a coherent idea of how to integrate different concerns into a comprehensive civics curriculum.

▶ Schooling and Democracy

"Schools, along with their teachers and curricula, have long been identified as the critical link between education and citizenship, as the locus from which democratic citizens emerge" (Niemi & Junn, 1998, pp. 2–3). Converse (1972) characterizes formal education as the "universal solvent" that explains more aspects of democratic citizenship than any other factor (p. 324). To quote him more fully:

> There is probably no single variable in the survey repertoire that generates as substantial correlations in such a variety of directions in political behavior material as level of formal education . . . whether one is dealing with cognitive matters such as level of factual information about politics or conceptual sophistication in assessment; or such motivational matters as degree of attention paid to politics and emotional involvement in political affairs; or questions of actual behavior, such as engagement in any of a variety of political activities from party work to vote turnout itself. (p. 324)

This statement summarizes consistent research findings that have accumulated over many decades, demonstrating the effect of formal education on a vast array of civic attitudes and behaviors (Almond & Verba, 1963; Barnes & Kaase, 1979; Berelson, Lazarsfeld, & McPhee, 1954; Campbell, Converse, Stokes, & Miller, 1969; Campbell, Gurin, & Miller, 1954; Dahl, 1961; Dalton, 1988; Delli Caprini & Keeter, 1996; Kamens, 1988; Nie, Powell & Prewitt, 1969; Verba, Nie & Kim, 1978; Wolfinger & Rosenstone, 1980).

The paradox about schooling and democracy is that while there is abundant evidence for the existence of a strong positive relationship between educational attainment and a variety of civic orientations and behaviors, how schooling does it remains an enigma, and the causal connection between formal education and democratic citizenship is pretty much an undeciphered "black box" (Torney-Purta, 1997).

I propose that sociological theories and research concerning schooling may provide helpful clues for understanding the link between education and citizenship. Sociologists attribute schooling effects in general mainly to two distinct but interrelated processes: socialization and allocation. From a socialization approach, schools are engaged in deliberate instruction and education of students. This is both their social mandate and their expertise. Differential outcomes are considered a consequence of the types, quality, and quantity of experiences that schools provide, holding students' ability and motivations constant. This leads to the expectation that students whose schools provided richer curricular and extracurricular experiences, and who were tutored by highly qualified teachers, will be more knowledgeable about politics and manifest greater commitment to democracy than students whose schooling experiences were less constructive.

Political socialization and citizenship education research have been dominated by the socialization approach to schooling (Dreeben, 1970; Easton & Dennis, 1969; Ehman, 1980; Gallatin & Adelson, 1970; Hahn, 1998; Hess & Torney, 1967; Jaros, 1973; Jennings & Niemi, 1968, 1974; Langton, 1969; Merelman, 1971, 1986; Niemi & Junn, 1998; Patrick, 1977; Sigel, 1970; Torney 1975; Weissberg, 1974).

I shall review the major findings of studies related to the quality and quantity of various schooling experiences. Civics courses are specifically designed to impart to students civic knowledge and competences and ware thus an obvious objective for study. Civics, however, is a marginal school subject in many countries (Torney-Purta, Schwille, & Amadeo, 1999). It is, therefore, not surprising that the overall effect of civics courses seems to be restricted and mixed. Delli Carpini and Keeter (1996) found that respondents' self-report of having studied civics in high school were weak predictors of political knowledge compared with other factors such as years of education, race, gender, and strength of party identification. The influence of civics instruction closely approached statistical significance on the knowledge of political institutions and processes, a knowledge domain that is central in civics courses. Conover and Searing (2000) found that civics courses bear virtually no relationship to students' sense of citizenship, with one exception—having a civics course makes students more aware of their legal duties as citizens. Other findings are slightly more encouraging. Several studies report that civics courses had a positive effect on students' efficacy and attitudes toward participation (Ehman, 1977; Jennings, Langton, & Niemi, 1974). Niemi and Junn (1998) found that amount and recency of civics coursework had a significant and positive effect on students' civic knowledge and on their attitudes about governmental responsiveness. Ichilov (2000) reports that eleventh-graders in Israel who were taking a civics course when the IEA civic education questionnaire was administered scored slightly better on the knowledge part than those who were not studying civics at that time. Niemi and Hepburn (1995) list seven other studies of students in the United States and abroad that identified positive effects of civics instruction.

Textbooks are another important component of civic education. Examination of textbooks, however, reveals that elementary and secondary school textbooks are typically designed for passive learning—transmission of facts and ideas rather than active involvement of learners in the pursuit of knowledge. Many topics, terms, and facts are mentioned, but few, if any, are developed in detail. Textbooks at all levels of schooling also tend to be supportive of the status quo (Carroll,. Broadnax, Contreras, Mann, Orenstein, & Stiehm, 1987; Patrick & Hoge, 1991; Larkins, Hawkins, & Gilmore, 1987; Ichilov, 1993). Israeli civics teachers were greatly dissatisfied with instructional materials. They claimed that textbooks emphasize the legal, structural, and procedural aspects of political institutions and neglect to consider central aspects of citizenship such as tolerance, equality, and respect for national symbols (Ichilov, 1989).

Additional studies reveal that altogether, variables related to formal instruction of civics, such as civic curriculum and teachers' qualifications, yield at best only moderate immediate and long-run effects on youngsters' citizenship orientations and knowledge (Diamond, 1960; Education Commission of the States, 1973; Jennings & Niemi, 1968, 1974; Kohlberg & Litt, 1963; Lockwood, 1970; Patrick, 1977; Tapp, 1971). In contrast, open classroom climate, measured by students' feeling that they can freely participate and express themselves in a supportive environment, seems to have a greater effect than formal instruction. This implies that classroom and school procedures can themselves be part of the learning process. Almond and Verba (1963) report that in a crossnational study of democratic culture, adults with the highest levels of political efficacy were those who remembered discussing and debating social and political issues in school. A favorable explanation is that through political discussions in schools students become more skillful and thus more willing to discuss politics in other settings as well. Political discussion also allows for the transmission of information through active learning and can thus enrich students' understanding of political issues (Conover & Searing, 2000). Taken together, research findings from the United States and western democracies suggest that when secondary school students discuss controversial issues in an open, supportive environment, there are often positive outcomes in terms of political interest, efficacy, confidence, and trust. Moreover, the teaching of controversial issues in a closed climate appears to be negatively correlated with those outcomes (Almond & Verba, 1963; Hahn, Tocci, & Angell, 1988; Torney, Oppenhein, & Farnen, 1975). However, no causal relations can be inferred from such studies. It's equally plausible to assume that students who initially have high levels of political interest, confidence, and efficacy are also attuned to controversial issues and engage in discussions.

Schools offer a variety of extracurricular activities, service learning programs, and an opportunity for students to participate in the governance of schools via school council, or the publishing of a school paper, for example. Some studies of participation in school governance and extracurricular activities have shown that active participation in school is likely to be transferred to new political situations (Almond & Verba, 1963; Barker & Gump, 1964; Beck & Jennings, 1982; Hanks, 1981; Lewis, 1962; Lindsay, 1984; Milbrath & Goel, 1977; Sigel & Hoskin, 1981; Trenfield, 1965). These studies suggest that school activities, although often nonpolitical, may help youngsters develop skills and orientations that could be transferred to the political world. Other studies found no such effects (Jones, 1974; Merelman, 1980; Ziblatt, 1965). Studies of service learning programs that engage students in community work indicate that overall an intensive and enduring engagement in such programs, in contrast to sporadic engagement, may positively contribute to students' political knowledge, ability to critically evaluate political events, and students' tendency to discuss politics with parents (Furco, 1997; Schlozman, Verba, Brady, & Erkulwater, 1998; Hodgkinson and Weitzman, 1996, 1997; Melchior, 1997; Niemi, Hepburn & Chapman, 2000; Verba, Scholzman, and Brady, 1995). Flanagan and Gill (1999) maintain that community work creates for youngsters a "bonding environment" that sensitizes participants to social issues, notably issues related to social justice (Barry, 1989; Jennings, 1989, 1991).

This brief review of major studies that represent the socialization process viewpoint leaves us with little clues for understanding the paramount effect of educational attainment on citizenship orientations. The explanatory power of curricular and extracurricular components of civic education, as far as citizenship knowledge, competences, attitudes, and behaviors are concerned, is fairly moderate.

From an allocation outlook, schools, as social institutions, do far more than impart knowledge, skills, traditions, and values to students. Though the form and substance of the educative process, schools also operate as "sorting machines" that select and certify individuals for adult roles at particular levels of the social hierarchy. The allocative perspective proposes that through schooling students accumulate "cultural capital." Symbolized by certificates, cultural capital becomes fixed assets by which individuals are assigned social positions and are initiated into class-related lifestyles (Bourdieu, 1971; Collins, 1979). Citizenship orientations and behaviors are clearly an important component of status-related lifestyles, as is indicated by studies that show a relationship between individuals' socioeconomic status and their voting behavior, sense of political efficacy, and involvement in public affairs (Easton, 1965; Humphries, Yaeger, & Katz, Himmelweit, 1981; Kohn, 1969; Lane, 1959; Lipset, 1960; Milbrath, 1965; Stouffer, 1965).

Nie, Junn, and Stehlik-Barry (1996) propose that by allocating scarce social and political ranks, formal education places individuals in their adult life either closer or further from the center of critical social and political networks. Increased educational attainment generally enables one to experience more diverse social relations and gain access to wider networks (Edwards & Foley, 1997). This, in turn, affects adult levels of political engagement. These observations no doubt enhance our understanding of the link between educational attainment and citizenship orientations. However, only the end product of education is considered, and no clues are provided concerning what happens in the course of schooling that could be related to the development of citizenship orientations.

Jennings and Niemi (1981) suggest that "educational stratification provides a fundamental early emerging, and persistent link between individuals and their political worlds" (p. 267). In other words, allocation processes operate in the course of schooling, not only on its completion. The most powerful manifestation of educational stratification, in my view, is the separation of students into different schools, programs, and tracks on the basis of their abilities, career aspirations, and socioeconomic backgrounds. Schools and educational programs enjoy dissimilar levels of esteem. This separation, therefore, symbolizes students' present status as well as future prospects. Thus, for example, students in academic tracks enjoy greater prestige among their peers and teachers and in the community outside school than students in vocational tracks, and the same holds true for students in the upper and lower ability groups (Keddie, 1971; Oakes, 1985; Oakes, Gamoran & Page, 1992; Rist, 1977).

Furthermore, educational stratification closely corresponds with social stratification in society. This means that students from better established families are often overrepresented in the more prestigious programs, while students belonging to minority groups and those representing lower socioeconomic echelons of society form the majority in the least prestigious programs (Ichilov, 1991; Oakes, 1985; Keddie, 1971). In other words, students representing marginal segments of society are often marginalized in schools as well.

Not only students are stratified and processed in schools. Knowledge too is stratified, and high-prestige knowledge is available almost exclusively to students in the high-status programs and tracks (Apple, 1990; Berenstein, 1971; Young, 1971).

Educational institutions convey to students normative descriptions of society and of their anticipated place in society as adults (Kamens, 1981). Already in school, students experience being placed closer or further away from the center where meaningful social assets are allocated. My argument is that the development of status-related citizenship orientations could be linked to individuals' placement in schools, and begin to emerge in the course of schooling. Educational stratification is related to the development of citizenship patterns through two distinct yet interrelated processes: placement of students in differentiated social networks and exposure of students to differentiated curricular and extracurricular schooling experiences.

Educational placement greatly determines whom students associate with in school and out of school. Association with peers from similar sociocultural background may solidify and reinforce status-related lifestyles that exist in the students' communities outside school (Ichilov, 1991). The concentration of minority and low-socioeconomic-status students in low-prestige programs may foster among them feelings of alienation, rejection, and marginality in school and of being discriminated against by being denied access to socially meaningful knowledge. Studies have shown that marginalized students are less engaged in school because they perceive fewer returns to education and limited opportunities for occupational mobility and for being politically effective and influential (Edwards & Foley, 1997; Fordhan & Ogbu, 1986; Johnson, Corsnoe, & Elder, 2001). Students recognize that the education they receive in school will not get them far ahead in society and will not enable them to escape insignificance and that prestigious occupations and further education are out of their reach. Such feelings toward school as a social agency can be generalized and result in civic apathy or militancy, distrust for societal institutions, and a feeling that democracy is a game played chiefly by the elites. Studies have shown that youth from working-class families are generally uninterested in politics (Bhavnani, 1991; Bynner & Ashford, 1994; Torney-Purta, 1990). This attitude could reflect both the influence of their family and community as well as their educational placement.

Interactions among students in the upper tracks may reinforce feelings of personal competence, acceptance, success, and prospects for belonging to the elites in the future as well. These feelings may be translated, for example, into greater anticipation of political engagement in adulthood and a stronger sense of political efficacy. Social networks, especially at the college level, are themselves a form of "social capital" that can be converted into future marital and business associations and "connections" with people in influential positions, for example.

Educational stratification results in differentiated curricular and extracurricular experiences for students. In England, for example, citizenship education used to be considered "practical" and therefore inferior to academic education grounded in liberal humanist conceptions of culture. Consequently, overt education for citizenship was designated largely for children of the working class. Such low-status citizenship courses were intended to foster "quietism," "domestication," and uncritical conforming citizens (Whitty, 1985, p. 279). Analysis of current curriculum materials designed for vocational and academic high schools in Israel has shown that the differentiated curriculum guides students into dissimilar citizenship roles. Academic school students are expected to acquire the capacity to perceive citizenship issues through broad, interdisciplinary, and multifaceted prism. Students in vocational schools, in contrast, are initiated into an unsophisticated and uncritical pattern of citizenship (Ichilov, 2002). Civic virtues such as critical thinking, problem solving, drawing conclusions, making generalizations, evaluating or synthesizing knowledge, and acting deliberatively in a pluralistic world are intimately related to high-stratified knowledge, notably to literacy, and access to such knowledge is unevenly allocated in schools. Students' uneven access to socially meaningful knowledge and educational experiences in school greatly determines their placement in the social hierarchy (Bowles, 1977; Bowles, & Gintis, 1976; Carnoy & Levin,

1985; Collins, 1979; Hargreaves, 1967; Keddie, 1971; Oakes, 1985; Rist, 1970; Sarup, 1978; Spring, 1980).

The way teachers observe, classify, and react to socioeconomic and cultural differences in children evidently results in differential learning experiences and opportunities (Davies, Gregory, & Riley, 1999; Keddie, 1971; Oakes, 1985). In schools dominated by academic curricula, teachers' reputation is often determined by teaching in high-status programs that cater to the "ablest" students (Young, 1971). In a study of Israeli high school teachers, Ichilov (1989) found that those who teach in academic programs and in schools that cater to well-established students are more open to discuss controversial issues and conflict situations and to expose students to criticism and pluralism, as compared with teachers who teach in schools with a majority of disadvantaged students. Educational placement could, thus, result in the preparation of students for dissimilar citizenship roles: students in high-status programs are initiated into a leadership role, while the "followership" role is reserved for the less-advantaged students (Apple, 1990; Ichilov, 2002).

Political scientists have overlooked the allocative processes of schooling, especially what happens to students in the course of schooling. However, some research findings suggest that educational stratification deserves to be examined and that this might expand our understanding of the connection between education and citizenship orientations. There is growing evidence that school placement affects a variety of political and social value orientations among students (Hyman & Wright, 1979; Ichilov, Haymann, & Shapira, 1990; Sullivan, Marcus, & Minns, 1975; Travers, 1982, 1983). Ichilov (1991) reports that program placement—academic or vocational— had a differential effect on students' expressed interest in politics, media use, willingness to become actively involved, discussion of politics with others, support of freedom of speech, and sense of political efficacy. Overall, the positive effect of academic programs, reinforcing a variety of civic orientations, was greater than that of vocational programs, where zero or negative effects more often prevailed. Evidence for the importance of an anticipated future for the formation of citizenship orientations and knowledge can be found in several studies. The recent report of the IEA International Civic Education Study (Torney-Purta, Lehmann, Oswald, & Schutz, 2001) reveals that "expected years of further education" had the strongest effect on civic knowledge among 14-year-old students in 28 countries, stronger than "home literacy resources" and "open classroom climate." A similar variable was an important predictor of civic knowledge in both the 1971 IEA Civic Education Study (Torney, Oppenhein, & Farnen, 1975) and in Niemi and Junn's (1998) analysis of the National Assessment of Civics in the United States. Niemi and Junn (1998) found that students' plans to attend four-year college was the strongest predictor of civics knowledge. In most instances it was stronger than amount and recency of course work in civics, participation in class discussions, participation in mock elections, and a variety of home environment variables. This was the case across racial groups—white, African American, and Hispanic—and across gender. It is reasonable to assume that educational aspirations are the outcome of a host of family, community, and personal factors that may become symbolized by students' placement in schools as well.

The exploration of the effects of educational stratification on the development of citizenship orientations seems to be a worthwhile endeavor. It should be a joint effort of behavioral scientists, in which political psychologists can play a prominent role. For example, psychologists could promote our understanding of the effects of educational stratification on citizenship orientations especially with reference to the role of marginality, alienation, labeling, stereotyping, self-image, aspirations, and expectations in the process of schooling. Are negative schooling experiences generalized into societal attitudes such as civic apathy, militancy, or distrust? If so, at what age do education-linked differences in civic orientations appear? Are differences diminishing or growing over the years? These are some of the queries that should be resolved in order to decipher the "black box" that conceals the connection between schooling and democratic citizenship.

Education and Democratic Citizenship in a Changing World

The preceding analysis of citizenship and citizenship education suggests that preparing the younger generation for the citizenship role is a formidable objective in our kaleidoscopic and fragmented world. However, it also suggests that citizenship education is, perhaps, needed more than ever to provide a sense of purpose, solidarity, and guidance to children who grow up in a great variety of political and social contexts (Ichilov, 1998; Pratte, 1988). Many societies today are witnessing rising levels of crime and violence, homelessness, racism, xenophobia, social inequality, abuse of the environment, and violations of human rights (Diamond & Plattner, 1994; Gitelman, 1992; Hannum, 1993; Kristeva, 1993; Kymlicka, 1995; Lerner, 1991; State of World Conflict Report, 1998; Taylor, 1994; Thornberry, 1991; Walzer, 1997; Weiner, 1998). In many western societies there is a trend among citizens to claim their rights and to retreat into their own privacy. However, in order to effectively cope with problems that arise at the local and international arenas, citizenship education should aim at creating conscientious, efficacious, interested, caring, and active citizens. Citizenship education should also help to redefine the public place by promoting global awareness and the realization that circumstances that affect our immediate moral and physical well-being are located on the transnational arena as well (Boulding, 1988; Ichilov, 1998).

Democratic societies place the heavy burden of citizenship education on the schools. A major conclusion of this chapter is that the schools' first moral obligation is "to give *all* children an education adequate to take advantage of their political status as citizens" (Gutmann, 1987, p. 288, emphasis added). Dewey (1916/1966) considers "equal opportunity to receive and to take from others . . . [and the exposure to] . . . shared undertakings and experiences" a hallmark of democratic education. "Otherwise, the influences which educate some into masters, educate others into slaves" (p. 84). My analysis of the unequal access to quality education for students representing minority and low socioeconomic families implies that schools often do not meet these societal expectations. Instead, schools frequently prepare students for dissimilar citizenship roles: leadership and followership. Inequality of educational opportunities, therefore, defies the basic tenets of democracy.

This analysis has also revealed that in terms of its contents, citizenship education is an eclectic and fragmented endeavor, encompassing a wide array of programs and approaches. Civics is a marginal school subject that is typically taught sporadically rather than consecutively throughout all the school grades and with little connection to other school subjects such as history and the social sciences. I would like to suggest that a more promising approach is to construct a comprehensive curriculum for citizenship education that would integrate the various concerns and schooling experiences into a coherent whole. It should be made available to students throughout their schooling, from grades K to 12.

This analysis also suggests that some important strides have been taken to explore how schooling affects so profoundly the development of citizenship orientations. However, much more theorizing and research are still needed in order to decipher the "black box" that conceals the connection between schooling and democratic citizenship. This should be a joint endeavor of all behavioral scientists.

It has been suggested that political psychology can offer important insights into the effects of educational stratification on citizenship orientations. Political psychology can also offer clues for understanding the development of citizenship in situations of multiple political allegiances, cultural diversity, and in instances of incongruence and conflict among one's allegiances and identities.

▲ References

Almond, G. A, & Verba, S. (1963). *The civic culture: Political attitudes and democracy in five nations*. Princeton: Princeton University Press.

Apple, M. W. (1990). *Ideology and curriculum* (2nd ed.). New York: Routledge.

Aristotle. (1943). *Politics* (B. Jowett, Trans.). New York: Walter J. Black.

Audigier, F. (2000). *Basic concepts and core competences for education for democratic citizenship*. Strasbourg: Council of Europe.

Barber, B. (1965). Some problems in the sociology of professions. In K. S. Lyn (Ed.), *The professions in America* (pp. 13–34). Boston: Houghton Mifflin.

Barber, B. (1995). *Jihad vs Mcworld.* New York: Times Books.

Barber, B. R. (1992). *An aristocracy for everyone.* New York: Ballantine.

Barker, R. G., & Gump, P. V. (1964). *Big school small school: High school size and student behavior.* Stanford, CA: Stanford University Press.

Barnes, C. A. (Ed.) (1992). *Critical thinking: Educational imperative.* San Francisco: Jossey-Bass.

Barnes, S. H., & Kaase, M. (1979). *Political action: Mass participation in five western democracies.* Beverly Hills, CA: Sage.

Barry, B. (1989). *Theories of justice.* Berkeley: University of California Press.

Beck, P. A., & Jennings, K. M. (1982). Pathways to participation. *American Political Science Review, 76,* 94–108.

Berelson, B. R., Lazarsfeld, P. F. & McPhee, W. N. (1954). *Voting: A study of opinion formation in a presidential campaign.* Chicago: University of Chicago Press.

Berenstein, B. (1971). On the classification and framing of educational knowledge. In M. F. D. Young (Ed.), *Knowledge and control* (pp. 47–70). London: Collier-Macmillan.

Bhavnani, K. K. (1991). *Talking politics: A psychological framing of views from youth in Britain.* Cambridge: Cambridge University Press.

Bîrzèa, C. (2000). *Education for democratic citizenship: A lifelong learning perspective.* Strasbourg: Council of Europe.

Boulding, E. (1988). *Building a global civic culture.* New York: Teachers College Press.

Bourdieu, P. (1971). Systems of education and systems of thought. In M. F. D. Young (Ed.), *Knowledge and control* (pp. 189–208). London: Collier-Macmillan.

Bowles, S. (1977). Unequal education and the reproduction of the social division of labor. In J. Karabel & A. H. Halsey (Eds.), *Power and ideology in education* (pp. 137–153). New York: Oxford University Press.

Bowles, S., & Gintis, H. (1976). *Schooling in capitalist America.* New York: Basic Books.

Boyne, R., & Rattansi, A.(1990). The theory and politics of postmodernism: By way of introduction. In R. Boyne & A. Rattansi (Eds.), *Postmodernism and society* (pp. 1–46). London: Macmillan.

Branson, M. (1998). *The role of civic education: A position paper.* Calabasas, CA: Center for Civic Education.

Bricker, D. C. (1989). *Classroom life as civic education.* New York: Teachers College Press.

Brownlie, I. (Ed.)(1992). *Basic documents on human rights* (3rd ed.). New York: Oxford University Press.

Bynner, J., & Ashford, S. (1994). Politics and participation: Some antecedents of young people's attitude to the political system and political activity. *European Journal of Social Psychology, 24,* 223–236.

Campbell, A., Converse, P. E., Stokes, D. E., & Miller, W. E. (1969). *The American voter.* New York: Wiley.

Campbell, A., Gurin, G. & Miller, W. E. (1954). *The voter decides.* Evanston, IL: Row, Peterson.

Carey, L., & Forrester, K. (2000). *Sites of citizenship: Empowerment, participation and partnership.* Strasbourg: Council of Europe.

Carnoy, M., & Levin, H. M. (1985). *Schooling and work in the democratic state.* Stanford, CA: Stanford University Press.

Carroll, J. D., Broadnax, W. D., Contreras, G., Mann, T. E., Orenstein, N. J., & Stiehm, J. (1987). *We the people: A review of U.S. government and civics textbooks.* Washington, DC: People for the American Way.

Clark, J. (1991). *Democratizing development: The role of voluntary agencies.* London: Kumarian Press.

Collins, R. (1979). *The credential society.* New York: Academic Press.

Conover, P., & Searing, D. D. (2000). A political socialization perspective. In L. M. McDonnell, P. M. Timpane, & R. Benjamine (Eds.), *Rediscovering the democratic purposes of education* (pp. 91–127). Lawrence: University of Kansas Press.

Convention on the Rights of the Child, 1989. (1992). In I. Brownlie (Ed.), *Basic documents on human rights* (3rd ed.). New York: Oxford University Press.

Converse, P. E. (1972). A change in the American electorate. In A. Campbell, & P. E. Converse (Eds.), *The human meaning of social change.* New York, NY: Russell Sage Foundation.

Crick, B. (2000). The English citizenship order: The temperate reply to critics. *School Field, 11*(3/4), 61–73.

Dahl, R. A. (1961). *Who governs? Democracy and power in an American city.* New Haven: Yale University Press.

Dahl, R. A. (1982). *Dilemmas of pluralistic democracy: Autonomy vs. control.* New Haven: Yale University Press.

Dahrendorf, R. (1994). The changing quality of citizenship. In B. van Steenberger (Ed.), *The condition of citizenship* (pp. 10–19). London: Sage.

Dahrendorf, R. (1996). Citizenship and social class. In M. Blumer & A. Rees (Eds), *Citizenship today: The contemporary relevance of T. H. Marshall.* London: University College.

Dalton, R. J. (1988). *Citizen politics in Western democracies.* Chatham, NJ: Chatham House.

Davies, I., Gregory, I., & Riley, S. C. (1999). *Good citizenship and educational provision.* London: Falmer Press.

Department for Education and Employment, Qualifications and Curriculum Authority. (1999). *Citizenship: The national curriculum for England.* London: Department for Education and Employment.

Delli Carpini, M. X., & Keeter, S. (1996). *What Americans know about politics and why it matters.* New Haven: Yale University Press.

Dewey, J. (1916/1966). *Democracy and education.* New York: Macmillan.

Diamond, L. & Plattner, M. F. (Eds.) (1994). *Nationalism, ethnic conflict, and democracy.* Baltimore: Johns Hopkins University Press.

Diamond, S. (1960). Studies and projects in citizenship education. In F. Patterson (Ed.), *The adolescent citizen.* New York: Free Press.

Dodds, S. (1998). Citizenship, justice and indigenous group-specific rights—Citizenship and indigenous Australia. *Citizenship Studies, 2*(1): 105–121.

Dreeben, R. (1970). "Schooling and citizenship." In R. Dreeben (Ed.), *On what is learned in schools.* Menlo Park, CA: Addison-Wesley.

Duerr, K., Spajic-Vrkaš V., & Martins, I. F. (2000). *Strategies for learning democratic citizenship.* Strasbourg: Council of Europe.

Durkheim, E. (1961). *Moral education.* Glencoe, IL: Free Press.

Easton, D. (1965). *A framework for political analysis.* Englewood Cliffs, NJ: Prentice-Hall.

Easton, D., & Dennis, J. (1969). *Children in the political system.* New York: McGraw-Hill.

Reading minds. (2001, February 24). *Economist, 358,* 91–94.

Education Commission of the States. (1973). *National assessment of educational progress: Political knowledge and attitudes.* Washington, DC: Government Printing Office.

Edwards, B., & Foley, M. W. (1997). Social capital and the political economy of our discontent. *American Behavioral Scientist, 40*(5), 669–679.

Edwards, M. (2001). Introduction. In M. Edwards & J. Gaventa (Eds.), *Global citizen action* (pp. 1–17). Boulder, CO: Lynne Rienner.

Edwards, M., & Gaventa, J. (Eds.). (2001). *Global citizen action.* Boulder, CO: Lynne Rienner.

Ehman, L. H. (1977). Research on social studies curriculum and instruction: Values. In F. P. Hunkins, Ehman, L. H., Hahn, C. L., Martorella, P. H. & Tucker, J. L. (Eds.), *Review of research in social studies education, 1970–1975.* Washington, DC: National Council for the Social Studies.

Ehman, L. H. (1980). The American school in the political socialization process. *Review of Educational Research, 50*(1), 99–119.

Ester, P., Halman, L., & de Moor, R. (1994). *The individualizing society: Value change in Europe and North America.* Tilberg: Tilberg University Press.

Etzioni, A. (1970). *Demonstration democracy.* New York: Gordon and Breach.

Etzioni, A. (1992). On the place of virtues in pluralistic democracy. In G. Marks & L. Diamond (Eds.), *Reexamining democracy* (pp. 70–79). Newbury Park, CA: Sage.

Flanagen, C. A., & Gill, S. (1999, April). *Adolescents' social integration and affection for the polity: Processes for different racial/ethnic groups.* Paper presented in symposium, "Who Gets Involved?" at the biennial meeting of the Society for Research in Child Development, Albuquerque, New Mexico.

Fordhan, S., & Ogbu, J. U. (1986). Black students' school success: Coping with the burden of "acting white." *Urban Review* 18, 176–206.

Frith, K. T. (1997). *Undressing the ad.* Berlin: Lang.

Furco, A. (1997). *School-sponsored service programs and the educational development of high school students.* Unpublished doctoral dissertation, University of California, Berkeley.

Gallatin, J., & Adelson, J. (1970). Individual rights and the public good: A cross-national study of adolescents. *Comparative Political Studies, 3,* 98–114.

Gibbins, J. (1989). Contemporary political culture: An introduction. In J. Gibbins (Ed.), *Contemporary political culture: Politics in a postmodern age.* London: Sage.

Gilbert, R. (1992). Citizenship, education and postmodernity. *British Journal of Sociology of Education, 13*(1), 51–68.

Giroux, H. A. (1983). *Theory and resistence in education: A pedagogy for the opposition.* Boston: Bergin and Garvey.

Gitelman, Z. (1992). Development and ethnicity in the Soviet Union. In A. J. Moytel (Ed.), *The post-Soviet nations* (pp. 220–240). New York: Columbia University Press.

Greenstein, F. I. (1973). Political psychology: A pluralistic universe. In J. N. Knutson (Ed.), *Handbook of political psychology* (pp. 438–471). San Francisco: Jossey Bass.

Gruber, J. E. (1987). *Controlling bureaucracies: Dilemmas in democratic governance.* Berkeley: University of California Press.

Gutmann, A. (1987). *Democratic education*. Princeton: Princeton University Press.

Gutmann, A. (2000). Why should schools care about civic education? In L. M. McDonnell, P. M. Timpane, & R. Benjamine (Eds.), *Rediscovering the democratic purposes of education* (pp. 73–91). Lawrence: University of Kansas Press.

Habermas, J. (1995). Citizenship and national identity: Some reflections on the future of Europe. In R. Beiner (Ed.), *Theorizing citizenship* (pp. 255–283). Albany: SUNY Press.

Hahn, C. L. (1998). *Becoming political.* Albany: SUNY Press.

Hahn, C. L., Tocci, C., & Angell, A. (1988). Civic attitudes and controversial issues discussion in five nations. Paper presented at the International meeting of the Social Studies, Vancouver.

Hanks, M. (1981). Youth, voluntary associations and political socialization. *Social Forces, 60,* 211–223.

Hannum, H. (1993). *Basic documents on autonomy and minority rights.* Boston: Nijhoff.

Hargreaves, D. (1967). *Social relations in a secondary school.* London: Routledge and Kegan Paul.

Heater, D. (1990). *Citizenship: The civic ideal in world history.* London: Longman.

Hepburn, M. A. (1998). A disquieting outlook for democracy: Mass media, news and citizenship education in the US. In O. Ichilov (Ed.), *Citizenship and citizenship education in a changing world* (pp. 130–149). London: Woburn Press.

Hess, R. D., & Torney, J. (1967). *The development of political attitudes in children.* Hawthorne, NY: Aldine.

Heying, C. H. (1997). Civic elites and corporate delocalization: An alternative explanation for declining civic engagement. *American Behavioral Scientist, 40*(5), 656–667.

Higgott, R., & Bieler, A. (Eds.). (1999). *Non-state actors and authority in the global system.* London: Routledge.

Himmelweit, H. T., Humphreys, P., Jaeger, M., & Katz, M. (1981). *How voters decide.* London: Academic.

Hochschild, J. L., & Scovronick, N. (2000). Democratic education and the American dream. In L. M. McDonnell, P. M. Timpane, & R. Benjamine (Eds.), *Rediscovering the democratic purposes of education* (pp. 209–43). Lawrence: University of Kansas Press.

Hodgkinson, V. A., & Weitzman, M. S. (1996). *Giving and volunteering in the U.S.* Washington, DC: Independent Sector.

Hodgkinson, V. A., & Weitzman, M. S. (1997). *Volunteering and giving among teenagers twelve to seventeen years of age.* Washington, DC: Independent Sector.

Hyman, H. H., & Wright, C. R. (1979). *Education's lasting influence on values.* Chicago: University of Chicago Press.

Ichilov, O. (1989). Perceptions and attitudes of Israeli high school civic education teachers concerning citizenship in democracy. *Studies in Education, 48,* 69–89. (In Hebrew).

Ichilov, O. (1990). Dimensions and role patterns of citizenship in democracy In O. Ichilov (Ed.), *Political socialization, citizenship education, and democracy* (pp. 11–25). New York: Teachers College Press.

Ichilov, O. (1991). Political socialization and schooling effects among Israeli adolescents. *Comparative Education Review, 35*(3), 430–447.

Ichilov, O. (1993). What textbooks teach Israeli youngsters about democracy. In R. F. Farnen (Ed.), *Re-conceptualizing politics, socialization and education: International perspectives for the next century* (pp. 315–329). Oldenburg, Germany: University of Oldenburg Press.

Ichilov, O. (1994). Political education. In T. Huson & T. N. Postlethwaite (Eds.), *The international encyclopedia of education* (2nd ed., vol. 8, pp. 4568–4572). New York: Pergamon.

Ichilov, O. (Ed.). (1998). *Citizenship and citizenship education in a changing world.* London: Woburn Press.

Ichilov, O. (2000). *Citizenhip orientations of 11th grade students and teachers in the Israeli Hebrew and Arab high schools.* Israel's National Research Report, IEA Civic Education Study. Tel Aviv: Tel Aviv University, School of Education.

Ichilov, O. (2002). Differentiated civics curriculum and patterns of citizenship education: Vocational and academic programs in Israel. In D. Scott & H. Lawson (Eds.), *Citizenship education and the curriculum.* International Perspectives on Curriculum Series, vol. 3, pp. 81–111. (Series editor: David Scott). Westport, CT: Greenwood.

Ichilov, O., Haymann, F., & Shapira, R. (1990). Social and moral integration and attachment to the nation-state: A case study of Israeli adolescents. *Urban Education, 25*(2), 143–57.

International Bureau of Education. (1994, December). *Educational Innovations and Information.* (No. 81). Author.

Janowitz, M. (1983). *The reconstruction of patriotism: Education for civic consciousness.* Chicago: University of Chicago press.

Jaros, D. (1973). *Socialization to politics.* New York: Praeger.

Jennings, K. M. (1989). Perceptions of social justice. In M. K. Jennings, J. van Deth, et al. (Eds.), *Continuities in political action.* Berlin: de Gruyter.

Jennings, K. M. (1991). Thinking about social justice. *Political Psychology, 12*(2), 187–205.

Jennings, K. M., Langton, K. P. & Niemi, R. G. (1974). Effects of the high school civics curriculum. In M. K. Jennings & R. G. Niemi (Eds.), *The political character of adolescence* (pp. 181–207). Princeton: Princeton University Press.

Jennings, K. M., & Niemi, R. G. (1968). Patterns of political learning. *Harvard Educational Review, 38*(3), 443–468.

Jennings, K. M., & Niemi, R. G. (1974). *The political character of adolescence.* Princeton: Princeton University Press.

Jennings, K. M. & Niemi, R. G. (1981). *Generations and politics: A panel study of young adults and their parents.* Princeton: Princeton University Press.

Johnson, M. K., Corsnoe, R., & Elder, G. H., Jr. (2001). Students' attachment and academic engagement: The role of race and ethnicity. *American Sociological Review, 74*(4), 318–341.

Jones, R. (1974). Changing student attitudes: The impact of community participation. *Social Science Quarterly, 55,* 439–450.

Kamens, D. H. (1981). Organizational and institutional socialization in education. *Research in Sociology of Education and Socialization, 2,* 208–19.

Kamens, D. H. (1988). Education and democracy: A comparative institutional analysis. *Sociology of Education, 61,* 114–127.

Keck, M., & Sikkink, K. (1998). *Activists beyond borders: Trans-national advocacy networks in international politics.* London: Cornell University Press.

Keddie, N. (1971). Classroom knowledge. In M. F. D. Young (Ed.), *Knowledge and control.* New York: Collier-Macmillan.

Kiernan, A. K. (1997). Citizenship: The real democratic deficit of the European Union? *Citizenship Studies, 1*(3), 323–335.

Klein, N. (1999). *No logo.* New York: Picador.

Kohlberg, L., & Lockwood, A. (1970). *The cognitive developmental psychology and political education: Progress in the sixties.* Cambridge, MA: Harvard Moral Development Project.

Kohn, M. (1969). *Class and conformity: A study in values.* Homewood, IL: Dorsey.

Kristeva, J. (1993). *Nations without nationalism.* New York: Columbia University Press.

Kymlicka, W. (1991). Liberalism and the politicization of ethnicity. *Canadian Journal of Law and Jurisprudence, 4*(2), 239–256.

Kymlicka, W. (1995). *Multicultural citizenship: A liberal theory of minority rights.* Oxford: Oxford University Press.

Lane, R. E. (1959). *Political life.* New York: Free Press.

Langton, K. P. (1969). *Political socialization.* London: Oxford University Press.

Larkins, A. G., Hawkins, M. L., & Gilmore, A. (1987). Trivial and noninformation content of elementary social studies: A review of primary texts in four series. *Theory and research in social education, 15*(4), 299–311.

Lerner, N. (1991). *Group rights and discrimination in international law.* Dordrecht: Nijhoff.

Lewis, H. (1962). *The teenager joiner and his orientations toward public affairs: A test of two multiple group membership hypothesis.* Unpublished doctoral dissertation, Michigan State University, East Lansing.

Lindsay, P. (1984). High school size, participation in activities, and young adult social participation: Some enduring effects of schooling. *Educational Evaluation and Policy Analysis, 6,*73–83.

Lipman, M. (1988). *Philosophy goes to school.* Philadelphia: Temple University Press.

Lipset, S. M. (1960). *Political man.* New York: Doubleday.

Litt, E. (1963). Civic education, community norms, and political indoctrination. *American Sociological Review, 28,* 69–75.

Lo, L. N. K., & Si-Wai, M. (1996). Introduction: Nurturing the moral citizen of the future. In L. N. K. Lo & M. Si-Wai (Eds.), *Moral and civic education* (pp. ix–1). Hong Kong: Hong Kong Institute of Educational Research.

Lovibond, S. (1990). Feminism and postmodernism. In R. Boyne & A. Rattansi (Eds.), *Postmodernism and society* (pp. 154–187). London: Macmillan.

Lybarger, M. B. (1991). The historiography of social studies: Retrospect, circumspect, and prospect. In J. P. Shaver (Ed.), *Handbook of research on social studies teaching and learning* (pp. 3–16). New York: Macmillan.

Lyotard, J. F. (1984). *The postmodern condition.* Manchester, England: Manchester University Press.

Luke, A., & Walton, C. (1994). Critical reading: Teaching and assessing. In T. Hus'n, & T. N. Postlethwaite (Eds.), *The international encyclopedia of education,* 2nd ed., vol. 2 (pp. 1194–1198). New York: Pergamon.

March, J. G., & Olsen, J. P. (2000). Democracy and schooling: An institutional perspective. In L. M. McDonnell, P. M. Timpane, & R. Benjamine (Eds.), *Rediscovering the democratic purposes of education* (pp. 148–174). Lawrence: The University of Kansas Press.

Marshall, T. H. (1977). *Class, citizenship and social development.* Chicago: University of Chicago Press.

Marshall, T. H. (1981). *The right to welfare and other essays.* London: Heinemann.

McDonnell, L. M. (2000). Defining democratic purposes. In L. M. McDonnell, P. M. Timpane, & R. Benjamine (Eds.), *Rediscovering the democratic purposes of education* (pp. 1–21). Lawrence: University of Kansas Press.

McPeck, J. E. (1981). *Critical thinking and education.* New York: Martin.

Mead, M. (1996). Ruling class strategies and citizenship. In M. Blumer & A. Rees (Eds.), *Citizenship today: The contemporary relevance of T. H. Marshall.* London: University College.

Melchior, A. (1997). *National evaluation of learn and serve America school and community-based programs: Interim report.* Waltham, MA: Brandeis University Center for Human Resources.

Merelman, R. M. (1971). *Political socialization and educational climates.* New York: Holt, Rinehart and Winston.

Merelman, R. M. (1980). Democratic politics and the culture of American education. *American Political Science Review, 74,* 319–332.

Merelman, R. M. (1986). Revitalizing political socialization. In M. G. Hermann (Ed.), *Political psychology: Contemporary problems and issues* (pp. 279–320). San Francisco: Jossey-Bass.

Milbrath, L. W. (1965). *Political participation.* Chicago: Rand McNally.

Milbrath, L. W., & Goel, M. L. (1977). *Political participation: How and why people get involved in politics.* Chicago: Rand McNally.

Moe, T. M. (2000). The two democratic purposes of public education. In L. M. McDonnell, P. M. Timpane, & R. Benjamine (Eds.), *Rediscovering the democratic purposes of education* (pp. 127–48). Lawrence: University of Kansas Press.

Motyl, A. J. (Ed.). (1992). *The post-Soviet nations.* New York: Columbia University Press.

Mouffe, C. (1992). Democratic politics today. In C. Mouffe (Ed.), *Dimensions of radical democracy* (pp. 1–14). London: Verso.

National Commission on Civic Renewal. (1998). *A nation of spectators: How civic disengagement weakens America and what we can do about it.* College Park: University of Maryland Press.

Nie, N. H., Powell, B., & Prewitt, K. (1969). Social structure and political participation. *American Political Science Review, 63,* 361–378.

Nie, N. H., Junn, J., & Stehlik-Barry, K. (1996). *Education and democratic citizenship in America.* Chicago: University of Chicago Press.

Niemi, R. G., & Hepburn, M. A. (1995). The rebirth of political socialization. *Perspectives on Political Science, 24*(1).

Niemi, R. G., Hepburn, M. A., & Chapman, C. (2000). Community service of high school students: A cure for civic ills? *Political Behavior, 22*(1).

Niemi, R. G., & Junn, J. (1998). *Civic education: What makes students learn.* New Haven: Yale University Press.

Nodia, G. (1994). Nationalism and democracy. In L. Diamond & M. F. Plattner (Eds.), *Nationalism, ethnic conflict, and democracy* (pp. 3–23). Baltimore: Johns Hopkins University Press.

Norris, P. (1999). Introduction: The growth of critical citizens? In P. Norris (Ed.), *Critical citizens: Global support for democratic government* (pp. 1–31). Oxford: Oxford University Press.

Oakes, Jeannie. (1985). *Keeping track: How schools structure inequality*. New Haven: Yale University Press.

Oakes, J., Gamoran, A., & Page, R. N. (1992). Curriculum differentiation: Opportunities, outcomes, and meanings. In P. W. Jackson (Ed.), *Handbook of research on curriculum* (pp. 570–626). New York: Macmillan.

Pangle, L. S., & Pangle, T. L. (2000). What the American founders have to teach us about schooling for democratic citizenship. In L. M. McDonnell, P. M. Timpane, & R. Benjamine (Eds.), *Rediscovering the democratic purposes of education* (pp. 21–47). Lawrence: The University of Kansas Press.

Patrick, J. J. (1977). Political socialization and political education in schools. In S. A. Renshon (Ed.), *Handbook of political socialization* (pp. 190–223). New York: Free Press.

Patrick, J. J., & Hoge, J. D. (1991). Teaching government, civics, and law. In J. P. Shaver (Ed.), *Handbook of research on social studies teaching and learning* (pp. 427–437). New York: Macmillan.

Paul, R. (1993). *Critical thinking: How to prepare students for rapidly changing world*. Santa Rosa, CA: Sonoma State University.

Pingel, F. (1999). *UNESCO guidebook on textbook research and textbook revision*. Strassburg: UNESCO.

Postman, N., & Powers, S. (1992). *How to watch TV news*. New York: Penguin Books.

Power, F. C., Higgins, A., & Kohlberg, L. (1989). *Lawrence Kohlberg's approach to moral education*. New York: Columbia University Press.

Pratte, R. (1988). *The civic imperative*. New York: Teachers College Press.

Putman, R. D. (1995). Bowling alone: America's declining social capital. *Journal of Democracy, 6,* 65–78.

Reading minds. (2001, February 24). *Economist, 358,* 91–94.

Reich, R. (1995, June). *Testing the boundaries of parental authority over education: The case of homeschooling*. Paper presented at conference "Fostering Youth's Civic Engagement and Participation in Free and Democratic Societies," Brown University, Providence, RI.

Rifkin, J. (1995). *The end of work*. New York: Putnam.

Rist, R. C. (1970). Student social class and teacher expectations: The self-fulfilling prophecy in ghetto education. *Harvard Educational Review, 40,* 411–451.

Rist, R. C. (1977). On understanding the process of schooling: The contributions of labeling theory. In J. Karabel & A. H. Halsey, *Power and ideology in education* (pp. 292–313). New York: Oxford University Press.

Rose, R. (1999). Eastern Europe a decade later: Another great transformation. *Journal of Democracy, 10*(1), 51–57.

Sartori, G. (1997). Understanding pluralism. *Journal of Democracy, 8*(4), 58–70.

Sarup, M. (1978). *Marxism and education*. London: Routledge and Kegan Paul.

Saunders, G. (1993). Citizenship in a liberal society. In B. S. Turner (Ed.), *Citizenship and social theory* (pp. 57–91). London: Sage.

Schild, V. (2000). Neo-liberalism's new gendered market citizens: The "civilizing" dimensions of social programmes in Chile. *Citizenship Studies, 4*(3), 275–307.

Schlozman, K. L., Verba, S., Brady, H., & Erkulwater, J. (1998). *Why can't they be like we are? Understanding the generation gap in participation*. Unpublished manuscript. Boston College.

Schneider, D. (2000). Symbolic citizenship, nationalism and the distant state: The United States Congress in the 1996 debate on immigration reform. *Citizenship Studies, 4*(3), 255–275.

Scholte, A. J. (2000). Global civil society. In N. Woods (Ed.), *The political economy of globalization* (pp. 173–201). Basingstoke, England: Macmillan.

Sigel, R. (Ed.). (1970). *Learning about politics.* New York: Random House.

Sigel, R., & Hoskin, M. (1981). *The political involvement of adolescents.* New Brunswick, NJ: Rutgers University Press.

Solomon, J. (1988). *The signs of our times.* Los Angeles: Tarcher.

Spring, J. (1980). *Educating the worker-citizen.* New York: Longman.

Spring, J. (2000). *The universal right to education.* Mahwah, NJ: Erlbaum.

State of world conflict report. (1998). Carter Center.

Stotsky, S. (1991). *Connecting civic education and language education: The contemporary challenge.* New York: Teachers College Press.

Stouffer, S. A. (1955). *Communism, conformity and civil liberties.* Garden City, NY: Doubleday.

Sullivan, J., Marcus, G., & Minns, D. (1975). The development of political ideology: Some empirical findings. *Youth and Society, 7,* 148–70.

Tapp, J. L. (1971) Developing sense of law and legal justice. *Journal of Social Issues, 27*(2), 65–91.

Taylor, C. (1994). The politics of recognition. In A. Gutmann (Ed.), *Multiculturalism: Examining the politics of recognition* (pp. 25–74). Princeton: Princeton University Press.

Thornberry, P. (1991). *International law and the rights of minorities.* Oxford: Oxford University Press.

Torney, J., Oppenheim, A., & Farnan, R. (1975). *Civic education in ten countries. An empirical study.* New York: Halsted Press.

Torney-Purta, J. (1990). Youth in relation to social institutions. In S. S. Feldman, & G. R. Elliott (Eds.), *At the threshold: The developing adolescent* (pp. 457–478). Cambridge, MA: Harvard University Press.

Torney-Purta, J. (1997). Links and missing links between education, political knowledge, and citizenship. *American Journal of Education, 105,* 447–57.

Torney-Purta, J., Lehmann, R., Oswald, H., & Schulz, W. (2001). *Citizenship and education in twenty-eight countries.* Amsterdam: IEA.

Torney-Purta, J., Schwille, J., & Amado, J. A. (1999). *Civic education across countries: Twenty-four national case studies from the IEA civic education project.* Amsterdam: IEA.

Travers, E. (1982). Ideology and political participation among high school students: Changes from 1970–1978. *Youth and Society, 13*(3), 327–352.

Travers, E. (1983). The role of school in political socialization reconsidered. *Youth and Society, 14*(4), 475–501.

Trenfield, W. G. (1965). An analysis of the relationship between selected factors and the civics interests of high school students. *Journal of Educational Research, 58,* 460–472.

Turner, B. S. (1993). *Citizenship and social theory.* London: Sage.

Turner, B. S. (1997). Citizenship studies: A general theory. *Citizenship Studies, 1*(1), 5–19.

UNESCO. (2000a). *The Dakar framework for action: Education for all: Meeting our collective commitments.*

UNESCO. (2000b, April). *Final report.* World Education Forum, Dakar, Senegal.

UNESCO. (2000c). World declaration on education for all: Meeting basic learning needs. In *The Dakar framework for action: Education for all: Meeting our collective commitments.*

Universal Declaration of Human Rights, 1948. (1992) In I. Brownlie (Ed.), *Basic documents on human rights* (3rd ed.). New York: Oxford University Press.

Verba, S., Nie, N., & Kim, J. (1978). *Participation and political equality: A seven nation comparison.* New York: Cambridge University Press.

Verba, S., Schlozman, K. L., & Brady, H. E. (1995). *Voice and equality.* Cambridge, MA: Harvard University Press.

Walzer, M. (1989). Citizenship. In T. Ball, J. Farr, & R. L. Hanson (Eds.), *Political innovation and conceptual change* (pp. 211–219). Cambridge: Cambridge University Press.

Walzer, M. (1997). *On toleration.* New Haven: Yale University Press.

Weiner, E. (1998). Coexistence work: A new profession. In E. Weiner (Ed.), *The book of international coexistence* (pp. 13–25). New York: Continuum.

Weinreich-Haste, H. (1986). Kohlberg and politics: A positive view. In S. Modgil & C. Modgil (Eds.), *Kohlberg: Consensus and controversy.* Lews, England: Falmer Press.

Weissberg, R. (1974). *Political learning, political choice & democratic citizenship.* Englewood Cliffs, NJ: Prentice-Hall.

Wexler, P. (1990). Citizenship in the semiotic society. In B. S. Turner (Ed.), *Theories of modernity and postmodernity* (pp. 164–176). London: Sage.

Whitty, G. (1985). Social studies and political education in England since 1945. In I. Goodson (Ed.), *Social histories of the secondary curriculum: Subjects for study* (pp. 269–289). London: Falmer Press.

Wolfinger, R. E., & Rosenstone, S. J. (1980). *Who votes?* New Haven: Yale University Press.

Wood, D. N. (1996). *Post-intellectualism and the decline of democracy.* Westport, CT: Praeger.

Young, M. F. D. (1971). An approach to the study of curricula as socially organized knowledge. In M. F. D Young (Ed.), *Knowledge and control* (pp. 19–47). London: Collier-Macmillan.

Ziblatt, D. (1965). High school extracurricular activities and political socialization. *Annals of the American Academy of Political and Social Science, 361,* 20–31.

19 Bert Klandermans

Collective Political Action

Participation in collective political action has always fascinated social scientists, perhaps because they have been amazed that people were prepared to make sacrifices for a cause, sometimes even risking their lives. Amazement may also have led to the view of participation in collective action as an irrational act carried out by isolated and marginal members of society (Hoffer, 1951; Kornhauser, 1959; Le Bon, 1903/1960). We have since moved far beyond theories that framed collective action participation as irrational. The theories and models of today are complex and sophisticated frameworks that take into account a multifaceted set of factors in explaining collective action participation. Indeed, it is a long way from the early studies that took feelings of relative deprivation or frustration as the single determinant of collective action participation to the complicated models of recruitment and participation of today.

In this chapter I will take stock of what we have learned so far. Compared to three or four decades ago—when the systematic empirical study of collective action participation began to take off—we know a lot more now about the dynamics of collective action participation. Most of the work during those years has been accomplished in the context of a specific form of collective political action, namely, action staged in the context of a social movement, for example, the student movement, the peace movement, the anti–Vietnam war movement, the women's movement, or the environmental movement. Therefore, I will concentrate in this chapter on social movement participation. In doing so I will focus on three issues. *First*, I will argue that movement participation has become a common way of doing politics. In the literature this has been referred to as the "movementization of politics." These developments have rendered the classical distinction between conventional and unconventional political participation obsolete. What used to be referred to as unconventional political participation in the literature has become as conventional as any other form of political participation. *Second*, I will elaborate on the dynamics of movement participation. I will borrow the concepts of demand and supply from economics to distinguish factors residing in the public (demand) from factors characterizing the movements that stage collective action (supply). I will define *mobilization* as the process that brings demand and supply together. Three perspectives on participation play a central role in my treatment of mobilization, briefly described as instrumentality, identity, and ideology. Each perspective emphasizes a different motivational mechanism in the explanation of movement participation. People participate because they want to change something, or because they want to show their identity, or because they want to express their views and to give meaning to their world. *Third*, I will discuss participation over the life course. The questions I will address in the last section all relate to long-term processes in participation. What are the dynamics of sustained participation, and how do some people's lives turn into activist careers? How is commitment to a social movement maintained, and why do people quit? I close the chapter with a brief discussion of the biographical consequences of movement participation.

◤ The Movementization of Politics

"Social movements are collective challenges by people with common purposes and solidarity in sustained interaction with elites and authorities" (Tarrow, 1994, p. 4). This definition of social movements includes three key elements that deserve some elaboration. First, social movements are *collective challenges*. They concern contentious action against elites, authorities, other groups, or cultural codes. There is an obvious reason why this is the case. Social movements typically encompass people who lack access to politics. Had they had access, there would have been no need for a social movement. Contentious collective action forces authorities to pay attention to the claims brought forward. Second, it concerns people with a *common purpose* and *solidarity*. Social movement participants rally behind common claims, they want authorities to *do* something, to change a state of affair or to undo changes. Such common claims are rooted in feelings of collective identity and solidarity. Third, isolated incidents of collective action are *not* social movements. Only by *sustaining* collective action does an actor turn a contentious episode into a social movement. Sustained collective action requires some organization. Social movements are loosely coupled networks of groups and organizations that individually or in collaboration stage the activities individuals can take part in (McAdam, McCarthy, & Zald, 1996).

Obviously, not every form of movement participation is contentious, nor are all forms of participation necessarily collective. Volunteering in the office of a movement organization, attending business meetings, or paying a membership fee are not contentious acts in and of themselves. Note, however, that it is not uncommon for such activities to generate the resources needed for more contentious action. Note also, that however modest activities might be, authorities might not even tolerate these activities. Apparently, it is not modesty or militancy of activities alone but their objectives that determine their meaning. Furthermore, some of these activities concern single individuals rather than collectives. In fact, people do not necessarily need to meet with others. Messages and goals can be relayed in many different ways. Yet the point of the matter is that individuals are identifying with and acting on behalf of a larger social category (Kelly & Breinlinger, 1996).

Meyer and Tarrow (1998) observe that movement-related action has become much more frequent over the last 30 years. These authors wonder whether this is because movement action has become part of the conventional repertoire of participation, in other words, whether movement activity has become institutionalized. Neidhardt and Rucht (1993) and Jenkins and Klandermans (1995) have made a similar observation. Increasingly, these authors have argued, social movement organizations are replacing political parties as intermediaries in interest representation between citizens and the state. These authors are not so much interpreting this as institutionalization of social movement action but rather as the "movementization" of politics. The following facts help to substantiate this claim: in the United States after the 1960s and 1970s (the years of the students' movement and the women's movement) a proliferation of all sorts of other movements took place: the anti-ERA campaign, Mothers Against Drunk Driving, the gay and lesbian movement, the Nuclear Freeze movement, the movement for divestment of U.S. investments in South Africa, and so on (see Meyer & Tarrow, 1998). In Great Britain, Russell Dalton (1996, p. 76) observes that in 1975, 22 percent of the British people signed some petition. In 1990 the figure was 75 percent. In 1974, 9 percent of the British participated in a demonstration, compared to 25 percent in 1990. Between 1979 and 1993 the number of protest events in the French city of Marseille more than doubled from 183 to 395 events per annum (Fillieule, 1998). Rucht (1998) reports considerable increases in protest events in Germany in the same period, a result that is confirmed by Kriesi, Koopmans, Duyvendak, and Guigni's (1995) study on new social movements in Europe. On the whole, then, Meyer and Tarrow's observation is supported by other empirical studies. In addition, they argue that this diffusion of protest is not only a matter of growing numbers, that is, of more protest events within a set amount of time, but of diffusion to broader sectors of the population as well. Across age groups, and gender lines, from the left to the right, among workers and students and in western and nonwestern societies alike, movement-related action has become a common phenomenon.

Why have social movements become commonplace? Although the reasoning varies, the answer to this question concerns the relative importance attributed to social movement organizations, interest groups, and political parties as intermediaries between citizens and the state (Jenkins & Klandermans, 1995). Thus conceived, an increased importance of one of the players necessarily implies a change in the significance of the others. Burstein (1999) suggests that as long as public opinion is unified and clear, politicians do not need social movement organizations or interest groups to define their politics. This implies that movement organizations gain significance if public opinion on an issue is divided and diffuse. In other words, according to this reasoning, the social movement sector has grown so much because western societies have become less hegemonic. Another reasoning takes the movement sector's relative effectiveness as its point of departure (Giugni, 1999; Jenkins, 1995). Compared to working one's way through the political institutions, contentious collective actions can be remarkably effective, provided that the right ingredients are in place. Some 10 years ago I estimated on the basis of various reviews that approximately one third of the instances of collective political action had some degree of success (Klandermans, 1989b). Similar estimates for political parties and interest groups are lacking, but we may assume that experiencing success encourages similar actions in the future, while seeing others succeed is certainly an incentive to try oneself.

The literature on political participation used to distinguish between conventional and unconventional political participation (see Barnes & Kaase, 1979). Conventional political participation concerned such forms of participation as voting, campaigning, canvassing, and participation in political parties; unconventional forms of participation concerned activities such as boycotts, blockades, site occupations, and protest demonstrations. The labels *conventional* and *unconventional* suggest that some forms of participation are more routinized, more common, more business-as-usual than others. Perhaps there was a time when this was a useful distinction. However, what was categorized as unconventional has become *more* common and *more* routinized than some so-called conventional forms of political participation. Sidney Tarrow (1994) coined the term "modal action repertoire" to emphasize that many forms of collective action have become part of the average citizens' repertoire of political activities. Interesting examples of research pertinent to this topic concern the policing of protest (Della Porta & Reiter, 1998). These studies—inter alia, of protest policing in Washington, D.C., at the Capitol (McPhail & McCarthy, 1998)—reveal that over the years organizers and police in mutual collaboration have developed elaborated routines to control mass demonstrations. Such developments have reduced the usefulness of the conventional-unconventional distinction. In fact, politically active citizens employ an extended repertoire that seems to render the conventional-unconventional divide obsolete. Theoretically, it is more useful to distinguish between individual and collective forms of political action, because the motivational dynamics of collective action are different from those of individual action, as I will show in the pages to come.

▶ Major Theoretical Approaches

This is not the place to answer the question of why social movements come into being and why they have become common practice. There is a rich literature available on that matter (for instance Buechler, 2000; Klandermans, 2000b, 2001; McAdam, McCarthy, & Zald, 1996; McAdam, Tarrow,

& Tilly, 2001; Meyer & Tarrow, 1998; Pichardo, 1997; Tarrow, 1998). For my purpose it suffices to summarize the global answers that have been forwarded, in brief: because people are aggrieved, because people have the resources to mobilize and seize the political opportunity to protest, and because of the politicization of collective identities. These answers parallel the history of theoretical approaches to collective action. Research began in the fifties and sixties with classical theories such as symbolic interactionism, structural functionalism, and relative deprivation theory. Buechler (2000) classified these theories as *classical collective behavior theories*, a category that he characterizes as theories that understand social movements as a reaction to social stress, strain, or breakdown. The direct causes of collective behavior are seen as rooted in individuals who are experiencing various forms of discontent or anxiety. Basically, discontent is viewed as the origins of protest. In social movement literature these theories have also been labeled *breakdown theories*, a term that alludes to the fact that these theories conceived of social movements as indicators of the existence of major cleavages in a society and of societal tension or even breakdown as a consequence. The work of Blumer (1951), Turner and Killian (1972), Smelser (1962), Davies (1962), and Gurr (1970) are classic examples of this research tradition. The first two are associated with symbolic interactionism, Smelser with structural functionalism, and the latter two with relative deprivation.

But it was obvious that many aggrieved people never engage in protest. Indeed, in the early seventies, advocates of *resource mobilization theory* began to argue that grievances are ubiquitous and that the real question is not so much what makes people aggrieved but what makes aggrieved people participate in social movements (McCarthy & Zald, 1976 ; Oberschall, 1973). Resource mobilization theorists saw social movements as normal, rational, institutionally rooted political challenges by aggrieved people. Differential availability of resources explained in their eyes why some aggrieved people become involved in social movements while others don't. It was argued that people need resources to stage collective political action, and a key resource for such action is organizations and networks that exist among the affected population (so-called indigenous organizations, Morris, 1982). Within the resource mobilization framework, participation in collective action was analyzed in terms of the costs and benefits associated with it. Rational choice models of behavior (Oberschall, 1973; Klandermans, 1984; Opp, 1989) and Olson's theory of collective action (Olson, 1968) were employed as models to explain individuals' participation and nonparticipation in collective action. When the potential benefits outweigh the anticipated costs, people opt to participate. Paradoxically, the same deprivation that might motivate people to stage collective action might deprive them of the resources needed for such action. Indeed, it was proposed that external resources could tip the balance.[1] Applying an economic metaphor, distinctions were made among social movements (beliefs that represent a preference for change in a society), social movement organizations (organizations that identify with a social movement), social movement industries (social movement organizations that belong to the same social movement), and the social movement sector (all social movement organizations in a society). Soon a variant of resource mobilization theory developed within political science— the political process approach—which proposed that political opportunities presented to aggrieved groups with the resources to take action make the difference. Political opportunities are "those consistent—but not necessarily formal or permanent—dimensions of the political environment that provide incentives for people to undertake collective action by affecting their expectations of success and failure" (Tarrow, 1994, p. 85). Among the many aspects of the political environment that have been referred to are the strength of the state, the level of repression, the party system, the degree of access to policy, and the dividedness of elites.

In the late 1980s and early 1990s, partly as the result of an exchange between American and European social movements scholars (Klandermans, Kriesi, & Tarrow, 1988), an interest began to develop in the cognitive and affective origins of social movements. In response to the structuralist approach of the then dominant paradigm—resource mobilization—social movement scholars from various angles began to highlight the processes of interaction, symbolic definition, and negotiation among participants, opponents, and bystanders of collective action. Grievances, resources, and opportunities are all relevant for social movements to develop, but they are both instigator and outcome of these processes; in other words, grievances, resources, and opportunities are all socially constructed. Moreover, researchers working from this perspective argued that aggrieved people might have the resources and opportunities to protest, but they still need to construct a politicized collective identity to engage in collective political action. Over the last decade and a half, this new approach to collective action has been elaborated in studies of framing, collective identity, and emotion in the context of social movements. Together they have been labelled *social constructionist approaches* to protest. Snow and his colleagues (Snow, Rochford, Burke, Worden, & Benford, 1986) were among the first to elaborate on the role of cognitive processes in their discussion of frame alignment—that is, attempts by movement organizers to persuade people to adopt the movement's reading of the situation, as I will discuss in a following section. At the same time, Melucci (1985) began to point to the importance of collective identity (also Cohen, 1985). Soon cognition and identity began to proliferate in social movement literature (see Morris & Mueller, 1992, for an overview). The most recent social constructionist attempt to move away from structural approaches such as resource mobilization and political process concerns the role of emotions in collective action (see Goodwin, Jasper, & Poletta, 2001 for an overview). Framing, identity, and emotion—key concepts of the social constructionist approach—will feature prominently in the pages to come. For this overview it suffices to conclude that social constructionism has carved out its own niche as a legitimate alternative approach to the analysis of social movements (Buechler, 2000, p. 54).

This brief overview of the three theoretical trends that have dominated the field alludes to the fact that the generation of a social movement is related to demand and supply factors in a society and to mobilization as the process that brings the two together. *Demand factors* relate to the interest in a society in a movement's goals. Is the movement addressing a problem people worry about? Is there a need for a movement on these issues? Usually, the people who participate in a movement are only a small proportion of those who care about the issue. This is not necessarily a sign of weakness. On the contrary, for a movement to be viable, a large reservoir of sympathizers is needed to nourish its activists. *Supply factors,* on the other hand, relate to the characteristics of the movement. Is it strong? Is it likely to achieve its goals at affordable costs? Does it have charismatic leaders? Is it an organization people can identify with? Does it stage activities that are appealing to people? Demand and supply do not automatically come together. In the market economy marketing is employed to make sure that the public is aware of a supply that might meet its demand. *Mobilization* is the marketing mechanism of the movement domain. Together demand, supply, and mobilization construct the dynamics of movement participation.

◣ The Dynamics of Movement Participation: Mobilization

An individual's participation in collective political action staged by a social movement organization is the end result of a sometimes lengthy process of mobilization. Successful mobilization gradually brings supply and demand together. Mobilization is a complicated process that can be broken down into several, conceptually distinct steps. Klandermans (1984) was the first to break the process of mobilization down into consensus and action mobilization. Consensus mobilization refers to dissemination of the views of the movement organization, and action mobilization refers to the transformation of those who have adopted the view of the movement into participants. Thus defined, action mobilization is, obviously, constrained by the results of consensus mobilization (Klandermans, 1997). An interesting recent illustration can be found in Walgrave and Manssens's (2000) study of the "White March" in Brussels, October 1996, in response to the government's failure to deal with the Dutroux kidnappings and killings. Moral outrage brought hundreds of thousands of people into the streets of Brussels. The authors demonstrate that the mass media played a crucial role in mobilizing consensus on the issue.

Consensus mobilization has been elaborated much further by Snow and Benford and their colleagues in their frame alignment approach to mobilization (see Benford, 1997 for a critical review). Frames are sets of beliefs, values, and views of the world. More specifically, collective action frames are "sets of collective beliefs that serve to create a frame of mind in which participation in collective action appears meaningful" (Klandermans, 1997, p. 17). Gamson (1992) distinguishes three components of collective action frames: (1) injustice, that is, moral indignation arising from grievances; (2) identity, a sense of identification with the group engaged in the action and a sense of antagonism vis-à-vis authorities held responsible for the averse situation; and (3) agency, that is, the belief that one can alter conditions or policies through collective action. Frame alignment is the process of linking a movement's frame to that of individual citizens. In its frame the movement provides a diagnosis and prognosis of the situation and describes possible routes to a better situation (Snow & Benford, 1988; Snow et al., 1986). Snow and his colleagues distinguish various types of frame alignment based on a declining fit between the movement's frame and that of an individual. Frame bridging is a form of frame alignment pertinent to situations where the movement's and the individual's frame overlap. In this situation, in order to mobilize individual citizens it suffices to inform them about the movement's frame. Frame transformation concerns the other end of the scale. In this situation the movement frame differs to such a degree from that of the individual that only a change of mind on the part of the individual would produce the required consensus. It is assumed that in the context of an average mobilization drive, frame transformation is unlikely to occur.

Klandermans and Oegema (1987) then broke the process of action mobilization further down into four separate steps, each step bringing the supply and demand of collective political action closer together until an individual eventually takes the final step to participate in an instance of collective political action. The first step in action mobilization builds on the results of consensus mobilization. It distinguishes the general public into people who sympathize with the cause and people who don't. The more successful consensus mobilization has been, the larger the pool of sympathizers from which a mobilizing movement organization can draw. A large pool of sympathizers is of strategic importance, because for a variety of reasons many sympathizers never turn into participants. The second step is an obvious one; it divides the sympathizers into those who have been a target of mobilization attempts and those who haven't. Naturally, it is also possible to distinguish qualitative and quantitative differences in targeting. People can be targeted more or less frequently and in more or less insistent ways. Evidence suggests that both reinforce participation. The third step concerns the social psychological core of the process. It divides people who have been targeted into those who are motivated to participate in the specific activity and those who aren't. Finally, the fourth step differentiates the people who are motivated into those who end up participating and those who don't. In our research on the mobilization efforts for a local peace demonstration (Klandermans & Oegema, 1987) we found that three quarters of the population of a small community south of Amsterdam felt sympathy for the movement's cause. Of these sympathizers again three quarters were somehow targeted by mobilization attempts. Of those targeted one sixth were motivated to participate in the demonstration. Finally, of those motivated one third participated.

The net result of these different steps is some (usually small) proportion of the general public that participates in collective action.[2] With each step, smaller or larger numbers drop out. The smaller the number of dropouts, the better the fit between demand and supply. The degree of fit can be assessed by responses to the following queries: (1) Does the cause of the movement appeal to concerns of individual citizens? (2) Do the movement's networks link to the individuals' networks? (3) Is the activity the movement is mobilizing for appealing to individual citizens? (4) Is the movement able to eliminate any remaining barrier to participation for individual citizens? Psychologically, the first and the third questions are the most interesting. I will elaborate on those questions in the next two sections. The fourth question is interesting from a social psychological perspective, although I am not aware of much relevant research. Obviously, we may assume that at this stage barriers to participation interact with an individual's strength of motivation. The stronger someone's motivation, the more likely it is that she will overcome the last barriers. Our own research suggests that friendship networks play an important role in this respect. Apparently, it is your friends that keep you to your promises (Oegema & Klandermans, 1994). But more research is needed to understand this final step in the process. The second question is about the structure of networks. The basic tenet is simple: the more an individual is tied into a movement's network, the more likely it is that he will become a target of mobilization attempts. Sophisticated analyses of a movement's multiorganizational field abound in the extensive literature on the role of networks in movement mobilization. The interested reader is referred to this literature for further information (see Knoke, 1990; Diani & McAdam, 2002).

◤ Demand and Supply in Movement Participation

Do the cause of the movement and the activities the movement is staging appeal to individual citizens? The answers to this question in the social movement literature can be distinguished in terms of the fundamental reason given for movement participation: people may want to change their circumstances, they may want to act as members of their group, or they may want to give meaning to their world and express their views and feelings. I suggest that together these three motives account for most of the demand for collective political action in a society. Social movements may supply the opportunity to fulfill these demands, and the better they do, the more movement participation turns into a satisfying experience. I refer to these three types of transactions of demand and supply as: instrumentality, identity, and ideology.[3] *Instrumentality* refers to movement participation as an attempt to influence the social and political environment; *identity* refers to movement participation as an expression of identification with a group; and *ideology* refers to movement participation as a search for meaning and an expression of one's views. Different theories are associated with these three angles (see Tarrow, 1998, and Klandermans, 1997, for overviews). Instrumentality is related to resource mobilization and political process theories of social movements (Buechler, 2000) and at the psychological level to rational choice theory and expectancy-value theories (Opp, 1989); identity is related to sociological approaches that emphasize the collective identity component of social movement participation and with the social psychological social identity theory (Stryker, Owen, & White, 2000); and ideology is related to approaches in social movement literature that focus on culture, meaning, narratives, moral reasoning, and emotion (Goodwin, Jasper & Poletta, 2001) and in psychology to theories of social cognition and emotions (Abelson, Ewing, & Roseman, 1986; Parkinson & Manstead, 1993; chapter 6). I am not suggesting that these are mutually exclusive motives, or competing views on social movement participation, although some parties in the debates in the literature seem to have taken that position. I do agree, however, with those who argue that approaches that neglect any of those three motives are fundamentally flawed. To be sure, individual participants may participate because of a single motive, but all three are needed to understand why people take part in collective political action.

I know of no study that has attempted to assess the relative weight of all three motives in their effect on participation. Simon and his students (Simon et al., 1998) have studied the relative influence of identity and instrumentality and shown that both instrumentality and identity play an independent role in the explanation of participation (see also Kelly & Breinlinger, 1996, Stürmer, 2000). In her study of farmers' protest in the Netherlands, De Weerd (1999) showed that injustice, identity, and agency—the three dimensions of collective action frames distinguished by Gamson (1992)—contributed independently to the explanation of participation in farmers' protest in that country. On the basis of these studies I would at the very least propose an additive model. If all three motives apply, participation is more likely than if only one or two apply. An additive model, of course, implies that the motives may compensate one another, perhaps even to the extent that in an individual case one or two motives may be irrelevant altogether. To complicate matters further, the three motives may interact. For example, a strong identification or ideology might alter cost-benefit calculations. Similarly, a strong ideology may reinforce levels of identification. These are thorny issues, and robust results from empirical studies are lacking. Obviously, we need to do more research based on more sophisticated models and methods to tackle the issue.

The Demand Side of Collective Political Action

Marwell and Oliver (1993) once observed that in view of significant changes in their environment, most people continue to do what they were doing, namely, nothing. This observation suggests that the demand for collective political action in a society is usually low. On the other hand, it has been argued that collective political action has become more common over the last decades. In this section I will further elaborate on the issue and discuss the demand side of instrumentality, identity, and ideology.

Instrumentality

A demand for change begins with dissatisfaction, be it the experience of illegitimate inequality, feelings of relative deprivation, feelings of injustice, moral indignation about some state of affairs, or a suddenly imposed grievance (Klandermans, 1997; Gamson, 1992).[4] Social psychological grievance theories such as relative deprivation theory or social justice theory have tried to specify how and why grievances develop (see Hegtvedt & Markovsky, 1995; Tyler, Boeckmann, Smith, & Huo, 1997; Tyler & Smith, 1998 for overviews). Despite the fact that grievances are at the roots of collective political action, they have not featured prominently in social movement literature since the early seventies. Resource mobilization theory and political process theory, the two approaches that have dominated the field in that period, have always taken as their point of departure that grievances are ubiquitous and that the key question in movement participation research is not so much why people are aggrieved but why aggrieved people participate.

In the seventies, in reaction to approaches that tended to picture movement participation as irrational Hoffer, 1951; Kornhauser, 1959; (Le Bon, 1903/1960), social movement scholars began to emphasize the instrumental character of movement participation. It was no longer depicted as behavior borne of resentment by marginalized and isolated individuals, or as an aggressive reaction to frustration, or as politics of impatience, but as politics with other means. In particular, resource mobilization (as illustrated by the work of such pioneers as McCarthy & Zald, 1976, and Oberschall, 1973) and political process approaches (McAdam, 1982; Tilly, 1978) took the assumed rationality of movement participants as their point of departure. According to these authors, movement participation is as rational or irrational as any other behavior. Movement participants are people who believe that they can change their political environment to their advantage, and the instrumentality paradigm holds that their behavior is controlled by the perceived costs and benefits of participation. It is taken for granted that they are aggrieved, but it is not so much the grievances per se but the belief that the situation can be changed at affordable costs that makes them participate. They have the resources and perceive the opportunities to have an impact.

From an instrumental perspective, a solution must be found to the dilemma of collective action. It was through the work of Olson that students of movement participation became aware of the problem. In 1968 Mancur Olson published *The Logic of Collective Action*; the core of the book was the argument that rational actors will *not* contribute to the production of a collective good unless selective incentives persuade them to do so. Collective goods are characterized by "jointness of supply." That is to say, if they are made available to one person, they become available to everybody, irrespective of whether people have contributed to the production of the collective good (for example, a law against discrimination, or measures against pollution). Therefore, according to Olson, a rational actor will choose to take a free ride, unless selective incentives (costs or benefits that are made contingent on participation in the production of the collective good) prevent him from doing so. Olson's argument was soon applied to social movement participation. It helped to explain why so often people do not participate in social movements despite the interest they have in the achievement of the movement's goals. Movement scholars argued that movement goals typically are collective goods. If the goal is achieved, people will enjoy the benefits, irrespective of whether they have participated in the effort. In view of a goal for which achievement is uncertain but for which benefits—if materialized—can be reaped anyway, rational actors will take a free ride, or so goes the Olsonian reasoning. Selective incentives are supposedly the solution to the dilemma of collective action. Such incentives are typically supply factors. Therefore, I will return to the issue when I discuss the supply side of participation.

Social movement scholars quickly discovered that reality was more complex than Olson's simple model suggested. The problem with Olson's logic of collective action is that it provides an explanation for why people do not participate but fares poorly in explaining why people *do* participate. Moreover, Oliver (1980) argued that Olson's solution that people participate for selective incentives is fundamentally flawed, as it does not give a satisfactory answer to the question of where the resources needed to provide selective incentives come from. If these must be collected from individual citizens, the same collective action dilemma arises again. This is not to say that selective incentives are irrelevant but that in the final instance they cannot solve the collective action dilemma. In other words, if collective and selective incentives do not provide a sufficient explanation of movement participation, what else might make the difference? A recurring criticism was that Olson's model assumes that individuals make their decisions in isolation, as if there are no other people with whom they consult, with whom they feel solidarity, and by whom they are kept to their promises. This pointed to the significance of collective identity as a factor in movement participation.

Identity

It soon became clear that instrumentality, that is, movement participation to achieve some external goal (social or political change), was not the only reason to participate. After all, many external goals are only reached in the long run, if at all. Similarly, when it comes to material benefits, costs frequently outweigh benefits. Apparently, there is more in being a movement participant than perceived costs and benefits. Indeed, one of those motives relates to belonging to a valued group.

Simon (1998, 1999) succinctly described identity as a place in society. People occupy many different places in society. One is a student, unemployed, a housewife, a soccer player, a politician, a farmer, and so on. Some of those places are exclusive, occupied only by a small number of people. The members of a soccer team are an example. Others are inclusive, encompassing large numbers of people, such as Europeans. Some places are mutually exclusive, such as male-female, or employed-unemployed; some are nested, for example, French, Dutch, German versus European; and some are crosscutting, such as female and student (Hornsey & Hogg, forthcoming; Turner 1999). All these different roles and positions a person occupies form her *personal identity*. At the same time, every place a person occupies is shared with other people. I am not the only professor of social psychology, nor the only Dutch or the only European. I share these identities with other people—a fact that turns them into collective identities. Thus a *collective identity* is a place shared with other people. This implies that personal identity is always collective identity at the same time. Personal identity is general, referring to a variety of places in society, whereas collective identity is always specific, referring to a specific place.

Most of the time collective identities remain latent. Self-categorization theory hypothesizes that an individual may act as a unique person, that is, display his personal identity, *or* as a member of a specific group, that is, display one of the many collective identities he has, depending on contextual circumstances (Turner, Hogg, Oakes, Reicher, & Wetherell, 1987; Turner 1999). Contextual factors may bring personal or collective identity to the fore. Obviously, this is often not a matter of free choice. Circumstances may force a collective identity into awareness whether people like it or not, as the Yugoslavian and South African histories have illustrated dramatically, and there are other equally or even more dramatic examples throughout human history. But in less extreme circumstances collective identities can also become significant. Take for example the possible effect of an announcement that a waste incinerator is planned next to a neighborhood. Chances are that within very little time the collective identity of the people living in that neighborhood will become salient.

Self-categorization theory proposes that people are more prepared to employ a social category in their self-definition the more they identify with that category. Identification with a group makes people more prepared to act as a member of that group (Turner, 1999). This assertion refers, of course, to identity strength. In her review of social identity theory, Huddy (2001, chapter 15) observes that social identity literature tends to neglect the fact that real-world identities vary in strength. She argues that identifying more or less strongly with a group may make a real difference especially in political contexts. Moreover, she suggests, strong identities are less affected by context. Following this reasoning, we may expect that strong identities make it more likely that people act on behalf of their group.

The basic hypothesis regarding collective identity and movement participation is fairly straightforward: a strong identification with a group makes participation in collective political action on behalf of that group more likely. The available empirical evidence overwhelmingly supports this assumption. Kelly and Breinlinger (1996) found that identification with a labor union and its members made it more likely that workers would participate in industrial action; while gender identification made participation in the women's movement more likely. Simon and colleagues (1998) and Stürmer (2001) observed that identification with other gay people, but especially with other members of the gay movement, reinforced involvement in the gay movement. A similar finding was reported with regard to participation in unions of the elderly in the same study. Finally, De Weerd and Klandermans (1999) reported that farmers who identified with other farmers were more likely to be involved in farmer's protest than those who did not display any identification with other farmers.

Ideology

The third motive—wanting to express one's views—refers simultaneously to a longstanding theme in the social movement literature and to a recent development. In classic studies of social movements the distinction was made between instrumental and expressive movements or protest (see Gusfield, 1963; Searles & Williams, 1962). In those days, instrumental movements were seen as movements that aimed at some external goal, for example, the implementation of citizenship rights. Expressive movements, on the other hand, were movements that had no external goals. Participation was a goal in itself, for example, the expression of anger in response to experienced injustice. Movement scholars felt increasingly uncomfortable with the distinction, because it was thought that most movements had both instrumental and expressive aspects and that the emphasis on the two could change over time. Therefore, the distinction lost its use. Recently, however, the idea that people might participate in movements to express their views has received renewed attention among movement scholars who were unhappy with the overly structural approach of resource mobilization and political process theory. These scholars began to put an emphasis on the creative, cultural, and emotional aspects of social movements, such as music, symbols, rituals, narratives, and moral indignation (see Goodwin, Jasper, &

Polletta, 2001 for a recent overview). People are angry, develop feelings of moral indignation about some state of affairs or some government decision, and wish to make that known. They participate in a social movement not only to enforce political change but to gain dignity in their lives through struggle and moral expression.

Ideology, be it the left-right distinction, as it is commonly defined in political science, or, as social psychologists define it, a relatively coherent set of cognition, attitudes, and feelings maintained by an individual, has a significant affective component. Acting on one's ideology is deemed to be one of the fundamental motives of movement participation, and as Marcus (chapter 6) argues, necessarily is charged with emotion. On the basis of his review of recent insights into the working of emotional systems, Marcus proposes that the capacity to enact behavior comes with emotion. Emotion systems have access to the sensory stream well before the brain systems that generate conscious awareness can complete their work, Marcus concludes. Furthermore, the emotion systems produce appraisals that then initiate emotional, cognitive, and behavioral actions. Goodwin and colleagues (2001) add to this reasoning that appraisal and action are socially constructed, that is to say, are formed in interpersonal interaction, especially in the case of politically relevant emotions. In their view, emotions that are politically relevant are more likely to be socially constructed than other emotions. For these emotions, cultural and historical factors play an important role in the interpretation of the state of affairs by which they are generated. Emotions, these authors hold, are important in the growth and unfolding of social movements and political protest. Obviously, appraisals can be manipulated. Activists work hard to create moral outrage and anger and to provide a target against which these can be vented. They must weave together a moral, cognitive, and emotional package of attitudes. But emotions also play an important role in the ongoing activities of the movements. Jasper (1997, 1998) distinguishes two kinds of collective emotions—reciprocal emotions and shared emotions—that reinforce each other. Each measure of shared outrage against an injustice reinforces the reciprocal emotion of fondness for others precisely because they feel the same way. They are like us; they understand. Conversely, mutual affection is a context in which new shared emotions are easily created. Anger and indignation are emotions that are related to a specific appraisal of the situation. At the same time, people might be puzzled by some aspects of reality and try to understand what's going on. They may look for others with similar experiences, and a social movement may provide an environment in which to exchange experiences, to tell their stories, and to express their ideologies.

The Supply Side of Participation

Social movement organizations are more or less successful in satisfying demands for collective political participation, and we may assume that movements that successfully supply what potential participants demand gain more support than movements that fail to do so. Movements and movement organizations can be compared in terms of their effectiveness in this regard.

Instrumentality

Instrumentality presupposes an effective movement that is able to enforce some wanted changes or at least to mobilize substantial support. Making an objective assessment of a movement's impact is not an easy task (see Giugni, McAdam, & Tilly, 1999; Giugni, 1998), but movement organizations will try to convey the image of an effective political force. They can do so by pointing to the impact they have had in the past or to the powerful allies they have. Of course, they may lack all this, but they might be able to show other signs of movement strength. A movement may command a large constituency as witnessed by turnout for demonstrations, membership figures, or large donations. It may comprise strong organizations with strong charismatic leaders who have gained respect, and so on. Instrumentality also implies the provision of selective incentives. The selective incentives for participation may vary considerably among movement organizations. Such variation depends—inter alia—on the resources a movement organization has at its disposal, its financial means, its professionalization, and the like (McCarthy & Zald, 1976; Oliver, 1980). Surprisingly, there has been little systematic comparison of movements, movement organizations, and campaigns in regard to the supply side of participation (but see Klandermans, 1993). In a similar vein, systematic documentation is lacking of the way in which the larger political system and the alliances and conflicts movement organizations engage in influencing the supply side of movement participation. Tilly (1978) coined the terms "repression" and "facilitation" to distinguish between political systems that increase or decrease the costs of participation. Indeed, repressive political environments may increase the costs of participation considerably: people may lose friends, they may risk their jobs or otherwise jeopardize their sources of income, they may be jailed, and they may even lose their lives. More research is needed, however, on this matter.

Klandermans (1984, 1997) has combined these factors into his model of movement participation. The model takes as its point of departure that movement goals are public goods. It belongs to the expectancy-value family (Ajzen & Fishbein, 1980; Feather & Norman, 1982) and links the supply of collective political action to the individual's demands. In doing so it combines insights from rational choice theory (Ferree, 1992; Rule, 1989) with those from collective action theory (Olson, 1968). The model makes a distinction between collective and selective incentives. Put simply, it asserts that people are motivated by an attractive public good—such as clean air, peace, or equal rights (collective incentives) to be achieved by participation in attractive action means—for example, a rally where their favorite music group performs (selective incentives). Collective incentives are further broken down into the value of the public good and the expectation that it will be produced. An important element of that expectation are beliefs about the behavior of others. This is what makes collective behavior different from individual behavior. The theory supposes an optimum: too many expected participants makes it unnecessary for the individual to participate; too few expected participants makes it useless for the individual to participate. Perceived selective incentives add to the explanation, especially so-called social incentives, which in Klandermans' model consist of the expected reaction of significant others if the individual decides to participate. Since its publication the model has found convincing empirical support (Brïet, Klandermans, & Kroon, 1987; Klandermans, 1984, 1993; Klandermans & Oegema, 1987; Kelly & Breinlinger, 1996; Simon et al., 1998; Stürmer, 2000; White, 1993).

Identity

Movements offer the opportunity to act on behalf of one's group. This is most attractive if people identify strongly with their group. The more farmers, identify with other farmers the more appealing it is to take part in farmers' protest (De Weerd & Klandermans, 1999; Klandermans, De Weerd, Sabucedo, & Rodriguez, 2001). The more women identify with other women, the more attractive it is to participate in the women's movement (Kelly & Breinlinger, 1996); and the more gay people identify with other gay people, the more they are attracted by the possibility of taking part in the gay movement (Simon et al., 1998; Stürmer, 2000). Interestingly, all these studies show that to the participants being part of the exclusive group of movement participants is far more attractive than being part of the inclusive category the movement tries to mobilize. In addition to the opportunity to act on behalf of the group, collective political action participation offers the opportunity to identify with the movement's cause, the people in the movement, the movement organization or the group one is participating in, and the leader of the movement. Not all these sources of identification are always equally appealing. Movement leaders can be more or less charismatic, or the people in the movement or in someone's group can be more or less attractive. Moreover, movements and movement organizations may be, and in fact often are, controversial. Hence becoming a participant in a movement organization does not mean adopting a positively valued group identity. However, in the context of the movement's networks, this identity as a member of the movement is positively valued. There the militant does have the status society is denying her. And for the militant, of course, ingroup-outgroup dynamics may turn the movement organization or group into a far more attractive group than any other group "out there" that is opposing the movement. Indeed, it is not uncommon for militants to refer to the movement organization as a second family, a substitute for the social and associative life that society was no longer offering them (Orfali, 1990; Tristan, 1987). Movement organizations not only supply sources of identification, they also offer all kinds of opportunities to enjoy and celebrate the collective identity: marches, rituals, songs, meetings, signs, symbols, and common codes.

Kelly and Breinlinger's (1996) study of union members and participants in the women's movement drew attention to group identification as a factor in the explanation of movement participation. More specifically, these authors demonstrate that movements provide the opportunity to form an activist identity, that is, an identity as somebody who engages in collective action. In a similar vein, Simon and colleagues (1998) have demonstrated that group identification is as important for participation in a social movement as cost-benefit considerations. Indeed, Simon and colleagues conclude that "There seem to exist two independent pathways to social movement participation, or at least to willingness to participate. One pathway seems to be *calculation* of the costs and benefits of participation. . . . The second pathway seems to be *identification* with the movement, or in other words adoption of a distinct activist identity" (p. 656, emphasis in original).

There is evidence that identity processes have both an indirect and a direct effect on protest participation (Sturmer, 2000). The effect is *indirect* in the sense that collective identity influences instrumental reasoning. For example, Kelly and Breinlinger (1996) observed that the calculated pathway to participation is of more importance to weak than strong group identifiers. Others suggested that strong identification makes it less attractive to take a free ride. Hirsch's (1990) study of the Columbia University divestment protest is a good example of how identification with fellow protestors increased the costs of defection for participants. Indeed, collective identity appears to be a way to overcome the social dilemma built into the instrumental route to movement participation (see also Klandermans 2000a). High levels of group identification increase the costs of defection and the benefits of cooperation. In other words, collective identity impacts on the instrumental pathway to protest participation. The effect is also *direct* because collective identity creates a shortcut to participation. People participate not so much because of the outcomes associated with participation but because they identify with the other participants. Stürmer advances the hypothesis that participation generated by the identity pathway is a form of automatic behavior, whereas participation brought forward by the instrumental pathway is a form of reasoned action.

Ideology

Social movements play a significant role in the diffusion of ideas and values. Rochon (1998) makes the important distinction between "critical communities" where new ideas and values are developed and "social movements" that are interested in winning social and political acceptance for those ideas and values. "In the hands of movement leaders, the ideas of critical communities become ideological frames" (p. 31), says Rochon, and he continues on to argue that social movements are not simply extensions of critical communities. After all, not all ideas developed in critical communities are equally suited to motivate collective action. Social movement organizations, then, are carriers of meaning. Through processes such as consensus mobilization (Klandermans, 1984, 1992b) or framing (Snow et al., 1986) they seek to propagate their definition of the situation to the public at large. Gerhards and Rucht's study (1992) of flyers produced by the various groups and organizations involved in the protests against the IMF and the World Bank in Berlin is an excellent example in this respect. These authors show how links are constructed between the ideological frame of the organizers of the demonstration and those of the participating organizations in order to create a shared definition of the situation. In the social movement literature, such definitions of the situation have been labeled "collective action frames" (Gamson, 1992; Klandermans, 1997). Collective action frames can be defined in terms of injustice—that is, some definition of what's wrong in the world; identity—that is, some definition of who is affected and who is responsible; and agency—that is, beliefs about the possibility of changing society. We may assume that people who join a movement come to share some part of the movement's action frame and that in the process of frame sharing they give meaning to their world.

Social movements do not invent ideas from scratch, they borrow from the history of ideas. They build on an ideological heritage as they relate their claims to broader themes and values in society. In so doing they relate to societal debates that have a history of their own, and that history is usually much longer than that of the movement itself. Gamson (1992), for example, refers to the "themes" and "counterthemes" that in his view exist in every society. One such pairing of theme and countertheme that he mentions is "self-reliance" verses "mutuality," that is, the belief that individuals have to take care of themselves verses the belief that society is responsible for its less fortunate members. Klandermans and Goslinga (1996) discuss how in the Netherlands these two beliefs became the icons that galvanized debate and spurred protest over disability payments. While "self-reliance" became the theme of those favoring restrictions in disability payment, "mutuality" was the theme of those who defended the existing system. Another example is what Tarrow (1998) calls "rights frames": human rights, civil rights, women's rights, animal rights, and so on—in other words, collective action frames that relate a movement's aims to some fundamental rights frame. For decades Marxism has provided an ideological heritage for movements to identify with, positively by embracing it or negatively by distancing themselves from it. In a similar vein, fascism and Nazism form the ideological heritage for right-wing extremists who must come to terms with it either by identifying with it or by keeping it at a distance. Some of those ideas from the past are more useful than others. For example, Kitschelt (1995) has argued that parties of the new radical right that overly identify with Nazism or fascism are doomed to failure (see also Ignazi & Ysmal, 1992).

Social movements reconstruct those old ideas, they are reinterpreting and repackaging them in such a way that they become attractive to potential movement participants. It is a process that Boudon (1986) has described as follows: "Just like mushrooms in the underwood, ideologies that seem to have disappeared for good may resurface at some better point in time. . . . The main difference between ideologies and mushrooms is that the first always reappear in a revised form. Pareto had a clear view on that: an old and discredited idea, can only take on anew, if it has undergone a meta-morphosis. Because it must be possible to perceive it as a new idea" (p. 283). It is this combination of old and new that gives the interpretative schemes of social movements their strength. But social movements are not just the conduit of the cognitive component of ideology. Emotions, that is, the affective component of ideology, are equally important. After all, people are angry and morally outraged, and movement organizations provide the opportunity to express and communicate those feelings.

In Sum

Obviously, movement organizations play a crucial role in the process of mobilization for collective action. To be sure, potential participants can be viewed as in demand of opportunities to affiliate with or engage in some movement, but nothing would happen without a supply that actually connects to these demands (unless someone is so motivated that he takes the initiative to start a movement). The supply side of the mobilization process depends on movement organizations, and I have argued that movement organizations may vary considerably in that regard. The success of a movement or the lack of it thus depends on both demand and supply. If movement organizations fail to frame and organize their activities such that they connect to some existing demand—be it along the instrumental, identity, or ideological dimension—they will stay small and insignificant. On the other hand, however appealing the protest opportunities supplied by a movement organization might be in the eyes of the organizers, without people who are actually in demand of these opportunities the organization won't get very far either.

◤ Participation in the Life Course

Most research on collective political action concerns a comparison of participants and nonparticipants in a specific instance of participation at a specific point in time—be it a demonstration, a boycott, a sit-in, a rally, or a petition. Psychologically speaking, this concerns a specific type of participation: short term and typically involving low risk or little effort, although occasionally participation involves high risk or effort. Elsewhere (Klandermans, 1997) I have applied the time and effort dimensions to distinguish four different types of action: low-effort/short-term—for example, signing a petition or giving a donation; high-effort/short-term—for example, a strike or a sit-in; low-effort/long-term—for example, paying a membership fee to an organization or manning a help phone once every fortnight; high-effort/long-term—for example, being a movement activist. I have always argued that different activities have different motivational dynamics. Effort, of course, influences cost-benefit evaluations, but in this setting of participation over the life course I am interested in the time dimension (see chapter 3 for further discussion of adult political development).

Marwell and Oliver (1993) have introduced the important distinction between a decelerative and accelerative production function in the social movement domain. Although it has been tested only through mathematical modeling, it draws attention to two fundamentally different forms of collective action. Production functions describe how much every additional participant adds to the likelihood that the collective good will be produced. Some forms of participation follow a decelerative production function, that is to say, every additional participant makes less of a difference. Such action forms tend to have a point beyond which the difference becomes negligible. The membership of the board of a movement organization is a typical example; some 10–15 people are needed, and beyond that additional participants in fact may be counterproductive. Other forms of collective action follow an accelerative production function, every additional participant makes more of a difference. Accelerative functions tend to have threshold values. Before the threshold is reached, additional participants add very little, but beyond the threshold the added value of an additional participant rapidly increases. It is not uncommon for action forms following accelerative functions to become decelerative at some point, resulting in an S-shaped curve. A strike is a typical example of a collective action form taking an accelerative production function. In a company of 1,000 production workers, it doesn't make much of a difference whether 50, 100, or 150 workers go on strike, the action would be a failure. But beyond a specific number, let's say 300, every additional striker increasingly adds more to the likelihood of success. Until some other number of participants is reached, let's say 800, beyond which additional strikers don't really matter any more, the company is on strike. Marwell and Oliver point to the fact that free riding is only a problem in collective action forms that follow decelerative production functions.

Why is this such an important distinction? Because individual participants face different dilemmas in the two types of activities. In the case of an accelerative function, their concern is, obviously, whether the threshold will be met. If not, participation is in vain. As indicated in the previous section, expectations about the behavior of others are crucial in this respect. In the case of a decelerative function, the important question is whether participants are prepared to give the others the free ride. It is the latter dilemma that interests me here, because most long-term commitments involve action with a decelerative production function.

Study of sustained participation is surprisingly absent in the social movement literature—surprisingly, because long-term participants keep the movement sector going. Kriesi and van Praag (1988) make the distinction between (1) sympathizers—people who are sympathetic toward the movement's cause but who do very little most of the time—occasionally they are mobilized for some moderate form of support (signing a petition, giving a donation); (2) active supporters—people who are mobilized on a more regular basis; and (3) core activists, who keep the movement going on a daily basis. In the course of time a movement expands and contracts because active supporters and occasionally sympathizers are mobilized and demobilized. It is the core activists who are responsible for this fluctuation. A movement has only a limited number of core activists. For example, 5–10 percent of the membership of the Dutch labor unions are core activists (Klandermans & Visser, 1995; Nandram, 1995), while the Dutch peace movement at its heyday counted approximately five hundred core groups with 15–20 members each (Oegema, 1993). The recruitment of these participants follows a decelerative function. Empirical evidence suggests that most core activists are perfectly aware of the fact that they are giving 90 percent or more of the movement's supporters a free ride, but don't care. On the contrary, this is what seems to motivate them to take the job. "If I don't do it, nobody else will do it" is the most frequently given motivation (Klandermans & Visser, 1995; Oliver, 1984). They are the true believers who care so much for the movement's cause that they are prepared to make that effort knowing that most others won't. Indeed, Nandram (1995) found that for 29 percent of the core activists within Dutch unions, this was the single most important motivation for their participation.

Sustained participation need not necessarily take the form of the same activity all the time. People often go from one activity to another, sometimes even from one movement to another, and in so doing build activist careers. It is these activist careers that concern my final section, on participation over the life course. In the pages to come I will address three topics: First, how do such activists' careers develop? How do people's life courses turn into activist careers? Second, how is the sometimes literally lifetime commitment to a movement maintained, and what makes some quit? Third, what are the biographical consequences of participation?

Becoming a Long-Term Activist: The Dynamics of Sustained Participation

Becoming a long term activist is to a large extent a matter of biographical availability. After all, sustained participation requires discretionary time for an extended period. The concept of biographical availability was proposed by McAdam (1986) in his study of participation in the Mississippi Freedom Summer. What McAdam had in mind was freedom from other societal commitments. "If college students are uniquely free of life-course impediments to activism, the Freedom Summer applicants were freer still. And the actual volunteers were the freest of all" (Goldstone & McAdam, 2001). Indeed, participants in the Mississippi Freedom Summer Campaign were students who were biographically available. But in terms of a life history, there is more than available time, there is also mental availability, that is, a readiness toward the ideas a movement is propagating. In trying to understand the interplay of socialization, movement mobilization, and the social and political context, I propose to use the concepts of contingency, biographical continuity, and conversion.

Contingency concerns the convergence in a person's life history of the potential to participate in a social movement as it has developed in the course of time and an event that turns that potentiality into actual participation. *Biographical continuity* and *conversion* are two concepts that further qualify contingency. Biographical continuity describes a life history whereby participation appears as the logical result of political socialization from someone's youth onward. Conversion, on the other hand, describes a life history whereby participation implies a change of someone's mind.

In her dissertation "Political Socialization, Bridging Organization, Social Movement Interaction: The Coalition of Labor Union Women," Silke Roth (1997) proposes the concept of biographical continuity to address how movement membership and participation is related to other social and political participation. Biographical continuity refers to the situation where movement membership and participation are the logical consequence of preceding political socialization. Conversion, on the other hand, relates to those situations where movement membership and participation imply a break with the past. Critical events are supposed to play a crucial role in both situations. In the context of biographical continuity, the event means the last push or pull in a direction in which the person is already going, in the context of conversion, the event means an experience that marks a change of mind. Obviously, such conversion does not come out of the blue. It is rooted in a growing dissatisfaction with life as it is. The critical event is the last push toward change. Teske (1997) describes the example of a journalist who ends up in front of the gate of a nuclear weapons plant and whose experience with the authorities' suppressive response to that demonstration turns him into an activist. The story of this journalist made clear that on the one hand it was no accident that he ended up at that gate, but on the other hand had the demonstration not taken that dramatic turn, it would not have had this impact on his life.

By way of illustration I will refer to material from life history interviews my colleagues and I conducted with extreme-right activists. Two patterns of mobilization emerged from those interviews. The first pattern concerned interviewees who had not been interested in politics in the past but later became involved in the extreme right. They can perhaps be best described as politically displaced persons who found a new political home. They could no longer identify with the parties they voted for, or they felt that politics or the government was not addressing the real problems of society. In terms of their parental milieu, no clear picture emerged. Some were from a social democratic background, some from a conservative background. The second pattern concerned interviewees who had always been interested in politics, some of them from very early on. Interestingly, all reported that they had always been interested in right-wing politics. All but one were from a politically conservative milieu, the remaining interviewee was from a social democratic milieu. There seems to be a generational pattern here: the former interviewees were from an older generation and became involved in politics later in their lives. Obviously, they are the ones whose right-wing activism is a matter of conversion. The latter were from a younger generation and were attracted to politics on the extreme right from the very beginning. They seem to constitute some kind of "new right" reacting to the new social movements of the eighties (see also Minkenberg, 1998). This group's political life history can be described in terms of biographical continuity, that is at least the way they describe it themselves.

Commitment and Disengagement

Socialization may be important to generate the readiness for long-term participation, but the real matter in sustained participation is commitment. Elsewhere I have discussed extensively the maintenance and decline of commitment (Klandermans 1997). In this section I will summarize the core argument. I draw the concept of commitment from organizational psychology and the social psychology of union participation, where a lively debate on commitment has taken place over the last two decades (Goslinga 2003). To date, the best-known conceptualization of organizational commitment is that developed by Meyer and Allen (Allen & Meyer, 1990, 1995; Meyer & Allen, 1991). These authors identify three distinct themes in the definition of commitment: "commitment as an affective attachment to the organization, commitment as a perceived cost associated with leaving the organization, and commitment as an obligation to remain in the organization" (Meyer, Allen, & Gellatly, 1993, p. 539). They refer to these three forms of commitment as affective, continuance, and normative commitment.

Meyer and colleagues (1993) emphasize that we must carefully distinguish different constituents of commitment. Indeed, we observed that in the case of the Dutch peace movement, levels of commitment to the national movement were lower than those of commitment to one's own core group (Klandermans, 1997, p. 94–97). But defection from the movement appears to be more related to commitment to the core group than to commitment to the national movement. Interestingly, however, commitment to the core group was less sensitive to the movement's successes and failures in the national political arena than was commitment to the national movement. In other words, in studying levels of movement commitment, we must always raise the question of what it is that the person is committed to: the movement, a movement organization, a leader, a group of activists, or some combination? The observation, in itself, that people are more committed to their own group than to the more distant movement organization is, of course, not so surprising. Nor is it very amazing that commitment to one's own group rather than the movement seems to determine whether someone stays a member. Yet as far as the maintenance of commitment is concerned, such findings do have important implications for sustained participation and disengagement.

Maintaining Commitment

Movement commitment does not last by itself. It must be maintained via interaction with the movement, and any measure that makes that interaction gratifying helps to maintain commitment. Downton and Wehr (1991, 1997) discuss mechanisms of social bonding that movements apply to maintain commitment. Leadership, ideology, organization, rituals, and social relations that make up a friendship network each contribute to sustaining commitment, and the most effective is, of course, a combination of all five. These authors refer to the "common devotion" that results from shared leadership; to group pressure as the primary means of maintaining a social movement's ideology; to "taking on a role within the organization itself" as a way of increasing people's investment in the organization; to rituals as patterns of behavior that are repeated over time to strengthen core beliefs of the movement; and to circles of friends that strengthen and maintain individual commitment by putting an individual's beliefs and behavior under greater scrutiny and social control. They develop their argument in the context of a study of sustained participation in the peace movement in the United States. They show how persisters—as they call long-term movement participants—continually cultivate the personal opportunity to stay actively involved by responding to new projects others invent or by creating their own. The full exploitation of this personal opportunity structure is a key factor in the formation and maintenance of commitment; other factors are: creating an activist identity, bonding to a peace group's ideology, maintaining the belief that peace action is urgent, integrating peace action into everyday life, gaining support from significant others, developing a strategy to avoid burnout, and so on.

Although not all of them are equally well researched, each of these five mechanisms are known from the literature on union and movement participation as factors that foster people's attachment to movements. For example, it is known from research on union participation that involving members in decision-making processes increases commitment to a union (Klandermans, 1986, 1992a). For such different groups as the lesbian movement groups (Taylor & Whittier, 1995) and a group called Victims of Child Abuse Laws (Fine, 1995) it was demonstrated how rituals strengthen the membership's bond to the movement. Unions and other movement organizations have developed all kind of services for their members to make membership more attractive. Selective incentives may seldom be sufficient reasons to participate in a movement, but they do increase commitment.

Despite its efforts, and with the possible exception of some religious sects and underground organizations, it is unlikely that a movement organization can prevent participants from exiting the organization if they are determined to do so. Turnover of supporters is, thus, part and parcel of the life of every movement. It is difficult, however, to estimate turnover rates in movements because movements do not carry membership administrations. Some movement organizations such as labor unions, Amnesty International, and Greenpeace do administer their membership, however. In the Netherlands, annual turnover rates of 10 percent are not unusual among those organizations.

Disengagement

What makes people defect? Insufficient gratification in combination with lack of commitment seems to be the answer. For example, more than 70 percent of the workers who left their unions did so because they were dissatisfied or frustrated or felt that they weren't treated well by their union (van de Putte, 1995). But discontent is not a sufficient condition. Obviously, movement commitment must also decline. Indeed, Moreland and Levine (1982) hypothesized that the level of commitment of those members who eventually leave a group develops in a cyclical way. Initially, it increases until some peak level is reached, then it declines until the level is reached at which people decide to quit.

That raises, of course, the questions of what causes insufficient gratification, and of why commitment declines? Psychologically speaking, it is too simple to assume that disengagement is the opposite of engagement, if only because, in the course of participation, a certain level of commitment develops that interacts with levels of gratification. Moreover, the three forms of commitment do not necessarily reach the same degree. Similarly, they may decline at different rates and for different reasons. Taking the results with regard to union commitment into account, normative commitment presumably is the most stable of the three. Meyer and Allen (1991) have argued that normative commitment has its roots in long-term socialization processes, which makes it understandable that it is more stable than the other forms of commitment that have more transitory bases. In the union context, continuance commitment appears to be the next most stable. Investments, of course, are made in the past and cannot be changed anymore, but new alternatives may appear, and existing alternatives may become more attractive so that commitment to continue may decline. Affective commitment appeared to be the most variable of the three. Supposedly it declines when interaction with the movement or its members becomes less gratifying. Affective commitment, continuance commitment, and normative commitment may balance each other out, and the more stable forms of commitment may compensate for a decline in those that are less stable. A person who sees no attractive alternatives, has invested heavily in the organization, and is truly committed to the values and goals of the movement may decide, that all things considered, he would rather continue to share the burden and make the necessary sacrifices than leave. Note that these are theoretical speculations, no empirical evidence have been collected thus far, to my knowledge, in support of these claims in the social movement context.

◤ Biographical Consequences of Participation

A final question of interest in regard to collective political action participation in the life course concerns that of the biographical consequences of participation. Obviously, participation in a movement—certainly when it is a highly controversial movement—leaves its traces in an individual's biography. For example, some extreme-right activists in the Netherlands lost their jobs or, if they had a business, lost clients; others lost their best friends when their participation in the movement became known. Movements are almost by definition controversial, and therefore we may expect participation to affect people's lives. At the same time, movements tend to create a total environment for people; they take people's discretionary time, the movement network begins to replace their friendship networks, and the movement begins to dominate their activities. This is carried to the extreme in underground movements. Della Porta's work on underground left-wing activists in Italy and Germany (1988, 1992a, 1992b) illustrates that clearly. This author (1992) shows how individuals "once having joined an underground group . . . would be required to participate at increasingly demanding levels of activity, whether in terms of risk or the time involved." She observes that "the result of this '24-hours-a day' commitment to the organization was, the lack of any time for thinking. . . . The biographies of the Italian and German militants demonstrate that this process of material and emotional involvement culminated in the militants' almost complete identification with a community of the armed struggle" (p. 18).

Through the years there has been a modest but persistent research interest in the biographical impact of social movement participation especially among so called New Left activists in the United States (Fendrich, 1993; Marwell, Aiken, & Demerath, 1987; McAdam, 1988; Whalen & Flacks, 1989). In their article "Contention in Demographic and Life-Course Context," Goldstone and McAdam (2001) summarize the major findings of this research. They conclude that "the former activists have tended to (1) remain politically active and leftist in their political orientations; (2) be employed in the 'helping' or social service professions; (3) have lower incomes; and are more likely than their peers to have (4) married later; (5) been divorced; and (6) to have experienced an episodic or nontraditional work history" (p. 215). Initially, these findings were predominantly based on high-risk activities such as participation in the Mississippi Freedom Summer or voter registration campaigns in the Deep South of the United States. But more recent studies also concerned run-of-the-mill participation and revealed very similar results (McAdam, Van Dyke, Munch, & Shockey, 1998; Sherkat and Blocker 1997). Goldstone and McAdam conclude from their review that participation in movement activities has a profound and enduring influence on people's lives.

◤ Conclusions

Collective political action has become a common strategy to influence government. However, the occurrence of collective political action is not just a matter of people who are pushed to act by some social psychological dynamic (the demand side of participation); it is also a matter of movement organizations pulling people into action (the supply side of participation) and a mobilization campaign that bring the two together. Different motives to participate come into play. Instrumentality, identity, and ideology have been mentioned as possible motives that contribute to the individual's decision to participate. I suggested that the three may compensate each other. Participation may not be immediately effective in bringing about changes. Participants understand that and will not expect government to give in at the first sight of contention. On the other hand, it may suffice for many participants to have the opportunity to meet with other like-minded people and to express their opinion. Collective political action is not only about effectiveness but also about passionate politics. This is not to say that effectiveness is likely to become irrelevant altogether. Obviously, sooner or later something should change. If nothing ever happens, a social movement will collapse, or fade, or turn into a social club or self-help organization.

Although collective action is most frequently aimed at governments, political authorities are certainly not the only targets. In fact, any institution can become the target of collective action. For example, Tarrow (1988) discussed collective action undertaken by an Italian church community against the clergy; Katzenstein (1998) studies feminist protest inside the church and the military; and recently Raeburn (2001) finished a study of the gay movement's struggle for gay rights within big companies. Finally, labor unions, of course, have always targeted authorities other than government, although in western Europe, as well as in countries such as South Africa or Zimbabwe, labor unions are significant political players as well.

When it comes to the explanation of collective action, I make the distinction between demand, supply, and mobilization. Often the reason no collective action takes place, despite widespread discontent, is that there is no viable movement organization to stage any action. At the same time, when present a movement organization does not get very far if there are no people who are concerned about the issues the organization tries to address. Finally, without effective mobilization, supply and demand may never meet. Understanding the supply side of participation involves theories from sociology and political science about the development and dynamics of social movements; understanding the demand side, however, requires social and political psychological models. As in economics, there is an intriguing interplay of demand and supply. Sometimes an appealing and well-timed action attracts an enormous turnout, that is to say, the supply reinforces the demand. Sometimes it is the other way around, massive discontent generates a strong movement, and demand triggers supply. But of course, most of the time demand and supply reinforce each other. Mobilization is the process where demand and supply meet. Theories of persuasion and network analysis are relevant in this realm.

I have deliberately drawn attention to participation over the life course. The emphasis on collective action in our research tends to obscure the fact that for many people participation in collective action is a step in an activist career. Looking at activism from a life course perspective brings a different kind of explanatory framework to the fore. In such a framework, activism becomes a phase in an individual's life that one tries to understand from the perspective of the individual's life history. Rather than ask what makes a participant in this specific collective action different from a nonparticipant, the question becomes: How does participation in this specific collective action fit into the life history of the individual? That automatically draws attention to sustained participation, because quite a few people are actively involved in a social movement for an extended period of time. It also highlights the biographical consequences of participation, because instances of collective action participation leave their traces in the individual's life course. At the same time, looking at participation in the life course orients our research to disengagement, because sooner or later participants will quit the movement or at least scale their participation down.

This discussion of the trends and turns in social movement research has alerted us also to many unanswered questions. Some of those are mentioned in Aminzade, Goldstone, and Perry's (2001) inventory of unexplored issues in the social movement literature. I will finish the chapter with a brief discussion of those unanswered questions.

A first set of unanswered questions concerns the dynamics of demand and supply. Mobilization as the process that connects demand to supply has been extensively studied. However, there has been less research on how demand evolves and how supply develops. Indeed, how a movement organization's attempts to mobilize consensus and the individual's experience work together in generating demand is understudied, as is the question of how such processes affect action mobilization. Yet it would be interesting to know whether a specific strategy of consensus mobilization would activate a specific group of people, or framing an issue in a specific way would make a difference in terms of action mobilization, to give a couple of examples.

Second, it would be worth the effort to explore the relative weight of instrumentality, identity, and ideology. Obviously, each motivation has its impact, but how do they work together? Do they add to each other, or do they interact? Are they correlated or independent determinants of participation?

Third, and more specifically, identity deserves more extensive attention from movement researchers. To be sure, a rapidly growing literature exists of identity and movement participation, but most of this literature is only conceptual and very little of it is empirical. Solid empirical studies on identity in the context of movement participation are still rare. The work of Simon and Klandermans and colleagues (De Weerd, 1999; De Weerd & Klandermans, 1999; Klandermans & De Weerd, 2000; Klandermans et al., 2002; Simon & Klandermans, 2001; Simon et al., 1998; and Stürmer, 2000) marks the beginning of a new research tradition, but much remains to be done. Especially important are questions in regard to multiple identities (Klandermans, Sabucedo, & Rodriguez, 2002; Kurtz, 2002; Roth 1997). Social movements mobilize people who share a collective identity, but typically people share many different collective identities that are sometimes competing. What determines which of those many identities becomes the core of a movement and how competing identities are reconciled?

Fourth, equally understudied is the role of ideology and its relationship to emotions. Strangely enough, very little systematic empirical work is available on ideology and on the way people's ideals and values generate passionate politics. Indeed, Oliver and Johnston (2000) have even argued that the frame alignment approach has replaced ideology with the frame concept, although Snow and Benford in their rebuttal (2000) emphasize that they never recommended replacing the term *ideology* with the term *frame*. Ideology in their view is a cultural resource for framing activities. Goodwin and colleagues (2001) point to the overly structural tendency of the ruling paradigm in social movement research. Be this as it may, undoubtedly more research is needed on these issues (see also Aminzade & McAdam, 2001).

Fifth, although a great deal of work has been done on the role of networks in mobilization, most studies are limited to questions of recruitment, more specifically, to questions regarding the ties between individuals and movement organizations that facilitate recruitment. But what role do networks play exactly? Are they merely conduits of mobilization attempts? Do they control costs and benefits of participation? Do they help people to overcome barriers? This and many other questions remain unanswered. Finally, very little is known about leadership in social movements. Klandermans (1989a) discussed the roles leaders take in a movement organization and how they facilitate the functioning of movement organizations. A decade later, Aminzade and colleagues (2001), in the context of a description of various types of leadership in social movements, still observe that empirical studies of leadership in social movement organizations are largely lacking.

In addition to these questions regarding the dynamics of supply and demand, a different set of questions concerns the expansion and contraction of the movement sector in a society (Goldstone & Tilly, 2001). Although expansion and contraction of the movement sector refers to processes that occur at the macro level, these processes are, of course, intimately related to dynamics at the micro level. Facilitation or repression of movements by the state, and the expansion or contraction of political opportunities, influence the supply side of participation and make participation in collective political action more or less attractive to people. Moreover, they influence processes of mobilization. Obviously, comparative designs are needed to investigate these influences. Such comparative research is rare, however (but see Irvin, 2000; Kurtz, forthcoming; and Schock, forthcoming). Such comparisons may involve comparisons over time (McAdam & Sewell, 2001) or space (Miller, 2000; Sewell, 2001). They may compare the demand side of participation, or the supply side of participation, or the political environment of social movements.

Finally, there are many unanswered questions regarding sustained participation, commitment, disengagement, and the life course (Goldstone & McAdam, 2001). Research on sustained participation, commitment in social movements, disengagement, and the life course is scarce. This is partly due to the fact that one needs longitudinal studies to answer questions with regard to these matters. One could also study sustained participation and the like cross-sectionally, but even these kinds of studies are rare. There are a few exceptions (Andrews, 1991; Downton & Wehr, 1997; Klandermans, 1997, pp. 93–97; Kelly & Breinlinger, 1996; Teske, 1997), but basically much is still to be explored. Relevant questions include How does commitment develop over time? How might it be related to different parts of a movement? How is it related to group identification? And so on. Sustained participation and disengagement are two sides of the same coin that are both poorly investigated. Obviously, commitment is related to continued participation and defection. Hirschman (1970) was among the first to elaborate on that link in his work on exit, voice, and loyalty. Many of the answers to the questions of why some people spend a lifetime in one and the same movement (or for that matter in various movements) while others quit are yet unknown. It would be worth the effort to follow long-term participants in social movements in order to find out what keeps them going. Or to find out how long-term participants differ from those who only participate in single events. Goldstone and McAdam (2001) point to the fact that there is no demographic/life course perspective on involvement in contentious movements, and they argue in favor of such a perspective. They propose that it should shed light on life-course factors that mediate entrance into activism and the biographical consequences of individual activism.

There is, of course, more that I could add, but I believe that the key questions have been mentioned. Collective political action has become an important part of political life. Political psychology is the discipline that should try to understand how and why it occurs.

◤ Notes

1. In South Africa, for instance, every nongovernmental organization of any significance received outside funding during the apartheid era.

2. A small proportion does not necessarily mean a negligible event. For example, although only 4 percent of the population participated in the peace demonstration, this mounted nevertheless into a demonstration with five hundred thousand participants—the largest demonstration the country had ever seen.

3. The instrumentality-identity-ideology triad is not invented for this field. Indeed, it has a long history in functional theories of attitudes and behavior (see Sears & Funk, 1991).

4. Suddenly imposed grievances are grievances generated by an event imposed on people. The term was coined by Walsh (1988) in his study of the popular response to the Three Mile Island nuclear accident, but it applies to a variety of events such as a railway track, a highway or a waste incinerator which is planned next to a community, a company closure, and so on.

◤ References

Abelson, R. P., Ewing, M. F., & Roseman, I. (1986). Emotion and political cognition: Emotion appeals in political communication. In R. R. Lau & D. O. Sears (Eds.), *The nineteenth Annual Carnegie Symposium on Cognition: Political cognition*. London: Erlbaum.

Allen, N. J., & Meyer, J. P. (1990). The measurement and antecedents of affective, continuance, and normative commitment to the organization. *Journal of Occupational Psychology, 63*, 1–18.

Allen, N., & Meyer, J. P. (1995, February). *Affective, continuance, and normative commitment to the organization: An examination of construct validity.* Paper presented at the Kurt Lewin Institute Masterclass, Schiermonnikoog, Netherlands.

Aminzade, R. R., Goldstone, J. A., Perry, E. (2001). Leadership dynamics and dynamics of contention. In R. R. Aminzade, J. A. Goldstone, D. McAdam, E. Perry, W. H. Sewell, Jr., S. Tarrow, & C. Tilly (Eds.), *Silence and voice in the study of contentious politics* (pp. 126–154). Cambridge, MA: Cambridge University Press.

Aminzade, R. R., & McAdam, D. (2001). Emotions and contentious politics. In R. R. Aminzade, J. A. Goldstone, D. McAdam, E. Perry, W. H. Sewell, Jr., S. Tarrow & C. Tilly (Eds.), *Silence and voice in the study of contentious politics* (pp. 14–50). Cambridge: Cambridge University Press.

Andrews, M. (1991). *Lifetimes of commitment: Aging, politics, psychology.* Cambridge: Cambridge University Press.

Barnes, S. H., & Kaase, M. (1979). *Political action: Mass participation in five western democracies.* London: Sage.

Benford, R. D. (1997). An insider's critique of the social movement framing perspective. *Sociological Inquiry, 67,* 409–430.

Blumer, H. (1951). The field of collective behavior. In A. M. Lee (Ed.), *Principles of sociology* (pp. 167–222). New York: Barnes and Noble.

Boudon, R. (1986). *L'idéologie ou l'origine des idées reçues.* Paris: Fayard.

Briet, M., Klandermans, B., & Kroon, F. (1987). How women become involved in the women's movement. In C. Mueller & M. Katzenstein (Eds.), *The women's movements of Western Europe and the United States: Changing theoretical perspectives* (pp. 44–67). Philadelphia: Temple University.

Buechler, S. (2000). *Social movements in advanced capitalism: The political economy and cultural construction of social activism.* Oxford: Oxford University Press.

Burstein, P. (1999). Social movement and public policy. In M. Guigni, D. McAdam, & C. Tilly (Eds.), *How social movements matter* (pp. 3–21). Minneapolis: University of Minnesota Press.

Dalton, R. (1996). *Citizen politics: Public opinion and political parties in advanced industrial democracies* (2nd ed.). Chatham, NJ: Chatham House.

De Weerd, M. (1999). *Sociaal psychologische determinanten van boerenprotest: Collectieve actie frames, identiteit en effectiviteit.* Unpublished dissertation. Free University, Amsterdam.

De Weerd, M., & Klandermans, B. (1999). Group identification and social protest: Farmer's protest in the Netherlands. *European Journal of Social Psychology, 29,* 1073–1095.

Della Porta, D. (1988). Recruitment into clandestine organizations: Leftwing terrorists in Italy. In B. Klandermans, H. Kriesi, & S. Tarrow (Eds.), *From structure to action: Comparing movement participation across cultures.* Greenwich, CT: JAI Press.

Della Porta, D. (1992a). On individual motivations in underground political organizations. In D. Della Porta (Ed.), *Social movements and violence: Participation in underground organizations, international social movement research* (Vol. 4, pp. 3–28). Greenwich, CT: JAI-Press.

Della Porta, D. (1992b). Political socialization in left-wing underground organizations: Biographies of Italian and German militants. In D. Della Porta (Ed.), *Social movements and violence: Participation in underground organizations, international social movement research* (Vol. 4, pp. 259–290). Greenwich, CT: JAI Press.

Della Porta, D., & Reiter, H. (1998). *The policing of protest in contemporary democracies.* Minneapolis: University of Minnesota Press.

Diani, M., & McAdam, D. (2002). *Social movements and networks: Relational approaches to collective action.* Oxford: Oxford University Press.

Downton, J. V., & Wehr, P. (1991). Peace movements: The role of commitment and community in sustaining member participation. *Research in Social Movements, Conflicts and Change, 13,* 113–134.

Downton, J., Jr., & Wehr, P. (1997). *The persistent activist: How peace commitment develops and survives.* Boulder, CO: Westview Press.

Fendrich, J. M. (1993). *Ideal citizens.* Albany: SUNY Press.

Ferree, M. M. (1992). The political context of rationality: Rational choice theory and resource mobilization. In A. Morris & C. M. Mueller (Eds.), *Frontiers in social movement theory* (pp. 29–52). New Haven: Yale University Press.

Fillieule, O. (1998). Plus ça change, moins ça change. Demonstrations in France in nineteen-eighties. In *Act of dissent. New developments in the study of protest* (pp. 199–226).

Fine, G. A. (1995). Public narration and group culture: Discerning discourse in social movements. In H. Johnston & B. Klandermans (Eds.), *Social movements and culture* (pp. 127–143). Minneapolis: University of Minnesota Press.

Friedhelm, N., & Rucht, D. (1993). Auf dem Weg in die Bewegungsgesellschaft? Uber die Stabilisierbarkeit sozialer Bewegungen. *Sozialer Welt, 44,* 305–326.

Gamson, W. A. (1992). The social psychology of collective action. In A. Morris & C. McClurg Mueller (Eds.), *Frontiers in social movement theory* (pp. 53–76). New Haven: Yale University Press.

Gerhards, J., & Rucht, D. (1992). Mesomobilization: Organizing and framing in two protest campaigns in West Germany. *American Journal of Sociology, 98,* 555–596.

Giugni, M. (1998). Was it worth the effort? The outcomes and consequences of social movements. *Annual Review of Sociology, 24,* 371–93.

Giugni, M., McAdam, D., & Tilly, C. (1999). *How social movements matter.* Minneapolis: University of Minnesota Press.

Goldstone, J. A., & Tilly, C. (2001). Threat (and opportunity): Popular action and state response in the dynamics of contentious action. In R. R. Aminzade, J. A. Goldstone, D. McAdam, E. Perry, W. H. Sewell, Jr., S. Tarrow, & C. Tilly (Eds.), *Silence and voice in the study of contentious politics* (pp. 179–194). Cambridge: Cambridge University Press.

Goldstone, R., & McAdam, D. (2001). Contention in demographic and life-course context. In R. R. Aminzade, J. A. Goldstone, D. McAdam, E. Perry, W. H. Sewell, Jr., S. Tarrow, & C. Tilly (Eds.), *Silence and voice in the study of contentious politics* (pp. 195–221). Cambridge: Cambridge University Press.

Goodwin, J., Jasper, J., & Polletta, F. (2001). Why emotions matter. In J. Goodwin, J. Jasper, & F. Polletta (Eds.), *Passionate politics, emotions and social movements* (pp. 1–24). Chicago: University Press of Chicago.

Goslinga, S. (2003). *Binding aan de vakbond. (Union Commitment).* Unpublished doctoral dissertation. Amsterdam: Free University.

Gurr, T. R. (1970). *Why men rebel.* Princeton: Princeton University Press.

Gusfield, J. R. (1963). *Symbolic crusade: Status politics and the American temperance movement*. Urbana: University of Illinois Press.

Hegtvedt, K. A., & Markovsky, B. (1995). Justice and injustice. In K. S. Cook, G. A. Fine, & J. S. House (Eds.), *Sociological perspectives in social psychology* (pp. 257–280). Boston: Allyn and Bacon.

Hirsch, E. L. (1990). Sacrifice for the cause: The impact of group processes on recruitment and commitment in protest movements. *American Sociological Review, 55*, 243–254.

Hirschman, A. O. (1970). *Exit, voice and loyalty: Responses to decline in firms, organizations and states*. Cambridge, MA: Harvard University Press.

Hoffer, E. (1951). *The true believer*. New York: Harper.

Hornsey, M. J., & Hogg, M. A. (forthcoming). Integroup similarity and subgroup relations: Some implications for assimilation. *Personality and Social Psychology Bulletin*.

Huddy, L. (2001). From social to political identity: A critical examination of social identity theory. *Political Psychology, 22*, 127–156.

Ignazi, P., & Ysmal, C. (1992). New and old extreme right parties. The French Front National and the Italian Movimento Sociale. *European Journal of Political Research, 22*, 101–121.

Irvin, C. (1999). *Militant nationalism: Between movements and party in Ireland and the Basque country*. Minneapolis: University of Minnesota Press.

Jasper, J. M. (1997). *The art of moral protest. Culture, biography, and creativity in social movements*. Chicago: University of Chicago Press.

Jasper, J. M. (1998). The emotions of protest: Affective and reactive emotions in and around social movements. *Sociological Forum, 13*, 397–424.

Jenkins, J. C., & Klandermans, B. (1995). *The politics of social protest: Comparative perspectives on states and social movements*. Minneapolis: University of Minnesota Press.

Jenkins, J. C. (1995). Social movements, political representation, and the state: An agenda and comparative framework. In J. C. Jenkins & B. Klandermans (Eds.), *The politics of social protest: Comparative perspectives on states and social movements* (pp. 14–35). Minneapolis: University of Minnesota Press.

Katzenstein, M. F. (1998). *Faithful and fearless: Moving feminist protest inside the church and military*. Princeton: Princeton University Press.

Kelly, C., & Breinlinger, S. (1996). *The social psychology of collective action*. Basingstoke, England: Taylor and Francis.

Kitschelt, H. (1995). *The radical right in western Europe*. Ann Arbor: Michigan University Press.

Klandermans, B. (1984). Mobilization and participation: Social psychological expansions of resource mobilization theory. *American Sociological Review, 49*, 583–600.

Klandermans, B. (1986). Psychology and trade union participation: Joining, acting, quitting. *Journal of Occupational Psychology, 59*, 189–204.

Klandermans, B. (1989a). Leadership and decision making. In B. Klandermans (Ed.), *Organizing for change: Social movement organizations in Europe and the United States. International Social Movement Research*, (Vol. 2, pp. 215–224). Greenwich, CT:JAI Press.

Klandermans, B. (1989b). Organizational effectiveness. In B. Klandermans (Ed.), *Or-*

ganizing for change: Social movement organizations in Europe and the United States. International Social Movement Research (Vol. 2, pp. 383–394). Greenwich, CT: JAI–Press.

Klandermans, B. (1992a). Trade union participation. In J. F. Hartley & G. M. Stephenson (Eds.), *Employment relations: The psychology of influence and control at work* (pp. 184–202). Oxford: Blackwell.

Klandermans, B. (1992b). The social construction of protest and multi-organizational fields. In A. Morris & Carol Mueller (Eds.), *Frontiers in social movement theory.* New Haven: Yale University Press.

Klandermans, B. (1993). A theoretical framework for comparisons of social movement participation. *Sociological Forum, 8,* 383–402.

Klandermans, B. (1997). *The social psychology of protest.* Oxford: Blackwell.

Klandermans, B. (2000a). Identity and protest: How group identification helps to overcome collective action dilemmas. In M. Van Vugt, M. Snyder, T. R. Tyler, & A. Biel (Eds.), *Cooperation in modern society: Promoting the welfare of communities, states, and organizations* (pp. 162–183). London: Routledge.

Klandermans, B. (2000b). Social movements: Trends and turns. In A. Sales & S. Quah (Eds.), *International handbook of sociology* (pp. 236–254). London: Sage.

Klandermans, B. (2001). Why movements come into being and why people join them. In J. Blau (Ed.), *Blackwell's compendium of sociology* (pp. 268–281). Oxford: Blackwell.

Klandermans, B., & De Weerd, M. (2000). Group identification and political protest. In S. Stryker, T. Owens, & R. W. White (Eds.), *Social psychology and social movements: Cloudy past and bright future* (pp. 68–92). Minneapolis: University of Minnesota Press.

Klandermans, B., De Weerd, M., Sabucedo, J. M., & Rodriguez, M. (2001). Framing contention: Dutch and Spanish farmers confront the EU. In D. Imig & S. Tarrow (Eds.), *Contentious Europeans: Protest and politics in an integrating Europe* (pp. 77–96). Boulder, CO: Rowman and Littlefield.

Klandermans, B., & Goslinga, S. (1996). Media discourse, movement publicity and the generation of collective action frames: Theoretical and empirical exercises in meaning construction. In D. McAdam, J. McCarthy, & M. Zald (Eds.), *Opportunities, mobilizing structures, and frames: Comparative applications of contemporary movement theory.* Cambridge: Cambridge University Press.

Klandermans, B., & Oegema, D. (1987). Potentials, networks, motivations and barriers: Steps toward participation in social movements. *American Sociological Review, 5,* 519–531.

Klandermans, B., Sabucedo, J. M., & Rodriguez, M. (2002). Politicization of collective identity: Farmer's identity and farmer's protest in the Netherlands and Spain. *Political Psychology, 23,* 235–251.

Klandermans, B., Sabucedo, J. M., & Rodriguez, M. (2001). Will the skin be nearer than the shirt? Multiple identities among farmers in the Netherlands and Spain. Unpublished paper, Amsterdam/Santiago de Compostela.

Klandermans, B., & Visser, J. (red.) (1995). *De vakbeweging na de welvaartsstaat.* Assen: Van Gorcum.

Knoke, D. (1990). *Political networks. The structural perspective.* New York: Cambridge University Press.

Kornhauser, W. (1959). *The politics of mass society.* Glencoe, IL: Free Press.

Kriesi, H., Koopmans, R., Duyvendak, J. W., & Guigni, M. G. (1995). *New social movements in Western Europe: A comparative analysis.* Minneapolis: University of Minnesota Press.

Kurtz, S. (2002). *All kinds of justice: Labor and identity politics.* Minneapolis: University of Minnesota Press.

Le Bon, G. (1903/1960). *The crowd: A study of popular mind.* New York: Viking Press.

Marwell, G., Aiken, M., & Demerath III, N. J. (1987). The persistence of political attitudes among 1960s civil rights activists. *Public Opinion Quarterly, 51,* 359–375.

Marwell, G., & Oliver, P. (1993). *The critical mass in collective action. A micro-social theory.* Cambridge: Cambridge University Press.

McAdam, D. (1982). *Political process and the development of black insurgency.* Chicago: University of Chicago Press.

McAdam, D. (1986). Recruitment to high risk activism: The case of freedom summer. *American Journal of Sociology, 92,* 64–90.

McAdam, D. (1988). *Freedom summer.* New York: Oxford University Press.

McAdam, D., McCarthy, J., & Zald, M. N. (1996). *Comparative perspectives on social movements. Political opportunities, mobilizing structures, and cultural framing.* Cambridge: Cambridge University Press.

McAdam, D., & Sewell, W. H., Jr. (2001). It's about time: Temporality in the study of social movements and revolutions. In R. R. Aminzade, J. A. Goldstone, D. McAdam, E. Perry, W. H. Sewell, Jr., S. Tarrow, & C. Tilly (Eds.), *Silence and voice in the study of contentious politics* (pp. 89–125). Cambridge, MA: Cambridge University Press.

McAdam, D., Van Dyke, N., Munch, A., & Shockey, J. (1998). *Social movements and the life-course.* Unpublished manuscript. Department of Sociology, University of Arizona, Tucson.

McCarthy, J. D., & Zald, M. (1976). Resource mobilization and social movements: A partial theory. *American Journal of Sociology, 82,* 1212–1241.

McPhail, C., & McCarthy, J. D. (1998). In D. Della Porta & H. Reiter (Eds.), *The policing protest* (p. 22). Minneapolis: University of Minnesota Press.

Meyer, D., & Tarrow, S. (1998). *The social movement society: Contentious politics for a new century.* Boulder, CO: Rowman and Littlefield.

Meyer, J. P., & Allen, N. J. (1991). A three component conceptualization of organizational commitment. *Human Resource Management Review, 1,* 61–89.

Meyer, J. P., Allen, N. J., & Gellatly, I. R. (1993). Affective and continuance commitment to the organization: Evaluation of measures and analysis of concurrent and time-lagged relations. *Journal of Applied Psychology, 75,* 710–720.

Miller, B. (2000). *Geography and social movements: Comparing antinuclear activism in the Boston area.* Minneapolis: University of Minnesota Press.

Minkenberg, M. (1998). *Die neue radikale rechte im vergleich, USA, Frankreich, Deutschland.* Opladen/Wiesbaden, Westdeutscher Verlag.

Moreland, R. L., & Levine, J. (1982). Socialization in small groups: Temporal changes in individual–group relations. *Advances in Experimental Social Psychology, 15,* 137–192.

Nandram, S. (1995). *Het beredeneerd aan-en afmelden als kaderlid. Een studie naar het vrijwilligerswerk binnen een vakbond.* [Reasoned application and defection as union militant. A study of volunteers within labor unions]. Unpublished doctoral dissertation, Free University, Amsterdam.

Neidhardt, F., & Rucht, D. (1993). Auf dem Weg in die Bewegungsgesellschaft? Uber die Stabilisierbarkeit sozialer Bewegungen. *Sozialer Welt, 44*, 305–326.

Oberschall, A. (1973). *Social conflict and social movements.* Englewood Cliffs, NJ: Prentice-Hall.

Oegema, D. (1993). *Tussen petitie en perestroika. De nadagen van de Nederlandse vredesbeweging.* Unpublished doctoral dissertation, Free University, Amsterdam.

Oegema, D., & Klandermans, B. (1994). Non-conversion and erosion: The unwanted effects of action mobilization. *American Sociological Review, 59*, 703–722.

Oliver, P. E. (1980). Rewards and punishments as selective incentives for collective action: Theoretical investigations. *American Journal of Sociology, 85*, 1356 375.

Oliver, P. E. (1984). If you don't do it, nobody else will: Active and token contributors to local collective action. *American Sociological Review, 49*, 601–610.

Oliver, P. E., & Johnston, H. (2000). What a good idea! Ideology and frames in social movement research. *Mobilization, 5*, 37–54.

Olson, M. (1968). *The logic of collective action. Public goods and the theory of groups.* Cambridge, MA: Harvard University Press.

Opp, K-D. (1989). *The rationality of political protest. A comparative analysis of rational choice theory.* Boulder, CO: Westview.

Orfali, B. (1990). *L'adhésion au Front national. De la minorité au mouvement social.* Paris: Kimé.

Parkinson, B., & Manstead, A. S. R. (1993). Making sense of emotions in stories and social life. *Cognition and Emotion, 7*, 295–323.

Pichardo, N. (1997). New social movements: A critical review. *Annual Review of Sociology, 23*, 411–430.

Raeburn, N. (2001). *The rise of lesbian, gay, and bisexual rights in the corporate workplace.* Unpublished doctoral dissertation, Ohio State University, Columbus.

Rochon, T. R. (1998). *Culture moves: Ideas, activism, and changing values.* Princeton: Princeton University Press.

Roth, S. (1997). *Political socialization, bridging organization, social movement interaction: The coalition of labor union women (1974–1996).* Unpublished dissertation, University of Connecticut, Hartford.

Rucht, D. (1998). The structure and culture of collective protest in Germany since 1950. In D. S. Meyer & S. Tarrow (Eds.), *The social movement society, contentious politics for a new century* (pp. 29–59). Lanham, MD: Rowman and Littlefield.

Rule, James B. (1989). Rationality and non-rationality in militant collective action. *Sociological Theory, 7*, 145–160.

Searles, R., & Williams, J. A., Jr. (1962). Negro college students' participation in sit-ins. *Social Forces, 40*, 215–220.

Sears, D. O., & Funk, C. (1991). The role of self-interest in social and political attitudes. *Advances in Experimental Psychology, 24*, 1–91.

Sewell, W., Jr. (2001). Space in contentious politics. In R. R. Aminzade, J. A. Goldstone, D. McAdam, E. Perry, W. H. Sewell, Jr., S. Tarrow, & C. Tilly (Eds.), *Silence and voice in the study of contentious politics* (pp. 51–88). Cambridge: Cambridge University Press.

Sherkat, D. E., & Blocker, T. J. (1997). Explaining the political and personal consequences of protest. *Social Forces, 75*, 1049–76.

Shock, K. (forthcoming). *The politics of people power: Nonviolent action and social movements in non-democracies.* Minneapolis: University of Minnesota Press.

Simon, B. (1998). Individuals, groups, and social change: On the relationship between individual and collective self-interpretations and collective action. In C. Sedikides, J. Schopler, & C. Insko (Eds.), *Intergroup cognition and intergroup behavior* (pp. 257–282). Mahwah, NJ: Erlbaum.

Simon, B. (1999). A place in the world: Self and social categorization. In T. R. Tyler, R. M. Kramer, & O. P. John (Eds.), *The psychology of the social self* (pp. 47–69). Mahwah, NJ: Erlbaum.

Simon, B., & Klandermans, B. (2001). Towards a social psychological analysis of politicized collective identity: Conceptualization, antecedents, and consequences. *American Psychologist, 56,* 319–331.

Simon, B., Loewy, M., Stürmer, S., Weber, U., Kampmeier, C., Freytag, P., Habig, C., & Spahlinger, P. (1998). Collective identity and social movement participation. *Journal of Personality and Social Psychology, 74,* 646–658.

Snow, D. A., & Benford, R. D. (1988). Ideology, frame resonance, and participant mobilization. In B. Klandermans, H. Kriesi, & S. Tarrow (Eds.), *From structure to action: Comparing movement participation across cultures, international social movement research* (Vol. 1, pp. 197–218). Greenwich, CT: JAI Press.

Snow, D., & Benford, R. D. (2000). Clarifying the relationship between framing and ideology. *Mobilization, 5,* 55–60.

Snow, D. A., Rochford, E. Burke Jr., Worden, S. K., & Benford, R. D. (1986). Frame alignment processes, micro-mobilization and movement participation. *American Sociological Review, 51,* 464–481.

Stürmer, S. (2000). *Soziale Bewegungsbeteiligung: Ein psychologisches Zwei-Wege Modell.* Unpublished doctoral dissertation, University of Kiel, Kiel Germany.

Tarrow, S. (1988). Old movements in new cycles: The career of a neighborhood religious movement in Italy. In B. Klandermans, H. Kriesi, & S. Tarrow (Eds.), *From structure to action: Comparing movement participation across cultures* (pp. 281–305). Greenwich, CT: JAI Press.

Tarrow, S. (1994). *Power in movement. Social movements, collective action and mass politics in the modern state.* Cambridge: Cambridge University Press.

Tarrow, S. (1998). *Power in movement. Social movements, collective action and mass politics in the modern state* (2nd ed.). Cambridge: Cambridge University Press.

Taylor, V., & Whittier, N. E. (1995). Analytical approaches to social movement culture: The culture of the women's movement. In H. Johnston & B. Klandermans (Eds.), *Social movements and culture* (pp. 163–187). Minneapolis: University of Minnesota Press.

Teske, N. (1997). *Political activists in America. The identity construction model of political participation.* Cambridge: Cambridge University Press.

Tilly, C. (1978). *From mobilization to revolution.* Reading, MA: Addison-Wesley.

Tristan, A. (1987). *Au Front.* Paris: Gallimard.

Turner, J. C. (1999). Some current issues in research on social identity and self-categorization theories. In N. Ellemers, R. Spears, & B. Doosje (Eds.), *Social identity* (pp. 6–34). Oxford: Blackwell.

Turner, J. C., Oakes, P. J., Haslam, A., & McGarty, C. (1994). Self and collective: Cognition and social context. *Personality and Social Psychology Bulletin, 20,* 454–463.

Turner, R. H., & Killian, L. M. (1972). *Collective behavior* (2nd ed.). Englewood Cliffs, NJ: Prentice-Hall.

Tyler, T. R., Boeckmann, R. R., Smith, H. J., & Huo, Y. J. (1997). *Social justice in a diverse society.* Boulder, CO: Westview Press.

Tyler, T. R., Smith, H. (1998). Social justice and social movements. In D. Gilbert, S. T. Fiske, & G. Lindzey (Eds.), *Handbook of social psychology* (4th ed., pp. 595–626). New York: McGraw-Hill.

Van den Putte, B. (1995). Uit de bond: Bedanken als vakbondslid. In B. Klandermans & J. Visser (Eds.), *De vakbeweging na de welvaartsstaat* (pp. 87–112). Meppel, Netherlands: Van Gorcum.

Walgrave, S., & Manssens, J. (2000). The making of the white march: The mass media as a mobilization alternative to movement organizations. *Mobilization, 5,* 217–240.

Walsh, E. J. (1988). *Democracy in the shadows: Citizen mobilization in the wake of the accident at Three Mile Island.* Westport, CT: Greenwood Press.

Whalen, J., & Flacks, R. (1980). The Isla Vista "bank burners" ten years later: Notes on the fate of student activism. *Sociological Focus, 13,* 215–236.

White, R. W. (1993). *Provisional Irish Republicans. An oral and interpretive history.* Westport, CT: Greenwood Press.

20 Ervin Staub and Daniel Bar-Tal

Genocide, Mass Killing, and Intractable Conflict

Roots, Evolution, Prevention, and Reconciliation

The twentieth century, as many commentators have noted, was a century of great mass violence in which many millions of people were killed. During the second half of the century, much of this violence was within states, between groups differing in ethnicity, religion, political ideology and agenda, and power and privilege. The Minorities at Risk study noted substantial decline in the number of new ethnically based protest campaigns and re-bellions since 1992, as well as a decline in the intensity of the ongoing ones (Gurr, 2001). But in spite of this observation, mass violence was very sub-stantial in the 1990s, as is shown by the cases of Rwanda, the former Yugoslavia, Sri Lanka, Angola, Sierra Leone and other places in Africa, violence in the Middle East, and elsewhere. One might predict that with continuous great changes in the world in technology, information systems, values, social organization, and political systems; with great differences be-tween rich and poor; with globalization, overpopulation, aspirations by groups for greater rights or self-determination; and with an increase in fun-damentalism, conflicts and violence between groups will be a significant problem in the new century (Staub, 1999a).

In view of this prediction, the prevention of mass violence and espe-cially intractable conflicts, genocides, and mass killings becomes an essential task. Beyond creating great human suffering at one place, conflict and vi-olence between groups often spill across borders, threatening the security of other nations as well as the moral status of the international community, which is frequently passive, even complicit, in cases when some nations support the perpetrators. Social scientists can greatly contribute to the un-derstanding of the origins, dynamics, and consequences of mass violence. They can and must also develop conceptions for and engage in efforts to bring about their prevention.

Intergroup mass violence is a broad category, with many acts and pro-cesses involved (see, for example, Brass, 1996; Brubaker & Laitin, 1998). It refers to two or more groups harming each other: minimally, one group acting against another, or two groups acting against each other, with these acts claiming a large number of lives. Acts by individuals who injure, kill, and murder may be considered intergroup violence when the individuals act as group members.

The focus of this chapter is on intractable conflict and on genocide/ mass killing. It is surprising, in view of the significant connections between these two phenomena, that there has been relatively little integration in studying them (Brown, 1995). We will attempt to provide connections between the two realms as we describe their origins, dynamics, cessation, and prevention. Taking an interdisciplinary approach, which is central to political psychology, we will identify influences that operate at the level of the system: structural conditions such as power arrangements and institutions, current social conditions, cultural factors, and particularly psychological dynamics involving beliefs, values, feelings, and motivations shared by group members. We will then consider the prevention of genocide and intractable conflict. We will especially focus on the role of bystander nations, and on healing and reconciliation after intractable conflict or genocide, which are important to prevent their recurrence.

▶ Definitions and Central Concepts

Intractable Conflict

Conflicts between ethnic, religious, or political groups, societies, or nations, which arise when their goals, intentions, values and/or actions are perceived as incompatible (Bar-Tal, Kruglanski, & Klar, 1989; Mitchell, 1981; Rubin, Pruitt, & Kim, 1994), are an integral part of intergroup relations. They are usually over tangible matters involving territory, material resources, and access to opportunity, power, and privilege (Gurr, 2001). But many of them also involve and may become primarily rooted in intangible issues or psychological forces such as values, ideals, identity, mistrust or perceived threat from the other (Ross, 1993: Staub, 1989). Our concern here is with conflicts that are intense and involve mass violence, like those in Northern Ireland between Protestants and Catholics, in Turkey between Turks and Kurds, in Rwanda between Hutus and Tutsis, in Kashmir, and in the Middle East. These are the kind of conflict that have been described as protracted (Azar, 1990; Brecher & Wilkenfeld, 1988; Crighton & MacIver, 1990), as enduring rivalries (e.g., Goertz & Diehl, 1993; Huth & Russett, 1993; Mor & Maoz, 1999), and as deep rooted (e.g., Burton, 1987; Mitchell, 1981). They have also been called ethnopolitical conflict or warfare (Chirot & Seligman, 2001). We will call these conflicts intractable, meaning that they involve mass violence and have not yielded to resolution either by negotiation or the use of force. We view intractability as the end point of a dimension. Kriesberg (1993, 1998b) identified the first four elements described here that place conflicts on the intractable end of this dimension, and Bar-Tal (1998) added the three that follow.

(1) Intractable conflicts are *protracted*. They last at least a generation, with many confrontations over time that generate much hatred and ani-

mosity. (2) They are *violent*. Not only soldiers or armed antagonists but also civilians (including women and children) may be killed, property destroyed, refugees created, and atrocities committed. (3) They are perceived as *irreconcilable*. The parties view their goals as radically opposite, adhere to them without compromise, and prepare for continuation of the conflict. (4) They demand *extensive investment*. The parties in the conflict make vast military, economic, and psychological investments in order to cope successfully with the situation. (5) They are *total*. Intractable conflicts are perceived as being over existential goals and needs, both material and intangible, involving many domains of individual and group life such as territory, resources, employment, identity, values, or religion. (6) They are of a *zero-sum nature*. The parties are reluctant to shift their own goals, they negate their rival's goals, and do not see possible compromise. Therefore, each party considers a gain by another as a loss, and a loss by another as a gain, and tries therefore to inflict losses on the opponent and prevent any gain (Ordeshook, 1986). (7) They are *central*, in two senses: first, in the psychological life of the individual group members, who are constantly preoccupied with the conflict in their thoughts and feelings (for example, a person may never feel safe from harm), and second, in public life, in the media, in the leaders' articulations, in its salience in the public agenda and debates. Members of the group are constantly involved with the intractable conflict, and it serves as an important consideration in individual and group decision-making. Totality, zero-sum nature, violence, and longevity are especially important indicators of intractable conflict (Doyle & Sambani, 2000).

Prolonged conflict has an immense effect on the parties involved. It generates a culture and ethos of conflict (Bar-Tal, 2000b; Ross, 1998), becomes imprinted in the collective memories of the societies involved (Fentress & Wickman, 1992; Halbswachs, 1992; Irwin-Zarecka, 1994), and is handed down through the generations, solidifying hostility and hatred and supporting the continuation of the conflict.

Genocide and Mass Killing

Genocide and/or mass killing may develop out of conflict, especially intractable conflict, as in the case of Rwanda. But it may be perpetrated without real conflict between groups, as in the case of the genocide against the Jews. Some of the processes described below, such as devaluation and scapegoating, can lead to the selection of a group as an ideological enemy, even when there is no real conflict.

Genocide is an attempt to eliminate a whole group of people, either directly by killing them, or indirectly by creating conditions that lead to their death or prevent reproduction (e.g., starvation or preventing births). The UN genocide convention considers genocide to be acts committed with the intent to destroy in whole or in part a national, ethnic, racial, or religious group as such. The extermination of political groups was not included under the genocide convention but can nonetheless be considered genocide, although it has also been referred to as *politicide* (Harff & Gurr, 1990).

The genocide convention refers to the destruction of a group "in part" as genocide. However, killing large numbers of people without the apparent intent to eliminate a whole group may best be regarded as *mass killing*. The motivation for mass killing may be similar to that for genocide (see below), but it may also be primarily to intimidate and establish dominance either over a subgroup of society, by eliminating its leadership or intimidating its members, or over a whole society. Mass killing may also be an aspect of intractable conflict. In mass killing, the specification of who is to be killed may be less precise than in genocide. The number of people killed may be relatively small or large. A great deal of scholarly effort has focused on the definition of genocide (see, for example, Bauer, 1984; Chalk and Jonassohn, 1990; Dadrian, 1974; Dobkowski & Wallimann, 1992; Fein, 1993; Hirsch, 1995; Kressel, 2002; Lemkin, 1944) as well as on naming mass killings (e.g, politicide; democide—see Rummel, 1994). A simple but effective definition was provided by Chalk and Jonassohn (1990, p. 23): "Genocide is a form of one-sided mass killing in which the state or other authority intends to destroy the group, as that group and membership in it are defined by the perpetrators." Consistent with our view, this definition includes political groups under the term *genocide* and both direct and indirect means of destruction.

One benefit of a precise definition might be that when violence against a group is defined as genocide, the international community, moved by the moral imperative of the genocide convention, would be more likely to act to stop the killings. But a precise definition may also mean less feeling of obligation to act in response to "mere" mass killing. This was dramatically shown in 1994, when the international community, including the United States, strongly resisted identifying the ongoing extermination of Tutsis in Rwanda as genocide, apparently to avoid the moral obligation to act (des Forges, 1999; Gourevich, 1998, Powers, 2001, 2002).

An important reason to distinguish between genocide and mass killing would be to develop the best theory of the origins and prevention of each. However, the influences leading to them are usually similar. Genocide is often the outcome of an evolution, with mass killing a way station to it (Staub, 1989). For example, there were mass killings in decades preceding the genocides both in Turkey against the Armenians and in Rwanda against the Tutsis. While good theory can be the basis for assessing the conditions that predict the likelihood of group violence in a particular instance, the exact form of it is probably not possible to predict.

A number of scholars have offered categorizations of genocides. For example, Smith (1999) has proposed five types, with different primary motives: retributive (motivated by blaming victims and revenge), institutional (genocide that is routinized, part of conquest or warfare), utilitarian (its purpose some form of gain, as in the case of colonial domination), monopolistic (to determine who will have power, who will rule) and ideological (the desire to create a perfect society, to eliminate all that is impure). Smith writes: "the most frequent source of genocide in the twentieth century has been the monopolization of power" (1999, p. 7). This is consistent with Fein's (1993) conclusion that demands by subordinate groups for greater rights and more resources have been the most frequent source of genocide since World War II. In such cases, genocide appears to grow out of conflict.

It is important to understand the driving forces behind a particular violent conflict, so that effective policy responses can be developed. But consistent with the preceding discussion, in our view it is best to develop a general conception of both origins and prevention, with careful application to specific instances. A general conception, combined with consideration of the specific elements of a situation, can best indicate which elements might be especially important in a particular instance.

◣ The Origin, Dynamics, and Maintenance of Mass Violence

On the basis of our own work (e.g., Bar-Tal, 1998, 2000b, in press-a; Staub, 1989; 1996b; 1999a; in press-b; see also references) and the work of others (e.g., Chalk and Jonassohn, 1990; Dadrian, 1995; Fein, 1979, 1993; Harff & Gurr, 1988; Melson; 1992; Smith, 1999; see also Charny, 1999), we will describe societal conditions, psychological processes, and cultural elements that contribute to genocide, as well as mass killing and the usually mutual violence that is part of intractable conflict, referring to them as mass violence. The following analysis suggests a probabilistic conception: the more of the influences we describe are present and the greater their intensity, the more likely it is that extreme violence will occur.

Instigating Conditions and Basic Human Needs

Certain social conditions are frequent starting points. They have powerful psychological effects. They frustrate important needs, which eventually may give rise to psychological and societal processes that begin an evolution toward mass violence. It is primarily in the presence of predisposing cultural characteristics (see later section) that instigators are likely to have such effects.

Difficult Life Conditions

This is a summary term (Staub, 1989) to describe economic hardship, political tension and disorganization, and great and rapid social change that separately and especially in combination are potential starting points for processes that may lead to mass violence. These different social conditions are grouped together because they can have similar psychological impact on individuals and as a result may generate similar social processes in groups.

As an example, difficult life conditions were greatly involved in bringing the Nazi party to power in Germany, the first phase of the genocidal process. Germany lost War World I, a peace treaty was imposed on Germany that reduced living standards and that Germans found humiliating, and there followed a revolution and system change, hyperinflation and depression, great internal political conflict, with private armies fighting against each other, and more (Craig, 1982; DeJonge, 1978; Staub, 1989). In Rwanda difficult life conditions and intractable conflict jointly exerted influence. There were severe economic problems, related to overpopulation and the substantial decline in the price of coffee and tin in world markets, Rwanda's primary exports. There were also deep political dissatisfaction and demands for change. There was also an intractable conflict between Hutus and Tutsis that turned into a civil war (des Forges, 1999; Prunier, 1995; Staub, 1999a).

Government or state failure has been described as a contributor to genocide (Melson, 1992; Harff and Gurr, 1990). A failing government means difficult life conditions, such as economic problems, or political disorganization and conflict that leaders are unable to manage. The failure impacts both the population and the leaders themselves. What may be regarded as government or state failure has preceded genocide in a number of instances, for example the Armenians in Turkey (Melson, 1992), Hitler coming to power in Germany, the Tutsis in Rwanda (des Forges, 1999).

Basic Human Needs

Difficult life conditions frustrate fundamental psychological needs. These needs are universal, although their exact form is shaped by culture, by the socialization of individuals and life experience in particular groups (Staub, 1989, 1996b, 1999b, 2001b, in press-b; see also Burton, 1990; Kelman, 1990). One basic need is the need for security, to feel that oneself, one's family, important others, one's whole group are safe from physical as well as psychological harm and that they will have food, shelter, and other basic necessities for survival. Another basic need is for a positive identity, for oneself and, to the extent that one is dependent on or identifies with one's group, for the group as well. Still another is the need for a feeling of effectiveness and control, the ability to protect oneself and one's family and group from harm and to achieve important goals. Another need is for connection to other individuals, as well as a community or group. A less evident basic need is for a comprehension of reality that makes the world and one's own place in it understandable. Finally, people also have spiritual needs, for meaning and for transcendence, to go beyond themselves, which can be deeply frustrated by difficulties of life and violence.

Difficult life conditions make people feel insecure, ineffective, and not in control, with their sense of self diminished. People tend to focus on themselves when life is difficult and feel disconnected from others at a time when they most need connection and support. Life problems, societal disorganization, and change generate challenge to traditional worldviews and frustrate the need for comprehension of reality.

Basic needs have an imperative quality. They demand satisfaction. If they cannot be fulfilled constructively, they will often be fulfilled destructively. That is, they may then be fulfilled at the cost of other people, or even at the cost of oneself, when fulfilling one need ends up frustrating another need. For example, needs for security, for effectiveness and control, and for maintaining a positive identity can lead to actions that bring forth reactions that lessen security (Staub, 1996b, in press-b). Instigators can give rise to social psychological processes in groups of people and to the evolution of societal beliefs that help fulfill basic needs but at the same time move the group toward turning against another group or, when there is already group conflict, intensify antagonism.

Conflict Between Groups

Conflicts can become violent and/or intractable with significant violence and can ultimately evolve into genocide. In an intractable conflict, a group considers its goals as of existential importance and views the other group as preventing their achievement (see Williams, 1994). The gap between conflicting goals is viewed as immense, not possible to resolve through compromise. Such perception may be generated speedily (see also Coleman, 2000) by words (statements about intentions or demands) or actions (embargo or attack).

But intractable conflicts may also evolve slowly through ideas that define the goals and interests of the two groups as contradictory (seeing one's group as exploited, discriminated against, or deserving self-determination or independence), as in the case of conflict between Palestinians and Israelis or in South Africa. The ideas (the epistemic basis to the conflict) may be initiated by a small group of people. They may lead to protest (Staub and Rosenthal, 1994) and then to violent actions to achieve group goals. The actions threaten the interests and security of the other group and create violent responses. Conceptualizations of the conflict or ideologies (see below) develop justifications and rationales but also further motivation for action. Group members become widely mobilized and committed to group goals.

An intractable conflict may begin with small-scale violence that claims life. Loss of life in a conflict has great emotional meaning, often being viewed as a result of the other group violating a fundamental moral code. The suffering caused by the violence is perceived as a collective issue, and the group takes the responsibility to treat and compensate the victims, to prevent the recurrence of physical violence, and to take revenge for it (Bar-Tal, in press-a; Frijda, 1994). Thus violent actions and retributions create an escalating cycle. Over time one or both parties may lose all moral restraint. As conflicts become violent and as violence intensifies, the evolution may lead to war (Goertz & Diehl, 1993), to one-sided or mutual mass killing, or to genocide. Such violence, in turn, adds to the intractability of the conflict.

War increases the likelihood of genocide. The genocide of the Tutsis in Rwanda took place in the context of a civil war, although during a cease-fire after seemingly successful peace negotiations (Des Forges, 1999; Staub, 1999a). Genocide may take place not against the enemy in the war but against a deeply devalued group or ideological enemy, as in the case of the Holocaust, which took place during World War II, and the genocide of the Armenians during World War I. War may provide a cover for such violence, the violence of war may lessen inhibitions, and the frustration of basic needs in war may add to the motivational base out of which genocide arises.

The preceding discussion primarily describes the nature and dynamics of intractable conflict. Its origins, and the conditions under which it is likely to lead to intense violence, will be further identified hereafter. One of them is a vital conflict of interest that is difficult to resolve. This may be partly for material reasons: territory needed by both parties for living space; scarce water supply needed by both groups; entrenched differences in power, wealth, and opportunity. It is also for psychological reasons: the territory being seen as part of the group's identity; worldviews or legitimizing ideologies claiming that the power differences are right (Sidanius & Pratto, 1998); a history of devaluation and fear of the other; hopelessness about the resolution of conflict by peaceful means; and evolving ideology and group beliefs that intensify enmity.

Frequently, conflict and difficult life conditions operate together. Structural conflict, such as inequalities in a society, may not be perceived as unjust and may not lead to action until life conditions contribute to the difficulties of life and intensify the experience of relative deprivation of an already less privileged group (Leatherman, DeMars, Gaffney, & Vayrynen, 1999). Alternately, intractable conflicts create difficulties in life conditions. They are by their nature stressful, threatening, create uncertainty, and demand large economic and military investments (Bar-Tal, 1998). They make it difficult to fulfill basic needs, like the needs for security, positive identity, and comprehension of reality (see Burton, 1990; Lederer, 1980; Kelman, 1990; Staub, 1989, 1999a, 1999b, in press-b).

Self-interest

Self-interest, or greed, can also lead to mass violence, even when the interests of one group, as historically defined, have not been in conflict with those of another group. However, one group now wants something that another group possesses. The want often expresses greed rather than need. A common historical instance is warfare for the sake of conquest. Self-interest has often entered in the mass killing or genocide of indigenous groups. The dominant group may want the territory on which an indigenous group lives, without historical claim to the territory, either as living space or for economic development (Hitchcock & Twedt, 1997). When European conquerors arrived in the Americas, the "conflict" consisted of the Europeans wanting what Native Americans possessed, such as gold or territory.

Psychological and Societal Processes and Cultural Characteristics That Contribute to Mass Violence

Persistent, difficult life conditions and persistent conflicts frustrate the fulfillment of basic needs (Burton, 1990; Kelman, 1990; Lederer, 1980; Staub, 1989, 1996b, 1999b, in press-b). They give rise to shared psychological reactions and social processes in response to them, such as increased identification with a group, scapegoating and the creation of destructive ideologies, described below. These serve, in part, to fulfill basic needs, but may turn the group to use violence against another group. This is especially likely when societal or group culture has certain characteristics, which we will describe. The instigating conditions and cultural characteristics join in giving rise to violence-generating psychological and social processes.

Strong Identification with a Group

Instigating conditions make it difficult for people to stand on their own and to face the problems they encounter as individuals. People tend to shift away from an individual identity that has become burdensome, as they are unable to provide for themselves and their families or are confused by the political and social chaos around them or are threatened by the conflict with the other group (Kecmanovic, 1996; Staub, 2001b; Worchel, 1999). They turn to an ideological movement for identity, like the Khmer Rouge in Cambodia, or increase their identification with an ethnic, political, or religious group they have previously been members of. Rather than being individuals, they become Nazis or communists, or more German, Serb, Hutu, Israeli, or Palestinian than they have been before (see also chapter 15). In response to the attacks on the World Trade Center and Pentagon, people in the United States became more American. This strengthens identity and connection, provides some feeling of security, and helps fulfill the other basic needs as well. Then, as social identity theorists have suggested (Tajfel, 1978, 1981), individuals elevate their group, initially by psychologically diminishing the other through devaluation, and ultimately by harming the other (see Crighton & MacIver, 1990).

Scapegoating

Blaming the other group for life problems is a common psychological response that turns a group against another. Over time it becomes a societal or group belief that the other is at fault. Believing that one is not responsible for economic and other difficulties of life strengthens individual identity, creates connection, since such blaming is a group process, and helps people gain a comprehension of current reality. The Germans blamed the Jews for the loss of World War I. The Nazis added to this by blaming them for the threat of communism, as well as any and all problems that affected Germans (Craig, 1982; DeJong, 1978). Hutus blamed Tutsis for economic and political problems in Rwanda, as well as for the civil war (des Forges, 1999; Staub, 1999a). When conflict leads to mutual harm-doing, it is common for each group to blame the other and not to acknowledge or even be aware of its own contribution.

Ideologies and Societal Beliefs

A seemingly universal effect of instigating conditions is the adoption or creation of an ideology (Cash, 1996; Galtung, 1990; Staub, 1989, 1999a). Ideologies are defined here as visions of ideal societal arrangement. People need positive visions in difficult times, but the ideologies that are precursors to group violence are destructive in that they identify enemies who stand in the way of the ideology's fulfillment. Such ideologies seem always to be present in genocide. Sometimes the vision describes an ideal arrangement for all humanity, such as communism, a "better world ideology" (Staub, 1989). The Cambodian communists, the Khmer Rouge, were guided by a belief in total societal equality (Staub, 1989). At other times it is nationalistic, in the sense of the desire to create one's own state or, more often in the case of genocide, to enhance its power, prestige, or purity. The Young Turks, the organizers of the genocide against the Armenians (Staub, 1989), had a vision of Turkey's renewed greatness. Often the ideology includes elements of both, as in the case of the Nazi ideology with its vision of racial purity as well as more living space for Germany (Hilberg, 1961).

Powerful groups often protect their power and privilege by developing a worldview or ideology—a legitimizing ideology (Sidanius & Pratto, 1998) or belief in comparative superiority (Gurr, 2001)—that makes it right for them to have power and privilege. As they act against the demands of a subordinate group, they are defending not only their privilege but also their worldview (Staub, 1989). Ideologies of development have been used to claim the land of and justify harmful actions against indigenous populations (Hitchock and Twedt, 1997).

Ideologies are a form of societal beliefs. Societal beliefs, which develop in every society (Bar-Tal, 2000b), can provide building bocks for destructive ideologies. German anti-Semitism and desire for expansion were incorporated into the Nazi ideology. Societal beliefs are beliefs shared by members of a society on topics and issues that are of special concern for the society: goals, myths, collective memory, self-image, views of other groups, and so on. They contribute to the sense of uniqueness of the group (Bar-Tal,

2000b) and serve to make sense of as well as to create a shared reality (see also Mannheim, 1952). They establish commonality of perceptions, norms, and values, as well as foster interdependence and coordination of social activities. They also create collective emotional orientations (Bar-Tal, 2001; Kemper, 1990; Markus & Kitayama, 1994), serve as a basis for group members' identity, and provide direction and goals for individual and group behavior (Bar-Tal & Oren, 2000). Central societal beliefs represent a societal ethos (Bar-Tal, 2000b), a coherent picture of the society that guides choices made by individuals, explains and justifies decisions by leaders, and imparts legitimacy to the social system (see concepts of political culture, Almond & Verba, 1963, and cultural climate, Gamson, 1988).

A History of Devaluation

Intense hostility and violence between groups may not be possible, intractable conflict is not likely to evolve, without a sharp differentiation between "us and them" and intense devaluation of "them." Varied concepts have been used to describe devaluation, and a number of distinctions have been made among its types. One scholar, while acknowledging the contribution of societal problems (difficult life conditions in our terminology) in Germany, has suggested that a special form of devaluation, eliminationist anti-Semitism, was *the* cause of the Holocaust (Goldhagen, 1996).

Profound devaluation is present in all genocides. Intense devaluation is especially likely to contribute to genocide if the devalued group does relatively well in terms of material well-being and status, as was the case with Armenians in Turkey, Jews in Germany, and Tutsis in Rwanda, their relative well-being intensifying hostility in the face of instigating conditions (Staub, 1989, 1996b, 1999a). However, while devaluation is centrally important, it is one of a variety of conditions in the generation of genocide, as well as in making a conflict intractable.

The differentiation between "us" and "them" (Tajfel, 1978; Brewer & Campbell, 1976) and ethnocentrism, the tendency to accept the ingroup and reject the outgroup (Sumner 1906), are common human tendencies (see also chapter 16). Ethnocentrism is one basis for the devaluation of another group and for its exclusion from the normal human community (Bar-Tal, 1990; Brewer, 1979). Devaluation of another group can become part of a group's culture in response to a variety of situations: due to the differentness of the other; a group becoming more powerful and using and exploiting the other, which has to be justified; a group intent to create a separate identity, a likely source of Christian anti-Semitism as Christians separated themselves from their Jewish origins; difficult life conditions leading to scapegoating; or conflict between groups (Staub, 1989, 1996b: Wistrich, 1999).

Bar-Tal (1989, 1990) has described *delegitimization.* as an extreme form of devaluation. It is an extreme negative categorization of a group, in five ways: *dehumanization* (e.g., savage, primitive, monster), *outcasting* (e.g., murderers, thieves, psychopaths), *trait characterization* (e.g., aggressors, idiots, parasites), use of *political labels* (e.g., Nazis, fascists, communists), and use of *group comparison* (e.g., Vandals or Huns). In essence, delegitimization suggests that a group violates basic human norms and values and denies its humanity, which allows violence against them (see also Bandura, 1999; Kelman, 1973; Opotow, 1990; Staub, 1989, 1990).

Indigenous groups have frequently been the object of extreme devaluation (Almaguer, 1994; Beuf, 1977; Forbes, 1964), because of differentness, justification of exploitation and bad treatment, and so on. The devaluation has made them easy targets for violence, including violence motivated by self-interest. Often the names of despised animals have been applied to them. Familiar examples include Native Americans in the United States (Almaguer, 1994; Beuf, 1977; Staub, 2000a) and in the Americas in general and black people in South Africa, where apartheid was justified by seeing black people as primitive, inferior, savage, and backward (Cornevin, 1980; Lever, 1978).

Devaluation, and labeling of an adversary group, play an essential function in intractable conflict (see Kelman 1997; Rieber, 1991). They help explain to group members why the conflict erupted, why it still continues, and why it is violent. They justify the violence and destruction inflicted on the rival group (Bar-Tal, 1990). Cecil (1993) and Hunter, Stringer, and Watson (1991) showed mutual delegitimization of Protestants and Catholics in Northern Ireland, and Bar-Tal and Teichman (in press) Arab delegitimization in the Israeli society.

In cases of intractable conflict, the other often comes to be seen as a mortal enemy and the identity of one's own group as partly defined by its enmity to the other. Staub has called this an ideology of antagonism. This creates the zero-sum psychology described earlier, in which a loss to the other is seen as gain to the self. The ideal vision of the world is one without the group that is identified as the enemy. Hutu power, a movement in Rwanda with a "Ten Commandments" that called for violent action against Tutsis, exemplifies such an ideology of antagonism (des Forges, 1999; Staub, 1999a).

Past Victimization and Collective Memory

Groups that have suffered great trauma, especially great harm and violence inflicted on them, are deeply affected (Montville, 1993; Staub, 1998a). Since individual identity is deeply rooted in group membership (Tajfel and Turner, 1979; Bar-Tal and Staub, 1997), this is true not only of direct survivors but also of members of groups who have not been physically present at the violent events (Staub, 1998a). Trauma, and especially intense victimization, diminishes people. Even if they consciously know that they are not at fault, at some level they tend to feel that something must be wrong with them as individuals (Herman, 1992; Pearlman and Saakvitne, 1995) or as members of groups (Staub, 1998a; Staub & Pearlman, 2001). Otherwise, how could such horrible things been done to them? Their self-worth is diminished, their feeling of vulnerability is greatly enhanced, people and the world look dangerous. Their sense of security in the world and trust in people, especially in other groups, is greatly impaired.

As a result, groups that have suffered severe persecution and violence and carry unhealed wounds are more likely to become perpetrators under certain conditions. When they face conflict, whether continuing conflict with the group that has inflicted violence on them or new conflict with another group, they focus on their own needs and have difficulty considering the needs of the other. Since threat and danger look greater to them, they are likely to react more intensely than is required by circumstance. They may strike out to defend themselves, even when self-defense is not necessary. Through such a process they may become perpetrators (Staub, 1998a). Or by their actions they may contribute to the development and escalation of intractable conflict and thus to vicious cycles of violence. The woundedness of Jews as well as Palestinians is likely to have contributed to the ongoing cycles of violence between them.

Past victimization of a group can lead to self-perception as a victim (Mack, 1990). Groups encode important experiences, especially extensive suffering, in their collective memory, which can maintain a sense of woundedness and past injustice through generations (Halbswachs, 1992; Connerton, 1989). Volkan (1997) suggests that groups tend to focus on a chosen trauma, that becomes an important guide for future acts. Serb violence in the course of the breakdown of Yugoslavia is one example of the role of past victimization and collective memory (see Glenny, 1992; Denich, 1994).

The traumatic collective memories are used to provide interpretation for and meaning to contemporary events and experiences (Connerton, 1989; Halbswachs, 1992; Kammen, 1991). In addition to insecurity, they can give rise to undue self-reliance, disregard of international rules, and violence as self-defense (Krystal, 1968; Pennebaker, Paez, & Rime, 1997). In extreme cases, past experiences may give rise to a siege mentality, a core societal belief that other groups have negative intentions toward the group, which stands alone in a hostile world (see Bar-Tal, 2000b). Russian society following the international intervention in a domestic war after the Bolshevik revolution in 1917 (Kennan, 1960) and Israeli society in the wake of anti-Semitism, the Holocaust (Liebman, 1978; Stein, 1978), and early Arab attacks seem examples of societies with such siege mentalities.

Strong Respect for Authority

For society to exist, there has to be respect for institutions and people in authority. But societies vary in their orientation to authority. Very strong respect for authority adds to the cultural potential for genocide (Staub,

1989; Kressel, 2002). People accustomed to follow seem to find it more difficult to stand on their own in the face of life problems or group conflict. They are likely to be more affected by them and to respond more by looking for leaders to follow and obey and by giving themselves over to a group. They are also less likely to oppose immoral, destructive policies and practices, allowing the evolution of violence to unfold. Finally, they are more likely to obey direct orders by authorities to harm others (Milgram, 1974).

Strong respect for authority may be part of the culture, and may be embodied in the hierarchical nature of institutions. For example, in Rwanda, authorities were appointed at many levels of society, starting with a small group of families in each village. The tradition of obedience to these authorities was an important reason for the participation by many members of the population in the killings during the genocide of 1994. People were ordered to kill at times as a form of customary communal labor (des Forges, 1999; Prunier, 1995; Staub, 1999a).

Monolithic, Nondemocratic Societies

The acceptance of varied beliefs, the free expression of views and public engagement with issues, and the access of all groups to the public domain makes it probable that there will be opposition to policies and actions that harm some group (Staub, 1989). This makes an evolution toward mass killing or genocide less likely. Pluralism also makes the transformation of conflict from one that is seemingly resolvable to one that is intractable less likely. Moreover, in repressive societies that are also traditional, great culture changes are especially difficult to integrate, thus frustrating basic needs (Staub, in press-a).

Research on democratic and nondemocratic societies has found that democracies are unlikely to engage in mass violence against a subgroup of their own population (Rummell, 1994, 1997). The greatest mass killings of the twentieth century have taken place in totalitarian societies, such as communist countries and Nazi Germany, and to a lesser extent in less restrictive, authoritarian societies. According to Rummel (1994, 1999; see also Charny, 1999; Pilisuk & Wong, 2002), the more absolute the power of a government and the elite associated with it, the more likely it is to engage in what he calls democide, the killing of masses of people in war, mass killing, or genocide. There are many reasons for this; one is that in such societies attempts to redress grievances often lead to violent responses. Mass killing and genocide are least likely in *mature* democracies (Staub, 1999a), with pluralistic cultures, and institutions of civic society that help maintain fully democratic systems. Weimar Germany, where this was not the case, collapsed in the face of intensely difficult life conditions. In Colombia, where democracy is shallow, there has been great violence between different segments of society. In Argentina, where elected governments were regularly replaced by the military, and differences between rich and poor were extreme, unsuccessful efforts to improve the life of less privileged groups led to terrorism, with mass killing by the government in response (Staub, 1989).

The Role of Leaders and Elites

One theme of this chapter has been that the combination of instigating conditions and culture have psychological effects that make groups of people inclined to violence against others. Especially when this combination exists, leaders and elites can and do play an important role in generating destructive processes. It is usually leaders who construct destructive ideologies. They call forth collective memories of past victimization. They create institutions that direct or perpetrate violence, such as government offices, channels of communication for propaganda, or paramilitary groups (Staub, 1999a). Rwanda is one of many places where such paramilitary groups were central in perpetrating genocide (des Forges, 1999).

A common view is that leaders do all this to gain followers, or strengthen their power and influence over followers (Allport, 1954), or to protect their position as members of elites (Sidanius & Pratto, 1998). However, leaders are also affected by the combination of culture and instigating conditions that create inclinations to blame and turn against others. In addition, groups so affected are more open to leaders who are inclined toward these destructive processes.

Some leaders may personally carry unhealed wounds from victimization their group has suffered. The parents of several Serb leaders, for example, General Mladic, the commander of the Serb army in Bosnia, were among those killed by Croats during World War II. This is likely to lead to an inclination for defensive violence, as described earlier. Thus destructive leadership can be based on the leaders' genuine feelings and beliefs, fulfilling their own basic needs in difficult times, or it can be self-interested manipulation by leaders, or some combination of the two (Staub, 1999a). Different preventive approaches may be required, depending on which it is (See also Gurr, 2001).

The Evolution of Increasing Violence and Intractable Conflict

Given instigating conditions and cultural preconditions, once violence by one group against another begins, without restraining forces such as active bystanders, an evolution is likely to follow. Individuals and groups learn by doing. They change as a result of their own actions. In the course of this evolution, conflict may become intractable, violence more intense. Violence by a dominant group or government may lead with "steps along a continuum of destruction" to genocide (Staub, 1989, in press-b).

Once violence begins, individuals and the whole group tend to justify their actions, not only to others but also to themselves. They explain their actions as due to the victims' blameworthy action or faulty character (Lerner, 1980). Their increasingly negative view of the victim and the "high" ideals of the ideology join to make new violence easier and more likely (Staub, 1989). Such an evolution has also been found in terrorist groups. They sometimes begin with political action, as for example the Baader-Meinfhof group in Germany, but as these seem ineffective, they turn to violence. Learning by doing and the dynamics within the group, for example members who strive for status by expressing more radical views, lead to increasing violence (McCauley & Segal, 1989).

As devaluation intensifies, the victim or enemy is progressively excluded from the moral and human realm (Opotaw, 1990; Staub, 1989, 1990) or, in another terminology, from the realm of moral obligation (Fein, 1979, 1993). As violence intensifies, there is often a reversal of morality, so that killing members of the other group becomes the right, moral thing to do. Killers may come to see themselves as able and willing to kill to fulfill higher ideals (Staub, 1989).

Following Milgram's work on obedience to authority, Zukier (1994) noted the role in such an evolution of authorities who order acts of violence. As people engage in these acts, the personal changes just described follow. Browning (1992) described a process of desensitization and personal change in the members of a reserve police battalion who were sent to Poland to kill Jews. But people who are ordered to engage in such violence, or volunteer for it, often do not start from scratch. The reserve police officers had engaged in violence in the course of their police work, in part preparing them for this greater violence (Staub, 1992, 2001c). Some of them had also engaged in previous violence dictated by the system (Rhodes, 2002). When they were first ordered in Poland to kill large numbers of people, many later reported to Browning that they were greatly distressed, even felt ill. Some said they did not act. But over time, they became efficient, calm, and dedicated killers. Support by their superiors in their "difficult" task, praise, being part of a like-minded group, and learning by doing helped them along. (However, in the view of Goldhagen, 1996, they were dedicated, cold-blooded killers from the start.)

Changes in societies include changes in societal beliefs, as well as in norms of conduct, so that previously unacceptable actions toward the enemy or victim group become normal, even desirable. Institutions change, or new institutions are created that serve discrimination, conflict, and violence (Staub, 1989). Such evolution may take place over a long historical period. Cultures retain memories of historical events, including their own past actions and collective memories that are created out of them. Views of and orientation to another group may become part of the deep structure of a culture. In response to new instigating conditions, the evolution of increasing violence may resume. For example, both in Turkey against the Armenians and in Rwanda against the Tutsis (des Forges, 1999), mass killings were followed by long periods without violence, and then the resumption of even more intense violence, genocide (Staub, 1999a). To prevent renewed violence, active efforts that address the influences leading to violence are required, rather than the mere passage of time.

Ethos of Intractable Conflict

In the course of intractable conflict, societal beliefs evolve that create an "ethos of conflict" (Bar-Tal, 2000b; or culture of conflict, Ross, 1998). This helps people adapt to and cope with their threatening and difficult situation but also feeds the violence. It fulfills basic needs, especially for comprehension of an uncertain reality (Berkowitz, 1968; Maddi, 1971; Reykowski, 1982) and a positive identity, including a view of the group as moral. It promotes devotion to the society and country, rationalizes harming the enemy, and encourages readiness for personal sacrifice. Bar-Tal has suggested *eight societal beliefs as themes in an ethos of conflict* (see Bar-Tal, 1998), as follows.

1. *About the just nature of group goals.* These beliefs justify goals that are challenged in the conflict. They show the supreme importance of these goals, stressing that failure to achieve them may threaten the existence of the group. For example, the Serbs held societal beliefs in the 1990s about the justice and importance of keeping Yugoslavia as one political entity (Glenny, 1992; White, 1996).
2. *About the negative image of the opponent.* These beliefs, which usually exist even before the conflict becomes intractable, or even an active conflict, intensify (Bar-Tal, 1990; Stagner, 1967; White, 1970).
3. *About positive self-image.* Societies in intractable conflicts develop and hold beliefs that maintain and enhance a positive self-image (Frank, 1967; Stagner, 1967; Sande, Goethals, Ferrari, & Worth, 1989). These include skills, virtues, positive actions performed in the past, possibly moral and heroic, and positive contributions to humankind and civilization. For example, during the Vietnam war Americans emphasized their positive characteristics as part of the justification for the war (White, 1970).
4. *About victimization.* A society in intractable conflict comes to believe that it is victimized by the opponent.
5. *About security.* These beliefs outline the necessary conditions for personal safety and national security, which often lead to intense violence against the other (Klare & Thomas, 1991; Ney & Lynn-Jones, 1988). Security becomes a central societal value in times of intractable conflict. Bar-Tal, Jacobson, and Klieman (1998) described security beliefs in the Israeli society as a result of the Arab-Israeli conflict as master symbols and determinative factors in many decisions and policies that contributed to the violence (See also Brecher, 1972; Yaniv, 1993).

6. *About patriotism.* Patriotism, defined as the attachment by group members to their group and the country in which they reside, is of crucial importance in times of intractable conflict. Patriotism maintains loyalty and mobilizes group members for action (see Reykowski, 1997; Rose, 1985; Stern, 1995). People are asked to sacrifice their own needs to help achieve society's goals (Somerville, 1981). Those who sacrifice their lives are glorified as heroes. A blind adherence to the group is demanded, while constructive patriotism, questioning the group's or leaders' policies and practices, is not tolerated (Staub, 1997; Schatz, Staub, & Levine, 1999). The emphasis on patriotism in Israeli society in the course of the Arab-Israeli conflict served the functions of solidarity, strengthening identity, loyalty, mobilization, and the willingness to sacrifice (Ben Amos & Bar-Tal, in press).

7. *About unity.* Beliefs about common goals, values, origins, history, and tradition emphasize the importance of maintaining unity by ignoring internal discords and disagreements in the face of external threat. They highlight that internal conflict can harm the common cause.

8. *About peace.* These beliefs hold peace as the ultimate goal and describe the society as peace loving. The presentation of peace as a supreme goal is usually done in utopian, general, and vague terms, like a dream or wish, without specifying the concrete meaning of peace or ways to achieve it.

The ethos of conflict is a prism through which group members look at the world, collect new information, interpret their experiences, and make decisions about their courses of action (e.g., Ross, 1995). It is maintained by societal, political, and cultural institutions and transmitted to new generations by the educational system. It is used to justify the society's policies, decisions, and action. While it makes better adaptation to the intractable conflict possible, it also fuels the conflict and violence. These societal beliefs seem to be present to some degree in the United States in the wake of the 9/11/01 attacks, perhaps to different extents in the public mind, the media, and in political processes.

The Role of Bystanders

The passivity, and at times complicity, of bystanders, witnesses who are in a position to act, is of great importance in allowing the evolution of the influences that lead to violence, and of violence itself (Staub, 1989, 1999a). Usually, *internal bystanders*, members of a population who themselves are not part of an ideological movement or perpetrator group, remain passive in the face of increasing enmity and violence. As part of the same group they are also affected by instigating conditions and culture, such as devaluation of the victim group.

External Bystanders

Outside groups and nations, also tend to remain passive, or even support perpetrators. Sometimes they do this actively, as the United States and other countries supported Iraq before its invasion of Kuwait, even while Iraq was using chemical weapons against its Kurdish population (Staub 1991). At other times they do it by going on with business as usual, as the world did during the 1930s in relation to Nazi Germany. For example, U.S. corporations (Simpson, 1993) were busy doing business in Germany. Even the passivity of bystanders encourages perpetrators, who take passivity for approval (Taylor, 1983). Early action, which is rare, has the greatest potential to inhibit the evolution of violence without the use of violence. As the resurgent Israeli-Palestinian conflict became increasingly violent starting in 2000, the United States, the potentially most influential bystander, did very little (see also Powers, 2001, 2002; Staub, 2000b).

At times, violence in intractable conflict is limited because of the behavior of bystanders (Staub, 2001a). In Northern Ireland, under British home rule, Britain took both police actions and other steps in trying to stop violence (Cairns & Darby, 1998). In the Israeli-Palestinian conflict, apart from actual wars and before the renewal of violence in 2000, the relationship to the United States, as well as the voice of varied views and parties in a pluralistic, democratic society, have exerted influence in Israel. In both coflicts, segments of the population worked to bring together small groups across the divide. The experience in both cases, perhaps especially Northern Ireland, suggests that while intractable conflict is volatile, under special circumstances it may become institutionalized at a certain level, just as discrimination against another group can be.

▲ Halting and Preventing Mass Violence

Halting Potential Mass Killing or Genocide

When violence against a group has already begun on a broad scale, or intense discrimination and limited violence indicate great danger, halting its further evolution becomes imperative. Usually at that point only powerful nations, or the international community, can exert sufficient influence. In the past, this has rarely happened. It did happen in Bosnia, after years of hesitation and minimal action. The intense military response in Kosovo was the result of the absence of early action as well as the lack of experience in constructively responding to such situations (Staub, 1999a). The later that bystanders act, the more difficult it is to halt violence without military action. The need for military action can probably be averted in most instances by early intervention—a proposition that needs to be tested by appropriate, committed actions by bystander nations.

The first stage of response, if violence is still limited, may be private communication with leaders. Autocratic leaders do not want to seem weak in the eyes of their followers and may refuse to cooperate in face of public demands. Private communications may include warnings, specific demands for changes in policies and practices, and offers of help. The engagement with leaders should be carried out with sensitivity to the culture, political processes, and psychological wounds of the group as well as of the leaders themselves (Staub, 1999a), which requires special training of emissaries. Initial success in communication should be followed by mediation and conflict resolution, economic help, and continued engagement with leaders. At times of crisis, the involvement of high-level leaders of countries important to the potential perpetrators may be necessary for success. This requires that such leaders take risks, since their efforts may be unsuccessful.

If ineffective, the second stage ought to be public condemnation and public warning of specific consequences. If this is ineffective, various sanctions should follow. Sanctions that affect the whole population may in the short run be counterproductive, with leaders using them to blame the outside world and to create increased group cohesion (Leatherman et al., 1999). Over the long run they can be successful, as according to many analysts they were in South Africa and to some extent in the former Yugoslavia. However, they can also create great suffering in the population, as they did in Iraq, without accomplishing their aims. Mixed goals may contribute to their failure, when in addition to aiming to stop human rights violations and violence they aim at removing leaders (Staub, 1999a).

Targeted sanctions aim at leaders and the elite (Carnegie Commission, 1997). They include confiscating foreign bank accounts and boycotts of goods of special interest to the elite. Sanctions that are responsive to specific circumstances, are flexible, and are changed in response to new conditions seem the best policy. As the last resort, in the face of intense violence, military action is required. Many have argued for the need of a UN force (Fein, 1994). If instead of a peacekeeping force with instructions not to fight, even a small fighting force had been available and active in Rwanda in 1994, the genocide almost certainly could have been prevented (Gourevich, 1998; Powers, 2001, 2002).

A tool that may help prevent future genocides has emerged in recent times: the prosecution of perpetrators outside their country, through ad hoc international tribunals and the newly created International Criminal Court. In addition, countries have begun to pass laws that enable them to try people accused of human rights violations elsewhere. Britain detained General Pinochet of Chile; Belgium tried Rwandese nuns for collaboration in the murder of Tutsis in Rwanda in 1994. While the international prosecution of perpetrators is important, only by addressing the varied forces that lead to mass killing or intractable conflict can intense violence be prevented.

Preventing Violence and Transforming Conflict

The presence and intensity of the influences that were identified as contributing to genocide or intractable conflict can be assessed and used to predict the likelihood of later violence. (Lundt, 1996; Staub, 1998b). Evidence of evolution, of increase in hostility and harm-doing, is an especially important indicator. External bystanders can have a positive role in affecting internal processes in a society involved in prevention and conflict transformation and in developing constructive leadership (Staub, 1999a; see also Ackermann, 2000).

However, bystanders—governments, international institutions, nongovernmental organizations (NGOs)—tend to become concerned about violence and conflict, if at all, only in response to already intense problems. While a great deal of recent attention has focused on early warning (Gurr & Harff, 1996; Harff, 1996), there is no effective system of early warning or of the use of early warning to activate a response (Staub, 1999a). Leatherman and colleagues (1999, p. 206) suggest that each situation requires the building of a coalition of many parties for prevention. Such coalitions are fluid and differ from case to case, reflecting the perception of interests by major powers and leading regional states. But the building of such a coalition requires time, and when states are disinterested, it may not happen.

It seems essential to build a system within governments of high-level institutions specifically charged with early warning and the *activation* of preventive actions. These institutions can connect with NGOs and international organizations. Social activism by civic groups may be essential to bring this about. It is also essential to influence the way these institutions function, to add psychological knowledge and skills to the practice of prevention, as delineated below (Staub, 1998b, 1999a).

Processes of Prevention

Leaders can help overcome devaluation and promote the positive image of an outgroup by both words and actions. For example, Richard Nixon did this by initiating friendly talk with Chinese leaders; Arafat and Rabin changed attitudes by shaking hands. After the Oslo agreement, support for suicide bombers declined among Palestinians (McCauley, in press). Whether beginning changes deepen depends on further events. The media has a powerful potential to create positive change (see Roach, 1994). However, the media often magnifies hostility. Sympathetic portrayal of the other group, its values, culture, and goals and the ways of life of its members, can promote positive attitudes.

Instead of scapegoating and divisive ideologies, in response to difficult life conditions, leaders can generate a vision of and plans for the future that include all groups, in shared efforts to improve life. The United States led by Roosevelt during the Great Depression is an example. However, societal problems in that case were not as great as in most genocidal situations. As in the Camp David agreement, the handshake between Rabin and Arafat, and the Oslo agreement, outsiders can play an important role.

Structural changes, such as changes in the economic situation of particular groups, are important. In Northern Ireland, greater economic opportunities and greater material well-being of the Catholic minority has contributed to the possibilities of peace. Enlightened elements of British home rule have fostered this change (Cairns & Darby, 1998). The United Nations has stressed economic development as a way to reduce group hostility (Carnegie Commission, 1997). Improving the life of less-privileged groups in a society, as well as reducing inequalities, are important in ameliorating conflict. However, in the short term, economic development can contribute to problems. Already privileged groups may be the primary beneficiaries, increasing a sense of injustice (Gordon, 1994). Economic development and modernization also create profound social changes, with attendant psychological effects. In addition, when conflict is already entrenched and groups have inflicted violence on each other, psychological changes are required for overcoming hostility. But without structural changes, psychological changes may not be possible to bring about or maintain.

Crosscutting relations (Deutsch, 1973; Staub, 1989), deep engagement by members of hostile groups with each other, can make a significant difference. Both in Northern Ireland (Cairns & Darby, 1998) and until the year 2000 in Israel, community organizations bringing members from the two sides together probably significantly limited the extent of violence. In Macedonia, journalists belonging to the different ethnic groups have joined to write stories about the lives of people in each group, publishing them in the newspapers of each of the groups (Manoff, 1996).

Social psychologists have long stressed the importance of contact and attempted to specify conditions under which contact needs to occur to lessen devaluation and hostility. Superficial contact, living in the same neighborhood, does not help. For contact to be effective, it has to involve significant engagement with the other (Deutch, 1973, Pettigrew, 1997, 1998; Staub, 1989). In addition, various conditions have been noted as necessary for contact to have positive effects, such as equality among those engaged with each other, the support of authorities, and others (Allport, 1954; Cook, 1970).

But these conditions often do not exist in the larger world. Instead, they may have to be created as processes within the interacting group: equality within the group, third parties facilitating the interaction and supporting the process in place of authorities, and so on (Staub, 2002). In a study in Northern Ireland, Cairns and Hewstone (2000; described in Lundwell, 2001) found that contact between Protestant and Catholic students reduced anxiety and prejudice when group affiliation was made explicit and students kept it in mind during the interaction.

▶ *Reconciliation*

Conflict resolution approaches, such as negotiation, bargaining, mediation, and arbitration have been important in preventing escalation or continuation of violence and in conflict transformation. Sometimes these bring about an agreement signed by the parties, representing a resolution and symbolizing the formal ending of the conflict (e.g., Bercovitch, 1995; Burton, 1987; Deutsch, 1973; Kriesberg, 1992; Ross, 1993). These processes are discussed in chapter 10. In other cases, as in Rwanda, violence may be stopped by the military defeat of the perpetrator group.

An end of active conflict or violence, even if it is the outcome of formal peace agreements, does not mean the start of genuinely peaceful relations (e.g., Knox & Quirk, 2000; Lederach, 1997; Lipschutz, 1998). Negotiated solutions may to some degree satisfy the leaders and some segments of a society. But some members of each group may not accept them, and even those who do often continue to hold beliefs and views that may reignite violence. In many cases a reconciliation process seems essential to prevent continued cycles of violence and allow the building of stable, peaceful relations between two groups after intractable conflict or mass violence (Ackermann, 1994; Arthur, 1999; Asmal, Asmal, & Roberts., 1997; Bar-Tal, 2000a; Chadha, 1995; Gardner-Feldman, 1999; Kriesberg, 1998a; Lederach, 1997; Lipschutz, 1998; Wilmer, 1998).

Reconciliation is both a process and an outcome. Its proximate aims are to bring about psychological changes in the orientation of members of groups toward each other, in their understanding of the past, in their vision of a joint future, and in who they are in relation to each other. Reconciliation as a naturally occurring process is usually slow. In many situations it requires active efforts to facilitate it and to overcome social, cultural, and psychological obstacles to it.

The nature of the process and the outcomes depend on characteristics of the groups and their circumstances (see examples in Whittaker, 1999). Are the groups part of the same political entity, so that they will continue to live together, as in Nicaragua, South Africa, or Rwanda, or are they separate political entities, as in Israel and Egypt? Was violence perpetrated by one group, or was it mutual?

Peace-making techniques have traditionally focused on the structural aspects of restoring or forming relations between former antagonists (see Charif, 1994; Lederach, 1997; Lipschutz, 1998; Murray & Greer, 1999; Wilmer, 1998). It was assumed that equality in the interaction of parties, together with economic and political restructuring, leads to cooperative links, which stabilize peaceful relations (Ackermann, 1994; Gardner-Feldman, 1999; Weiwen & Deshingkar, 1995). The literature focused on such structural elements as maintaining channels of communication and consultation between the leaders and representatives of the groups; reducing threat and tension by disarmament and demilitarization; developing free and open trade; cooperative economic ventures; inclusion of all groups in the power system; establishment of structural equality and justice; human and civil rights and democratic political governance; the creation of equal opportunity and redistribution of wealth (Arnson, 1999; Corm, 1994; Kriesberg, 1998a; Lederach, 1998; Murray & Greer, 1999; Wilmer, 1998; Zalaquett, 1999).

Unfortunately, these approaches do not guarantee lasting peaceful relations (Arnson, 1999; Arthur, 1999; Kriesberg, 1998a; Simpson, 1997; and see Wilmer, 1998, on the former Yugoslavia). Over time they might promote significant reconciliation and lasting peace, especially if they foster deep contact between group members in the context of joint efforts, but often violence reemerges before this has happened. Moreover, these approaches are themselves impeded by the still-existing feelings of hostility.

We define reconciliation as mutual acceptance by members of hostile or previously hostile groups of each other and the societal structures and psychological processes directly involved in the development and maintenance of such acceptance (Staub, 1998a; Staub & Pearlman, 2001). Genuine acceptance means trust in and positive attitude toward the other, and sensitivity to and consideration of the other party's needs and interests (Bar-Tal & Bennink, in press). Given where the parties usually start, these ideal outcomes are difficult to achieve. Reconciliation is a process that moves participants toward these outcomes (Staub & Pearlman, 2001), usually with regressions along the way (see Bar-Tal, in press-b).

Elements of Reconciliation

Reconciliation requires basic psychological changes in large segments of both groups (Asmal et al., 1997; Bar-Tal, 2000a; Kriesberg, 1998a; Lederach, 1997). A distinction may be made between elements or building blocks of reconciliation and methods to bring them about. Elements that have been proposed include truth and justice (see under methods), healing, forgiveness, and shared views of history.

Shared Collective Memory

During the mass killing or conflict, the parties had divergent and often opposing views about the conflict and the history of their relations. Creating a common view seems important in reconciliation (Hayes, 1998; Hayner, 1999; Kopstein, 1997; Lederach, 1997; Volkan, 1998; Whittaker, 1999), although what its nature should be is not necessarily clear (see Asmal et al., 1997; Bar-Tal, 2000a; Kelman, 1999; Marrow, 1999). We will call this common view a *shared collective memory* (Staub & Pearlman, 2002). Its formation requires establishing a shared truth (Staub & Pearlman, 2001, 2002) and the parties accepting this truth about the past (Asmal et al., 1997; Hayes, 1998; Lederach, 1998; Norval, 1998, 1999). The two conflicting narratives of the past (Hayner, 1999; Kopstein, 1997; Norval, 1999), which support the continuation of the conflict and serve as obstacles to peace-making (Bar-Tal, in press-a), are to be recognized and reconciled.

For this to happen, each group must admit and take responsibility for its role in creating the conflict and engaging in violence. One avenue to this is a process of negotiation, in which the story of the two groups is synchronized and a new narrative is generated (Asmal et al., 1997; Hayes, 1998; Norval, 1998). With time, this new historical account can replace the reigning collective memory. One example of such negotiation was the Franco-German commission of historians that by the 1950s had critically scrutinized the myths of hereditary enmity between the French and German peoples and revised the existing history textbooks. As a final product the commission provided new accounts of the history of the two nations (Willis, 1965). However, such negotiations are usually impossible when wounds are fresh and hurt and anger still intense. Other processes, such as healing, must precede them. In Rwanda, a group of leaders has strongly affirmed the importance of a shared collective memory but regarded it as an ideal that may not be possible to achieve, at least at this time (Staub & Pearlman, 2002).

Healing, Forgiveness, and Reconciliation

Many scholars argue that the psychological wounds that result from years of violence, the grief, sorrow, and sense of victimhood, as well as anger and the will to revenge, must be perceived and acknowledged by outsiders (Staub, 1998a), including the other party (Asmal et al., 1997; Kriesberg, 1998a; Ross, 1995; Wilmer, 1998). Others suggest that the process of reconciliation, to be effective, requires collective healing, and even forgiveness of the adversary's misdeeds (Arthur, 1999; Hayner, 1999; Lederach, 1998; Staub & Pearlman, 2001).

Acknowledging a group's pain and suffering, helping its members relive their painful experiences under safe conditions, supporting them in mourning their losses, validating their experience of pain and grief, and offering empathy and support are all essential elements of healing (Lederach, 1998; Minow, 1998; Montville, 1993; Staub, 1998a, Staub & Pearlman, 2001). Healing in turn creates a space where forgiveness can be offered and accepted (see Shriver, 1995). Forgiveness is of special importance in cases of unequal responsibility, when one party is seen as responsible for the outbreak or maintenance of the conflict or violence. Forgiveness symbolizes a psychological departure from the past (Lederach, 1998; Norval, 1999).

Some scholars see collective reconstruction of the past as a primary element in reconciliation and regard healing and forgiveness, especially in severely divided societies like South Africa and Northern Ireland, as very hard, if not impossible, to achieve (Gardner-Feldman, 1999; Hayes, 1998; Horowitz, 1993). Hayes (1998) argues that reconciliation is not about the forgiveness of the dreadful acts committed under apartheid but about how all will participate in building a new society (p. 33).

It is important to distinguish between healing and forgiveness. Following extreme violence, the latter is difficult to contemplate, and its very nature is not well understood. The timing, degree, and object of forgiveness (Is it the perpetrators who are to be forgiven, or more likely members of the perpetrator group who are not themselves perpetrators? see Staub & Pearlman, 2001) are all important to explore. While forgiveness adds to the possibility of reconciliation, it is healing from the past that seems primary. However, forgiveness does seem inherent in full reconciliation, the genuine acceptance of the other. Understanding the influences that have led to the perpetrators' action, however horrible, contributes to healing (see below) and may be an avenue as well to acceptance of the other.

Healing from past victimization is essential to prevent new violence. As noted earlier, without healing, when groups continue to live together, anger and the desire for revenge can lead to violence by former victims. In addition, without healing, former victims may respond to threat in ways that lead them to become perpetrators of violence, even against groups other than the one that has harmed them. Healing by perpetrators is also necessary. The perpetrators may have been themselves wounded, this leading to their actions. In addition, direct perpetrators, or even members of the perpetrator group, are likely to be wounded by the extreme violence that they themselves or their group have engaged in. Their actions, and their own defensive reactions to them, limit their capacity for empathy or guilt and therefore their ability to later reconcile. Instead, even if they are stopped or defeated or an agreement brings the intractable conflict to a halt, they tend to continue to blame their prior victims or adversaries (Staub, 1998a; Staub & Pearlman, 2001).

Without some healing, which helps affirm the self and increase trust in other people and the world, it may be impossible for reconciliation to begin. Without the beginning of reconciliation, especially when previously hostile groups continue to live together, healing, which requires some degree of safety, might not proceed (Staub, 1998a, 2000a; Staub & Pearlman, 2001). It is also likely that the creation of a shared history, a new collective memory, requires prior healing.

Methods of Reconciliaton

A variety of methods to facilitate reconciliation have been proposed (see examples in Bronkhorst, 1995; Whittaker, 1999). Some are part of formal policies while others are carried out informally. We will describe several methods, especially those that can be used in situations of genocide, mass killing, and intractable conflict, for intrastate but also for interstate reconciliation

Apology

Apology offered to another group accepts responsibility for harm done to it and appeals to the victims for forgiveness (Scheff, 1994). It implies a commitment to the pursuit of truth and justice (Asmal et al., 1997; Gardner-Feldman, 1999; Kriesberg, 1998a; Norval, 1999). Apology creates a psychological shift in victims that fosters healing and also forgiveness. The Czech-German Declaration on Mutual Relations and Their Future Development, signed in January 1997, is an example of mutual apology. Germany accepted the responsibility for the events of World War II and expressed regret for the sufferings and wrongs brought on the Czech people, while the Czechs expressed regret for the suffering and wrongs done to Germans expelled from the Sudeten Area after the war (Handl, 1997). As in this case, it requires time and probably prior healing to enable groups to apologize.

Truth and Reconciliation Commissions

These commissions explore what has actually happened. They expose violation of human and civil rights, discrimination, and violence by formal institutions of the state, groups, and individuals (Asmal et al., 1997; Kaye, 1997; Kriesberg, 1998a; Liebenberg & Zegeye, 1998). In recent years, variations on such commissions have been undertaken in South Africa, Chile, Argentina, El Salvador, Honduras, Uruguay, and Rwanda. Among them, the South African Truth and Reconciliation Commission (TRC) has received the most attention (Asmal et al., 1997; Chirwa, 1997; De la Rey & Owens, 1998; Hayes, 1998; Hamber, 1998; Liebenberg & Zegeye, 1998; Norval, 1998).

Establishing the truth, and thereby acknowledging the victims' suffering, helps them heal. Documenting the actions of perpetrators makes it less likely that they will feel, or claim to have been, the victims. It also provides the basis for a collective history that takes everyone's role into consideration (Staub & Pearlman, 2001, 2002). However, the truth is often complex and difficult to establish.

Public Trials

These provide the opportunity to establish the truth, acknowledge the victims' suffering, fulfill a deep-seated desire for retribution, and satisfy the need for justice. By laying the responsibility for crimes on particular individuals, such trials reduce the collective responsibility of the group to which the perpetrators belong. The punishment of perpetrators may help prevent the recurrence of mass violence, as it shows that criminals can be found, tried, and punished (Kriesberg, 1998a; Kritz, 1996; Liebenberg & Zegeye,

1998). It may help satisfy the basic needs of victims for security, positive identity, and a meaningful comprehension of reality. The Nuremberg tribunals, the War Crimes Tribunal set up to try perpetrators from the former Yugoslavia and Rwanda, and the permanent International Criminal Court established in 2002 are intended, in part, to serve these functions.

Payment of Reparations

The offer of reparation indicates admission of guilt and regret on the part of the perpetrator (see Shriver, 1995). Its acceptance may be a step by victims toward a readiness to reconcile. An example is the compensation paid to Czech victims by the German government for their suffering during the German occupation of 1939–45 (Handl, 1997; Kopstein, 1997). The improvement of the economic condition of people impoverished in the course of violence against their group is an important contributor to a feeling of justice and openness to reconciliation (Gibson, in press).

Education

Education is an important avenue toward reconciliation (Asmal et al., 1997; Calleja, 1994; Chetkow-Yanoov, 1986; Gordon, 1994). It refers mostly to peace education in the schools. However, it can also involve fostering among adults an understanding of the roots of the violence (Staub, Pearlman, Hagengimana, & Gubin, 2002; see below). Peace education aims to affect knowledge, perceptions, feelings, attitudes, and motives (Salomon & Nevo, 2002). To be effective it must include both instruction and experiential learning (Staub, 2002). Both require the training of teachers. The former requires setting educational objectives and the preparation of a curriculum. Experiential learning requires the development of a climate in schools (Bar-Tal, 2002; Bjerstetd, 1988, 1993; Burns & Aspelagh, 1996; Harris, 1988; Hicks, 1988; Reardon, 1988; Staub, 2002, in press-b) involving positive relationship between students and teachers and among peers. It requires the creation of classroom and school communities, and participation by students in a system that promotes positive attitudes toward people in general and toward people in the other group if they are present, and feelings of responsibility for taking action in behalf of others and, by extension, in behalf of peace (Staub, 1996a, 2002, in press-b). Genuine peace education requires the kind of socialization of children that develops inclusive caring, caring for people beyond one's own group, including a formerly devalued group (Staub, 2002, in press-a, in press-b).

In South America's conflict-ridden societies, peace education addresses issues of human rights and the prevention of structural violence and economic inequality (Garcia, 1984). In Northern Ireland, peace education employs Mutual Understanding programs that aim to create genuine cultures of peace in the Protestant and Catholic school systems (Duffy, 2000). In Japan it deals with the atrocities carried out by the Japanese during War World II and with the meaning of apology ((Murakami, 1992).

Joint Projects

As noted earlier, joint projects can develop links between members of two groups. The projects can involve elites and professionals, as well as the broad community. They provide an opportunity for personal encounters through which past opponents can form personal relations (Brown, 1988; Chadha, 1995; Chetkow-Yanoov, 1986; Kriesberg, 1998a; Pettigrew, 1997, 1998; Volpe, 1998). The more they lead to deep engagement, under positive conditions, the more effective they are likely to be in overcoming past hostility (Deutch, 1973; Pettigrew, 1997; Staub, 1989). In addition, the joint projects may create interdependence, common goals and outcomes that benefit the members of both groups.

Joint projects can take many forms. For example, in the French-German reconciliation process, a project of town twinning between 1950 and 1962 formed 125 partnerships between French and German towns. By 1989, this project had expanded to include over 1,300 towns and went beyond towns to the establishment of twin relations between secondary schools and universities (Ackermann, 1994).

Healing, Forgiveness and Reconciliation in the Real World: An "Intervention" in Rwanda

We will briefly describe a practical intervention to promote healing, forgiveness, and reconciliation in Rwanda in the aftermath of the genocide, together with an experimental evaluation of its effectiveness (Staub, 2000a; Staub & Pearlman, 2001, 2002; Staub et al., 2002).

Healing requires engagement with traumatic experience, with support and empathy from other people. It requires reconnecting with other people, which can happen in part through such support and empathy (Herman, 1992; Pearlman & Saakvitne, 1995; Staub, 1998a). People talking about their experiences in small groups and receiving support from each other can further healing and prepare the way for reconciliation, especially when it is possible to have members of both groups included. This was one element of the training used in Rwanda. People talked about the killing of their loved ones and how they themselves survived. They talked about coming from mixed families, hiding during the genocide because of a Tutsi mother and being seen as member of the perpetrator group after the genocide because of a Hutu father. The provided empathy and support for each other.

The training also included psychoeducational elements, brief lectures followed by extensive discussion. The topics included the effects of trauma on individuals, to help participants understand their own experience, and paths to healing. It also included learning about how genocide originates (see Staub, 1989, 1999a, as well as this chapter) with examples from other genocides and mass killings. Participants themselves effectively applied the conception of the origins of genocide to Rwanda.

Tutsi participants seemed to feel humanized: if genocide has also happened at other places, and tragic and horrible as it is, if it is an understandable human processes, than what happened in Rwanda does not exclude them from the human realm. In addition, considering the forces that operate in leading perpetrators to their actions seemed to create some shift in their attitude toward perpetrators. Participants also said that if they can understand the roots of genocide, they can take preventive action.

Interventions intended to promote reconciliation, such as dialogue and conflict resolution in small groups, are rarely evaluated, and when they are the evaluation is primarily anecdotal (Ross & Rothman, 1999). A formal evaluation of this intervention was done, not with participants, but with people once removed. The participants in the training worked for local NGOs that worked with groups in the community. Some of them subsequently worked with newly created groups, for two hours twice a week for three weeks, *integrating* the approach used in the training with their traditional approach. Other facilitators who did not receive the training worked with newly created groups using their *traditional* approach. Participants in these groups had measures of trauma experiences, trauma symptoms, and a newly created measure of "other orientation" administered before the training, immediately afterward and two months later. People in control groups received no training but had these measures administered to them about the same time. The groups had both Hutu and Tutsi members.

The trauma symptoms of the participants in the integrated group decreased from the first to the third administration and in comparison to the other groups. Their orientation to members of the other ethnic group became more positive both from the first to the last administration and in comparison to the participants in the traditional and control groups. The increase in positive orientation consisted of seeing the genocide as having had complex origins, expressing willingness to work with the other group for important goals such as a peaceful future, and "conditional forgiveness," the expression of willingness to forgive if members of the other group acknowledged their actions and apologized (Staub, 2000a; Staub & Pearlman, 2001; Staub et al., 2002).

In summary, there are different methods to promote the process of psychological reconciliation, as well as the specific elements that contribute to it. For example, healing can take place through testimonials, commemoration, and ceremonies in large group settings, which promote engagement with experience and can provide support. However, testimonials and ceremonies have to be the right kind. Otherwise they may maintain woundedness, as the commemorations of the battle that the Serbs lost to Turkey in the fourteenth century apparently did (Leatherman et al., 1999). For healing and reconciliation to occur, commemoration has to connect people and point to a shared, hopeful future (Staub & Pearlman, 2001).

The more the processes of reconciliaton described here are supported by policies and practices of the institutions of the state(s) and of the leadership, the more effective are they likely to be. The cognitive and emotional changes of reconciliation require a combination of methods. The ideal combination probably depends on the nature of conflict and magnitude of mass violence, the extent to which one side or both sides to the violence are responsible for its outbreak and for misdeeds performed, the preceding history of relations between the groups, the culture of the groups involved, the availability of economic resources, the involvement of the international community, and so on. An important task is to develop knowledge about what methods are most useful under particular conditions.

▶ References

Ackermann, A. (1994). Reconciliation as a peace-building process in post-war Europe: The Franco-German case. *Peace and Change, 19*, 229–250.

Ackermann, A. (2000). *Making peace prevail.* Syracuse, NY: Syracuse University Press.

Allport, G. W. (1954). *The nature of prejudice.* Reading, MA: Addison-Wesley.

Almaguer, T. (1994). *Racial fault lines: The historical origins of white supremacy in California.* Berkeley: University of California Press.

Almond, G. A., & Verba, S. (1963). *The civic culture: Political attitudes and democracy in five nations.* Boston: Little, Brown.

Arnson, C. J. (1999). Conclusion: Lessons learned in comparative perspective. In C. J. Arnson (Ed.), *Comparative peace processes in Latin America* (pp. 447–463). Stanford: Stanford University Press.

Arthur, P. (1999). The Anglo-Irish peace process: Obstacles to reconciliation. In R. L. Rothstein (Ed.), *After the peace: Resistance and reconciliation* (pp. 85–109). Boulder: Lynne Rienner.

Asmal, K., Asmal, L., & Roberts, R. S. (1997). *Reconciliation through truth: A reckoning of apartheid's criminal governance.* Capetown, South Africa: David Phillips.

Azar, E. E. (1990). *The management of protracted social conflict.* Hampshire, England: Dartmouth.

Bandura, A. (1999). Moral disengagement in the perpetration of inhumanities. *Personality and Social Psychological Review, 3*, 193–209.

Bar-Tal, D. (1989). Delegitimization: The extreme case of stereo-typing and prejudice. In D. Bar-Tal, C. Graumann, A. W. Kruglanski, & W. Stroebe (Eds.), *Stereotyping and prejudice: Changing conceptions* (pp. 169–188). New York: Springer-Verlag.

Bar-Tal, D. (1990). Causes and consequences of delegitimization: Models of conflict and ethnocentrism. *Journal of Social Issues, 46*(1), 65–81.

Bar-Tal, D. (1998). Societal beliefs in times of intractable conflict: The Israeli case. *International Journal of Conflict Management, 9*, 22–50.

Bar-Tal, D. (2000a). From intractable conflict through conflict resolution to reconciliation: Psychological analysis. *Political Psychology, 21*, 351–365.

Bar-Tal, D. (2000b). *Shared beliefs in a society: Social psychological analysis*. Thousand Oaks, CA: Sage.

Bar-Tal, D. (2001). Why does fear override hope in societies engulfed by intractable conflict, as it does in the Israeli society? *Political Psychology, 22,* 601–627.

Bar-Tal, D. (2002). The elusive nature of peace education. In G. Salomon & B. Nevo (Eds.), *Peace education: The concept, principles and practice around the world* (pp. 27–36). Mahwah, NJ: Erlbaum.

Bar-Tal, D. (in press-a). Collective memory of physical violence: Its contribution to the culture of violence. In E. Cairns & M. D. Roe (Eds.). *Memories in conflict.* London: Macmillan.

Bar-Tal, D., & Bennink, G. (in press). Nature of reconciliation as an outcome and as a process. In Y. Bar-Siman-Tov (Ed.), *From conflict resolution to reconciliation.* New York: Oxford University Press.

Bar-Tal, D., Jacobson, D., & Klieman, A. (Eds.). (1998). *Security concerns: Insights from the Israeli experience.* Stamford, CT: JAI Press.

Bar-Tal, D., Kruglanski, A. W., & Klar, Y. (1989). Conflict termination: An epistemological analysis of international cases. *Political Psychology, 10,* 233–255.

Bar-Tal, D., & Oren, N. (2000). *Ethos as an expression of identity: Its changes in transition from conflict to peace in the Israeli case.* Discussion Paper No. 83. Jerusalem: Leonard Davis Institute for International Relations, Hebrew University of Jerusalem.

Bar-Tal, D., and Staub, E. (1997). Introduction: The nature and forms of patriotism. In D. Bar-Tal & E. Staub (Eds.), *Patriotism in the lives of individuals and groups.* Chicago: Nelson-Hall.

Bar-Tal, D., & Teichman Y. (in press). *Stereotypes and prejudice: The case of the perceptions of Arabs in the Israeli society.* Cambridge: Cambridge University Press.

Bauer, Y. (1984). The place of the Holocaust in contemporary history. In J. Frankel (Ed.), *Studies in contemporary jewry* (Vol. 1, pp. 201–224). New York: Oxford University Press.

Ben-Amos, A., & Bar-Tal, D. (Eds.). (in press). *Patriotism in Israel.* (Tel-Aviv: Dyonon in Hebrew).

Bercovitch, J. (Ed.). (1995). *Resolving international conflicts.* Boulder, CO: Lynne Rienner.

Berkowitz, L. (1968). Social motivation. In G. Lindzey & E. Aronson (Eds.), *The Handbook of social psychology* (2nd ed., vol. 3, pp. 50–135). Reading, MA: Addison-Wesley.

Beuf, A. (1977). *Red children in white America.* Philadelphia: University of Pennsylvania Press.

Bjerstedt, A. (1988). *Peace education in different countries.* Malmo, Sweden: Educational Information and Debate.

Bjerstedt, A. (Ed.). (1993). *Peace education: Global perspective.* Malmo, Sweden: Almqvist and Wiksell.

Brass, P. R. (Ed.). (1996). *Riots and pogroms.* New York: New York University Press.

Brecher, M. (1972). *The foreign policy system of Israel: Setting, images, processes.* London: Oxford University Press.

Brecher, M., & Wilkenfeld, J. (1988). Protracted conflicts and crises. In M. Brecher & J. Wilkenfeld (Eds.), *Crisis, conflict and instability* (pp. 127–140). Oxford: Pergamon.

Brewer, M. B.(1979). In-group bias in the minimal intergroup situation: Cognitive-motivational analysis. *Psychological Bulletin, 17,* 575–482.

Brewer, M. B.,& Campbell, D. T. (1976) *Ethnocentrism and intergroup attitudes: East African evidence.* New York: Halstead Press.

Bronkhorst, D. (1995). *Truth and reconciliation: Obstacles and opportunities for human rights.* Amsterdam: Amnesty International.

Brown, R. (1995) *Prejudice: Its social psychology.* Oxford: Blackwell.

Brown, R. (1988). *Group processes: Dynamics within and between groups.* Oxford: Blackwell.

Browning, C. R. (1992). *Ordinary men: Reserve Battalion 101 and the final solution in Poland.* New York: HarperCollins.

Brubaker, R., & Laitin, D. (1998). Ethnic and nationalist violence. *Annual Review of Sociology, 24,* 423–452.

Burns, R. J., & Aspeslagh, R. (Eds.).(1996). *Three decades of peace education around the world.* New York: Garland.

Burton, J. W. (1987). *Resolving deep-rooted conflict: A handbook.* Lanham, MD: University Press of America.

Burton, J. W. (1990). *Conflict: Resolution and prevention.* New York: St. Martin's Press.

Cairns, E., & Darby, J. (1998). The conflict in Northern Ireland. *American Psychologist, 53,* 754–760.

Cairns, E., & Hewstone, M. (2000). *Forgiveness and the reduction of intergroup conflict in Northern Ireland: A progress report.* Unpublished manuscript.

Calleja, J. (1994). Educating for peace in the Mediterranean: A strategy for peace building. In E. Boulding (Ed.), *Building peace in the Middle East: Challenges for states and civil society* (pp. 279–285). Boulder: Lynne Rienner.

Carnegie Commission on the Prevention of Deadly Conflict. (1997). *Preventing deadly conflict: Final report.* New York: Carnegie Corporation of New York.

Cash, J. D. (1996). *Identity, ideology and conflict.* Cambridge: Cambridge University Press.

Cecil, R. (1993). The marching season in Northern Ireland: An expression of politico-religious identity. In S. MacDonald (Ed.), *Inside European identities* (pp. 146–166). Providence, RI: Berg.

Chadha, N. (1995). Enemy images: The media and Indo-Pakistani tensions. In M. Krepon & A. Sevak (Eds.), *Crisis prevention, confidence building and reconciliation in South Asia* (pp. 171–198). New York: St. Martin's Press.

Chalk, F. R., & Jonassohn, K. (1990). *The history and sociology of genocide: Analyses and case studies.* New Haven: Yale University Press.

Charif, H. (1994). Regional development and integration. In D. Collings (Ed.), *Peace for Lebanon? From war to reconstruction* (pp. 151–161). Boulder: Lynne Rienner.

Charny, I. (1999). (Ed.). *The encyclopedia of Genocide.* Santa Barbara, CA: ABC-CLIO.

Chetkow-Yanoov, B. (1986). Improving Arab-Jewish relations in Israel: The role of voluntary organizations. *Social Development Issues, 10,* 58–70.

Chirot, D., & Seligman, M. (Eds.). (2001). *Ethnopolitical warfare: Causes, consequences and possible solutions.* Washington, DC: American Psychological Association.

Chirwa, W. (1997). Collective memory and the process of reconciliation and reconstruction. *Development in Practice, 7,* 479–482.

Coleman, P. (2000). Intractable conflict. In M. Deutsch, & P. T. Coleman (Eds.), *The handbook of conflict resolution: Theory and practice* (pp. 428–450). San Francisco: Jossey Bass.

Connerton, P. (1989). *How societies remember.* Cambridge: Cambridge University Press.

Cook, S. W. (1970). Motives in conceptual analysis of attitude-related behavior. In W. J. Arnold & D. Levine (Eds.), *Nebraska symposium on motivation.* Lincoln: University of Nebraska Press.

Corm, G. (1994). The war system: Militia hegemony and reestablishment of the state. In D. Collings (Ed.), *Peace for Lebanon? From war to reconstruction* (pp. 215–230). Boulder: Lynne Rienner.

Cornevin, M. (1980). *Apartheid: Power and historical falsification.* Paris: UNESCO.

Craig, G. A. (1982). *The Germans.* New York: New American Library.

Crighton, E., & MacIver, M. A. (1990). The evolution of protracted ethnic conflict. *Comparative Politics, 23,* 127–142.

Dadrian, V. N. (1974). A typology of genocide. *International Review of Modern Sociology, 5*(2), 201–212.

Dadrian, V. N. (1995). *The history of the Armenian genocide: Ethnic conflict from the Balkans to Anatolia to the Caucasus.* Providence, RI: Oxford Berghahn Books.

DeJong, A. (1978). *The Weimar chronicle: Prelude to Hitler.* New York: New American Library.

De la Rey, C., & Owens, I. (1998). Perceptions of psychological healing and the Truth and Reconciliation Commission in South Africa. *Peace and Conflict: Journal of Peace Psychology, 4,* 257–270.

Denich, B. (1994). Dismembering Yugoslavia: Nationalist ideologies and the symbolic revival of genocide. *American Ethnologist, 21,* 367–390.

Des Forges, A. (1999). *Leave none to tell the story: Genocide in Rwanda.* New York: Human Rights Watch.

Deutsch, M. (1973). *The resolution of conflict: Constructive and destructive processes.* New Haven: Yale University Press.

Dobkowski, M. N., & Wallimann, I. (1992) *Genocide in our time: An annotated bibliography with analytical introduction.* Ann Arbor, MI: Pierian.

Doyle, M. W., & Sambani, N. (2000). International peace building: A theoretical and quantitative analysis. *American Political Science Review, 94,* 779–801.

Duffy, T. (2000). Peace education in divided society: Creating a culture of peace in Northern Ireland. *Prospects, 30,* 15–29.

Fein, H. (1979). *Accounting for genocide: Victims and survivors of the Holocaust.* New York: Free Press.

Fein, H. (1993). Accounting for genocide after 1945: Theories and some findings. *International Journal of Group Rights, 1,* 79–106.

Fein, H. (1994). *The prevention of genocide.* Working Paper of the Institute for the Study of Genocide, City University of New York.

Fentress, J., & Wickham, C. (1992). *Social memory.* Oxford: Blackwell

Fisher, R. J. (1990). *The social psychology of intergroup and international conflict resolution.* New York: Springer-Verlag.

Forbes, J. D. (1964). *The Indian in America's past.* Englewood Cliffs, NJ: Prentice Hall.

Frank, J. D. (1967). *Sanity and survival: Psychological aspects of war and peace.* New York: Vintage.

Frijda, N. H. (1994). The lex talionis: On vengeance. In S. H. M. van Goozen, N. E.

Van de Poll, & J. A. Sergeant (Eds.), *Emotions: Essays on emotion theory* (pp. 263–289). Hillsdale, NJ: Erlbaum.

Galtung, J. (1990). Cultural violence. *Journal of Peace Research, 27,* 291–305.

Gamson, W. A. (1988). Political discourse and collective action. *International Social Movement Research, 1,* 219–244.

Garcia, C. (1984). Latin America traditions and perspectives. *International Review of Education, 29*(3), 369–390.

Gardner-Feldman, L. (1999). The principle and practice of reconciliation in German foreign policy: Relations with France, Israel, Poland and the Czech Republic. *International Affairs, 75,* 333–356.

Gibson, J. L. (in press). Truth, justice and reconciliation: Judging the fairness of amnesty in South Africa. *American Journal of Political Science.*

Glenny, M. (1992). *The fall of Yugoslavia.* London: Penguin.

Goertz, G., & Diehl, P. F. (1993). Enduring rivalries: Theoretical constructs and empirical patterns. *International Studies Quarterly, 37,* 147–171.

Goldhagen D. J. (1996). *Hitler's willing executioners: Ordinary Germans and the Holocaust.* New York: Knopf.

Gordon, R. (1994). Article 2 (7) Revisited: The post cold-war Security Council. Reports and Papers, No. 5. In Abiodum Williams, *Article 2 (7) Revisited* (Eds.), (pp. 21–36). Providence, RI: Academic Council of the United Nations Systems.

Gourevich, P. (1998). *We wish to inform you that tomorrow we will be killed with our families.* New York: Farrar Straus and Giroux.

Gurr, T. R. (2001). Minorities and Nationalists: Managing Ethnopolitical Conflict in the New Century. Chester A. Crocker, Fen Osler Hampson, & Pamela Aall (Eds.), *Turbulent peace: The challenges of managing international conflict.* Washington, DC: United States Institute of Peace Press.

Gurr, T. R., & B. Harff, (1996). *Early warning of communal conflicts and genocide: Linking empirical research to international responses.* Tokyo: United Nations Press.

Halbwachs, M.(1992). *On collective memory.* Chicago: University of Chicago Press.

Hamber, B. (1998). The burdens of truth: An evaluation of the psychological support services and initiatives undertaken by the South African Truth and Reconciliation Commission. *American Imago, 55,* 9–28.

Handl, V. (1997). Czech-German declaration on reconciliation. *German Politics, 6,* 150–167.

Harff, B. (1996). Early warning of potential genocide: The cases of Rwanda, Burundi, Bosnia, and Abkhazia. In T. R. Gurr & B. Harff (Eds.), *Early warning of communal conflicts and genocide: Linking empirical research to international responses* (pp. 47–78). Tokyo: United Nations Press.

Harff, B., & Gurr, T. R. (1990). Victims of the state genocides, politicides and group repression since 1945. *International Review of Victimology, 1,* 1–19.

Harff, B., Gurr, T. R., & Unger, A. (1999, November). *Preconditions of genocide and politicide: 1955–1998.* Paper presented at the Conference on Differing Approaches to Assessing Potential Genocide, Politicides and Mass Killings, Vienna, Virginia.

Harris, I. M. (1988). *Peace education.* Jefferson, NC: McFarland.

Hayes, G. (1998). We suffer our memories: Thinking about the past, healing, and reconciliation. *American Imago, 55,* 29–50.

Hayner, P. B. (1999). In pursuit of justice and reconciliation: Contributions of truth telling. In C. J. Arnson (Ed.), *Comparative peace processes in Latin America* (pp. 363–383). Stanford, CA: Stanford University Press.

Herman, J. (1992). *Trauma and recovery.* New York: Basic Books.

Hicks, D. W. (Ed.). (1988). *Education for peace: Issues, principles and practices in the classroom.* London: Routledge.

Hilberg, R. (1961). *The destruction of the European Jews.* New York: Harper and Row.

Hirsch, H. (1995). *Genocide and the politics of memory.* Chapel Hill: University of North Carolina Press.

Hitchcock, R. K., & Twedt, T. M. (1997). Physical and cultural genocide of various indigenous peoples. In S. Totten, W. S. Parsons, & I. W. Charny (Ed.). *Century of genocide: Eyewitness accounts and critical views.* New York: Garland.

Horowitz, D. L. (1993). Conflict and the incentives to political accommodation. In D. Keogh & M. H. Haltzel (Eds.), *Northern Ireland and the politics of reconciliation* (pp. 173–188). Washington, DC: Woodrow Wilson Center Press.

Hunter, J. A., Stringer, M., & Warson, R. P. (1991). Intergroup violence and intergroup attributions. *British Journal of Social Psychology, 30,* 261–266.

Huth, P., & Russett, B. (1993). General deterrence between enduring rivals: Testing three competing models. *American Political Science Review, 87,* 61–72.

Irwin-Zarecka, I. (1994). *Frames of remembrance: The dynamics of collective memory.* New Brunswick, NJ: Transaction.

Kammen, M. (1991). *Mystic chords of memory: The transformation of tradition in American culture.* New York: Knopf.

Kaye, M. (1997). The role of the Truth Commissions in the search for justice, reconciliation and democratization: The Salvadorean and Honduran cases. *Journal of Latin American Studies, 29,* 693–716.

Kecmanovic, D. (1996). *The mass psychology of ethnonationalism.* New York: Plenum.

Kelman, H. C. (1973). Violence without moral restraint: Reflections on the dehumanization of victims and victimizers. *Journal of Social Issues, 29*(4), 25–61.

Kelman, H. C. (1990). Applying a human needs perspective to the practice of conflict resolution: The Israeli-Palestinian case. In J. Burton (Ed.), *Conflict: Human needs theory.* New York: St. Martin's Press.

Kelman, H. C. (1997). Social-psychological dimensions of international conflict. In I. W. Zartman & J. L. Rasmussen (Ed.), *Peacemaking in international conflict: Methods and techniques* (pp. 191–237). Washington, DC: United States Institute of Peace Press.

Kelman, H. C. (1999). Transforming the relationship between former enemies: A social-psychological analysis. In R. L. Rothstein (Ed.), *After the peace: Resistance and reconciliation* (pp. 193–205). Boulder, CO: Lynne Rienner.

Kemper, T. D (Ed.). (1990). *Research agendas in the sociology of emotions.* Albany, NY: SUNY Press.

Kennan, G. F. (1960). *Russia and the West under Lenin and Stalin.* Boston: Little, Brown.

Klare, M. T., & Thomas, D. C. (Eds.). (1991). *World security: Trends and challenges at century's end.* New York: St. Martin Press.

Knox, C., & Quirk, P. (2000). *Peace building in Northern Ireland, Israel and South Africa: Transition, transformation and reconciliation.* London: Macmillan.

Kopstein, J. S. (1997). The politics of national reconciliation: Memory and institutions in German-Czech relations since 1989. *Nationalism and Ethnic Politics, 3,* 57–78.

Kressel, N. J. (2002). *Mass hate: The global rise of genocide and terror.* Cambridge, MA: Westview Press

Kriesberg, L. (1992). *International conflict resolution.* New Haven: Yale University Press.

Kriesberg, L. (1993). Intractable conflict. *Peace Review, 5,* 417–421.

Kriesberg, L. (1998a). Coexistence and the reconciliation of communal conflicts. In E. Weiner (Ed.), *The handbook of interethnic coexistence* (pp. 182–198). New York: Continuum.

Kriesberg, L. (1998b). Intractable conflicts. In E. Weiner (Ed.), *The handbook of interethnic coexistence* (pp. 332–342). New York: Continuum.

Kritz, N. J. (1996). The rule of law in the postconflict phase. In C. A. Crocker, F. O. Hampson, & P. Aall (Eds.), *Managing global chaos: Sources of conflict of and responses to international conflict* (pp. 587– 606). Washington, DC: United States Institute of Peace Press.

Krystal, H. (Ed.). (1968). *Massive psychic trauma.* New York: International Universities Press.

Leatherman, J., DeMars, W., Gaffney, P. D., & Vayrynen, R. (1999). *Breaking cycles of violence: Conflict prevention in intrastate cries.* Bloomfield, CT: Kumarian Press.

Lederach, J. P. (1997). *Building peace: Sustainable reconciliation in divided societies.* Washington, D.C.: United States Institute of Peace Press.

Lederach, J. P. (1998). Beyond violence: Building sustainable peace. In E. Weiner (Ed.), *The handbook of interethnic coexistence* (pp. 236–245). New York: Continuum.

Lederer, K. (Ed.). (1980). *Human needs.* Cambridge, MA: Oelgeshager, Gunn and Hain.

Lemkin, R. (1944). *Axis rule in occupied Europe: Laws of occupation, analysis of government, proposals for redress.* Washington, DC: Carnegie Endowment of International Peace.

Lerner, M. (1980). *The belief in a just world: A fundamental delusion.* New York: Plenum Press.

Lever, H. (1978). *South African society.* Johannesburg, South Africa: Jonathan Ball.

Liebenberg, I. & Zegeye, A. (1998). Pathway to democracy? The case of the South African Truth and Reconciliation process. *Social Identities, 4,* 541–558.

Liebman, C. (1978). Myth, tradition and values in Israeli society. *Midstream, 24,* 44–53.

Lipschutz, R. D. (1998). Beyond the neoliberal peace: From conflict resolution to social reconciliation. *Social Justice: A Journal of Crime, Conflict and World Order, 25* (4), 5–19.

Lundt, M. S. (1996). *Preventing violent conflicts: A strategy for preventive diplomacy.* Washington, DC: United States Institute of Peace Press.

Lundwell, K. (2001). *Psychological aspects of collective violence and reconciliation: A survey of current research.* Centre for Multiethnic Research, Uppsala University. Uppsala, Sweden.

Mack, J., E. (1990) The psychodynamics of victimization among national groups in conflict. In V. D. Volkan, D. A. Julius, & J. V. Montville (Eds.), *The psychodynamics of international relationships* (pp. 119–129). Lexington, MA: Lexington.

Maddi, S. R. (1971). The search for meaning. In W. J. Arnold, & M. M. Page (Eds.), *Nebraska symposium on motivation 1970* (pp. 137–186). Lincoln: University of Nebraska Press.

Manoff, R. (1996). *The mass media and social violence: Is there a role for the media in preventing and moderating ethnic, national, and religious conflict?* Unpublished manuscript. Center for War, Peace, and News Media, Department of Journalism and Mass Communication, New York University, New York.

Mannheim, K. (1952). *Ideology and utopia.* New York: Harcourt, Brace.

Markus, H. R., & Kitayama, S. (1994). The cultural shaping of emotion: A conceptual framework. In S. Kitayama & H. R. Markus (Eds.), *Emotion and culture: Empirical studies of mutual influence* (pp. 339–351). Washington, DC: American Psychological Association.

Marrow, D. (1999). Seeking peace amid memories of war: Learning form the peace process in Northern Ireland. In R. L. Rothstein (Ed.), *After the peace: Resistance and reconciliation* (pp. 111–138). Boulder, CO: Lynne Rienner.

McCauley, C. (in press). Making sense to terrorism after 9/11. In R. Moser (Ed.), *Shocking violence II: Violent disaster, war and terrorism affecting our youth.* Charles C. Thomas.

McCauley, C. R., & Segal, M. D. (1989). Terrorist individuals and terrorist groups: The normal psychology of extreme behavior. In J. Groebel & J. F. Goldstein (Eds.), *Terrorism.* Seville, Spain: Publicaciones de la Universidad de Sevilla.

Melson, R. (1992). *Revolution and genocide: On the origins of the Armenian genocide and the Holocaust.* Chicago: University of Chicago Press.

Milgram, S. (1974). *Obedience to authority: An experimental view.* New York: Harper and Row.

Minow, M. (1998). *Between vengeance and forgiveness.* Boston: Beacon Press.

Mitchell, C. R. (1981). *The structure of international conflict.* London: Macmillan.

Montville, J. V. (1993). The healing function in political conflict resolution. In D. J. D. Sandole & H. van der Merve (Eds.), *Conflict resolution theory and practice: Integration and application* (pp. 112–127). Manchester, England: Manchester University Press.

Mor, B. D., & Maoz, Z. (1999) Learning and the evolution of enduring rivalries: A strategic approach. *Conflict Management and Peace Science, 17,* 1–48

Murakami, T. (1992). *Peace education in Britain and Japan.* Kyoto, Japan: Office of Sociology of Education, Kyoto University of Education.

Murray, M. R., & Greer, J. V. (1999). The changing governance of rural development: State-community interaction in Northern Ireland. *Policy Studies, 20,* 37–50.

Ney, J. S., & Lynn-Jones, S. M. (1988). International security studies: A report of a conference on the state of the field. *International Security, 12,* 5–27.

Norval, A. J. (1998). Memory, identity and the (im)possibility of reconciliation: The work of the Truth and Reconciliation Commission in South Africa. *Constellations, 5,* 250–265.

Norval, A. J. (1999). Truth and reconciliation: The birth of the present and the reworking of history. *Journal of African Studies, 25,* 499–519.

Opotaw, S. (Ed.). (1990). Moral exclusion and injustice. *Journal of Social Issues, 46* (1).

Ordeshook, P. C. (1986). *Game theory and political theory.* Cambridge: Cambridge University Press.

Pearlman, L. A., & Saakvitne, K. (1995). *Trauma and the therapist.* New York: Norton.

Pennebaker, J. W., Paez, D., & Rimé, B. (Eds.). (1997). *Collective memory of political events: Social psychological perspectives.* Mahwah, NJ: Erlbaum.

Pettigrew, T. F. (1997). Generalized intergroup contact effects on prejudice. *Personality and Social Psychology Bulletin, 23*(2), 173–185.

Pettigrew, T. F. (1998). Intergroup contact theory. *Annual Review of Psychology, 49,* 65–85.

Pilisuk, M., & Wong, A. (2002). State terrorism: When the perpetrator is the government. In C. Stout (Ed.), *Psychology of terrorism.* Westport, CT: Praeger.

Powers, S. (2001, September). Bystanders to genocide. *Atlantic Monthly.*

Powers, S. (2002). *A problem from hell: America and the age of genocide.* New York: Basic Books.

Prunier, G. (1995). *The Rwanda crisis: History of a genocide.* New York: Columbia University Press.

Reardon, B. A. (1988). *Comprehensive peace education: Educating for global responsibility.* New York: Teachers College Press.

Reykowski, J. (1982). Social motivation. *Annual Review of Psychology, 33,* 123–154.

Reykowski, J. (1997). Patriotism and the collective system of meanings. In D. Bar-Tal & E. Staub (Eds.), *Patriotism in the lives of individuals and nations* (pp. 108–128). Chicago: Nelson-Hall.

Rhodes, R. (2002). *Masters of death: The SS-Einsatzgruppen and the invention of the Holocaust.* New York: Knopf.

Rieber, R. W. (Ed.).(1991). *The psychology of war and peace: The image of the enemy.* New York: Plenum.

Rose, R. (1985). National pride in cross-national perspective. *International Social Science Journal, 37,* 85–96.

Ross, M. H. (1993). *The management of conflict: Interpretations and interests in comparative perspective.* New Haven: Yale University Press.

Ross, M. H. (1995). Psychocultural interpretation theory and peacemaking in ethnic conflicts. *Political Psychology, 16,* 523–544.

Ross, M. H. (1998). The cultural dynamics of ethnic conflict. In D. Jacquin, A. Oros, & M. Verweij (Eds.), *Culture in world politics* (pp. 156–186). Houndmills, England: Macmillan.

Ross, M. H. & Rothman, J. (1999). *Theory and practice in ethnic conflict management: Theorizing success and failure.* New York: Macmillian.

Rubin, J. Z., Pruitt, D. G., & Kim, S. (1994). *Social conflict: Escalation, stalemate, and settlement.* New York: McGraw-Hill.

Rummel, R. J. (1994). *Death by government.* New Brunswick, NJ: Transaction.

Rummel, R. J. (1997). *Power kills: Democracy as a method of nonviolence.* New Brunswick, NJ: Transaction.

Rummel, R. J. (1999). *Statistics of democide: Genocide and mass murder since 1900.* New Brunswick, NJ: Transaction.

Salomon G., & Nevo, B. (Eds.). (2002). *Peace education for the twenty-first century.* Mahwah, NJ: Erlbaum.

Sande, G. N., Goethals, G. R., Ferrari, L., & Worth, L. T. (1989). Value-guided attributions: Maintaining the moral self-image and the diabolical enemy-image. *Journal of Social Issues, 45*(2), 91–118.

Schatz, R. T., Staub, E., & Lavine, H. (1999). On the varieties of national attachment: Blind versus constructive patriotism. *Political Psychology, 20,* 151–175.

Scheff, T. J. (1994). *Bloody revenge: Emotions, nationalism, and war.* Boulder, CO: Westview.

Shriver, D. W., Jr. (1995). *An ethic for enemies: Forgiveness in politics.* New York: Oxford University Press.

Sidanius, J., & Pratto, F. (1998). *Social dominance.* Cambridge: Cambridge University Press.

Simpson, C. 1993. *The splendid blond beast.* New York: Grove Press.

Simpson, G. (1997). Reconstruction and reconciliation: Emerging from transition. *Development in Practice, 7,* 475–478.

Smith, R. W. (1999). State power and genocidal intent: On the uses of genocide in the twentieth century. In L. Chorbajian & G. Shirinian (Eds.), *Studies in comparative genocide.* New York: St. Martin's Press.

Somerville, J. (1981). Patriotism and war. *Ethics, 91,* 568–578.

Stagner, R. (1967). *Psychological aspects of international conflict.* Belmont, CA: Brooks/ Cole.

Staub, E. (1989). *The roots of evil: The origins of genocide and other group violence.* New York: Cambridge University Press.

Staub, E. (1990). Moral exclusion, personal goal theory and extreme destructiveness. In S. Opotaw (Ed.), Moral exclusion and injustice (special issue). *Journal of Social Issues, 46,* 47–65.

Staub, E. (1991). Persian Gulf conflict was reflection of stormy undercurrents in U.S. psyche. *Psychology International,* 1–9. Washington, DC: American Psychological Association.

Staub, E. (1992). Understanding and preventing police violence. *Center Review, 6,* 1–7. A Publication of the Center of Psychology and Social Change, Harvard Medical School, Cambridge, MA.

Staub, E. (1996a). Altruism and aggression in children and youth: Origins and cures. R. Feldman (Ed.), *The psychology of adversity.* Amherst: University of Massachusetts Press.

Staub, E. (1996b). Cultural-societal roots of violence: The examples of genocidal violence and of contemporary youth violence in the United States. *American Psychologist, 51,* 117–132.

Staub, E. (1997). Blind versus constructive patriotism: Moving from embeddedness in the group to critical loyalty and action. In E. Staub & D. Bar-Tal (Eds.), *Patriotism in the lives of individuals and groups.* Chicago: Nelson-Hall.

Staub, E. (1998a). Breaking the cycle of genocidal violence: Healing and reconciliation. In J. Harvey (Ed), *Perspectives on loss.* Washington, DC: Taylor and Francis.

Staub, E. (1998b). Early intervention: Prediction and action. In H. J. Langholtz (Ed.), *The psychology of peacekeeping.* Westport, CT: Praeger.

Staub, E. (1999a). The origins and prevention of genocide, mass killing and other collective violence. *Peace and Conflict: Journal of Peace Psychology, 5,* 303–337.

Staub, E. (1999b). The roots of evil: personality, social conditions, culture and basic human needs. *Personality and Social Psychology Review, 3,* 179–192.

Staub, E. (2000a). Genocide and mass killing: Origins, prevention, healing and reconciliation. *Political Psychology, 21,* 2, 367–382.

Staub, E. (2000b). Mass murder: Origins, prevention and U.S. involvement. In R. Gottesman (Ed.), *Violence in America: An encyclopedia.* New York: Scribner's.

Staub, E. (2001a). Ethnopolitical and other group violence: Origins and prevention.

In D. Chirot & M. Seligman (Eds.), *Ethnopolitical warfare: Causes, consequences and possible solutions*. Washington, DC: American Psychological Association.

Staub, E. (2001b). The role of individual and group identity in genocide and war. In R. D. Ashmore, L. Jussim, & D. Wilder (Eds.), *Social identity, intergroup conflict and conflict reduction*. New York: Oxford University Press.

Staub, E. (2001c). Understanding and preventing police violence. In S. Epstein & M. Amir (Eds.), *Policing, security and democracy*. Huntsville, TX: Office of Criminal Justice Press.

Staub, E. (2002). From healing past wounds to the development of inclusive caring: Contents and processes of peace education. In G. Solomon & B. Nevo (Eds.), *Peace Education for the twenty-first Century*. Mahwah, NJ: Erlbaum.

Staub, E. (in press-a). Preventing terrorism: Raising "inclusively" caring children in the complex world of the twenty-first century. In C. Stout (Ed), *Psychology of Terrorism*. Westport, CT: Praeger.

Staub, E. (in press-b). *The psychology of good and evil: Why children, adults and groups help and harm others*. New York: Cambridge University Press.

Staub, E., & Pearlman, L. (2001). Healing, reconciliation and forgiving after genocide and other collective violence. In S. J. Helmick & R. L. Petersen (Eds.), *Forgiveness and reconciliation: Religion, public policy and conflict transformation*. Radnor, PA: Templeton Foundation Press.

Staub, E., and Pearlman, L. A. (2002). *Facilitators' summary of observations and recommendations from leaders' seminar: Preventing renewed violence*, Kigali, Rwanda. August 2001. Unpublished manuscript. (see www.heal-reconcile-rwanda.org)

Staub, E., Pearlman, A. L., Gubin, & Hagengimana, A., (2002). *Healing, forgiving and reconciliation: an intervention and its experimental evaluation in Rwanda*. Unpublished manuscript. University of Massachusetts, Amherst.

Staub, E., & Rosenthal, L. (1994). Mob violence: Societal-cultural sources, group processes and participants. In L. Eron & J. Gentry (Eds.), *Reason to hope: A psychosocial perspective on violence and youth*. Washington, DC: American Psychological Association.

Stein, H. F. (1978). Judaism and the group-fantasy of martyrdom: The psychodynamic paradox of survival through persecution. *Journal of Psychohistory, 6*, 151–210.

Stern, P. C. (1995). Why do people sacrifice for their nations? *Political Psychology, 16*, 117–235.

Sumner, W. G. (1906). *Folkways*. New York: Ginn.

Tajfel, H. (1978). Social categorization, social identity and social comparison. In H. Tajfel (Ed.), *Differentiation between social groups* (pp. 61–76). London: Academic Press.

Tajfel, H. (1981). *Human groups and social categories: Studies in social psychology*. Cambridge: Cambridge University Press.

Tajfel, H., & Turner, J. C. (1979). An integrative theory of intergroup conflict. In W. G. Austin & S. Worchel (Eds.), *The social psychology of intergroup relations*. Monterey, CA: Brooks-Cole.

Taylor, F. (Ed.). (1983). *The Goebbels diaries: 1939–1941*. New York: Putnam.

Volkan, V. (1997). *Blood lines: From ethnic pride to ethnic terrorism*. New York: Farrar, Straus and Giroux.

Volkan, V. D. (1998). The tree model: Psychopolitical dialogues and the promotion of coexistence. In E. Weiner (Ed.), *The handbook of interethnic coexistence* (pp. 343–358). New York: Continuum.

Volpe, M. R. (1998). Using town meetings to foster peaceful coexistence. In E. Weiner (Ed.), *The handbook of interethnic coexistence* (pp. 382–396). New York: Continuum.

Weiwen, Z., & Deshingkar, G. (1995). Improving Sino-Indo relations. In M. Krepon & A. Sevak (Eds.), *Crisis prevention, confidence building and reconciliation in South Asia* (pp. 227–238). New York: St. Martin's Press.

White, R. K. (1970). *Nobody wanted war: Misperception in Vietnam and other wars.* Garden City, NY: Doubleday.

White, R. K. (1996). Why the Serbs fought: Motives and misperceptions. *Peace and Conflict: Journal of Peace Psychology, 2*(2), 109–128.

Whittaker, D. J. (1999). *Conflict and reconciliation in the contemporary world.* London: Routledge.

Williams, R. M., Jr. (1994). The sociology of ethnic conflicts: Comparative international perspective. *Annual Review of Sociology, 20,* 49–79.

Willis, F. R. (1965). *France, Germany, and the New Europe, 1945–1963.* Palo Alto, CA: Stanford University Press.

Wilmer, F. (1998). The social construction of conflict and reconciliation in the former Yugoslavia. *Social Justice: A Journal of Crime, Conflict & World Order, 25* (4), 90–113.

Wistrich, R. S. (Ed.). (1999). *Demonizing the other: Antisemitism, racism and xenophobia.* Amsterdam: Harwood.

Worchel, S. (1999). *Written in blood: Ethnic identity and the struggle for human harmony.* New York: Worth.

Yaniv, A. (Ed.). (1993). *National security and democracy in Israel.* Boulder, CO: Lynne Rienner.

Zalaquett, J. (1999). Truth, justice, and reconciliation: Lessons for the international community. In C. J. Arnson (Ed.), *Comparative peace processes in Latin America* (pp. 341–361). Stanford, CA: Stanford University Press.

Zukier, H. (1994). The twisted road to genocide: On the psychological development of evil during the Holocaust. *Social Research, 61*(2), 423–455.

Epilogue

21 Robert E. Lane

Rescuing Political Science from Itself

Political science is a discipline only in the sense that, like literature, it is listed in college catalogs, but not in the sense of a body of phenomena analyzed by a coherent set of theories, or even competing coherent theories, like physics. I once got a grant for my department by telling the inquiring foundation that we did not pretend that political science was a discipline but only that it lays claim to a set of problems for which many approaches and theories are relevant. But, of course, even without a central theory, it must have a subject matter.

Recently, Ian Shapiro (1999) recaptured and defended an earlier focus. Arguing against a then current emphasis on "the deliberative process" (Gutman & Thompson, 1996), he said that political science was basically about *interests* and power, illustrating the point with the example of the Hillary Clinton–Magaziner health policy fiasco in 1994–95: the cause of the failure, he said, was not the lack of deliberative processes, as alleged, but the overwhelming resources brought to bear against the proposed health policy reform by the insurance industry. So my first treatment here will deal with the contribution of psychology to the study of political interests.

For most of us, interests were what institutions were all about, their powers and modus operandi. Some, like Hegel and Marx, have thought that such institutions as the state and the "capitalist" economy had some immanent properties that permitted predictions of outcomes, but more modest analysts have recently investigated what they call "the logic of institutions." Given psychology's greater interest in individuals and their relations, one might have thought psychology has little to say about such institutional logics. Not so. My second theme will be the contribution of psychology to the study of the logic of political institutions.

In the 1930s and 1940s it would have been said that political science was distinguished by its unique concern for *political processes:* electoral, parliamentary, constitutional, legal. That was true, although the only unifying theme associated with the concept of process was decision-making (e.g., Lindblom, 1965; Simon, 1979). To treat decision-making with proper sophistication, however, required theories of such psychological processes as cognitive balancing, schema formation, emotional self-regulation, and so forth. I will look at a simple effort here to analyze the intersection of political and psychological processes.

In the 1950s, under the influence of Harold Lasswell (1950a, 1950b) we used to say that political science was the study of *power* in all its settings, but it turned out that power in the family, in the church, as well as in government, was not what we were talking about; settings made too much of a difference. Still, from Machiavelli to Hobbes to Acton to Lasswell, power themes were central to political analysis, and it will be worth examining what psychology adds to political science as the study of power. To summarize, in this first part I will examine psychology's contribution to the study of (1) interests, (2) the logic of institutions, (3) political processes, and (4) power.

The second major part of this chapter is the study of political ends or goals, the subject of political philosophy as well as political theory. Although far less evaluative than political science, psychology has implicit concepts of good and bad, of cherished values that might inform political science in a useful way. What are they? First, in this part, I will suggest ways that psychology as an explanatory science can contribute to the stipulation and explication of ends. I will argue that the usual ends of political philosophy, say freedom and equality, are not ends at all but rather means to ends that psychology can itself defend. As it turns out, these ends are also implicit in most theories of democracy, and if psychology can become self-conscious about them, its spokespersons can contribute to the normative aspects of political science. In this second part, a part devoted to political ends, I will show how political psychology (5) adds causal inference to philosophy's verbal implication, (6) increases our understanding of freedom by explication of the process of choosing, (7) reveals equality to be a state with both costs and benefits; and, most important (8), offers a fresh assessment of the ultimate values at stake in political life.

▶ Political Science as the Study of Interests

The concept of interests became almost a fad in the Enlightenment when, according to Hirschman (1977), by appearing to give rational control over the feared passions, the new concept of interests licensed the release of government controls to markets. As Helvetius commented, "interests rule the world. . . . Men are not bad; they are merely subject to their own interests" (*De l'esprit, Oeuvres* 2.5; in Sabine, 1963, p. 564): Although it was Adam Smith who made self-interest respectable, it was the Encyclopedists and the physiocrats who first gave self-interest its rational character (Bury, 1955/1920, pp. 163–164). The concept of interest was materialist as well, as we see from the list of interests that James Madison (1894/1787), an American child of the Enlightenment, provided: "those with and without property, mercantile and landed and manufacturing interests, debtors and creditors" (p. 55). Thus, at the very beginning, interests were *rational, material,* and appropriately, in Mill's later phrase, *self-regarding.*

These three qualities made interests objectively observable, able to be inferred from almost all situations, motivated by a standard human endowment, and, since each person was similarly endowed, understandable by everyone. Legislators could perceive and cater to interests of this kind, parents could teach children how to behave with respect to them, and, although ministers might deplore them, the sins committed in pursuit of material self-interest were more or less forgivable. Indeed, in the seventeenth century the Protestant clergyman Richard Baxter scolded those who might "choose the less gainful way" as failing in their duties as "God's Stewards" (in Weber, 1958, p. 162).

The problem with the interests approach to politics is that these three qualities are, at best, misleading. Although political scientists understood some of the reasons for this source of error, psychologists understood them better and showed how they falsified our interpretations of experience. That is the gist of this section

Relaxing the Materialist Assumptions

There is no intrinsic reason why interests need be material interests; after all, as a verb, the word "interest" has no such implication. In his initial definition, Jeremy Bentham (1954) said, "a man is said to have an interest in any subject, in so far as that subject could be a source of pain or pleasure" (p. 424). But Bentham (pp. 437–438) also thought that money was the best measure of pain and pleasure. In this century, in an often-quoted passage, the distinguished philosopher Ralph Barton Perry (1954) explains that by "interest" he means something more than "attention or curiosity": that an interest is present when we have attitudes toward it that "have the common characteristic of *being for or against [it]*" (p. 7). Usage is otherwise. Another philosopher, Nicholas Rescher (1969), lets the cat out of the bag when he says: "certain resources, almost reducible to money in certain highly articulated societies, and health, are plausibly the chief constituents of the category of interests" (pp. 200–201). Since economics defines its field as embracing only those things compatible with "the measuring rod of money" (Pigou, (1948/1932], p. ix), they agree with Rescher. Very slowly economists are changing (e.g., Frey, 1997), but the standard paradigm is, of course, materialist. Law and political science followed this usage, from the time of Arthur Bentley (1911) identifying interests more or less as Madison did.

Perhaps—it is not clear—the materialist version of humankind was justified in a period of scarcity, but in advanced societies it is no longer justified. At least four lines of research undermine the economists' assumption of the primacy of greed. First, there are the studies of subjective well-being (SWB) showing that beyond the poverty level—that is, for most of us—level of income is unrelated to SWB or happiness (Veenhoven, 1993; Diener, Diener, & Diener, 1995; Lane, 2000a). Of course, these do not prove anything about what people *think* makes them happy, and therefore about their pursuit of happiness, but it does suggest that in the absence of scarcity, materialist pursuits are relatively unrewarding for most people. This inference is reinforced by research with a "materialism scale" (e.g., "Buying things gives me a lot of pleasure"; "Some of the most important achievements in life include acquiring material possessions"; (Richins & Dawson, 1992, p. 310). People who score high on this measure are unhappier than low scorers.

In a third, more oblique, line of research, studies where motives of fairness are set against motives of profit, find that fairness often wins, even among merchants (e.g., Frank, 1990; Thaler, 1987). Finally, studies of procedural justice (Lind & Tyler, 1988; Thibaut & Walker, 1975) find that the outcomes of a trial, the sentence or settlement, affected a defendant's satisfaction far less than the sense of being heard by a concerned authority who listened to her case. As I (Lane, 1988) once said, "it is how you are treated, not what you get" that makes the difference. Motives of love, honor, and duty are equally strong.

Relaxing the Assumptions of Rationality

In contrast to "the group mind" (McDougall, 1920) and "the crowd instinct" (Le Bon, 1920/1895]), interest politics seemed to offer support to rational democracy. As Bentham might have said, unlike the passions, interests "calculate." This concept of interest gave Downs's *Economic Theory of Democracy* (1957) an easy, and, it must be admitted, sometimes fruitful, entry to political science. But because people have allegiances to processes and rituals, national symbols, and multiple conflicting groups, the economic theory with its rationality assumptions turned out to be fatally incomplete (Green & Shapiro, 1994; Lane, 1995; Hogarth & Reder, 1987; Sen, 1987).

People have great trouble perceiving the relative frequency of events and therefore in drawing inductive inferences about causes, in performing logical transformation, as in (Piaget's (Piaget & Inhelder, 1969) "formal operations"—a level few people reach—and in subsuming cases under appropriate general rules (McGuire, 1990; Nisbett & Ross, 1980). Because of these incapacities, individuals are often mistaken about their own interests and how to pursue them. At the very least, end-means rationality cannot be assumed. Of the two systems that Zajonc (1980) finds operating somewhat independently, the affective system gives its answers first and is more trusted than the more deliberate cognitive system.

Relaxing the Self-interest Assumptions

There is no major philosopher since Plato who has not wrestled with the problem of human self-centeredness, if not outright selfishness. Of course, as Parfit (1984), Elster (1985) and Rosenberg (1979) remind us, the self is not all of a piece. Of all our multiple selves (the ideal self, the rejected self, the self we know and may accept) perhaps the conflict between the current and the future self, the continuity of the self, is the most troublesome.

Whose self-interest is to be pursued? Those with weak identification with the future self may well bind themselves now for the sake of the future self (insurance contracts, Ulysses' binding himself to the mast to avoid yielding to the Sirens). Psychology makes two major contributions to this problem of present versus future self: work on deferred gratification (e.g., Mischel, Shoda, & Rodriguez, 1989) finding, inter alia, that the kind of visibility of a desired object that television presents impedes deferrals; and research on people's conceptions, and uses, of time (Doob, 1971).

In this connection, a finding by Rokeach (1970) that I always thought was underappreciated may help. When one's values and attitudes conflict, it is not that values trump attitudes but that the most precious thing to be preserved is the integrity and continuity of the self ("What kind of a person am I?")—unless, as Curtis Hardin (1995) believes, the self is a protean figure, changing with circumstances. Conflicts in identities derived from group affiliation have been thought equally troublesome, but research shows that mere membership in a group is not enough to decide for whom one votes (Herring, 1938). On the other hand, the current themes of "identity politics" are given both nourishment and support by the shift from "objective" interests to concepts of the self as bases for political analysis (e.g., Bennett, 1998; Norton, 1988). For the past 20 years we have been able to read less and less about a person's political attitudes from his social class, occupation, religion, and ethnicity (Abramson, Aldrich, Paolino, & Rohde, 1992). If neither imputed interests nor social identities characterize political man, he becomes volatile and less predictable. When demographics fail, we call on psychology.

A delightful pair of articles by Dale Miller and his colleague (Miller, 1999; Miller & Rather, 1998) helps to answer Stigler's (1981, p. 176) proposition: if one were to test people in situations where ethical choices were opposed to material self-interest, "much of the time, most of the time in fact, the self-interest theory (as interpreted on Smithian lines) will win." In the first of Miller's pieces (Miller & Rather, 1998) he tests whether or not other people make the same attribution that Stigler makes. They do, but they are wrong where people are asked to give blood and in favoring groups they belong to. And in the second study Miller (1999) argues with some evidence that usually when people behave in self-interested ways they think that is what is expected of them, that they are only following the norms of their society. If this is true, then appealing to behavior in a commercial society tells us more about people's desire to comply with social norms than of their self-regardingness.

The emphasis on the self loses its egocentric quality when it is realized that the self in question is the self-in-relation-to-others. We know from the works of Runciman (1966) and Crosby (1982) that people are politically aroused less by the sense of self-deprivation than by "fraternal deprivation," deprivation to others like the self. In psychology, themes of identity (again) are characterized by social attachments (Wicklund & Gollwitzer, 1982; Yardley & Honess, 1987). Because it is companionship that contributes the most to happiness, especially in the West, where it is sorely missed (Lane 2000a), we may be sure that the self in isolation from others is not the happy, desired self, not the subject of most people's self-interest. As Kenneth Boulding (1973, p. 94) once said, the economists' idea that people are interested only in their own welfare is a "preposterous limitation."

The justification for self-interest in markets is the beneficence of the hidden hand; there is no hidden hand in elections. Furthermore, Sen (1987, pp. 21, 52) holds that an economy dominated entirely by self-interest would neither maximize utility nor, if analysts employ this version of humankind, lead to an accurate prediction of economic outcomes. But even without that justification or precedent, political analysts who borrow their models from economics (e.g., Riker & Ordshook, 1973; Ferejohn & Fiorina, 1974), have thought that they were safely within the bounds of a universally understood human nature. That is not the case, either as a biological proposition (Hoffman, 1981; Zahn-Waxler, Cummings, & Ianotti, 1986) or as a cultural finding. For example, crosscultural measures of the "individualism-collectivism" dimension contrast primarily western attitudes that give priority to people's own goals with the primarily Asian and African collectivist priority of group goals (Hofstede 1984; Triandis 1995). The dominance of self-interest turns out to be a culture-bound, western concept; in collectivist societies group goals and group harmony take precedence.

Because of the work of David Sears and his colleagues and students (Sears & Funk, 1983; 1991; Sears & Citrin, 1982; Sears, Hensler, & Speer, 1979), I can explicate in more detail the incidence of self-interest in elections and opinion formation.

Self-Interest in Opinions and Elections

The interesting story of electoral self-interest could be captured by that familiar little verse:

> Last night upon the stair
> I met a man who wasn't there.
> He wasn't there again today,
> Oh how I wish he'd go away.

The basic form of Sears's and his colleagues' and students' research is to examine attitudinal and voting differences between those who are personally or through their families affected by a policy and those who are not so affected. The first studies were on attitudes toward school busing issues; as it turned out, the attitudes of white parents with children who were or were likely be bused were no different from those who were not. It was not their busing experiences but their basic ideologies, especially on race, that made the difference (Sears et al., 1979). Later, the political scientist Martin Gilens

(1999) was to confirm this pattern with evidence on attitudes toward welfare.

Sears and Funk (1991) then extended the analysis of self-interest to a review of a remarkably diverse array of issues, again comparing those affected by a policy and those not directly affected: toughness on crime, affirmative action, bilingual education, tax and transfer policies, abortion, the war in Vietnam. In each of these cases, there were no differences in attitudes by those affected (or with fear of being affected) and those who were not or did not have relevant fears. Only in the cases of large property owners affected by California's Proposition 13 and state employees' reactions to proposals to reduce state revenues was there evidence of self-interested opinions or votes. In sum, say Sears and Funk (1991).

> the general conclusion is quite clear: self-interest ordinarily does not have
> much effect upon the ordinary citizen's sociopolitical attitudes. There are
> only occasionally exceptions, as when there are quite substantial and
> clear stakes (especially regarding personal tax burdens) or ambiguous and
> dangerous threats. Moreover, self-interest effects generally turn out to be
> quite small, specific to the policies most narrowly linked to the self-
> interest dimension in question. (p. 76)

The more successful alternative theory relied on basic ideological positions dealing mainly with affectively freighted feelings about party identities, basic liberal or conservative values, ethnic identities, and racist or nonracist attitudes, which were then triggered by some issue in the political agenda. For rational choice as well as self-interest theories, Sears's research is fatal: if people use internal referents, as contrasted to the contingent, stimulus-response theory implied by rational choice and self-interest theories, the meanings of rationality and self-interest change and threaten circularity and tautology.

Five considerations interpret and modify this account of the failure of self-interest to shape opinion and influence voting. First, the apparent support for pocketbook voting (Kramer, 1983) turns out to be mainly "sociotropic voting," that is, voting influenced not by the voter's perception of her own benefits but rather by perception of the social benefits and costs of the given policy. It is headlines and ideology, not personal gain and loss, that make the difference (Kinder & Kiewiet, 1981). Second, self-interest has an influence in *priming* interest (Iyengar & Kinder, 1987), guiding attention, which is, in turn, further guided by the symbolic ideologies and identities that Sears found to bear the major explanatory weight for sociopolitical attitudes. Third, because self-interest has a narrow focus on specific issues as they arise, it does not organize general beliefs about government or policies. As John Stuart Mill (1910/1861), said, "interests by which they [human beings] will be led when they are thinking only of self-interest will be almost exclusively those which are obvious at first sight, and which operate on their present condition" (p. 153). Similarly, fourth, there is no reverse effect whereby symbolic or ideological interests are modified by later experience with issues that affect the self. Sears and Funk (1991) do not find this to be the case. Finally, the failure of self-interest to account for opinions on political affairs does not mean that people are selfless, for part of this lack of expression of *political* self-interest stems from people's sense that, at least in the United States, they are themselves responsible for solving their own problems: "What can I do to help myself?" (Brody & Sniderman, 1977). It is a paradox that self-attribution diminishes the expression of self-interest in political affairs.

The Larger Contributions of Psychology

With a grateful salute to the psychologists, we have relaxed the assumptions of materialism, rationalism, and self-regardingness attached to the political study of interests. Have we sufficiently clarified the politics of interests? Rescher (1969) is prescient: "what we now need more urgently is a better understanding of the *nature of the person* whose welfare is of interest and a conceptually more coherent and compelling welfare theory. We could also benefit from a richer understanding of the ... ways in which our tastes, preferences, and other values are formed" (p. 207). Without information on what people want and what is satisfying to them and what helps them understand their situations and cope effectively with them, the analysis of interests must necessarily be based on the opinions of outsiders, inferences from both current social values and beliefs about why people act as they do (Bem, 1972). In short, although psychology rarely uses the general concept of interests (except for self-interest) in its analysis,[1] psychology can rescue the politics of interests from itself.

◣ The Logic of Institutions

Political science is not just about individual attitudes and decisions; it is even more about institutions: parliaments, bureaucracies, courts, executives. Because people in institutions adopt *roles*, their individual attributes may be greatly modified by their acceptance (or rejection) of institutional goals and values. Of the many ways to study institutions (legal, organizational, recruitment and personnel policies, social impact, cost-benefit analysis, etc.) I will use the recently reinvigorated idea of "the logic of institutions." This is by no means home turf for psychologists (Himmelweit, 1990), although applied psychology has greatly illuminated behavior in the workplace (e.g., Lawler, 1982; Vroom, 1964)), consumer behavior (e.g., Jacoby 1976; Jacoby, Speller, & Kohn, 1974; McGuire, 1977; Mullen & Johnson, 1990), and, of course, political institutions. But even in these areas psychology focuses on individual (and group), not institutional, behavior. How then can psychology help with the logic of institutions?

The term "logic of institutions" has recently emerged from work on "the new institutionalism" (Friedland & Robertson, 1990; Powell & DiMaggio, 1991), although the idea is much older. Roger Friedland and Robert Alford (1991) define it as "a set of material practices and symbolic constructions—which constitutes its organizing principles and which is available to organizations and individuals to elaborate" (p. 248). Because I want to focus on outcomes, in this chapter I will define the logic of an institution as: *the intended and unintended consequences of the particular people, rules, practices, and resources devoted in a given context to a given organizational mission.* The logic for a market firm implies expanding business until marginal costs equal marginal revenues. On a grander scale, the logic of capitalism, said Marx (not his term), is its immanent tendency to concentrate income among the owners of capital to the point where workers (proletariat) can no longer buy the products of their own labor.

Much of the work of analyzing psychology's contribution to the logic of institutions has been done by undermining the assumptions of economic man, his materialism, rationalism, and exclusively self-interested behavior. Beyond that, however, there is the fundamental epistemological assault on the ready application of deductive logic, the basis of most economic analysis. The logic of institutions shares something of this tendency. Thus, in dealing with that logic there is an incompatibility arising "from the fact that economics is largely a deductive science and psychology an inductive one." Whereas economists assume their models of the human personality, psychologists "tend to derive their model of man from the observations that they make" (Lewis, 1982, p. viii). Economics took its methods from physics and mathematics; psychology from something closer to what was to be studied, the variable world of human beings. Deduction is a valuable scientific tool, of course, but deduction from false premises is not.

All "Logics" Must Be Interpreted

Since many institutions have multiple missions (as a legislature's mission is both to reflect the wishes of its various constituencies and to serve overall national interests), (1) agents inevitably have to choose which mission to serve (DiMaggio & Powell, 1991, pp. 29–30). In addition, (2) for the logic of an institution to be meaningful, agents must be assumed to identify with the interests of their institutions; otherwise these loosely allied agents of institutions experience none of the force of the "logic's" imperatives. But we know from the general analysis of agent-principal problems that this is frequently not the case. Liebenstein (1976), for example, shows the consequences to a firm of an agent's conflict between her own and the institution's interest. Furthermore, (3) the outcome of the logic of any one institution is unpredictable, for two reasons: (a) the internal conflict within an institution has uncertain outcomes and cannot be predicted from the institution's imputed logic, and (b) conflict between institutions takes two forms, ideological (symbolic) and structural, that is, the rationales defending the various institutional missions challenge each other while the structures struggle for turf and resources in more concrete ways (Friedland & Alford, 1991, p. 249). Finally, (4) "when social scientists import the dominant institutional logics into their analyses of individuals and organizations in unexamined ways, they . . . risk becoming ideolog[ists] of the institutions they study" (p. 262). *Quis custodiet custodes ipsos?* Who will interpret the interpreters themselves?

The point is that the use of that inviting word "logic" is misleading because of the difficulty of making valid inferences about an institution's behavior from the logic of that institution. Psychologists, with their inductive methods, can help expose this pretension. Two cases make this clear: the logic of democracy and the logic of bureaucracy.

The Logic of Democracy

Given that each voter in a democratic election is assumed to vote for his own self-interest and that the interests most prominently at stake are thought to be material, it is logical that all voters with incomes below the mean will vote for redistribution from the rich to the less rich. Because the income distribution is skewed, there are many more voters below the mean than above it. If the poorer voters vote, there will be redistribution. Q.E.D.

If, however, enough poor people believe that they or their children will be rich someday, they may resist distribution. So much is accepted by economic analysts of the polity, but they seem unaware of other impediments to this logic. For example, almost two thirds (62 percent) of the American public believe that their circumstances are better than average, while only 13 percent believe they are worse off (Andrews & Withey, 1976, p. 317). The distribution of beliefs on this score is similar in Germany (Glatzer, 1991, p. 268). Other beliefs also contribute to this reluctance to redistribute.

A second source of redistribution would be people's "natural" feelings of sympathy for the poor and disadvantaged—the almsgiving recommended by all major religions. But the belief that we are each of us responsible for our own fate is a major impediment to redistribution. For example, it is more characteristic of North Americans than Europeans (Katona, Strumpel, & Zahn, 1971, pp. 55–57) or Latin Americans and people in other less developed countries (Reitz & Groff, 1974), or most Asian countries (Brislin, 1983, p. 384). The belief in people's control over their own fates is part of a larger pattern of attribution: one can explain human behavior by reference to *circumstances* (accidents, persecution, exploitation—the kinds of things Barrington Moore (1972) believes cause "human misery") or to *dispositions* (incompetence, moral obtuseness, greed). This distinction between explaining behavior by circumstance or by disposition has been said to be "the most important global psychological view" in the entire arsenal of causal theories. And in the West, especially in the United States, it is the dispositional theories that prevail (Nisbett & Ross, 1980, pp. 30, 31).

The belief that people are the origins of their own outcomes and not the pawns of fate or powerful others influences three important mediating attitudes: (1) beliefs about justice, (2) emotional responses to the disadvantaged, and (3) more directly, willingness to help the disadvantaged.

A belief in a just world (BJW; Lerner, 1980) is directly shaped by dispositional attributions. For example, a test of this widely shared belief includes such items as: "People who get 'lucky breaks' have usually earned their good fortune" and "People who meet with misfortune often have brought it on themselves." Those who score high on the BJW scale bias their perceptions of reality to accommodate their justice beliefs. In short, the poor deserve their poverty.

Interpretation of generalized, nonspecific arousal is a second step in this explanation. People may be aroused yet uncertain which emotion is the right one: pity, anger, irritation, despair, hope? The interpretation of the arousal then requires an explanation of what happened or is happening, that is, attribution (Weiner, 1985). Thus the dispositional attributions that characterize the West generally and the United States in particular shape all manner of emotions, including those that influence attitudes toward the poor and the ill. Again, the attribution to dispositions rather than circumstances turns the arousal to blame rather than pity.

The third step in this tripartite theory is the consequent willingness or unwillingness to help. In brief, if the victim's situation arouses anger, observers are unwilling to help; if it arouses pity, they are willing. Thus dispositional attributions led to emotions that permitted observers either to blame the victim and withhold help or to blame circumstances beyond the victim's control and so to pity and help (Schwarzer & Weiner, 1991).

The logic of democracy says that in pursuing their self-interest, voters below the national income mean will be likely to vote for tax and transfer plans. Rosy perceptions of their own positions in this income ladder tend to undermine this logic. And the tendency to employ dispositional explanations to account for poverty, leading to blame instead of pity, further undermines support for redistribution (Lane, 2001).

The Logic of Bureaucracy

The logic of bureaucracy has three facets. When Weber (1909, in Mayer 1944) said that bureaucracy was one of the two main sources of rationality in modern society (the other was the market), he was not complimenting bureaucracy. On the contrary, for him the rationality of bureaucracy was a "parceling out of the soul" and a stifling of curiosity, the Faustian spirit of man. Most people think Weber was prescient about the causes of the failure of the great communist experiments of eastern Europe, seeing what Marx never did see. What is the logic of bureaucracy that so offended Weber and also permitted him to predict an outcome hidden to those who thought they understood "the logic of capitalism"? Before answering that question, I must clarify one point about the logic of bureaucracy: it is not to be confounded with the logic of the market. Evidence of the greater efficiency of private as compared to public bureaucracies (Borcherding, Pommerehne, & Schneider, 1982; Wolf, 1988) is impressive but not conclusive: a municipal bus line loses money running buses to thinly populated areas because the city wants to create incentives to deconcentrate the urban population. Which is more efficient? Efficiency has many dimensions beyond the balance sheet, as in the Prussian army and the Society of Jesus.

Distilling from Crozier (1964), Merton (1968), Kamenka (1989), and Wilson (1990), one might characterize the logic of bureaucracy in the following terms: (1) impersonality of official-client relations (to reduce favoritism); (2) interchangeability of personnel (to achieve a standardized product); (3) rule-bound decision-making processes (implying insensitivity to particular cases); (4) hierarchical organization; (5) relative security of tenure of officeholders, and (6) incentives to expand staff and budgets, not because the services are "needed" but because a larger organization justifies greater power and salary for the head of an agency and pleases subordinates (Niskanen, 1971). Less formally, one might say that these characteristics, in turn, imply (7) officious behavior by clerks who wrap themselves in the majesty of government to cloak their lack of individual significance; (8) inability to change means to serve overall ends prescribed by the charter of the organization; (9) higher rewards to prudence and caution than to daring and innovation (see Powell & DiMaggio, 1991, p. 249).

These inferences about the logic of bureaucracy are so familiar as to seem like an itemization of the ingredients of a stereotype. And like a stereotype, this interpretation of the logic of bureaucracy is, indeed, misleading. In the first place, studies of actual bureaucrats find them much more flexible than the above caricature claims (Kohn, 1971). Put differently, if the agent internalizes the purposes of the organization, she may serve the purpose as well as the rule (Zeitz, 1984). Second, Heclo's (1974) crossnational studies of welfare and health agencies found that the expansion of these agencies followed careful analysis of certain needs not served at the time—and not just padded payrolls. Third, in an article entitled "The Logic of Public Sector Growth," Aaron Wildavsky (1985) explores in depth the various theories of the growth of the state relative to the growth of the economy. He concludes that each country gets the level of government its people want (or wanted): "cultural change precedes and dominates budgetary change: the size of the state today is a function of its political culture yesterday" (p. 257). The "logic" of bureaucracy is not just an immanent unfolding of the structure of its incentives but a response to changes in technology, ideology, and wealth as these are reflected in its culture.

In violation of the "logic of bureaucracy," bureaucratic encounters are much more satisfying to clients than the stereotype would lead us to expect. In 1973 Daniel Katz and his colleagues (Katz, Gutek, Kahn, & Barton, 1975) studied the experiences reported by a national sample of almost 1,500 people with seven service agencies (welfare, pension, health, employment, etc.) and four "control" agencies (tax, police, driver's licenses, traffic regulation). They found that the public's personal experiences with nonregulative government bureaucracies are actually experienced by subjects as rather benign: there were usually agents available to handle a person's inquiry or complaint, these agents took personal responsibility for the case presented and pursued the matter to a conclusion, the agents were usually courteous and informed, and so forth. But do these favorable bureaucratic encounters change people's attitudes toward "government bureaucracy"? No. The default values of the familiar stereotypes of bureaucracy prevail: ideology triumphs over experience.

As in the case of the failed logic of self-interest in democratic elections, so the logic of bureaucracy seems to be a poor predictor of bureaucratic behavior in a democracy. In both cases, the substance of psychology makes an important contribution to setting things straight, but so does the skeptical empiricism that informs psychological theory and research, the unwillingness to accept "logics" where plural influences are at work undermining one such "logic" to establish another. The psychologist's preference for inductive reasoning based on observation, mentioned earlier, saves political science from its inferences from principles that overlap and confound each other.

▶ Political Processes and Psychological Processes

Political science sometimes stakes out a claim to a turf characterized as *political processes*. Psychology is about intra- and interindividual (including group) processes. They intersect where individuals and their interrelationships influence institutional behavior, that is, most of the time. As mentioned, institutions create *roles* that modify individual behavior, but the interpretation of roles is partly an individual matter, as we know from the differences between authoritarian and democratic teachers in the same role. But setting this aside for the moment, would it be fruitful to create a matrix where political processes are crossed by psychological processes? To simplify, consider table 21.1, with only three political processes—electoral, legislative, and judicial—and three loosely defined types of psychological processes: selected cognitive processes, personality (e.g., "big five") expression (the remnant of the old personality and politics literature), and emotional and motivational arousal. Please understand that this is at best illustrative; other psychological themes, such as internal-external attribution, concrete versus formal operations, and types of justice beliefs might serve equally well. I do not know, but such intersections may be the basic, if unacknowledged, paradigm of political psychology.

Would it be possible to summarize and interpret the rows as accounts of political processes and the columns as accounts of psychological processes in different political situations? Let us try. The electoral row says that electoral outcomes are influenced by tendencies to attend to the vivid, personal, and immediate (Tversky & Kahneman, 1981), possibly producing "nonattitudes" (Converse, 1964) on the more pallid issues in the campaign, a tendency competing with the influence of affectively loaded symbols learned in late adolescence. (Sears, 1983). Extroverts will receive more information of these kinds than introverts or those who are anxious and fearful ("neuroticism"—see Lubinski, 2000). All of this occurs in a sphere that is unusually marked by negative affectivity, risking cynicism and withdrawal (Lau, 1985; 2002). But if the people were happy, these risks are minimized (Isen, 1987). As an agenda for research, this is not bad but it is only a sampling of what a psychological theory of electoral processes might look like.

The legislative process illustrated in table 21.1 is influenced by the conflict in legislators' minds over service to their constituents and parties and to their concepts of the public interest, a conflict marked by the tendency to reduce dissonance by interpreting the public interest as identical with the interests of their parties and their constituents (Abelson Aronson, McGuire, Newcomb, Rosenberg, & Tannenbaum 1968; see Festinger,

Table 21.1
Matrix of Political and Psychological Processes

	Psychological		
Political	Selected cognitive processes	"Personality and Politics"	Emotional-motivational
Electoral	Availability heuristic v. symbolic salience v. nonattitudes; linear v. lateral thinking	Extroversion v. neuroticism, e.g., 2 of big 5 = approach v. avoid others	Negative affectivity v. positivity bias; happy v. unhappy
Legislative	Cognitive dissonance, e.g., party loyalty v. ideology; solidarity or task leader?	Authoritarian v. egalitarian personality; traits & multiple demands	n-achieve v. n-affiliation v. n-power
Judicial	Linear v. associative thinking	Egalitarianism, e.g., debtors v. creditors	Cognitive assessment of emotions

1957). Quite apart from the official leadership of each house (majority leader, speaker, etc.), leadership will be informally divided between a task leader and a group solidarity leader (Bales, 1950). Although it seems that public officials are not more authoritarian than are comparable others (McConaughy, 1950), they must find some comfort in exercising power, as well as having a strong achievement motive to be successful in public life (Browning & Jacob, 1954). The trait approach to predicting legislative behavior, however, is complicated by the multiple demands of the legislators' situations (Gibb, 1979).

On civil rights decisions, judges might reflect the differences that Zellman and Sears (1971) found between the linear thinking of those less favorable to civil rights and the lateral or associative thinking of those more favorable. In the perpetual contest between the debtors and creditors noted by Madison, the egalitarianism of judges would probably affect their decisions (Sinclair & Mark, 1991). Finally, because sympathy and anger toward a victim depend on whether a judge thinks the victim brought misfortune on herself, the habits of attribution of the judge will greatly affect the outcome (Weiner, 1985).

Has this illustrative matrix said anything new about electoral, legislative, and judicial processes? Nothing that psychologists wouldn't guess, although possibly the matrix offers insights for political scientists. But why are the columns so much less satisfactory as research agenda for psychological research? One reason is that our publics are interested in political processes, however they are affected, rather than psychological processes in special settings, political or otherwise. But there is, I think, a possible opening here, for example, political thinking across various political roles (see Tetlock, 1981, 1983), a Piagetian interpretation of politics (Rosenberg, Ward, & Clinton, 1989), a script theory (Abelson, 1981), and perhaps a theory of politics as "mindless" (Langer, 1990)—to take the place of the now defunct but once almost dominant Freudian theories (e.g., Lasswell, 1930).

Politics as the Study of Power

One turns with relief from the wordy, often taxonomic, heavily moralized political treatments of power (e.g., Bachrach & Baratz, 1962; Lasswell, Merriam, & Smith, 1950; Lukes, 1975; Poulantzas, 1978; Rogow & Lasswell, 1963; Sampson, 1965). To psychological discussion of power, dominance, and obedience. Although political psychology offers interpretations of power motivation (McClelland, 1975; Winter, 1973; but see Foster & Rusbult, 1999), it is more successful in its accounts of what happens to people engaged in both sides of a power relationship (see hereafter). It also offers well-founded accounts of less coercive but no less asymmetrical methods of influence and persuasion (e.g., Hovland, Janis, & Kelley, 1953; Katz & Lazarsfeld 1965/1955). Oddly, although there is a substantial political science literature on the distribution of power and its justification (e.g., Hobbes (1950/1650; *Federalist*, 1894/1790), one must turn to psychology (and primatology) for studies of dominance and obedience (but see Somit & Peterson, 1995).

A few words on the sometimes elusive literature on attitudes toward power and power orientation are in order. First, among other features: the psychology of power distinguishes between *outcome* orientation (focus on instrumental power to get something done) and *process* orientation (the enjoyment of using power in directing others) partly because outcome orientation modifies the universal antipathy toward power seekers (McClelland, 1975, pp. 7, 17). In economics, process orientation has a curious unmarketlike effect: it is associated with the growth but not the profitability of a firm (McClelland & Winter, 1971). More generally, power-oriented people (Machiavellians) do tend to manipulate others, to have few intimates but many acquaintances, to be regarded as leaders by others, and to be successful in games but not in life (Christie & Geis, 1970). Power-oriented people are unpopular for good reasons: they suffer from an atrophy of conscience—but we would be in a bad way if the indignation of those who have witnessed some injustice did not lead them to seek power to redress these wrongs (Foster & Rusbult 1999).

As everyone knows, Lord Acton (1904/1887) said that "power tends to corrupt and absolute power corrupts absolutely." It is an interesting thesis, widely and artfully quoted, but in what sense is it true? One sense comes from political psychology's studies of the effects of power on an authority's self-attribution: the person issuing a command believes that the command is the reason for the obedience of the commanded, whether or not they would have done that particular commanded act if there had been no such command. The desire to see the self as a cause means that authorities tend to deprive their subjects of their own senses of autonomy, taking a narrow post hoc, propter hoc view of their own actions (Gilbert, Jones, & Pelham, 1987). Milgram's (1974) experiments in malignant obedience shed further light: if an authority is clothed in the legitimacy of office, most people will obey conscience-violating orders because they can shed responsibility for their acts and because virtue then lies in performing well the task undertaken rather than in conscientious action. Protection against yielding to malignant obedience comes from a well-founded sense of internal locus of control (Lefcourt, 1976, 1984).

A study by David Kipnis (1972) helps to show in further detail what Acton might have meant by his famous aphorism. Twenty-eight undergraduates studying business administration were given jobs supervising "workers" in tasks with speed criteria. One half of the supervisors were given coercive power (adjusting pay and imposing fines) while the other half had no such power, relying only on their skills in persuasion. Strength of desire for social relations with the workers was also measured. The supervisors endowed with coercive power used their powers with the following sequential effects (p. 40):

1. Power increased the temptations to use it to influence subordinates' behavior.
2. Using power increased the belief that others' behavior is controlled only by the authority's orders.
3. Hence powerful authorities devalue others' performances and persons.
4. Devaluation increased the social distance with subordinates, who were then viewed as objects of manipulation and deserving of contempt for not controlling their own behavior.

If the political scientist's analysis of the uses of power and the political philosopher's justification of various distributions are important, so are the psychologists' studies of the effects of power on the powerful and the powerless. And feelings of powerlessness, well covered by research in attribution (e.g., Lefcourt, 1976, 1984; Seligman, 1973), turn out to be among the most important sources of political apathy and mental illness (Mirowski & Ross, 1989). In addition, the high incidence of psychosocial disorders among aborigines in Australia and the United States is at least partly owing to their sense of powerlessness (Kahn, 1986).

In all primate societies power is unevenly distributed, with sometimes tragic effects on the personalities and apparent happiness of those who are low in the order of dominance. The neuroscientist and primatologist Robert Sapolsky (1999) traces the sources and consequences of "stress-response," a physiological response that gives temporary energy and relief from pain to animals where survival (fight or flight) is at stake but that in humans can be chronically present when symbolic, cognitive skills evoke it. "Many studies of social primates," says Sapolsky, "suggest that low ranking individuals have chronically activated stress-response and are more prone to stress related diseases" (p. 453). This is partly owing to their lack of resources, the greater unpredictability of their lives, and to more fragile sense of personal control. What is so fascinating about this account is that it gives a physiological foundation to the study of power, powerlessness, and the analysis of social class.

◤ Political Philosophy and Political Psychology

Political psychology contributes to political philosophy through its research on the very kinds of ends and goals that distinguish most political philosophy and some political theory. *En passant*, one might note that psychology can also explicate the evaluative process itself (Mandler, 1982) in ways that supplement the more familiar philosophy of science (Hempel, 1952; Popper, 1959). But that is not one of the main points.

Political Philosophy and Causal Analysis

The first point I would like to make is the problem philosophy has in dealing with causes. Political philosophy (and often political theory) retains many of the humanistic characteristics of philosophy, the mother of all the social (and natural) sciences. Philosophy is very good at "unpacking" meanings: "What do we mean when we say . . . 'responsibility,' 'fair,' 'freedom'?" No one does it better. Although philosophy also deals well with *verbal* implication, it has no way to handle causal analysis, which is always the province, implicitly or explicitly, of science: at its core: if *a*, then *b because* of prior occurrence of *a* and, most important, because of some forcing relationship between *a* and *b*. "Because" is tricky, for it may mean verbal implication, for example, the right to vote is implied by the concept of democracy. Or causal implication: for example, if poor people are given the right to vote, they will redistribute income from the rich to the poor. As a science, psychology adds causal theory to these ethical judgments (Lane, 2000b).

The Contribution of Psychology to Normative Analysis

Political science is, rather more than psychology, a normative discipline, justifying as much as it explains. Not just "who gets what, when, how" (Lasswell, 1936) but who *should* get what. Not just the uses of free choice but the justification of free choice. One might have thought that this area of justification, lying closer to philosophy, was more distant from psychology, but in several respects that is not so, for four reasons. (1) All good justifications are implicitly consequential, that is, they deal with cause-and-effect relations. Often psychology has a theory of the causes and consequences of, say, choice, as in Jack Brehm's (1972) reactance theory (told that they cannot have *C*, those who preferred *B* to *C* now prefer *C*). In addition, (2), psychology explains normative judgments themselves: "just-world" beliefs (Lerner, 1980), equity beliefs (Walster, Berscheid, & Walster, 1976), moral judgment (Kohlberg, 1981). This is quite different from ethics itself—saying what *is* fair and unfair. (3) Because philosophers since Aristotle (*Ethics,* 1961/1952) appeal to the norms of the time—in modern versions calling these norms "our intuitions"—psychology can appropriately contribute to this facet of ethical discussion by helping us understand how norms are formed and used (Miller, 1999; Miller & Rattner, 1998); an understanding that also helps avoid circularity (each people's "intuitions" generally confirm the norms of their own societies and oppose the different norms of other societies). Finally, (4) psychology makes its own contribution to the ends of government, as I will show in the final section of this chapter.

People as Ends, as Means, and as Causes

There is an ethical and a causal or explanatory boundary to the treatment of humans as means and causes. From Kant (1949/1797]) we learn that people are to be treated only as ends and never purely as means, but this is often innocently breached, as in political theories of agency and psychological theories of attribution. Because of his devotion to autonomy, Kant surely approved of humans as causes. But one cannot be a cause without also being a means to the effect consequent to the cause. If I decide something autonomously, I am both a cause of and a means to the outcome following from my decision. Anyone who is a cause of something is also a means to its realization. The ethical limit, then, allows that people should be treated as means but insists that by the same act they should also be treated as ends.

The explanatory limit hinges on the nature of social and historical causation. It is not the Kantian proscription that governs the interpretation of human causation so much as the rules for accounting for variance in human behavior. As mentioned, explanations of human behavior may emphasize dispositions or circumstances, but they will usually explain more if they account for *interaction* between the two (Bem & Funder, 1978). Psychologists will excuse me if I point out to others that political psychology in no way implies a greater emphasis on dispositions (Mischel, 1968) and indeed honors the view that exclusively dispositional analyses represent "the fundamental attributional error" (Ross, 1977). In this way psychology also avoids "methodological individualism" (Lukes, 1973), which says that everything is explainable in terms of human properties, as in great man theories of history. What are sacred are the ends, human well-being and human development (see hereafter), and not human agency—certainly a desideratum but not a necessary cause.

◤ Freedom and Choice

Freedom is the external circumstance extending human choice. As negative freedom, it means lack of constraint on choices; as positive freedom, it is opportunity to exercise a degree of control over one's own fate (Berlin, 1969). It is appropriate in this discussion of political psychology, however, to focus on the subjective phenomena that freedom facilitates, choice itself. Like market economics, political science makes a fetish of choice (Schwartz, 2000): its presence justifies many evils that follow because, after all, people *chose* those evils. Majority decisions are justified because more people chose a particular outcome than opposed it; rights to free expression are justified as protections for minorities to choose something else at another time— and to express themselves at all times. Fetish? Choices must be made; if not by the self, then by others for the self. It is perilous territory. Let me say at the outset of this discussion that what is at stake is not the value of freedom but rather the conditions for making choices more fruitful. What can psychology tell us about the value and perils and mechanisms of the choices offered by such freedom?

Freedom as Capability

Although it was Christian Bay (1965/1958) who, to my knowledge, was the first to formally define freedom in terms of *capacity* to choose, more recently Amartya Sen (1999) has elaborated this argument for a human development approach to economic development. These are philosophers and economists. To achieve the same kind of capacities, psychologists, I believe, would give priority to a belief that one is, indeed, able to influence the circumstances of one's life: internal locus of control (Kelley, 1973; Lefcourt, 1976, 1984; Strickland, 1989; Weiner, 1995). People without that belief will probably avoid choices or choose unfreedom, consonant with their belief that others already control their fates. One implication is that to expand freedom (choices), policy must expand people's sense of internality, and one way to do that is to increase the number of choices that teach them that when they act, their little environments do, in fact, respond (Seligman, 1973). Neither industrial democracy (Lafferty, 1989) nor national elections (Lane, 2000a) do this very well, but perhaps, going back a step in the causal sequence, giving the franchise to people who have been denied it serves that purpose rather well (Cataldo, Johnson, & Kellstadt, 1968). The hypothesis here is that exercising a familiar franchise does not increase one's sense of competence, but being included in the franchise after having been excluded from it does.

Capability as Emotional Maturity

Enhancing capacities for choice as a means of promoting effective freedom goes beyond cognitive abilities and beliefs to the regulation of emotions, not suppressing them, of course, but developing emotional intelligence: " 'Emotional intelligence' refers to *the capacity for recognizing our own feelings and those of others, for motivating ourselves, and for managing emotions within ourselves and in our relationships*" (Goleman, 1998, pp. 317, emphasis in original). Physiologically, it coordinates the processing of the emotional centers of the brain (in the subcortex) with the intellectual centers in the neocortex. Practically, it restores to the concept of rationality the capacity to know what one really wants: "using our deepest preferences to move and guide us toward our goals, to help us take initiative and strive to improve and to persevere in the face of setbacks and frustration" (Goleman, 1998, p. 318; see also Mayer & Salovey, 1993). The associated improvement in interpersonal relations and self-control has another payoff: it answers Zimbardo's (1969) plea for emotional control when people are tempted to abuse freedom, yielding to "impulse, and chaos."

Freedom as Source and Beneficiary of Complex Thinking

In a paean to free discussion that is reminiscent of John Stuart Mill, Walter Bagehot (n.d./1869) argued that "nothing promotes intellect like intellectual discussion and nothing promotes intellectual discussion so much as government by discussion" (p. 199) Plausible enough, and consonant with the amazing rise in IQ throughout the West (Flynn, 1987), but, like Acton's dictum about power, at best a research proposal. Could it be true? In the first place, the cause is rather distant from the alleged effect of promoting intellect. What promotes intellect? Much, perhaps 40 percent, of the variance, is given by genes (Jencks et al., 1979, p. 188) while much of the remainder is shaped early in childhood (Vernon, 1969)—as Bagehot acknowledges. And there are many kinds of "intellect," some, like "practical intelligence" (Sternberg, 1998) have little to do with the forms of intellect that may be learned by watching or participating in government by discussion.

On a gross level, how would Bagehot explain the high "intellect" of both mainland Chinese (without benefit of government by discussion) and overseas Chinese in Taiwan and the United States who share those benefits? Democratic theorists wish Bagehot to be right—but that is not enough for political psychologists. For example, Barry Schwartz (2000) argues with evidence that "freedom, autonomy, and self-determination can become excessive, and that when that happens, freedom can be experienced as a kind of tyranny. . . . Influenced by the ideology of economics and rational-choice theory, modern American society has created an excess of freedom, with resulting increases in people's dissatisfaction with their lives and in clinical depression" (p. 79).

On the other hand, the presence of alternatives does promote an increase in what some psychologists call "cognitive complexity" (Harvey, Hunt, & Schroder, 1961), that is, "holding in mind several elements or dimensions of a situation or problem and the use of some integrating rules to select among them" (p. 10) In contrast, cognitive simplicity employs a single or at most two opposing rules and responds in a stimulus-bound, binary manner. Such complexity has been found to be a condition for democratic group operations, since these involve multiple points of view that require integration (Schroder & Harvey, 1963, p. 161). As Bagehot (1869) says, for government by discussion to have the desired effect, people must want to discuss—and if they then do discuss, they must meet the conditions for such discussion. Finally, to the extent that more freedom is associated with more complex environments, it should produce greater dendritic arborization and heavier brain mass in humans, as in other mammals

(Kolb & Whishaw, 1998). If we do not take too literally Bagehot's "intellect" but rather translate it as "intelligent political decisions," we find a plausible hypothesis, devoid of unwarranted generalization, that seems supported by experiments on deliberative democracy (Fishkin, 1991; Gutman & Thompson, 1996). Good, but the blessed tendency of the experimental method to examine preferred outcomes raises some questions.

Where Increasing Choice Makes for Poorer Choices

In a provocative article on the expansion of choice, Sheena Iyengar and Mark Lepper (2000, p. 995) ask: "Can one desire too much of a good thing?" Their experiments in both laboratory and field settings show that people are more likely to show a refined "gourmet" taste in their shopping and students are more likely to "undertake optional class essay assignments when, in each case, subjects are offered a limited array of 6 choices rather than a more extensive array of 24 or 30 choices" (p. 995). Moreover, participants enjoyed the shopping more and wrote better essays when given fewer choices. In another experiment using shopping as the opportunity for more or fewer choices, Jacoby, Speller, and Kohn (1974) offered 4 or 6 or 12 different detergents to shoppers. The authors found that, according to the shoppers' own criteria of the kinds of things they wanted, they chose *worse* with more options than with fewer. Unlike the Iyengar and Lepper experiment, however, Jacoby and colleagues' shoppers liked the greater number of options better. The possibility that the more options offered, the poorer the quality of choice has gone into consumer behavior textbooks as a more or less reliable, counterintuitive finding (Engel, Blackwell, & Kollat, 1978, p. 602). For political scientists, experience with the Australian long ballot (proliferating choices) makes this tendency of the quality of choice to deteriorate with increased options—with consequent declining information on each option—a familiar political problem.

Cognitive Overload

Few complaints about modernity are more familiar than the allegation of its tendency to impose on people more stimuli and information than they can assimilate or handle. Stimulus overload is said to be a cause of lack of friendliness in cities (Milgram, 1974), of lower rates of prosocial behavior at busy intersections (Korte, Ytema, & Toppen, 1975), of low influence of advertising (Mullen & Johnson, 1990), and of political withdrawal: for example, the following item was frequently included in the annual surveys of the National Election Studies (NES): "Sometimes politics and government seem so complicated that a person like me can't really understand what's going on." From 1952 to 1992 about 75 percent of the public agreed with that statement (NES data bank). More generally, "more information is estimated to have been produced in the last 15 years than in the whole of previous history" (London *Independent,* August 4, 1991, p. 18).

The perverse effects of information overload are documented in consumer studies, managerial studies, and political studies. A study of consumer choices of breakfast cereals shows that with 16 brands and 35 dimensions (sweetness, nutrition, texture, etc.—$16 \times 35 = 560$ cells), the mean number of dimensions used was 4.9, while a fifth of the shoppers paid attention only to familiar brands (Jacoby, 1976). At the managerial level: "when inundated with data, [managers] make more mistakes, misunderstand others and snap at co-workers. The result can be flawed conclusions and foolish decisions, causing potentially great financial loss to companies" (Murray, 1998, p. 42). In the study of level of thinking in a political problem-solving experiment mentioned earlier, it was found that complexity of thought tracked complexity of problem up to a breaking point (different for each participant) and then sharply declined to the most simple-minded heuristics (Schroder, Driver, & Streufert, 1967).

Informed Choices

In their defense of freedom, philosophers, dimly aware of the pitfalls in the choice process, like to specify that they don't mean any old choices but rather "informed choices" (e.g., Griffin, 1986). How this criterion for acceptable choices copes with information overload is not clear. But perhaps it refers to some special kind of knowledge, like self-knowledge or contemplative knowledge. In one experiment, Wilson and Schooler (1991) asked students to analyze all their reasons for choosing a certain food and in a second experiment to evaluate the relevant attributes of a list of courses they might take. "Both kinds of introspection caused people to make choices that, compared with control [subjects'], corresponded less with expert opinion" (p. 2). What seems to have happened is that focusing on reasons and itemizing attributes distracted people from the objective qualities of the objects they were choosing among. Like rational choice, "informed choice" is a desideratum without a method, a cognitive state without a cognitive process to implement it. Here is where the political psychologist can be most helpful.

The field of pitfalls when choosing is a rich expanse: use of stereotypes as default schemas; search for shortcut decision rules that, in the event, mislead; inability, by power of will; to *not* think about an attribute (e.g., skin color), inability to decide once one's preferences have been clarified, and so forth. Reading John Stuart Mill (1910/1859), Isaiah Berlin (1969), or Stuart Hampshire (1975) on freedom gives the liberal conscience a pleasant glow; reading Richard Nisbett and Lee Ross (1980) on the many "shortcomings" in human inference, or Robert Zajonc (1980) on the priority of emotional evaluation over cognitive evaluation, one wonders how humankind has done as well as it has in creating and sustaining democracies over the years. Knowing the pitfalls, perhaps we can do better.

◣ Equality as a Political Goal

Equality has an epistemological standing different from that of freedom, for, like R. M. Hare (1981), we might say that it is logical for like things to be treated in like manner, or we might provide a theological justification for treating God's creatures with identical concern, or, like Kant (1949/ 1797), we might say that because human dignity is not to be bartered it has no exchange rate, or like Rawls (1971) that because justice itself is defined by equal treatment, any departure from equality needs to be justified. Like all science, psychology is speechless in the face of such defenses. But once a consequential argument is entered, then we are in empirical territory and cannot rely only on a priori justifications of ethics but rather must follow causal chains to achieve a cost-benefit analysis (with all its implicit norms) for egalitarian policies. Does, for example, equality of circumstances contribute to subjective well-being? Veenhoven's (1993, pp. 48, 50, 132) analysis of the relation between income equality and well-being across 23 nations finds no such relation. To support this finding, a later study of 55 nations (Diener et al., 1995, p. 861) finds that with level of income controlled, income equality correlates at only a nonsignificant .04 level with measures of SWB.

The known positive hedonic effect of downward comparisons (Wills, 1981) may also inhibit equality from maximizing SWB in any given population (Brickman & Campbell, 1971). Stripped of their a priori standing, arguments for equality must also confront its effects on striving and motivation, the possible rise of envy over small differences as equality becomes the standard (Tocqueville, 1945, vol. 2, p. 135), and whether or not people want income equality. I found (Lane, 1959) that the idea of income equality frightened working-class people who did not care about the higher income of elites but resented the idea that the underclass people down the street would have as much income as they.

The point is that the values that seem to justify making such democratic goals as freedom and equality the standards by which we judge our institutions and practices are not ultimate goods but rather means to the ultimate goods that we have not yet explored.

◣ The Psychology of Political Ends

"Personality psychologists have long been aware that their work was saturated with values, either their own or the values of the cultures in which they worked" (Haan, 1977, p. 64). In speaking of mental health "one asserts that these psychological attributes are 'good.' And, inevitably, the question is raised: Good for what? Good in terms of middle class ethics? Good for democracy? For the social *status quo?* . . . The list could be continued" (Jahoda, 1958, p. 77). So psychologists have a set of values of which they are (sometimes) aware and toward which their science is (sometimes) pointed. Probably because of selective forces in recruitment (including selecting out antiintraceptive biases), "most psychologists are politically liberal and conservatives are vastly underrepresented" (Redding, 2001, p. 205). How would the application of the (sometimes) admitted values and the publicly unacknowledged liberalism be reflected in shaping political ends?

Political Ends in the Period of the New Humanism

Although "humanism" has recently been used in contrast to science; I want to use it in the older Enlightenment's sense of placing human beings, not God nor Mammon, at the center of our value system; and, perversely, I wish to call it the *New* Humanism, new in the sense of applying to the postindustrial and postmodernization period. There is philosophical authority for this emphasis, as, for example, when David Ross (1930) says of ultimate values, "contemplate any imaginary universe from which you suppose mind entirely absent, and you will fail to find anything in it that you can call good in itself" (p. 140). Earlier, the utilitarian Henry Sidgewick (1907, vol. 1, p. ix) said: "if we consider carefully such permanent results as are commonly judged to be good, other than qualities of human beings, we can find nothing that, on reflection, appears to possess this quality of goodness." For reasons well understood by the sociology of knowledge, just as economists value the market and political theorists value democracy above other goods, so psychologists will value their subject matter, human beings, above other goods. They are apostles of the New Humanism.

But I want to go further and specify just what it is about human beings that psychologists can, with some authority, add to the roster of political ends. These qualities are human development and subjective well-being. Like claims for all ultimate goods, in the last analysis these are merely reasoned assertions, but the reasoning would claim that if it is human beings who are valuable, then their value must have specified qualities, qualities that are better if developed than otherwise. For moralists, note that a prime human quality is virtue (conscientiousness, empathy, and benevolence). And if people's lives are so valuable, so (by a process of reasoning that is not quite linear) one might infer that the quality of their lives shares in that value.

Government and Subjective Well-Being

Even the Enlightenment thinkers who wrote the Declaration of Independence and drafted the Constitution of the United States proposed only that government facilitate individual *pursuit* of happiness, with no promise that government should or could actually make people happier. It is just as well: crosscultural studies show that after GDP per capita is controlled, there is no relationship between level of democratic practices and happiness (Veenhoven, 1993, p. 50; Diener et al., 1995, p. 861). Although there is a relationship in Europe between years of stable democracy and happiness (Inglehart & Rabier, 1986, p. 52), these authors hold that while happiness makes for stable democracy, they cannot claim that democracy makes people happy. The main point here, however, lies in another direction. In spite of Aristotle, is it really true that people in all societies value happiness in the same way and to the same degree? Apparently not: using various measures of "individualism" and interdependence ("collectivism"), Suh, Diener, Oishi, and Triandis (1998) found that while the idea of the pursuit of happiness had high priority in individualist societies, it did not in collectivist (mostly Asian) societies, where the idea of interpersonal harmony and doing one's duty received priority. Asking themselves if they were happy, many Asians simply had not thought about it. There is, of course, a conundrum here: If doing one's duty is internally rewarding, isn't that simply another way of pursuing happiness? If so, then the dour Puritan was a happy man, all cheery inside behind that black frock coat and sour visage. Without strain, I think, we may distinguish the feelings arising from the pacification of a minatory conscience and the feelings of happiness that, all over the world, lead people to laugh and feel good—let alone activate the left subcortex where the pleasure center lies (Davidson & Fox, 1982).

But the answer is obvious: by relieving the pains of economic insecurity, discrimination and rejection, intrusion into privacy, and punitive acts both within and outside the penal system, government can at least relieve sorrow.

Human Development as a Political End

Is human development a political end as well as a psychological one? Among others, Aristotle (*Politics,* 1280b), Durkheim (in Lukes, 1973, p. 324), and J. S. Mill (1910/1861, p. 127) have made the quality of the people in a political system the criterion for assessing the quality of its government, but these authors' understandings of how to develop the desired qualities has been weak. Nor has political psychology drawn its talents from those psychologists who specialize in human development, a failing that "turning political psychology upside down" (Lane, 2002) might remedy. For political scientists, most of the beliefs about how government influences the character of its citizens are based on simple isomorphism of social structure and personality response (e.g., Norton, 1991): If the polity is more inclusive, fewer people will have the low self-esteem of the excluded; if people are given voting rights, they will gain new feelings of empowerment; if tax policies are more progressive, people will feel more equal and treat each other more equally. In each case, there is research falsifying these commonsense assumptions—and other research supporting them. We do not have a science or much of a theory of how governments can help people to become more self-confident, psychologically secure, humane, empathic, responsible citizens—if, indeed, it is in the power of governments to do these things. The degree and manner of government influence over personality qualities is not settled: Frey and Stutzer (2000) find that compared to those in other Swiss cantons, people in cantons with more control over their local governments (direct democracy) are generally happier; Stone, Kaminer, and Durrheim (2000) report that degree of exposure by both white and black youths to stressful political events in South Africa is linearly related to level of symptoms of personal distress.

Note, too, that government can do a number of things to improve cognitive skills, emotional self-regulation, and sense of efficacy (Lane, 1994). But rather than enter a programmatic discussion, let me take up the central, thorny question of standards of "better people." Have the goals developed by western (mostly American) psychologists a universal appeal? The tentative answer is inevitably mixed.

Can Human Development be a Meaningful Crosscultural Goal?

In the early 1970s, D. H. Heath (1977) studied concepts of mature (male) personality in five settings in three countries (United States, Italy, Turkey), giving his informants the following criteria for assessing maturity that were developed after extended discussion with informants in the three countries (pp. 65–66): (1) Reliability of behavioral control; (2) presence of a sense of direction with firm but flexible controls; (3) unity of action, feeling, and intellect; and (4) an accurate and favorable sense of identity.

The global assessments by those who knew their subjects well were followed by detailed inquiry into the cognitive, emotional, and behavioral characteristics of the "mature" and the "immature" personalities. In the end, Heath found that "if agreement on meanings and evaluations can be said to be a form or validation, these concepts and criteria were intersubjectively and cross-culturally validated" (p. 66). "Maturity" had pretty much the same meaning in the American, Italian, and Turkish samples. But of course, there were differences, too: behavior that Americans thought was normal self-assertion Turkish respondents thought was "pushy" and "aggressive." And what southern Italians thought was appropriate modesty, Americans thought was passivity.

Klaus Scherer and associates (1986) studied the self-reported emotional experiences of joy, sadness, fear, and anger in eight European countries, analyzing the antecedents, intensity, situational stimuli, and personality correlates of these emotions among 779 subjects. They found very few significant differences by national culture (p. 189), although to the authors' surprise, the British were more sensitive than others to physical pleasure and the Swiss were more emotionally expressive.

Similarly, Schwartz and Bardi (2001, p. 268) found a remarkable cross-cultural consistency in the ordering of values among schoolteachers in 56 countries, of college students in 54 countries, and representative samples in 13 countries. In all these samples, "benevolence," "self-direction," and "universalism" values were consistently most important, whereas "power," "tradition," and "stimulation" values were least important; and "security," "conformity," "achievement," and "hedonism" were in between. Calling this ordering "pancultural," these authors found that the "value hierarchies of 83 percent of samples correlate at least .80 with this pancultural hierarchy" (p. 268).

But, of course, cultural differences in cognitive styles (Li-Jun, Peng, & Nisbett, 2000), other values (Inglehart, 1990, 1997; Schwartz & Bilsky, 1990; Triandis, 1995), moral prescriptions (Schweder, Mahapatra, & Miller, 1990), internal locus of control (Brislin, 1983; Feather, 1967; Lao, 1977; Price-Williams, 1985) all vary and make hazardous any claim to universal standards of human development. Tetlock, Kristel, Elson, Green, and Lerner (2000) help explain why: "in many contexts, people are striving to achieve neither epistemic nor utilitarian goals, but rather . . . are struggling to protect sacred values from secular encroachments by increasingly powerful societal trends toward market capitalism (and the attendant pressure to render everything fungible) and scientific naturalism (and the attendant pressure to pursue inquiry wherever it logically leads)" (p. 853). Human development will be differently interpreted in different societies, but not only is a westernization process taking place (perhaps the gravamen of the charge against globalization) but also, as Inglehart (1997) points out in a kind of anticipatory response to Tetlock, a worldwide postmodenizing trend is taking place, from traditional sources of authority (religion and custom) to electoral and bureaucratic sources and from the values implicit in the struggle for security and for life itself to values embodied in increasingly consensual concepts of a better quality of life. The New Humanism has taken a few steps on a long journey, a journey whose agent and tour guide may be political psychology.

"What is man that Thou art mindful of him?" Well, as David Ross (1930) and Henry Sidgewick (1907) said, the human mind and person represent the sum total of all that is valuable in our cosmos. Do we lose sight of this value in our studies of attribution, self-regulation, interpersonal relations, and so forth? I think so. For very good reasons, psychology does not ask, "What is Man?" or "Why are humans valuable?" It would lose its scientific credentials if it did. But under cover of this marriage with political science, let the unscientific question emerge and, however discreetly, let psychologists help answer the urgent question: How can governments help people to become more self-confident, psychologically secure, humane, empathic, responsible citizens?

◣ Note

1. The concept of *interests* seems unfamiliar to psychology; at least the term is not in the index of the third edition (1985) of the *Handbook of Social Psychology*, edited by Gardner Lindzay and Elliot Aronson, and is mentioned only as vocational interests in *PsyInfo* on the Internet.

◣ References

Abelson, R. P. (1981). Psychological status of the script concept. *American Psychologist, 36,* 715–721.

Abelson, R. P., Aronson, E., McGuire, W. J., Newcomb, T. M., Rosenberg, M. J., & Tannenbaum, P. H. (Eds.). (1968). *Theories of cognitive consistency: A sourcebook.* Chicago: Rand-McNally.

Abramson, P. R., Aldrich, J. H., Paolino, P., & Rohde, D. (1992). "Sophisticated" voting in the 1988 presidential primaries. *American Political Science Review, 86,* 55–69.

Acton, Lord (J. Emmerich). (1904/1887). Letter to Bishop Mandell Creighton 1 April 1887. In *Life and letters of Mandell Creighton* (Vol. 1, p. 172). London: Longmans, Green.

Andrews, F. M., & Withey, S. B. (1976). *Social indicators of well-being: Americans' perceptions of life quality.* New York: Plenum.

Aristotle. (1961/1952). *Nichomachean ethics.* (H. Rackham, Trans.). Oxford: Blackwell. Selections reprinted in R. B. Brandt (Ed.), *Value and obligation* (pp. 57–85). New York: Harcourt, Brace and World.

Aristotle. (1909). *Politics.* (B. Jowett, Trans.). Oxford: Clarendon Press.

Bachrach, P. & Baratz, M. S. (1962). Two faces of power. *American Political Science Review, 56,* 947–952.

Bagehot, W. (n.d. 1869]). *Physics and politics* (new ed.). London: Kegan Paul, Trench, Trubner.

Bales, R. F. (1950). *Interaction process analysis: A method for the study of small groups.* Reading, MA: Addison-Wesley.

Bay, C. (1965/1958). *The structure of freedom.* New York: Atheneum.

Bem, D. J. (1972). Self-perception theory. In L. Berkowitz (Ed.), *Advances in experimental social psychology* (Vol. 6, pp. 1–62). New York: Academic Press.

Bem, Daryl J., & David C. Funder. (1978). Predicting more of the people more of the time: Assessing the personality of situations. *Psychological Review, 85,* 485–501.

Bennett, L. (1998). The uncivic culture: Communications, identity, and the rise of lifestyle politics. *PS: Political Science and Politics, 31,* 741–761.

Bentham, J. (1954). *Jeremy Bentham's economic writings* (W. Stark, Ed.). Vol. 3. London: Royal Economic Society.

Bentley, A. (1911). *The process of government.* Chicago: University of Chicago Press.

Berlin, I. (1969). *Four essays on liberty.* London: Oxford University Press.

Borcherding, T. E., Pommerehne, W., & Schneider, F. (1982). *Comparing the efficiency of private and public production: The evidence from five countries.* Zurich: Institute for Empirical Research in Economics, University of Zurich.

Boulding, K. E. (1973). *The economy of love and fear: A preface to grants economics.* Belmont, CA: Wadsworth.

Brehm, J. W. (1972). *Responses to the loss of freedom: A theory of psychological reactance.* Morristown, NJ: General Learning Press.

Brickman, P., & Campbell, D. T. (1971). Hedonic relativism and planning the good society. In M. H. Appley (Ed)., *Adaptation-level theory: A symposium* (pp. 278–302). New York: Academic Press.

Brislin, R. W. (1983). Cross-cultural research in psychology. *Annual Review of Psychology, 34,* 363–400.

Brody, R. A., & Sniderman, P. M. (1977). From life space to polling place: The relevance of personal concerns for voting behavior. *British Journal of Political Science, 7,* 337–360.

Browning, R. P., & Jacob, H. 1954. Power motivation and the political personality, *Public Opinion Quarterly, 28,* 75–90.

Bury, J. B. (1955/1920). *The idea of progress.* New York: Dover.

Cataldo, E. F., Johnson, R. M., & Kellstadt, L. A. (1968). Social strain and urban violence. In L. H. Masotti & D. R. Bowen (Eds.), *Riots and rebellion: Civil violence in the urban community* (pp. 285–298). Beverly Hills, CA: Sage.

Christie, R., & Geis, F. L. (1970). *Studies in Machiavellianism.* New York: Academic Press.

Converse, P. E. (1964). The nature of belief systems in mass publics. In D. Apter (Ed.), *Ideology and discontent* (pp. 206–261). New York: Free Press.

Crosby, F. J. (1982). *Relative deprivation and working women.* New York: Oxford University Press.

Crozier, M. (1964/1963). *The bureaucratic phenomenon.* Chicago: University of Chicago Press.

Davidson, R. J., & Fox, N. A. (1982). Asymmetrical brain activity discriminates between positive versus negative affective stimuli in human infants. *Science, 218,* 1235–1237.

Diener, E., Diener, M., & Diener, C. (1995). Factors predicting the subjective well-being of nations. *Journal of Personality and Social Psychology, 69,* 851–864.

DiMaggio, P. J., & Powell, W. W. (1991). Introduction. In W. W. Powell & P. J. DiMaggio (Eds.), *The new institutionalism in organizational analysis* (pp. 3–33). Chicago: Chicago University Press.

Doob, L. (1971). *The patterning of time.* New Haven: Yale University Press.

Downs, A. (1957). *An economic theory of democracy.* New York: Harper.

Elster, J. (Ed.). (1985). *The multiple self.* Cambridge: Cambridge University Press.

Engel, J. F., Blackwell, R., & Kollat, D. R. (1978). *Consumer behavior* (3rd ed). Hinsdale, IL: Dryden Press.

Feather, N. T. (1967). Some personality correlates of external control. *Australian Journal of Psychology, 19,* 253–260

The Federalist. (1894/1790). *The Federalist and other constitutional papers* (E. H. Scott, Ed.) Chicago: Albert, Scott.

Ferejohn, J. A., & Fiorina, M. P. (1974). The paradox of not voting: A decision theoretic analysis. *American Political Science Review, 68,* 525–546.

Festinger, L. (1957). *A theory of cognitive dissonance.* Stanford, CA: Stanford University Press.

Fishkin, J. S. (1991). *Democracy and deliberation: New directions for democratic reform.* New Haven: Yale University Press.

Flynn, J. R. (1987). Massive IQ gains in 14 nations: What IQ tests really measure. *Psychological Bulletin, 101*, 171–191.

Foster, C. A., & Rusbult, C. E. (1999). Injustice and powerseeking. *Personality and Social Psychology Bulletin, 25*, 834–849.

Frank, R. H. (1990). Rethinking rational choice. In R. Friedland & A. F. Robertson (Eds.), *Beyond the marketplace: Rethinking economy and society* (pp. 53–87). New York: de Gruyter.

Frey, B., & Stutzer, A. (2000). Happiness, economy, and institutions. *Economic Journal, 220*, 918–938.

Frey, B. S. (1997). *Not just for the money: An economic theory of personal motivation.* Cheltenham, England: Elgar.

Friedland, R., & Robertson, A. F. (1990). Beyond the marketplace. In R. Friedland & A. F. Robertson (Eds.), *Beyond the marketplace: Rethinking economy and society* (pp. 3–49). New York: de Gruyter.

Friedland, R., & Alford, R. R. (1991). Bringing society back in: Symbols, practices, and institutional contradictions. In W. W. Powell & P. J. DiMaggio (Eds.), *The new institutionalism in organizational analysis* (pp. 232–263). Chicago: University of Chicago Press.

Gibb, C. A. (1979). Leadership. In G. Lindzey & E. Aronsons (Eds.), *The handbook of social psychology* (2nd ed., vol. 4, pp. 26–27). Reading, MA: Addison-Wesley.

Gilbert, D. T., Jones, E. E., & Pelham, B. W. (1987). Influence and inference: What the active perceiver overlooks. *Journal of Personality and Social Psychology, 52*, 861–870.

Gilens, M. (1999). *Why Americans hate welfare: Race, media, and the politics of antipoverty policy.* Chicago: University of Chicago Press.

Glatzer, W. (1991). Quality of life in advanced industrialized countries: The case of West Germany. In F. Strack, M. Argyle, & N. Schwarz (Eds.), *Subjective well-being: An interdisciplinary perspective* (pp. 261–279). Oxford: Pergamon.

Goleman, D. (1998). *Working with emotional intelligence.* New York: Bantam.

Green, D. P., & Shapiro, I. (1994). *Pathologies of rational choice: A critique of applications in political science.* New Haven: Yale University Press.

Griffin, J. (1986). *Well-being: Its meaning, measurement, and moral importance.* Oxford: Clarendon Press.

Gutman, A., & Thompson, D. (1996). *Democracy and disagreement.* Cambridge, MA: Belknap Press.

Haan, N. (1977). *Coping and defending: Processes of self-environment organization.* New York: Academic Press.

Hampshire, S. (1975). *Freedom of the individual* (Rev. ed.). Princeton: Princeton University Press.

Hardin, C. D. (1995, January). The influence of the immediate situation on memory for previous self-evaluations. *Dissertation Abstracts International, 55* (7-B), 3062. University Microfilms.

Hare, R. M. (1981). *Moral thinking: Its levels, method and point.* Oxford: Clarendon,

Harvey, O. J., Hunt, D., & Schroder, H. M. (1961). *Conceptual systems and personality organization.* New York: Wiley.

Heath, D. H. (1977). *Maturity and competence: A transcultural view.* New York: Wiley.

Heclo, H. (1974). *Modern social politics in Britain and Sweden.* New Haven: Yale University Press.

Hempel, C. G. (1952). *Fundamentals of concept formation in empirical science.* In *Foundations of the unity of science.* Vols. 1–2 of *International encyclopedia of unified science.* Chicago: University of Chicago Press.

Herring, E. P. (1938). How does the voter make up his mind? *Public Opinion Quarterly, 2,* 31–50.

Himmelweit, H. T. (1990). Societal psychology: Implications and scope. In H. T. Himmelweit & G. Gaskell (Eds.), *Societal psychology* (pp. 17–45). London: Sage.

Hobbes, T. (1950/1650). *Leviathan.* New York: Dutton.

Hoffman, M. L. (1981). Is altruism part of human nature? *Journal of Personality and Social Psychology, 40,* 121–137.

Hofstede, G. (1984). *Culture's consequences: International differences in work-related values.* (Abridged ed.). Beverly Hills, CA: Sage.

Hogarth, R. M., & Reder, M. W. (1987). Introduction: Perspectives from economics and psychology. In R. M. Hogarth & M. W. Reder (Eds.), *Rational choice: The contrast between economics and psychology* (pp. 1–23). Chicago: University of Chicago Press.

Hovland, C. I., Janis, I., & Kelley, H. H. (1953). *Communication and persuasion: Psychological studies of opinion change.* New Haven: Yale University Press.

Inglehart, R. (1997). *Modernization and postmodernization: Cultural, economic, and political change in forty-three societies.* Princeton: Princeton University Press.

Inglehart, R. (1990). *Culture shift in advanced industrial society.* Princeton: Princeton University Press.

Inglehart, R., & Rabier, J-R. (1986). Aspirations adapt to situations—but why are the Belgians so much happier than the French? A cross-cultural analysis of the subjective quality of life. In F. M. Andrews (Ed.), *Research on the quality of life* (pp. 2–55). Ann Arbor, MI: Institute for Social Research.

Isen, A. M. (1987). Positive affect, cognitive processes, and social behavior. In L. Berkowitz (Ed.), *Advances in experimental social psychology* (Vol. 20, pp. 203–253). New York: Academic Press.

Iyengar, S., & Kinder, D. R. (1987). *News that matters.* Chicago: Chicago University Press.

Iyengar, S. S., & Lepper, M. R. (2000). When choice is demotivating: Can one desire too much of a good thing. *Journal of Personality and Social Psychology, 79,* 995–1006.

Jacoby, J. (1976). Perspectives on a consumer information program. In M. L. Ray & S. Ward (Eds.), *Communicating with consumers* (pp. 12–20). Beverly Hills, CA: Sage.

Jacoby, J., Speller, D. E., & Kohn, C. A. (1974). Brand choice behavior as a function of information load. *Journal of Marketing Research, 11,* 63–69.

Jahoda, M. (1958). *Current concepts of positive mental health.* New York: Basic Books.

Jencks, C., Bartlett, S., (1979). *Who gets ahead? The determinants of economic success in America.* New York: Basic Books.

Kahn, M. W. (1986). Psychosocial disorders of aboriginal people of the United States and Australia. *Journal of Rural Community Psychology, 7,* 45–59.

Kamenka, E. (1989). *Bureaucracy.* Oxford: Blackwell.

Kant, I. (1949/1797). *Fundamental principles of the metaphysic of morals.* (T. K. Abbott, Trans.). Indianapolis: Bobbs-Merrill.

Katona, G. (1975). *Psychological economics.* New York: Elsevier.

Katona, G., Strumpel, B., & Zahn, E. 1971. *Aspirations and affluence: Comparative studies in the U.S. and Western Europe.* New York: McGraw Hill.

Katz, D., Gutek, B. A., Kahn, R. L., & Barton, E. (1975). *Bureaucratic encounters: A pilot study in the evaluation of government services.* Ann Arbor, MI: Institute for Social Research.

Katz, E., & Lazarsfeld, P. F. (1965/1955). *Personal influence: The part played by people in the flow of mass communications,* Glencoe, IL: Free Press.

Kelley, H. H. (1973). The processes of causal attribution. *American Psychologist, 28,* 107–128.

Kinder, D. R., & Kiewiet, D. R. (1981). Sociotropic politics: The American case. *British Journal of Political Science, 11,* 129–161.

Kipnis, D. (1972). Does power corrupt? *Journal of Personal, and Social Psychology, 14,* 33–41.

Kohlberg, L. (1964). Development of moral character and ideology. In M. L. Hoffman & L. W. Hoffman (Eds.), *Review of child development research* (Vol. 1, pp. 383–431). New York: Russell Sage.

Kohlberg, L. (1981). *The philosophy of moral development: Moral stages and the idea of justice.* New York: Harper and Row.

Kohn, M. L. (1971). Bureaucratic man: A portrait and an interpretation. *American Sociological Review, 36,* 461–474.

Kolb, B., & Whishaw, I. Q. (1998). Brain plasticity and behavior. *Annual Review of Psychology, 49,* 43–64.

Korte, C., Ytema, I., & Toppen, A. (1975). Helpfulness in Dutch society as a function of urbanization and environmental input level. *Journal of Personality and Social Psychology, 32,* 996–1003.

Kramer, G. H. (1983). The ecological fallacy revisited: aggregate vs. individual level findings on economics and elections and sociotropic voting. *American Political Science Review, 77,* 92–111.

Lafferty, W. M. (1989). Work as a source of political learning among wage-laborers and lower-level employees. In R. S. Sigel (Ed.), *Adult political socialization* (pp. 102–142). Chicago: University of Chicago Press.

Lane, R. E. (1959). The fear of equality. *American Political Science Review, 53,* 35–51.

Lane, R. E. (1988). Procedural goods in a democracy: How one is treated vs. what one gets. *Social Justice Research, 2,* 177–192.

Lane, R. E. (1994). Quality of life and quality of persons: A new role for government? *Political Theory, 22,* 219–252.

Lane, R. E. (1995). What rational choice explains. *Critical Review, 9,* 107–126. Reprinted in J. Friedman (Ed.), *The rational choice controversy: Economic theories of politics reconsidered.* New Haven: Yale University Press, 1996.

Lane, R. E. (2000a). *The loss of happiness in market democracies.* New Haven: Yale University Press.

Lane, R. E. (2000b). Moral blame and causal explanation. *Journal of Applied Philosophy, 17,* 45–58.

Lane, R. E. (2001). Self-reliance and empathy: The enemies of poverty—and of the poor. *Political Psychology, 22,* 473–492.

Lane, R. E. (2002). Turning political psychology upside down. In K. R. Monroe (Ed.), *Political psychology* (pp. 367–384). Hillsdale, NJ: Erlbaum.

Langer, E. J. (1990). *Mindfulness.* Reading, MA: Addison-Wesley.

Lao, R. C. (1977). Levenson's IPC (Internal Control) Scale: A comparison of Chinese and American students, *Journal of Cross-Cultural Psychology, 9,* 113–124.

Lasswell, H. D. (1930). *Psychopathology and politics.* Chicago: University of Chicago Press.

Lasswell, H. D. (1936). *Politics: Who gets what, when, how.* New York: McGraw-Hill.

Lasswell, H. D., & Kaplan, A. (1950). *Power and society: A framework for political inquiry.* New Haven: Yale University Press.

Lasswell, H. D., Merriam, C. E., & Smith, T. V. (1950). *A study of power.* Glencoe, IL: Free Press.

Lau, R. R. (1985). Two explanations for negativity affects in political behavior. *American Journal of Political Science, 29,* 119–138.

Lau, R. R. (2003). Decision making models. In D. O. Sears, L. Huddy, & R. Jervis (Eds.), *Handbook of political psychology.* New York: Oxford University Press.

Lawler, E. E., III. (1982). Strategies for improving the quality of work life. *American Psychologist, 37,* 486–493.

Le Bon, G. (1920/1895). *The crowd.* London: Unwin.

Lefcourt, H. M. (1976). *Locus of control: Current trends in theory and research.* Hillsdale, NJ: Erlbaum.

Lefcourt, H. M. (Ed.). (1984). *Research with the locus of control construct. Extensions and limitations* (Vol. 3). Orlando, FL: Academic.

Lerner, M. J. (1980). *The belief in a just world: A fundamental delusion.* New York: Plenum.

Lewis, A. 1982. *The psychology of taxation.* Oxford: Martin Robertson.

Li-Jun, J., Peng, K., & Nisbett, R. E. (2000). Culture, control, and perceptions of relationships in the environment. *Journal of Personality and Social Psychology, 78,* 943–955.

Liebenstein, (1976). *Beyond economic man: A new foundation for microeconomics.* Cambridge, MA: Harvard University Press.

Lind, E. A., & Tyler, T. R. (1988). *The social psychology of procedural justice.* New York: Plenum.

Lindblom, C. E. (1965). *The intelligence of democracy.* New York: Free Press.

Lindzay, G., & Aronson, E. (Eds.). (1985). *The handbook of social psychology.* (3d ed). New York: Random House.

Lubinski, D. (2000). Scientific and social significance of assessing individual differences: Sinking shafts at a few critical points. *Annual Review of Psychology, 51,* 405–444.

Lukes, S. (1973). *Individualism.* Oxford: Blackwell.

Lukes, S. (1975). *Power: A radical view.* Atlantic Highlands, NJ: Humanities Press.

Madison, J. (1894/1787). *Federalist* X. Against faction . . . The subject continued. *The Federalist.* In E. H. Scott (Ed.), *The Federalist and other constitutional papers* (Vol. 1, pp. 53–60). Chicago: Albert, Scott.

Mandler, G. (1982). The structure of value: Accounting for taste. In M. S. Clark & S. T. Fiske (Eds.), *Affect and cognition* (pp. 1–20). Hillsdale, NJ: Erlbaum.

Mayer, J. D., & Salovey, P. (1993). The intelligence of emotional intelligence, *Intelligence, 17,* 433–442.

McClelland, D. C. (1975). *Power: The inner experience.* New York: Halsted.

McClelland, D. C., & Winter, D. C. (1971). *Motivating economic achievement.* New York: Free Press.

McConaughy, J. B. (1950). Certain personality factors of state legislators in South Carolina. *American Political Science Review, 44*, 879–903.

McDougall, W. (1920). *The group mind.* Cambridge: Cambridge University Press.

McGuire, W. J. (1977). Psychological factors influencing consumer choice. In R. Ferber (Ed.), *Selected aspects of consumer behavior* (pp. 319–359). Washington, DC: Government Printing Office.

Merton, R. K. (1968). Bureaucratic structure and personality. In R. K. Merton (Ed.), *Social theory and social structure* (Rev. ed., pp. 249–260). New York: Free Press.

Milgram, S. (1974). *Obedience to authority: An experimental view.* New York: Harper and Row.

Mill, J. S. (1910/1859). On liberty. In *Utilitarianism, liberty, and representative government* (pp. 65–170). London: Dent.

Mill, J. S. (1910/1861). Considerations on representative government. In *Utilitarianism, liberty, and representative government* (pp. 173–393). London: Dent.

Miller, D. T. (1999). The norm of self-interest. *American Psychologist, 54*, 1053–1060.

Miller, D. T., & Rattner, R. K. (1998). The disparity between the actual and assumed power of self-interest. *Journal of Personality and Social Psychology. 74*, 53–62.

Mirowski, J., & Ross, C. E. (1989). *Social causes of psychological distress.* New York: de Gruyter.

Mischel, W. (1968). *Personality assessment.* New York: Wiley.

Mischel, W. (1969). Continuity and change in personality. *American Psychologist, 24*, 1012–1018.

Mischel, W., Shoda, Y., Rodriguez, M. L. (1989). Delay of gratification in children. *Science, 244* 933–938.

Moore, B., Jr. (1972). *Reflections on the causes of human misery and upon certain proposals to eliminate them.* Boston: Beacon Press.

Mullen, B., & Johnson, C. (1990). *The psychology of consumer behavior.* Hillsdale, NJ: Erlbaum.

Murray, B. (March 1998). Data smog: newest culprit in brain drain. *APA Monitor, 29*, 42.

Nisbett, R., & Ross, L. (1980). *Human inference: Strategies and shortcomings of social judgment.* Englewood Cliffs, NJ: Prentice-Hall.

Niskanen, W. A. (1971). *Bureaucracy: Servant or master?* Chicago: Aldine.

Norton, A. (1988). *Reflections on political identity.* Baltimore: Johns Hopkins University Press.

Norton, D. L. (1991). *Democracy and moral development: A politics of virtue.* Berkeley: University of California Press.

Parfit, D. (1984). *Reasons and persons.* Oxford: Clarendon Press.

Perry, R. B. (1954). *Realms of value: A critique of human civilization.* Cambridge, MA: Harvard University Press.

Piaget, J., & Inhelder, B. (1969). *The psychology of the child* (H. Weaver, Trans.). New York: Basic Books.

Pigou, A. C. (1948/1932). *The economics of welfare* (4th ed.). London: Macmillan.

Popper, K. R. (1959). *The logic of scientific discovery.* New York: Basic Books.

Poulantzas, N. (1978). *State, power, socialism.* London: New Left.

Powell, W. W., & DiMaggio, P. J. (Eds.), (1991). *The new institutionalism in organizational analysis.* Chicago: Chicago University Press.

Price-Williams, D. R. (1985). Cultural psychology. In G. Lindzey & E. Aronson

(Eds.), *Handbook of social psychology* (Vol. 2, pp. 993–1042). New York: Random House.

Rawls, J. (1971). *A theory of justice.* Cambridge, MA: Harvard University Press.

Redding, R. E. (2001). Sociopolitical diversity in psychology. *American Psychologist, 56,* 205–215.

Reitz, H. J., & Groff, G. K. (1974). Economic development and belief in locus of control among factory workers in four countries. *Journal of Cross-Cultural Psychology, 15,* 344–355.

Rescher, N. (1969). *Introduction to value theory.* Englewood Cliffs, NJ: Prentice-Hall.

Richins, M. L., & Dawson, S. (1992). A consumer values orientation for materialism and its measurement: Scale development and validation. *Journal of Consumer Research, 19,* 303–316.

Riker, W. H., & Ordshook, P. C. (1973). *An introduction to positive political theory.* Englewood Cliffs, NJ: Prentice-Hall.

Rogow, A. A., & Lasswell, H. D. (1963). *Power, corruption, and rectitude.* Englewood Cliffs, NJ: Prentice-Hall.

Rokeach, M. (1970). *The nature of human values.* New York: Free Press.

Rosenberg, M. (1979). *Conceiving the self.* New York: Basic Books.

Rosenberg, S., Ward, D., & Chilton, S. (1989). *Political reasoning and cognition: A Piagetian view.* Durham, NC: Duke University Press.

Ross, L. (1977). The intuitive psychologist and his shortcomings. In L. Berkowitz (Ed.), *Advances in experimental psychology* (Vol. 10, pp. 173–220). New York: Academic.

Ross, W. D. (1930). *The right and the good.* Oxford: Clarendon Press.

Runciman, W. G. (1966). *Relative deprivation and social justice.* Berkeley: University of California Press.

Sabine, G. H. (1961). *A history of political theory* (3rd. ed.) New York: Holt, Rinehart and Winston.

Sampson, R. V. (1965). *Equality and power.* London: Heineman.

Sapolsky, R. M. (1999). The physiology and pathophysiology of unhappiness. In D. Kahneman, E. Diener, & N. Schwarz (Eds.), *Well-being: The foundations of hedonic psychology* (pp. 453–469). New York: Russell Sage Foundation.

Scherer, K. R. (1986). Emotion experiences across European cultures: A summary statement. In K. R. Scherer, H. L. Wallbott, & A. B. Summerfield (Eds.), *Experiencing emotion: A cross-cultural study* (pp. 173–189). Cambridge: Cambridge University Press.

Schroder, H. M., Driver, M. J., & Streufert, S. (1967). *Human information processing.* New York: Holt, Rinehart and Winston.

Schroder, H. M., & Harvey, O. J. (Eds.). (1963). *Motivation and social interaction: Cognitive developments.* New York: Ronald.

Schwartz, B. (2000). Self-determination: The tyranny of freedom. *American Psychologist, 55,* 79–88.

Schwartz, S. H., & Bardi, A. 2001. Value hierarchies across cultures: Taking a similarities perspective. *Journal of Cross-Cultural Psychology, 22,* 268–290

Schwartz, S. H., & Bilsky, W. (1990). Toward a theory of the universal content and structure of values: Extensions and cross-cultural replications. *Journal of Personality and Social Psychology, 58,* 878–891.

Schwarzer, R., & Weiner, B. (1991). Stigma controllability and coping as predictors of emotions and social support. *Journal of Social and Personal Relationships, 18,* 133–140.

Schweder, R. A., Mahapatra, M., & Miller, J. G. (1990). Culture and moral development. In J. W. Stigler, R. A. Schweder, & G. Herdt (Eds.), *Cultural psychology: Essays on comparative human development* (pp. 130–204) New York: Cambridge University Press.

Sears, D. O. (1983). The persistence of early political predispositions. In L. Wheeler & P. Shaver (Eds.), *Review of personality and social psychology* (Vol. 4, pp. 79–116). Beverly Hills, CA: Sage.

Sears, D. O., & Citrin, J. (1982). *Tax revolt: Something for nothing in California.* Cambridge, MA.: Harvard University Press.

Sears, D. O., & Funk, C. L. 1991. The role of self-interest in social and political attitudes. In *Advances in experimental social psychology* (Vol. 24, pp. 1–91). New York: Academic Press.

Sears, D. O., Hensler, C. P., & Speer, L. K. (1979). Whites' opposition to "busing": Self-interest or symbolic politics. *American Political Science Review, 73,* 369–384.

Seligman, M. E. P. (1973). *Helplessness: On depression, development, and death.* San Francisco: Freeman.

Sen, A. (1987). *On ethics and economics.* Oxford: Blackwell.

Sen, A. (1999). *Development as freedom.* New York: Knopf.

Shapiro, I. (1989). Gross concepts in political argument. *Political Theory, 17,* 51–76.

Shapiro, I. (1999). Enough of deliberation: Politics is about interests and power. In S. Macedo (Ed.), *Deliberative politics: Essays on democracy and disagreement* (pp. 28–38). New York: Oxford University Press.

Sidgewick, H. (1907). *The methods of ethics* (7th ed.). London: Macmillan.

Simon, H. A. (1979). *Models of thought.* New Haven: Yale University Press.

Sinclair, R. C., & Mark, M. M. (1991). Mood and the endorsement of egalitarian macrojustice versus equity-based microjustice principles. *Personality and Social Psychology Bulletin, 17,* 369–375.

Smith, A. (1937/1776). *An inquiry into the nature and causes of the wealth of nations* (E. Cannan, Ed.). New York: Modern Library.

Somit, A., & Peterson, S. A. (1995). Darwinism, dominance, and democracy, *Research in Biopolitics, 3,* 19–34.

Sternberg, R. J., Wagner, R. K. Williams, W. M., & Horvath, J. A. (1995). Testing common sense. *American Psychologist 50,* 912–925.

Stigler, G. J. (1981). Economics or ethics? In S. McMurrin (Ed.), *Tanner lectures on human values* (Vol. 2). Cambridge: Cambridge University Press.

Stone, M., Kaminer, D., & Durrheim, K. (2000). The contribution of political life events to psychological distress among South African adolescents. *Political Psychology, 21,* 465–487.

Strickland, B. R. (1989). Internal-external control expectancies: From contingency to creativity. *American Psychologist, 44,* 1–12.

Suh, E., Diener, E., Oishi, S., & Triandis, H. C. (1998). The shifting basis of life satisfaction judgments across cultures: Emotions versus norms. *Journal of Personality and Social Psychology, 74,* 482–493.

Tetlock, P. E. (1983). Accountability and complexity of thought. *Journal of Personality and Social Psychology, 45,* 74–83.

Tetlock, P. E., Kristel, O. V., Elson, S. B., Green, M. C., & Lerner, J. S. (2000). The psychology of the unthinkable: Taboo trade-offs, forbidden base rates, and heretical counterfactuals. *Journal of Personality and Social Psychology, 78,* 853–870.

Tetlock, P. E. (1981). Pre- to post-election shifts in presidential rhetoric: Impression management or cognitive adjustment. *Journal of Personality and Social Psychology, 41,* 207–212.

Thaler, R. H. (1987). The psychology and economics conference handbook: Comments on Simon, on Einhorn and Hogarth, and on Tversky and Kahneman. In R. M. Hogarth & M. W. Reder (Eds.), *Rational choice: The contrast between economics and psychology* (pp. 95–100). Chicago: University of Chicago Press.

Thibaut, J., & Walker, L. (1975). *Procedural justice: A psychological analysis.* Hillsdale, NJ: Erlbaum.

Tocqueville, Alexis de. 1945. *Democracy in America* (Phillips Bradley, Ed.). Vol. 1. New York: Knopf. (First published in French, vol. 1 in 1835 and vol. 2 in 1840)

Triandis, H. C. (1995). *Individualism and collectivism.* Boulder, CO: Westview Press.

Tversky, A., & Kahneman, D. (1981). The framing of decisions and the psychology of choice. *Science, 211,* 453–458.

Veenhoven, R. (1993). *Happiness in nations: Subjective appreciation of life in fifty-six nations 1946–1992.* Rotterdam: RISBO Press.

Vernon, P. E. (1969). *Intelligence and cultural environment.* London: Methuen.

Vroom, V. H. (1964). *Work and motivation.* New York: Wiley.

Walster, E., Berscheid, E., & Walster, G. W. (1976). New directions in equity research. In L. Berkowitz & E. Walster (Eds.), *Advances in experimental social psychology* (Vol. 9, pp. 1–42). New York: Academic Press.

Weber, M. (1944). On bureaucratization in 1909. In J. P Mayer (Ed.), *Max Weber and German politics* (App. 1). London: Faber.

Weber, M. (1958). *The protestant ethic and the spirit of capitalism* (T. Parsons, Trans.). New York: Scribner's. (From articles first published 1904–1906)

Weiner, B. (1995). *Judgments of responsibility: A foundation for a theory of social conduct.* New York: Guilford Press.

Weiner, B. (1985). An attributional theory of achievement motivation and emotion. *Psychological Review, 92,* 548–573.

Wicklund, R. A., & Gollwitzer, P. M. (1982). *Symbolic self-completion.* Hillsdale, NJ: Erlbaum.

Wildavsky, A. (1985). The logic of public sector growth. In J-E. Lane (Ed.), *State and market: The politics of the public and private* (pp. 231–270). Beverly Hills, CA: Sage.

Wills, T. A. (1981). Downward comparison principles in social psychology. *Journal of Personality and Social Psychology, 90,* 245–271.

Wilson, J. Q. (1990). *Bureaucracy: What government agencies do and why they do it.* New York: Basic Books.

Wilson, T. D., & Schooler, J. W. (1991). Thinking too much: Introspection can reduce the quality of preferences and decisions, *Journal of Personality and Social Psychology, 60,* 181–192

Winter, D. G. (1973). *The power motive.* New York: Free Press.

Wolf, C., Jr. (1988). *Markets or governments: Choosing between imperfect alternatives.* Cambridge, MA: MIT Press.

Yardley, K., & Honess, T. (Eds.), (1987). *Self and identity: Psychological perspectives.* Chichester, England: Wiley.

Zahn-Waxler, C. E., Cummings, M., & Iannotti, R. J. (1986). *Altruism and aggression: Social and biological origins.* New York: Cambridge University Press.

Zajonc, R. B. (1980). Feeling and thinking: Preferences need no inferences. *American Psychologist, 35,* 151–175.

Zeitz, G. (1984). Bureaucratic role characteristics and member affective response in organizations. *Sociological Quarterly, 25,* 301–318.

Zellman, G. L., & Sears, D. O. (1971). Childhood origins of tolerance for dissent. *Journal of Social Issues, 27,* 109–136.

Zimbardo, P. G. (1969). The human choice: Individuation, reason, and order versus deindividuation, impulse, and chaos. In *Nebraska symposium on motivation.* (Vol. 17, pp. 237–307). Lincoln: Nebraska University Press.